THE LAW OF
TAX-EXEMPT ORGANIZATIONS

BRUCE R. HOPKINS

Member of the
District of Columbia Bar

THE LAW OF
TAX-EXEMPT ORGANIZATIONS

FOURTH EDITION

A RONALD PRESS
PUBLICATION

JOHN WILEY & SONS
New York · Chichester
Brisbane · Toronto
Singapore

Library of Congress Cataloging in Publication Data

Hopkins, Bruce R.
  The law of tax-exempt organizations.

  "A Ronald Press publication."
  Includes index.
    1. Corporations, Nonprofit—Taxation—United States.
  2. Charitable uses, trusts, and foundations—Taxation—
  United States.   I. Title.
  KF6449.H6   1983   343.7206′6   82-21815
  ISBN 0-471-87538-4   347.30366

To my daughter Natalie and my son Christopher

Preface

This book evolved out of the materials developed for the course in tax-exempt organizations at the George Washington University National Law Center, in Washington, D.C., which I have been privileged to teach since 1973. Thus the book grew from a desire to provide an introduction to the law of tax-exempt organizations that is sufficiently general to present the field in its entirety, yet with enough particularity to give the reader the specifics needed to gain access to more detailed information where required.

Lawyers, accountants, managers, and others interested in tax-exempt organizations can use this book to familiarize themselves with a particular aspect of the subject matter or refresh their minds about one rule or another. Even the practitioner who considers himself or herself an expert in the area can, it is hoped, find this volume useful on many occasions. Because of size limitations, the book cannot and does not answer all the questions in this volatile field, but what is considered a helpful documentation of regulations, rulings, cases, and literature has been included.

There is a feature of this edition of the book that merits note, which is that I have removed from the principal text nearly all references to Internal Revenue Code sections, and all references to cases and rulings, in an effort to make the text more readable. This information instead appears in footnotes.

It is the author's belief that the policy of exempting certain organizations from taxation furthers many other national policies and that tax incentives to charitable giving are essential and require the sustenance of further encouragement. Tax reform and tax equity will become empty and counterproductive "accomplishments" if achieved at the expense of diminishing voluntary charitable giving in furtherance of the programs and objectives of innumerable worthwhile institutions.

I thank those who typed (and retyped) the pages of the editions of this book (principally Judith Pickford Barse and Catherine Burcin), those who helped me with the research (principally Barbara S. Anderson, Joseph Henderson, and Shelley Pumphrey) and my friends at John Wiley & Sons.

BRUCE R. HOPKINS

Washington, D.C.
January 1983

Contents

PART III

OTHER TAX-EXEMPT ORGANIZATIONS

PART IV

PRIVATE FOUNDATIONS

PART V

QUALIFICATION OF TAX-EXEMPT ORGANIZATIONS: SUBSTANCE AND PROCEDURE

PART VI

FEEDER ORGANIZATIONS AND UNRELATED INCOME TAXATION

APPENDICES

PART I

INTRODUCTION TO TAX-EXEMPT ORGANIZATIONS

1

Rationale for Tax-Exempt
Organizations

The institutions of society within the United States are generally classified as governmental, for-profit, or nonprofit entities. Governmental entities are the branches, departments, agencies, and bureaus of the federal, state, and local governments. For-profit entities comprise the business sector of this society. Nonprofit organizations constitute what is frequently termed the "third sector," the "voluntary sector," the "private sector," or the "independent sector" of United States society. For a variety of reasons, the organizations making up the nation's independent sector have been granted exemption from tax liability and, in some instances, have been accorded the status of entities contributions to which are tax deductible.

Federal, state, and usually local law provide exemption from income tax for (and, where appropriate, deductibility of contributions to) a wide variety of organizations such as churches, colleges, universities, health care providers, various charities, civic leagues, labor unions, trade associations, social clubs, political organizations, veterans' groups, fraternal organizations, and certain cooperatives. Yet despite the longevity of most of these exemptions, the underlying rationale therefor is vague and varying. Nonetheless, the rationales for exemption appear to be (1) long-standing public policy, (2) inherent tax theory, and (3) unique and specific reasons giving rise to a particular tax provision.

§ 1.1 Historical Considerations

One commentator[1] has correctly observed that the various categories of tax-exempt organizations (described in Internal Revenue Code of 1954[2] §§ 501, 521, 526, 527, and 528) "are not the result of any planned legislative scheme"

[1]McGovern, "The Exemption Provisions of Subchapter F," 29 *Tax Lawyer* 523 (1976).
[2]Title 26, United States Code. Hereinafter the Internal Revenue Code is cited as the "Code."

3

but were "enacted over a period of eighty years by a variety of legislators for a variety of reasons."[3]

This author points out that, prior to 1894, all customs and other tax legislation enacted by Congress specified the entities subject to taxation. Thus, until that date, tax "exemption" existed by virtue of statutory omission. However, when the income tax of 1894 imposed a flat two percent rate on corporate income, Congress was required to face the task of defining the appropriate subjects of tax exemption. Consequently, section 32 of the Tariff Act of 1894 provided exemption for nonprofit charitable, religious, and educational organizations, fraternal beneficiary societies, certain mutual savings banks, and certain mutual insurance companies. Although the 1894 Act succumbed to a constitutional challenge, the Sixteenth Amendment subsequently was ratified and the Revenue Act of 1913 and comparable measures subsequently were enacted, permanently establishing the principles of progressive taxation and tax exemption.

This writer concluded that there were three basic considerations underlying the concept of tax exemption, particularly for charitable entities. The first of these considerations was "heritage;" he wrote that the "history of mankind reflects that our early legislators were not setting precedent by exempting religious or charitable organizations."[4] The second of these considerations was "morality;" he noted that "[l]egislative history clearly indicates, for example, that Congress has generally been willing to exempt the income of organizations formed for the mutual benefit of members so long as they are primarily financed by such members"[5] (this is a restatement of the inherent tax theory underlying exemption, discussed below). As a prime example of a tax exemption based on "policy" grounds, the writer cited a senator in 1894 pleading the case for exemption of mutual savings banks:

> Argument ought not to be necessary to sustain the proposition that mutual savings banks should be absolutely exempt from any income taxation.
>
> They represent the savings of the poor; they are not established for ordinary business purposes; the earnings—aside from those necessary for legitimate expenses—belong to the depositors, and are paid to them from time to time in the shape of interest or dividends; they ordinarily have no capital stock, and the managers are simply the agents or trustees of the depositors.
>
> . . . This Government cannot afford to permit the savings of the poor to be taxed through a Federal income tax. It would be the crowning infamy of this bill.[6]

He cites "special interest legislation" as the third consideration underlying the concept of exemption.

In the conclusion of this analysis, this author wrote that "[w]hile it is clear, in retrospect, that many of the [exemption] provisions have long outlived their

[3]McGovern, *supra*, n. 1 at 524.
[4]*Ibid*. at 527.
[5]*Ibid*.
[6]26 Cong. Rec. 6622 (1894).

historic justification, it is also clear in contemporary application that many of them continue to play a very crucial role in the law of tax-exempt organizations."[7]

§ 1.2 Public Policy and National Heritage

The public policy rationale for exempting organizations from tax is best illustrated by the category of organizations described in Code § 501(c)(3), namely, charitable, educational, religious, scientific, literary and similar entities, and, to a lesser extent, the "social welfare" organization, exempted by virtue of Code § 501(c)(4). The federal tax exemption for charitable and other organizations may be traced to the origins of the income tax,[8] although most of the committee reports accompanying the 1913 act and subsequent revenue acts are silent on the reasons for initiating and continuing the exemption.

One may nevertheless safely venture that the exemption for charitable organizations in the federal tax statutes is largely an extension of comparable practice throughout the whole of history.[9] Presumably, Congress simply believed that these organizations should not be taxed and found the proposition sufficiently obvious as to not warrant extensive explanation. Some clues may be found in the definition of "charitable" activities in the income tax regulations,[10] wherein is included such purposes as relief of the poor, advancement of education or science, erection or maintenance of public buildings, and lessening of the burdens of government. Clearly then, the exemption for charitable organizations is a derivative of the concept that they perform functions which, in the organizations' absence, government would have to perform; therefore, government is willing to forego the otherwise tax revenues in return for the public services rendered.

Since the founding of the United States and beforehand in the colonial period, tax exemption—particularly with respect to religious organizations—was common.[11] The churches were openly and uniformly spared taxation.[12] This practice has been sustained throughout the nation's history—not only at the federal but at the state and local levels, most significantly with property taxation.[13] The Supreme Court, in upholding the constitutionality of the reli-

---

[7]McGovern, *supra,* n. 1 at 547. Another overview of the various tax exemption provisions appears in Bittker and Rahdert, "The Exemption of Nonprofit Organizations from Federal Income Taxation," 85 *Yale L. J.* 299 (1976).

[8]38 Stat. 166. The income tax charitable contribution deduction originated in the 1894 statute (28 Stat. 556, § 32) which was declared unconstitutional in *Pollock* v. *Farmers' Loan and Trust Co.*, 157 U.S. 429 (1895).

[9]See Chapter 4.

[10]Reg. § 1.501(c)(3)-1(d)(2).

[11]See Cobb, *The Rise of Religious Liberty in America* 482–528 (1902); Lecky, *History of European Morals* (1868).

[12]Torpey, *Judicial Doctrines of Religious Rights in America* 171 (1948).

[13]See *Trustees of the First Methodist Episcopal Church* v. *City of Atlanta*, 76 Ga. 181 (1886); *Trinity Church* v. *City of Boston*, 118 Mass. 164 (1875).

gious tax exemption, observed that "[t]he State has an affirmative policy that considers these groups as beneficial and stabilizing influences in community life and finds this classification [exemption] useful, desirable, and in the public interest."[14]

The Supreme Court early concluded that the foregoing rationalization was the basis for the federal tax exemption for charitable entities. In 1924, the Court noted that "[e]vidently the exemption is made in recognition of the benefit which the public derives from corporate activities of the class named, and is intended to aid them when not conducted for private gain."[15]

The U. S. Court of Appeals for the Eighth Circuit has observed, as respects the exemption for charitable organizations, that "[o]ne stated reason for a deduction or exemption of this kind is that the favored entity performs a public service and benefits the public or relieves it of a burden which otherwise belongs to it."[16] One of the rare congressional pronouncements on this subject is further evidence of the public policy rationale. In its committee report accompanying the Revenue Act of 1938, the House Ways and Means Committee stated:

> The exemption from taxation of money or property devoted to charitable and other purposes is based upon the theory that the government is compensated for the loss of revenue by its relief from financial burden which would otherwise have to be met by appropriations from public funds, and by the benefits resulting from the promotion of the general welfare.[17]

One federal court observed that the reason for the charitable contribution deduction has "historically been that by doing so, the Government relieves itself of the burden of meeting public needs which in the absence of charitable activity would fall on the shoulders of the Government."[18]

Other aspects of the public policy rationale are reflected in caselaw and the literature. Charitable organizations are regarded as fostering voluntarism and pluralism in the American social order.[19] That is, society is regarded as benefiting not only from the application of private wealth to specific purposes in the public interest but also from the variety of choices made by individual philanthropists as to which activities to further.[20] This decentralized choice-making is arguably more efficient and responsive to public needs than the cumbersome and less flexible allocation process of government administration.[21]

[14]*Walz* v. *Tax Commission*, 397 U.S. 664, 673 (1970).

[15]*Trinidad* v. *Sagrada Orden de Predicadores*, 263 U.S. 578, 581 (1924).

[16]*St. Louis Union Trust Company* v. *United States*, 374 F.2d 427, 432 (8th Cir. 1967). Also *Duffy* v. *Birmingham*, 190 F.2d 738, 740 (8th Cir. 1951).

[17]H. Rep. No. 1860, 75th Cong., 3d Sess. (1939), at 19.

[18]*McGlotten* v. *Connally*, 338 F.Supp. 448, 456 (D.D.C. 1972).

[19]See *Green* v. *Connally*, 330 F.Supp. 1150, 1162 (D.D.C. 1971), aff'd sub nom. *Coit* v. *Green*, 404 U.S. 997 (1971).

[20]See Rabin, "Charitable Trusts and Charitable Deductions," 41 *N.Y.U.L. Rev.* 912, 920–925 (1966).

[21]See Saks, "The Role of Philanthropy: An Institutional View," 46 *Va. L. Rev.* 516 (1960).

The principle of pluralism was stated by John Stuart Mill, in *On Liberty* (1859), as follows:

> In many cases, though individuals may not do the particular thing so well, on the average, as the officers of government, it is nevertheless desirable that it should be done by them, rather than by the government, as a means to their own mental education—a mode of strengthening their active faculties, exercising their judgment, and giving them a familiar knowledge of the subjects with which they are thus left to deal. This is a principal, though not the sole, recommendation of jury trial (in cases not political); of free and popular local and municipal institutions; of the conduct of industrial and philanthropic enterprises by voluntary associations. These are not questions of liberty, and are connected with that subject only by remote tendencies; but they are questions of development . . . The management of purely local businesses by the localities, and of the great enterprises of industry by the union of those who voluntarily supply the pecuniary means, is further recommended by all the advantages which have been set forth in this Essay as belonging to individuality of development, and diversity of modes of action. Government operations tend to be everywhere alike. With individuals and voluntary associations, on the contrary, there are varied experiments, and endless diversity of experience. What the State can usefully do is to make itself a central depository, and active circulator and diffuser, of the experience resulting from many trials. Its business is to enable each experimentalist to benefit by the experiments of others; instead of tolerating no experiments but its own.

This same theme was echoed by then-Secretary of the Treasury George P. Shultz, in testimony before the House Committee on Ways and Means in 1973, when he observed:

> These organizations ["voluntary charities, which depend heavily on gifts and bequests"] are an important influence for diversity and a bulwark against over-reliance on big government. The tax privileges extended to these institutions were purged of abuse in 1969 and we believe the existing deductions for charitable gifts and bequests are an appropriate way to encourage those institutions. We believe the public accepts them as fair.[22]

The principle of voluntarism in the United States was expressed by another commentator as follows:

> Voluntarism has been responsible for the creation and maintenance of churches, schools, colleges, universities, laboratories, hospitals, libraries, museums, and the performing arts; voluntarism has given rise to the private and public health and welfare systems and many other functions and services that are now an integral part of the American civilization. In no other country has private philanthropy become so vital a part of the national culture or so effective an instrument in prodding government to closer attention to social needs.[23]

[22]"Proposals for Tax Change," Department of the Treasury, April 30, 1973, at 72.

[23]Fink, "Taxation and Philanthropy—A 1976 Perspective," 3 *J. Coll. & Univ. L.* 1, 6–7 (1975).

Charitable organizations, maintained by tax exemption and nurtured by the ability to attract deductible contributions, are reflective of the American philosophy that all policy-making should not be reposed in the governmental sector. "Philanthropy," wrote one jurist,

> is the very possibility of doing something different than government can do, of creating an institution free to make choices government cannot—even seemingly arbitrary ones—without having to provide a justification that will be examined in a court of law, which stimulates much private giving and interest.[24]

The public policy rationale for tax exemption (particularly for charitable organizations) was reexamined and reaffirmed by the Commission on Private Philanthropy and Public Needs in its findings and recommendations in 1975.[25] The Commission observed:

> Few aspects of American society are more characteristically, more famously American than the nation's array of voluntary organizations, and the support in both time and money that is given to them by its citizens. Our country has been decisively different in this regard, historian Daniel Boorstin observes, "from the beginning." As the country was settled, "communities existed before governments were there to care for public needs." The result, Boorstin says, was that "voluntary collaborative activities" were set up to provide basic social services. Government followed later.

> The practice of attending to community needs outside of government has profoundly shaped American society and its institutional framework. While in most other countries, major social institutions such as universities, hospitals, schools, libraries, museums and social welfare agencies are state-run and state-funded, in the United States many of the same organizations are privately controlled and voluntarily supported. The institutional landscape of America is, in fact, teeming with nongovernmental, noncommercial organizations, all the way from some of the world's leading educational and cultural institutions to local garden clubs, from politically powerful national associations to block associations—literally millions of groups in all. This vast and varied array is, and has long been widely recognized as part of the very fabric of American life. It reflects a national belief in the philosophy of pluralism and in the profound importance to society of individual initiative.

> Underpinning the virtual omnipresence of voluntary organizations, and a form of individual initiative in its own right, is the practice—in the case of many Americans, the deeply ingrained habit—of philanthropy, of private giving, which provides the resource base for voluntary organizations. Between money gifts and the contributions of time and labor in the form of volunteer work, giving is valued at more than $50 billion a year, according to Commission estimates.

> These two interrelated elements, then, are sizable forces in American society, far larger than in any other country. And they have contributed immeasurably to

[24]Friendly, "The Dartmouth College Case and the Public–Private Penumbra," 12 *Texas Q*. (2d Supp.) 141, 171 (1969).

[25]*Giving in America—Toward A Stronger Voluntary Sector* (1975). All quotations herein from the Commission's report are by permission.

this country's social and scientific progress. On the ledger of recent contributions are such diverse advances as the creation of noncommercial "public" television, the development of environmental, consumerist and demographic consciousness, community-oriented museum programs, the protecting of land and landmarks from the often heedless rush of "progress." The list is endless and still growing; both the number and deeds of voluntary organizations are increasing. "Americans are forever forming associations," wrote de Tocqueville. They still are: tens of thousands of environmental organizations have sprung up in the last few years alone. Private giving is growing, too, at least in current dollar amounts.[26]

The Commission described the dimensions of the philanthropic community (the "voluntary sector") as follows:

Most giving—79 percent in 1974—comes from living individuals, and the main focus of the Commission's research has been on such giving. The Commission's largest single research effort was a Commission-sponsored sample survey of 2,917 taxpayers conducted jointly by the University of Michigan's Survey Research Center and by the U.S. Census Bureau. Extensive questioning of respondents was conducted in 1974, covering giving for the previous year. In 1973, according to projections based on the respondents' answers, individuals may have given as much as $26 billion.

In addition, nearly six billion womanhours and manhours of volunteer work were contributed to nonprofit organizations in 1973, the survey indicates, and the total value placed on this contributed labor is another $26 billion. (Bequests accounted for $2.07 billion in 1974, foundations for $2.11 billion and corporations for $1.25 billion in direct dollar giving.)

Estimating the sources of giving by individuals is still more art than science, but even by conservative reckonings, $50 billion a year is the very large round-number total of the value of contributed time and money in the mid-1970's. A disproportionate amount of giving comes from contributors with the highest income, at least 13 percent of individual giving from this 1 percent of the population. Yet at the same time the bulk of giving, more than half, comes from households with income below $20,000.

Other Commission findings: college graduates give six times as much on the average as do those with only high school educations. Small town residents give more than city dwellers. The married give more than the single, the old more than the young. The giving of time was also found to correlate closely with the giving of money; the contributor of one is likely to be a contributor of the other.[27]

What are the dimensions of this sector? To the extent that they have been measured at all, the measurement has usually been only a partial one that looks at the amount of private giving and volunteer activity that goes into nonprofit organizations. Even on this incomplete scale, however, it is clear that the nonprofit sector accounts for a very large amount of time and money. According to estimates based on surveys made for the Commission, . . . at least $25 billion annually is given to various causes and organizations, and an equal amount worth of volunteer work is devoted to philanthropic activity. Yet these figures require some subtraction, and a good deal of addition. For one, a small but significant and growing

[26]*Ibid*. at 9–10.
[27]*Ibid*. at 13–14.

amount of private giving goes to public institutions, mainly state colleges and universities. On the other hand, a sizable share of the funding of the nonprofit sector comes from the government nowadays, and considerable additional funds come from endowment and other investment income and from operating revenues, including payments to nonprofit organizations by those who use their services—students' tuitions, medical patients' fees and the like. Government funding, endowment income and service charges must be added to the overall ledger of the voluntary sector. When they are, a rough extrapolation from available data indicates the total annual receipts of the private nonprofit sector to be in the range of $80 billion, or half as much as Americans spend on food in a year. Here is an approximate breakdown, again based on rough estimations, of what the major areas within the nonprofit sector receive and spend. (Only money inputs are indicated; volunteer work, free corporate services and the like are not included.)

REVENUES OF THE VOLUNTARY SECTOR
Estimates of Amounts of Private and Government Funds
Received by Private Nonprofit Organizations in
Major Recipient Areas, 1974
(In billions of dollars)

	PRIVATE FUNDS			GOVERN-MENT FUNDS	TOTAL
	Philan-thropy	Service Charges and Endowment Income	Total		
Health	$ 4.0	$17.8	$21.8	$15.7	$37.5
Education	4.2	7.5	11.7	1.6	13.3
Other (Welfare, Culture, etc.)	5.4	6.0	11.4	5.9	17.3
Total (except Religion)	$13.6	$31.3	$44.9	$23.2	$68.1
Religion	11.7	0.8	12.5	—	12.5
Grand Total	$25.3	$32.1	$57.4	$23.2	$80.6

Source: Commission on Private Philanthropy and Public Needs

One Commission report calculates that a "core group" of traditional philanthropic organizations includes 350,000 religious organizations, 37,000 human service organizations, 6,000 museums, 5,500 private libraries, 4,600 privately supported secondary schools, 3,500 private hospitals, 1,514 private institutions of higher education, and 1,100 symphony orchestras. Some other recent calculations: There are 1,000 national professional associations. New York City alone has around 6,000 block associations. And a study of voluntary groups in the town of Arlington, Mass., identified some 350 such groups there, serving a population of around 52,000. This last finding confirms earlier estimates of proportions between community size and the number of voluntary groups, and gives support to the extrapolation that in all, counting local chapters of regional or national groups, there may be as many as six million private voluntary organizations in the United States. . . .

ULTIMATE BENEFICIARIES

The arithmetic of the nonprofit sector finds much of its significance in less quantifiable and even less precise dimensions—in the human measurements of who is served, who is affected by nonprofit groups and activities. In some sense, everybody is: the contributions of voluntary organizations to broadscale social and scientific advances have been widely and frequently extolled. Charitable groups were in the forefront of ridding society of child labor, abolitionist groups in tearing down the institution of slavery, civic-minded groups in purging the spoils system from public office. The benefits of nonprofit scientific and technological research include the great reduction of scourges such as tuberculosis and polio, malaria, typhus, influenza, rabies, yaws, bilharziasis, syphilis and amoebic dysentery. These are among the myriad products of the nonprofit sector that have at least indirectly affected all Americans and much of the rest of the world besides.

Perhaps the nonprofit activity that most directly touches the lives of most Americans today is noncommercial "public" television. A bare concept twenty-five years ago, its development was underwritten mainly by foundations. Today it comprises a network of some 240 stations valued at billions of dollars, is increasingly supported by small, "subscriber" contributions and has broadened and enriched a medium that occupies hours of the average American's day.

More particularly benefited by voluntary organizations are the one quarter of all college and university students who attend private institutions of higher education. For hundreds of millions of Americans, private community hospitals, accounting for half of all hospitals in the United States, have been, as one Commission study puts it, "the primary site for handling the most dramatic of human experiences— birth, death, and the alleviation of personal suffering." In this secular age, too, it is worth noting that the largest category in the nonprofit sector is still very large indeed, that nearly two out of three Americans belong to and evidently find comfort and inspiration in the nation's hundreds of thousands of religious organizations. All told, it would be hard to imagine American life without voluntary nonprofit organizations and associations, so entwined are they in the very fabric of our society, from massive national organizations to the local Girl Scouts, the parent–teachers association or the bottle recycling group.[28]

Subsequent portraits of the philanthropic sector show an increase in its development and diversity. For example, while charitable giving in 1974 totaled $25.3 billion according to the Commission, it reached $43.3 billion in 1979 according to the American Association of Fund-Raising Counsel, Inc.[29] Nearly 85 percent of this giving (or $36.5 billion) was provided by living individuals, with the balance from corporations ($2.3 billion), foundations ($2.24 billion), and bequests ($2.23 billion). Of these contributions, 46.5 percent ($20.14 billion) went to religious organizations and institutions. The balance was devoted to education ($5.99 billion), health and hospitals ($5.95 billion), social welfare ($4.35 billion), arts and humanities ($2.7 billion), civic and public ends ($1.24 billion), and other philanthropic causes ($2.94 billion).

[28]*Ibid.* at 34–38.
[29]*Giving USA* (1980). The data attributed to the AAFRC in this portion of the text are derived from this publication.

This body of data for 1979 also reflects the current state of the philanthropic sector as defined by the number of certain organizations and institutions. For example, the religious community is composed of 300,676 Protestant churches, 3,550 Jewish synagogues and temples, 421 Catholic churches, 1,583 Eastern churches, 60 Buddhist churches, and 188 other categories of churches; the educational community includes 10,373 parochial educational institutions; the health care component of philanthropy includes 7,015 hospitals; and the social welfare aspect of the sector includes 2,200 United Ways. The AAFRC measures the philanthropic sector less in terms of numbers of organizations and more in terms of the involvement of people, and thus estimates 133.75 million church-goers, 58.4 million school and college students, 3.3 million teachers, 37.2 million hospital patients (in 1978), and 3 million Girl Scouts (in 93 countries), with the total number of volunteers for philanthropic purposes perhaps as high as 68 million persons.[30]

This public policy rationale likewise largely underpins the exemption for social welfare organizations contained in Code § 501(c)(4). The social welfare organization exemption also originated in 1913 and the income tax regulations include the promotion of social welfare within the definition of "charitable."[31] However, gifts to social welfare organizations are generally not deductible as charitable contributions.[32]

The public policy rationale also relates to other categories of exempt organizations. For example, while charitable and social welfare organizations operate to promote the general welfare, trade associations and other forms of business leagues act to promote the welfare of the business and industrial community. Thus, exemption from federal income tax is accorded "business leagues" under Code § 501(c)(6),[33] presumably on the theory that a healthy business climate advances the public welfare.[34]

The public policy rationale for and the general tax status of membership associations are largely misunderstood. Frequently such an association is tax-exempt—if exempt at all—by reason of Code § 501(c)(3) or 501(c)(6).[35] For the most part, an association is founded to provide services to its members or otherwise advance their interests, which is the prime reason for its members' joining. The tax classification of an association should be dependent on its purposes and objectives rather than on the composition of its membership.

---

[30]A survey by The Gallup Organization, Inc., released in 1981, indicates that 31 percent of Americans engage in some volunteer service on a regular, active basis and that 52 percent of American adults and about the same proportion of teenagers volunteered over a one-year period.

[31]Reg. § 1.501(c)(3)-1(d)(2).

[32]See, in general, Chapter 16. See, however, Code §§ 170(c)(3), 2055(a)(4), and 2522(a)(4).

[33]See Chapter 17.

[34]See, e.g., *Retail Credit Association of Minneapolis* v. *United States*, 30 F.Supp. 855 (D. Minn. 1938).

[35]See Chapters 6 and 17.

However, most analyses of associations' tax categorizations by the Internal Revenue Service[36] and the courts place great emphasis on the membership and services to it.[37]

As will be discussed, if an association's voting membership is comprised of individuals—particularly individuals who are practitioners of a profession—the tendency of the IRS is to regard the association as a business league.[38] If an association's membership is composed of "charitable" institutions or agencies, such as nonprofit colleges, universities, hospitals, or social service organizations, it will likely be treated as a "charitable" organization. Although the latter rationale is assuredly correct, the former is a false distinction. An association of individuals may well be properly classified as a "charitable" entity (as a charitable, educational, scientific, religious, or similar organization) or as a trade association or other form of business league. As noted, the important factor as a rationale for tax exemption is the association's purposes and objectives, not the nature of its membership.

The same may be said about services to an association's membership. There is no inherent incompatibility between services to members and tax-exempt status. Yet there is all-too-frequent expression of the belief that services to members are activities that *per se* constitute non-exempt activities. However, services to members can well be part of the process by which an organization achieves and maintains tax exemption. A difficulty nonetheless persists in distinguishing between services to members that advance exempt purposes and services that constitute private inurement[39] or otherwise advance private interests.[40]

Exemption from taxation for certain types of not-for-profit organizations is a principle that is larger than the Internal Revenue Code. Citizens combating problems and reaching solutions on a collective basis—in "association"—is inherent in the very nature of American societal structure. Nonprofit associations are traditional in the United States and their role and responsibility is not diminished in modern society. Rather, some contend that the need for the efforts of nonprofit organizations is greater today then previously, in view of the growing complexity and inefficiency of government. To tax these entities would be to flatly repudiate and contravene this doctrine which is so much a part of the nation's heritage.

This view of nonprofit associations operating in the United States has been the most eloquently stated by Alexis de Tocqueville. He, too, espoused the principle of pluralism, as expressed in his *Democracy in America:*

---

[36]Hereinafter, "the IRS" or "the Service."

[37]See, e.g., *National Association for the Legal Support of Alternative Schools,* 71 T.C. 118 (1978).

[38]See Chapter 17 § 2.

[39]See Chapter 12.

[40]See Chapter 17 § 6.

Feelings and opinions are recruited, the heart is enlarged, and the human mind is developed only by the reciprocal influence of men upon one another. I have shown that these influences are almost null in democratic countries; they must therefore be artificially created, and this can only be accomplished by associations. . . . A government can no more be competent to keep alive and to renew the circulation of opinions and feelings among a great people than to manage all the speculations of productive industry. No sooner does a government attempt to go beyond its political sphere and to enter upon this new track than it exercises, even unintentionally, an insupportable tyranny; for a government can only dictate strict rules, the opinions which it favors are rigidly enforced, and it is never easy to discriminate between its advice and its commands. Worse still will be the case if the government really believes itself interested in preventing all circulation of ideas: it will then stand motionless and oppressed by the heaviness of voluntary torpor. Governments, therefore, should not be the only active powers; associations ought, in democratic nations, to stand in lieu of those powerful private individuals whom the equality of conditions has swept away.

But de Tocqueville's classic formulation on this subject came in his portrayal of the use by Americans of "public associations" in civil life:

Americans of all ages, all conditions, and all dispositions constantly form associations. They have not only commercial and manufacturing companies, in which all take part, but associations of a thousand other kinds, religious, moral, serious, futile, general or restricted, enormous or diminutive. The Americans make associations to give entertainments, to found seminaries, to build inns, to construct churches, to diffuse books, to send missionaries to the antipodes; in this manner they found hospitals, prisons, and schools. If it is proposed to inculcate some truth or to foster some feeling by the encouragement of a great example, they form a society. Wherever at the head of some new undertaking you see the government in France, or a man of rank in England, in the United States you will be sure to find an association.

One of the modern-day exponents of the role and value of the independent sector in the United States is John W. Gardner, former Secretary of Health, Education, and Welfare, founder of Common Cause, and one of the founders of Independent Sector. Mr. Gardner has written extensively on the subject of the necessity for and significance of the nation's nonprofit sector. He writes that "[t]he area of our national life encompassed by the deduction for religious, scientific, educational, and charitable organizations lies at the very heart of our intellectual and spiritual strivings as a people, at the very heart of our feeling about one another and about our joint life."[41] He adds that "[t]he private pursuit of public purpose is an honored tradition in American life"[42] and believes that "[a]ll elements in the private sector should unite to maintain a tax policy that preserves our pluralism."[43] Likewise, Robert J. Henle, formerly president of Georgetown University and presently a professor at St. Louis University, writes

[41]Gardner, "Bureaucracy vs. The Private Sector," 212 *Current* 17–18 (May 1979).
[42]*Ibid*. at 17.
[43]*Id*. at 18.

of how "[t]he not-for-profit, private sector promotes the free initiative of citizens and gives them an opportunity on a nonpolitical basis to join together to promote the welfare of their fellow citizens or the public purpose to which they are attracted."[44]

Consequently, it is erroneous to regard tax exemption (or, where appropriate, the charitable contribution deduction) as anything other than a reflection of this larger doctrine. Congress is not "giving" such organizations any "benefits"; the exemption (or deduction) is not a loophole," a "preference," or a "subsidy"—it certainly is not an "indirect appropriation." Rather, the various Internal Revenue Code provisions comprising the tax-exemption system exist basically as a reflection of the affirmative policy of American government to not inhibit by taxation the beneficial activities of qualified exempt organizations acting in community and other public interests.

§ 1.3   Inherent Tax Theory

Aside from considerations of public policy, there exists an inherent tax theory for tax exemption. The essence of this rationale appears to be that the receipt of what otherwise might be deemed income by an exempt organization is not a taxable event, in that the organization is merely a convenience or means to an end, a vehicle whereby those participating may receive and expend money in much the same way as they would if the money was expended by them individually.

This rationale chiefly underlies the exemption for certain social clubs, which enable individuals to pool their resources for the purpose of provision of recreation and pleasure more effectively than can be done on an individual basis.[45] This tax rationale was well summarized by one federal court:

> Congress has determined that in a situation where individuals have banded together to provide recreational facilities on a mutual basis, it would be conceptually erroneous to impose a tax on the organization as a separate entity. The funds exempted are received only from the members and any "profit" which results from overcharging for the use of the facilities still belongs to the same members. No income of the sort usually taxed has been generated; the money has simply been shifted from one pocket to another, both within the same pair of pants.[46]

This rationale has also been reflected in congressional committee reports.[47] It was most recently involked by Congress when enacting the specific tax ex-

[44]Henle, "The Survival of Not-for-Profit, Private Institutions," *America* 252 (October 23, 1976).

[45]See Chapter 18.

[46]*McGlotten* v. *Connally*, supra, n. 18 at 458.

[47]H. Rep. No. 91-413, at 48, 91st Cong., 1st Sess. (1969); S. Rep. No. 91-552, at 71, 91st Cong., 1st Sess. (1969). A similar rationale for the income tax exemption of churches (see Chapter 8) has been advanced. Bittker, "Churches, Taxes, and the Constitution," 78 *Yale L. J.* 1285 (1969).

emption for homeowners' associations.[48] Thus the Senate Finance Committee observed:

> Since homeowners' associations generally allow individual homeowners to act together in order to maintain and improve the area in which they live, the committee believes it is not appropriate to tax the revenues of an association of homeowners who act together if an individual homeowner acting alone would not be taxed on the same activity.[49]

This rationale, however, operates only where "public" money is not unduly utilized for private gain.[50]

Inherent perhaps in this rationale is something parallel to the First Amendment right of "association."[51] This right has been expressed as including "the right to express one's attitudes or philosophies by membership in a group . . . ."[52]

§ 1.4 Other Rationales

By no means, however, can each provision exempting a category of organizations from tax be neatly correlated with one or both of the above-discussed rationales.

Some of the exemptions were enacted in the spirit of being merely declaratory of or to further then-existing law. The House Ways and Means Committee, in legislating a forerunner to the provision that exempts certain voluntary employees' beneficiary associations,[53] commented that these associations "are common today [1928] and it appears desirable to provide specifically for their exemption from ordinary corporation tax."[54] The exemption for nonprofit cemetery companies[55] was enacted to parallel existing state and local property tax exemption.[56] The exemption for farmers' cooperatives[57] has been characterized as part of the federal government's posture of supporting agriculture.[58] The provision exempting certain U.S. corporate instrumentalities,[59] is declaratory of the exemption already provided in the particular enabling statute.[60]

---

[48]See Chapter 20.

[49]S. Rep. No. 94-938, 94th Cong., 2d Sess. (1976), at 394.

[50]See *West Side Tennis Club* v. *Commissioner*, 111 F.2d 6 (2d Cir. 1940), cert. den. 311 U. S. 674 (1940).

[51]See *N.A.A.C.P.* v. *Button*, 371 U. S. 415 (1963); *N.A.A.C.P.* v. *Alabama*, 347 U. S. 449 (1958).

[52]*Griswold* v. *Connecticut*, 381 U. S. 479, 483 (1965).

[53]Code § 501(c)(6). See Chapter 17.

[54]H. Rep. No. 72, 78th Cong., 1st Sess. (1928), at 17.

[55]Code § 501(c)(13). See Chapter 20.

[56]See Lapin, "The Golden Hills and Meadows of the Tax-Exempt Cemetery," 44 *Taxes* 744, 746–748 (1966).

[57]Code § 521. See Chapter 20.

[58]Comment, 27 *Iowa L. Rev.* 128, 151–155 (1941).

[59]Code § 501(c)(1). See Chapter 20.

[60]See H. Rep. No. 704, 73rd Cong., 2d Sess. (1934), at 21–25.

Other federal tax exemption provisions may be traced to an effort to achieve a particular, stated objective. These provisions tend to be of more recent vintage, testimony to the fact of a more complex Internal Revenue Code. Thus, the exemption for veterans' organizations[61] was enacted to create a category of organizations entitled to use a particular exemption from the unrelated business income tax.[62] Similarly, the exemption for college and university investment vehicles[63] is the result of Congress's effort to preserve the exempt status of The Common Fund in the face of a determination by the IRS to the contrary.[64]

All of the foregoing rationales for tax-exempt organizations have been described in philosophical, historical, political, policy, or technical tax terms. Yet another approach to an understanding of exempt organizations can be found in economic theory.

Principles of economics are essentially founded on the laws of supply (production) and demand (consumption). Using the foregoing analyses, exempt organizations appear to have arisen in response to the pressures of the supply side, namely, the need for the goods and services provided, and the force of pluralistic institutions and organizations in society. But others view tax-exempt organizations as responses to sets of social needs that can be described in demand-side economic terms, a "positive theory of consumer demand."[65]

According to the demand-side analysis, consumers in many contexts prefer to deal with nonprofit, tax-exempt organizations in purchasing goods and services. The reason for this is that a nonprofit organization has a "legal commitment to devote its entire earnings to the production of services,"[66] while for-profit organizations have a great incentive to raise prices and cut quality. Generally it is too difficult for consumers to monitor these forces. This means that consumers have a greater basis for trusting tax-exempt organizations to provide the services—a restatement, in a way, of the fiduciary concept. Thus, the consumer "needs an organization that he can trust, and the non-profit, because of the legal constraints under which it must operate, is likely to serve that function better than its for-profit counterpart."[67]

This phenomenon has been described as "market failure" as far as for-profit organizations are concerned, in that, in certain circumstances, the market is unable to police the producers by means of ordinary contractual devices.[68] This,

---

[61]Code § 501(c)(19). See Chapter 20.

[62]Code § 512(a)(4).

[63]Code § 501(f).

[64]See Chapter 10. In general, see Symposium, "Federal Taxation and Charitable Organizations," 39 *Law and Contemp. Probs.* 1 (1975); Symposium, "Non-Profit Organizations' Impact on U. S. Society," 19 *Clev. St. L. Rev.* 207 (1970); Note, "Tax Exemption: Firmly Rooted," 41 *Notre Dame Lawyer* 695 (1966); Webster, "Certain inconsistencies and discrimination in the taxation of exempt organizations," 21 *J. Tax.* 102 (1964).

[65]Hansmann, "The Role of Nonprofit Enterprise," 89 *Yale Law J.* 835, 896 (1980).

[66]*Ibid.* at 844. See Chapter 12.

[67]*Ibid.* at 847.

[68]*Id.* at 845.

in turn, has been described as "contract failure," which occurs where "consumers may be incapable of accurately evaluating the goods promised or delivered" and "market competition may well provide insufficient discipline for a profit-seeking producer."[69] Hence, according to this theory, the consuming public selects the nonprofit organization, which operates without the profit motive[70] and offers the consumer the "trust element" that the for-profit organizations cannot always provide.

However, although the economic demand-side theory is fascinating and undoubtedly contains much truth, it probably overstates the aspect of consumer demand and downplays historical realities, tax considerations, and human frailties. The nonprofit organization antedates the for-profit corporation and many of today's tax-exempt organizations may be nonprofit because their forebears started out as such. And the forces of pluralism of institutions and organizations continue to shape much of the contemporary independent sector.

§ 1.5 Fate of Exempt Organizations

Tax-exempt organizations, particularly those that qualify as recipients of deductible charitable contributions, and the charitable contribution deduction continue to be buffeted by the traditional litany of alleged abuses.[71] Worse, tax "reformers" are relentlessly pursuing revisions that would insidiously undermine the tax incentives for nonprofit organizations by changing the law in ways that only indirectly affect charitable giving and tax exemption in general. Such reformers are furthered in their goals by the general pressures to expand tax bases and thereby reduce tax rates (as evidenced by the adoption of "Proposition 13" in California and the embracement of it by top national and state government officials), the tax "simplification" movement, and the "tax expenditures" concept.[72]

During his campaign for the presidency, Jimmy Carter labeled the U.S. tax system a "disgrace" and pledged simplification of the tax law and returns. His actual proposals did not challenge the philanthropic community head-on but would have had the effect of substantially reducing the number of taxpayers who have a tax incentive for giving. This would occur because of increased use of the standard deduction (the "zero bracket amount"), caused by repeal or consolidation of certain itemized deductions. This process has been occurring over past years—by increases in the standard deduction itself—with a commensurate loss in charitable giving of billions of dollars. According to Department of the Treasury data,[73] President Carter's tax proposals would have con-

---

[69]*Id.* at 843.

[70]See Chapter 11 § 3.

[71]See Chapter 3.

[72]See Hopkins, "Carter's Coming Tax Proposals—The Impact on Philanthropy," X *The Philanthropy Monthly* (No. 11) 14 (Nov. 1977).

[73]"The President's 1978 Tax Program, Detailed Descriptions and Supporting Analyses of the Proposals," Department of the Treasury, Jan. 30, 1978, at 18.

verted six million taxpayers from deduction itemization to use of the standard deduction, which would have meant that 84 percent of the American tax-paying public was deprived of tax motivation to make charitable contributions. These proposals would have so narrowed the constituency for the charitable deduction as to create the impression that it is merely a "tax dodge" for the wealthy.

Another manifestation of unfolding law changes that could have an indirect but important adverse impact on philanthropy is the nation's evolution toward a tax system that places decreasing reliance on income taxation as a revenue source. Illustrative of this is the apparent inevitability of adoption of a value-added tax (VAT)—somewhat of a national sales tax that would be imposed on sales of property and services at every stage of the production and distribution process. One VAT proposal receiving serious study would generate $130 billion in tax revenue, resulting in a $50 billion reduction in federal income taxation of individuals. This would be accomplished by reducing rates (for example, lowering the highest rate from 70 percent to 50 percent), slashing the maximum capital gains rate to 20 percent, expanding the earned income credit, providing individual savings incentives, and increasing deductible contributions to pension plans. Irrespective of their merit when viewed independently, these and related tax revisions collectively threaten to erode further the shrinking tax base of taxpayers who itemize deductions and have tax reasons for giving.[74]

The foregoing thus posits a conflict between the goal of tax simplification and the preservation of an effective and broad-based incentive for charitable giving. In an effort to resolve this conflict, many charitable groups endorse a concept termed the "above-the-line" charitable deduction. Pursuant to this concept, the charitable deduction is made an offset against gross income, rather than adjusted gross income as is the case under general rules. This approach enables a taxpayer to utilize the charitable contribution deduction as well as the standard deduction. In this way, the tax incentive for giving is restored to a broad base of taxpayers.

Due to an extraordinary amount of effort by the nation's philanthropic community, spearheaded by an organization named "Independent Sector,"[75] the above-the-line charitable contribution deduction became a reality when, on August 13, 1981, President Ronald Reagan signed the Economic Recovery Tax Act of 1981[76] into law. This expansion of the utility of the charitable deduction is intended to stimulate charitable giving and voluntarism and to pump addi-

[74]Tax Restructuring Act of 1979, H.R. 5665, 96th Cong., 1st Sess. (1979).

[75]The Independent Sector, formed in 1980, terms itself "a national forum to encourage giving, volunteering and not-for-profit initiative." As of January 26, 1982, the organization had 358 members, representing a wide spectrum of America's voluntary institutions and groups. Independent Sector is the successor to the Coalition of National Voluntary Organizations and the National Council on Philanthropy.

[76]95 Stat. 172 (1981); P.L. 97-34, 97th Cong., 1st Sess. (1981). This particular change in the law was occasioned by enactment of § 121 of the 1981 Act and appears as Code § 170(i).

tional billions of dollars into the American nonprofit sector, thereby increasing the range and extent of the thousands of services and programs supported by the nation's nonprofit organizations.

This new deduction, as finally enacted, reflects the political and economic realities that overshadowed its consideration. Two features of the measure were grudgingly accepted by the independent sector as conditions for its enactment: a phase-in of the extent of the deduction (which first takes effect for 1982) and a "sunsetting" of the rules (which are set to expire after 1986). By accepting these compromises, the independent sector headed off one of the principal goals of the Department of the Treasury, which was establishment of a "floor" consisting of an amount above which contributions would only be deductible,[77] and defused the greatest concern of the Treasury Department, which was (and is) the revenue loss associated with the expanded deduction.[78]

As a result, the charitable deduction for nonitemizers is presently written so that: (1) in 1982 and 1983, a donor can deduct 25 percent of the first $100 contributed to charity (thus, a maximum deduction of $25), (2) in 1984, a donor can deduct 25 percent of the first $300 contributed to charity (a maximum deduction of $75), (3) in 1985, a donor can deduct 50 percent of all contributions, and (4) in 1986, a donor can deduct all charitable contributions without otherwise itemizing deductions. However, the extent of allowability of any charitable deduction is governed by certain overall percentage limitations.[79]

In the author's opinion, the principal rationale for the above-the-line charitable deduction is that support for the nation's charitable sector is a matter of fundamental policy and philosophy underlying the very nature of the American system of government, which should give free play to private initiative and voluntarism. From this standpoint, the new deduction is not revolutionary tax legislation but merely tax policy being shaped in light of overall governmental policy and structure. This view was stated on the floor of the Senate during that body's consideration of the charitable contributions legislation by one of its principal proponents, Senator Daniel P. Moynihan (D–N.Y.), as follows:

> It [the new legislation] would . . . restore a bit more independence and vitality to the voluntary sector. It will add a bit to the ability of the ordinary working men and woman [sic] to determine how, and on what, some of his or her money is spent. It will in some small measure retard the process that has been described as the slow but steady conquest of the private sector by the public.

[77]A principal concern within the philanthropic community was that enactment of a "floor" under the charitable deduction (as is the case with the medical deduction) for nonitemizers would inevitably lead to a floor under the deduction for itemizers—a dreaded possibility (see Chapter 3 § 7).

[78]These "revenue losses" (see Chapter 3 § 6) are estimated to be $33 million for fiscal year 1982, $280 million for fiscal year 1983, $390 million for fiscal year 1984, $1.291 billion for fiscal year 1985, and $2.827 billion for fiscal year 1986.

[79]See Chapter 3 § 2.

Accompanying a mounting wariness toward Government monopoly, there is a widening appreciation by the American people of the unique and vital role played by private, nonprofit organizations in our Nation's economy.

This appreciation predates the present administration. It constitues the fundamental rationale for this legislation, which we first introduced in the 95th Congress. Moreover, it is familiar to every American as the basic principle of federalism: that the National Government should assume only those responsibilities that cannot satisfactorily be carried out by the States, by the localities, and by the myriad private structures and organizations, both formal and informal, that comprise the American society: structures that include the family itself, the neighborhood, the church, and the many private nonprofit agencies found in every community in this land.

*   *   *

While I am in the Senate, this legislation will not be undone. For it will be shown to be among the most significant social policy advances of recent years. It will reinforce the fiscal underpinnings of the tens of thousands of voluntary organizations that embody this society's devotion to community, its dedication to common provision, and its predilection for what [de] Tocqueville called association. It will enhance one of mankind's noblest impulses: to give voluntarily of one's own earnings so that the lives of others will be better. It will retard the tendency to rely solely on Government to meet the needs of individuals and communities.[80]

Another rationale advanced by advocates of the expanded charitable contributions deduction was somewhat the same as the more philosophic justification but was more straightforward: that the portion of an individual's income that is given to charity should not be taxed. Still another contention advanced was that the various increases in the standard deduction (the "zero bracket amount") in recent years outpaced the equivalent level of itemized deductions, so that a consequence was a relative decline in the amount of charitable giving. Yet another rationale was that government's best interests lie in adoption of the provision, in that, in the words of its other principal sponsor, Senator Bob Packwood (R–Ore.), it provides a considerable "bang for the buck,"[81] since the expanded deduction embodies a multiplier effect; for example, one estimate has been that the availability of the expanded deduction in 1975 would have resulted in increased gifts to charity of $3.8 billion with an attendant revenue loss to the government of $3.2 billion.

A further rationale for the charitable contributions legislation was advanced—one that is peculiar to the circumstances in which it was considered. Congressional consideration of the tax legislation (and hence the new charitable deduction) came shortly after passage of the Reagan Administration's budget cuts, which, it has been estimated,[82] will cause a loss during fiscal years 1981

[80]127 Cong. Rec. S7962 (daily ed., July 20, 1981).

[81]*Ibid.* at S7960.

[82]Salamon and Abramson, "The Federal Government and the Non-Profit Sector: Implications of the Reagan Budget Proposals" (Urban Institute, May 1981), reproduced at 127 Cong. Rec. S7964 (daily ed., July 20, 1981).

through 1984 of about $110.4 billion to charitable organizations. There has been much hope expressed in and out of Congress that the expanded deduction will inject funding into private sector programs to enable that sector to continue the provision of some of the social services that heretofore have been the responsibility of government. Although it is readily apparent that the independent sector cannot shoulder all of these financial commitments, the hope has been expressed that the expanded charitable deduction can help to nurture support for continuation of at least some of these services.

The adverse impact on tax-exempt organizations and deductible charitable giving occasioned by the tax reform/tax simplification movement may culminate in enactment of a version of the so-called "flat rate" tax. Under this approach, the existing progressive tax rates would be abolished and replaced by a flat tax, measured by a single percentage rate, payable by all persons at all income levels. In exchange for this single rate (usually proposed to be between 10 and 20 percent), the concept contemplates the repeal of many (if not all) of the present deductions, credits, exemptions, and the like that permeate the federal income tax laws. While proposed as a means to simplify tax return filing requirements and curb tax abuses, the flat-rate approach could result in loss or curtailment of tax exemptions for nonprofit organizations and/or the charitable deductions. The proposal is said to be under serious study by the Reagan Administration and is attracting considerable interest in Congress.

The charitable contribution deduction is not an anachronism, nor is it a loophole. Rather, it is a bulwark against overdomination by government and a hallmark of a free society, in the author's opinion; it helps nourish the voluntary sector of this nation and preserve individual initiative and reflects the pluralistic philosophy which has been the guiding spirit of democratic America. The charitable deduction has been proven to be fair and efficient, and without it the philanthropic sector of our society would be rendered unrecognizable by present standards.

Landrum R. Bolling, Chairman of the Council on Foundations, has written in a pamphlet entitled "Philanthropy and the Private Sector in American Life" that "the survival of this incredibly pluralistic society is tied to the broad use of volunteer institutions, activities, and programs to deal with the great variety of our needs and interests." Mr. Bolling, following a description of the "importance of encouraging voluntarism" and the "wisdom of decentralization," urged the development of a "comprehensive, coherent, and consistent public policy to encourage private philanthropy."[83] Likewise, Gordon Manser, Chairman, Board of Pensions, the United Presbyterian Church, has observed: "What is of transcendent importance is recognition of the vital role of voluntary organizations in our society and willingness to shape and strengthen philanthropy so that its mission may be carried forward."[84]

[83]This pamphlet is reproduced at 121 Cong. Rec. 19472 (1975).
[84]Manser, "Philanthropy: At a watershed point?," X *The Philanthropy Monthly* (No. 3) (March 1977).

The charitable contribution deduction thus may be deteriorating incrementally; some fear that its opponents are succeeding by chipping away at its foundation with the passage of each "tax reform" act. Without a strong and affirmative defense, tax incentives for charitable giving may succumb some more again, this time at the hands of another Tax Reform Act. It is to be hoped that Congress will soon realize the folly of more tinkering in this area and will come to see the virtue of encouraging charitable giving instead of stymying it. One distinguished philanthropist believes that if the leadership of the government and business sectors of U.S. society were to assume the responsibility for support of the private sector, including support by means of the tax system, "[w]e would surprise ourselves and the world, because American democracy, which all too many observers believe is on a downward slide, would come alive with unimagined creativity and energy."[85]

There should be no doubt that the nation's independent sector is operating in a hostile world. The philanthropic community must be ever vigilant, for there are public opinion-forming commentators who continually offer up criticisms of the independent sector, many suggesting that the sector is an anachronism with its services more properly undertaken by government.[86] Another line of attack is that recipients of charitable gifts are misusing funds and/or are soliciting contributions with inexcusably high fund raising costs.[87]

In sum, there needs to be a realization that the charitable deduction (and exemption) is predicated on principles that are more fundamental than tax doctrines and are larger than the technical considerations of the Code. The federal tax provisions enhancing charity exist as a reflection of the affirmative national policy of not inhibiting by taxation the beneficial activities of qualified organizations striving to advance the quality of the American social order.

[85]Rockefeller, "America's Threatened Third Sector," *The Reader's Digest* 105, 108 (April 1978).

[86]See, e.g., Bakal, "The American Way of Giving—Inside the World of Charity," 135 *Town and Country* 207 (Nov. 1981), 201 (Dec. 1981); Nielsen, "The Crisis of the Nonprofits," 12 *Change* 22 (Jan. 1980).

[87]See, e.g., Hazard, "Making Your Donation Count," *U.S. News & World Report* 88 (Oct. 12, 1981); "Bearing Alms," *Time* 66 (Jan. 28, 1980); Quinn, "Caveat Donor," *Newsweek* 65 (Dec. 18, 1978); Etzioni, "Defrocking Sacred Cows," 7 *Human Behavior* 16 (July 1978); "A Record Year for Charities—But Where Does the Money Go?," *U.S. News & World Report* (Oct. 18, 1976). In general, see Bakal, *Charity U.S.A.* (1980, Katz, *Give! Who Gets Your Charity Dollar?* (1974). Cf. Hopkins, *Charity Under Siege: Government Regulation of Fund Raising* (1980).

2

Advantages and Disadvantages of Tax Exemption

As subsequent chapters indicate, there are many categories of tax-exempt organizations and, accordingly, the advantages and disadvantages of tax exemption will differ, depending upon the particular category.

§ 2.1 Source of Tax Exemption

Section 61(a) of the Internal Revenue Code provides that "[e]xcept as otherwise provided in this subtitle [Subtitle A—income taxes], gross income means all income from whatever source derived . . .," including items such as interest, dividends, compensation for services, and receipts derived from business. The Code provides for a variety of deductions, exclusions, and exemptions in computing taxable income. Many of these are contained in Code Subtitle A, Subchapter B, entitled "Computation of taxable income." However, of pertinence in the tax-exempt organizations context is the body of exemption provisions—and exceptions thereto—contained in Subtitle A, Subchapter F, captioned "Exempt organizations."

Exemption from federal income taxation is derived from a specific provision to that end in the Code. "Derivation" of exemption is here used in the sense of "recognition" of exemption by the appropriate administrative agency ((the IRS) or as a matter of law, as opposed to exemption which is a by-product (albeit a resolutely sought one) of some other tax status (such as a cooperative or a state instrumentality).

A federal tax exemption is a privilege (a matter of legislative grace) and being an exception to the norm of taxation is strictly construed.[1] Such an exemption must be by enactment of Congress and will not be granted by implication.[2] At the same time, provisions giving tax exemption for charitable organizations are liberally construed.[3] Similarly, the exemption of income devoted to charity by means of the charitable contribution deductions has been held not to be narrowly construed,[4] as are most other deductions.[5] These provisions respecting income destined for charity are accorded favorable construction since they are "begotten from motives of public policy"[6] and any ambiguity therein has been traditionally resolved against taxation.[7]

The provision in the Code which is the general source of the federal income tax exemption is Code § 501(a),[8] which states, "[a]n organization described in subsection (c) or (d) or section 401(a) shall be exempt from taxation under this subtitle [Subtitle A—income taxes] unless such exemption is denied under section 501 or 503."

The Supreme Court has characterized Code § 501 as "the linchpin of the statutory benefit system."[9] The Court has summarized the exemption of Code § 501(a) as according "advantageous treatment to several types of nonprofit corporations, including exemption of their income from taxation and [for those also eligible charitable donees] deductibility by benefactors of the amounts of their donations."[10]

Thus, to be recognized as exempt under Code § 501(a), an organization must conform to the appropriate descriptive provisions of Code §§ 501(c), 501(d), or 401(a). The exemption, however, does not extend to an organization's unrelated business taxable income.[11]

---

[1]See, e.g., *Alfred I. duPont Testamentary Trust* v. *Commissioner*, 514 F.2d 917 (5th Cir. 1975); *Conference of Major Religious Superiors of Women, Inc.* v. *District of Columbia*, 348 F.2d 783 (D.C. Cir. 1965); *American Automobile Association* v. *Commissioner*, 19 T.C. 1146 (1953); *Associated Industries of Cleveland* v. *Commissioner*, 7 T.C. 1449 (1946); *Deputy* v. *DuPont*, 308 U. S. 488 (1940); *Bingler* v. *Johnson*, 394 U. S. 741 (1969) and authorities cited therein. In general, see Murtagh, "The Role of the Courts in the Interpretation of the Internal Revenue Code," 24 *Tax Lawyer* 523 (1971).

[2]See, e.g., *Mescalero Apache Tribe* v. *Jones*, 411 U. S. 145 (1973).

[3]See *American Institute for Economic Research* v. *United States*, 302 F.2d 934 (Ct. Cl. 1962), cert. den. 372 U. S. 976 (1963), reh. den. 373 U. S. 954 (1963); *Harrison* v. *Barker Annuity Fund*, 90 F.2d 286 (7th Cir. 1937).

[4]See *Sico Foundation* v. *United States*, 295 F.2d 924, 930, n. 19 (Ct. Cl. 1962) and cases cited therein.

[5]See *White* v. *United States*, 305 U. S. 281, 292 (1938).

[6]*Helvering* v. *Bliss*, 293 U. S. 144, 151 (1934).

[7]*C. F. Mueller Co.* v. *Commissioner*, 190 F.2d 210 (3d Cir. 1951).

[8]Also see Code §§ 521, 526, 527, 528.

[9]*Simon* v. *Eastern Kentucky Welfare Rights Organization*, 426 U. S. 26, 29, n. 1 (1976).

[10]*Ibid.* at 28.

[11]Reg. § 1.501(a)-1(a)(1). See Chapters 40–43.

As will be discussed,[12] an organization that seeks to obtain tax-exempt status, therefore, bears a heavy burden to prove that it satisfies all the requirements of the exemption statute.[13]

§ 2.2 Advantages

Tax Relief

Of course, the one advantage shared by all categories of exempt organizations is that, barring loss of exemption or imposition of the tax on income other than exempt function income, the unrelated business income tax, the tax on excessive legislative activities, the tax on certain "political" activities, or (if private foundations) the tax on net investment income, they are spared federal income taxation. Generally, tax-exempt status under federal law will mean comparable status under state and local law.

Federal income tax exemption may also involve exemption from certain federal excise and employment taxes. However, if an exempt organization is deemed to be a private foundation, it will be subject to a special excise tax on investment income and, if it chooses to dissolve, perhaps a termination tax. Generally, the private foundation rules carry sanctions in the form of taxes.[14]

Many organizations exempt under federal law also qualify for exemption from state and local sales, use, property, and other forms of tax.[15]

Deductibility of Contributions

Exempt organizations which qualify as entities described in Code § 170(c) are eligible to attract deductible charitable contributions from individual and corporate donors. In large part, this advantage is extended only to organizations described in Code § 501(c)(3).[16] Occasionally, an exempt organization whose exemption is based on a section of the Code other than § 501(c)(3) can achieve the same results with respect to deductibility of contributions, even if not classified as charitable donees. The most common example of this is the ability of trade associations to be exempt under Code § 501(c)(6)[17] and yet have contributions deductible as business expenses under Code § 162.

---

[12]See Chapter 37.

[13]*Harding Hospital* v. *United States*, 505 F.2d 1068, 1071 (6th Cir. 1974); *Haswell* v. *United States*, 500 F.2d 1133, 1140 (Ct. Cl. 1974).

[14]See Chapters 25–30 and 32.

[15]As respects the local property tax exemption, see Balk (ed.), *The Free List* (1971).

[16]Code § 170(c)(2). But see Code §§ 170(c)(1), (3)–(5), 170(h).

[17]See Chapter 17.

Grants

Many tax-exempt organizations are the likely subject of grants from private foundations. This is especially the case with charitable organizations, which have achieved public charity status, since a foundation generally may distribute funds to such an organization in satisfaction of the mandatory payout requirements[18] without having to assume expenditure responsibility for the grant.[19] In many instances, federal agencies only make grants to or enter into contracts with nonprofit, tax-exempt organizations, oftentimes only those organizations determined to be charitable entities.

Other

Numerous other advantages to be derived from exemption exist. For example, the employees of a charitable organization may take advantage of special rules providing favorable tax treatment for contributions for annuities.[20] Services performed for an organization described in Code § 501(a) may be exempt from taxation under the Federal Insurance Contributions Act (Social Security) and Federal Unemployment Tax Act.[21] Further, exempt organizations often have the privilege of preferred second or third class mailing rates.[22] In one instance, an organization (unsuccessfully) sought categorization as a charitable entity so that its child day care centers would qualify for the food reimbursement program administered by the U.S. Department of Agriculture.[23]

Although obviously relatively minor in scope, another advantage to the exemption for charitable organizations is that it provides exemption from the Organized Crime Control Act,[24] which prohibits illegal gambling businesses. Specifically, the Act exempts from its application "any bingo game, lottery, or similar game of chance conducted by an organization exempt from tax under paragraph (3) of subsection (c) of section 501 of the Internal Revenue Code of 1954, as amended, if no part of the gross receipts derived from such activity

---

[18]See Chapter 26.

[19]See Chapter 29.

[20]Code § 403(b).

[21]See Code §§ 3121(b) and 3306(c).

[22]39 U.S.C. §§ 4355(a), 4452(d). The organizations entitled to the preferential postage rates (essentially those described in Code § 501(c)(3)) are defined in the Domestic Mail Manual §§ 423.13, 623.2. These definitions were adopted in 1973 (38 Fed. Reg. 1566 (Jan. 15, 1973)), with the U.S. Postal Service essentially adhering to the federal tax law definition of the eligible organizations, although as to "charitable" entities the Postal Service originally proposed a totally different definition (37 Fed. Reg. 17423 (Aug. 26, 1972)).

[23]*Baltimore Regional Joint Board Health and Welfare Fund, Amalgamated Clothing and Textile Workers Union* v. *Commissioner*, 69 T.C. 554 (1978).

[24]18 U.S.C. § 1955.

inures to the benefit of any private shareholder, member, or employee of such organization except as compensation for actual expenses incurred by him in the conduct of such activity."[25]

Another advantage of general tax exemption for some organizations is the availability of exemption from the windfall profit tax. The Crude Oil Windfall Profit Tax Act of 1980 imposes a windfall profit tax, which is a temporary levy, retroactive to March 1, 1980. The tax applies to the "windfall profit" derived from the sale of domestically produced crude oil. The windfall profit is the selling price of the oil less an adjusted base price and a deduction for state severance taxes on the profit. Taxable oil is classified into one of three "tiers." The tiers differ in several respects, including the tax rate that is applied and the adjusted base price that is used. The rates range as high as 70 percent.

Oil produced from properties owned by educational institutions[26] and medical facilities[27] is exempt from the windfall profit tax where the properties were held by the organizations on January 21, 1980. Educational institutions are described as those that maintain a faculty and curriculum and have a regularly enrolled student body at the place where the educational activities are conducted. Related "foundations" for state colleges and universities are included in this description. Medical facilities are described as hospitals and certain medical research organizations.[28]

Oil produced from interests held by a church[29] on January 21, 1980, is exempt from the tax—but only if the net proceeds from production of the oil were dedicated to the support of an educational institution or medical facility prior to January 22, 1980. Proceeds from an oil interest received after January 21, 1980, such as a bequest, are not eligible for the exemption.

The windfall profit tax exemption for specified charitable and educational organizations and medical facilities was extended in 1981 to cover oil production attributable to economic interests held by a charitable organization "which is organized and operated primarily for the residential placement, care or treatment of delinquent, dependent, orphaned, neglected, or handicapped children."[30] To qualify for this exemption, the oil interest must have been held by the organization on January 21, 1980, and at all times thereafter before the last day of the calendar quarter. If the interest is not held by the organization, the exemption may apply if the interest was held by a church for the benefit of the organization and if all the proceeds from the interest were dedicated on January 21, 1980, and at all times thereafter before the close of the calendar quarter, to the qualifying child care agency.

Still another advantage of income tax exemption is the exemption that an

---

[25]See *United States* v. *Hawes*, 529 F.2d 472, 481 (5th Cir. 1976).

[26]Code § 170(b)(1)(A)(ii) or (iv). See Chapter 22 § 1.

[27]Code § 170(b)(1)(a)(A)(iii). See Chapter 22 § 1.

[28]See Code § 4994(b)(1)(A).

[29]Code § 170(b)(1)(a)(A)(i). See Chapter 22 § 1.

[30]See Code § 4994(b)(1)(A)(ii).

organization may have from the federal price discrimination law, known as the Robinson–Patman Act. The Act, in essence, makes it "unlawful for any person engaged in commerce, in the course of such commerce, either directly or indirectly, to discriminate in price between different purchasers of commodities of like grade and quality, where either or any of the purchasers involved in such discrimination are in commerce, or such commodities are sold for use, consumption, or resale within the United States . . . , and where the effect of such discrimination may be substantially to lessen competition or tend to create a monopoly in any line of commerce. . . ."[31] Exempted from coverage of this Act are certain nonprofit institutions that purchase supplies for their own use at lower prices than can be obtained by other purchasers. This exemption is accorded to "schools, colleges, universities, public libraries, churches, hospitals, and charitable institutions not operated for profit."[32] The purpose of the exemption is to enable nonprofit institutions to operate as inexpensively as possible.[33]

§ 2.3 Disadvantages

Qualification as a tax-exempt organization may impose certain disadvantages. Thus, certain categories of exempt organizations are prohibited from engaging in substantial legislative activities[34] and in campaign or other political activities.[35] In other instances, most notably in the field of private foundations, qualification as an exempt organization brings with it a host of limitations which must be adhered to if exempt status is to be maintained. Exempt status also will likely entail extensive annual reporting requirements.[36] The requirement of adherence to these limitations may not be worth qualification as an exempt organization, especially where more preferable alternatives are available.

§ 2.4 Alternatives to Exempt Status

An organization may elect or be required to operate without formal recognition as a tax-exempt entity and yet achieve the same basic objective: the nonpayment of income tax. However, the legitimate alternatives to tax-exempt status are few.

Perhaps the simplest illustration of this principle is the organization (nonprofit or not) that is operated so that its deductions equal or exceed income in any taxable year. In essence, this is the basis upon which cooperatives function without having to pay tax.

---

[31]15 U.S.C. § 13(a).
[32]15 U.S.C. § 13(c).
[33]See *Logan Lanes, Inc.* v. *Brunswick Corp.*, 378 F.2d 212 (9th Cir. 1967).
[34]See Chapter 13.
[35]See Chapter 14.
[36]See Chapter 38.

The tax treatment of nonexempt cooperatives is the subject of Code §§ 1381–1383. These sections apply to any "corporation operating on a cooperative basis" (with exceptions) and to farmers' cooperatives exempt under Code § 521.[37] Basically, a qualified cooperative escapes taxation because, in computing taxable income, a deduction is available for "patronage dividends" and qualified and nonqualified "per unit retain allocations."[38] Moreover, a farmers' cooperative is entitled to certain deductions for nonpatronage dividends.[39] Generally amounts received as patronage dividends and qualified per-unit retain certificates are includible in the patrons' gross income.

An organization which loses its tax-exempt status may continue to operate without taxation by conversion to operation as a cooperative.[40] Similarly, an organization that cannot qualify as a tax-exempt entity may choose to function as a cooperative.[41]

If a nonexempt organization that does not operate on a cooperative basis seeks to avoid taxation by matching deductions and income, federal tax law may foil the scheme if the organization is a social club or other membership organization operated to furnish goods or services to its members.[42] In this situation, the expenses of furnishing services, goods or other items of value (e.g., insurance) to members are deductible only to the extent of income from members (including income from institutes or trade shows primarily for members' education). This means that any expenses attributable to membership activities in excess of membership income may not be deducted against membership income (although the increment may be carried forward). Prior to enactment of these rules, the courts had upheld contrary treatment.[43]

There is a line of law that permits nontaxability of an organization where it is merely a conduit for the expenditure of a fund established for a specific purpose. Thus, a soft drink manufacturer that received funds from bottlers for a national advertising fund was held not taxable on such funds since they were earmarked for advertising purposes; the manufacturer was considered only an administrator of a trust fund.[44] Initially, the IRS took the position that this

---

[37]See Chapter 20.

[38]Code §§ 1382(b), 1388.

[39]Code § 1382(c).

[40]See, e.g., A. Duda & Sons Cooperative Ass'n v. United States, 495 F.2d 193 (5th Cir. 1974). This decision was subsequently withdrawn and superseded by the decision reported at 504 F.2d 970 (5th Cir. 1975).

[41]See, e.g., Rev. Rul. 69–633, 1969–2 C.B. 121.

[42]Code § 277.

[43]See, e.g., Anaheim Union Water Company v. Commissioner, 321 F.2d 253 (9th Cir. 1963). For an application of Code § 277, see Boating Trade Association of Metropolitan Houston v. United States, 75–1 U.S.T.C. ¶ 9398 (S.D. Tex. 1975).

[44]The Seven-Up Company v. Commissioner, 14 T.C. 965 (1950). Also Rev. Rul. 69–96, 1969–1 C.B. 32; Ford Dealers Advertising Fund, Inc. v. Commissioner, 55 T.C. 761 (1971), aff'd 456 F.2d 255 (5th Cir. 1972); Park Place, Inc. v. Commissioner, 57 T.C. 767 (1972); Greater Pittsburgh Chrysler Dealers Association of Western Pennsylvania v. United States, 77–1 U.S.T.C. ¶ 9293 (W.D. Pa. 1977); Broadcast Measurement Bureau v. Commissioner, 16 T.C. 988 (1951).

precept would be followed only where the recipient of the funds receives them with the obligation to expend them solely for a particular purpose.[45] However, this position was subsequently superseded by a ruling which taxes to the recipient organization the amounts received and permits related deductions, subject to the previously discussed expense allocation rules.[46] Also, the IRS has distinguished the above-described factual setting involving a soft drink manufacturer from that where the participants (dealers, bottlers and the like) form an unincorporated organization to conduct a national advertising program; the Service ruled that the organization is separately taxable as a corporation.[47]

If exempt status is unavailable, lost, or not desired, and if deductions do not or cannot equal income and cooperative status is either unavailable or unwanted, and if the organization is not formally incorporated, perhaps the entity can escape taxation by contending it is nonexistent for tax purposes. This is generally unlikely, in view of the authority of the IRS to treat an unincorporated entity as a taxable corporation.[48] Yet this is what political campaign committees did for many years, as the Service failed or refused to assert tax liability. However, early in 1974, the IRS ruled that campaign committees are to be treated as taxable corporations (although contributions remain nontaxable).[49] This ruling was in turn superseded by the enactment of Code § 527 and related sections[50] late in 1974.[51] Nonetheless, even after its 1974 ruling, the IRS continued to uphold the per donee gift tax exclusion of $3,000 for separate fund-raising campaign committees,[52] despite opposition in the courts.[53] However, in 1974, Congress exempted contributions to political parties or committees from the gift tax.[54]

---

[45]Rev. Rul. 58–209, 1958–1 C.B. 19.

[46]Rev. Rul. 74–318, 1974–2 C.B. 14.

[47]Rev. Rul. 74–319, 1974–2 C.B. 15. Also *Dri-Power Distributors Association Trust* v. *Commissioner*, 54 T.C. 460 (1970); *N.Y. State Ass'n Real Est. Bd. Group Ins. Fund* v. *Commissioner*, 54 T.C. 1325 (1970); *Angelus Funeral Home* v. Commissioner, 47 T.C. 391 (1967), aff'd 407 F.2d 210 (9th Cir. 1969), cert. den. 396 U. S. 824 (1969).

[48]See, e.g., Rev. Rul. 75–258, 1975–2 C.B. 503, where the IRS ruled that the "Family Estate" trust is an association taxable as a corporation under Code § 7701 and Rev. Rul. 77–214, 1977–1 C.B. 408, where the IRS determined that a certain type of German unincorporated business organization ("Gesellschaft mit beschrankter Haftung" or "GmbH") is taxable as a corporation. Also, the U. S. Tax Court has concluded that real estate syndicates organized under the California limited partnership act are associations to be taxable as corporations with the meaning of Code § 7701 (a)(3). *Larson* v. *Commissioner*, 65 T.C. No. 10 (1975) (withdrawn), 66 T.C. 159 (1976). In general, see *Morrissey* v. *Commissioner*, 296 U. S. 344 (1935); Reg. § 301.7701–2(a)(1).

[49]Rev. Rul. 74–21, 1974–1 C.B. 14.

[50]See Code §§ 41 (as amended), 84, 2501(a)(5).

[51]See Chapter 20.

[52]Rev. Rul. 72–355, 1972–2 C.B. 532; Rev. Rul 74–199, 1974–1 C.B. 285.

[53]See *Tax Analysts and Advocates* v. *Shultz*, 376 F.Supp. 889 (D.D.C. 1974), aff'd 75–1 U.S.T.C. ¶ 13,052 (D.C. Cir. 1975).

[54]Code § 2501(a)(5).

Thus, to be exempt from federal income taxation, an organization generally must make an affirmative effort to be recognized as exempt from tax, operate as a cooperative, legally marshall deductions against income, or seek a change in the law. Otherwise, it is nearly certain that the entity will be liable for tax as a taxable corporation.

3

Criticisms of Tax Exemption and Charitable Contribution Deductions

The related concepts of tax exemption and deductions for charitable giving in the tax structure of the United States are receiving increasing attention and review and, in some quarters, criticism. The focus is by far on those organizations exempt under Code § 501(a) as described in Code § 501(c)(3), which are eligible to attract deductible charitable contributions under Code § 170(c)(2). The technicalities of Code provisions aside, what is at stake in this continuing tax "reform" dialog is the role of "charity" in the American society in the future. Stated another way, many are reexamining the approaches to charity built into the U. S. tax system and speculating on alternative approaches: further encouragement, redirection of the charitable dollar, other means of stimulating giving, or abandonment of the charitable gift as a tax-related event altogether.

§ 3.1 Criticisms in General

The pressure on tax exemption is severe, though the charitable contribution deduction is being subjected to an even greater barrage. The reasons for this stem largely from the need of government, on all levels, for additional revenues. Tax exemption shrinks the tax base, forcing the remaining taxpayers to bear an increasing tax burden as the demand for tax revenue rises. This is most vividly demonstrated in metropolitan centers, where acres of valuable land owned by government, churches, and the like escape property taxation, forcing such taxation at higher rates on adjoining parcels.

Aside from the drain on government revenues, tax exemption is frequently attacked as being a "loophole." Probably the best example of this attitude is that widely held of private foundations, particularly in the years immediately preceding the 1969 reforms.[1]

The Commission on Private Philanthropy and Public Needs (Filer Commission) summarized the challenges to the federal income tax charitable contribution deduction as follows:

> The charitable deduction has been part of the tax law since 1917, four years after the income tax itself became a basic fixture of American life. It was instituted to sustain the level of giving in the face of new steep tax rates and because it was held that personal income that went to charitable purposes should not be taxed because it did not enrich the giver. These remain the two principal rationales of the charitable deduction, under which a contributor can subtract the amount of yearly giving from income upon which income taxes are computed. In recent years, however, partly as a result of a growing tendency to look at tax immunities as forms of government subsidy, the charitable deduction has been criticized, along with other personal income tax deductions, as inequitable. This is because, under the progressive income tax, the higher the deductor's tax bracket, the greater the tax savings he or she receives from taking a deduction. Thus, high tax bracket contributors have a significantly greater incentive to give than those at the other end of the income scale.
>
> At the same time that the charitable deduction is being challenged philosophically, it is being eroded, in very concrete terms, by liberalizations of the standard deduction, the income tax provision that allows taxpayers to deduct a set amount or a proportion of their income in lieu of taking specific, itemized deductions. The maximum standard deduction has increased greatly in recent years—from $1,000 for a couple in 1970 to $2,600 in 1975. This has so diminished the advantage of taking itemized deductions that as of 1975's returns less than one third of all taxpayers are expected to be taking the charitable deduction.[2]

At any rate, the tax exemption is generally deemed worthy of continuance, despite the revenue "loss" and occasional abuses, because of the basic acceptance of the importance of individual, pluralistic endeavors in our society.[3] Moreover, the U.S. tax laws contain increasingly sophisticated rules for taxation of income derived by exempt organizations from nonexempt sources.[4]

§ 3.2 Charitable Contribution Rules

As the following pages indicate, the tax laws pertaining to tax exemption and deductible giving are closely intertwined, the more so since enactment of the Tax Reform Act of 1969.[5] Many exempt organizations, especially those that are charitable in nature, are heavily dependent upon contributions for their

[1]See Chapter 21.

[2]*Giving in America—Toward a Stronger Voluntary Sector* 18 (1975).

[3]See Chapter 1.

[4]See Chapters 40–43.

[5]See Golden, "Charitable Giving in the 70's: The Impact of the 1969 Act," 48 *Taxes* 787 (1970).

activities. Without the continuous gift dollar, nearly all charitable organizations would be severely crippled and some would wither away.

The basic concept of the federal income tax charitable contribution deduction is that an individual taxpayer who itemizes deductions and corporate taxpayers can deduct, subject to varying limitations, an amount equivalent to the value of a contribution made to a qualified donee. A "charitable contribution" for income tax purposes is a gift to or for the use of one or more qualified donees.

Aside from the nature of the donee, the other basic element in determining whether a charitable contribution is deductible is the nature of the property given. Basically, the distinctions are between current giving and deferred giving, between gifts of cash and of property, and between outright gifts and those of partial interests or in trust. The value of a qualified charitable contribution generally is its fair market value.[6]

The deductibility of charitable contributions is confined by certain percentage limitations, which in the case of individuals are a function of the taxpayer's "contribution base," which is essentially the same as adjusted gross income.[7] These percentage limitations are (1) 50 percent of contribution base in any taxable year for contributions to public charities and certain private foundations,[8] (2) 20 percent of contribution base for contributions to organizations other than the 50 percent charities, including most private foundations,[9] (3) 30 percent of contribution base for contributions of appreciated property to public charities,[10] and (4) 50 percent of contribution base for contributions of appreciated property to public charities where the amount of the contribution is reduced by 40 percent of unrealized appreciation.[11]

Deductible charitable contributions by corporations in any tax year beginning after December 31, 1981, may not exceed 10 percent of taxable income, as adjusted; for prior years the limitation is 5 percent of corporate taxable income.[12] A corporation on the accrual method of accounting can elect to treat a contribution as having been paid in a tax year if it is actually paid during the first 2½ months of the following year.[13] While corporate gifts of property are generally subject to the rules discussed below, special rules apply to the deductibility of gifts of inventory.[14] The making of a charitable gift by a business corporation is not an *ultra vires* act and may be deductible where the general interests of the corporation and its shareholders are advanced.[15]

[6]Reg. § 1.170A–1(c).
[7]Code § 170(b)(1)(E).
[8]Code § 170(b)(1)(A). See Chapters 22 and 23.
[9]Code § 170(b)(1)(B).
[10]Code § 170(b)(1)(C)(i).
[11]Code § 170(b)(1)(C)(iii).
[12]Code § 170(b)(2).
[13]Code § 170(a)(2).
[14]Code § 170(e)(3).
[15]See, e.g., *A. P. Smith Mfg. Co.* v. *Barlow*, 98 A.2d 581 (Sup. Ct. N.J. 1953), app. dis. 346 U.S. 861 (1953).

The tax treatment of gifts of property is dependent upon whether the property is "capital gain property," that is, a capital asset, appreciated in value, which if sold would result in long-term capital gain.[16] If not, the property is "ordinary income property" (including short-term capital gain property).

A donor (individual or corporate) who makes a gift of ordinary income property to any charity (public or private) must reduce the deduction by the full amount of any gain.[17] Any donor who makes a gift of capital gain property to a public charity generally can compute the deduction at the property's fair market value at the time of the gift, regardless of basis and with no taxation of the appreciation.[18] An individual donor who makes a gift of capital gain tangible personalty to a public charity must reduce the deduction by 40 percent (28/46 in the case of corporations) of the long-term capital gain which would have been recognized had the donor sold the property at its fair market value as of the date of contribution, where the use by the donee is unrelated to its exempt purposes.[19] An individual donor who makes a gift of capital gain property to a private foundation must reduce the deduction by 40 percent of the appreciation (28/46 in the case of corporations).[20]

A deduction for a contribution of less than the donor's entire interest in property (that is, a partial interest), including the right to use property, is generally denied.[21] The exceptions are gifts of interests in trust,[22] gifts of an outright remainder interest in a personal residence or farm,[23] gifts of an undivided portion of one's entire interest in property,[24] gifts of a lease on, option to purchase, or easement with respect to real property granted in perpetuity to a public charity exclusively for conservation purposes,[25] and a remainder interest in real property which is granted to a public charity exclusively for conservation purposes.[26]

Contributions of income interests in property in trust are basically confined to the use of charitable lead trusts.[27] Aside from the charitable gift annuity and gifts of remainder interests in personal residences or farms, there is no deduction for a contribution of a remainder interest in property unless it is in

---

[16]Code § 170(b)(1)(C)(iv).
[17]Code § 170(e)(1)(A). See, e.g., Code § 1221(3).
[18]Code § 170(e).
[19]Code § 170(e)(1)(B)(i).
[20]Code § 170(e)(1)(B)(ii).
[21]Code § 170(f)(3).
[22]Code § 170(f)(3)(A).
[23]Code § 170(f)(3)(B)(i).
[24]Code § 170(f)(3)(B)(ii).
[25]Code § 170(f)(3)(B)(iii).
[26]Code § 170(f)(3)(B)(iv).
[27]Code § 170(f)(2)(B).

trust and the trust is one of three types[28]: a charitable remainder annuity trust or unitrust[29] or a pooled income fund.[30]

Other notable features of the income tax charitable contribution deduction are the carryover rules,[31] the phase-out of the "unlimited deduction,"[32] lack of deduction for contributions of services,[33] and the requirement of the filing of an information return with respect to certain transfers of income-producing property to charity.[34]

Charitable gifts are not subject to the gift tax[35] nor to the estate tax.[36] There is no percentage ceiling on the amount of an estate that may be subject to the estate tax charitable deduction and appreciated property may pass to charity from estates without any taxation on the appreciation element.[37]

§ 3.3   The "Equity" Argument

Of the criticisms of the income tax charitable contribution deduction, the one generating the most approbation falls under the rubic of "equity." In essence, the complaint is that a taxpayer in the 50 percent tax bracket has 50 percent of his or her charitable gift "subsidized" by the federal government, while a taxpayer in the 30 percent tax bracket can only avail himself or herself of a 30 percent "subsidy" and the taxpayer using the standard deduction receives no "subsidy" at all. The catch-phrase here is "directing federal funds," meaning that the high-income donor can allegedly unilaterally "direct" a substantial portion of federal funds (that is, the revenues "lost" because of the deduction) to a chosen charitable purpose, while the lower-income taxpayer cannot or at least can do so only to a lesser extent.

Two principal solutions are being propounded to restore "equity" to the income tax charitable contribution deduction. One is to substitute a tax credit for the deduction, in an effort to "democratize" the tax benefit derived from charitable giving, by equalizing the tax advantage for taxpayers in all brackets,

---

[28]Code § 170(f)(2)(A).
[29]Code § 664(d).
[30]Code § 642(c)(5).
[31]Code § 170(d).
[32]Code § 170(f)(6), 170(g).
[33]Reg. § 1.170A–1(g).
[34]Code § 6050.
[35]Code § 2522.
[36]Code § 2055.
[37]Enactment of the Economic Recovery Tax Act of 1981 wrought many changes in the federal tax law relating to charitable giving. These changes are the subject of a separate volume by the author, *Charitable Giving and Tax-Exempt Organizations: The Impact of the 1981 Tax Act* (New York: John Wiley & Sons, 1982).

including those who do not itemize deductions.[38] However, it must be recognized that a tax credit for charitable giving would reallocate charitable dollars—away from education, the arts, and cultural institutions (for example, museums) and to religious groups and the social service agencies.

§ 3.4   The "Matching Grant" Argument

The second solution to the allegedly iniquitous feature of the charitable deduction requires a belief that its effect is comparable to that of a federal "matching grant" program.[39] That is, the proponents of this approach contend that a donor in the 50 percent tax bracket who gives $100 really only gives $50, while the government "matches" his or her gift with $50. Thus, the adherents of this approach would scrap the charitable deduction and institute a formal matching grant system, where a donor to charity would have his or her gift matched by the government, up to varying limitations. The matching grant approach would have a reallocation effect similar to that of the credit approach, although the champions of such a matching grant program say that Congress would appropriate funds directly to those educational and charitable organizations whose gift revenues are thereby reduced. The pressures and demands on the federal budget and the formidable task of securing sufficient and continuous appropriations, however, offer scant hope for full "restoration" of funds to those charities not favored by matched contributions.

§ 3.5   Filer Commission Recommendations

The recommendations of the Commission on Private Philanthropy and Public Needs as respects the charitable contribution deduction are as follows:

The Commission examined the existing governmental inducement to giving and considered several proposed alternatives, including tax credits for giving and matching grant systems. In doing so, it kept these six objectives in mind:

—To increase the number of people who contribute significantly to and participate in nonprofit activities.

[38]See Davies, "The Charitable Contributions Credit: A Proposal to Replace Section 501(c)(3) Tax-Exempt Organizations," 58 Cornell L. Rev. 304 (1973); McDaniel, "Alternatives to Utilization of the Federal Income Tax System to Meet Social Problems," 11 B.C. Ind. & Com. L. Rev. 867 (1970).
[39]See Bittker, "Charitable Contributions: Tax Deductions or Matching Grants?," 28 Tax L. Rev. 27 (1972); McDaniel, "Federal Matching Grants for Charitable Contributions: A Substitute for the Income Tax Deduction," 27 Tax L. Rev. 377 (1972); McDaniel, "Federal Financial Assistance to Charity: An Alternative to the Tax Deduction," 55 Mass. L.Q. 243 (1970). Also see Brown, "Towards Equity and Efficiency in Federal Taxation," 36 Univ. Pittsburg L. Rev. 835 (1975); Freeman and Baland, "The Rich Get Richer and the Poor Get Taxes: Toward a Democratic Theory of Tax Reform," 2 Hastings Const. L.Q. 681 (1975).

—To increase the amount of giving.

—To increase the inducements to giving by those in low- and middle-income brackets.

—To preserve private choice in giving.

—To minimize income losses of nonprofit organizations that depend on the current pattern of giving.

—To be as "efficient" as possible. In other words, any stimulus to giving should not cost significantly more in foregone government revenue than the amount of giving actually stimulated.

A. Continuing The Deduction

In light of these criteria, the Commission believes that the charitable deduction should be retained and added onto rather than replaced by another form of governmental encouragement to giving. The Commission affirms the basic philosophical rationale of the deduction, that giving should not be taxed because, unlike other uses of income, it does not enrich the disburser. Also, the deduction is a proven mechanism familiar to donor and donee, easy to administrate and less likely than credits or matching grants to run afoul of constitutional prohibitions as far as donations to religious organizations are concerned.

The deduction has been shown, furthermore, to be a highly "efficient" inducement. Computerized econometric analyses based on available tax and income data were made for the Commission and they indicate that for every dollar of taxes uncollected because of the charitable deduction, more than one dollar in giving is stimulated. The Commission's sample survey of taxpayers also indicates that itemizers who take the charitable deduction give substantially more, at every income level, than nonitemizers.

The deduction is seen as inviting the least amount of government involvement in influencing the direction of giving. And, finally, eliminating the deduction or replacing it with a tax credit or matching grant system would significantly shift giving away from several current recipient areas at a time when these areas are already undergoing severe economic strains.

B. Extending And Amplifying The Deduction

The Commission recognizes that the charitable deduction is used by fewer and fewer taxpayers—now fewer than one third—because of the liberalized standard deduction. So, to broaden the reach of the charitable deduction and to increase giving, the Commission recommends:

> That all taxpayers who take the standard deduction should also be permitted to deduct charitable contributions as an additional, itemized deduction.

This extension of the deduction would, it is calculated, provide an inducement to give to nearly 60 million nonitemizers, and would thereby result in increased giving, according to econometric projections, of $1.9 billion in 1976 dollars.

This amount is still relatively modest in terms of the amount of giving that would be needed to restore giving to its level in 1960 before its decline in relative purchasing power set in—an increase in giving, in current dollars, of around $8 billion would be required. Moreover, while extending the deduction to nonitemizers would provide many millions of taxpayers with some inducement to give, the inducement would still be tied to the progressive rate structure of the income tax and would be markedly lower at low- and middle-income levels that it is at upper levels. Therefore, the Commission recommends as an additional new incentive for low- and middle-income contributors:

That families with incomes below $15,000 a year be allowed to deduct twice the amount of their giving, and those with incomes between $15,000 and $30,000 be allowed to deduct 150 percent of what they contribute.

The "double deduction" and the 150 per cent deduction would have the effect of doubling the proportion of tax savings for charitable giving for low-income families and increasing the proportion by one half for middle-income families and would thus appreciably narrow the range in savings between these brackets and high-income taxpayers. The amount of giving induced and the efficiency of inducing it might, moreover, be impressive. According to econometric projections, $9.8 billion more in giving would be stimulated, at a cost of only $7.4 billion in tax revenue lost.

C. INCREASING CORPORATE GIVING

Corporate giving is still a relatively new element in American philanthropy; the corporate charitable deduction itself has been in effect only for forty years. And there are those on both the left and right who question whether corporations should be involved in philanthropy at all. While recognizing that such can only be a minor element in the corporation's role in society, the Commission also notes that only 20 per cent of corporate taxpayers in 1970 reported any charitable contributions and only 6 per cent made contributions of over $500. The record of corporate giving is an unimpressive and inadequate one, the Commission believes. Therefore, the Commission recommends:

That corporations set as a minimum goal, to be reached no later than 1980, the giving to charitable purposes of 2 per cent of pre-tax income, and that further studies of means to stimulate corporate giving be pursued.[40]

§ 3.6   Tax Expenditures

Perhaps the development that has most singlehandedly threatened the present-day tax treatment of the charitable contribution is the growing respectability of the "tax expenditures" concept.[41] This concept has come to the fore because of the search for additional sources of tax revenues and Congress' recent zeal for reclaiming a meaningful control over the budget formulation and priorities-

---

[40]*Supra*, n. 2, at 19–21.

[41]See Surrey, *Pathways to Tax Reform* (1974); Surrey, "Federal Income Tax Reform: The Varied Approaches Necessary to Replace Tax Expenditures with Direct Governmental Assistance," 84 *Harv. L. Rev.* 352 (1970); Surrey, "Tax Incentives as a Device for Implementing Government Policy: A Comparison with Direct Government Expenditures," 83 *Harv. L. Rev.* 705 (1969); Bittker, "Accounting for Federal 'Tax Subsidies' in the National Budget," 22 *Nat. Tax J.* 244 (1969), Surrey and Hellmuth reply, 22 *Nat. Tax J.* 244 (1969), Bittker reply, *Nat. Tax J.* 528 (1969).

setting processes. In essence, "tax expenditures" are revenue "losses" attributable to tax deductions, exemptions, preferential tax rates, deferrals of tax liability, exclusions, and credits. The charitable contribution, then, is treated as merely one of many tax expenditures but is jeopardized by the regarding of it as the cause of revenue "losses," which is frequently done without due regard for the positive aspects of private charitable works (the furtherance of pluralism and the like) and the greater efficiency of the privately spent dollar compared to the governmentally spent dollar, although both are for public ends.[42]

Long the subject of approval in the literature, the tax expenditures concept was given congressional sanction in the Congressional Budget Act enacted in 1974. This Act directs the Budget Committees of the U.S. Senate and House of Representatives to study and devise methods of coordinating tax expenditures with direct congressional appropriations. Also, under House rules revisions adopted in 1974, each of its standing committees now has the task of analyzing the probable impact of tax policy affecting the subject matter within the committee's jurisdiction. As a result of the 1974 Budget Act, tax expenditures were presented for the first time in the President's budget request, for fiscal year 1976.

With the tax expenditures approach, economists try to ascertain the revenue the federal government has foregone by category of deduction, exemption, credit and the like; the sums thus derived are frequently referred to as the results of "back-door spending." While the tax expenditures concept is a useful budgetary evaluation and planning tool, it generates much misunderstanding when applied to the charitable deduction. The tax revenues ostensibly "lost" by virtue of the charitable deduction are not "lost" at all but are devoted to public ends, albeit more efficiently than the federally spent dollar. (Research performed for the Filer Commission shows that, for each $1.00 that the federal government "loses" because of the charitable deduction, the charitable sector gains between $1.15 and $1.29, depending upon the donor's tax bracket.)

However, a focus on this subject solely from an economic standpoint is, in the author's opinion, inappropriate. The issue is the vitality and future of this nation's voluntary sector. The heritage and political philosophy of this country strongly emphasizes individual initiative and private institutions working for public ends. Pluralism and voluntarism are what the charitable deduction is all about; it is private giving stimulated by tax incentives that fuels our nonprofit institutions and agencies. The issue in connection with continuation of the charitable contribution deduction comes down to whether this nation's private sector is to have a role in the allocation of resources to public purposes—the definition of a free society—or whether all of the decisions are going to be made, priorities set, and monies expended by the national government.

---

[42]There is nothing particularly innovative about this concept; in *State v. Alabama Education Foundation*, 163 So. 527 (Sup. Ct. Ala. 1935), the court expressed the view that "[t]o exempt from taxation is akin to appropriating the amount of the tax" (at 531).

§ 3.7 Other "Reforms"

Other proposals to "reform" the charitable contribution deduction include the following: (1) availing taxpayers of an optional credit or deduction approach, (2) place a "floor" under the deduction, such as 3 percent (like the medical deduction), and (3) subject the appreciation element in property given to charity to tax at the time of the gift (like gifts to political organizations).

The estate tax charitable contribution deduction does not generate nearly as much attention as the income tax deduction, although proposed revisions in this area include taxation of unrealized appreciation in property passing to charity by bequests and devises and placing a ceiling (for example, 50 percent of the estate) on the amount of the deduction.

Some are urging that the private foundation rules, particularly those with respect to excess business holdings and self-dealing,[43] be imposed upon public charities.[44] However, even if these rules are modified to take account of the very different situation obtaining with respect to public charities, the imposition of these rules and others (for example, jeopardizing investments)[45] could, at a minimum, greatly increase the liability of trustees and officers for their actions taken as such in the management of colleges, universities, hospitals, and other public charities.

While many of these reforms do not lend themselves to precise policy formulations and statistical analyses, the recommendations of the Commission on Private Philanthropy and Public Needs[46] may be quite influential in providing a definitive rationale and justification for many features of the present system of tax exemptions and charitable deductions, and may chart the course for future legislative action in these areas. Congress in the 1980's, may enact reforms in these fields having dramatic impact on the whole of the philanthropic concept, perhaps nearly as extensive as the sweeping changes wrought in 1969.

[43]See Chapters 25 and 27.
[44]See Chapter 35.
[45]See Chapter 28.
[46]See Chapter 1.

PART II

CHARITABLE
ORGANIZATIONS

4

Scope of Term "Charitable"

Organizations exempt from federal income tax under Code § 501(c)(3) are popularly referred to simply as "charitable" organizations. The pertinent portion of Code § 501(c)(3) provides exemption for:

> Corporations, and any community chest, fund or foundation, organized and operated exclusively for religious, charitable, scientific, testing for public safety, literary, or educational purposes, or to foster national or international amateur sports competition (but only if no part of its activities involve the provision of athletic facilities or equipment), or for the prevention of cruelty to children or animals . . .

The term "charitable" is often used in this broader context notwithstanding the fact that "charitable" is only one of the eight descriptive words and phrases used in the federal tax law to describe the various organizations of Code § 501(c)(3). That is, the term "charitable" may be considered a generic term and, in its expansive sense, may be read to include "religious," "scientific," "educational," and like purposes.[1]

The use of the term "charitable" to describe all Code § 501(c)(3) organizations has arisen in part because, with one exception, all Code § 501(c)(3) organizations are also qualified charitable donees[2] and thus are eligible to attract charitable contributions which are deductible for federal tax purposes. (The exception is public safety testing organizations.) Thus, the focus of this chapter is on the parameters of the term "charitable" as it is used to portray all of the organizations described in Code § 501(c)(3).

---

[1] See *United States* v. *Proprietors of Social Law Library*, 102 F.2d 481 (1st Cir. 1939). Frequently, therefore, throughout the text of this book, the term "charitable" will be used to reference any category of organization described in Code § 501(c)(3).

[2] Code § 170(c)(2) (income tax exemption), § 2055(a)(2) (estate tax exemption), § 2522(b)(2) (gift tax exemption).

§ 4.1   Legal Definitions of Term "Charitable"

Most individuals, when they formulate a definition of the term "charitable," conceive of the "soup kitchen" meaning of the term, namely, aid to the destitute. This is usually their exclusive perception of "charity." Thus, individuals frequently do not regard their churches, synagogues, universities, colleges, hospitals, and similar institutions as "charitable" entities—even though they receive a "charitable" deduction for the gift support they provide.

This concept of "charity" is known in the law as the "popular and ordinary" usage of the term. In this setting, the word "charitable" means "relief of the poor."

The term "charitable" has been given formal recognition in the law for centuries, as the term emanates from the common law of charitable trusts. This definition is rather broad, meaning essentially that a function promoting the general welfare is "charitable." The general rule is that the word "charitable" at common law encompassed "trusts for the relief of poverty; trusts for the advancement of education, trusts for the advancement of religion; and trusts for other purposes beneficial to the community, not falling under any of the preceding heads."[3]

A corollary of this definition is that an organization that in some manner violates "public policy" cannot be "charitable."[4]

§ 4.2   Historical Background

The term "charitable," under the English common law, was a most encompassing term, yet it remained a definable legal concept. The definition of the term "charitable" dates back to the definition of charitable purposes in the Preamble to the Statute of Charitable Uses of 1601.[5] The Statute itself is based upon holdings of the English Court of Chancery before 1601 and upon earlier experiences (such as the Codes of Justinian) of previous civilizations including those of Rome and Greece and in early Judaism, as well as in many other early cultures and religions. (In the Bible, for example, one reads "also we certify you, that, touching any of the priests and Levites, singers, porters, Nethinim, or Ministers of this House of God, it shall not be lawful to impose toll, tribute, or customs upon them."[6] The Statute enumerates certain "charitable" purposes, as follows:

> . . . some for relief of aged, impotent and poor people, some for maintenance of sick and maimed soldiers and mariners, schools of learning, free schools, and scholars in universities, some for repair of bridges, ports, havens, causeways, churches, seabanks and highways, some for education and preferment of orphans, some for or towards relief, stock or maintenance for houses of correction, some for marriages of poor maids, some for supportation, aid and help of young trades-

---

[3]*Commissioners for Special Purposes of Income Tax* v. *Pemsel*, A.C. 531, 583 (1891).

[4]See *Green* v. *Connally*, 330 F. Supp. 1150 (D.D.C. 1971), aff'd sub nom. *Coit* v. *Green*, 404 U.S. 997 (1971).

[5]Stat. 43 Eliz. I, c.4.

[6]Ezra 7:24.

men, handicraftsmen and persons decayed, and others for relief or redemption of prisoners or captives, and for aid or ease of any poor inhabitants concerning payments of fifteens, setting out of soldiers and other taxes.

These and other classifications of the concept of charity were discussed by Lord Macnaghten in 1891, who said:

Of all words in the English language bearing a popular as well as a legal significance I am not sure that there is one which more unmistakably has a technical meaning in the strictest sense of the term, that is a meaning clear and distinct, peculiar to the law as understood and administered in this country, and not depending upon or coterminous with the popular or vulgar use of the word.[7]

Lord Macnaghten's discussion has been cited with approval by the U.S. Supreme Court.[8]

The English common law concept of "philanthropic" is considerably broader than the term "charitable." The basic opinion on this point was authored in 1896, wherein Lindley, L.J., wrote: "Philanthropy and benevolence both include charity; but they go further, and include more than mere charitable purposes. 'Philanthropic' is a very wide word, and includes many things which are only for the pleasure of the world, and cannot be called 'charitable.' "[9] In the case, Sterling, J., wrote that the word "philanthropic," in meaning "goodwill to mankind at large," is "wide enough to comprise purposes which are not charitable in the technical sense."[10] This approach is traceable into the common law of the United States.[11]

Consequently, the categories of organizations described in Code § 501(c)(3) may be referred to on occasion as "philanthropic" or also as "benevolent" or "eleemosynary."[12] These terms, however, are generally regarded, from a legal standpoint, as inappropriate for Code § 501(c)(3) organizations, as being less descriptive, being too broad, or invoking peculiarities of local law.[13] The term

[7]*Commissioners for Special Purposes of Income Tax* v. *Pemsel, supra, n, 3.*

[8]*Evans* v. *Newton*, 382 U. S. 296, 303 (1966). In general, see Bogart, *Trusts and Trustees* § 369.

[9]2 Ch. 451, 459 (1896).

[10]*Ibid.* at 457.

[11]See, e.g., *Drury* v. *Inhabitants of Natick*, 10 Allen 169 (Mass. 1865). A minority view evident in English common law and reflected in U. S. cases was that the terms "philanthropic" and "charitable" are synonymous. *Commissioners for Special Purposes of Income Tax* v. *Pemsel, supra*, n. 3; *Jackson* v. *Phillips*, 14 Allen 539 (Mass. 1867); *Rotch* v. *Emerson*, 105 Mass. 431 (1870).

[12]In general, see Clark, "Charitable Trusts, the Fourteenth Amendment and the Will of Stephen Girard," 66 *Yale L. J.* 979 (1957).

[13]See *Westchester County Society for Prevention of Cruelty to Animals* v. *Mengel*, 54 N.E. 329, 330 (Ct. App. N.Y. 1944); *Schall* v. *Commissioner*, 174 F.2d 893, 894 (5th Cir. 1949); *Allebach* v. *City of Friend*, 226 N.W. 440, 441 (Sup. Ct. Neb. 1929); *In re Downer's Estate*, 142 A. 78 (Sup. Ct. Ver. 1938); *Thorp* v. *Lund*, 116 N.E. 946 (Sup. Ct. Mass. 1917).

"charitable," then, has a legal meaning and is regarded as a term of art, while terms such as "philanthropy" remain popularized words lacking in legal significance.[14]

§ 4.3   Federal Tax Law Definition of "Charity"

Congress, in enacting and perpetuating tax exemption for organizations now described in Code § 501(c)(3), did not and has not given much guidance as to whether it was influenced by the common law definition of the term "charitable" or the use of that term in its "popular and ordinary" sense. This fact has two ramifications: the meaning to be ascribed to the term "charitable" as used in Code § 501(c)(3) and whether the entirety of that section is intended to describe organizations that are in some sense "charitable."

As to the latter point, the matter can be regarded as an exercise in construing the statute itself. That is, pursuant to the canons of statutory construction, the search for congressional intent is to begin with the express words of the statute.[15]

The provision—Code § 501(c)(3)—describes as organizations that are eligible for federal income tax exemption those that are "organized and operated exclusively for" eight specifically enumerated purposes or functions. These purposes or functions include those that are considered "charitable," "educational," "religious," and "scientific." However—and this is absolutely fundamental to those who in these regards place heavy emphasis on the statutory construction argument—the enumeration of the exempt functions or purposes is framed in the disjunctive: the law describes "religious, charitable, scientific . . . or educational purposes . . ." This use of the disjunctive can be regarded as evidence of congressional intent to accord tax exemption to any organization organized and operated for any *one* of the designated purposes or functions. As the U.S. Supreme Court has noted: "Canons of construction ordinarily suggest that terms connected by a disjunctive be given separate meanings, unless the context dictates otherwise."[16] Thus, the distinct references in Code § 501(c)(3) to "charitable" *or* "educational" *or* "scientific" *or* like organizations can be read as confirming "Congress' intent that [for example] not all educational institutions must also be charitable institutions (as that term was used in the common law) in order to receive tax-exempt status."[17]

There is another applicable canon of statutory construction, which is that related statutory provisions should be interpreted together.[18] This has consid-

---

[14]See Bogert, *Trusts and Trustees* § 370.

[15]For example, *Northwest Airlines, Inc.* v. *Transport Workers Union*, 451 U.S. 77 (1981); *United States* v. *Oregon*, 366 U.S. 643 (1961).

[16]*Reiter* v. *Sonotone Corp.*, 442 U.S. 330, 339 (1979).

[17]*Prince Edward School Foundation* v. *United States*, 450 U.S. 944, 947 (1981) (dissent from denial of certiorari).

[18]For example, *Kokoska* v. *Belford*, 417 U.S. 642 (1974); *United States* v. *Cooper Corp.*, 312 U.S. 600 (1941).

erable relevance in this context, inasmuch as sister provisions of Code § 501(c)(3) (both those in existence and those since repealed) reiterate the separate and disjunctive purposes or functions described in Code § 501(c)(3).[19] The principal one of these sister provisions is Code § 170(c)(2)(B), which defines the term "charitable contribution" for purposes of the federal income tax charitable contribution deduction. This provision also recites the eight separate and independent categories of exempt functions, thereby providing further support for the proposition that Congress intended to recognize each category of purpose or function enumerated in Code § 501(c)(3) as distinct bases for tax exemption.[20]

Thus, one can argue that, in Code § 501(c)(3) and its sister provisions, Congress "has spoken in the plainest of words"[21] in intending to accord tax exemption to any organization organized and operated exclusively for any one of the purposes or functions enumerated in Code § 501(c)(3).

A review of the legislative history of the tax law provisions according tax exemption and eligibility to receive deductible contributions to charitable, educational and like organizations[22] provides support for a construction of these provisions that leads to the conclusion that each of the eight exempt purposes is an independent basis for qualification for the two tax benefits.[23]

The tax exemptions contained in Code § 501(c)(3) originated as a part of the Tariff Act of 1894.[24] The provision stated that "nothing herein contained shall apply to . . . corporations, companies, or associations organized and conducted solely for charitable, religious, or educational purposes."[25]

After ratification of the Sixteenth Amendment, Congress enacted the Tariff Act of 1913, exempting from the income tax "any corporation or association organized and operated exclusively for religious, charitable, scientific, or ed-

---

[19]For example, phraseology in the disjunctive similar to that in Code § 501(c)(3) can be found in Code §§ 503(b)(3) (references to Code § 501(c)(3) organizations repealed in 1969), 504(a)(1) and (3) (repealed in 1969), 513(a) (defining the term "unrelated trade or business"), 2055(a)(2) (estate tax charitable contribution deduction), and 2522(a)(2) (gift tax charitable contribution deduction).

[20]A contrasting argument is stated in *Bob Jones University* v. *United States*, 639 F.2d 147 (4th Cir. 1980), where, in part because contributions to all organizations described in Code § 170(c)(2)(B) are referred to as "charitable contributions," the court concluded that each of the separately enumerated purposes are to be considered as within a broad classification of "charitable."

[21]*TVA* v. *Hill*, 437 U.S. 153, 194 (1978).

[22]Code §§ 501(c)(3) and 170(c)(2)(B), respectively.

[23]Those who contend that the language of Code §§ 170(c)(2)(B) and 501(c)(3) is facially clear on this point also assert that such clarity makes an examination of the legislative history of Code § 501(c)(3) unnecessary. For example, *Ernst & Ernst* v. *Hochfelder*, 425 U.S. 199 (1976); *United States* v. *Oregon*, 366 U.S. 643 (1961).

[24]28 Stat. 556 (Act ch. 349).

[25]The income tax enacted in 1894 was declared unconstitutional by the Supreme Court in *Pollock* v. *Farmers' Loan And Trust Co.*, 158 U.S. 601 (1895).

ucational purposes, no part of the net income of which inures to the benefit of any private shareholder or individual."[26]

In the Revenue Act of 1918, the enumeration of exempt organizations was expanded to include those organized "for the prevention of cruelty to children or animals."[27] The Revenue Act of 1921 expanded the statute to exempt "any community chest, fund, or foundation" and added "literary" groups to the list of exempt entities.[28] The Revenue Acts of 1924,[29] 1926,[30] 1928,[31] and 1932[32] did not provide for any changes in the law of tax-exempt organizations.

The Revenue Act of 1934 carried forward the exemption requirements as stated in the prior revenue measures and added the rule that "no substantial part" of the activities of an exempt organization can involve the carrying on of "propaganda" or "attempting to influence legislation."[33] The Revenue Acts of 1936[34] and 1938[35] brought forward these same rules, as did the Internal Revenue Code of 1939.[36]

Code § 501(c)(3) came into being upon enactment of the Internal Revenue Code in 1954.[37] The previous rules were retained and two additions to the statute were made: the listing of tax-exempt organizations was amplified to include entities that are organized and operated for the purpose of "testing for public safety" and organizations otherwise described in Code § 501(c)(3) became expressly forbidden to "participate in, or intervene in (including the publishing or distributing of statements), any political campaign on behalf of any candidate for public office."

Subsequent revisions of Code § 501, in relation to Code § 501(c)(3), were enactment, as part of the Revenue and Expenditure Control Act of 1968, of the requirements for "cooperative hospital service organizations"[38] and enactment of the rules for "cooperative service organizations of operating educational organizations",[39] and the addition, by enactment of the Tax Reform Act of 1976, to the listing of tax-exempt organizations of those that "foster national or international sports competition (but only if no part of its activities involve the

[26]38 Stat. 114, 166 (Act ch. 16, Section II(G)(a)).
[27]40 Stat. 1076 (Act ch. 18, Section 231(6)).
[28]42 Stat. 253 (Act ch. 136, Section 231(6)).
[29]43 Stat. 282 (Act ch. 234, Section 231(6)).
[30]44 Stat. 40 (Act ch. 27, Section 231(6)).
[31]45 Stat. 813 (Act ch. 852, Section 103(6)).
[32]47 Stat. 193 (Act ch. 209, Section 103(6)).
[33]48 Stat. 700 (Act ch. 277, Section 101(6)).
[34]49 Stat. 1674 (Act ch. 690, Section 101(6)).
[35]52 Stat. 481 (Act ch. 289, Section 101(6)).
[36]53 Stat. 1 (ch. 2).
[37]68A Stat. 163 (ch. 736).
[38]82 Stat. 269 (Act Title I, Section 109).
[39]88 Stat. 235 (Act Section 3).

provision of athletic facilities or equipment)[40] and of rules providing "safe harbor" guidelines for measuring permissible legislative activities.[41]

For example, it can be readily asserted that if Congress had intended that all organizations now embraced by Code § 501(c)(3) must qualify as charitable entities in the common law sense of the term, it would not have made reference in 1894 to "charitable, religious, or educational purposes," since the references to "religious" and "educational" purposes would have been subsumed within the references to the term "charitable." Likewise, the subsequent additions of the references to "scientific" purposes (in 1913), the "prevention of cruelty to children or animals" (in 1918), "literary" purposes (in 1921), the "testing for public safety" (in 1934), and for certain amateur sports organizations (in 1976) arguably would have been unnecessary if the term "charitable" has been used in its common law sense. Similarly, it can be contended that if Congress had intended to condition tax exemption on satisfaction of the requirements of a common law charity, there would have been no need to add to the statutory law (as was done in 1913) the prohibition concerning the inurement of net earnings to private persons, inasmuch as, under the common law, the income of a charitable organization cannot inure to the benefit of private persons.[42] The same can be said of the limitation on legislative activities (enacted in 1934).[43]

Therefore, one can utilize the overall structure of the federal tax law regarding tax exemption and charitable giving as evidence that each of the eight purposes enumerated in Code § 501(c)(3) are not overlain with a requirement that all organizations, to be exempt under that section, must qualify as entities that are "charitable" in the common law sense.[44]

Aside from the matter as to whether the entirety of Code §§ 170(c)(2)(B) and 501(c)(3) is overlain with one or more requirements imposed by the common law of charitable trusts, there is the question as to the intent of Congress when it employed the term "charitable" in those two, and related, provisions. That is, did Congress have in mind the common law definition of the term "charitable" or did it intend to apply the word in its "popular and ordinary" sense?

[40]90 Stat. 1730 (Act Title XIII, Section 1313). As discussed in Chapter 10 § 6, the restriction that no part of a sports organization's activities can involve the provision of athletic facilities or equipment no longer applies to a "qualified sports organization," pursuant to Code § 501 (j) enacted by section 286 of the Tax Equity and Fiscal Responsibilty Act of 1982.
[41]90 Stat. 1720 (Act Title XIII, Section 1307).
[42]4 Scott, *The Law of Trusts* § 376 (2d ed. 1956).
[43]*Ibid* at § 376.6.
[44]This reading of the law is in conformance with still another axiom of statutory construction, which is that statutes are to be construed to give effect to each word and that no one part of a statute should be interpreted so as to render another part of the statute redundant. For example, *Jarecki* v. *G.D. Searle & Co.*, 367 U.S. 303 (1961); *United States* v. *Menasche*, 348 U.S. 528 (1955).

There is little concrete evidence to support a proposition that Congress intended the application of either definition.

The strongest argument that Congress did not intend the use of the common law definition of the term "charitable" is the statutory construction argument, discussed above, which is that application of the broad, common law definition of the word would render other words and phrases in the provisions redundant.[45] There is no legislative history, however, that gives much (if any) support for the proposition that Congress intended use of the narrower, "popular" meaning of the term.

In fact, what little legislative history there is is usually cited in support of the view that the common law/"public policy" definition is the one to be applied. The chief component of this legislative history is a portion of a report of the House of Representatives issued in 1939, explaining the theory that animated Congress to exempt from taxation organizations devoted to charitable and other purposes, which is as follows:

> The exemption from taxation of money or property devoted to charitable and other purposes is based upon the theory that the Government is compensated for the loss of revenue by its relief from financial burdens which would otherwise have to be met by appropriations from other public funds, and by the benefits resulting from the promotion of the general welfare.[46]

This phraseology—inasmuch as it uses words such as "public" and "general welfare"—can thus be read as evidencing the need to follow the dictates of the common law meaning of "charitable," including the "public policy" doctrine. (At the same time, this legislative history speaks of "charitable and other purposes," which can be read as evidence of an intent to invoke a narrower meaning of the term "charitable.")

As noted below, the courts will occasionally look to contemporaneous administrative agency interpretation of a statute in an attempt to divine the statute's true meaning.[47] It is, therefore, instructive to note that, as early as 1923, in reviewing the law that is now Code § 501(c)(3), the IRS interpreted the word "charitable" in its "popular and ordinary sense" and not in its common law sense.[48] As revenue acts were subsequently enacted, the accompanying regulations stated: "Corporations organized and operated exclusively for char-

---

[45]*Ibid.*

[46]H.R. Rep. No. 1860, 75th Cong., 3d Sess. 19 (1938).

[47]See text accompanying ns. 56–58, *supra.*

[48]I.T. 1800, II-2 C.B. 152, 153 (1923), which discusses the intended meaning of the word "charitable" in section 231(6) of the Revenue Acts of 1918 and 1921. As the Supreme Court has observed, "a consistent and contemporaneous construction of a statute by the agency charged with its enforcement is entitled to great deference." *NLRB* v. *Boeing Co.*, 412 U.S. 67, 75 (1973). Also *Power Reactor Development Co.* v. *Electricians*, 367 U.S. 396 (1961).

itable purposes comprise, in general, organizations for the relief of the poor"[49]—clearly the "popular and ordinary" meaning of the term "charitable." During the fifteen years that the Internal Revenue Code of 1939[50] was in effect, three sets of regulations were issued, each of which defined the term "charitable" in its popular and ordinary sense.[51] When the Internal Revenue Code of 1954 was enacted, Code § 501 was derived from the 1939 Code.[52] As to Code § 501, a report of the House Committee on Ways and Means stated that "[n]o change in substance has been made . . ."[53] Consequently, it appears rather apparent that, as of the adoption of the Internal Revenue Code of 1954, the "popular and ordinary" meaning of the term "charitable" governed the definition of that word for federal tax purposes.

Nonetheless, in 1959, new regulations were promulgated which vastly expanded the federal tax definition of the term "charitable." This regulation (which is presently in effect) reads as follows:

> The term 'charitable' is used in section 501(c)(3) in its generally accepted legal sense and is, therefore, not to be construed as limited by the separate enumeration in section 501(c)(3) of other tax-exempt purposes which may fall within the broad outlines of 'charity' as developed by judicial decisions. Such term includes: Relief of the poor and distressed or of the underprivileged; advancement of religion; advancement of education or science; erection or maintenance of public buildings, monuments, or works; lessening of the burdens of Government; and promotion of social welfare by organizations designed to accomplish any of the above purposes, or (i) to lessen neighborhood tensions; (ii) to eliminate prejudice and discrimination; (iii) to defend human and civil rights secured by law; or (iv) to combat community deterioration and juvenile delinquency***.[54]

This regulation has several striking features. One of these is that the definition of the term "charitable" as stated therein is said to be used in its "generally accepted legal sense"—which is at least somewhat akin to its common law meaning. Another is that "[r]elief of the poor" is now only one of several ways in which an organization may qualify as a "charitable" entity.

Thus, the above-quoted tax definition of the term "charitable," as supplemented and amplified by subsequent court cases and IRS rulings, is the existing

---

[49]Treas. Reg. 65, Art. 517 (Revenue Act of 1924, *supra*, n. 29); Treas. Reg. 69, Art. 517 (Revenue Act of 1926, *supra*, n. 30); Treas. Reg. 74, Art. 527 (Revenue Act of 1928, *supra*, n. 31); Treas. Reg. 77, Art. 527 (Revenue Act of 1932, *supra*, n. 32); Treas. Reg. 86, Art. 101(6)–1 (Revenue Act of 1934, *supra*, n. 33); Treas. Reg. 94, Art. 101(6)–1 (Revenue Act of 1936 *supra*, n. 34); Treas. Reg. 101, Art. 101(6)–1 (Revenue Act of 1938, *supra*, n. 35).

[50]See n. 36, *supra*.

[51]Treas. Reg. 103, § 19.101(6)–1; Treas. Reg. 111, § 29.101(6)–1; Treas. Reg. 118, § 39.101(6)–1(b).

[52]Specifically, 1939 Code §§ 101 and 421.

[53]H.R. Rep. No. 1337, 83d Cong., 2d Sess. A165 (1954).

[54]Reg. § 1.501(c)(3)–1(d)(2).

law on the subject. To that extent, any concern as to the original intended meaning of the term "charitable" for federal tax purposes may be academic. However, it may be that the 1959 regulations are of suspect validity because they are so inconsistent with the intent of Congress at the time.[55] On the other hand, the sheer passage of time since promulgation of the 1959 regulations may give these regulations ongoing validity simply because Congress has— despite many opportunities to do so—refrained from enacting a statutory definition of the term "charitable" and thus has tacitly accepted the broader meaning of the word as articulated by the Department of the Treasury and the IRS.

In construing a statute, courts frequently place emphasis on the interpretation accorded the statute in the regulations promulgated by the governmental agency or agencies charged with the administration and enforcement of the statute. In this case, the relevant regulations are those promulgated in 1959 by the Department of the Treasury and enforced by the IRS.

These regulations clearly reflect an interpretation of Code § 501(c)(3) that affords tax-exempt status to any organization qualifying under *one* of the eight categories enumerated in the statute, without regard to whether it also accords with the characteristics of a common law charity. Under the regulations, an organization may be exempt "if it is organized and operated exclusively for *one or more of the following purposes:* (a) Religious, (b) Charitable, (c) Scientific, (d) Testing for public safety, (e) Literary, (f) Educational, or (g) Prevention of cruelty to children or animals."[56] As if this regulation was not adequately clear as to the independence of the separate exempt purposes, the regulations continue with the observations that "*each* of the[se] purposes . . . is an exempt purpose in itself" and that "an organization may be exempt if it is organized and operated exclusively for any one or more of such purposes."[57]

Therefore, the pertinent regulations take the position that each purpose or function stated in Code §§ 170(c)(2)(B) and 501(c)(3) is an independent basis for qualification as a tax-exempt charitable donee. However, as noted, these regulations were adopted in 1959 and thus cannot be reflective of congressional intent in, for example, 1894 or 1913.[58]

Despite the fact that it is probable that (1) Congress, in employing the term "charitable" when initially formulating the federal income tax rules, intended its use to be in conformance with the narrower, "popular and ordinary" meaning

[55]As the Supreme Court has observed, an administrative agency only has the authority "to adopt regulations to carry into effect the will of Congress as expressed by the statute" and that a regulation "which does not do this, but operates to create a rule out of harmony with the statute, is a mere nullity." *Manhattan General Equipment Co.* v. *Commissioner*, 297 U.S. 129, 134 (1936).

[56]Reg. § 1.501(c)(3)–1(d)(1)(i) (emphasis supplied).

[57]Reg. § 1.501(c)(3)–1(d)(1)(iii) (emphasis supplied).

[58]Cf. *National Muffler Dealers Association* v. *United States*, 440 U.S. 472, 477 (1979), where the Supreme Court wrote of "a substantially contemporaneous construction of the statute by those presumed to have been aware of congressional intent."

and thus intended the words "educational," "religious," "scientific," and the like to be independent bases for qualification for exemption and charitable donee status and (2) the common law definition of the term "charitable" does not impose "public policy" requirements that govern the conduct of all organizations described in Code §§ 170(c)(2)(B) and 501(c)(3), the question as to whether there are some overall requirements imposed on such organizations by the tax law (other than by statute) is not thereby fully answered. This is because there may be other applicable law that requires application of all tax exemptions, deductions, credits, exclusions, and the like in adherence to the dictates of a "public policy" standard.

The principal authority for such a proposition is a 1958 U.S. Supreme Court case, holding that tax benefits such as deductions and exclusions generally are subject to limitation on public policy grounds.[59] At issue in that case was the deductibility of fines paid for violation of state maximum weight laws applicable to motor vehicles (enacted to protect state highways from damage and to ensure the safety of highway users) as "ordinary and necessary" business expenses.[60] The Supreme Court held that an expense is not "necessary" to the operation of a business "if allowance of the deduction would frustrate sharply defined national or state policies proscribing particular types of conduct, evidenced by some governmental declaration thereof."[61] Observing that "[d]eduction of fines and penalties uniformly has been held to frustrate state policy in severe and direct fashion by reducing the 'sting' of the penalty prescribed by the state legislature," the Court concluded that Congress did not intend to allow income tax deductions for fines incurred to punish violations of state penal laws.[62]

On its face, this decision appears to place an overall "public policy" constraint on the extent of all tax "benefits," including deductions pursuant to Code § 170(c)(2) and exemptions pursuant to Code § 501(c)(3).

However, upon closer examination, this decision is arguably to be accorded less weight than may initially appear.

First, the case concerned the deduction of expenses paid pursuant to the requirements of penal statutes—fines and penalties. Rules relevant to stark criminal laws may not necessarily be applicable when considering the reach of tax exemptions.

Second, while there is the "ordinary and necessary" standard in the business expense context, there is no comparable standard in the tax-exemption context. Thus, the statutory construction considerations present in the penal statute setting may not be applicable in the tax-exemption setting.

Third, subsequently the Supreme Court has admonished that the "public

---

[59]*Tank Truck Rentals, Inc.* v. *Commissioner,* 356 U.S. 30 (1958).
[60]The deduction there at issue was that available pursuant to the predecessor of Code § 162(a).
[61]*Tank Truck Rentals, Inc.* v. *Commissioner, supra,* n. 59, at 33.
[62]*Ibid.* at 35–36.

policy" exception to the general rule of deductibility is "sharply limited and carefully defined."[63] The Court added:

> [T]he federal income tax is a tax on net income, not a sanction against wrongdoing. That principle has been firmly imbedded in the tax statute from the beginning. One familiar facet of the principle is the truism that the statute does not concern itself with the lawfulness of the income that it taxes.[64]

Fourth, Congress acted after these cases to circumscribe the denial of tax deductions on public policy grounds. In 1969 and 1971, Congress enacted rules explicitly limiting the public policy doctrine of nondeductibility to fines paid for violations of law and to illegal bribes, kickbacks, and similar payments.[65] Thus, in 1969, a Senate Finance Committee report stated: "Public policy, in other circumstances, generally is not sufficiently clearly defined to justify the disallowance of deductions."[66]

Thus, any "public policy" grounds arguably applicable in the tax-exemption/charitable donee context by reason of this 1958 opinion appear to have been subsequently displaced by other opinions and congressional action.

Those who contend that the entirety of Code § 501(c)(3) and its sister provisions is overlain with a "public policy" requirement start with an assertion that has many ramifications in other tax contexts, namely, that tax-exempt status and eligibility for tax-deductible charitable contributions constitute forms of government support (frequently cast as "indirect subsidies").[67] From this argument follows the logical next argument that the federal tax laws make the federal government a partner in the national system of private philanthropy. This, in turn, logically leads to the conclusion that congressional expectations dictate that a qualifying organization must promote the general welfare. As discussed, this approach then invokes the "public policy" doctrine, either on the basis of the common law of charitable trusts or the inherent characteristics of tax exemptions, deductions, and the like.[68]

Advocates of this approach basically assert two positions: (1) that Congress intended the common law of charitable trusts to apply to all Code § 501(c)(3) organizations and (2) that this is (at least in part) evidenced by the fact that Congress characterized a contribution to almost all organizations described in Code § 501(c)(3) as a "charitable contribution."[69]

As to the former point, those advancing this approach must assert that

---

[63]*Commissioner* v. *Tellier*, 383 U.S. 687, 691, 693–694 (1966).

[64]*Ibid.*

[65]Code § 162(c) and (f).

[66]S. Rep. No. 91-552, 91st Cong., 1st Sess. (1969), at 2 *U.S. Code Cong. Ad. News* 2311 (1969).

[67]See Chapter 3 § 3.

[68]See text accompanying ns. 59–66, *supra*.

[69]Code § 170(c)(2)(B). The exception is the organization that tests for public safety (see Chapter 10 § 2).

congressional action in 1894[70] was reflective of the common law definition of the term "charitable"[71] and that the use of the term as stated in the regulations adopted in 1959[72] is reflective of the intended definition by Congress throughout the decades.[73]

From the standpoint of applicable legislative history on this point, the provision most usually cited is that of the House Committee on Ways and Means in 1938.[74] Also, such proponents sometimes refer to a statement by the sponsor of the 1909 tax exemption statute[75] that the provision was designed to relieve from the income tax (then only on corporations) those organizations "devoted exclusively to the relief of suffering, to the alleviation of our people, and to all things which commend themselves to every charitable and just impulse."[76]

In a sense, the strongest argument available to advocates is the position taken by various courts since the inception of the income tax exemption and deduction for "charitable" entities. That is—perhaps without realizing the full implications of the principle—some court opinions have emphasized the breadth of the meaning of the term "charitable."

For example, the Supreme Court seemingly emphasized the overarching application of the term "charitable" in the Code § 170(c)(2) context when it observed that "Congress, in order to encourage gifts to religious, educational *and other charitable objects*, granted the privilege of deducting such gifts from gross income."[77] Earlier, the Court wrote, concerning a predecessor provision to Code § 501(c)(3), that "[e]vidently the exemption [was] made in recognition of the benefit which the public derives from corporate activities of the class named, and [was] intended to aid them when not conducted for private gain."[78]

This approach is also reflected in a variety of appellate court opinions. Thus, the First Circuit Court of Appeals has written that "[t]he term 'charitable' is a generic term and includes literary, religious, scientific and educational institutions."[79] Likewise, the District of Columbia Circuit has stated: "That Congress had in mind these broader definitions is confirmed by the words used in the [District of Columbia Code] for by its terms it embraces religious, charitable, scientific, literary, or educational corporations, thus including within the exemption clause every nonprofit organization designed and operating for the

---

[70]See n. 24, *supra*.

[71]See text accompanying § 1 hereof.

[72]See text accompanying ns. 54–58, *supra*.

[73]In other words, this approach must reject the thought that Congress ever intended application of the term "charitable" in its "popular and ordinary" sense. See § 1 hereof.

[74]See text accompanying n. 46, *supra*.

[75]H.R. 1438, 61st Cong., 1st Sess. (1909).

[76]44 Cong. Rec. 4150 (1909).

[77]*Helvering* v. *Bliss*, 293 U.S. 144, 147 (1934) (emphasis supplied).

[78]*Trinidad* v. *Sagrada Orden de Predicadores*, 263 U.S. 578, 581 (1924). Likewise, *St. Louis Union Trust Company* v. United States, 374 F.2d 427, 432 (8th Cir. 1967).

[79]*United States* v. *Proprietors of Social Law Library, supra* n. 1, at 483.

benefit and enlightenment of the community, the State, or the Nation."[80] Similarly, in the context of the private school controversy,[81] the Fourth Circuit held that the structure of the statutory framework (Code §§ 170 and 501(c)) demonstrates that an organization seeking tax exemption under Code § 501(c)(3) must show that it is "charitable," irrespective of the particular nature of its activities (e.g., religious, educational, or scientific).[82]

If it is assumed that the requirement of being "charitable" is the threshold test for qualification for tax exemption[83] and eligibility for deductible contributions,[84] then one must next confront the question as to the applicable meaning of the term "charitable." As discussed,[85] the word "charitable" is susceptible of (at least) two definitions: the "common law" meaning and the "popular and ordinary" meaning. The courts that have concluded that all organizations that are to be tax exempt under Code § 501(c)(3) and eligible for deductible contributions must satisfy the basic requirement of being "charitable" have applied the term in its broad, common law sense—an activity or purpose that benefits society as a whole.

On this point, the District of Columbia Circuit Court of Appeals once observed that "we must look to established [trust] law to determine the meaning of the word 'charitable' ".[86] Subsequently, the same court stated that Congress intended to apply these tax rules "to those organizations commonly designated charitable in the law of trusts."[87]

This approach thus invokes the "public policy" doctrine[88] and makes it applicable to all Code §§ 501(c)(3) and 170(c)(2) organizations. As the Supreme Court observed over 100 years ago: "A charitable use, where neither law nor public policy forbids, may be applied to almost any thing that tends to promote the well-doing and well-being of social man."[89] A federal district court later held, in application of the doctrine to educational entities, that "[t]his public policy doctrine operates as a necessary exception to or qualifier of the precept that in general trusts for education are considered to be for the benefit of the community."[90] The Restatement, Trusts, puts the matter this way: "A trust for

---

[80]*International Reform Federation* v. *District Unemployment Board,* 131 F.2d 337, 339 (D.C. Cir. 1942).

[81]See Chapter 6.

[82]*Bob Jones University* v. *United States, supra,* n. 20.

[83]Code § 501(c)(3).

[84]Code § 170(c)(2).

[85]See § 1 hereof.

[86]*Pennsylvania Co. for Insurance on Lives* v. *Helvering,* 66 F.2d 284, 285 (D.C. Cir. 1933).

[87]*International Reform Federation* v. *District Unemployment Board, supra,* n. 80 at 339.

[88]See n. 4, *supra*.

[89]*Ould* v. *Washington Hospital for Foundlings,* 95 U.S. 303, 311 (1877).

[90]*Green* v. *Connally, supra,* n. 4 at 1160.

a purpose the accomplishment of which is contrary to public policy, although not forbidden by law, is invalid."[91]

In conclusion, the view that all organizations described in Code §§ 501(c)(3) and 170(c)(2) are subject to overall charitable/public policy requirements is best supported by the gloss placed on these provisions by a variety of court opinions. Little, if any, support for this view can be found in the thought that all deductions, exemptions, and the like are bound up in public policy considerations. And, the application of canons of statutory construction and strict analysis of the relevant legislative history offer no support for this view.

Conversely, those who assert that, of the organizations described in Code §§ 501(c)(3) and 170(c)(2), only the "charitable" entities need meet the test as to what is "charitable," find the most support in the literary application of the statutes and their early administrative interpretations. Subsequent court opinions—assuming they represent today's law—nonetheless do much to undermine that assertion.

§ 4.4   Some General Concepts

Conceptually, the term "charitable" has—as it has always had—a broad, wide-ranging, multifaceted meaning. While specific applications of the concept are continually generating new illustrations of "charitable" organizations, the basic categories of "charity" are encompassed by the common law definition of the term[92] as opposed to terms such as "philanthropy," "eleemosynary," or "benevolent."[93] The IRS has observed that the provisions in the Code relating to charitable organizations "do not reflect any novel or specialized tax concept of charitable purposes, and that . . . [those provisions] should be interpreted as favoring only those purposes which are recognized as charitable in the generally accepted legal sense."[94] The concept of charitable thus includes (1) relief of poverty by assisting the poor, distressed, and underprivileged, (2) advancement of religion, (3) advancement of education and science, (4) performance of government functions and lessening of the burdens of government, (5) promotion of health, and (6) promotion of social welfare for the benefit of the community. Viewing the foregoing categories as in essence the totality of the concept of "charitable," there is a striking similarity between the Preamble to the Statute of Charitable Uses enacted in 1601 and the Department of the Treasury regulation under Code § 501(c)(3).[95]

[91]*Restatement of Trusts* 2d § 377, Comment c (1959).
[92]Reg. § 1.501(c)(3)-1(d)(2). See n. 54, *supra.*
[93]See, e.g., *People v. Thomas Walters Chapter of Daughters of American Revolution,* 142 N.E. 566 (Sup. Ct. Ill. 1924); *In re Dol's Estate,* 187 P. 428 (Sup. Ct. Cal. 1920); *Hamburger v. Cornell University,* 166 N.Y.S. 46 (Sup. Ct. Sara. Cty. 1917).
[94]Rev. Rul. 67-325, 1967-2 C.B. 113.
[95]Also see *Restatement of Trusts* 2d §§ 368–374.

The scope of these six categories in relation to tax law requirements is discussed in Chapter 7. However, there are some collateral principles derived from the law of charitable trusts with respect to the concept of "charity" that should be distilled at this point.[96]

First, the persons who are to benefit from the purported charitable activity must constitute a sufficiently large or indefinite class. Thus, it is inadequate if the beneficiaries of the alleged charitable works are specifically named, are solely relatives of the donor or donors, or are organizations such as social clubs and fraternal organizations.[97] Conversely, an adequate class may be present even where the beneficiaries are confined to the inhabitants of a particular town or are employees of a particular company. Thus, a foundation established to award scholarships solely to members of a designated fraternity was ruled exempt as an educational organization.[98] However, another foundation lost its tax-exempt status because it expended a considerable portion of its funds on a scholarship grant to the son of a trustee of the foundation.[99] Basically, where a class of persons is involved as beneficiaries, the sufficiency of the class for purposes of ascertaining whether charitable activities are being engaged in becomes a question of degree.[100]

A case in point is the regard of the IRS for the elderly. Until the 1970s, the Service's position was that the aged were not a charitable class *per se*, even the unemployed aged.[101] There was some support for this stance from the courts.[102] When an organization operated to assist the elderly, any exemption as a charitable entity was tied to the concept that they were also impoverished, as illustrated by the charitable and educational status accorded an organization to aid elderly unemployed persons of limited means in obtaining employment by providing such persons with free counseling and placement services and by educating the general public in the employment capabilities of the elderly.[103]

This position of the IRS began to soften in the early 1970s, as evidenced by its change of heart as respects homes for the aged, when the Service first

---

[96]It is commonplace for the law of charitable trusts to be analogized to in exploring the meaning of terms used in Code § 501(c)(3). See, e.g., *Green v. Connally supra*, n. 90, 330 F. Supp. at 1157–1159.

[97]Rev. Rul. 56-403, 1956-2 C.B. 307.

[98]*Ibid.*

[99]*Charleston Chair Company v. United States*, 203 F. Supp. 126 (E.D.S. Car. 1962). Also Rev. Rul. 67-367, 1967-2 C.B. 188.

[100]See *Restatement of Trusts* 2d § 375; Bogert, *Trusts and Trustees* § 365; Rev. Rul. 57-449, 1957-2 C.B. 622. Also see Rev. Rul. 67-325, *supra*, n. 94, where the IRS discusses this concept in the context of ruling, following the decision in *Peters v. Commissioner*, 21 T.C. 55 (1953), that community recreational facilities may be classified as charitable if they are provided for the use of the general public in the community. Cf. Rev. Rul. 59-310, 1959-2 C.B. 146; IRS Private Letter Ruling 8024109.

[101]Rev. Rul. 68-422, 1968-2 C.B. 207; Rev. Rul. 56-138, 1956-1 C.B. 202.

[102]See *Watson v. United States*, 355 F.2d 269 (3rd Cir. 1965).

[103]Rev. Rul. 66-257, 1966-2 C.B. 212.

articulated the thought that the elderly face forms of distress other than financial distress and have special needs for housing, health care, and economic security in general.[104] Thereafter, the IRS held that charitable status could be extended to an organization that established a service center providing information, referral, counseling services relating to health, housing, finances, education, employment, and recreational facilities for a particular community's senior citizens,[105] that operates a rural rest home to provide, at a nominal charge, two-week vacations for elderly poor people,[106] and that provides home delivery of meals to elderly and handicapped people by volunteers.[107]

In 1977, the IRS first recognized that the elderly can constitute a charitable class *per se.* In so doing, the Service continued to impose as a touchstone the corollary requirement that the elderly also be distressed but the facts reveal that the presence of this element was minimal. The circumstances involved an organization that provides low cost bus transportion to senior citizens and the handicapped in a community where public transportation is unavailable or inadequate. Observed the IRS: "Providing the elderly and the handicapped with necessary transportation within the community is an activity directed toward meeting the special needs of these charitable classes of individuals."[108] Subsequently, the Service ruled that an organization that provides specially designed housing "that is within the financial reach of a significant segment of the community's elderly persons" qualifies as a charitable entity.[109]

The IRS ruled that a law library qualifies as an exempt educational organization, even though the organization's rules limit "access to and use of the library facilities . . . to a designated class of persons . . ."[110] The Service, on this point, said that "[w]hat is of importance is that the class benefited be broad enough to warrant a conclusion that the educational facility or activity is serving a broad public interest rather than a private interest." The rationale for the favorable ruling was that the library facilities are available to a "significant number" of people and that the restrictions were placed on use of the library because of the limited size and scope of the facilities.[111]

Therefore, the requirements as to what is "charitable" generally contemplate the presence of a sufficient class or community. On occasion, however, the IRS will attempt to use this requirement as a basis for denial of exemption, by characterizing the beneficiaries as being too small in number or too limited in interests, such as where benefits are confined to an organization's membership.

[104]Rev. Rul. 72-124, 1972-1 C.B. 145.
[105]Rev. Rul. 75-198, 1975-1 C.B. 157.
[106]Rev. Rul. 75-385, 1975-2 C.B. 205.
[107]Rev. Rul. 76-244, 1976-1 C.B. 155.
[108]Rev. Rul. 77-246, 1977-2 C.B. 190.
[109]Rev. Rul. 79-18, 1979-1 C.B. 194.
[110]Rev. Rul. 75-196, 1975-2 C.B. 155.
[111]See Rev. Rul. 68-504, 1968-2 C.B. 211, and Rev. Rul. 65-298, 1965-2 C.B. 163, which hold that an organization formed to conduct educational programs for a specific group is entitled to Code § 501(c)(3) qualification.

But there are reasonable limitations on the reach by the IRS in applying this doctrine. As one court has observed: "To our knowledge, no charity has ever succeeded in benefiting *every* member of the community. If to fail to so benefit *everyone* renders an organization noncharitable, then dire times must lie ahead for this nation's charities."[112]

Second, a charitable purpose may be served regardless of whether corpus is immediately distributed or is continued indefinitely, or whether the number of persons actually relieved is small as long as they are selected from a valid charitable class. Nor is the economic status of the individuals benefited necessarily a factor, except where relief of poverty is the basis for designation of the purpose as "charitable." That is, it is not necessary that the beneficiaries of a charitable organization's program be members of a "charitable class" in the colloquial sense of that term (such as the poor or the distressed). Rather, the essential requirement for achieving charitable status is that benefits be accorded the general public or the community, or some sufficiently general subgroup thereof, such as students, patients, or the aged.[113] For example, the IRS determined that community recreational facilities are classifiable as charitable if they are provided for the use of the general public of a community.[114] As one court stated, "[r]elief of poverty is not a condition of charitable assistance. If the benefit conferred is of sufficiently widespread social value, a charitable purpose exists."[115] Likewise, another court accorded tax exemption to an organization that functions primarily as a crop seed certification entity, despite the government's contention that its activities only incidentally benefit the public, with the court observing that "[t]he fact that the majority of persons interested in seed technology may well come from the agricultural community does not mean that farmers and gardeners are not an important part of the general public. . . ."[116]

Third, a limited number of persons may be benefited as the result of an organization's activities and the assistance considered "charitable" in nature as long as the effect is to benefit the community rather than merely individual recipients. Thus, the funding of a chair at a university will benefit individual professors although the actual effect is to promote education, and is therefore an exempt activity. In such instances, the individuals benefited are frequently regarded as "means" or "instruments" to a charitable end. As an illustration, an organization was ruled exempt as a charitable entity for providing substantially free legal services to low-income residents of economically depressed communities by providing financial and other assistance to legal interns; the IRS recognized that the interns themselves are not members of a charitable

---

[112]*Sound Health Association v. Commissioner*, 71 T.C. 158, 185 (1978).

[113]See, e.g., Rev. Rul. 68-422, *supra*, n. 101.

[114]Rev. Rul. 67-325, *supra* n. 94

[115]*In re Estate of Henderson*, 112 P.2d 605, 607 (Sup. Ct. Cal. 1941).

[116]*Indiana Crop Improvement Association, Inc. v. Commissioner*, 76 T.C. 394, 400 (1981).

class but held that they are "merely the instruments by which the charitable purposes are accomplished."[117] Likewise, proxy contests when conducted in the public interest are "charitable" activities, in that there is a "community benefit" (i.e., the "beneficiary of this activity and educational process to promote socially responsible corporations will be the public"), even though the exempt organization's resources are being devoted to direct participation in the processes of corporate management.[118] The same principle obtains as respects the operation of "public interest law firms."[119] The IRS has accepted the view that a charitable organization may provide services or make distributions to nonexempt organizations where done in furtherance of its exempt purpose.[120]

Thus, the IRS ruled that an organization did not fail to qualify as a charitable and educational entity because its exempt function (the training of unemployed and under-employed individuals) is carried out through the manufacturing and selling of toy products.[121] The Service observed:

> The question in this case is whether the organization is conducting its manufacturing and merchandising operation as an end in itself or as the means by which it accomplished a charitable purpose other than through the production of income. Here, the facts clearly support the conclusion that the manufacturing and merchandising operation is the means of accomplishing the organization's declared charitable objectives. Thus, there is a clear and distinct causal relationship between the manufacturing activity and the training of individuals for the purpose of improving their individual capabilities. There is likewise no evidence that the scale of the endeavor is such as to suggest that it is being conducted on a larger scale than is reasonably necessary to accomplish the organization's charitable purpose.

Similarly, the Service has stated that:

> The performance of a particular activity that is not inherently charitable may nonetheless further a charitable purpose. The overall result in any given case is dependent on why and how that activity is actually being conducted.[122]

Fourth, the concept of what is "charitable" is continually changing and evolving. This principle may be illustrated by the abandonment by the IRS of its prior rule that homes for the aged may be exempt only where services are provided free or below cost to be replaced by the requirement that housing,

---

[117]Rev. Rul. 72-559, 1972-2 C.B. 247.

[118]*Center on Corporate Responsibility, Inc. v. Shultz*, 368 F. Supp. 863, 874, n. 21 (D.D.C. 1973).

[119]See Rev. Proc. 71-39, 1971-2 C.B. 575. See Chapter 6.

[120]Rev. Rul. 81-29, 1981-1 C.B. 329; Rev. Rul. 68-489, 1968-2 C.B. 210.

[121]Rev. Rul. 73-128, 1973-1 C.B. 222.

[122]Rev. Rul. 69-572, 1969-2 C.B. 119. Also Rev. Rul. 80-279, 1980-2 C.B. 176; Rev. Rul. 80-278, 1980-2 C.B. 175; Rev. Rul. 67-4, 1967-1 C.B. 121. Cf. *Senior Citizens Stores, Inc. v. United States*, 79-2 U.S.T.C. ¶ 9592 (5th Cir. 1979).

health care, and financial security needs be met.[123] Thus, the old law which
focused solely upon relief of financial distress of the aged has been supplanted
by a recognition of other forms of "distress": need for housing, health care
services, and financial security. Changes in the concept are expounded, *inter
alia*, in constitutions, statutes, and, for the most part, court decisions. In the
latter instance, the changes "are wrought by changes in moral and ethical
precepts generally held, or by changes in relative values assigned to different
and sometimes competing and even conflicting interests of society."[124]

Fifth, a particular "charitable" activity may partake of more than one of the
basic six categories, such as a scholarship program for impoverished youths
which constitutes both the relief of poverty and the advancement of education.

Sixth, the motive of the founder in initiating the alleged charitable activity
is immaterial in terms of ascertaining whether the activity is in fact "charitable"
in nature.[125] This principle was illustrated by the case of a decedent's bequest
to a cemetary association formed to maintain a cemetary and sell burial plots.
In the absence of proof that the cemetary was operated exclusively for charitable
purposes or that the bequest was to be used exclusively for such purposes, the
U.S. Tax Court held that the bequest was not a charitable bequest for federal
estate tax purposes.[126] The court stated that "[i]t is the use to which a bequest
is to be applied that determines its deductibility and not the motive prompting
the bequest."[127]

Seventh, a "charitable" purpose cannot be served where the property involved or the income therefrom is directed to a private use.[128] Thus, a charitable
organization cannot be one organized and operated for a profit or for other
private ends. For example, a book publishing venture was denied exemption
as a "charitable and/or educational organization because a substantial purpose
of the organization was found to be the derivation of substantial profits by the
organization and the authors to which it made grants.[129] Other illustrations
include an organization that was denied exemption because its principal activity
was the making of research grants for the development of new machinery to
be used in a commercial operation[130] and an association that was denied ex-

---

[123]Rev. Rul. 72-124, *supra*, n. 104, superseding Rev. Rul. 57-467, 1957-2 C.B. 313.

[124]*Green v. Connally, supra*, n. 90, 330 F. Supp. at 1159; see Bogert, *Trusts and
Trustees* § 369 and Scott, *The Law of Trusts* §§ 368, 374.2.

[125]Bogert, *Trusts and Trustees* §§ 366.

[126]*Estate of Amick v. Commissioner*, 67 T.C. 924 (1977).

[127]*Ibid* at 928. Also *Wilbur National Bank v. Commissioner*, 17 B.T.A. 654 (1929);
Estate of Wood v. Commissioner, 39 T.C. 1 (1962); Rev. Rul. 67-170, 1967-1 C.B. 272.
Cf. *Estate of Audenried v. Commissioner*, 26 T.C. 120 (1956).

[128]See *Restatement of Trusts* 2d § 376.

[129]Rev. Rul. 66-104, 1966-1 C.B. 135; *Christian Manner International, Inc. v. Commissioner*, 71 T.C. 661 (1979).

[130]Rev. Rul. 65-1, 1965-1 C.B. 226.

emption as a business league because its "research program" benefited its members rather than the public.[131]

It was for this reason that the IRS refused to recognize an organization as being charitable where its primary purpose was to encourage individuals to contribute funds to charity and its primary activity was the offering of free legal services for personal tax and estate planning to individuals who wish to make current and deferred gifts to charity as part of their overall tax and estate planning. Stating that "[a]iding individuals in their tax and estate planning is not a charitable activity in the generally accepted legal sense," the IRS ruled that "the benefits to the public are tenuous in view of the predominantly private purpose served by arranging individuals' tax and estate plans."[132]

However, the fact that private individuals or organizations incidentally derive a benefit from a "charitable" undertaking does not destroy the "charitable" nature of the endeavor. For example, an organization of educational institutions which accredits schools and colleges was found to foster excellence in education and to qualify as a charitable and educational entity even though its membership contained a small number of proprietary schools, since "[a]ny private benefit that may accrue to the few proprietary members because of accreditation is incidental to the purpose of improving the quality of education."[133] Thus, the IRS, which accorded status as a charitable entity to an organization formed and supported by residents of an isolated rural community to provide a medical building and facilities at reasonable rent to attract a doctor who would provide medical services to the community, stated:

> In these circumstances, any personal benefit derived by the doctor (the use of the building in which to practice his profession) does not detract from the public purpose of the organization nor lessen the public benefit flowing from its activities and is not considered to be the type of private interest prohibited by the regulations.[134]

Likewise, the IRS ruled that the fact that attorneys use a tax-exempt library to derive personal benefit in the practice of their profession is incidental to the exempt purpose of the library and is, in most instances, a "logical by-product" of an educational process.[135] Similarly, the U.S. Tax Court held that a day care center qualified as an educational organization and that the provision of custodial care was "merely a vehicle for or incidental to achieving petitioner's only substantial purpose, education of the children, and is not ground for disqual-

---

[131]Rev. Rul. 69-632, 1969-2 C.B. 120.

[132]Rev. Rul. 76-442, 1976-2 C.B. 148. See Note, "The Twilight Zone of Charity: The IRS Denies Exemption for a Free Tax Planning Service under Section 501(c)(3)," 55 N. Car. L. Rev. 721 (1977).

[133]Rev. Rul. 74-146, 1974-1 C.B. 129.

[134]Rev. Rul. 73-313, 1973-2 C.B. 174.

[135]Rev. Rul. 75-196, supra, n. 109. See also Rev. Rul. 75-471, 1975-2 C.B. 207; also Rev. Rul. 78-85, 1978-1 C.B. 150.

ification from exemption."[136] The Tax Court subsequently reiterated this position, holding that a early childhood center is a tax-exempt educational organization, "with custodial care being incidental only because of the needs of the children for such care if they are to receive the education offered."[137] Still another illustration is the ability of an exempt organization to provide services (such as research) in furtherance of an exempt function where nonexempt entities are among the recipients of the services.[138] In still another illustration of this point, the IRS has determined that a professional standards review organization can qualify as a charitable entity, as promoting health and lessening the burdens of government, because the benefits accorded by it to members of the medical profession are "incidental" to the charitable benefits it provides.[139]

Eighth, a "charitable" purpose cannot be one which is illegal or contrary to public policy.[140] The IRS determined that an organization formed to promote world peace and disarmament cannot qualify as either a charitable or social welfare organization, because its primary activity is the sponsoring of antiwar protest demonstrations, where it urges its participants to commit violations of local ordinances and breaches of public order.[141] The Service held:

In this case the organization induces or encourages the commission of criminal acts by planning and sponsoring such events. The intentional nature of this encouragement precludes the possibility that the organization might unfairly fail to qualify for exemption due to an isolated or inadvertent violation of a regulatory statute. Its activities demonstrate an illegal purpose which is inconsistent with charitable ends. Moreover, the generation of criminal acts increases the burdens of government, thus frustrating a well recognized charitable goal, i.e., relief of the burdens of government. Accordingly, the organization is not operated exclusively for charitable purposes and does not qualify for exemption from Federal income tax under section 501(c)(3) of the Code.

* * *

Illegal activities, which violate the minimum standards of acceptable conduct necessary to the preservation of an orderly society, are contrary to the common good and the general welfare of the people in a community and thus are not permissible means of promoting the social welfare for purposes of section 501(c)(4) of the Code. Accordingly, the organization in this case is not operated exclusively for the promotion of social welfare and does not qualify for exemption from Federal income tax under section 501(c)(4).

However, the fact that a particular purpose requires efforts to bring about a change in the statutory law does not preclude the purpose from being char-

[136]*San Francisco Infant School, Inc v. Commissioner*, 69 T.C. 957, 966 (1978).
[137]*Michigan Early Childhood Center, Inc. v. Commissioner*, 37 T.C.M. 808, 810 (1978).
[138]See Rev. Rul. 81-29, *supra*, n. 120.
[139]Rev. Rul. 81-276, 1981-2 C.B. 128.
[140]See *Restatement of Trusts* 2d § 377; *Tank Truck Rentals, Inc. v. Commissioner, supra*, n. 59.
[141]Rev. Rul. 75-384, 1975-2 C.B. 204.

itable. Thus, the proscription on substantive legislative activities by "charitable" organizations is a statutory constraint on otherwise permissible charitable activities rather than a declaration of a feature of "charitable" at common law.[142]

In conclusion, the "common element of all charitable purposes is that they are designed to accomplish objects which are beneficial to the community."[143] A frequently cited case on this point is an 1877 U.S. Supreme Court pronouncement, where the court stated: "A charitable use, where neither law nor public policy forbids, may be applied to almost any thing that tends to promote the well-doing and well-being of social man."[144]

[142]See Chapter 13.

[143]See Restatement of *Trusts* 2d § 368, comment a.

[144]*Ould* v. *Washington Hospital for Foundlings, supra,* n. 89, at 311. See, in general, Reiling, "What is a Charitable Organization," 44 *A.B.A.J.* 528 (1958); Annot. 12 A.L.R. 2d 849, 855 (1950). Also *Peters v. Commissioner, supra,* n. 100, at 59.

5

Organizational and Operational Tests

An organization, to be exempt as a "charitable" entity, must be both organized and operated exclusively[1] for one or more of the permissible exempt purposes. If an organization fails to meet either the organizational test or the operational test, it will not qualify for exemption from federal income taxation as a charitable entity.[2] (The organizational and operational tests of other categories of tax-exempt organizations are discussed in the respective chapters.)

§ 5.1 Organizational Test

An organization is organized exclusively for one or more exempt purposes only if its articles of organization (i.e., its corporate charter, articles of association, trust instrument, or other written instrument by which it is created)[3] limit its purposes to one or more exempt purposes[4] and do not expressly empower it to engage, otherwise than as an insubstantial part of its activities, in activities which in themselves are not in furtherance of one or more exempt purposes.[5] Additional requirements are imposed for the governing instruments of private foundations.[6]

In meeting the organizational test, the organization's purposes, as stated in its articles of organization, may be as broad as, or more specific than, the particular exempt purposes, such as religious, charitable, or educational ends.

---

[1]See Chapter 11.
[2]Reg. § 1.501(c)(3)-1(a); *Levy Family Tribe Foundation* v. *Commissioner*, 69 T.C. 615, 618 (1978).
[3]Reg. § 1.501(c)(3)-1(b)(2).
[4]See Reg. § 1.501(c)(3)-1(d).
[5]Reg. § 1.501(c)(3)-1(b)(1)(i).
[6]Code § 508(e). See Chapter 31.

Therefore, an organization which, by the terms of its articles, is formed "for literary and scientific purposes within the meaning of section 501(c)(3) of the Internal Revenue Code" shall, if it otherwise meets the requirements of the organizational test, be considered to have met the test. Similarly, articles stating that the organization is created solely "to receive contributions and pay them over to organizations which are described in section 501(c)(3) and exempt from taxation under section 501(a) of the Internal Revenue Code" are sufficient for purposes of the organizational test. If the articles state that the organization is formed for "charitable purposes," such articles ordinarily will be sufficient for purposes of the organizational test.[7]

Articles may not empower the carrying on of nonexempt activities (unless they are insubstantial), even though such organization is, by the terms of its articles, created for a purpose that is no broader than the specified charitable purposes.[8] Thus, an organization that is empowered by its articles "to engage in a manufacturing business" or "to engage in the operation of a social club" does not meet the organizational test, regardless of the fact that its articles may state that the organization is created "for charitable purposes within the meaning of section 501(c)(3) of the Internal Revenue Code."[9]

In no case will an organization be considered to be organized exclusively for one or more exempt purposes if, by the terms of its articles, the purposes for which such organization is created are broader than the specified charitable purposes. The fact that the actual operations of such an organization have been exclusively in furtherance of one or more exempt purposes is not sufficient to permit the organization to meet the organizational test. Similarly, such an organization will not meet the organizational test as a result of statements or other evidence that the members thereof intend to operate only in furtherance of one or more exempt purposes.[10]

An organization is not considered organized exclusively for one or more exempt purposes if its articles expressly empower it to (1) devote more than an insubstantial part of its activities to attempting to influence legislation by propaganda or otherwise,[11] (2) directly or indirectly participate in. or intervene in (including the publishing or distributing of statements), any political campaign on behalf of or in opposition to any candidate for public office,[12] or (3) have objectives and engage in activities which characterize it as an "action" organization (see below).[13]

It is the position of the IRS that only a "creating document" may be looked to in meeting the organizational test:

[7]Reg. § 1.501(c)(3)-1(b)(1)(ii).
[8]See Rev. Rul. 69-279, 1969-1 C. B. 152; Rev. Rul. 69-256, 1969-1 C.B. 151.
[9]Reg. § 1.501(c)(3)-1(b)(iii). Also *Santa Cruz Building Association* v. *United States,* 411 F.Supp. 871 (E.D. Mo. 1976).
[10]Reg. § 1.501(c)(3)-1(b)(1)(iv).
[11]See Chapter 13.
[12]See Chapter 14.
[13]Reg. § 1.501(c)(3)-1(b)(3).

Accordingly, the organizational test cannot be met by reference to any document that is not the creating document. In the case of a corporation, the bylaws cannot remedy a defect in the corporate charter. A charter can be amended only in accordance with state law, which generally requires filing of the amendments with the chartering authority. In the case of a trust, operating rules cannot substitute for the trust indenture. In the case of an unincorporated association, the test must be met by the basic creating document and the amendments thereto, whatever that instrument may be called. Subsidiary documents that are not amendments to the creating document may not be called on.[14]

An organization is not organized exclusively for one or more exempt purposes unless its assets are dedicated to an exempt purpose. An organization's assets will be considered dedicated to an exempt purpose, for example, if, upon dissolution, the assets would, by reason of a provision in the organization's articles or by operation of law, be distributed for one or more exempt purposes, or to the federal government, or to a state or local government, for a public purpose or would be distributed by a court to another organization to be used in a manner as in the judgment of the court will best accomplish the general purposes, for which the dissolved organization was organized. However, an organization does not meet the organizational test if its articles or the law of the state in which it was created provide that its assets would, upon dissolution, be distributed to its members or shareholders.[15] Consequently, tax exemption as a charitable organization will be denied where, upon dissolution of the organization, its assets would revert to the individual founders rather than to one or more qualifying charities.[16]

The dedication of assets requirement contemplates that, notwithstanding the dissolution of a charitable entity, the assets will continue to be devoted to a charitable purpose (albeit a substituted one). Under the cy pres rule, a state court, in the exercise of its equity power, may modify the purpose of a charitable trust or place the funds of a charitable corporation in a new entity.[17] Organizations which are organized for both exempt and nonexempt purposes fail to satisfy the organizational test.[18]

The income tax regulations contemplate two types of governing instruments for a "charitable" organization: the instrument by which the organization is created (termed the "articles of organization") and the instrument stating the rules pursuant to which the organization is operated (the "bylaws"). For the incorporated organization, the articles of organization are the "articles of incorporation." For the unincorporated entity, the articles of organization may

[14]IRS Exempt Organizations Handbook (IRM 7751) § 332(2).

[15]Reg. § 1.501(c)(3)-1(b)(4).

[16]*Truth Tabernacle* v. *Commissioner,* 41 T.C.M. 1405 (1981); *Calvin K. of Oakknoll* v. *Commissioner,* 69 T.C. 770 (1978), aff'd 79-1 U.S.T.C. ¶ 9328(2d Cir. 1979); *General Conference of the Free Church of America v. Commissioner,* 71 T.C. 920 (1979).

[17]Scott, *The Law of Trusts* §§ 397, 339.3; IRS Exempt Organizations Handbook (IRM 7751) § 335(4), (6).

[18]Rev. Rul. 69-256, *supra,* n. 8; Rev. Rul. 69-279, *supra,* n. 8.

be so termed or may be termed otherwise, such as the "constitution." The IRS has privately ruled that an unincorporated organization may combine these two types of instruments in a single document.

As discussed, the regulations require the articles of organization of a charitable organization to (1) limit its purposes to one or more exempt (i.e., charitable, educational, and the like) purposes, (2) not expressly empower it to engage (other than insubstantially) in nonexempt activities, and (3) provide that upon dissolution its assets will be distributed for one or more exempt purposes.

The articles of organization or bylaws of a charitable organization *may but need not* contain provisions such as the following:

No part of the net earnings, gains or assets of the corporation [or organization] shall inure to the benefit of or be distributable to its directors [or trustees], officers, other private individuals, or organizations organized and operated for a profit (except that the corporation [or organization] shall be authorized and empowered to pay reasonable compensation for services rendered and to make payments and distributions in furtherance of the purposes as hereinabove stated). No substantial part of the activities of the corporation [or organization] shall be the carrying on of propaganda or otherwise attempting to influence legislation, and the corporation [or organization] shall be empowered to make the election authorized under section 501(h) of the Internal Revenue Code of 1954. The corporation [or organization] shall not participate in or intervene in (including the publishing or distribution of statements) any political campaign on behalf of or in opposition to any candidate for public office. Notwithstanding any other provision herein, the corporation [or organization] shall not carry on any activities not permitted to be carried on—

(a) by an organization exempt from federal income taxation under section 501(a) of the Internal Revenue Code of 1954 as an organization described in section 501(c)(3) of such Code,

(b) by an organization described in sections 509(a)(1),(2), or (3) of the Internal Revenue Code of 1954 (as the case may be), and/or

(c) by an organization, contributions to which are deductible under sections 170(c)(2), 2055(a)(2), or 2522 (a)(2) of the Internal Revenue Code of 1954.

*   *   *

References herein to sections of the Internal Revenue Code of 1954, as amended, are to provisions of such Code as those provisions are now enacted or to corresponding provisions of any future United States revenue law.

An organization *must*, if it is to satisfy the federal tax law organizational requirements for charitable entities, have in its articles of organization provisions substantially equivalent to the following:

The corporation [or organization] is organized and operated exclusively for [charitable, educational, etc.] purposes within the meaning of section 501(c)(3) of the Internal Revenue Code of 1954.

*   *   *

In the event of dissolution or final liquidation of the corporation [or organization], the board of directors [or trustees] shall, after paying or making provision for the payment of all the lawful debts and liabilities of the corporation [or organization], distribute all the assets of the corporation [or organization] to one or more of the following categories of recipients as the board of directors [or trustees] of the corporation [or organization] shall determine:

(a) a nonprofit organization or organization which may have been created to succeed the corporation [or organization], as long as such organization or each of such organizations shall then qualify as a governmental unit under section 170(c) of the Internal Revenue Code of 1954 or as an organization exempt from federal income taxation under section 501(a) of such Code as an organization described in section 501(c)(3) of such Code; and/or

(b) a nonprofit organization or organizations having similar aims and objects as the corporation [or organization] and which may be selected as an appropriate recipient of such assets, as long as such organization or each of such organizations shall then qualify as a governmental unit under section 170(c) of the Internal Revenue Code of 1954 or as an organization exempt from federal income taxation under section 501(a) of such Code as an organization described in section 501(c)(3) of such Code.

The law of the state in which an organization is created is controlling in construing the terms of its articles.[19] However, any organization which contends that such terms have under state law a different meaning from their generally accepted meaning must establish the special meaning by clear and convincing reference to relevant court decisions, opinions of the state attorney general, or other evidence of applicable state law.[20]

Because of these considerations, an organization is best advised to include in its organizing document an express provision for the distribution of assets for "charitable" purposes upon the occasion of the organization's liquidation or dissolution. Nonetheless, this type of provision is technically not required where state law itself satisfies the organizational test requirements. In this regard, the applicable state law is dependent upon the form of the organization: whether the entity is an *inter vivos* charitable trust, a testamentary charitable trust, a nonprofit corporation, or an unincorporated association.[21]

The IRS has published guidelines for identification of states and circumstances where an express dissolution clause for charitable organizations is not required. Basically, these guidelines are a function of the type of organization that is involved. For example, the IRS has determined that the cy pres doctrine in any jurisdiction is insufficient to prevent an *inter vivos* charitable trust or an unincorporated association from failing, and thus that an adequate dissolution clause is essential for satisfaction of the organizational test. By contrast, the law of several states applies the cy pres doctrine to testamentary charitable trusts and the law of a few states applies the doctrine to nonprofit charitable corporations.[22] Consequently, from the standpoint of the IRS, an organization

---

[19]See *Estate of Sharf* v. *Commissioner*, 38 T. C. 15 (1962), aff'd 316 F.2d 625 (7th Cir. 1963); *Holden Hospital Corp.* v. *Southern Illinois Hospital Corp..* 174 N. E. 2d 793 (Sup. Ct. Ill. 1961).

[20]Reg. § 1.501(c)(3)-1(b)(5).

[21]See Chapter 36.

[22]Rev. Proc. 82-2, 1982-3 I.R.B. 9.

in a jurisdiction where the cy pres doctrine is inapplicable must have an express, qualifying distribution or liquidation clause to satisfy the organizational test.[23]

In most respects, the courts have adhered to these specific requirements of the organizational test. However, prior to the effective date of the organizational test requirements in the income tax regulations (July 27, 1959[24]), there was a tendancy to read into the term "organized" in the federal tax law rules for charitable organizations a greater flexibility than is contemplated by the regulations.[25] That is, the courts tended to blur the technical distinction between the organizational test and the operational test by viewing the former in the light of the predominant purpose for forming the organization and its manner of operations.[26] In one case,[27] for example, a court concluded that the word "organized" does not state a "narrowly limited formal requirement" and that the term largely requires only the requisite inurement:

> Our conclusion is that a corporation satisfies the requirement of being "organized" for a charitable purpose if, at the time in question, its setup or organization of ownership, directors, and officers is such that its earnings must inure to a charity.[28]

The organization in this case remained organized as a business corporation with stockholders. However, once all of its stock became held by an exempt hospital and the hospital's trustees assumed control over it, the organization was deemed qualified as a charitable entity even though the corporate charter was never amended—with the court finding that it was properly organized "for all practical purposes."[29]

By contrast, another court had elected to follow the "reasonable interpretation" of the word "organized."[30] The organization involved was organized as a business corporation and the fact that it was a holding company for an exempt art museum was considered insufficient for passage of the organizational test.

---

[23]The IRS will accept the following phraseology of a dissolution clause:
Upon the dissolution of [this organization], assets shall be distributed for one or more exempt purposes within the meaning of section 501(c)(3) of the Internal Revenue Code, or corresponding section of any future Federal tax code, or shall be distributed to the Federal government, or to a state or local government, for a public purpose. [*Ibid.* § 3.05.]

[24]Reg. § 1.501(c)(3)-1(b)(6).

[25]See Rev. Rul. 60-193, 1969-1 C. B. 195.

[26]See *Passiac United Hebrew Burial Association* v. *United States*, 216 F.Supp. 500 (D. N.J. 1963).

[27]*Dillingham Transportation Building* v. *United States*, 146 F.Supp. 953 (Ct. Cl. 1957).

[28]*Ibid.* at 955.

[29]Also see *Roche's Beach, Inc.* v. *Commissioner*, 96 F.2d 776 (2d Cir. 1938).

[30]*Sun-Herald Corp.* v. *Duggan*, 73 F.2d 298 (2d Cir. 1934), cert. den. 294 U. S. 719 (1934). Also see *Sun-Herald Corp.* v. *Duggan*, 160 F.2d 475 (2d Cir. 1947). Cf. *Universal Oil Products Co.* v. *Campbell*, 181 F.2d 451 (7th Cir. 1950).

The court held that the term " 'organized' means 'incorporated' and not 'operated' " and that, in line with the IRS requirements, the "right of the corporation to an exemption is to be determined by the powers given it in its charter."[31]

Some courts sought a middle ground. In one case, the court said:

> The better view, based in part upon the doctrine of liberality of construction respecting charitable exemptions which resolves ambiguities in favor of the taxpayer and in part upon a refusal to allow form to control over substance, is that "organized" means "created to perform" or "established to promote" charitable purposes rather than meaning merely "incorporated" with powers limited solely to charitable activities.[32]

Thus, this court dismissed the approach that focuses only on "recitations in a charter or certificate" and held that the analysis must extend to the "actual objects motivating the organization and the subsequent conduct of the organization" and the "manner in which the corporation has been operated."[33]

Since promulgation of the regulations containing the organizational test, the courts have been rather silent on the subject. However, one court has hinted that a provision in an organization's articles which is contrary to the requirements of the organizational test (i.e., permitting lobbying activities) may not be a bar to tax exemption where that aspect of the organization's activities is "dormant."[34] Another court has observed that the "mere existence of power to engage in activities other than those set out in section 501(c)(3) does not in itself prevent . . . [an organization] from meeting the organizational test."[35]

In the final analysis, however, prudence dictates compliance with the regulation's organizational test whenever possible. There are many barriers to tax-exempt status and the organizational test is one of the easiest to clear. This point is underscored by the approach of the IRS that, since articles of organization that fail to meet the organizational test are ordinarily amendable and since after amendment the exemption may be retroactive to the period before amendment, the "resolution of an organizational test question is only the first step in determining whether an organization is exempt."[36] Even if doing battle with the IRS over the tax-exempt status of an organization appears inevitable, presumably the struggle can be joined over matters of greater substance.

---

[31]*Sun-Herald Corp.* v. *Duggan, supra* n. 30, 73 F.2d at 300.

[32]*Samuel Friedland Foundation* v. *United States*, 144 F.Supp. 74, 84 (D. N.J. 1956).

[33]*Ibid.* at 85. Also see *Commissioner* v. *Battle Creek, Inc.*, 126 F.2d 405 (5th Cir. 1942); *Forest Press, Inc.* v. *Commissioner*, 22 T.C. 265 (1954); *Lewis* v. *United States*, 189 F.Supp. 950 (D. Wyo. 1961).

[34]*Center on Corporate Responsibility* v. *Shultz*, 368 F.Supp. 863, 878, n. 31 (D. D. C. 1973).

[35]*Peoples Translation Service/Newsfront International* v. *Commissioner*, 72 T.C. 42, 48 (1979).

[36]IRS Exempt Organizations Handbook (IRM 7751) § 338(2).

§ 5.2 Operational Test

An organization, to qualify as a "charitable" organization, is regarded as operated exclusively for one or more exempt purposes only if it engages primarily in activities which accomplish one or more of the exempt purposes specified therein. The IRS has observed that, to satisfy the "operational test," the "organization's resources must be devoted to purposes that qualify as exclusively charitable within the meaning of section 501(c)(3) of the Code and the applicable regulations."[37] An organization will not be so regarded if more than an insubstantial part of its activities is not in furtherance of an exempt purpose.[38] An organization is not considered as operated exclusively for one or more exempt purposes if its net earnings inure in whole or in part to the benefit of private shareholders or individuals.[39]

A deficiency in an organization's operations that causes failure of the operational test cannot be cured by language in its governing instruments. Thus, the IRS has stated that "[a]n organization whose activities are not within the statute cannot be exempt by virtue of a well-written charter."[40]

An organization may meet the federal tax law requirements for charitable entities even though it operates a trade or business as a substantial part of its activities.[41] However, if the organization has as its primary purpose the carrying on of a trade or business, it may not be exempt.[42] (The existence of an operating profit is not conclusive as to a business purpose.[43]) Even though the operation of a business does not deprive an organization of classification as a charitable entity, there may be unrelated trade or business tax consequences.[44]

In one instance, the operational test was said to look more toward an organization's purposes rather than its activities, in recognition of the fact that an organization may conduct a business in furtherance of a tax-exempt purpose and qualify as a charitable entity:

Under the operational test, the purpose towards which an organization's activities are directed, and not the nature of the activities themselves, is ultimately dispositive of the organization's right to be classified as a section 501(c)(3) organization exempt from tax under section 501(a). . . . [I]t is possible for . . . an activity to be carried on for more than one purpose. . . . The fact that . . . [an] activity may constitute a trade or business does not, of course, disqualify it from classification

[37]Rev. Rul. 72-369, 1972-2 C. B. 245.
[38]Reg. § 1.501(c)(3)-1(c)(1).
[39]Reg. §§ 1.501(c)(3)-1(c)(2), 1.501(a)-1(c). Also *Levy Family Tribe Foundation* v. *Commissioner, supra* n. 2. See Chapter 12.
[40]IRS Exempt Organizations Handbook (IRM 7751) § 320(2).
[41]See, e.g., Rev. Rul. 64-182, 1964-1 (Part 1) C. B. 186.
[42]Reg. § 1.501(c)(3)-1(e)(1).
[43]See Rev. Rul. 68-26, 1968-1 C. B. 272; *Elisian Guild, Inc.* v. *United States,* 412 F.2d 121 (1st Cir. 1969). Cf. *Fides Publishers Association* v. *United States,* 263 F.Supp. 924 (N.D. Ind. 1967).
[44]See Chapter 40.

under section 501(c)(3), provided the activity furthers or accomplishes an exempt purpose. . . . Rather, the critical inquiry is whether . . . [an organization's] primary purpose for engaging in its . . . activity is an exempt purpose, or whether its primary purpose is the nonexempt one of operating a commercial business producing net profits for . . . [the organization] . . . Factors such as the particular manner in which an organization's activities are conducted, the commercial hue of those activities and the existence and amount of annual or accumulated profits are relevant evidence of a forbidden predominant purpose.[45]

This important distinction between activities and purpose is frequently overlooked by the IRS and the courts. For example, in one case the court concluded that the operational test was not satisfied because the organization failed to describe its activities in sufficient detail in its application for recognition of tax exemption.[46]

An illustration of the application of the operational test rules is provided by a case concerning the tax-exempt status of an organization established to provide a fund for the purpose of giving scholarships to contestants in the Miss Georgia Pageant.[47] As a condition for qualifying for the scholarships, the organization requires the participants to enter into a contract obligating them, in the event they are selected to participate in the Pageant, to abide by its rules and regulations. The Tax Court ruled that the "scholarships" are compensatory in nature, being payment for the contestants' agreement to perform the requirements of the contract, thus not constituting tax-excludable[48] scholarships. Because the grant of the scholarships was the organization's sole activity, and because the primary purpose of the payments was to provide compensation, the court concluded that the organization does not qualify for tax exemption under the federal tax rules for charitable entities.

An organization is not operated exclusively for one or more exempt purposes if it is an "action" organization.[49]

An organization is an action organization if a substantial part of its activities is attempting to influence legislation by propaganda or otherwise. For this purpose, an organization will be regarded as attempting to influence legislation if the organization contacts, or urges the public to contact, members of a legislative body for the purpose of proposing, supporting, or opposing legislation or if it advocates the adoption or rejection of legislation. The term "legislation" includes action by the U.S. Congress, by any state legislature, by any local council or similar governing body, or by the public in a referendum, initiative, constitutional amendment, or similar procedure. An organization will not fail

---

[45]*B.S.W. Group, Inc.* v. *Commissioner*, 70 T.C. 352, 356-357 (1978). Also see *Ohio Teamsters Trust Fund* v. *Commissioner*, 77 T.C. 189 (1981).

[46]*General Conference of the Free Church of America* v. *Commissioner*, 71 T.C. 920 (1979).

[47]*Miss Georgia Scholarship Fund, Inc.* v. *Commissioner*, 72 T.C. 267 (1979).

[48]Code § 117.

[49]Reg. § 1.501(c)(3)-1(c)(i).

to meet the operational test merely because it advocates, as an insubstantial part of its activities, the adoption or rejection of legislation.[50]

An organization is an action organization if it participates or intervenes, directly or indirectly, in any political campaign on behalf of or in opposition to any candidate for public office. The term "candidate for public office" means an individual who offers himself or herself, or is proposed by others, as a contestant for an elective public office, whether the office be national, state, or local. Activities which constitute participation or intervention in a political campaign on behalf of or in opposition to a candidate include, but are not limited to, the publication or distribution of written or printed statements or the making of oral statements on behalf of or in opposition to the candidate.[51]

An organization is an action organization if it has the following two characteristics: (1) its main or primary objective or objectives (as distinguished from its incidental or secondary objectives) may be attained only by legislation or a defeat of proposed legislation and (2) it advocates or campaigns for the attainment of this main or primary objective or objectives as distinguished from engaging in nonpartisan analysis, study or research, and making the results thereof available to the public. In determining whether an organization has these characteristics, all the surrounding facts and circumstances, including the articles and all activities of the organization, are considered.[52]

The IRS recognizes that the regulations' terms "exclusively," "primarily," and "insubstantial" present "difficult conceptual problems."[53] The Service concludes that "[q]uestions involving the application of these terms can more readily be resolved on the basis of the facts of a particular case."[54]

Application of the operational test is, therefore, intertwined with the proscriptions on private inurement and legislative and political activities.[55] In essence, however, to meet the operational test, an organization must be engaged in activities which further public rather than private purposes.[56]

The entwining of the operational test with the other requirements of the federal tax rules governing charitable organizations was explicitly recognized by the U.S. Tax Court in a decision refusing to reclassify a health and welfare fund exempt as an employee beneficiary association[57] as a charitable organization.[58] The court ruled against the organization on the ground that it is not operated exclusively for charitable purposes[59] and that its activities are fur-

---

[50]Reg. § 1.501(c)(3)-1(c)(3)(ii).
[51]Reg. § 1.501(c)(3)-1(c)(3)(iii).
[52]Reg. § 1.501(c)(3)-1(c)(3)(iv).
[53]IRS Exempt Organizations Handbook (IRM 7751) § 341.1(2).
[54]*Ibid*.
[55]See Chapters 12–14.
[56]Reg. § 1.501(c)(3)-1(d)(1)(ii).
[57]See Chapter 20.
[58]*Baltimore Regional Joint Board Health and Welfare Fund, Amalgamated Clothing and Textile Workers Union* v. *Commisioner*, 69 T.C. 554 (1978).
[59]See Chapter 11.

thering private interests[60] but cloaked its opinion in the mantle of the operational test. (The organization's activities consist of operating child day care centers—which the court seems to imply is not a charitable activity[61]—and providing services to members, and the organization charged the employees less tuition for the day care services than it charged other parents.)

An organization deemed an action organization, other than because of more than merely incidental political campaign activities, though it cannot qualify as a charitable organization, may nonetheless qualify as a social welfare organization.[62]

[60]See Chapter 12.

[61]See Rev. Rul. 70-533, 1970-2 C. B. 112; *San Francisco Infant School, Inc.* v. *Commissioner*, 69 T.C. 957 (1978). *Michigan Early Childhood Center, Inc.* v. *Commissioner*, 37 T.C.M. 808 (1978).

[62]Reg. § 1.501(c)(3)-1(c)(3)(v). See Chapters 15 and 16.

6

The Charitable Organization

Section § 501(c)(3) of the Internal Revenue Code provides exemption for organizations organized and operated exclusively for "charitable" purposes.

The term "charitable," which has the most extensive history and the broadest meaning of any of the terms in Code § 501(c)(3), is used in the section in its "generally accepted legal sense" and is, therefore, not to be construed as limited by the other purposes stated in the section which may fall within the broad outlines of "charity" as developed by judicial decisions.[1] The various categories of purposes comprehended by the term "charitable" in the federal tax law are discussed in this chapter.

§ 6.1 Relief of Poverty

The regulations accompanying the federal tax law concerning charitable organizations define the term "charitable" as including "[r]elief of the poor and distressed or of the underprivileged."[2]

The relief of poverty is perhaps the most basic and historically founded form of "charitable" activity. Assistance to the poor (but not necessarily the absolutely destitute) is the layman's concept of "charity"—assistance in the form of "the distribution of money or goods among the poor, by letting land to them at low rent, by making loans to them, by assisting them to secure employment, by the establishment of a home or other institution, by providing soup kitchens and the like."[3] If anything characterizes the 20th century brand of relieving poverty, it is the trend away from providing direct financial assistance (more and more the province of government) and to the provision of services.

Organizations deemed exempt because they relieve the poor, distressed, or underprivileged may be categorized as providing certain types of services. Some

[1]Reg. § 1.501(c)(3)-1(d)(2). See Reg. § 1.501(c)(3)-1(d)(1)(i)(b).
[2]Reg. § 1.501(c)(3)-1(d)(2).
[3]Restatement of *Trusts* 2d §369, comment a.

organizations provide assistance to enable the impoverished to secure employment, such as vocational training,[4] establishment of a market for products of
the needy,[5] or employment assistance for the elderly,[6] while others provide
assistance to maintain employment, such as operation of a day care center,[7]
promote the rights and welfare of public housing tenants,[8] provide technical
and material assistance under foreign self-help programs,[9] provide financial
assistance in securing a private hospital room,[10] or operate a service center
providing information, referral, and counseling services relating to health, housing, finances, education, and employment, as well as a facility for specialized
recreation, for a particular community's senior citizens.[11] Other such organizations provide services more personal in nature, such as provision of low-
income housing,[12] legal services,[13] money management advice,[14] vacations for
the elderly poor at a rural rest home,[15] home delivery of meals to the elderly,[16]
and transportation services for the elderly and handicapped.[17] Still other such
organizations seek to render assistance to the poor and distressed by helping
them at a point in time when they are particularly needy, as are prisoners
requiring rehabilitation,[18] the elderly requiring specially designed housing,[19]
the physically handicapped requiring such housing,[20] hospital patients needing
the visitation and comfort provided by their relatives and friends,[21] and widow(er)s
and orphans of police officers and firefighters killed in the line of duty.[22]
Similarly, exemption on that basis was accorded to an organization which posts
bail for persons who are otherwise incapable of paying for bail as part of its

[4]Rev. Rul. 73-128, 1973-1 C. B. 222.

[5]Rev. Rul. 68-167, 1968-1 C. B. 255; *Industrial Aid for the Blind* v. *Commissioner*, 73 T. C. 96 (1979).

[6]Rev. Rul. 66-257, 1966-2 C. B. 212.

[7]Rev. Rul. 70-533, 1970-2 C. B. 112; Rev. Rul. 68-166, 1968-1 C. B. 255.

[8]Rev. Rul. 75-283, 1975-2 C. B. 201.

[9]Rev. Rul. 68-117, 1968-1 C. B. 251; Rev. Rul. 68-165, 1968-1 C. B. 253.

[10]Rev. Rul. 79-358, 1979-2 C. B. 225.

[11]Rev. Rul. 75-198, 1975-1 C. B. 157. Also Rev. Rul. 77-42, 1977-1 C. B. 142.

[12]Rev. Rul. 70-585, 1970-2 C. B. 115; Rev. Rul. 68-17, 1968-1 C. B. 247; Rev. Rul. 67-250, 1967-2 C. B. 182; Rev. Rul. 67-138, 1967-1 C. B. 129.

[13]Rev. Rul. 78-428, 1978-2 C. B. 177; Rev. Rul. 72-559, 1972-2 C. B. 247; Rev. Rul. 69-161, 1969-1 C. B. 149.

[14]Rev. Rul. 69-441, 1969-2 C. B. 115.

[15]Rev. Rul. 75-385, 1975-2 C. B. 205.

[16]Rev. Rul. 76-244, 1976-1 C. B. 155.

[17]Rev. Rul. 77-246, 1977-2 C. B. 190.

[18]Rev. Rul. 70-583, 1970-2 C. B. 114, Rev. Rul. 67-150, 1967-1 C. B. 133.

[19]Rev. Rul. 79-18, 1979-1 C. B. 194.

[20]Rev. Rul. 79-19, 1979-1 C. B. 195.

[21]Rev. Rul. 81-28, 1981-1 C. B. 328.

[22]Rev. Rul. 55-406, 1955-1 C. B. 73.

integrated program for their release and rehabilitation,[23] to a legal aid society which provides free legal services and funds to pay fees of commercial bondsmen for indigent persons who are otherwise financially unable to obtain such services,[24] and to an organization which provides rescue and emergency services to persons suffering because of a disaster.[25] And, under appropriate circumstances,[26] an organization can qualify as "charitable" where the impoverished being assisted are in countries other than the United States.[27]

The lingering view of charity as being nearly confined to assistance to the poor was dramatically illustrated in the litigation that followed the 1969 IRS pronouncement of what constitutes a charitable hospital.[28] In that year, the IRS issued a ruling to the effect that the promotion of health was itself a charitable purpose as long as the requisite charitable class was present; specifically, the ruling enables a hospital to qualify for exemption where it simply provides emergency room services to all persons requiring such care irrespective of their ability to pay.[29] A lawsuit ensued, with a federal district court holding that a hospital, to be exempt, must significantly serve—without full or any charge—the poor. The court concluded that "Congress and the judiciary have consistently insisted that the application of sections 501 and 170 to hospitals be conditioned upon a demonstration that ameliorative consideration be given poor people in need of hospitalization."[30] To find otherwise, said the court, would be "to disregard what has been held to be the underlying rationale for allowing charitable deductions."[31] On appeal, however, this construction of the term "charitable" was reversed. Upon finding that the law of charitable trusts has promotion of health as a charitable purpose and noting the IRS citation of the appropriate authority, the appeals court held that the term "charitable" is "capable of a definition far broader than merely relief of the poor."[32] After reviewing the changes in the financing of health care in the United States over past decades (including the advent of Medicare and Medicaid), the court found that the rationale by which hospitals' charitable status is confined to the extent they provide for the poor "has largely disappeared."[33] Indeed, the court noted,

---

[23]Rev. Rul. 76-21, 1976-1 C. B. 147.

[24]Rev. Rul. 76-22, 1976-1 C. B. 148. Also Rev. Rul. 69-161, *supra*, n. 13.

[25]Rev. Rul. 69-174, 1969-1 C. B. 149. Cf. Rev. Rul. 77-3, 1977-1 C. B. 140.

[26]See text accompanying ns. 406–427, *infra*.

[27]See, e.g., Rev. Rul. 68-165, *supra*, n. 9, Rev. Rul. 68-117, *supra*, n. 9.

[28]See this chapter § 6, *infra*.

[29]Rev. Rul. 69-545, 1969-2 C. B. 117.

[30]*Eastern Kentucky Welfare Rights Organization* v. *Shultz*, 370 F.Supp. 325, 332 (D.D.C. 1973).

[31]*Ibid*. at 333.

[32]*Eastern Kentucky Welfare Rights Organization* v. *Simon*, 506 F.2d 1278, 1287 (D.C. Cir. 1974).

[33]*Ibid*. at 1288.

"[t]oday, hospitals are the primary community health facility for both rich and poor."[34]

As noted,[35] a charitable undertaking may be present where the beneficiaries thereof are the "poor and distressed." Yet, in what may be a notable departure, the IRS based a finding of "charitable" status for an organization solely on the ground that it relieves the "distressed" irrespective of whether they are also poor. The occasion was the Service's consideration of the tax treatment of a nonprofit hospice that operates on both inpatient and outpatient bases, to assist persons of all ages who have been advised by a physician that they are terminally ill in coping with the distress arising from their condition.[36] Thus, the classification of the organization as a charitable entity was predicated on the fact that the hospice "alleviat[es] the mental and physical distress of persons terminally ill."

The IRS continues to revert to this outdated doctrine in an effort to deny charitable status to various categories of otherwise qualified organizations. A case in point was the treatment accorded the nation's nonprofit consumer credit counseling agencies, which are organized and operated to provide consumer credit counseling services and information on personal money management. These agencies offer their credit counseling services to the general public. That is, the individuals and families eligible for assistance are not limited to those who are in need of such assistance solely by reason of the fact that they are low-income individuals. Late in 1976, the IRS privately ruled that certain of these agencies do not qualify as charitable organizations because, *inter alia*, their services are not limited to low-income individuals. This determination was contested, with the agencies urging the view that the provision of assistance by them to individuals and families who constitute members of the general public does not preclude charitable status for them.

There is no requirement, in the Code or in the income tax regulations, that an organization must provide services only to low-income individuals (i.e., the poor and distressed or the underprivileged), to qualify as a charitable organization. In fact, the only requirement in this regard is that such an organization be operated for a public rather than for a private interest. For example, one

---

[34]*Ibid*. The *Eastern Kentucky* case was heard by the Supreme Court, which ruled only that the plaintiffs lacked standing to bring the action. 426 U. S. 26 (1976). This conclusion was also reached by the Sixth Circuit Court of Appeals in *Lugo* v. *Miller*, 640 F.2d 823 (6th Cir. 1981), rev'g (on the issue) *Lugo* v. *Simon*, 453 F. Supp. 677 (N.D. Ohio). See Chapter 38.

[35]See text accompanying n. 2, *supra*.

[36]Rev. Rul. 79-17, 1979-1 C. B. 193. A similar discussion, concerning similar forms of distress facing the elderly, appears in the IRS ruling concerning homes for the aged (see § 6 *infra*). Also see Rev. Rul. 79-19, *supra*, n. 20, which discusses the distress confronting the physically handicapped.

writer stated that "[i]t is a general rule in the construction of exemptions from taxation that the word 'charity' is not to be restricted to the relief of the sick or the poor, but extends to any form of philanthropic endeavor or public benefit."[37]

Thus, as discussed below, an organization may achieve charitable status if it functions, for example, to advance education or to promote social welfare. These are independent grounds for acquiring classification as a charitable organization and do not require proof that the organization is also operated to relieve the poor and distressed or the underprivileged. This principle was noted by the IRS in 1975 when it observed, when considering tax-exempt public interest law firms, that such organizations are regarded "as charities because they provide a service which is of benefit to the community as a whole."[38]

The question of the tax-exempt status of the consumer credit counseling agencies as charitable groups was resolved in court, where it was held that the IRS cannot condition a nonprofit organization's tax status solely on the extent to which it provides assistance to the indigent.[39] Thus, said the court, the status of consumer credit counseling agencies as charitable groups cannot be regarded by the IRS as dependent on whether they confine their assistance to low-income individuals (or provide services at no charge). The agencies were found to be entitled to classification as charitable organizations as long as they can demonstrate that they satisfy at least one of the definitions of the term "charitable" (or one of the definitions of the term "educational").

The outcome of this case recalls the words of one writer, authored decades ago: "Although the relief of the poor, or benefit to them is, in its popular sense a necessary ingredient in the charity, this is not so in the view of the law."[40]

Thus, it should now be clear that a "charitable" purpose is not necessarily dependent on a showing that the poor are being relieved. Functions such as promotion of health, advancement of education, and lessening of the burdens of government are, therefore, charitable enterprises which need not involve any nexus with relief of the poor. At the same time, the belief persists that a charitable activity must involve free or reduced-cost services to indigents, and that a charitable purpose cannot be present where "the rich, the poor and the in-between are treated alike."[41]

[37]Black, *A Treatise in the Law of Income Taxation* 40 (2d ed. 1950).
[38]Rev. Rul. 75-74, 1975-1 C. B. 152.
[39]*Consumer Credit Counseling Service of Alabama, Inc.* v. *United States*, 78-2 U.S.T.C ¶ 9660 (D.D.C. 1978). Also *Credit Counseling Centers of Oklahoma, Inc.* v. *United States*, 79-2 U.S.T.C. ¶ 9468 (D.D.C. 1979).
[40]Zollman, *American Law of Charity*, 135–136 (1924).
[41]*Child* v. *United States*, 540 F.2d 579, 582 (2d Cir. 1976); *Bank of Carthage* v. *United States*, 304 F.Supp. 77, 80 (W.D. Mo. 1969).

§ 6.2 Advancement of Religion

The regulations accompanying the federal tax law concerning charitable organizations provide that the term "charitable" includes the "advancement of religion."[42]

The "advancement of religion" has long been considered a "charitable" purpose, although, like the "advancement of education," the scope of this category of "charitable" endeavors is imprecise due to the separate enumeration in federal tax law of other "charitable" purposes (in this case "religious"). The concept of "advancement of religion" includes the construction or maintenance of a church building, monument, memorial window, or burial ground, and collateral services such as the provision of music, payment of salaries, dissemination of religious doctrines, maintenance of missions, or distribution of religious literature.[43] The "charitable" exemption includes organizations whose works extend to the advancement of particular religions, religious sects, or religious doctrines, as well as religion in general.[44]

Organizations deemed exempt as charitable entities because they advance religion include those maintaining a church newspaper,[45] providing material for a parochial school system,[46] affording young adults counseling,[47] and undertaking genealogical research.[48] The IRS has ruled that an organization that supervises the preparation and inspection of food products prepared commercially in a particular locality to ensure that they satisfy the dietary rules of a particular religion is exempt as advancing religion.[49] An organization that provides funds for the defense of members of a religious sect in legal actions which involve a substantial constitutional issue of a state's abridgement of religious freedom was ruled exempt as a "charitable" organization in that it is "promoting social welfare by defending human and civil rights secured by law" although it would seem that it is also advancing religion.[50] An organization formed and controlled by an exempt conference of churches, that borrows funds from individuals and makes mortgage loans at less than the commercial rate of interest to affiliated churches to finance the construction of church buildings, qualified as a charitable organization because it advances religion.[51] An organization that provides a continuing educational program in an atmosphere conducive to

---

[42]Reg. § 1.501(c)(3)-1(d)(2).

[43]*Restatement of Trusts* 2d §371, comment a.

[44]*Ibid.*, comments b, d.

[45]Rev. Rul. 68-306, 1968-1 C. B. 257. Cf. *Foundation for Divine Meditation, Inc.* v. *Commissioner*, 24 T.C.M. 411 (1965), aff'd sub nom. *Parker* v. *Commissioner*, 365 F.2d 792 (8th Cir. 1966), cert. den. 385 U. S. 1026 (1967).

[46]Rev. Rul. 68-26, 1968-1 C. B. 272.

[47]Rev. Rul. 68-72, 1968-1 C. B. 250.

[48]Rev. Rul. 71-580, 1971-2 C. B. 235.

[49]Rev. Rul. 74-575, 1974-2 C. B. 161.

[50]Rev. Rul. 73-285, 1973-2 C. B. 174.

[51]Rev. Rul. 75-282, 1975-2 C. B. 201.

spiritual renewal for ministers, members of churches, and their families may qualify as an exempt organization because it advances religion.[52] An organization that provides traditional religious burial services, which directly support and maintain basic tenets and beliefs of a religion regarding burial of its members, was ruled to advance religion.[53] Likewise, an organization that conducts week-end religious retreats, open to individuals of diverse Christian denominations, at a rural lakeshore site at which the participants may enjoy recreational facilities in their limited amount of free time, qualifies as an organization that advances religion.[54]

Religion may be advanced by an organization that operates a noncommercial broadcasting station presenting programming on religious subjects.[55] Similarly, a nonprofit religious broadcasting station may acquire classification as a charitable organization even though it operates on a commercial license, as long as it does not sell commercial or advertising time[56] or, if it does so, sells the time as an incidental part of its activities.[57]

The IRS determined that an organization established to provide temporary low-cost housing and related services for missionary families on furlough for recuperation or training in the United States from their assignments abroad qualified as a charitable organization acting to advance religion because the assistance to the missionaries was provided them in their official capacities for use in furtherance of and as part of the organized religious program with which they were associated.[58] The Service cautioned, however, that "the providing of assistance to individuals in their individual capacities solely by reason of their identification with some form of religious endeavor, such as missionary work, is not a charitable use."

§ 6.3   Advancement of Education or Science

The regulations accompanying the federal tax law concerning charitable organizations include among the definitions of "charitable" the "advancement of education or science."[59]

The advancement of education includes the establishment or maintenance of nonprofit educational institutions, financing of scholarships and other forms of student assistance, establishment or maintenance of institutions such as public libraries and museums, advancement of knowledge through research,

---

[52]See Rev. Rul. 77-366, 1977-2 C. B. 192.
[53]Rev. Rul. 79-359, 1979-2 C. B. 226.
[54]Rev. Rul. 77-430, 1977-2 C. B. 194.
[55]See Rev. Rul. 66-220, 1966-2 C. B. 209.
[56]Rev. Rul. 68-563, 1968-2 C. B. 212.
[57]Rev. Rul. 78-385, 1978-2 C. B. 174.
[58]Rev. Rul. 75-434, 1975-2 C. B. 205. The IRS also ruled that an organization formed to aid immigrants in the U. S. qualified under Code § 501(c)(3). Rev. Rul. 76-205, 1976-1 C. B. 154.
[59]Reg. § 1.501(c)(3)-1(d)(2).

and dissemination of knowledge by publications, seminars, lectures and the like. The advancement of science includes comparable activities devoted to the furtherance or promotion of science and the dissemination of scientific knowledge. However, inasmuch as the federal tax law exemption for "charitable" organizations also contains the terms "educational" and "scientific," organizations coming within one or both of these two terms are likely to also qualify as "charitable" in nature.

For tax purposes, the more traditional forms of advancement of education, such as the establishment or maintenance of educational institutions, libraries, museums, and the like, will fall within the scope of the term "educational," leaving to the broader term "charitable" related concepts of "advancement" of education in the collateral sense. Nonetheless, the IRS, in ruling an organization to be "educational," frequently also finds it to be "charitable."[60]

For example, while the operation of a college or university is more in the nature of "educational" than "charitable," many satellite endeavors may be regarded as "charitable." Thus the provision of scholarships is a "charitable" activity,[61] as in the making of low-interest college loans,[62] and the provision of free housing, books, or supplies.[63] Other such "charitable" activities include publication of student journals such as law reviews,[64] maintenance of a training table for athletes,[65] provision of assistance to law students to obtain experience with public interest law firms and legal aid societies,[66] operation of a foreign student center,[67] selection of students for enrollment at foreign universities,[68] operation of an alumni association,[69] provision of work experience in selected trades and professions to high school graduates and college students,[70] the operation of interscholastic athletic programs,[71] and the provision of housing for students of a college.[72] Still other "charitable" *qua* "educational" activities are more institutionally oriented, such as bookstores,[73] organizations that accredit schools and colleges[74] or provide financial and investment assistance[75]

---

[60]See, e.g., Rev. Rul. 77-272, 1977-2 C. B. 191.

[61]Rev. Rul. 69-257, 1969-1 C. B. 151; Rev. Rul. 66-103, 1969-1 C. B. 134.

[62]Rev. Rul. 63-220, 1963-2 C. B. 208; Rev. Rul. 61-87, 1969-1 C. B. 191.

[63]Rev. Rul. 64-274, 1964-2 C. B. 141.

[64]Rev. Rul. 63-235, 1963-2 C. B. 610.

[65]Rev. Rul. 67-291, 1967-2 C. B. 184.

[66]Rev. Rul. 78-310, 1978-2 C. B. 173.

[67]Rev. Rul. 65-191, 1965-2 C. B. 157.

[68]Rev. Rul. 69-400, 1969-2 C. B. 114.

[69]Rev. Rul. 60-143, 1960-1 C. B. 192; Rev. Rul. 56-486, 1956-2 C. B. 309; *Estate of Thayer* v. *Commissioner*, 24 T.C. 384 (1955).

[70]Rev. Rul. 75-284, 1975-2 C. B. 202; Rev. Rul. 70-584, 1970-2 C. B. 114.

[71]Rev. Rul. 55-587, 1955-2 C. B. 261.

[72]Rev. Rul. 76-336, 1976-2 C. B. 143.

[73]*Squire* v. *Students Book Corp.*, 191 F.2d 1018 (9th Cir. 1951).

[74]Rev. Rul. 74-146, 1974-1 C. B. 129.

[75]Rev. Rul. 71-529, 1971-2 C. B. 234; Rev. Rul. 67-149, 1967-1 C. B. 133.

or computer services[76] to educational organizations. However, one type of organization operated closely with colleges and universities—fraternities and sororities—generally is not regarded as being charitable or educational in nature.[77]

Colleges and universities frequently utilize affiliated organizations in connection with the carrying out of their charitable and educational activities. It is clear that these related organizations are "charitable" in character. As illustrations, the IRS has ruled exempt an organization the operates a book and supply store that sells items only to students and faculty of the college,[78] that operates a cafeteria and restaurant on the campus of a university primarily for the convenience of its students and faculty,[79] and that provides housing and food service exclusively for students and faculty of a university.[80]

The attitude of the IRS regarding organizations the functions of which are oriented toward assistance to other organizations which are clearly exempt shifts radically where the assistance is directed to two or more such entities. Exempt organizations, such as colleges, universities and hospitals, are turning ever more frequently to cooperative ventures to reduce costs and improve the quality of performance. Universities often find it productive and more efficient to share, for example, data processing or library resources, while hospitals are likely to share laundry facilities.[81] (The tax treatment of consortia is discussed below.)

Organizations not affiliated with any formal institution of learning but which provide instruction may also be deemed to "advance education," such as those which teach industrial skills,[82] conduct work experience programs,[83] provide apprentice training,[84] act as a clearinghouse and course coordinator for instructors and students,[85] instruct in the field of business,[86] evaluate the public service obligations of broadcasters,[87] and provide services to relieve psychological tensions and improve the mental health of children and adolescents.[88]

Education may be advanced through such modes as the publication and

[76]Rev. Rul. 74-614, 1974-2 C. B. 164, amplified by Rev. Rul. 81-29, 1981-1 C. B. 329.

[77]Rev. Rul. 69-573, 1969-2 C. B. 125; *Phinney, Dougherty* v. 307 F.2d 357 (5th Cir. 1962); *Davison* v. *Commissioner*, 60 F.2d 50 (2d Cir. 1932). See also Rev. Rul. 64-117, 1964-1 (Part 1) C. B. 180 (student clubs), and Rev. Rul. 64-118, 1964-1 (Part 1) C. B. 182 (fraternity housing corporations).

[78]Rev. Rul. 69-538, 1969-2 C. B. 116.

[79]Rev. Rul. 58-194, 1958-1 C. B. 240.

[80]Rev. Rul. 67-217, 1967-2 C. B. 181.

[81]See Patterson, *Colleges in Consort* (1974).

[82]Rev. Rul. 72-101, 1972-1 C. B. 144. Cf. Rev. Rul. 78-42, 1978-1 C. B. 158.

[83]Rev. Rul. 78-310, *supra* n. 66; Rev. Rul. 76-37, 1976-1 C. B. 146; Rev. Rul. 75-284, *supra*, n. 70; Rev. Rul. 70-584, *supra* n. 70.

[84]Rev. Rul. 67-72, 1967-1 C. B. 125.

[85]Rev. Rul. 71-413, 1971-2 C. B. 228.

[86]Rev. Rul. 68-16, 1968-1 C. B. 246.

[87]Rev. Rul. 79-26, 1979-1 C. B. 196.

[88]Rev. Rul. 77-68, 1977-1 C. B. 142.

dissemination of research,[89] maintenance of collections,[90] the provision of anthropological specimens,[91] the operation of a foreign exchange program,[92] and the operation of an honor society.[93] Likewise the IRS determined that the provision of bibliographic information by means of a computer network to researchers at both exempt and nonexempt libraries constitutes the advancement of education.[94] Similarly, the IRS held that an organization formed to preserve the natural environment by acquiring ecologically significant undeveloped land and to maintain the land or to transfer it to a government conservation agency qualifies for exemption at least in part for the reason that it is advancing education and science.[95]

§ 6.4 Lessening the Burdens of Government

The regulations accompanying the federal tax law concerning charitable organizations define the term "charitable" as including "lessening of the burdens of Government" and also the "erection or maintenance of public buildings, monuments, or works."[96] This first concept relates more to the provision of governmental or municipal services rather than facilities, because of inclusion in the regulations of the exempt activity of erection or maintenance of public facilities.

Some organizations exempt under this category of "charitable" provide services directly in the context of governmental activity, such as assisting in the preservation of a public lake,[97] beautifying a city,[98] operating a prisoner correctional center,[99] assisting in the operation of a mass transportation system,[100] maintaining a volunteer fire company,[101] conserving natural resources,[102] or encouraging plantings of public lands.[103] In the latter case, the IRS observed that "[p]roviding fire and rescue service for the general community has been held to be a charitable purpose because it lessens the burden of government."

Other such organizations provide services in tandem with existing governmental agencies. As examples, an organization which makes funds available to

[89]Rev. Rul. 67-4, 1967-1 C. B. 121.
[90]Rev. Rul. 70-321, 1970-1 C. B. 129.
[91]Rev. Rul. 70-129, 1970-1 C. B. 128.
[92]Rev. Rul. 80-286, 1980-2 C. B. 179.
[93]Rev. Rul. 71-97, 1971-1 C. B. 150.
[94]Rev. Rul. 81-29, supra, n. 76.
[95]Rev. Rul. 76-204, 1976-1 C. B. 152. Cf. Rev. Rul. 78-384, 1978-2 C. B. 174.
[96]Reg. § 1.501(c)(3)-1(d)(2).
[97]Rev. Rul. 70-186, 1970-1 C.B. 128.
[98]Rev. Rul. 68-14, 1968-1 C.B. 243. Cf. Rev. Rul. 75-286, 1975-2 C.B. 210.
[99]Rev. Rul. 70-583, supra, n. 18.
[100]Rev. Rul. 71-29, 1971-1 C.B. 150.
[101]Rev. Rul. 74-361, 1974-2 C.B. 159.
[102]Rev. Rul. 67-292, 1967-2 C.B. 184.
[103]Rev. Rul. 66-179, 1966-1 C.B. 139.

a police department for use as reward money is exempt as charitable,[104] as is an organization that assists firefighters, police, and other personnel to perform their duties more efficiently during emergency conditions,[105] an organization that provides bus transportation to isolated areas of a community not served by the existing city bus system as a Model Cities demonstration project performed under the authority of the federal and local governments,[106] and an organization which provides expert opinions to local government officials concerning traffic safety.[107] A government internship program may likewise come within this category of charitable activities,[108] as would a program of awards to citizens for outstanding civic achievements.[109] Likewise, professional standards review organizations[110] can qualify as charitable entities because they enable the medical profession to assume the government's responsibility for reviewing the appropriateness and quality of services provided under the Medicare and Medicaid programs.[111]

In a recent application of these rules, an organization that certifies crop seed within the State of Indiana was found to be performing a service required by federal and state law—a service performed in other states by a governmental agency—and thus to be charitable because it is lessening the burdens of government. The organization, functioning in conjunction with Purdue University, was held to be protecting the "purchasing public—generally farmers and gardeners—from perceived abuses in the sale of agricultural and vegetable seed which is impure, mislabeled or adulterated" and therefore to be undertaking a "public service" and a "recognized governmental function."[112]

Organizations that qualify for "charitable" status as performing governmental functions are those which supply a community with facilities ordinarily provided at the taxpayers' expense or maintain the facilities, such as town halls, bridges, streets, parks, trees, and monuments.[113] Examples of organizations in this category include those which engage in activities such as solid waste recycling,[114] community improvement,[115] and community land-use analysis,[116] as

---

[104]Rev. Rul. 74-246, 1974-1 C.B. 130.

[105]Rev. Rul. 71-99, 1971-1 C.B. 151.

[106]Rev. Rul. 78-68, 1978-1 C.B. 149. Cf. Rev. Rul. 78-69, 1978-1 C.B. 156.

[107]Rev. Rul. 76-418, 1976-2 C.B. 145. Cf. Rev. Rul. 70-79, 1970-1 C.B. 127.

[108]Rev. Rul. 70-584, *supra* n. 70.

[109]Rev. Rul. 66-146, 1966-1 C. B. 136.

[110]See §§ 6 and 9 hereof, *infra*.

[111]Rev. Rul. 81-276, 1981-2 C.B. 128.

[112]*Indiana Crop Improvement Association, Inc.* v. *Commissioner*, 76 T.C. 394, 398, 399 (1981).

[113]*Restatement of Trusts* 2d § 373, comment a.

[114]Rev. Rul. 72-560, 1972-2 C. B. 248; IRS Private Letter Ruling 7823052.

[115]Rev. Rul. 68-15, 1968-1 C. B. 244.

[116]Rev. Rul. 67-391, 1967-2 C. B. 190.

well as those which provide public parks,[117] other recreational facilities,[118] and public parking lots.[119]

A corollary of the foregoing is that an organization that frustrates attempts to relieve the burdens of government and thereby increases such burdens cannot qualify as a charitable organization.[120]

§ 6.5   Community Beautification and Maintenance

A category of charitable purpose somewhat akin to the category just discussed is the purpose of community beautification and maintenance and the preservation of natural beauty. However, the IRS did not expressly recognize this purpose as a separate category of charitable endeavor until 1978.

As discussed, prior IRS rulings have recognized as charities organizations that devote their assets to the maintenance and improvement of community recreational facilities and parklands. Thus, charitable status was accorded an organization formed to preserve a lake as a public recreational facility and to improve the condition of the water in the lake to enhance its recreational features[121] and an organization formed to promote and assist in city beautification projects and to educate the public in the advantages of street planning.[122]

In 1978, the IRS ruled with respect to a membership organization that was formed to help preserve, beautify and maintain a public park located in a city.[123] The organization plants trees, flowers, and shrubs, maintains the park facilities, and mows the grass and picks up litter, thereby ensuring "the continued use of the park for public recreational purposes." In so ruling, the IRS cited charity trust law precedents in the court decisions and the literature.[124]

§ 6.6   Promotion of Health

The promotion of health as a "charitable" purpose includes the establishment or maintenance of hospitals, clinics, homes for the aged, and the like; advancement of medical and similar knowledge through research; and the maintenance of conditions conducive to health. "Health," for this purpose, includes "mental

---

[117]Rev. Rul. 66-358, 1966-2 C. B. 218.

[118]Rev. Rul. 70-186, *supra*, n. 97; Rev. Rul. 59-310, 1959-2 C. B. 332.

[119]*Monterey Public Parking Corp.* v. *United States*, 481 F.2d 175 (9th Cir. 1973).

[120]Rev. Rul. 75-384, 1975-2 C. B. 204.

[121]Rev. Rul. 70-186, *supra* n. 97.

[122]Rev. Rul. 68-14, *supra* n. 98.

[123]Rev. Rul. 78-85, 1978-1 C. B. 150.

[124]IV *Scott on Trusts* (3d ed. 1967) § 374.10; *Restatement of Trusts* 2d § 374 (comment f) (1959); Bogert, *Trusts and Trustees* (2d ed. 1959) § 378 at 179, 180; *President and Fellows of Middlebury College* v. *Central Power Corp. of Vermont*, 143 A. 384 (Sup. Ct. Vt. 1928); *Noice* v. *Schnell*, 137 A. 582 (Ct. Err. App. N.J. 1927); *Cresson's Appeal*, 30 Pa. 437 (1858).

health" and would include, were it not for a separate enumeration in the federal tax law description of charitable organizations, the prevention of cruelty to children.[125] The regulations defining the types of charitable entities do not contain any specific reference to the promotion of health as a charitable purpose but this aspect of "charitable" activity has been reaffirmed by the IRS on several occasions.[126]

The most obvious example of an organization established and operated for the promotion of health is a hospital.[127] To qualify for exemption as a charitable organization, however, a hospital must demonstrate that it serves a public rather than a private interest.[128] The Supreme Court has noted that "[n]on-profit hospitals have never received these benefits [tax exemption and eligibility to receive deductible contributions] as a favored general category, but an individual nonprofit hospital has been able to claim them if it could qualify" as a charitable entity.[129] The Court added: "As the Code does not define the term *charitable*, the status of each nonprofit hospital is determined on a case-by-case basis by the IRS" (emphasis in original).[130]

The initial position of the IRS in this regard was published in 1956, in which the Service set forth requirements for exemption, including a rule requiring patient care without charge or at below cost.[131] At that time, the IRS stated that a hospital, to be "charitable," "must be operated to the extent of its financial ability for those not able to pay for the services rendered and not exclusively for those who are able and expected to pay." This approach was a reflection of the charitable hospital as it once was—an almshouse, providing health care more for the poor than for the sick.

Today's hospital now provides health services for the entire community, with a commensurate increase in patient care revenue (especially in relation to private contributions) and health care costs. Prepayment plans now cover hospital expenses for much of the citizenry and reimbursement programs under Medicare and Medicaid are reducing the number of patients who lack an ability to "pay" for health services. Thus, in 1969, the IRS modified its 1956 position by recognizing that the promotion of health is inherently a charitable purpose and is not obviated by the fact that the cost of services is borne by patients or

[125]*Restatement of Trusts* 2d § 372, comment b.
[126]See, e.g., Rev. Rul. 69-545, *supra*, n. 29; also see *Restatement of Trusts* 2d §§368, 372 (1959); IV *Scott on Trusts* §§368, 372 (3d ed. 1967).
[127]See Code § 170(b)(1)(A)(iii); Bogert, *Trusts and Trustees* § 374 (2d ed. 1967).
[128]Reg. § 1.501(c)(3)-1(d)(1)(ii); *Restatement of Trusts* 2d § 372, comment b.
[129]*Simon v. Eastern Kentucky Welfare Rights Organization*, *supra*, n. 34 at 29.
[130]*Ibid*. at 29. See Comment, "Income Taxation—A Pauper a Day Keeps the Taxman Away: Qualification of Hospitals as Charitable Institutions Under Section 501 (c)(3)," 54 N. Car. L. Rev. 1195 (1976); Note, "Federal Income Tax Exemptions for Private Hospitals," 36 Fordham L. Rev. 747 (1968). Cf. Congdon, "With Charity for All: Did the I.R.S. Comply With the Administrative Procedure Act in Changing the Requirements for Charitable Exemptions of Hospitals?," 1 ISL L. Rev. (No. 1) 41 (1976).
[131]Rev. Rul. 56-185, 1956-1 C. B. 202.

third party payors.[132] Under the 1969 ruling, to be exempt, a hospital must promote the health of a class of persons broad enough to benefit the community and must be operated to serve a public rather than a private interest. Basically, this means that the emergency room must be open to all and that hospital care is provided to all who can pay, directly or indirectly. The hospital may generate a surplus of receipts over disbursements and nonetheless be exempt. The requirement that health care be provided free or at reduced costs has been dropped.

Other factors which may indicate that a hospital is operating for the benefit of the public include control of the institution in a board of trustees composed of individuals who do not have any direct economic interest in the hospital; maintenance by the hospital of an open medical staff, with privileges available to all qualified physicians, consistent with the size and nature of the facilities; a hospital policy enabling any member of the medical staff to rent available office space; hospital programs of medical training, research, and education; and involvement by the hospital in various projects and programs to improve the health of the community.[133]

However, even if an organization provides health care, it will not be exempt if it is a proprietary institution, is operated for the benefit of private individuals (for example, owners, doctors), is operated for benefit of a closed medical staff, enters into favorable rental agreements with a limited group of doctors, or limits its emergency room care and hospital admissions substantially to patients of such a group.[134] Other factors which may indicate that a hospital is operating for the benefit of private interests are whether the hospital is controlled by members of the medical staff or by the original owners of the institution when in proprietary form; the hospital enters into contractual arrangements enabling the controlling physicians or original owners to realize direct economic benefits from the operation of certain of its departments; the hospital has a record of negligible uncollectible accounts and charity cases; and, if a sale is involved, the purchase price paid for the proprietary hospital is less than the reasonable value of the facility to the nonprofit organization.[135] The prospects of private

---

[132]Rev. Rul. 69-545, *supra* n. 29. See *Restatement of Trusts* 2d § 372, comment b. This ruling was upheld in *Eastern Kentucky Welfare Rights Organization* v. *Simon*, *supra*, n. 32. See Recent Decision, 9 *Ga. L. Rev.* 729 (1975).

[133]See IRS Exempt Organizations Handbook (IRM 7751) § 343.5(2).

[134]See *Harding Hospital, Inc.* v. *United States*, 505 F.2d 1068 (6th Cir. 1974); *Sonora Community Hospital* v. *Commissioner*, 46 T.C. 519 (1966) aff'd 397 F.2d 814 (9th Cir. 1968); *Burgess* v. *Four States Memorial Hospital*, 465 S.W.2d 693 (Sup. Ct. Ark. 1971); *Maynard Hospital, Inc.* v. *Commissioner*, 52 T.C. 1006 (1969). In general, see Bromberg, "Tax Problems of Nonprofit Hospitals," 47 *Taxes* 524 (1969). Cf. IRS Private Letter Ruling 7821141.

[135]See IRS Exempt Organizations Handbook (IRM 7751) § 343.5(3). Cf. IRS Private Letter Ruling 7825036.

inurement will be of particular concern where a proprietary hospital or similar organization is transferred to a nonprofit, ostensibly tax-exempt, entity.[136]

A doctor's relationship with an otherwise "charitable" hospital can raise private inurement problems.[137] Of prime concern are contractual arrangements for compensation between the hospital and a hospital-based specialist. In one instance, the head of a hospital's radiology department received a fixed percentage of the department's gross income; the amount paid him was reasonable, the specialist had no control over the hospital, the agreement was an arm's-length negotiated arrangement, and thus no private inurement was found.[138] Presumably, a contractual arrangement outside the scope of such a situation (such as where compensation is based on net income) could preclude the hospital's exemption on private inurement grounds. However, organizations created by the medical staff of an exempt hospital may, under appropriate circumstances, qualify as charitable entities.[139] By contrast, a percentage compensation agreement destroyed an organization's exemption as a charitable entity where the arrangement transformed its principal activity into a joint venture between it and a group of physicians or became merely a device for distributing profits to persons in control.[140]

Another well-recognized health provider institution is the home for the aged. Until 1972, the chief basis for exemption of a home for the aged as a "charitable" entity was that free or below cost services must be provided, in conformance with the early IRS view as to hospitals.[141] This approach was abandoned in 1972 and replaced with a requirement that the charitable home for the aged be operated so as to satisfy the primary needs of the aged: housing, health care, and financial security.[142] The need for housing is generally satisfied if the home "provides residential facilities that are specifically designed to meet some combination of the physical, emotional, recreational, social, religious, and similar needs" of the aged. As for health care, that need is generally satisfied where the home "either directly provides some form of health care, or in the alternative, maintains some continuing arrangement with other organizations, facilities, or health personnel, designed to maintain the physical, and if necessary, mental well-being of its residents." Satisfaction of the financial security need has two aspects: the home must (1) maintain in the residence "any persons who become unable to pay their regular charges" and (2) provide its services "at the lowest feasible cost." A home for the aged will qualify for exempt status as

---

[136]See *State* v. *Wilmar Hospital*, 2 N.W.2d 564 (Sup. Ct. Minn. 1942).
[137]See Chapter 12.
[138]Rev. Rul. 69-383, 1969-2 C.B. 113.
[139]See Rev. Rul. 69-631, 1969-2 C. B. 119.
[140]*Lorain Avenue Clinic* v. *Commissioner*, 31 T. C. 141 (1958); *Birmingham Business College* v. *Commissioner*, 276 F.2d 476 (5th Cir. 1960), aff'g, mod. and rem'g 17 T.C.M. 816 (1958).
[141]Rev. Rul. 56-185, *supra*, n. 131. See also Rev. Rul. 57-467, 1957-2 C. B. 313.
[142]Rev. Rul. 72-124, 1972-1 C. B. 145. See Rev. Rul 75-198, 1975-1 C. B. 157.

a charitable organization, assuming it otherwise qualifies, if it operates in a manner designed to meet these primary needs of the aged. However, a home for the aged may, in the alternative, qualify under prior IRS rulings for exempt status, if the home is primarily concerned with providing care and housing for financially distressed aged persons.[143]

One of the most controversial of the health provider institutions—from the standpoint of federal tax categorization—is the health maintenance organization (HMO).[144] The HMO provides health care services by means of facilities and programs, in a manner comparable to that of an exempt hospital. It is a membership organization; its services are provided to members on a prepaid basis and to nonmembers on a fee-for-service basis. In most instances, the HMO handles emergency cases without regard to whether the patient is a member and annually provides care either free or at reduced rates to a limited number of indigent patients. Frequently, HMO's sponsor education programs and research efforts to study ways to deliver better health care services. The HMO governing board is usually elected by and from its membership.

The position of the IRS has been that an HMO may qualify for tax exemption as a social welfare organization[145] but cannot qualify for exemption as a charitable organization because the preferential treatment accorded its member-subscribers constitutes the serving of private interests and because the prepayment feature constitutes a form of insurance that is not a charitable activity. However, this position was rejected by the U.S. Tax Court, which held that (1) the persons benefited by an HMO represent a class large enough to constitute a requisite community,[146] (2) the HMO meets all of the IRS criteria applied to determine charitable status for hospitals,[147] and (3) while the risk of illness is spread throughout its entire membership, the HMO does not operate for commercial purposes but for charitable purposes and thus the risk spreading feature[148] is not a bar to designation of an HMO as a charitable organization.[149]

Various other types of health provider institutions which qualify as charitable

---

[143]See Rev. Rul. 64-231, 1964-2 C. B. 139; Rev. Rul. 61-72, 1961-1 C. B. 188. In general, see Bromberg, "Non-profit homes for the aged: an analysis of their current tax exempt status," 38 J. Tax. 54, 120 (1973); Bromberg, "Tax Exemption of Homes for the Aged," 46 Taxes 68 (1968).

[144]HMOs are authorized under federal law pursuant to Title XIII of the Public Health Service Act, 42 U.S.C. § 300e.

[145]See Chapter 15 § 5.

[146]See Chapter 4 § 2. The court, in dismissing the Service's private inurement rationale, held that the concept of private benefit is limited to situations where an organization's "insiders" are benefited. See Chapter 12 § 2.

[147]Rev. Rul. 69-545, supra n. 29.

[148]The IRS has ruled that prepaid group practice plans are not insurance companies for federal tax law purposes (Code Subchapter L). Rev. Rul. 68-27, 1968-1 C. B. 315.

[149]Sound Health Association v. Commissioner, 71 T.C. 158 (1978). In general, see Bromberg, "Obtaining a 501(c)(3) exemption for an HMO should be easier now despite IRS objections," 50 J. Tax. 302 (1979).

organizations for federal tax purposes exist. These include entities such as drug rescue centers,[150] blood banks,[151] halfway houses,[152] organizations which minister to the nonmedical needs of patients in a proprietary hospital,[153] nursing bureaus,[154] senior citizens centers,[155] organizations which provide private hospital rooms when medically necessary,[156] Christian Science medical care facilities,[157] and medical research organizations.[158] Moreover, exempt status has been accorded several types of organizations providing specialized health care services. Thus, for example, the "home health agency," an organization which provides low cost health care to patients in their homes, is a charitable entity.[159] Similarly, an organization created to attract a doctor to a medically underserved community by providing a medical building and facilities was ruled exempt, notwithstanding the fact that the doctor would generally charge for his services and receive some personal benefit (use of building) under the arrangement.[160] Also, an organization, that built and leased a public hospital and related facilities to an exempt charitable association which operates the facilities, for an amount sufficient only to retire indebtedness and meet necessary operating expenses, was determined to be furthering the charitable purpose of promoting the health of the community.[161] Likewise, organizations which conduct medical research are frequently ruled exempt as charitable organizations, although such organizations may instead be considered as engaged in "scientific" research.[162] As another illustration, an organization that operates a free computerized donor authorization retrieval system to facilitate transplantation of body organs upon a donor's death qualified as a charitable organization as engaged in the promotion of health.[163] Still another example is an organization that provides

---

[150]Rev. Rul. 70-590, 1970-2 C. B. 116.

[151]Rev. Rul. 66-323, 1966-2 C. B. 216, as modified by Rev. Rul. 78-145, 1978-1 C. B. 169.

[152]Rev. Rul. 72-16, 1972-1 C. B. 143. Also Rev. Rul. 75-472, 1975-2 C. B. 208.

[153]Rev. Rul. 68-73, 1968-1 C. B. 251.

[154]Rev. Rul. 55-656, 1955-2 C. B. 262.

[155]Rev. Rul. 75-198, *supra*, n. 142.

[156]Rev. Rul. 79-358, *supra*, n. 10.

[157]Rev. Rul. 80-114, 1980-1 C. B. 115, superseding Rev. Rul. 78-427, 1978-2 C.B. 176. This determination is consistent with the Service's position that payments to Christian Science practitioners for services rendered are deductible medical expenses. Rev. Rul. 55-261, 1955-1 C.B. 307.

[158]Code § 170(b)(1)(A)(iii).

[159]Rev. Rul. 72-209, 1972-1 C. B. 148.

[160]Rev. Rul. 73-313, 1973-2 C. B. 174; see also *In re Carlson's Estate*, 358 P.2d 669 (Sup. Ct. Kan. 1961); cf. Rev. Rul. 69-266, 1969-2 C. B. 151.

[161]Rev. Rul. 80-309, 1980-2 C. B. 183.

[162]See, e.g., Rev. Rul. 69-526, 1969-2 C. B. 115. See Chapter 10. See, in general, Bromberg, "The Charitable Hospital," 20 *Cath. Univ. L. Rev.* 237 (1970); Rose, "The IRS Contribution to the Health Problems of the Poor," 21 *Cath. Univ. L. Rev.* 35 (1971).

[163]Rev. Rul. 75-197, 1975-1 C. B. 156.

services (e.g., housing, transportation, and counseling) for relatives and friends who have traveled to the organization's community to visit and comfort patients at local health care facilities.[164] Further, the IRS has conceded that, under certain conditions, a professional standards review organization can qualify as a charitable entity for the reason that it is promoting health.[165]

In 1977, the IRS stated that the term "charitable" includes the promotion of "public health," in ruling that an organization formed to provide individual psychological and educational evaluations, as well as tutoring and therapy, for children and adolescents with learning disabilities qualifies as a charitable organization.[166] The organization's psychologists and other professionals administer tests designed to determine intellectual capacity, academic achievement, psychological adjustment, speech and language difficulties, and perceptual-motor abilities. Therapy is available through staff professionals who have special training in the various areas of learning disabilities.

Application of the concept that the term "charitable" embraces the function of promoting health continues to trouble the IRS as the courts persist in allowing various forms of the practice of medicine (generally, a for-profit endeavor) to lodge within its ambit. Of course, the practice of medicine occurs in hospitals but, as noted, the law has rationalized the classification of most non-profit hospitals as charitable. Thereafter, also as noted, charitable entities have been determined to include a variety of clinics, centers, research agencies, plans, and—most recently—health maintenance organizations. Even more recently, however, the Service has been confronted with another type of noncommercial health provider: the incorporation of clinical departments of teaching hospitals associated with medical schools.

In nearly every hospital, there is tension surrounding the issue of who actually operates the hospital: the physicians or the administrative staff. While in fact both groups play essential roles, the physicians have readily persisted in achieving superiority of departmental management roles. This is significant for several reasons, including the fact that a considerable portion of the compensation of a physician is derived from fees generated out of the department in which he or she renders the clinical care. Consequently, the participating physicians have been quite concerned about the form of the management vehicle, wanting it to be an entity they control, a nonprofit organization, and, necessarily, an organization that can engage in the practice of medicine.

In one instance, at issue was the exempt status of a professional corporation, all of the stockholders (who were also its employees) of which were physicians on the clinical staff of a teaching hospital operated by a state university and full-time members of the faculty of the university's school of medicine. The corporation consisted of four departments of the medical school and—in addition to the provision of medical care—was empowered to provide academic

---

[164]Rev. Rul. 81-28, *supra*, n. 21.
[165]Rev. Rul. 81-276, *supra*, n. 111. See § 9 hereof, *infra*.
[166]Rev. Rul. 77-68, *supra*, n. 88.

and clinical instruction of medical students, medical research, and ancillary administrative services solely for the benefit of the medical school and the teaching hospital. The financial support of the organization was derived from the receipt of fees for medical care performed by its employees at the teaching hospital; approximately 25 percent of the billable value of the services performed by the employees was rendered to patients who were unable to pay and were not required to pay for the services.

Rejecting the position of the IRS, the Tax Court found that the corporation was organized and operated for charitable, educational, and scientific purposes, in that it, *inter alia*, "delivers health care to the general public."[167] The fact that the organization was authorized to engage in the general practice of medicine did not deter the court, in that the organization's activities were limited to serving the interests of the medical school and hospital involved; thus, it was not authorized to practice medicine for profit. The court also excused the form of the professional corporation, rationalizing it as necessary because that is the only corporate entity permitted to practice medicine in the state. Further, the court tolerated the existence of stockholders and dismissed the fact that each shareholder was entitled to receive the par value of his or her single share ($1.00) in the event of dissolution as being insubstantial and thus not a violation of the rule requiring dedication of assets for a charitable purpose.[168]

Consequently, on the basis of this and prior Tax Court decisions,[169] the court appears firmly committed to the proposition that this type of corporate collective of physicians is tax-exempt, even though it generates fees for the performance of medical care services and pays such funds to individuals who are its stockholders. In these instances, of course, it is the close nexus with a medical school and teaching hospital that provides the underlying basis for the tax exemption.

Occasionally, the IRS will rule that an organization is a charitable entity because it is carrying out an integral part of the activities of another charitable organization.[170] The Service used this rationale to find that a trust created by an exempt hospital to accumulate and hold funds to be used to satisfy malpractice claims against the hospital, and from which the hospital directs the trustee to make payments to claimants, is a charitable organization for federal tax purposes.[171]

---

[167]*University of Maryland Physicians, P.A.* v. *Commissioner*, 41 T.C.M. 732, 735 (1981). Other exempt activities were held to be the rendering of services without charge to the indigent (§ 1 hereof), provision of clinical training to the students, interns, and residents of the medical school (§ 3 hereof; Chapter 7§ 2), and medical research for the advancement of the healing arts (§ 3 hereof; Chapter 9).

[168]See Chapter 5 § 1.

[169]*University of Massachusetts Medical School Group Practice* v. *Commissioner*, 74 T.C. 1299 (1980); *B.H.W. Anesthesia Foundation* v. *Commissioner*, 72 T.C. 681 (1979).

[170]See Rev. Rul. 75-282, *supra*, n. 51.

[171]Rev. Rul. 78-41, 1978-1 C. B. 148. Unfortunately (because it may make a difference), the IRS in this ruling did not indicate whether the trust is irrevocable or revocable.

§ 6.7 Promotion of Social Welfare

The "promotion of social welfare" is the most indefinite category of "charitable" purposes. In the general law of charitable trusts, the concept includes such wide-ranging activities as the promotion of temperance, prevention or alleviation of suffering of animals, promotion of national security, inculcation of patriotism, promotion of the happiness or well-being of the members of the community, promotion of the happiness or well-being of persons who have few opportunities for recreation and enjoyment, and (perhaps) the erection or maintenance of a tomb or monument.[172] As has been observed, "[n]o attempt . . . can successfully be made to enumerate all of the purposes which fall within the scope" of this category of "charitable" purpose and the question in each case is whether "the purpose is one the accomplishment of which might reasonably be held to be for the social interest of the community."[173]

The regulations defining charitable purposes state five types of promotion of social welfare endeavors: activities "designed to [(1)] accomplish any of the above [charitable] purposes," (2) "lessen neighborhood tensions," (3) "eliminate prejudice and discrimination," (4) "defend human and civil rights secured by law," and (5) "combat community deterioration and juvenile delinquency."[174]

The types of organizations exempt as charitable organizations because they are operated to eliminate prejudice and discrimination may be illustrated by three rulings by the IRS in 1968. One of the organizations discussed in the rulings worked to educate the public about integrated housing and conducted programs to prevent panic selling because of the introduction of blacks into a formerly all-white neighborhood.[175] Another conducted investigations and research to obtain information regarding discrimination in housing and public accommodations against minority groups.[176] Still another operated to advance equal job opportunities in a particular community for qualified workers discriminated against because of race or creed.[177] An organization formed to eliminate discrimination against members of minorities seeking employment in the construction trades by recruiting, educating, and counseling workers, providing technical assistance to attorneys involved in suits to enforce workers' rights, and acting as a court-appointed monitor after successful suits, qualified as a charitable organization because it acts to eliminate prejudice and discrimination.[178] Combating community deterioration in the "charitable" sense involves remedial action leading to the elimination of the physical, economic and social causes of the deterioration,[179] such as by purchasing and renovating deterio-

---

[172]*Restatement of Trusts* 2d § 374, comments b-h. See Chapter 15.
[173]*Ibid.*, comment a.
[174]Reg. § 1.501(c)(3)-1(d)(2).
[175]Rev. Rul. 68-655, 1968-2 C. B. 613.
[176]Rev. Rul. 68-438, 1968-2 C. B. 609.
[177]Rev. Rul. 68-70, 1968-1 C. B. 248.
[178]Rev. Rul. 75-285, 1975-2 C. B. 203.
[179]Rev. Rul. 67-6, 1967-1 C. B. 135.

rating residences and selling or leasing them to low-income families on a non-profit basis[180] and by operating a self-help home building program.[181] The charitable activity of combating community deterioration can be present "whether or not the community is in a state of decline."[182]

"Discrimination" in this context is not confined to racial discrimination. Thus, an organization formed to promote equal rights for women in employment and other economic contexts was ruled exempt as promoting social welfare by eliminating prejudice and discrimination.[183] Also, an organization created to aid immigrants to the United States in overcoming social, cultural, and economic problems by personal counseling or referral to appropriate agencies was granted exemption on the same basis.[184]

The position of the IRS once was that the phrase "human and civil rights secured by law" refers only to those individual liberties, freedoms, and privileges involving human dignity that are either specifically guaranteed by the U.S. Constitution or by a special statutory provision coming directly within the scope of the Thirteenth or Fourteenth Amendment or some other comparable constitutional provision, or that otherwise fall within the protection of the Constitution by reason of their long-established recognition in the common law as rights that are essential to the orderly pursuit of happiness by free people. Consequently, tax exemption as a charitable organization was denied to an organization the primary activity of which is the provision of legal assistance to employees whose rights are violated under compulsory unionism arrangements, on the theory that its criterion for intervention in a case is whether there is a grievance arising out of a compulsory union membership requirement and that the right to work is not a protected constitutional right. Upon review, a court disagreed, holding that the right to work is an individual liberty involving a human dignity that is guaranteed by the Constitution, and is therefore a human and civil right secured by law. The organization is thus exempt as a charitable entity.[185]

As regards the promotion of social welfare by combating juvenile delinquency, the IRS has upheld the activity of an organization that promotes sports for children. The organization involved in the case develops, promotes, and regulates a sport for individuals under 18 years of age, and generally provides a recreational outlet for young people.[186] Similarly, an organization that provides teaching of a particular sport to children, by holding clinics conducted

---

[180]Rev. Rul. 68-17, *supra*, n. 12; also Rev. Rul. 76-408, 1976-2 C. B. 145; Rev. Rul. 70-585, *supra*, n. 12.

[181]Rev. Rul. 67-138, *supra*, n. 12.

[182]Rev. Rul. 76-147, 1976-1 C. B. 151.

[183]Rev. Rul. 72-228, 1972-1 C. B. 148.

[184]Rev. Rul. 76-205, *supra*, n. 58.

[185]*National Right to Work Legal Defense and Education Foundation, Inc.* v. *United States*, 487 F.Supp. 801 (E.D. N. Car. 1979).

[186]Rev. Rul. 80-215, 1980-2 C. B. 174.

by qualified instructors and by providing free instruction, equipment, and facilities, was found to be combating juvenile delinquency and thus charitable.[187]

Obviously, these five categories of "social welfare" activities tend to overlap. Thus, one organization ruled to be engaged in the elimination of prejudice and discrimination was also found to operate to "lessen neighborhood tensions" and "prevent deterioration of neighborhoods,"[188] while another was ruled to also act to lessen neighborhood tensions and to defend "human and civil rights secured by law."[189] An organization that counseled residents of a community and city officials in the best use of vacant lots in order to eliminate potential gathering places for "unruly elements" was held to be engaged in combating juvenile delinquency, as well as, because of other activities, the elimination of prejudice and discrimination, the lessening of neighborhood tensions, and the combating of community deterioration.[190]

Once again, categories of exempt organizations can overlap—here, as regards efforts to eliminate prejudice and discrimination and to educate the public. Thus, an organization educating the public as to how to invest in housing made available to the public on a nondiscriminatory basis was ruled exempt.[191] Similar illustrations include an organization that informed the public, through lectures and discussions, of the advantages of nondiscriminatory hiring[192] and an organization that operated programs to prevent panic selling as the result of blacks moving into a formerly all-white neighborhood.[193]

As noted, the regulation defining "charitable" endeavors states that the promotion of social welfare includes activities which seek to accomplish otherwise "charitable" ends. By nature, the most likely other category of charitable endeavor to be accomplished in this matter is the lessening of the burdens of government. Thus, an organization created to assist local governments of a metropolitan region by studying and recommending regional policies directed at the solution of mutual problems was held to be involved in both the combating of community deterioration and lessening of the burdens of government.[194] Yet, such social welfare activities may range the gamut of charitable works, as in the case of an organization that makes awards to individuals who have made outstanding contributions and achievements in the field of commerce, com-

[187]Rev. Rul. 65-2, 1965-1 C. B. 227. Cf. Rev. Rul. 70-4, 1970-1 C. B. 126, holding that an organization promoting and regulating a sport for amateurs qualifies under Code § 501(c)(4) (see Chapter 15) but not under Code § 501(c)(3) because it directs its activities to all members of the general public regardless of age.

[188]Rev. Rul. 68-655, *supra*, n. 175.

[189]Rev. Rul. 68-438, *supra*, n. 176. Also see Rev. Rul. 73-285, *supra*, n. 50.

[190]Rev. Rul. 68-15, *supra*, n. 115. Also Rev. Rul. 81-284, 1981-2 C. B. 130; Rev. Rul. 76-419, 1976-2 C. B. 146; Rev. Rul. 74-587, 1974-2 C. B. 162. Cf. Rev. Rul. 77-111, 1977-1 C. B. 144.

[191]Rev. Rul. 67-250, *supra*, n. 12.

[192]Rev. Rul. 68-70, *supra*, n. 177.

[193]Rev. Rul. 68-655, *supra*, n. 175.

[194]Rev. Rul. 70-79, *supra*, n. 107.

munications, creative arts and crafts, education, finance, government, law, medicine and health, performing arts, religion, science, social services, sports and athletics, technology, and transportation.[195]

§ 6.8   Other Categories

Occasionally, the IRS will issue a ruling to the effect that an organization is exempt as a charitable entity without much attempt to pidgeonhole its activities within one or more of the traditional definitions of a charitable function. A case in point is the determination that an organization established to promote environmental conservancy is a charitable entity.[196] Said the IRS: "It is generally recognized that efforts to preserve and protect the natural environment for the benefit of the public serve a charitable purpose." The Service concluded that, by its activities, "the organization is enhancing the accomplishment of the express national policy of conserving the nation's unique natural resources."[197] However, the Service refused to classify an organization as a charitable entity, because it merely restricts land to uses that do not change the environment, where the land lacks any "distinctive ecological significance" and where any public benefit is "too indirect and insignificant."[198]

Nonetheless, the position of the IRS that only land of "distinctive ecological significance" can qualify as an exempt function holding of an environmental conservation organization was implicitly rejected by the U.S. Tax Court when it accorded classification as a charitable organization to a model farm operated as a conservation project.[199] The facts of the case state that the organization's land "is generally representative of the surrounding farmland in the county" and that the organization "readily admits its land does not have special environmental attributes, nor is the land part of an ecologically significant undeveloped area such as a swamp, marsh, forest, or other wilderness tract."[200] Instead, the organization's "goal is to test and demonstrate the restoration of over-cultivated, exhausted land to a working ecological balance."[201] The organization simply "encourages more local practice of the farming and conservation techniques it is developing."[202] Rather than focus on the nature of the land as such, the court emphasized the use of the land: the organization's

[195]Rev. Rul. 66-146, *supra*, n. 109; also see *Bok* v. *McCaughn*, 42 F.2d 616 (3rd Cir. 1930).

[196]Rev. Rul. 76-204, *supra*, n. 95; Rev. Rul. 80-279, 1980-2 C. B. 176; Rev. Rul. 80-278, 1980-2 C. B. 175. Also see Rev. Rul. 75-207, 1975-1 C. B. 361; Rev. Rul. 70-186, *supra*, n. 97; Rev. Rul. 67-292, *supra*, n. 102; IRS Private Letter Ruling 7823052.

[197]Rev. Rul. 76-204, *supra* n. 196.

[198]Rev. Rul. 78-384, *supra*, n. 95.

[199]*Dumaine Farms* v. *Commissioner*, 73 T.C. 650 (1980).

[200]*Ibid.* at 653.

[201]*Id*.

[202]*Id*.

"agricultural program seeks to demonstrate the commercial viability of ecologically sound farming techniques not yet practiced in the surrounding community."[203]

Similarly, the IRS in 1978, concluded that the promotion of patriotism is a recognized charitable objective. The ruling came in the case of a membership organization, formed by citizens of a community to promote "civic pride in the community, the state, and the country," by providing a color guard and conducting flag-raising and other ceremonies at patriotic and community functions.[204] As authority for this position, the Service stated that "[t]rusts created for the purpose of inculcating patriotic emotions have been upheld as charitable, as have trusts for the purchase and display of a flag, and for the celebration of a patriotic holiday."[205]

The U.S. Tax Court, in a case of first impression for the court, held that the promotion, advancement, and sponsoring of recreational and amateur sports is a charitable activity.[206] The organization involved owns and operates an amateur baseball team that plays in a semiprofessional league, leases and maintains a baseball field used by its team and other teams, furnishes instructors and coaches for a baseball camp, and provides coaches for Little League teams. The players are not paid for their participation on the team, although they do receive free lodging and are guaranteed employment in local industries during the season. The government's contention that the team is semiprofessional, and thus that the operation of it is a nonexempt activity, was rejected.[207]

In 1980, the IRS ruled that the term "charitable" includes the "care of orphans."[208] The occasion was consideration of the tax status of an organization that arranges for the placement of orphan children living in foreign countries with adoptive parents in the United States. The Service has also determined that "facilitating student and cultural exchanges" is a charitable activity.[209]

[203]*Id.* at 656.

[204]Rev. Rul. 78-84, 1978-1 C. B. 150.

[205]Citing IV *Scott on Trusts* (3d ed. 1967) § 374.3; Bogert, *Trusts and Trustees* (2d ed. 1964) § 378.

[206] *Hutchinson Baseball Enterprises, Inc.* v. *Commissioner*, 73 T.C. 144 (1979). However, where the sports organization is primarily established to further the recreational interests of its creators, tax exemption as a charitable organization will not be available. See *North American Sequential Sweepstakes* v. *Commissioner*, 77 T.C. 1087 (1981).

[207]This case did not involve the Code § 501(c)(3) provision for certain amateur sports organizations. See Chapter 10 § 6.

[208]Rev. Rul. 80-200, 1980-2 C. B. 173.

[209]Rev. Rul. 80-286, *supra*, n. 92. The U.S. Tax Court concluded that the purpose of "maintain[ing] public confidence in the legal system" through "various means of improving the administration of justice" is "charitable." *Kentucky Bar Foundation, Inc.* v. *Commissioner*, 78 T.C. 921 (1982).

§ 6.9 Contemporary Issues

Aside from the foregoing adherence to a classification of "charitable" activities into six basic categories, there are several contemporary problem areas that warrant brief highlighting.

Fees for Services

A difficult aspect of the law of charitable organizations has long been the tax treatment and consequences of receipt by them of fees for services performed as part of one or more activities substantially related to exempt purposes.[210] While it is clear that a charitable organization may charge a fee for services and not jeopardize tax exemption for that reason, the issue is raised by the IRS from time to time when the Service sees fit to contend that an organization, to be charitable in nature, must provide its services, information, or the like without charge.

The charging of a fee by an organization is not a bar to categorization of it as a charitable or educational entity.[211] The absence of a requirement in law that an organization, to qualify as a charitable entity, must provide its services without charge is manifested by many provisions of the income tax regulations. For example, one regulation states that an educational organization includes "[a]n organization, such as a primary or secondary school, [or] a college, . . . which has a regularly scheduled curriculum, a regular faculty, and a regularly enrolled body of students in attendance at a place where the educational activities are regularly carried on."[212] It is generally understood and accepted that schools, colleges, and universities do not have to provide teaching and other educational services to students without charge to obtain or retain classification as "charitable" organizations. In fact, such institutions levy a variety of charges for their services, in amounts which are far more than "nominal" and which range up to thousands of dollars per semester, including tuition, charges for room and board, and registration, laboratory and other fees. The IRS does not challenge the tax status of these institutions simply because charges are imposed for the services provided.

The same may be said for the tax status of nonprofit health care institutions. For example, the IRS does not deprive a hospital of its classification as a charitable organization solely because patients are charged for the services rendered, even though the charges can amount to hundreds of dollars per day.[213] Likewise, institutions and organizations of a nonprofit nature such as

---

[210]Fees for services performed in the context of unrelated activities are subject to the tax on unrelated business income. See Chapters 40–42.

[211]See, e.g., Rev. Rul. 80-200, *supra* n. 208; Rev. Rul. 78-99, 1978-1 C. B. 152; Rev. Rul. 77-365, 1977-2 C. B. 192; Rev. Rul. 77-246, *supra*, n. 17; Rev. Rul. 77-68, *supra*, n. 88.

[212]Reg. § 1.501(c)(3)-1(d)(3)(ii), Example (1).

[213]Rev. Rul. 69-545, *supra*, n. 29.

medical clinics, homes for the aged, and blood banks impose charges for their services and are not deprived of tax exemption as charitable organizations as a result.[214] For example, the revenue ruling discussing the status of homes for the aged as charitable organizations expressly notes that the "operating funds [of such homes] are derived principally from fees charged for residence in the home."[215]

The income tax regulations also make it clear that the "educational" classification extends to organizations such as "[m]useums, zoos, planitariums, [and] symphony orchestras."[216] Of course, these organizations frequently impose a charge for the services they provide and can do so at no detriment to their status as charitable entities. The IRS has expressly ruled, for example, that a nonprofit theater may charge admission for its performances and nonetheless qualify as a charitable organization.[217]

Congress also has expressly recognized the tax-exempt status of the foregoing and similar types of organizations as charitable entities for purposes of non-private foundation classification. Thus, the instructional institutions are regarded as "educational" entities.[218] Similarly, hospitals and other health care organizations are regarded as "charitable" entities.[219] Likewise, the Department of the Treasury has expressly recognized museums, symphony orchestras, theaters, and the like as "charitable" entities.[220]

The foregoing types of nonprofit organizations are accorded classification as charitable entities notwithstanding the fact that they impose a charge for their services. Thus, there is nothing inherently inconsistent between classification of an organization as a "charitable" entity and the charging of a fee. One set of commentators observed:

[T]he test of a charitable institution in many jurisdictions is not the extent of the free services rendered . . . but whether those who operate it are doing so for private profit, directly or indirectly. . . . Free service is not a prerequisite to tax exemption, and the legal meaning of charitable purposes is not limited to the care of the indigent.[221]

It becomes a matter of illogical and unfair discrimination for the IRS to freely permit some categories of charitable organizations to charge substantial fees for their services and yet question or deprive charitable status for other cate-

[214]See, e.g., Rev. Rul. 72-124, *supra*, n. 142; Rev. Rul. 70-590, *supra*, n. 150; and Rev. Rul. 66-323, *supra*, n. 151.
[215]Rev. Rul. 72-124, *supra*, n. 142.
[216]Reg. § 1.501(c)(3)-1(d)(3)(ii), Example (4).
[217]Rev. Rul. 73-45, 1973-1 C. B. 220.
[218]Code § 170 (b)(1)(A)(ii).
[219]Code § 170 (b)(1)(A)(iii).
[220]Code § 170 (b)(1)(A)(vi); Reg. § 1.170A-9(e)(1)(ii).
[221]Hayt, Hayt, and Groeschel, *Law of Hospital, Physician and Patient*, 65–69 (2d ed. 1952).

gories of otherwise qualified organizations that do so, such as consumer credit counseling agencies.

The services provided by these agencies are clearly charitable and educational in nature. The consumer credit counseling services provided by the agencies to individuals and families are themselves educational in nature, inasmuch as the agencies are instructing the public on subjects useful to the individual and beneficial to the community.[222] Other educational activities are undertaken by the agencies for the benefit of the general public when they provide information to the public on consumer credit and budgeting by means of speakers and publications. The activities of the agencies are also charitable in nature because they are designed to advance education and promote social welfare.[223] Despite these facts, the IRS sought—unsuccessfully—to deny these agencies classification as charitable organizations because, *inter alia*, they charge a nominal fee for certain services, which fee is waived in instances of economic hardship.[224]

Notwithstanding its restrictive stance with respect to consumer credit counseling agencies and other organizations, the IRS soon thereafter ruled that an organization that is operated to provide legal services to indigents may charge, for each hour of legal assistance provided, a "nominal hourly fee determined by reference to the client's own hourly income."[225] And, as discussed, exempt health care institutions are allowed to charge fees as a principal source of their revenue. This exception from its general anti-fee stance was reiterated by the Service early in 1979 in a ruling providing classification as a charitable entity for a hospice,[226] an organization providing specially designed housing for the elderly,[227] and an organization providing housing to the physically handicapped.[228]

There have been instances in the past where the IRS has determined that an organization is charitable in nature because it provides services that are free to the recipients. However, this is a separate and independent basis for finding a charitable activity, usually invoked only where the services, assistance, or benefits provided are not themselves charitable or educational in nature. An illustration of the use of this rationale is the public interest law firm which provides legal services (which is not inherently an exempt purpose), yet nonetheless can qualify as a charitable organization.[229] As noted above, the free services rationale is not an essential, and the only, basis for determining whether an organization is a charitable entity, and, indeed, were this the law, the vast

---

[222]Reg. § 1.501(c)(3)-1(d)(3)(i)(d).

[223]Reg. § 1.501(c)(3)-1(d)(2).

[224]See *Consumer Credit Counseling Service of Alabama, Inc.* v. *United States*, 78-2 U.S.T.C. ¶ 9660 (D.D.C. 1978).

[225]Rev. Rul. 78-428, *supra*, n. 13.

[226]Rev. Rul. 79-17, *supra*, n. 36.

[227]Rev. Rul. 79-18, *supra*, n. 19.

[228]Rev. Rul. 79-19, *supra*, n. 20.

[229]Rev. Proc. 71-39, 1971-2 C. B. 575.

majority of organizations presently exempt as "charitable" entitles would face revocation of exemption.

This distinction was made by the IRS in its treatment of cooperative organizations established by colleges and universities. In one instance, a computer services sharing organization was granted status as a charitable organization because the IRS determined that the services provided to the participating colleges and universities were themselves charitable in nature; no requirement was imposed that the services be provided without charge.[230] In another instance, a similar organization was accorded status as a charitable entity even though the services it rendered to the participating educational institutions were regarded as "administrative" in nature (that is, noneducational); the distinguishing feature was that the organization received less than 15 percent of its financial support from the entities which received the services.[231] Thus, as far as the recipient entities were concerned, they were receiving the services at no cost or at the most for a nominal charge. Had this organization been providing only an insubstantial amount of administrative services and a substantial level of educational services, its tax exemption would have been predicated on the basis that it is engaging in inherently exempt activities; the 15 percent-85 percent rule was used only as an alternative rationale for the exemption as a charitable entity.

In conclusion, the law does not require, as a condition to qualification as a charitable organization, that the organization provide services without charge. In fact, it has been held that the "position that the test of a charitable institution is the extent of free services rendered, is difficult of application and unsound in theory."[232] The only requirements in this regard, in the Internal Revenue Code and the income tax regulations, are that the organization not be operated with a profit motive and not for private interests. The law looks to the benefits flowing to the general public in assessing the presence of a charitable purpose. The feature of an organization providing benefits without charge should be used by the IRS only as an alternative rationale, in the absence of an inherently exempt purpose, to assess the organization's status in relation to the requirements for qualification as a charitable entity.

Promotion of the Arts

It is now clearly established that organizations devoted to promotion of the arts may qualify for exemption as "charitable" (and perhaps "educational" and "literary") entities. For example, an organization that functions to arouse and give direction to local interest in a given community for the establishment of

---

[230]Rev. Rul. 74-614, *supra*, n. 76, amplified by Rev. Rul. 81-29, *supra*, n. 76.
[231]Rev. Rul. 71-529, *supra*, n. 75.
[232]*Southern Methodist Hosp. & Sanatorium of Tucson* v. *Wilson*, 77 P.2d 458, 462 (Sup. Ct. Ariz. 1943).

a repertory theater qualifies as a charitable entity.[233] The repertory theater company itself may be "charitable" in nature.[234] This type of charitable activity was initially recognized by the IRS as being "cultural," with emphasis on the musical arts.[235]

One feature of this aspect of "charitable" endeavor is the effort akin to advancement of education, that is, to promote public appreciation of one of the arts. Thus, an organization formed to perpetuate group harmony singing and to educate the general public as to this type of music is exempt.[236] Similarly, an organization formed to promote an appreciation of jazz music as an American art form is an exempt organization,[237] as is a nonprofit school of contemporary dancing.[238] The tax exemption for charitable groups may likewise extend to an organization that seeks to encourage the creative arts and scholarship by making grants to needy artists,[239] by promoting interest in and appreciation of contemporary symphonic and chamber music,[240] or by sponsoring public exhibits of art works by unknown but promising artists.[241]

Other organizations are exempt because they function to promote and encourage the talent and ability of young artists. The scope of types of these activities include the training of young musical artists in concert technique,[242] the promotion of filmmaking by conducting festivals to provide unknown independent filmmakers with opportunities to display their films,[243] and the encouragement of musicians and composers through commissions and scholarships and the opportunity for students to play with accomplished professional musicians.[244] Organizations in this category frequently promote (and finance) their charitable function through the sponsorship of public festivals, concerts, exhibits, and other productions. In nearly all such instances, the artists are amateurs, performing solely for the on-stage experience or to enable the charitable organization to meet expenses.

Organizations operated to promote the arts, which otherwise qualify as charitable entities, may easily find themselves engaging in an activity the IRS regards as serving a private interest. Thus, while the preservation of classical music programming can be a charitable purpose,[245] an organization that un-

---

[233]Rev. Rul. 64-174, 1964-1 (Part I) C. B. 183.
[234]Rev. Rul. 64-175, 1964-1 (Part I) C. B. 185.
[235]See S.M. 176, 1 C. B. 147 (1919); I.T. 1475, 1-2 C. B. 184 (1922).
[236]Rev. Rul. 66-46, 1966-1 C. B. 133.
[237]Rev. Rul. 65-271, 1965-2 C. B. 161.
[238]Rev. Rul. 65-270, 1965-2 C. B. 160.
[239]Rev. Rul. 66-103, *supra*, n. 61.
[240]Rev. Rul. 79-369, 1979-2 C. B. 226.
[241]Rev. Rul. 66-178, 1966-1 C. B. 138.
[242]Rev. Rul. 67-392, 1967-2 C. B. 191.
[243]Rev. Rul. 75-471, 1975-2 C. B. 207.
[244] Rev. Rul. 65-271, *supra*, n. 237.
[245]See Rev. Rul. 64-175, *supra*, n. 234.

dertook a variety of activities to enable a for-profit radio station to continue broadcasting classical music was denied exemption.[246] Likewise, although the displaying of art works may be a charitable activity,[247] an organization will not achieve exemption as a charitable entity where it sells the art works it exhibits and remits the proceeds to the artists.[248] (However, the fact that exhibited art works are available for sale will not necessarily deprive the organization sponsoring the show of tax exemption as a charitable group.[249])

In recent years, status as charitable organizations has been accorded organizations that sponsor professional presentations, such as plays, musicals, and concerts. The chief rationale for extending the exemption to these organizations is that they operate to foster the development in a community of an appreciation for the dramatic and musical arts, such as by staging theatrical productions that are not otherwise available in the community.[250] At the same time, these exempt theaters may place the commercial theaters in the same locale at a competitive disadvantage. Defenders of the exempt cultural centers claim that they put on theatrical presentations that otherwise would never be produced, while their critics insist that they are frequently presenting popular entertainment in unfair competition with privately owned theater.

In some instances, the two types of theater (privately owned and tax-exempt) operate in relative harmony. This, for example, has been the case with New York City's nonprofit Lincoln Center, which traditionally stages shows which could never appear on Broadway. By contrast, however, the commercially operated National Theater in Washington, D.C., competes directly with the John F. Kennedy Center for the Performing Arts and the Arena Stage, which are tax-exempt theater organizations.

It is not clear as to how or whether this dilemma can be resolved; perhaps the answer lies in this observation: "In the final analysis, of course, what the [private] theater owners want is not so much to do away with the cultural centers but to keep them in their place—and that place, the owners believe, is to serve as the setting for staging works that might not be performed elsewhere, at least [not] in commercial theaters."[251]

One court has discussed the distinctions between tax-exempt performing arts organizations and commercial theaters as follows:

> Admittedly, the line between commercial enterprises which produce and present theatrical performances and nonprofit, tax-exempt organizations that do the same is not always easy to draw. Indeed, the theater is the most prominent area of the performing arts in which commercial enterprises co-exist, often in the same city,

---

[246]Rev. Rul. 76-206, 1976-1 C. B. 154.

[247]Rev. Rul. 66-178, *supra*, n. 241.

[248]Rev. Rul. 76-152, 1976-1 C. B. 151. Also Rev. Rul. 71-395, 1971-2 C. B. 228.

[249]See Rev. Rul. 78-131, 1978-2 C. B. 156.

[250]See Rev. Rul. 73-45, *supra*, n. 217.

[251]"Is a Cultural Center An Appropriate Setting For Lawrence Welk?," *Wall St. J.*, May 7, 1973 at 1.

with nonprofit, tax-exempt charitable organizations that also sponsor professional presentations. . . .

However, there are differences. Commercial theaters are operated to make a profit. Thus, they choose plays having the greatest mass audience appeal. Generally, they run the plays so long as they can attract a crowd. They set ticket prices to pay the total costs of production and to return a profit. Since their focus is perennially on the box office, they do not generally organize other activities to educate the public and they do not encourage and instruct relatively unknown playwrights and actors.

Tax-exempt organizations are not operated to make a profit. They fulfill their artistic and community obligations by focusing on the highest possible standards of performance; by serving the community broadly; by developing new and original works; and by providing educational programs and opportunities for new talent. Thus, they keep the great classics of the theater alive and are willing to experiment with new forms of dramatic writing, acting, and staging. Usually nonprofit theatrical organizations present a number of plays over a season for a relatively short specified time period. Because of a desired quality in acoustics and intimacy with the audience, many present their performances in halls of limited capacity. The combination of the shortness of the season, the limited seating capacity, the enormous costs of producing quality performances of new or experimental works coupled with the desire to keep ticket prices at a level which is affordable to most of the community means that except in rare cases, box office receipts will never cover the cost of producing plays for non-profit performing arts organizations. . . . We feel that petitioner has shown that it is organized and operated similar to other nonprofit theatre organizations, rather than as a commercial theatre.[252]

Public Interest Law Firms

One of the relative newcomers to the realm of charitable organizations is the "public interest law firm." The proliferation of public interest law firms has raised many questions—chiefly, in federal tax law and in lawyers' canons of ethics. They pose tax problems because they can mirror the private practice of law in some respects and because of the definitional problems of identifying the requisite charitable class or community. On this latter point, the public interest law firms are not necessarily in a "pro bono publico" practice, representing the impoverished in the nature of the legal aid programs. Rather, these firms provide legal representation for important citizen interests which are unrepresented because the cases are not economically feasible for private firms. These interests typically are environmental policies, the tax system, freedom of information, and the federal government's regulatory attitude toward food, drugs and the airwaves—interests which inevitably pit the public interest law firms against the "establishment" (including prestigious law firms), with resulting "political" consequences. Organizations which otherwise qualify as public interest law firms are regarded "as charities because they provide a service which is of benefit to the community as a whole," with "[c]haritability . . . also

---

[252]*Plumstead Theatre Society, Inc.* v. *Commissioner*, 74 T.C. 1324 (1980) aff'd 675 F.2d 244 (9th Cir. 1982).

dependent upon the fact that the service provided by public interest law firms is distinguishable from that which is commercially available."[253]

With the advent of the public interest law firm, the IRS adopted a policy of granting them exempt status as "charitable" organizations. But their overwhelming and well-publicized successes and their encouragement by many, as well as opposition to them, forced the Service to reexamine its policy of exempting them from tax and permitting them to attract deductible contributions. Thus, a controversy was touched off in October of 1970 when the IRS announced that it had temporarily stopped granting tax-exempt status, as charitable groups, to public interest law firms. The reaction to the announcement included great outcries of protest and prompted congressional hearings.[254] The IRS retreated somewhat, later in the month, by announcing that contributions to public interest law firms would remain deductible during the study period. But the public furor continued to mount. In November, 1970, the Service issued guidelines on the subject, indicating that a favorable ruling would be issued to a public interest law firm if it represents a broad public interest and if private inurement is incidental.

Subsequently, the IRS promulgated guidelines for the issuance of advance rulings providing exemption for public interest law firms and for testing organizations holding favorable rulings.[255] In these guidelines, the IRS acknowledged that legal representation for disadvantaged minorities, victims of racial discrimination, and those denied human and civil rights either in criminal or civil matters has been long recognized as a "charitable" activity. But the IRS said it found no "clear set of precedents" for exempting an organization operating in support of the interests of a majority of the public. Therefore, the Service declared it necessary to develop guidelines for organizations with a program designed to serve the public interest through litigation, although it held open the possibility that the facts and circumstances as to a particular organization may demonstrate its "charitable" nature even though the guidelines are not adhered to in certain respects.

These guidelines state that the "engagement of the organization in litigation can reasonably be said to be in representation of a broad public interest rather than a private interest." In addition to generally complying with the requirements of the federal tax law rules concerning charitable organizations, the IRS guidelines for the public interest law firm require the following: (1) it may accept fees for services rendered but only in accordance with specific IRS procedures, (2) it may not have a program of "disruption of the judicial system, illegal activity, or violation of the applicable canons of ethics," (3) it files with its annual information return (Form 990) a description of cases litigated and the "rationale for the determination that they would benefit the public gen-

---

[253]Rev. Rul. 75-74, *supra*, n. 38.

[254]See "Tax Exemptions for Charitable Organizations Affecting Poverty Programs," Hearings Before Senate Subcommittee on Employment, Manpower, and Poverty, 91st Cong., 2d Sess. (1970).

[255]Rev. Proc. 71-39, *supra*, n. 229.

erally," (4) its policies and programs are the responsibility of a "board or committee representative of the public interest," not controlled by its employees or those who litigate on its behalf nor by noncharitable organizations, (5) it is not operated so as to create "identification or confusion with a particular private law firm," and (6) "[t]here is no arrangement to provide, directly or indirectly, a deduction for the cost of litigation which is for the private benefit of the donor."

However, these guidelines failed to resolve one substantial lingering question: when may a public interest law firm accept fees for services? The IRS grappled with this question when it promulgated procedures for the acceptance of attorneys' fees by such firms.[256] In essence, these procedures (1) forbid a firm from seeking attorneys' fees from clients, (2) allow the acceptance of attorneys' fees where paid by opposing parties under court or agency award, (3) require the firm to use awarded fees solely to defray normal operating expenses, with no more than one-half of such costs (calculated over five years) so defrayed, and (4) require the firm to file with its annual information return a report of all fees sought and recovered.

The IRS has recognized that the awarding of attorneys' fees serves to effectuate a legislative or judicial policy in deterring or encouraging certain actions.[257] Thus, concluded the IRS, "the award or acceptance of attorneys' fees by public interest law firms in these situations is consistent with and tends to support the statutory and public policy objectives in awarding such fees," and such a firm constitutes a charitable organization as long as it is "clear that neither the expectation nor the possibility, however remote, of an award of fees is a substantial motivating factor in the selection of cases."[258] By contrast, where the firm "has an established policy of charging or accepting attorneys' fees from its clients, the representation provided cannot be distinguished from that available through traditional private law firms" and the exemption as a charitable entity will be denied or revoked.[259] Similarly, a public interest law firm will lose exemption if it enters into a fee-sharing arrangement with a private attorney who will keep a portion of a court-awarded fee that exceeds the amount paid by the firm to the private attorney for services rendered.[260]

---

[256]Rev. Proc. 75-13, 1975-1 C. B. 662.

[257]Citing *Mills* v. *Electric Auto-Lite Co.*, 396 U.S. 375 (1970); *Newman* v. *Piggie Park Enterprises, Inc.*, 309 U.S. 400 (1968).

[258]Rev. Rul. 75-76, 1975-1 C. B. 154.

[259]Rev. Rul. 75-75, 1975-1 C. B. 154.

[260]Rev. Rul. 76-5, 1976-1 C. B. 146. In general, see Note, "Public Interest Law Firms and Client-Paid Fees," 33 *Tax Law*. 915 (1980); Hobbet, "Public Interest Law Firms—To Fee or Not to Fee," 27 *Nat'l Tax J*. 45 (1974); Note, "Tax-Exempt Status of Public Interest Law Firms," 45 *So. Cal. L. Rev*. 228 (1972); Note, "IRS Man Cometh: Public Interest Law Firms Meet the Tax Collector," 13 *Ariz. L. Rev*. 857 (1971); Goldberg and Cohen, "Does higher authority than IRS guidelines exist for public interest law firms?," 34 *J. of Tax*. 77 (1971); "Tax Exemption for 'Public Interest Law Firms'," Report of The Committee on Civil Rights, 26 *Record of the Assoc. of the Bar of the City of New York* 91 (1971).

Consortia

As noted above, exempt organizations are frequently utilizing cooperative ventures to further their purposes. The early position of the IRS toward cooperative venturing by or for charitable and educational organizations was relatively favorable. This may be seen as late as 1969, when the Service ruled in connection with an organization which was created to construct and maintain a building to house member agencies of a community chest.[261] The purpose of this organization was to facilitate coordination among the agencies and to make more efficient use of the available voluntary labor force. The rental rate charged the agencies was substantially less than commercial rates for comparable facilities (the organization leased the land from a city and itself paid only a nominal rental) and the organization's annual rental income was approximately equal to its total annual operating costs. Citing the concept that the "performance of a particular activity that is not inherently charitable may nonetheless further a charitable purpose,"[262] the IRS ruled the organization to be exempt as a "charitable" entity, emphasizing the low rental rates and the close relationship between its purposes and functions and those of the tenant organizations.[263]

However, the present policy of the IRS in this regard is to presume such cooperative ventures to be fully taxable entities, as being engaged in a trade or business, even where the venture is controlled by and performs a function for its members that each institution would otherwise have to undertake for itself, without incidence of tax. The Service has two narrow exceptions to this policy, in that exemption will be granted where the consortium conducts substantive programs which the IRS regards as inherently exempt in nature[264] or where at least 85 percent of the organization's revenue is derived from outside sources.[265] The IRS also bases its position on a passage in the regulations accompanying the federal tax rules pertaining to feeder organizations.[266] The IRS policy toward cooperative ventures had, for many years, been rejected in the courts on nearly every occasion when it was considered[267] and Congress

[261]Rev. Rul. 69-572, 1969-2 C. B. 119.

[262]See Rev. Rul. 67-4, *supra*, n. 89.

[263]Also see Rev. Rul. 64-182, 1964-1 C. B. (Part 1) 186; Rev. Rul. 58-147, 1958-2 C. B. 275.

[264]See Rev. Rul. 74-614, *supra*, n. 76, amplified by Rev. Rul. 81-29, *supra*, n. 76; IRS Private Letter Ruling 7816061. But see IRS Private Letter Rulings 7951134 and 7905129.

[265]Rev. Rul. 72-369, 1972-2 C. B. 245; Rev. Rul. 71-529, *supra*, n. 75. A corollary policy of the IRS is that, where neither of the exceptions is present, the provision of services by one exempt organization to one or more other exempt (or nonexempt) organizations is the conduct of an unrelated trade or business (see Part VI). Rev. Rul. 69-528, 1969-2 C. B. 127; IRS Private Letter Ruling 7902019 (issue no. 4).

[266]Rev. Rul. 69-528, *supra*, n. 265.

[267]See *Hospital Bureau of Standards and Supplies* v. *United States*, 158 F.Supp. 560 (Ct. Cl. 1958); *United Hospital Services, Inc.* v. *United States*, 384 F.Supp. 776

has specifically legislated in this area, contravening the Service's policy three times.[268]

An instance in which a court upheld the position of the IRS regarding consortia occurred when the U.S. Tax Court first considered the issue. The case involved a cooperative hospital laundry service owned and operated by tax-exempt hospitals. Finding the regulations under the feeder organization rules[269] to have the force of law because of long-standing congressional awareness of them, and concluding that the legislative history of related statutes evidences congressional intent to not allow tax exemption for hospital-controlled laundries, the court found that the hospital laundry service organization is a feeder organization and thus not exempt from taxation.[270] Because of the emphasis placed on this legislative history, however, it is not clear whether consortia other than hospital laundry enterprises would receive like treatment by the Tax Court. Shortly after the Tax Court reached this decision, the U.S. Court of Appeals for the Third Circuit arrived at the same conclusion,[271] as did the Ninth Circuit[272] and later the Sixth Circuit.[273]

Despite this strict policy, the IRS has recognized the necessity and utility of cooperative endeavors in the field of higher education for over a decade. Thus, the Service has stated:

> Many activities normally carried on by colleges and universities can be more effectively accomplished through the combined efforts of a group of such institutions. . . . Associations composed entirely of privately supported non-profit

---

(S.D. Ind. 1974); *Hospital Central Services Association* v. *United States*, 77-2 U.S.T.C. ¶ 9601 (W.D. Wash. 1977); *Metropolitan Detroit Area Hospital Services, Inc.* v. *United States*, 445 F.Supp. 857 (E.D. Mich. 1978); *Northern California Central Services, Inc.* v. *United States*, 591 F.2d 620 (Ct. Cl. 1979); *Community Hospital Services, Inc.* v. *United States*, 79-1 U.S.T.C. ¶ 9301 (E.D. Mich. 1979); *HCSC-Laundry* v. *United States*, 473 F.Supp. 250 (E.D. Pa. 1979). In general, see Gailey, "Tax-Exempt Auxiliary Corporations and Major Public Institutions," 14 *Bus. Off.* (No. 5) 24 (1980); Hopkins, "Cooperative Ventures of Colleges and Universities: The Current Tax Law Developments," 4 *Coll. & Univ. Bus. Off.* (No. 5) (1975); Whaley, "Interinstitutional Cooperation Among Educational Organizations," 1 *J. of Coll. & Univ. Law* (No. 2) 93 (1973).

[268]See Code §§ 501(e), (f), 513(e).

[269]See Chapter 39.

[270]*Associated Hospital Services, Inc.* v. *Commissioner*, 74 T.C. 213 (1980).

[271]*HCSC-Laundry* v. *United States*, 624 F.2d 428 (3d Cir. 1980), rev'g 473 F.Supp. 250 (E.D. Pa. 1979), aff'd 450 U.S.1 (1981).

[272]*Hospital Central Services Association* v. *United States*, 623 F.2d 611 (9th Cir. 1980), cert. den. 450 U.S. 911 (1980), rev'g 77-2 U.S.T.C. ¶ 9601 (W.D. Wash. 1977). Also *Community Hospital Services, Inc.* v. *United States*, 81-1 U.S.T.C. ¶ 9198 (6th Cir. 1981), rev'g 79-1 U.S.T.C. ¶ 9301 (E.D. Mich 1979).

[273]*Metropolitan Detroit Area Hospital Services* v. *United States*, 634 F.2d 330 (6th Cir. 1980), rev'g 445 F.Supp. 857 (E.D. Mich. 1978).

colleges and universities have been created and are operated exclusively to carry out these activities.

[These associations] aid and promote the educational endeavors of their members and interpret to the public the aims, functions, and needs of the institutions, with a view to better understanding and cooperation.[274]

This view has been repeatedly but inconsistently subscribed to by the IRS in the intervening years.[275]

Some IRS rulings are flatly contradictory to its announced position on college, university and similar consortia. For example, the IRS has ruled that an organization, the membership of which is educational (including some proprietary) institutions, qualifies as a charitable organization because it accredits these institutions.[276] The rationale for the exemption is that the organization advances education and thus is "charitable"; it engages in activities which "support and advance education by providing significant incentive for maintaining a high quality educational program." The act of accreditation is not inherently a charitable activity; it is the fact that service was rendered for educational institutions that gave rise to the exemption.

Similarly, the IRS has accorded status as a charitable entity to an organization controlled by an exempt conference of churches, where its purpose was solely to make mortgage loans to the churches to enable them to finance the construction of church buildings.[277] The rationale for the exemption is that the organization is advancing religion. Surely the making of mortgage loans is not an inherently religious activity. Rather, the exemption was derived from the fact that the loans were made at less than commercial interest rates to churches of the conference to enable them to construct buildings at reduced cost for religious purposes.

Also, the IRS has granted charitable status to a consortium of counties all located in the same state.[278] This exemption was accorded simply on the ground that the organization's activities contribute to the "more efficient operation of

[274]Rev. Rul. 63-15, 1963-1 C. B. 189. In general, see Welzenbach, "Consortia: A Means of Saving Money and Expanding Services," X *Bus. Off.* (No. 11) 10 (1977).

[275]See, e.g., Rev. Rul. 63-208, 1963-2 C. B. 468, and Rev. Rul. 63-209, 1963-2 C. B. 469 (offices formed by an exempt religious entity to administer its statewide parochial school system and a convent to house teachers in parochial schools organized by the religious institution functioned as integral parts of the educational activities of the schools); Rev. Rul. 64-286, 1964-2 C. B. 401 (general board of a church which made purchases for the exclusive use of parochial schools and missions shared the exempt status of the primary educational organization); Rev. Rul. 71-553, 1971-2 C. B. 404 (student government association was an integral part of a university); and IRS Private Letter Ruling 7816061 (organization formed to furnish the services of a computerized card catalog system to its member libraries).

[276]Rev. Rul. 74-146, *supra*, n. 74.

[277]Rev. Rul. 75-282, *supra*, n. 51.

[278]Rev. Rul. 75-359, 1975-2 C. B. 79.

county government." Efficiency of operation is, as noted, one of the principal reasons for establishment of consortia.

Further, it has long been the position of the IRS that an organization formed and operated for the purpose of providing financial assistance to organizations that are regarded as charitable, educational, and the like is itself qualified for tax exemption as a charitable entity.[279]

The Court of Claims has had occasion to reaffirm its original position (in 1958) concerning consortia.[280] In a 1975 case,[281] the court stated:

> This court has held in the past that where one organization provides a service which is necessary and indispensable to the operations of another, the first will take on the tax status of the second.[282]

Invoking an "adjunct theory," the court added:

> These cases clearly indicate that where one organization serves as a mere adjunct for a primary organization by providing services which are essential to the functioning of the primary organization and which would be normally performed by it, the adjunct will acquire the tax status of the primary company.[283]

The "adjunct" theory was initially invoked by the U.S. Court of Appeals for the Second Circuit in 1934.[284] The first application of this theory to adjuncts of charitable organizations occurred in 1951. In that year, the Ninth Circuit Court of Appeals reviewed the tax status of a corporation organized to operate a bookstore and restaurant on the campus of a state college. Despite the fact that these operations are not inherently "charitable" or "educational" activities, the Ninth Circuit invoked the rationale of the "adjunct" theory as follows:

> [T]he business enterprise in which taxpayer is engaged obviously bears a close and intimate relationship to the functioning of the College itself.[285]

The Ninth Circuit concluded that this corporation was entitled to exemption as an "educational" organization.

The "adjunct" theory was espoused by the U.S. Tax Court in 1970, in concluding that a museum in San Francisco was an exempt "educational" or-

[279]Rev. Rul. 67-149, *supra*, n. 75. See, e.g., Rev. Rul. 78-310, *supra*, n. 66.
[280]See *supra*, n. 267.
[281]*Trustees of Graceland Cemetery Improvement Fund* v. *United States*, 515 F.2d 763 (Ct. Cl. 1975).
[282]*Ibid*. at 770.
[283]*Ibid*. at 771.
[284]*Produce Exchange Stock Clearing Association* v. *Helvering*, 71 F.2d 142 (2d Cir. 1934).
[285]*Squire* v. *Students Book Corp*., 191 F.2d 1018, 1020 (9th Cir. 1951). See Rev. Rul. 78-41, *supra*, n. 171.

ganization because it was an integral part of and a valuable adjunct to the San Francisco public school system.[286] At issue in this case was the availability of the pre-1969 additional charitable contribution deduction of 10 percent of a taxpayer's adjusted gross income for contributions to operating educational institutions which engage in the presentation of formal instruction.[287] The Tax Court concluded that gifts to the museum qualified for the bonus charitable contribution deduction, even though the museum itself did not satisfy the statutory requirements, because it was an integral part of the school system and thus was clothed with the system's "educational" status.[288]

The Court of Claims was presented with the opportunity to review and restate its position as to the exempt status of consortia, in a case initiated in 1975.[289] However, this opportunity was lost when the IRS mooted that case in 1976 by issuing a private ruling that the consortium qualifies as a charitable organization.

One of the principal reasons that the Treasury Department and the IRS have opposed tax-exempt status for a consortium arrangement is their fear that an organization, that is not formed and controlled by charitable entities, will by its own choice confine its services to such entities and thereby itself acquire charitable status, even where the provision of such services is in competition with commercial enterprises. Of course, this factual situation is easily distin-

---

[286]*Brundage* v. *Commissioner*, 54 T.C. 1468 (1970). Cf. *Miller* v. *United States*, 527 F.2d 231 (8th Cir. 1975).

[287]See Code § 170(b)(1)(A)(ii).

[288] Also see *Rosehill Cemetery Co.* v. *United States*, 285 F.Supp. 21 (N.D. Ill. 1968); *Industrial Aid for the Blind* v. *Commissioner*, 73 T.C. 96 (1979).

[289]*Illinois Educational Consortium* v. *United States* (No. 317-75). The Illinois Educational Consortium has as its membership the four systems of higher education in that state which administer the state's eleven universities. The Consortium renders services to these universities for the purpose of supporting and advancing the collective activities of the members as a means to improve management. The Consortium renders services to its members which are inherently charitable and educational in nature, whereby it furthers the universities' instructional and research programs and functions. Among its services are activities which increase cooperation, coordination and sharing in the utilization of computer equipment, systems, facilities and personnel. The Consortium also engages in cooperative purchasing of software and training aids, finances the acquisition of computer equipment, leases such equipment to its members, and transfers such equipment between its member universities to increase its utility. A result of the Consortium's activities has been the sharing of computing resources among several of the state universities, thereby enabling the state's higher education systems to achieve cost savings. The Consortium is controlled by a board of directors composed solely of representatives of its member universities. Its services are rendered wholly to its member universities and are services which the institutions would have to render themselves in the Consortium's absence. Its support is derived from members' dues and contributions, state agency grants and payments from members for services rendered. The IRS private ruling in this case is directly contrary to its public position, summarized above.

guishable from the normal consortium arrangement but the government's fear persists nonetheless.

The government's concerns in this regard were presumably largely alleviated by a 1978 decision by the U.S. Tax Court, holding that an organization that plans to offer consulting services for a fee to a class of nonprofit (but not all tax-exempt) organizations does not qualify as a charitable entity but is taxable as a business.[290] The Court's opinion might have come out the other way, however, had the organization (1) confined its clientele to charitable organizations (even though not controlled by them), (2) not set its fees to return an 11 percent net profit, and (3) been able to include within the evidentiary base some demonstration that its services would not be in competition with commercial businesses.

A private letter ruling issued by the IRS in 1979 seems largely at odds with its public pronouncements and positions to date. The matter concerned an organization, the members of which are nonprofit universities and municipal libraries, that operates a computer network to enable its members to exchange information concerning the availability of books and other research materials in the libraries throughout a particular state. The Service had previously determined that the organization is exempt as a charitable entity apparently for the reason that its programs are inherently exempt in nature.[291] The issue was whether the organization could, without jeopardy to its tax-exempt status or incurrence of unrelated income, extend its resource services to various private businesses (such as banks, utilities, and automotive, chemical, and pharmaceutical industries). The Service held that "in making your information dissemination services available to private institutions on the same basis, and for the same fee, as services are provided to your members you are serving your exempt purpose of disseminating useful bibliographic information to researchers."[292]

In certain instances, a consortium of colleges, universities, hospitals, or the like may confine its membership to institutions operated by a particular state, in which case the consortium may qualify as a political subdivision of that state, with the result that its income would be excluded from federal taxation. The IRS has informally rejected this approach, although such a consortium may be able to qualify as an instrumentality of the particular state. (If a consortium could so qualify, it would achieve an added advantage, in that interest paid on its borrowings would be exempt income to the lenders.[293]) It should be noted that, were it not for a minor aspect of an existing provision in the Internal Revenue Code,[294] such a consortium would automatically be considered a public charity.[295] This provision, in effect, extends exempt status to "an organization

[290]B.S.W. Group, Inc. v. Commissioner, 70 T.C. 352 (1978).
[291]See Rev. Rul. 74-614, supra, n. 76.
[292]IRS Private Letter Ruling 7951134.
[293]Code § 103.
[294]Code § 170(b)(1)(A)(iv).
[295]Code § 509(a)(1).

which normally receives a substantial part of its support . . . from any state or political subdivision thereof . . . and which is organized and operated exclusively to receive, hold, invest, and administer property and to make expenditures to or for the benefit of a [state] college or university." There is no basis for assuming that Congress intended to legislate a requirement that only organizations that serve merely one state institution of higher education qualify as charitable entities to the exclusion of comparable entities that serve more than one state college or university.

Among the most well-known of the consortia is The Common Fund, a cooperative arrangement formed by a large group of colleges and universities for the collective investment of their funds, which was ruled to be a charitable organization in 1970. During its formative years, the management and administrative expenses of the Fund were largely met by start-up grants from a private foundation. However, as the Fund became more reliant upon payments from its member institutions, it became unqualified for status as a charitable entity, according to the IRS, because of the "donative element" test, in that the Fund's services were no longer being provided to members at a charge of no more than 15 percent of costs. In the face of loss of the Fund's exemption, Congress made it clear that the cooperative arrangements for investment of the type typified by The Common Fund are exempt charitable organizations.[296]

The legislative history of The Common Fund provision states that it applies only to cooperative organizations formed and controlled by the participating institutions themselves, rather than to private organizations furnishing the same services even where those services might be made available only to educational organizations. In a significant passage, Congress announced that, in enacting this statute, "it is not intended that any inference be drawn as to the exempt status of other organizations formed by educational institutions or by other charities on their behalf to carry out their normal functions in a cooperative manner."[297]

Congress changed the law in this area in one respect in 1976.[298] As the foregoing indicates, it has been the position of the IRS that income which an exempt hospital derives from providing services to other exempt hospitals constitutes unrelated business income to the hospital providing the services, on the theory that the provision of services to other hospitals is not an activity which is substantially related to the tax-exempt purposes of the hospital providing the services.[299] By enactment of the Tax Reform Act of 1976, Congress acted to reverse this position in the case of small hospitals.

[296]Code § 501(f).

[297]S. Rep. No. 93-888, 93d Cong., 2d Sess. (1974) at 3.

[298]Code § 513(e). See Chapter 42.

[299]Rev. Rul. 69-633, 1969-2 C. B. 121. However, in 1980, the IRS issued a technical advice memorandum that held that the provision by an exempt organization of administrative services for other "unrelated" exempt organizations constitutes the performance of an unrelated business (8032039), which holds open the possibility that services to "related" organizations may, for that reason, be considered related activities.

Congress enacted this law change to overrule the IRS position taxing income as from an unrelated trade or business where a tax-exempt hospital[300] provides services only to other tax-exempt hospitals, as long as each of the recipient hospitals has facilities to serve not more than 100 inpatients and the services would be consistent with the recipient hospitals' exempt purposes if performed by them on their own behalf.[301]

This law change was implemented to enable a number of small hospitals to receive services from a single institution instead of providing them directly or creating a tax-exempt organization to provide the services. However, language in the legislative history is somewhat broader than the specifics of this rule, inasmuch as the Senate Finance Committee explanation states that "a hospital is not engaged in an unrelated trade or business simply because it provides services to other hospitals if those services could have been provided, on a tax-free basis, by a cooperative organization consisting of several tax-exempt hospitals."[302]

The U.S. Supreme Court in 1981 held that a cooperative hospital laundry organization does not qualify for tax exemption as a "charitable" entity.[303] Such an organization is, of course, a type of "consortium." However, the Court ruled adversely to the organization because the facts necessitated application of the rules concerning cooperative hospital organizations—a unique and narrow set of circumstances[304]—and not because the tax law is generally in opposition to tax exemption for consortia. Thus, the opinion should not be construed as meaning that tax exemption, as charitable organizations, is no longer available to consortia in general.

Local Economic Development Corporations

New forms of nonprofit organizations continually come into being, in response to the needs and desires of society, inevitably posing questions as to their eligibility for classification as charitable entities. This is the case with the "local economic development corporation" ("LEDC"). LEDCs engage in a variety of activities, including investment in local businesses; direct operation of job-training, housing, and other programs; business counseling; and encouragement to established national businesses to open plants or offices in economically depressed areas. A prime purpose of a LEDC is to alleviate poverty—clearly a charitable purpose. However, by necessity, LEDCs render assistance to commercial business enterprises and make investments in businesses as part of their principal function. While such activities are not normally

---

[300]Code § 170(b)(1)(A)(iii). See Chapter 22.
[301]The services provided must be confined to those described in Code § 501(e)(1)(A). See Chapter 10.
[302]S. Rep. No. 94-938 (Part 2), 94th Cong., 2d Sess. (1976) at 76.
[303]*HCSC-Laundry* v. *United States*, 450 U.S. 1 (1981).
[304]See Chapter 10 § 4.

regarded as "charitable" in nature, there is recent authority for a determination that such LEDCs engage in charitable endeavors.

The investment aspects of LEDCs may be of less concern than the assistance aspects, principally because of the rules adopted in 1969 permitting private foundations to make "program-related investments."[305] Suffice it to say that if a private foundation may undertake such investments then so may other "charitable" organizations. Thus, for LEDCs in relation to the requirements for qualifying as charitable organizations, the focus may be on the activity of providing services to private business enterprises. In large part, resort must be made to the doctrine that private individuals or organizations may be benefited and the activity is nonetheless "charitable" where such immediate beneficiaries are merely means or instruments to a charitable end.[306] Perhaps a fitting analogy can be made to a 1973 IRS pronouncement, where an organization created to attract a doctor to a medically underserved community by providing a medical building and facilities was ruled to be a "charitable" entity, notwithstanding the fact that the organization was subsidizing the doctor in his private practice.[307]

Because it provides its services to private enterprise, even if minority-owned or located in economically depressed areas, the IRS may regard a LEDC itself as being a trade or business and thus not exempt. This raises a serious problem, even though it is clear that an exempt organization may conduct charitable activities by means of a trade or business.[308] Will the IRS require the LEDC to provide such services at substantially below cost (i.e., with a "donative intent") or can it operate at cost or even generate a surplus? Another 1973 IRS ruling indicates that, under appropriate circumstances, the answer may be that a donative element is unnecessary. In that ruling, an organization which operated a toy manufacturing enterprise for the purpose of providing on-the-job training for unskilled workers in an economically depressed area was granted exemption.[309] Otherwise, a LEDC would only be able to have its expenses covered from returns on investments or operations to the extent of 15 percent of costs, even though no commercial enterprise would consider such an investment or operation.[310] Similarly, for those LEDCs that assume debt rather than equity positions in private enterprises, the IRS may require that the loans

[305]See Chapter 28.

[306]See, e.g., Rev. Rul. 72-559, *supra*, n. 13. See Chapter 5.

[307]Rev. Rul. 73-313, *supra*, n. 160.

[308]See Reg. § 1.501(c)(3)-1(e)(1). These same considerations obtain with respect to LEDCs which actually conduct rather than assist qualified businesses. "An activity that would be a business if carried on by a commercial organization may nevertheless, in some circumstances, be the necessary means of achieving exempt purposes." IRS Exempt Organizations Handbook (IRM 7751) § 381.1(2).

[309]Rev. Rul. 73-128, *supra*, n. 4. Also Rev. Rul. 68-167, 1968-1 C. B. 255; Rev. Rul. 70-585, *supra*, n. 12; Rev. Rul. 61-72, *supra*, n. 143.

[310]See Rev. Rul. 71-529, *supra*, n. 75.

be made at less than the commercial rate of interest (or perhaps under circumstances in which no commercial institution would make the loan).[311]

The position of the IRS that "charitable" status requires the provision of services at substantially below cost—if it has any validity at all—may be regarded as only one method by which to ascertain "charitable" status. Thus, a LEDC may be able to achieve exemption as a charitable entity on some other basis. There is authority for the proposition that this "donative intent" prerequisite does not extend to other categories of "charitable" groups. For example, the Tax Court has held that "profitable or even competitive activities in furtherance of petitioner's religious purpose do not affect its right to exemption."[312] Similarly, an organization that made and sold anthropological casts was ruled to be both "educational" and "scientific," with no mention made of the relationship of sales price to cost.[313]

In 1974, the IRS ruled that an organization is exempt as a charitable entity (as promoting social welfare) where it maintains a program of providing low-cost financial assistance and other aid designed to improve economic conditions and economic opportunities in economically depressed areas.[314] The organization undertakes to combat such conditions by providing funds and working capital to business corporations or individual proprietors who are unable to obtain funds from conventional commercial sources because of the poor financial risks involved. The Service noted that "these loans and purchases of equity interest are not undertaken for purpose of profit or gain but for the purpose of advancing the charitable goals of the organization and are not investments for profit in any conventional business sense."

It is possible for a LEDC to qualify for tax exemption as a charitable entity even though it is licensed as a nonprofit small business investment company ("SBIC") under the Small Business Investment Act.[315] A SBIC licensee is required to comply with certain regulations promulgated by the Small Business Administration ("SBA"), which set requirements as to the level of interest rates charged by a licensee and impose various restrictions on the degree of financial support that may be offered to a prospective recipient. The difficulty is that an SBA-regulated SBIC may be prevented from engaging in certain loan transactions in which it would otherwise be able to engage in furtherance of charitable purposes. However, even though "a narrower range of permissible transactions" is available to an SBIC than to non-SBA-regulated LEDCs, the IRS concluded that the SBIC "may still provide loans to businesses that cannot secure financing through conventional commercial sources, the operation of which businesses will achieve charitable purposes. . . ."[316] Thus, although this ruling does not

---

[311]See Rev. Rul. 63-220, *supra*, n. 62; Rev. Rul. 61-87, *supra*, n. 62.
[312]*A.A. Allen Revivals, Inc.* v. *Commissioner*, 22 T.C.M. 1435 (1963).
[313]Rev. Rul. 70-129, *supra*, n. 91.
[314]Rev. Rul. 74-587, *supra*, n. 190.
[315]15 U.S.C. § 681(d).
[316]Rev. Rul. 81-284, *supra*, n. 190.

mean that all SBA-regulated SBICs are automatically tax-exempt LEDCs, it does mean that the mere fact that the organization is subject to the SBA regulations does not preclude it from tax exemption.

Subsequently, the IRS distinguished the situation involved in its 1974 ruling from that where the primary purpose of the organization is to promote business in general rather than to provide assistance only to businesses owned by minority groups or to businesses experiencing difficulty because of their location in a deteriorated section of the community. Thus, the IRS denied classification as a charitable entity to an organization formed to increase business patronage in a deteriorated area mainly inhabited by minority groups by providing information on the area's shopping opportunities, local transportation, and accommodations, and to an organization the purpose of which is to revive retail sales in an area suffering from continued economic decline by constructing a shopping center in the area to arrest the flow of business to competing centers in outlying areas.[317]

Assuming that a LEDC is otherwise exempt as a charitable organization, the question arises as to what must happen if a LEDC-assisted enterprise becomes successful. Does the requirement that a "charitable" organization be "primarily" engaged in an exempt activity[318] mean that such a LEDC would have to divest itself of its investment position in the enterprise or discontinue services to it? Or could the LEDC continue to support it on the theory that the enterprise continues to alleviate unemployment in an economically depressed area and that the LEDC's support of that enterprise is directed toward increased employment opportunities?[319]

Professional Standards Review Organizations

Another new category of organization posing problems as regards eligibility for tax exemption is the "Professional Standards Review Organization" ("PSRO"), which was given statutory authorization in 1972.[320] PSROs are qualified groups of doctors that establish mandatory cost and quality controls in connection with medical treatment rendered in hospitals and financed under Medicare and Medicaid and that monitor this care. PSROs were conceived of as part of a larger effort to curb the rising costs of health care, in this instance by minimizing or eliminating unnecessary services (the services being termed "overutilization") by assuring that payments under these governmental health care pro-

[317]Rev. Rul. 77-111, *supra*, n. 190.

[318]Reg. § 1.501(c)(3)-1(c)(1).

[319]In general, see Weinman, "New opportunities opening up for 501(c)(3) organizations to assist profitable business," 41 *J. Tax.* 102 (1974); Note, "Tax Exemptions for Organizations Investing in Black Businesses," 78 *Yale L.J.* 1212 (1969).

[320]Social Security Amendments of 1972 (P.L. 603) § 249F, 86 Stat. 1429 (adding new Title XI to the Social Security Act); 42 U.S.C. § 1320c *et seq.*

grams are made only when and to the extent that the health care services provided are medically necessary.

Clearly, Congress views PSROs as organizations acting in the public interest, their chief purpose being to generally improve the quality of medical care in the U.S. and to obtain maximum value for every federal health dollar expended.[321] Assuming that the tax law requirements for charitable organizations are otherwise satisfied, this purpose would seem to clearly constitute a "charitable" activity: the promotion of health, lessening of the burdens of government, and promotion of social welfare. However, there may also be a "private" purpose being served by PSROs, namely, enhancement of and establishment of confidence in the medical profession (even though much of the medical community was bitterly opposed to the PSRO concept).

The law requires PSROs to be nonprofit organizations and they are reimbursed by the federal government for administrative costs. Members of a PSRO must be licensed practitioners of medicine or osteopathy. Basically, therefore, the question must be—as respects charitable status—whether a PSRO functions primarily to benefit the general public or to serve the interests of the medical profession. The inclination of the IRS is to treat certain health care organizations as business leagues rather than charitable organizations.[322] The Service has recognized that incidental benefit to physicians will not defeat exemption as a charitable organization,[323] but has also made it clear that, when it concludes a profession is itself receiving substantial benefit from an organization's activities, status as a business league is the likely result.[324] Prior to the ensuing litigation, it was not overly venturesome to speculate that the Service would find that the public benefits flowing from PSRO activities are overshadowed by the benefits ostensibly accorded physicians in their professional capacities.[325]

---

[321]Social Security Act § 1151 states that the purpose of PSROs is to "promote the effective, efficient, and economical delivery of health care services of proper quality for which payment may be made (in whole or in part) under this Act." In general, see Gosfield, *PSROs: The Law and the Health Consumer* (1975); Welch, "Professional Standards Review Organizations—Problems and Prospects," *N. Eng. J. Med.* 289 (Aug., 1973).

[322]See Chapter 17.

[323]Rev. Rul. 73-313, *supra*, n. 160.

[324]See Rev. Rul. 74-553, 1974-2 C. B. 168; Rev. Rul. 73-567, 1973-2 C. B. 178; Rev. Rul. 70-641, 1970-2 C. B. 119. See "Point to Remember" No. 5, 28 *Tax Lawyer* 625 (1975). Cf. *Kentucky Bar Foundation, Inc.* v. *Commissioner, supra*, n. 209. This posture of the IRS may be contrasted with the fact that the medical profession instituted an (unsuccessful) action to enjoin implementation of the PSRO law and to declare the 1972 act unconstitutional. *Association of American Physicians & Surgeons* v. *Weinberger*, 395 F. Supp. 125 (N.D. Ill. 1975). Cf. *American Association of Councils of Medical Staffs* v. *Mathews*, 421 F. Supp. 848 (E.D. La. 1976).

[325]See Bromberg, "The Effect of Tax Policy on the Delivery and Cost of Health Care," 53 *Taxes* 452, 475–478 (1975); Somers, "PSRO: Friend or Foe?," *N. Eng. J. Med.* 289 (Aug., 1973).

By contrast, the IRS has recognized a health systems agency, an organization established by federal law[326] to establish and maintain a system of health planning and resources development aimed at providing adequate health care for a specified geographic area, to be a charitable organization.[327] Among the functions of the agency is the establishment of a health systems plan after appropriate consideration of the recommended national guidelines for health planning policy issued by the Department of Health and Human Services. The agency receives planning and matching grants from the federal government. Finding the basis of the designation of the agency as a charitable entity to be the promotion of health, the IRS observed that, "[b]y establishing and maintaining a system of health planning and resources development aimed at providing adequate health care, the HSA is promoting the health of the residents of the area in which it functions."

Nonetheless, the adverse position of the IRS regarding PSROs was rejected by the U.S. District Court for the District of Columbia, in a case involving PSRO support centers.[328] The court held that Congress' principal purpose in establishing PSROs was to ensure the economical and effective delivery of health care services under Medicare and Medicaid, and that any benefits that physicians and others may derive (including reimbursement for services, limitation on tort liability, or promotion of esteem for the medical profession) have only a "tenuous, incidental, and non-substantial connection with the PSRO scheme."[329] On this latter point, the court added that the PSRO support centers do not engage "in financial transactions designed to benefit the members of the organizations or the organizations themselves, activities in the nature of a patient referral service, or other potential money-making activities designed to benefit members or participants."[330]

As an interesting sidelight of this PSRO decision, the court found it "difficult to reconcile" the position of the IRS against PSROs and the ruling granting classification as charitable entities to health systems agencies. Said the court: "The similarity between HSAs and PSROs and PSRO support centers is obvious. PSROs collect and analyze data, establish regional norms and criteria of care, and coordinate activities with HSAs and other federal and state health planning entities."[331]

As the result of these two court decisions,[332] the IRS revised its position concerning PSROs and concluded that, in certain circumstances, a PSRO is a

---

[326]National Health Planning and Resources Development Act of 1974, 42 U.S.C. § 300k *et seq.*

[327]Rev. Rul. 77-69, 1977-1 C. B. 143.

[328]*Virginia Professional Standards Review Foundation* v. *Blumenthal*, 466 F.Supp. 1164 (D.D.C. 1979).

[329]*Ibid.* at 1170.

[330]*Ibid.* at 1173. Also see *Professional Standards Review Organization of Queens County, Inc.* v. *Commissioner*, 74 T.C. 240 (1980).

[331]Rev. Rul. 77-69, *supra*, n. 327.

[332]See ns. 328 and 330, *supra.*

charitable organization because it "is promoting the health of the beneficiaries of governmental health care programs by preventing unnecessary hospitalization and surgery."[333] However, the IRS regards these factors as essential for exemption of a PSRO as a charitable entity: (1) membership in it is open by law to all physicians without charge, (2) it is an organization mandated by federal statute as the exclusive method of assuring appropriate quality and utilization of care provided to Medicare and Medicaid patients, (3) the composition of the board of directors of the PSRO is not tied to any membership or association with any medical society, and (4) the PSRO has the authority to make final decisions regarding quality and utilization of medical care for purposes of payment under the Medicare and Medicaid programs. The fact that the activities of the PSRO "may indirectly further the interests of the medical profession by promoting public esteem for the medical profession, and by allowing physicians to set their own standards for the review of medicare and medicaid claims and thus prevent outside regulation" was dismissed as being "incidental" to the charitable benefits provided by the organization.

Racial Discrimination

The IRS has taken the position that private educational institutions may not, to be tax exempt, have racially discriminatory policies. In a 1971 case,[334] the Secretary of the Treasury and the Commissioner of Internal Revenue were enjoined from approving any application for recognition of exemption, continuing any current exemption, or approving charitable contribution deductions for any private school in Mississippi which does not show that it has a publicized policy of nondiscrimination. The court found a "Federal public policy against support for racial segregation of schools, public or private" and held that the Code "does not contemplate the granting of special Federal tax benefits to trusts or organizations . . . whose organization or operation contravene Federal public policy."[335] Thus, this decision is essentially founded on the principle that the statutes providing tax deductions and exemptions are not construed to be applicable to actions that are either illegal or contrary to public policy.[336] The court in this case concluded: "Under the conditions of today they [the federal tax law rules allowing tax exemption for and deductibility of gifts to "charitable" organizations] can no longer be construed so as to provide to private

---

[333]Rev. Rul. 81-276, *supra*, n. 111.

[334]*Green* v. *Connally*, 330 F.Supp. 1150 (D.D.C. 1971), aff'd sub nom *Coit* v. *Green*, 404 U.S. 997 (1971).

[335]*Ibid*., 330 F.Supp. at 1163, 1162.

[336]For discussion of the "public policy" rationale, see Note, "Charities, Exempt Status and Public Policy," 50 *Texas L. Rev.* 544 (1972); also Notes at 19 *Wayne L. Rev.* 1629 (1973); 72 *Col. L. Rev.* 1215 (1972); 23 *Syracuse L. Rev.* 1189 (1972); 68 *Mich. L. Rev.* 1410 (1970); 23 *Tax L. Rev.* 399 (1968); 68 *Col. L. Rev.* 992 (1968); 21 *Vand. L. Rev.* 406 (1968).

schools operating on a racially discriminatory premise the support of the exemptions and deductions which Federal tax law affords to charitable organizations and their sponsors."[337]

The IRS in 1971 stated that it would deny tax-exempt status to any private school, that otherwise meets the requirements for tax exemption and charitable donee status, which "does not have a racially nondiscriminatory policy as to students."[338] Subsequently, the Service has identified private schools lacking such a policy in several states to which contributions can no longer be assured to be tax deductible.

The Service initially announced its position on the exempt status of private nonprofit schools in 1967, stating that exemption and deductibility of contributions would be denied if the school is operated on a segregated basis.[339] This position was basically reaffirmed early in 1970 and the IRS began announcing denials of exemption later that year. But a clamor began for stricter guidelines when the granting of exemptions resumed to allegedly segregated schools.[340]

The Service, in 1972,[341] issued guidelines and record keeping requirements for determining whether private schools that have exemption rulings or are applying for such exemption have racially nondiscriminatory policies as to students. The definition of such a policy remained that of the 1971 ruling, namely, that the school "admits the students of any race to all the rights, privileges, programs, and activities generally accorded or made available to students at that school" and that the school "does not discriminate on the basis of race in administration of its educational policies, admissions policies, scholarship and loan programs, and athletic and other school-administered programs."

Under these guidelines, a school had to show that it had a "meaningful number of students from racial minorities enrolled," that is, that it had an acceptable admissions policy. But this was not alone sufficient to demonstrate "a racially nondiscriminatory policy as to students." Unless a school had "clearly established" that it was operating under this policy, it was required—to qualify as a "charitable" organization—to "take affirmative steps to demonstrate that it will so operate in the future." Once the policy was adopted, it had to be made known to "all racial segments of the community served by the school." This could be accomplished by publication of a notice in a newspaper of general circulation, use of the broadcast media, use of brochures and catalogs, or ad-

[337]*Green* v. *Connally, supra,* n. 334, 330 F.Supp. 1164. See Note, "Constitutionality of Federal Tax Benefits to Private Segregated Schools," 11 *Wake Forest L. Rev.* 289 (1975).

[338]Rev. Rul. 71-447, 1971-2 C. B. 230.

[339]See Rev. Rul. 67-325, 1967-2 C. B. 113. See Spratt, "Federal Tax Exemption for Private Segregated Schools: The Crumbling Foundation," 12 *Wm. & Mary L. Rev.* 1 (1970).

[340]See, e.g., "Equal Educational Opportunity," Hearings Before the Senate Select Committee on Equal Educational Opportunity, at 1991–2038, 91st Cong., 2d Sess. (1970).

[341]Rev. Proc. 72-54, 1972-2 C. B. 834.

vising leaders of racial minorities so that they in turn will make the policy known to other members of their race.

In 1975, the IRS promulgated new guidelines on the subject,[342] which superseded the 1972 rules.

Under the 1975 guidelines, the racially nondiscriminatory policy of every private school must be stated in its governing instruments or governing body resolution, and in its brochures, catalogs, and similar publications. This policy must be publicized to all segments of the general community served by the school, either by notice in a newspaper or by use of broadcast media. All programs and facilities must be operated in a racially nondiscriminatory manner and all scholarships or comparable benefits must be offered on this basis. Each school must annually certify its racial nondiscrimination policy.[343]

The 1975 guidelines state the information that every school filing an application for recognition of exempt status must provide. Also included are an assortment of record-keeping requirements, mandating the retention for at least three years of records indicating the racial composition of the school's student body, faculty and administrative staff; records documenting the award of financial assistance, copies of all brochures, catalogs, and advertising dealing with student admissions, programs, and scholarships; and copies of all materials used by or on behalf of the school to solicit contributions. Failure to maintain or to produce the required reports and information ostensibly creates a presumption that the school has failed to comply with the guidelines and thus has a racially discriminatory policy as to students.

In general, a private school must be able to affirmatively demonstrate (for example, as upon audit) that it has adopted a racially nondiscriminatory policy as to students that is made known to the general public and that since the adoption of that policy it has operated in a bona fide manner in accordance therewith.

It is the position of the IRS that church-related schools that teach secular subjects and generally comply with state law requirements for public education for the grades for which instruction is provided may not rely on the First Amendment to avoid the bar on tax exemption to those educational institutions that practice racial discrimination.[344]

However, one federal district court rejected this position of the federal government, holding that the refusal by a private university to admit minority applicants did not preclude its status as a "charitable" organization because it primarily is a religious entity and its admissions policies are predicated upon its religious beliefs. The court reasoned that the IRS policies on this point apply only to educational, and thus not religious, organizations. The above-described

[342]Rev. Proc. 75-50, 1975-2 C. B. 587.
[343]See TIR-1449 (Mar. 19, 1976); also Ann. 76-57, 1976-16 I.R.B. 24.
[344]Rev. Rul. 75-231, 1975-1 C. B. 158. In general, see *Brown v. Dade Christian Schools, Inc.*, 556 F.2d 310 (5th Cir. 1977); *Goldsboro Christian Schools, Inc. v. United States*, 436 F.Supp. 1314 (E.D. N.C. 1977), aff'd in unpublished opinion (4th Cir. Feb. 24, 1981).

federal public policy doctrine cannot, according to the court, be utilized to evaluate the university's tax status, since to do so would transgress its First Amendment right to the free exercise of religion and to its establishment clause protections. Moreover, the court held that the public policy test is applicable to "charitable," but not necessarily to "educational" or "religious" organizations, and concluded that the Service's approach was improperly "a use by the IRS of the federal tax law as a sanction for what it considers a wrongdoing, or its idea of proper social conduct of persons of different races."[345]

Nonetheless, on appeal, the U.S. Court of Appeals for the Fourth Circuit reversed the lower court's decision, concluding that the IRS acted correctly in denying the private university tax-exempt status because of its practices of racial discrimination. The appellate court held that the entirety of the federal tax rules concerning "charitable" organizations "is rooted in public policy considerations" and that the federal government's policy of refusing tax exemption for racially discriminatory schools "assures that Americans will not be providing indirect support for any educational organization that discriminates on the basis of race." The court also found that such application of the nondiscrimination policy to the university does not violate the Free Exercise and Establishment clauses of the First Amendment. Consequently, if this case is an accurate statement of the law on the point, private educational institutions are subject to the government's nondiscrimination policy in tax matters, irrespective of whether the institution is a "religious" one.[346]

The Supreme Court has held that private schools are barred by federal law from denying admission to children solely for the reason of race.[347] The Court held that a statute, which grants equal rights to make and enforce contracts, is contravened where a black applicant is denied a contractual right which would have been granted to him or her if he or she were white. This statute has been characterized as a limitation on private discrimination and, by virtue of the Court's decision, applies to private schools irrespective of state action or tax exemption.[348]

The IRS ruled that an organization that was formed to conduct an apprentice training program offering instruction in a skilled trade is a charitable entity, even though it confines its instruction to American Indians. Admissions were so limited in accordance with the Adult Vocational Training Act (which authorizes programs of vocational and on-the-job training to help adult American Indians living on or near Indian reservations obtain gainful employment) and with a Bureau of Indian Affairs funding contract. The IRS concluded that the organization's "admission policy is designed to implement certain statutorily defined Federal policy goals that are not in conflict with Federal public policy against racial discrimination in education" and that "[i]t is not a type of racial restriction that is contrary to Federal public policy."[349]

---

[345]*Bob Jones University v. United States*, 468 F.Supp. 890, 905 (D.S.C. 1978).
[346]*Bob Jones University v. United States*, 639 F.2d 147 (4th Cir. 1980), cert. gr.
[347]This position is based upon 42 U.S.C. § 1981.
[348]*Runyon v. McCrary*, 424 U.S. 941 (1976).
[349]Rev. Rul. 77-272, *supra*, n. 60.

At the same time, however, the IRS has also determined that the federal public policy against racial discrimination in education "pervades every aspect of the educational arena," including privately created and administered scholarship trusts. In this instance, the Service ruled that racial discrimination was occurring with respect to a trust because it limited scholarships to students of "Finnish extraction."[350]

In an effort to further regulate in this field, the IRS proposed controversial guidelines, on August 21, 1978, [351] and again in revised form on February 13, 1979,[352] for ascertaining whether private schools have racially discriminatory policies toward students. These rules would establish certain presumptions as to discriminatory practices by a private school, such as the nature of its minority enrollment and the relationship between formation or expansion of the school and local public school desegregation.

While these guidelines were pending, Congress, in enacting the fiscal year 1980 appropriations act for the Department of the Treasury,[353] prohibited the IRS from using funds appropriated thereunder to implement the guidelines. In addition to specifically precluding the use of these appropriations to carry out the proposed guidelines, the legislation states that none of the appropriations "shall be used to formulate or carry out any rule, policy, procedure, guideline, regulation, standard, or measure which would cause the loss of tax-exempt status to private, religious, or church-operated schools under section 501(c)(3) of the Internal Revenue Code of 1954 unless in effect prior to August 22, 1978."[354]

The position of the IRS in this regard became particularly aggravated when, notwithstanding the prohibition on the use of appropriated funds, a court ordered the Service to refrain from according or continuing tax-exempt status for racially discriminatory private schools in the state of Mississippi.[355] This court order likewise uses certain criteria concerning the timing of establishment of the school to raise an inference of discrimination, to be overcome only by clear and convincing evidence to the contrary. This prohibition was dropped from the House version of the measure to provide the fiscal year 1981 appropriations for the Department of the Treasury.[356]

---

[350]IRS Private Letter Ruling 7851096.

[351]43 Fed. Reg. 37296.

[352]44 Fed. Reg. 9451. In general, see Sanders, "Exemptions for private schools threatened by Service's latest controversial guidelines," 50 *J. Tax.* 234 (1979); Wilson, "An Overview of the IRS's Revised Proposed Revenue Procedure on Private Schools as Tax-Exempt Organizations," 57 *Taxes* 515 (1979).

[353]P.L. 96-74, 93 Stat. 559 (1979).

[354]Congress, in this legislation, also barred the IRS from carrying out any ruling to the effect "that a taxpayer is not entitled to a charitable deduction for general purpose contributions which are not used for educational purposes by [an exempt] religious organization," thereby prohibiting enforcement of Rev. Rul. 79-99, 1979-1 C. B. 108, during fiscal year 1980.

[355]*Green* v. *Miller*, 80-1 U.S.T.C. ¶ 9401 (D.D.C. 1980).

[356]H.R. 7583, 96th Cong., 2d Sess. (1980).

The U.S. District Court for the District of Columbia subsequently gave considerable impetus to the philosophy underlying the proposed IRS guidelines, when it upheld the Service's revocation of tax-exempt status of a private school on the ground that the institution maintains a racially discriminatory admissions policy. In so holding, the court noted that the school did not directly prove a nondiscriminatory admissions policy and that the government did not directly prove that the policy was discriminatory. Nonetheless, the court inferred from the circumstances surrounding the establishment of the school that it administers a racially discriminatory policy. The court also upheld the revocation of tax exemption retroactive to 1970.[357]

Although this area of law had seemed relatively settled, on January 8, 1982, the Reagan Administration announced that it had decided to abandon the 12-year-old effort to deny tax exemption and the eligibility to receive deductible contributions to private schools that have racially discriminatory practices. As part of this announcement, the Reagan Administration stated that it was going to accord tax-exempt and charitable donee status to Bob Jones University and Goldsboro Christian Schools, and claimed that these cases before the Supreme Court were thereby rendered moot. Ten days later, the Administration submitted legislation on the subject. The legislation was intended to place regulation in this field on a statutory basis, rather than on the amorphous foundation of "federal public policy."[358]

---

[357]*Prince Edward School Foundation* v. *United States*, 80-1 U.S.T.C. ¶ 9295 (D.D.C. 1980), aff'd in unpublished opinion (1981), cert. den. 450 U.S. 944 (1981).

[358]The proposed legislation would have created a new Code § 501(j), which would state the following general rule:

"An organization that normally maintains a regular faculty and curriculum (other than an exclusively religious curriculum) and normally has a regularly enrolled body of students in attendance at the place where its educational activities are regularly carried on shall not be deemed to be described in subsection [501](c)(3), and shall not be exempt from tax under subsection [501](a), if such organization has a racially discrim-inatory policy."

A definitional rule was proposed as follows:

"(i) An organization has a 'racially discriminatory policy' if it refuses to admit students of all races to the rights, privileges, programs, and activities generally accorded or made available to students by that organization, or if the organization refuses to administer its educational policies, admission policies, scholarship and loan programs, athletic programs, or other programs administered by such organizations in a manner that does not discriminate on the basis of race. The term 'racially discriminatory policy' does not include an admissions policy of a school, or a program of religious training or worship of a school, that is limited, or grants preferences or priorities, to members of a particular religious organization or belief, *provided,* that no such policy, program, preference, or priority is based upon race or upon a belief that requires discrimination on the basis of race.

"(ii) The term 'race' shall include color or national origin."

Comparable revisions would be made in the rules concerning charitable giving to discriminatory private schools (Code §§ 170(f)(7), 642(c)(7), 2055(e)(4), and 2522(c)(3)).

The move to rescind this administrative policy brought a barrage of assertions that the Administration was endorsing the practices of racist private education. Attempting to mitigate the political damage, the President, on January 12, 1982, issued a statement that read: "I am unalterably opposed to racial discrimination in any form. I would not knowingly contribute to any organization that supports racial discrimination."

Both during and following House Ways and Means Committee and Senate Finance Committee hearings on the proposed legislation, it was clear that there was little appetite in Congress for legislation concerning tax exemption for private schools with racially discriminatory policies. Many members of Congress were concerned about the collateral issues that would be raised during debate, and about the political sensitivities that surround this subject. There was a brief period when it appeared that Congress would slip out of the tight spot in which the President had placed it by passing a "sense of the Congress" resolution, but that approach also failed to engender much support.

Then, on February 18, 1982, the U.S. Circuit Court of Appeals in Washington, D.C., ordered the Reagan Administration not to grant tax exemption to any private schools with racially discriminatory practices.[359] The order applied to Bob Jones University and Goldsboro Christian Schools. This order appeared to erase any basis the Reagan Administration may have had for contending that the cases before the Supreme Court were mooted by the administrative decision on January 8, 1982.

Much speculation arose thereafter as to what the Reagan Administration would do next. Many believed that the President would not reverse his mootness claim, and wait for Congress or the courts to act. On February 25, 1982, however, the Reagan Administration asked the Supreme Court to consider the private school issue and suggested that a third party argue the position that the IRS has the authority to deny tax exemption to discriminatory schools. On April 19, 1982, the Supreme Court accepted these cases and announced the appointment of William T. Coleman, Jr., former U.S. Secretary of Transportation and past Chairman of the NAACP Legal Defense and Educational Fund, as an advocate of the IRS position. Oral arguments on the cases occurred on October 12, 1982.

As the issue of the appropriate tax policy for private schools with racially discriminatory policies continues to fester, its ramifications also continue to grow. This is amply illustrated by a case involving an organization known as the National Alliance; this case is on cross-appeals to the United States Court of Appeals for the District of Columbia Circuit.[360] The appeals are being taken from an order by the United States District Court for the District of Columbia, which granted summary judgment to the National Alliance and remanded the case to the IRS for further proceedings.

The National Alliance was formed as a nonprofit organization in 1974 to,

[359]*Wright v. Regan*, 49 A.F.T.R. 2d 82-757 (D.C. Cir. 1982).
[360]*National Alliance v. United States*, 81-1 U.S.T.C. ¶ 9464 (D.D.C. 1981).

according to its articles of incorporation, develop "in those with whom communication is established" an "understanding of and a pride in their racial and cultural heritage and an awareness of the present dangers to that heritage," with a view to establishing an "effective force for building a new order in American life." According to court records, its membership is confined to "persons of the European race." Its primary activities are the publication and distribution of a newspaper, a bulletin, and books and pamphlets. In the words of an amici curiae brief filed by the American Jewish Congress, the Anti-Defamation League, and the National Association for the Advancement of Colored People, the organization is engaged in the "propagation of racial hatred and advocacy of the extermination of Jews and Blacks (as well as other 'non-European' peoples)."

The IRS determined that the National Alliance could not qualify for tax exemption because it is neither "charitable" nor "educational." In return, the organization took the matter to court, contending that denial of the tax exemption is an infringement of its constitutional rights. This argument was largely based on the fact that the U.S. Court of Appeals has concluded that the tax regulations defining the term "educational" are unconstitutionally vague.[361]

The correlation with this case and the private school issue is the reach of the doctrine that an organization cannot be "charitable" where it engages in an activity that is contrary to "public policy."[362] In the school context, the position reflected in court decisions is that racially discriminatory policies are contrary to public policy. The counterargument has been that schools are "educational," not "charitable," so that the public policy doctrine is inapplicable.

The National Alliance case is presenting somewhat the same issue. In the minds of the above amici, the matter is clear. They state: "The propagation of doctrines of racial hatred and mass murder can hardly be classified as a charitable or educational activity." One might assume that statement to be reflective of fact but, in actuality, the matter is not quite so simple.

Leaving aside the category of "charitable" to which the public policy doctrine applies (and thus precludes the conduct of activities such as "mass murder"), the focus in the National Alliance case (as in the private school cases) is whether the public policy doctrine (or something approximating it) is applicable to "educational" organizations.

It must be said there is no direct precedent for resolving this issue. There is caselaw holding that organizations that engage in political agitation or in propagandizing cannot be "educational."[363] The political agitation cases may not be on point. The cases concerning propaganda are closer in applicability but "propaganda" is usually portrayed as a one-sided presentation of opinion. The tax regulations defined "educational" in a way that allowed an organization to disseminate opinion as long as it was preceded by a balanced discussion of

[361]*Big Mama Rag, Inc.* v. *United States*, 631 F.2d 1030 (D.C. Cir. 1980).
[362]See Chapter 4 § 2.
[363]See Chapters 13 and 14.

the facts. Given this definition, can an organization advocate "racial hatred" and "mass murder" and be educational as long as the advocacy is preceded by the "pros and cons" of these types of activity? Technically, it is hard to answer that question because that definition is part of the regulations that have been struck down as unconstitutional.

There are also First Amendment considerations. The case again raises the question as to whether a denial of tax exemption can contravene free speech rights. From the organization's point of view, it is advocating views, not committing deeds. Thus, these amici urge the court to hold that "inflammatory speech" cannot be educational. No authority is cited for that position.

Those who urge that federal income tax exemption be denied the National Alliance may well have the better of the policy argument. Rather eloquently, the above amici state that, for the court to rule otherwise "would simply make a grotesque travesty of the tax exemption statute." However, the state of the law does not yet match the policy being urged. It may well be that an activity that is protected by the free speech doctrine is automatically "educational" as long as it is not "propagandizing." If the Supreme Court resolves the private school issue, perhaps it will resolve this question also.

It is important to view this developing aspect of the law of tax-exempt organizations in a larger context.

A close look at the arguments for and against the granting of tax exemption and charitable donee status to racially discriminatory private schools, on the basis of existing law, finds that a pivotal issue is the "worth" to be accorded these tax classifications. This is an old argument that ebbs and flows as circumstances change. For example, when the widespread application of the "tax expenditures" concept developed, it gave many people a renewed opportunity to contend that charitable tax exemptions and deductions are tangible economic items to be recognized as forms of "quasi appropriations" and "back-door spending."[364]

Those who argue that the IRS has the authority under present law to revoke or deny tax exemption to discriminatory private schools assert that it was, and continues to be, congressional policy in granting tax exemption and eligibility for deductible charitable contributions that each qualifying organization must promote the general welfare and benefit the community at large. It is the furtherance of these "public ends," so the argument unfolds, that causes the government to be a "partner" in the process by which private philanthropic undertakings are supported. The argument thus concludes that these tax provisions amount to a substantial financial benefit that is a form of government support or subsidy.

Thus, in the draft brief prepared for the government for filing with the U.S. Supreme Court in the days when it was arguing that the IRS possesses the authority to revoke or deny tax exemption and charitable donee status to discriminatory private schools, the government flatly states that these two tax

[364]See Chapter 3.

preferences "constitute a substantial financial benefit and form of indirect government support." The brief also states that "the tax laws make the government a partner in the multiple forms of private philanthropy that abound in the nation." (Consequently, this argument concludes that private schools must be "charitable" to enjoy these tax benefits and that when they practice discrimination they violate notions of Federal public policy and therefore forfeit their entitlement to this form of government subsidy.)

By contrast, in the brief actually filed with the Supreme Court, the government argued precisely the opposite point. The contention there was that the tax laws do not make the government "a partner or joint venturer" in the affairs of tax exempt organizations. Rather, the government advised the Court, the existence of tax exemption is merely "a decision by Congress to refrain from collecting taxes from certain classes of organizations."

This latter brief considers whether a tax exemption is a form of "Federal financial assistance" for purposes of Title VI of the Civil Rights Act of 1964, which prohibits racial discrimination in any program or activity receiving such assistance. That assistance is defined as "assistance to any program or activity by way of grant, loan, or contract other than a contract of insurance or guaranty." The point is made in the brief that the statute does not indicate that Congress intended tax exemptions to be this type of assistance, that the legislative history of the Act lacks any evidence of this intent, and that the proposition to the contrary is inconsistent with the overall structure of the Act.

The tax-exempt organizations community in general thus has a considerable stake in the outcome of this litigation. First, if tax exemption is in fact "Federal financial assistance," there are some far-reaching implications as regards application of the Civil Rights Act. Second, such a conclusion would erode the concept of tax exemption (and the charitable deduction) as being reflective of the higher principle of the essential role of pluralism and voluntarism in a democratic society, and reduce it to merely a government subsidy to be reduced or revoked at Congress' will. Third, that conclusion would advance the idea (already nurtured by the tax expenditures concept) that government is entitled to all property and earnings of private parties, and a decision by (or failure of) Congress not to tax is "Federal financial assistance."[365]

---

[365]*Ibid.* In general, see Nevin and Bills, *The Schools That Fear Built* (1977); Comment, "The Tax Exempt Status of Sectarian Educational Institutions That Discriminate on the Basis of Race," 65 *Iowa L. Rev.* 258 (1979); Note, "Racial Exclusion by Religious Schools, Brown v. Dade Christian Schools, Inc.," 91 *Harv. L. Rev.* 879 (1978); Note, "Constitutionality of Federal Tax Benefits to Private Segregated Schools," 11 *Wake Forest L. Rev.* 289 (1975); Horvitz, "Tax Subsidies to Promote Affirmative Action in Admission Procedures for Institutions of Higher Learning—Their Inherent Danger," 52 *Taxes* 452 (1974); Comment, "Denial of Tax Exempt Status to Southern Segregation Academies," 6 *Harvard Civil Rights—Civil Liberties L. Rev.* 179 (1970); Note, "Federal Tax Exempt Status of Private Segregated Schools," 7 *Wake Forest L. Rev.* 121 (1970).

Sex Discrimination

While there is a recognized federal public policy against support for racial segregation in private schools (and, presumably, other varieties of racial discrimination[366]), there is developing a comparable federal public policy against support for institutions that engage in sex discrimination.[367] The question is whether this is a sufficiently established federal policy so that its contravention would have an impact on the tax status of these institutions and other "charitable" organizations.[368] The issue has been raised, with the courts concluding that sex discrimination does not bar tax exemption.[369] However, at least one court—having concluded that the charitable contribution deduction is equivalent to a federal matching grant—has found that by allowing the deduction of charitable contributions the federal government has conferred a "benefit" on the recipient organization and that the Fifth Amendment is applicable.[370]

It may also be quite validly asserted that there is a federal public policy, either presently in existence or in the process of development, against other forms of discrimination, such as discrimination on the basis of marital status, national origin, religion, handicap, and age.[371] Thus, the law may develop to the point where a "charitable" organization will jeopardize its tax status where it engages in one or more of these forms of discrimination. The IRS itself has displayed some sensitivity to these matters, such as by including discrimination

[366]See *Bob Jones University* v. *Simon*, 416 U.S. 725 (1974); *Crenshaw County Private School Foundation* v. *Connally*, 474 F.2d 1185 (3rd Cir. 1973), cert. den. 417 U.S. 908 (1973).

[367]See, e.g., *McGlotten* v. *Connally*, 338 F.Supp. 448 (D.D.C. 1972). See Bittker and Kaufman, "Taxes and Civil Rights: 'Constitutionalizing' the Internal Revenue Code," 82 *Yale L.J.* 51 (1972).

[368]See, e.g., Executive Order 11246, as amended, 30 Fed. Reg. 12319 (1965); Title VII of the Civil Rights Act of 1964, as amended, 42 U.S.C. § 2000e *et seq.*; Equal Employment Opportunity Commission regulations, 29 C.F.R. § 1604 *et seq.*; Title IX of the Education Amendments of 1972, 20 U.S.C. § 1681 *et seq.*; the Equal Pay Act of 1963, 29 U.S.C. § 206 *et seq.*; *Califano* v. *Webster*, 430 U.S. 313 (1977); *Alexander* v. *Louisiana*, 405 U.S. 625 (1972); *Reed* v. *Reed*, 404 U.S. 71 (1971).

[369]See *McCoy* v. *Shultz*, 73-1 U.S.T.C. ¶ 9233 (D.D.C. 1973); *Junior Chamber of Commerce of Rochester, Inc., Rochester, New York* v. *U.S. Jaycees, Tulsa, Oklahoma*, 495 F.2d 883 (10th Cir. 1974), cert. den. 419 U.S. 1026 (1974); *New York City Jaycees, Inc.* v. *United States Jaycees, Inc.*, 512 F.2d 856 (2d Cir. 1975).

[370]*McGlotten* v. *Connally*, *supra*, n. 367 at 456–457, n. 37. See *Stearns* v. *Veterans of Foreign Wars*, 500 F.2d 788 (D.C. Cir. 1974) (remand). In general, see Comment, "Taxing Sex Discrimination: Revoking Tax Benefits of Organizations Which Discriminate on the Basis of Sex," 1976 *Ariz. State L.J.* 641 (1976); Note, "Sex Restricted Scholarships and the Charitable Trust," 59 *Iowa L. Rev.* 1000 (1974).

[371]See, e.g., Title VII of the Civil Rights Act of 1964, as amended, 42 U.S.C. § 2000e *et seq.*; Executive Order 11246, as amended, 30 Fed. Reg. 12319 (1965); Title IX of the Education Amendments of 1972, 20 U.S.C. § 1681 *et seq.*; the Rehabilitation Act Amendments of 1974, 29 U.S.C. §§ 793 and 794; the Age Discrimination in Employment Act, 29 U.S.C. § 621 *et seq.*; and the Age Discrimination Act of 1975, 89 Stat. 713.

on the ground of national origin as being within the scope of racial discrimination for purposes of the nondiscrimination rules applicable to private educational institutions[372] and by evidencing concern that a 1965 ruling carries overtones of a condonation of age discrimination.[373]

Government Instrumentalities

A wholly owned state or municipal instrumentality that is a separate entity may qualify for exemption as a "charitable" entity if it is a "clear counterpart" of a charitable, educational, religious, or like organization.[374] The test set by the IRS is the scope of the organization's purposes and powers, that is, whether the purposes and powers are beyond those of a charitable organization. For example, a state or municipality itself cannot qualify as a charitable organization since its purposes are not exclusively those described therein, nor would an integral component of the state or municipality.[375]

An otherwise qualified instrumentality meeting the "counterpart" requirement would be deemed a charitable organization, such as a school, college, university, or hospital.[376] But if an instrumentality is clothed with powers other than those described in the federal tax rules for charitable groups, such as enforcement or regulatory powers in the public interest (for example, health, welfare, safety), it would not be a requisite "clear counterpart" organization. Two 1974 rulings draw the contrast. In one ruling,[377] a public housing authority was denied exemption as a charitable organization, even though its purpose was to provide safe and sanitary dwelling accommodations for low income families in a particular municipality. The state statute under which it was incorporated conferred upon it the power to conduct examinations and investigations, administer oaths, issue subpoenas, and make its findings and recommendations available to appropriate agencies; these powers were ruled to be regulatory or enforcement powers. By contrast, in the other ruling,[378] a public library organized under a state statute was ruled to be a counterpart to a charitable organization and hence tax exempt. The organization has the power to determine the tax rate necessary to support its operations within specified maximum and minimum rates; since the organization lacked the power to impose or levy taxes, the power was deemed not regulatory or enforcement in nature.

Thus, the "clear counterpart" type of state instrumentality may qualify for

---

[372]Rev. Proc. 75-50, *supra*, n. 342.

[373]Rev. Rul. 77-365, *supra*, n. 211.

[374]Rev. Rul. 60-384, 1960-2 C. B. 172; Rev. Rul. 55-319, 1955-1 C. B. 172; *Estate of Slayton* v. *Commissioner*, 3 B.T.A. 1343 (1926).

[375]But see Code § 115(a).

[376]See Rev. Rul. 67-290, 1967-2 C. B. 183.

[377]Rev. Rul. 74-14, 1974-1 C. B. 125.

[378]Rev. Rul. 74-15, 1974-1 C. B. 126.

exemption as a "charitable" organization, while the instrumentality having enforcement or regulatory powers (presumably a "political subdivision"[379]) will
not so qualify. While both "instrumentalities" and "political subdivisions" constitute qualified charitable donees,[380] the non-"clear counterpart" instrumentality apparently does not.

Until 1975, the IRS had not specifically distinguished between state instrumentalities and state political subdivisions. In that year, the IRS made the
distinction, ruling that an association of counties in a state constituted an instrumentality of the state or the counties (themselves political subdivisions) but
not a political subdivision of the state.[381]

In 1957,[382] the IRS promulgated criteria for identifying *both* state instrumentalities and political subdivisions:

> In cases involving the status of an organization as an instrumentality of one or
> more states or political subdivisions, the following factors are taken into consid-
> eration: (1) whether it is used for a governmental purpose and performs a gov-
> ernmental function; (2) whether performance of its function is on behalf of one
> or more states or political subdivisions; (3) whether there are any private interests
> involved, or whether the states or political subdivisions involved have the powers
> and interests of an owner; (4) whether control and supervision of the organization
> is vested in public authority or authorities; (5) if express or implied statutory or
> other authority is necessary for the creation and/or use of such an instrumentality
> and whether such authority exists; and (6) the degree of financial autonomy and
> the source of its operating expenses.

According to the government, however, one additional characteristic separates a political subdivision from a state instrumentality: the former has been
delegated the right to exercise part of the sovereign power of the governmental
unit of which it is a division (or is a municipal corporation).[383] Thus, the association of counties discussed above was denied status as a political subdivision
of the state because it was not delegated any of the counties' or state's sovereign
powers. However, the IRS ruled that the association was nonetheless a qualified
donee for charitable contribution purposes, with contributions deductible as
being "for the use of" political subdivisions (that is, the counties), subject to
the annual limitation of 20 percent of the donor's "contribution base."[384]

The tax-exempt status of this association is not clear; presumably it is exempt
as a state instrumentality under the U.S. constitutional system of government;
because of the position of the IRS on consortia and related entities (see above),
the association may not be regarded by the IRS as a "clear counterpart" instrumentality exempt as a charitable organization.

[379]See Code §§ 103(a)(1), 115(a)(1), 170(c)(1).
[380]Code §§ 170(c)(2), 170(c)(1), respectively.
[381]Rev. Rul. 75-359, *supra*, n. 278.
[382]Rev. Rul. 57-128, 1957-1 C. B. 311.
[383]Reg. § 1.103(b).
[384]Code § 170(b)(1)(B).

Presumably, a state law characterization of an entity's status as a type of governmental unit is overridden for federal tax purposes by the criteria established in 1957. For example, the University of Illinois has been determined by the Supreme Court of that state to be a "public corporation."[385] But because the University of Illinois meets the criteria promulgated in 1957 and has been delegated the right to exercise part of the sovereign power of the State of Illinois, it constitutes a political subdivision of the State. (Both the IRS and the courts have recognized that the education of its citizens is an essential governmental function of a state.[386]) Thus it is that a state college or university (and comparable entities such as state hospitals) may qualify as both a "clear counterpart" state instrumentality (and thus have tax exemption as a charitable entity) and a political subdivision because its activities in addition to those described in the 1957 criteria are neither regulatory nor enforcement powers.[387] However, it is the position of the IRS that most state universities cannot qualify as political subdivisions.[388]

The foregoing analysis by the IRS does not take into account the consequence of operation of the "adjunct" theory (discussed above). By this theory, the association of counties should be regarded as a political subdivision of the state rather than an instrumentality of the state, inasmuch as the characteristics of the counties are attributable to the association.[389]

The IRS has ruled on several occasions as to whether an entity is a political subdivision or a state instrumentality. The IRS characterized a county board of education as an instrumentality of a state in the fact statement of a 1970 ruling but then concluded that the board qualified as a political subdivision.[390] Similarly, the IRS ruled a governor's conference to be a political subdivision of a state.[391] Also, an organization created by the governors of eleven states to foster interstate cooperation and to otherwise coordinate action among these states was ruled to be an instrumentality of the states.[392] Likewise, the Service held that an industrial commission established by a state legislature to study the problems of industrial life in a geographic area qualifies as a charitable donee.[393]

Reversing an earlier position, the IRS ruled that an incorporated integrated state bar, which engages in a variety of activities with respect to attorneys,

[385]The People ex rel, The Board of Trustees of the University of Illinois v. George F. Barrett, Attorney General, 46 N.E.2d 951 (Sup. Ct. Ill. 1943).

[386]Rev. Rul. 75-436, 1975-2 C. B. 217; Gilliam v. Adams, 171 S.W.2d 813 (Sup. Ct. Tenn. 1943).

[387]Cf. Rev. Rul. 74-14, supra, n. 377.

[388]Rev. Rul. 77-165, 1977-1 C. B. 21. See discussion in Chapter 20 § 22.

[389]See, e.g., Brundage v. Commissioner, supra, n. 286; cf. Miller v. United States, supra, n. 286; Puerto Rico Marine Management, Inc. v. International Longshoremen's Association, AFL-CIO, 398 F.Supp. 118 (D.P.R. 1975).

[390]Rev. Rul. 70-562, 1970-2 C. B. 63.

[391]Rev. Rul. 69-459, 1969-2 C. B. 35.

[392]IRS Private Letter Ruling 7935043.

[393]Rev. Rul. 79-323, 1979-2 C. B. 106.

does not qualify as an instrumentality or political subdivision of a state.[394] The Service reasoned that the state bar is a "dual purpose" organization, in that it has public purposes (such as admission, suspension, disbarment and reprimand of licensed attorneys) and private purposes (such as the protection of professional interests of its members), and thus that it "is not an arm of the state because it is a separate entity and has private as well as public purposes." The Service also held that the state bar "is not a political subdivision because it has no meaningful sovereign powers."

A committee, created by joint resolution of a state legislature, established to receive and expend contributions to provide state units for a parade incident to a presidential inauguration, was ruled to be a political subdivision.[395] A committee which was created by a governor's executive order, to educate the public about the activities of the United Nations, was considered a political subdivision of the state.[396] Under appropriate circumstances, a nonprofit corporation may qualify as a political subdivision of a state.[397]

In 1963, the IRS considered the question as to whether a nonprofit membership corporation qualifies as a political subdivision.[398] The members of the corporation consisted of representatives of the local chambers of commerce and other private business groups in a particular county, the county commissioners, and officials of participating municipalities. There was no private inurement and the corporation's articles provided that upon any dissolution of the corporation the beneficial interest in any property owned by the corporation would pass to the county.

The IRS held that obligations of such a corporation would be considered issued "on behalf of" the state or a political subdivision thereof, provided each of the following requirements is met: (1) the corporation must engage in activities which are essentially public in nature; (2) the corporation must be one which is not organized for profit (except to the extent of retiring indebtedness); (3) the corporate income must not inure to any private person; (4) the state or a political subdivision thereof must have a beneficial interest in the corporation while the indebtedness remains outstanding and it must obtain full legal title to the property of the corporation with respect to which the indebtedness was incurred upon the retirement of such indebtedness; and (5) the corporation must have been approved by the state or a political subdivision thereof.[399]

---

[394]Rev. Rul. 77-232, 1977-2 C. B. 71, revoking Rev. Rul. 59-152, 1959-1 C. B. 54. This change in classification also means that contributions to such state bars are not deductible under Code §§ 170(c)(1), 2055(a)(1) and 2522(a)(1). However, Rev. Rul. 77-232 is inapplicable to contributions made prior to July 5, 1977. Rev. Rul. 78-129, 1978-1 C. B. 67.

[395]Rev. Rul. 58-265, 1958-1 C. B. 127.

[396]Rev. Rul. 62-66, 1962-1 C. B. 83.

[397]Rev. Rul. 59-41, 1959-1 C. B. 13; Rev. Rul. 54-296, 1954-2 C. B. 59.

[398]Rev. Rul. 63-20, 1963-1 C. B. 24.

[399]Also see Rev. Rul. 60-243, 1960-2 C. B. 35, and Rev. Rul. 57-187, 1957-1 C. B. 65. Regulations proposed in 1976 would supersede these and like rulings. Prop. Reg. § 1.103-1 (41 Fed. Reg. 4829 (1976)).

State liquor stores are generally considered political subdivisions, as being part of the states' effort to regulate the use of alcohol.[400]

The United States Court of Appeals for the Second Circuit has held that a "political subdivision" is any division of any state which has been delegated the right to exercise part of the sovereign power of the unit.[401] The Second Circuit stated that:

> The term "political subdivision" is broad and comprehensive and denotes any division of the State made by the proper authorities thereof, acting within their constitutional powers, for the purpose of those functions of the State which by long usage and the inherent necessities of government have always been regarded as public.[402]

Similarly, the Supreme Court of North Carolina has observed that:

> . . . [i]mportant factors, among others, which must be considered in determining that . . . [a]n agency is an instrument of government are: [whether] (1) It was created by the government; (2) it is wholly owned by the government; (3) it is not operated for profit; (4) it is primarily engaged in the performance of some essential governmental function; [and] (5) the proposed tax will impose an economic burden upon the government, or it serves to materially impair the usefulness or efficiency of the agency, or to materially restrict it in the performance of its duties.[403]

An organization may seek instrumentality status rather than tax exemption as a charitable entity to avoid the annual reporting requirements, the private foundation rules, other federal tax limitations on charitable groups, or because it cannot qualify as "charitable" in nature. Contributions to instrumentalities are deductible as long as they qualify as a "governmental unit" and the gift is made for exclusively public purposes,[404] and the interest they pay on their borrowings is exempt from the lender's gross income.[405]

Charitable Works in Foreign Countries

A U.S. organization that otherwise qualifies as a charitable entity and that carries on part or all of its charitable activities in foreign countries is not

---

[400]Rev. Rul. 71-132, 1971-1 C. B. 29; Rev. Rul. 71-131, 1971-1 C. B. 28.

[401]*Commissioner* v. *Shamberg's Estate*, 44 F.2d 998, 1004–1006 (2d Cir. 1944).

[402]*Ibid*. at 1004.

[403]*Unemployment Compensation Commission of North Carolina* v. *Wachovia Bank and Trust Co.*, 2 S.E.2d 592, 596 (Sup. Ct. N.C. 1939). Also see *City of Cincinnati* v. *Gamble*, 34 N.E.2d 226, 231 (Sup. Ct. Ohio 1941); *City of Bay Minette* v. *Quinly*, 82 So.2d 192, 194 (Sup. Ct. Ala. 1955); *War Memorial Hospital of District No. 1, Park County* v. *Board of County Commissioners of County of Park*, 279 P.2d 472, 475 (Sup. Ct. Wyo. 1955); *Gebhardt* v. *Village of La Grange Park*, 188 N.E. 372, 374 (Sup. Ct. Ill. 1933).

[404]Code §§ 170(c)(1), 170(b)(1)(A)(v).

[405]Code § 103(a)(1).

precluded because of such activities from qualifying as a "charitable" organization.[406] For example, the "charitable" activity of "relief of the poor and distressed or of the underprivileged" is nonetheless charitable where the beneficiaries of the assistance are outside the U.S. Thus, the IRS has ruled exempt as a charitable group an organization formed to help poor rural inhabitants of developing countries[407] and an organization created for the purpose of assisting underprivileged people in Latin America to improve their living conditions through educational and self-help programs.[408]

The foregoing distinctions are well illustrated by the tax treatment accorded the so-called "friends" organization. This is an organization formed to solicit and receive contributions in the United States and to expend the funds on behalf of a charitable organization in another country. Its support may be provided in a variety of ways, including program or project grants, provision of equipment or materials, or scholarship or fellowship grants.

Charitable contributions made directly to an organization not created or organized in the United States, a state or territory, the District of Columbia, or a possession of the United States are not deductible.[409] Also, contributions to a United States charity which transmits the funds to a foreign charity are deductible only in certain limited circumstances.

An IRS ruling issued in 1963 sets forth five illustrations of supporting domestic charities and the tax treatment to be given contributions thereto.[410] Example (1) involves a mere conduit entity formed by the foreign organization. Example (2) involves a mere conduit entity formed by individuals in the United States. Example (3) involves an exempt U.S. charity that agrees to solicit and funnel contributions to a foreign organization. Example (4) involves a U.S. charity that frequently makes grants to charities in a foreign country in furtherance of its exempt purposes, following review and approval of the uses to which the funds are to be put. Example (5) involves a U.S. charity that formed a subsidiary organization in a foreign country to facilitate its exempt operations there, with certain of its funds transmitted directly to the subsidiary.

This 1963 ruling states a rationale of earmarking and of nominal as opposed to real donees, and thus concludes that contributions to the U.S. entities in examples (1), (2), and (3) therein are not deductible. Contributions to the U.S. organization described in example (4) are deductible because there is no earmarking of contributions and "use of such contributions will be subject to control by the domestic organization." Contributions to the U.S. organization described in example (5) are deductible because "the foreign organization is merely an administrative arm of the domestic organization," with the domestic organization considered "the real recipient" of the contributions.

The 1963 test was amplified in 1966, with the IRS describing the necessary attributes of the "friends" organization (in essence, the entity in example (4)

[406]Rev. Rul. 71-460, 1971-2 C. B. 231.
[407]Rev. Rul. 68-117, *supra*, n. 9.
[408]Rev. Rul. 68-165, *supra*, n. 9. Also Rev. Rul. 80-286, *supra*, n. 92.
[409]Code § 170(c)(2)(A); Rev. Rul. 63-252, 1963-2 C. B. 101, and cases cited therein.
[410]Rev. Rul. 63-252, *supra*, n. 409.

of the 1963 ruling) in some detail.[411] Again, the IRS emphasized the "ear-marking" problem,[412] stating that "[t]he test in each case is whether the organization has full control of the donated funds, and discretion as to their use, so as to insure that they will be used to carry out its functions and purposes." The point of example (4) of the 1963 ruling was also illustrated in 1975.[413]

However, these rules concerning prohibited "earmarking" and "conduits" contemplate two separate organizations: the "domestic" (United States) entity and the "foreign" entity. Where, therefore, the domestic and foreign activities are housed in one entity (such as a corporation), and that entity qualifies as a domestic charitable organization, the rules do not apply and the contributions to the organization are deductible as charitable gifts. Thus, in one case, the U.S. Tax Court held that a corporation (a recognized charitable entity) organized under the law of the State of Delaware and operating a private school in Paris, France, is fully qualified as a recipient of deductible contributions from U.S. sources.[414] The organization has no employees, activities, or assets in the United States and all expenditures are in France. These facts led the IRS to contend that the U.S. corporation is a mere "shell" and functions solely to funnel contributions to a foreign organization (namely, the school). But the court refused to go much beyond the fact that the corporation is a valid legal entity[415] and that the charitable giving rules do not require a substantial operational nexus in the United States in order to qualify as an eligible recipient of deductible gifts.[416]

[411]Rev. Rul. 66-79, 1966-1 C. B. 48.
[412]Citing Rev. Rul. 62-113, 1962-2 C. B. 10.
[413]Rev. Rul. 75-65, 1975-1 C. B. 79.
[414]*Bilingual Montessori School of Paris, Inc.* v. *Commissioner*, 75 T.C. 480 (1980).
[415]Code § 170(c)(2)(A).
[416]This holding creates a substantial exception to the Service's conduit rationale and exalts much form over substance (see, e.g., *Maryland Savings-Share Insurance Corp.* v. *United States*, 644 F.2d 16, 31 (Ct. Cl. 1981), where the Court writes of mere "different mechanics for achieving the same result"). The charitable giving rules do not differentiate between corporations but rather between organizations, and in any event a corporation for tax purposes can be different from a corporation for state law purposes. Thus, irrespective of the status of the U.S. corporation, it would not have been difficult for the Court to find the school to be a "corporation" for federal tax law purposes. The fact that the domestic entity was recognized as a Code § 501(c)(3) organization eligible for gifts deductible for estate and gift tax purposes should not preclude such a finding. Also, the Court explored the legislative history and found that the rationale expressed therein—that the charitable deduction for gifts to foreign charities is not available because there are no economic and social benefits for the U.S. government—supports its conclusions. However, there can be no such U.S. "benefits" resulting from the conduct of a school in France, whether operated by a U.S. entity or not. Also, the legislative history states that if the gift recipient "is a domestic organization the fact that some portion of its funds is used in other countries for charitable and other purposes . . . will not affect the deductibility of the gift" (H. Rep. No. 1860, 75th Cong., 3d Sess. (1938)) but this statement does not necessarily mean that the same result occurs where *all* of the funds, and assets, are so used in other countries.

Assuming, however, that the "friends" organization has been properly created and operated so as to qualify as a "charitable" entity for purposes of charitable giving and tax exemption, a determination must also be sought as to whether it is a private foundation.[417] This type of entity can qualify as a publicly supported organization if it can demonstrate sufficient support from the general public.[418] However, since grants from substantial contributors cannot be utilized in computing the public support fraction, such public charity status may not be available. This leaves the supporting organization rules.

These rules require, *inter alia*, the supporting organization to stand in one of three required relationships to the supported organization (the foreign organization). Because the charitable giving rules stress the independence of the qualified "friends" organization from the foreign charity, the weakest of the supporting relationships should be relied upon in establishing its nonprivate foundation status. This is the relationship defined in the regulations accompanying the supporting organization rules as "operated in connection with." In connection with this relationship, the "responsiveness test" can be met by causing one or more of the officers of the foreign organization to be a director or officer of the U.S. organization.[419] The "integral part test" can be met by demonstrating that the U.S. entity makes payments of substantially all of its income to the foreign entity.[420] In essence, the difficulty is to show independence between the U.S. and foreign entities to achieve tax-exempt status and to qualify for deductible contributions but to establish a sufficient relationship between them to satisfy the requirements of the supporting organization rules.

As to the charitable contribution deduction, however, the IRS has ruled that contributions to a U.S. charity that solicits contributions for a specific project of a foreign charity are deductible only under certain circumstances. Contributions made directly to a foreign organization are not deductible.[421] Organizations formed in the U.S. for the purpose of raising funds and transmitting them to a foreign charity are not eligible to attract deductible charitable contributions.[422] Conversely, where a domestic organization makes grants to foreign charities out of its general fund following review and approval of the specific grant or where the foreign organization is merely an administrative arm of the domestic organization, contributions to the domestic charity would be deductible.[423] The test is whether the domestic organization is the real recipient of the contributions, as it must be for the charitable contribution deduction to be allowed. The domestic organization must exercise care that it does not, as

---

[417]See Chapters 21 and 22.
[418]See Code §§ 509(a)(1) (§ 170(b)(1)(A)(vi)) and 509(a)(2).
[419]Reg. § 1.509(a)-4(i)(2)(ii)(b).
[420]Reg. § 1.509(a)-4(i)(3)(iii)(a).
[421]Code § 170(c)(2)(A).
[422]Rev. Rul. 63-252, *supra*, n. 409.
[423]*Ibid*.

part of its solicitation of funds, earmark the funds for foreign charities and must have full control over the donated funds and have discretion as to their use.[424]

As a general rule, a contribution by a corporation to a charitable organization is deductible only if the gift is to be used within the United States or its possessions exclusively for permissible charitable purposes.[425] However, where the recipient charitable organization is itself a corporation, this restriction is inapplicable.[426]

Because of the United States–Canada tax treaty, the general rule that contributions to a foreign charity are not deductible does not apply in the case of certain contributions to Canadian charities.[427] In order for the contribution to be deductible, the Canadian organization must be one which, if it were a U.S. organization, would be eligible for deductible charitable contributions. In addition, the deduction may not exceed the charitable deduction allowable under Canadian law, computed as though the corporation's taxable income from Canadian sources was its aggregate income.

Auxiliary Charitable Organizations

Many categories of tax-exempt organizations have found or are finding a variety of advantages to the creation of an auxiliary tax-exempt organization. The auxiliary organization functions in tandem with the sponsoring organization—although the nature of the relationship varies—to achieve common objectives.

The most common pattern is for a noncharitable organization to establish a charitable auxiliary. If properly designed, the charitable organization becomes eligible to receive deductible charitable contributions and can, in turn, make grants to the noncharitable organization. This approach also has the advantage of concentrating the fund-raising function in a separate organization with a separate governing board—a device that is sometimes used by sponsoring organizations that have charitable status themselves.

Another pattern is for a charitable organization, that is engaging in or planning to engage in an activity that may jeopardize its tax status, to spin off the disabling function into a separate organization that will qualify under another

---

[424]Rev. Rul. 75-434, *supra*, n. 58; Rev. Rul. 66-79, *supra*, n. 411. Also see Rev. Rul. 75-65, *supra*, n. 413. A related issue is the availability of the estate tax deduction for charitable transfers to foreign governments or political subdivisions thereof. See Rev. Rul. 74-523, 1974-2 C. B. 304, and the cases cited therein. In general, see Sanders, "Support and Conduct of Charitable Operations Abroad," *1st Annual Notre Dame Institute on Charitable Giving, Foundations, and Trusts* 33 (1976).

[425]Code § 170(c)(2), last sentence.

[426]This results from the fact that Code § 170(c)(2) opens with the phrase that a "corporation, trust, or community chest, fund, or foundation" may qualify as a charitable donee, while the restriction in the last sentence of Code § 170(c)(2) applies to a gift to a "trust, chest, fund, or foundation."

[427]Rev. Proc. 59-31, 1959-2 C. B. 949.

category of tax exemption. For example, a charitable organization may conclude that it is engaging in legislative activities to a substantial extent[428] and thus spin off such activities into a social welfare organization.[429] Similarly, a charitable organization may want to help advance the cause of certain political candidates, an objective that it cannot pursue itself,[430] so it may establish a business league[431] which in turn would establish a political action committee.[432]

The above-noted pattern of the noncharitable organization creating a charitable organization is most typically demonstrated by the situation where a trade association establishes an auxiliary charitable organization. The charitable organization may undertake certain activities previously conducted by the sponsoring organization (such as seminars, conferences, and publications) and receive deductible contributions which are used to advance its programs. For example, a medical society may wish to attract deductible charitable contributions to a scholarship fund for medical students, which it can do by placing the fund in a separate organization which would qualify as a charitable organization for both tax exemption and charitable giving purposes.

Other categories of tax-exempt organizations may also effectively utilize a charitable auxiliary organization, most likely the social welfare organization and the labor or agricultural organization.[433] The best example of an auxiliary charitable organization serving another "charitable" organization is the supporting foundation attached to a state university.[434]

There are certain criteria that must be adhered to so as to be certain that the appropriate relationship between a noncharitable organization and an auxiliary charitable organization is maintained. For the most part, the criteria are dependent upon whether the "charitable" organization is to be operated as a subsidiary of the business league or other category of noncharitable organization, or whether the two organizations are to operate as free-standing, independent entities. The subsidiary type of charitable organization is likely to qualify as a supporting organization, as discussed elsewhere herein,[435] while the "brother–sister" type of arrangement is the one treated in this context.

Of all of the pertinent criteria, the clearest is that the two organizations may not commingle funds. This means that both organizations must be financially self-supporting and must keep their funds in separate accounts. As discussed below, however, this does not preclude one organization from reimbursing the other for legitimate expenses incurred on its behalf.

Probably the most vexing question is the composition of the governing boards

[428]See Chapter 13.
[429]See Chapter 15.
[430]See Chapter 14.
[431]See Chapter 17.
[432]See Chapter 20.
[433]See Chapter 19.
[434]Code § 170(b)(1)(A)(iv). See Chapter 22.
[435]Code § 509(a)(3). See Chapter 22.

of the two organizations. While some brother–sister organizations do so, it is not advisable to have the directors and officers of both organizations be the same individuals. Such an arrangement may tempt the IRS to contend that, for tax status purposes, the two organizations should be treated as one, thereby endangering the charitable status of the auxiliary. As a generalization, the objective should be to minimize the extent to which the boards of the two organizations are overlapping. There can be interlocking of these directorates without jeopardizing the status of the charitable entity[436] but the more prudent practice is likely to be to keep these positions in the minority. (Again, these observations relate to the brother–sister arrangement and not to the supporting organization.[437])

In connection with the brother–sister arrangement, one organization may reimburse the other for expenses incurred in its behalf without jeopardizing the tax status of either. For example, the sponsoring organization could incur an expense for and be reimbursed by the charitable organization without endangering the latter's tax classification. This presumes the reimbursement process occurs on an "arms' length" basis, including payment from an invoice. This means that the two organizations may share office space, personnel, equipment costs, and the like,[438] and one organization would bill the other for its allocable portion of the expenses. It would be preferable to have the charitable organization be the billed entity.

Nonetheless, the more such sharing occurs, the greater is the likelihood that the IRS will raise questions. This is a somewhat cosmetic or superficial aspect of these considerations, rather than an authentic problem in law. An extensive sharing arrangement may invite inquiry but should not trigger any adverse consequences, even if examined, as long as the "arms' length" feature of the relationship is preserved.

The fact that the two organizations have common members, interests, and/or objectives will not endanger the tax status of either. Of course, this commonality forms the backdrop by which the IRS is put on notice that the two organizations are operating at least partially in tandem and thus sensitizes the IRS to the possibility that fund commingling or some other impermissible practice is taking place.

The auxiliary charitable organization may properly make grants to the sponsoring organization as long as it can be clearly demonstrated that the grants

---

[436]See *Center on Corporate Responsibility, Inc.* v. *Shultz*, 368 F.Supp. 863, 876-877 (D.D.C. 1973); Rev. Rul. 66-79, *supra*, n. 411; Rev. Rul. 63-252, *supra*, n. 409; Rev. Rul. 58-293, 1958-1 C. B. 146; Rev. Rul. 54-243, 1954-1 C. B. 92.

[437]In *Greater United Navajo Development Enterprises, Inc.* v. *Commissioner*, 74 T.C. 69 (1980), aff'd in unpublished opinion (9th Cir. Dec. 23, 1981), two corporations with the same directors, officers, and staff were regarded by both the IRS and the court as one organization.

[438]*Center on Corporate Responsibility, Inc.* v. *Shultz, supra*, n. 436, at 866, n. 2.

are for one or more qualifying ("charitable") purposes. Such grants must be targeted for specific purposes and not used by the recipient (unless it, too, is a charitable entity) to defray the cost of general operations.

Circumstances in which a charitable organization desires to establish another charitable entity are well illustrated by the growing trend whereby a tax exempt hospital creates a supporting "foundation." The prime reasons for establishing such a related support vehicle generally are the following: the foundation (1) provides for a primary focus on fund raising, rather than intermixing fund raising with the overall responsibilities of operation of the hospital, (2) enables its leadership to be persons with expertise principally in fund raising and finance, (3) can attract gifts where the hospital cannot and can effectively accommodate a full-scale planned giving program, (4) can facilitate the acquisition of an endowment fund, relatively immune from pressures to currently utilize unrestricted gifts for ongoing hospital operations, and (5) permits the hospital to not include gifts as part of its operating income, which can be of immense advantage to the hospital when calculating such income for third-party payor, labor negotiation, and like purposes.[439] Of particular concern must be the basis for seeking to acquire public charity status for the foundation, that is, whether it is to be a publicly supported organization or a supporting organization.[440]

The decision to establish and utilize an auxiliary charitable organization is not one to be made lightly, since considerable decision-making and administrative responsibilities are involved. The auxiliary must be created with attention to all of the requisite formalities: development of the governing instruments, design of a board of directors or trustees, planning of financial support, and application for recognition of tax exemption. The same may be said with respect to operation: selection of physical location, acquisition of staff, and compliance with the paperwork demands—minutes of meetings, state annual reports, federal annual information returns, and other governmental forms.

On balance, however, in many instances, the advantages associated with an auxiliary charitable organization will outweigh the disadvantages. The ability of the auxiliary to attract charitable contributions means that, for the objectives served by the two organizations, there is access to cash contributions and property gifts that otherwise would not be forthcoming. Also, the use of an auxiliary makes support of the charitable programs by private foundations much

---

[439]There is nothing in law that would prevent consolidation of the finances of a charitable organization and its supporting foundation, such as consolidation of the receipts of a hospital and its foundation for Medicare reimbursement purposes or of a state university and its foundation (see text accompanying note 434) for purposes of determining the level of annual appropriations. Nonetheless, developing accounting principles and reporting practices for nonprofit organizations may require, in most cases, presentation of combined financial statements by an organization and a related support vehicle.

[440]See Chapter 22.

more likely, since (assuming the recipient qualifies as a public charity[441]) the administrative rigors of the expenditure responsibility requirements are thereby avoided.

As the law of tax-exempt organizations becomes more complex and more flexibility is required, the use of the auxiliary charitable organization becomes more attractive. Nonetheless, at the present, there is very little law to guide those who administer these exempt organizations and their charitable auxiliaries, and who must devise the correct operating relationship between them.

[441]See Chapter 22.

7

The Educational Organization

Code § 501(c)(3) provides that an organization may be exempt from federal income tax if it is organized and operated exclusively for an "educational" purpose.[1] The term "educational" is a broad term and many educational organizations are also charitable in nature, as the term "charitable" includes the "advancement of education."[2]

The government has—quite properly—adopted a definition of the term "educational" as encompassing far more than formal schooling. Basically, the concept of "educational" as used for federal tax purposes is defined as relating to the "instruction or training of the individual for the purpose of improving or developing his capabilities" or the "instruction of the public on subjects useful to the individual and beneficial to the community."[3]

§ 7.1 Formal Educational Organizations

Obviously, nonprofit educational institutions, such as primary, secondary, and postsecondary schools, colleges and universities, early childhood centers,[4] and professional trade schools, are "educational" organizations.[5] These organizations all have, as required, "a regularly scheduled curriculum, a regular faculty, and a regularly enrolled body of students in attendance at the place where the educational activities are regularly carried on."[6] To be so exempt, however, the schools must, like all "charitable" organizations, meet all of the

[1]See Reg. § 1.501(c)(3)-1(d)(1)(i)(f).

[2]See Chapter 6.

[3]Reg. § 1.501(c)(3)-1(d)(3)(i). As discussed in § 5 hereof, the income tax regulations defining the term "educational" have been declared unconstitutional.

[4] *Michigan Early Childhood Center, Inc.* v. *Commissioner*, 37 T.C.M. 808 (1978); *San Francisco Infant School, Inc.* v. *Commissioner*, 69 T.C. 957 (1978); Rev. Rul. 70-533, 1970-2 C. B. 112.

[5]Reg. § 1.501(c)(3)-1(d)(3)(ii)(1).

[6]*Ibid*. See Code § 170(b)(1)(A)(ii).

tax law requirements pertaining to these entities, including a showing that they are operated for public, rather than private, interests.

Museums, zoos, planetariums, symphony orchestras, and other similar organizations are also considered institutions providing formal instruction and training and therefore are "educational."[7] In this regard, tax-exempt status has been accorded entities such as a sports museum,[8] a bird and animal sanctuary,[9] an international exposition,[10] and a bar association library.[11] The IRS has noted that an organization established to maintain and operate a museum facility, which offers, in sponsorship with a university, a degree program in museology, is an educational organization.[12]

An illustration of what the IRS regards as an institution "similar" to a museum and the like was provided in 1977 when the Service so categorized an organization formed to create and operate a replica of an early American village.[13] The organization, which makes the village open to the public, was determined by the IRS to be "engaging in activities similar to those of a museum" and thus to be "educational" in nature. In so finding, the Service relied upon a determination made in 1975 in which an organization was found to be "educational" because it promotes an appreciation of history through the acquisition, restoration and preservation of homes, churches, and public buildings having special historical or architectural significance and opens the structures for viewing by the general public.[14]

§ 7.2   Instruction of Individuals

As noted, the term "educational" for federal tax law purposes relates to the instruction or training of the individual for the purpose of improving or developing his or her capabilities.

Coming within this category of educational organizations are those entities the primary function of which is to provide instruction or training for a general purpose or on a particular subject, although they may not have a regular curriculum, faculty or student body. Thus an organization providing educational and vocational training and guidance to nonskilled persons to improve employment opportunity is an "educational" organization,[15] as is an organization conducting an industrywide apprentice training program,[16] operating com-

---

[7]Reg. § 1.501(c)(3)-1(d)(3)(ii)(4).
[8]Rev. Rul. 68-372, 1968-2 C. B. 205.
[9]Rev. Rul. 67-292, 1967-2 C. B. 184.
[10]Rev. Rul. 71-545, 1971-2 C. B. 235.
[11]Rev. Rul. 75-196, 1975-1 C. B. 155.
[12]Rev. Rul. 76-167, 1976-1 C. B. 329.
[13]Rev. Rul. 77-367, 1977-2 C. B. 193.
[14]Rev. Rul. 75-470, 1975-2 C. B. 207.
[15]Rev. Rul. 73-128, 1973-1 C. B. 222.
[16]Rev. Rul. 67-72, 1967-1 C. B. 125. Cf. Rev. Rul. 59-6, 1959-1 C. B. 121.

munity correctional centers for the rehabilitation of prisoners,[17] providing a facility and program for the rehabilitation of individuals recently released from a mental institution,[18] providing apprentice training in a skilled trade to American Indians,[19] offering instruction in basic academic subjects, speech, perceptual motor coordination, and psychological adjustment for children and adolescents with learning disabilities,[20] and providing room, board, therapy, and counseling for persons discharged from alcoholic treatment centers.[21] Similarly, the IRS ruled exempt as educational in nature an organization that maintains a government internship program for college students,[22] that provides assistance to law students to obtain experience with public interest law firms and legal aid societies,[23] and that promotes student and cultural exchanges.[24] As for instruction on a particular subject, organizations providing instruction in securities management,[25] dancing,[26] sailboat racing,[27] drag car racing,[28] and the promotion of sportsmanship[29] have been ruled tax-exempt as "educational" entities. However, the training of animals is not regarded as an educational activity, even where the animals' owners also receive some instruction.[30]

Another category of educational organizations that relate to the instruction or training of individuals are those that conduct discussion groups, panels, forums, lectures, and the like.[31] For example, the operation of a "coffee house" by a number of churches, where church leaders, educators, businesspersons, and young people discuss a variety of topics, is an "educational" endeavor.[32] Comparable organizations include those which instruct individuals to improve their business or professional capabilities, such as the conduct of seminars and training programs on the subject of managing credit unions (for individuals in developing nations),[33] the practice of medicine (for physicians),[34] and banking

---

[17] See Rev. Rul. 70-583, 1970-2 C. B. 114; Rev. Rul. 67-150, 1967-1 C. B. 133.

[18] Rev. Rul. 72-16, 1972-1 C. B. 143.

[19] Rev. Rul. 77-272, 1977-2 C. B. 191.

[20] Rev. Rul. 77-68, 1977-1 C. B. 142.

[21] Rev. Rul. 75-472, 1975-2 C. B. 208.

[22] Rev. Rul. 70-584, 1970-2 C. B. 114. Also see Rev. Rul. 75-284, 1975-2 C. B. 204.

[23] Rev. Rul. 78-310, 1978-2 C. B. 173.

[24] Rev. Rul. 68-165, 1968-1 C. B. 253; Rev. Rul. 80-286, 1980-2 C. B. 179.

[25] Rev. Rul. 68-16, 1968-1 C. B. 246.

[26] Rev. Rul. 65-270, 1965-2 C. B. 160.

[27] Rev. Rul. 64-275, 1964-2 C. B. 142.

[28] *Lions Associated Drag Strip* v. *United States*, 64-1 U.S.T.C. ¶ 9283 (S.D. Cal. 1963).

[29] Rev. Rul. 55-587, 1955-2 C. B. 261. Also IRS Private Letter Ruling 7851004.

[30] *Ann Arbor Dog Training Club, Inc.* v. *Commissioner*, 74 T.C. 207 (1980); Rev. Rul. 71-421, 1971-2 C. B. 229.

[31] Reg. § 1.501(c)(3)-1(d)(3)(ii), Example (2).

[32] Rev. Rul. 68-72, 1968-1 C. B. 250.

[33] Rev. Rul. 74-16, 1974-1 C. B. 126.

[34] Rev. Rul. 65-298, 1965-2 C. B. 163.

(for bank employees).[35] Other tax-exempt organizations in this category include an organization that conducts discussion groups and panels in order to acquaint the public with the problems of ex-convicts and parolees,[36] an organization sponsoring public workshops for training artists in concert technique,[37] and an organization that conducts clinics for the purpose of teaching a particular sport.[38] Organizations that present courses of instruction by means of correspondence or through the utilization of television or radio may qualify as "educational" in nature.[39]

However, if the functions of a "discussion group" are to a significant extent fraternal or social and where the speeches and discussions are deemed subjective and more akin to the exchanges of personal opinions and experiences in the informal atmosphere of a social group or club, the organization will not qualify as organized and operated exclusively for educational purposes.[40] Likewise, an organization that employs no faculty and provides no classes, lectures, or instructional material may be regarded as a social or recreational group rather than an educational organization, as was the case with a flying club that merely provides its members with an opportunity for unsupervised flight time.[41]

A third category of educational organizations that instruct individuals are those which primarily engage in study and research. As an illustration, educational status has been accorded an organization that undertook a program of study, research and assembly of materials relating to court reform in a particular state.[42] Other organizations ruled exempt under this category of "educational" include an organization that researches and studies Civil War battles[43] and one that conducts and publishes research in the area of career planning and vocational counseling.[44] An organization that conducts travel study tours for the purpose of educating individuals about the culture of the U.S. and other countries has been ruled tax-exempt,[45] although the commercial travel industry challenged the policy of the IRS in granting tax-exempt status to organizations substantially providing commercial travel services, claiming a competitive dis-

[35]Rev. Rul. 68-504, 1968-2 C. B. 211. See IRS Private Letter Ruling 7852007 (issue no. 2).

[36]Rev. Rul. 67-150, *supra*, n. 17.

[37]Rev. Rul. 67-392, 1967-2 C. B. 191.

[38]Rev. Rul. 65-2, 1965-1 C. B. 227, as amplified by Rev. Rul. 77-365, 1977-2 C. B. 192. Also see *Hutchinson Baseball Enterprises, Inc.* v. *Commissioner*, 73 T.C. 144 (1979).

[39]Reg. § 1.501(c)(3)-1(d)(3)(ii)(3).

[40]Rev. Rul. 73-439, 1973-2 C. B. 176. Also see Rev. Rul. 77-366, 1977-2 C. B. 192.

[41]*Syrang Aero Club, Inc.* v. *Commissioner*, 73 T.C. 717 (1980); *North American Sequential Sweepstakes* v. *Commissioner*, 77 T.C. 1087 (1981).

[42]Rev. Rul. 64-195, 1964-2 C. B. 138.

[43]Rev. Rul. 67-148, 1967-1 C. B. 132.

[44]Rev. Rul. 68-71, 1968-1 C. B. 249.

[45]Rev. Rul. 70-534, 1970-2 C. B. 113; Rev. Rul. 69-400, 1969-2 C. B. 114.

advantage.[46] Of course, where an exempt educational program involving travel (such as winter-time ocean cruises) is intermixed with substantial social and recreational activities, tax-exempt status will not be forthcoming.[47] Thus, an organization, the sole purpose and activity of which is to arrange group tours for students and faculty members of a university, was ruled to not be educational,[48] while an organization that arranges for and participates in the temporary exchange of children between families of a foreign country and the United States was found tax-exempt because it is fostering the cultural and educational development of children.[49]

Although it appears obvious, the IRS was constrained to rule that the definition of the term "educational" relating to the instruction of individuals (and, presumably, also as respects instruction of the public) "contains no limitation with regard to age in defining that term."[50] The issue arose when the Service, in ruling that an organization organized and operated for the purpose of teaching a particular sport qualified as an educational entity,[51] observed in the facts that the program of instruction is offered only to children. This earlier ruling was amplified to make it clear that the concept of "educational" extends to the instruction of individuals "of all ages."

§ 7.3 Instruction of the Public

As noted, the income tax regulations state that the term "educational" as used for federal tax purposes relates, *inter alia*, to the "instruction of the public on subjects useful to the individual and beneficial to the community." In many instances, an organization is considered "educational," both because it is regarded as instructing the public as well as the individual. Nonetheless, even though it is difficult (and probably unnecessary) to formulate rigid distinctions between the two types of educational purposes, three categories of the former purpose emerge.

One category of this type of educational organization is the one that provides certain "personal services" deemed beneficial to the general public. The IRS, under this rationale, has ruled exempt an organization that provides marriage counseling services,[52] that disseminates information concerning hallucinatory drugs,[53] that conducts personal money management instruction,[54] that educates

---

[46]*American Society of Travel Agents, Inc.* v. *Simon*, 36 A.F.T.R. 2d 75-5142 (D.D.C. May 23, 1975) (complaint dismissed), aff'd 566 F.2d 145 (D.C. Cir. 1977) (finding of no standing to sue), cert. den. 435 U.S. 947 (1978). See discussion in Chapter 38, § 7.

[47]Rev. Rul. 77-366, *supra,* n. 40.

[48]Rev. Rul. 67-327, 1967-2 C. B. 187.

[49]Rev. Rul. 80-286, *supra,* n. 24.

[50]Rev. Rul. 77-365, *supra,* n. 38.

[51]Rev. Rul. 65-2, *supra,* n. 38.

[52]Rev. Rul. 70-640, 1970-2 C. B. 117.

[53]Rev. Rul. 70-590, 1970-2 C. B. 116.

[54]Rev. Rul. 69-441, 1969-2 C. B. 115.

expectant mothers and the public in a method of painless childbirth,[55] that counsels women on methods of resolving unwanted pregnancies,[56] that counsels widows to assist them in legal, financial, and emotional problems caused by the death of their husbands,[57] and that counsels men concerning methods of voluntary sterilization.[58] Similarly, an organization that functions primarily as a crop seed certification entity was held to be educational because of its adult education classes, seminars, newsletter, and lending library.[59]

Another category of educational organizations are those which endeavor to instruct the public in the field of civic betterments. In this regard, this type of organization frequently also qualifies under one or more varieties of the concept of "charitable" or "social welfare." Thus an organization that disseminates information, in the nature of results of its investigations, in an effort to lessen racial and religious prejudice in the fields of housing and public accommodations has been ruled tax-exempt.[60] Other organizations in this category include ones that distribute information about the results of a model demonstration housing program for low-income families conducted by it,[61] disseminate information on the need for international cooperation,[62] educate the public as to the means of correcting conditions such as community tension and juvenile delinquency,[63] enlighten the public in a particular city as to the advantages of street planning,[64] develop and distribute a community land-use plan,[65] and educate the public regarding environmental deterioration due to solid waste pollution,[66] radio and television programming,[67] and accuracy of news coverage by newspapers.[68]

The third category of educational organizations that exists to instruct the public are those that conduct study and research. The variety of efforts encompassed by these organizations is nearly limitless. As illustrations, these organizations include those which conduct analyses, studies, and research into the problems of a particular region (pollution, transportation, water resources, waste disposal) and publish the results,[69] instruct the public on agricultural

[55]Rev. Rul. 66-255, 1966-2 C. B. 210.
[56]Rev. Rul. 73-569, 1973-2 C. B. 178. Also see Rev. Rul. 76-205, 1976-1 C. B. 178.
[57]Rev. Rul. 78-99, 1978-1 C. B. 152.
[58]Rev. Rul. 74-595, 1974-2 C. B. 164.
[59]*Indiana Crop Improvement Association, Inc.* v. *Commissioner*, 76 T.C. 394 (1981).
[60]Rev. Rul. 68-438, 1968-2 C. B. 209. Also see Rev. Rul. 75-285, 1975-2 C. B. 203; Rev. Rul. 68-70, 1968-1 C. B. 248; Rev. Rul. 67-250, 1967-2 C. B. 182.
[61]See Rev. Rul. 68-17, 1968-1 C. B. 247; Rev. Rul. 67-138, 1967-1 C. B. 129.
[62]Rev. Rul. 67-342, 1967-2 C. B. 187.
[63]Rev. Rul. 68-15, 1968-1 C. B. 244.
[64]Rev. Rul. 68-14, 1968-1 C. B. 243.
[65]Rev. Rul. 67-391, 1967-2 C. B. 190.
[66]Rev. Rul. 72-560, 1972-2 C. B. 248. Also IRS Private Letter Ruling 7823052.
[67]Rev. Rul. 64-192, 1964-2 C. B. 136.
[68]Rev. Rul. 74-615, 1974-2 C. B. 165.
[69]Rev. Rul. 70-79, 1970-1 C. B. 127.

matters by conducting fairs and exhibitions,[70] and publish a journal to disseminate information about specific types of physical and mental disorders.[71]

On this final point, the publication of printed material can be an educational activity in a variety of other contexts. For example, an organization that surveyed scientific and medical literature and prepared, published, and distributed abstracts thereof was deemed tax-exempt.[72] Similarly, an organization was ruled exempt for assisting the National Park Service by preparing, publishing, and distributing literature concerning a particular park.[73] Likewise, a nonprofit corporation that compiled and published a manual on the standard library cataloguing system was ruled to be engaged in educational activities.[74] Of course, where a publication effort is operated by an entity akin to normal commercial practices, exemption as an educational organization will be denied (see below).[75] Thus, the IRS held that an organization, the only activities of which are the preparation and publication of a newspaper of local, national, and international news articles with an ethnic emphasis, soliciting advertising and selling subscriptions to the newspaper in a manner indistinguishable from ordinary commercial publishing practices, was not operated exclusively for educational purposes.[76]

In general, an organization engaged in publishing can qualify as an educational entity where (1) the content of the publication is educational, (2) the preparation of the material follows methods generally accepted as educational in character, (3) the distribution of the materials is necessary or valuable in achieving the organization's exempt purposes, and (4) the manner in which the distribution is accomplished is distinguishable from ordinary commercial publishing practices.[77] The IRS relied on these criteria in concluding that the recording and sale of musical compositions that are not generally produced by the commercial recording industry is educational because it is a means for presenting new works of unrecognized composers and the neglected works of more recognized composers.[78]

The educational activities of organizations in this third category may be carried on through a club, such as a gem and mineral club[79] or a garden club,[80]

---

[70]Rev. Rul. 67-216, 1967-2 C. B. 180.
[71]Rev. Rul. 67-4, 1967-1 C. B. 121.
[72]Rev. Rul. 66-147, 1966-1 C. B. 137.
[73]Rev. Rul. 68-307, 1968-1 C. B. 258.
[74]*Forest Press, Inc.* v. *Commissioner*, 22 T. C. 265 (1954).
[75]Rev. Rul. 60-351, 1960-2 C. B. 169.
[76]Rev. Rul. 77-4, 1977-1 C. B. 141. Also *Christian Manner International, Inc.* v. *Commissioner*, 71 T.C. 661 (1979).
[77]Rev. Rul. 67-4, *supra*, n. 71. See, e.g., IRS Private Letter Rulings 8031045 and 7902019 (issue nos. 8 and 9).
[78]Rev. Rul. 79-369, 1979-2 C. B. 226.
[79]Rev. Rul. 67-139, 1967-1 C. B. 129.
[80]Rev. Rul. 66-179, 1966-1 C. B. 139.

or by means of public lectures and debates.[81] These organizations may function as broad-based membership organizations,[82] as organizations formed to promote a specific cause,[83] or as a transitory organization, such as one to collect and collate campaign materials of a particular candidate for ultimate donation to a university or public library.[84]

Perhaps the most notable ruling from the IRS concerning this last category of educational organizations is one issued in 1971, where a society of heating and air conditioning engineers and others having a professional interest in this field was held to be "educational" in nature.[85] Its educational purposes were deemed to be the operation of a library, dissemination of the results of its scientific research, and the making available of model codes of minimum standards for heating, ventilating, and air conditioning. The IRS went to considerable lengths to distinguish this type of professional society from a business league.[86]

There are innumerable organizations that are charitable, educational, or scientific societies and that hold rulings from the IRS that they are "charitable" organizations. Frequently, their membership base is comprised of individuals (rather than other organizations) and these persons share common professional and/or disciplinary interests. In most instances, these organizations satisfy the criteria for classification as charitable, educational, or like entities but, because they provide services to individual members, the increasing tendency of the IRS is to categorize or reclassify them as business leagues, on the ground that they serve to enhance the professional development of the members rather than advance a charitable purpose.[87] This tendency was manifested early in 1978 when the Service, following field audits, advised some scientific associations that they are being reclassified as business leagues.

An otherwise tax-exempt organization that produces and distributes free, or for small, cost-defraying fees, educational, cultural, and public interest programs for public viewing via public-educational channels of commercial cable television companies is operated for educational purposes and thus qualifies for tax exemption because an organization may achieve its educational purposes through the production of television programs where it does so in a noncommercial manner.[88] Similarly, a nonprofit organization established to operate a noncommercial educational broadcasting station presenting educational, cultural, and public interest programs qualifies as an exempt educational entity,[89]

[81]Rev. Rul. 66-256, 1966-2 C. B. 210.
[82]Rev. Rul. 68-164, 1968-1 C. B. 252.
[83]Rev. Rul. 72-228, 1972-1 C. B. 148.
[84]Rev. Rul. 70-321, 1970-1 C. B. 129.
[85]Rev. Rul. 71-506, 1971-2 C. B. 233.
[86]Cf. Rev. Rul. 70-641, 1970-2 C. B. 119.
[87]See Chapter 17 § 2.
[88]Rev. Rul. 76-4, 1976-1 C. B. 145.
[89]Rev. Rul. 66-220, 1966-2 C. B. 209.

as does an organization which produces educational films concerning a particular subject and which disseminates its educational material to the public by means of commercial television, where the films are presented in a noncommercial manner.[90]

With these three rulings as precedent, the IRS considered the case of an organization which makes facilities and equipment available to the general public for the production of noncommercial educational or cultural television programs intended for communication to the public via the public and educational access channels of a commercial cable television company. The programs involved do not support or oppose specific legislation and, where a particular viewpoint is advocated, the organization ensures that the program will present a full and fair exposition of the pertinent facts (see below). The organization is informally affiliated with, but does not control and is not controlled by, the commercial cable television company. The IRS ruled that, "[b]y providing members of the general public with the opportunity to produce television programs of an educational or a cultural nature for viewing on the public access channels of a commercial cable television company," the organization is operating exclusively for educational purposes.[91]

In this ruling, the IRS characterized the prior three rulings as "clearly indicat[ing] that an organization may achieve its educational purposes through the production of television programs, regardless of whether the programs are to be broadcast over the airwaves or over a cable system, so long as the programs are presented in a noncommercial manner." The Service added: "The absence of commercial advertising is a key factor in determining the noncommercial nature of the programming activity."[92] However, where the organization engages in educational programming via television to a substantial extent, it can be accorded designation as an educational entity, even though the organization owns and operates the station under a commercial broadcasting license.[93]

§ 7.4 "Educational" Activity or Trade or Business

The IRS frequently asserts, and the courts less frequently agree, that a particular activity is not "educational" but is, rather, a trade or business. Admittedly, the line is often difficult to draw. What may be an exempt educational activity in one context may be a trade or business in another. Certainly, for example, in the general world of commerce, operation of a restaurant, bookstore, broadcasting station, portfolio management service, publishing company, and the like is a trade or business. But such an operation may qualify as an

[90]Rev. Rul. 67-342, *supra*, n. 62.
[91]Rev. Rul. 76-443, 1976-2 C. B. 149.
[92]With regard to programs prepared for cable television, Federal Communications Commission regulations prohibit cable operators from commercially advertising on their educational or "public access" channels.
[93]Rev. Rul. 78-385, 1978-2 C. B. 174.

exempt educational organization, as, for example, has a university restaurant,[94] a university store,[95] a broadcasting station,[96] an endowment fund management service,[97] a retail sales enterprise,[98] a money lending operation,[99] and an organization publishing a law school journal.[100]

Therefore, it is difficult to formulate guidelines to determine when a given purpose is "educational" or a business. Of course, an exempt purpose must be one which benefits the public rather than any private individual or individuals and the organization must not be operated for the benefit of private shareholders or individuals.[101] But even these rules, aside from the essential questions as to what constitutes an "educational" activity, require some subjective judgments.

The task of making these judgments befell the Court of Claims, in a case involving an organization created to disseminate knowledge of economics with a view to advancing the welfare of the American people. The court concluded that the primary purpose of the organization was not educational but was a business or commercial one.[102] The organization published two periodicals containing analyses of securities and industries and of general economic conditions; no forecasting of stock market trends was made, although the publications did contain recommendations as to the purchase and sale of securities. These publications were sold at subscription at a cost above production expenses, as was a separate service providing advice for sales and purchases of securities in a particular portfolio; the organization also published special studies prepared by its research staff and maintained fellowship and scholarship programs.

In this case, the Court of Claims went through an instructive process of reasoning. First, it noted that "education" is an "extremely broad concept."[103] Second, recognizing that the tax exemption provision is to be liberally construed, the court "first assume[d] *arguendo* an educational purpose without giving definitive meaning to that concept."[104] Third, the court then "ascertain[ed] whether or not the taxpayer has an additional commercial purpose."[105] Fourth, upon finding a commercial purpose, the court had to decide "whether

---

[94]Rev. Rul. 67-217, 1967-2 C. B. 181.

[95]Rev. Rul. 68-538, 1968-2 C. B. 116; Rev. Rul. 58-194, 1958-1 C. B. 240; *Squire v. Students Book Corp.*, 191 F.2d 1018 (9th Cir. 1951).

[96]Rev. Rul. 66-220, *supra*, n. 89.

[97]Rev. Rul. 71-529, 1971-2 C. B. 234.

[98]Rev. Rul. 68-167, 1968-1 C. B. 255.

[99]Rev. Rul. 63-220, 1963-2 C. B. 208; Rev. Rul. 61-87, 1961-1 C. B. 191. Cf. Rev. Rul. 69-177, 1969-1 C. B. 150.

[100]Rev. Rul. 63-234, 1963-2 C. B. 210. Cf. Rev. Rul. 66-104, 1966-1 C. B. 135; Rev. Rul. 60-351, *supra*, n. 75.

[101]Reg. §§ 1.501(c)(3)-1(c)(ii), 1.501(c)(3)-1(c)(2).

[102]*American Institute for Economic Research* v. *United States*, 302 F.2d 934 (Ct. Cl. 1962).

[103]*Ibid*. at 937.

[104]*Ibid*. at 938. See *Griess* v. *United States*, 146 F.Supp. 505 (N.D. Ill. 1956).

[105]*Ibid*. 302 F.2d at 938.

the commercial purpose is primary or incidental to the exempt purpose."[106] The court found the commercial purpose to be primary and not incidental to any tax-exempt purpose, and thus held the organization not to be exempt as an educational organization.

The holding of the Court of Claims in this case is that the required element of "exclusivity" was absent and that the exemption was thus unavailable, citing the Supreme Court that "the presence of a single [nonexempt] . . . purpose, if substantial in nature, will destroy the exemption regardless of the number or importance of truly [exempt] . . . purposes."[107] The court, in concluding that the publications of the organization merely provide investment advice to subscribers for a fee, noted that the existence of profits, while not conclusive, is some evidence that the business purpose is primary[108] and that the services of the organization are those "commonly associated with a commercial enterprise."[109] Of course, the argument of the organization that any profits gained from the sale of its publications are used for exempt purposes was unavailing.[110]

Subsequently, the IRS determined that an association of investment clubs, formed for the mutual exchange of investment information among its members and prospective investors to enable them to make sound investments, is not an "educational" organization, inasmuch as the association is serving private economic interests.[111]

The same result occurred with respect to a nonprofit organization that clearly engaged in educational activities, namely, the sponsorship of "est" programs involving training, seminars, lectures, and the like in areas of intrapersonal awareness and communication.[112] However, the educational activities were conducted pursuant to licensing arrangements with for-profit corporations which amounted to substantial control over the functioning of the nonprofit organization. In rejecting tax-exempt status for the nonprofit organization, the court held that it "is part of a franchise system which is operated for private benefit and that its affiliation with this system taints it with a substantial commercial purpose."[113] Thus, the organization's entanglements with for-profit corporations were such that commercial ends were imbued to it notwithstanding the nature of its activities when viewed alone.

Likewise, an organization, originally exempted as an (in part) educational

---

[106]*Ibid.* This line of reasoning was followed in, for example, *Pulpit Resource* v. *Commissioner,* 70 T.C. 594 (1978).

[107]*Ibid.* at 937. The quote is from *Better Business Bureau* v. *United States,* 326 U.S. 279, 283 (1945). See Chapter 11.

[108]See *Scripture Press Foundation* v. *United States,* 285 F.2d 800 (Ct. Cl. 1961), cert. den. 368 U.S. 985 (1962).

[109]*American Institute for Economic Research* v. *United States, supra,* n. 102 at 938.

[110]See Code § 502; Chapter 39.

[111]Rev. Rul. 76-366, 1976-2 C. B. 144.

[112]*est of Hawaii* v. *Commissioner,* 71 T.C. 1067 (1979).

[113]*Ibid.* at 1080.

(missionary) entity, had its exemption revoked as it evolved into a publishing entity.[114] Both the IRS and the court concluded that the publishing activities had taken on a "commercial hue" and the organization had "become a highly efficient business venture."[115] In reaching this conclusion, the court noted that the organization (1) follows publishing and sales practices followed by comparable nonexempt commercial publishers, (2) has shown increasing profits in recent years,[116] (3) is experiencing a growth in accumulated surplus, and (4) has been paying substantially increased salaries to its top employees.[117]

This line of law will likely prove troublesome for many tax-exempt organizations. For many years, nonprofit organizations (particularly charitable organizations) have been criticized for not operating more efficiently and prudently (that is, for not functioning "like a business"). Many organizations that elected to operate in a more "businesslike" fashion realized some changes, such as a surplus of receipts over expenses, creation of reserves for operations, and acquisition of capital, including equipment and perhaps real estate. Some organizations acquired employees for the first time and others added professional managers and advisors to their roster of employees. The result has generally been more cost-effective management and prudent use of funds and property by nonprofit groups. Another result has been that the IRS and the courts, seeing nonprofit organizations paying higher salaries (required to attract competent assistance) and achieving net receipts, reserves, real estate holdings, and the like, now contend and hold that these organizations should be denied tax-exempt status, or have it revoked, because the organization is "competing" with for-profit organizations and is operating in a "commercial" manner. At some point, the law must accommodate the reality that tax-exempt organizations are required to function in contemporary economic society just as other organizations must, and this means professional management, compensated staff, assets, and a meaningful flow of revenue. For the most part, the concept of a charity operated solely by volunteers, expending every dollar every year for charitable purposes, and struggling through annual deficits is a quaint notion that, to the extent it was ever suitable, is now an anachronism.

The IRS, as noted, frequently concludes that an asserted exempt purpose is instead a trade or business. For example, the Service considered the status of an organization that operates a retail grocery store to sell food to residents in a poverty area at substantially lower-than-usual prices, that maintains a free delivery service for the needy, and that allocates about four percent of its earnings for use in a training program for the hard-core unemployed. The IRS held that the operation of the grocery store as an end in itself is a substantial nonexempt purpose, since it was conducted on a scale larger than reasonably

---

[114]*The Incorporated Trustees of the Gospel Worker Society v. United States*, 510 F.Supp. 374 (D.D.C. 1981).

[115]*Ibid.* at 381.

[116]See Chapter 11 § 3.

[117]See Chapter 12 § 3.

necessary for the training program (a recognized exempt activity) and since the operation may not be characterized as an investment or business undertaking for the production of income for use in carrying on qualified charitable purposes, and denied the exemption.[118] Similarly, the IRS ruled nonexempt an organization, wholly owned by an exempt college, that manufactures and sells wood products primarily to employ students of the college to enable them to continue their education, on the ground that the enterprise itself was not an instructional or training activity.[119] Conversely, the Service has recognized that an exempt organization may engage in a commercial activity without endangering its tax status where the business is not an end in itself but is a means by which charitable purposes are accomplished and where the endeavor is not conducted on a scale larger than is reasonably necessary to accomplish the organization's tax-exempt purpose.[120] Likewise, an organization that provides training of procurement officials for countries receiving United States aid was found to be educational, despite an IRS contention that procurement activity is not inherently exempt, since the procurement activity furthered the organization's educational and training program.[121]

Although the matter generates more attention than is warranted, often the outcome of a case involving an organization's tax-exempt status, where the IRS is claiming that the organization is operated for a substantial commercial purpose, is dependent upon the organization's charges for services or products in relation to its costs. Where the fees are set at a level less than costs, the courts and sometimes the IRS will be spurred on to the conclusion that the organization is not operated in an ordinary commercial manner.[122] Other considerations govern where a nonprofit organization is actually experiencing net receipts.[123]

§ 7.5 "Education" vs. "Propaganda"

Inherent in the concept of "educational" is the requirement that an organization is not educational in nature where it zealously propagates particular ideas or doctrines without presentation of the ideas or doctrines in any reasonably objective or balanced manner. The requirement is reflected in the income tax regulations that define the term "educational," wherein it is stated that:

> An organization may be educational even though it advocates a particular position or viewpoint so long as it presents a sufficiently full and fair exposition of the pertinent facts as to permit an individual or the public to form an independent

[118]Rev. Rul. 73-127, 1973-1 C. B. 221.
[119]Rev. Rul. 69-177, *supra*, n. 99.
[120]Rev. Rul. 73-128, *supra*, n. 15.
[121]*Afro-American Purchasing Center, Inc.* v. *Commissioner*, 37 T.C.M. 184 (1978).
[122]See *Peoples Translation Service/Newsfront International* v. *Commissioner*, 72 T.C. 42 (1979).
[123]See Chapter 11 § 3.

opinion or conclusion. On the other hand, an organization is not educational if its principal function is the mere presentation of unsupported opinion.[124]

This requirement is designed to exclude from the concept of "educational" the technique of the dissemination of "propaganda," a term which is to be considered in the context of the rules governing legislative activities by charitable organizations.[125] For present purposes, it can be said that the term "educational" does not extend to "public address with selfish or ulterior purpose and characterized by the coloring or distortion of facts."[126]

An organization may avoid the charge that its principal function is the mere presentation of unsupported opinion either by presenting a sufficiently full and fair exposition of the pertinent facts in the materials it prepares and disseminates or by circulating copies of materials that contain such an exposition.[127]

These regulations were applied by the IRS in a case involving an organization that endeavors to educate the public concerning the obligations of the broadcast media to serve the public interest. Periodically, the organization prepares evaluations of the performance of local broadcasters and makes the evaluations available to the general public and governmental agencies. The IRS ruled that these evaluations are "objective" (members of the organization with a personal, professional, or business interest in a particular evaluation do not participate in the consideration) and that the organization qualifies as an educational entity.[128]

Also, an "educational" organization, for federal tax purposes, may not so carry on its work as to become an "action" organization.[129] Thus the income tax regulations provide as follows:

> The fact that an organization, in carrying out its primary purpose, advocates social or civic changes or presents opinion on controversial issues with the intention of molding public opinion or creating public sentiment to an acceptance of its views does not preclude such organization from qualifying under section 501(c)(3) so long as it is not an "action" organization of any one of the types described in paragraph (c)(3) of this section.[130]

The foregoing points are illustrated by a cautious ruling by the IRS holding that an organization operated to educate the public about homosexuality in order to foster an understanding and tolerance of homosexuals and their problems qualifies as an educational entity.[131] The Service was careful to note that

[124]Reg. § 1.501(c)(3)-1(d)(3)(i).

[125]See Chapter 13.

[126]*Seasongood* v. *Commissioner*, 227 F.2d 907, 911 (6th Cir. 1955).

[127]See *National Association for the Legal Support of Alternative Schools* v. *Commissioner*, 71 T.C. 118 (1978).

[128]Rev. Rul. 79-26, 1979-1 C. B. 196.

[129]See Chapters 5, 13, and 14.

[130]Reg. § 1.501(c)(3)-1(d)(2).

[131]Rev. Rul. 78-305, 1978-2 C. B. 172.

the information disseminated by the organization was "factual" and "independently compiled," and that the materials distributed "contain a full documentation of the facts relied upon to support conclusions contained therein." Further, the Service observed that the organization "does not advocate or seek to convince individuals that they should or should not be homosexuals."

By contrast, an organization, the principal activity of which was publication of a feminist monthly newspaper, was found by a federal district court to not qualify as an educational entity because it fails to meet the "full and fair exposition" standard. The newspaper contains material designed to advance the cause of the women's movement; the organization refuses to publish items it considers damaging to that cause. The court, characterizing the organization as an "advocate" that has eschewed a policy of offering any balancing facts, said that its holding "is not to say that a publication may not advocate a particular point of view and still be educational, or that it must necessarily present views inimical to its philosophy, only that in doing so it must be sufficiently dispassionate as to provide its readers with the factual basis from which they may draw independent conclusions."[132] The court rejected the assertion that the standard is a *per se* violation of the First Amendment,[133] although it did observe that the regulation does not allow the IRS to censor views with which it does not agree.

On appeal, in a startling upset of the tax regulations concerning educational organizations, the U.S. Court of Appeals for the District of Columbia concluded that the "full and fair exposition" requirement is so vague as to violate the First Amendment. The appellate court conceded that the terms in the tax-exempt organizations field, such as "religious," "charitable," and "educational," readily "lend themselves to subjective definition at odds with the constitutional limitations."[134] However, the court said that the "full and fair exposition test" lacks the "requisite clarity, both in explaining which applicant organizations are subject to the standard and in articulating its substantive requirements."

The regulations state that only an organization that "advocates a particular position or viewpoint" must pass the test. The rules looked to by the IRS classify such an organization as one that is "controversial."[135] That, held the court, is too vague to pass First Amendment muster, because the IRS lacks any "objective standard by which to judge which applicant organizations are advocacy groups," in that the determination is made solely on the basis of one's subjective evaluation of what is "controversial."

Also, the court found wanting the requirements of the "full and fair exposition" standard. The court posed these questions: (1) what is a "full and fair"

---

[132]*Big Mama Rag, Inc.* v. *United States*, 79-1 U.S.T.C. ¶ 9362 (D.D.C. 1979).

[133]In so doing the court relied largely upon *Cammarano* v. *United States*, 358 U.S. 498 (1959), and *Hannegan* v. *Esquire*, 327 U.S. 146 (1946).

[134]*Big Mama Rag, Inc.* v. *United States*, 631 F.2d 1030 (D.C. Cir. 1980).

[135]E.g., Exempt Organizations Handbook § 345 (12); Rev. Rul. 78-305, *supra*, n. 131.

exposition, (2) can an exposition be "fair" but not "full," (3) what is a "pertinent" fact, (4) when is the exposition "sufficient" to permit persons to form an independent opinion, and (5) who makes these determinations? Noting the "futility of attempting to draw lines between fact and unsupported opinion," the appeals court observed that the district court did not actually apply the test but instead found the organization too "doctrinaire." This approach was severely criticized, with the higher court writing that it "can conceive of no value-free measurement of the extent to which material is doctrinaire, and the district court's reliance on that evaluative concept corroborates for us the impossibility of principled and objective application of the fact/opinion distinction."

Summarizing its findings (in words with implications reaching far beyond the specific case), the court said: "Applications for tax exemption must be evaluated, however, on the basis of criteria capable of neutral application. The standards may not be so imprecise that they afford latitude to individual IRS officials to pass judgment on the content and quality of an applicant's views and goals and therefore to discriminate against those engaged in protected First Amendment activities."[136]

On the basis of this appellate court decision, the U.S. District Court for the District of Columbia vacated a determination by the IRS and remanded the matter to the Service for reconsideration. The organization involved, which applied for recognition of tax exemption as a charitable and/or educational entity, publishes a monthly newsletter and a monthly membership bulletin, holds lecture and film meetings, and distributes books and other publications. The IRS took the position that the organization "spread[s] . . . racial propaganda which is often inflammatory and unsupported opinion under the guise of being educational," presents articles that are "exceptionally controversial," and advances a "partisan viewpoint of the issues." Consequently, the case was sent back to the Service for further proceedings, including application of the concept of "educational" in the absence of valid regulations.[137]

[136]In general, see Comment, "Tax Exemptions for Educational Institutions: Discretion and Discrimination," 128 *U. Pa. L. Rev.* 849 (1980).

[137]*National Alliance* v. *United States*, 81-1 U.S.T.C. ¶ 9464 (D.D.C. 1981).

8

The Religious Organization

Code § 501(c)(3) provides that an organization may be exempt from federal income tax under Code § 501(a) if it is organized and operated exclusively for a "religious" purpose.[1] In recent years, the government and the courts have been quite outspoken in attempting to define, for tax purposes, what is or is not a "religious" activity or organization—despite obvious policy and constitutional law constraints. The income tax regulations do not contain any definition of the term "religious."

§ 8.1 The Constitutional Law Framework

Until recently, governmental agencies and the courts have either refused to, or been quite cautious in attempting to, define what is a "religious" activity or organization. This reticence at the federal level stems largely from First Amendment considerations, as articulated in judicial opinions in tax, labor, and other cases.

The First Amendment provides, in the so-called "religion clauses," that "Congress shall make no law respecting an establishment of religion, or prohibiting the free exercise thereof . . ." While most First Amendment cases involve either the "establishment clause" or the "free exercise clause," both of these religion clauses are directed toward the same goal: the maintenance of government neutrality with regard to affairs of religion. Thus, the Supreme Court has observed that "the First Amendment rests upon the premise that both religion and government can best work to achieve their lofty aims if each is left free from the other within its respective sphere."[2]

Free exercise clause cases generally arise out of conflict between secular

---

[1]See Reg. § 1.501(c)(3)-1(d)(1)(i)(a). In general, see Paulsen, "Preferment of Religious Institutions in Tax and Labor Legislation," 14 *Law & Contemporary Problems* 144 (1949); Zollman, *American Church Law* 328–329 (1933).

[2]*Illinois ex rel. McCollum* v. *Board of Education*, 333 U.S. 203, 212 (1948).

laws and individual religious beliefs. The free exercise clause has been characterized by the Supreme Court as follows:

> The door of the Free Exercise Clause stands tightly closed against any governmental regulation of religious beliefs as such. [citations omitted] Government may neither compel affirmation of a repugnant belief, [citation omitted] nor penalize or discriminate against individuals or groups because they hold religious views abhorrent to the authorities.. . . On the other hand, the Court has rejected the challenges under the Free Exercise Clause to governmental regulations of certain overt acts prompted by religious beliefs or principles, for "even when the action is in accord with one's religious convictions, [it] is not totally free from legislative restrictions."[3]

The Court added that "in this highly sensitive constitutional area, '[o]nly the gravest abuses, endangering paramount interest, give occasion for permissible limitation.' "[4]

The more significant free exercise cases include the clash between the secular law prohibiting polygamy and the precepts of the Morman religion,[5] military service requirements and conscientious objectors' principles,[6] state unemployment compensation law requiring Saturday work and the dictates of the Seventh Day Adventists' religion,[7] compulsory school attendance laws and the doctrines of the Amish religion,[8] and a license tax on canvassing and the missionary evangelism objectives of Jehovah's Witnesses.[9] Where there is to be government regulation, notwithstanding free exercise claims, there must be a showing by the government of "some substantial threat to public safety, place or order."[10] Thus, courts have upheld a compulsory vaccination requirement,[11] prosecution of faith healers practicing medicine without a license,[12] and a prohibition of snake handling as part of religious ceremonies.[13]

Short of such a "substantial threat," however, the government may not investigate or review matters of ecclesiastical cognizance. This principle frequently manifests itself in the realm of alleged employment discrimination in

---

[3]*Sherbert* v. *Verner*, 374 U.S. 398, 402–403 (1963).
[4]*Ibid*. at 406, quoting from *Thomas* v. *Collins*, 323 U.S. 516, 530 (1937).
[5]*Reynolds* v. *United States*, 98 U.S. 145 (1878).
[6]*Gillette* v. *United States*, 401 U.S. 437 (1971).
[7]*Sherbert* v. *Verner, supra*, n. 3.
[8]*Wisconsin* v. *Yoder*, 406 U.S. 205 (1972).
[9]*Murdock* v. *Pennsylvania*, 319 U.S. 105 (1943).
[10]*Sherbert* v. *Verner, supra*, n. 3, at 403.
[11]*Jacobson* v. *Massachusetts*, 197 U.S. 11 (1905).
[12]*People* v. *Handzik*, 102 N.E.2d 340 (Sup. Ct. Ill. 1964).
[13]*Kirk* v. *Commonwealth*, 44 S.E.2d 409 (Sup. Ct. App. Va. 1947).

violation of the Civil Rights Act of 1964.[14] Thus, there must be a compelling governmental interest in regulation before free exercise rights may be infringed.[15]

While the free exercise clause cases usually involve alleged unwarranted intrusions of government into the sphere of individuals' religious beliefs, the establishment clause cases usually involve governmental regulation of religious institutions. These cases frequently arise as attacks on the propriety of state aid (often to religious schools) or special treatment (such as tax exemption) to religious organizations.[16] This clause is designed to prohibit the government from establishing a religion, or aiding a religion, or preferring one religion over another. Thus, the Supreme Court has observed that the establishment clause is intended to avoid "sponsorship, financial support, and active involvement of the sovereign in religious activity."[17]

The Supreme Court has repeatedly held that the First Amendment is intended to avoid substantial entangling church–state relationships. In one case, where state aid to religious schools, conditioned on pervasive restrictions, was held to be excessive entanglement, the Court stated:

> . . . [a] comprehensive, discriminating, and continuing state surveillance will inevitably be required to ensure that these restrictions are obeyed and the First Amendment otherwise respected.. . . This kind of state inspection and evaluation of religious content of a religious organization is fraught with the sort of entanglement that the Constitution forbids. It is a relationship pregnant with dangers of excessive government direction of church schools and hence of churches . . . and we cannot ignore here the danger that pervasive modern governmental power will ultimately intrude on religion and thus conflict with the Religion Clauses.[18]

Thus, where there is significant government investigation and/or surveillance, particularly analysis of the sincerity or application of religious beliefs, of a religious institution, there is likely to be a violation of the establishment clause.[19]

In a posture of particular significance to the law of tax-exempt organizations, the Supreme Court has articulated the possibility of permissible government involvement with religious organizations, but in a manner that furthers neu-

---

[14]See, e.g., *McClure* v. *Salvation Army*, 460 F.2d 553 (5th Cir. 1972).

[15]In general, see Clark, "Guidelines for the Free Exercise Clause," 83 *Harv. L. Rev.* 327 (1969).

[16]See, e.g., *Committee for Public Education* v. *Nyquist*, 413 U.S. 756 (1973); *Lemon* v. *Kurtzman*, 403 U.S. 602 (1971); *Walz* v. *Tax Commission*, 397 U.S. 664 (1970); *Engle* v. *Vitale*, 370 U.S. 421 (1962); *Abington School District* v. *Schempp*, 374 U.S. 203 (1953); *Zorach* v. *Clausen*, 343 U.S. 306 (1952); *Illinois ex rel. McCollum* v. *Board of Education, supra*, n. 2; and *Everson* v. *Board of Education*, 330 U.S. 1 (1946).

[17]*Lemon* v. *Kurtzman, supra*, n. 16, at 612.

[18]*Ibid.* at 619–620.

[19]See, e.g., *Presbyterian Church* v. *Hull Church*, 393 U.S. 440 (1969); *Caulfield* v. *Hirsh*, 95 L.R.R.M. 3164 (E.D. Pa. 1977).

trality. Thus, the Court, in a case concerning an attack on tax exemption for religious properties as being violative of the establishment clause, has said that the government may become involved in matters relating to religious organizations so as "to mark boundaries to avoid excessive entanglement" and to adhere to the "policy of neutrality that derives from an accommodation of the Establishment and Free Exercise Clauses that has prevented that kind of involvement that would tip the balance toward government control of Church or governmental restraint on religious practice.. . . ."[20] Consequently, the current stance of the law as articulated by the Supreme Court is that tax exemption for religious organizations is not violative of the First Amendment since it promotes neutrality, inasmuch as the alternative of nonexemption would necessarily lead to prohibited excessive entanglements (such as valuation of property, imposition of tax liens, and foreclosures).

As regards nonprofit organizations seeking tax exemption as religious entities, it is difficult to mark the boundary between proper government regulation and unconstitutional entanglement. Not infrequently, for example, a religious organization will claim a violation of its constitutional rights when the IRS probes too extensively in seeking information about it in the context of evaluation of an application for recognition of exemption. However, the courts appear to agree that the IRS is obligated, when processing an exemption application, to make inquiries and gather information to determine whether the organization's purposes and activities are in conformance with the statutory requirements, and that such an investigation is not precluded by the First Amendment's guarantee of freedom of religion.[21]

It is against this constitutional law backdrop that the regulatory agencies' and courts' difficulties in defining and regulating religious entities may be viewed.

§ 8.2   Concept of "Religious" in General

Although the federal income tax law provides tax exemption for "religious" organizations, there is no statutory or regulatory definition of the terms "religious" or "religion" for tax purposes. Indeed, by reason of the establishment clause and the free exercise clause of the First Amendment, it would undoubtedly be unconstitutional for the federal government to adopt and apply a strict definition of these terms. Nonetheless, in specific cases, government officials, judges, and justices have had to grapple with the meaning of the term "reli-

---

[20]*Walz* v. *Tax Commission, supra,* n. 16, at 669–670.

[21]See *United States* v. *Toy National Bank,* 79-1 U.S.T.C. ¶ 9344 (N.D. Ia. 1979); *General Conference of the Free Church of America* v. *Commissioner,* 71 T.C. 920, 930–932 (1979); *Coomes* v. *Commissioner,* 572 F.2d 554 (6th Cir. 1978); *United States* v. *Holmes,* 614 F.2d 985 (5th Cir. 1980); *United States* v. *Freedom Church,* 613 F.2d 316 (1st Cir. 1980); *Bronner* v. *Commissioner,* 72 T.C. 368 (1979). Cf. *United States* v. *Dykema,* 80-2 U.S.T.C. ¶ 9735 (E.D. Wis. 1980).

gious." In other than the constitutional law and federal tax law contexts, these instances have arisen in cases concerning, for example, conscientious objector status,[22] employment discrimination,[23] state and local real property tax exemptions,[24] and zoning restrictions.[25]

[22]E.g., *Welsh v. United States,* 398 U.S. 333 (1970); *United States v. Seeger,* 380 U.S. 163 (1965); *Berman v. United States,* 156 F.2d 377 (9th Cir. 1946), cert. den. 329 U.S. 795 (1946); *United States ex rel. Phillips v. Downer,* 135 F.2d 521 (2d Cir. 1943); *United States v. Kauten,* 133 F.2d 703 (2d Cir. 1943).

[23]E.g., *Braunfield v. Brown,* 366 U.S. 599 (1961); *Johnson v. U.S. Postal Service,* 364 F.Supp. 37 (N.D. Fla. 1973); *Powers v. State Department of Social Welfare,* 493 P.2d 590 (Sup. Ct. Kan. 1972); *Martin v. Industrial Acc. Commission,* 304 P.2d 828 (D.C. App. Cal. 1956).

[24]*Walz v. Tax Commission, supra,* n. 16; *Washington Ethical Society v. District of Columbia,* 249 F.2d 127 (D.C. Cir. 1957); *American Bible Society v. Lewisohn,* 351 N.E.2d 697 (Ct. App. N.Y. 1976); *Watchtower Bible and Tract Society, Inc. v. Lewisohn,* 315 N.E.2d 801 (Ct. App. N.Y. 1974); *People ex rel. Watchtower Bible and Tract Society, Inc. v. Haring,* 170 N.E.2d 677 (Ct. App. N.Y. 1960); *Fellowship of Humanity v. County of Alameda,* 315 P.2d 394 (D.C. App. N.Y. 1957).

[25]*In re Community Synagogue v. Bates,* 136 N.E.2d 488 (Ct. App. N.Y. 1956). An oft-cited case holds that the term "religion" has "reference to one's views of his relations to his Creator, and to the obligations they impose of reverence for his being and character, and of obedience to his will." *Davis v. Beason,* 133 U.S. 333, 342 (1890). Another court stated that "religion" has "reference to man's relation to Divinity; to reverence, worship, obedience, and submission to the mandates and precepts of supernatural or superior beings" and in its broadest sense "includes all forms of belief in the existence of superior beings, exercising power over human beings by volition, imposing rules of conduct with future rewards and punishments." *McMasters v. State of Oklahoma,* 29 A.L.R. 292, 294 (Ok. Crim. Ct. App. 1922). From a strict legal standpoint, however, the word "religion" is not defined in the U.S. Constitution. See *Reynolds v. United States, supra,* n. 5 at 162. Nonetheless, many courts have advanced definitions, including the following: "Religion as generally accepted may be defined as a bond uniting man to God and a virtue whose purpose is to render God the worship due to him as the source of all being and the principle of all government of things" (*Nikulnikoff v. Archbishop and Consistory of Russian Orthodox Greek Catholic Church,* 255 N.Y.S. 653, 663 (Sup. Ct. N.Y. Cty. 1932)); "[t]he essence of religion is belief in a relation to God involving duties superior to those arising from any human relation" (*United States v. Macintosh,* 283 U.S. 605, 633 (1931)); and "the Christian religion, in its most important ultimate aspect, recognizes, has faith in and worships a Divine Being or Spirit—one Father of all mankind—who has the power to and will forgive the transgressions of repentants and care for the immortal souls of the believers, and which belief brings earthly solace and comfort to and tends to induce right living in such believers" (*Taylor v. State,* 11 So.2d 663, 673 (Sup. Ct. Miss. 1943)). A summary definition of the term is: "Religion is squaring human life with superhuman life. . . . What is common to all religions is belief in a superhuman power and an adjustment of human activities to the requirements of that power, such adjustment as may enable the individual believer to exist more happily." Hopkins, *The History of Religions* 2, quoted in *Minersville School District v. Gobitis,* 108 F.2d 683, 685 (3d Cir. 1939).

The government and the courts have generally been loathe to take the position that an allegedly "religious" activity, function or purpose is not "religious" in nature. One court succinctly stated the reason why:

> Neither this Court, nor any branch of this Government, will consider the merits or fallacies of a religion. Nor will the Court compare the beliefs, dogmas, and practices of a newly organized religion with those of an older, more established religion. Nor will the Court praise or condemn a religion, however excellent or fanatical or preposterous it may seem. Were the Court to do so, it would impinge upon the guarantees of the First Amendment.[26]

The U.S. Tax Court has evidenced a like attitude, as when it wrote that, "[a]s a judicial body, we are loathe to evaluate and judge ecclesiastical authority and duties in the various religious disciplines."[27]

This approach has been sanctioned by the U.S. Supreme Court, which has repeatedly held[28] that freedom of thought and religious belief "embraces the right to maintain theories of life and of death and of the hereafter which are rank heresy to followers of the orthodox faiths," and that, if triers of fact undertake to examine the truth or falsity of the religious beliefs of a sect, "they enter a forbidden domain."[29]

An illustration of the courts' "hands off" policy toward determining what is and is not "religious" is an opinion of the U.S. Tax Court concerning an organization the founder of which received "revelations' from "Ascended Masters," principally Saint Germain.[30] His wife continued to receive the revelations after his death. The entity was organized and operated to propagate the teachings of the "'I AM' Religious Activity." In this case, the IRS did not allege that the organization was not religious but principally sought to convince the court that net income of the organization was inuring to the benefit of private individuals. The Tax Court devoted little effort to finding the organization "religious" in nature but largely relied on its statement in a prior case:

> Religion is not confined to a sect or a ritual. The symbols of religion to one are anathema to another. What one may regard as charity another may scorn as foolish waste. And even education is today not free from divergence of view as to its validity. Congress left open the door of tax exemption to all corporations meeting the test, the restriction being not as to the species of religion, charity, science or education under which they might operate, but as to the use of its profits and the exclusive purpose of its existence.[31]

[26]*Universal Life Church, Inc.* v. *United States*, 372 F.Supp. 770, 776 (E.D. Cal. 1974).
[27]*Colbert* v. *Commissioner*, 61 T.C. 449, 455 (1974).
[28]See ns. 2–21, *supra.*
[29]*United States* v. *Ballard*, 322 U.S. 78, 86, 87 (1943). Also see *United States* v. *Seeger*, n. 22, *Supra*, at 174–176).
[30]*Saint Germain Foundation* v. *Commissioner*, 26 T.C. 648 (1956).
[31]*Unity School of Christianity* v. *Commissioner*, 4 B.T.A. 61, 70 (1926).

The court, noting that it was not "compelled to decide whether the objectives of the petitioner are worthy or desirable," concluded that the organization was established exclusively for "religious" purposes.[32]

The Court of Claims reflected the same degree of caution when deciding a case involving an organization formed as the parent church of "scientology."[33] The court concluded that the organization was not exempt from tax—not because it was not "religious" (that issue was not even considered)—but because the net income of the entity was held to have inured to the founders in their private capacity.[34]

In one instance, an organization attempted to become recognized as a religious organization by virtue of its operation of a retreat facility.[35] The facility is a mountain lodge; the activities available at the lodge—being religious, recreational, and social—are not regularly scheduled nor required. The religious activities revolve around individual prayer and contemplation, with optional daily devotions and occasional Sunday services available. The IRS asserted that the organization's "substantial, if not sole, purpose is to provide a facility where guests can relax, socialize and engage in recreational activities, or, in other words, to operate a vacation resort."[36] Conversely, the organization contended that "its primary purpose is to provide a religious retreat facility for Christian families where they may come to reflect upon and worship the Lord in a setting free from the outside interferences of everyday life."[37] The U.S. Tax Court, holding that the organization failed to sustain its burden of proof that the facilities were not used in more than an insubstantial manner for recreational purposes, concluded that tax exemption as a religious organization could not be found, in that "[w]holesome family recreation or just sitting on a rock contemplating nature may well provide a family or an individual with a religious, or at least a spiritually-uplifting experience, but it is difficult to see how that experience differs, if it does, from the same experience one can have at any quiet inn or lodge located in the beautiful mountains of Colorado."[38]

---

[32]*Saint Germain Foundation v. Commissioner, supra,* n. 30, at 657. Also Rev. Rul. 68-563, 1968-2 C. B. 212, as amplified by Rev. Rul. 78-385, 1978-2 C. B. 174; Rev. Rul. 68-26, 1968-1 C. B. 272.

[33] *Founding Church of Scientology v. United States,* 412 F.2d 1197 (Ct. Cl. 1969), cert. den. 397 U.S. 1009 (1970). Cf. *Church of Scientology of Hawaii v. United States,* 485 F.2d 313 (9th Cir. 1973); *Church of Scientology of California v. United States,* 75-2 U.S.T.C. ¶ 9584 (9th Cir. 1975); *Founding Church of Scientology of Washington, D.C. v. United States,* 409 F.2d 1146 (D.C. Cir. 1968), cert. den. 396 U.S. 963 (1969).

[34]The U.S. Tax Court has held that the expenses of scientology processing and United States, 75-2 U.S.T.C. ¶ 9586 (9th Cir. 1975); Rev. Rul. 78-188, 1978-1 C. B. missioner, 62 T.C. 551 (1974), aff'd 523 F.2d 365 (8th Cir. 1975). Cf. *Handeland v. United States,* 75-2 U.S.T.C. ¶ 9586 (9th Cir. 1975); Rev. Rul. 78-188, 1978-1 C. B. 40; Rev. Rul. 78-189, 1978-1 C. B. 68; and Rev. Rul. 78-190, 1978-1 C. B. 74.

[35]*The Schoger Foundation v. Commissioner,* 76 T.C. 380 (1981).

[36]*Ibid.* at 386.

[37]*Ibid.* at 387.

[38]*Ibid.* at 388.

The Postal Service has not been as reticent as the IRS and Treasury Department about promulgating some general definition of a "religious" organization in the exemption context. Thus, for purposes of preferred mailing privileges for qualified nonprofit organizations, the Postal Manual states that a religious organization is an organization the primary purpose of which is one of the following: (1) to conduct religious worship, for example, churches, synagogues, temples, or mosques, (2) to support the religious activities of nonprofit organizations the primary purpose of which is to conduct religious worship, or (3) to perform instruction in, to disseminate information about, or otherwise to further the teaching of particular religious faiths or tenets.[39]

Typically, a court, when finding an alleged "religious" organization not tax-exempt, generally does so not on the ground that the purpose is not religious but rather on a finding that the activity smacks too much of a commercial enterprise operated for private gain or that the organization is an "action" organization.[40] In one case, the taxpayers operated a restaurant as a private business for profit with the net profits going to a church, which itself was engaged in commercial activities; the taxpayers' contributions to the church were held not deductible because the organization's business activities defeated the requisite status.[41] Another purported "religious" organization's tax-exempt status was precluded because its primary activity was the operation of a (religious) publishing house.[42]

In still another variant of this same approach, a court found that an organization's social aspects were so predominant as to relegate any religious activities to secondary status.[43] The organization, formed to further the doctrine of "ethical egoism," was found to have as its principal purpose the social functions of sponsoring dinner meetings and publishing a newsletter. While "church meetings" were also held, the court believed they were in reality merely an extension of the social meetings. In general, the court concluded that the "religious aspects of such conclaves seems . . . indistinct." Likewise, an organization was determined to not qualify as a religious organization because its

---

[39]Chapter 1, Part 134.5.

[40]See Chapter 5.

[41]*Riker* v. *Commissioner*, 244 F.2d 220 (9th Cir. 1957), cert. den. 355 U.S. 839 (1957). Also see *Parker* v. *Commissioner*, 365 F.2d 792 (8th Cir. 1966).

[42]*Scripture Press Foundation* v. *United States*, 285 F.2d 800 (Ct. Cl. 1961), cert. den. 368 U.S. 985 (1962). Also see *Christian Manner International, Inc.* v. *Commissioner*, 71 T.C. 661 (1979); *Fides Publishers Association* v. *United States*, 263 F.Supp. 924 (N.D. Ind. 1967); *Unitary Mission Church of Long Island* v. *Commissioner*, 74 T.C. 507 (1980), aff'd in unpublished opinion (2d Cir., Jan. 19, 1981); *Bubbling Well Church of Universal Love, Inc.* v. *Commissioner*, 74 T.C. 531 (1980). But see *Elisian Guild, Inc.* v. *United States*, 412 F.2d 121 (1st Cir. 1969); Rev. Rul. 68-26, *supra*, n. 32.

[43]*First Libertarian Church* v. *Commissioner*, 74 T.C. 396 (1980).

primary activity was the investment and accumulation of funds, albeit for the purpose of eventually building a church.[44]

The IRS is invoking the private inurement doctrine in still another context involving religious organizations: the tax treatment of communal groups. This type of religious organization is becoming more commonplace in American society. Typically the member commits all or some of his or her possessions to the community. The organization in turn provides shelter and food, and sometimes clothing, medical care, or children's schooling. In some cases, the members are employed outside the community and contribute their salaries and earnings to the organization. In all cases, the primary purposes of the organization are to conduct religious services, provide a place of worship, offer instruction in religious tenets, and otherwise further the organization's "message." The communal structure is perceived as the most effective way to conduct the ministry, particularly on an outreach basis. Frequently, these organizations perceive themselves to be churches.

The IRS position is that, where individuals reside in a communal setting in the context of professing religious beliefs, with room, board, and other costs provided by the organization, the result is unwarranted private benefit to the individuals which precludes tax exemption. This position has been upheld by the courts on two occasions.[45]

These and similar cases have enormous implications. Certainly, the "traditional" church, for example, may provide lodging, food, and the like to its ministers and family,[46] or operate a school, and not attract any difficulties with the IRS. Parsonages and parochial schools are not likely to be the foundation for IRS revocation of a church's tax-exempt status. Perhaps the publicity recently given to "cults" and the uncovering of immense property holdings of and substantial government infiltration by controversial "churches" have influenced the IRS to shy away from any aid and comfort to burgeoning "nontraditional" churches by merely denying them tax exemption.

Regardless of individual attitudes toward new religions or new religious structures, the consequences of the government's position are yet to unfold. As respects the tax status of monasteries, nunneries, and religious orders, the IRS has previously recognized that support of monks, nuns, and other clerics (in the form of shelter, food, clothing, medical care, and other necessities) is an exempt function. Will these groups now face the loss of tax exemption because they provide this type of "private" support?

The repercussions of this IRS attitude toward communal groups have only begun to be felt. The decision in the above-noted cases may not represent the

---

[44]*Western Catholic Church* v. *Commissioner*, 73 T.C. 196 (1979), aff'd 631 F.2d 736 (7th Cir. 1980).

[45]*Beth-El Ministries, Inc.* v. *United States*, 79-2 U.S.T.C. ¶ 9412 (D.D.C. 1979); *Martinsville Ministries, Inc.* v. *United States*, 80-2 U.S.T.C. ¶ 9710 (D.D.C. 1979).

[46]See, e.g., Code § 107.

final resolution of these matters, if only because the court would not permit oral argument and did not write full opinions to accompany its decisions. Yet if these cases reflect the true state of the law, it does not bode well for a wide variety of religious groups.

As concerns the "action" organization rules, perhaps the best illustration is the government's successful revocation of the tax-exempt status of Billy James Hargis' corporation called "Christian Echoes." Christian Echoes maintains religious radio and television broadcasts, authors publications, engages in evangelistic campaigns and meetings, operates the Summer Anti-Communist University, and conducts other activities. All parties (IRS and courts) recognized Christian Echoes as being "religious"; its exemption was lost on the grounds that a substantial part of its activities consists of carrying on propaganda, attempting to influence legislation, and intervening in political campaigns.[47] Similarly, the IRS successfully revoked the tax-exempt status of Americans United, an organization the purpose of which is to defend and maintain religious liberty in the United States by the dissemination of knowledge concerning the constitutional principle of the separation of church and state, on the ground that the organization engaged in a substantial amount of lobbying.[48]

The U.S. Supreme Court has concluded that tax exemption (specifically, for New York state property tax purposes) for religious organizations does not constitute excessive entanglement by the state with religion as proscribed by the First Amendment.[49] Recognizing that either taxation or tax exemption of churches "occasions some degree of involvement with religion," the Court held that "[g]ranting tax exemptions to churches necessarily operates to afford an indirect economic benefit and also gives rise to some, but yet a lesser, involvement than taxing them."[50] This argument was presaged in the literature[51] and in state court cases.[52] An unavoidable aspect of this process is that the state is placed in the position of deciding which organizations qualify as being "reli-

[47]*Christian Echoes National Ministry, Inc.* v. *United States*, 470 F.2d 849 (10th Cir. 1972), cert. den. 414 U.S. 864 (1973).

[48]*Alexander* v. *"Americans United," Inc.*, 416 U.S. 752 (1974).

[49]*Walz* v. *Tax Commission, supra*, n. 16. See Note, 16 *Vill. L. Rev.* 374 (1970).

[50]*Ibid.* at 674. See *Committee for Public Education* v. *Nyguist*, 413 U.S. 756 (1973).

[51]See, e.g., Harpster, "Religion, Education, and the Law," 36 *Marq. L. Rev.* 24, 66 (1952); Note, "Exemption of Property Owned and Used by Religious Organizations," 11 *Minn. L. Rev.* 541, 550 (1927).

[52]See, e.g., *Murray* v. *Comptroller of Treasury*, 216 A.2d 897 (Ct. App. Md. 1966), cert. den., 385 U.S. 816 (1966); *General Finance Corp.* v. *Archetto*, 176 A.2d 73 (Sup. Ct. R.I. 1961), app. dis., 369 U.S. 424 (1962); *Fellowship of Humanity* v. *County of Alameda, supra* n. 24, *Lundberg* v. *County of Alameda*, 298 P.2d 1 (Sup. Ct. Cal. 1956), app. dis. sub nom. *Heisey* v. *County of Alameda*, 352 U.S. 921 (1956); *Franklin St. Society* v. *Manchester*, 60 N.H. 342 (1880). But see *Sostre* v. *McGinnes*, 334 F.2d 906 (2d Cir. 1964); *Washington Ethical Society* v. *District of Columbia, supra*, n. 24, *Cooke* v. *Tramburg*, 205 A.2d 889 (Sup. Ct. N.J. 1964).

gious" in nature—a difficult decision to make, particularly where "unorthodox" beliefs are involved.

The difficulties confronting the IRS in deciding whether organizations can qualify for tax exemption as religious organizations, and in some cases as churches, have become nearly overwhelming. Instances involving blatant abuses are generating numerous court opinions and thus are forming the evolving law. The concerns of the IRS about mail-order ministries, real estate tax exemption frauds, and questionable tax deductions are leading the IRS to many adverse decisions which, in turn, are causing like decisions by the courts, so that the law is shaping up as being appropriately tough as regards the sham situations but it is formulating some legal principles that are highly questionable when applied outside the areas of abuse.

A case in point is a U.S. Tax Court decision concerning the Southern Church of Universal Brotherhood Assembled, a Maryland nonprofit corporation.[53] The Church described as its "text" for its "continuing sermon" the "Chesapeake Bay, its rivers and estuaries to demonstrate the indiscriminate provision of food, energy, water and minerals to all mankind resident within the tide water areas of the Bay by our bountiful Father." Among the Church's programs are "marine learning institutes" which are boat outings to, in the language of the Court opinion, "collect material from the Chesapeake Bay to demonstrate the laws of God by which things work and the divine rules for getting things done." To accomplish these ends, the Church owns a Ventura Cat sailboat and intends to purchase a larger craft. The Church's minister, who also is its president and a trustee, was ordained by The Aquarian Church of the Brothers and Sisters of Jesus Christ (known as "TACT"). TACT has one requirement for ordination, which is that the minister speak English. (According to the court, TACT advocates affiliation with it "as a way to protect one's tax freedom and lead a holy tax-free life.") While the minister owns the parsonage and the facility where the services are held, the Church pays the utilities, fuel, maintenance, and repair expenses of the parsonage and provides the minister's family with food, postage, stationery, pots and pans, dishes, glassware, sheets, blankets, towels, and curtains. In one year, the total receipts of the Church were $6,987.84. Of that, its minister contributed $6,573.00. In another year, the total receipts were $14,373.33, of which the minister contributed $14,372.00. The Court concluded that the Church could not be tax-exempt because it serves the private interests of its minister. While this is undoubtedly the case, the problem with the opinion is that it disregards the fact that most "conventional" churches provide parsonages whereby the minister and family members are provided lodging, food, clothing, and the like. Why is that not private inurement that deprives the church of its tax exemption? This and comparable court opinions bless the most egregious of discrimination, whereby "orthodox" churches are protected but

[53]*The Southern Church of Universal Brotherhood Assembled, Inc.* v. *Commissioner*, 74 T.C. 1223 (1980).

new ones are held taxable.[54] There must be a basis for differentiating between the charlatans and the authentically religious, but the tax law is contributing to some unfortunate precedent. Perhaps the Court in the instant case would have been more sympathetic if the Church's "text" were the Bible instead of the Chesapeake Bay. The outcome may have been different if the Church's chief asset were not a sailboat that can carry a combined passenger and crew weight of 500 pounds. But then, the Church's acronym is SCUBA.

As one court stated, "[t]he lack of a precise definition [of the term "religious"] is not surprising in light of the fact that a constitutional provision is involved."[55] Most of what caselaw there is on the subject finds the courts' rejection of a narrow definition, rather than an affirmative statement of an encompassing definition. Thus, a court has observed that, "[i]n implementing the establishment clause, the Supreme Court has made clear that an activity may be religious even though it is neither part of nor derives from a societally recognized religious sect."[56] Occasional attempts made in the literature to define "religion"[57] usually become criticized for being incomplete or outdated.[58]

There are, nonetheless, some explicit discussions of what may constitute "religion" or "religious belief." In one case, it was said that "[r]eligious belief . . . is a belief finding expression in a conscience which categorically requires the believer to disregard elementary self-interest and to accept martyrdom in preference to transgressing its tenets."[59] Another court found an activity religious because it was centered around belief in a higher being "which in its various forms is given the name 'god' in common usage" and because a form of prayer was involved.[60] The U.S. Supreme Court has placed emphasis on belief in a "supreme being," and has looked to see whether "a given belief that is sincere and meaningful occupies a place in the life of its possessor parallel to that filled by the orthodox belief in God"[61] and whether the belief occupies in the life of the individual involved "'a place parallel to that filled by . . . God' in traditional religious persons."[62] But some courts have been reluctant to confine the concept of "religious belief" to theistic beliefs. For example, one court held that the permissible inquiry on this subject is "whether or not the

[54]E.g., *Basic Bible Church* v. *Commissioner*, 74 T.C. 846 (1980); *Truth Tabernacle* v. *Commissioner*, 41 T.C.M. 1405 (1981). Cf. *McGahen* v. *Commissioner*, 76 T.C. 468 (1981).
[55]*Malnak* v. *Yogi*, 440 F.Supp. 1284 (D.N.J. 1977), aff'd 592 F.2d 197 (3d Cir. 1979).
[56]*Ibid.*, 440 F.Supp. at 1313.
[57]E.g., Note, "Toward a Constitutional Definition of Religion," 91 *Harv. L. Rev.* 1056 (1978).
[58]E.g., Worthing, " 'Religion' and 'Religious Institutions' Under the First Amendment," 7 *Pepperdine L. Rev.* 313, 320–321 (1980).
[59]*United States* v. *Kauten, supra*, n. 22 at 708.
[60]*Malnak* v. *Yogi, supra*, n. 55, 440 F.Supp. at 1320, 1323.
[61]*United States* v. *Seeger, supra*, n. 22, 380 U.S. at 165–166.
[62]*Welsh* v. *United States, supra*, n. 22, 398 U.S. at 340.

belief occupies the same place in the lives of its holders that the orthodox beliefs occupy in the lives of believing majorities, and whether a given group that claims the exemption conducts itself the way groups conceded to be religious conduct themselves."[63] This same court added that the appropriate test is whether the activities of the organization in question "serve the same place in the lives of its members, and occupy the same place in society, as the activities of the theistic churches."[64] Indeed, this court developed what is apparently the most expansive, yet definitional, statement as to the general characteristics of the concept of "religion":

> Religion simply includes: (1) a belief, not necessarily referring to supernatural powers; (2) a cult, involving a gregarious association openly expressing the beliefs; (3) a system of moral practice directly resulting from an adherence to the belief; and (4) an organization within the cult designed to observe the tenets of belief.[65]

Consequently, federal tax law lacks a crisp and workable definition of the term "religious." There is, nonetheless, an approach to application of the term that adheres to the admonition offered concerning the meaning of the term "obscenity," that one "knows it when one sees it."[66] As the foregoing citations reflect, there are unabashed references in the court opinions to "traditional," "orthodox," and "majority" religious beliefs, and at least one opinion differentiates between groups "conceded to be religious" and others. Also, as noted, it is relatively clear that "religious belief" is not confined to "theistic belief." Indeed, the best one-sentence summary on point is that the term "religion" as employed in federal and state statutes "has been held to encompass non-theistic beliefs which occupy a place in the lives of their possessors parallel to that occupied by belief in God in persons with traditional religious faith."[67]

An organization that is deemed to be a "religious" entity may well engage in activities that by themselves may not be regarded as religious, such as charitable, educational, social welfare, and community activities. It appears generally recognized that the conduct of these activities will not deprive an otherwise "religious" organization of its classification as a "religious" group. For example, one court has held that "[s]trictly religious uses and activities are more than prayer and sacrifice" and include social activities, study, and community service.[68] Another commentator has observed that "[r]eligious activities

---

[63]*Fellowship of Humanity* v. *County of Alameda, supra,* n. 24, 315 P.2d at 406.

[64]*Ibid.*, 315 P.2d at 409–410.

[65]*Id.*, 315 P.2d at 406.

[66]In *Jacobellis* v. *Ohio,* 378 U.S. 184 (1964), Justice Stewart, conceptualizing as to the meaning of the word "obscene," observed that one may not succeed in intelligibly defining the term but would "know it when I see it" (at 197).

[67]Worthing, " 'Religion' and 'Religious Institutions' Under the First Amendment," *supra,* n. 58 at 332.

[68]*In re Community Synagogue* v. *Bates, supra,* n. 25, 136 N.E.2d at 493.

or uses have been held to include incidental social, charitable, and maintenance activities (for both persons and property) as well as religious worship."[69]

There is no question but that the current state of the law on this subject poses perplexing and probably unbearable burdens on regulatory officials and judges. These difficulties are exacerbated as new religions emerge (for example, the Unification Church and Scientology movements) and as new forms of approach to the practice of religion emerge (for example, the "electronic churches" and the "mail-order ministries"). Yet policymakers must tread carefully even when confronting the "nontraditional," "minority," and/or "unorthodox" religious groups. The First Amendment applies to them as well. As one court has noted, "[n]ew religions appear in this country frequently and they cannot stand outside the first amendment merely because they did not exist when the Bill of Rights was drafted."[70]

§ 8.3 "Churches"

The matter of what is a "religious" organization can be approached in another, yet somewhat supplemental, way. That is, rather than a focus on the meaning of the term "religious," an inquiry can be made as to the categories of entities that are eligible for designation as "religious" organizations.

This subclassification of religious groups yields the following (not necessarily inclusive) categories:

• Churches,[71]

---

[69]Worthing, " 'Religion' and 'Religious Institutions' Under the First Amendment," *supra*, n. 58 at 332.

[70]*Malnak* v. *Yogi, supra*, n. 55, 440 F.Supp. at 1315.

[71]Code § 170(b)(1)(A)(i). The term "church" has been defined in a variety of ways. One of the most straightforward definitions is that a "church" is "an organization for religious purposes, for the public worship of God." *Bennett* v. *City of La Grange*, 112 S.E. 482, 485 (Sup. Ct. Ga. 1922). Other definitions of the term "church" include the following: "A body or community of Christians, united under one form of government by the same profession of the same faith, and the observance of the same ritual and ceremonies" (*McNeilly* v. *First Presbyterian Church in Brookline*, 137 N.E. 691 (Sup. Jud. Ct. Mass. 1923)); "The term may denote either a society of persons who, professing Christianity, hold certain doctrines or observances which differentiate them from other like groups, and who use a common discipline, or the building in which such persons habitually assemble for public worship" (*Baker* v. *Fales*, 16 Mass. 488, 498, quoted in *First Independent Missionary Baptist Church of Chosen* v. *McMillan*, 153 So.2d 337, 342 (D.C. App. Fla. 1963)); and "A church society is a voluntary organization whose members are associated together, not only for religious exercises, but also for the purpose of maintaining and supporting its ministry and providing the conveniences of a church home and promoting the growth and efficiency of the work of the general church of which it forms a co-ordinate part" (*First Presbyterian Church of Mt. Vernon* v. *Dennis*, 161 N.W. 183, 187 (Sup. Ct. Ia. 1917). Thus, the term "church" carries many meanings,

- Conventions of churches,[72]
- Associations of churches,[73]
- Church-run organizations, such as schools, hospitals, orphanages, nursing homes, publishing entities, broadcasting entities, and cemeteries
- Religious orders
- Apostolic groups[74]
- Integrated auxiliaries of churches[75]
- Missionary organizations
- Bible and tract societies

Of these, the meaning of the term "church" has received the most consideration.

Federal tax authorities have had to apply the term "church" in a variety of tax contexts. For example, a regulation issued in 1958 (and applicable for tax years before 1970) defined the term in the unrelated income tax (and charitable contribution deduction) context as follows:

> The term "church" includes a religious order or a religious organization if such order or organization (a) is an integral part of a church, and (b) is engaged in carrying out the functions of a church, whether as a civil law corporation or otherwise. In determining whether a religious order or organization is an integral part of a church, consideration will be given to the degree to which it is connected with, and controlled by, such church. A religious order or organization shall be considered to be engaged in carrying out the functions of a church if its duties include the ministration of sacerdotal functions and the conduct of religious worship. If a religious order or organization is not an integral part of a church, or if such an order or organization is not authorized to carry out the functions of a church (ministration of sacerdotal functions and conduct of religious worship) then it is subject to the tax imposed by section 511 [on unrelated income] whether or not it engages in religious, educational, or charitable activities approved by a church. What constitutes the conduct of religious worship or the ministration of sacerdotal functions depends on the tenets and practices of a particular religious

---

including the congregation and the physical facilities themselves. As one court observed, the term "may refer only to the church building or house of worship; it may mean in a more consecrated way the great body of persons holding the Christian belief, or in a restricted sense confined to those adhering to one of the several denominations of the Christian faith, at large or in a definite territory; and it may mean the collective membership of persons constituting the congregation of a single permanent place of worship" (*Forsberg v. Zehm*, 143 S.E. 284, 286 (Sup. Ct. App. Va. 1928)).

[72]Code § 170(b)(1)(A)(i).

[73]*Id*. For the legislative history of this phrase, see *De La Salle Institute v. United States*, 195 F.Supp. 891, 897–910 (N.D. Cal. 1961). See Chapter 22. See Reg. § 1.170A-9(a).

[74]See §4 hereof.

[75]See ns. 89-91, *infra*.

body constituting a church. If a religious order or organization can fully meet the requirements stated in this subdivision, exemption from the tax imposed by section 511 will apply to all its activities, including those which it conducts through a separate corporation (other than a corporation described in section 501(c)(2)) a title-holding entity or other separate entity which it wholly owns and which is not operated for the primary purpose of carrying on a trade or business for profit. Such exemption from tax will also apply to activities conducted through a separate corporation (other than a corporation described in section 501(c)(3)) or other separate entity which is wholly owned by more than one religious order or organization, if all such orders or organizations fully meet the requirements stated in this subdivision and if such corporation or other entity is not operated for the primary purpose of carrying on a trade or business for profit.[76]

Basically, under this regulation, a "church" is an organization the "duties" of which include the "ministration of sacerdotal [i.e., priestly] functions and the conduct of religious worship." The existence of these elements depends on the "tenets and practices of a particular religious body." A church may also include a religious order or other organization which is an "integral part" of a church and is engaged in carrying out the functions of a church.[77]

Concerning the term "convention or association of churches," the IRS recognizes that the term has a historical meaning generally referring to a cooperative undertaking by a church of the same denomination.[78] However, the Service has ruled that the term also applies to a cooperative undertaking by churches of differing denominations, assuming that the convention or association otherwise qualifies as a religious organization.[79]

The IRS has formulated criteria that it uses to ascertain whether or not an organization qualifies as a "church." The IRS position is that, to be a church for tax purposes, an organization must satisfy at least some of the following criteria: (1) a distinct legal existence, (2) a recognized creed and form of worship, (3) a definite and distinct ecclesiastical government, (4) a formal code of doctrine and discipline, (5) a distinct religious history, (6) a membership not associated with any other church or denomination, (7) a complete organization of ordained ministers ministering to their congregations and selected after completing prescribed courses of study, (8) a literature of its own, (9) established places of worship, (10) regular congregations, (11) regular religious services, (12) Sunday schools for the religious instruction of the young, and (13) schools for the preparation of its ministers.[80]

---

[76]Reg. §§ 1.170-2(b)(2), 1.511-2(a)(3)(ii).
[77]See *Guam Power Authority* v. *Bishop of Guam*, 383 F.Supp. 476 (D. Guam 1974).
[78]Rev. Rul. 74-224, 1974-1 C.B. 61. Cf. *Vaughn* v. *Commissioner*, 48 T.C. 358 (1967).
[79]*Ibid*.
[80]Internal Revenue Manual § 321.3.

In remarks delivered in early 1977,[81] the Commissioner of Internal Revenue reiterated the fact that the IRS is utilizing these criteria. However, he added that "few, if any, religious organizations—conventional or unconventional—could satisfy all of these criteria" and that the Service does "not give controlling weight to any single factor." Further, he asserted that "[t]his is obviously the place in the decisional process requiring the most sensitive and discriminating judgment." He concluded with the observation that the IRS has "been criticized for the scope and breadth of the criteria we use and it has been implied that the Service has been trying in recent years to discourage new religions and new churches" and with the assurance "that that is not the case with the IRS." The IRS continues to utilize these criteria.

As has been discussed, the courts have been reluctant to pass on the question as to what is a "religious" organization, let alone what is a "church." Still, an extreme factual setting may embolden a court to make a distinction between religious activities and personal codes of conduct that lack spiritual import. This was the case with the Neo-American Church, the chief precept of which was that psychedelic substances, such as LSD and marihuana, are the "true Host of the Church," thereby specifying that it is "the Religious *duty* of all members to partake of the sacraments on regular occasions." The Church had the equivalent of bishops (known as "Boo Hoos"), a symbol (a three-eyed toad), official songs (e.g., "Puff, the Magic Dragon"), a Church key (a bottle opener), a Catechism and Handbook (excerpt: "we have the *right* to practice our religion, even if we are a bunch of filthy, drunken bums"), and a motto ("Victory over Horseshit"). Recognizing that judges "must be ever careful not to permit their own moral and ethical standards to determine the religious implications of beliefs and practices of others," a court nonetheless concluded that the Neo-American Church is not "religious," in the absence of any "solid evidence of a belief in a supreme being, a religious discipline, a ritual, or tenets to guide one's daily existence."[82]

Nonetheless, as the issue is being pressed more frequently, some courts are becoming more willing to enunciate criteria for a qualifying "church." Thus, in the view of the U.S. Tax Court, a church is an organization that, in addition to having a "religious-type function," (1) holds services or meetings on a regular

---

[81]"Difficult Definitional Problems in Tax Administration: Religion and Race," remarks by then-IRS Commissioner Jerome Kurtz before the Practising Law Institute Seventh Biennial Conference on Tax Planning for Foundations, Tax-Exempt Status and Charitable Contributions, on Jan. 9, 1977, reproduced at Bureau of National Affairs, *Daily Executive Report*, Jan. 11, 1977, at p. J.8.

[82]*United States* v. *Kuch*, 288 F.Supp. 439, 443–444 (D.D.C. 1968). Also *Puritan Church of America* v. *Commissioner*, 10 T.C.M. 485 (1951), aff'd 209 F.2d 306 (D.C. Cir. 1953), cert. den. 347 U.S. 975 (1954), 350 U.S. 810 (1955). Cf. *Malnak* v. *Yogi, supra*, n. 55; *People* v. *Woody*, 394 P.2d 813 (Sup. Ct. Cal. 1964); *Baker* v. *Commissioner*, 40 T.C.M. 983 (1980); *Clippinger* v. *Commissioner*, 37 T.C.M. 484 (1978).

basis, (2) has ministers or other "representatives," (3) has a record of performance of "marriages, other ceremonies or sacraments," (4) has a place of worship, (5) ordains ministers, (6) requires some financial support by its members,
(7) has a form of "formal operation," and (8) satisfies all other requirements of
the federal tax law rules for religious organizations.[83]

In the first instance of a court's utilization of the IRS criteria as to the
definition of the term "church," it concluded that an organization, albeit religious, could not qualify as a church because there is no "congregation," nor
requisite "religious instruction" or "conduct of religious worship."[84] Laying
down a "minimum" definition of a church as including "a body of believers or
communicants that assembles regularly in order to worship," the court said
that of "central importance" is "the existence of an established congregation
served by an organized ministry, the provision of regular religious services and
religious education for the young, and the dissemination of a doctrinal code."
In the case, no "congregation" was found present, in that the only communicants
were the founder of the church and his wife who "pray together in the physical
solitude of their home"; the organization's "religious instruction" consists of "a
father preaching to his son"; and its "organized ministry" is a "single self-
appointed clergyman." Because, in the opinion of the court, the organization
"does not employ recognized, accessible channels of instruction and worship"
and is merely a "quintessentially private religious enterprise," the court concluded that it is not a "church."

The U.S. Supreme Court has offered a partial definition of the term "church"
in the tax context, in an opinion construing an exemption from unemployment
compensation taxes imposed by the Federal Unemployment Tax Act and com-
plementary state law. The issue was the eligibility for the exemption for services
performed for church-related schools that do not have a separate legal existence,
pursuant to provision of exemption for employees "of a church or convention
or association of churches."[85] The Court rejected the view that the term "church"
means no more than "the actual house of worship used by a congregation" and
held that the word "must be construed, instead, to refer to the congregation
or the hierarchy itself, that is, the church authorities who conduct the business
of hiring, discharging, and directing church employees."[86] Thus, in one instance, a church-operated day school, financed by the church's congregation
and controlled by a board of directors elected from that congregation, was

---

[83]*Pusch* v. *Commissioner*, 39 T.C.M. 838 (1980), aff'd 628 F.2d 1353 (5th Cir. 1980).
Also *Abney* v. *Commissioner*, 39 T.C.M. 965 (1980); *Manson* v. *Commissioner*, 40
T.C.M. 972 (1980); *Lynch* v. *Commissioner*, 41 T.C.M. 204 (1980). Cf. *Morey* v. *Riddell*,
205 F.Supp. 918 (S.D. Cal. 1962); *Peek* v. *Commissioner*, 73 T.C. 912 (1980); *Vaughn*
v. *Commissioner*, *supra*, n. 78.

[84]*American Guidance Foundation, Inc.* v. *United States*, 80-1 U.S.T.C. ¶ 9452 (D.D.C.
1980).

[85]Code § 3309 (b)(1)(A).

[86]*St. Martin Evangelical Lutheran Church* v. *South Dakota*, 451 U.S. 772 (1981).

considered part of the church, and a secondary school owned, supported, and controlled by an Evangelical Lutheran Synod was considered part of a convention or association of churches; neither school was separately incorporated. Although the Court recognized that the issue carries with it potential constitutional law questions,[87] it also expressly "disavow[ed] any intimations in this case defining or limiting what constitutes a church under FUTA or under any other provision of the Internal Revenue Code."[88]

The IRS published regulations providing a definition of an "integrated auxiliary" of a church;[89] an integrated auxiliary is treated the same as a church in that it is not required to file annual information returns.[90] Basically, the regulations, which were adopted over the opposition of the church community, define an integrated auxiliary of a church as being an exempt organization the principal activity of which is exclusively religious and which is controlled by or associated with a church or a convention or association of churches. As proposed in 1976, the regulations were more stringent, in that they would have required an integrated auxiliary of a church to be an organization (1) the primary purpose of which is to carry out the tenets, functions, and principles of faith of the church with which it is "affiliated" (as defined) and (2) the operations of which in implementing the primary purpose directly promote religious activity among the members of the church.

Integrated auxiliaries of a church, under the regulations, include men's and women's fellowship associations, mission societies, theological seminaries, and religious youth organizations. Schools of a general academic or vocational nature, hospitals, orphanages, old age homes, and the like are not considered to be integrated auxiliaries, even though they have a religious environment or promote a church's teaching. However, schools that are operated, supported, and controlled by a church or a convention or association of churches are clearly integrated auxiliaries, and if they lack a separate legal existence are probably part of the related church or convention or association of churches.[91]

Traditionally, courts have enunciated only two guides as to what constitutes a "church" in the tax context: it must be a "religious" organization and it must be the equivalent of a "denomination" or a "sect." For example, in 1967, the U.S. Tax Court held that "though every church may be a religious organization, every religious organization is not per se a church" and that "the concept of 'church' appears to be synonymous with the concept of 'denomination'."[92] But then the court hastened to add that its holding "is not to imply, however, that

---

[87]*Ibid.* at 780.
[88]*Ibid.* at 784, n. 15.
[89]Reg. § 1.6033-2(g)(5).
[90]See Chapter 38.
[91]*St. Martin Evangelical Lutheran Church v. South Dakota, supra,* n. 86.
[92]*Vaughn v. Commissioner, supra,* n. 78 at 363. As to the latter element, the court observed that the organization involved is "merely a religious organization comprised of individual members who are already affiliated with various churches." *Id.* at 364.

in order to be constituted a church, a group must have an organizational hierarchy or maintain church buildings."[93]

If the definition stated in the now-withdrawn unrelated income tax regulation is employed, the conclusion becomes that the primary function of a "church" is "sacerdotal" activities, while a "religious" organization may permissibly engage in a broader range of activities, and a charitable and educational organization may engage in a still wider range of activities that may nonetheless have a nexus with religious undertakings (for example, the charitable purpose of advancement of religion[94]).

From this standpoint, a "church" is, in the absence of a statutory definition, an organization that is a "church" under the "common meaning and usage of the word."[95] Pursuant to this approach, "[a]n organization established to carry out 'church' functions, under the general understanding of the term, is a 'church.'"[96] Such functions, according to this view, principally are forms of conduct of religious worship (such as a mass or communion) but are not activities such as the operation of schools, religious orders, wineries, and missions, even where these "religious organizations . . . [or functions are] formed [or conducted] under church auspices."[97] If the latter categories of activities predominate, the organization cannot be a "church," inasmuch as "[t]he tail cannot be permitted to wag the dog" and the conduct of such "incidental activities" cannot make an organization a church.[98] Some subsequent cases follow this approach, such as the 1980 Tax Court finding that an organization is not a church because "there is no showing in the record of any marriages, other ceremonies or sacraments performed by any 'minister' or representative of the Church."[99] Other cases reject this narrow reading of the term and embrace within the ambit of "church" function activities such as "mission or evangelistic program[s]" and efforts for "the care of the needy, the sick, or the imprisoned, traditionally the beneficiaries of the ministration of churches."[100]

In the meantime, in the absence of a statutory definition of the term "church" or much guidance on the subject from the courts, the IRS is actively applying its fourteen points to determine if a religious organization can qualify as a "church." These criteria are taken from a speech by an IRS Commissioner; they are not even embodied in a regulation (with an opportunity for public comment) or a revenue ruling.

One commentator has offered this observation on these criteria:

[93]*Ibid*. at 363.
[94]See Chapter 6.
[95]*De La Salle Institute* v. *United States, supra,* n. 73 at 903.
[96]*Ibid*. at 903.
[97]*Id*. at 902.
[98]*Id*. at 901.
[99]*Pusch* v. *Commissioner, supra,* n. 83, 39 T.C.M. at 841.
[100]*Bubbling Well Church of Universal Love, Inc*. v. *Commissioner, supra,* n. 42 at 536.

These criteria tend to require an organization to be a developed denomination according to the pattern reflected in the most accepted mainline churches. They do not recognize the substantial departure from this structure among a number of religious organizations which have long been recognized as American churches. Furthermore, over more than the last decade, there has been the development of "house churches" among Protestants, Catholics, and some Jews, who seek community, less structure, and hopefully, more authentic spirituality. Few could argue that these churches do not embody the religion of most of those who belong, yet such churches may not meet many of the criteria established by the IRS National Office.

Christ and His band of disciples certainly did not meet these criteria. An examination of the relevant references indicates that the Biblical church which was in the home of Priscilla and Aquila would not qualify for tax exemption under these tests. It is perhaps never wise to define a religion based on its developed state, since its early state is not only its most fluid, but usually its most delicate and important. It is precisely then, in this larval stage, that a particular religion needs to have the benefits of religious protections.

These criteria provide the basis for an unconstitutional establishment of religion. They do not establish a particular creed, to be sure, but they establish a finely specified structure as a requirement for the protections afforded to churches. There seems to be no constitutionally compelling argument that organizations with this structure should receive religious protections while other less organized "churches"—as that word is commonly understood—are denied them. What these criteria tend to do is limit the religious scene to the denominations already in existence, in violation of the establishment clause.[101]

Thus, just as the law cannot formulate an appropriate tax definition of the term "religion," it seems incapable of formulating an appropriate definition of the term "church." Probably the entanglement doctrine precludes the application of such definitions in any event.[102]

§ 8.4 Religious or Apostolic Organizations

Certain "religious or apostolic" organizations are exempt from federal income taxation, even though they are not embraced by the general reference to "religious" organizations.[103] These are "religious or apostolic associations or corporations, if such associations or corporations have a common treasury or community treasury, even if such associations or corporations engage in business

[101]Worthing, " 'Religion' and 'Religious Institutions' Under the First Amendment," *supra*, n. 58 at 344–345.

[102]See, in general, Whelan, " 'Church' in the Internal Revenue Code: The Definitional Problems," 45 *Fordham L. Rev.* 885 (1977); Worthing, "The Internal Revenue Service as a Monitor of Church Institutions: The Excessive Entanglement Problem," 45 *Fordham L. Rev.* 929 (1977); Schwarz, "Limiting Religious Tax Exemptions: When Should the Church Render Unto Caesar," 29 *Univ. Flor. L. Rev.* 50 (1976); Burns, "Constitutional Aspects of Church Taxation," 9 *Col. J. Law Social Problems* 646 (1973).

[103]Code § 501(d).

for the common benefit of the members, but only if the members thereof include (at the time of filing their returns) in their gross income their entire pro rata shares, whether distributed or not, of the taxable income of the association or corporation for such year." Any amount so included in the gross income of a member is treated as a dividend received.[104]

For purposes of determining the pro rata shares of the taxable income of a religious or apostolic organization (to be included in the members' gross income), the membership in the organization is to be determined in accordance with the rules of the organization itself and applicable state law. Individuals qualified to be members of such an organization must consent to such membership status, and parents may consent to the membership on behalf of their minor children to the extent allowed under applicable state law.[105]

The origins of these rules (in 1936) are reflected in the following excerpt from its legislative history:

> It has been brought to the attention of the committee that certain religious and apostolic associations and corporations, such as the House of David and the Shakers, have been taxed as corporations, and that since their rules prevent their members from being holders of property in an individual capacity the corporations would be subject to the undistributed-profits tax. These organizations have a small agricultural or other business. The effect of the proposed amendment is to exempt these corporations from the normal corporations tax and the undistributed-profits tax, if their members take up their shares of the corporations' income on their own individual returns. It is believed that this provision will give them relief, and their members will be subject to a fair tax.[106]

Subsequently, the Court of Appeals for the Ninth Circuit, in commenting on the type of organization contemplated by these rules, said: "One might assume, then, that Congress intended an association somewhat akin to the ordinary association or partnership in which each member has a definite, though undivided, interest in the business conducted for the common benefit of the members, as well as a common interest in the community treasury and property."[107]

Also, the statute's beginnings are traceable to the fact that "apostolic" organizations were early found to not qualify for tax exemption under the general rules for religious organizations because of the presence of commercial activities and private inurement, as discussed in the cases concerning the tax status of the Hutterische Church.[108] Few exemptions under this provision have been

---

[104]See Reg. § 1.501(d)-1(a); Rev. Rul. 58-328, 1958 1 C. B. 327; Rev. Rul. 57-574, 1957-2 C. B. 161; *Riker* v. *Commissioner, supra*. n. 41; IRS Private Letter Ruling 7740009.

[105]Rev. Rul. 77-295, 1977-2 C. B. 196.

[106]80 Cong. Rec. 9074 (1936).

[107]*Riker* v. *Commissioner, supra*, n. 41 at 230.

[108]*Hofer* v. *United States*, 64 Ct. Cl. 672 (1928); *Hutterische Bruder Gemeinde* v. *Commissioner*, 1 B. T. A. 1208 (1925).

granted; the most notable example may be the 1939 determination of exemption thereunder accorded the Israelite House of David.[109] The courts appear to prefer to cope with organizations of this nature in the context of the law applicable to religious groups generally.[110]

Organizations contemplated by these rules are those that are supported by internally operated businesses in which all the members have an individual interest. In one instance, a communal religious organization did not conduct any business activities and instead was supported by the wages of some of its members who were engaged in outside employment and thus was ruled to not qualify as a religious or apostolic organization.[111]

It is the position of the IRS (general counsel) that failure to qualify as an apostolic organization under these rules does not preclude the possibility that an organization may qualify as a communal religious organization.[112] In other words, the Service does not believe that Congress occupied the field with respect to tax exemption of all communal religious organizations in enacting the rules for apostolic organizations.

[109]See *Blume* v. *Gardner*, 262 F.Supp. 405, 408 (W.D. Mich. 1966), aff'd 397 F.2d 809 (6th Cir. 1968). Also *Israelite House of David* v. *United States*, 58 F.Supp. 862 (W.D. Mich. 1945); *People* v. *Israelite House of David*, 225 N.W. 638 (Sup. Ct. Mich. 1929).

[110]See *Golden Rule Church Association* v. *Commissioner*, 41 T.C. 719 (1964); *State* v. *King Colony Ranch*, 350 P.2d 841 (Sup. Ct. Mont. 1960).

[111]Rev. Rul. 78-100, 1978 1 C. B. 162.

[112]GCM 38827 (Dec. 7, 1981). In general, see Note, "Mail Order Ministries, the Religious Purpose Exemption, and the Constitution," 33 *Tax Law.* 959 (1980); Kelley, "Why Churches Do Not Pay Taxes," XIII *The Philanthropy Monthly* 20 (Nov. 1980); Jackson, "Are Churches Charitable or Public Trusts?," XIII *The Philanthropy Monthly* 21 (Nov. 1980); Brancato, "Characterization in Religious Property Tax-Exemption: What is Religious? A Survey and a Proposed Definition and Approach," 44 *Notre Dame Law.* 60 (1968); Consedine and Whelan, "Church Tax Exemptions," 15 *Catholic Law.* 93 (1969); Hurvich, *Religion and the Taxing Power,*" 35 *U. Cinn. L. Rev.* 531 (1966); Katz, "Radiations from Church Tax Exemption," 1970 *Sup. Ct. Rev.* 93 (1970); Korbel, "Do the Federal Income Tax Laws Involve an 'Establishment of Religion?'," 53 *A. B. A. J.* 1018 (1967); Note, "Aid to Religion Through Taxation," 43 *Notre Dame Law.* 756 (1968); Boyan, "Defining Religion in Operational and Institutional Terms," 116 *U. Pa. L. Rev.* 479 (1967–1968); Note, "Constitutionality of Tax Exemptions Accorded American Church Property," 30 *Albany L. Rev.* 58 (1966); Van Alstyne, "Tax Exemption of Church Property," *Ohio State L. J.* 461 (1959); Stimson, "The Exemption of Churches from Taxation," 18 *Taxes* 361 (1940); Zollman, "Tax Exemption of American Church Property," 14 *Mich. L. Rev.* 646 (1916).

9

The Scientific Organization

Code § 501(c)(3) provides federal income tax exemption for organizations organized and operated exclusively for "scientific" purposes.[1]

Basically, a "scientific" organization is one engaged in scientific research or otherwise operated for the dissemination of scientific knowledge. A fundamental requirement underlying this form of tax exemption is that the organization must serve a public rather than a private interest.[2] Thus, the tax-exempt scientific organization must, among the other criteria for the exemption, be organized and operated in the public interest.[3]

§ 9.1 Concept of "Research"

In this area, the focus is largely on the concept of "research." "Research," when taken alone, is a word with various meanings—it is not synonymous with "scientific." Inasmuch as the nature of particular research depends upon the purpose which it serves, for research to be "scientific," it must be carried on in furtherance of a scientific purpose. Thus, the term "scientific" includes the carrying on of scientific research in the public interest.

The determination as to whether research is scientific does not depend on whether the research is classified as "fundamental" or "basic" as contrasted with "applied" or "practical." However, federal tax law excludes from unrelated business taxable income, in the case of an organization operated primarily for purposes of carrying on fundamental research the results of which are freely available to the general public, all income derived from research performed for any person and all deductions directly connected therewith.[4] For purposes of the unrelated income rules, therefore, it is necessary to determine whether

[1]Reg. § 1.501(c)(3)-1(d)(1)(i)(c).
[2]Reg. §§ 1.501(a)-1(c), 1.501(c)(3)-1(c)(2).
[3]Reg. § 1.501(c)(3)-1(d)(5)(i).
[4]Code § 512(b)(9).

the organization is operated primarily for purposes of carrying on "fundamental," as contrasted with "applied," research.[5]

Consequently, scientific research does not include activities ordinarily carried on incident to commercial operations, as, for example, the testing or inspection of materials or products or the designing or construction of equipment or buildings.[6] For example, an organization which fosters the development of machinery in connection with a commercial operation, and is empowered to sell, assign and grant licenses with respect to its copyrights, trademarks, trade names, or patent rights, is not engaged in scientific research.[7] Similarly, an organization that tests drugs for commercial pharmaceutical companies was held to not qualify for tax exemption because the testing was regarded as principally serving the private interests of the manufacturers.[8] Likewise, an organization that inspects, tests, and certifies for safety shipping containers used in the transport of cargo, and engages in related research activities, is not engaged in scientific research because these activities are an incident to commercial or industrial operations.[9]

Scientific research is regarded as carried on in the public interest if the results of the research (including any patents, copyrights, processes, or formulas) are made available to the public on a nondiscriminatory basis, if the research is performed for the United States, or any of its agencies or instrumentalities, or for a state or political subdivision thereof, or if the research is directed toward benefiting the public.[10] Examples of scientific research which is considered as meeting this last criterion include scientific research carried on for the purpose of aiding in the scientific education of college or university students, obtaining scientific information which is published in a form that is available to the interested public, discovering a cure for a disease, or aiding a community or geographical area by attracting new industry thereto or by encouraging the development of, or retention of, an industry in the community or area. Scientific research is regarded as carried on in the public interest even though research is performed pursuant to a contract or agreement under which the sponsor of the research has the right to obtain ownership or control of any patents, copyrights, processes, or formulas resulting from research.[11] Thus, an organization formed by physicians to research heart disease was ruled to be exempt as a scientific organization.[12] An organization engaged in conducting research programs in the social sciences may qualify as a scientific organization.[13]

[5]Reg. § 1.501(c)(3)-1(d)(5)(i).
[6]Reg. § 1.501(c)(3)-1(d)(5)(ii). See Rev. Rul. 68-373, 1968-2 C. B. 206.
[7]Rev. Rul. 65-1, 1965-1 C. B. 226.
[8]Rev. Rul. 68-373, *supra*, n. 6; IRS Private Letter Ruling 8020009.
[9]Rev. Rul. 78-426, 1978-2 C. B. 175.
[10]Reg. § 1.501(c)(3)-1(d)(5)(iii).
[11]*Ibid*.
[12]Rev. Rul. 69-526, 1969-2 C. B. 115. Also see *Commissioner* v. *Orton*, 173 F.2d 483 (6th Cir. 1949).
[13]Rev. Rul. 65-60, 1965-1 C. B. 231.

The IRS unsuccessfully asserted that an organization that conducts a crop seed certification program and scientific research in seed technology is engaged in activities of a type ordinarily conducted incident to commercial operations and serves the private interests of commercial seed producers and commercial farmers. But a court concluded that the scientific research involved qualified the organization for tax exemption because the research is being conducted either pursuant to its delegated authority as the official seed certification agency for a state or in conjunction with the state's designated agency for agricultural research and experimentation. Also, the research was considered carried on for public rather than private interests because the research is performed for a state or political subdivision thereof, because the results of the research are made available to the public on a nondiscriminatory basis, and because the research is directed toward benefiting the public. While conceding that "the majority of persons interested in seed technology may well come from the agricultural community," the court stated that that "does not mean that farmers and gardeners are not an important part of the general public."[14]

The IRS accorded categorization as a scientific organization to a membership organization formed to encourage and assist in the establishment of nonprofit regional health data systems, conduct scientific studies and propose improvements with regard to quality, utilization, and effectiveness of health care and health care agencies, and to educate those involved in furnishing, administering and financing health care.[15] The Service observed that "[b]y improving and enlarging the body of knowledge concerning current usage of health facilities and methods of treatment, the organization seeks to create a more efficient use of the nation's health facilities, and to aid in the planning of better care for future health needs." The IRS also ruled that an organization formed to develop scientific methods for the diagnosis, prevention, and treatment of diseases, and to disseminate the results of its developmental work to members of the medical profession and the general public, qualifies for tax exemption as a scientific entity.[16]

§ 9.2   Requirement of "Public Interest"

An organization is not regarded as organized or operated for the purpose of carrying on scientific research in the public interest and, consequently, will

[14]*Indiana Crop Improvement Association, Inc.* v. *Commissioner,* 76 T.C. 394, 400 (1981).

[15]Rev. Rul. 76-455, 1976-2 C. B. 150.

[16]Rev. Rul. 65-298, 1965-2 C. B. 163. Cf. Rev. Rul. 74-553, 1974-2 C. B. 168. When Congress enacted the Economic Recovery Tax Act of 1981 (95 Stat. 172), it created a 25 percent tax credit for certain research and experimental expenditures paid in carrying on a trade or business. Code § 44F. This credit is available for, *inter alia,* "basic research" expenses. That term is defined to mean "any original investigation for the advancement of scientific knowledge not having a specific commercial objective, except that such term shall not include (A) basic research conducted outside the United States, and (B) basic research in the social sciences or humanities."

not qualify as a "scientific" organization for federal tax purposes if (1) it performs research only for persons which are (directly or indirectly) its creators and which are not "charitable" organizations or (2) it retains (directly or indirectly) the ownership or control of more than an insubstantial portion of the patents, copyrights, processes, or formulas resulting from its research and does not make the items available to the public on a nondiscriminatory basis. In addition, although one person is granted the exclusive right to the use of a patent, copyright, process, or formula, it is considered as made available to the public if the granting of the exclusive right is the only practicable manner in which the patent, copyright, process, or formula can be utilized to benefit the public. In such a case, however, the research from which the patent, copyright, process, or formula resulted will be regarded as carried on in the public interest only if it is carried on for the United States (or instrumentality thereof) or a state (or political subdivision thereof) or if it is scientific research which is directed toward benefiting the public.[17]

These distinctions were the subject of a 1976 IRS ruling discussing the exempt organizations tax treatment of commercially sponsored scientific research, which is scientific research undertaken pursuant to contracts with private industries.[18] Under these contracts, the sponsor pays for the research and receives the right to the results of the research and all ownership rights in any patents resulting from work on the project.

Where the results and other relevant information of the commercially sponsored projects are "generally published in such form as to be available to the interested public either currently, as developments in the project warrant, or within a reasonably short time after completion of the project," the organization is considered to be engaging in scientific research in the public interest. Publication of the research is not required in advance of the time at which it can be made public without jeopardy to the sponsor's right by reasonably diligent action to secure any patents or copyrights resulting from the research. By contrast, the carrying on of sponsored research is considered the conduct of an unrelated trade or business[19] where the organization agrees, at the sponsor's request, to "forego publication of the results of a particular project in order to protect against disclosure of processes or technical data which the sponsor desires to keep secret for various business reasons" or where the research results are withheld beyond the time reasonably necessary to obtain patents or copyrights.

§ 9.3   "Scientific" as "Educational" or "Charitable"

Organizations qualifying as "scientific" may also be exempt as educational or charitable. For example, an organization formed to survey scientific and medical literature published throughout the world and to prepare and distribute free abstracts of the literature was ruled to be both charitable and scientific in

---

[17]Reg. § 1.501(c)(3)-1(d)(5)(iv).
[18]Rev. Rul. 76-296, 1976-2 C. B. 141. Cf. IRS Private Letter Ruling 8020009.
[19]See Chapter 42.

nature.[20] An organization engaged in research on human diseases, developing scientific methods for treatment, and disseminating its results through physicians' seminars was determined to be an educational organization.[21] Also, an engineering society created to engage in scientific research in the areas of heating, ventilating, and air conditioning for the benefit of the general public was deemed to qualify as an educational and scientific organization.[22]

However, an organization composed of members of an industry to develop new and improved uses for products of the industry was ruled to not be an exempt scientific organization on the ground that it was serving the private interests of its creators.[23] By contrast, an organization formed by a group of physicians specializing in heart disease to research the cause and publish treatments of heart defects was found to be an exempt scientific organization.[24] In the latter instance, any personal benefit (in the form of increased prestige and enhanced reputation) derived by the physician-creators was deemed not to lessen the public benefits flowing from the organization's operations.

[20]Rev. Rul. 66-147, 1966-1 C. B. 137. Also *Science & Research Foundation, Inc.* v. *United States*, 181 F.Supp. 526 (S.D. Ill. 1960); *Forest Press, Inc.* v. *Commissioner*, 22 T.C. 265 (1954).

[21]Rev. Rul. 65-298, *supra*, n. 16.

[22]Rev. Rul. 71-506, 1971-2 C. B. 233. Also *American Kennel Club, Inc.* v. *Hoey*, 148 F.2d 920 (2d Cir. 1945).

[23]Rev. Rul. 69-632, 1969-2 C. B. 120. Also see *Medical Diagnostic Association* v. *Commissioner*, 42 B. T. A. 610 (1940).

[24]Rev. Rul. 69-526, *supra*, n. 12. In general, see Sugarman and Mancino, "Tax Aspects of University Patent Policy," 3 *J. Coll. Univ. L.* (No. 1) 41 (1976); Wolfman, "Federal Tax Policy and the Support of Science," 114 *Univ. Pa. L. Rev.* 171 (1965); Gray, "What Is 'Research' For the Purpose of Exemption?," *5th Biennial N.Y.U. Conf. on Char. Fdns.* 233 (1961).

10

Other Code § 501(c)(3) Organizations

Aside from the organizations discussed in the previous four chapters, Code § 501(c)(3) provides exemption for certain organizations which are organized and operated for literary purposes, test for public safety, prevent cruelty to children and animals, operate on a cooperative basis, or qualify as amateur sports organizations.

§ 10.1 The "Literary" Organization

The IRS rarely rules that an organization is tax-exempt because it is a "literary" organization.[1] Presumably, the concept is encompassed by the terms "charitable" and "educational."

§ 10.2 Public Safety Testing Organizations

In 1943, the U.S. Court of Appeals for the Seventh Circuit held that an organization, which conducted tests, experiments, and investigations into the causes of losses against which insurance companies provide coverage, was neither charitable, scientific, nor educational.[2] Congress responded by providing tax-exempt status for organizations which engage in "testing for public safety." This term includes "the testing of consumer products, such as electrical products, to determine whether they are safe for use by the general public."[3]

This provision was the basis for tax exemption for an organization which

---

[1]See Reg. § 1.501(c)(3)-1(d)(1)(i)(e). In general, see Trenberry, "A Literary Pilgrim's Progress Along Section 501(c)(3)," 51 *A.B.A.J.* 252 (1965).

[2]*Underwriters' Laboratory, Inc.* v. *Commissioner*, 135 F.2d 371 (7th Cir. 1943), cert. den. 320 U.S. 756 (1943).

[3]Reg. § 1.501(c)(3)-1(d)(4). Also Reg. § 1.501(c)(3)-1(d)(1)(i)(d).

tested boating equipment and established safety standards for products used aboard pleasure craft by the boating public.[4] However, an organization which clinically tested drugs for commercial pharmaceutical companies was denied tax exemption under this provision, on the ground that the testing principally served the private interests of the manufacturer and that a drug is not a "consumer product" until it is approved for marketing by the Food and Drug Administration.[5] Similarly, an organization, the activities of which include the inspection, testing, and safety certification of cargo shipping containers, and research, development, and reporting of information in the field of containerization, was denied tax exemption under this provision because these activities serve the private interests of manufacturers and shippers by facilitating their operations in international commerce.[6]

These organizations are expressly exempted from classification as private foundations.[7] However, contributions, bequests, or gifts to public safety testing organizations (as such) are not deductible, inasmuch as no provision has been made therefor in the charitable contribution deduction rules.[8]

§ 10.3   Prevention of Cruelty Organizations

Code § 501(c)(3) provides tax exemption for organizations which are organized and operated exclusively for the "prevention of cruelty to children or animals."[9]

An organization which acts to prevent the birth of unwanted animals and their eventual suffering by providing funds for pet owners who cannot afford the spaying or neutering operation was ruled tax-exempt under this provision,[10] as was an organization which seeks to secure humane treatment of laboratory animals.[11]

An organization to protect children from working at hazardous occupations in violation of state laws and in unfavorable work conditions is an organization established to prevent cruelty to children.[12]

§ 10.4   Cooperative Hospital Service Organizations

"Cooperative hospital service organizations" are deemed to be charitable organizations[13] and are not private foundations.[14]

---

[4]Rev. Rul. 65-61, 1965-1 C. B. 234.
[5]Rev. Rul. 68-373, 1968-2 C. B. 206; IRS Private Letter Ruling 8020009.
[6]Rev. Rul. 78-426, 1978-2 C. B. 175.
[7]Code § 509(a)(4). See Chapter 22.
[8]Code §§ 170, 2055, 2106, and 2522.
[9]Reg. § 1.501(c)(3)-1(d)(1)(i)(g).
[10]Rev. Rul. 74-194, 1974-1 C. B. 129.
[11]Rev. Rul. 66-359, 1966-2 C. B. 219.
[12]Rev. Rul. 67-151, 1967-1 C. B. 134.
[13]Code § 501(e).
[14]Code §§ 170(b)(1)(A)(iii) and 509(a)(1). See Chapter 22.

These organizations must be organized and operated solely for two or more tax-exempt member hospitals and must be organized and operated on a cooperative basis. They must perform certain specified services[15] on a centralized basis for their members, namely, data processing, purchasing,[16] warehousing, billing and collection, food, clinical,[17] industrial engineering,[18] laboratory, printing, communications, records center, and personnel (including selection, testing, training, and education of personnel) services. To qualify, these services must constitute exempt activities if performed on its own behalf by a participating hospital.[19]

The IRS takes the position that, to qualify as a cooperative hospital service organization, the organization may provide only the services specified in the specific authorizing legislation.[20] This position is based upon the legislative history of the provision.[21] Thus, the Service has ruled that a cooperative hospital laundry service cannot be tax-exempt as a "charitable" organization by reason of these specific rules, and has observed that such an entity may qualify as a tax-exempt cooperative.[22] However, it has been expressly held by a court that an organization that qualifies under the cooperative hospital service organizations rules may nonetheless also qualify as charitable organizations.[23]

One court, in a case involving a centralized laundry service operated for tax-exempt hospitals, has held that the organization qualifies for status as a char-

---

[15]Code § 501(e)(1)(A).

[16]An organization performs the service of "purchasing" when it buys equipment for one of its patron hospitals, even though it holds legal title to the equipment, where that arrangement is used merely as a convenience to the hospital, which remains the beneficial owner of and solely responsible for paying for the equipment. Rev. Rul. 80-316, 1980-2 C. B. 172.

[17]The term "clinical" was added to the list of specified services by the Tax Reform Act of 1976.

[18]See Rev. Rul. 74-443, 1974-2 C. B. 159.

[19]See Rev. Rul. 69-633, 1969-2 C. B. 121. In general, see Tuthill, "Qualifying as a Tax Exempt Cooperative Hospital Service Organization," 50 *Notre Dame Law.* 448 (1975).

[20]Rev. Rul. 69-160, 1969-1 C. B. 147.

[21]H. Rep. No. 1533, 90th Cong., 2d Sess. (1968) at 1, 20. Also see S. Rep. No. 744, 90th Cong., 1st Sess. (1967) at 200–201; H. Rep. No. 1030, 90th Cong., 1st Sess. (1967) at 73.

[22]Rev. Rul. 69-633, *supra*, n. 19. (The rules concerning cooperative organizations are at Code §§ 1381–1383.) The enactment of Code § 501(e) in 1968 does not nullify the holding of the Court of Claims in *Hospital Bureau of Standards and Supplies, Inc.* v. *United States*, 158 F.Supp. 560 (Ct. Cl. 1958) (see Chapter 6). See, e.g., *American Potash & Chemical Corp.* v. *United States*, 399 F.2d 194 (Ct. Cl. 1968). Services performed in the employ of a cooperative hospital service organization described in Code § 501(e) are exempted from "employment" for purposes of the F.I.C.A. and the F.U.T.A.; however, for purposes of the F.I.C.A., the exemption may be waived by the organization if it files a waiver certificate (Form SS-15). Rev. Rul. 74-493, 1974-2 C. B. 327.

[23]*Chart, Inc.* v. *United States*, 491 F.Supp. 10 (D.D.C. 1979).

itable entity, notwithstanding these specific rules.[24] The court maintained that the "question of whether it [the plaintiff organization] is organized and operated for an exempt purpose is a question of fact for this Court to decide." Commenting on the rules for certain hospital cooperatives, the court said: "The clearly expressed Congressional purpose behind the enactment of § 501(e) was to enlarge the category of charitable organizations under § 501(c)(3) to include certain cooperative hospital service organizations, and not to narrow or restrict the reach of § 501(c)(3)." Since the organization was operational prior to the enactment of these rules, the court, having concluded that it is charitable in nature, found the specific rules irrelevant to the case.[25]

The Senate Finance Committee's version of the Tax Reform Act of 1976 contained a provision,[26] which would have inserted "laundry" services in the statutory enumeration of permissible services. The Finance Committee had observed that "it is appropriate to encourage the creation and operation of cooperative service organizations by exempt hospitals because of the cost savings to the hospitals and their patients that result from providing certain services, such as laundry and clinical services, on a cooperative basis."[27] However, this provision was defeated on the floor of the Senate.[28]

Since the enactment of these specific rules in 1968,[29] there has been considerable controversy as to the meaning and scope of the provision in relation to the general rules defining "charitable" entities.[30] In essence, there have been two competing views: the hospital cooperative rules were enacted to (1) provide the exclusive and controlling means by which a cooperative hospital service organization can achieve tax exemption, so that such an organization that fails to satisfy the requirements of the rules thereby fails to qualify as a charitable organization[31] or (2) enlarge the category of charitable organizations to include certain types of cooperative hospital service organizations, so that it does not narrow or restrict the reach of the rules defining "charitable" organizations generally.[32]

---

[24]*United Hospital Services, Inc.* v. *United States*, 384 F.Supp. 776 (S.D. Ind. 1974).

[25]Also see *Northern California Central Services, Inc.* v. *United States*, 591 F.2d 620 (Ct. Cl. 1979).

[26]H.R. 10612 (1976) (as reported by the Senate Committee on Finance) § 2509.

[27]S. Rep. No. 94-938 (Part 2), 94th Cong., 2d Sess. (1976) at 76.

[28]Amendment No. 315, 122 Cong. Rec. 25915 (1976).

[29]P.L. 90-374, 90th Cong., 2d Sess. (1968), § 109(a), 82Stat. 269.

[30]Code § 501(c)(3).

[31]See, e.g., *HCSC-Laundry* v. *United States*, 624 F.2d 428 (3d Cir. 1980), rev'g 473 F.Supp. 250 (E.D. Pa. 1979); *Metropolitan Detroit Area Hospital Services, Inc.* v. *United States*, 634 F.2d 330 (6th Cir. 1980), rev'g 445 F.Supp. 857 (E.D. Mich. 1978); *Community Hospital Services, Inc.* v. *United States*, 47 AFTR 2d 81-999 (6th Cir. 1981), rev'g 43 AFTR 2d 79-934 (E.D. Mich. 1979); *Hospital Central Services Assn.* v. *United States*, 623 F.2d 611 (9th Cir. 1980), rev'g 40 AFTR 2d 77-5646 (W.D. Wash. 1977).

[32]See, e.g., *Northern California Central Services, Inc.* v. *United States*, 591 F.2d 620 (Ct. Cl. 1979); *United Hospital Services, Inc.* v. *United States, supra*, n. 24; *Chart, Inc.* v. *United States, supra*, n. 23.

In a 1981 per curiam decision, the U.S. Supreme Court ruled that the first of these two views is the correct one.[33] In reaching this conclusion, the Court utilized a statutory construction rationale (namely, the rule that a specific statute controls over a general provision, particularly where the two are interrelated and closely positioned[34]), but principally relied on the legislative history underlying the rules for hospital cooperatives. The case involved a cooperative laundry organization serving tax-exempt entities and, as noted, laundry service is not specifically referenced in the rules despite efforts in 1978 and 1976 to include such a reference.[35] The Court thus determined that:

> In view of all this, it seems to us beyond dispute that subsection (e)(1)(A) of § 501, despite the seemingly broad general language of subsection (c)(3), specifies the types of hospital service organizations that are encompassed within the scope of § 501 as charitable organizations. Inasmuch as laundry service was deliberately omitted from the statutory list and, indeed, specifically was refused inclusion in that list, it inevitably follows that petitioner is not entitled to tax-exempt status. The Congress easily can change the statute whenever it is so inclined.[36]

This decision is accompanied by a dissent (which, in the author's view, is the correct interpretation of the law) that holds that the proper analysis commences with an evaluation of the overall statutory scheme, without reference to any legislative history. The dissent notes that the rules for these cooperatives are not structured as an exception to the rules providing tax exemption for "charitable" entities[37] and concludes that its purpose is to enlarge the category of charitable organizations. As regards the legislative history, the dissent concludes that enactment of these rules "unambiguously granted a tax exemption to certain entities that arguably already were entitled to an exemption under [Code] § 501(c)(3)" and that "[t]here is absolutely no evidence that the 1968 statute was intended to withdraw any benefits that were already available under the 1954 Act."[38] The dissent views the congressional actions in 1968 and 1976 as meaning that hospital laundry cooperatives cannot qualify under these specific rules but not that they cannot qualify under the rules concerning charitable organizations in general.

The principal flaw in the Supreme Court majority opinion is its holding that these specific rules represent a determination by Congress as to the types of cooperative hospital organizations that can qualify for tax exemption as "charitable" entities. If that is in fact the law, then a cooperative hospital organization created before 1968 and recognized as having tax exemption would, if it cannot satisfy the specific rules, have its recognition of tax exemption revoked; there

---

[33]*HCSC-Laundry* v. *United States*, 450 U.S. 1 (1981), aff'g 624 F.2d 428 (3d Cir. 1980).

[34]Citing *Bulova Watch Co.* v. *United States*, 365 U.S. 753, 761 (1961).

[35]Ns. 21, 26–28, *supra*.

[36]*HCSC-Laundry* v. *United States*, *supra*, n. 33, at 8.

[37]Code §§ 501(a) and 501(c)(3). Cf. Code §§ 502 and 503.

[38]*HCSC-Laundry* v. *United States*, *supra*, n. 36 at 20.

is no legislative history indicating that Congress intended such a result.[39] More significantly, the logic of this majority opinion is that Congress, in enacting the rules for hospital service cooperatives and educational service cooperatives[40] legislated as to the entire subject of the tax status of cooperative organizations and thus that a cooperative organization that cannot satisfy either set of rules for service cooperatives cannot qualify as a "charitable" entity. This a result is clearly not the law.[41] The fact is that Congress enacted the hospital cooperative rules solely in the hope of forestalling adverse IRS policy concerning hospital cooperatives but did so in a way that enabled the Service to circumvent the intent of Congress by devising a unique interpretation of the legislative history and then by convincing the appellate courts of the efficacy of this interpretation.[42]

§ 10.5   Cooperative Educational Service Organizations

"Cooperative service organizations of operating educational organizations" are deemed to be charitable organizations.[43]

These organizations must be organized and controlled by and comprised solely of members which are private or public educational institutions.[44] They must be organized and operated solely to hold, commingle, and collectively invest and reinvest (including arranging for and supervising the performance by independent contractors of investment services related thereto), in stocks and securities, the monies contributed thereto by each of the members of the organization, and to collect income therefrom and turn over the entire amount, less expenses, to its members.

These rules were enacted to forestall the contemplated revocation by the IRS of the tax-exempt status of The Common Fund, a cooperative arrangement formed by a large group of colleges and universities for the collective investment of their funds. During its formative years, the management and administrative expenses of the Fund were largely met by start-up grants from a private foundation. However, as the Fund became more reliant upon payments from its member institutions, the IRS decided that this factor alone disqualified the Fund for tax-exempt status.[45] In the face of loss of the Fund's tax exemption,

[39]See *United Hospital Services, Inc.* v. *United States, supra,* n. 24.

[40]See § 5 hereof, *infra.*

[41]See Chapter 6 § 9 at 112-119.

[42]The decision in *HCSC-Laundry* v. *United States, supra,* n. 38, should be contrasted with another 1981 Supreme Court decision, where the Court went out of its way to ignore directly pertinent legislative history and to interpret a statute in a manner wholly inconsistent with congressional intent, so as to avoid constitutional law difficulties, finding that approach "simpler and more reasonable." *St. Martin Evangelical Lutheran Church* v. *South Dakota,* 451 U.S. 772, 782 (1981).

[43]Code § 501(f).

[44]This means organizations defined in Code § 170(b)(1)(A) (ii) or (iv). See Chapter 22.

[45]See S. Rep. No. 93-888, 93d Cong. 2d Sess. (1974) at 2–3. See Chapter 6, § 7 thereof.

Congress made it clear that cooperative arrangements for investment of the type typified by The Common Fund are eligible for tax exemption as "charitable" entities.

§ 10.6　Amateur Sports Organizations

The newest category of "charitable" organization is the amateur athletic organization, added by the Tax Reform Act of 1976. This exemption was accomplished by adding to the tax-exempt organizations rules[46] and the charitable contribution deduction rules[47] the following phraseology: " . . . or to foster national or international amateur sports competition (but only if no part of its activities involve the provision of athletic facilities or equipment)."

The legislative history of this provision contains the observation that, under prior law, organizations which "teach youth or which are affiliated with charitable organizations" may qualify as charitable entities and may receive charitable contributions but that organizations which foster national or international sports competition may be granted tax exemption as social welfare organizations[48] or business leagues[49] and hence are ineligible to receive deductible contributions. This history also states, as respects the parenthetical limitation, that "[t]his restriction . . . is intended to prevent the allowance of these benefits for organizations which, like social clubs, provide facilities and equipment for their members."[50]

The parenthetical prohibition is a limitation only upon the purpose added in 1976, that is, it is not a limitation on the tax exemption and charitable contribution provisions generally. Thus, a private foundation was advised by the IRS that it may make a grant to a state university-related foundation for the purpose of constructing an aquatic complex as an integral part of the university's educational program, with the grant constituting a qualifying distribution,[51] because it will be made to accomplish educational and charitable purposes.[52]

---

[46]Code § 501(c)(3).

[47]Code §§ 170(c)(2)(B), 2055(a)(2), and 2522(a)(2).

[48]Code § 501(c)(4). See Chapter 15.

[49]Code § 501(c)(6). See Chapter 17.

[50]Joint Committee on Taxation, "General Explanation of the Tax Reform Act of 1976," 94th Cong., 2d Sess. (1976) at 423–424.

[51]See Chapter 26, § 2.

[52]IRS Private Letter Ruling 8037103. Congress, upon enactment of the Tax Equity and Fiscal Responsibility Act of 1982, created Code § 501(j), which states that, in the case of a "qualified amateur sports organization" (as defined in Code § 501(j)(2)), the requirement in Code § 501(c)(3) that no part of its activities involve the provision of athletic facilities or equipment shall not apply (Code § 501(j)(1)).

This provision, which was not intended to adversely affect the qualification for charitable status of any organization which would qualify under the standards of preexisting law, became effective on October 4, 1976.[53]

[53]Tax Reform Act of 1976, § 2702(c), (d).

11

Concept of "Exclusively"

Code § 501(c)(3) provides that an organization must, to qualify thereunder, be organized and operated "exclusively" for an exempt purpose. Invocation of the concept of "exclusively" is infrequent, inasmuch as the focus is generally on the existence of an exempt purpose, evidence of private inurement, or taxation of unrelated business income. However, it is clear that the term "exclusively" as employed in this context does not mean "solely" but rather "primarily" in the sense of "substantially."[1]

§ 11.1 "Primary Purpose" Rule

The general rule, as stated by the Supreme Court in 1945, is that the "presence of a single . . . [nonexempt] purpose, if substantial in nature, will destroy the exemption regardless of the number or importance of truly . . . [exempt] purposes."[2] The U.S. Court of Appeals for the Eighth Circuit has held that nonexempt activity will not result in loss or denial of exemption where it is "only incidental and less than substantial" and that a "slight and comparatively unimportant deviation from the narrow furrow of tax approved activity is not fatal."[3] In the words of the IRS, the rules applicable to "charitable" organizations in general have "been construed as requiring all the resources of the organization [other than an insubstantial part] to be applied to the pursuit of one or more of the exempt purposes therein specified."[4] So, the existence of one or more truly exempt purposes of an organization will not be productive

[1]See Reg. § 1.501(c)(3)-1(c)(1). Also see Reg. § 1.501(c)(3)-1(a)(1).

[2]*Better Business Bureau of Washington, D. C.* v. *United States*, 326 U.S. 279, 283 (1945).

[3]*St. Louis Union Trust Co.* v. *United States*, 374 F.2d 427, 431–432 (8th Cir. 1967). Also see *Seasongood* v. *Commissioner*, 227 F.2d 907, 910 (6th Cir. 1955).

[4]Rev. Rul. 77-366, 1977-2 C. B. 192.

of tax exemption as a "charitable" entity if there is present in its operations a substantial nonexempt purpose.[5]

It is essential to observe at the outset that the doctrine of "exclusively" looks—in a rule frequently honored in its breach—to an organization's purposes rather than its activities.[6] The focus should not be on an organization's primary activities as the test of tax exemption but on whether the activities accomplish one or more tax-exempt purposes.[7] This is why, for example, an organization may engage in nonexempt or profit making activities and nonetheless qualify for tax exemption.[8]

The proper approach to be taken, therefore, when determining whether an organization qualifies as a "charitable" entity, is to assume *arguendo* one or more tax-exempt purposes and endeavor to ascertain whether the organization has a commercial or other nonexempt purpose. Upon finding a nonexempt purpose, an inquiry need be made as to whether it is primary or incidental to the exempt purposes.[9] Then, if there is a nonexempt purpose that is substantial in nature, the exemption would be precluded.

This approach is not always taken, however, as illustrated by the case involving a would-be religious organization that was denied tax exemption on the ground of the exclusivity doctrine.[10] The disqualifying aspect of its activities was that the organization made grants that "carried with them no legal obligation to repay any interest or principal" and as to which the organization was "unable to furnish any documented criteria which would demonstrate the selection process of a deserving recipient, the reason for specific amounts given, or the purpose of the grant."[11] However, the statutory and regulatory law contains no criteria by which public charities are to consider and award grants.[12]

The difficulties inherent in applying the "exclusively" test are amply illustrated by a 1979 U.S. Tax Court case, where the opinion initially prepared as the majority holding was converted by the full court into a dissenting opinion. At issue was the tax status of an organization that operates a pharmacy which sells prescription drugs at cost to the elderly and handicapped. The court held

[5]*Stevens Bros. Foundation* v. *Commissioner*, 324 F.2d 633 (8th Cir. 1963), cert. den. 376 U.S. 969 (1964); *Scripture Press Foundation* v. *United States*, 285 F.2d 800, 806 (Ct. Cl. 1961), cert. den. 368 U.S. 985 (1962); *Fides Publishers Association* v. *United States*, 263 F.Supp. 924, 935 (N.D. Ind. 1967); *Edgar* v. *Commissioner*, 56 T.C. 717, 755 (1971).

[6]See Reg. § 1.501(c)(3)-1(c)(1).

[7]*Aid to Artisans, Inc.* v. *Commissioner*, 71 T.C. 202 (1978).

[8]See Chapter 4 § 2; § 3 hereof, *infra*.

[9]*American Institute for Economic Research* v. *United States*, 302 F.2d 934 (Ct. Cl. 1962); *Edward Orton, Jr., Ceramic Foundation* v. *Commissioner*, 56 T.C. 147 (1971); *Pulpit Resource* v. *Commissioner*, 70 T.C. 594 (1978); *Aid to Artisans, Inc.* v. *Commissioner, supra*, n. 7.

[10]*Church In Boston* v. *Commissioner*, 71 T.C. 102 (1978).

[11]*Ibid.* at 106–107.

[12]Cf. Code § 4945(d), applicable only to private foundations (see Chapter 29 § 3).

that the organization did not constitute a charitable entity, inasmuch as it did not use its surplus receipts to provide drugs to these persons below cost and it is in competition with profit-making drug stores. Contrary arguments that the organization operates to promote health and relieve the financial distress of a charitable class were unavailing. The dissenting opinion took the position that an organization's activities are not to be evaluated in a vacuum but in the context of accomplishment of tax-exempt purposes, that generation of a profit is not a *per se* bar to tax exemption, and that the organization is not being operated for commercial ends but rather to promote health.[13]

This doctrine was subsequently applied in an opinion denying tax-exempt status as a religious entity to an organization that operates a mountain lodge as a retreat facility.[14] While the organization contended that "its primary purpose is to provide a religious retreat facility for Christian families where they may come to reflect upon and worship the Lord in a setting free from the outside interferences of everyday life," the government asserted that its "substantial, if not sole, purpose is to provide a facility where guests can relax, socialize and engage in recreational activities, or, in other words, to operate a vacation resort."[15] The court held that the organization is not operated "exclusively" for religious (or other tax-exempt) purposes largely because of the organization's inability to demonstrate that "the recreational facilities were not used extensively and were not used in more than an insubstantial manner."[16] The court also appeared concerned with the fact that a guest at the lodge is not required to participate in any type of religious activity and that the organization is governed and was initially funded by members of the same family.[17]

§ 11.2   Erosion of the Concept

Some recent cases would indicate that the concept of "exclusively" is declining in relative importance. Perhaps this erosion is most detectable in an opinion from the U.S. Court of Appeals for the Ninth Circuit where a public parking facility was accorded categorization as a charitable organization.[18] The organization was formed by several private businesses and professional persons

[13]*Federation Pharmacy Services, Inc.* v. *Commissioner,* 72 T.C. 687 (1979), aff'd 80-2 U.S.T.C. ¶ 9553 (8th Cir. 1980).

[14]*The Schoger Foundation* v. *Commissioner,* 76 T.C. 380 (1981).

[15]*Ibid.* at 386.

[16]*Id.* at 388.

[17]At the same time, in a showing as to how the "exclusivity" doctrine can dictate the outcome of a case, the court observed that "[i]n a proper factual case, the operation of a lodge as a religious retreat facility would no doubt constitute an exempt religious purpose under section 501(c)(3), and the presence of some incidental recreational or social activities might even be found to be activities to further or accomplish that exempt purpose" (*Id.* at 389).

[18]*Monterey Public Parking Corp.* v. *United States,* 431 F.2d 175 (9th Cir. 1973), aff'g 321 F.Supp. 972 (N.D. Cal. 1970).

to construct and operate the facility, utilizing a validation stamp system, in an effort to attract shoppers to a center city. The government contended that the operation of a commercial parking facility is not an exempt activity and that a substantial objective of the organization is to encourage the general public to patronize the businesses which participate in the validation stamp system, which is direct private inurement and only incidental public benefit.[19] Concluding that the city involved was the primary beneficiary of the organization's activities, the district court had held that the "business activity itself is similar to that which others engage in for profit, but it is not carried on in the same manner; it is carried on only because it is necessary for the attainment of an undeniably public end."[20] On appeal, the Ninth Circuit observed that the lower court "made a quantitative comparison of the private versus the public benefits derived from the organization and operation of the plaintiff corporation" and determined that the requirements for exemption were "adequately fulfilled." The opinion is not illustrative of blind adherence to the "exclusivity" doctrine.[21]

The IRS does not subscribe to the principles of the public parking corporation case and has announced that it will not follow the decision.[22] The Service asserts that this type of a public parking corporation does not operate exclusively for charitable purposes and carries on a business with the general public in a manner similar to organizations that are operated for profit. This position was made clear earlier when the Service ruled that an organization formed to revive retail sales in an area suffering from continued economic decline by constructing a shopping center that would complement the area's existing retail facilities could not qualify for exemption as a charitable entity. The IRS, then taking no notice of the Ninth Circuit decision, said that the activities of the organization "result in major benefits accruing to the stores that will locate within the shopping center," thereby precluding the exemption.[23] (However, an organization that provides free parking to persons visiting a downtown area can qualify as a social welfare organization.[24])

Nonetheless, the Ninth Circuit and other like-minded courts remain subject to the dictates of the Supreme Court's interpretation of the exclusivity doctrine, so the future may see a minimization of the concept of "substantiality" and a rationalization of allegedly private purposes as being in the long run for public gain. As another appellate court has noted: "Charitable purposes are those

---

[19]See Chapter 12.

[20]*Monterey Public Parking Corp.* v. *United States, supra,* n.18, 321 F.Supp. at 977.

[21]But see Rev. Rul. 73-411, 1973-2 C. B. 180. The declining importance of the "exclusively" concept may also be seen in *Edward Orton, Jr., Ceramic Foundation* v. *Commissioner, supra,* n. 9.

[22]Rev. Rul. 78-86, 1978-1 C. B. 151.

[23]Rev. Rul. 77-111, 1977-1 C. B. 144. Also Rev. Rul. 64-108, 1964-1 (Part I) C. B. 189.

[24]Rev. Rul. 81-116, 1981-1 C. B. 333.

which benefit the community by relieving it *pro tanto* from an obligation which it owes to the objects of the charity as members of the community."[25]

Application of the concept of "exclusively" in contemporary times may require even more flexibility than has been previously displayed. This may be particularly unavoidable as respects organizations performing services which are considered necessary in today's society, even where the services bear a parallel with those rendered in commercial settings. For example, the provision of medical services can obviously be an enterprise for profit, yet the IRS was able to rule that an organization formed to attract a physician to a medically underserved rural area, by providing him with a building and facilities at a reasonable rent, qualifies as a charitable organization.[26] "In these circumstances," said the Service, "any personal benefit derived by the doctor (the use of the building in which to practice his profession) does not detract from the public purpose of the organization nor lessen the public benefit flowing from its activities."[27] Similarly, an organization formed to provide legal services for residents of economically depressed communities was ruled to be engaged in charitable activities.[28] Even though those providing the services were subsidized by the organization, the Service minimized this personal gain by the rationale that they are merely the instruments by which the charitable purposes are accomplished.[29]

Thus the U.S. Tax Court considered the tax status of an organization the primary purpose of which is to promote, improve, and expand the handicraft output of disadvantaged artisans in developing societies of the world.[30] The organization's primary activities are the purchase, import, and sale of handicrafts—taken alone, clearly commercial activities—undertaken to alleviate economic deficiencies in communities of disadvantaged artisans, educate the American public in the artistry, history, and cultural significance of handicrafts from these communities, preserve the production of authentic handicrafts, and achieve economic stabilization in disadvantaged communities where handicrafts are central to the economy. The court found that these activities advance charitable and educational objectives[31] and that the furtherance of nonexempt purposes (benefit to nondisadvantaged artisans) is an insubstantial part of the organiza-

---

[25]*Duffy* v. *Birmingham*, 190 F.2d 738, 740 (8th Cir. 1951). Cf. *The Leon A. Beeghly Fund* v. *Commissioner*, 35 T.C. 490 (1960).

[26]Rev. Rul. 73-313, 1973-2 C. B. 174.

[27]Citing *In re Estate of Carlson*, 358 P.2d 669 (Sup. Ct. Kan. 1961). Cf. Rev. Rul. 69-266, 1969-1 C. B. 151.

[28]Rev. Rul. 72-559, 1972-2 C. B. 247. Also Rev. Rul. 70-640, 1970-2 C. B. 117; *Golf Life World Entertainment Golf Championship, Inc.* v. *United States*, 65-1 U.S.T.C. ¶ 9174 (S.D. Cal. 1964). Cf. Rev. Rul. 72-369, 1972-2 C. B. 245.

[29]See Chapter 4.

[30]*Aid to Artisans, Inc.* v. *Commissioner, supra*, n. 7.

[31]The court held that the first of these activities relieves the poor and distressed or the underprivileged (see Chapter 6 § 1) and that the fourth of these activities promotes social welfare (see Chapter 6 § 7).

tion's activities. Probably the essence of the case is captured in the following excerpt: "Thus, the sale of handicrafts to exempt organizations [museums] is neither an exempt purpose as argued by petitioner nor a non-exempt purpose as argued by respondent. Rather, such sale is merely an activity carried on by . . . [the organization] in furtherance of its exempt purposes."[32] This case is one of the few court decisions to fully explore and properly apply the "exclusively" requirement at being a focus on purposes, rather than activities.

As noted at the outset, however, whatever the continuing vitality or meaning of the term "exclusively" in this context, this consideration will usually be overshadowed by inquiries into the presence of any tax-exempt activities (if not, the sanction may well be denial or loss of exemption, notwithstanding the organization's purposes), the presence of any private inurement, or unrelated business activity (in which case, the basic exemption may nonetheless be sustained).

§ 11.3 Operations for Profit

The IRS, when alleging that an organization is not operated exclusively for an exempt purpose, frequently bases its contention on a finding that the organization's operation is similar to a commercial enterprise operated for profit. But, one court observed that "the presence of profitmaking activities is not *per se* a bar to qualification of an organization as exempt if the activities further or accomplish an exempt purpose."[33]

The question as to whether, and if so to what extent, an exempt organization (particularly one that is classified as a "charitable" entity) can earn a profit is at once difficult and easy to answer. The question is easy to answer in the sense that it is clear that the mere showing of a profit for one or more tax years will not bar tax exemption. However, if the profit is from what is perceived as a business activity and the fact of a profit is used to show the commercial hue of the activity, the answer to the question will depend upon the facts and circumstances of the particular case. That is, the decisive factor is likely to be the nature of the activities that give rise to the profits.

An illustrative body of law is that concerning organizations that prepare and sell publications at a profit.[34]

In one case, an organization sold religious publications to students attending classes it sponsored and to members of its religious following, for a relatively small profit.[35] In rejecting the government's argument that the receipt of the income indicated that the organization was not operated exclusively for religious purposes, the U.S. Tax Court held that the sale of religious literature is an activity "closely associated with, and incidental to," the organization's tax-

---

[32]*Aid to Artisans, Inc.* v. *Commissioner, supra,* n. 7 at 214.
[33]*Ibid.* at 211.
[34]See Chapter 7 § 4.
[35]*Saint Germain Foundation* v. *Commissioner,* 26 T.C. 648 (1956).

exempt purposes and bears "an intimate relationship to the proper functioning" of it, and thus that the receipt of the income does not prevent the organization from being an organization organized and operated exclusively for religious purposes.[36]

By contrast, in a subsequent case, a court denied status as a charitable entity to an organization that prepared and sold religious literature on a nondenominational basis. Because the organization's materials were competitively priced and the sales over a seven-year period yielded substantial accumulated profits which greatly exceeded the amount expended for its activities, the Court of Claims concluded that the sales activities were the organization's primary concern and that it was engaging in the conduct of a trade or business for profit.[37] Another organization met the same fate, namely, denial of exemption for publishing for profit, with the court observing that, were the law otherwise, "every publishing house would be entitled to an exemption on the ground that it furthers the education of the public."[38] Likewise, an organization was denied exemption because its primary activity, the publication and sale of books which are religiously inspired and oriented and written by its founder, is conducted in a commercial manner, at a profit.[39]

Each case on this point, therefore, must reflect one of these two analyses. In a 1978 case, the U.S. Tax Court accepted the contention by an organization that its publishing activities further its religious purpose of improving the preaching skills and sermons of the clergy of the Protestant, Roman Catholic, and Jewish faiths. Subscriptions for the publications are obtained by advertising and direct mail solicitation and the publications are sold at a modest profit. The court found that the organization was not in competition with any commercial enterprise and that the sale of religious literature was an integral part of the organization's religious purposes. Said the court: "The fact that petitioner intended to make a profit, alone, does not negate that petitioner was operated exclusively for charitable purposes."[40]

By contrast, an organization was denied tax exemption as a charitable entity because it was directly engaged in the conduct of a commercial leasing enterprise for the principal purpose of realizing profits. The enterprise was regarded as its principal activity (measured by total gross income), in which it was an active participant, and not related to an exempt purpose. Further, its charitable activities were deemed to be of relatively minimal consequence.[41]

---

[36]*Ibid.* at 658. Also see *Elisian Guild, Inc.* v. *United States*, 412 F.2d 121 (1st Cir. 1969), rev'g 292 F.Supp. 219 (D. Mass. 1968).

[37]*Scripture Press Foundation* v. *United States, supra*, n. 5.

[38]*Fides Publishers Association* v. *United States, supra*, n. 5, at 936.

[39]*Christian Manner International, Inc.* v. *Commissioner*, 71 T.C. 661 (1979).

[40]*Pulpit Resource* v. *Commissioner, supra* n. 9 at 611. Also *Industrial Aid for the Blind* v. *Commissioner*, 73 T.C. 96 (1979).

[41]*Greater United Navajo Development Enterprises, Inc.* v. *Commissioner*, 74 T.C. 69 (1980).

Similarly, a court reflected upon a nonprofit organization's accumulated profits and decided that this was evidence that the primary function of the organization was commercial in nature.[42]

Thus, the mere fact of profit-making activities is not supposed to adversely affect an organization's tax-exempt status. As the U.S. Court of Appeals for the First Circuit has noted, the "pertinent inquiry" is "whether the [organization's] exempt purpose transcends the profit motive rather than the other way around."[43] However, the IRS may use the existence of a profit to characterize the activity as being commercial in nature, thus placing at issue the question as to whether the organization's activities are devoted exclusively to tax-exempt purposes. This approach is sometimes also taken by the courts, such as in a case where the publications of an organization were held to produce an unwarranted profit, thereby depriving it of qualification as an educational organization.[44]

[42]*Elisian Guild, Inc.* v. *United States, supra*, n. 36 at 124.

[43]*The Incorporated Trustees of The Gospel Worker Society* v. *United States*, 510 F. Supp. 374 (D.D.C. 1981) aff'd 672 F.2d 894 (D.C. Cir. 1981), cert. den. 102 S. Ct. 2010 (1982).

[44]*American Institute for Economic Research* v. *United States*, 302 F.2d 934 (Ct. Cl. 1962). See Chapter 7 § 4.

12

Private Inurement

An organization, to be qualified as an entity described in Code § 501(c)(3) or in certain other categories of tax-exempt organizations, must be organized and operated so that "no part of . . . [its] net earnings . . . inures to the benefit of any private shareholder or individual."[1] That is, aside from being organized and operated exclusively for an exempt purpose and otherwise meeting the appropriate statutory requirements, a charitable organization must comport with the law proscribing "private inurement."

§ 12.1 Essence of Private Inurement

The concept of private inurement, although it lacks precise definition, is broad and wide ranging. The essence of the concept is to ensure that an exempt charitable organization is serving a public interest and not a private interest.[2] That is, to be tax-exempt, it is necessary for an organization to establish that it is not organized and operated for the benefit of private interests such as designated individuals, the creator or his or her family, shareholders of the organization, persons controlled (directly or indirectly) by such private interests,[3] or any persons having a personal and private interest in the activities of the organization.[4]

---

[1] The private inurement proscription is also expressly applicable to other tax-exempt organizations, such as social welfare organizations (Chapter 15), business leagues (Chapter 17), social clubs (Chapter 18), and labor, agriculture, and horticultural organizations (Chapter 19).

[2] See *Ginsburg v. Commissioner*, 46 T.C. 47 (1966); Rev. Rul. 76-206, 1976-1 C.B. 154.

[3] Reg. § 1.501(c)(3)-1(c)(1)(ii).

[4] Reg. § 1.501(a)-1(c). Also see Reg. § 1.501(c)(3)-1(c)(2).

In essence, in determining the presence of any proscribed private inurement, the law looks to the ultimate purpose of the organization: if the basic purpose of the organization is to benefit private individuals, then it cannot be tax-exempt, even though exempt activities may also be performed; conversely, incidental benefits to private individuals will not defeat the exemption, if the organization otherwise qualifies under the appropriate exemption provision.[5]

Private inurement is not necessarily the same as commercial activities. As has been discussed, a "charitable" organization may engage in commercial activities where done so for a larger exempt purpose;[6] otherwise, however, the existence of a single commercial or otherwise nonexempt substantial purpose will destroy the exemption.[7] In this sense, the concept relating to commercial activities is more whether the organization is organized and operated "exclusively" for an exempt purpose[8] rather than private inurement. Private inurement is less a question of "commercial" undertakings and is more akin to "self-dealing" in the private foundation field.[9]

In essence, the private inurement doctrine embodies the unique difference between nonprofit and for-profit organizations. That is, for the most part, the characteristics of both categories of organization are identical: both require a legal form,[10] pay compensation, face essentially the same expenses, are able to receive a profit[11] and make investments, and produce goods and services. But, unlike the for-profit entity, the nonprofit organization cannot distribute its profits (net earnings) to those who control it and/or financially support it, that is, there may not be any authentic[12] equity ownership in a nonprofit organization. Thus, the private inurement doctrine—elsewhere termed the "nondistribution constraint"[13]—is the substantive dividing line between the nonprofits and the for-profits and has been heralded as one of the chief reasons a service is provided or a product is produced by a nonprofit rather than a for-profit organization.[14]

[5]Reg. § 1.501(c)(3)-1(d)(1)(ii).

[6]See Chapter 6.

[7]See Chapter 11.

[8]*Ibid.*

[9]See Chapter 25. See *Northwestern Municipal Ass'n* v. *United States*, 99 F.2d 460 (8th Cir. 1938).

[10]See Chapter 36.

[11]See Chapter 11 § 3.

[12]A few states still permit a nonprofit corporation to issue stock but these anomalous situations are somewhat at odds with the federal tax law requirements imposed on tax-exempt organizations.

[13]Hansmann, "The Role of Nonprofit Enterprise," 89 *Yale Law J.* 835, 838 (1980).

[14]See Chapter 1 § 4.

§ 12.2 The Requisite "Insider"

It appears relatively clear that the statutory concept of private inurement, with its emphasis on inurement of "net earnings,"[15] contemplates a type of transaction between a tax-exempt organization and an individual in the nature of an "insider," the latter able to cause the application of the organization's net earnings for private purposes as the result of his or her exercise of control or influence. Thus, the statute speaks of inurement to the benefit of any "private shareholder or individual." It is for this reason that the self-dealing analogy[16] becomes useful: certain types of transactions are proscribed, being between the charitable or other tax-exempt organization and one or more insiders ("disqualified persons").

This reference to "insider" in this context has been discussed by the IRS, with the Service stating that, as a general rule, "[a]n organization's trustees, officers, members, founders, or contributors may not, by reason of their position, acquire any of its funds."[17] Stating the proposition another way, the Service has observed that "[t]he prohibition of inurement, in its simplest terms, means that a private shareholder or individual cannot pocket the organization's funds except as reasonable payment for goods or services."[18] Similarly, the Service has made it clear that proscribed private inurement involves a transaction or series of transactions, such as unreasonable compensation, unreasonable rental charges, or deferred or retained interests in the organization's assets.

Thus, impermissible private inurement would seem to involve two necessary components: That the private individual (insider) to whom the benefit inures has the ability to control or otherwise influence the actions of the tax-exempt organization so as to cause the benefit and that the benefit conferred be intentionally conferred by the influenced exempt organization and not result coincidentally from happenstance.

A variety of cases and rulings in this field confirm the observation that private inurement in essence entails the presence of certain transactions involving insiders.

The Court of Claims held that the Founding Church of Scientology failed to demonstrate entitlement to tax exemption because of the presence of im-

---

[15]The Revenue Act of 1909, Chapter 7, § 38, FIRST (2)(D), and subsequent reenactments through 1917 contained the language "no part of the net income of which inures to the benefit of any private shareholder or individual. . . ." In the Revenue Act of 1918 (§ 231(6)), the word "earnings" was substituted for the word "income." There is nothing in the statutory history to suggest that this change had any substantive significance and the comparability of the meanings of "income" and "earnings" indicates that none was intended. See § 4, *infra*.

[16]See § 3, *infra*.

[17]IRS Exempt Organizations Handbook (IRM 7751) § 342.1(1).

[18] *Ibid.* at § 342.1(3).

permissible private inurement.[19] An individual (the creator of Scientology) was the founder of the Church and he and his wife were two of its three trustees. The Church disbursed substantial sums to its founder and to members of his family, with such payments denominated as fees, commissions, royalties, compensation for services, rent, and reimbursement of expenses and expenditures made on the Church's behalf. The Church maintained a personal residence for its founder, paid him ten percent of its earnings, and made loans to him and members of his family.

The court observed that "[w]hat emerges from these facts is the inference that the . . . [founder's] family was entitled to make ready personal use of the corporate earnings. . . . [N]othing we have found in the record dispels the substantial doubts the court entertains concerning the receipt of benefit by . . . [this family] from plaintiff's net earnings."[20] It was obvious that 'the court regarded these various disbursements as inurement of the Church's net earnings to private individuals; as respects certain of the disbursements, the court stated that "the logical inference can be drawn that these payments were disguised and unjustified distributions of plaintiff's earnings."[21]

The U.S. Court of Appeals for the Fifth Circuit denied tax exemption to the Birmingham Business College, in part because its net earnings were distributed to its shareholders for their personal benefit.[22] The founder of the College and his two sisters were the only shareholders; these three and two of their spouses were the College's trustees.

The court was concerned about the "constant commingling of the funds of the shareholders and BBC."[23] The court found that the College "was operated as a business producing, or ultimately producing, substantial revenues for its operators . . . [T]he net earnings, or substantial portions, were to be, and were in fact, distributed to these shareholders for their own personal benefit."[24] The College's charter limited compensation so that it could not exceed a ratable distribution based on stock ownership; "[i]t was, and was intended to be, a means by which to assure an equal distribution of the earnings."[25]

The U.S. Tax Court refused to recognize the Texas Trade School as a tax-exempt educational institution because of the presence of private inurement.[26] Five individuals leased property to the School and the School constructed improvements on property which was owned by the five and leased to the

---

[19]*Founding Church of Scientology* v. *United States*, 412 F.2d 1197 (Ct. Cl. 1969), cert. den. 397 U.S. 1009 (1970).

[20]*Ibid.* at 1202.

[21]*Ibid.* at 1201.

[22]*Birmingham Business College, Inc.* v. *Commissioner*, 276 F.2d 476 (5th Cir. 1960).

[23]*Ibid.* at 479.

[24]*Ibid.* at 480.

[25]Id.

[26]*Texas Trade School* v. *Commissioner*, 30 T.C. 642 (1958), aff'd 272 F.2d 168 (5th Cir. 1959).

School. Of this group, one was president of the School, two were vice-presidents, and one was secretary-treasurer; these four constituted the School's executive committee and four of its nine directors. The rents paid by the School were found to be "excessive and unreasonable."[27]

The court found that, "as a result of these excessive rent payments part of the net earnings of . . . [the School] inured to the benefit of the members of the . . . group . . . and that part of the net earnings of . . . [the School] also inured to their benefit because of the construction at its expense of buildings and improvements on real estate owned by them."[28]

The Tax Court also declined to accord a foundation tax-exempt status as a charitable organization because part of its net earnings was found to have inured to its creator and controller.[29] The foundation made loans for the personal benefit of its creator and his family members and friends, made research expenditures to carry out a personal hobby of his, and purchased stock in a corporation owned by a friend of its creator as a personal favor to the latter.

The court concluded that the foundation "was organized in such a fashion that . . . [its creator] held control of its activities and expenditures; it was operated to carry out projects in which . . . [he] was interested and some of its funds were expended for . . . [his] benefit . . . or [for the benefit of] members of his family."[30]

Likewise, the Tax Court ruled that the Cranley Research Foundation did not qualify as a charitable organization, because of inurement of its net earnings to private individuals.[31] The Foundation was established by Cranley (a vascular surgeon), who was one of its three trustees; his father was another. The Foundation's principal activities were the treatment of patients (chiefly Cranley's) and the conduct of scientific research. A nurse employed by the Foundation was used by Cranley in his private practice without additional compensation.

The court concluded that Cranley was benefited in his private capacity from activities of the Foundation. The Foundation's laboratory (located next door to Cranley's office) was, according to the government, used "on numerous occasions in his practice;" the court accepted the government's charge that Cranley's "practice and the income therefrom were materially enhanced by the establishment of the laboratory."[32] Cranley received consultation fees from patients making use of the laboratory.

In another case, the Tax Court found that the Western Catholic Church fails to qualify as a religious organization, because of inurement of net earnings to its founder. The founder (its minister) and his wife and daughter comprised the organization's board of directors. The Church's primary activity was seen

[27]*Ibid*, 30 T.C. at 647.
[28]*Ibid*.
[29]*Best Lock Corp.* v. *Commissioner*, 31 T.C. 1217 (1959).
[30]*Ibid*. at 1236.
[31]*Cranley* v. *Commissioner*, 20 T.C.M. 20 (1961).
[32]*Ibid*. at 25.

by the court as the making of investments to accumulate money for a building fund.

The Church had no place of worship and conducted no public religious services. It did conduct some ministry through its founder, who was also its principal donor, and distribution of some grants to needy individuals, who were selected by the founder. The court concluded that the founder's "activities were more personal than church oriented."[33]

The Court of Claims declined to accord the Horace Heidt Foundation charitable status because of the private gain derived by Heidt therefrom.[34] The Foundation was established to provide musical instruction, proper living quarters, and medical assistance to "young people interested in the entertainment field and who were featured in Mr. Heidt's shows."[35]

The court found that, "[i]n these circumstances Horace Heidt received a great benefit by establishing an organization whereby the recipients of the organization's charitable services were in his employ and benefiting him" and that "it was to Mr. Heidt's advantage as a director of a radio program and as an employer to provide these services."[36]

Another application of the private inurement doctrine by the courts appears in a case concerning the Harding Hospital.[37] The Hospital's tax exemption was barred by a court, in part because of the advantages that the doctors, who organized the Hospital, obtained from its operation. Most of the patients admitted by the Hospital were attended by the founding physicians. Also the court was concerned about the arrangement for management services and the lease of office space.

Speaking of the concentration of these doctors' patients in the Hospital, which the court found to be "the primary source of the doctors' professional income," the court found that (even though net earnings were not paid over to them) "this virtual monopoly by the . . . [doctors] of the patients permitted benefits to inure to . . . [them] within the intendment of the statute."[38] There was an agreement between the doctors and the Hospital, whereunder they were paid to supervise the Hospital, which the court concluded conveyed private benefits to the doctors.[39]

The IRS revoked the tax-exempt status of a hospital organized and operated by a physician. The hospital distributed its earnings to the physician in the

---

[33]*Western Catholic Church* v. *Commissioner*, 73 T.C. 196 (1979), aff'd 631 F.2d 736 (7th Cir. 1980).

[34]*Horace Heidt Foundation* v. *United States*, 170 F.Supp. 634 (Ct. Cl. 1959).

[35]*Ibid.* at 637.

[36]*Ibid.* at 638.

[37]*Harding Hospital, Inc.* v. *United States*, 505 F.2d 1068 (6th Cir. 1974).

[38]*Ibid.* at 1078.

[39]Citing *Maynard Hospital, Inc.* v. *Commissioner*, 52 T.C. 1006 (1969), and *Sonora Community Hospital* v. *Commissioner*, 46 T.C. 519 (1967), aff'd 397 F.2d 814 (9th Cir. 1968).

form of direct payments, improvements to his corporation's property, and the free use of its facilities. The U.S. Tax Court upheld the revocation on the theory that a part of the hospital's net earnings inured to the benefit of a private individual. Therefore, the court ruled that gain realized on the sale of the hospital's property was properly taxable. The court disallowed deductions for a portion of certain administrative, service, and professional fees which related to the physician's private practice, as well as interest payments for unexplained loan, mortgage and other obligations, and additions to a bad-debt reserve where the reserve method of accounting was not elected. The physician was held to be in receipt of ordinary income for the improvements made by the hospital to property owned by his corporation. The hospital was held liable for penalties for not filing income tax returns for four years, although it was contesting in good faith the revocation of its tax-exempt status for earlier years at that time.[40]

A chiropractor established an organization to study chiropractic methods and the organization received a ruling that it qualified as a charitable organization. The chiropracter engaged in various self-dealing activities with the organization, including the sale of his home, car, and medical equipment to the organization, and caused the organization to pay his personal expenses and a salary while he continued his normal medical practice. The organization did not engage in research and did not grant scholarships, as it had been set up to do. The Tax Court upheld the revocation of the organization's exempt status.[41]

A tax-exempt organization engaged in several transactions with its founder, including the receipt of property from his mother and paying her an annuity and her son's college education, paying the founder's personal expenses, and purchasing and leasing the founder's realty. The Tax Court held that the organization's income inured to the benefit of private individuals and that it served a private rather than a public purpose, and that the IRS properly revoked its tax-exempt status.[42]

The IRS has likewise adopted the viewpoint that the private inurement prohibition relates only to insider-controlled benefits. In 1969, the Service found no private inurement in a situation where an exempt hospital compensated a hospital-based radiologist on the basis of a fixed percentage of the income of the radiology department.[43] This conclusion was arrived at, in part, because the "radiologist did not control the organization."

Similarly, a trust, which was required to pay out its net income for exempt purposes for a period of years or the lives of specified individuals, was ruled not to qualify for tax-exempt status.[44] At the end of the period, the trust terminated and the principal reverted to the creator of the trust or his estate.

[40]*Kenner v. Commissioner*, 33 T.C.M. 1239 (1974).
[41]*The Labrenz Foundation, Inc. v. Commissioner*, 33 T.C.M. 1374 (1974).
[42]*Rueckwald Foundation, Inc. v. Commissioner*, 33 T.C.M. 1383 (1974). Also *Human Engineering Institute v. Commissioner*, 37 T.C.M. 619 (1978).
[43]Rev. Rul. 69-383, 1969-2 C.B. 113.
[44]Rev. Rul. 66-259, 1966-2 C.B. 214.

The disqualifying feature was the reversionary interest, which resulted in inurement of investment gains over the trust's life to the creator's benefit.[45]

Thus, in the absence of a self-dealing-like transaction involving one or more individuals with control or other influence over the tax-exempt organization, impermissible private inurement is probably not present. Aside from the somewhat elusive question as to whether, in a given situation, there is inurement of "net earnings," an activity of an exempt organization that produces only an incidental and/or unintended benefit to a private individual (there rarely will be a "shareholder") should not be regarded as proscribed private inurement.

Of course, an exempt organization frequently confers benefits to private individuals (even other than its employees and agents and independent contractors with whom it does business) on a daily basis. An illustration of this would be a college or university. Its very location and the fact that it attracts students throw off great benefits to a variety of private businesses (stores, restaurants, service establishments, and the like), real estate dealers, and more. Its graduates frequently spend their adult lives toiling in private industry, which reaps untold benefits from the education provided. Such illustrations are manifold. But no one could seriously suggest that such a situation involves private inurement that jeopardizes the institution's tax-exempt status.

This is the case even though the benefits may be more than incidental. The result obtains from the fact that the private benefits are mere happenstance, are an unintended byproduct of the carrying out of an exempt purpose. This rationale was applied in 1975 in a case involving a social welfare organization which conferred most of its benefits on the employees of one corporation, with which the organization's founder had been affiliated, and the board of directors of which was composed solely of employees of the same corporation.[46] The IRS has also espoused this rationale.[47] Thus the Service ruled, with respect to a tax-exempt social club, that the awarding of prizes paid from tournament entry fees does not constitute inurement of the organization's net income but is in furtherance of the members' pleasure and recreation.[48]

Consequently, a "charitable" organization should be concerned with the "charitable leakage" doctrine awkwardly embodied in the private inurement rationale largely where there is a transaction or transactions akin to private foundation self-dealing involving one or more "insiders."[49]

---

[45]Also *Alfred I. DuPont Testamentary Trust* v. *Commissioner*, 514 F.2d 917 (5th Cir. 1975); *Scholarship Endowment Foundation* v. *Nicholas*, 106 F.2d 552 (10th Cir. 1939); *Northwestern Municipal Ass'n* v. *United States*, supra, n. 9; *Smith* v. *Reynolds*, 43 F.Supp. 510 (D. Minn. 1942); *Chattanooga Automobile Club* v. *Commissioner*, 182 F.2d 551 (6th Cir. 1950).

[46]*Eden Hall Farm* v. *United States*, 389 F. Supp. 858 (W.D. Pa. 1975).

[47]See, e.g., Rev. Rul. 75-196, 1975-1 C.B. 155; Rev. Rul. 71-580, 1971-2 C.B. 235; Rev. Rul. 70-533, 1970-2 C.B. 112; Rev. Rul. 66-358, 1966-2 C.B. 218.

[48]Rev. Rul. 74-148, 1974-1 C.B. 138.

[49]See, e.g., *Sound Health Association* v. *Commissioner*, 71 T.C. 158 (1978); *Leon A. Beeghly Fund* v. *Commissioner*, 35 T.C. 490 (1960).

The doctrine of private inurement is not to be confused with other, similar maxims: A charitable organization (1) must be operated exclusively for tax-exempt purposes, (2) must be operated for public rather than private purposes, and (3) may not be operated for a noncharitable (other than insubstantial) purpose.

§ 12.3   Private Inurement—Scope and Types

It is thus clear that, under the rules concerning "charitable" organizations, an organization may not be organized and operated for the benefit of any individual in his or her own private capacity, unless, as discussed below, the private benefit is considered merely "incidental." Individuals can be privately benefited in many ways and thus "private inurement" has many manifestations. Moreover, the fact that the benefit conveyed may be relatively small does not change the basic element of potential impermissible inurement.[50] Of course, an organization may incur ordinary and necessary expenditures in its operations without losing its tax-exempt status.[51] Although the concepts of private inurement and private foundation self-dealing are by no means precisely the same, the following summary of self-dealing transactions offers a useful sketch of the scope of transactions that may, in appropriate circumstances, amount to instances of private inurement: (1) sale or exchange, or leasing, of property between an organization and a private individual, (2) lending of money or other extension of credit between an organization and a private individual, (3) furnishing of goods, services or facilities between an organization and a private individual, (4) payment of compensation (or payment or reimbursement of expenses) by an organization to a private individual, and (5) transfer to, or use by or for the benefit of, a private individual of the income or assets of an organization.[52]

The IRS has invoked the self-dealing rationale in a situation involving a charitable organization—not a private foundation—in at least one instance.[53] The occasion was in the context of an IRS discussion of when a nonprofit school which is a successor to a former for-profit school is regarded as substantially serving the private interests of the directors of the school. The IRS determined that the a school was operating to serve a public interest where it purchased

---

[50]See *Spokane Motorcycle Club* v. *United States*, 222 F.Supp. 151 (E.D. Wash. 1963).

[51]See, e.g., *Birmingham Business College, Inc.* v. *Commissioner, supra*, n. 22; *Enterprise Ry. Equip. Co.* v. *United States*, 161 F.Supp. 590 (Ct. Cl. 1958); *Mabee Petroleum Corp.* v. *United States*, 203 F.2d 872 (5th Cir. 1953); *Broadway Theatre League of Lynchburg, Va., Inc.* v *United States*, 293 F.Supp. 346 (W.D. Va. 1968).

[52]Code § 4941(d)(A)-(E).

[53]Rev. Rul. 76-441, 1976-2 C.B. 147. Cf. Rev. Rul. 76-91, 1976-1 C.B. 149. Also *Church In Boston* v. *Commissioner*, 71 T.C. 102 (1978); *Vnuk* v. *Commissioner*, 38 T.C.M. 710 (1979); IRS Private Letter Ruling 7904041.

the for-profit school's personal property at fair market value in an arm's-length transaction, is paying a fair rental value for use of the land and buildings, and is paying the former owners of the for-profit school (who were retained to provide supervision and care of the students) reasonable compensation for their services. By contrast, in a situation where a nonprofit organization, which has received all of the stock in a for-profit school as a gift, took over the former school's assets and assumed all of its liabilities including notes owned to the former owners, the IRS denied the organization qualification as a charitable entity, holding that it was operating for the directors' (the former school's stockholders) private interests because the liabilities assumed by the organization exceeded the fair market value of the for-profit school's assets. Said the IRS: "The directors were, in fact, dealing with themselves and will benefit financially from the transaction."

Compensation for Services

It is clear that payment of reasonable compensation by an exempt organization does not result in the inurement of net earnings to the benefit of private individuals.[54] Conversely, excessive compensation can result in such inurement.[55] Of course, whether the compensation paid is reasonable is a question of fact, to be decided in the context of each case.[56]

A large salary or wage (in absolute dollar amount, not as a percentage of gross receipts) will likely be considered the receipt of benefit by the employee of the organization's net earnings, particularly where the employee is concurrently receiving other forms of compensation from the organization (for example, fees, commissions, royalties) and more than one member of the same family are compensated employees.[57] Thus, where the control of an organization was in two ministers who contributed all of its receipts, all of which was paid to them as housing allowances, the tax exemption of the organization was revoked; the court said that the compensation was not "reasonable" although

[54]Code § 4941(d)(2)(E).

[55]See, e.g., *Harding Hospital, Inc.* v. *United States, supra*, n. 37; *Birmingham Business College, Inc.* v. *Commissioner, supra*, n. 22; *Mabee Petroleum Corp.* v. *United States, supra*, n. 51; *Texas Trade School* v. *Commissioner, supra*. n. 26; *Northern Illinois College of Optometry* v. *Commissioner*, 2 T.C.M. 664 (1943).

[56]See, e.g., *Jones Bros. Bakery, Inc.* v. *United States*, 411 F.2d 1282 (Ct. Cl. 1969); *Home Oil Mill* v. *Willingham*, 68 F. Supp. 525 (N.D. Ala. 1945), aff'd 181 F.2d 9 (5th Cir. 1950), cert. den. 340 U.S. 852 (1950).

[57]See, e.g., *Founding Church of Scientology* v. *United States, supra* n. 19; *Bubbling Well Church of Universal Love, Inc.* v. *Commissioner*, 74 T.C. 531 (1980); *Unitary Mission Church of Long Island* v. *Commissioner*, 74 T.C. 507 (1980), aff'd in unpublished opinion (2d Cir. Jan. 19, 1981).

it may not be "excessive."[58] Yet large salaries and noncash benefits received by an organization's employees can be reasonable, considering the nature of their services and skills, such as payments to physicians by a nonprofit group that is an incorporated department of anesthesiology of a hospital.[59] For example, a court considered a case where three executives of a nonprofit organization had salaries in 1970 of $25,000, $16,153, and $5,790, and in 1978 of $100,000, $72,377, and $42,896, respectively. This was held to be an "abrupt increase" in the salaries and a "substantial amount" of compensation, leading to the conclusion that the salaries "are at least suggestive of a commercial rather than nonprofit operation."[60]

A pension trust that pays benefits to retired employees of a particular company, regardless of their economic resources or financial needs, does not qualify as a charitable entity.[61] Nonetheless, tax-exempt organizations may pay reasonable pensions to retired employees without adversely affecting their tax-exempt status.[62]

Equity Distributions

In most states, nonprofit corporations, especially charitable and educational organizations, may not be organized as stock corporations. Even in the instances where tax-exempt organizations may have formal stockholders, the organizations may not pay dividends. Where the individual stockholders derive income from the organization's operations through the medium of dividend payments, the organization cannot qualify as a "charitable" or many other types of tax-exempt organization.[63]

Retained Interests

The IRS takes the position that a "charitable" organization may not be organized so that an individual or individuals retains a reversionary interest,

---

[58]*Church of the Transfiguring Spirit, Inc.* v. *Commissioner*, 76 T.C. 1, 6 (1981). Cf. *Universal Church of Scientific Truth, Inc.* v. *United States*, 74-1 U.S.T.C. ¶ 9360 (N.D. Ala. 1973), where the organization retained tax exemption in part because its revenues came from charges for published materials and the expenses were not entirely for the compensation of its ministers.

[59]*B.H.W. Anesthesia Foundation, Inc.* v. *Commissioner*, 72 T.C. 681 (1979). Also *University of Massachusetts Medical School Group Practice* v. *Commissioner*, 74 T.C. 1299 (1980).

[60]*The Incorporated Trustees of the Gospel Worker Society* v. *United States*, 510 F. Supp. 374, 379 (D.D.C. 1981).

[61]Rev. Rul. 68-422, 1968-2 C.B. 207.

[62]Rev. Rul. 73-126, 1973-1 C.B. 220.

[63]See, e.g., *Maynard Hospital, Inc.* v. *Commissioner*, 52 T.C. 1006 (1969). For a discussion of the applicability of this type of private inurement in the context of Code § 501(c)(13), see Chapter 19, § 9.

whereby the principal would flow to a private individual upon dissolution or liquidation; instead, in such event net assets must pass for charitable or public, governmental purposes.[64] However, the acceptance of an income-producing asset subject to a reserved life estate will not result in inurement, because only the charitable remainder interest is acquired; likewise, annuity payments in return for a gift of an income-producing asset is not undue inurement, because the payment of the annuity merely constitutes the satisfaction of the charge upon the transferred asset.[65]

Rental Arrangements

As in the case of payment of compensation, a "charitable" organization generally may lease property and make rental payments therefor.[66] However, the rental payments must be reasonable and the arrangement must be beneficial and desirable to the organization. That is, inflated rental prices may well amount to a private benefit inuring to the lessor.[67]

Loans

A loan arrangement involving the assets of a "charitable" organization will always be skeptically reviewed.[68] Like rental arrangements, the terms of such a loan should be financially advantageous to the organization and should be commensurate with the organization's purposes.[69] If a loan is not timely repaid, questions of private inurement will almost assuredly be raised.[70] As has been noted, "the very existence of a private source of loan credit from an organization's earnings may itself amount to inurement of benefit."[71] Thus, for example, a school's tax exemption was revoked in part because two of its officers were provided by the school with interest-free, unsecured loans that subjected the school to uncompensated risks for no business purpose.[72]

[64]Rev. Rul. 66-259, 1966-2 C.B. 214. See Chapter 6.

[65]Rev. Rul. 69-176, 1969-1 C.B. 150. Also see Code §§ 642(c)(5) and 664 (treatment of pooled income funds and charitable remainder trusts).

[66]However, a rental arrangement between a disqualified person and a private foundation may constitute an act of self-dealing. See Chapter 25

[67]See, e.g., *Founding Church of Scientology* v. *United States, supra,* n. 19 at 1202; *Texas Trade School* v. *Commissioner, supra,* n. 26.

[68]A loan arrangement between a disqualified person and a private foundation may constitute an act of self-dealing. See Chapter 25.

[69]See *Griswold* v. *Commissioner,* 39 T.C. 620 (1962).

[70]See *Best Lock Corp.* v. *Commissioner, supra,* n. 29; Rev. Rul. 67-5, 1967-1 C.B. 123.

[71]*Founding Church of Scientology* v. *United States, supra,* n. 19 at 1202. Also see *Unitary Mission Church of Long Island* v. *Commissioner, supra,* n. 57; *Western Catholic Church* v. *Commissioner, supra,* n. 33; *Church in Boston* v. *Commissioner, supra,* n. 53 at 106–107.

[72]*John Marshall Law School* v. *United States,* 81-2 U.S.T.C. ¶ 9514 (Ct. Cl. 1981).

The U.S. Tax Court found private inurement as the result of a loan where a non-profit corporation, formed to take over the operations of a school conducted up to that time by a for-profit corporation, required parents of its students to make interest-free loans to the for-profit corporation. Private inurement was detected in the fact that the property to be improved by the loan proceeds would revert to the for-profit corporation after a 15-year term and that the interest-free feature of the loans was an unwarranted benefit to private individuals.[73]

The Tax Court earlier found private inurement in a case involving a tax-exempt hospital and its founder, who was a physician who operated a clinic located in the hospital building.[74] The hospital and the clinic shared supplies and services, and most of the hospital's patients were also patients of the founding physician and his partner. The hospital made a substantial number of unsecured loans to a nursing home owned by the physician and a trust for his children at below-market interest rates. The court held that there was private benefit to the physician because this use of the hospital's funds reduced his personal financial risk in and lowered the interest costs for the nursing home. The court also found inurement in the fact that the hospital was the principal source of financing for the nursing home, since an equivalent risk incurred for a similar duration could be expected to produce higher earnings elsewhere. In general, the court observed, "[w]here a doctor or group of doctors dominate the affairs of a corporate hospital otherwise exempt from tax, the courts have closely scrutinized the underlying relationship to insure that the arrangements permit a conclusion that the corporate hospital is organized and operated *exclusively* for charitable purposes without any private inurement."[75]

Provision of Goods, Refreshments

A "charitable" organization cannot have as its primary purpose the provision of goods or refreshments (in the nature of social or recreational activities) to private individuals. Of course, the organization may incidentally bear the expense of meals and refreshments (for example, working luncheons, annual banquets) and the like, but, in general, "[r]efreshments, goods and services furnished to the members of an exempt corporation from the net profits of the business enterprise are benefits inuring to the individual members."[76] Thus a discussion group that held closed meetings at which personally oriented speeches were given, followed by the serving of food and other refreshments, was ruled not to be tax-exempt since the public benefits were remote at best and the "functions of the organization are to a significant extent fraternal and designed to stimulate fellowship among the membership."[77] Likewise, a school's tax

[73]*Hancock Academy of Savannah, Inc.* v. *Commissioner*, 69 T.C. 488 (1977).
[74]*Lowry Hospital Association* v. *Commissioner*, 66 T.C. 850 (1976).
[75]*Ibid.* at 859.
[76]*Spokane Motorcycle Club* v. *United States, supra*, n. 50 at 1202.
[77]Rev. Rul. 73-439, 1973-2 C.B. 176.

exemption was revoked in part because the school paid for a variety of household items and furnishings used in the home of one of its officers.[78]

This aspect of private inurement frequently surfaces in the context of tax-exempt social clubs. Such clubs must be organized and operated for pleasure, recreation and other nonprofitable purposes and the private inurement prohibition applies.[79] They must have an established membership of individuals, personal contacts and fellowship and a commingling of members must play a material part in the life of the organization.[80] For example, this commingling requirement is satisfied in the case of a membership organization that provides bowling tournaments and recreational bowling competition for its members.[81] However, in this case, the IRS ruled that the awarding of cash prizes paid from entry fees does not constitute inurement of the organization's net income but is in furtherance of the members' pleasure and recreation.

Services Rendered

An organization, the primary purpose of which is to render services to individuals in their private capacity, generally cannot qualify as a "charitable" entity. There are exceptions to this principle, such as where the individuals benefited constitute a bona fide charitable class, the individual beneficiaries are considered merely instruments or means to a charitable objective, or the private benefit is merely incidental.

This type of private inurement takes many forms and involves judgments governing in individual cases that are difficult to quantify. For example, the advancement of the arts has been seen to be a charitable activity.[82] But a cooperative art gallery that exhibits and sells only its members' works was ruled to be serving the private purposes of its members ("a vehicle for advancing their careers and promoting the sale of their work") and hence not tax-exempt, even though the exhibition and sale of paintings may otherwise be an exempt purpose.[83]

Similarly, although the rendering of housing assistance for low income families may qualify as an exempt purpose,[84] an organization that provides such assistance but gives preference for housing to employees of a farm proprietorship operated by the individual who controls the organization was ruled not to be a charitable organization.[85] Also, a school's tax exemption was revoked in

---

[78]*John Marshall Law School* v. *United States, supra*, n. 72.
[79]Code § 501(c)(7). See Chapter 18.
[80]Rev. Rul. 58-589, 1958-2 C.B. 266.
[81]Rev. Rul. 74-148, *supra*, n. 48.
[82]See Chapter 6.
[83]Rev. Rul. 71-395, 1971-2 C.B. 228.
[84]See Chapter 6.
[85]Rev. Rul. 72-147, 1972-1 C.B. 147.

part because the school awarded scholarships to the children of two of its officers, yet made no scholarship awards to anyone else.[86]

The provision of services to individuals, as precluded by the private inurement proscriptions, takes many forms. For example, an organization created to provide bus transportation for school children to an exempt private school was ruled to not be tax-exempt.[87] The IRS said that the organization serves a private rather than a public interest, in that it enables the participating parents to fulfill their individual responsibility of transporting children to school. The Service concluded: "When a group of individuals associate to provide a cooperative service for themselves, they are serving a private interest." A testamentary trust established to make payments to charitable organizations and to use a fixed sum from its annual income for the perpetual care of the testator's burial lot was ruled to be serving a private interest.[88] Further, an organization that operates a subscription "scholarship" plan, whereby "scholarships" are paid to preselected, specifically named individuals designated by subscribers, was ruled to not be tax-exempt, since it is operated for the benefit of designated individuals.[89] Likewise, the furnishing of farm laborers for individual farmers, as part of the operation of a labor camp to house transient workers, was held not to be an "agricultural" purpose under federal tax law but rather the provision of services to individual farmers that they would otherwise have to provide for themselves.[90] Also, a nonprofit corporation was deemed to be serving private purposes where it was formed to dredge a navigable waterway, little used by the general public, fronting the properties of its members.[91] Further, an organization that provides travel services, legal services, an insurance plan, an antitheft registration program, and discount programs to its members was held to be serving the interests of the members, thereby precluding the organization from qualifying as an educational organization.[92]

On occasion, the rule that unwarranted services to members can cause denial or loss of an organization's tax-exempt status leads to bizarre consequences. This general limitation is, from time to time, stretched—to bring about adverse consequences for the organization involved—far beyond what Congress surely intended in legislating the proscription on private inurement.

A classic illustration of this expansionist reading of the private inurement clause is the holding by the U.S. Tax Court that a genealogical society, the membership of which is comprised of those interested in the migrations of persons with a common name (by birth or marriage) to and within the United

[86]*John Marshall Law School* v. *United States, supra,* n. 22.

[87]Rev. Rul. 69-175, 1969-1 C.B. 149. See *Chattanooga Automobile Club* v. *Commissioner,* 182 F.2d 551 (6th Cir. 1950).

[88]Rev. Rul. 69-256, 1969-1 C.B. 150.

[89]Rev. Rul. 67-367, 1967-2 C.B. 188.

[90]Rev. Rul. 72-391, 1972-2 C.B. 249. See Chapter 19.

[91]*Ginsburg* v. *Commissioner, supra,* n. 1. Cf. Rev. Rul. 70-186, 1970-1 C.B. 128.

[92]*U.S. CB Radio Association, No. 1, Inc.* v. *Commissioner,* 42 T.C.M. 1441 (1981).

States, failed to qualify as a "charitable" organization on the ground that its genealogical activities serve the private interests of its members.[93] The society's activities include research of the "family's" development (primarily by collecting and abstracting historical data), preparation and dissemination of publications containing the research, promotion of scholarly writing, and instruction (by means of lectures and workshops) in the methodology of compiling and preserving historical, biographical, and genealogical research. The organization's underlying operational premise is that the growth and development of the continental United States can be understood by tracing the migratory patterns of a typical group of colonists and their descendants.

While the IRS and the court conceded that some of the society's activities are charitable and educational, they determined that the compilation and publication of the genealogical history of this "family" group was an activity that serves the private interests of the organization's members. The court "note[d] specifically petitioner's emphasis on compiling members' family lives and the . . . [group's] family history" and held that "[a]ny educational benefit to the public created by petitioner's activities is incidental to this private purpose."[94] This rationale ignores the discipline of "kinship studies" by which social history focuses extensively on families and family-related institutions and strains to place a negative, private orientation on the term "family" when in fact the use of a family is merely a research technique whereby the tracings of genealogy are done pursuant to an objective standard. This case presents a major threat to genealogical societies—particularly "family associations"—because of the opinion's characterizing of genealogical study as private inurement.[95]

[93]*The Callaway Family Association, Inc.* v. *Commissioner*, 71 T.C. 340 (1978). This opinion presumably reinforces the published IRS ruling that genealogical societies in general qualify as Code § 501(c)(7) organizations (see Chapter 18 § 1). Rev. Rul. 67-8, 1967-1 C.B. 142. However, in an opinion handed down less than one month prior to the *Callaway Family Association* case, the U.S. Tax Court expressly recognized that a membership organization can qualify under Code § 501(c)(3) where it provides information and services to both members and nonmembers. *National Association for the Legal Support of Alternative Schools* v. *Commissioner*, 71 T.C. 118 (1978).

[94]*Ibid.* at 344. Also see *Benjamin Price Genealogical Association* v. *Internal Revenue Service*, 79-1 U.S.T.C. ¶9361 (D.D.C. 1979).

[95]The U.S. Tax Court distinguished the general family association from the type of family association that engages in genealogical activities for religious purposes, usually one that is operated to collect and furnish information needed by the Mormon Church to advance its religious precepts. *Ibid.* at 345. The IRS has ruled that the latter type of family association is a charitable entity because it advances religion (see Chapter 6 § 2). Rev. Rul. 71-580, 1971-2 C.B. 235. Yet the definition of the term "charitable" also includes the advancement of education (see Chapter 6 § 3) and the private inurement restrictions apply equally to all categories of charitable and other classes of tax-exempt organizations. The court's attempted distinction of these two categories is baseless and discriminatory, and, if the *Callaway Family Association* case is good law, it should defeat the tax-exempt status granted to the organizations in Rev. Rul. 71-580, *supra*, and Rev. Rul. 67-8, *supra*, n. 93.

Following this Tax Court holding, the IRS publicly ruled that a genealogical society may qualify as an educational organization by conducting lectures, sponsoring public displays and museum tours, providing written materials to instruct members of the general public on genealogical research, and compiling a geographical area's pioneer history. However, the organization's membership is open to all interested persons in the area, rather than members of any one "family," and the society does not conduct genealogical research for its members, although its members research genealogies independently using the society's research materials.[96] By contrast, the Service also ruled that an organization cannot qualify as a charitable or educational entity where its membership is limited to descendants of a particular family, it compiles family genealogical research data for use by its members for reasons other than to conform to the religious precepts of the family's denomination, it presents the data to designated libraries, it publishes volumes of family history, and it promotes occasional social activities among family members.[97]

A charitable organization frequently provides services to individuals in their private capacity when it dispenses financial planning advice in the context of designing planned gifts. This type of personal service made available by an exempt organization has never been regarded as jeopardizing the organization's tax-exempt status. But the IRS refused to accord tax exemption to an organization that engages in financial counseling by providing tax planning services (including charitable giving considerations) to wealthy individuals referred to it by subscribing religious organizations. The U.S. Tax Court upheld the government's position, finding that tax planning is not an exempt activity and that the primary effect of the advice is to reduce individuals' liability for taxes—a private benefit.[98] The court rejected the contention that the organization was merely doing what the subscribing members can do themselves without endangering their tax exemption: fund raising.[99]

The private inurement proscription may operate not only with separate individuals in their private capacity but also with corporations, industries, professions, and the like. Thus, an organization primarily engaged in the testing of drugs for commercial pharmaceutical companies was ruled not to be engaged in scientific research or testing for public safety but to be serving the private interests of the manufacturers[100] Similarly, an organization composed of members of a particular industry to develop new and improved uses for existing products of the industry was ruled to be operated primarily to serve the private interests of its creators and thus not tax-exempt.[101] And, an association of

[96]Rev. Rul. 80-301, 1980-2 C.B. 180.

[97]Rev. Rul. 80-302, 1980-2 C.B. 182.

[98]*Christian Stewardship Assistance, Inc.* v. *Commissioner*, 70 T.C. 1037 (1978).

[99]But see discussion in Chapter 6, pp. 112–119.

[100]Rev. Rul. 68-373, 1968-2 C.B. 206. Also see Rev. Rul. 65-1, 1965-1 C.B. 226; IRS Private Letter Ruling 8020009.

[101]Rev. Rul. 69-632, 1969-2 C.B. 120.

professional nurses which operates a nurses' registry was ruled to be affording greater employment opportunities for its members and thus to be substantially operated for private ends.[102]

Assumption of Liability

As a general proposition, an exempt organization can incur debt to purchase an asset at fair market value and subsequently retire the debt with its receipts and not thereby violate the private inurement proscription.[103] However, if the purchase price for the asset is in excess of the property's fair market value, private inurement may result.[104]

In one instance, a nonprofit corporation was formed to take over the operations of a school conducted up to that time by a for-profit corporation. The organization assumed a liability for goodwill which the U.S. Tax Court determined was an excessive amount. The Court held that this assumption of liability was a violation of the prohibition on private inurement because it benefited the private interests of the owners of the for-profit corporation.[105] (In a footnote, the Court strongly suggested that any payment by a nonprofit corporation for goodwill constitutes a private inurement, since goodwill is generally a measure of the profit advantage in an established business and the profit motive is, by definition, not supposed to be a factor in the operation of a nonprofit organization.[106])

Employee Benefits

The IRS looks skeptically on allegedly charitable organizations established to benefit employees, particularly where the entity is controlled and funded by the employer. Thus, a trust created by an employer to pay pensions to retired employees was ruled not a charitable organiation.[107] This same result would obtain where the recipients are present employees,[108] in part because they do not constitute a charitable class.[109] Perhaps the best example of this rule is that of the foundation that lost its exemption because it devoted its funds

---

[102]Rev. Rul. 61-170, 1961-2 C.B. 112.

[103]See *Shiffman* v. *Commissioner*, 32 T.C. 1073 (1959); *Estate of Howes* v. *Commissioner*, 30 T.C. 909 (1958), aff'd sub nom. *Commissioner* v. *Johnson*, 267 F.2d 382 (1st Cir. 1959); *Ohio Furnace Co., Inc. v. Commissioner*, 25 T.C. 179 (1955), app. dis. (6th Cir. 1956).

[104]See *Kolkey* v. *Commissioner*, 27 T.C. 37 (1956), aff'd 254 F.2d 51 (7th Cir. 1958).

[105]*Hancock Academy of Savannah, Inc.* v. *Commissioner*, *supra*, n. 73.

[106]*Ibid.* at 494, n. 6.

[107]Rev. Rul. 56-138, 1956-1 C.B. 202.

[108]See *Watson* v. *United States*, 355 F.2d 269 (3d Cir. 1965); Rev. Rul. 68-422, 1968-2 C.B. 207.

[109]See Chapter 4.

to the payment of expenses of young performers employed by the foundation's founder who was in show business.[110] However, organizations such as these (and also those that are supported by employees) may nonetheless qualify for tax exemption under other aspects of federal tax law.[111]

Of course, benefits can be accorded to employees in conformance with charitable standards, particularly where the benefits are not vested in the participants and are awarded on the basis of merit as determined in individual cases.[112] In these instances, the IRS will be seeking assurance that the benefits are not a form of indirect compensation.[113]

In one case, a school's tax exemption was revoked because, for one or more of its officers, it provided interest-free, unsecured loans; paid for household items and furnishings used in the private residence; made scholarship awards to their children; paid personal travel expenses; paid for their personal automobile expenses; paid the premiums on life and health insurance policies (where such premiums were not paid for anyone else); and purchased season tickets to sports events.[114]

Tax Avoidance Schemes

The IRS classifies tax avoidance schemes involving nonprofit organizations as representing another category of private benefit. Here, the Service is concerned about the business or professional person who transfers his or her business assets to a controlled nonprofit entity solely for the purpose of avoiding taxes and then continues to operate the business or profession as an employee of the transferee organization. The IRS characterizes such schemes as follows:

Transactions of this type are lacking in substance in the sense that the transferor is still, in effect, engaging in his business or profession in his individual capacity. Since the organization is operated by the transferor essentially as an attempt to reduce his personal Federal income tax liability while still enjoying the benefits of his earnings, the organization's primary function is to serve the private interest of its creator rather than a public interest.[115] In one instance, a physician transferred his medical practice and other assets to a controlled organization, which then hired him to conduct "research," that is, examine and treat patients; tax exemption for the organization was denied.[116] In another case, an organization characterized as a church was formed by a professional nurse (who was the organization's minister, director, and principal officer). It held assets and liabilities

---

[110]*Horace Heidt Foundation* v. *United States, supra,* n. 34.
[111]See Code § 501(c)(9),(17). See Chapter 20, §§ 5 and 13.
[112]G.C.M. 19028, 1937-2 C.B. 125.
[113]*Chase* v. *Commissioner,* 19 T.C.M. 234 (1960).
[114]*John Marshall Law School* v. *United States, supra,* n. 72.
[115]IRS Exempt Organizations Handbook (IRM 7751) § 343.4.
[116]Rev. Rul. 69-266, 1969-1 C.B. 151. Also *Nittler* v. *Commissioner,* 39 T.C.M. 422 (1979); *Walker* v. *Commissioner,* 37 T.C.M. 1851 (1978); *Boyer* v. *Commissioner,* 69 T.C. 521 (1977).

formerly owned and assumed by the nurse and provided the nurse with a living allowance and use of the assets (including a house and automobile). The organization was ruled to not be tax-exempt because the corporation "serves as a vehicle for handling the nurse's personal financial transactions."[117]

Joint Ventures with Commercial Entities

The IRS is becoming increasingly concerned about the growing propensity of tax-exempt organizations to become involved in partnerships or joint ventures with individuals and/or nonexempt entities. Real estate ventures, with the tax-exempt organization as the general partner in a limited partnership, is a common manifestation of this practice. The Service is known to have a concern that some of these ventures may be a means for conferring unwarranted benefit on the private participants.

Nonetheless, one court decision sanctions the involvement of a charitable organization as a general partner in a limited partnership. The case concerns an arts organization that, to generate funds to pay its share of the capital required to produce a play with a tax-exempt theater, sold a portion of its rights in the play to outside investors by means of a limited partnership. The arts organization was the general partner, with two individuals and a for-profit corporation as limited partners. Only the limited partners were required to contribute capital and they collectively received a share of any profits or losses resulting from production of the play. In disagreeing with the IRS position that the organization, solely by involvement in the limited partnership, was being operated for private interests, the court noted that the sale of the interest in the play was for a reasonable price, the transaction was at arm's-length, the organization was not obligated for the return of any capital contribution made by the limited partners, the limited partners had no control over the organization's operations, and none of the limited partners nor any officer or director of the for-profit corporation was an officer or director of the arts organization.[118]

In one instance, the IRS approved of a joint undertaking between a blood plasma fractionation facility and a commercial laboratory, whereby the parties would acquire a building site and construct a blood fractionation facility on it. This arrangement enabled the facility to become self-sufficient in its production of blood fractions, to reduce the costs of fractionating blood, and thus to be able more effectively to carry out its charitable blood program. Each party had an equal ownership of, and shared equally in the production capacity of, the facility. The Service concluded that the organization's participation in the joint undertaking was substantially related to its tax-exempt purposes.[119]

---

[117]Rev. Rul. 81-94, 1981-1 C.B. 330. Also Rev. Rul. 78-232, 1978-1 C.B. 69. These two rulings concern the so-called "ABC Church."

[118]*Plumstead Theatre Society, Inc.* v. *Commissioner*, 74 T.C. 1324 (1980). Cf. *Broadway Theatre League of Lynchburg, Va., Inc.* v. *United States, supra*, n. 51.

[119]IRS Private Letter Ruling 7921018.

§ 12.4 "Net Earnings"

The meaning of the term "net earnings" in this context—undefined in the statute—has largely been framed in the courts.

In general, the term "net earnings" refers to gross earnings less expenses—a meaning that applies the phrase in a technical, accounting sense. The Supreme Court of Tennessee, for example, repeatedly wrote about such a definition throughout the early decades of the federal tax law. In one case, the court said that, where the term is not defined in the applicable act, it "must be given its usual and ordinary meaning of what is left of earnings after deducting necessary and legitimate items of expense incident to the corporate business."[120] This approach was followed in the early years by other state courts[121] and by federal courts.[122]

However, in the tax-exempt organizations setting, the technical meaning of the term never caught on as its sole meaning. Some courts applied the term in this manner, where the facts particularly lent themselves to this approach.[123] But most decisions on the point reflect the contemporary approach that there can be inurement of "net earnings" in the absence of transfers of net equity (such as by means of dividends).[124] An early proponent of this view was the Supreme Court of Washington, which observed that the "net earnings" phraseology "should not be given a strictly literal construction, as in the accountant's sense" and that the "substance should control the form," so that tax exemption should be denied where private inurement is taking place, "irrespective of the means by which that result is accomplished."[125] Likewise, the U.S. Court of Appeals for the Eighth Circuit foresaw today's application of the term when it held that it "may include more than the term net profits as shown by the books of the organization or than the difference between the gross receipts and disbursements in dollars" and that "[p]rofits may inure to the benefit of shareholders in other ways than dividends."[126] This view basically represents the

---

[120]*Bank of Commerce & Trust Co.* v. *Senter*, 260 S.W. 144, 151 (Sup. Ct. Tenn. 1924). Also *Southern Coal Co.* v. *McCanless*, 192 S.W.2d 1003, 1005 (Sup. Ct. Tenn. 1946); *National Life & Accident Ins. Co.* v. *Dempster*, 79 S.W.2d 564, 567 (Sup. Ct. Tenn. 1935).

[121]E.g., *Inscho* v. *Mid-Continent Development Co.*, 146 P. 1014, 1023 (Sup. Ct. Kan. 1915).

[122]E.g., *United States* v. *Riely*, 169 F.2d 542, 543 (4th Cir. 1948); *Winkelman* v. *General Motors Corporation*, 44 F. Supp. 960, 1000 (S.D.N.Y. 1942).

[123]E.g., *Birmingham Business College, Inc.* v. *Commissioner, supra*, n. 22 at 480–481; *Gemological Institute of America* v. *Commissioner*, 17 T.C. 1604, 1609 (1952), aff'd 212 F.2d 205 (9th Cir. 1954); *Putnam* v. *Commissioner*, 6 T.C. 702, 706 (1946).

[124]E.g., *Gemological Institute of America* v. *Riddell*, 149 F. Supp. 128, 130 (S.D. Cal. 1957); *Edward Orton, Jr. Ceramic Foundation* v. *Commissioner*, 9 T.C. 533 (1947), aff'd 173 F.2d 483 (6th Cir. 1949).

[125]*Virginia Mason Hospital Ass'n* v. *Larson*, 114 P.2d 978, 983 (Sup. Ct. Wash. 1941).

[126]*Northwestern Municipal Ass'n* v. *United States, supra*, n. 9 at 463.

current application of the term "net earnings"—today, a more generalized "private benefit" test.[127]

In one instance, the U.S. Tax Court, in concluding that an organization that purchases and sells products manufactured by blind persons constitutes an exempt organization, was not deterred in reaching this finding because of the fact that the organization distributes a portion of its "net profits" to qualified workers at a state agency.[128] The court appeared to hold that these profit distributions were in furtherance of exempt purposes and were insubstantial.

§ 12.5   "Incidental" Private Inurement

Even though private inurement may be present in a given factual situation, tax exemption will not be denied for that reason if the private inurement is considered "incidental." As an illustration, the IRS, having reversed an initial decision, ruled that an organization of accredited educational institutions is exempt as a "charitable" entity because the development of standards for accreditation of colleges is a charitable activity in that it constitutes the advancement of education.[129] The relevance of this ruling is that, although a "very few" schools that have been approved for membership in the organization are proprietary institutions, the Service ruled that any private benefit that may accrue to them because of accreditation is incidental to the purpose of improving the quality of education.[130]

Similarly, where a business donated lands and money to a charitable entity to establish a public park, its exemption was not jeopardized because the donor retained the right to use a scenic view in the park as a brand symbol.[131] Also, in a situation involving a business corporation that provided a substantial portion of the support of a charitable organization operating a replica of a 19th century village, where the corporation benefited by having the village named after it, by having its name associated with the village in conjunction with its own advertising program, and by having its name mentioned in each publication of the organization, the IRS ruled that "such benefits are merely incidental to the benefits flowing to the general public . . ."[132] Likewise, the IRS determined that a children's day-care center, operated in conjunction with an industrial

[127]E.g., *Harding Hospital, Inc.* v *United States, supra,* n. 37 at 1072.

[128]*Industrial Aid for the Blind* v. *Commissioner,* 73 T.C. 96 (1979). For an analysis of the applicability of the private inurement rationale in a contemporary context, i.e., in relation to hospitals' "productivity incentive programs," see Bromberg, "The Effect of Tax Policy on the Delivery and Cost of Health Care," 53 *Taxes* 452, 469–475 (1975).

[129]Rev. Rul. 74-146, 1974-1 C.B. 129. Also see Rev. Rul. 74-575, 1974-2 C.B. 161. Cf. Rev. Rul. 81-29, 1981-1 C.B. 329.

[130]The IRS subsequently held that a Code § 501(c)(3) organization may have a "relatively small" (defined as 5 percent or less) number of proprietary institutions as members without jeopardizing its tax exemption. IRS Private Letter Ruling 7816061.

[131]Rev. Rul. 66-358, *supra,* n. 47.

[132]Rev. Rul. 77-367, 1977-2 C.B. 193.

company that enrolls children on the basis of financial need and the children's needs for the care and development program of the center, is tax-exempt because any private benefit derived by the company or the parents of enrolled children was incidental to the public benefits resulting from the center's operation.[133] In another example, the IRS concluded that an otherwise exempt educational organization may produce public interest programs for viewing via public educational channels of commercial cable television companies because any benefit to the companies is "merely incidental."[134] Also, the Service concluded that the sale of items on consignment by a thrift shop does not result in the loss of tax-exempt status, in that any benefit to the consignors is "clearly incidental" to the organization's charitable purposes.[135] Likewise, a consortium of universities and libraries was advised by the IRS that it may, without jeopardizing its tax exemption, make its information dissemination services available to private businesses, since "[a]lthough there is some benefit to the private institutions such benefit is incidental to this activity and, in fact, may be said to be a logical by-product of it."[136]

Notwithstanding this general rule, some courts—particularly the U.S. Tax Court—take the position that any element of private inurement can cause an organization to lose or be deprived of tax exemption. For example, in one opinion, the Court stated that "even if the benefit inuring to the members is small, it is still impermissible."[137] This interpretation of the law is reflected in other opinions as well.[138]

[133]Rev. Rul. 70-533, 1970-2 C.B. 112.
[134]Rev. Rul. 76-4, 1976-1 C.B. 145.
[135]Rev. Rul. 80-106, 1980-1 C.B. 113.
[136]IRS Private Letter Ruling 7951134.
[137]*McGahen v. Commissioner*, 76 T.C. 468, 482 (1981).
[138]E.g., *Unitary Mission Church of Long Island* v. *Commissioner, supra,* n. 57; *Beth-El Ministries, Inc.* v. *United States*, 79-2 U.S.T.C. ¶ 9412 (D.D.C. 1979). In general, see Etzioni and Doty, "Profit In Not-For-Profit Institutions," 9 *Philanthropy Monthly* (No. 2) 22 (1976); Note, "Section 501(c)(3) and Incidental Social and Recreational Activities," 22 *St. Louis Univ. L. J.* 225 (1967); Note, " 'Inurement of Earnings to Private Benefit' Clause of Section 501(c)(3): A Standard Without Meaning?," 48 *Minn. L. Rev.* 1149 (1964).

13

Legislative Activities

Organizations described in Code § 501(c)(3) (and the contributions deduction sections[1]) are deemed to meet four basic criteria, one of which is that "no substantial part of the activities" of such organizations may constitute "carrying on propaganda, or otherwise attempting, to influence legislation." This provision was added to the federal tax law in 1934, without benefit of Congressional hearings, in the form of a floor amendment in the Senate. The sponsor of the amendment made it clear that the intent of his provision was to curb a maverick organization known as the National Economy League and stated during the debate that he did not wish to adversely affect the legislative activities of "any of the worthy institutions."

An organization is regarded as attempting to influence legislation, according to the regulations, if it (1) contacts, or urges the public to contact, members of a legislative body for the purpose of proposing, supporting, or opposing legislation, or (2) advocates the adoption or rejection of legislation.[2] Under these general rules, if a substantial part of an organization's activities is attempting to influence legislation, the organization is denominated an "action" organization and hence cannot qualify as a "charitable" entity.[3]

Generally, as discussed,[4] a contribution to a charitable organization results in a charitable contribution deduction. However, where a charitable organization receives a contribution that is earmarked for use in influencing specific legislation, the contribution is not deductible as a charitable gift.[5]

---

[1]Code §§ 170(c)(2)(B), 2055(a)(2), 2106(a)(2)(A)(ii) and (iii), and 2522(a)(2) and (b)(2).
[2]Reg. § 1.501(c)(3)-1(c)(3)(ii).
[3]See Chapter 5.
[4]See Chapter 3 § 2.
[5]Rev. Rul. 80-275, 1980-2 C. B. 69. Also Rev. Rul. 79-81, 1979-1 C.B. 107; Rev. Rul. 68-484, 1968-2 C. B. 105; Rev. Rul. 62-113, 1962-2 C. B. 10; and Rev. Rul. 56-329, 1956-2 C. B. 125.

§ 13.1 "Legislative Activities"

Legislative activities take many forms, including the presentation of testimony at public hearings held by legislative committees, correspondence and conferences with legislators and their staffs, publication of documents advocating specific legislative action, and appeals to the general public to contact legislators or take other specific action as regards legislative matters (so-called "grass-roots" lobbying).[6] In the view of the IRS, it is irrelevant, for purposes of classification as a "charitable" organization, that the legislation advocated would advance the charitable purposes for which the organization was created to promote.[7] This position should be contrasted with the state of the law prior to enactment of the Revenue Act of 1934.[8]

However, for an organization to be denied or lose tax-exempt status because of lobbying activity, the legislative activities must be undertaken as an act of the organization itself. Thus, for example, the IRS has recognized that the legislative activities of a student newspaper are not attributable to the sponsoring university.[9] Similarly, during the course of the anti-Indochina War efforts on many college and university campuses, which included legislative activities, the principle was established that the activities by students and faculty were not official acts of the particular institution.[10]

§ 13.2 "Legislation"

The term "legislation" has several manifestations, principally action by Congress, a state legislative body, a local council or similar governing body, and the general public in a referendum, initiative, constitutional amendment, or similar procedure.[11]

"Legislation" does not include action by the executive branch, such as the

---

[6]*Roberts Dairy Co.* v. *Commissioner*, 195 F.2d 948 (8th Cir. 1952), cert. den. 344 U. S. 865 (1952); *American Hardware and Equipment Co.* v. *Commissioner*, 202 F.2d 126 (4th Cir. 1953), cert. den. 346 U. S. 814 (1953).

[7]Rev. Rul. 67-293, 1967-2 C. B. 185. See *Cammarano* v. *United States*, 358 U. S. 498 (1959).

[8]See *Slee* v. *Commissioner*, 42 F.2d 184, 185 (2d Cir. 1930).

[9]Rev. Rul. 72-513, 1972-2 C. B. 246.

[10]See American Council on Education guidelines, CCH *Stand. Fed. Tax Rep.* ¶ 3033.197. In general, see Hopkins and Myers, "Governmental Response to Campus Unrest," 22 *Case Western Res. L. Rev.* 408 (1971); Broughton, "New Politics on the Campus, Reconstitution, The Princeton Plan," VI *The College Counsel* 119 (1971); Field, "Tax Exempt Status of Universities: Impact of Political Activities by Students," 24 *Tax Lawyer* 157 (1970); Goldberg, "Guarding against loss of tax exempt status due to campus politics," 33 *J. Tax.* 232 (1970); Note, "Taxation—University Political Activities and Federal Tax Exemption: American Council on Education Guidelines," 84 *Harv. L. Rev.* 463 (1970).

[11]Reg. § 1.501(c)(3)-1(c)(3)(ii). But see *Smith* v. *Commissioner*, 3 T. C. 696 (1944).

promulgation of rules and regulations, nor does it include action by the independent regulatory agencies.[12] It seems to be generally assumed that appropriations bills are "legislation" for tax purposes, although the term is a derivative of the word "law," which generally refers to rules of conduct. By contrast, the enactment of an appropriations measure merely amounts to the establishment of budget authority—basically authority in the executive branch to obligate and expend funds. Also, the term "legislation" includes foreign as well as domestic laws.[13]

§ 13.3 The Concept of "Substantial"

A determination as to whether a specific activity or category of activities of an exempt organization is "substantial" must basically be a factual one and, until enactment of the elective rules, discussed below, the law offered no formula for computing "substantial" or "insubstantial" legislative undertakings. Thus, the Senate Finance Committee, in its report accompanying the Tax Reform Act of 1969, said that "the standards as to the permissible level of [legislative] activities under the present law are so vague as to encourage subjective application of the sanction."[14] In its report accompanying the Tax Reform Act of 1976, the Senate Finance Committee portrayed the dilemma this way: "Many believe that the standards as to the permissible level of [legislative] activities under present law are too vague and thereby tend to encourage subjective and selective enforcement."[15]

One approach for attempting to measure substantiality in this context is to determine what percentage of an organization's spending is devoted on an annual basis to efforts to "influence legislation." (As discussed below, this is the approach eventually adopted by Congress.) Yet the prohibition against legislative influencing may have been intended to involve more than simply an expenditure or diversion of funds and to include restrictions on certain levels of activity. A portion of an organization's efforts and activities devoted to legislative activities may well be regarded as more important than the organization's expenditures for the purpose.[16] It was once suggested that five percent of an organization's time and effort which involves legislative activities is not "substantial."[17]

However, in the context of activities, a percentage standard may be of less utility. An exempt organization enjoying considerable prestige and influence

[12]See Gellhorn, "Public Participation in Administrative Proceedings," 81 *Yale L. J.* 359 (1972).

[13]Rev. Rul. 73-440, 1973-2 C. B. 177.

[14]S. Rep. No. 91-552, 91st Cong., 1st Sess. (1969), at 47.

[15]S. Rep. No. 94-938 (Part 2), 94th Cong., 2d Sess. (1976), at 80.

[16]See *League of Women Voters* v. *United States*, 180 F.Supp. 379 (Ct. Cl. 1960), cert. den. 364 U. S. 822 (1960).

[17]*Seasongood* v. *Commissioner*, 227 F.2d 907, 912 (6th Cir. 1955).

might be considered as having a "substantial" impact on the legislative process solely on the basis of a single official position statement, an activity considered negligible when measured according to a percentage standard of time expended.[18] A standard such as this, however, would tend to place undue emphasis on whether or not a particular legislative effort was successful.[19]

In 1972, the U.S. Court of Appeals for the Tenth Circuit gave a new dimension to the concept of "attempting to influence legislation," when it upheld the revocation of tax exemption of the Christian Echoes National Ministry.[20] The court, after holding that the pertinent income tax regulations properly interpret the intent of Congress (before enactment of the elective rules), found the following "substantial" legislative activities: articles constituting appeals to the public to react to certain issues, support or opposition to specific terms of legislation and enactments, and efforts to cause members of the public to contact members of Congress on various matters. Of particular consequence was the court's explicit rejection of a percentage test in determining "substantiality," which was dismissed as obscuring the "complexity of balancing the organization's activities in relation to its objectives and circumstances."[21] Said the court: "The political [i.e., legislative] activities of an organization must be balanced in the context of the objectives and circumstances of the organization to determine whether a *substantial* part of its activities was to influence or attempt to influence legislation."[22]

§ 13.4   The Elective Rules

Because of the considerable and continuing uncertainty as to the meaning and scope of the rules proscribing legislative activities by charitable organizations, Congress, in enacting the Tax Reform Act of 1976, sought to clarify and amplify the proscription. While the difficulties of compliance with the legislative activities limitation have been manifold, perhaps the greatest dilemma has been in relation to ascertainment of the method by which "substantial" activities are determined, that is, whether such activities are a function of time expended, funds spent, or some other criterion.

The effort to clarify the legislative activities prohibition by statute occupied several years. There were several reasons for favoring legislative revision in

[18]See *Kuper* v. *Commissioner*, 332 F.2d 562 (3d Cir. 1964), cert. den. 379 U. S. 920 (1964).

[19]See *Haswell* v. *United States*, 500 F.2d 1133, 1142 (Ct. Cl. 1974), cert. den. 419 U. S. 1107 (1974); *Dulles* v. *Johnson*, 273 F.2d 362, 367 (2d Cir. 1959), cert. den. 364 U. S. 834 (1960).

[20]*Christian Echoes National Ministry, Inc.* v. *United States*, 470 F.2d 849 (10th Cir. 1972), cert. den. 414 U. S. 864 (1973).

[21]*Ibid*. at 855.

[22]*Ibid*.

this area, not the least of which was the discrepancy in federal tax law which fully allowed business and industry groups favorable tax treatment in connection with presentation of their views to Congress[23] but denied the same access (other than "incidentally") to "charitable" organizations.

The 1976 law change is traceable to a proposal from the American Bar Association, recommending that charitable organizations be permitted to engage in legislative activities akin to those allowed business and industry groups, that is, legislative efforts as respects matters of direct interest to the organization and its members (if any).[24] In 1971, then-Senator Edmund Muskie (D-Me.) introduced a bill to permit publicly supported exempt organizations to communicate directly with Congress and the state legislatures, as well as with the organizations' members, to affect legislation of direct interest to them.[25] This proposal would not have had any impact on the law which prohibits grass-roots (public) lobbying (other than to an "insubstantial" extent) nor would the existing prohibition on participation or intervention in any political campaign on behalf of any candidate for public office have been affected.

Specifically, the bill would have allowed public charities to, without endangering their tax-exempt status, "[appear] before, [submit] statements to, or [send] communications to, the committees, or individual members, of Congress or of any legislative body of a State, a possession of the United States, or a political subdivision of any of the foregoing with respect to legislation or proposed legislation of direct interest to the organization." The measure also would have permitted "communication of information between the organization and its members or contributors with respect to legislation or proposed legislation of direct interest to the organization." The term matters "of direct interest to the organization" would have been defined as those matters "directly affecting any purpose for which it is organized and operated." However, the foregoing changes would not have applied to "any attempt to influence the general public, or segments thereof, with respect to legislative matters, elections, or referendums."

Senator Muskie said that "if we are to maintain a democratic form of government in practice, and if the Congress is to reach reasoned judgments on the important issues before it, we must assure that every segment of our society is able to communicate with Congress. With its present restrictions, the Tax Code seriously impedes such communication."[26] Added Muskie: "It makes no sense to decide that these [charitable, educational, etc.] organizations operate in the public interest and grant them tax-exempt status and then silence them when they attempt to speak to those who must decide public policy." He concluded:

---

[23]See Code § 162(e).
[24]See 21 *Tax Law.* 915, 967 (1968).
[25]S. 1408, 92d Cong., 1st Sess. (1971). Also H. R. 8176, 8920 (1971).
[26]117 Cong. Rec. 8517 (1971).

Why should the Government encourage private business to communicate with Congress by making lobbying a business expense which can be deducted from taxes, while preventing strong efforts of public-interest groups to speak to lawmakers by removing their tax-exempt status when they raise their voices?

The Muskie measure was subsequently reintroduced to provide that public charities had to have a substantial purpose other than lobbying.[27]

A subsequent bill introduced by then-House Ways and Means Committee Chairman Al Ullman (D-Ore.), which bears considerable resemblance to the statute ultimately adopted, introduced the concepts of a percentage qualification of what constitutes substantial legislative activities and a feature giving public charities the option to elect to be covered by the statutory tests.[28]

The bills introduced thereafter became more detailed and perhaps unnecessarily intricate as the sponsors and their staff continued to imagine more and more ways in which public charities would ostensibly misuse their new lobbying authority. The subsequent measures include a refined version of the Ullman bill, which contained a sliding scale of percentages for assessing substantiality of legislative efforts,[29] and a bill introduced by Rep. Barber Conable (R-N.Y.), which also embodied a sliding scale and an exclusion for certain types of communications on legislative matters between an organization and its members.[30]

Provisions to these effects were contained in the proposed Tax Reform Act of 1974 which died aborning in the House Committee on Ways and Means. Once again, however, the efforts to produce some statutory clarification in this area persisted, with the result that the House passed a measure to this end in 1976.[31] This bill was eventually subsumed within the Tax Reform Act of 1976, which introduced four new federal tax law provisions.[32]

These provisions define a permissible range of legislative activities in terms of the expenditure of funds. (The legislative history of these provisions indicates, however, that the basic concept that legislative activities cannot be a "substantial" portion of the efforts of a "charitable" organization has not been disturbed.) However, "charitable" organizations must elect to come under the new standards, and can do so on a year-to-year basis.[33] Those that choose to not make the election are governed by the pre-existing tests, with all of their

---

[27]S. 3063, 92d Cong. 2d Sess. (1972). See 118 Cong. Rec. 843 (1972).

[28]H.R. 13720, 92d Cong., 2d Sess. (1972). See "Legislative Activity By Certain Types of Exempt Organizations," Hearings Before House Committee on Ways and Means, 92d Cong., 2d Sess. (1972).

[29]H.R. 5095, 93d Cong., 1st Sess. (1973).

[30]H.R. 10237, 93d Cong., 1st Sess. (1973). Also S. 1036, 93d Cong., 1st Sess. (1973); 119 Cong. Rec. 5746 (1973).

[31]H.R. 13500, 94th Cong. 2d Sess. (1976). Also H.R. 8021, S. 2832, 94th Cong., 1st Sess. (1975).

[32]Code §§ 501(h), 504, 4911, 6033(b)(8).

[33]This election, and any revocation thereof, is made by filing IRS Form 5768.

uncertainties. Churches, conventions or associations of churches, integrated auxiliaries thereof, certain supporting entities of noncharitable organizations, and private foundations may not elect to come under the new rules—the latter having been subjected to stringent regulation in this regard in 1969.[34]

These standards are formulated in terms of declining percentages of total expenditures. The basic permitted annual level of expenditures for legislative efforts (the "lobbying nontaxable amount") is 20 percent of the first $500,000 of an organization's expenditures for an exempt purpose (including legislative but not fund-raising activities), plus 15 percent of the next $500,000, 10 percent of the next $500,000, and 5 percent of any remaining expenditures. However, the total amount spent for legislative activities in any one year by an organization may not exceed $1,000,000. A specific limitation—amounting to one-fourth of the foregoing amounts—is imposed on attempts to influence the general public on legislative matters ("grass-roots lobbying").

A charitable organization that has elected these limitations and that exceeds them becomes subject to an excise tax in the amount of 25 percent of the excess lobbying expenditures. As respects these two limitations, the tax falls on the greater of the two excesses. If an electing organization's lobbying expenditures normally (that is, on an average over a four-year period) exceed 150 percent of the limitation, it will lose its tax-exempt status as a "charitable" entity. The statute provides that such an organization may not convert to a tax-exempt social welfare organization.[35]

The term "legislation" is defined to include "action with respect to Acts, bills, resolutions, or similar items by the Congress, any State legislature, any local council or similar governing body, or by the public in a referendum, initiative, constitutional amendment, or similar procedure."[36] The term "action" is "limited to the introduction, amendment, enactment, defeat, or repeal of Acts, bills, resolutions, or similar items."[37]

The rules define the term "influencing legislation" as meaning any attempt to influence any legislation through an attempt to affect the opinion of the general public (as noted, "grass-roots lobbying") and through communication with any member or employee of a legislative body or any other governmental official or employee who participates in the formulation of the legislation ("direct lobbying").[38] Five categories of activities are excluded from the term "influencing legislation": (1) making available the results of nonpartisan analysis, study, or research, (2) providing technical advice or assistance in response to a written request by a governmental body, (3) appearances before, or communications to, any legislative body with respect to a possible decision of that body which might affect the existence of the organization, its powers and duties,

---

[34]Code § 4945(d)(1), (e). See Chapter 29.
[35]See Chapters 15 and 16. Cf. Reg. § 1.501(c)(3)-1(c)(3)(v).
[36]Code § 4911(e)(2).
[37]Code § 4911(e)(3).
[38]Code § 4911(d)(1).

its tax-exempt status, or the deduction of contributions to it, (4) communications between the organization and its bona fide members, unless the communications directly encourage the members to influence legislation or directly encourage the members to urge nonmembers to influence legislation, and (5) routine communications with government officials or employees.[39]

The rules contain a method of aggregating the expenditures of related organizations, so as to forestall the creation of numerous organizations for the purpose of avoiding the foregoing tests. Where two or more "charitable" organizations are members of an affiliated group and at least one of the members has elected coverage under these provisions, the calculations of lobbying and exempt purpose expenditures must be made by taking into account the expenditures of the group. If these expenditures exceed the permitted limits, each of the electing member organizations must pay a proportionate share of the penalty excise tax, with the nonelecting members treated under preexisting law.[40]

Generally, under these rules, two organizations are deemed "affiliated" where (1) one organization is bound by decisions of the other on legislative issues pursuant to its governing instrument or (2) the governing board of one organization includes enough representatives of the other (that is, there is an "interlocking directorate") to cause or prevent action on legislative issues by the first organization. Where a number of organizations are affiliated, even in chain fashion, all of them are treated as one group of affiliated organizations. However, if a group of autonomous organizations controls an organization but no one organization in the controlling group alone can control that organization, the organizations are not considered an affiliated group by reason of the interlocking directorates rule.

In order to make information about the legislative activities of (electing) charitable organizations obtainable by the public, Congress expanded the required contents for annual information returns.[41] Thus an electing organization must disclose in the information return the amount of its lobbying expenditures (total and grass-roots), together with the amount that it could have spent for legislative purposes without becoming subject to the 25 percent excise tax. An electing organization that is a member of an affiliated group must provide this information with respect to both itself and the entire group.[42]

In general, these rules became effective for tax years beginning after December 31, 1976. However, the rule precluding a charitable organization which has engaged in excessive lobbying from converting to an exempt social welfare organization applies to activities occurring after October 4, 1976 (the date of enactment of the Tax Reform Act of 1976).

Even though these rules were enacted in 1976, the interpretative regulations

[39]Code § 4911(d)(2).
[40]Code § 4911(f).
[41]See Chapter 38.
[42]Code § 6033(b)(8).

have not as yet been promulgated (as of early 1983). Consequently, in the absence of any court decisions or IRS public rulings, the myriad issues raised by the rules remain unanswered. However, as to one issue—the question as to the degree of allocations of expenses required in ascertaining the lobbying amounts—some private letter rulings indicate that the IRS is going to be rather strict on the subject. In one ruling, in ascertaining an amount of nondeductible grass-roots lobbying expenses by a corporation, the IRS took into account not only items as the costs of writing materials, postage, and other office supplies but also the allocable portion of managers' and employees' salaries.[43] In another ruing, the IRS allocated to (and held nondeductible) the operational expenses of a political action committee the portion of a corporation's officers' and employees' salaries devoted to the committee's activities, based in part on the time expended by these individuals after regular business hours.[44]

§ 13.5   The "Action" Organization

A charitable organization found to have engaged in legislative activities to a prohibited extent is deemed an "action" organization and thus is not entitled to continuing tax exemption. Likewise, legislative activities may preclude tax exemption. One form of action organization is one as to which a "substantial part of its activities is attempting to influence legislation by propaganda or otherwise."[45] Another type of action organization is one as to which its "main or primary objective or objectives (as distinguished from its incidental or secondary objectives) may be attained only by legislation or a defeat of proposed legislation," and "it advocates, or campaigns for, the attainment of such main or primary objective or objectives as distinguished from engaging in nonpartisan analysis, study or research and making the results thereof available to the public."[46]

The IRS conceded in 1970 that a charitable organization which does not initiate any action with respect to pending legislation but merely responds to a request from a legislative committee to testify is not, solely because of such activity, an "action" organization.[47] To sustain this "exception," the IRS stated that (1) proscribed attempts to influence legislation "imply an affirmative act and require something more than a mere passive response to a Committee invitation" and (2) "it is unlikely that Congress, in framing the language of this position [Code § 501(c)(3)], intended to deny itself access to the best technical expertise available on any matter with which it concerns itself."[48]

[43]IRS Private Letter Ruling 8202021.

[44]IRS Private Letter Ruling 8202019.

[45]Reg. § 1.501(c)(3)-1(c)(3)(ii).

[46]Reg. § 1.501(c)(3)-1(c)(3)(iv). In general, see *McClintock-Trunkey Co.* v. *Commissioner*, 19 T. C. 297 (1952), rev'd on other issue, 217 F.2d 329 (9th Cir. 1955).

[47]Rev. Rul. 70-449, 1970-2 C. B. 111.

[48]See Curtis, "The House Committee on Ways and Means: Congress Seen Through a Key Committee," 1966 *Wis. L. Rev.* 121, 132 (1966).

§ 13.6 Nonpartisan Analysis/Research or Propaganda

An organization may engage in nonpartisan analysis, study, and research and publish its results (that is, perform "educational" activities[49]), where some of the plans and policies formulated can only be carried out through legislative enactments, without being an "action" organization, as long as it does not advocate the adoption of legislation or legislative action to implement its findings.[50] That is, an organization may evaluate a subject of proposed legislation or a pending item of legislation and present to the public an objective analysis of it, as long as it does not participate in the presentation of suggested bills to the legislature and does not engage in any campaign to secure enactment of the legislation.[51] But if the organization's primary objective can be attained only by legislative action, it is an "action" organization.[52] In general, promoting activism instead of promoting educational activities can deny an organization classification as a "charitable" entity.[53]

As for the specific connotation of the term "propaganda," it appears quite clear that the term is not as expansive as merely spreading particular beliefs, opinions, or doctrines. Rather, the word "connotes public address with selfish or ulterior purpose and characterized by the coloring or distortion of facts."[54] To avoid stigmatization as "propaganda," therefore, a presentation must be fairly well balanced as to stating alternative viewpoints and solutions, and be motivated more by a purpose to educate than by a "selfish" purpose.[55]

§ 13.7 Constitutional Law Considerations

It has been asserted that the proscription on substantial legislative activities contained in Code § 501(c)(3) is violative of constitutional law principles.[56] While the issues have been repeatedly presented to the courts, until 1982 none of the litigants had been successful in securing a decision finding that this provision is constitutionally deficient.

Representative of these decisions was that handed down in 1979 in a case

---

[49]See Chapter 7.

[50]Reg. § 1.501(c)(3)-1(c)(3)(iv); Rev. Rul. 70-79, 1970-1 C. B. 127; *Weyl* v. *Commissioner*, 48 F.2d 811 (2d Cir. 1931).

[51]Rev. Rul. 64-195, 1964-2 C. B. 138; I. T. 2654, XI-2 C. B. 39 (1932).

[52]Rev. Rul. 62-71, 1962-1 C. B. 85; *Haswell* v. *United States*, *supra*, n. 19 at 1143–1145.

[53]Rev. Rul. 60-193, 1960-1 C. B. 195, as modified by Rev. Rul. 66-258, 1966-2 C. B. 213.

[54]*Seasongood* v. *Commissioner*, *supra*, n. 17 at 910-912. Also see *Cochran* v. *Commissioner*, 78 F.2d 176, 179 (4th Cir. 1935).

[55]See Rev. Rul. 68-263, 1968-1 C. B. 256.

[56]See, e.g., Troyer, "Charities, Law-Making, and the Constitution: The Validity of the Restrictions on Influencing Legislation," 31 *N.Y.U. Inst. on Fed. Tax.* 1415 (1973); Note, "Regulating the Political Activities of Foundations," 83 *Harv. L. Rev.* 1843 (1970).

initiated by Taxation With Representation of Washington.[57] The issues involved were the following: does this tax limitation on legislative activities (1) impose an unconstitutional condition upon the exercise of First Amendment rights (i.e., the right to engage in legislative activity), (2) restrict the exercise of First Amendment rights as being a discriminatory denial of tax exemption for engaging in speech, (3) deny organizations so restricted the equal protection of the laws in violation of the Fifth Amendment, and/or (4) lack a compelling governmental interest which would justify the restrictions on First Amendment rights?

The approach of the courts on the First Amendment question has been to recognize that the lobbying of legislators constitutes an exercise of the First Amendment right of petition[58] and thus that the Amendment protects legislative activities. Oft-cited in this context is the Supreme Court declaration that the general advocacy of ideas is constitutionally protected as part of this nation's "profound national commitment to the principle that debate on public issues should be uninhibited, robust, and wide-open."[59] However, the courts inevitably go on to observe that the tax law does not violate First Amendment rights because it does not on its face prohibit organizations from engaging in substantial efforts to influence legislation.[60]

This position is based on a 1959 Supreme Court pronouncement upholding the constitutionality of a regulation which excluded from deduction as business expenses amounts expended for the promotion or defeat of legislation.[61] There, the Court stated that the "[p]etitioners are not being denied a tax deduction because they engage in constitutionally protected activities, but are simply being required to pay for these activities entirely out of their own pocketbook, as everyone else engaging in similar activities is required to do under the provisions of the Internal Revenue Code."[62] Thus, when it comes to substantial legislative activities, charitable organizations are required to fund these efforts from their own resources, and such a result is not regarded as a denial of a deduction for engaging in constitutionally protected activities.

As regards the second aspect of the First Amendment question, this argument is premised upon the fact that several categories of tax-exempt organizations are free to lobby[63] and that certain types of outlays by business cor-

---

[57]*Taxation With Representation of Washington* v. *Blumenthal*, 79-1 U.S.T.C. ¶ 9185 (D.D.C. 1979).

[58]E.g., *Eastern Railroad Presidents Conference* v. *Noerr Motor Freight, Inc.*, 365 U. S. 127 (1961); *Liberty Lobby, Inc.* v. *Pearson*, 390 F.2d 489 (D.C. Cir. 1968).

[59]*New York Times Co.* v. *Sullivan*, 376 U. S. 254, 270 (1964).

[60]See *Taxation with Representation* v. *United States*, 585 F.2d 1219 (4th Cir. 1978), cert. den. 441 U. S. 905 (1979).

[61]*Cammarano* v. *United States, supra* n. 7.

[62]*Ibid.* at 513.

[63]See, e.g., the organizations described in Code §§ 501(c)(4), (5), (6), (8), (9), and (19).

porations for lobbying are deductible.[64] Thus, the proposition is that the lobbying condition on charitable groups is a discriminatory denial of a tax exemption for engaging in speech. The courts hold that this principle relates to legislative efforts "aimed at the suppression of dangerous ideas"[65] and not to denials or revocation of tax exemptions for charitable organizations.

Similar short shrift has been given to the equal protection challenge, which is based upon the fact that similarly situated (i.e., tax-exempt) organizations are accorded different treatment with respect to lobbying activities. The courts usually concede that this involves a classification that accords differing treatment to classes but that it is permissible since the classification does not affect a "fundamental" right nor involve a "suspect" class.[66] The applicable standard of scrutiny—which this statutory limitation has been repeatedly ruled to satisfy— is whether the challenged classification is reasonably related to a legitimate governmental purpose.[67]

This standard is also deemed met where the courts evaluate the constitutionality of the proscription on legislative activity as respects legislative activities in relation to the requirement that it be rationally related to a legitimate government purpose.[68] Several of these purposes are usually found served: "assurance of governmental neutrality with respect to the lobbying activities of charitable organizations; prevention of abuse of charitable lobbying by private interests; and preservation of a balance between the lobbying activities of charitable organizations and those of non-charitable organizations and individuals."[69]

Thus, until 1982, all courts that considered the matter had made it clear that there is no constitutional imperfection in the federal tax anti-lobbying clause.[70] But, in that year, the U.S. Court of Appeals for the District of Columbia Circuit changed the complexion of the constitutional law concerning the anti-lobbying rule applicable to "charitable" organizations. The appellate court agreed that this restriction on legislative activities is not violative of free speech (First Amendment) rights but—after concluding that an organization

---

[64]See Chapter 17 § 5.

[65]*Speiser v. Randall,* 357 U. S. 513, 519 (1958), where the U. S. Supreme Court struck down a state statute that required veterans to take a loyalty oath as a condition to the receipt of a veterans' property tax exemption.

[66]See, e.g., *San Antonio Independent School District v. Rodriguez,* 411 U. S. 1 (1973); *Dunn v. Blumstein,* 405 U. S. 330 (1972); *Shapiro v. Thompson,* 394 U. S. 618 (1969).

[67]See, e.g., *United States Department of Agriculture v. Moreno,* 413 U. S. 528 (1973); *Frontiero v. Richardson,* 411 U. S. 677 (1973).

[68]See, e.g., *United States v. O'Brien,* 391 U. S. 367 (1968); *Schenk v. United States,* 249 U. S. 47 (1919).

[69]*Taxation With Representation of Washington v. Blumenthal, supra,* n. 57.

[70]See *Haswell v. United States, supra,* n. 19 at 500 F.2d 1147–1150; *Tax Analysts and Advocates v. Shultz,* 74-2 U.S.T.C. ¶ 9601 (D.D.C. 1974), aff'd 512 F.2d 992 (D.C. Cir. 1975)(suit to declare legislative activities provision of Code § 501(c)(3) dismissed).

which acquires tax exemption and charitable donee status is thereby receiving a government subsidy—held that this subsidy cannot constitutionally be accorded on a discriminatory basis and that to do so is violative of equal protection (Fifth Amendment) rights.[71] Therefore, the court held, the fact that "charitable" organizations are required to limit their lobbying to an "insubstantial" extent, while certain other organizations—such as veterans' organizations—can lobby without such limits, is an unconstitutionally discriminatory allocation of this "government subsidy."[72]

The appellate court held that "[b]y subsidizing the lobbying activities of veterans' organizations while failing to subsidize the lobbying of . . . charitable groups, Congress has violated the equal protection guarantees of the Constitution."[73] While the court decided that the challenge to the lobbying restriction is "weak" if based solely on free speech claims and is "weak" if based solely on equal protection claims,[74] it concluded that "the whole of . . . [the] argument well exceeds the sum of its parts" and that "a First Amendment concern must inform the equal protection analysis in this case."[75]

As a prelude to its findings, the court concluded that a "high level of scrutiny is required" because the lobbying restriction on charitable organizations "constitutes a limitation on protected First Amendment activity" and because the equal protection argument involves "what is clearly a fundamental right."[76] Under law, this "scrutiny" requires a determination as to whether "a substantial governmental interest supports the classification."[77] The court based its conclusion on the premise that nonprofit organizations that embody both features of tax exemption and eligibility to attract tax-deductible contributions are essentially alike. Inasmuch as the court was unpersuaded that there is a valid governmental interest to be served by treating charitable groups and veterans' groups differently on the matter of lobbying, the court ruled that the distinctions between the two classes of entities are "post hoc rationales" that are "constitutionally illegitimate."[78] Hence, the court found an unconstitutional denial of equal protection rights.

The remedy desired by the plaintiff in this case was the invalidation of the

[71]*Taxation With Representation of Washington* v. *Regan*, 676 F.2d 715 (D.C. Cir. 1982).

[72]"Charitable" organizations are those that are tax-exempt by reason of Code § 501(c)(3) and that are charitable donees by reason of Code § 170(c)(2); veterans' organizations are tax-exempt by reason of Code § 501(c)(3), (4), or (19), and are charitable donees by reason of Code § 170(c)(3).

[73]*Taxation With Representation of Washington* v. *Regan, supra,* n. 71 at 717.

[74]*Ibid.* As to the equal protection aspect, the court conceded that "Congress has vast leeway under the Constitution to classify the recipients of its benefits and to favor some groups over others." *Id.* at 740.

[75]*Id.* at 715.

[76]*Id.* at 730.

[77]*Id.* at 731.

[78]*Id.* at 739.

lobbying restrictions on charitable organizations. This the court was disinclined to do. First, it wrote that unfettered lobbying by charitable organizations would increase the likelihood of "selfish" contributions made solely to advance the donors' personal legislative interests.[79] Second, the court concluded that Congress believes that the public interest requires limitations on lobbying by charitable organizations and that "[e]ven when they attempt to remedy constitutional violations, courts must resist ordering relief that clearly exceeds the legitimate expectations of Congress."[80] The reverse approach—to place the same restrictions on veterans' groups as are presently imposed upon charitable groups—was far more appealing to the court and received serious consideration. But the court hesitated to strike down what it termed the "preferential treatment now accorded the lobbying of veterans' organizations" since veterans' groups were not parties to the litigation.[81] Instead, the case was ordered remanded to the district court "with the instruction that it cure the constitutionally invalid operation of Section 501(c) after inviting veterans' organizations to participate in framing the relief."[82] However, before the remand could occur, the decision was appealed to the U.S. Supreme Court.[83]

It is unlikely that the enactment of the rules in 1976 liberalizing the ability of public charities to engage in legislative activities will stem the flow of comment and proposed legislation on the subject. In fact, a call for further legislative action in this area appeared within days of adoption of the 1976 tax act.[84] For example, practitioners are likely to protest the uncertainties and other troubles lurking in the percentage calculation and attribution rules. This segment of the law of tax-exempt organizations has always been a fertile field for the commentators[85] and is likely to remain so.

[79]*Id*. at 742.

[80]*Id*.

[81]*Id*. at 743.

[82]*Id*. at 744.

[83]*Regan* v. *Taxation With Representation of Washington, appeal docketed*, No. 81-2338 (U. S. Sup. Ct. 1982). A fuller analysis of this decision appears in Hopkins, "Nonprofit Lobbying: Are the Rules Changing?," 23 *Foundation News* (No. 3) 46 (May/June 1982).

[84]Note, "Lobbying by Section 501(c)(3) Organizations Under the Tax Reform Act of 1976: A Proposal for Change," 30 *Tax Lawyer* 214 (1976).

[85]See Webster and Krebs, *Associations and Lobbying Regulation* (1979). Washburn, "New Tax Act Defines 'Substantial' Lobbying—But Charities Must Elect to be Covered," 55 *Taxes* 291 (1977); Bostick, "Lobbying By Non-Profit Groups," 1 *District Lawyer* (No. 3) 21 (1977); Whaley, "Political Activities of Section 501(c)(3) Organizations," *Proceedings of Univ. S. Cal. Law Center 29th Tax Institute* 195 (1977); Weithorn, "Practitioners' planning guide to the new lobbying rules for public charities," 46 *J. Tax.* 294 (1977); Hyslop and Ebell, "Public Interest Lobbying and the Tax Reform Act of 1976," 7 *Environmental Law* 283 (1977); Moore, Washburn and Goldman, "Restrictions on Lobbying Activities by Charitable Organizations: Proposed Legislative Remedies," 3 *Notre Dame J. Legis.* 17 (1976); Fogel, "To the I.R.S., 'Tis Better to Give Than to

Lobby," 61 *A.B.A. J.* 960 (1975); Caplin and Timbie, "Legislative Activities of Public Charities," 39 *Law and Contemporary Problems* 183 (1975); Note, "Political Speech of Charitable Organizations Under the Internal Revenue Code," 41 *Univ. Chi. L. Rev.* 352 (1974); Geske, "Direct Lobbying Activities of Public Charities," 26 *Tax Lawyer* 305 (1973); Green, "Activism and the Tax Status of Exempt Organizations," 44 *Penn. B.A.Q.* 500 (1973); Wachtel, "David Meets Goliath in the Legislative Arena: A Losing Battle for an Equal Charitable Voice?," 9 *San Diego L. Rev.* 933 (1972); Garrett, "Federal Tax Limitations on Political Activities of Public Interest and Educational Organizations," 59 *Geo. L. J.* 561 (1971); Goldberg, "Guarding against loss of tax exempt status due to campus politics," 33 *J. Tax.* 232 (1970); Hauptman, "Tax-Exempt Private Educational Institutions: A Survey of the Prohibition Against Influencing Legislation and Intervening in Political Matters," 37 *Brooklyn L. Rev.* 107 (1970); Lehrfeld, "The Taxation of Ideology," 19 *Cath. Univ. L. Rev.* 50 (1969); Note, "Sierra Club, Political Activity, and Tax-Exempt Charitable Status," 55 *Geo. L. J.* 1128 (1967); Note, "Income Taxes-Deductions: In General—IRS Proposes to Revoke Sierra Club's Eligibility to Receive Deductible Contributions Because of the Club's Political Activities," 80 *Harv. L. Rev.* 1793 (1967); Borod, "Lobbying for the Public Interest—Federal Tax Policy and Administration," 42 *N.Y.U.L. Rev.* 1087 (1967); Grant, "Sierra Club: The Procedural Aspects of the Revocation of its Tax Exemption," 15 *U.C.L.A. L. Rev.* 200 (1967); Boehm, "Taxes and Politics," 22 *Tax L. Rev.* 369 (1967); Clark, "The Limitation on Political Activities: A Discordant Note in the Law of Charities," 46 *Va. L. Rev.* 439 (1960); Note, "The Effect of Legislative Activity on the Tax Status of Religious, Charitable and Scientific Organizations," 10 *Ohio State L. J.* 414 (1957); Note, "Tax Treatment of Lobbying Expenses and Contributions," 67 *Harv. L. Rev.* 1408 (1954).

14

Political Activities

Organizations described in Code § 501(c)(3) (and the contributions deduction sections) are deemed to meet four basic criteria, one of which is that these organizations must "not participate in, or intervene in (including the publishing or distributing of statements), any political campaign on behalf of any candidate for public office."

This criterion has an origin remarkably similar to that of the proscription on substantial legislative activities by charitable groups.[1] This provision was added, during Senate debate, as a floor amendment offered by then-Senator Lyndon B. Johnson to the bill which subsequently became the Internal Revenue Code of 1954. The proposal was made in an attempt to curb the activities of a private foundation in Texas that Senator Johnson believed had provided indirect financial support to his opponent in an election.

§ 14.1   Scope of Proscription

The prohibition on involvement by an exempt charitable organization in a political campaign is generally supposed to be absolute, although neither the legislative history of the provision nor the regulations provide much clarification.[2] The IRS states that "this is an absolute prohibition," adding that "[t]here is no requirement that political campaigning be substantial".[3] However, analogy may be made to a comparable statute which is also absolute on its face: § 610 of the Federal Corrupt Practices Act. That Act makes "[i]t . . . unlawful for . . . any corporation whatever . . . to make a contribution or expenditure in connection with" various federal elections. Nonetheless, the courts have read a substantiality test into the absolute proscription of § 610.[4] Further, it has

[1]See Chapter 13.
[2]See Reg. §§ 1.501(c)(3)-1(b)(3)(ii), 1.501(c)(3)-1(c)(iii).
[3]IRS Exempt Organizations Handbook (IRM 7751) § 370(2).
[4]See *United States* v. *Construction Local 264*, 101 F. Supp. 873 (W. D. Mo. 1951); *United States* v. *Painters Local 481*, 172 F.2d 854 (2d Cir. 1949).

been stated that "a slight and comparatively unimportant deviation from the narrow furrow of tax approved activity is not fatal."[5]

An exempt organization which is found to have engaged in political activities would be deemed an "action" organization, because "it participates or intervenes, directly or indirectly, in any political campaign on behalf of or in opposition to any candidate for public office."[6]

§ 14.2 "Political Campaign" Activities

The requirement that a "charitable" organization not engage in political campaign activities is relatively clear as to meaning, particularly as compared to the questions raised by the limitation on legislative activities. Because of this relative clarity, the matter has infrequently been the subject of discussion in the cases or in IRS rulings. However, the IRS has ruled that a "charitable" organization may not evaluate the qualifications of potential candidates in a school board election and then support particular slates in the campaign.[7] Also, the Tax Court has held that an organization established with the dominant aim of bringing about world government as rapidly as possible does not qualify as a charitable organization.[8] On the other hand, the IRS has ruled that a university is not participating in a political campaign by providing a political science course that required the students' participation in political campaigns of their choice[9] nor by provision of faculty advisors and facilities for a campus newspaper that publishes the students' editorial opinions on political matters.[10] Also, an exempt broadcasting station that provides equal air time to all electoral candidates in compliance with the Federal Communications Act does not violate the proscription against partisan political activities.[11]

Despite the requirement of a "political campaign" and a "candidate for public office," the IRS has denominated as an action organization (and thus denied exemption to) an organization formed for the purpose of implementing an orderly change of administration of the office of governor of a particular state in the most efficient and economical fashion possible by assisting the governor-elect during the period between his election and inauguration.[12] The Service ruled that the organization's "predominant purpose is to effectuate changes in the government's policies and personnel which will make them correspond with the partisan political interests of both the Governor-elect and the political party he represents." Without any statement of its reasoning, the IRS ruled that a

---

[5]St. Louis Union Trust Co. v. United States, 374 F.2d 427, 431–432 (8th Cir. 1967).
[6]Reg. § 1.501(c)(3)-1(c)(3)(iii). See Chapter 5.
[7]Rev. Rul. 67-71, 1967-1 C. B. 125.
[8]Estate of Blaine v. Commissioner, 22 T. C. 1195 (1954).
[9]Rev. Rul. 72-512, 1972-2 C. B. 246.
[10]Rev. Rul. 72-513, 1972-2 C. B. 246.
[11]Rev. Rul. 74-574, 1974-2 C. B. 160.
[12]Rev. Rul. 74-117, 1974-1 C. B. 128.

presidential inaugural committee that sponsors inaugural activities, some of which are open to the public and some by invitation only, where donations to it were commingled with the proceeds from various fund-raising affairs and activities, is not an organization organized and operated exclusively for charitable purposes.[13] It appears, however, that an inaugural committee would qualify as a social welfare organization[14] under the law governing tax exemption for such entities.[15]

Such an expansion of this prohibition on political activities was furthered even more by the U.S. Court of Appeals for the Tenth Circuit, in denying tax-exempt status to the Christian Echoes National Ministry for engaging in legislative activities and intervening in political campaigns.[16] Christian Echoes did not formally endorse specific candidates for office; rather, by means of publications and broadcasts, it attacked candidates and incumbents (presidents, congressmen) considered too liberal and endorsed conservative officeholders. The court summarized the offense: "These attempts to elect or defeat certain political leaders reflected Christian Echoes' objective to change the composition of the federal government."[17] However, it would appear that open criticism of an elected public official, even one who is eligible for reelection, is not violative of this proscription, unless done in the context of a "political campaign." But such a distinction was not made by the Court of Appeals in this case.

On May 1, 1978, the IRS issued a ruling[18] that alarmed a wide range of nonprofit organizations. This ruling—which was unquestionably a misapplication of the law—would have substantially broadened the scope of the proscription on political campaign activities applicable to charitable organizations.

However, in a rare reversal, the IRS revoked this ruling on June 2, 1978. In substitution, the IRS issued a new ruling[19] which properly attempts to confine impermissible "voter education" activities to those that are partisan in nature.

Generally, it was thought that dissemination of the views, voting records, and the like of candidates was permissible when total neutrality was observed. However, the IRS dashed this belief with the May, 1978, ruling when it announced that an organization cannot qualify for tax exemption as a "charitable" entity if it publishes in its newsletter the responses received from candidates for public office in an upcoming election, in reply to a questionnaire sent by the organization to all of the candidates. The Service, which expressly noted that the organization otherwise qualifies as an exempt educational entity, ob-

[13]Rev. Rul. 77-283, 1977-2 C. B. 72.

[14]See Chapter 15.

[15]See opinion of law to Carter Inaugural Committee at BNA, *Daily Report for Executives* (No. 230) J-6 (Nov. 29, 1976).

[16]*Christian Echoes National Ministry, Inc.* v. *United States*, 470 F.2d 849 (10th Cir. 1972), cert. den. 414 U. S. 864 (1973).

[17]*Ibid.* at 856. Also see *Monsky* v. *Commissioner*, 36 T.C.M. 1046 (1977); *Giordano* v. *Commissioner*, 36 T.C.M. 430 (1977).

[18]Rev. Rul. 78-160, 1978-1 C. B. 153.

[19]Rev. Rul. 78-248, 1978-1 C. B. 154.

served that the fact that the questions put to the candidates were on topics of concern to the organization's educational, research, and publishing activities and that the responses were published without editorial comment did not preclude deprivation of its tax exemption. The organization's newsletter is distributed to numerous individuals and organizations on its membership list and to others on request.

In this ruling, the IRS stated that this prohibition on involvement in political campaigns "do[es] not refer only to participation or intervention with a partisan motive, but to *any* participation or intervention which affects voter acceptance or rejection of a candidate." Consequently, determined the Service, "the organization's solicitation and publication of candidates' views on topics of concern to the organization can reasonably be expected to influence voters to accept or reject candidates."

This unwarranted stretching of this proscription on campaign activities went far beyond the intent of Congress in enacting this provision and represented a significant departure from the previous administrative law. This ruling meant that nearly any activity involving a nonprofit organization and political candidates would cause the organization to lose or fail to acquire tax-exempt status. Thus, the import of this ruling extended not only to an organization's publishing activities but to similar programs involving political candidates such as seminars and debates, or the mere act of making facilities available to candidates. (On one point, the IRS stayed within the previously understood boundaries—unlike the Tenth Circuit Court of Appeals—by relating the ruling to candidates "in an upcoming election," which, however, raises the not unimportant question as to how much in the offing an election must be to not be "upcoming.")

Prior to the issuance of this ruling, it was generally believed that this type of "involvement" by an exempt organization in political campaign activities did not rise to the level of participation or intervention on behalf of a political candidate that is contemplated by this and similar proscriptions. This belief stemmed from the definition of the term "educational," which permits advocacy of particular positions or viewpoints as long as a full and fair exposition of the pertinent facts is also presented.[20] This understanding was furthered by the IRS in 1974 when it published a ruling allowing organizations operating a broadcasting station to provide equal air time to political candidates.[21] But the Service distinguished the 1974 ruling from its position in the May, 1978, ruling on the ground that, as respects the former, the organizations were required by the Federal Communications Act to provide free air time to political candidates, whereas, as respects the latter, there was no legal necessity to publish the candidates' statements.

This ruling would have particularly adversely impacted the political education organizations (such as the League of Women Voters Education Fund) which provide the public service of disseminating the views of political can-

[20]Reg. § 1.501(c)(3)-1(d)(3)(1). See Chapter 7.
[21]Rev. Rul. 74-574, *supra*, n. 11.

didates on a nonpartisan basis. However, this type of activity was thought to have been outside the grasp of this prohibition on charitable groups, as exemplified by the enactment in 1969 of the law which explicitly excludes from the prohibition on public election activities by private foundations certain "nonpartisan" campaign activities.[22]

The import of this ruling would have extended far beyond the voter education organizations and would likely have affected hundreds of issue-oriented groups that frequently publish but do not comment upon the views of political candidates. Moreover, this new position could have jeopardized the tax status of noncommercial broadcasting stations that are not subject to the federal equal time requirement. Even a school that permits candidates to participate in a public debate in its auditorium could, according to the effect of the May, 1978, ruling, have endangered its tax-exempt and charitable donee status.

There are, of course, First Amendment considerations involved in these restrictions. After the ruling was issued, there was a great outcry and a flurry of communications to the IRS, and there was much talk of a court challenge to the ruling.

The June 2, 1978, ruling contains two examples of "voter education" activities that a "charitable" organization may carry on without loss of tax exemption. These examples indicate that a charitable organization can (1) prepare and disseminate a compilation of the voting records of all members of Congress on a wide variety of major subjects, as long as there is no editorial comment and no approval or disapproval of the voting records is implied, and (2) publish the responses to its questionnaire on a wide variety of subjects from all candidates for an office, as long as no preference for a candidate is expressed. This second example presents a set of facts essentially identical to those in the May, 1978, ruling—but an opposite legal conclusion.

The June, 1978, ruling also contains two illustrations of prohibited activities: an organization may not (1) publish candidates' answers to questions that indicate a bias on the issues or (2) publish a voter guide reflecting the voting records of members of Congress on selected issues of interest to the organization. Probably the most troubling aspect of this ruling is the suggestion that the mere reproduction of candidates' views on a "narrow range" of issues (however defined) will somehow constitute an exemption-threatening activity.

Notwithstanding these latter two illustrations, the IRS subsequently ruled that a charitable organization may publish a newsletter containing the voting records of congressional incumbents on selected issues without prohibited involvement in political campaigns. The Service indicated that the format and content of the publication need not be neutral, in that each incumbent's votes and the organization's views on selected legislative issues can be reported, and the publication may indicate whether the incumbent supported or opposed the organization's view. Nonetheless, the IRS considered the following factors as demonstrating the absence of political campaign activity: (1) the voting records

[22]See Chapter 29.

of all incumbents will be presented, (2) candidates for reelection will not be identified, (3) no comment will be made on an individual's overall qualifications for public office, (4) no statements expressly or impliedly endorsing or rejecting any incumbent as a candidate for public office will be offered, (5) no comparison of incumbents with other candidates will be made, (6) the organization will point out the inherent limitations of judging the qualifications of an incumbent on the basis of certain selected votes, by stating the need to consider such unrecorded matters as performance on subcommittees and constituent service, (7) the organization will not widely distribute its compilation of incumbents' voting records, (8) the publication will be distributed to the organization's normal readership (who number only a few thousand nationwide), and (9) no attempt will be made to target the publication toward particular areas in which elections are occurring nor to time the date of publication to coincide with an election campaign.[23]

The organization named "Independent Sector" was, in recent years, engaged in a variety of activities in support of legislation that would enable taxpayers who do not itemize their deductions to nonetheless have the advantages of the charitable contribution deduction (the so-called "above-the-line" deduction).[24] It reported in its newsletter the votes in Congress on this legislation, along with copies of debate transcripts and a brief description of the background of each vote. This activity continued during the 1980 elections, with some of the candidates advocating passage of the legislation. Independent Sector also presented testimony on the subject to the platform committees of the Democratic and Republican parties.

The IRS ruled in 1980 that these lobbying activities did not constitute participation or intervention by Independent Sector in one or more political campaigns.[25] Of importance to the Service were the facts that the lobbying activities are engaged in without reference to the timing of political campaigns and that its newsletter is regularly published and not distributed widely throughout the electorate. The presentation of testimony before the platform committees of the political parties was also deemed to be a legislative effort, not a political effort.

On the heels of the letter ruling to Independent Sector approving publication of voting lists by charitable organizations, the IRS sanctioned the practice of some charitable groups of issuing "report cards" on the voting of legislators. But it took a lawsuit to reverse the original position of the IRS and bring the Service to this conclusion. At issue was the publication by the Office for Church in Society (OCS), an arm of the United Church of Christ, of lists of votes on selected issues, in which a legislator receives a " + " if his or her vote coincides with the OCS position and a " − " when it does not. The organization thereby injects into the presentation an element of editorial comment that was absent

[23]Rev. Rul. 80-282, 1980-2 C. B. 178.
[24]See Chapter 1 § 5.
[25]Ruling dated September 4, 1980.

in the facts involved in the Independent Sector ruling and discouraged by the IRS in 1978. Nonetheless, the "report card" technique used by the OCS does not include any appeal for any candidate's election or defeat.

The case began when, in January of 1979, the OCS requested the IRS to rule that the publication of its report cards was not a form of prohibited participation or intervention in a political campaign. When the ruling was not forthcoming, the OCS filed its suit on First Amendment grounds. Nine days later, the ruling was issued as requested. As with the ruling issued to Independent Sector, the IRS conditioned its position on the fact that the publications will continue to be distributed to subscribers and will not be targeted to the locations of specific campaigns.[26]

Despite these dramatic turns of events, the fact remains that the IRS sought to resurrect the political campaign issue. Organizations should constantly monitor all of their activities in this area, because these rulings may have ramifications far beyond the types of activities discussed in them.

§ 14.3 Educational or Political Activities

The government does permit a "charitable" organization to instruct the public on matters useful to the individual and beneficial to the community.[27] In carrying out such an "educational" purpose, an organization may cautiously enter the political milieu. Thus, organizations have been permitted to assemble and donate to libraries the campaign speeches, interviews, and other materials of an individual who was a candidate for a "historically important elective office,"[28] conduct public forums at which debates and lectures on social, political, and international questions are considered,[29] and disseminate information for the purpose of elevating the standards of ethics and morality in the conduct of campaigns for political office.[30] However, the organization will imperil its tax exemption if it solicits the signing or endorsing of a fair campaign practices code by political candidates.[31]

However, in performing activities such as these, the organization must present a sufficiently full and fair exposition of pertinent facts to permit the public to form its own opinion or conclusion independent of that presented by the organization, although the organization may also advocate a particular position or viewpoint.[32] Thus, while a charitable organization may seek to educate the public on patriotic, political, and civic matters and even alert the citizenry to

---

[26]Ruling dated October 8, 1980.
[27]Reg. § 1.501(c)(3)-1(d)(3). See Chapter 7.
[28]Rev. Rul. 70-321, 1970-1 C. B. 129.
[29]Rev. Rul. 66-256, 1966-2 C. B. 210.
[30]Rev. Rul. 66-258, 1966-2 C. B. 213.
[31]Rev. Rul. 76-456, 1976-2 C. B. 151. Also Rev. Rul. 60-193, 1960-1 C. B. 195.
[32]Reg. § 1.501(c)(3)-1(d)(3). See *Haswell* v. *United States*, 500 F.2d 1133, 1143-1145 (Ct. Cl. 1974), cert. den. 419 U.S. 1107 (1974).

the dangers of an extreme political doctrine, it may not do so by the use of disparaging terms, insinuations, innuendoes, and suggested implications drawn from incomplete facts.[33]

§ 14.4   Treatment of Activist Organizations

Aside from the types of activity traditionally considered by the federal tax laws to be "action" efforts—legislative and political campaign activities—there is a broad range of clearly "action" or "political" undertakings which may be described as the type of speech or activities sheltered by the First Amendment. These undertakings may be manifested in a variety of ways, such as writings, demonstrations, boycotts, and litigation, all protected by the rights of free speech and association and the right to petition (assuming the absence of any illegal activities). These activities frequently give the IRS pause in evaluating the status of an organization as a "charitable" entity but, unless the activities may be fairly characterized as being impermissible lobbying or electioneering, there is no basis in the law concerning action organizations (as that term is used in its technical sense) for denying an organization engaging in such activities tax-exempt status or for revoking such an organization's tax-exempt status.

The tolerance of the courts in this area in general was classically illustrated by a federal district court finding that the anticonvention boycott orchestrated by the National Organization for Women, in states the legislatures of which had not ratified the proposed Equal Rights Amendment, was not in violation of antitrust laws, even though the boycott or concerted refusal to deal has been held to be an unlawful combination in restraint of trade.[34] Because the objective of NOW's convention boycott campaign was the ratification of the ERA, by means of demonstrating support and generating widespread publicity for the proposed amendment, the court found that the boycott activities "were not intended as punitive . . . and were not motivated by any type of anticompetitive purpose."[35] NOW was successful in asserting that the antitrust laws do not apply to boycotts that take place in a political rather than a commercial context.[36] The essence of the NOW case is summed up in one sentence from an article quoted by the court: "There are areas of our economic and political life in which the precepts of antitrust must yield to other social values."[37]

Coincidentally, at the same time the NOW litigation was unfolding, the IRS had before it the tax status of an organization that conducts a consumer boycott.

[33]Rev. Rul. 68-263, 1968-1 C. B. 256.

[34]*State of Missouri* v. *National Organization for Women, Inc.*, 467 F.Supp. 289 (W. D. Mo. 1978).

[35]*Ibid.* at 296.

[36]Also *Eastern Railroad Presidents Conference* v. *Noerr Motor Freight, Inc.*, 365 U. S. 127 (1961); *Register of Wills for Baltimore City* v. *Cook*, 216 A.2d 542 (Ct. App. Md. 1966).

[37]Handler, "Annual Review of Antitrust Developments," 71 *Yale L. J.* 75, 88 (1961).

Prior to the decision in the NOW case, the IRS concluded that the organization, which conducts a national campaign against the purchase of products by companies that manufacture infant formula and market it in developing countries by means of allegedly unethical business practices, could not qualify as a charitable entity because it is an "action" organization. Consequently, the organization took the matter into court,[38] but just before the case reached the briefing stage, the IRS suddenly reversed its position and issued a favorable ruling, thereby mooting the case.

Presumably, therefore, the case stands as precedent for the proposition that an organization may conduct a boycott in furtherance of charitable ends.[39] The operative legal principle appears to be that, while the conduct of a boycott may not itself be an exempt function, a boycott can further an exempt purpose and thereby lead to charitable status. As the IRS has recognized, "[t]he performance of a particular activity that is not inherently charitable may nonetheless further a charitable purpose [and the] . . . overall result in any given case is dependent on why and how that activity is actually being conducted."[40]

Moreover, the IRS has formally conceded that an otherwise tax-exempt charitable organization can further its exempt purposes by instituting litigation, even where the organization employs private attorneys to represent it in bringing and maintaining the litigation. The Service does insist, however, that an organization's litigation activities be a "reasonable means" of accomplishing its tax-exempt purposes, and that the program of litigation not be illegal, contrary to a clearly defined and established public policy, or violative of express statutory provisions.[41]

This means-to-an-end principle thus characterizes activities like demonstrations, boycotts, and litigation as "neutral" activities—from a federal tax standpoint—and allows the tax status of the organization conducting them to depend on its ability to show how tax-exempt purposes are thereby furthered. (In some instances, the IRS has publicly recognized the tax-exempt status of organizations engaging in this type of activity, such as litigation conducted by public interest law firms.)

This principle has also been recognized in the courts. As the U.S. Tax Court recently noted, "the purpose towards which an organization's activities are directed, and not the nature of the activities themselves, is ultimately dispo-

---

[38]*The Infant Formula Action Coalition* v. *United States* (D.D.C. No. 79-0129).

[39]Some organizations, already possessing Code § 501(c)(3) classification, engage in consumer boycotts (relating to, for example, the purchase of tuna, products that exploit animals, and products produced in whaling nations) but *The Infant Formula Action Coalition* case, *supra*, n. 38, involved an organization that conducts a boycott as its primary activity and that had its tax status reviewed by the IRS at the outset of its existence.

[40]Rev. Rul. 69-572, 1969-2 C. B. 119.

[41]Rev. Rul. 80-278, 1980-2 C. B. 175. The IRS, in Rev. Rul. 80-279, 1980-2 C. B. 176, has taken a like stance with respect to an organization that conducts mediation of international environmental disputes.

sitive of the organization's right to be classified as a section 501(c)(3) organization."[42] In a similar case, the same court found that an activity (sale of handicrafts) was neither an exempt purpose nor a nonexempt purpose but "an activity carried on by . . . [the organization] in furtherance of its exempt purposes."[43]

The U.S. Supreme Court has applied this principle in an analogous context. Perhaps the most applicable of the Court's opinions is the holding that litigation activities as conducted in the public interest context of that case are modes of expression and association protected by constitutional law and may not be barred by state authority to regulate the legal profession.[44] The Court distinguished this type of litigation from that normally instituted to resolve private differences, stating that the former is "a means for achieving lawful objectives."[45] In that case, litigation activities were perceived as neutral activities, engaged in as a means for accomplishment of the organization's ends. Likewise, boycotts, demonstrations, and the like can serve as vehicles for carrying forward charitable purposes. As the Court has repeatedly observed, the First Amendment protects advocacy, certainly of lawful ends, against governmental intrusion.[46]

A court has specifically held that litigation is an "appropriate vehicle for an organization to accomplish" its tax-exempt purpose, in a case involving the tax-exempt status of an organization that provides legal assistance to employees whose rights are violated under compulsory unionism arrangements.[47]

In one case, the IRS had taken the position that engaging in proxy contest activities was not a charitable activity. There was no dispute over the fact that proxy contests are not inherently charitable or educational endeavors. However, upon review, the court placed the organization's activities in context, that is, in light of its overall purposes.[48] The court recognized that the purpose of

[42]*Pulpit Resource* v. *Commissioner*, 70 T. C. 594 (1978).

[43]*Aid to Artisans, Inc.* v. *Commissioner*, 71 T. C. 202 (1978).

[44]*N.A.A.C.P.* v. *Button*, 371 U. S. 415 (1963).

[45]*Ibid.* at 429.

[46]For example, *Thomas* v. *Collins*, 323 U. S. 516 (1945); *Herndon* v. *Lowry*, 301 U. S. 242 (1937). Also *Pratt* v. *Robert S. Odell & Co.*, 122 P.2d 684, 692 (D.C. App. Cal. 1942), where it was held that a corporation may expend funds in the prosecution of litigation to which it is not a party where the expenditure is a means for furthering its objects; and *Register of Wills for Baltimore City* v. *Cook, supra*, n. 36 at 546, where it was held that advocacy of passage of the Equal Rights Amendment is one method of accomplishing the charitable objectives of a tax-exempt trust. In this context, it should be noted that, in *Village of Schaumburg* v. *Citizens for a Better Environment*, 444 U. S. 620 (1980), the Supreme Court held that acts of fund raising are among the most protected forms of free speech.

[47]*National Right to Work Legal Defense and Education Foundation, Inc.* v. *United States*, 487 F. Supp. 801 (E. D. N. Car. 1979). Cf. *Retired Teachers Legal Defense Fund, Inc.* v. *Commissioner*, 78 T.C. 280 (1982).

[48]*Center on Corporate Responsibility, Inc.* v. *Shultz*, 368 F.Supp. 863 (D.D.C. 1973).

the organization "is to make corporate management, and thus corporations, responsible."[49] The court continued:

> It is only reasonable that corporations begin to realize that they have duties beyond simply making money for their stockholders. A corporation does not exist in a vacuum, but is part of the community for better or for worse. In the past, it has been for worse. Large corporations have contributed to many of the social problems affecting the community both directly, in hiring practices, effects on the environment, non-compliance with regulations, indifference to the consumer safety, etc. and indirectly through use of their economic power in socially irresponsible ways. As a member of the community, it is incumbent upon corporations to use their substantial economic power for the community good, rather than solely for self-enrichment, at the community's expense.
>
> The need for a swift re-orientation of the corporate perspective to its community responsibilities is imperative. The general public is in no financial organizational or power position to undertake the task with any effectiveness.[50]

With that as background, the court in this case discussed the proxy voting process and its impact on corporate management. After commenting that proposals to promote socially responsible programs and policies may not be voted in by stockholders, the court concluded:

> But the questions will have been raised, the shareholders will have been educated to the wider horizon, and the seed may have been planted for future change that will require the corporation to assume some of its duties as a member of the community. The beneficiary of this activity and educational process to promote socially responsible corporations will be the public. . . .
>
> As the Court views them, proxy contests appear to be the more direct and effective instrument of achieving the Plaintiff's purposes, and when conducted in the public interest, as the Plaintiff has done, they are charitable activities, in that they are the instruments (both legal and not against public policy) by which the charitable purposes are accomplished for the public good.[51]

It may be anticipated that this new breed of action—perhaps better put, "activist"—organizations will be proliferating. The consumerism movement, public reaction to nuclear power plant accidents and fuel shortages, and similar

---

[49]*Ibid.* at 874, n. 21.

[50]*Ibid.* at 874–875, n. 21.

[51]*Ibid.* at 875, n. 21. In general, see Crumplar, "Tax Consequences of Political Activity by Religious Organizations," V *The Christian Lawyer* (No. 2) 29 (1975); Garrett, "Federal Tax Limitations on Political Activities of Public Interest and Educational Organizations," 59 *Geo. L. J.* 561 (1971); Note, "Political Activity and Tax-Exempt Organizations Before and After The Tax Reform Act of 1969," 38 *G. W. U. L. Rev.* 1114 (1970); Amer. Ent. Inst., *Political Activities of Colleges and Universities* (1970); Lehrfeld, "How much 'politicking' can a charitable organization engage in?," 20 *J. Tax.* 236 (1968); Boehm, "Political Expenditures by Tax-Exempt Organizations," 14 *Prac. Law.* 13 (1968); Note, "Income Tax Disadvantages of Political Activities," 57 *Col. L. Rev.* 273 (1957).

developments are likely to spawn new forms of activist groups. Unlike some of their forebears, these groups will conduct heavy direct mailing efforts, both for dissemination of information and for fund raising. Thus, their tax and postal status will be of great concern to them. It will also be of concern to the IRS and the Service's natural reluctance to grant tax preferences to unorthodox groups or those with unorthodox practices will readily manifest itself. But, with easy access to the courts, with the courts' steadiness in protecting speech, petition, and association rights, and with the flourishing of the "means-to-an-end" doctrine, these activist organizations should be able to secure their desired federal law status.

§ 14.5   Taxation of Political Activities

An organization that engages in political campaign activities but not to the degree that its tax exemption is endangered may nonetheless be required to pay a special tax. While this presumably would not be possible for a charitable organization, it could occur in the case of an organization such as a social welfare group.[52] Charitable organizations may nonetheless engage in activities that are considered "political" activities[53]—but not "political campaign" activities and, as a result, attract this tax.

In the case of most tax-exempt organizations,[54] where there is an expenditure for a political activity, this tax will likely apply. The tax is determined by computing an amount equal to the lesser of the organization's net investment income[55] for the year involved or the amount expended for the political end. This amount must be treated as "political organization taxable income"[56] and taxed[57] at the highest corporate rates.[58]

[52]See Rev. Rul. 81-95, 1981-1 C. B. 332.
[53]See Code § 527(e)(2). In general, see Chapter 21 § 18.
[54]That is, those described in Code § 501(c).
[55]Code § 527(f)(2).
[56]Code § 527(c).
[57]Code § 527(b).
[58]Code § 11(b).

PART III

OTHER TAX-EXEMPT ORGANIZATIONS

15

Social Welfare Organizations

An organization may be created to carry out its purposes through the development and implementation of programs designed to have an impact on community, state, or national policymaking. These endeavors may range over a wide spectrum of matters, such as environmental protection, housing, minority and civil rights, poverty, adult education, manpower training, and urban transportation, or a host of other current problems and concerns. Those planning the undertakings of this type of an organization may envision activities that are more activist in nature than the IRS is likely to tolerate in considering tax exemption for the organization as a "charitable" entity. Under these circumstances, such an "action" organization[1] may qualify as a "social welfare" organization or civic league, pursuant to Code § 501(c)(4).

Code § 501(c)(4) provides tax exemption for "[c]ivic leagues or organizations not organized for profit but operated exclusively for the promotion of social welfare . . ."[2]

§ 15.1 Concept of "Social Welfare"

There is no precise definition of the term "social welfare," and the regulations accompanying this category of tax exemption offer only two basic precepts: (1) "social welfare" is commensurate with the "common good and general welfare" and "civic betterments and social improvements,"[3] and (2) the promotion of social welfare does not include activities that primarily constitute "carrying on a business with the general public in a manner similar to organizations which are operated for profit."[4] The regulations also contain a prohibition on political campaign activity[5] and state that an organization is not operated primarily for

[1]See Chapter 5.
[2]See Reg. § 1.50(c)(4)-1(a)(1).
[3]Reg. § 1.501(c)(4)-1(a)(2)(i).
[4]Reg. § 1.501(c)(4)-1(a)(2)(ii).
[5]See Chapter 14.

the promotion of social welfare "if its primary activity is operating a social club for the benefit, pleasure, or recreation of its members."[6] However, the conduct of social functions for the benefit of its members will not defeat social welfare status for an organization, where these activities are something less than primary,[7] or are otherwise incidental to a primary function.[8]

Like the "charitable" organization, the "social welfare" organization, to be operated "exclusively" for the promotion of social welfare, must be operated "primarily" for that purpose.[9] The key principle in this area is that, to qualify as a social welfare organization, the activities of the organization must be such as will benefit the community as a whole, rather than merely benefit the organization's membership or other select group of individuals or organizations.[10] Thus, an organization that restricted its membership to individuals of good moral character and health belonging to a particular ethnic group residing in a geographical area and that provided sick benefits to members and death benefits to their beneficiaries was ruled not tax-exempt as a social welfare organization, as it was essentially a mutual, self-interest type of organization.[11]

For example, a nonprofit organization, incorporated for the purpose of furnishing television reception to its members on a cooperative basis in an area not adaptable to ordinary reception, where the members contracted for services and the payment of installment fees, was deemed not to be a social welfare organization because it was "operate[d] for the benefit of its members rather than for the promotion of the welfare of mankind."[12] Yet, a similar organization, which obtained memberships and contributions on a voluntary basis, was found to be a social welfare organization since it "operates its system for the benefit of all television owners in the community."[13]

Similarly, because of the lack of sufficient benefit to the entire community, a trust formed to provide group life insurance only for members of an association was not considered a social welfare organization.[14] Likewise, a resort operated for a school's faculty and students was held not to be a social welfare organization.[15] In the latter instance, the U.S. Court of Appeals for the Second Circuit held that "the exemption granted to social welfare . . . organizations is made in recognition of the benefit which the public derives from their social welfare

---

[6]Reg. § 1.501(c)(4)-1(a)(2)(ii).
[7]Rev. Rul. 66-179, 1966-1 C. B. 139; Rev. Rul. 63-190, 1963-2 C. B. 212.
[8]Rev. Rul. 66-221, 1966-2 C. B. 220.
[9]See Chapter 11.
[10]Reg. § 1.501(c(4)-1(a)(2)(i).
[11]Rev. Rul. 75-199, 1975-1 C. B. 48.
[12]Rev. Rul. 54-394, 1954-2 C. B. 131. Also Rev. Rul. 55-716, 1955-2 C. B. 263.
[13]Rev. Rul. 62-167, 1962-2 C. B. 142.
[14]*New York State Ass'n. of Real Estate Boards Group Ins. Fund v. Commissioner,* 54 T. C. 1325 (1970).
[15]*People's Educational Camp Society, Inc.* v. *Commissioner,* 331 F.2d 923 (2d Cir. 1964).

activities."[16] Conversely, a consumer credit counseling service, which assisted families and individuals with financial problems, was ruled to qualify as a social welfare organization because its objectives and activities "contribute to the betterment of the community as a whole" by checking the rising incidence of personal bankruptcy in the community.[17] Also, social welfare status was accorded an organization that processes consumer complaints concerning products and services provided by businesses, meets with the parties involved to encourage resolution of the problem, and recommends an appropriate solution, and (where the solution is not accepted) informs the parties about the administrative or judicial remedies available to resolve the dispute.[18] Likewise, an organization created to maintain a system for the storage and distribution of water to raise the underground water level in a community was ruled a social welfare organization because of the benefits to those whose wells were thereby supplied.[19]

Organizations which operate in a manner inimical to precepts of what constitutes the common good and the general welfare of the people in a community will not, of course, qualify as a social welfare organization. In part for that reason, the IRS denied tax exemption to an antiwar protest organization which urged demonstrators to commit violations of local ordinances and breaches of public order.[20] Said the Service: "Illegal activities, which violate the minimum standards of acceptable conduct necessary to the preservation of an orderly society, . . . are not a permissible means of promoting social welfare . . ."

Other examples of social welfare organizations include an organization that provided a community with supervised facilities for the teaching of the safe handling and proper care of firearms,[21] that encouraged industrial development to relieve unemployment in an economically depressed area,[22] that helped to secure accident insurance for the students and employees in a school district,[23] that provides bus transportation between a community and the major employment centers in a metropolitan area during rush hours when the regular bus service is inadequate,[24] that conducts a community art show for the purpose of encouraging interest in painting, sculpture, and other art forms,[25] and that established and maintained a roller-skating rink for residents of a particular

---

[16]*Ibid*. at 932.

[17]Rev. Rul. 65-299, 1965-2 C. B. 165.

[18]Rev. Rul. 78-50, 1978-1 C. B. 155.

[19]Rev. Rul. 66-148, 1966-1 C. B. 143.

[20]Rev. Rul. 75-384, 1975-2 C. B. 204.

[21]Rev. Rul. 66-273, 1966-2 C. B. 222.

[22]Rev. Rul. 67-294, 1967-2 C. B. 193.

[23]Rev. Rul. 61-153, 1961-2 C. B. 114. Cf. Rev. Rul. 66-354, 1966-2 C. B. 207.

[24]Rev. Rul. 78-69, 1978-1 C. B. 156. Cf. Rev. Rul. 78-68, 1978-1 C. B. 149; Rev. Rul. 55-311, 1955-1 C. B. 72.

[25]Rev. Rul. 78-131, 1978-1 C. B. 156. Cf. Chapter 6 § 8.

county.[26] Junior chambers of commerce usually qualify as social welfare organizations.[27]

Organizations formed to promote sports frequently are a type of nonprofit organization likely to gain status as a social welfare organization. A corporation formed to initiate programs designed to stimulate the interest of youth in organized sports, by furnishing youths virtually free admission and encouraging their attendance at sporting events, was considered a social welfare organization because it provided "wholesome entertainment for the social improvement and welfare of the youths of the community."[28] But sports organizations can go too far, as illustrated by the fate of a nonprofit corporation that was organized to provide facilities for training men and horses for use in emergencies, and obtained qualification as a social welfare organization, only to subsequently lose its tax exemption because it evolved into a commercial riding stable.[29] Said the court: "[T]he few persons eligible to use petitioner's facilities as members or on any basis other than by paying a regular commercial fee for such use causes petitioner's operation (no matter how laudable) to be such as not to come within the meaning of 'social welfare.'"[30]

In one case, a corporation maintained a vacation home for "working girls and women of proper character."[31] All of the trustees were required to be employees of a particular business corporation; the use of the farm's facilities was by invitation only to a select and limited number of women who were predominantly (80 percent) employees of the same business corporation. The government unsuccessfully asserted that the vacation home did not benefit the community as a whole, by virtue of the predominance of the employees of a single business or the invitational process. Indeed, the court concluded that the organization "is an institution which has served a broad community need in the sense that Congress intended, that is, that when one segment or slice of the community, in this case thousands of working women . . ., are [sic] served, then the community as a whole benefits."[32]

---

[26]Rev. Rul. 67-109, 1967-1 C. B. 136.

[27]See Rev. Rul. 65-195, 1965-2 C. B. 164.

[28]Rev. Rul. 68-118, 1968-1 C. B. 261. Also see Rev. Rul. 70-4, 1970-1 C. B. 126; Rev. Rul. 69-384, 1969-2 C. B. 122; Rev. Rul. 68-224, 1968-1 C. B. 262. As discussed in Chapter 10, Congress amended Code § 501(c)(3) in 1976 to provide tax exemption thereunder for organizations the primary purpose of which is to foster national or international sports competition.

[29]*Los Angeles County Remount Ass'n*. v. *Commissioner*, 27 T. C. M. 1035 (1968).

[30]*Ibid*. at 1044. Also see Rev. Rul. 55-516, 1955-2 C. B. 260.

[31]*Eden Hall Farm* v. *United States*, 389 F. Supp. 858 (W. D. Penn. 1975).

[32]*Ibid*. at 866. The IRS has said that it will not follow the *Eden Hall Farm* decision, *supra* n. 31, on the ground that an organization providing recreational facilities to the employees of selected corporations cannot qualify as an exempt social welfare organization. Rev. Rul. 80-205, 1980-2 C. B. 184.

§ 15.2   The Requisite "Community"

As discussed, a social welfare organization may not—if it is to qualify for tax exemption—operate for the benefit of a select group of individuals but must be engaged in the promotion of the common good and general welfare of those in a "community."[33] It has proved difficult to quantify the meaning of the term "community," as can be seen, for example, as respects the question of the appropriate tax status of community associations, principally, homeowners' associations. The typical homeowners' association is a nonprofit membership corporation composed of landowners and tenants in a housing development. The association may have been created by the real estate developer or subsequently by the homeowners themselves. These associations are normally supported by annual assessments or membership dues; membership therein may be voluntary or involuntary. A homeowners' association typically engages in one or more of the following functions: (1) it owns and/or maintains common green areas, streets, and sidewalks for the use of all residents, (2) it administers and enforces covenants for preserving the architecture and general appearance of the development, and/or (3) it participates in the formulation of public policies having an impact on the development, such as the expansion of nearby principal roads, development of nearby lands, encroachment of commercial enterprises, and the like. In this latter capacity, the association is functioning much as a conventional civic league.[34]

The IRS ruled, in relation to an association performing the first two of the above functions, that the association is exempt from federal income tax as a social welfare organization.[35] The association was found to be "serving the common good and the general welfare of the people of the entire development," noting that a "neighborhood, precinct, subdivision, or housing development" may constitute the requisite "community." Any private inurement was deemed incidental. Thus, even though the association was established by the developer and its existence may have aided him in selling housing units, any benefits to the developer were dismissed as "incidental." Also deemed incidental were the benefits that accrue to the individual members, such as the preservation and protection of property values.[36]

Following issuance of this ruling in 1972, the IRS quickly concluded that its "increasing experience" with homeowners' associations demonstrated that the ruling was being misconstrued as to its scope. Consequently, in 1974, the Service issued a "clarifying" ruling.[37] The IRS said that homeowners' associations, as described in the 1972 ruling, are *prima facie* presumed to be essentially and primarily formed and operated for the benefit of the individual members

[33]Reg. § 1.501(c)(4)-1(a)(2)(i). See Rev. Rul. 76-147, 1976-1 C. B. 8; *Erie Endowment v. United States*, 316 F.2d 151 (3d Cir. 1963).

[34]See Rev. Rul. 67-6, 1967-1 C. B. 135.

[35]Rev. Rul. 72-102, 1972-1 C. B. 149.

[36]Cf. Rev. Rul. 69-280, 1969-1 C. B. 152.

[37]Rev. Rul. 74-99, 1974-1 C. B. 131.

and hence not tax-exempt—a position wholly absent from the 1972 ruling. But then the IRS ruled that an organization with membership limited to the residents and business operators within a city block and formed to preserve and beautify the public areas in the block, thereby benefiting the community as a whole as well as enhancing the members' property rights, may qualify as a social welfare entity.[38] Moreover, a membership organization formed to help preserve, beautify, and maintain a public park was ruled to qualify as a charitable organization.[39]

The position of the IRS as to the definition of "community," as stated in this 1974 ruling, is that the term "has traditionally been construed as having reference to a geographical unit bearing a reasonably recognizable relationship to an area ordinarily identified as a governmental subdivision or a unit or district thereof." Thus, the Service held that a "community" is "not simply an aggregation of homeowners bound together in a structured unit formed as an integral part of a plan for the development of a real estate subdivision and the sale and purchase of homes therein."[40] Among other things, this statement places undue emphasis on the homeowners' association formed by a developer rather than initiated by the homeowners.

The IRS, in the 1974 ruling, also held that, where the association's activities include those directed to exterior maintenance of private residences, the above *prima facie* presumption is reinforced. Moreover, the 1974 ruling states that, as far as ownership and maintenance of common areas is concerned, the Service's approval is only extended to those areas "traditionally recognized and accepted as being of direct governmental concern in the exercise of the powers and duties entrusted to governments to regulate community health, safety, and welfare." That is, the Service's "approval" was extended only to ownership and maintenance by a homeowners' association of areas such as "roadways and parklands, sidewalks and street lights, access to, or the use and enjoyment of which is extended to members of the general public, as distinguished from controlled use or access restricted to the members of the homeowners' association."

Subsequent pronouncements by the IRS in this area illustrate that the Service continues to issue inconsistent determinations as to the meaning of the term "community." In 1975, the IRS issued a ruling which, assuming the presence of a community, accorded social welfare status to an organization formed to provide the community with security protection, improved public services, recreational and holiday activities, and a community newspaper.[41] Because these services clearly redound to the benefit of the individual residents in the community, it is difficult to reconcile this ruling with the foregoing 1974 ruling. This is particularly the case in view of still another ruling, this one

[38]Rev. Rul. 75-286, 1975-2 C. B. 210. Cf. Rev. Rul. 68-14, 1968-1 C. B. 243.
[39]Rev. Rul. 78-85, 1978-1 C. B. 150.
[40]See *Commissioner* v. *Lake Forest, Inc.*, 305 F.2d 814, 820 (4th Cir. 1962); Rev. Rul. 56-225, 1956-1 C. B. 58.
[41]Rev. Rul. 75-386, 1975-2 C. B. 211.

denying classification as a social welfare entity to an organization formed to promote the common interest of tenants in an apartment complex, by negotiating with the apartment management and engaging in litigation activities.[42]

Thereafter, the IRS moderated its position in these regards somewhat, by stating that whether a particular homeowners' association meets the requirements of conferring benefit on a community must be determined according to the facts and circumstances of each case. Also, the Service indicated that, although an area represented by an association may not be a community, the association may nonetheless still qualify for tax exemption if its activities benefit a community (such as owning and maintaining common areas and facilities for the use and enjoyment of the general public). But the government continues to insist that the exemption as a social welfare organization is not available to a homeowners' association (that does not represent a community) if it restricts the use of its facilities (such as parking and recreational facilities) to its members.[43]

Consequently, a homeowners' association, to qualify for exemption under the foregoing IRS rules, must (1) serve a "community," (2) not conduct or at least minimize exterior maintenance of private residences activities, and (3) must at best minimize the ownership and maintenance of common areas not for the use and enjoyment of the general public.

The tax status of homeowners' associations has become even more important with the popularity of condominiums and the condominium management corporation. Basically, a condominium involves an ownership arrangement whereby individuals own a unit in a building and—with the other owners—the underlying land and commonly used improvements. The condominium management corporation, formed and supported by the unit owners, performs the maintenance and repair activities of the commonly owned properties.[44]

The position of the IRS is that condominium management corporations do not qualify as social welfare organizations inasmuch as the organizations' activities are for the private benefit of the members.[45] The Service's rationale underlying this position is of two parts. First, the IRS has ruled that, because of the essential nature and structure of the condominium system of ownership, the rights, duties, privileges, and immunities of the members are "inextricably and compulsorily tied to the owner's acquisition and enjoyment of his property in the condominium." Second, the IRS notes that "condominium ownership necessarily involves ownership in common by all condominium unit owners of a great many so-called common areas, the maintenance and care of which necessarily constitutes the provision of private benefits for the unit owners."

---

[42]Rev. Rul. 73-307, 1973-2 C. B. 186.

[43]Rev. Rul. 80-63, 1980-1 C. B. 116.

[44]See, e.g., Garrett, "The Taxability of Condominium Owners' Associations," 12 *San Diego L. Rev.* 778 (1975); Curry, "Tax Considerations of Condominiums," 19 *Tul. Tax Inst.* 347 (1970); Anderson, "Tax Aspects of Cooperative and Condominium Housing," 25 *N.Y.U. Inst. on Fed. Tax.* 79 (1967).

[45]Rev. Rul. 74-17, 1974-1 C. B. 130. Cf. Rev. Rul. 70-604, 1970-2 C. B. 9.

The IRS traces its position as to condominium management organizations back to a 1962 federal court of appeals opinion.[46] There, the court held that a cooperative housing corporation was not an exempt social welfare organization since its activities were in the nature of an economic and private cooperative undertaking. In 1965, the IRS ruled that a cooperative organization operating and maintaining a housing development and providing housing facilities does not qualify as a tax-exempt organization.[47] Again, in 1969, the Service ruled that a nonprofit organization formed to provide maintenance of exterior walls and roofs of members' homes in a development is not tax-exempt as a social welfare entity.[48]

The homeowners' association and condominium management organization may, if attempts to qualify as a social welfare organization fail, qualify as a tax-exempt social club. That is, an organization may have as its primary purpose the establishment and operation of social facilities, such as a swimming pool, for the benefit of the homeowners in a community.[49]

Also, a homeowners' association may establish a separate but affiliated organization, to own and maintain recreational facilities and restrict their use to members of the association, as long as the organization is operated totally separate from the association.[50]

Congress, in 1976, enacted Code § 528 in an attempt to bring some clarification to the tax law concerning homeowners' associations. This provision provides an elective tax exemption for condominium management and residential real estate management associations.[51]

§ 15.3   Prohibition on Private Gain

Notwithstanding the laudatory goals envisioned by groups organized to promote the common good and general welfare, they must avoid activities that parallel commercial business operations or that extend benefits only to a limited few.

As noted, a tax-exempt social welfare organization may not be organized or operated for profit. Yet, organizations seeking the status of (or seeking to preserve the status of) a social welfare organization often are denied or lose that status because their activities intrude too much into the sphere of commercial activities, causing them to be considered organized or operated for profit. Thus,

[46]*Supra*, n. 40.

[47]Rev. Rul. 65-201, 1965-2 C. B. 170.

[48]Rev. Rul. 69-280, *supra*, n. 36. See Rev. Rul. 74-563, 1974-2 C. B. 38. Also *Eckstein v. United States*, 452 F.2d 1036 (Ct. Cl. 1971).

[49]See Rev. Rul. 69-281, 1969-1 C. B. 155. But see Rev. Rul. 75-494, 1975-2 C. B. 214. In general, see Frank, "IRS takes harsh position on exempting condominium and homeowners' association," 44 *J. Tax*. 306 (1976); Snowling, "Federal Taxation of Homeowners' Associations," 28 *Tax Lawyer* 117 (1974).

[50]Rev. Rul. 80-63, *supra*, n. 43.

[51]See Chapter 20.

the regulations state, as noted, that the promotion of social welfare does not include activities that constitute "carrying on a business with the general public in a manner similar to organizations which are operated for profit."[52]

In a ruling denying charitable status to a nonprofit corporation, and which is presumably applicable in the social welfare context, the IRS held that publication of a foreign language magazine alleged to be of literary, scientific, and educational character, available to the general public through paid subscriptions, was a business activity *per se*.[53] The Service said that the corporation was engaged in "ordinary commercial publishing practices" and that there was "no showing that the operations fulfill a corporate role which in and of itself is exclusively charitable, scientific, literary or educational." A nonprofit corporation formed to provide managerial, developmental, and consultation services for low and moderate income housing projects for a fee on behalf of tax-exempt organizations was determined not to be a social welfare organization because its "primary activity is carrying on a business . . . in a manner similar to organizations operated for profit."[54] Likewise, an organization that provides security services for residents and property owners of a particular community, on a regular basis in return for certain compensation, was ruled to be carrying on a business and thus not exempt as a social welfare entity.[55] An organization, once engaging in social welfare activities, lost the categorization because its principal activities became the promotion of public dances for profit, the proceeds from which were used for speculative real estate dealings.[56]

The IRS granted social welfare classification to an organization that operates an airport which is used by the public.[57] In the face of the prohibition in the income tax regulations on according social welfare classification to an organization carrying on a business with the general public,[58] the Service decided that the rule is not contravened because the organization uses volunteer services and receives government grants. The requirement of a served community was held met because the airport serves a rural area that has no other airport facilities; at the same time, most of the airplanes berthed at the airport are owned by key local businesses that are essential to the area's economy and the airport is used predominantly by executives, employees, and clients of the companies.[59] The organization was deemed responsive to the community because it is supervised by a city council, inasmuch as the airport is located on land owned by a muncipality.

A related criterion of the social welfare organization is that it must not be operated primarily for the economic benefit or convenience of its members.

---

[52]Reg. § 1.501(c)(4)-1(a)(2)(ii).
[53]Rev. Rul. 60-351, 1960-2 C. B. 169.
[54]Rev. Rul. 70-535, 1970-2 C. B. 117; Rev. Rul. 74-298, 1974-1 C. B. 133.
[55]Rev. Rul. 77-273, 1977-2 C. B. 195.
[56]*Club Gaona, Inc.* v. *United States*, 167 F. Supp. 741 (S. D. Cal. 1958).
[57]Rev. Rul. 78-429, 1978-2 C. B. 178.
[58]See text accompanying n. 4.
[59]Cf. Chapter 11 § 2.

Thus a corporation that purchased and sold unimproved land, invested proceeds received from the sales, and distributed profits to members, was deemed not a social welfare organization.[60] Similarly, as noted, an organization formed to manage low and moderate income housing property for a fee was ruled to not qualify for social welfare status.[61] Likewise, the U. S. Court of Appeals for the Second Circuit held that a consumer and producer membership co-operative, which rebated a percentage of net income to members as patronage dividends, made such disbursements "primarily to benefit the taxpayer's membership economically" and not exclusively for promotion of social welfare,[62] and that a membership corporation comprised of buyers of ready-to-wear apparel and accessories was not a social welfare organization, since its functions were largely social and many of its activities were designed to enable presently employed members to earn more money.[63]

Many other types of membership service groups have been denied categorization as social welfare organizations, such as an automobile club,[64] an organization that operated a dining room and bar for the exclusive use of the members,[65] and a national sorority controlled by a business corporation that furnished the member chapters with supplies and services.[66] In another instance, an organization formed to purchase groceries for its membership at the lowest possible prices on a cooperative basis was denied social welfare status.[67] The rationale: "The organization . . . is a private cooperative enterprise [operated primarily] for the economic benefit or convenience of the members." Similarly, the IRS denied classification as a social welfare entity to a cooperative organization providing home maintenance services to its members, even though payments for the services are made in kind.[68] In another instance, an organization the membership of which is limited to persons who own shares of public utility companies was ruled to not qualify as a social welfare entity because it is operated to serve private interests, in that it promotes the interests of the public utility industry and its stockholders by preparing and filing statements concerning public utility matters pending before state and federal agencies and legislative bodies, and by publishing a newsletter about matters affecting the stockholders.[69]

However, the rendering of services to members does not necessarily work a denial or loss of social welfare status. For example, a memorial association

[60]Rev. Rul. 69-385, 1969-2 C. B. 123.
[61]Rev. Rul. 70-535, supra, n. 54.
[62]Consumer-Farmer Milk Cooperative v. Commissioner, 186 F.2d 68 (2d Cir. 1950).
[63]American Women Buyers Club, Inc. v. United States, 338 F.2d 526 (2d Cir. 1964).
[64]Smyth v. California State Automobile Ass'n., 175 F.2d 752 (9th Cir. 1949).
[65]Rev. Rul. 61-158, 1961-2 C. B. 115.
[66]Rev. Rul. 66-360, 1966-2 C. B. 228.
[67]Rev. Rul. 73-349, 1973-2 C. B. 179.
[68]Rev. Rul. 78-132, 1978-1 C. B. 157.
[69]Rev. Rul. 80-107, 1980-1 C. B. 117.

formed to develop methods of achieving simplicity and dignity in funeral services and to maintain a registry for the wishes of its members in regard to
funeral arrangements qualified for exemption,[70] as did an organization engaged
in rehabilitation and job placement of its members.[71] Likewise, an organization
that promotes the legal rights of all tenants in a particular community and
occasionally initiates litigation to contest the validity of legislation adversely
affecting tenants was held to qualify as a social welfare organization because its
activities are directed toward benefiting all tenants in the community.[72] By
contrast, a tenants' rights group was denied social welfare organization status
because its activities are directed primarily toward benefiting only tenants who
are its members.[73]

Also, qualification as a social welfare entity will not be precluded where an
organization's services are equally available to members and nonmembers. As
an illustration, the IRS accorded social welfare classification to an organization
formed to prevent oil and other liquid spills in a city port area, and to contain
and clean up any spills that do occur.[74] The organization's membership includes
business firms, primarily oil and chemical companies, which store or ship liquids
in the port area. Because the organization cleans up spills of both members
and nonmembers, the IRS found that it is acting to prevent deterioration of
the port community and not merely to prevent damage to the facilities of its
members, so that any benefits to its members are incidental. Had the organization confined its repairs to property damaged by its members, the tax
exemption would not have been available.[75]

Veterans' organizations frequently qualify as social welfare organizations;[76]
however, the IRS has also ruled to the contrary.[77] Organizations that have a
membership of veterans may qualify as social welfare groups,[78] although tax
exemption may also be available under a separate category of tax exemption
enacted for the benefit of veterans' groups.[79] A subsidiary organization must
establish tax-exempt status on its own rather than on the basis of the functions
of the parent veterans' organization.[80]

[70]Rev. Rul. 64-313, 1964-2 C. B. 146.
[71]Rev. Rul. 57-297, 1957-2 C. B. 307.
[72]Rev. Rul. 80-206, 1980-2 C. B. 185.
[73]Rev. Rul. 73-306, 1973-2 C. B. 179.
[74]Rev. Rul. 79-316, 1979-2 C. B. 228.
[75]See *Contracting Plumbers Cooperative Restoration Corp.* v. *United States*, 488
F.2d 684 (2d Cir. 1973), cert. den. 419 U. S. 827 (1974).
[76]See Rev. Rul. 66-150, 1966-1 C. B. 147. Cf. Rev. Rul. 58-117, 1958-2 C. B. 196.
[77]Rev. Rul. 68-46, 1968-1 C. B. 260. Also see *Veterans Foundation* v. *United States*,
281 F.2d 912 (10th Cir. 1960).
[78]See Rev. Rul. 68-455, 1968-2 C. B. 215; Rev. Rul. 68-45, 1968-1 C. B. 259; Rev.
Rul. 55-156, 1955-1 C. B. 292; *Polish Army Veterans Post 147* v. *Commissioner*, 236
F.2d 509 (3d Cir. 1956).
[79]Code § 501(c)(19) See Chapter 20 § 15.
[80]Rev. Rul. 66-150, *supra*, n. 76.

§ 15.4 Legislative and Political Activities

As will be discussed,[81] the social welfare organization is not circumscribed as to legislative activities, as is the case with "charitable" organizations.[82] That is, it may be the type of "action" organization which advocates the passage or defeat of legislation.[83]

Also, "charitable" organizations are precluded from engaging in any political campaign activities.[84] By contrast, a social welfare organization can engage in some political campaign activities as long as the principal purpose of the organization is to advance social welfare.[85] Any political activities may, however, attract the tax imposed upon "political organization taxable income."[86]

§ 15.5 Prepaid Health Care Plans

Historically, prepaid health care plans (including the Blue Cross and Blue Shield programs) have been categorized as tax-exempt social welfare organizations. As the prepaid medical care concept developed in the mid-1900s, the plans were organized so as to avoid treatment under state law as insurance and to provide health care services at the community level. It has been suggested, however, that many of these plans in operation today do not meet the requirements for exemption as social welfare entities, because they provide benefits to members rather than to the requisite community and because they carry on their activities with the general public in a manner similar to for-profit organizations.[87]

The most generally known form of these plans is the "fee-for-service plan," which provides the administrative function of arranging for the provision of medical services by health care providers to patients constituting a "group" who subscribe for the services by prepaying premiums to the plan. These plans traditionally have not been considered insurance companies for federal tax purposes because they issue service contracts rather than indemnity.[88] Also, the earlier plans were "community-rated," that is, they provided benefits to all members of the community at the same rate. However, because many of these plans are now issuing indemnity and are no longer community-rated, one commentator has observed that "apparently the fee-for-service plans are not only losing their historical justification for exemption, but also are failing

---

[81]See Chapter 16.

[82]See Chapter 13.

[83]See, e.g., Rev. Rul. 68-656, 1968-2 C. B. 216; Rev. Rul. 71-530, 1971-2 C. B. 237; but see Rev. Rul. 70-79, 1970-1 C. B. 127.

[84]See Chapter 14.

[85]Rev. Rul. 81-95, 1981-1 C. B. 332.

[86]Code § 527(f). See Chapter 20 § 18.

[87]McGovern, "Federal tax exemption of prepaid health care plans," 7 *The Tax Adviser* 76 (1976).

[88]See Rev. Rul. 68-27, 1968-1 C. B. 315.

to meet today's social welfare standards. The facts suggest that these plans are engaging in a competitive commercial insurance operation."[89]

Another of these health care delivery forms is the "prepaid group practice plan," known today as the "health maintenance organization" ("HMO"). Pursuant to the HMO concept, members pay a fixed premium for comprehensive medical services and the health care providers receive a fixed rate of compensation. At the outset, the IRS treated HMOs as social welfare organizations because these plans actually provide medical care and are community-rated, although some plans may not satisfy the requirement of serving the requisite community.[90] In many instances, however, HMOs can qualify for tax exemption as "charitable" organizations.[91]

A third category of prepaid health care plan is the "foundation for medical care." This is a nonprofit organization, founded and controlled by physicians, that provides medical care through contracts with physicians and other providers. A commercial insurance carrier underwrites and markets the plan of coverage. The participating physicians are obligated to accept fee schedules and peer review procedures. One commentator has questioned the appropriateness of tax exemption for these foundations, claiming that they came into existence, "not for community benefit, but to protect local physicians and their traditional mode of delivering health care."[92]

In general, this commentator has concluded "that there is no present, legal basis for the exemption of prepaid health care plans under Sec. 501(c)(4)" and called upon Congress to "determine whether and to what extent the health care industry merits an exemption from federal income tax."[93] Thus it is, as discussed throughout,[94] that organizations claiming to be promoting health may qualify as tax-exempt organizations, as "charitable" entities, social welfare organizations, or professional organizations (business leagues).

[89]McGovern, "Federal tax exemption of prepaid health care plans," *supra*, n. 87 at 79.

[90]*Ibid.* at 80.

[91]See discussion at Chapter 6 § 8.

[92]McGovern, "Federal tax exemption of prepaid health care plans," *supra*, n. 87 at 80.

[93]*Ibid.* at 81.

[94]See Chapter 6 §§ 5 and 8; Chapter 17 § 3. In general, see Hopkins, "The Social Welfare Organization Under the Internal Revenue Code," 17 *Prac. Lawyer* (No. 6) 15 (1971); Amdur, "Tax Exemption of Social Welfare Organizations," 45 *Taxes* 292 (1967).

16

Social Welfare and
Charitable Organizations:
Comparisons and
Distinctions

In several ways, the tax-exempt "charitable" organization and the tax-exempt "social welfare" organization are identical. Neither may be organized nor operated for private gain.[1] Neither may, to any appreciable degree, participate or intervene in any political campaign on behalf of or in opposition to any candidate for public office. Both are liable for taxation on unrelated business income. Moreover, of greatest importance, the concepts of what is "charitable" and what constitutes "social welfare" can be very much alike. Thus, the same organization may simultaneously qualify under both categories of tax exemption.[2]

§ 16.1 Comparisons and Distinctions

As noted,[3] the promotion of social welfare is one of the definitions of a charitable activity for purposes of tax exemption.[4] Thus, a variety of activities and programs may be characterized as tax-exempt functions for purposes of either "charitable" entities or social welfare entities. For example, the following charitable efforts have been treated as promoting social welfare: furnishing

[1]See Rev. Rul. 69-385, 1969-2 C. B. 123; *Amalgamated Housing Corp.* v. *Commissioner*, 37 B.T.A. 817 (1938), aff'd 108 F.2d 1010 (2d Cir. 1940).
[2]See, e.g., Rev. Rul. 74-361, 1974-2 C. B. 159. In general, see Reg. § 1.501(c)(4)-1(a)(2)(i).
[3]See Chapter 6.
[4]Reg. § 1.501(c)(3)-1(d)(2).

of housing to low-income groups,[5] relieving unemployment by area development,[6] rehabilitating the elderly unemployed,[7] and inducing industry to locate
in a community.[8]

The principal distinction, as regards its federal tax status, between a charitable and social welfare organization is that the former is prohibited from
"carrying on propaganda, or otherwise attempting to influence legislation" as
a "substantial part" of its activities.[9] Conversely, a social welfare organization,
while not so circumscribed as to permissible legislative activities, cannot attract
charitable contributions that are deductible for income, gift, and estate tax
purposes. However, federal tax law provides that a "charitable contribution"
includes a gift to a "state, a possession of the United States, or any political
subdivision of the foregoing, or the United States or the District of Columbia,
but only if the contribution or gift is made for exclusively public purposes."[10]
Thus, contributions to a social welfare organization that was organized to build
a stadium and lease it to a school district, which would eventually get title,
were ruled deductible as charitable contributions.[11] But deductible charitable
contributions in this context are infrequent.

Thus the basic trade-off between these two types of tax-exempt organizations
is a greater scope of permissible legislative activities as opposed to deductible
contributions as a source of revenue.

§ 16.2   Action Organizations

The basic operational difference between charitable and social welfare organizations is embodied in the regulations accompanying both sections by the
concept of the so-called "action" organization. A charitable organization must
not have any of the characteristics of an action organization,[12] while a social
welfare organization may be a certain type of action organization.[13] Stated
another way, a social welfare organization may qualify for tax exemption as a
charitable organization, as long as it is not deemed an "action" organization.[14]

As discussed earlier, an action organization is defined as being any one of
three types of organizations.[15] In contrast to the charitable organization, the

[5]Rev. Rul. 55-439, 1955-2 C. B. 257; *Garden Homes Co.* v. *Commissioner*, 64 F.2d
593 (7th Cir. 1932).
[6]Rev. Rul. 64-187, 1964-1 (Part 1) C. B. 187.
[7]Rev. Rul. 57-297, 1957-2 C. B. 307.
[8]*Industrial Addition Association* v. *Commissioner*, 1 T. C. 378 (1942), aff'd 149 F.2d
294 (6th Cir. 1945).
[9]See Chapter 13.
[10]Code § 170(c)(1).
[11]Rev. Rul. 57-493, 1957-2 C. B. 314.
[12]See Reg. § 1.501(c)(3)-1(c)(3).
[13]Reg. § 1.501(c)(4)-1(a)(2)(ii).
[14]Reg. § 1.501(c)(4)-1(a)(2)(i).
[15]See Chapter 5.

social welfare organization may be an action organization, as long as it is not the type of action organization that is substantively involved in political campaigns.[16]

§ 16.3   Legislative Activities

A social welfare organization can undertake legislative activities within the general framework established by the regulations describing the two types of action organizations which may engage in activities involving legislation.

Specifically, a social welfare organization may draft proposed legislation, present petitions for the purpose of having legislation introduced, and circulate speeches, reprints and other material concerning legislation.[17] Such an organization may appear before a federal or state legislative body, or a local council, administrative board or commission, and may encourage members of the community to contact legislative representatives in support of its programs.[18]

The IRS has ruled that a social welfare organization can operate to inform the public on controversial subjects, "even though the organization advocates a particular viewpoint." The Service has noted that "seeking of legislation germane to the organization's program is recognized by the regulations . . . as permissible means of attaining social welfare purposes." Offering a rationale for allowing a social welfare organization to engage in legislative activities, the Service has stated: "The education of the public on [controversial subjects] is deemed beneficial to the community because society benefits from an informed citizenry."[19] Likewise, the Service extended status as a charitable entity to an organization formed to educate the public on the subject of abortions, promote the rights of the unborn, and support legislative and constitutional changes to restrict women's access to abortions, recognizing that the organization "advocates objectives that are controversial."[20]

Similarly, an organization that engaged in attempts to influence legislation intended to benefit animals, animal owners, persons interested in the welfare of animals, and the community at large was considered a social welfare organization, although it was denied status as a "charitable" entity (as an organization operated for the prevention of cruelty to animals) because it was deemed to be an action organization.[21]

§ 16.4   Political Activities

Like charitable organizations, social welfare organizations generally are forbidden from participating or intervening in any political campaign on behalf of

[16]Reg. §§ 1.501(c)(3)-1(c)(3)(v), 1.501(c)(4)-1(a)(2)(ii).
[17]Rev. Rul. 68-656, 1968-2 C. B. 216.
[18]Rev. Rul. 67-6, 1967-1 C. B. 135.
[19]Rev. Rul. 68-656, *supra*, n. 17.
[20]Rev. Rul. 76-81, 1976-1 C. B. 156.
[21]Rev. Rul. 67-293, 1967-2 C. B. 185.

or in opposition to any candidate for public office.[22] The IRS has traditionally been particularly strict in applying this restriction, as illustrated by the denial of classification as a social welfare organization to a group that rated candidates for public office on a nonpartisan basis and disseminated its ratings to the general public, on the theory that its rating process was intervention or participation on behalf of those candidates favorably rated and in opposition to those less favorably rated.[23]

Nor will objectivity necessarily ward off an unfavorable determination, as evidenced by the nonprofit group that selected slates of candidates for school board elections and engaged in campaigns on their behalf, and that was accordingly denied tax exemption as a "charitable" organization (and thus presumably as a social welfare organization) because of such "political" activities, "even though its process of selection may have been completely objective and unbiased and was intended primarily to educate and inform the public about the candidates."[24]

The foregoing does not mean, however, that a social welfare organization is completely foreclosed from participation in governmental and political affairs. An organization the activities of which were primarily directed, on a nonprofit and nonpartisan basis, toward encouraging businessmen and women to become more active in politics and government and toward promoting business, social, or civic action was held to qualify for tax exemption as a social welfare organization.[25] Likewise, a group that engaged in nonpartisan analysis, study and research, made the results available to the public, and publicized the need for a code of fair campaign practices, was ruled to be an educational organization.[26] Also, an organization that recruited college students for an internship program providing employment with local municipal agencies qualified as an educational and charitable organization.[27] Thus, a social welfare organization could similarly undertake these activities.

The IRS, therefore, in determining an organization's tax status in light of the requirements for a social welfare entity, carefully adheres to the distinction between those groups that actively participate or intervene in a political campaign for or against candidates and those that more passively seek to stimulate public interest in improved government, better campaign practices, and the like.

However, this prohibition on political campaign activities by tax-exempt social welfare organizations is not absolute, in that the requirement is that these

[22]See Chapter 14.
[23]Rev. Rul. 67-368, 1967-2 C. B. 194.
[24]Rev. Rul. 67-71, 1967-1 C. B. 125.
[25]Rev. Rul. 60-193, 1960-1 C. B. 145.
[26]Rev. Rul. 66-258, 1966-2 C. B. 213.
[27]Rev. Rul. 70-584, 1970-2 C. B. 114.

organizations must be "primarily" engaged in activities that promote social welfare. Thus, an organization primarily engaged in social welfare functions may carry on activities (such as financial assistance and in-kind services) involving participation and intervention in political campaigns on behalf of or in opposition to candidates for nomination or election to public office.[28]

[28]Rev. Rul. 81-95, 1981-1 C. B. 332. However, such political campaign activities will cause the organization to be subject to the tax imposed by Code § 527(f) on the expenditures for political activities that are within the meaning of Code § 527(e)(2). See Chapter 20 § 18.

17

Business Leagues and Similar Organizations

Code § 501(c)(6) exempts from federal income taxation "[b]usiness leagues . . . not organized for profit and no part of the net earnings of which inures to the benefit of any private shareholder or individual." This exemption also extends to chambers of commerce, real estate boards, boards of trade, and professional football leagues (whether or not administering a pension fund for football players).

§ 17.1 Business Leagues in General

A business league is an association of persons having some common business interest, the purpose of which is to promote such common interest and not to engage in a regular business of a kind ordinarily carried on for profit. Its activities are directed to the improvement of business conditions of one or more lines of business as distinguished from the performance of particular services for individual persons. An organization whose purpose is to engage in a regular business of a kind ordinarily carried on for profit, even though the business is conducted on a cooperative basis or produces only sufficient income to be self-sustaining, cannot be a business league.[1] A business league is not required to promote the general commercial welfare.[2]

The term "business" is broadly construed and includes nearly any activity carried on for the production of income,[3] including the professions[4] and con-

---

[1] Reg. § 1.501(c)(6)-1. See *Retailers Credit Association* v. *Commissioner*, 90 F.2d 47 (9th Cir. 1937). For a discussion of the legislative history of this exemption, see *National Muffler Dealers Association, Inc.* v. *United States*, 440 U.S. 472, 477–479 (1979).

[2] Rev. Rul. 59-391, 1959-2 C. B. 151; *Commissioner* v. *Chicago Graphic Arts Federation, Inc.*, 128 F.2d 424 (7th Cir. 1942).

[3] See Code § 513(c).

[4] Rev. Rul. 70-641, 1970-2 C. B. 149; I.T. 3182, 1938-1 C. B. 168.

sumer cooperatives.[5] Exemption has been denied for lack of a sufficient common business interest in situations involving an organization of individuals engaged in different trades or professions not in competition who exchanged business information,[6] an association of motorists,[7] and an association of dog owners, most of whom were not in the business of raising dogs.[8] At a minimum, to qualify as a tax-exempt business league, an organization must have some sort of a program directed to the improvement of business conditions; for example, the provision of bar and luncheon facilities is insufficient.[9] Organizations that promote the common interests of hobbyists do not qualify as business leagues, although tax exemption may be found within some other category of tax-exempt organization.[10]

In this context, a line of business is a "trade or occupation, entry into which is not restricted by a patent, trademark, or similar device which would allow private parties to restrict the right to engage in the business."[11]

The "line of business" requirement was upheld by the U.S. Supreme Court in 1979 as being consistent with the intent of Congress in granting tax exemption to business leagues. The occasion for the Court's review of the pertinent regulations was a case involving the tax status of a trade organization of muffler dealers that confines its membership to dealers franchised by Midas International Corporation and that has as its principal activity the bargaining with the corporation on behalf of its members. The Court held that Midas Muffler franchisees do not constitute a "line of business," in that their efforts do not benefit a sufficiently broad segment of the business community, as would the efforts of the entire muffler industry.[12] Thus, concluded the Court, tax exemption as a business league "is not available to aid one group in competition with another within an industry."[13]

[5]Rev. Rul. 67-264, 1967-2 C. B. 196.

[6]Rev. Rul. 59-391, *supra*, n. 2.

[7]*American Automobile Association* v. *Commissioner*, 19 T.C. 1146 (1953).

[8]*American Kennel Club* v. *Hoey*, 148 F.2d 920 (2d Cir. 1945).

[9]Rev. Rul. 70-244, 1970-1 C. B. 132.

[10]See Rev. Rul. 66-179, 1966-1 C. B. 144.

[11]IRS Exempt Organizations Handbook (IRM 7751) § 652(1).

[12]*National Muffler Dealers Association, Inc.* v. *United States*, *supra*, n. 1, aff'g 565 F.2d 845 (2d Cir. 1977). The Supreme Court thus rejected the contrary view of the U.S. Court of Appeals for the Seventh Circuit, which had held that an association composed solely of bottlers of a single brand of soft drink was an exempt business league. *Pepsi-Cola Bottlers' Association* v. *United States*, 369 F.2d 250 (7th Cir. 1966).

[13]*National Muffler Dealers Association, Inc.* v. *United States*, *supra*, n. 1 at 488. Three justices dissented from the majority view, in part because the pertinent regulation originally promulgated (in force from 1919 to 1929) embodied a position opposite to the one contained in the present regulation and they believed that was "strong evidence of the understanding of the meaning of the law at the time it was enacted" in 1913. *Ibid.* at 489. However, the Court majority deferred to the revised regulation, which has been the administrative law on the point since 1929 and which reflects the view of

Consequently, the "line of business" rule generally requires that a trade group represent an entire industry.[14] Thus, in one instance, an organization was held not entitled to tax exemption as a business league because "[n]othing is done to advance the interests of the community or to improve the standards or conditions of a particular trade."[15] However, the courts (including the U.S. Supreme Court) have recognized as tax-exempt a business league that represents all components of an industry within a geographic area.[16]

Where business groups have a narrower range of purposes and/or membership base, classification as a business league will not be forthcoming. For example, the IRS has denied tax exemption to groups composed of businesses that market a single brand of automobile[17] or bottle one type of soft drink.[18] In these and similar cases, the IRS has reasoned that such groups are not designed to better conditions in an entire industrial "line" but rather are devoted to the promotion of a particular product at the expense of others in the industry.[19]

Thus, exemption was denied an association composed of the licensees of a patent on a particular product since its activities did not benefit those who manufactured competing products of the same type as that covered by the patent.[20] By contrast, an organization formed by members of an industry which contracts with research organizations to develop new and improved uses for existing products was granted tax exemption, in part because none of the organization's patents and trademarks were licensed to any member on an exclusive basis.[21]

As the U.S. Court of Appeals for the Second Circuit has observed, the "line of business" requirement "is well suited to assuring that an organization's efforts do indeed benefit a sufficiently broad segment of the business community."[22]

---

those who originally advocated tax exemption for business leagues. *Ibid.* at 472–484. For an analysis of this case, see Statham and Buek, "S. Ct.'s holding in National Muffler precludes exemption for franchisee associations," 51 *J. Tax.* 80 (1979).

[14]See, e.g., *American Plywood Association* v. *United States*, 267 F. Supp. 830 (W.D. Wash. 1967); *National Leather & Shoe Finders Association* v. *Commissioner*, 9 T.C. 121 (1947).

[15]*Produce Exchange Stock Clearing Association* v. *Helvering*, 71 F.2d 142, 144 (2d Cir. 1934). See Note, 35 *Ford. L. Rev.* 738, 741 (1967).

[16]See, e.g., *Commissioner* v. *Chicago Graphic Arts Federation, Inc.*, *supra* n. 2; *Crooks* v. *Kansas City Hay Dealers Association*, 37 F. 83 (8th Cir. 1929); *Washington State Apples, Inc.* v. *Commissioner*, 46 B.T.A. 64 (1942).

[17]Rev. Rul. 67-77, 1967-1 C. B. 138.

[18]Rev. Rul. 68-182, 1968-1 C. B. 263 (wherein the IRS announced its nonacquiescence in *Pepsi-Cola Bottlers' Association* v. *United States*, *supra*, n. 12).

[19]See Rev. Rul. 76-400, 1976-2 C. B. 153.

[20]Rev. Rul. 58-294, 1958-1 C. B. 244.

[21]Rev. Rul. 69-632, 1969-2 C. B. 120.

[22]*National Muffler Dealers Association* v. *United States*, *supra*, n. 12 at 565 F.2d 847.

Activities which promote a common business interest include the presentation of information and opinions to government agencies,[23] promotion of improved business standards and methods and uniform business practices,[24] advocacy of the open shop principle,[25] attempts to influence legislation germane to the members' common business interests,[26] and even the mere holding of luncheon meetings for the purpose of discussing the problems of a particular industry.[27] In other instances, the IRS has ruled that an organization formed to promote the acceptance of women in business and the professions is a tax-exempt business league because it attempts to seek to improve conditions in one or more lines of business,[28] as is an organization formed to attract conventions to a city for the benefit of the economic interest of business throughout the community.[29]

Even though it is essential, to qualification as a tax-exempt business league, that the organization be an association of persons having a common business interest, the persons do not necessarily have to be engaged in a business at the time they are acting in association. As an illustration, an organization of persons studying for a degree in a particular profession can qualify as a tax-exempt business league if the purpose of the organization is to promote their common interests as future members of that profession and if it otherwise qualifies.[30] Also, a tax-exempt association will not jeopardize its business league status if it characterizes as nonvoting "associate members" persons who are merely sponsors of the organization and lack a common business interest with the regular members.[31]

The typical business league has as its membership—in conformance with the requirement that it be an "association of persons"—business corporations or individuals. However, a tax-exempt business league may have tax-exempt organizations as its membership, even where there are only two entities as members. For example, the IRS held that a trust created by a labor union and a business league qualifies as a tax-exempt business league.[32] Likewise, a trust created pursuant to collective bargaining agreements between a labor union and several business leagues is itself tax exempt as a business league.[33]

The requirement that a business league not engage in business for profit had more significance before enactment of the unrelated business income rules

[23]*American Refractories Institute* v. *Commissioner*, 6 T.C.M. 1302 (1947); *Atlanta Master Printers Club* v. *Commissioner*, 1 T.C.M. 107 (1942).
[24]Rev. Rul. 68-657, 1968-2 C. B. 218.
[25]*Associated Industries of Cleveland* v. *Commissioner*, 7 T.C. 1449 (1946).
[26]Rev. Rul. 61-177, 1961-2 C. B. 117.
[27]Rev. Rul. 67-295, 1967-2 C. B. 197.
[28]Rev. Rul. 76-400, *supra*, n. 19.
[29]Rev. Rul. 76-207, 1976-1 C. B. 158.
[30]Rev. Rul. 77-112, 1977-1 C. B. 149.
[31]IRS Private Letter Ruling 7938003.
[32]Rev. Rul. 70-31, 1970-1 C. B. 130.
[33]Rev. Rul. 82-138, 1982-29 I.R.B. 5.

in 1950. Before that date, business activities could preclude tax exemption, as occurred with respect to an organization selling credit information and collection services,[34] operating an employment agency,[35] and testing the safety of electrical products.[36] But tax exemption will not be threatened where a business is not an organization's principal activity, such as a chamber of commerce operating a credit bureau as one of fifteen departments,[37] a chamber of commerce developing an industrial park to attract new industry to the community,[38] and an association of insurance agents collecting (as an insubstantial activity) commissions on municipal insurance placed through its members.[39] Even where a principal purpose is not the operation of a business, an association may nonetheless be subject to liability for the unrelated business income tax, notwithstanding the fact that the business is conducted with its members.[40]

Varieties of tax-exempt business leagues abound, in part because the term lacks a well-defined meaning or common usage outside the parameters of the federal tax law rules concerning business leagues.[41]

For example, an organization created under state statute to pay claims against (i.e., act as guarantor for) insolvent insurance companies, where the companies are mandatory members of the organization, was ruled to be a tax-exempt business league, with the IRS holding that "the organization is serving a quasi-public function imposed by law which is directed at relieving a common cause of hardship and distress of broad public concern in the field of insurance protection."[42] Likewise, an association of insurance companies created pursuant to a state's no-fault insurance statute to provide personal injury protection for residents of the state who sustain injury and are not covered by any insurance was ruled to qualify as an exempt business league because its activities "promote the common business interests of its members by fulfilling an obligation that the state has imposed upon the insurance industry as a prerequisite for doing business within the state and by enhancing the image of the industry."[43] Business league status was accorded an organization of representatives of diversified businesses that own or lease one or more digital computers produced by various manufacturers; the IRS found that the "primary objective of the organization is to provide a forum for the exchange of information which will lead to the

[34]*Credit Bureau of Greater New York v. Commissioner*, 162 F.2d 7 (2d Cir. 1947).

[35]*American Association of Engineers Employment, Inc. v. Commissioner*, 11 T.C.M. 207 (1952).

[36]*Underwriters Laboratories, Inc. v. Commissioner*, 135 F.2d 371 (7th Cir. 1943). But see Chapter 10.

[37]*Milwaukee Association of Commerce v. United States*, 72 F.Supp. 310 (E.D. Wis. 1943).

[38]Rev. Rul. 70-81, 1970-1 C. B. 131. Also see Rev. Rul. 81-138, 1981-1 C. B. 358.

[39]*King County Insurance Association v. Commissioner*, 37 B.T.A. 288 (1938).

[40]Rev. Rul. 66-151, 1966-1 C. B. 152.

[41]See *Helvering v. Reynolds Co.*, 306 U.S. 110, 114 (1939).

[42]Rev. Rul. 73-452, 1973-2 C. B. 183.

[43]Rev. Rul. 76-410, 1976-2 C. B. 155.

more efficient utilization of computers by its members and other interested users, and thus improve the overall efficiency of the business operations of each."[44] Similarly, an organization that operates a "plan room" and publishes a news bulletin that contains information about plans available at the plan room, bid results and activities of concern to persons in the industry was ruled to be an exempt business league.[45]

Other tax-exempt business leagues include an organization composed of members of a particular industry formed to develop new and improved uses for existing products of the industry,[46] an organization composed of advertising agencies which verifies the advertising claims of publications selling advertising space and makes reports available to members of the advertising industry generally,[47] and an organization formed to improve the business conditions of financial institutions by offering rewards for information leading to the arrest and conviction of individuals committing crimes against its members.[48] Also, an organization the members of which are involved in the commercial fishing industry in a state, that publishes a monthly newspaper of commercial fishing technical information and news, and that derives its income primarily from membership dues and sales of advertising may qualify as a business league.[49]

As discussed below, the performance of particular services for individuals can cost an otherwise qualified business league its tax-exempt status. However, an activity may be found to benefit a common business interest even though services are being rendered to members, as long as a member's benefit is incidental. Examples of this include organizations which conduct negotiations for members and nonmembers in an industry,[50] mediate and settle disputes affecting an industry,[51] operate a bid registry,[52] investigate criminal aspects of claims against members,[53] subsidize litigation,[54] operate an insurance rating bureau,[55] negotiate the sale of broadcast rights,[56] conduct fire patrols and salvage operations for insurance companies,[57] provide for equitable distribution

---

[44]Rev. Rul. 74-147, 1974-1 C. B. 136. Cf. Rev. Rul. 74-116, 1974-1 C. B. 127.

[45]Rev. Rul. 72-211, 1972-1 C. B. 150, clarifying Rev. Rul. 56-65, 1956-1 C. B. 199. See *Builder's Exchange of Texas, Inc.* v. *Commissioner*, 31 T.C.M. 844 (1972).

[46]Rev. Rul. 69-632, *supra*, n. 21.

[47]Rev. Rul. 69-387, 1969-2 C. B. 124.

[48]Rev. Rul. 69-634, 1969-2 C. B. 124.

[49]Rev. Rul. 75-287, 1975-2 C. B. 211.

[50]*American Fisherman's Tuna Boat Association* v. *Rogan*, 51 F.Supp. 933 (S.D. Cal. 1943).

[51]Rev. Rul. 65-164, 1965-1 C. B. 238.

[52]Rev. Rul. 66-223, 1966-2 C. B. 224.

[53]Rev. Rul. 66-260, 1966-2 C. B. 225.

[54]Rev. Rul. 67-175, 1967-1 C. B. 139.

[55]*Oregon Casualty Association* v. *Commissioner*, 37 B.T.A. 340 (1938).

[56]IRS Private Letter Ruling 7922001.

[57]*Minneapolis Board of Fire Underwriters* v. *Commissioner*, 38 B.T.A. 1532 (1938).

of high-risk insurance policies among member insurance companies,[58] and publish a magazine containing information of interest to an entire industry.[59]

§ 17.2 Professional Organizations

In many instances, principally those involving professional societies or other organizations operating for the benefit of a profession, the rules concerning business leagues serve as the basis for tax exemption rather than the rules concerning charitable organizations. For example, the IRS presumes that bar associations and medical societies are business leagues, even though some of these organizations' activities are clearly charitable and educational.[60] That is, the Service presumes that these organizations' activities are directed primarily at the promotion of the particular profession and that they are operated to further the common business purpose of their members.

A medical society may engage in the following charitable and educational activities: meetings where technical papers are presented, maintenance of a library, publication of a journal, provision of lecturers and counseling services at medical schools, and the support of public health programs. The society may also undertake the following activities: provision of a patient referral service, maintenance of a grievance committee, meetings concerned with the promotion and protection of the practice of medicine, operation of a legislative committee, and conduct of a public relations program. Where the latter category of activities is primary, charitable status is denied, under the "exclusively" doctrine,[61] and business league status is accorded.[62] A bar association may likewise engage in comparable charitable and educational activities (e.g., law institutes, law review journal, moot court program, speakers' panels, and legal assistance to indigents). But the bar association will be a business league where the following activities predominate: promulgation of minimum fee schedules, preparation of studies on the economics of law office administration, programs directed toward making the practice of law more profitable, enforcement of standards of conduct, and sponsorship of social events (e.g., holiday parties, golf tournaments, and travel plans).[63] However, some court decisions have implied that bar associations may qualify as charitable organizations.[64] In fact, a 1982 U.S. Tax Court decision holds that the maintenance of "public confidence in the legal system" is a "goal

---

[58]Rev. Rul. 71-155, 1971-1 C. B. 152.

[59]*National Leather & Shoe Finders Association* v. *Commissioner, supra,* n.14.

[60]See Chapters 6 and 7. See IRS Private Letter Ruling 7852007 (issue no. 2).

[61]See Chapter 11.

[62]Rev. Rul. 71-504, 1971-2 C. B. 231. Also see Rev. Rul. 77-232, 1977-2 C. B. 71; IRS Private Letter Ruling 7930044.

[63]Rev. Rul. 71-505, 1971-2 C. B. 232. Also *Hammerstein* v. *Kelley,* 349 F.2d 928 (8th Cir. 1965); *Colonial Trust Co.* v. *Commissioner,* 19 B.T.A. 174 (1930).

[64]See *St. Louis Union Trust Co.* v. *United States,* 374 F.2d 427 (8th Cir. 1967); *Dulles* v. *Johnson,* 273 F.2d 362 (2d Cir. 1959); *Rhode Island Hospital Trust Co.* v. *United States,* 159 F.Supp. 204 (D.R.I. 1958).

of unquestionable importance in a civil and complex society" and that activities such as the operation of a client security fund, an inquiry tribunal, a fee arbitration plan, and a lawyer referral service "are devoted to that goal through various means of improving the administration of justice."[65]

These distinctions become particularly acute in the context of the categorization for tax purposes of professional societies. If the society's dominant activities are noncommercial research, maintenance of a library, publication of a journal, and the like, it will qualify for tax exemption as being charitable, educational, or perhaps scientific, as long as no substantial activities are directed at or are concerned with the protection or promotion of the professional practice or business interests of any of the professions represented by its membership.[66] A professional society, then, may fail to qualify as a charitable organization and will be deemed a business league where it, other than incidentally, (1) engages in public relations activities, (2) polices a profession, (3) seeks to improve the condition of its members, (4) seeks to develop good will or fellowship among its members, (5) engages in social and recreational activities, (6) maintains facilities (e.g., restaurant, lounge, or club house) for its members or (7) engages in legislative or political campaign activities. In one instance, an organization of individuals from various public health and welfare professions (seemingly charitable undertakings) was ruled a business league, for the reasons that its "activities promote the business and professional interests of the members by increasing the effectiveness of the interaction among the various professions, by developing greater efficiency in the professions, and by solving problems common to the professions."[67]

§ 17.3 Health Care Organizations

Various organizations concerned with the provision of quality health care in the United States appear destined for tax status as business leagues, notwithstanding the long-standing acceptance of the promotion of health as a charitable purpose.[68] Because of the potential of forms of commensurate benefit to the participating physicians, the approach of the IRS to the categorization of these entities has been made a part of its approach to accrediting organizations. The IRS has recognized that programs of testing and certification of an industry's products is an exempt function for a business league.[69] In a speech in 1973, the Commissioner of Internal Revenue, analogizing to organizations that accredit television repairmen and automobile mechanics, commented that or-

---

[65]*Kentucky Bar Foundation, Inc.* v. *Commissioner*, 78 T.C. 921, 930 (1982).

[66]See Rev. Rul. 71-506, 1971-2 C. B. 233.

[67]Rev. Rul. 70-641, *supra*, n. 4. Also see I.T. 3182, *supra*, n. 4; G.C.M. 4805, VII-2 C. B. 58.

[68]See Chapter 6.

[69]Rev. Rul. 70-187, 1970-1 C. B. 131; Rev. Rul. 81-127, 1981-1 C. B. 357; IRS Private Letter Ruling 7922001.

ganizations that accredit physicians in their fields of specialization will be treated as business leagues and not charitable organizations.[70] Thus, in the eyes of the IRS, enhancement of the medical profession, not delivery of adequate health care, is the primary objective of these groups. The Commissioner's observations are memorialized in a ruling published in 1973.[71]

Similarly, the IRS has ruled that an organization formed by physicians of a state medical society to operate peer review boards for the purpose of establishing and maintaining standards for quality, quantity, and reasonableness of the costs of medical services qualifies as a business league.[72] The Service recognized that these organizations are being established in response to concern over the rising costs of medical care, in an effort to curb the costs by reviewing medical procedures and utilization of medical facilities. Nonetheless, ruled the IRS, "[a]though this activity may result in a measurable public benefit, its primary objective is to maintain the professional standards, prestige, and independence of the organized medical profession and thereby furthers the common business interest of the organization's members." However, as the IRS has acknowledged, the promotion of health is a charitable purpose[73] and some courts seem to believe that improvements in the delivery of health care is a charitable function, even if the profession is somewhat benefited.[74]

As the result of the many opinions flowing from the cases decided pursuant to the special declaratory judgment procedure,[75] the position of the IRS concerning health care organizations is being materially modified. Described previously,[76] the courts are making it clear that organizations such as professional standards review organizations and health maintenance organizations are "charitable" entities because they promote health. The doctrines enunciated in these cases are dramatically shaping the law concerning the tax exemption of health care entities and are enhancing the ability of these organizations to qualify as "charitable" organizations rather than as business leagues.

§ 17.4   Trade Associations

The most common form of business league is the trade association. The typical trade association has as its membership companies or persons engaged in the same line of business or operating within the same industry. Its purpose is to promote and improve the conditions of the business or industry. One non-

---

[70]Remarks of Donald C. Alexander, August 29, 1973, before the American Society of Association Executives (IR-1326).

[71]Rev. Rul. 73-567, 1973-2 C. B. 178. Cf. *Kentucky Bar Foundation, Inc.* v. *Commissioner, supra,* n. 65.

[72]Rev. Rul. 74-553, 1974-2 C. B. 168.

[73]See, e.g., Rev. Rul. 69-545, 1969-2 C. B. 117.

[74]See *San Antonio District Dental Society* v. *United States,* 340 F.Supp. 11 (W.D. Tex. 1972); *Huron Clinic Foundation* v. *United States,* 212 F.Supp. 847 (S.D. 1962).

[75]Code § 7428. See Chapter 37.

[76]See Chapter 6.

tax-law definition of a trade association characterizes it as "a nonprofit, cooperative, voluntarily-joined, organization of business competitors designed to
assist its members and its industry in dealing with mutual business problems."[77]

The regulations' criteria for the tax-exempt trade association are generally
followed by the courts. But there has been disagreement, such as over the
scope of the proscription in the regulations that a trade association's activities
should not be the "performance of particular services for individual persons."
However, in one case, a court did not deny a trade association tax exemption
even though it maintained laboratories for quality control testing and promoted
the association's trademark through television advertising.[78] Nonetheless, the
IRS has ruled that a trade association of manufacturers, the principal activity
of which is the promotion of its members' products under its required trademark, does not qualify for tax exemption.[79] Further, the regulations maintain
that an exempt trade association's activities must be directed to the "improvement of business conditions of one or more lines of business" and not just for
a limited group (such as a single brand or product)[80] within a line of business.
Nonetheless, an association of bottlers of a particular brand of soft drink has
been held to be an exempt trade association.[81]

An organization may fail to qualify as a business league because it disseminates advertising carrying the name of its members. Illustrations of this include
an association created to attract tourism to a particular area, the principal activity
of which was publication of a yearbook consisting primarily of paid advertise-
ments by its members[82] and an association that published catalogs which listed
only products manufactured by the members.[83] Conversely, if the organization
advertises the products and services of an entire industry, tax exemption will
not be denied,[84] even if the advertising incidentally results in the performance
of services by occasionally mentioning the names of its members.[85]

Other areas of controversy as respects the tax status of trade associations
include the requisite availability of association research,[86] operation of trade

---

[77]Judkins, *National Associations of the United States*, vii (1949).

[78]*American Plywood Association* v. *United States*, 267 F.Supp. 830 (W.D. Wash.
1967). But see Rev. Rul. 56-65, *supra*, n. 45.

[79]Rev. Rul. 70-80, 1970-1 C. B. 130.

[80]See Rev. Rul. 68-182, 1968-1 C. B. 263; Rev. Rul. 58-294, *supra*, n. 20.

[81]*Pepsi-Cola Bottlers' Association, Inc.* v. *United States*, 369 F.2d 250 (7th Cir. 1966).
See Note, "Pepsi-Cola Bottler's Ass'n Case," 35 *Fordham L. Rev.* 738 (1965); Note,
"Business League Exemption Granted to Association of Bottlers of One Brand-Name
Product," 16 *Kan. L. Rev.* 113 (1967).

[82]Rev. Rul. 65-14, 1965-1 C. B. 236.

[83]*Automotive Electric Association* v. *Commissioner*, 168 F.2d 366 (6th Cir. 1948).
Also Rev. Rul. 56-84, 1956-1 C. B. 201.

[84]*Washington State Apples, Inc.* v. *Commissioner*, *supra* n. 16.

[85]Rev. Rul. 55-444, 1955-2 C. B. 258.

[86]Rev. Rul. 69-106, 1969-1 C. B. 153; *Glass Container Industry Research Corp.* v.
United States, 70-1 U.S.T.C. ¶9214 (W.D. Pa. 1970).

shows,[87] provision of credit information,[88] and provision of group insurance for the employees of employer-members.[89] Concerning the tax treatment of association trade shows, once under extensive study by the IRS,[90] the Senate Finance Committee stated, in the context of comment on the unrelated income tax rules,[91] that:

> The Committee does not intend that this provision modify the treatment under the regulations of the status of institutes and trade shows. Thus it is not intended that a tax apply where an industry trade association derives income from trade shows based on charges made to exhibitors for exhibit space and admission fees charged patrons or viewers of the show. This is only true, however, where the show is not a sales facility for individual exhibitors; its purpose must be the promotion and stimulation of interest in, and demand for, the industry's products in general, and it must be conducted in a manner reasonably calculated to achieve that purpose. Also, for the income from the trade show to be free of tax, the stimulation of demand for the industry's products in general must be one of the purposes for which exemption was granted the industry trade association. In such cases, the activities producing the income for the association from the show— that is, the promotion, organization and conduct of the exhibition—contribute importantly to the achievement of the association's exempt purpose, and as a result the income is related to its exempt purpose.

> Consistent with this policy, the conduct of a trade show by a trade association consisting of members who use the type of products exhibited at the show, or consisting of both this type of member and members who produce or sell the products exhibited, for the purpose of exhibiting and explaining the products, is a related trade or business, provided the show is not used as a sales facility for individual exhibitors.[92]

[87]See, e.g., Rev. Rul. 58-224, 1958-1 C. B. 242; Rev. Rul. 67-219, 1967-2 C. B. 212; *Orange County Builders Association, Inc.* v. *United States*, 65-2 U.S.T.C. ¶9679 (S.D. Cal. 1956); *Texas Mobile Home Association* v. *Commissioner*, 324 F.2d 691 (5th Cir. 1963); *American Institute of Interior Designers* v. *United States*, 204 F.Supp. 201 (N.D. Cal. 1962); *American Woodworking Machinery and Equipment Show* v. *United States*, 249 F.Supp. 392 (M.D.N. Car. 1966); *Men's and Boys' Apparel Club of Florida* v. *United States*, 64-2 U.S.T.C. ¶9840 (Ct. Cl. 1964); *National Association of Display Industries* v. *United States*, 64-1 U.S.T.C. ¶9285 (S.D.N.Y. 1964).

[88]See, e.g., Rev. Rul. 70-591, 1970-2 C. B. 118; Rev. Rul. 68-265, 1968-1 C. B. 265; *Oklahoma City Retailers Association* v. *United States*, 331 F.2d 328 (10th Cir. 1964).

[89]Rev. Rul. 70-95, 1970-1 C. B. 137; Rev. Rul. 67-176, 1967-1 C. B. 140; Rev. Rul. 66-151, *supra*, n. 40; *Oklahoma Cattlemen's Association* v. *United States*, 310 F.Supp. 320 (W.D. Okla. 1969).

[90]Ann. 69-3, 1969-5 I.R.B. 37.

[91]Code § 513(c). The changes in this area wrought by the Tax Reform Act of 1976 are discussed in Chapter 42.

[92]S. Rep. No. 91-552, 91st Cong., 1st Sess. (1969), at 76. See Kannry, "Trade Shows Must Bar All Selling To Avoid Unrelated Income Tax," 44 *J. Tax* 300 (1976); McKinney, "The Application of Section 277 to Business Leagues and Income Derived from Trade Shows," 48 *Taxes* 266 (1970).

The pre-1976 Tax Reform Act position of the IRS was that income received by tax-exempt organizations from the rental of display space to exhibitors at trade shows is not taxable as unrelated business income where the purpose of the display is not to furnish a sales facility for exhibitors.[93]

§ 17.5 Legislative Activities of Business Leagues

There is no restriction, from the standpoint of business leagues' tax exemption, on the amount of legislative activity these organizations may conduct. Indeed, as noted, the IRS has recognized attempts to influence legislation as a valid function for a tax-exempt business league.[94]

However, the federal tax law rules concerning deductible business expenses[95] place limitations as respects the business expense deduction for lobbying expenses. These rules operate as a limitation on lobbying activities by business leagues, particularly trade associations, because these associations are heavily dependent for their financial support on dues from members (usually business corporations), which members deduct the dues payments as business expenses. The restrictions on the use of the dues payments for legislative activities that attach by reason of the rules governing deductible business expenses thus apply to the use of the funds by the business league.

The business expense deduction rules permit the deduction for two categories of ordinary and necessary business expenses paid or incurred for legislative efforts. The first category permits the deduction for expenses in direct connection with appearances before, submission of statements to, or sending communications to, members or committees of legislative bodies with respect to legislation or proposed legislation of direct interest to the taxpayer.[96] The second category of deduction is for expenses in direct connection with communication of information between the taxpayer and an organization of which the taxpayer is a member with respect to legislation or proposed legislation of direct interest to the taxpayer and to the organization.[97] As noted, these rules apply to the portion of dues paid or incurred by the taxpayer with respect to an organization of which it is a member that is attributable to the expenses of legislative activities.[98]

However, there is no business deduction for amounts paid or incurred in

---

[93]Rev. Ruls. 75-516–75-520, 1975-2 C. B. 220-226; also see Rev. Rul. 58-224, *supra*, n. 87. The position expressed in these 1975 rulings remains the rule for Code § 501(c)(3) organizations.

[94]Rev. Rul. 61-177, *supra*, n. 26.

[95]Code § 162(e).

[96]Code § 162(e)(1)(A). The "direct interest" concept is discussed in Reg. § 1.162-20(c)(2)(ii)(b).

[97]Code § 162(e)(1)(B).

[98]Code § 162(e)(1).

connection with any attempt to influence the general public, or segments thereof, with respect to legislative matters, elections, or referendums.[99] Thus, no deduction is allowed for any expenses incurred in connection with "grass-roots" campaigns or any other attempt to urge or encourage the public to contact members of a legislative body for the purpose of proposing, supporting, or opposing legislation.[100] Communications between a business league and its members generally do not, as noted, constitute the influencing of the general public. But the employees and customers of members of a business league constitute a segment of the general public. Consequently, a communication from a business league that is intended to go beyond its members and is either directly, or through its membership, directed at a segment of the public will constitute "grass-roots" lobbying. For example, according to a 1978 IRS ruling, an appeal by a trade association to its members to contact segments of the general public to support a legislative effort is grass-roots lobbying and the expenses attributable thereto (including the allocable portion of members' dues) are not deductible as business expenses.[101] Moreover, a communication from a trade association, regarding legislation of direct interest to it or to its members, to prospective members was ruled in 1978 to constitute grass-roots lobbying.[102]

These 1978 rulings were issued amid congressional investigations of ostensible abuses of the lobbying expense deduction. In early 1978, the Senate Subcommittee on Administrative Practice and Procedure launched an investigation of "image" and "advocacy" advertising by large corporations. Beforehand, the House Subcommittee on Commerce, Consumer and Monetary Affairs initiated an investigation of "grass-roots" corporation and trade association lobbying. The latter probe involved a review of the information returns of 61 tax-exempt organizations (nearly all major trade associations) and the results of a survey of 467 major corporations. Moreover, the IRS subsequently conducted a study to analyze the deductibility of expenditures for advocacy advertising and audited about one-half of the information returns filed by the larger trade associations.[103]

---

[99]Code § 162(e)(2)(B).

[100]Reg. § 1.162-20(c)(4).

[101]Rev. Rul. 78-113, 1978-1 C. B. 43.

[102]Rev. Rul. 78-114, 1978-1 C. B. 44. For illustrations of grass-roots lobbying by a corporation (rather than by an organization of which it is a member), see Rev. Rul. 78-111, 1978-1 C.B. 41, and Rev. Rul. 78-112, 1978-1 C. B. 42. An effort to enjoin enforcement of Rev. Ruls. 78-111 through 78-114 failed, with the court finding that Code § 7421(a) (see Chapter 38 § 6) prohibits the requested injunctive relief. *National Association of Manufacturers* v. *Blumenthal*, 466 F.Supp. 905 (D.D.C. 1979).

[103]Letter dated December 2, 1977, from then-IRS Commissioner Jerome Kurtz to the General Accounting Office, reproduced at BNA, *Daily Tax Report* (No. 48) (Mar. 10, 1978) at p. G-4. In general, see Webster and Krebs, *Associations and Lobbying Regulation* (1979).

§ 17.6   Nonqualifying Business Leagues

There are several bases on which the IRS may deny tax-exempt business league status to an organization. One is the prohibition on business activities for profit. Thus, an organization that issued shares of stock carrying the right to dividends was denied exemption.[104] Also, an association of insurance companies that provides medical malpractice insurance to doctors, nurses, hospitals, and other health care providers in a particular state, where that type of insurance is not available from for-profit insurers in the state, was denied classification as a business league on the ground that the provision of medical malpractice insurance is a business of a kind ordinarily carried on for profit.[105] Similarly, an association of insurance companies that accepts for reinsurance high-risk customers who would ordinarily be turned down by the member companies was ruled not to qualify as a business league because reinsurance is a business ordinarily carried on by commercial insurance companies for a profit.[106] Another basis for nonqualification as a business league is a finding that the organization is not structured along particular business or industry lines.

The chief basis on which exemption as a tax-exempt business league may be denied is, as noted, a finding that the organization is performing particular services for its members, as distinguished from the improvement of business conditions in the particular business or industry.[107] Thus, the IRS denied tax-exempt business league status to a telephone answering service for tow truck operators, on the ground that it provides its members with economy and convenience in the conduct of their individual businesses.[108] A nurses' registry was denied categorization as a tax-exempt business league on a finding that it was no more than an employment service for the benefit of its members.[109] By contrast, a lawyer referral service was ruled to be a tax-exempt business league, since (because of the manner in which it is operated) it is more than a mere business referral service and serves to improve the image and functioning of the legal profession in general.[110]

Other organizations providing services to individual persons and denied tax exemption as business leagues include entities providing insurance,[111] operating

---

[104]*Northwestern Jobbers Credit Bureau v. Commissioner*, 37 F.2d 880 (8th Cir. 1930). Cf. *Crooks v. Kansas City Hay Dealers Association*, 37 F.2d 83 (8th Cir. 1929).

[105]Rev. Rul. 81-174, 1981-1 C. B. 335.

[106]Rev. Rul. 81-175, 1981-1 C. B. 337.

[107]*Southern Hardware Traffic Association v. United States*, 283 F.Supp. 1013 (W.D. Tenn. 1968), aff'd 411 F.2d 563 (6th Cir. 1969).

[108]Rev. Rul. 74-308, 1974-2 C. B. 168.

[109]Rev. Rul. 61-170, 1961-2 C. B. 112. See also Rev. Rul. 71-175, 1971-1 C. B. 153, concerning a telephone-answering service for physicians. Cf. Rev. Rul. 55-656, 1955-2 C. B. 262.

[110]Rev. Rul. 80-287, 1980-2 C. B. 185. Also *Kentucky Bar Foundation, Inc.* v. *Commissioner, supra*, n. 65.

[111]Rev. Rul. 74-81, 1974-1 C. B. 135.

a traffic bureau,[112] appointing travel agents to sell passages on members' ships,[113] making interest-free loans to member credit unions,[114] operating commodity and stock exchanges,[115] promoting its members' writings,[116] supplying management services and supplies and equipment,[117] operating a multiple listing service,[118] conducting a trading stamp plan,[119] operating a laundry and dry cleaning plant,[120] operation of a warehouse,[121] promoting the exchange of orders by wire,[122] acting as a receiver and trustee for a fee,[123] appraising properties,[124] performing services in connection with bond investments,[125] estimating quantities of building materials for members' projects,[126] ensuring the discharge of members' obligations to pay taxes,[127] publishing and distributing a directory of members to businesses likely to require the members' services,[128] and maintaining a library for members' use.[129]

In one case, the U.S. Tax Court held that an organization did not qualify as a tax-exempt business league because it both (1) engaged in a regular business of a kind ordinarily carried on for profit and (2) its activities were directed to the performance of particular services for individual members.[130] As respects the business activity, the court found that the organization was engaging in an insurance business to a substantial extent (measured in terms of time and finances), as its officers and employees were involved on a daily basis with record-keeping, processing claims for benefits, paying claims, and performing other administrative duties in connection with the insurance activities. The

[112]Rev. Rul. 68-264, 1968-1 C. B. 264.

[113]Rev. Rul. 74-228, 1974-1 C. B. 136.

[114]Rev. Rul. 76-38, 1976-1 C. B. 157.

[115]Reg. § 1.501(c)(6)-1. But see Rev. Rul. 55-715, 1955-2 C. B. 263.

[116]Rev. Rul. 57-453, 1957-2 C. B. 310.

[117]Rev. Rul. 66-338, 1966-2 C. B. 226; *Indiana Retail Hardware Association* v. *United States*, 366 F.2d 998 (Ct. Cl. 1966); *Apartment Operations Association* v. *Commissioner*, 136 F.2d 435 (9th Cir. 1943); *Uniform Printing and Supply Co.* v. *Commissioner*, 33 F.2d 445 (7th Cir. 1929), cert. den. 280 U.S. 69 (1929).

[118]Rev. Rul. 59-234, 1959-2 C. B. 149. See *Evanston-North Shore Board of Realtors* v. *United States*, 320 F.2d 375 (Ct. Cl. 1963).

[119]Rev. Rul. 65-244, 1965-2 C. B. 167.

[120]*A-1 Cleaners and Dyers Co.* v *Commissioner*, 14 B.T.A. 1314 (1929).

[121]*Growers Cold Storage Warehouse Co.* v. *Commissioner*, 17 B.T.A. 1279 (1929).

[122]*Florists Telegraph Delivery Association* v. *Commissioner*, 47 B.T.A. 1044 (1942).

[123]O.D. 786, 4 C. B. 269 (1921).

[124]*Central Appraisal Bureau* v. *Commissioner*, 46 B.T.A. 1281 (1942).

[125]*Northwestern Municipal Association* v. *United States*, 99 F.2d 460 (8th Cir. 1938).

[126]*General Contractors Association* v. *United States*, 202 F.2d 633 (7th Cir. 1953).

[127]Rev. Rul. 66-354, 1966-2 C. B. 207.

[128]Rev. Rul. 76-409, 1976-2 C. B. 154.

[129]Rev. Rul. 67-182, 1967-1 C. B. 141.

[130]*Associated Master Barbers and Beauticians of America, Inc.* v. *Commissioner*, 69 T.C. 53 (1977). See Dye, "Tax Court Revokes Exemption Based on Association Self-Insurance Program," 29 *Association Management* 16 (Dec. 1977).

court distinguished this insurance activity from that conducted by associations only on a passive basis (that is, mere sponsorship of the insurance program) and where a self-insurance program was not involved.[131] With respect to the provision of services, the court observed that the organization offered its members, in addition to the many insurance programs, an eyeglass and prescription lens replacement service, and sold its local chapters and members various supplies, charts, books, shop emblems, and association jewelry. The court concluded that the organization was undertaking activities that "serve as a convenience or economy to . . . [its] members in the operation of their businesses" and was not promoting a common business interest or otherwise conducting itself like a qualified business league.

In reliance upon this case, the IRS denied tax exemption as a business league to two types of associations of insurance companies because they (1) engaged in a business of a kind ordinarily carried on for profit and (2) are performing particular services for their members. In one instance, an association of insurance companies in a state that provides medical malpractice insurance to health care providers where the insurance is not available from for-profit insurers in the state was held to be "performing particular services for its member companies and policyholders" because its "method of operation involves it in its member companies' insurance business, and since the organization's insurance activities serve as an economy or convenience in providing necessary protection to its policyholders engaged in providing health care."[132] The same rationale was applied to the activities of an association of insurance companies that accepts for reinsurance high-risk customers who would ordinarily be turned down by its member companies.[133] (However, the rule remains that an association of insurance companies that assigns applications for insurance to member companies which perform the actual insurance functions can qualify as a business league because it does not assume the risk on the policies.[134])

It is frequently difficult in a specific instance to distinguish between the performance of particular services and activities directed to the improvement of business conditions. Perhaps the best illustration of this difficulty is the case of the organization that maintains a "plan room." In one case, an organization of contractors operated a plan room, containing information about plans available, bid results, and activities of concern to persons in the industry. The IRS ruled that the organization was an exempt business league because its activities improve the business conditions of the line of business served inasmuch as it makes the information on construction projects freely available to the construction industry as a whole. Clearly, the existence of this type of a plan room is

---

[131]*Oklahoma Cattlemen's Association, Inc.* v. *United States, supra,* n. 89; *San Antonio District Dental Society* v. *United States,* 340 F.Supp. 11 (W.D. Tex. 1972).

[132]Rev. Rul. 81-174, *supra,* n. 103.

[133]Rev. Rul. 81-175, *supra,* n. 104.

[134]Rev. Rul. 71-155, *supra,* n. 55.

a significant convenience or economy for the member contractors. But the IRS dismissed this aspect of the facts on the ground that the information on file at the plan room generally duplicates the information already available to its members—hardly a positive commentary on the actual effectiveness or usefulness of the organization.[135]

Business leagues should be contrasted with organizations operating to better the conditions of persons engaged in agriculture or to improve the grade of their products. These organizations may qualify for tax exemption as labor, agricultural, or horticultural organizations[136] rather than as business leagues. However, if the organization is promoting the common business interests of persons in an industry related to agricultural pursuits, business league designation would be appropriate assuming the organization otherwise qualifies.[137]

Still another basis precluding tax exemption as a business league is, as noted, the inurement of net earnings to private individuals. This is somewhat related to the proscription on services to members. For example, private inurement was deemed present with respect to an organization which used its funds to provide financial assistance and welfare benefits to its members,[138] which paid its members for expenses incurred in malpractice litigation,[139] and which distributed royalties to its members.[140]

A related inurement concept concerns the impact on the level of members' dues as the result of the organization's receipt of nonmember income (i.e., income other than membership dues). Basically, the question resolves itself on the issue of whether the activity is an unrelated trade or business,[141] although prior to the advent of those rules (in 1950) it had been held that a dues reduction occasioned by business earnings constituted private inurement.[142] Also, a business league may receive income from nonmember sources without deprivation of tax exemption where the income-producing activity is related to the exempt purpose, such as a sports organization operating public championship tournaments,[143] a veterinarians' association operating a public rabies clinic,[144] an insurance agents association receiving commissions from handling insurance programs,[145] and a professional association conducting a training program for nonmembers.[146] Thus, for example, an otherwise qualified business league can

[135]Rev. Rul. 72-211, *supra*, n. 45. See Rev. Rul. 56-65, *supra*, n. 45.

[136]See Chapter 19.

[137]See Rev. Rul. 70-31, *supra*, n. 32; Rev. Rul. 67-252, 1967-2 C. B. 195.

[138]Rev. Rul. 67-251, 1967-2 C. B. 196.

[139]*National Chiropractor Association* v. *Birmingham*, 96 F.Supp. 874 (N.D. Iowa 1951).

[140]*Wholesale Grocers Exchange* v. *Commissioner*, 3 T.C.M. 699 (1944).

[141]See Chapter 42.

[142]*National Automobile Dealers Association* v. *Commissioner*, 2 T.C.M. 291 (1943).

[143]Rev. Rul. 58-502, 1958-2 C. B. 271.

[144]Rev. Rul. 66-222, 1966-2 C. B. 223.

[145]Rev. Rul. 56-152, 1956-1 C. B. 56.

[146]Rev. Rul. 67-296, 1967-2 C. B. 22.

derive its support primarily from the sale of television broadcasting rights to the tournaments it conducts without imperiling its tax exemption, because the "sponsorship of tournaments and the sale of broadcasting rights with respect thereto by the organization directly promotes the interests of those engaged in the sport by encouraging participation in the sport and by enhancing awareness of the general public of the sport as a profession."[147]

Another private inurement issue of pertinence to trade associations concerns the tax consequences of cash rebates to exhibitors who participate in their trade shows. As a general principle, a qualified business league may make cash distributions to its members without loss of tax exemption where the distributions represent no more than a reduction in dues or contributions previously paid to the league to support its activities.[148] The IRS extrapolated from this principle in ruling that a trade association may, without adversely affecting its tax-exempt status, make cash rebates to member and nonmember exhibitors who participate in the association's annual trade show, where the rebates (1) represent a portion of an advance floor deposit paid by each exhibitor to insure the show against financial loss, (2) are made to all exhibitors on the same basis, and (3) may not exceed the amount of the deposit.[149] Because "the effect of refunding a portion of the floor deposits is to reduce the exhibitors' cost of participating in the trade show," the Service concluded that such a return of funds did not constitute inurement of net earnings. If, however, a business league sponsoring an industry trade show, involving both member and nonmember exhibitors who are charged identical rates, makes space rental rebates only to its member-exhibitors, the rebates are considered proscribed inurements of income.[150]

§ 17.7 Chamber of Commerce, Board of Trade, Etc.

A chamber of commerce or a board of trade that is tax-exempt pursuant to Code § 501(c)(6) is an organization the "common business interest" of which is the general economic welfare of a community. That is, it is an organization the efforts of which are directed at promoting the common economic interests of all the commercial enterprises in a given trade community. For example, the attraction of business to a particular community is an appropriate tax-exempt activity in this context, even where it necessitates the development of an industrial park.[151] Similarly, an organization formed for the purpose of encouraging national organizations to hold their conventions in a city was accorded tax-exempt status as a chamber of commerce.[152]

[147]Rev. Rul. 80-294, 1980-2 C. B. 19.
[148]See, e.g., *King County Insurance Association* v. *Commissioner, supra*, n. 39.
[149]Rev. Rul. 77-206, 1977-1 C. B. 149. Also Rev. Rul. 81-60, 1981-1 C. B. 335.
[150]*Michigan Mobil Home and Recreational Vehicle Institute* v.*Commissioner*, 66 T.C. 770 (1976).
[151]Rev. Rul. 70-81, *supra*, n. 38; Rev. Rul. 81-138, *supra*, n. 38.
[152]Rev. Rul. 76-207, *supra*, n. 29.

One court has observed that the terms "chamber of commerce" and "board of trade" are "nearly synonymous" although there is a "slight distinction" between their meanings. The court explained: "The former relates to all businesses in a particular geographic location, while the latter may relate to only one or more lines of business in a particular geographic location, but need not relate to all."[153]

By contrast, a business league serves only the common business interests of the members of a single line of business or of closely related lines of business within a single industry. Also, as respects a chamber of commerce or a board of trade, membership is voluntary and generally open to all business and professional persons in the community.

The IRS ruled that a tenants' association (specifically, an association of shopping center merchants) does not qualify as a tax-exempt chamber of commerce or a board of trade.[154] The IRS noted that membership in the association is compulsory, imposed by the landlord owner of the shopping center, and that the requisite "community" is not being served, as "[t]he community represented by the membership of the present organization is a closed, non-public aggregation of commercial enterprises having none of the common characteristics of a community in the usual geographical or political sense."[155] Finally, the IRS invoked a private inurement rationale, holding that the organization was designed to serve the tenants' business interests in the center. (Exempt status as a business league was denied because the association was not structured along particular industry or business lines.[156]) Similarly, a board of trade was denied tax exemption because its principal activity is to provide services to individuals (grain analysis laboratory services to both members and nonmembers) and because the board is supported almost entirely from the substantial profits of the laboratory.[157] Likewise, the term "board of trade" does not encompass "organizations which provide conveniences or facilities to certain persons in connection with buying, selling, and exchanging goods."[158]

However, a "neighborhood community association" may qualify for tax exemption in this context where the following criteria are satisfied: (1) the organization has a voluntary membership, (2) it is not concerned with tenants' matters, and (3) the organization is operated to improve the business conditions of a community (rather than a single one-owner shopping mall).[159] This may be the case even though a majority of the association's member businesses is located in one shopping center.

[153]*Retailers Credit Association* v. *Commissioner, supra,* n. 1 at 51.
[154]Rev. Rul. 73-411, 1973-2 C. B. 180.
[155]*Ibid.* Also see Rev. Rul. 59-391, *supra,* n. 2.
[156]See Rev. Rul. 64-315, 1964-2 C. B. 147, clarified by Rev. Rul. 73-411, *supra,* n. 154.
[157]Rev. Rul. 78-70, 1978-1 C. B. 159. Also *Fort Worth Grain and Cotton Exchange* v. *Commissioner,* 27 B.T.A. 983 (1933).
[158]L. O. 1123, III-1 C. B. 275 (1924).
[159]Rev. Rul. 78-225, 1978-1 C. B. 159.

Tax exemption for real estate boards, added in 1928, came into being as an overturning of a court decision. The Board of Tax Appeals in 1927 denied tax exemption as a business league to a corporation organized by associations of insurance companies to provide printing services for member companies.[160] Thereafter, the statute was revised so as to specifically exempt real estate boards from taxation.

Tax exemption for professional football leagues was added in 1966. This was done to forestall any claim that a football league's pension plan would be considered inurement of benefits to a private individual. The amendment was part of a larger legislative package that paved the way for a merger which created an "industry-wide" professional football league.

§ 17.8   Consequences of Abandonment of Code § 501(c)(6) Status

The advantages and benefits of Code § 501(c)(6) classification are many: (1) exemption from federal income taxation (thereby sheltering from tax the receipt of dues and other items of income, except with respect to any tax on unrelated income, (2) exemption from taxation (such as income, sales, excise, franchise, and property taxes) at state and local levels, (3) access to contract and grant funds under programs where contractees and grantees must be nonprofit organizations, (4) enhancement of the public's perception and acceptance of the organization and its programs as the result of being designated tax-exempt, (5) much greater flexibility as respects accumulation of funds without adverse tax consequences, and (6) a deduction of $1,000[161] in computing taxable income.[162]

Nonetheless, a business league with a membership base may contemplate abandonment of its tax exemption under Code § 501(c)(6), usually in the hope that it can avoid the tax on unrelated income,[163] and conversion to a taxable organization.

Prior to 1969, this stratagem may have worked, because the income from business activities (including services to nonmembers) and investments could have been offset by deductions in the form of expenses of providing services to members, thereby not generating any overall net income. This approach was tolerated by the U.S. Court of Appeals for the Ninth Circuit, which held that the investment income of a nonexempt water company could be offset by

---

[160]*Uniform Printing & Supply Co.* v. *Commissioner, supra,* n. 117.

[161]See Chapter 41 § 3.

[162]Classification of an organization under Code § 501(c)(3) also brings the same advantages and benefits as classification under Code § 501(c)(6), along with the preferences of charitable donee status and various postal privileges. See Chapter 2 § 2.

[163]See Chapter 40.

its losses in supplying water to its members.[164] However, other courts were not permitting this result.[165]

Congress, in enacting the Tax Reform Act of 1969, created special rules in an attempt to resolve the matter.[166] These rules are applicable with respect to any membership organization which is not exempt from taxation and which is operated primarily to furnish services or goods to its members. This provision allows deductions for a tax year attributable to the furnishing of services, insurance, goods, or other items of value to the organization's membership only to the extent of income derived during the year from members or transactions with members (including income derived during the year from institutes and trade shows which are primarily for the education of members).

The intent of these rules is to preclude the result previously sanctioned by the Ninth Circuit, that is, to prevent a taxable membership organization from offsetting its business and investment income with deductions created by the provision of services to members. Stated another way, these rules are designed to make taxable membership organizations allocate their deductions to the corresponding sources of income.[167] As a result, an organization that operated in a particular year at an overall loss may still have to pay tax if its business and investment activities produced net income. In this fashion, these rules are intended to serve as a deterrent to the abandonment of tax-exempt status by membership organizations, particularly those that are serving their members at less than cost.[168]

Where, for a tax year, a taxable membership organization's deductions attributable to the furnishing of items of value to members exceed income from its members, the excess may be carried forward and used as such a deduction against income from its members in the succeeding tax year.[169]

---

[164]*Anaheim Union Water Co.* v. *Commissioner*, 321 F.2d 253 (9th Cir. 1963), rev'g 35 T.C. 1972 (1961). Also *Bear Valley Mutual Water Co.* v. *Riddell*, 283 F.Supp. 949 (C.D. Cal. 1968), aff'd 427 F.2d 713 (9th Cir. 1970); *San Antonio Water Co.* v. *Riddell*, 285 F. Supp. 297 (C.D. Cal. 1968), aff'd 427 F.2d 713 (9th Cir. 1970).

[165]See *Adirondack League Club* v. *Commissioner*, 55 T.C. 796 (1971), aff'd 458 F.2d 506 (2d Cir. 1972); *Five Lakes Outing Club* v. *United States*, 468 F.2d 443 (8th Cir. 1972); *Iowa State University of Science & Technology* v. *United States*, 500 F.2d 508 (Ct. Cl. 1974).

[166]Code § 277.

[167]See, e.g., *Armour-Dial Men's Club, Inc.* v. *Commissioner*, 77 T.C. 1 (1981).

[168]See H. Rep. No. 91-413 (Part 1), 91st Cong., 1st Sess. (1969) at 49; S. Rep. No. 91-552, 91st Cong., 1st Sess. (1969) at 74.

[169]Certain nonprofit membership organizations that receive prepaid dues income (such as the American Automobile Association) are not subject to the Code § 277 restrictions on deductions. See Code §§ 277(b)(2), 456(c). Code § 277 is applicable to any nonexempt membership organization that otherwise meets the requirements of the section and was previously tax-exempt under any provision of Code § 501(c), including Code § 501(c)(3),(4),(5),(6), or (7). In general, see Brittain and Crotty, "Creation of Tax-

Exempt Business Leagues: For the Section 501(c)(6) 'First Timer'," 16 *Washburn L. J.* 628 (1977); Crawford, "The Money Side: Associations," XXX *Golf J.* (No. 2) 24 (1977); Denny, "Professional and Social Organizations," 25 *Tulane Tax Inst.* 2200 (1975); Combs, "Tax Implications of Association Efforts for Members," 69 *The Brief* 155 (1974); Fox and Jackson, "Trade Associations: Present and Future Problems," 26 *Tax L. Rev.* 781 (1971); Bodner, "Antitrust Restrictions on Trade Association Membership and Participation," 54 *A.B.A.J.* 37 (1968); Cooper, "The Tax Treatment of Business Grassroots Lobbying: Defining and Attaining the Public Policy Objectives," 68 *Col. L. Rev.* 801 (1968); "Tax-Exempt Business League and Its Functions," 8 *B.C. Ind. & Com. L. Rev.* 953 (1967); Orrick, "Risks Inherent in Trade Associations," *Nat'l Oil Jobber* 11 (May 1967); Note, "Tax-Exempt Business League and Its Functions," 8 *B.C. Ind. & Com. L. Rev.* 953 (1967); Note, "Taxation—Business Leagues—Noncompetitive Membership Does Not Preclude Exempt Status," 13 *Wayne L. Rev.* 611 (1967); Van De Linder, "Trade associations: Retaining exemption, unrelated business income problems," 24 *J. Tax.* 250 (1966); Webster, "Current Federal Tax Aspects of Association Activities," 27 *A.B.A. Sec. Antitrust Law* 150 (1965); Webster, "Should a trade association give up its tax exemption? The pros and cons," 23 *J. Tax.* 358 (1962); Teschner, "Business Leagues, Tax Exemption v. Service to Members," 37 *Taxes* 669 (1959).

18

Social Clubs

The tax-exempt social club has as the essential prerequisite of its exemption the provision of pleasure and recreation to its members. By contrast, many other tax-exempt organizations find their classification as such rationalized by a concept of community service (charitable works, promotion of social welfare, economic betterment, or the like).

§ 18.1 General Rules

The tax exemption for social clubs is the subject of Code § 501(c)(7), which describes clubs "organized for pleasure, recreation, and other nonprofitable purposes, substantially all of the activities of which are for such purposes and no part of the net earnings of which inures to the benefit of any private shareholder." Generally, this tax exemption extends to social and recreation clubs which are supported solely by membership fees, dues, and assessments.[1] However, an organization which otherwise qualifies as a tax-exempt social club will not be denied exemption solely because it adopts a method of raising revenue from members by means other than fees, dues, and assessments.[2]

Social clubs are tax-exempt in part because Congress has recognized that these organizations are generally not appropriate subjects of taxation, that is, that the operation of a social club does not involve the requisite shifting of income.[3] One court has summarized the rationale as follows:

Congress has determined that in a situation where individuals have banded to-gether to provide recreational facilities on a mutual basis, it would be conceptually erroneous to impose a tax on the organization as a separate entity. The funds exempted are received only from the members and any "profit" which results

[1]Reg. § 1.501(c)(7)-1(a). See *Maryland Country Club, Inc.* v. *United States*, 539 F.2d 345 (4th Cir. 1976).
[2]Rev. Rul. 44, 1953-1 C. B. 109.
[3]See Chapter 1.

301

from overcharging for the use of the facilities still belongs to the same members. No income of the sort usually taxed has been generated; the money has simply been shifted from one pocket to another, both within the same pair of pants.[4]

The Department of the Treasury has acknowledged the legitimacy of the social club exemption for essentially the same reason:

> [T]he tax exemption for social clubs is designed to allow individuals to join together to provide recreational or social facilities on a mutual basis, without further tax consequences . . . [where] the sources of income of the organization are limited to receipts from the membership . . . the individual is in substantially the same position as if he had spent his income on pleasure or recreation without the intervening separate organization.[5]

To qualify as a tax-exempt social club, an organization must not only be nonprofit[6] but must meet both an organizational test and an operational test.[7] To satisfy the requirement of a pleasure, recreation, or other permissible purpose,[8] the club must have an established membership of individuals, personal contacts and fellowship.[9] A commingling of the members must play a material part in the life of the organization.[10]

Where the requisite degree of fellowship is absent, tax exemption may be denied, as occurred with respect to an organization formed to furnish television antenna service to its members[11] and associations composed wholly of "artificial" persons or other clubs.[12] Thus, a club operated to assist its members in their business endeavors through study and discussion of problems and similar activities at weekly luncheon meetings was denied tax exemption on the ground that any social activities at the meetings were merely incidental to the business purpose of the organization.[13] A related concept is that a club, to be tax-exempt, must have members actively sharing interests or goals, as evidenced, for example, by appropriate prerequisite conditions or limitations upon members.[14]

---

[4]*McGlotten* v. *Connally*, 338 F.Supp. 448, 458 (D.D.C. 1972).

[5]Treasury Department, *Tax Reform Studies and Proposals* (Comm. Print), 91st Cong., 1st Sess. (1969) at 317.

[6]See *West Side Tennis Club* v. *Commissioner*, 111 F.2d 6 (2d Cir. 1940), cert. den. 311 U.S. 674 (1940).

[7]See, e.g., Rev. Rul. 70-32, 1970-1 C. B. 140.

[8]For discussions of the scope of the phrase "other nonprofitable purposes," see *Allgemeiner Arbeiter Verein* v. *Commissioner*, 237 F.2d 605 (3d Cir. 1956); *Allied Trades Club* v. *Commissioner*, 228 F.2d 906 (3d Cir. 1956).

[9]*Barstow Rodeo and Riding Club* v. *Commissioner*, 12 T.C.M. 1351 (1953).

[10]Rev. Rul. 58-589, 1958-2 C. B. 266.

[11]Rev. Rul. 55-716, 1955-2 C. B. 263.

[12]Rev. Rul. 67-428, 1967-2 C. B. 204.

[13]Rev. Rul. 69-527, 1969-2 C. B. 125.

[14]See *Arner* v. *Rogan*, 40-2 U.S.T.C. ¶9567 (D.C. 1940).

It is insufficient, for purposes of this exemption, for an organization to be able to demonstrate a common objective or interest of the members; commingling is essential. Consequently, for example, most nonprofit automobile clubs are denied tax exemption as social clubs.[15]

To the IRS, the criterion of providing pleasure or recreation by a social club to its members is paramount to the qualification of the club for tax exemption. Thus, gambling can be an exempt purpose for a social club, even where substantial income is derived therefrom, as long as the source of the revenue is its members and their guests. The IRS will refrain from denying or revoking an organization's tax exemption on this basis, notwithstanding the fact that the gambling activities are illegal under state or local law.[16]

While country clubs, dinner clubs, variety clubs, local women's clubs, swim, golf, and tennis clubs,[17] and the like may set the norm for the tax-exempt social club, the concept of an exempt social club is considerably broader. Thus, a flying club was ruled to qualify, where the members are interested in flying as a hobby, commingle in informal meetings, maintain and repair aircraft owned by the club, and fly together in small groups,[18] as opposed to a club which is operated primarily to provide flying facilities suitable for members' individual business or personal use.[19] Social club status was accorded an organization composed solely of persons who are members of a political party and those interested in party affairs,[20] and of members of a specific family to bring them into closer communication through social, family history, and newsletter activities.[21] Gem and mineral clubs or a federation thereof may qualify as tax-exempt social clubs.[22] Other illustrations of tax-exempt social clubs include dog clubs,[23] garden clubs,[24] fraternity chapter houses,[25] and a sponsor of bowling tournaments.[26]

---

[15]Rev. Rul. 69-635, 1969-2 C. B. 126; *Keystone Automobile Club* v. *Commissioner*, 181 F.2d 402 (3d Cir. 1950); *Chattanooga Automobile Club* v. *Commissioner*, 182 F.2d 551 (6th Cir. 1950); *Automobile Club of St. Paul* v. *Commissioner*, 12 T.C. 1152 (1949).

[16]Rev. Rul. 69-68, 1969-1 C. B. 153. See *State ex rel. Sanborn* v. *Kalb*, 543 P.2d 872 (Sup. Ct. Kan. 1975).

[17]See Rev. Rul. 69-281, 1969-1 C. B. 155.

[18]Rev. Rul. 74-30, 1974-1 C. B. 137. Also see *Syrang Aero Club, Inc.* v. *Commissioner*, 73 T.C. 717 (1980).

[19]Rev. Rul. 70-32, *supra*, n. 7.

[20]Rev. Rul. 68-266, 1968-1 C. B. 270.

[21]Rev. Rul. 67-8, 1967-1 C. B. 142.

[22]Rev. Rul. 67-139, 1967-1 C. B. 129.

[23]Rev. Rul. 73-520, 1973-2 C. B. 180; Rev. Rul. 71-421, 1971-2 C. B. 229.

[24]Rev. Rul. 66-179, 1966-1 C. B. 139.

[25]Rev. Rul. 69-573, 1969-2 C. B. 125; Rev. Rul. 64-118, 1964-1 C. B. (Part 1) 182; *Phinney* v. *Dougherty*, 307 F.2d 357 (5th Cir. 1962).

[26]Rev. Rul. 74-148, 1974-1 C. B. 138.

§ 18.2   Private Inurement Doctrine

As is the case in the field of tax-exempt organizations generally, the private inurement doctrine can operate to deprive an organization of tax exemption as a social club. For the most part, as discussed below, the application of this doctrine to tax-exempt social clubs focuses on the question as to whether non-member use is generating revenue the use of which (such as for maintenance and improvement of club facilities) is unduly redounding to the personal advantage of the members (as represented by reduced dues, improved facilities, and the like).[27] Even in this context, however, use of club facilities by the general public may not constitute proscribed inurement where the club contributes any net profits from a function (for example, a steeplechase[28]) to charity.[29] Infrequent public use if permissible as long as it is incidental and basically in furtherance of the club's purposes[30]—although, as to be noted, considerable effort has gone into the matter of defining what is "incidental."

The private inurement doctrine in this context can also become applicable where an otherwise tax-exempt social club has more than one class of members. It is the position of the IRS that where membership classes in a club that enjoy the same rights and privileges in the club facilities are treated differently as respects dues and initiation fees, there is prohibited private inurement because the membership class that pays the lower dues and fees is being subsidized by the members of the other class(es).[31] Similarly, private inurement can arise where a club increases its services without a corresponding increase in dues or other fees paid for club support.[32]

Another dimension to the private inurement doctrine in this context invokes undue dealings between the club and its members. For example, one social club was denied tax exemption because it regularly sold liquor to its members, for consumption off the premises.[33] Likewise, a club that leased building lots to its members in addition to providing them recreation facilities was deemed not entitled to tax exemption.[34] In a somewhat comparable set of circumstances, the IRS ruled nonexempt a club operating a cocktail lounge and cafe as an integral part of a motel and restaurant business; about one-fourth of the club's "membership" was comprised of persons temporarily staying at the motel.[35] However, private inurement is not involved where an exempt social club pays

---

[27]See *Aviation Club of Utah* v. *Commissioner*, 162 F.2d 984 (10th Cir. 1947).

[28]Rev. Rul. 68-119, 1968-1 C. B. 268.

[29]Rev. Rul. 69-636, 1969-2 C. B. 126.

[30]Rev. Rul. 60-323, 1960-2 C. B. 173.

[31]Rev. Rul. 70-48, 1970-1 C. B. 133.

[32]Rev. Rul. 58-589, *supra*, n. 10.

[33]Rev. Rul. 68-535, 1968-2 C. B. 219. Also *Santa Barbara Club* v. *Commissioner*, 68 T.C. 200 (1977).

[34]Rev. Rul. 68-168, 1968-1 C. B. 269; *Lake Petersburg Association* v. *Commissioner*, 33 T.C.M. 259 (1974).

[35]Rev. Rul. 66-225, 1966-2 C. B. 227.

a fixed fee to each club member who brings a new member into the club, as long as the payments are "reasonable compensation for performance of a necessary administrative service."[36]

A club may provide social and recreational facilities to its members who are limited to homeowners of a housing development and nonetheless qualify for tax exemption. However, the exemption will be precluded where any of the following services are provided by the club: (1) owning and maintaining residential streets, (2) administering and enforcing covenants for the preservation of the architecture and appearance of the housing development, or (3) providing police and fire protection and a trash collection service to residential areas.[37]

§ 18.3   Public Use of Club Facilities

Under the income tax regulations (which antedate the 1976 statutory revision, discussed below) a "club which engages in business, such as making its social and recreational facilities available to the general public . . . , is not organized and operated exclusively for pleasure, recreation, and other non-profitable purposes, and is not exempt under section 501(a)."[38] Solicitation of the general public to utilize club facilities will disqualify the club for tax exemption.[39]

The IRS in 1971 promulgated guidelines for determining the effect on a social club's exemption of gross receipts derived from nonmember use of the club's facilities,[40] in so doing superseding earlier guidelines announced in 1964.[41] The concern in this regard is not with the situation where a club member entertains a few guests at his or her club, but where a club's facilities are made available to the general public on a regular and recurring basis,[42] thereby removing that segment of the public from the marketplace of competing commercial operations. Of course, "infrequent" use of an exempt club by the general public is permissible since it is an "incidental" use.[43]

---

[36]Rev. Rul. 80-130, 1980-1 C. B. 117.

[37]Rev. Rul. 75-494, 1975-2 C. B. 214.

[38]Reg. § 1.501(c)(7)-1(b).

[39]*Keystone Automobile Club* v. *Commissioner, supra,* n. 15; *United States* v. *Fort Worth Club of Fort Worth, Texas,* 345 F.2d 52 (5th Cir. 1965), mod. and reaff'd 348 F.2d 891 (5th Cir. 1965); *Polish American Club, Inc.* v. *Commissioner,* 33 T.C.M. 925 (1974).

[40]Rev. Proc. 71-17, 1971-1 C. B. 683. See *The Minnequa University Club* v. *Commissioner,* 30 T.C.M. 1305 (1971).

[41]Rev. Proc. 64-36, 1964-2 C. B. 962.

[42]See Rev. Rul. 60-324, 1960-2 C. B. 173. Also see Rev. Rul. 69-217, 1969-1 C. B. 115; Rev. Rul. 68-638, 1968-2 C. B. 220; Rev. Rul. 65-63, 1965-1 C. B. 240; Rev. Rul. 69-220, 1969-1 C. B. 154; *Spokane Motorcycle Club* v. *United States,* 222 F.Supp. 151 (E.D. Wash. 1963).

[43]Rev. Rul. 60-323, *supra,* n. 30; Rev. Rul. 66-149, 1966-1 C. B. 146; *Town and Country Club* v. *Commissioner,* 1 T.C.M. 334 (1942).

The IRS guidelines make it clear that use of a club's facilities by the general public may indicate the existence of a nonexempt purpose, which if substantial would cause loss of tax exemption, or may make the club liable for the unrelated business income tax. These guidelines establish a basic set of assumptions (which are also utilized for audit purposes) regarding member-sponsored income and a complex record-keeping system to substantiate them. Detailed records are also required to determine under what circumstances and to what extent the club makes its facilities available to nonmembers.

Essentially, the guideline assumptions are that:

1. Where a group of no more than eight individuals, at least one of which is a member, uses club facilities, it is assumed that the nonmembers are the guests of the member, provided payment for the use is received by the club directly from the member or his or her employer.

2. Where at least 75 percent of a group using club facilities are members, a similar assumption will be made. The validity of this test was rejected by a federal district court in 1975 as being "unreasonable," with the court opining that "revenue from member-sponsored occasions involving attendance of nonmembers should not be considered as outsider transactions with respect to their impact on exempt status if it would be reasonable and normal, in the ordinary course of the activities usually pursued by social clubs, to utilize club premises or services for such occasions."[44]

3. Payment by a member's employer is assumed to be for a use that serves a direct business objective of the employee-member. It may be noted here that a corporation may pay for individual club memberships without jeopardizing the club's tax exemption,[45] although an organization the membership of which was entirely in corporations' names would not qualify.[46] However, to the extent an exempt social club has corporate members, the individuals who use the club's facilities under the memberships are treated as the general public for purpose of the guidelines.[47]

4. In all other situations, a host-guest relationship is not assumed but must be substantiated. As to these occasions, the club must maintain books and records containing specific information (as stated in the guidelines) about each use and the income derived therefrom. However, even as to items (1) and (2), adequate records must be maintained.

[44]*Pittsburgh Press Club* v. *United States*, 388 F.Supp. 1269, 1276 (W.D. Pa. 1975), rev. and rem. 536 F.2d 572 (3d Cir. 1976), 426 F.Supp. 553 (W.D. Pa. 1977), rem. 579 F.2d 751 (3d Cir. 1978), 462 F.Supp. 322 (W.D. Pa. 1978), rev. 615 F.2d 600 (3d Cir. 1980).
[45]Rev. Rul. 74-168, 1974-1 C. B. 139.
[46]Rev. Rul. 67-428, *supra*, n. 12.
[47]Rev. Rul. 74-489, 1974-2 C. B. 169.

As well as stating the above assumptions, the 1971 revenue procedure details bookkeeping requirements which tax-exempt social clubs must follow. They are more specific and detailed than the previous requirements.

Where the group includes eight or less individuals, the club must maintain records which substantiate that the group included no more than eight individuals, at least one of whom was a member and that payment was received from the member or his or her employer.

Where 75 percent or more of the group are members of the club, records must be maintained which substantiate that at least 75 percent of the group were club members and that payment was received directly from members or members' employers.

On all other occasions involving nonmembers, the club must maintain records showing each use and the income derived therefrom, even though a member pays initially for such use. The club's records must also include the following: (1) date, (2) number in the party, (3) number of nonmembers therein, (4) total charges, (5) charges attributable to nonmembers, and (6) charges paid by nonmembers. If a member pays all or part of the charges, there must be a statement signed by the member whether he or she has been or will be reimbursed and to what extent by the nonmembers.

Further, where a member's employer reimburses the member, or pays the club directly for nonmember charges, there must be a statement indicating the name of the employer, the amount attributable to nonmember use, the nonmember's name and business or other relationship to the member, and the business, personal, or social purpose of the member served by the nonmember use. If a nonmember (other than a member's employer) makes payment to the club or reimburses a member and claims the amount was paid gratuitiously, the member must sign a statement indicating the donor's name, relationship to the member, and information demonstrating the gratuitous nature of the payment.

Thus, it is apparent that the requirements for record-keeping under the 1971 revenue procedure are burdensome. However, the penalty for failing to maintain adequate records is severe. If these records are not maintained, the Service will not apply the minimum gross receipts standard or the audit assumptions and all income will be treated as unrelated business income. Therefore, tax-exempt clubs must maintain adequate records for the purpose of labeling income from members as "exempt function income."

Excessive use of club facilities by the general public is not the only way in which a club may be considered as engaging in business. In one instance, a swim club was held to be operated as a commercial venture for the financial benefit of its manager and thus was denied tax exemption.[48] In another case, a club had such a large number of "associate members" that the IRS treated it as selling services for profit to these individuals.[49]

---

[48]Rev. Rul. 65-219, 1965-2 C. B. 168. Cf. Rev. Rul. 67-302, 1967-2 C. B. 203.
[49]Rev. Rul. 58-588, 1958-2 C. B. 265.

As discussed, one of the statutory requirements for tax exemption of social clubs has been that they must be organized and operated "exclusively" for pleasure, recreation, and other nonprofitable purposes. Congress in 1976 changed this rule so that now "substantially all" of a club's activities must be for these purposes.[50] This will allow a social club to receive some outside income (including investment income) and a higher level of income from nonmembers using its facilities or services than the IRS previously allowed without losing its tax-exempt status. The intent of Congress is that a tax-exempt social club can receive up to 35 percent of its gross receipts (other than unusual amounts) from investment income and receipts from nonmembers as long as the latter do not exceed 15 percent of total receipts.[51]

In computing this percentage, a club need not take into consideration "unusual amounts of income." This rule was generally intended to cover receipts from the sale of a clubhouse or similar facility. Presumably, the rule is also applicable to receipts from a major sporting event (such as a golf or tennis tournament) which is open to the public but is held by the club on an irregular basis. This interpretation would be in conformance with prior caselaw.[52]

However, some clubs hold tournaments on a regularly recurring basis (e.g., once each year). In this situation, the exclusion for unusual amounts is presumably unavailable. Thus, such a club's tax exemption would be adversely affected if the 15 percent limitation was exceeded[53] but, even if the level of receipts did not trigger revocation of tax exemption, the return from the tournament would nonetheless be subject to taxation as non-"exempt function income."

It is clear that a club that makes its facilities available to the general public in hosting an athletic tournament generates receipts from nonmember use of the facilities, with such receipts subject to the 15 percent test. For example, the IRS privately ruled in 1977 that a country club that hosts a nationally recognized golf tournament about every twenty years does not jeopardize its tax status, although the income therefrom is taxable as unrelated income. In 1980, in another private ruling, the IRS extended this holding to apply to a club that annually hosts a publicly attended golf tournament. This latter ruling was somewhat presaged by a 1978 ruling, holding that an association of professional tournament golfers that maintains a championship course may make the course available to the general public when the tournament is not being held, without disturbing its tax-exempt status but with the income from the use subject to taxation as unrelated business income.[54]

---

[50]P. L. 94-568, 94th Cong., 2d Sess. (1976).

[51]H. Rep. No. 94-1353, 94th Cong., 2d Sess. (1976) at 4; S. Rep. No. 94-1318, 94th Cong., 2d Sess. (1976) at 4. See I.R. 1731 (Jan. 11, 1977).

[52]E.g., *Santee Club* v. *White*, 87 F.2d 5 (1st Cir. 1936).

[53]See *West Side Tennis Club* v. *United States*, 111 F.2d 6 (2d Cir. 1940); Rev. Rul. 68-638, *supra*, n. 42.

[54]IRS Private Letter Ruling 7838108.

§ 18.4 Taxation of Social Clubs

The income tax regulations deprive tax exemption for a club which "engages in business, such as by selling real estate, timber or other products," unless a sale of property is incidental.[55] Nonetheless, abuses were prevalent, perhaps fostered by the courts' willingness to salvage a club's tax exemption. For example, the U.S. Court of Appeals for the Fifth Circuit held that two golf clubs did not lose tax exemption because of the execution of oil leases on their properties that generated substantial income, on the theory that the leases were "incidental" to club operations.[56] Of course, the profits from the oil leases went completely untaxed.

In 1969, Congress adhered to the Department of the Treasury's recommendation for reform in this area. The Treasury Department had, in effect, relied on the basic rationale for tax exemption and ran the rationale in reverse, contending that the investment income of social clubs was equivalent to income earned by the club members in their individual capacity. Thus the Senate Finance Committee stated:

> Since the tax exemption for social clubs and other groups is designed to allow individuals to join together to provide recreational and social facilities or other benefits on a mutual basis, without tax consequences, the exemption operates properly only when the sources of income of the organization are limited to the receipts from the membership. . . . However where the organization receives income from sources outside the membership, such as income from investments . . . upon which no tax is paid, the membership receives a benefit not contemplated by the exemption in that untaxed dollars can be used by the organization to provide pleasure or recreation (or other benefits) to its membership.[57]

In enacting the Tax Reform Act of 1969, Congress subjected income unrelated to the normal operation of a social club to the tax on unrelated business income.[58] However, the approach of Congress in determining the amount of club income to be taxed was, at the time, unique.[59] Generally, an exempt organization's net income from unrelated activities is isolated from other receipts and taxed, with the remaining receipts exempt from tax. But, the income of social clubs is taxed in the opposite manner: rather than isolate unrelated business income, the law isolates "exempt function income" and taxes the balance of the income.[60] All income of a social club other than exempt function income is taxed, regardless of whether or not it was produced from an unrelated

---

[55]Reg. § 1.501(c)(7)-1(b); Rev. Rul. 69-232, 1969-1 C. B. 154.

[56]*Scofield* v. *Corpus Christi Golf & Country Club*, 127 F.2d 452 (5th Cir. 1942); *Koon Kreek Klub* v. *United States*, 108 F.2d 616 (5th Cir. 1940). But see *The Coastal Club, Inc.* v. *Commissioner*, 43 T.C. 783 (1965).

[57]S. Rep. No. 91-552, 91st Cong., 1st Sess. (1969) at 71; also see H. Rep. No. 91-413, 91st Cong., 1st Sess. (1969) (Part 1) at 47; Rev. Rul. 69-220, *supra*, n. 42.

[58]See Chapters 40–42.

[59]Also see Code §§ 527 and 528 (Chapter 20).

[60]Code § 512(a)(3).

activity.[61] This income is computed for tax purposes by deducting all expenses directly connected with production of the income and by applying certain of the modifications generally used in determining unrelated business taxable income.[62]

"Exempt function income" is gross income from dues, fees, charges, or similar amounts paid by members of the organization in connection with the purposes constituting the basis for the tax exemption of the club.[63] Also, the passive income of an exempt social club is generally not taxed if it is set aside to be used for charitable and similar purposes.[64]

It has been the view of the Department of the Treasury that the dividends received deduction is not allowed in computing the taxable income of these organizations.[65] Believing that the reason for this deduction is inapplicable in the context of these organizations, Congress clarified this point by agreeing to the Treasury's Department position.[66] (A similar law change was made for nonexempt membership organizations.[67])

§ 18.5   Sale of Club Assets

Congress in 1969 also relegated to statute the law governing nonrecurring sales of club assets. A common example of this is a golf club that sells land which has become encroached upon by developers to buy land further out in the countryside for new facilities.[68] Where the purpose of such a sale is not profit but to facilitate relocation or a comparable purpose, the law provides a carryover of basis, that is, nonrecognition of gain.[69] Specifically, where property used directly in the performance of the club's tax-exempt function is sold and

---

[61]Code § 512(a)(3)(A); Prop. Reg. § 1.512(a)-3(a),(b). Thus, in one case, the interest earned by a social club on deposits required for its charter flights was held taxable as unrelated income. *Council of British Societies in Southern California* v. *United States*, 78-2 U.S.T.C. ¶9744 (C.D. Cal. 1978).

[62]Code § 162, 512(b). The foregoing rules are also applicable to employees' associations described in Code § 501(c)(9). See Chapter 20. It is the position of the IRS that the expenses associated with activities that are not profit-motivated cannot be deducted in determining unrelated business income under Code § 512(a)(3). Rev. Rul. 81-69, 1981-1 C. B. 351.

[63]Code § 512(a)(3)(B); Prop. Reg. § 1.512(a)-3(c)(1),(2). See, e.g., IRS Private Letter Ruling 7930007.

[64]Code § 170(c)(4); Prop. Reg. § 1.512(a)-3(c)(3), (4).

[65]Prop. Reg. § 1.512(a)-3(b)(2).

[66]P.L. 94-568, *supra*, n. 50; H. Rep. No. 1353, 94th Cong. 2d Sess. (1976) at 6.

[67]Code § 277.

[68]See Rev. Rul. 69-232, *supra*, n. 55; Rev. Rul. 65-64, 1965-1 C. B. 241; Rev. Rul. 58-501, 1958-2 C. B. 262; *Santee Club* v. *White*, *supra*, n. 52; *Mill Lane Club* v. *Commissioner*, 23 T.C. 433 (1954); *Juniper Hunting Club, Inc.* v. *Commissioner*, 28 B.T.A. 525 (1933).

[69]Code § 513(a)(3)(D).

the proceeds reinvested in exempt function property, within a period beginning one year before the sale date and ending three years thereafter, any gain from the sale is recognized only to the extent that the sale price of the old property exceeds the purchase price of the new property.[70]

§ 18.6 Racial Discrimination

The U.S. Constitution, in the Fifth and Fourteenth Amendments, prohibits racial discrimination by government and government-supported private institutions. Private organizations may lawfully discriminate, such as private clubs on the basis of race in membership, absent applicability of the "state action" doctrine by which government is deemed to have sufficiently supported or encouraged the private discrimination as to amount to a constitutional violation.[71]

The relationship between the state action doctrine and tax exemptions has been the focus of several cases. This relationship as regards social clubs was the subject of a 1972 case where a black, allegedly denied membership in a lodge of the Benevolent and Protective Order of Elks solely because of his race, brought a class action to enjoin the granting of tax benefits to nonprofit fraternal organizations which exclude nonwhites from membership.[72] The issue thus became whether tax exemptions and deductions cause the benefited private organizations to have the requisite imprimatur of government, that is, whether exemptions and deductions amount to a grant of federal funds to them. Where such a "grant" is involved, the state action doctrine will bring the protections of the Constitution to such private acts.

[70]Prop. Reg. § 1.512(a)-3(e). Cf. Code § 1034.

[71]Cases discussing the "state action" doctrine (in areas other than but including the private club context) have flourished in recent years. See, for example, *Burton v. Wilmington Parking Authority*, 356 U.S. 715 (1961); *United States v. Texas Education Agency*, 532 F.2d 380 (5th Cir. 1976); *Golden v. Biscayne Bay Yacht Club*, 530 F.2d 16 (5th Cir. 1976); *Doe v. Charleston Area Medical Center, Inc.*, 529 F.2d 638 (4th Cir. 1975); *New York City Jaycees, Inc. v. United States Jaycees, Inc.*, 512 F.2d 856 (2d Cir. 1975); *Greenya v. George Washington University*, 512 F.2d 556 (D.C. Cir. 1975); *Barrett v. United Hospital*, 375 F.Supp. 791 (S.D. N.Y. 1974), aff'd 506 F.2d 1395 (2d Cir. 1974); *Coleman v. Wagner College*, 429 F.2d 1120 (2d Cir. 1970); *Taylor v. Maryland School For the Blind*, 409 F.Supp. 148 (D. Md. 1976); *Hollenbaugh v. Board of Trustees of Carnegie Free Library, of Connellsville, Pennsylvania*, 405 F.Supp. 629 (W.D. Pa. 1975); *McMenamin v. Philadelphia County Democratic Executive Committee of Philadelphia*, 405 F.Supp. 998 (E.D. Pa. 1975); *Berrios v. Inter American University*, 409 F.Supp. 769 (D. P. R. 1975); *Falkenstein v. Department of Revenue*, 350 F.Supp. 887 (D. Ore. 1972), app. dis. 409 U.S. 1099 (1973); Note, "State Action and the United States Junior Chamber of Commerce," 43 *Geo Wash. L. Rev.* 1407 (1975). Further, see *Reitman v. Mulkey*, 387 U.S. 369 (1967); *Evans v. Newton*, 382 U.S. 296 (1966); *Pennsylvania v. Board of City Trusts*, 353 U.S. 230 (1957); *Shelley v. Kraemer*, 334 U.S. 1 (1948); *Steele v. Louisville and Nashville Railroad*, 323 U.S. 192 (1944); *Civil Rights Cases*, 109 U.S. 3 (1883).

[72]*McGlotten v. Connally, supra*, n. 4.

In this case, the court concluded that a social club's policy of racial discrimination would not preclude tax exemption, although the exemption given to fraternal organizations[73] requires the absence of discriminatory practices. The rationale underlying this distinction in treatment turns on the peculiar manner in which social clubs are taxed: since they are taxed on all receipts other than exempt function income, there is no state action-type "benefit" but only a matter of defining appropriate subjects of taxation, whereas fraternal organizations, being taxed only on unrelated business taxable income, do receive a government benefit in that investment income goes untaxed.[74]

Congress in 1976 concluded that it is "inappropriate" for an exempt social club to have a "written policy" of discrimination on account of race, color, or religion. Accordingly, Congress enacted a rule that bars tax exemption for social clubs maintaining such a discriminatory policy.[75]

In 1980, Congress refined this requirement to allow social clubs that are affiliated with fraternal beneficiary societies[76] to retain tax exemption even though membership in the clubs is limited to members of a particular religion. Also, this law change will allow certain alumni clubs which are limited to members of a particular religion in order to further the religion's teachings or principles to retain their exemption as social clubs.[77]

[73]Code § 501(c)(8). See Chapter 20 § 4.

[74]See *Golden* v. *Biscayne Bay Yacht Club, supra*, n. 71; *Olzman* v. *Lake Hills Swim Club, Inc.*, 495 F.2d 1331 (2d Cir. 1974); *Cornelius* v. *Benevolent Protective Order of Elks*, 382 F.Supp. 1182 (D. Conn. 1974); *Moose Lodge* v. *Irvis*, 407 U.S. 163 (1972). Cf. *Pitts* v. *Department of Revenue*, 333 F.Supp. 662 (E.D. Wis. 1971).

[75]P.L. 94-568, *supra*, n. 50.

[76]See Chapter 20 § 4.

[77]P.L. 96-601, 96th Cong., 2d Sess. (1980). Among the intended beneficiaries of these rules are the social clubs operated by the Knights of Columbus. In general, see Graham, "Social Clubs: Establishing the Right to Exemption Under Section 501(c)(7) and a Proposal for Expanding the Scope of Exemption," 33 *Tax Law.* 881 (1980); Crawford, "New laws indicate scope of exempt clubs' revenues from investments, nonmembers," 47 *J. Tax.* 48 (1977); Crawford, "Country Clubs: The Money Side," XXIX *Golf J.* (No. 2) 28 (1976) Moffet, "The Problems of Section 501(c)(7) Organizations," 54 *Taxes* 4 (1976); Denny, "Professional and Social Organizations," 25 *Tulane Tax Inst.* 2200 (1975); Horn, "Unrelated Business Income of Social Clubs," 49 *Taxes* 738 (1971); Carlson, "The Little Known Repeal of the Income Tax Exemption of Social Clubs," 26 *Tax L. Rev.* 45 (1970); Ginstling, "Social clubs coming under closer IRS scrutiny: nonmember use can kill exemption," 23 *J. Tax.* 162 (1966); Gasperow, "Tax Problems of Country Clubs," *J. Accountancy* 60 (Oct. 1964).

19

Labor, Agricultural, and
Horticultural Organizations

Code § 501(c)(5) exempts from federal income tax "labor, agricultural, or horticultural organizations." Under the income tax regulations, no part of the net earnings of such an organization may inure to the benefit of any member.[1] Moreover, such an organization must have as its object the betterment of the conditions of those engaged in the exempt pursuits, the improvement of the grade of their products, and the development of a higher degree of efficiency in the particular occupation.[2]

§ 19.1 Labor Organizations

While the most common example of the tax-exempt labor organization is a labor union, the exempt labor organization category encompasses a broader range of entities. This classification includes, for example, an organization of tax-exempt labor unions representing public employees,[3] an organization to provide strike and lockout benefits,[4] the so-called "labor temple" (offices, meeting rooms, auditoriums, and the like for labor union members),[5] and an organization publishing a labor newspaper.[6]

According to the IRS, "[g]eneral usage defines a labor organization as an

[1] Reg. § 1.501(c)(5)-1(a)(1). The pro rata refund of excess dues to members by an exempt agricultural organization does not constitute private inurement and thus does not disqualify the organization from continuing tax exemption. Rev. Rul. 81-60, 1981-1 C.B. 335.
[2] Reg. § 1.501(c)(5)-1(a)(2).
[3] Rev. Rul. 74-596, 1974-2 C. B. 167.
[4] Rev. Rul. 67-7, 1967-1 C. B. 137.
[5] *Portland Co-Operative Labor Temple Association* v. *Commissioner*, 39 B. T. A. 450 (1939).
[6] Rev. Rul. 68-534, 1968-2 C. B. 217.

association of workmen who have combined to protect or promote the interests of the members by bargaining collectively with their employers to secure better working conditions, wages, and similar benefits."[7] Thus, a tax-exempt labor organization must have authority to represent or speak for its members in matters relating to their employment, such as wages, hours of labor, conditions, or economic benefits. An organization that does not function, or directly support the efforts of any labor organization, to better employment conditions cannot qualify as an exempt labor organization. For example, an organization (controlled by individuals in their private capacity) that provides weekly income to its members in the event of a lawful strike by the member's labor union by reason of its contractual agreements with and payments from the workers was ruled to not qualify as an exempt labor organization.[8]

A labor organization is generally composed of employees or representatives of the employees (such as collective bargaining agents) and similar groups. But an organization the membership of which is composed principally of laborers will not, for that reason alone, qualify as a labor organization.[9] An exempt labor organization's membership must be composed of those who are, in law, "employees." For example, an organization the members of which are independent contractors and entrepreneurs (persons engaged in harness racing in a specific geographical area as drivers, trainers, and horse owners) was held to not qualify as a labor organization because the members are not employees.[10]

The IRS accorded labor organization status to a committee formed pursuant to a collective bargaining agreement to improve working conditions for apprentices in various skilled crafts and to aid in the settlement of disputes between employers and apprentices.[11] The Service so held, even though the committee's membership consists of an equal number of employer and employee representatives, and the committee is financed primarily by employer and union contributions.[12] Labor organization classification was also extended to a trust organized pursuant to a collective bargaining agreement, funded and administered solely by the employers in an industry, because the purpose of the trust is to compensate a multiemployer steward who is under a union's direct control with responsibility to settle disputes, investigate complaints, and otherwise encourage compliance with the agreement throughout the entire industry.[13] Similarly, the IRS determined that a nurses' association, which has as its primary purposes the acting as a collective bargaining agent for its mem-

[7]IRS Exempt Organizations Handbook (IRM 7751) § 521.

[8]Rev. Rul. 76-420, 1976-2 C. B. 153.

[9]See *Workingmen's Co-Operative Ass'n of the United States Insurance League of New York* v. *Commissioner*, 3 B. T. A. 1352 (1926). Cf. Rev. Rul. 78-287, 1978-2 C. B. 146.

[10]Rev. Rul. 78-288, 1978-2 C. B. 179. On this point, the IRS will look to see whether the members are self-employed for purposes of Code § 1402.

[11]Rev. Rul. 59-6, 1959-1 C. B. 121. Also Rev. Rul. 78-42, 1978-1 C. B. 158.

[12]Rev. Rul. 75-473, 1975-2 C. B. 213.

[13]Rev. Rul. 77-5, 1977-1 C. B. 146.

bers in contract negotiations between various institutions and the nurses employed by them and the operation of a health and welfare fund for its membership, constitutes a tax-exempt labor organization.[14]

In another illustration, the IRS ruled that a city school teachers' association is a tax-exempt labor organization.[15] The organization was formed to improve the professional abilities of its members and to secure for them better salaries and working conditions. It sponsors seminars and courses for its members, participates in teacher conventions, bargains collectively and processes grievances, and keeps its members informed of its activities through regular meetings and a newsletter.

Generally, an exempt labor organization is one which operates to better the conditions of those (frequently its members) engaged in a particular trade, such as by striking for better wages and working conditions. Where the labor organization has members, they will mostly be employees, although the inclusion of some self-employed persons in the membership will not deprive the organization of its classification as an exempt labor group if it otherwise qualifies.[16] Similarly, the payment by a labor organization of death, sick, accident, and similar benefits to its members generally will not preclude the tax exemption.[17] However, the payment by an organization of law enforcement officers for its members' legal defense in actions brought against them in connection with the performance of their official duties did not adversely affect the organization's tax-exempt status as a labor organization.[18]

The IRS had occasion to consider the tax status of a nonprofit organization which was established pursuant to a collective bargaining agreement between a union and an employers' association to enable members of the union to save money under a plan by which a fixed amount is withheld from their pay and deposited in a bank account. The funds are paid to the union's members annually, along with any interest remaining after payment of administrative expenses. In determining that this organization does not qualify as a labor organization, the Service noted that, to so qualify, the activities of such an organization must "be those commonly or historically recognized as characteristic of labor organizations, or be closely related and necessary to accomplishing the principal purposes of exempt labor organizations." Thus the IRS concluded that "savings plans that disburse money on an annual basis are not closely related to the labor organization's principal activities of negotiating wages, hours, and working conditions nor are such savings plans closely related and necessary to providing the mutual benefits characteristically associated with labor organizations."[19]

[14]Rev. Rul. 77-154, 1977-1 C. B. 148.
[15]Rev. Rul. 76-31, 1976-1 C. B. 157.
[16]Rev. Rul. 77-154, *supra*, n. 14; Rev. Rul. 74-167, 1974-1 C. B. 134.
[17]Rev. Rul. 62-17, 1962-1 C. B. 87. Cf. Rev. Rul. 77-46, 1977-1 C. B. 147.
[18]Rev. Rul. 75-288, 1975-2 C. B. 212.
[19]Rev. Rul. 77-46, *supra*, n. 17.

As noted, one of the purposes of an exempt labor organization may be the development among its members of a higher degree of efficiency in their occupations. To this end, a labor organization may administer bona fide skill-improvement or self-improvement programs as part of its tax-exempt activity, as long as the programs are administered by the organization specifically for, and involve substantial participation by, its members. Thus, this doctrine does not embrace programs substantially developed and administered by other organizations (even though they improve the skills of the labor organization's membership) or that require only insubstantial participation by a labor organization's members in educational activities. For example, a labor organization was advised that its conduct of travel tours for nonmembers and members who do not substantially participate in educational programs administered by it is not an exempt activity.[20]

A labor union owned- and-controlled company organized to provide employment to the union's members did not qualify for tax exemption, even though its net profits were turned in to the union's treasury.[21] Exemption was also denied an organization established by an employer and a union under a collective bargaining agreement to ensure the efficient discharge of the employer's obligation to pay withheld employment taxes to federal and state authorities.[22] An organization of farmers formed to furnish farm laborers for individual farmers also did not qualify for tax exemption as a labor organization.[23] With the advent of the unrelated business income taxation scheme,[24] labor organizations may engage in some nonexempt activities, in the nature of "business" functions or services, and nonetheless continue to remain exempt from federal income taxation.[25]

The effectiveness of labor organizations, particularly unions, on the legislative and political fronts continually generates controversy. The matter came before the courts in 1972 and 1973 in a case brought by aerospace workers covered by compulsory union-shop contracts and thus required to pay union dues to enjoin the government from continuing to recognize tax exemption in the case of any labor organization that expends membership dues for partisan political campaigns.[26] The court rejected the idea that the tax exemption of unions should be terminated where union dues are used in political campaigns, stating that Congress has considered and not adopted that result.[27] The court also rejected the argument that the tax exemption amounts to a federal subsidy and consequently that general political activity of labor organizations should

[20]IRS Private Letter Ruling 7944018.
[21]Rev. Rul. 69-386, 1969-2 C. B. 123.
[22]Rev. Rul. 66-354, 1966-2 C. B. 207.
[23]Rev. Rul. 72-391, 1972-2 C. B. 249.
[24]See Chapters 40–42.
[25]See, e.g., Rev. Rul. 62-191, 1962-2 C. B. 146; Rev. Rul. 59-330, 1959-2 C. B. 153.
[26]*Marker* v. *Schultz*, 485 F.2d 1003 (D. C. Cir. 1973), aff'g 337 F.Supp. 1301 (D. D. C. 1972).
[27]See 18 U. S. C. § 610.

be proscribed, finding that the exemption is "benevolent neutrality" and that there is not the requisite "nexus" between the exemption and any government "involvement" in union activities.[28]

§ 19.2 Agricultural Organizations

As respects agricultural organizations, the principal issue is likely to be the scope of the term "agricultural." Until recently, the IRS relied on the narrow dictionary definition of the term "agriculture" as meaning "the science or art of cultivating the soil, harvesting crops and raising livestock."[29] That is, the Service relied on the traditional meaning of the term, without much recognition given to some modern realities.

Prior to 1976, neither the federal statutory tax law nor the income tax regulations defined the term "agricultural." In the absence of such a defined meaning, those advocating a more realistic approach to this area of tax policy contended that this term must, for tax purposes, be given its "normal and customary" meaning.[30] This advocated approach did not entail mere reference to dictionary definitions, inasmuch as statutes are to be interpreted in effectuation of intended congressional policy, which may not be identical to the meaning of certain words in lay terms. Certainly, the principal dictionary meaning of "agriculture" is the cultivation of land, as in the raising of crops. However, "agriculture" also means "husbandry" which connotes "farming" as well as "agriculture." "Agriculture" means "farming (in a broad sense, including . . . stock raising, etc.)."[31] Certainly, "stock" raising can be interpreted as broader than the raising of "livestock."[32] Thus, it was contended that the statutory scheme should be relied upon, rather than dictionary definitions.[33]

An illustration of the foregoing was the Service's refusal to accord tax-exempt status to organizations engaged in the harvesting of aquatic resources (popularly termed "aquaculture"). Yet it appeared that, in the face of contemporary food, health, and related needs, any distinction in this context between land farming and sea resource gathering is artificial—in reality, both are "agricultural" endeavors. In other statutory and regulatory contexts, this distinction has disappeared. For example, the Farm Credit Act, as amended, provides that fish-

---

[28]Citing *Watz* v. *Tax Commission*, 397 U. S. 664 (1970). See Chapter 38. In general, see Graves, "When will political activities of unions and associations cost them their exemption?," 35 *J. Tax*. 254 (1971); Albert and Hansell, "The Tax Status of the Modern Labor Union," 111 *Univ. of Pa. L. Rev.* 137 (1962).

[29]Citing Webster's Third New International Dictionary. Also *Dorrell* v. *Norida Land & Timber Co.*, 27 P.2d 960 (Sup. Ct. Id. 1933).

[30]See *United States* v. *Byrum*, 408 U. S. 125, 136 (1972). Also *Commissioner* v. *Caulkins*, 144 F.2d 482, 484 (6th Cir. 1944).

[31]See The American College Dictionary.

[32]See *Fromm Bros.* v. *United States*, 35 F.Supp. 145 (W. D. Wis. 1940); Rev. Rul. 57-588, 1957-2 C. B. 305.

[33]See *Mitchell* v. *Cohn*, 333 U. S. 411 (1948).

erman may qualify for the benefits of the Act as "producers or harvesters of aquatic products." The Rural Development Act of 1972 authorizes individuals involved in producing fish and fishery products to obtain loans in the same manner as farmers. Additionally, the Federal Energy Office's Petroleum Allocation and Price Regulations include fishing under the definition of "agricultural production." In other contexts, the IRS has readily turned, in the process of assessing organizations' claims to tax exemption, to nontax statutes to divine congressional intent or the basis for federal public policy bearing on the organizations' activities.[34]

Unlike the term "farmer,"[35] it is clear that the term "agriculture," for federal tax purposes, is to be liberally construed. Thus, for example, an organization which annually hosted a rodeo was deemed an agricultural organization.[36] An organization which is concerned with methods of raising fur-bearing animals and marketing pelts was ruled an agricultural organization,[37] as was an organization which tests soil for farmers and nonfarmers and furnishes test results for educational purposes.[38] It is not even mandatory that the membership of the organization desiring categorization as "agricultural" be engaged in agricultural pursuits.[39] Therefore, an organization of women who had no relationship to agriculture other than the fact that their husbands are farmers in a particular state was ruled an agricultural organization.[40]

Effectuation of rational contemporary tax policy called for a broader interpretation of the term "agriculture." The U.S. Court of Appeals for the First Circuit provided precedent for such a view:

> According to the lexicographers, agriculture is defined as the art or science of cultivating the ground including the harvesting of crops and *in a broader sense the science or art of the production of plants and animals useful to man*, including in a variable degree the preparation of these products for man's use (emphasis supplied).[41]

It was thought that if the distinctions attempted by the IRS in this regard did not advance tax policy, a court would likely find the activities of an organization engaged in or associated with aquatic harvesting to be "agricultural" in nature. It was significant that the sole authority cited by the Service for its position was a dictionary. Yet, in a comparable setting, a court using the same authority held that the raising and trapping of muskrats constitutes an "agricultural" pursuit.[42] However, the IRS remained steadfast in its resolve, con-

---

[34]See Rev. Rul. 76-204, 1976-1 C. B. 152.

[35]See Code § 521; Chapter 20.

[36]*Campbell* v. *Big Spring Cowboy Reunion*, 210 F.2d 143 (5th Cir. 1954).

[37]Rev. Rul. 56-245, 1956-1 C. B. 204.

[38]Rev. Rul. 54-282, 1954-2 C. B. 126.

[39]See Rev. Rul. 60-86, 1960-1 C. B. 198.

[40]Rev. Rul. 74-118, 1974-1 C. B. 134.

[41]*Sancho* v. *Bowie*, 93 F.2d 323, 324 (1st Cir. 1937).

[42]*Bonham & Young Co.* v. *Martin*, 11 A.2d. 371, 372 (N.J. State Bd. Tax App. 1940).

ceding only that an organization formed for the purpose of encouraging better and more economical methods of fish farming is an agricultural organization.[43] Also, the Service determined that an organization the members of which are involved in the commercial fishing industry in a state, that publishes a monthly newspaper of commercial fishing technical information and news, and that derives its income primarily from membership dues and sale of advertising, did not qualify as an agricultural organization but instead as a business league.[44]

In an attempt to settle this controversy, Congress in enacting the Tax Reform Act of 1976, authored a federal tax law provision[45] to provide that, for purposes of tax exemption as an "agricultural" organization, the term "agriculture" includes (but is not limited to) the act or science of cultivating land, harvesting crops or aquatic resources, or raising livestock. The insertion of the phrase "harvesting . . . aquatic resources" is designed to encompass fishing and related pursuits (such as the taking of lobsters and shrimp), the cultivation of underwater vegetation, and the cultivation or growth of any edible organism. This change resulted from Congress' realization that there is no tax policy to be served under the provision for tax-exempt agricultural groups for differentiating between occupations devoted to the production of foodstuffs and other items from the earth and from the waters. The statutory definition is effective for tax years beginning after 1975, although inasmuch as the statute is believed to be declaratory of what Congress perceived the law should have been beforehand,[46] it may be contended that the definition is of utility with respect to pre-1976 tax years.

Another dimension of this dilemma for organizations engaged in or associated with aquatic harvesting is that the Postal Service followed the position of the IRS and categorized them as business leagues rather than agriculture organizations, thereby depriving them of the preferential postal rates under the second and third classes. Congress also remedied this aspect of the problem in 1976, when it enacted the Postal Reorganization Act Amendments of 1976.[47] Section 11 of the Amendments added a definition of the term "agriculture" to the postal laws, as including "the art or science of cultivating land, harvesting crops or marine resources, or raising of livestock," thereby removing these organizations from business league status under the postal laws as well.[48] For postal law

[43]Rev. Rul. 74-488, 1974-2 C. B. 166. Cf. Rev. Rul. 76-241, 1976-1 C. B. 131.
[44]Rev. Rul. 75-287, 1975-2 C. B. 211. See Chapter 17.
[45]Code § 501(g).
[46]See 121 Cong. Rec. 34442 (1975).
[47]P. L. 94-421, 94th Cong., 2d Sess. (1976).
[48]39 U. S. C. § 3626(d). While the tax law definition of the term "agricultural" encompasses the "harvesting . . . [of] aquatic resources," the postal law definition of the term includes the "harvesting . . . [of] marine resources." The dictionary definition of "aquatic" is "of or pertaining to water," whereas the dictionary definition of "marine" is "of or pertaining to the sea," thereby holding open the possibility that an organization engaged in or associated with the harvesting of fresh waters will acquire classification as an "agricultural" organization for federal tax purposes but as a business league for postal law purposes.

purposes, this definition also extends to "any organization or association which collects and disseminates information or materials relating to agricultural pursuits."

Other tax-exempt agricultural organizations include an association engaged in the promotion of the artificial insemination of cattle,[49] an association formed to guard the purity of Welsh ponies,[50] an organization, established to advance agriculture, which buys supplies and equipment for resale to its members,[51] a local association of dairy farmers participating in the U.S. Department of Agriculture's National Cooperative Dairy Herd Improvement Program,[52] a local association of farmers formed to promote more effective agricultural pest control,[53] and an organization of agricultural growers and producers formed principally to negotiate with processors for crop prices.[54]

The IRS will not grant agricultural status to an organization the principal purpose of which is to provide a direct business service for its members' economic benefit. Thus, an organization engaged in the management, grazing, and sale of its members' cattle was denied tax-exempt status.[55] The same fate befell an organization composed of agricultural producers the principal activity of which is marketing livestock for its members.[56] Similarly, the Service denied an organization classification as an "agricultural" entity where it furnished farm laborers for individual farmers, ruling that the organization is "merely providing services to individual farmers that they would have to provide for themselves or get someone else to provide for them."[57] In another illustration of this rule, the IRS denied agricultural status to an organization that owns and operates a livestock facility and leases it to local members of a nonexempt national association of farmers for use in implementing the association's collective bargaining program with processors. The facility was used to collect, weigh, sort, grade, and ship livestock marketed through the program. The IRS determined that the operation and leasing of the facility "is the providing of a business service to those members who make use of the national association's collective bargaining program" and that this service "merely relieves the members of the organization of work they would either have to perform themselves or have performed for them."[58]

As noted, to be tax-exempt as an "agricultural" organization, the organization must, *inter alia*, have its objective the betterment of the conditions of those "engaged in" agricultural pursuits. The IRS on one occasion used this rule as

[49]*East Tennessee Artificial Breeders Association* v. *United States*, 63-2 U. S. T. C. ¶ 9748 (E. D. Tenn. 1963).
[50]Rev. Rul. 55-230, 1955-1 C. B. 71.
[51]Rev. Rul. 57-466, 1957-2 C. B. 311. But see Rev. Rul. 67-252, 1967-2 C. B. 195.
[52]Rev. Rul. 74-518, 1974-2 C. B. 166, clarifying Rev. Rul. 70-372, 1970-2 C. B. 118.
[53]Rev. Rul. 81-59, 1981-1 C. B. 334.
[54]Rev. Rul. 76-399, 1976-2 C. B. 152.
[55]Rev. Rul. 74-195, 1974-1 C. B. 135.
[56]Rev. Rul. 66-105, 1966-1 C. B. 145. See also Rev. Rul. 70-372, *supra*, n. 52.
[57]Rev. Rul. 72-391, *supra*, n. 23.
[58]Rev. Rul. 77-153, 1977-1 C. B. 147.

the rationale for denying "agricultural" status to an institute of butter and cheese manufacturers, concluding that those who benefit directly from its activities were not engaged in agricultural pursuits (allowing, however, that it may qualify as a business league).[59] Similarly, the IRS was successful, using the rationale that activities only remotely promoting the interests of those engaged in agricultural pursuits cannot qualify an organization for this exemption, in refusing an organization tax exemption where it was organized to hold agricultural fairs, stock shows, and horse race meets but actually devoted itself solely to horse racing.[60]

As has been pointed out, the IRS may conclude that an organization is being operated in the furtherance of interests other than agriculture and that, consequently, it is more properly classifiable as a business league rather than as an agricultural organization.[61] The exemptions for agricultural and "charitable" organizations may also overlap, such as where an organization conducts a state or county fair or otherwise presents expositions and exhibitions in an educational manner.[62]

§ 19.3   Horticultural Organizations

"Horticulture" is the art or science of cultivating fruits, flowers, and vegetables.[63]

Exemption as a horticultural organization was accorded a garden club formed for the purpose of bettering the conditions of persons engaged in horticultural pursuits and improving their products, by publishing a monthly journal, reporting new developments in horticultural products to its members, and encouraging the development of such products through a system of awards.[64]

§ 19.4   Unrelated Income Considerations

An organization finding tax exemption as a labor, agricultural, or horticultural entity may nonetheless carry on activities subjecting it to the tax on unrelated business income.[65] As illustration of those rules in this context, the IRS has ruled as taxable income received by an agricultural organization from the sale of supplies and equipment to members,[66] income derived by a labor organi-

[59]Rev. Rul. 67-252, *supra*, n. 51.
[60]*Forest City Live Stock and Fair Co.* v. *Commissioner*, 26 B. T. A. 1494 (1932).
[61]See, e.g., Rev. Rul. 67-252, *supra*, n. 51; Rev. Rul. 56-245, *supra*, n. 37.
[62]Rev. Rul. 67-216, 1967-2 C. B. 180. See *Indiana Crop Improvement Association, Inc.* v. *Commissioner*, 76 T.C. 394 (1981).
[63]See *Guerrero* v. *United States Fidelity and Guaranty Co.*, 98 S. W. 2d 796 (Sup. Ct. Tex. 1936).
[64]Rev. Rul. 66-179, 1966-1 C. B. 139.
[65]See Chapters 40–42.
[66]Rev. Rul. 57-466, *supra*, n. 51.

zation from the operation of semiweekly bingo games,[67] income obtained by an agricultural organization as commissions from the sale of members' cattle,[68] income derived by a labor organization from the performance of accounting and tax services for some of its members,[69] and income received by an agricultural organization from the operation of club facilities for its members and their guests.[70] Also, federal tax law provides an exclusion from the unrelated income taxation rules for income received by a tax-exempt organization used to establish, maintain, or operate a retirement home, hospital, or similar facility for the exclusive use and benefit of the aged and infirm members of the organization, where the income is derived from agricultural pursuits and conducted on grounds contiguous to the facility and where the income does not provide more than 75 percent of the cost of maintaining and operating the facility,[71] although this provision was removed from the Code (but not from law) as part of the "deadwood" provisions of the Tax Reform Act of 1976.

[67]Rev. Rul. 59-330, *supra*, n. 25.
[68]Rev. Rul. 69-51, 1969-1 C. B. 159.
[69]Rev. Rul. 62-191, *supra*, n. 25.
[70]Rev. Rul. 60-86, *supra*, n. 39.
[71]Pre-1976 Code § 512(b)(14).

20

Other Tax-Exempt Organizations

There are several categories of organizations, exempt from federal income tax, other than those which have been discussed in previous chapters. These categories are summarized in this chapter, in order of the accompanying Internal Revenue Code section numbers.

§ 20.1 United States Instrumentalities

Code § 501(c)(1) describes "[c]orporations organized under Act of Congress, if such corporations are instrumentalities of the United States and if, under such Act, as amended and supplemented, such corporations are exempt from Federal income taxes." Thus, this provision is extraneous, because the particular enabling act itself provides exemption, although the federal tax law reference provides a specific tax law underpinning for the exemption.

Organizations exempt from federal tax under this section include the Federal Deposit Insurance Corporation, the Reconstruction Finance Corporation, Federal Land Banks, Federal National·Mortgage Association, Federal Reserve Banks, Federal Savings and Loan Insurance Corporation, and the Pennsylvania Avenue Development Corporation.

Federal credit unions organized and operated under the Federal Credit Union Act are instrumentalities of the United States[1] and therefore are entitled to tax exemption under this provision. These credit unions are includible in a group exemption letter issued to the Bureau of Federal Credit Unions, then-Department of Health, Education and Welfare.[2] Certain other credit unions,

[1]Rev. Rul. 55-133, 1955-1 C. B. 138.
[2]IRS Exempt Organizations Handbook (IRM 7751) § (50)32.1. Also see Rev. Rul. 60-169, 1960-1 C. B. 621.

which fail to qualify under this provision, may secure tax exemption under Code § 501(c)(14) (see below).[3]

When Congress enacted the Employee Retirement Income Security Act of 1974 (ERISA), it established the Pension Benefit Guaranty Corporation (PBGC) primarily to administer a pension plan termination program. ERISA exempted the PBGC from state and local taxation but was silent on the matter of federal taxation. By enactment of the Tax Reform Act of 1976, Congress also exempted the PBGC from federal taxation.

Congress amended the ERISA[4] to specifically exempt the PBGC from taxation by the United States. (However, the PBGC remains subject to the taxes imposed under the Federal Insurance Contributions Act and the Federal Unemployment Tax Act.) This action by Congress qualified the PBGC for tax-exempt status as an instrumentality of the United States. The applicability of the PBGC provision is retroactive to September 2, 1974 (the date of enactment of ERISA).

§ 20.2   Title-Holding Corporations

Code § 501(c)(2) describes "[c]orporations organized for the exclusive purpose of holding title to property, collecting income therefrom, and turning over the entire amount thereof, less expenses,[5] to an organization which itself is "tax-exempt." Title-holding corporations were originally established to circumvent the laws of states which restricted the ability of certain exempt organizations to themselves hold title to property; they have also proved useful as a device to limit liability, facilitate administration, and increase borrowing power.[6] This type of organization cannot accumulate income and cannot engage in any business other than that of holding title to property.[7] Should one of the organizations to which a holding corporation makes income distributions cease to qualify for tax exemption, the holding corporation will lose its exemption.[8]

Despite the general prohibition on income accumulation, however, an exempt title-holding corporation may retain part of its income each year to apply to indebtedness on property to which it holds title.[9] The transaction is treated as if the income had been turned over to the parent and the parent had used the income to make a capital contribution to the title-holding corporation which, in turn, applied the contribution to the indebtedness. In rationalizing this flexibility, the IRS observed that the title-holding corporation "is by its nature

---

[3]See Rev. Rul. 69-283, 1969-1 C. B. 156.

[4]§ 4002(g)(1).

[5]See Rev. Rul. 66-102, 1966-1 C. B. 133.

[6]See IRS Exempt Organizations Handbook (IRM 7751) § 230.

[7]Reg. § 1.501(c)(2)-1. Also see Rev. Rul. 58-566, 1958-2 C. B. 261.

[8]Rev. Rul. 68-371, 1968-2 C. B. 204.

[9]Rev. Rul. 77-429, 1977-2 C. B. 189, superseding Rev. Rul. 67-104, 1967-1 C. B. 120.

responsive to the needs and purposes of its exempt parent which established it mainly to facilitate the administration of properties" and that, without the benefit of this ruling, the "subsidiary will be restricted in serving the needs of the parent in connection with the administration of properties."

The IRS ruled that an organization formed as a subsidiary of a tax-exempt title-holding corporation, organized for the exclusive purpose of holding title to investment property that would otherwise be held by the parent, itself qualifies as a tax-exempt title-holding corporation, since it collects the income from the property and turns it over to its parent (which is, of course, a tax-exempt organization.)[10]

While the renting of real estate is usually treated as a business, the IRS has determined that income from the rental of realty is a permissible source of income for exempt title-holding corporations.[11] However, the rental of personal property (unless leased with realty) is treated as the conduct of business.[12] Thus organizations engaging in business activity—other than rental of real property—will be denied or lose their exemption.[13]

Consequently, the characterization of the nature of the property being rented can be determinative of an organization's status as a title-holding corporation. In one instance, a corporation that otherwise qualified for tax exemption as a title-holding entity held a leasehold interest in an office building, with all of its income derived from the subleasing of space in the building to the general public. Even though a leasehold of real property is generally classified as personal property, income derived from subleasing an office building is treated as income derived from the rental of real property.[14] The IRS reasoned that such income is similarly treated as rental income from real property for purposes of qualification for tax exemption as a title-holding corporation,[15] thereby concluding that the corporation is tax-exempt.[16]

IRS rulings amplify the permissive powers of a tax-exempt title-holding

---

[10]Rev. Rul. 76-335, 1976-2 C. B. 141.

[11]Rev. Rul. 69-381, 1969-2 C. B. 113. See Reg. § 1.512(b)-1(c)(2); Rev. Rul. 66-295, 1966-2 C. B. 207.

[12]Rev. Rul. 69-278, 1969-1 C. B. 148.

[13]*Stanford University Bookstore* v. *Commissioner*, 29 B. T. A. 1280 (1934); *Sand Springs Railway Co*. v. *Commissioner*, 21 B. T. A. 1291 (1931).

[14]Code § 512(b)(3). See Chapter 40 § 3.

[15]This reasoning proceeded as follows: A Code § 501(c)(2) corporation generally cannot have unrelated business taxable income. Reg. § 1.501(c)(2)-1(a). For unrelated income purposes, the term "real property" includes property described in Code § 1250(c). Reg. § 1.512(b)-1(c)(3)(i). That provision encompasses certain real property which is or has been property of a character subject to the depreciation allowance rules of Code § 167. Qualifying depreciable real property includes intangible real property, which in turn includes a leasehold of land of Code § 1250 property. Accordingly, such a leasehold is Code § 1250 property and thus is real property for purposes of Code § 501(c)(2).

[16]Rev. Rul. 81-108, 1981-1 C. B. 327.

corporation,[17] and contain illustrations of organizations which will qualify[18] and do not qualify[19] thereunder.

§ 20.3 Local Employees' Associations

Code § 501(c)(4) provides exemption not only for social welfare organizations[20] but also for "local associations of employees, the membership of which is limited to the employees of a designated person or persons in a particular municipality, and the net earnings of which are devoted exclusively to charitable, educational or recreational purposes." The word "local" has the same meaning as under Code § 501(c)(12) (see below).[21]

A local association of employees can assume a variety of forms, such as the association that operated a gasoline station on property owned by its members' employer[22] and the organization that engaged only in social and recreational activities that met the approval of the members' employer.[23] A local employees' association the membership of which was limited to the employees of a particular employer and which operated a bus for the convenience of its members was denied tax exemption,[24] as was an organization the purpose of which was to pay lump-sum retirement benefits to its members or death benefits to their survivors.[25] The term "employees" can include retirees who were members of the association at the time of retirement.[26]

The IRS considered the tax status of an organization, the membership of which is limited to the employees of an employer in a particular municipality. The organization arranges with businesses to extend discounts to its members on their purchases of specified goods and services, and sells tickets to recreational and entertainment activities to them at a discount. Basing its position on legislative history,[27] the IRS dismissed the organization as a "cooperative

---

[17]Rev. Rul. 74-362, 1974-2 C. B. 170; Rev. Rul. 69-381, *supra*, n. 11; Rev. Rul. 68-490, 1968-2 C. B. 241; Rev. Rul. 66-295, *supra*, n. 11; Rev. Rul. 66-150, 1966-1 C. B. 147.

[18]Rev. Rul. 68-222, 1968-1 C. B. 243. Also see *N.P.E.F. Corp.* v. *Commissioner*, 5 T. C. M. 313 (1946).

[19]Rev. Rul. 71-544, 1971-2 C. B. 227. Also see *Citizens Water Works, Inc.* v. *Commissioner*, 33 B. T. A. 201 (1935). Cf. *Return Realty Corp.* v. *Ranieri*, 359 N. Y. S. 2d 611 (Sup. Ct. N.Y. Cty. 1974).

[20]See Chapter 15.

[21]Reg. § 1.501(c)(4)-1(b); Reg. § 1.501(c)(12)-1.

[22]Rev. Rul. 66-180, 1966-1 C. B. 144.

[23]Rev. Rul. 70-202, 1970-1 C. B. 130. Also see *T. J. Moss Tie Co.* v. *Commissioner*, 18 T. C. 188 (1952); *Weil Clothing Co.* v. *Commissioner*, 13 T. C. 873 (1949).

[24]Rev. Rul. 55-311, 1955-1 C. B. 72.

[25]Rev. Rul. 66-59, 1966-1 C. B. 142.

[26]Rev. Rul. 74-281, 1974-1 C. B. 133.

[27]Hearings Before House Ways and Means Committee on Revenue Revision of 1924, 68th Cong., 1st Sess. (1924) at 5-12; 65 *Cong. Rec.* 2905-2906 (1924).

buying service for members" and denied it tax exemption as an employees' association.[28]

The IRS took the position that a voluntary employees' beneficiary association which met all of the express requirements of Code § 501(c)(9) but could not meet the 85 percent source-of-income test (deleted by the Tax Reform Act of 1969) (see below) could not qualify for exemption as an employees' association.[29] Thus, the IRS does not follow a case holding that a cooperative electric company is tax-exempt as an employees' association even though it met all of the requirements for exemption under Code § 501(c)(12) (see below) except for the 85 percent source of-income test.[30]

§ 20.4 Fraternal Beneficiary Societies

Code § 501(c)(8) provides tax exemption for fraternal beneficiary societies, orders, or associations operating under the lodge system or for the exclusive benefit of the members of a fraternity itself operating under the lodge system and providing for the payment of life, sick, accident, or other benefits to the members of such society, order, or association or their dependents.[31]

The classic definition of a fraternal beneficiary society was formulated by the U.S. Court of Appeals for the Eighth Circuit:

We must accordingly assume that the words "fraternal-beneficial" were used in their ordinary sense—to designate an association or society that is engaged in some work that is of a fraternal and beneficial character. According to this view, a fraternal-beneficial society . . . would be one whose members have adopted the same, or a very similar, calling, avocation, or profession, or who are working in unison to accomplish some worthy object, and who for that reason have banded themselves together as an association or society to aid and assist one another, and to promote the common cause. The term "fraternal" can properly be applied to such an association, for the reason that the pursuit of a common object, calling or profession usually has a tendency to create a brotherly feeling among those who are thus engaged. It is a well-known fact that there are at the present time many voluntary or incorporated societies which are made up exclusively of persons who are engaged in the same avocation. As a general rule such associations have been formed for the purpose of promoting the social, moral, and intellectual welfare of the members of such associations, and their families, as well as for advancing their interests in other ways and in other respects. . . . Many of these associations make a practice of assisting their sick and disabled members, and of extending substantial aid to the families of deceased members. Their work is at the same time of a beneficial and fraternal character, because they aim to improve the condition of a class of persons who are engaged in a common pursuit, and to unite them by a stronger bond of sympathy and interest. . . .[32]

[28]Rev. Rul. 79-128, 1979-1 C. B. 197.
[29]Rev. Rul. 57-494, 1957-2 C. B. 315.
[30]*United States* v. *Pickwick Electric Membership Corp.*, 158 F.2d 272 (6th Cir. 1946).
[31]See Reg. § 1.501(c)(8)-1; *Banner Building Co., Inc.* v. *Commissioner*, 46 B. T. A. 857 (1942); *Royal Highlanders* v. *Commissioner*, 1 T. C. 184 (1942).
[32]*National Union* v. *Marlow*, 74 F. 775, 778 (8th Cir. 1896). Also *Employees Benefit Association of American Steel Foundries* v. *Commissioner*, 14 B. T. A. 1166 (1929).

On the basis of this definition, an organization of employees of a railroad company was denied tax exemption as a fraternal beneficiary society.[33] The organization was established to administer a relief fund for the payment of benefits to its members in case of sickness, accident, or death. The Board of Tax Appeals characterized the organization's deficiencies in this regard as follows:

> [The organization] is entirely without any social features. Its membership is made up of individuals whose vocations are as numerous and diverse as the classifications of employment of a great railway system; the section hand, the freight hustler, the brakeman, the conductor in charge of a fast trans-continental train, the locomotive engineer, the train dispatcher, the clerk in the office, all are entitled to membership in the Association for the mere asking, expressed in written application, provided no disability exists; and yet none of these look to the petitioner for any betterment in social and laboring conditions. There is no fraternal object which moves them to seek membership in the Association, but rather the motive is mercenary. The petitioner has neither lodges, rituals, ceremony, or regalia; and it owes no allegiance to any other authority or jurisdiction. It is not a "fraternal beneficiary association" operating under the lodge system . . . and, therefore, is not entitled to exemption. . . .[34]

Thus an organization will not be classified as "fraternal" in nature where the only common bond between the majority of its members is the fact of membership in the organization.[35] Moreover, mere recitation of common ties and objectives in an organization's governing instrument is insufficient; there must be specific activities in implementation of such purposes.[36]

As noted, a fraternal beneficiary organization, to qualify for tax exemption, must operate under the lodge system or for the exclusive benefit of members that so operate. The regulations state that "operating under the lodge system" means "carrying on its activities under a form of organization that comprises local branches, chartered by a parent organization and largely self-governing, called lodges, chapters, or the like."[37] Therefore, an organization without a parent organization or subordinate branches does not operate under the lodge system and cannot find tax exemption as a fraternal beneficiary society.[38] (Moreover, such a mutual, self-interest type of organization that may otherwise qualify as a tax-exempt fraternal beneficiary society cannot, for tax years beginning after June 2, 1975, qualify as a tax-exempt social welfare organization.[39]) Fur-

---

[33]*Philadelphia & Reading Relief Association* v. *Commissioner*, 4 B. T. A. 713 (1926).

[34]*Ibid.* at 726.

[35]See *Polish Army Veterans Post 147* v. *Commissioner*, 24 T. C. 891 (1955). aff'd 236 F.2d 509 (3d Cir. 1956).

[36]See *Fraternal Order of Civitans of America* v. *Commissioner*, 19 T. C. 240 (1952).

[37]Reg. § 1.501(c)(8)-1. See *Western Funeral Benefit Association* v. *Hellmich*, 2 F.2d 367 (E. D. Mo. 1924).

[38]Rev. Rul. 55-495, 1955-2 C. B. 259.

[39]Rev. Rul. 75-199, 1975-1 C. B. 160, mod. Rev. Rul. 55-495, *supra*, n. 38. Also Rev. Rul. 81-58, 1981-1 C. B. 331.

ther, the parent and local organizations must be active, with mere provision for them in governing instruments insufficient.[40] Notwithstanding this requirement, however, an organization that does not operate under the lodge system was granted tax exemption as a fraternal beneficiary society because it operates exclusively for the benefit of the members of a fraternal beneficiary society that itself operates under the lodge system, by providing life, sick, and accident benefits to the members of the society or their dependents.[41]

Also, as noted, an exempt fraternal beneficiary society must have an established system for the payment to its members or their dependents of life, sick, accident, or other benefits. While not every member of the society need be covered by the program of benefits,[42] a substantial number of members must be extended such coverage.[43] According to the U.S. Court of Appeals for the Ninth Circuit, the term "benefits" in this context is not confined to insurance for members against personal risks such as disability or death but may also extend to insuring them against property loss.[44] This decision overruled the U.S. Tax Court's determination that permissible benefits include only those insuring members against mishap to the person.[45]

Consequently, an exempt fraternal beneficiary organization must both operate under the lodge system and provide for the payment of benefits to members or their dependents—although one of these features does not have to predominate over the other.[46] However, both features must be present in substantial form and neither may be a sham.[47]

As noted, the tax-exempt fraternal beneficiary society must be operated for the exclusive benefit of its members. However, where benefits to others are incidental to the accomplishment of the society's exempt purpose, the organization's tax exemption will not be jeopardized. Thus, for example, a society that conducts an insurance operation for its members in all 50 states was determined to not lose its tax exemption because it participates in a state-sponsored reinsurance pool that protects participating insurers from excessive losses on major medical health and accident insurance, since any benefit derived by other insurers from participation in the pooling arrangement is "incidental" to the society's exempt purpose.[48] Similarly, the re-insurance of its policies is a fraternal beneficiary society's tax-exempt function.[49]

[40]I. T. 1516, 1-2 C. B. 180 (1922).

[41]Rev. Rul. 73-192, 1973-1 C. B. 224.

[42]Rev. Rul. 64-194, 1964-2 C. B. 149.

[43]*Polish Army Veterans Post 147* v. *Commissioner, supra,* n. 35.

[44]*Grange Insurance Association of California* v. *Commissioner,* 317 F.2d 222 (9th Cir. 1963).

[45]37 T. C. 582 (1961).

[46]Rev. Rul. 73-165, 1973-1 C. B. 224.

[47]See *Commercial Travelers Life & Accident Association* v. *Rodway,* 235 F. 370 (N.D. Oh. 1913).

[48]Rev. Rul. 78-87, 1978-1 C. B. 160.

[49]IRS Private Letter Ruling 7937002.

One federal district court has held that fraternal organizations that are otherwise tax-exempt which practice racial discrimination as to membership may not be tax-exempt.[50] This holding was based on the fact that, unlike organizations that are tax-exempt as social clubs or voluntary employees' beneficiary associations,[51] the passive investment income of fraternal beneficiary organizations is not taxed; this the court found to be a governmental "benefit" warranting invocation of the Fifth Amendment. The case was initiated as a class action by a black individual allegedly denied membership in a local lodge of the Benevolent and Protective Order of Elks.

Individuals' gifts to a domestic fraternal beneficiary organization are deductible where the gift is to be used exclusively for religious, charitable, scientific, literary, or educational purposes, or for the prevention of cruelty to children and animals.[52]

§ 20.5 Voluntary Employees' Beneficiary Associations

Code § 501(c)(9) describes voluntary employees' beneficiary associations "providing for the payment of life, sick, accident or other benefits to the members of such association or their dependents or designated beneficiaries," absent private inurement.[53]

One of the basic requirements for achievement of tax exemption as a voluntary employees' beneficiary association is that the organization be an association of employees.[54] Typically, those eligible for membership in such an association are defined by reference to a common employer (or affiliated employers), to coverage under one or more collective bargaining agreements (with respect to benefits provided by reason of the agreement(s)), to membership in a labor union, or to membership in one or more locals of a national or international labor union. Employees of one or more employers engaged in the same line of business in the same geographic locale are considered to share an employment-related bond for purposes of an organization through which their employers provide benefits. Employees of a labor union are considered to share an employment-related common bond with members of the union, and employees of an association are considered to share an employment-related common bond with members of the association. Whether a group of individuals is defined by reference to a permissible standard or standards is a question to be determined with regard to all the pertinent facts and circumstances.[55]

Eligibility for membership may be restricted by geographic proximity, or by objective conditions or limitations reasonably related to employment, such

---

[50]*McGlotten* v. *Connally*, 338 F. Supp. 448, 459 (D. D. C. 1972).
[51]See Code § 512(a)(3); Chapters 18 and 41.
[52]Code § 170(c)(4).
[53]See Reg. § 1.501(c)(9)-1.
[54]Reg. § 1.501(c)(9)-2(b).
[55]Reg. § 1.501(c)(9)-2(a)(1).

as a limitation to a reasonable classification of workers, a limitation based on a reasonable minimum period of service, a limitation based on maximum compensation, or a requirement that a member be employed on a full-time basis. Also, eligibility for benefits may be restricted by objective conditions relating to the type or amount of benefits offered. Any objective criteria used to restrict eligibility for membership or benefits may not, however, be selected or administered in a manner that limits membership or benefits to officers, shareholders, or highly compensated employees of an employer contributing to or otherwise funding the employees' association. Similarly, eligibility for benefits may not be subject to conditions or limitations that have the effect of entitling officers, shareholders, or highly compensated employees of an employer contributing to or otherwise funding the employees' association to benefits that are disproportionate in relation to benefits to which other members of the association are entitled. Whether the selection or administration of objective conditions has the effect of providing disproportionate benefits to officers, shareholders, or highly compensated employees generally is to be determined on the basis of all the facts and circumstances.[56] The tax exemption does not apply to pension funds distributing benefits to partners.[57]

Membership in this type of association must be "voluntary." Membership is voluntary if an affirmative act is required on the part of an employee to become a member rather than the designation as a member due to employee status. However, an association is considered "voluntary" even though membership is required of all employees, as long as the employees do not incur a detriment (such as deductions from compensation) as the result of membership in the association. An employer is not deemed to have imposed involuntary membership on the employee if membership is required as the result of a collective bargaining agreement or as an incident of membership in a labor organization.[58]

The life, sick, accident, or other benefits provided by a voluntary employees' beneficiary association must be payable to its members, their dependents, or their designated beneficiaries.[59] Life, sick, accident, or other benefits may take the form of cash or noncash benefits. To be tax-exempt, the association must function so that substantially all of its operations are in furtherance of the provision of the requisite benefits.[60] The income tax regulations define the

---

[56]Reg. § 1.501(c)(9)-2(a)(2)(i). The income tax regulations enumerate certain generally permissible restrictions or conditions. Reg. § 1.501(c)(9)-2(a)(2)(ii); also Reg. § 1.501(c)(9)-4(b). Cf. Rev. Proc. 66-30, 1966-2 C. B. 1212; Rev. Rul. 59-28, 1959-1 C. B. 120.

[57]See *Nelson* v. *Joyce*, 404 F.Supp. 489 (N. D. Ill. 1975); Rev. Rul. 70-411, 1970-2 C. B. 91; Rev. Rul. 69-144, 1969-1 C. B. 115.

[58]Reg. § 1.501(c)(9)-2(c)(2).

[59]See, e.g., Rev. Rul. 65-81, 1965-1 C. B. 225; Rev. Rul. 59-28, *supra*, n. 56; *Milwaukee Sign Painters Welfare Fund* v. *United States*, 66-1 U.S.T.C. ¶ 9170 (E.D. Wis. 1965).

[60]Reg. § 1.501(c)(9)-3(a).

terms "life benefit"[61] and "sick and accident benefit,"[62] and provide that the term "other benefits" includes only benefits that are "similar to" life, sick, or accident benefits, namely, a benefit that is intended to safeguard or improve the health of a member or a member's dependents, or that protects against a contingency that interrupts or impairs a member's earning power.[63] "Other benefits" include paying vacation benefits, providing vacation facilities, reimbursing vacation expenses, subsidizing recreational activities, the provision of child-care facilities for preschool and school-age dependents, and personal legal service benefits.[64] "Other benefits" do not include the payment of commuting expenses, the provision of accident or homeowner's insurance benefits for damage to property, the provision of malpractice insurance, the provision of loans to members (except in times of distress), or the provision of savings facilities for members.[65]

Illustrations of these associations, under the law prior to the promulgation of the pertinent income tax regulations, include an organization which reimburses its members for premiums paid under the Medicare program[65a] and a trust established for the purpose of furnishing supplemental unemployment benefits to a designated class of employees during a period of temporary layoff.[66] An association that merely ensures the discharge of an obligation imposed by law upon an employer corporation (e.g., workmen's compensation benefits) was held to not qualify for tax exemption because the employees do not receive any additional benefits.[67]

The private inurement doctrine as applied to voluntary employees' beneficiary associations means not only a prohibition on matters such as unreasonable compensation or self-dealing, but also the payment to any member of disproportionate benefits.[68] The IRS has ruled that there was no private inurement where an insurance company paid excess insurance premiums to a voluntary employees' beneficiary association which proportionately distributed the excess to its members.[69]

Congress, as part of the Tax Reform Act of 1969, removed a limitation that no more than 15 percent of such an association's annual receipts could be in the form of investment income, thereby enabling these trusts to accumulate

[61]Reg. § 1.501(c)(9)-3(b).

[62]Reg. § 1.501(c)(9)-3(c).

[63]Reg. § 1.501(c)(9)-3(d).

[64]Reg. § 1.501(c)(9)-3(e).

[65]Reg. § 1.501(c)(9)-3(f). E.g., Rev. Rul. 57-61, 1957-1 C. B. 197; G.C.M. 22554, 1941-1 C. B. 243.

[65a]Rev. Rul. 66-212, 1966-2 C. B. 230.

[66]Rev. Rul. 58-442, 1958-2 C. B. 194.

[67]Rev. Rul. 74-18, 1974-1 C. B. 139. Also Rev. Rul. 66-354, 1966-2 C. B. 207.

[68]Reg. § 1.501(c)(9)-4(a), (b).

[69]Rev. Rul. 64-258, 1964-2 C. B. 134. See Note, "Self-Insured Employee Welfare Plans and the 501(c)(9) Trust: The Spector of State Regulation," 43 Univ. Cincinnati L. Rev. 325 (1974).

reserves at reasonable levels. (These trusts must conform to the requirements of the Employee Retirement Income Security Act, however, including those governing investment practices.) With this restriction eliminated, major business corporations are utilizing these trusts to provide employee benefits on the self-insurance basis, because the benefits program can be fashioned to meet the employers' desires and because it is less expensive than insurance premium costs.[70]

§ 20.6　Domestic Fraternal Societies

Code § 501(c)(10) provides tax exemption for domestic fraternal societies, orders, or associations, operating under the lodge system, the net earnings of which are devoted exclusively to religious, charitable, scientific, literary, educational, and fraternal purposes, and which do not provide for the payment of life, sick, accident, or other benefits to its members.[71] An organization not providing these benefits but otherwise qualifying as a fraternal beneficiary society[72] qualifies as a domestic fraternal society. Thus, a domestic fraternal beneficiary society of farmers, which met all of the requirements of the fraternal beneficiary society rules except that it did not provide for the payment of the requisite benefits, although it did make its members eligible for favorable insurance rates, was denied classification as a fraternal beneficiary society and ruled to be a domestic fraternal society.[73] However, a social welfare organization[74] (e.g., a national college fraternity) does not qualify for exemption under this section.[75]

A domestic fraternal society meeting these basic requirements was organized to provide a fraternal framework for social contact among its members who are interested in the use of and the philosophy behind a method used in attempting to divine the future. The net income of the organization is used to provide instruction on the use of the method, supply information on the method to the public, and maintain a reference library—all charitable and educational uses. The IRS ruled that the organization qualifies for tax exemption.[76]

The IRS ruled that an organization formed by a local lodge of a fraternal beneficiary society, both tax-exempt as domestic fraternal societies, to carry on the activities of the society in a particular geographical area, is itself exempt

---

[70]See Cirino, "Benefits: The quiet debut of 501(c)(9) trusts," 11 *Institutional Investor* (No. 5) 57 (1977); Haneberg, "The 501(c)(9) Trust Revisited," 114 *Trusts & Estates* 622 (1975). In general, see the *501(c)(9) Trust Primer,* published by Northwestern National Life Insurance Co.; Stuchiver, "Using a 501(c)(9) Trust to Fund Employee Benefits," 112 *Trusts & Estates* 242 (1973).

[71]Reg. § 1.501(c)(10)-1.

[72]Code § 501(c)(8).

[73]Rev. Rul. 76-457, 1976-2 C. B. 155.

[74]See Chapter 18.

[75]Reg. § 1.501(c)(10)-1.

[76]Rev. Rul. 77-258, 1977-2 C. B. 195.

as a domestic fraternal society.[77] Because the organization was chartered and supervised by the local lodge and was subject to the laws and edicts of the parent society, it was deemed to function "as part of the lodge system" of the fraternal society and hence qualify for the exemption.

The IRS also ruled that an organization that does not conduct any fraternal activities and does not operate under the lodge system, but operates exclusively for the benefit of the members of certain related domestic fraternal societies operating under the lodge system, cannot qualify as an exempt domestic fraternal society.[78] The rationale for the denial is that the tax rules for domestic fraternal societies lack the language in the tax rules for fraternal beneficiary societies providing exemption for an organization operating for the benefit of the members of an exempt fraternity (a provision enacted to cover the separately organized insurance branches of a fraternal beneficiary society).[79]

§ 20.7   Teachers' Retirement Fund Associations

Code § 501(c)(11) provides tax exemption for teachers' retirement fund associations of a purely local character, if there is no private inurement (other than through payment of retirement benefits) and the income consists wholly of amounts received from public taxation, amounts received from assessments on the teaching salaries of members, and income in respect of investments.

No income tax regulations have been issued under this provision nor have there been any IRS rulings or court decisions, leading the Service to conclude that the section "has very limited application."[80] The phrase "of a purely local character" apparently has the same meaning in this context as it does with respect to benevolent or mutual organizations.[81]

§ 20.8   Benevolent or Mutual Organizations

Code § 501(c)(12) describes benevolent life insurance associations of a purely local character, mutual ditch or irrigation companies, mutual or cooperative telephone companies, or like organizations, if 85 percent or more of the income is collected from members for the sole purpose of meeting losses and expenses.

Thus, one type of organization described in these rules is the benevolent life insurance association of a purely local character. These associations basically

---

[77]Rev. Rul. 73-370, 1973-2 C. B. 184. In *Hip Sing Association, Inc. v. Commissioner*, 43 T.C.M. 1092 (1982), an organization was found to be operating under the lodge system, even though the parent organization was created after the branches.

[78]Rev. Rul. 81-117, 1981-1 C. B. 346.

[79]See § 4, *supra*.

[80]IRS Exempt Organizations Handbook (IRM 7751) § (11)12(1).

[81]Reg. § 1.501(c)(12)-1(b).

operate to provide life insurance coverage to their members, albeit at cost because of the requirement that income be collected solely for the purpose of meeting losses and expenses.[82] Organizations "like" benevolent life insurance associations include burial and funeral benefit associations which provide benefits in cash,[83] but not in the form of services and supplies (although the latter type of organization may qualify for tax exemption as a mutual insurance company[84]), and an organization furnishing light and water to its members on a cooperative basis.[85] IRS rulings and court decisions provide examples of organizations considered not "like" benevolent life insurance associations.[86]

The phrase "of a purely local character" means "confined to a particular community, place, or district, irrespective, however, of political subdivisions,"[87] that is, a single identifiable locality.[88] An organization is not local in character where its activities are limited only by the borders of a state,[89] although state lines are not controlling as to what constitutes a single locality. One organization lost its tax exemption as a benevolent life insurance association by advertising in four states.[90] Another organization was denied tax exemption because it operated in 14 counties, as did another conducting its affairs in 32 counties, including three separate metropolitan trade centers.[91]

The other type of organization exempt from federal income tax by virtue of these rules encompasses mutual ditch or irrigation companies, mutual or cooperative telephone companies, and like organizations.[92] These organizations are commonly mutual or cooperative electric companies and water companies.[93] Exemption has been accorded an organization established to protect certain

---

[82]See IRS Exempt Organizations Handbook (IRM 7751) § (12)21.

[83]*Thompson* v. *White River Burial Association*, 178 F.2d 954 (8th Cir. 1950), aff'g 81 F. Supp. 18 (E. D. Ark. 1948).

[84]See § 11, *infra*.

[85]Rev. Rul. 67-265, 1967-2 C. B. 205.

[86]See Rev. Rul. 65-201, 1965-2 C. B. 170; *Consumers Credit Rural Electric Cooperative Corp.* v. *Commissioner*, 319 F.2d 475 (6th Cir. 1963); *Shelby County Mut. Relief Association* v. *Schwaner*, 21 F.2d 252 (S. D. Ill. 1927); *New Jersey Automobile Club* v. *United States*, 181 F. Supp. 259 (Ct. Cl. 1960); *Swedish Mission Friends' Aid Association* v. *Commissioner*, 12 B. T. A. 1152 (1928).

[87]Reg. § 1.501(c)(12)-1(b).

[88]*Hardware Underwriters and National Hardware Service Corp.* v. *United States*, 65 Ct. Cl. 267 (1928).

[89]Reg. § 1.501(c)(12)-1(b).

[90]*Huff-Cook Mutual Burial Association, Inc.* v. *United States*, 327 F. Supp. 1209 (W. D. Va. 1971).

[91]Rev. Rul. 64-193, 1964-2 C. B. 151.

[92]See Rev. Rul. 72-36, 1972-1 C. B. 151; Rev. Rul. 65-174, 1965-2 C. B. 169.

[93]Rev. Rul. 67-265, 1967-2 C. B. 205. Also Rev. Rul. 73-453, 1973-2 C. B. 185.

river banks against erosion[94] and an organization which provided and maintained a two-way radio system for its members.[95] The membership of cooperative companies need not be restricted to ultimate consumers,[96] nonmembers may be charged a higher rate for service than members,[97] and a government agency may be a member of a cooperative.[98] IRS rulings provide examples of organizations considered not "like" mutual and cooperative organizations.[99]

The IRS has utilized a rather unusual rationale to allow a mutual ditch company tax exemption, notwithstanding the fact that it does not satisfy all of the requirements enunciated by the Service in 1972.[100] The organization, created in 1874 to maintain and operate an irrigation system for the use and benefit of its members, was unable to meet standards concerning forfeiture of a member's rights and interest upon withdrawal or termination and distribution of gains from the sale of an appreciated asset upon dissolution, in that former shareholders are not entitled to any funds. However, the IRS said that it is nonetheless "necessary to give some consideration to the historical context within which mutual ditch and irrigation companies were created and have operated," because prior to the enactment of these rules in 1916 organizations such as the one at issue "were well established entities in a number of western states." The Service noted that, under applicable state law, these organizations (1) "issued stock representing both water rights and equitable interest in the organization's assets," which "was considered personal property and freely available" and (2) "had the power to assess the outstanding stock for the costs of operation and maintenance and to enforce any assessment lien through foreclosure and forced sale, thereby transferring a delinquent shareholder's interest to the purchaser." Therefore, the IRS concluded that "[i]n view of the fact that such organizations were operating in this manner when Congress originally enacted legislation providing for their exemption from federal income tax, and the fact that there have been no major changes in the applicable federal tax provisions in the intervening years, it is clear that Congress intended and still intends that mutual ditch and irrigation companies operated in the manner and under the circumstances described above would qualify for exemption from federal income tax under section 501(c)(12) of the Code." The requirements promulgated in 1972 were consequently modified accordingly.[101]

In another case, a mutual company formed for the purpose of supplying

---

[94]Rev. Rul. 68-564, 1968-2 C. B. 221.
[95]Rev. Rul. 57-420, 1957-2 C. B. 308.
[96]Rev. Rul. 65-174, *supra*, n. 92.
[97]Rev. Rul. 70-130, 1970-1 C. B. 133.
[98]Rev. Rul. 68-75, 1968-1 C. B. 271.
[99]See Rev. Rul. 65-201, *supra*, n. 86; Rev. Rul. 55-311, *supra*, n. 24.
[100]Rev. Rul. 72-36, *supra*, n. 92.
[101]Rev. Rul. 81-109, 1981-1 C. B. 347.

electric power to its members was recognized by IRS as qualifying as a tax-exempt entity. Subsequently, part of the organization's distribution system located within a county was purchased by the county's public utility district. The organization's members located in that utility district were given back their membership fee in full payment for their interest in the company, since they became served by the new utility. The company refused to meet the demand of the IRS that it distribute the gains realized from the sale on a patronage basis and thus had its tax-exempt status revoked. Upon review, the U.S. Court of Appeals for the Ninth Circuit held that the company need not credit or distribute its surplus or net gains on a patronage basis to maintain its classification as a tax-exempt mutual company.[102]

All organizations, to be exempt from tax under these rules, must obtain at least 85 percent of their income from amounts collected from members for the sole purpose of meeting losses and expenses. This requirement is applied on the basis of annual accounting periods.[103] Income from all sources is taken into account, including capital gains from the sale of assets[104] and investments;[105] amounts received as gifts or contributions are not regarded as income.[106] In one instance, the IRS ruled that, where an electric cooperative leased power facilities to a nonmember power company which in turn sold power to the cooperative, the entire rental income was income from a nonmember for purposes of the 85 percent requirement rather than an offset against the cost of acquiring power.[107] In another case, an organization in good faith failed to elect the installment method of treating gain from the sale of real property, with the result that the receipt of the entire gain caused less than 85 percent of its income to be derived from its members; over the government's objection, a court allowed the organization to amend its annual information return to make the election and thus preserve its tax exemption.[108] By contrast, the Service determined that the income derived by an exempt electric cooperative from the annual sale of its excess fuel to a commercial pipeline company that was not a member of the cooperative is not to be taken into account in determining compliance with the 85-percent-of-income requirement, in that the excess fuel was sold at cost and thus no gross income was derived from the sales.[109] Court

---

[102]*Peninsula Light Co., Inc.* v. *United States*, 552 F.2d 878 (9th Cir. 1977). The IRS, in Rev. Rul. 78-238, 1978-1 C. B. 161, announced that it would not follow this decision.

[103]Rev. Rul. 65-99, 1965-1 C. B. 242.

[104]See *Cate Ditch Co.* v. *United States*, 194 F. Supp. 688 (S. D. Cal. 1961); *Mountain Water Co. of La Crescenta* v. *Commissioner*, 35 T. C. 418 (1960).

[105]Reg. § 1.501(c)(12)-1(a).

[106]G. C. M. 5921, VIII-1 C. B. 179 (1929).

[107]Rev. Rul. 65-174, *supra*, n. 92.

[108]*Sunny Slope Water Co.* v. *United States*, 78-2 U.S.T.C. ¶ 9685 (C. D. Cal. 1978).

[109]Rev. Rul. 80-86, 1980-1 C. B. 118.

decisions provide examples of organizations which failed to meet the 85 percent-of-income requirement.[110]

In 1978, Congress enacted legislation which revised the 85 percent-of-income requirement, as it relates to mutual or cooperative telephone companies, so that the requirement is applied (for taxable years beginning after December 31, 1974) "without taking into account any income received or accrued from a nonmember telephone company for the performance of communication services which involve members of such mutual or cooperative telephone company, that is, involving the completion of long-distance calls to, from, or between members of the mutual or cooperative company."[111] This provision was occasioned in response to (and to overrule) a ruling by the IRS in 1974, holding that a cooperative telephone company, providing only local telephone service to its members but obtaining connecting long-distance service by agreement with a nonmember company, could not adjust its gross income by offsetting income due from long-distance tolls collected by both companies against expenses for services rendered by the nonmember company to the cooperative's members but had to include as part of its gross income all the member and nonmember income from the long-distance service, to determine whether member income meets the 85 percent-of-income requirement.[112] Congress indicated its belief that the performance of the "call-completion services" is a related activity and that the "payments" from another telephone company for such services should not disqualify otherwise eligible telephone cooperatives from tax-exempt status.[113]

Then, in 1980, Congress enacted rules providing that, in connection with the 85 percent member-income requirement, any income from the rental of poles used in the tax-exempt activities of mutual or cooperative telephone and electric companies or from display listings in a directory is to be disregarded,

---

[110]See *Allgemeiner Arbeiter Verein* v. *Commissioner*, 237 F.2d 604 (3d Cir. 1956); *Family Aid Association of the United States House of Prayer for All People* v. *United States*, 36 F. Supp. 1017 (Ct. Cl. 1941). In *Dial-Cab Taxi Owners Guild Association, Inc.* v. *Commissioner*, 42 T. C. M. 590 (1981), the organization was held to not qualify under Code § 501(c)(12) because it was unable to carry its burden of proving that 85 percent of its income in the tax years involved was collected solely to cover losses and expenses. The court said the organization was "acquiring a substantial net worth far in excess of its reasonably anticipated needs" and that it failed to show that the retained earnings will be used to meet losses and expenses. The court also indicated that the organization—which provides a radio dispatching service to its member taxicab owners and operates a two-way radio station to dispatch its members—may not otherwise qualify as a "like organization" because its reliance on the *Peninsula Light Co., Inc.* decision, *supra*, n. 102, is "tenuous."

[111]P.L. 95-345; see H. Rep. No. 95-742, 95th Cong., 1st Sess. (1977); S. Rep. No. 95-762, 95th Cong., 2d Sess. (1978). See Reg. § 501(c)(12)-1.

[112]Rev. Rul. 74-362, *supra*, n. 17.

[113]Consequently, the 1974 Revenue Ruling (*supra*, n. 17) was obsoleted with respect to tax years beginning after December 31, 1974. Rev. Rul. 81-291, 1981-2 C. B. 131.

as is pole rental income (where the poles are used in exempt activities) of mutual or cooperative companies generally.[114]

The IRS is of the opinion that an organization which meets all of the requirements for tax exemption under these rules except for the 85 percent-of-income test cannot qualify for exemption as a social welfare organization.[115] Also, an organization carrying on two functions, one qualifying under the social club rules[116] and the other under these rules, cannot qualify for exemption under either statute.[117]

§ 20.9 Cemetery Companies

Code § 501(c)(13) describes cemetery companies owned and operated exclusively for the benefit of their members and which are not operated for profit. As a result of a 1970 statutory change,[118] this tax exemption also extends to a corporation chartered solely for the purpose of the disposal of bodies by burial or cremation which may not engage in any business not necessarily incident to that purpose. Thus, there are three types of cemetery companies which may gain tax exemption under this section.

According to the IRS, a tax-exempt cemetery company is generally "one which owns a cemetery, sells lots therein for burial purposes, and maintains these and the unsold lots in a state of repair and upkeep appropriate to a final resting place."[119] With respect to the membership category of cemetery companies, its members are those who are "its lot owners who hold such lots for bona fide burial purposes and not for purpose of resale."[120] According to the U.S. Tax Court, an exempt cemetery company need not be public nor serve exclusively public interests but may be a family cemetery organization.[121] Under certain circumstances, a cemetery company may be tax-exempt even though

---

[114]P. L. 96-541, 96th Cong., 2d Sess. (1980). This enactment also provides that income from the rental of such poles by mutual or cooperative telephone and electric companies is not subject to the tax on unrelated business income (see Chapters 40–42).

[115]Cf. *United States* v. *Pickwick Electric Membership Corp., supra*, n. 30. See Rev. Rul. 57-494, *supra*, n. 29.

[116]See Chapter 18.

[117]*Allgemeiner Arbeiter Verein* v. *Commissioner, supra*, n. 110.

[118]P. L. 91-618, 84 Stat. 1855.

[119]IRS Exempt Organizations Handbook (IRM 7751) § (13) 22.1. See, e.g., *Resthaven Memorial Park and Cemetery Association* v. *United States*, 155 F. Supp. 539 (W. D. Ky. 1957); *Forest Lawn Memorial Park Association, Inc.* v. *Commissioner*, 5 T. C. M. 738 (1946).

[120]Reg. § 1.501(c)(13)-1(a)(1). Also *West Laurel Hill Cemetery Co.* v. *Rothensies*, 139 F.2d 50 (3d Cir. 1943).

[121]See *The John D. Rockefeller Family Cemetery Corp.* v. *Commissioner*, 63 T. C. 355 (1974); *Du Pont de Nemours Cemetery Co.* v. *Commissioner*, 33 T. C. M. 1438 (1974). Cf. Rev. Rul. 65-6, 1965-1 C. B. 229; *Provident National Bank* v. *United States*, 325 F. Supp. 1187 (E. D. Pa. 1971).

it has private preferred stockholders.[122] The tax exemption applies only to organizations providing for the burial or cremation of the remains of human bodies—not pets.[123]

An organization receiving and administering funds for the perpetual care of a nonprofit cemetery itself qualifies as a tax-exempt cemetery company.[124] A nonprofit organization that provides for the perpetual care of a burial area in a community may also become so classified, even though it is not associated with a nonprofit cemetery.[125]

One of the requirements for tax exemption as a cemetery company is that the company may not be permitted by its charter to engage in any business not necessarily incident to its tax-exempt (burial) purposes.[126] The IRS has construed this requirement to extend to actual activities, thereby ruling, for example, that operation by a cemetery company of a mortuary will deprive the company of the tax exemption.[127] Under this rule, the IRS also held that operation of a crematorium would likewise adversely affect the exemption,[128] although this determination was subsequently withdrawn in view of the 1970 modification of the statute.[129] However, a cemetery company may sell monuments, markers, vaults, and flowers solely for use in the cemetery, where the sales proceeds are used for maintenance of the cemetery.[130]

The regulations provide that no part of the net earnings of an exempt cemetery company may inure to the benefit of any private shareholder or individual.[131] The private inurement doctrine frequently is at play where a newly organized cemetery company is involved, in relation to payments to and other relationships with the organizers. The reasoning of the IRS is that (1) where a cemetery company acquires land at an indeterminable price, to be paid for on the basis of a percentage of the proceeds from the sale of individual lots from the tract, the vendor of the land has a continuing interest in the land, (2) any appreciation in value, whether it be due to the state of the market generally or the cemetery's own efforts to undertake capital improvements, etc., will result in a benefit to the vendor of the land, and (3) continuing participation in the earnings of the cemetery company will also ordinarily result in receipt by the vendor of a total price substantially in excess of the reasonable value of the land at the time of its sale to the cemetery company.[132]

---

[122]Reg. § 1.501(c)(13)-1(b).
[123]Rev. Rul. 73-454, 1973-2 C. B. 185.
[124]Rev. Rul. 58-190, 1958-1 C. B. 15.
[125]Rev. Rul. 78-143, 1978-1 C. B. 161.
[126]Reg. § 1.501(c)(13)-1(b).
[127]Rev. Rul. 64-109, 1964-1 (Part 1) C. B. 190.
[128]Rev. Rul. 69-637, 1969-2 C. B. 127.
[129]Rev. Rul. 71-300, 1971-2 C. B. 238.
[130]Rev. Rul. 72-17, 1972-1 C. B. 151.
[131]Reg. § 1.501(c)(13)-1(b).
[132]See Rev. Rul. 61-137, 1961-2 C. B. 118.

Perhaps the most important issue in relation to these rules is that which has emerged as many American cemeteries became transformed from noncommercial operations (such as by religious institutions and municipal governments) to commercial businesses. As part of that process, profit-oriented enterprises sought favorable tax consequences from bootstrap sales of assets to ostensibly tax-exempt cemetery companies. When this issue was first litigated, the courts were highly tolerant of these transactions,[133] thereby generating substantial criticism.[134] Subsequently, the courts began to scrutinize more carefully the substance of these transactions, concluding that the cemetery company was causing private inurement of net earnings by the creation of equity interests. That is, in considering transactions by which a cemetery acquires land under the terms of an open-ended or percentage arrangement contract in which the transferor receives a percentage of the sale price of each lot, the courts came to conclude that the substance of the transaction was to create an equity interest in the transferor because all the traditional elements of a true debt are missing: (1) there is no unqualified obligation on the part of the cemetery company to pay because the installments depend upon the sale of lots, (2) there is no maturity date because the obligation is to continue until all lots are sold, (3) there is no sum certain since the price of the lots is subject to change, (4) there is no stated interest rate, (5) there is no minimum annual payment, (6) there is no right to share with general creditors, (7) there is no paid-in capitalization of the company, and (8) the transferors have control of the cemetery company.[135] Thus, the IRS ruled that a nonprofit cemetery company that acquires land from a for-profit cemetery company, under an agreement providing payment to the former owners on the basis of a percentage of the sales price of each cemetery lot sold, is not a tax-exempt cemetery company because the transferors acquired an equity interest in the cemetery company, which constitutes prohibited private inurement.[136]

[133]*Forest Lawn Memorial Park Association, Inc.* v. *Commissioner*, 45 B. T. A. 1091 (1941); *Kensico Cemetery* v. *Commissioner*, 35 B. T. A. 498 (1937), aff'd 96 F.2d 594 (2d Cir. 1938). Also *Rose Hill Memorial Park, Inc.* v. *Commissioner*, 23 T. C. M. 1434 (1964); *Washington Park Cemetery Association, Inc.* v. *Commissioner*, 22 T. C. M. 1345 (1963).

[134]See Note, "Special Treatment of Cemeteries," 40 *So. Cal. L. Rev.* 716 (1967); Lanning, "Tax Erosion and the Bootstrap Sale of a Business," 108 *U. Pa. L. Rev.* 623 (1960). In general, see Mitford, *The American Way of Death* (1963).

[135]See *Restland Memorial Park of Dallas* v. *United States*, 509 F.2d 187 (5th Cir. 1975); *Evergreen Cemetery Association* v. *United States*, 375 F.Supp. 166 (W. D. Ky. 1974); *Rose Hills Memorial Park Association* v. *United States*, 463 F.2d 425 (Ct. Cl. 1972), cert. den. 414 U. S. 822 (1973); *Arlington Memorial Park Association* v. *United States*, 327 F.Supp. 344 (W. D. Ark. 1971); *Knellwood Memorial Gardens* v. *Commissioner*, 46 T. C. 764 (1966); Prop. Reg. § 1.501(c)(13)-1(d). See Tracy, "Proposed Regulations Narrow Statutory Exemptions For Cemeteries," 54 *Taxes* 396 (1976).

[136]Rev. Rul. 77-70, 1977-1 C. B. 150.

Another issue concerns the ability of a commercial cemetery to sequester funds in a "perpetual care trust fund" which would qualify as an exempt cemetery company. The matter seemed to have been resolved in 1975 when the Court of Claims, enunciating the "adjunct" theory,[137] held that such tax exemption was present by reason of the fact that such a fund, which renders services normally provided by the cemetery company, has the same tax status as the cemetery company itself.[138] This rationale had been espoused earlier by the IRS.[139] However, Congress in 1976 enacted a provision providing a deduction for amounts distributed by perpetual care trust funds to taxable cemetery companies for the care and maintenance of gravesites.[140] To qualify under this provision, the fund would have to be a trust established pursuant to local law by a taxable cemetery for the care and maintenance of the cemetery.[141]

Contributions to tax-exempt cemetery companies are deductible for federal income tax purposes.[142] The contributions must be voluntary and made to or for the use of a nonprofit cemetery, the funds of which are irrevocably dedicated to the care of the cemetery as a whole. Contributions made to a cemetery company for the perpetual care of a particular lot or crypt are not deductible.[143] Bequests or gifts to tax-exempt cemetery companies are not deductible for federal estate or gift tax purposes.[144]

§ 20.10   Credit Unions and Mutual Reserve Funds

Code § 501(c)(14) describes credit unions without capital stock organized and operated for mutual purposes and without profit.[145] As noted, federal credit unions organized and operated in accordance with the Federal Credit Union

[137]See Chapter 6.

[138]*Trustees of Graceland Cemetery Improvement Fund* v. *United States*, 515 F.2d 763 (Ct. Cl. 1975). Also *Laurel Hill Cemetery Association* v. *United States*, 427 F.Supp. 679 (E. D. Mo. 1977), aff'd 566 F.2d 630 (8th Cir. 1977); *Endowment Care Trust Fund of Inglewood Park Cemetery Association Board of Trustees* v. *United States*, 76-2 U.S.T.C. ¶ 9516 (Ct. Cl. 1976); *Au* v. *United States*, 76-1 U.S.T.C. ¶ 9370 (Ct. Cl. 1976); *Albuquerque National Bank* v. *United States*, 75-1 U.S.T.C. ¶ 9294 (D. N. Mex. 1975).

[139]Rev. Rul. 64-217, 1964-2 C. B. 153; Rev. Rul. 58-190, *supra*, n. 124. Cf. *Washington Trust Bank* v. *United States*, 444 F.2d 1235 (9th Cir. 1971), cert. den. 404 U.S. 1059 (1972); *Evergreen Cemetery Association of Seattle* v. *United States*, 444 F.2d 1232 (9th Cir. 1971); *Mercantile Bank and Trust Co.* v. *United States*, 441 F.2d 364 (8th Cir. 1971); *Arlington Memorial Park Association* v. *United States*, *supra*, n. 135.

[140]P. L. 94-528, 94th Cong., 2d Sess. (1976). Also see H. Rep. No. 94-1344, 94th Cong., 2d Sess. (1976).

[141]Code § 642(j); Reg. § 1.642(j).

[142]Code § 170(c)(5).

[143]Rev. Rul. 58-190, *supra*, n. 124.

[144]Rev. Rul. 67-170, 1967-1 C. B. 272. In general, see Frederick and Porcano, "Taxation of Cemetery Organizations," 57 *Taxes* 186 (1979); Lapin, "Golden Hills and Meadows of the Tax-Exempt Cemetery," 44 *Taxes* 744 (1966).

[145]See Reg. § 1.501(c)(14)-1. See *United States* v. *Cambridge Loan & Building Co.*, 278 U. S. 55 (1928).

Act are tax-exempt as instrumentalities of the United States.[146] Credit unions exempt from federal tax under these rules generally are those chartered under state law,[147] although in one instance the IRS granted exemption under this provision to an organization formed by a group at a United States military base in a foreign country.[148] However, in addition to being chartered under a state credit union law, a credit union, to qualify under these rules, must operate without profit and for the mutual benefit of its members.[149]

The first credit union in the United States was chartered in New Hampshire in 1909 and was recognized by the Treasury Department as a tax-exempt organization in 1935. The government attempted to revoke its tax-exempt status in 1966, contending that the organization was operating as a commercial savings and loan association, because of the nature of its services and the alleged absence of the requisite "common bond" among its members. The issues were litigated, with the courts finding that the organization did not lose its tax-exempt credit union status because it offers services such as checking accounts and real estate loans and that the members of the credit union in fact have a common bond (it primarily serves the French-speaking residents of Manchester, New Hampshire) even though this commonality was not reduced to a written requirement.[150] The U. S. Court of Appeals for the First Circuit used the occasion of its decision to define a credit union as follows:

> A credit union is a democratically controlled, cooperative, nonprofit society organized for the purpose of encouraging thrift and self-reliance among its members by creating a source of credit at a fair and reasonable rate of interest in order to improve the economic and social conditions of its members. A credit union is fundamentally distinguishable from other financial institutions in that the customers may exercise effective control.[151]

This tax exemption also extends to certain mutual organizations organized before September 1, 1957.[152] Prior to 1951, all savings and loan associations were exempt from taxation, as were the nonprofit corporations that insured these savings institutions. In that year, the tax exemption for savings and loan associations was repealed because Congress determined that the purpose of the exemption, which was to afford savings institutions which had no capital stock the benefit of a tax exemption so that a surplus could be accumulated to provide the depositors with greater security, was no longer applicable because the savings and loan industry had developed to the point where the ratio of

---

[146]Rev. Rul. 55-133, *supra*, n. 1.

[147]Rev. Rul. 69-282, 1969-1 C. B. 155.

[148]Rev. Rul. 69-283, *supra*, n. 3.

[149]Rev. Rul. 72-37, 1972-1 C. B. 152.

[150]*La Caisse Populaire Ste. Marie v. United States*, 425 F.Supp. 512 (D. N. H. 1976), aff'd 563 F.2d 505 (1st Cir. 1977).

[151]*Ibid.*, 563 F.2d at 509.

[152]Code § 501(c)(14)(B).

capital account to total deposits was comparable to commercial banks, which did not have an exemption. However, the tax exemption for the insurers of these associations was continued for those that were organized prior to September 1, 1951.[153] In 1960, Congress extended the expiration date to September 1, 1957, to accommodate the Ohio Deposit Guaranty Fund, since that entity had been organized at a time when the savings and loan associations were essentially not taxed, due to generous bad debt reserve provisions.[154]

In 1962, a nonprofit corporation was established by the legislature of the State of Maryland for the purpose of insuring the accounts of depositors in savings and loan associations doing business in the state, which were not insured by the Federal Savings and Loan Insurance Corporation. Legislation was introduced and considered to advance the termination date to January 1, 1963,[155] but was never enacted, in part because Congress did not want to recreate a discrimination in favor of such financial institutions.[156] (This nonaction on the part of Congress was challenged, with the U.S. Supreme Court holding that Congress did not function in an arbitrary and unconstitutional manner in declining to extend the exemption beyond 1957.[157]) Similar legislation, to extend the cut-off period to January 1, 1969, for the benefit of the Maryland entity and a comparable North Carolina insurer, was introduced and considered in 1976 and 1978 but not enacted.[158] Thereafter, the Maryland organization attempted to secure a judicial determination that it was entitled to a deduction from its income for an addition to its loss reserves but this was rejected on the ground that such a deduction would be the equivalent of exemption of the income from tax—a result Congress has repeatedly rejected.[159]

§ 20.11   Mutual Insurance Companies

Code § 501(c)(15) describes mutual insurance companies or associations other than life or marine (including interinsurers and reciprocal underwriters) if the gross amount received during the tax year from certain items and premiums

---

[153]At that time, Congress understood that the exemption would be limited to four private insurers (two in Massachusetts, one in Connecticut, and one in New Hampshire). See S. Rep. No. 781, 82d Cong., 1st Sess. (1951), at 22–29.

[154]See S. Rep. No. 1881, 87th Cong., 2d Sess. (1962), at 40.

[155]H. R. 3297, 88th Cong., 1st Sess. (1963). See H. Rep. No. 3297, 88th Cong., 1st Sess. (1963).

[156]Savings and loan associations, like other financial institutions, were entitled to establish tax-free reserves from their earnings for losses on loans; there was opposition to exemption of these insurers from tax on the earnings of their members' capital deposits because it would, in effect, provide a method whereby the associations could accumulate reserves free of tax. Also, there was concern about the financial stability of the FSLIC.

[157]*Maryland Savings-Share Insurance Corp.* v. *United States*, 400 U. S. 4 (1970).

[158]H. R. 10612 (Senate version). 94th Cong., 1st Sess. (1976); H. R. 6989, 95th Cong., 1st Sess. (1978).

[159]*Maryland Savings-Share Insurance Corp.* v. *United States*, 644 F.2d 16 (Ct.Cl. 1981).

(including deposits and assessments) does not exceed $150,000. These items[160] are (1) interest, dividends, rents, and royalties, (2) amounts received from entering into leases, mortgages, or other instruments or agreements from which the organization derives interest, rents, or royalties, (3) amounts received from altering or terminating these instruments or agreements (4) gross income from a business (other than the insurance business) carried on by the company or by a partnership of which it is a partner, and (5) premiums,[161] including deposits and assessments.[162]

An insurance company exempt from federal tax under these rules must be a mutual organization; all of its policyholders must be members having common equitable ownership.[163] Also, the members must control the company; it will lose tax exemption if a substantial number of policyholders are denied the right to vote for management[164] or if nonpolicyholders enjoy voting rights equal to policyholders.[165] Further, the tax-exempt mutual company must provide its members with insurance at substantially actual cost, with any excess premiums eventually returned to the policyholders (as dividends or premium reductions).[166] The issuance of policies on a nonassessable basis (i.e., at fixed premiums) is not a necessary prerequisite to mutuality.[167]

The requirement that insurance be provided at substantially actual cost can operate to deny this tax exemption where the company has a guaranty fund evidenced by dividend-bearing stock entitling the holders to share in the profits of the organization or to share beyond the face amount of the certificates in the assets of the organization upon dissolution. Nonetheless, the holders of the certificates may have voting rights without endangering the company's tax exemption as long as control in fact remains with its policyholder members.[168] Further, this requirement means that exempt mutual companies may not accumulate unreasonable reserves.[169]

[160]See Code § 822(b)(1)(A)-(C), (2).

[161]See Reg. § 1.821-4(a).

[162]Reg. § 1.501(c)(15)-1(a). Cf. *Young Men's Christian Ass'n Retirement Fund, Inc.* v. *Commissioner*, 18 B. T. A. 139 (1929).

[163]Rev. Rul. 74-196, 1974-1 C. B. 140.

[164]*Keystone Automobile Club Casualty Co.* v. *Commissioner*, 122 F.2d 886 (3d Cir. 1941), cert. den. 315 U. S. 814 (1942).

[165]Rev. Rul. 55-240, 1955-1 C. B. 406; Rev. Rul. 58-616, 1958-2 C. B. 928.

[166]*Penn Mutual Life Insurance Co.* v. *Lederer*, 252 U. S. 523 (1920); *Safeguard Mutual Fire Insurance Co.* v. *Commissioner*, 4 T. C. 75 (1944). Also *Estate of Moyer* v. *Commissioner*, 32 T. C. 515 (1959).

[167]See *Ohio Farmers Indemnity Co.* v. *Commissioner*, 108 F.2d 665 (6th Cir. 1940).

[168]See *Property Owners Mutual Insurance Co.* v. *Commissioner*, 28 T. C. 1007 (1957); *Holyoke Mutual Fire Insurance Co.* v. *Commissioner*, 28 T. C. 112 (1957).

[169]*Mutual Fire Ins. Co. of Germantown* v. *United States*, 142 F.2d 344 (3d Cir. 1944); *Keystone Mutual Casualty Co.* v. *Driscoll*, 137 F.2d 907 (3d Cir. 1943); *MacLaughlin* v. *Philadelphia Contributionship for Ins. of Houses From Loss by Fire*, 73 F.2d 582 (3d Cir. 1934), cert. den. 294 U. S. 718 (1935); *The Mutual Fire, Marine and Inland Insurance Co.* v. *Commissioner*, 8 T. C. 1212 (1947); *Baltimore Equitable Soc.* v. *United States*, 3 F.Supp. 427 (Ct. Cl. 1933), cert. den. 290 U. S. 662 (1933).

§ 20.12   Crop Operations Finance Corporations

Code § 501(c)(16) provides tax exemption for corporations organized by a tax-exempt farmers' cooperative or association[170] or members thereof, for the purpose of financing the ordinary crop operations of the members or other producers, and operated in conjunction with such an association.[171] This type of finance corporation may retain its tax exemption even though it issues capital stock, where certain statutory conditions are met, or it accumulates and maintains a reasonable reserve. An exempt crop financing corporation may own all the stock of a business corporation without jeopardizing its tax-exempt status.[172]

The U.S. Tax Court denied tax exemption under these rules to a crop financing corporation, which was organized by fruit growers who were members of tax exempt cooperatives, because the growers did not perform their activities as members of the cooperatives.[173]

§ 20.13   Supplemental Unemployment Benefit Trusts

Code § 501(c)(17) provides tax exemption for certain trusts forming part of a plan providing for the payment of supplemental unemployment compensation benefits, which satisfy five basic requirements.[174] Among other criteria, the trust must be part of a plan the eligibility conditions and benefits of which do not discriminate in favor of supervisory or highly compensated employees and which requires that benefits be determined according to objective standards. Also, the trust must be a part of a plan which provides that the corpus and income of the trust cannot (before the satisfaction of all liabilities to employees covered by the plan) be used for, or diverted to, any purpose other than the provision of supplemental unemployment compensation benefits; termination of a trust, with distribution of its remaining assets to employees covered by the plan (after the satisfaction of all liabilities) will not result in loss of its tax-exempt status (even though technically the assets will not be used solely for the purpose of providing benefits).[175]

These supplemental plans are intended to provide benefits to laid-off (or perhaps ill) employees, frequently in conjunction with other payments such as state unemployment benefits.

The term "supplemental unemployment compensation benefits" means separation-from-employment benefits and sick and accident benefits which are subordinate to the separation benefits.[176] These benefits encompass short-week

---

[170]See § 16, *infra*.
[171]See Reg. § 1.501(c)(16)-1.
[172]Rev. Rul. 78-434, 1978-2 C. B. 179.
[173]*Growers Credit Corp.* v. *Commissioner*, 33 T. C. 981 (1970).
[174]See Reg. § 1.501(c)(17)-1(a).
[175]Rev. Rul. 81-68, 1981-1 C. B. 349.
[176]Code § 501(c)(17)(D); Reg. § 1.501(c)(17)-1(b)(1).

benefits paid to employees not wholly separated from employment[177] and relocation payments to employees who would otherwise be separated from employment.[178] However, payments from a trust to union members to compensate them for anticipated lost wages because of the adoption of a new industrial process were ruled to not qualify as this type of benefits since there was no showing that all union members receiving the benefits were involuntarily separated from employment or actually incurred a reduction in the number of hours worked because of the new process.[179]

An otherwise qualified trust can invest in low-risk, income-producing investments that serve social purposes, do not accrue for the benefit of related parties, and are not contrary to the employees' interests without jeopardizing its tax exemption.[180] However, distribution to employees of funds representing contributions in excess of maximum funding will adversely affect a trust's tax-exempt status.[181] The trustee of an exempt plan may, upon authorization from an employee, deduct and pay the employee's union dues from his or her benefit payments.[182]

§ 20.14   Certain Funded Pension Trusts

Code § 501(c)(18) describes a trust or trusts, created before June 25, 1959, forming part of a plan providing for the payment of benefits under a pension plan funded only by employees' contributions, where three basic requirements are satisfied.[183]

§ 20.15   Veterans' Organizations

Code § 501(c)(19), as amended in 1982, provides tax exemption for a post or organization of past or present members of the armed forces of the United States, or an auxiliary unit or society thereof, or a trust or foundation therefor, where (1) it is organized in the United States or any of its possessions, (2) at least 75 percent of its members are past or present members of the U.S. armed forces and substantially all of the other members are individuals who are cadets or spouses, widows or widowers of such past or present members or of cadets and (3) there is no private inurement. These rules were revised in 1982 to enable certain veterans' organizations to qualify for tax exemption

---

[177]Rev. Rul. 70-189, 1970-1 C. B. 134.
[178]Rev. Rul. 70-188, 1970-1 C. B. 133.
[179]Rev. Rul. 77-43, 1977-1 C. B. 151.
[180]Rev. Rul. 70-536, 1970-2 C. B. 120.
[181]Rev. Rul. 71-156, 1971-2 C. B. 153.
[182]Rev. Rul. 73-307, 1973-2 C. B. 185.
[183]See Reg. § 1.501(c)(18)-1.

without having a principal amount of members who are war veterans.[184] Some veterans groups may nonetheless continue to have tax exemption as social welfare organizations.[185]

Although the accompanying tax regulations have not been revised to reflect revision of the statute, presumably, a veterans organization, to qualify for tax exemption under these rules, must operate exclusively to (1) promote the social welfare of the community, (2) assist disabled and needy veterans and members of the U.S. armed forces and their dependents, and the widows or widowers and orphans of deceased veterans, (3) provide entertainment, care, and assistance to hospitalized veterans or members of the U.S. armed forces, (4) carry on programs to perpetuate the memory of deceased veterans and members of the armed forces and comfort their survivors, (5) conduct programs for religious, charitable, scientific, literary, or educational purposes, (6) sponsor or participate in activities of a patriotic nature, (7) provide insurance benefits for their members or dependents thereof or both, or (8) provide social and recreational activities for their members.[186]

Exempted from the unrelated business income tax is income derived from members of these organizations attributable to payments for life, accident, or health insurance with respect to its members or their dependents, where the net profits are set aside for charitable purposes.[187] The enactment of this general income tax exemption thus provides a category of organizations entitled to use the unrelated business income tax exemption.

A contribution to a post or organization of war veterans, or an auxiliary unit or society of, or trust or foundation for, any such post or organization is deductible as a charitable gift, if the donee is organized in the United States or any of its possessions and none of its net earnings inures to the benefit of any private shareholder or individual.[188]

In 1982, by enactment of Code § 501(c)(23), Congress established another category of tax-exempt veterans' organization, which is available for any association organized before 1880, more than 75 percent of the members of which are present or past members of the U.S. Armed Forces and a principal purpose of which is to provide insurance and other benefits to veterans or their dependents.[189]

---

[184]Code § 501(c)(19) was amended by § 354(a) of the Tax Equity and Fiscal Responsibility Act of 1982. Under prior law, the membership of a tax-exempt veterans' organization had to be comprised of at least 97.5 percent of war veterans or the other qualifying individuals (Reg. § 1.501(c)(19)-1(b)(2)). The term "war veteran" was defined at Reg. § 1.501(c)(19)-1(b)(1) and a war period was defined in Rev. Rul. 78-239, 1978-1 C. B. 162.

[185]See Chapter 15.

[186]See Reg. § 1.501(c)(19)-1(c).

[187]Code § 512(a)(4); Reg. § 1.512(a)-4.

[188]Code § 170(c)(3).

[189]Tax Equity and Fiscal Responsibility Act of 1982 § 354(b).

Prior to enactment of the specific exemption for war veterans' organizations in 1972, veterans' organizations found their tax exemption as social welfare organizations,[190] social clubs,[191] or charitable and educational organizations.[192] It is not clear from the legislative history underlying the specific exemption whether the exemption is to be the exclusive basis for tax exemption for veterans' groups or whether they may continue to be eligible for exemption under one or more of the other categories. One judicial opinion treats this specific exemption as if it is the exclusive ground for tax exemption for veterans' organizations,[193] although the better view appears to be that this exemption was originally written for "war veterans'" organizations and that other veterans' organizations may, if they are otherwise qualified to do so, base their tax exemption upon the social welfare organization, social club, or charitable and educational organization categories.[194]

When this tax exemption category was first proposed in the House of Representatives,[195] the descriptive language was the same as that in the provision making veterans' groups eligible charitable donees.[196] In both the House Committee on Ways and Means report[197] and in statements on the House floor,[198] there are repeated references to creation of a separate category of exemption for "veterans' organizations." The House-passed measure was amended by the Senate, which added the 75 percent membership requirement.[199] This membership requirement was added by the Senate Committee on Finance, which regarded the amendment as an expansion of the specific exemption. (The Senate Finance Committee report characterized the House bill as providing the exemption for "war veterans' organizations."[200]) The Finance Committee report also states that "[t]he committee intends this provision to cover any veterans organization whose membership is composed almost exclusively of military associated individuals."[201]

---

[190]See Chapter 15.

[191]See Chapter 18.

[192]See Chapter 6 and 7.

[193]*Taxation With Representation of Washington* v. *Regan*, 676 F. 2d 715 (D.C. Cir. 1982).

[194]Legislation introduced as the "Veterans' Organizations Tax Reform Act" (S. 2570, H. R. 6483, 97th Cong., 2d Sess. (1982)) would create a Code § 501(j) which would expressly allow "an organization of war veterans" unlimited lobbying authority as long as the legislative activities are related to veterans' affairs; such an organization is not confined to one described in Code § 501(c)(19). See remarks of Senator Sasser at 128 *Cong. Rec.* S6003 (May 25, 1982) (daily ed.).

[195]H. R. 11185, 92d Cong., 2d Sess. (1972).

[196]Code § 170(c)(3). See n. 189, *supra*.

[197]H. Rep. No. 92-851, 92d Cong., 2d Sess. (1972).

[198]118 *Cong. Rec.* 6033 (1972).

[199]118 *Cong. Rec.* 29076 (1972).

[200]S. Rep. No. 92-1082, 92d Cong., 2d Sess. (1972) at 1,3.

[201]*Ibid.* at 5.

Nonetheless, there is nothing in the legislative history of this specific exemption for certain types of veterans' organizations that expressly precludes a veterans' organization that cannot or may not qualify under it from tax exemption pursuant to some other classification of tax-exempt organization where the criteria for that classification are satisfied. In related contexts, there is authority for the proposition that an organization that does not qualify under a specific exemption category is not thereby rendered ineligible for tax exemption on the basis of another, broader category of tax-exempt organization.[202]

§ 20.16   Farmers' Cooperatives

Under Code § 521, a farmers' cooperative organization is exempt from federal income taxation, except as otherwise provided in the nonexempt cooperative rules of Code §§ 1381–1388. These farmers' cooperatives are farmers', fruit growers', or like associations organized and operated on a cooperative basis for the purpose of (1) marketing the products of members or other producers and returning to them the proceeds of sales, less the necessary marketing expenses, on the basis of either the quantity or the value of the products furnished by them, or (2) purchasing supplies and equipment for the use of members or other persons and turning over the supplies and equipment to them at actual cost plus necessary expenses.[203] A farmers' cooperative may pay dividends on its capital stock in certain circumstances,[204] may permit proxy voting by its shareholders,[205] and may maintain a reasonable reserve.[206] The earnings of cooperatives generally are taxed to them or their patrons; these rules give tax-exempt farmers' cooperatives certain advantages in computing the tax that are not available to other cooperatives.

Farmers' cooperatives came into being because of the economic fact that "[a] farmer sells his products in a producers' market and makes his purchases in a retail market."[207] Thus, a farmers' marketing cooperative markets farmers' products at a price nearer retail price and makes their purchases at wholesale rather than retail. A farmers' purchasing cooperative sells supplies and equipment to its patrons at a price which leaves a balance after expenses. The cooperative's net earnings or savings are distributed to the patrons on the basis of the amount of business transacted by them, in the form of "patronage dividends."

Farmers' cooperatives are associations of individuals such as farmers, fruit

---

[202]E.g., *Chart, Inc.* v. *United States*, 491 F. Supp. 10 (D.D.C. 1979).

[203]Reg. § 1.521-1.

[204]Code § 521(b)(2); Reg. § 1.521-1(a)(2). See Rev. Rul. 75-388, 1975-2 C. B. 227; Rev. Rul. 73-148, 1973-1 C. B. 294. Also see *Agway, Inc.* v. *United States*, 524 F.2d 1194 (Ct. Cl. 1975).

[205]Rev. Rul. 75-97, 1975-1 C. B. 167.

[206]Code § 521(b)(3); Reg. § 1.521-1(a)(3). See Rev. Rul. 76-233, 1976-1 C. B. 173.

[207]IRS Exempt Organizations Handbook (IRM 7751) § (44)12(1).

growers, livestock growers, and dairymen. Illustrations of these organizations include associations operated to facilitate the artifical breeding of members' livestock,[208] acquire and apportion the beneficial use of land for the grazing of members' livestock,[209] furnish its members a place to market their farm products,[210] process and market poultry for members and other producers,[211] market farm-raised fish,[212] operate a grain elevator and feed yard and process soybeans,[213] purchase raw materials for processing into completed products before their transfer to patrons,[214] and produce and market range grasses.[215] The term "like association" is limited to associations that market agricultural products or purchase supplies and equipment for those engaged in producing agricultural products.[216] Thus, the admission to membership of a substantial number of nonproducers in an otherwise tax-exempt producers' cooperative would destroy the association's tax exemption.[217] This, in turn, raises questions as to what constitutes a "farm"[218] and a "farmer."[219]

Examples of organizations denied this tax exemption as not being "like" a farmers' cooperative include an association that maintained its patrons' orchards and harvested their crops,[220] that markets lumber for the independent lumber-producing companies which control it,[221] and that marketed building materials on a cooperative basis,[222] and an association of advertising agencies[223] and of garbage collectors.[224] An organization may be recognized as a cooperative association under state law and still be denied this tax exemption.[225]

Other requirements must be met to achieve this tax exemption, including the requirements that the association be organized and operated on a "coop-

---

[208]Rev. Rul. 68-76, 1968-1 C. B. 285.

[209]Rev. Rul. 67-429, 1967-2 C. B. 218.

[210]Rev. Rul. 67-430, 1967-2 C. B. 220.

[211]Rev. Rul. 58-483, 1958-2 C. B. 277.

[212]Rev. Rul. 64-246, 1964-2 C. B. 154.

[213]Rev. Rul. 74-567, 1974-2 C. B. 174.

[214]Rev. Rul. 54-12, 1954-1 C. B. 93.

[215]Rev. Rul. 75-5, 1975-1 C. B. 166.

[216]See *Sunset Scavenger Co., Inc.* v. *Commissioner*, 84 F.2d 453 (9th Cir. 1936).

[217]*Cooperative Central Exchange* v. *Commissioner*, 27 B. T. A. 17 (1932).

[218]See Rev. Rul. 64-246, *supra*, n. 212.

[219]See Rev. Rul. 55-611, 1955-2 C. B. 270.

[220]Rev. Rul. 66-108, 1966-2 C. B. 154.

[221]Rev. Rul. 73-570, 1973-2 C. B. 195.

[222]Rev. Rul. 73-308, 1973-2 C. B. 193.

[223]*National Outdoor Advertising Bureau, Inc.* v. *Helvering*, 89 F.2d 878 (2d Cir. 1937).

[224]*Sunset Scavenger Co., Inc.* v. *Commissioner*, *supra*, n. 216.

[225]*Lyeth* v. *Hoey*, 305 U. S. 188 (1938).

erative" basis,[226] that there be bona fide "members,"[227] and that (where appropriate) there be "producers."[228]

The IRS has issued guidelines[229] to determine whether a patron is a producer patron of a farmers' cooperative for purposes of applying certain stock ownership requirements.[230] These guidelines provide, in part, that the Service will consider stock owned by persons who market more than 50 percent of particular products they have produced and marketed through the cooperative, or who purchase from the cooperative more than 50 percent of their supplies and equipment of the type handled by the cooperative, during the cooperative's taxable year, as being owned by qualified producers for purpose of the stock ownership requirement. A person who does not meet this 50 percent standard for a specific year can nonetheless be considered a producer for purposes of the ownership requirements if certain permissible facts and circumstances are present whereby the person was unable to comply with the marketing or purchasing tests in a particular year. Some of the acceptable facts and circumstances are indicated in the guidelines and in a 1977 ruling.[231]

Still other requirements concern the nature of permissible activities. As respects marketing cooperatives, questions have been raised as to what constitutes "marketing."[232] The IRS has a long-standing policy of allowing farmers' cooperatives, in connection with their marketing function, to manufacture or otherwise change the basic form of their member's products, as illustrated by the tax-exempt farmers' cooperative operating a cannery and facilities for drying fruit and a cooperative operating a textile mill, both of which market the processed or unprocessed products of their member growers and distribute the proceeds to them on the basis of the quantity of product furnished, less a charge to cover the cost of processing.[233] Subsequently, this policy was further illustrated by a ruling from the IRS allowing qualification as an exempt farmers' cooperative of a cooperative association that, in connection with its marketing function, processes its members' agricultural products into alcohol.[234]

[226]See Reg. § 1.521-1(a)(1); Rev. Rul. 71-100, 1971-1 C. B. 159; Rev. Rul. 68-496, 1968-2 C. B. 251; Rev. Rul. 55-558, 1955-2 C. B. 270; *Eugene Fruit Growers Association v. Commissioner*, 37 B. T. A. 993 (1938).

[227]See § 1.521-1(a)(3); *Producers Livestock Marketing Association of Salt Lake City v. Commissioner*, 45 B. T. A. 325 (1941).

[228]Rev. Rul. 72-589, 1972-2 C. B. 282; Rev. Rul. 67-422, 1967-2 C. B. 217; Rev. Rul. 58-483, *supra*, n. 211; *Farmers Cooperative Creamery Association of Cresco, Iowa v. United States*, 81-1 U.S.T.C. ¶ 9457 (N. D. Iowa 1981); *Dr. P. Phillips Cooperative v. Commissioner*, 17 T. C. 1002 (1951).

[229]Rev. Proc. 73-39, 1973-2 C. B. 502.

[230]Code § 521(b)(2). See note 204, *supra*.

[231]Rev. Rul. 77-440, 1977-2 C. B. 199.

[232]See *Treasure Valley Potato Bargaining Association v. Ore-Ida Foods, Inc.*, 497 F.2d 203 (9th Cir. 1974); Rev. Rul. 67-430, *supra*, n. 210; Rev. Rul. 66-108, *supra*, n. 220; Mim. 3886, X-2 C. B. 164 (1931).

[233]Rev. Rul. 77-384, 1977-2 C. B. 198.

[234]Rev. Rul. 81-96, 1981-1 C. B. 359.

Concerning the purchasing cooperative, the issue may be what is encompassed by the term "supplies and equipment."[235] Business done for or with the United States or any of its agencies is to be disregarded in determining right to the tax exemption.[236] Because hedging is an activity that is incidental to the marketing function of an exempt farmer's cooperative, it may establish a commodity trading division to serve as a commodity broker to facilitate hedging transactions for its marketing patrons without affecting its tax exemption.[237]

An exempt farmers' cooperative may establish and control a subsidiary corporation so long as the activities of the subsidiary are activities that the cooperative itself might engage in as an integral part of its operations without affecting its exempt status.[238] For this reason, the IRS ruled that a cooperative may establish and control a Domestic International Sales Corporation.[239]

One rule that has generated considerable attention is the limitation on the purchasing of supplies and equipment for nonmembers and nonproducers to 15 percent of the value of all of the cooperative's purchase of supplies and equipment.[240] By contrast, a marketing cooperative will generally not qualify for the tax exemption if it markets the goods of nonproducers.[241] However, there are exceptions to the limitation on marketing nonproducer goods, which may be categorized into sideline,[242] ingredient,[243] and emergency[244] purchases from nonproducers.

Still another requisite for entitlement to this tax exemption is that any excess of gross receipts over expenses and payments to patrons (termed "earnings") must be returned to the patrons in proportion to the amount of business done for them. The income and expenses for each function (primarily marketing and purchasing) must be accounted for separately.[245] In computing earnings, the

---

[235]See Rev. Rul. 68-76, *supra*, n. 208; Rev. Rul. 67-429, *supra*, n. 209; Rev. Rul. 54-12, *supra*, n. 214; S. M. 2288, III-2 C. B. 223 (1924); *Farmers Union Cooperative Association, Fairbury, Nebraska* v. *Commissioner*, 44 B. T. A. 34 (1941).

[236]Code § 521(b)(5); Rev. Rul. 65-5, 1965-1 C. B. 244.

[237]Rev. Rul. 76-298, 1976-2 C. B. 179.

[238]Rev. Rul. 69-575, 1969-2 C. B. 134.

[239]Rev. Rul. 73-247, 1973-1 C. B. 294.

[240]Code § 521(b)(4). See Rev. Rul. 69-417, 1969-2 C. B. 132; Rev. Rul. 67-346, 1967-2 C. B. 216; Rev. Rul. 67-223, 1967-2 C. B. 214. As for the effect of the use of subsidiaries in relation to this limitation, see Rev. Rul. 73-148, *supra*, n. 204; Rev. Rul. 69-575, *supra*, n. 238.

[241]Code § 521(b)(1). See Rev. Rul. 67-152, 1967-1 C. B. 147.

[242]See Rev. Proc. 67-37, 1967-2 C. B. 668; *Land O'Lakes, Inc.* v. *United States*, 362 F.Supp. 1253 (S. D. Minn. 1973), rev. and rem. 514 F.2d 134 (8th Cir. 1975), cert. den. 423 U. S. 926 (1975); *Eugene Fruit Growers Association* v. *Commissioner*, *supra*, n. 226.

[243]See Rev. Rul. 75-4, 1975-1 C. B. 165; Rev. Rul. 67-152, *supra*, n. 241; *Dr. P. Phillips Cooperative* v. *Commissioner*, *supra*, n. 228.

[244]See Rev. Rul. 69-222, 1969-1 C. B. 161; *Producers' Produce Co.* v. *Crooks*, 2 F.Supp. 969 (W. D. Mo. 1932).

[245]Rev. Rul. 67-253, 1967-2 C. B. 214; see Rev. Rul. 75-110, 1975-1 C. B. 167.

tax-exempt cooperative must experience only "necessary" expenses associated with marketing and purchasing (frequently undertaken in different "departments" or "branches"), rather than for items such as the purchase of life insurance for members.[246] Nonpatronage income may be allocated to the appropriate department of the cooperative.[247]

Also, a farmers' cooperative must treat its nonmember patrons the same as member-patrons as respects patronage dividends. There have been several cases where an association has been denied tax exemption because of this type of discrimination,[248] as well as a number of instances where inequality among patrons was deemed to be not present.[249]

A discussion of the circumstances under which a federated farmers' cooperative (an association the membership of which includes farmers' cooperative associations) may qualify for this tax exemption is the subject of a 1969 IRS ruling.[250] Two 1972 revenue procedures set forth methods acceptable for a federated cooperative and its members to establish exemption (involving the "look through" principle[251]) and setting forth the general requirements in this regard.[252]

§ 20.17 Shipowners' Protection and Indemnity Associations

Code § 526 provides that "[t]here shall not be included in gross income the receipts of shipowners' mutual protection and indemnity associations not organized for profit, and no part of the net earnings of which inures to the benefit

[246]Rev. Rul. 55-558, *supra*, n. 226. Also Rev. Rul. 73-93, 1973-1 C. B. 292.

[247]Rev. Rul. 67-128, 1967-1 C. B. 147; *Juanita Farmers Cooperative Association* v. *Commissioner*, 43 T. C. 836 (1965). See Rev. Rul. 75-228, 1975-1 C. B. 278; Rev. Rul. 74-327, 1974-2 C. B. 66.

[248]See, e.g., *Farmers Cooperative Creamery Association of Cresco, Iowa* v. *United States*, *supra*, n. 228; *Fertile Cooperative Dairy Association* v. *Huston*, 119 F.2d 274 (8th Cir. 1951); *Farmers Cooperative Co. of Wahoo, Nebraska* v. *United States*, 23 F.Supp. 123 (Ct. Cl. 1938); Rev. Rul. 73-59, 1973-1 C. B. 292.

[249]See, e.g., Rev. Rul. 69-52, 1969-1 C. B. 161; Rev. Rul. 66-152, 1966-1 C. B. 155. Also see Rev. Rul. 76-388, 1976-2 C. B. 180.

[250]Rev. Rul. 69-651, 1969-2 C. B. 135.

[251]See Rev. Ruls. 72-50, 51, 52, 1972-1 C. B. 163, 164, 165.

[252]Rev. Procs. 72-16, 17, 1972-1 C. B. 738, 739. In general, see Katz, "Buying through cooperatives has tax benefits for the cooperative and its owners," 16 *Taxation for Accountants* 115 (1976); Comment, "Agricultural Cooperative Associations and the Equal Treatment Requirement of Section 521," 27 *Alabama L. Rev.* 611 (1976); Note, "Section 521—Exemption of Farmers Cooperatives from Tax," 25 *Drake L. Rev.* 705 (1976); Schrader and Goldberg, *Farmers' Cooperatives and Federal Income Taxes* (1975); Pearson, "Farm Cooperatives and the Federal Income Tax," 44 *N. D. L. Rev.* 490 (1968); Logan, "Federal Income Taxation of Farmers' and Other Cooperatives," 44 *Tex. L. Rev.* 250, 1269 (1965–1966); Wile, "Taxation of Farmers' Cooperatives and Their Patrons," 18 *So. Cal. Tax Inst.* 449 (1966); Blair, "Farmers' cooperatives and their patrons face new problems in reporting income," 28 *J. Tax.* 180 (1968); Asbill, "Cooperatives: Tax Treatment of Patronage Refunds," 42 *Va. L. Rev.* 1087 (1956).

of any private shareholder; but such corporations shall be subject as other persons to the tax on their taxable income from interest, dividends, and rents."

The return of excess dues by a fishing vessel owners' association to its members was ruled by the IRS to not be inurement of earnings to the members; therefore, the dues paid to the association were not includible in its gross income.[253] The amount paid by a member of a tax-exempt association to its reserve fund to provide certain insurance protection was deemed deductible.[254]

§ 20.18 Political Organizations

Code § 527 provides tax exemption for the "political organization." Effective with respect to tax years beginning in 1975, these rules statutorily override previous IRS determinations on the point, to the effect that an unincorporated campaign committee is not exempt from federal income taxation and must file tax returns showing as gross income interest, dividends, and net gains from the sale of securities and related deductions.[255]

A political organization is a party, committee, association, fund, or other organization organized and operated primarily for the purpose of directly or indirectly accepting contributions or making expenditures, or both, for an "exempt function."[256] An exempt function is the function of influencing or attempting to influence the selection, nomination, election, or appointment of any individual to any federal, state, or local public office or office in a political organization, or the election of presidential or vice-presidential electors. Thus, for example, a bank account used by a candidate for depositing political contributions and disbursing bona fide political campaign expenses qualifies as a tax-exempt political organization.[257]

Political organizations are subject[258] to the applicable rate of corporate tax on their "taxable income," which is their gross income, less "exempt function income" and direct expenses, subject to certain modifications.[259] Exempt function income means (1) contributions of money or other property, (2) membership dues, membership fees, or assessments from a member of the organization, (3)

[253]Rev. Rul. 70-566, 1970-1 C. B. 128.

[254]Rev. Rul. 55-189, 1955-1 C. B. 265.

[255]See Rev. Rul. 74-21, 1974-1 C. B. 14, and Rev. Rul. 74-23, 1974-1 C. B. 17, as modified and clarified by Rev. Rul. 74-475, 1974-2 C. B. 22. Also see Rev. Proc. 68-19, 1968-1 C. B. 810; I. T. 3276, 1939-1 (Part 1) C. B. 108. Cf. *Communist Party of the U. S. A.* v. *Commissioner*, 373 F.2d 682 (D. C. Cir. 1967). Political organizations generally cannot qualify under any of the other categories of tax-exempt organizations, such as, for example, Code § 501(c)(3). *Lonsdale* v. *Commissioner*, 41 T. C. M. 1106 (1981); *Cavell* v. *Commissioner*, 40 T. C. M. 395 (1980).

[256]Code § 527(e). See, e.g., IRS Private Letter Ruling 7922051.

[257]Rev. Rul. 79-11, 1979-1 C. B. 207. Also see Rev. Rul. 79-12, 1979-1 C. B. 208, and Rev. Rul. 79-13, 1979-1 C. B. 208.

[258]Code § 527(b).

[259]Code § 527(c). These organizations' tax return is Form 1120-POL. See Reg. 1.6012-6; IRS Private Letter Ruling 7839123.

proceeds from a political fundraising or entertainment event, or (4) proceeds from the sale of political campaign materials, which are not received in the ordinary course of any trade or business, to the extent such amount is segregated for use only for the exempt function of the political organization.[260] The House of Representatives, in 1976, voted to liberalize these rules to provide that, under certain circumstances, income received by a political organization from the conduct of games of chance would not be taxable, but the measure has never been considered by the Senate.[261]

Under the law, prior to its revision in 1981, political organizations were subject to the highest rate (46 percent), rather than the graduated rates, of corporate tax on their taxable income. However, by enactment of the Economic Recovery Tax Act of 1981, Congress changed the law (for tax years beginning after December 31, 1981) so that the generally applicable corporate income tax rates apply to political organization taxable income of a congressional candidate's principal campaign committee.[262] Thus, in 1982, the lowest rate is 16 percent as to taxable amounts of $25,000 or less, and the highest rate continues to be 46 percent on taxable amounts over $100,000.[263]

Related provisions provide for the tax treatment of newsletter funds,[264] exempt contributions to political parties or committees from the gift tax,[265] and

---

[260]Code § 527(c)(3). See, e.g., Rev. Rul. 80-103, 1980-1 C. B. 120, where the IRS ruled that the proceeds received by a political organization from the sales of art reproductions do not qualify as exempt function income, because the sales activity was considered to be a trade or business.

[261]H. R. 10155; see H. Rep. No. 94-1355, 94th Cong., 2d Sess. (1976); H. R. 8533, H. R. 9429, 95th Cong., 1st Sess. (1977).

[262]This change in the law was occasioned by enactment of § 128 of the 1981 Act. A "principal campaign committee" is that designated by a candidate pursuant to 2 U. S. C. § 432(e).

[263]See Chapter 40.

[264]Code § 527(g).

[265]Code § 2501(a)(5). The effective date of this provision was set at May 8, 1974. The IRS has contended that gifts to political organizations made before May 8, 1974, are subject to the gift tax. Litigation ensued, with the U.S. Tax Court holding that the gift tax did not apply to amounts contributed for political purposes during the period there at issue (1967–1971). *Carson* v. *Commissioner*, 71 T.C. 252 (1978), aff'd 641 F.2d 864 (10th Cir. 1981). A similar decision had been reached by the U.S. Court of Appeals for the Fifth Circuit, for years 1959–1961. *Stern* v. *United States*, 426 F.2d 1327 (5th Cir. 1971). The *Carson* decision rejected the government's contention that the enactment of this gift tax exclusion represented a change in the law. The IRS subsequently acquiesced in the *Carson* decision. Rev. Rul. 82-216, 1982-50 I.R.B. 12. However, this acquiescence is in the result of the decision and not necessarily in the rationale of the decision. That is, in the acquiescence/ruling, the IRS states that it "continues to maintain that gratuitous transfers to persons . . . [other than political organizations] are subject to the gift tax absent any specific statute to the contrary, even though the transfers may be motivated by a desire to advance the donor's own social, political or charitable goals." For example, the IRS states that the gift tax exclusion in the charitable gift context

tax to the donor, at the time of transfer, the appreciation element in gifts of appreciated property to political organizations.[266]

If a tax-exempt organization[267] expends any amount during a tax year for what would be a political organization exempt function, it must include in its gross income for the year an amount equal to the lesser of its net investment income for the year or the aggregate amount so expended during the year for the function.[268] This amount is taxed in accordance with special rules.[269] However, an organization will not be taxed where it merely receives contributions from its members for political action and promptly transfers the funds to the unrelated (except for common interest) political organization that solicited them.[270] These rules are not intended to change the prohibition on political activities applicable to charitable organizations and social welfare organizations.[271] However, the concept of political organization exempt function is broader than the electioneering limitation in those laws.[272]

§ 20.19   Homeowners' Associations

Congress interceded to bring some clarification to the burgeoning body of law concerning the tax treatment of homeowners' associations that developed while these associations were treated as social welfare organizations.[273] It is now commonplace for these associations to be formed as part of the development of a real estate subdivision, a condominium project, or a cooperative housing project. These associations enable their members (individual homeowners and the like) to act together in managing, maintaining, and improving areas where they live. The associations' purposes include the administration and enforce-

---

(Code § 2522(a)) is not available for transfers to organizations that have been disqualified from qualification under Code § 501(c)(3) for engaging in legislative or political campaign activities.

[266]Code § 84.

[267]That is, one described in Code § 501(c).

[268]Code § 527(f)(1).

[269]Code § 527(b).

[270]IRS Private Letter Ruling 7903079.

[271]See S. Rep. No. 93-1357, 93d Cong., 2d Sess. (1974), at 29. For example, in Rev. Rul. 81-95, 1981-1 C. B. 332, the IRS ruled that a tax-exempt social welfare organization may, without adversely affecting its exempt status, participate in political campaign activities as long as it is primarily engaged in the promotion of social welfare but that the amounts expended for the activities may be treated as political organization taxable income.

[272]In general, see Prop. Reg. §§ 1.527-1 et seq. In general, see Streng, "The Federal Tax Treatment of Political Contributions and Political Organizations," 29 Tax Law. 139 1975); Kaplan, "Taxation and Political Campaigns: Interface Resolved," 53 Taxes 340 (1975).

[273]See Chapter 15.

ment of covenants for preserving the physical appearance of the development, the ownership and management of common areas (e.g., sidewalks, parks), and the exterior maintenance of property owned by the members.

Originally, the IRS regarded homeowners' associations as tax-exempt social welfare organizations.[274] But the Service, concerned that the requisite "community" was not being served, issued a countervailing ruling in 1974.[275] Most homeowners' associations found it difficult to meet the requirements in the 1974 determination.[276] The IRS also ruled that condominium management associations do not qualify for tax exemption.[277]

Several bills were introduced during 1974–1976 to rectify this situation and the 1974 aborted House Ways and Means Committee tax reform measure contained an exemption provision for homeowners' associations. Congress' solution as regards the appropriate tax treatment for homeowners' associations came in the form of Code § 528, enacted as part of the Tax Reform Act of 1976, which provides an elective tax exemption for condominium management and residential real estate associations.[278] This provision is in the mode of the present tax treatment of exempt social clubs[279] and political organizations,[280] in that only "exempt function income" escapes taxation.

To qualify under these rules, a homeowners' association must meet certain requirements: (1) it must be organized and operated to provide for the acquisition, construction, management, maintenance, and care of association property, (2) an income test, whereby at least 60 percent of the association's gross income for a tax year consists of exempt function income, (3) an expenditure test, whereby at least 90 percent of the annual expenditures of the association must be to acquire, construct, manage, maintain, and care for or improve its property, (4) no part of the association's net earnings inures to the benefit of any private shareholder or individual, and (5) substantially all of the dwelling units in the condominium project or lots and buildings in a subdivision, development, or similar area must be used by individuals for residences. The acts of acquiring, constructing, or providing management, maintenance, and care of association property, and of rebating excess membership dues, fees, or assessments, do not constitute private inurement. Association property means not only property held by it but also property commonly held by its members, property within the association privately held by the members, and property owned by a governmental unit and used for the benefit of residents of such unit.

[274]Rev. Rul. 72-102, 1972-1 C. B. 149.

[275]Rev. Rul. 74-199, 1974-1 C. B. 131.

[276]See Frank, "IRS takes harsh position on exempting condominium and homeowners' associations," 44 *J. Tax.* 306 (1976).

[277]Rev. Rul. 74-17, 1974-1 C. B. 130.

[278]The manner and time for making this election, and other rules in amplification of the statutory requirements, are stated at Reg. § 1.528-1 *et seq*.

[279]Code § 512(a)(3). See Chapter 18.

[280]Code § 527.

In this context, exempt function income means any amount received as membership dues, fees, or assessments from persons who are members of the association, namely, owners of condominium housing units (in the case of a condominium management association) or owners of real property (in the case of a residential real estate management association).[281] Taxable income includes investment income and payments by nonmembers for the use of the association's facilities, subject to a specific $100 deduction and deductions directly connected with the production of gross income (other than exempt function income).[282] By an enactment in 1980, the taxable income of a qualified homeowners' association is taxable at a rate of 30 percent, rather than the regular corporate rates (46 percent, with long-term capital gains taxed at a 28 percent rate).[283]

The House version of the 1969 Act would have also applied the foregoing rules to cooperative housing corporations.[284] But the 1969 Act in its final form followed the Senate bill in not allowing the exemption for such corporations. Instead, the Act clarified existing law to ensure that a cooperative housing corporation is entitled to a deduction for depreciation[285] with respect to property it leases to a tenant-stockholder even though the tenant-stockholder may be entitled to depreciate his or her stock in the corporation to the extent the stock is related to a proprietary lease or right of tenancy which is used by the tenant-stockholder in a trade or business or for the production of income.[286]

These rules apply to payments received after December 31, 1973, in tax years ending after that date.[287]

---

[281]Annual assessments paid to a homeowners' association by its members are not deductible as real property taxes. Rev. Rul. 76-495, 1976-2 C. B. 43.

[282]Qualified homeowners' associations that elect to be taxed under Code § 528 (see Code § 6012(a)(7)) file tax return Form 1120-H. Ann. 77-42, 1977-13 I. R. B. 23.

[283]P. L. 96-605, 96th Cong., 2d Sess. (1980). Inasmuch as these changes affect tax years ending after December 31, 1980, homeowners' associations with tax years beginning in 1980 and ending after December 31, 1980, must prorate their tax on Form 1120-H-FY (1980-1981) instead of using Schedule A—Tax Computation Schedule of the 1980 Form 1120-H. Ann. 81-28, 1981-8 I. R. B. 86.

[284]Code § 216(b).

[285]Code § 167(a).

[286]See *Park Place, Inc.* v. *Commissioner*, 57 T. C. 767 (1972).

[287]In general, see Cowan, "Working with new rules for condominiums, cooperatives and homeowners associations," 46 *J. Tax.* 204 (1977); IRS Publication 588 (rev. ed. 1980), which includes discussion of the treatment of individual condominium owners' tax situations and homeowners' associations' tax alternatives; Reinstein, "Federal Tax Implications of Condominium Associations," 50 *Fla. Bar J.* 219 (1976); Redemske, "Income tax considerations for the condominium corporation," 7 *Tax Adviser* 608 (1976); Garrett, "The Taxability of Condominium Owners' Associations," 12 *San Diego L. Rev.* 778 (1975); O'Connell, "Federal Income Tax Consequences for Condominium Homeowners: A Request for Equitable Tax Treatment," 15 *Santa Clara Lawyer* 384 (1975); Jackson, "Why You Should Incorporate a Homeowners Association," 3 *Real Estate L. J.* 311 (1975).

§ 20.20   Prepaid Legal Services Trusts

Congress, in adopting the Tax Reform Act of 1976, enacted another category of tax-exempt organization, namely, an entity as described in Code § 501(c)(20) established to form part of a qualified group legal services plan or plans. This provision is a portion of an overall scheme providing favorable tax treatment of prepaid group legal services provided by employers to their employees. To provide a tax incentive for such plans, the law excludes from an employee's income (1) amounts contributed by an employer to a qualified group legal services plan for employees, their spouses, or their dependents and (2) the value of services received by an employee or any amounts paid to an employee under the plan as reimbursement for legal services for the employee or his or her spouse or dependents.[288] To be a qualified plan, a group legal services plan must fulfill several requirements with regard to its provisions, the employer, and the covered employees.

A qualified group legal services plan must be a separate written plan of an employer for the exclusive benefit of his or her employees or their spouses or dependents. The plan must supply the employees (or their spouses or dependents) with specified benefits consisting of personal (i.e., nonbusiness) legal services through prepayment of, or provision in advance for, all or part of an employee's, his or her spouse's or dependents' legal fees.[289] Also, to be qualified, the group legal services plan must meet requirements with respect to nondiscrimination in contributions or benefits and in eligibility for enrollment.[290]

Amounts contributed by employers under a plan may be paid only (1) to insurance companies, (2) to qualified tax-exempt organizations, (3) as prepayments to providers of legal services under the plan, or (4) to a combination of the foregoing types of eligible payment recipients.[291] The entity referenced in category (2) is the tax-exempt prepaid legal services organization, described as "an organization or trust created or organized in the United States, the exclusive function of which is to form part of a qualified group legal services plan or plans, within the meaning of section 120." An organization is not to be deprived of tax exemption by reason of these rules because "it provides legal services or indemnification against the cost of legal services unassociated with a qualified group legal services plan" in addition to receiving contributions from employers.

To be treated as a qualified group legal services plan, the plan must timely notify the IRS that it is applying for recognition of the status.[292] The provisions concerning these organizations were originally applicable to tax years beginning

---

[288]Code § 120(a).
[289]Code § 120(b).
[290]Code § 120(c).
[291]Code § 120(c)(5).
[292]Code § 120(c)(4), (d)(7).

after December 31, 1976, and ending before January 1, 1982, but were extended in 1981 through tax years ending after December 31, 1984.[293]

§ 20.21   Black Lung Benefits Trusts

Another type of tax-exempt organization is the Black Lung Benefits Trust, as described in Code § 501(c)(21). This organization was added to the listing of exempt organizations by enactment of the Black Lung Benefits Revenue Act of 1977.[294] The provisions are effective for tax years beginning after December 31, 1977.

The purpose of these rules is to provide income tax exemption for a qualifying trust used by a coal mine operator to self-insure for liabilities under federal and state black lung benefits laws. Under the federal black lung benefits statute, a coal mine operator in a state not deemed to provide adequate workmen's compensation coverage for pneumoconiosis must secure the payment of benefits for which the operator may be found liable under the statute, either by means of commercial insurance or through self-insuring. Since no state laws are presently deemed adequate for this purpose, all operators subject to such liability must obtain insurance or self-insure. Because such insurance is unavailable or is of high cost, Congress established this form of self-insurance program, with similar tax consequences (from the point of view of the operator) as would result if the operator had purchased noncancellable accident and health insurance.[295]

A qualified Black Lung Benefits Trust must be irrevocable, must be established by a written instrument, must be created or organized in the United States, and may be contributed to by any person (other than an insurance company).

The trust must have as its exclusive purpose the (1) satisfaction, in whole or in part, of the liability of a contributor to the trust for, or with respect to, claims for compensation for disability or death due to pneumoconiosis under Black Lung Acts,[296] (2) payment of premiums for insurance exclusively covering this type of liability, and (3) payment of administrative and other incidental expenses of the trust (including legal, accounting, actuarial and trustee ex-

---

[293]This change in the law was occasioned by enactment of § 802 of the Economic Recovery Tax Act of 1981. In general, see Leaming, "Planning and Establishing a Prepaid Legal Plan," 3 *Legal Econ.* (No. 3) 9 (1977); Johnson, "Group Legal Services Plans and Section 2134 of the Tax Reform Act of 1976," 52 *Los Angeles Bar Bull.* (No. 9) 474 (1977); BNA Tax Management, Inc., Memorandum on Prepaid Legal Services, reproduced at BNA *Daily Report for Executives*, Jan. 28, 1977 at J-1.

[294]P. L. 95-227 § 4, 95th Cong., 2d Sess. (1978).

[295]See S. Rep. No. 95-336, 95th Cong., 2d Sess. (1978), at 11-12.

[296]These laws are part C, title IV of the Federal Coal Mine Health and Safety Act of 1969 and any state law providing compensation for disability or death due to pneumoconiosis.

penses) in connection with the operation of the trust and the processing of claims under Black Lung Acts against a contributor to the trust.[297]

No part of the assets of a Black Lung Benefits Trust may be used for, or diverted to, any purpose other than the foregoing three purposes or investment.[298] However, investment can occur only to the extent that the trustee determines that the invested assets are not currently needed for the trust's tax-exempt purposes. Moreover, the investment may only be in (1) public debt securities of the United States, (2) obligations of a state or local government which are not in default as to principal or interest, or (3) time or demand deposits in a bank[299] or an insured credit union located in the United States.[300]

The assets of a Black Lung Benefits Trust may also be paid into the Black Lung Disability Trust Fund[301] or into the general fund of the United States Treasury (other than in satisfaction of any tax or other civil or criminal liability of the person who established or contributed to the trust).

The income of a qualified Black Lung Benefits Trust is not taxable to the operator making contributions to it. Similarly, the trust's income is not taxable thereto, except that the trust is subject to tax on any unrelated business taxable income.[302] The trust must, however, file annual information returns with the IRS.[303]

The contributions by a coal mine operator to a Black Lung Benefits Trust are deductible by the operator for federal income tax purposes.[304] This provision imposes alternative limitations on the deductibility of such contributions for a tax year, based on actual benefit claims approved or filed during the taxable year as well as on the amount of anticipated liabilities for claims filed or expected to be filed in the future by past or present employees of the operator determined by using reasonable actuarial methods and assumptions, and any excess contributions may be taxable.[305] A contribution of property will be treated as a sale or exchange of the property for tax purposes, unless it is transferred without consideration and is not subject to a mortgage or similar lien.

A trust that is exempt under these rules is subject to prohibitions on self-

---

[297]Code § 501(c)(21)(A).

[298]Code § 501(c)(21)(B).

[299]As defined in Code § 581.

[300]As defined in the Federal Credit Union Act, 12 U. S. C. § 1752(b).

[301]See § 3 of the Black Lung Benefits Revenue Act of 1977, *supra*, n. 294.

[302]See Chapters 39–42.

[303]See Chapter 37. Although the exemption application and annual information returns of a Code § 501(c)(21) trust are subject to the public disclosure requirements (Code § 6104(a)(1), (b); see Chapter 38 § 5), disclosure is not required of confidential business information of a coal mine operator who establishes and contributes to such a trust (P. L. 95-488, 95th Cong., 2d Sess. (1978) § (e); H. Rep. No. 95-1656, 95th Cong., 2d Sess. (1978), at 6).

[304]Code § 192.

[305]See Code § 4953.

dealing[306] and the making of certain expenditures[307] (and is the only type of tax-exempt organization, other than a private foundation,[308] to be governed by such statutory restrictions). These prohibitions are similar to those imposed upon private foundations and are sanctioned by excise taxes upon the trust, its trustees, and/or the disqualified person(s) involved. The Senate Finance Committee has observed that the investment limitations imposed on these trusts "are intended to preclude speculative or other investments of corpus or income which might jeopardize the carrying out of the trust's exempt purposes and permit the [C]ommittee [which authored these provisions] to simplify the self-dealing restrictions and avoid the necessity of certain other restrictions to prevent potential abuses."[309]

§ 20.22   Multiemployer Pension Plan Trusts

Another type of tax-exempt organization, authorized by Code § 501(c)(22), is a trust established by the sponsors of a multiemployer pension plan as a vehicle to accumulate funds in order to provide withdrawal liability payments to the plan. This entity was added to the statutory enumeration of exempt organizations by enactment of the Multiemployer Pension Plan Amendments Act of 1980, legislation to improve retirement income security under private multiemployer pension plans.[310] The provisions are effective for tax years beginning after September 26, 1980.

§ 20.23   States, Political Subdivisions, Instrumentalities, Etc.

Still another type of tax-exempt entity is a state. This tax exemption derives not from any specific provision in the federal tax law, but is the result of the doctrine of intergovernmental immunity—the doctrine implicit in the U.S. Constitution that the federal government will not tax the states. The general principle is that "the United States may not tax instrumentalities which a state may employ in the discharge of her essential governmental duties."[311]

This tax exemption extends not only to the states but to integral parts thereof: "political subdivisions," "instrumentalities," "agencies," and the like. This tax exemption is also available to the District of Columbia and to any territory.

The constitutional basis for tax exemption or immunity is not unlimited;

---

[306]Code § 4951. Cf. Code § 4941.

[307]Code § 4952. Cf. Code § 4945.

[308]See Chapters 25 and 29.

[309]S. Rep. No. 95-336, *supra*, n. 295, at 14.

[310]P. L. 96-364, 96th Cong., 2d Sess. (1980).

[311]*Helvering v. Therrell*, 303 U. S. 218, 223 (1938). In general, see Tucker and Rombro, "State Immunity from Federal Taxation: The Need for Re-examination," 43 *Geo. Wash. L. Rev.* 501 (1975).

however, its scope has not been specifically delineated. The position of the U.S. Supreme Court was first that all "governmental" functions of a state were encompassed by the immunity and that only its "proprietary" activities could be taxed by the federal government.[312] Subsequently, the Supreme Court ruled that Congress could tax any "source of revenue by whomsoever earned and not uniquely capable of being earned only by a State," even though the tax "incidence falls also on a State."[313] Apparently, the "uniquely capable" test remains the standard.[314]

Notwithstanding the existence of a constitutional immunity, Congress in 1913 enacted a broader statutory immunity, which is manifested today in Code § 115. In its relevant portions,[315] this statutory immunity is available only for entities which exercise an "essential governmental function," and where the income thereby generated accrues to a state or political subdivision thereof. The IRS has long maintained that, by enacting the statutory immunity, "Congress did not desire in any way to restrict a State's participation in enterprises which might be useful in carrying out those projects desirable from the standpoint of the State Government . . ."[316]

The question thus becomes: what type of entity can avail itself of the broader immunity? Recent commentators write that only a state or political subdivision thereof, and not a private corporation, may invoke this immunity, because only the former can perform an essential governmental function.[317] The courts appear to have reached the same conclusion, albeit for a different reason, namely, on the theory that the interposition of a corporation operates to prevent the requisite "accrual" from taking place.[318] Such analyses, however, leave unanswered the question as to whether a corporation, such as a not-for-profit corporation, can qualify for tax purposes as a "political subdivision." The answer to this question has several ramifications, not the least of which is such an entity's ability to incur debt the interest on which is excludable from the recipient's gross income.[319]

In its narrowest sense, the term "political subdivision" connotes a jurisdictional or geographical component of a state, such as counties, cities, sewer districts, and so forth. Perhaps a more realistic definition of the term was provided by the U.S. Court of Appeals for the Second Circuit: The term "political subdivision" is broad and comprehensive and denotes any division of

---

[312]*South Carolina* v. *United States*, 199 U. S. 437 (1905).

[313]*New York* v. *United States*, 326 U. S. 572, 582 (1946).

[314]*Massachusetts* v. *United States*, 435 U. S. 444 (1978); *Willmette Park District* v. *Campbell*, 388 U. S. 411 (1949). Also *Flint* v. *Stone Tracy Co.*, 220 U. S. 107, 172 (1911).

[315]Code § 115(a)(1).

[316]G. C. M. 14407, XIV-1 C. B. 103.

[317]Tucker and Rombro, *supra*, n. 311 at 546–547.

[318]See, e.g., *Troy State University* v. *Commissioner*, 62 T. C. 493, 497 (1974).

[319]Code § 103.

the state made by the proper authorities thereof, acting within their constitutional powers, for the purpose of carrying out a portion of these functions of
the state which by long usage and the inherent necessities of government have
always been regarded as public.[320]

These considerations take on greater coloration when applied in the context
of organizations that are state-owned but have "charitable" counterparts, such
as state schools, colleges, universities, hospitals, and libraries.[321] Certainly these
entities are generally exempt from tax; the exemption derives in part, of course,
from the constitutional immunity accorded the revenue of integral units of
states; can the exemption be likewise traced to this statutory immunity? Presumably, there is the requisite "accrual"; the provision of education has been
regarded as the exercise of an essential governmental function.[322] By contrast,
courts have held that, under certain circumstances, operation of a hospital is
not an essential governmental function.[323] There is no case that specifically
holds that, for example, a state college or university is a "political subdivision,"
although such a conclusion may be reached by a process of negative implication.[324] However, the IRS has asserted that a state university cannot qualify as
a political subdivision because it fails to possess a substantial right to exercise
the power to tax, the power of eminent domain, or the police power.[325] This

[320]*Commissioner* v. *Shamburg's Estate*, 144 F.2d 998, 1005 (2d Cir. 1944), cert. den.
323 U. S. 792 (1944). Cf. Rev. Rul. 76-550, 1976-2 C. B. 331; Rev. Rul. 76-549, 1976-
2 C. B. 330. Also *Crilly* v. *Southeastern Pennsylvania Transportation Authority*, 529
F.2d 1355 (3d Cir. 1976); *Popkin* v. *New York State Health and Mental Hygiene Facilities
Improvement Corp.*, 409 F.Supp. 430 (S. D. N. Y. 1976).

[321]See Chapter 6.

[322]*Page* v. *Regents of University System of Georgia*, 93 F.2d 887 (5th Cir. 1937), rev.
on other grounds sub nom. *Allen* v. *Regents of the University System of Georgia*, 304
U. S. 339 (1938).

[323]*Liggett & Myers Tobacco Co.* v. *United States*, 13 F.Supp. 143 (Ct. Cl. 1936),
aff'd 299 U. S. 383 (1937), reh. den. 300 U. S. 686 (1937); *Cook* v. *United States*, 26
F.Supp. 253 (D. Mass. 1939). Cf. IRS Private Letter Ruling 7835065.

[324]*Troy State University* v. *Commissioner, supra*, n. 318; *Iowa State University of
Science and Technology* v. *United States*, 500 F.2d 508 (Ct. Cl. 1974).

[325]Rev. Rul. 77-165, 1977-1 C. B. 21. In an IRS National Office Technical Advice
Memorandum (Private Letter Ruling 8119061), the Service held that a state university
is not a political subdivision of the state (for purposes of eligibility for the interest
exclusion for the university's obligations) because the university possesses no more than
an insubstantial part of any sovereign power. The university does not have the power
to tax nor the power of eminent domain, and the Service concluded that the possession
of certain powers to promulgate and enforce regulations in the areas of health and safety
on the university's campus does not constitute the police power (citing *Manigault* v.
Springs, 119 U. S. 473 (1905); *Barbier* v. *Connelly*, 113 U. S. 27 (1885)). The IRS noted
that the campus police operate at the university under a scope of authority defined by
state law rather than by the university, and that the campus police have the power to
make arrests only for violations of the state's criminal law and not for violations of the
university's rules and regulations that are not criminal in nature. The university also

ruling does not mean that all state colleges and universities fail to constitute political subdivisions, as the IRS has privately ruled on a number of occasions that a state educational institution is a political subdivision because it posseses a substantial power of eminent domain and certain police powers.

All of this has certain related tax consequences. For example, a state college or university does not have to file an annual information return (Form 990), although no such exempton from the requirement may be found in the Code. This exemption is confirmed, however, by the fact that such an exception is provided in the regulations for state institutions that have a ruling granting them "charitable" status.[326] This regulation specifically invokes the statutory immunity in this context, referencing a "State institution, the income of which is excluded from gross income under [Code] section 115(a)."

Another consideration is the applicability of the tax on unrelated business income. Although state colleges and universities are generally tax-exempt, a special statutory provision[327] brings them within the ambit of the unrelated income tax. This statutory definition of a state college or university gives little comfort to those who contend that such an institution is a political subdivision: ". . . any college or university which is an agency or instrumentality of any government or any political subdivision thereof, or which is owned or operated by a government or any political subdivision thereof." Also, if a state college or university is a political subdivision of a state, one could posit a conflict between imposition of the unrelated income and the tax exclusion effected by the statutory immunity.

The IRS in 1979 issued a private ruling in an attempt to reconcile this conflict. The Service concluded that the provision applying the unrelated income tax should be interpreted to limit the applicability of the tax immunity in the case of governmental colleges and universities that have unrelated business taxable income, without regard to a business carried on primarily for their students,[328] rather than to supersede completely the applicability of the immunity in any case involving a governmental college or university. Thus, the Service decided that a governmental college or university deriving income from the exercise of an essentially governmental activity, with such income accruing to a state or political subdivision of a state, is doing so from the conduct of a related business. As a consequence of this interpretation, the IRS found that the doctrine of

---

failed with its argument that the interest on its obligations should be tax-excludable because the obligations were issued "on behalf of" the state (principally inasmuch as the university is a state instrumentality and a land grant institution), with the Service determining that the requisite degree of control by the state is absent, in that fewer than one-third of the university's board of trustees are government officials or appointees of the governor of the state (see Chapter 6 § 9, pp. 136–140). In general, see Henze, "State Universities As Political Subdivisions," 9 *J. Coll. & U.L.* 341 (1982–83).

[326]Reg. § 1.6033-2(g)(1)(v).

[327]Code § 511(a)(2)(B).

[328]See Code § 513(a)(2).

intergovernmental immunity does not bar the federal government from taxing income earned by a state university from the provision of hotel and utility services to the general public.[329] By contrast, the operation of a public airport by a state university was considered not to be an unrelated activity.[330]

Inasmuch as its tax exemption is not necessarily dependent upon a finding of the existence of a political subdivision, a state college, university, hospital, and the like will probably be more concerned about political subdivision status in the context of the exclusion of interest income,[331] where the feature of tax-exempt interest enhances the institution's borrowing capacity. Frequently, however, the state college or university is prohibited by state law from incurring debt; oftentimes, the borrowing for state higher education, health care, and the like is accomplished through "authorities" which themselves qualify as political subdivisions. Also, a state college or university may use one or more support organizations.[332]

The IRS has issued private rulings that such a support organization is a political subdivision for purposes of the interest exclusion. This presumably results from the fact that the support organizations are controlled by and wholly serve the state institutions.

Assuming that such a support organization is appropriately categorized as a political subdivision, can the organization find tax exemption pursuant to the statutory immunity rule? Since these organizations are not-for-profit corporations, the authorities discussed above indicate that they cannot exercise essential governmental functions and that revenue received by them does not accrue to the state. But this does not necessarily mean that such an organization cannot qualify as a political subdivision.

As regards the interest exclusion, however, the government once attempted to redefine the term "political subdivision" to exclude the private corporation from its purview. On February 2, 1976, the Department of the Treasury issued proposed regulations to provide that only a duly constituted authority of a state or local governmental unit may issue obligations the interest on which qualifies for the exclusion.[333] This regulation would supersede a number of revenue rulings which accorded political subdivision status to private corporations which incurred debt "on behalf of" a state or local governmental unit.

The types of nonprofit corporations that have been treated as political subdivisions by the IRS in the past are represented by four revenue rulings; these corporations would lose their political subdivision status under the proposed regulation.

In 1963,[334] the IRS allowed the interest exclusion for bonds issued by a

---

[329]IRS Private Letter Ruling 7904006.
[330]IRS Private Letter Ruling 7930043.
[331]Code § 103.
[332]Code § 170(b)(1)(A)(iv). See Chapter 22.
[333]Prop. Reg. § 1.103-1.
[334]Rev. Rul. 63-20, 1963-1 C. B. 24.

nonprofit corporation, formed to stimulate industrial development within a particular county. The IRS held that obligations of a nonprofit corporation organized pursuant to the general nonprofit corporation law of a state will be considered issued on behalf of the state or political subdivision thereof for purposes of the interest exclusion where each of the following requirements is met: (1) the corporation must engage in activities which are essentially public in nature, (2) the corporation must be one which is not organized for profit, (3) the corporate income must not inure to any private person, (4) the state or political subdivision thereof must have a beneficial interest in the corporation, and (5) the corporation must have been approved by the state or a political subdivision thereof.

In 1960,[335] the IRS allowed the interest exclusion with respect to the New York State Housing Finance Agency, a "public benefit corporation" established by statute. In favorably ruling in this instance, the Service noted the "substantial control which . . . [the State of New York] has over the management and operation of the agency."

In 1957,[336] the IRS allowed the interest exclusion with respect to "industrial development boards" established by the legislature of the state of Alabama. These boards are "public corporations" designed to promote industry and develop trade by inducing manufacturing, industrial, and commercial enterprises to locate in the state. The board of directors of each industrial development board is elected by the governing body of the municipality concerned; the obligations issued by the boards were considered to be issued on behalf of the particular municipality, a political subdivision of the state.

In 1973,[337] the IRS ruled that a "public corporation" established by the legislature of a state was a political subdivision for purposes of the interest exclusion. This entity, formed to acquire and administer a rapid transit system within several counties of the state, was governed by a board of directors appointed by the participating governmental bodies.

This proposed regulation thus represents an attempted abandonment by the government of its long-standing policy determination that, for tax purposes, private corporations can qualify as political subdivisions or otherwise act on behalf of a state. This rationale was expressed years ago by the IRS when it characterized the statutory immunity as applying to "that part of the income of a corporation engaged in the . . . performance of some governmental function which accrues to a State or municipality by virtue of its ownership of such corporation."[338]

---

[335]Rev. Rul. 60-248, 1960-2 C. B. 35.

[336]Rev. Rul. 57-187, 1957-1 C. B. 65. Also Rev. Rul. 54-106, 1954-1 C. B. 28.

[337]Rev. Rul. 73-563, 1973-2 C. B. 24.

[338]G. C. M. 14407, *supra*, n. 316. The federal tax law definition of the term "political subdivision" may be clarified by decisions of the U. S. Tax Court pursuant to the declaratory judgment procedure of Code § 7478 as enacted by the Revenue Act of 1978. The procedures for submission of requests for rulings involving Code §§ 103 and 7478 are described in Rev. Proc. 79-4, 1979-1 C. B. 483.

This concept of tax exemption for political entities has been extended to apply to Indian tribes, so that tax liability is not asserted against a tribe with respect to tribal income from activities carried on within the boundaries of the tribal reservation.[339] These tribes generally have governing instruments, a council, operational rules, a formal membership arrangement, and various governmental powers (such as the rights to levy taxes, enact ordinances, and maintain a police force).[340] The assets of an Indian tribe are owned by the tribe as a community (and not by the members) and the right to participate in the enjoyment of tribal property depends on continuing membership in the Indian tribe.[341] The fact that an Indian tribe is incorporated does not affect its tax-exempt status.[342]

§ 20.24 Retirement Plans

Code § 501(a) provides that "[a]n organization described in . . . [Code] section 401(a) shall be exempt from taxation under this subtitle . . ." Code § 401(a) defines the qualified trust fund which is part of a stock bonus, pension, or profit-sharing plan[343] of an employer for the exclusive benefit of his or her employees or their beneficiaries. While the fund is the tax-exempt organization, the principal focus of the law in this area is on the terms and conditions of the retirement plan.

The law of retirement plans was substantially modified by the Employee Retirement Income Security Act of 1974.[344] Government supervision of retirement plans is largely the responsibility of the IRS and the Department of Labor. The Act imposes requirements as respects employee participation, coverage, vesting of interests, funding, portability of benefits, fiduciary responsibility, prohibited transactions, preparation of plan summaries, and annual reporting and disclosure to the Department of Labor. The Pension Benefit Guaranty Corporation administers a program of plan termination insurance.

Pursuant to this Act, there has been established within the IRS an Office of Employee Plans and Exempt Organizations under the direction of an Assistant Commissioner of Internal Revenue. A Joint Pension Task Force is authorized to undertake studies in connection with continuing pension reform.

§ 20.25 Other Exempt Organizations

There are several other types of organizations or entities which may be regarded as "tax-exempt organizations" in the broadest sense of the term.

[339]*Mescalero Apache Tribe* v. *Jones*, 411 U. S. 145 (1973).
[340]Some Indian tribes are formally organized pursuant to the Indian Organization Act of 1934, 25 U. S. C. § 476.
[341]*Gritts* v. *Fisher*, 224 U. S. 640 (1912).
[342]*Maryland Casualty Co.* v. *Citizens National Bank of West Hollywood*, 361 F.2d 517 (5th Cir. 1966); *Parker Drilling Co.* v. *Metlakatla Indian Community*, 451 F.Supp. 1127 (D. Alas. 1978); Rev. Rul. 81-295, 1981-2 C. B. 15.
[343]See Reg. § 1.401-1(b)(1).
[344]P. L. 93-406, 93rd Cong., 2d Sess. (1974).

For example, federal law provides that property is held in trust by the United States for the benefit of certain Indian tribes and that the property held therein is exempt from federal taxation.[345] Similarly, property may be placed in a tax-exempt trust by Osage Indians.[346]

Some organizations are, as a matter of practice, tax exempt, not because of any specific grant of tax exemption but because of the ability to utilize sufficient deductions to effectively eliminate taxation. As noted, this is the principle on which the general "tax exemption" for cooperatives is premised.[347] Likewise, a pooled income fund[348] is generally a nontaxpaying entity because it is entitled to a deduction for distributions to beneficiaries and for long-term capital gain.[349] (By contrast, a charitable remainder annuity trust or unitrust[350] is an organization expressly exempt from tax except in years in which it has unrelated business taxable income.[351]) As discussed earlier, this approach will also provide "tax exemption" for perpetual care trust funds operated in conjunction with taxable cemeteries.[352]

Other entities achieve tax exemption because the law regards them as organizations which, while they may have to file tax returns, do not have taxable income but instead pass that liability on to others. It is this principle which operates to "exempt" partnerships[353] and small business ("Subchapter S") corporations[354] from federal taxation.

§ 20.26 Proposed Exempt Organizations

Proposals continue to abound for statutory authorization of new types of tax-exempt organizations. These proposals include the following:

1. Tax exemption for public utilities which furnish electrical power. S. 2213 (9975).

2. Same tax exemptions and other tax treatment to recognized Indian tribes as are available for governmental units. H.R. 8989 (1975); H. Rep. No. 94-1693 (1976).

---

[345]P. L. 95-498, 95th Cong., 2d Sess. (1978) § 6; P. L. 95-499, 95th Cong., 2d Sess. (1978) § 6.

[346]See P. L. 95-496, 95th Cong., 2d Sess. (1978) § 6.

[347]See Chapter 2.

[348]Code § 642(c)(5).

[349]See Reg. § 1.642(c)-5(a)(2).

[350]Code § 664.

[351]See Reg. § 1.664-1(c).

[352]Also see Code § 852(a) (concerning regulated investment companies).

[353]Code § 701.

[354]Code § 1372.

3. Tax exemption for a trust established by a taxpayer for the purpose of providing care for certain mentally incompetent relatives. H.R. 584 (1979); H.R. 10582 (1978); H. R. 3932 (1977); H.R. 9736 (1975).

4. Tax credit for contributions to "neighborhood corporations." S. 2192 (1975).

5. Tax exemption for certain nonprofit corporations all of the members of which are tax-exempt credit unions. H.R. 1153 (1977); H.R. 13532 (1976).

6. Tax exemption for certain nonprofit organizations operated for mutual purposes to provide reserve funds for and insurance of shares or deposits in certain credit unions and domestic building and loan associations. H.R. 14039 (1976); H.R. 6989 (1978).

7. Tax exemption for certain state and local government retirement systems. S. 1587 (1977); H.R. 9109 (1977).

8. Tax exemption for associations operated exclusively to provide workmen's compensation for state and local employees. H.R. 1074 (1979); H.R. 8470 (1977).

9. Tax exemption for a product liability self-insurance reserve trust. H.R. 394, 1677, 1678, 1947, 2341, 2693, 2926, 2935, 3252, 4729, and 6489 (1979–1980); H.R. 12471 (1978); H.R. 7711 (1977).

10. Tax exemption for certain organizations furnishing computer and fiscal management services to social service organizations. H.R. 7207 (1978).

11. Tax exemption for an Energy Company of America. H.R. 3885, 4649, and 5622 (1979).

12. Tax exemption for organizations of professionals. H.R. 990, 4724 (1979).

13. Tax exemption for professional liability insurance organizations. H.R. 4427 (1979).

PART IV

PRIVATE FOUNDATIONS

21

Introduction to Private Foundations

Private foundations have long been much-maligned entities, not only in the tax laws but in society at large. Their history, which is extensive, is rich with many successes and is strewn with far less abuses.[1] They are vehicles for some of the most humanitarian and progressive acts, yet whenever a list of tax "reforms" is compiled, private foundations seem to always attract much attention.

A private foundation is a unique breed of tax-exempt organization, in that while it is recognized as charitable, educational, or the like, it is usually controlled and supported by a single source, for example, one donor, a family, a company. This single characteristic, which the IRS has recognized as an indirect but nonetheless qualifying means of support of charity,[2] spawns several criticisms, including alleged irresponsive governance and inadequate responses to perceived needs. Private foundations are similarly chastized for being elitist, playthings of the wealthy, and havens of "do-gooders" assuaging their inner needs by dispensing beneficence to others.[3]

More serious criticisms of private foundations are that they further various tax inequities, are created for private rather than philanthropic purposes, and do not actually achieve charitable ends.[4] As will be developed in immediately subsequent chapters, nearly all of the abuses—perceived or otherwise—involving private foundations were eradicated as the result of enactment of the Tax Reform Act of 1969.

[1]See Wormser, *Foundations: Their Power and Influence* (1958); Andrews, *Philanthropic Foundations* (1956).

[2]Rev. Rul. 67–149, 1967-1 C. B. 133.

[3]See, e.g., Branch, "The Case Against Foundations," *The Washington Monthly* 3 (July, 1971).

[4]See, e.g., Stern, *The Great Treasury Raid* 242–246 (1964). Cf. Stern, *The Rape of the Taxpayer* (1973).

The origins of private foundations are traceable to the genesis of philanthropy itself. Foundations as legal entities were recognized in the Anglo-Saxon legal system and were fostered in the United States by the law of charitable trusts. Charitable endowments in America are essentially a creature of common law, although amply sustained in statutory laws concerning taxes, corporations, decedents' estates, trusts, and property.[5] The modern American foundation is of relatively recent vintage, dating back to the mid-nineteenth century. Many of the well-known foundations are reflective of the great fortunes established as of the advent of the 1900s. Foundations proliferated after World War II, in large part due to favorable economic conditions and tax incentives.

Foundations were not defined in the Internal Revenue Code (nor in any other federal statute) until 1969—though not because of lack of interest by Congress in them. They were investigated, for example, by the "Walsh Committee" (the Senate Industrial Relations Committee) in 1913–1915 for allegedly large stockholdings, by the "Cox Committee" (House Select Committee to Investigate and Study Educational and Philanthropic Foundations) in 1952, by Rep. B. Carroll Reece in 1954 (the House Special Committee to Investigate Tax-Exempt Foundations and Comparable Organizations) for alleged support of subversives, and by Rep. Wright Patman throughout the 1960s for allegedly tending more to private interests than public benefit. Patman's inquiries and others' culminated in the extensive foundation provisions of the Tax Reform Act of 1969,[6] which introduced the first statutory definition of the term "private foundation." Yet a more expressive definition is the following: ". . . a nongovernmental, nonprofit organization, with funds and program managed by its own trustees or directors, and established to maintain or aid social, educational, charitable, religious, or other activities serving the common welfare."[7]

Controversy persists over the appropriate role for foundations in America— or whether they should exist at all. Foundations are attacked by some as too uninvolved in current issues and problems, and by others as too effective in fomenting social change.[8] The federal government is now spending billions of dollars in the realms of health, education, and welfare—formerly the preserves of private philanthropy. Recent years have also borne witness to intensified drives for tax "reform," tax "equality," and tax "simplification." These and other

---

[5]See Fremont-Smith, *Foundations and Government* (1965), expecially Chapter 1.

[6]See Andrews, *Patman and Foundations; Review and Assessment* (1968); Myers, "Foundations and Tax Legislation," VI *Bull. of Found. Lib. Center* (No. 3) 51 (1965). Following a preliminary survey in 1961, Rep. Patman caused publication of "Tax Exempt Foundations and Charitable Trusts: Their Impact on Our Economy," Chairman's Report to (House) Select Committee on Small Business, First Installment, 87th Cong., 1st Sess. (1962). Six additional installments were published over the period 1963–1968.

[7]The Foundation Center, *The Foundation Directory*, Edition 4 vii (1971).

[8]See, e.g., Miller, "Are Foundations an Endangered Species?," *Reader's Digest* 191 (July, 1974); Yarmolinsky, "The Foundation as an Expression of the Democratic Society," 5 *N.Y.U. Conf. on Char. Fdns.* 65 (1961).

developments have made the tax treatment for private foundations and their donors even more vulnerable.

Notwithstanding a variety of antifoundation developments in the regulatory context, Congress and the executive branch of the federal govenment have, on occasion, affirmed their support for private foundations. For example, the Department of the Treasury has had this to say about the value of foundations:

> Private philanthropy plays a special vital role in our society. Beyond providing for areas into which government cannot or should not advance (such as religion), private philanthropic organizations can be uniquely qualified to initiate thought and action, experiment with new and untried ventures, dissent from prevailing attitudes, and act quickly and flexibly.

> Private foundations have an important part in this work. Available even to those of relatively restricted means, they enable individuals or small groups to establish new charitable endeavors and to express their own bents, concerns, and experience. In doing so, they enrich the pluralism of our social order. Equally important, because their funds are frequently free of commitment to specific operating programs, they can shift the focus of their interest and their financial support from one charitable area to another. They can, hence, constitute a powerful instrument for evolution, growth, and improvement in the shape and direction of charity.[9]

Private foundations are an integral component of a society that values individual responsibility and private efforts for the public good. One organization championing foundations advances the following rationale:

> . . . foundations have the particular characteristic of serving as sources of available capital for the private philanthropic service sector of our society in all its range and variety. They thus help make possible many useful public services that would in most cases otherwise have to be provided by tax monies. They offer "the other door on which to knock," without which many volunteer activities would not be initiated and others could not be continued. They are there to respond both to new ideas and shifting social needs with a freedom and flexibility that is not common to or easy for government agencies. Finally, as centers of independent thought and judgment in their own right, they help support freedom of thought, experimentation, and honest criticism directed at pressing needs of the society, including even the scrutiny and evaluation of governmental programs and policies. [10]

Nonetheless, the average person's view of private foundations is probably that as expressed by then-Sen. Vance Hartke, when he was Chairman of the Senate Subcommittee on Foundations: "There are many examples of private foundations in this country which do an excellent job, but they are outnumbered

[9]Treasury Department Report on Private Foundations, Committee on Finance, United States Senate, 89th Cong., 1st Sess. (1965), at 5 (also 11–13).

[10]Council on Foundations, *Report and Recommendations to the Commission on Private Philanthropy and Public Needs on Private Philanthropic Foundations*, I-8 (1974).

at least five to one by foundations which are failing to serve the public purpose adequately."[11]

Despite the stiff blows inflicted in 1969, private foundations continue. There are an estimated 23,000 grant-making private foundations in the United States, representing about $41.4 billion in assets. Approximately 15 percent of the foundations have assets of $1 million or more or made contributions of at least $100,000 annually. This category of foundation accounts for about 93 percent of the assets of all foundations in the United States and more than 89 percent of all foundation giving. There are 114 foundations with assets of $50 million and more, accounting for one-half of all foundation assets and 37 percent of all grants made by foundations in 1981. Total giving by America's private foundations in 1981 was about 2.62 billion, representing 4.9 percent of philanthropy in the United States in that year.[12]

Whatever the future holds for foundations,[13] the law presently governing them remains an essential topic for consideration as respects the law of tax-exempt organizations generally. Some of the concepts introduced in 1969, by which foundations are regulated far more stringently than are other charitable organizations, may be harbingers of laws to be enacted for all charitable organizations.[14]

In the meantime, as will be seen in subsequent chapters and as the U.S. Tax Court has observed, "classification as a private foundation is burdensome."[15]

---

[11]Speech entitled "Foundations at the Crossroads," reproduced at 121 *Cong. Rec.* 3035 (1975).

[12]American Association of Fund-Raising Counsel, *Giving USA* 17–21 (1982).

[13]See Iadarola and Brown, "The Private Foundation: Still Viable in the Post-1969 Era," 20 *National Public Accountant* (No. 2) 18 (1975); Hale, "How Firm a Foundation?," 60 *A.B.A.J.* 85 (1974); Heimann (ed.), *The Future of Foundations* (1973); Thrower, "Future of the Private Foundation—A Tax Analysis," 110 *Trust & Estates* 824 (1971); Grants, "Is the Small Foundation Viable?," 10 *N.Y.U. Conf. on Char. Fdns.* 273 (1971).

The House Subcommittee on Oversight, a unit of the House Committee on Ways and Means, is expected to open hearings sometime in 1983, to examine the impact of the existing law pertaining to private foundations on their continuing vitality.

[14]See Chapter 14; Morris, "Public Charities: Maintaining Their Favored Public Status," 11 *N.Y.U. Conf. on Char. Fdns.* 179 (1973); Troyer, "Public Charities and 1969 Act: A Look Ahead," 10 *N.Y.U. Conf. on Char. Fdns.* 109 (1971).

[15]*Friends of the Society of Servants of God* v. *Commissioner*, 75 T.C. 209 (1980). For more background on private foundations and the federal tax laws, see Southeastern Council of Foundations, *Why Establish a Private Foundation?* (1980); Pekkanen, "The Great Givers: Inside America's Top Foundations" (Part I), 133 *Town & Country* (No. 4996) 141 (Dec. 1979), (Part II) 134 *Town & Country* (No. 4997) 37 (Jan. 1980); Russell, *Giving and Taking: Across the Foundation Desk* (1977); Nason, *Trustees & The Future of Foundations* (1977); Lloyd, "Private foundations still a useful tool despite their potential for being taxed," 3 *Estate Planning* 106 (1976); Kennedy, "Financial Problems of Foundations Today," 12 *N.Y.U. Conf. on Char. Fdns.* 15 (1975); Stone, "The Charitable Foundation: Its Governance," 39 *Law and Contemporary Problems* 57 (1975); Worthy, "The Tax Reform Act of 1969: Consequences for Private Foundations," 39 *Law*

and Contemporary Problems 232 (1975); Wadsworth, "Private Foundations and the Tax Reform Act of 1969," 39 *Law and Contemporary Problems* 255 (1975); "Tax Information for Private Foundations and Foundation Managers," IRS Pub. 578 (rev. 1975); Smith and Chiechi, *Private Foundations: Before and After the Tax Reform Act of 1969* (1974); Bandy, "Survey of Foundation Advisors and Foundation Managers," 51 *Taxes* 4 (1973); Wagner, "Private foundations still have a place in planning to save taxes," 2 *Tax. for Lawyers* 38 (1973); Nielsen, *The Big Foundations* (1972); Guthery, "New Private Foundation Provisions," 58 *A.B.A.J.* 70 (1972); Hochberg and Stein, "Private foundations: A tour through the labyrinth created by the '69 act," 37 *J. Tax.* 49 (1972); Hochberg and Stein, "Classification as a private foundation has many tax ramifications," 37 *J. Tax.* 88 (1972); Lehrfeld, "Private foundations in post-1969 era: Have controls spawned new trend to orthodoxy?," 36 *J. Tax.* 292 (1972); Moore, "Private Foundations—Their Present Tax Status," 7 *Real Prop. Prob. & Tr. J.* 552 (1972); DeWind and Luey, "Some of the Things You Always Wanted to Know About Private Foundations," 24 *Tax Lawyer* (No. 3) 551 (1971); Weithorn (ed.), *Private Charitable Foundations* (1971); Note, "Private Foundations and the 1969 Tax Reform Act," 7 *Col. J. of Law and Soc. Prob.* 240 (1971); Hauser, "How Infirm a Foundation," 49 *Taxes* 750 (1971); Goulden, *The Money Givers* (1971); Goldstein and Sharpe, "Private Charitable Foundations After Tax Reform," 56 *A.B.A.J.* 447 (1970); Rudy, *The Foundations: Their Use and Abuse* (1970); Reeves (ed.), *Foundations Under Fire* (1970); Lehrfeld, Liles, and Middleditch, "Private Foundations," 23 *Tax Lawyer* 435 (1970); Eliasburg, "New law threatens private foundations: An analysis of the new restrictions," 32 *J. Tax.* 156 (1970); Eliasberg, "Tax Reform and Section 501 (c)(3)—The Private Foundation Goes Public," 4 *J. Bev. Hills Bar Assn.* (No. 2) 27 (1970); Kahn, "Regulation of Privately Supported Foundations—Some Anomalies," 4 *Indiana L. Rev.* 271 (1970); Backus, "The Private Foundation Faces the Tax Reform Act of 1969—What To Do," 16 *Prac. Lawyer* (No. 6) 13 (1970); Lundberg, *The Rich and the Super-Rich*, 382–432 (1968).

22

"Private Foundations" and "Public Charities"

Prior to enactment of the Tax Reform Act of 1969, there was no statutory definition of the term "private foundation." However, up to that time, a private foundation generally was recognized as a charitable organization to which contributions could be made which were deductible in an amount up to 20 percent of an individual donor's adjusted gross income, in contrast to contributions to churches, schools, hospitals, and other public charities, which were deductible to the extent of 30 percent the donor's of adjusted gross income.[1]

This 30 percent/20 percent distinction was introduced in the federal tax law in 1964. Before that, it was not until 1954 that Congress acted in recognition of the fact that there are distinctive differences in the nature of charitable organizations. In that year, Congress permitted an extra ten percent deduction (from 20 to 30 percent) for contributions to operating educational institutions, churches, and hospitals, and enacted other provisions in their favor. In 1964, the privileged class of "30 percent organizations" was expanded to include other public and publicly supported organizations and a five-year carryover of excess contributions was added for gifts to these organizations.

By the mid-1960s, the likelihood that alleged private foundation abuses would eventually result in statutory modifications was on the increase. A Treasury Department Report on Private Foundations, issued in 1965, emphasized the view that there was a need for more public involvement in the operation of philanthropic institutions that benefit from preferential treatment under the tax laws. Failing such direct public involvement, the Treasury Report stated that there must be an assurance through other means (namely, governmental regulation) that funds set aside for appropriate charitable purposes will find their way promptly into the hands of those institutions where there is assurance of public control and operation.

[1]Code § 170(b)(1) (pre-1969 Act).

Congress, having become convinced that there were problems concerning charitable organizations that needed remedy, believed that these problems were especially prevalent in the case of organizations in the 20 percent deduction category. On the other hand, it was also apparent that certain organizations in the 30 percent deduction group were not involved in these problems. Consequently, in enacting a definition of the term "private foundation," Congress conjured up a statute which provides that a private foundation is any domestic or foreign charitable organization, other than four categories of organizations.[2] The classification of the organizations which are deemed not to be private foundations—and hence are "public charities"—is the subject of Code § 509(a).

The organizations which fall into the categories of Code § 590(a)(1), (2), or (3) are those which either have broad public support or actively function in a supporting relationship to public charities.[3] The fourth category of nonprivate foundation is the organization organized and operated exclusively for testing for public safety, as described in Code § 509(a)(4). Contributions to public safety testing organizations are not deductible and therefore, according to the 1965 Treasury Report, they are more analogous to business leagues, social welfare organizations, and similar tax-exempt groups than to private foundations.

§ 22.1   "Public" Institutions

Organizations which are deemed not to be private foundations by reason of Code § 509(a)(1) are essentially those in the old 30-percent deduction category.[4] These organizations, that may be termed the "public" institutions, are described in Code §§ 170(b)(1)(A)(i) through (v). Other organizations in other categories of nonprivate foundation status may also have the attributes of "institutions" but the entities in the "public" institution classification are those that are there because they satisfy—per se—the requirements of at least one category of "public" institution.

Churches

A "church or a convention or association of churches" is a public charity.[5] These entities have been discussed in the analysis of religious organizations.[6]

The IRS has ruled that an exempt organization, the membership of which is comprised of churches of different denominations, qualifies as an association of churches.[7]

[2]See Reg. §§ 1.509(d)-1, 1.509(e)-1.
[3]Reg. § 1.509(a)-1.
[4]See Reg. §§ 1.170A-9(a)(3), 1.509(a)-2.
[5]Code § 170(b)(1)(A)(i); Reg. § 1.170A-9(a).
[6]See Chapter 8.
[7]Rev. Rul. 74-224, 1974-1 C. B. 61.

Educational Organizations

An "educational organization which normally maintains a regular faculty and curriculum and normally has a regularly enrolled body of pupils or students in attendance at the place where its educational activities are regularly carried on" is a public charity.[8] This type of organization must have as its primary function the presentation of formal instruction.[9] Thus, an organization that has as its primary function the presentation of formal instruction, has courses that are interrelated and given in a regular and continuous manner (thereby constituting a regular curriculum), normally maintains a regular faculty, and has a regularly enrolled student body in attendance at the place where its educational activities are regularly carried on, qualifies as a "public" educational institution.[10]

It is pursuant to these rules that institutions such as primary, secondary, preparatory, high schools, and colleges and universities, that are tax exempt as "educational" entities, derive public charity status. (For purposes of the charitable contribution deduction and nonprivate foundation status, these organizations also encompass federal, state, and other publicly supported schools which otherwise qualify, although their tax exemption may be a function of their status as state instrumentalities.) However, an organization may not achieve public charity status as an operating education institution where it is engaged in both educational and noneducational activities (for example, a museum operating a school), unless the latter activities are merely incidental to the former.[11] Thus, the IRS denied public charity status to an organization the primary function of which was not the presentation of formal instruction but the maintenance and operation of a museum.[12]

An organization may be regarded as presenting formal instruction even though it lacks a formal course program or formal classroom instruction. Thus, an organization that provides elementary education on a full-time basis to children at a facility maintained exclusively for that purpose, with a faculty and enrolled student body, is a public charity despite the absence of a formal course program.[13] Similarly, an organization that conducts a survival course was granted public charity classification, although its course periods were only 26 days and it used outdoor facilities more than classrooms, since it had a regular curriculum, faculty, and student body.[14] By contrast, an exempt organization, the primary

---

[8] Code § 170(b)(1)(A)(ii).

[9] Reg. § 1.170A-9(b).

[10] Rev. Rul. 78-309, 1978-2 C. B. 123.

[11] Reg. § 1.170A-9(b).

[12] Rev. Rul. 76-167, 1976-1 C. B. 329.

[13] Rev. Rul. 72-430, 1972-2 C. B. 105.

[14] Rev. Rul. 73-434, 1973-2 C. B. 71. Also see Rev. Rul. 79-130, 1979-1 C. B. 332; Rev. Rul. 73-543, 1973-2 C. B. 343; Rev. Rul. 75-215, 1975-1 C. B. 335; Rev. Rul. 72-101, 1972-1 C. B. 144; Rev. Rul. 69-492, 1969-2 C. B. 36; Rev. Rul. 68-175, 1968-1 C. B. 83; IRS Private Letter Ruling 7926119.

activity of which was providing specialized instruction by correspondence and a five- to ten-day seminar program of personal instruction for students who have completed the correspondence course, was ruled not to be an operating educational organization "[s]ince the organization's primary activity consists of providing instruction by correspondence."[15] In another instance, tutoring on a one-to-one basis in the students' homes was ruled insufficient to make the tutoring organization an operating entity.[16]

The fact that an otherwise qualifying organization offers a variety of lectures, workshops, and short courses concerning a general subject area, open to the general public and to its members, is not sufficient for it to acquire nonprivate foundation status as an educational institution.[17] This because such an "optional, heterogeneous collection of courses is not formal instruction" and does not constitute a "curriculum."[18] Where the attendees are members of the general public and can attend the functions on an optional basis, there is no "regularly enrolled body of pupils or students."[19] Further, where the functions are led by various invited authorities and personalities in the field, there is no "regular faculty."[20]

Medical Care and Research Organizations

An "organization the principal purpose or functions of which are the providing of medical or hospital care or medical education or medical research, if the organization is a hospital," is a public charity.[21]

The general criteria for an exempt hospital have been discussed previously.[22] For these purposes, the term "hospital" includes federal hospitals, state, county, and municipal hospitals which are instrumentalities of governmental units, rehabilitation institutions, outpatient clinics, extended care facilities, or community mental health or drug treatment centers, and cooperative hospital service organizations,[23] if they otherwise qualify. However, the term does not include convalescent homes, homes for children or the aged, or institutions the principal purpose or function of which is to train handicapped individuals to puruse a vocation,[24] nor does it include free clinics for animals.[25]

For these purposes, the term "medical care" includes the treatment of any

---

[15]Rev. Rul. 75-492, 1975-2 C. B. 80.
[16]Rev. Rul. 76-384, 1976-2 C. B. 57. Also see Rev. Rul. 76-417, 1976-2 C. B. 58.
[17]Rev. Rul. 78-82, 1978-1 C. B. 70.
[18]See Rev. Rul. 62-23, 1962-1 C. B. 200.
[19]See Rev. Rul. 64-128, 1964-1 (Part I) C. B. 191.
[20]Rev. Rul. 78-82, *supra*, n. 17.
[21]Code § 170(b)(1)(A)(iii).
[22]See Chapter 6. In general, see Bromberg, "Tax Problems of Nonprofit Hospitals," 47 *Taxes* 524 (1969).
[23]See Chapter 10. Cf. Rev. Rul. 76-452, 1976-2 C. B. 60.
[24]Reg. § 1.170A-9(c)(1).
[25]Rev. Rul. 74-572, 1974-2 C. B. 82.

physical or mental disability or condition, whether on an inpatient or outpatient basis, provided the cost of the treatment is deductible[26] by the person treated.[27]

A public charity is also an organization which is a "medical research organization directly engaged in the continuous active conduct of medical research in conjunction with a hospital."" Medical research" means the conduct of investigations, experiments, and studies to discover, develop, or verify knowledge relating to the causes, diagnosis, treatment, prevention, or control of physical or mental diseases and impairments of man. To qualify, the organization must have the appropriate equipment and professional personnel necessary to carry out its principal function.[28] Medical research encompasses the associated disciplines spanning the biological, social, and behavioral sciences.

The organization must have the conduct of medical research as its principal purpose or function[29] and be primarily engaged in the continuous active conduct of medical research in conjunction with a hospital, which itself is a public charity. The organization need not be formally affiliated with a hospital to be considered primarily engaged in the active conduct of medical research in conjunction with a hospital. However, there must be a joint effort on the part of the research organization and the hospital pursuant to an understanding that the two organizations will maintain continuing close cooperation in the active conduct of medical research.[30] An organization will not be considered to be "primarily engaged directly in the continuous active conduct of medical research" unless it, during the applicable computation period,[31] devotes more than one-half of its assets to the continuous active conduct of medical research or it expends funds equaling at least 3.5 percent of the fair market value of its endowment for the continuous active conduct of medical research.[32] If the organization's primary purpose is to disburse funds to other organizations for the conduct of research by them or to extend research grants or scholarships to others, it is not considered directly engaged in the active conduct of medical research.[33]

---

[26]Code § 213.

[27]Reg. § 1.170A-9(c)(1).

[28]Reg. § 1.170A-9(c)(2)(iii).

[29]See Reg. § 1.170A-9(c)(2)(iv).

[30]Reg. § 1.170A-9(c)(2)(vii).

[31]See Reg. § 1.170A-9(c)(2)(vi)(a).

[32]Reg. § 1.170A-9(c)(2)(v)(b).

[33]Reg. § 1.170A-9(c)(2)(v)(c). For purposes of the charitable contribution deduction, the organization must be committed, during the calendar year in which the contribution is made, to expend the contribution for medical research before January 1 of the fifth calendar year which begins after the date the contribution is made. See Reg. § 1.170A-9(c)(2)(ii), (viii). In general, see Eaton, "Tax problems of medical organizations: An examination, diagnosis and prognosis," 24 J. Tax. 102 (1966). Undoubtedly the most generally well-known of the medical research organizations is the Howard Hughes Medical Institute, which was accorded public charity status as the result of publication in 1976 of regulations under Code § 170(b)(1)(A)(iii). Within two months of publication of the regulations, Howard Hughes died, reportedly leaving most of his wealth to the Institute.

Supporting Foundations

Public charity status is provided for certain organizations providing support for public colleges and universities.[34] These entities are quite useful in attracting private giving for these institutions, with the gifts not subject to the direction of the particular state legislature.

Specifically, the organization must normally receive a substantial part of its support (exclusive of income received in the exercise or performance of its exempt activities) from the United States or from direct or indirect contributions from the general public. It must be organized and operated exclusively to receive, hold, invest, and administer property and to make expenditures to or for the benefit of a college or university (including a land grant college or university) which is a public charity and which is an agency or instrumentality of a state or political subdivision thereof, or which is owned or operated by a state or political subdivision thereof or by an agency or instrumentality of one or more states or political subdivisions.

These expenditures include those made for any one or more of the regular functions of colleges and universities, such as the acquisition and maintenance of real property comprising part of the campus area; the erection of college or university buildings; the acquisition and maintenance of equipment and furnishings used for, or in conjunction with, regular functions of colleges and universities; or expenditures for scholarships, libraries, and student loans.[35]

Another frequently important feature of the state college or university related foundation is its ability to borrow money for or on behalf of the supported institution, with the indebtedness bearing tax-excludable interest.[36]

Governmental Units

A governmental unit is a public charity.[37] A "governmental unit" is defined to include a state, a possession of the United States, or any political subdivision of either of the foregoing, or the United States or the District of Columbia.[38]

The term "governmental unit" presumably encompasses not only "political subdivisions" of states and the like but also government "instrumentalities," "agencies," and entities referenced by similar terms. These have been discussed previously.[39] The distinction between a "political subdivision" and "instrumentality" was made by the IRS in 1975, when it observed that a county is a political subdivision of a state and that an association of counties is a "wholly-

---

[34]Code § 170(b)(1)(A)(iv).

[35]Reg. § 1.170A-9(b)(2).

[36]Code § 103. Regulations proposed in 1976 would have placed this function by a Code § 170(b)(1)(A)(iv) organization in serious jeopardy. Prop. Reg. § 1.103-1.

[37]Code § 170(b)(1)(A)(v); Reg. § 1.170A-9(d).

[38]Code § 170(c)(1).

[39]See Chapters 6, 20.

owned instrumentality" of the counties,[40] on the basis of criteria promulgated in 1957.[41]

§ 22.2   Publicly Supported Organizations—Type I

General Rules

An organization is not a private foundation if it is a charitable entity[42] which "normally receives a substantial part of its support" (other than income from an exempt function) from a governmental unit[43] or from direct or indirect contributions from the general public.[44]

Organizations which qualify as "Type I" publicly supported entities generally are publicly or governmentally supported museums of history, art, or science, libraries, community centers to promote the arts, organizations providing facilities for the support of an opera, symphony orchestra, ballet, or repertory drama, or for some other direct service to the general public, and organizations such as the American Red Cross or the United Givers Fund.[45]

One way for an organization to achieve nonprivate foundation status under these rules is for it to normally derive at least one-third of its support from qualifying public and/or governmental sources.[46] Thus, an organization qualifying as a public entity under these rules must maintain a support fraction, the denominator of which is total eligible support and the numerator of which is the amount of support from eligible public and/or governmental sources.

In computing the eligible amount of public support (the numerator of the fraction), contributions from individuals, trusts, or corporations constitute public support to the extent that the total amount of contributions from any donor during the computation period does not exceed an amount equal to two percent of the organization's total support for the period.[47] Therefore, the total amount of support by a donor is included in full in the denominator of the support fraction and the amount determined by application of the two percent limitation is included in the numerator of the support fraction. The latter amount is the

[40]Rev. Rul. 75-359, 1975-2 C. B. 79.

[41]Rev. Rul. 57-128, 1957-1 C. B. 311.

[42]Code § 170(c)(2).

[43]Code § 170(c)(1).

[44]Code § 170(b)(1)(A)(vi). The U.S. Tax Court, faced with interpreting the regulations accompanying Code § 170(b)(1)(A)(vi), found them "almost frighteningly complex and technical." *Friends of the Society of Servants of God v. Commissioner*, 75 T.C. 209, 213 (1980).

[45]Reg. § 1.170(A)-9(e)(1)(ii). An organization otherwise qualifying as a public institution (see § 1, *supra*) may nonetheless qualify under Code § 170(b)(1)(A)(vi). Rev. Rul. 76-416, 1976-2 C. B. 57.

[46]Reg. § 1.170A-9(e)(2).

[47]Reg. § 1.170A-9(e)(6)(i). For example, Rev. Rul. 77-255, 1977-2 C. B. 74.

amount of support in the form of direct or indirect contributions from the general public. Donors who stand in a defined relationship to one another[48] must share a single two percent limitation. For example, the IRS ruled that contributions made by a business league[49] to a charitable organization seeking designation as a "Type I" publicly supported entity are subject to this two percent limitation.[50]

However, this two percent limitation does not generally apply to support received from other publicly supported organizations[51] nor to support from governmental units[52]—that is, this type of support is, in its entirety, public support.[53] Because an organization can be classified as not being a private foundation (such as by being a "public institution"), pursuant to a categorization other than a "Type I" publicly supported organization, and nonetheless meet the requirements of a "Type I" publicly supported organization,[54] this two percent limitation does not apply with respect to contributions from these organizations. For example, the limitation does not apply to support from a church, since "[i]n general, churches derive substantial amounts of their support from the general public" and, therefore, the contributions from a church are considered indirect public support.[55] Assistance from a foreign government may be considered allowable support in determining an organization's qualifications as a Type I publicly supported entity.[56]

Nonetheless, the two percent limitation will apply with respect to support received from a publicly supported charitable organization or governmental unit if the support represents an amount that was expressly or impliedly earmarked by a donor to the publicly supported organization or unit of government as being for or for the benefit of the organization asserting status as a publicly supported charitable organization.[57]

A matter that can be of considerable significance in enabling a charitable organization to qualify as a publicly supported organization is the meaning of the term "support." For this purpose, the term "support" means amounts received as gifts, grants, contributions, membership fees, net income from unrelated business activities, gross investment income,[58] tax revenues levied for the benefit of the organization and either paid to or expended on behalf of

---

[48]See Code § 4946(a)(1).

[49]See Chapter 18.

[50]Rev. Rul. 77-255, *supra*, n. 47.

[51]For this purpose, a publicly supported organization is one described in Code § 170(b)(1)(A)(vi) ("Type I").

[52]Code § 170(c)(1).

[53]Reg. § 1.170A-9(e)(6)(i).

[54]See Rev. Rul. 76-416, *supra*, n. 45.

[55]Rev. Rul. 78-95, 1978-1 C. B. 71.

[56]Rev. Rul. 75-435, 1975-2 C. B. 215.

[57]Reg. § 1.170A-9(e)(6)(v).

[58]Code § 509(e).

the organization, and the value of services or facilities (exclusive of services or facilities generally furnished to the public without charge) furnished by a governmental unit to the organization without charge.[59] All of the foregoing items are amounts that, if received by the organization, comprise the denominator of the support fraction.

In constructing the support fraction, an org.   exclude from both the numerator and the denominator of the supp.rt   n amounts received from the exercise or performance of its exempt purpose or function and contributions of services for which a deduction is not allowable.[60] However, an organization will not be treated as meeting the support test if it receives almost all of its support from gross receipts from related activities and an insignificant amount of its support from governmental units and the general public.[61] Also, the organization may exclude from both the numerator and the denominator of the support fraction an amount equal to one or more qualifying "unusual grants."[62]

In computing the support fraction, review must be made of the organization's support "normally" received. This means that the organization must meet the one-third support test for a period encompassing the four tax years immediately preceding the year involved, on an aggregate basis. Where this is done, the organization will be considered as meeting the one-third support test for its current tax year and for the tax year immediately succeeding its current tax year.[63]

There are several issues that can arise in computing the public support component (the numerator) of the support fraction, including (1) whether or not a contribution or grant is from a qualifying publicly supported charity,[64] (2) whether or not a contribution or grant from a qualifying publicly supported charity or governmental unit is a pass-through transfer from another donor or grantor,[65] (3) whether or not a receipt is a membership fee rather than revenue from a related activity,[66] (4) whether or not a payment pursuant to a government contract is support from a governmental unit rather than revenue from a related

[59]Code § 509(d); Reg. § 1.170A-9(e)(7)(i).

[60]Reg. § 1.170A-9(e)(7)(i).

[61]Reg. § 1.170A-9(e)(7)(ii).

[62]Reg. § 1.170A-9(e)(6)(ii), (iii). For example, Rev. Rul. 76-440, 1976-2 C. B. 58.

[63]Reg. § 1.170A-9(e)(4)(i).

[64]Code § 170(b)(1)(A)(vi) ("Type I").

[65]See Chapter 23 § 2.

[66]Reg. § 1.170A-9(e)(7)(iii). See, e.g., *The Home for Aged Men* v. *United States*, 80-2 U.S.T.C. ¶9711 (N.D.W.Va. 1980), where the court found that funds provided to a home for the aged by new admittees are not "membership fees" but are items constituting "exempt function income," with the result that the organization was determined to be a private foundation.

activity,[67] or (5) whether or not an organization is primarily dependent upon gross receipts from related activities.[68]

The foregoing rules may be illustrated by assuming a charitable organization that in one tax year received support totaling $100,000 as follows:

	Total Support	Amounts in Numerator	Amounts in Denominator
Public charity grant	$ 15,000	$15,000	$15,000
Receipts from performance of related services	15,000		
General public gifts	20,000	20,000	20,000
Gifts over 2% limitation	35,000		35,000
Gross investment income	15,000		15,000
Totals	$100,000	$35,000	$85,000

The numerator of the support fraction is $35,000 and the denominator of the fraction is $85,000; therefore, the organization meets the 33⅓ percent-of-support requirement for that year (although, as discussed, the requirement generally must be met over a four-year period).

[67] Reg. § 1.170A-9(e)(8). An amount paid by a governmental unit to an organization is not regarded as received from the exercise or performance of its tax-exempt functions (and thus can qualify as eligible "support") if the purpose of the payment is primarily to enable the organization to provide a service to the direct benefit of the public rather than to serve the direct and immediate needs of the payor. Reg. § 1.170A-9(e)(8)(ii). In application of this rule, the IRS determined that payments by the U.S. Department of Health and Human Services to a professional standards review organization are not excludable "gross receipts" but are includible "support," thus enabling the organization to be classified as an entity described in Code § 170(b)(1)(A)(vi). Rev. Rul. 81-276, 1981-2 C. B. 128.

[68] Reg. § 1.170A-9(e)(7)(ii). One of the similarities between a "Type I" publicly supported organization and a state-university related "foundation" (see § 1, supra) is that both must normally receive a substantial part of its support from governmental sources and/or contributions from the general public. However, there is a difference as respects the measurement of allowable governmental support. For purposes of publicly supported organizations (Code § 170(b)(1)(A)(vi)), governmental sources are a state, a U.S. possession, a political subdivision of the foregoing, or the U.S. or the District of Columbia (Code § 170(c)(1)), while for purposes of the state-university related "foundation" (Code § 170(b)(1)(A)(iv)), governmental sources are the U.S. or a state, or any political subdivision thereof. Thus, the sources of qualifying government support for a Code § 170(b)(1)(a)(vi) entity are broader than those for a Code § 170(b)(1)(A)(iv) organization. Rev. Rul. 82-132, 1982-27 I.R.B. 10.

In making these computations, care must be taken in a situation where the organization being evaluated under these rules previously had to make changes in its operations to qualify as a "charitable" entity. The position of the IRS is that the rules which require, as discussed, a determination of the extent of broad public financial support in prior years, "presuppose" that the organization was organized and operated exclusively for charitable purposes and otherwise qualified as a "charitable" entity during those years. Consequently, support received by an organization in these circumstances in one or more years in which it failed to meet the requirements for a "charitable" entity cannot be considered in ascertaining its status as a publicly supported charitable organization.[69]

This ruling seems inconsistent with congressional intent in enacting the definition of the term "private foundation." For example, the last sentence of that section permits a supporting organization[70] to so qualify by reference to the public support of an organization that is tax-exempt by reason of being other than a "charitable" organization.[71] For example, an organization that failed to qualify as a "charitable" entity for one year because it ran afoul of the prohibitions on legislative or political activities[72] but nonetheless had broad public support in that year, and subsequently abandoned the disqualifying activity, should still be able to utilize that year for purposes of qualifying as a publicly supported charitable organization.

"Facts and Circumstances" Test

Notwithstanding all of the foregoing, an organization may qualify as a publicly supported organization—where it cannot satisfy the one-third requirement—by meeting a "facts and circumstances" test, as long as the amount normally received from governmental and/or public sources is "substantial."[73] To meet this test, the organization must demonstrate the existence of three elements: (1) the total amount of governmental and public support normally received by the organization is at least ten percent of its total support normally received, (2) the organization has a continuous and bona fide program for solicitation of funds from the general public, governmental units, or public charities, and (3)

---

[69]Rev. Rul. 77-116, 1977-1 C.B. 155. The IRS likewise asserts that support received by an organization prior to the date of the filing of its application for recognition of tax exemption, where the application was filed after the fifteen-month period (see Chapter 37) cannot be used in ascertaining public charity status. Rev. Rul. 77-469, 1977-2 C.B. 196; Rev. Rul. 77-208, 1977-1 C.B. 153.

[70]See § 4 hereof, *infra*.

[71]*Ibid*.

[72]See Chapters 13 and 14.

[73]Reg. § 1.170A-9(e)(3). For an illustration of an organization which failed both the general rules and the facts and circumstances test, see *Collins* v. *Commissioner*, 61 T.C. 693 (1974).

all other pertinent facts and circumstances, including the percentage of its support from governmental and public sources, the "public" nature of the organization's governing board, the extent to which its facilities or programs are publicly available, its membership dues rates, and whether its activities are likely to appeal to persons having some broad common interest or purpose.[74] (The higher the percentage of support from public or governmental sources, the lesser is the burden of establishing the publicly supported nature of the organization through the other factors—and the converse is also true.)

Concerning the governing board factor, the organization's nonprivate foundation status will be enhanced where it has a governing body which represents the interests of the public, rather than the personal or private interests of a limited number of donors. This can be accomplished by the election of board members by a broadly based membership or otherwise by having the board comprised of public officials, persons having particular expertise in the field or discipline involved, community leaders, and the like.

As noted, one of the important elements of the facts and circumstances test is the availability of public facilities or services. Examples of entities meeting this requirement are a museum that holds its building open to the public, a symphony orchestra that gives public performances, a conservation organization that provides educational services to the public through the distribution of educational materials, and an old age home that provides domiciliary or nursing services for members of the general public.[75]

Community Trusts

A community trust (or community "foundation") may qualify as a public charity if it attracts, receives, and depends on financial support from members of the general public on a regular, recurring basis. Community foundations are designed primarily to attract large contributions of a capital or endowment nature from a small number of donors. They are generally identified with a particular community or area and are controlled by a representative group of persons from that community or area. Individual donors relinquish control over the investment and distribution of their contributions and the income therefrom, although donors may designate the purposes for which the assets are to be used, subject to change by the governing body of the community trust.[76] A community foundation may establish public charity status in accordance with the general requirements of the foregoing rules.[77] Failing that, it may still be

[74]Reg. § 1.170A-9(e)(3).
[75]The "reliance" rules (see § 7, infra) for "Type I" publicly supported organizations are in Reg. §§ 1.170A-9(e)(4)(v), 1.170A-9(e)(6)(iv).
[76]Reg. § 1.170A-9(e)(10)(i).
[77]Code § 170(b)(1)(A)(vi); Reg. § 1.170A-9(e)(1)-(9).

treated as publicly supported if it meets the support test, the structural test, the administration test, and the distribution test of the regulations.[78]

The support test sets limitations on the amount of contributions, gifts, and grants a community foundation may receive from one person, or two or three persons, as of the close of varying periods, and requires a bona fide continuous program of solicitation for new and additional gifts and bequests from a wide range of potential donors in the community it serves.[79] The structural test requires the community foundation to be recognized as a capital or endowment fund for charity, contains organizational and operational requirements, defines the composition of the governing body, requires a public annual financial report, and applies the self-dealing rules,[80] the expenditure responsibility rules,[81] and the excess business holdings rules,[82] with additional requirements.[83] The administration test states the required administration of gifts and bequests and investment of funds, imposes fiduciary responsibilities, and requires the existence of certain authority in the governing body.[84] The distribution test contains a payout requirement,[85] requires flexibility as to the fulfillment of specified charitable purposes, and mandates an absence of donor restrictions as respects at least one-half of the foundation's total income available for distribution each year.[86]

Grantors, contributors, and distributors to community trusts may rely on the public charity status of such trusts under circumstances that are the same as those applicable to reliance in the case of other categories of public charities[87] or of private operating foundations.[88]

§ 22.3   Publicly Supported Organizations—Type II

An organization is not a private foundation if it is a charitable entity[89] that is broadly, publicly supported and thus is responsive to the general public,

---

[78]Reg. § 1.170A-9(e).

[79]Reg. § 1.170A-9(e)(11). The support test involves, in part, certain requirements concerning governing instrument provisions and governing body resolutions. Examples of these provisions and resolutions appear in Rev. Rul. 77-333, 1977-2 C.B. 75, and Rev. Rul. 77-334, 1977-2 C.B. 77, respectively.

[80]See Chapter 26.

[81]See Chapter 30.

[82]See Chapter 28.

[83]Reg. § 1.170A-9(e)(12).

[84]Reg. § 1.170A-9(e)(13).

[85]See Chapter 27.

[86]Reg. § 1.170A-9(e)(14).

[87]See 7, *infra*.

[88]See Chapter 24 § 1. The reliance rule for community trusts appears at Reg. § 1.508-1(b)(4)(i). See Rev. Proc. 77-20, 1977-1 C. B. 585. In general, see Struckhoff, *The Handbook For Community Foundations: Their Formation, Development, and Operation* (1977).

[89]Code § 170(c)(2).

rather than to the private interests of a limited number of donors or other persons.[90]

Support Test

For an organization to achieve nonprivate foundation status under these rules, it must normally receive more than one-third of its support from any combination of (1) gifts, grants, contributions, or membership fees[91] and (2) gross receipts from admissions, sales of merchandise, performance of services, or furnishings of facilities in activities related to its tax-exempt function,[92] subject to certain limitations,[93] as long as the support in either category is from so-called "permitted sources." Thus, an organization seeking to qualify under this one-third support test must construct a "support fraction," with the amount of support received from these two sources constituting the numerator of the fraction and the total amount of support received being the denominator.[94] "Permitted sources" are governmental units,[95] certain public and publicly supported organizations,[96] and persons other than disqualified persons[97] with respect to the organization.

The term "support"[98] means (in addition to the two categories of "public" support referenced above) (1) net income from unrelated business activities, (2) gross investment income,[99] (3) tax revenues levied for the benefit of the organization and either paid to or expended on behalf of the organization, and (4) the value of services or facilities (exclusive of services or facilities generally furnished to the public without charge) furnished by a governmental unit to the organization without charge. The term does not include any gain from the disposition of property which would be considered as gain from the sale or exchange of a capital asset, or the value of exemption from any federal, state, or local tax or any similar benefit.[100] These six items of "support" are combined to constitute the denominator of the "support fraction."

[90]Code § 509(a)(2); Reg. § 1.509(a)-3(a)(4).
[91]Code § 509(a)(2)(A)(i).
[92]Code § 509(a)(2)(A)(ii). See, e.g., IRS Private Letter Ruling 7948113, holding that income from the operation of a post-season all-star college football game constitutes Code § 509(a)(2)(A)(ii) support.
[93]See text accompanying ns. 126-130, *infra*.
[94]Code § 509(a)(2)(A); Reg. § 1.509(a)-3(a)(2).
[95]Code § 170(c)(1).
[96]These are the organizations described in Code § 509(a)(1)("public" and "Type I") entities described in §§ 1 and 2, *supra*.
[97]See Chapter 24.
[98]Code § 508(d).
[99]Code § 509(e).
[100]Code § 509(d).

Investment Income Test

An organization, to avoid private foundation classification under these rules, also must normally receive not more than one-third of its support from the sum of (1) gross investment income,[101] including interest, dividends, payments with respect to securities loans, rents, and royalties and (2) any excess of the amount of unrelated business taxable income over the amount of the tax thereon.[102] To qualify under this test, an organization must construct a "gross investment income fraction," with the amount of gross investment income received constituting the numerator of the fraction and the total amount of support received being the denominator.[103] In certain instances, it may be necessary to distinguish between "gross receipts" and "gross investment income."[104]

For these purposes, amounts received by a would-be publicly supported organization ("Type II") from (1) an organization seeking classification as a supporting organization by reason of its support of the would-be publicly supported organization or from (2) a charitable trust, corporation, fund, or association or a split-interest trust,[105] which is required by its governing instrument or otherwise to distribute or which normally does distribute at least 25 percent of its adjusted net income to the would-be publicly supported organization and where the distribution normally comprises at least five percent of the would-be publicly supported organization's adjusted net income, retain their character as gross investment income (i.e., are not treated as gifts or contributions) to the extent that such amounts are characterized as gross investment income in the possession of the distributing organization. Where an organization, as above-described, makes distributions to more than one would-be publicly supported organization ("Type II"), the amount of gross investment income deemed distributed is prorated among the distributees.[106] Also, where an organization, as above-described, expends funds to provide goods, services, or facilities for the direct benefit of a would-be publicly supported organization, the amounts are treated as gross investment income to the beneficiary organization to the extent that such amounts are so characterized in the possession of the organization spending the funds.[107]

These rules were amended in 1975,[108] to provide that an organization having or seeking nonfoundation status under these rules may not normally receive more than one-third of its support each tax year, from not only gross investment income, but also not from any excess of unrelated business taxable income over

---

[101]Code § 509(e).
[102]Code § 509(a)(2)(B).
[103]Reg. § 1.509(a)-3(a)(3).
[104]See Reg. § 1.509(a)-3(m).
[105]See Code § 4947(a)(2); Chapter 33.
[106]Reg. § 1.509(a)-5(a)(1).
[107]Reg. § 1.509(a)-5(a)(2).
[108]Code § 509(a)(2)(B)(ii).

the tax thereon.[109] This provision arose because the Senate adopted amendments to postpone depreciation recapture where a controlled subsidiary operating an unrelated trade or business is liquidated into a parent tax-exempt corporation.[110] The Senate acted in this regard for the benefit of the Colonial Williamsburg Foundation, which liquidated a wholly-owned subsidiary in 1970 so as to qualify as a public charity under these rules. However, the House of Representatives responded with another amendment,[111] to treat income from an unrelated trade or business acquired by an organization after June 30, 1975, the same as investment income for these purposes.[112] The House amendment was designed to prevent a change of form as to the operation of an unrelated business from converting a "charitable" organization from a private foundation to a public charity—albeit grandfathering in prior transactions such as the Colonial Williamsburg liquidation.

Concept of "Normally"

These support and investment income tests are computed on the basis of the nature of the organization's "normal" sources of support. An organization is considered as "normally" receiving one-third of its support from permitted sources and not more than one-third of its support from gross investment income for its current tax year and immediately succeeding tax year if, for the four tax years immediately preceding its current tax year, the aggregate amount of support received over the four-year period from permitted sources is more than one-third of its total support and the aggregate amount of support over the four-year period from gross investment income is not more than one-third of its total support.[113] For example, if an organization's current tax year is calendar year 1983, the computation period is calendar years 1982, 1981, 1980, and 1979.

If, in an organization's current tax year, there are "substantial and material changes" in its sources of support (e.g., an unusually large contribution or bequest), other than changes arising from "unusual grants," the computation period becomes the tax year of such substantial and material changes and the four immediately preceding tax years.[114]

A substantial and material change in an organization's support may cause it to no longer meet one of the two tests of these rules and thus no longer qualify as a public charity. Nonetheless, its status as a public charity with respect to

---

[109]P.L. 94-81, 94th Cong., 1st Sess. (1975).
[110]Code §§ 1245(b)(7) and 1250(d)(9). See 121 *Cong. Rec.* 22264 (1975).
[111]Code § 509(a)(2)(B)(ii).
[112]See 121 *Cong. Rec.* 24812 (1975). See Reg. § 1.509(a)-3(a)(3).
[113]Reg. § 1.509(a)-3(c)(1)(i).
[114]Reg. § 1.509(a)-3(c)(1)(ii). For the rules with respect to "new" (i.e., post-1969) organizations in relation to the preceding two paragraphs, see Reg. § 1.509(a)-3(c)(1)(iv). Also see Reg. § 1.509(a)-3(d), (e).

a grantor or contributor will not be affected until notice of a change of status is communicated to the public. However, if the grantor or contributor was either aware of or was responsible for the substantial and material change or acquired knowledge that the IRS had given notice to the organization that it had lost its designation as a publicly supported charitable organization, then the status would be affected.[115] But, the foregoing rule does not apply if, under appropriate circumstances, the grantor or contributor acted in reliance upon a written statement by the grantee organization that the grant or contribution would not cause the organization to lose its nonprivate foundation classification.[116] This statement must be signed by a responsible officer of the organization and must set forth sufficient information to assure a reasonably prudent person that the grant or contribution will not cause loss of the organization's classification as a publicly supported entity.

Under the "unusual grant" rule, a contribution may be excluded from the numerator of the one-third support fraction and from the denominator of both the one-third support and one-third gross investment income fractions. These contributions will generally be substantial contributions and bequests from disinterested parties, which were attracted by reason of the publicly supported nature of the organization, were unusual or unexpected with respect to the amount, and would adversely affect the status of the organization in relation to the one-third support test.[117] Thus, the receipt of an unusual grant will not cause the recipient charitable organization to experience a substantial and material change in the organization's sources of financial support for purposes of the one-third support test. No item of gross investment income may be excluded under this "unusual grant" exception.

The IRS provided an illustration of the unusual grant rule in the case of a publicly supported charitable organization that received a large *inter vivos* gift of undeveloped land from a distinterested party, with the condition that the land be used in perpetuity to further the organization's tax-exempt purpose of preserving the natural resources of a particular town. The Service ruled that the gift constituted an unusual grant and thus that the organization's nonfoundation status was not adversely affected, even though all of the above factors were not satisfied and the organization had previously received an "unusual grant" ruling. The IRS cited the following facts as being of "particular importance": the donor was a disinterested party, the organization's operating expenses are paid for primarily through public support, the gift of the land furthered the exempt purpose of the organization, and the contribution was in the nature of new endowment funds because the organization was relatively new.[118]

In determining whether a contribution may be excluded under the "unusual

---

[115]Reg. § 1.509(a)-3(c)(1)(iii)(a).

[116]Reg. § 1.509(a)-3(c)(1)(iii)(b).

[117]Reg. § 1.509(a)-3(c)(3). Similar rules for Code § 170(b)(1)(A)(vi) organizations ("Type I"—see § 2, *supra*) are stated in Reg. § 1.170A-9(e)(6)(ii), (iii).

[118]Rev. Rul. 76-440, *supra* n. 62.

grant" exception, all pertinent facts and circumstances are taken into consideration, although no single factor is necessarily determinative.[119] Among the factors to be considered are whether (1) the contribution was made by a disqualified person, (2) the contribution was in the form of cash, readily marketable securities, or assets which further the tax-exempt purposes of the organization, (3) the organization met the one-third support test in the past, without the benefit of any exclusions of unusual grants, (4) the contribution was a bequest or an *inter vivos* transfer, (5) the organization carried on an active program of public solicitation and exempt activities, and was able to attract a significant amount of public support prior to the unusual gift, and (6) material restrictions or conditions have been imposed on the transfer. A potential grantee organization may request an advance ruling from the IRS as to whether an unusually large grant may be excluded under this exception[120]

The IRS has promulgated so-called "safe haven" criteria that, if satisfied, automatically cause a contribution or grant to be considered "unusual," if the gift or grant, by reason of its size, would otherwise adversely affect the status of a charitable entity as a publicly supported organization. These guidelines are intended to provide advance assurance to grantors and contributors that they will not, as the result of the unusual grant or gift, be considered to be responsible for any substantial and material changes in the sources of an organization's financial support. Pursuant to these guidelines, a gift or grant is unusual if (in addition to the fact that it would otherwise adversely affect an organization's public charity status) it meets six tests, including the requirements that (1) the gift or grant is made by a person who is not a substantial contributor prior to the transfer, or a foundation manager, or a related party, (2) the gift or grant is in the form of cash, readily marketable securities, or assets that directly further the organization's tax-exempt purposes, (3) there are no material restrictions imposed by the contributor or grantor on the organization in connection with the gift or grant, and (4) if the gift or grant is intended to underwrite operating expenses rather than to finance capital items, the terms and amount of the gift or grant are expressly limited to underwriting no more than one year's operating expenses.[121]

These rules may be illustrated as follows:

During the years 1975–1978, A, a publicly supported organization,[122] received total support of $350,000. Of this amount, $105,000 was received from grants, contributions, and receipts from admissions that constitute qualifying public support.[123] $150,000 was received in the form of grants and contributions from persons

[119]Nine factors to be considered are enumerated in Reg. § 1.509(a)-3(c)(4).

[120]Reg. § 1.509(a)-3(c)(5)(ii).

[121]Rev. Proc. 81-7, 1981-1 C. B. 621. These new rules do not preclude a potential donee or grantee organization from requesting a ruling from the IRS as to whether a proposed gift or grant, with or without the six characteristics, will constitute an unusual gift or grant.

[122]In this example, an organization described in Code § 509(a)(2).

[123]Code § 509(a)(2)(A)(i) and (ii).

who are disqualified persons because they are substantial contributors.[124] The remaining $95,000 was gross investment income.[125] Among the contributions from substantial contributors was a contribution of $50,000 from X, who was not a substantial contributor to A prior to the making of this contribution. All of the other requirements of the guidelines were met with respect to X's contribution. If X's contribution is excluded from A's support as an unusual grant, A will have received, for the years 1975–1978, $105,000 from public sources, $100,000 in grants and contributions from disqualified persons, and $95,000 in gross investment income. Therefore, if X's contribution is excluded from A's support, A meets the requirements for being a publicly supported organization for the year 1979 because more than one-third of its support is from "public" sources and no more than one-third of its support is gross investment income. Thus, X's contribution would adversely affect the public status of A and, since the guidelines are met, the contribution is excludable as an unusual grant. X will not be considered responsible for a "substantial and material" change in A's support.

The computations to show the effect of excluding X's contribution from A's support are as follows:

Total support for A during 1975–1978	$350,000
Less: Contribution from X	50,000
Total support of A less X's contribution	$300,000

Gross investment income received by A as a percentage of A's total support (less X's contribution) $\dfrac{\$\ 95,000}{\$300,000} = 31.67\%$

Public support received by A as a percentage of A's total support (less X's contribution) $\dfrac{\$105,000}{\$300,000} = 35\%$

Under the same facts, except that for the years 1975–1978 A received $100,000 in grants and contributions from disqualified persons, the result would be different. In this case, if X's contribution is excluded as an unusual grant, A will have received $105,000 from public sources, $50,000 in grants and contributions from disqualified persons, and $95,000 in gross investment income. If X's contribution is excluded from A's support, A will have received more than one-third of its support from gross investment income and thus not meet all of the requirements of the support test for 1979. Consequently, even though the guidelines are satisfied, X's contribution is not excludable as an unusual grant because it would not adversely affect the status of A as a publicly supported organization.

The computations to show the effect of excluding X's contribution from A's support are as follows:

Total support for A during 1975–1978	$300,000
Less: Contribution from X	50,000
Total support of A (less X's contribution)	$250,000

Gross investment income received by A as a percentage of A's total support (less X's contribution) $\dfrac{\$\ 95,000}{\$250,000} = 38\%$

[124]See Chapter 25 § 1.
[125]Code § 509(e).

Limitations on Support

There is no limitation on the amount of support which may be taken into account in determining the numerator of the support fraction under these rules concerning gifts, grants, contributions, and membership fees, except that this support must, as noted, come from permitted sources. However, in computing the amount of support received from gross receipts that is allowable toward the one-third requirement, gross receipts from related activities received from any person or from any bureau or similar agency of a governmental unit are includible in any tax year only to the extent that such receipts do not exceed the greater of $5,000 or one percent of the organization's support for the year.[126]

In one instance, a nonprofit blood bank entered into agreements with hospitals it supplied with blood, whereunder the hospitals were responsible for collecting charges from the patients and reimbursing the blood bank. Because of the existence of an agency relationship, the amounts paid to the hospitals were treated as though paid directly by the patients to the blood bank. Thus, each patient was considered a separate payor for purposes of the $5,000 or one percent support test.[127]

The phrase government "bureau or similar agency"[128] means a specialized operating (rather than policy-making or administrative) unit of the executive, judicial, or legislative branch of government, usually a subdivision of a department of government. Therefore, an organization receiving gross receipts from both a policy-making or administrative unit (e.g., the Agency for International Development) and an operational unit of a department (e.g., the Bureau for Latin America, an operating unit within AID) is treated as receiving gross receipts from two bureaus, with the amount from each separately subject to the $5,000 or one percent limitation.

A somewhat comparable limitation is derived from the "permitted sources" rules, in that one "source" that is not "permitted" is a "disqualified person" and one type of disqualified person is a "substantial contributor."[129] A substantial contributor is a person who contributes or bequeaths an aggregate amount of more than $5,000 to a charitable organization, where that amount is more than two percent of the total contributions and bequests received by the organization before the close of its tax year in which the contribution or bequest from the person is received by the organization.[130] Thus, transfers from a substantial contributor cannot qualify as public support.

The income tax regulations define the various forms of support referenced in these rules: "gift," "contribution," or "gross receipts;"[131] "grant" or "gross

---

[126]Reg. § 1.509(a)-3(b)(1).
[127]Rev. Rul. 75-387, 1975-2 C. B. 216.
[128]See Reg. § 1.509(a)-3(i).
[129]See Chapter 24 § 1.
[130]Code § 507(d)(2)(A).
[131]Reg. § 1.509(a)-3(f).

receipts;"[132] "membership fees;"[133] "gross receipts" or "gross investment income;"[134] and "grant" or indirect contribution.[135] For example, the term "gross receipts" means amounts received from a related activity where a specific service, facility, or product is provided to serve the direct and immediate needs of the payor, while a "grant" is an amount paid to confer a direct benefit on the general public. Any payment of money or transfer of property without adequate consideration is generally considered a "gift" or "contribution." The furnishing of facilities for a rental fee or the making of loans as part of an exempt purpose will likely give rise to "gross receipts" rather than "gross investment income." The fact that a membership organization provides services, facilities, and the like to its members as part of its overall activities will not result in the fees received from members being treated as "gross receipts" rather than "membership fees."

These rules may be illustrated by using essentially the same example as was used earlier in the discussion of the other category of publicly supported organization, namely, a charitable organization that in one tax year received support totaling $100,000 as follows:

	Total Support	Amounts in Numerator	Amounts in Denominator
Public charity grant	$ 15,000	$15,000	$ 15,000
Receipts from performance of related services	15,000	5,000	15,000
General public gifts	20,000	20,000	20,000
Disqualified persons gifts	35,000		35,000
Gross investment income	15,000		15,000
Totals	$100,000	$40,000	$100,000

The numerator of the support fraction is $40,000 and the denominator of the fraction is $100,000. Thus, the organization that met the support requirement under the previously discussed rules ("Type I") for a tax year also satisfied (for one tax year) the comparable requirement under these rules describing a type of publicly supported organization ("Type II"). (Again, as discussed, the requirement generally must be met over a four-year period.)

---

[132]Reg. § 1.509(a)-3(g). See IRS Private Letter Rulings 7852007 (issue no. 5) and 7851003.

[133]Reg. § 1.509(a)-3(h).

[134]Reg. § 1.509(a)-(3)(m).

[135]Reg. § 1.509(a)-3(j).

The rules concerning these two categories of publicly supported organizations are much the same, in that both types of entities generally must receive at least one-third of their support from "public" sources. However, there are material differences in the manner in which the one-third support fraction is computed. For example, an organization that has receipts from the conduct of related activities may find it advantageous to select the "Type II" category, inasmuch as the first $5,000 of the receipts (or one percent of total support, if greater) will constitute public support, whereas the receipts are excluded from the "Type I" support fraction altogether and may even preclude nonprivate foundation classification under the "Type I" category. Amounts from government contracts and/or membership dues may more readily be eligible public support under the "Type II" category. Conversely, an organization that receives financial support from those who would be substantial contributors under the "Type II" rules may well find preferable the "Type I" classification, in that at least the amount of support up to the two percent limitation constitutes qualifying public support, whereas none of the support from a substantial contributor can be public support. Also, the "Type II" category rules contain a specific limitation on the amount of allowable gross investment income, while the "Type I" rules do not.

As discussed above in connection with the rules pertaining to the "Type I" publicly supported charitable organization,[136] care must be taken in making these computations in relation to an organization that failed to qualify as a "charitable" entity during one or more years, since the IRS asserts that support received by the organization during the period of its disqualification cannot be taken into account in determining its foundation/public charity status.[137]

§ 22.4　Supporting Organizations

Another category of charitable organization that is deemed to not be a private foundation is the supporting organization.[138]

Organizations which are deemed not to be private foundations because they are supporting organizations are those which are not themselves publicly supported but are sufficiently related to organizations that are publicly supported or are otherwise "public" entities so that the requisite degree of public control and involvement is considered present. Thus, the supported organization must be one of the "public" institutions or one of the types of publicly supported organizations,[139] while the organization that is not a private foundation by virtue of these rules is characterized as a "supporting organization."[140] The supported

---

[136]Code § 170(b)(1)(A)(vi) (see § 2, *supra*).
[137]Rev. Rul. 77-116, *supra*, n. 69.
[138]Code § 509(a)(3).
[139]See §§ 1 and 2, respectively, *supra*.
[140]Reg. § 1.509(a)-4(a)(5).

organization may be a foreign organization, as long as it otherwise qualifies as a public or publicly supported entity.[141]

A supporting organization must be organized, and at all times thereafter operated, exclusively for the benefit of, to perform the functions of, or to carry out the purposes of one or more public charities.[142] A supporting organization must be operated, supervised, or controlled by or in connection with one or more public charities.[143] Thus, the relationship must be one of three types: (1) "operated, supervised or controlled by," (2) "supervised or controlled in connection with," or (3) "operated in connection with."[144] A supporting organization must not be controlled directly or indirectly by one or more disqualified persons (other than foundation managers), excluding public charities.[145]

Organizational Test

A supporting organization must be organized exclusively to support or benefit one or more specified public or publicly supported charitable organizations.[146] Its articles of organization[147] must limit its purposes to one or more of the purposes that are permissible for a supporting organization,[148] may not expressly empower the organization to engage in activities which are not in furtherance of such purposes, must state the specified public charities on whose behalf it is to be operated, and may not expressly empower the organization to operate to support or benefit any other organizations.[149]

Operational Test

A supporting organization must also be operated exclusively to support or benefit one or more specified public or publicly supported charitable organizations.[150] Unlike the definition of the term "exclusively" as applied in the context of charitable organizations generally, which means "primarily,"[151] the term "exclusively" in this context means "solely."[152]

The supporting organization must engage solely in activities which support or benefit the specified organizations.[153] These activities may include making

---

[141]Rev. Rul. 74-229, 1974-1 C. B. 142.
[142]Code § 509(a)(3)(A), Reg. § 1.509(a)-4(a)(2).
[143]Reg. §§1.509(a)-4(a)(3), 1.509(a)-4(f)(2).
[144]Code § 509(a)(3)(B).
[145]Code § 509(a)(3)(C), Reg. § 1.509(a)-4(a)(4).
[146]Code § 509(a)(3)(A).
[147]See Reg. § 1.501(c)(3)-1(b)(2).
[148]Code § 509(a)(3)(A).
[149]Reg. § 1.509(a)-4(c).
[150]Code § 509(a)(3)(A).
[151]See Chapter 11.
[152]Reg. § 1.509(a)-4(e)(1).
[153]See Reg. § 1.509(a)-4(e)(1), (2).

payments to or for the use of, or providing services or facilities for, individual members of the charitable class benefited by the specified public or publicly supported organization. A supporting organization may make a payment indirectly through another unrelated organization to a member of a charitable class benefited by a specified public or publicly supported organization, but only where the payment constitutes a grant to an individual rather than a grant to an organization. The supporting organization need not pay over its income to the public or publicly supported organizations but may carry on an independent program or activity which supports or benefits the specified supported organizations. A supporting organization may also engage in fund-raising activities, such as solicitations, dinners, and unrelated trade or business activities to raise funds for the supported organizations or for permissible beneficiaries.

"Specified" Public Charities

As noted, a supporting organization must be organized and operated to support or benefit one or more "specified" public charities.[154] This specification must be in the supporting organization's articles of organization, although the manner of the specification depends upon which of the three types of relationships with public charities is involved.[155]

Generally, it is expected that the articles of the supporting organization will designate each of the "specified" public charities by name. However, if the relationship is one of "operated, supervised or controlled by" or "supervised or controlled in connection with," designation by name is not required as long as the articles of organization of the supporting organization require that it be operated to support or benefit one or more beneficiary organizations which are designated by class or purpose and which include one or more public charities as to which there is one of the foregoing two relationships or public charities which are closely related in purpose or function to public charities as to which there is one of the two relationships.[156] Conversely, if the relationship is one of "operated in connection with," the supporting organization must designate the "specified" public charity or charities by name.[157]

These rules have been illustrated in the reasoning followed by the IRS in according supporting organization classification to a tax-exempt community

---

[154]Code § 509(a)(3)(A).

[155]Reg. § 1.509(a)-4(c)(1).

[156]Reg. § 1.509(a)-4(d)(2); also see Reg. § 1.509(a)-4(d)(3). The IRS denied an organization supporting organization/public charity classification where, after payment of a certain amount to qualified supported organizations, the supporting requirements would not be met. Rev. Rul. 79-197, 1979-2 C. B. 204.

[157]Reg. § 1.509(a)-4(d)(4). In one case, the U.S. Tax Court generally ignored these regulations and found compliance with the specificity requirement of Code § 509(a)(3)(A) merely by reading the statutory provision in light of the facts of the case. *Warren M. Goodspeed Scholarship Fund* v. *Commissioner*, 70 T.C. 515 (1978).

trust.[158] The community trust was created by a publicly supported community chest to hold endowment funds and to distribute the income therefrom to support public charities in a particular geographic area. A majority of the trustees of the community trust were appointed by the governing body of the community chest. The trust was required by the terms of its governing instrument to distribute its income to public charities in a particular area, so that, the IRS held, even though the public charities were not specified by name, the trust qualified as a supporting organization because the community chest was specified by the requisite class or purpose, in that the trust was organized and operated exclusively for the benefit of such class of organizations. Inasmuch as the community chest appointed a majority of the trust's trustees, the trust was "operated, supervised, or controlled by" the community chest, so that the "specification" requirement was met.[159]

An organization that is "operated in connection with" one or more public charities can satisfy the "specification" requirement even if its articles of organization permit a public charity which is designated by class or purpose (rather than by name) to be substituted for the public charities designated by name in its articles, but "only if such substitution is conditioned upon the occurrence of an event which is beyond the control of the supporting organization."[160] In one case, the trustee of a charitable entity had the authority to substitute other charitable beneficiaries for those named in its articles whenever, in the trustee's judgment, the charitable uses have become "unnecessary, undesirable, impracticable, impossible or no longer adapted to the needs of the public." The U.S. Tax Court held that the organization failed the organizational test, and hence is a private foundation, because the events which can trigger the substitution of beneficiaries are "within the trustee's control for all practical purposes" since the standard "requires the trustee to make a judgment as to what is desirable and what are the needs of the public."[161] The court stated that the organizational test is essential to qualification of organizations as supporting entities because the "public scrutiny [necessary to obviate the need for governmental regulation as a foundation] derives from the publicly supported beneficiaries, which, in turn, oversee the activities of the supporting organization" and "[t]his oversight function is substantially weakened if the trustee has broad authority to substitute beneficiaries and, thus, it is essential that such authority be strictly limited."[162]

A grandfather provision states that a supporting organization will be deemed to meet the requirement of "specificity" even though its articles do not designate each supported organization by name—despite the nature of the relationship—

---

[158]Reg. § 1.170A-9(e)(11). See n. 79, *supra*.

[159]Rev. Rul. 81-43, 1981-1 C. B. 350.

[160]Reg. § 1.509(a)-4(d)(4)(i)(a).

[161]*William F., Mable E. and Margaret K. Quarrie Charitable Fund* v. *Commissioner*, 70 T.C. 182, 187 (1978), aff'd 79-2 U.S.T.C.¶ 9534 (7th Cir. 1979).

[162]*Ibid.*, 70 T.C. at 190.

if there has been an historic and continuing relationship between the supporting organization and the public charities and, by reason of the relationship, there has developed a substantial identity of interests between the organizations.[163]

Required Relationships

As noted, to meet these requirements, an organization must be operated, supervised, or controlled by or in connection with one or more publicly supported organizations. Thus, if an organization does not stand in at least one of the three required relationships to one or more public charities, it cannot qualify as a supporting organization.[164] Regardless of the applicable relationship, it must be ensured that the supporting organization will be "responsive" to the needs or demands of one or more public charities and that the supporting organization will constitute an "integral part" of or maintain a "significant involvement" in the operations of one or more public charities.[165]

"Operated, Supervised, or Controlled by"

The distinguishing feature of the relationship between a supporting organization and one or more public charities encompassed by the phrase "operated, supervised or controlled by" is the presence of a substantial degree of direction by one or more public charities over the policies, programs, and activities of the supporting organization—a relationship comparable to that of a subsidiary and a parent.[166]

This relationship is established by the fact that a majority of the officers, directors, or trustees of the supporting organization are either comprised of representatives of the supported public charities or at least are appointed or elected by the governing body, officers acting in their official capacity, or the membership of the supported public charities.[167] This relationship will be considered to exist with respect to one or more public charities and the supporting organization considered to operate "for the benefit of" one or more different public charities only where it can be demonstrated that the purposes of the former organization are carried out by benefiting the latter organizations.[168]

"Supervised or Controlled in Connection with"

The distinguishing feature of the relationship between a supporting organization and one or more public charities encompassed by the phrase "supervised or controlled in connection with" is the presence of common supervision or control by the persons supervising or controlling both the supporting or-

---

[163]Reg. § 1.509(a)-4(d)(2)(iv).
[164]Reg. § 1.509(a)-4(f)(1).
[165]Reg. § 1.509(a)-4(f)(3).
[166]Reg. §§ 1.509(a)-4(f)(4), 1.509(a)-4(g)(1)(i).
[167]Reg. § 1.509(a)-4(g)(1).
[168]Reg. § 1.509(a)-4(g)(1)(ii).

ganization and the public charities to ensure that the supporting organization will be responsive to the needs and requirements of the public charities.[169] Therefore, in order to meet this requirement, the control or management of the supporting organization must be vested in the same persons that control or manage the public charities.

A supporting organization will not be considered to be in this relationship with a public charity (or charities) if it merely makes payments (mandatory or discretionary) to one or more named public charities, regardless of whether the obligation to make payments to the named beneficiaries is enforceable under state law and the supporting organization's governing instrument contains the requisite provisions.[170] According to the regulations, such an arrangement does not provide a sufficient connection between the payor organization and the needs and requirements of the public charities to constitute supervision or control in connection with such organizations.[171]

"Operated in Connection with"

The distinguishing feature of the relationship between a supporting organization and one or more public charities encompassed by the phrase "operated in connection with" is that the supporting organization is responsive to and significantly involved in the operation of the public charity or charities.[172] Generally, to satisfy the criteria of this relationship, a supporting organization must meet both a "responsiveness test" and an "integral part test."[173]

A supporting organization will be considered to meet the responsiveness test if it is responsive to the needs or demands of one or more public charities.[174] This test may be satisfied in either of two ways.

First, this test is met where the supporting organization and the supported organization(s) are in close operational conjunction. This is manifested by a showing that (1) one or more officers, directors, or trustees of the supporting organization are elected or appointed by the officers, directors, trustees, or membership of the supported organization(s), (2) one or more members of the governing bodies of the supported organization(s) are also officers, directors, or trustees of, or hold other important offices in, the supporting organization, or (3) the officers, directors, or trustees of the supporting organization maintain a close and continuous working relationship with the officers, directors, or trustees of the supported organization(s). Not only must at least one of these three subtests be met, but also it must be demonstrated that the officers, directors, or trustees of the supported organization(s) have a significant voice in the investment policies of the supporting organization, the timing of grants,

---

[169]Reg. § 1.509(a)-4(f)(4).
[170]Code § 509(e)(1)(A), (B).
[171]Reg. § 1.509(a)-4(h)(2).
[172]Reg. § 1.509(a)-4(f)(4).
[173]Reg. § 1.509(a)-4(i)(1).
[174]Reg. § 1.509(a)-4(i)(2)(i).

the manner of making them, and the selection of recipients by the supporting organization, and in otherwise directing the use of the income or assets of the supporting organization.[175]

The responsiveness test may also be met where (1) the supporting organization is a charitable trust under state law, (2) each specified publicly supported organization is a named beneficiary under the charitable trust's governing instrument, and (3) the beneficiary organization has the power to enforce the trust and compel an accounting under state law.[176]

A supporting organization will be considered to meet the integral part test if it maintains a significant involvement in the operations of one or more public charities and the public charities are in turn dependent upon the supporting organization for the type of support which it provides.[177] This test may be satisfied in either of two ways.

First, this test is met where the activities engaged in by the supporting organization for or on behalf of the supported organization(s) are activities to perform the functions of, or to carry out the purposes of, the supported organization(s), and, but for the involvement of the supporting organization, would normally be engaged in by the supported organization(s) itself.[178]

The second way to meet the integral part test involves a set of requirements considerably more complex. This package of rules represents the furthest and least demanding reaches under which a charitable organization can avoid private foundation status, particularly where it has met the responsiveness test solely because it is a charitable trust.[179]

The second way in which the integral part test can be met is where the supporting organization makes payments of substantially all of its income to or for the use of one or more supported organizations and the amount of support received by one or more of the supported organizations is sufficient to ensure the attentiveness of the organizations to the operations of the supporting organization. In addition, a substantial amount of the total support of the supporting organization must go to those supported organizations which meet the attentiveness requirement with respect to the supporting organization. In general, the amount of support received by a supported organization must represent a sufficient part of its total support so as to ensure the necessary attentiveness. (In applying this rule, if the supporting organization makes payments to, or for the use of, a particular department or school of a university, hospital, or church, the total support of the department or school is substituted for the total support of the beneficiary organization.[180])

The IRS has ruled that the term "substantially all" means at least 85 percent,

---

[175]Reg. § 1.509(a)-4(i)(2)(ii).
[176]Reg. § 1.509(a)-4(i)(2)(iii).
[177]Reg. § 1.509(a)-4(i)(3)(i); also see Reg. § 1.509(a)-4(i)(4).
[178]Reg. § 1.509(a)-4(i)(3)(ii).
[179]See *Nellie Callahan Scholarship Fund* v. *Commissioner*, 73 T.C. 626 (1980).
[180]Reg. § 1.509(a)-4(i)(3)(iii)(a).

because that was the meaning given to the same term in the rules concerning private operating foundations.[181] In that ruling, the IRS decided that the integral part test was violated by a charitable trust that distributed 75 percent of its income annually to a church, accumulating the balance until the original corpus is doubled, at which time all of the organization's income is to be distributed to the church.[182]

However, even where the amount of support received by a supported beneficiary organization does not represent a sufficient part of the beneficiary organization's total support, the amount of support received from a supporting organization may be sufficient to meet the requirements of the integral part test if it can be demonstrated that, in order to avoid the interruption of the carrying on of a particular function or activity, the beneficiary organization will be sufficiently attentive to the operations of the supporting organization. This may be the case where either the supporting organization or the beneficiary organization earmarks the support received from the supporting organization for a particular program or activity, even if the program or activity is not the beneficiary organization's primary program or activity so long as such program or activity is a substantial one.[183]

All pertinent factors, including the number of beneficiaries, the length and nature of the relationship between the beneficiary and supporting organization, and the purpose to which the funds are put, will be considered in determining whether the amount of support received by a beneficiary organization is sufficient to ensure the attentiveness of it to the operations of the supporting organization. Inasmuch as, in the government's view, the attentiveness of a beneficiary organization is motivated by reason of the amounts received from the supporting organization, the more substantial the amount involved (in terms of a percentage of the supported organization's total support) the greater the likelihood that the required degree of attentiveness will be present. However, in satisfaction of this test, evidence of actual attentiveness by the beneficiary organization is of almost equal importance. The regulations give as an example of acceptable evidence in this regard the imposition of a requirement that the supporting organization furnish reports at least annually to the beneficiary organization to assist the latter in ensuring that the former has invested its endowment in assets productive of a reasonable rate of return (taking appreciation into account) and has not engaged in any activity which would give rise to liability for any of the private foundation excise taxes if the supporting organization were a private foundation. The imposition of this requirement is, however, merely one of the factors used in determining whether a supporting organization is complying with the requirements of this test and the absence of the requirement will not necessarily preclude an organization from classification as a supporting organization based on other factors.[184] Thus, the IRS

---

[181]Code § 4942(j)(3)(A); Reg. § 53.4942(b)-1(c). See Chapter 23.
[182]Rev. Rul. 76-208, 1976-1 C. B. 161.
[183]Reg. § 1.509(a)-4(i)(3)(iii)(b).
[184]Reg. § 1.509(a)-4(i)(3)(iii)(d).

has ruled that reports, submitted by a trustee to each of the beneficiaries of a charitable trust, will not alone satisfy the attentiveness requirement of the integral part test.[185]

However, where none of the beneficiary organizations is dependent upon the supporting organization for a sufficient amount of the beneficiary organization's support within the meaning of these requirements, this test will not be satisfied, even though the beneficiary organizations have enforceable rights against the organization under state law.[186]

Limitation on Control

A supporting organization may not be controlled directly or indirectly by one or more disqualified persons, other than foundation managers and one or more public charities.[187] An individual who is a disqualified person with respect to the supporting organization (e.g., a substantial contributor) does not lose that status because a beneficiary public charity appoints or designates him or her a foundation manager of the supporting organization to serve as the representative of the public charity.

A supporting organization is considered "controlled" if the disqualified persons, by aggregating their votes or positions of authority, may require the organization to perform any act which significantly affects its operations or may prevent the supporting organization from performing the act. Generally, a supporting organization will be considered to be controlled directly or indirectly by one or more disqualified persons if the voting power of these persons is 50 percent or more of the total voting power of the organization's governing body or if one or more disqualified persons have the right to exercise veto power over the actions of the organization. All pertinent facts and circumstances, including the nature, diversity, and income yield of an organization's holdings, the length of time particular stocks, securities, or other assets are retained, and its manner of exercising its voting rights with respect to stocks in which members of its governing body also have some interests, will be taken into consideration in determining whether a disqualified person does in fact indirectly control an organization.[188] Supporting organizations are permitted to establish to the satisfaction of the IRS that disqualified persons do not directly or indirectly control it.[189]

For example, this control element may be the difference between the qualification of an organization as a supporting organization and as a "common fund"

---

[185]Rev. Rul. 76-32, 1976-1 C. B. 160.

[186]Reg. § 1.509(a)-4(i)(3)(iii)(e). Calling these regulations "fantastically intricate and detailed," one court concluded that a charitable organization failed both the "responsiveness test" and the "integral part test," in *Windsor Foundation* v. *United States*, 77-2 U.S.T.C. ¶9709 (E.D. Va. 1977).

[187]Code § 509(a)(3)(C).

[188]Reg. § 1.509(a)-4(j)(1).

[189]Reg. § 1.509(a)-4(j)(2).

private foundation.[190] This is because the right of the donors to designate the recipients of the organization's gifts can constitute control of it by disqualified persons, namely, substantial contributors.[191]

In one instance, the IRS found indirect control of a supporting organization by, in effect, "legislating" a new definition of the term "disqualified person." The matter involved a charitable organization that makes distributions to a university. The organization's board of directors is composed of a substantial contributor to the organization, two employees of a business corporation of which more than 35 percent of the voting power is owned by the substantial contributors, and one individual selected by the university. None of the directors has a veto power over the organization's actions. Conceding that the organization is not directly controlled by disqualified persons, the Service said that "one circumstance to be considered is whether a disqualified person is in a position to influence the decisions of members of the organization's governing body who are not themselves disqualified persons." Thus, the IRS decided that the two directors who are employees of the disqualified person corporation should be considered disqualified persons for purposes of applying in the 50 percent control rule. This position in turn led to the conclusion that the organization is indirectly controlled by disqualified persons and therefore cannot be a nonprivate foundation by virtue of being a qualifying supporting organization.[192]

The operation of these rules in general is illustrated by two rulings issued by the IRS in 1975.

One instance concerned a charitable trust formed to grant scholarships to students graduating from a particular public high school. The sole trustee of the trust was the council of the city in which the school was located and its funds were managed by the city's treasurer. The school system was an integral part of the city's government. One of the purposes of the city as outlined in its charter is to provide for the education of its citizens. The IRS granted the trust classification as a supporting organization (and thereby determined it is not a private foundation),[193] using the following rationale: (1) the city, being a governmental unit,[194] is a qualified supported entity,[195] (2) because of the involvement of the city council and treasurer, the trust satisfied the requirements of the "operated, supervised, or controlled by" relationship, (3) the organizational test was met because of the similarity of educational purpose between the trust and the city, (4) the "exclusive" operation requirement was deemed met because the trust benefited individual members of the charitable

[190]See Chapter 23 § 3.
[191]Rev. Rul. 80-305, 1980-2 C. B. 71. For a discussion of the definition of a "substantial contributor," see Chapter 24 § 1.
[192]Rev. Rul. 80-207, 1980-2 C. B. 193.
[193]Rev. Rul. 75-436, 1975-2 C. B. 217.
[194]Code §§ 170(c)(1), 170(b)(1)(A)(v).
[195]Code § 509(a)(1).

class aided by the city through its school system, and (5) the trust was not controlled by a disqualified person (other than a public charity).

By contrast, the IRS considered the public charity status of a charitable trust formed to grant scholarships to students graduating from high schools in a particular county. The scholarship recipients were selected by a committee comprised of officials and representatives of the county. The trustee of the trust was a bank. The IRS denied the trust classification as a supporting organization (and thereby determined that it is a private foundation),[196] using the following rationale: (1) the high schools are qualified supported organizations,[197] (2) since the trustee was independent of the county, neither the "operated, supervised, or controlled by" nor the "supervised or controlled in connection with" relationship was present, (3) the integral part test of the "operated in connection with" relationship was not met because of the independence of the trustee, the county's lack of voice in the trust's investment and grant-making policies, and the absence of the necessary elements of significant involvement, dependence upon support, and sufficient attentiveness, (4) the responsiveness test of the same relationship was not met because the beneficiary organizations were not named and lacked the power to enforce the trust and compel an accounting, and (5) the trust failed the organizational test because its instrument lacked the requisite statement of purpose and did not "specify" the publicly supported organizations.

The U.S. Tax Court has demonstrated a disposition to avoid such a stringent reading of these requirements. In finding a scholarship-granting charitable trust to be a public charity pursuant to the "operated in connection with" requirements, the court ruled that it satisfied the responsiveness and integral part tests even though the school was not a named beneficiary of the trust and the funds are paid directly to the graduates rather than to the school or a school system.[198] This and a prior Tax Court holding[199] indicate that the courts will not be giving these exceedingly complex and intricate regulations an overly technical interpretation but will apply them in a common-sense manner to effectuate the intent of Congress.

§ 22.5   Non-charitable Supported Organizations

A rather cryptic passage in the Internal Revenue Code states that, for purposes of the supporting organization rules, "an organization described in paragraph (2) [namely, a "Type II" publicly supported organization] shall be deemed to include an organization described in section 501(c)(4), (5), or (6) which would be described in paragraph (2) if it were an organization described in section

---

[196]Rev. Rul. 75-437, 1975-2 C. B. 218.
[197] Code §§ 170(b)(1)(A)(ii) or (v); 509(a)(1)
[198]*Nellie Callahan Scholarship Fund* v. *Commissioner, supra,* n. 179.
[199]*Warren M. Goodspeed Scholarship Fund* v. *Commissioner, supra,* n. 157.

501(c)(3)."[200] This means that a supporting organization (itself tax-exempt as a "charitable" organization) may be operated in conjunction with a social welfare organization, labor or agricultural organization, business league, or the like and qualify as a supporting organization and thus not be a private foundation (assuming the requirements of the law are otherwise met) if the beneficiary organization(s) meets the one-third support test of the rules concerning the "Type II" publicly supported organization.[201] This provision is largely designed to preserve nonprivate foundation status for related "foundations" and other "charitable" organizations such as endowment funds (e.g., scholarship and research funds) operated by trade and professional associations, other types of business leagues, social welfare organizations, labor groups, and the like.

§ 22.6 Relationships Created for Avoidance Purposes

The income tax regulations contain rules to ensure that the requirements concerning "Type II" publicly supported organizations and supporting organizations are not manipulated to avoid private foundation status for charitable organizations. Thus if a relationship between a would-be "Type II" publicly supported organization and a would-be supporting organization is established or availed of after October 9, 1969, and one of the purposes of the relationship is to avoid classification as a private foundation with respect to either organization, the character and amount of support received by the ostensible supporting organization will be attributed to the would-be publicly supported organization for purposes of determining whether the latter meets the one-third support test and the one-third gross investment income test.[202]

If an organization seeking qualification as a "Type II" publicy supported organization fails to meet either the one-third support test or the one-third gross investment income test by reason of the application of the foregoing rules or the rules with respect to retained character of gross investment income, and the organization is one of the specified organizations[203] for whose support or benefit an organization seeking the qualification is operated, the would-be supporting organization will not be considered to be operated exclusively to support or benefit one or more eligible public or publicly supported organizations.[204]

For purposes of determining whether an organization meets the gross investment income test in the rules concerning the "Type II" publicly supported organization,[205] amounts received by the organization from an organization

[200]This provision is frequently cited as an example of rampant complexity in the Internal Revenue Code. See, e.g., Younger, "In Praise of Simplicity," 62 *A.B.A.J.* 632, 633 (1976).

[201]Reg. § 1.509(a)-4(k). See Rev. Rul. 76-401, 1976-2 C. B. 175.

[202]Reg. § 1.509(a)-5(b).

[203]Code § 509(a)(3)(A).

[204]Reg. § 1.509(a)-5(c).

[205]Code § 509(a)(2)(B).

seeking categorization as a supporting organization by reason of its support of the would-be publicly supported organization retain their character as gross investment income (rather than gifts or contributions) to the extent that the amounts are characterized as gross investment income in the possession of the distributing organization. The rule is also applicable with respect to support of a would-be publicly supported organization from a charitable trust, corporation, fund, association, or similar organization, which is required by its governing instrument or otherwise to distribute or which normally does distribute at least 25 percent of its adjusted net income to the organization and the distribution normally comprises at least five percent of the distributee organization's adjusted net income.[206]

§ 22.7   Reliance by Grantors and Contributors

Once an organization has received a determination from the IRS classifying it as a publicly supported organization, the treatment of grants and contributions and the status of grantors and contributors to it generally are not affected by reason of a subsequent revocation of the determination by the IRS until notice of the revocation is communicated to the general public. However, this is not the case where the grantor or contributor had knowledge of the revocation or was in part responsible for or was aware of the act, the failure to act, or the substantial and material change on the part of the organization which gave rise to the revocation of status.[207]

A principal and fundamental difficulty with the reliance rules is that a grantor or contributor may not in fact be able to rely on the ruling that the grantee or donee is a public charity (or private operating foundation). Instead, the grantor or donor must solicit information from the grantee or donee and make an independent determination of the effect of the gift or grant on the grantee's or donee's nonfoundation status. The grantor or donor is expected to obtain a written statement and pertinent financial data from the grantee or donee and review the information under the constraints of a reasonably prudent person test. The concern is that the gift or grant may constitute a substantial and material change in the support of the recipient entity, thereby causing loss of

---

[206]In general, see Gallagher and Jarchow, "How to organize and meet the tax requirements of public charities and private foundations," 8 *Tax. for Lawyers* 302 (1980); Hart, "Section 509 supporting organizations may now qualify as public foundations," 47 *J. Tax.* 174 (1977); Parrs, "Avoiding Private Foundation Status as a Supporting Organization," 115 *Trusts & Estates* 800 (1976); Paluska, "Transforming a private foundation to a supporting organization: Why and how," 42 *J. Tax.* 248 (1975); Paluska, "The Supporting Organization as an Alternative to Private Foundation Status," 49 *Los Angeles Bar Bull.* 142 (1974).

[207]Reg. § 1.509(a)-7. As discussed throughout, the reliance rules are essentially the same as respects Code §§ 170(b)(1)(A)(vi) and 509(a)(2) organizations, and private operating foundations.

its public charity or private operating foundation status, with the attendant adverse consequences to the grantor or donor.[208] That is, for a contributor, the loss by a charitable entity of its classification as a public or publicly supported organization would likely mean that the contributor's deduction is confined by the 20 percent limitation rather than the 50 or 30 percent limitation[209] and, for a grantor that is a private foundation, the change in the grantee's classification may cause the grant to be a taxable expenditure.[210]

These requirements, by imposing the need for an extensive investigation and analysis, frequently eliminate any authentic "reliance" opportunity for grantors and contributors. Many of these grantors are private foundations that lack the resources to conduct the necessary investigations and consequently confine their grants to institutions that are clearly public charities so as to avoid the expenditure responsibility requirements.[211] The only alternatives, before the IRS provided some relief in this regard in 1981, which are likely to be time-consuming and expensive, were for the grantor or donor to seek an unusual grant ruling or to voluntarily undertake to assume expenditure responsibility.

The IRS in 1981 promulgated guidelines for determining when a contributor or grantor will not be considered responsible for "substantial and material" changes in the sources of financial support for an organization that, as the result of the transfer, loses its classification as a publicly supported organization. (In the parlance of the law, such a shift from categorization as a publicly supported charity to a private foundation is known as "tipping.") The essence of these guidelines, which are designed to provide a "safe haven" rule in this regard for donors and grantors to publicly supported charities, is this: a grantor or donor will not be considered to be responsible for a substantial and material change in a recipient's support if the total of the grants or gifts from a grantor or donor for a tax year is no more than 25 percent of the total support received by the recipient organization—other than the grant or gift from the grantor or donor, a foundation manager, or related parties—during the immediately preceding four tax years. In the case of an organization in existence for less than five tax years, the number of years of its existence immediately preceding the tax year at issue is substituted for the four-year period, as long as the organization has been in existence at least one tax year consisting of at least eight months.[212]

The following example illustrates the application of this rule:

A was determined by the IRS in 1974 to be a publicly supported charity and received total support of $340,000 in 1975 through 1978, the period immediately preceding its 1979 tax year. X, a private foundation, granted A $30,000 in 1979. X had contributed $40,000 of A's total support during 1975–1978. Even if A is later determined to be a private foundation for 1979, X will not be considered to

---

[208]Reg. § 1.509(a)-3(c)(1)(iii). Also Reg. § 1.170A-9(e)(4)(v).
[209]See Chapter 3 § 2.
[210]See Chapter 29 § 4.
[211]*Ibid.*
[212]Rev. Proc. 81-6, 1981-1 C. B. 620.

be responsible for a substantial and material change in A's sources of support, resulting in the loss of A's public charity status. The grant in 1979 was only 10 percent of A's total support during 1975–1978, less the grants·from X during that period ($300,000).

The computations are as follows:

Total support received by A during 1975–1978	$340,000
Less: Total support provided by X during 1975–1978	40,000
Total support, for purposes of guidelines, received by A during 1975–1978	$300,000
Total support provided by X during 1979 as a percentage of A's total support, for purposes of guidelines, during 1975–1978	$\frac{\$\ 30,000}{\$300,000} = 10\%$

To an extent, contributors may rely on the listing of an organization in the publication by the IRS of its cumulative list of "charitable" organizations.[213] As a general rule, a contribution by a donor who is unaware of the recipient organization's loss of "charitable" status will give rise to a charitable deduction where made on or before the date of a public announcement (such as by publication in the Internal Revenue Bulletin) stating that the contributions are no longer deductible. The same is true with respect to the recipient organization's "public charity" status. However, as noted previously, the IRS reserves the authority to disallow the charitable deduction where the donor (1) had knowledge of the revocation of status, (2) was aware that the revocation was imminent, or (3) was in part responsible for or was aware of the activities or deficiencies on the part of the organization that gave rise to the loss of qualification.[214]

§ 22.8 Other Rules

If a "charitable" organization was a private foundation on October 9, 1969, it will be treated as a private foundation for all periods thereafter (or until terminated[215]) even though it may also qualify as some other type of tax-exempt organization.[216] In other words, an organization cannot hope to avoid private foundation status by claiming it also qualifies, for example, as a social welfare organization.[217]

If an organization was a private foundation on October 9, 1969, and it is

[213]Publication No. 78, "Cumulative List of Organizations Described in Section 170(c) of the Internal Revenue Code."
[214]Rev. Proc. 82-39, 1982-27 I.R.B. 18.
[215]See Chapter 32.
[216]Reg. § 1.509(b)-1(a).
[217]See Chapter 15.

subsequently determined that it no longer qualifies as a "charitable" entity, it will continue to be treated as a private foundation (until terminated).[218] In other words, an organization cannot avoid private foundation status by converting to a taxable entity.

§ 22.9   Public Safety Organizations

Another category of organization that is deemed to not be a private foundation is an organization which is organized and operated exclusively for testing for public safety.[219] These entities are described in the analysis of "charitable" organizations.[220]

[218]Reg. § 1.509(b)-1(b).

[219]Code § 509(a)(4). See Chapter 10.

[220]For more information on the definitional distinctions between private foundations and public charities, see Raattama, Jr., and Ullman, "Private Foundations and Public Charities: Another View," 114 *Trusts & Estates* 611 (1975); Bandy, "Planning techniques to avoid the taxes on private foundations and related entities," 40 *J. Tax.* 244 (1974); Vacin, "Guidelines for Foundation Administration Under the Tax Reform Act," 52 *Taxes* 277 (1974); Moorehead, "Private Foundations and Public Charities: Handling Definitional Problems Under the Tax Reform Act," 31 *N.Y.U. Inst. Fed. Tax.* 1267 (1973); Halperin, "Private Foundations—Definition and Termination," 29 *N.Y.U. Inst. Fed. Tax.* 1783 (1971); Sugarman, "Conduct of the 'Business' of a Private Foundation under the Tax Reform Act of 1969," 26 *Bus. Law.* 1493 (1971); Sugarman, "Foundation Operations Under the Tax Reform Act," 48 *Taxes* 767 (1970).

23

Types of Private Foundations

As discussed, the federal tax law definition of the term "private foundation" embraces all "charitable" entities other than those that are expressly classified as not being private foundations.[1] Although the "standard" private foundation is the most predominant, there are several other varieties of foundations.

§ 23.1 Private Operating Foundations

Private operating foundations, while not statutorily defined until the enactment of Code § 4942(j)(3) in 1969, have long been recognized as nonpublicly supported organizations which devote most of their earnings and much of their assets directly to the conduct of their tax-exempt purposes, as opposed to merely making grants to other organizations.

Income Test

A private operating foundation must meet an income test.[2] To satisfy the income test for tax years beginning after December 31, 1981, a foundation must annually expend an amount equal to substantially all of the lesser of its adjusted net income[3] or its minimum investment return,[4] in the form of qualifying distributions,[5] directly for the active conduct of its tax-exempt activities. For prior years, the income test required a foundation to expend substantially all of its adjusted net income in the form of qualifying distributions directly for the active conduct of its tax-exempt activities.[6]

[1]See Chapter 22.
[2]Code § 4942(j)(3)(A); Reg. § 53.4942(b)-1(a).
[3]Code § 4942(f).
[4]Code § 4942(e)(1). See Chapter 26 § 1.
[5]Code § 4942(g). See Chapter 26 § 2.
[6]This change in the law was occasioned by enactment of § 823 of the Economic Recovery Tax Act of 1981.

The funds expended must be used by the foundation itself rather than by or through one or more grantee organizations. An amount set aside by a foundation for a specific project involving the active conduct of its tax-exempt activities will qualify as a direct expenditure if the initial setting aside of the funds constitutes a qualifying set-aside.[7] An example of this involves a private operating foundation, organized to restore and perpetuate wildlife and game on the North American continent, which converted a portion of newly acquired land into an extension of its existing wildlife sanctuary and a public park under a four-year construction contract pursuant to which payments are mainly during the last two years.[8] The making or awarding of grants, scholarships, or similar payments to individual beneficiaries to support active tax-exempt programs will qualify the grantor as a private operating foundation only if it maintains some significant involvement in the programs.[9]

The term "significant involvement" has two basic meanings. The requisite involvement is present where payments to accomplish the foundation's tax-exempt purpose are made directly and without the assistance of an intervening organization or agency, and the foundation maintains a staff (for example, administrators or researchers) which supervises and directs the exempt activities on a continuing basis. To utilize this meaning of the term, the foundation must have as an exempt purpose the relief of poverty or human distress and its tax-exempt purposes must be designed to ameliorate conditions among a poor or distressed class of persons or in an area subject to poverty or natural disaster (for example, providing food or clothing to indigents or residents of a disaster area). This involvement is also present where the foundation has developed some specialized skills, expertise, or involvement in a particular discipline, and it maintains a staff which supervises or conducts programs or activities which support its work, if the foundation makes grants or other payments to individuals to encourage their involvement in its field of interest and in some segment of the activities it carries on. An example of the latter would be grants to engage in scientific research projects under the general direction and supervision of the foundation.

This prohibition against mere distributions to grantees and the requirement of a significant involvement by the foundation in its programs nearly deprived one organization of operating foundation status but for a liberal construction by the IRS of the rules. A foundation (a trust) that operates a cultural center formed a corporation controlled by it to act in a fiduciary capacity on its behalf in conducting the operations of the center. An amount equal to substantially all of the foundation's net income is turned over each year to the corporation and disbursed in the operation of the center. The corporation holds income and property from the foundation as a fiduciary and not as an absolute owner. The IRS ruled that the corporation is not a grantee organization that receives

[7] Code § 4942(g)(2); Reg. § 53.4942(b)-1(b)(1).
[8] Rev. Rul. 74-450, 1974-2 C.B. 388.
[9] Reg. § 53.4942(b)-1(b)(2).

qualifying distributions from the trust but is a trustee of the trust, thereby enabling the foundation to qualify as an operating foundation.[10]

The term "substantially all," as used in the private operating foundation income test, means 85 percent. Thus, under the law for pre-1982 tax years, the income test required that at least 85 percent of the foundation's adjusted net income be devoted to the active conduct of one or more tax-exempt functions. Also, under prior law, qualification under the income test was not lost if the operating foundation made grants to organizations or engaged in other activities with the remainder of its adjusted net income and other funds.[11] However, under the law for tax years beginning after December 31, 1981, the amount that need be distributed by a private operating foundation may be less than 85 percent of its adjusted net income.

For a private operating foundation, its minimum investment return is 5 percent (the same as the standard private foundation minimum investment return) of its noncharitable assets.[12] Under the new definition, therefore, the amount that must be annually expended by an operating foundation for the active conduct of charitable activities is one of the following: (1) where the amount equal to 85 percent of an operating foundation's adjusted net income is less than the applicable portion of minimum investment return (4.25 percent), the foundation's payout requirement would be the same as under prior law, and (2) where the amount equal to 85 percent of an operating foundation's adjusted net income is greater than the applicable portion of minimum investment return, the amount that must be distributed is equal to 4.25 percent of the value of the noncharitable assets of the foundation.

The new rules add a cryptic sentence at the end of the definition of the term "private operating foundation," reading: "Notwithstanding the provisions of subparagraph (A) [the "income test" provision], if the qualifying distributions . . . of an organization for the taxable year exceed the minimum investment return for the taxable year, clause (ii) of subparagraph (A) [the new substantially-all-of-minimum-investment-return limitation on the payout amount] shall not apply unless substantially all of such qualifying distributions are made directly for the active conduct of the activities constituting the purpose or function for which it is organized and operated." This means that the new—and in this case lower—ceiling on the required operating foundation payout amount will not be applicable if the foundation's qualifying distributions in excess of the year's minimum investment return are not expended in conformance with the income

---

[10]Rev. Rul. 78-315, 1978-2 C.B. 271.

[11]Reg. § 53.4942(b)-1(c).

[12]A private operating foundation must, in addition to satisfying the income test, meet one of three other tests. One of these is the "endowment" test (*infra*) requiring a foundation to normally make qualifying distributions directly for the active conduct of charitable activities equal to at least two-thirds of the minimum investment return (Code § 4942(j)(3)(B)(ii)). This payout amount, which is 3⅓ percent (⅔ of 5 percent), remains unaffected by the change in the law in 1981.

test requirements. That is, in such an instance, the prior law applies, namely, the requirement becomes—once again—that a minimum of 85 percent of adjusted net income must go to the active conduct of the charitable activities.

Moreover, this rule is intended to expand the "substantially all" test to embrace not just an amount equal to adjusted net income but all amounts expended in the form of qualifying distributions (cash and/or property). The design of this rule is to preclude the opportunity for a private nonoperating foundation to qualify for operating foundation status while funding substantial grant programs out of distributions that exceed an amount equal to 4.25 percent of the value of noncharitable assets. A private operating foundation that engages in such a practice will likely lose its operating foundation classification for the year involved.[13]

As an illustration, assume a private operating foundation X, with $500,000 of noncharitable assets, operating on the calendar year basis, with annual adjusted net income of $50,000 (10 percent of the assets). For 1981, X is required to expend for the active conduct of its charitable activities at least $42,500 (85 percent of $50,000). For 1982 (assuming the same value of assets and same income), the mandatory payout for X would be considerably smaller, namely, $21,250, that being the lesser of substantially all of adjusted net income ($42,500) or substantially all of minimum investment return (85 percent of 5 percent of $500,000, or $21,250). Concerning the new rule relating to "excess" qualifying distributions, assume that in 1982 X distributed $30,000. This amount is in excess of the minimum investment return ($25,000), so the new rule is activated. The intention of the new rule is to require—to assure continuity of X's operating foundation status—that X expend at least $25,500 (85 percent of $30,000) for the active conduct of its tax-exempt activities. In fact, however, the new rule does not work that way. Suppose that X expended $25,200 of the $30,000 (84 percent) for the active conduct of its tax-exempt activities. This would trigger the new rule, because the actual distributions for the active conduct of exempt activities ($25,200) exceed the minimum investment return ($25,000). Since the amount expended in 1982 for the active conduct of its exempt activities ($25,200) is less than 85 percent of its total distributions (of $30,000), the

---

[13]The entire rule does not become operative until a foundation's annual distributions exceed its minimum investment return. Where the rule is activated, the new substantially-all-of-minimum-investment-return limitation on the payout amount (Code § 4942(j)(3)(A)(ii)) will not apply unless substantially all of the total distributions meet the income test. If that test is thus met, the new limitation applies (although, in that context, it does not matter, since the larger actual payout meets the substantially-all test continued from prior law). However, if that test is not met, because substantially all of the total distributions do not meet the income test requirement, the new limitation does not apply. This would leave only the 85-percent-of-adjusted-net-income test (Code § 4942(j)(3)(A)(i)), which—since it applies only to adjusted net income, an amount that may be lower than "qualifying distributions"—may not cause the desired result of imposing the percent test on all the distributions of the year, and may cause the operating foundation to be in violation of the income test payout requirements.

minimum investment return limitation is eliminated, resulting in a payout requirement of $42,500. This requirement is not satisfied ($25,200 < $42,500) nor is the intended result of requiring X to expend $25,500 of the $30,000 for the active conduct of tax-exempt activities, leaving the new rule not operating as intended and X in violation of the payout rule.

Thus, this new rule carries with it a substantial sanction. If it is violated (namely, if 85 percent of total qualifying distributions in excess of minimum investment return are not devoted to the active conduct of charitable activities), the payout requirement probably cannot be met, and the organization will likely lose its operating foundation status for the year involved and become classified as a private foundation.

The IRS has privately ruled that qualifying distributions from an operating foundation to a charitable corporation that it controls were not expenditures made directly for the active conduct of the tax-exempt functions of the operating foundation. The rationale for this conclusion was that the recipient organization was a "separate entity" that would utilize the foundation's payments in furtherance of its own programs. The operating foundation, which operates a museum and library, wanted to conduct certain educational programs by means of a corporation, so as to provide a shield against liabilities and to have personnel policies for the corporation's staff that were different from those for the foundation's staff. The new corporation was to be wholly owned by the foundation. Under the facts, the IRS was able to conclude that the payments by the operating foundation would have constituted qualifying distributions. However, the Service noted that an operating foundation is required to conduct charitable programs on its own rather than by means of grantee organizations. If this private ruling accurately reflects the law, private operating foundations may not operate charitable programs through separate corporations (subsidiaries) but, at best, may utilize separate but unincorporated entities that are integral parts of the foundation (e.g., divisions or branches).

Amounts paid to acquire or maintain assets used directly in the conduct of the foundation's tax-exempt activities constitute qualifying distributions. Examples of these expenditures are payments for the operating assets of a museum, public park, or historic site. Reasonable administrative expenses (for example, salaries and travel outlays) and other necessary operating costs are likewise the subject of qualifying distributions. However, administrative expenses and operating costs which are not attributable to tax-exempt activities, such as expenses in connection with the production of investment income, do not qualify. Expenses attributable to both exempt and nonexempt activities must be allocated to each activity on a reasonable and consistently applied basis.

In addition to the income test, to qualify as an operating foundation, an organization must satisfy either the "assets test," the "endowment test," or the "support test."[14]

---

[14]Reg. § 53.4942(b)-1(a).

Assets Test

An organization will satisfy the assets test[15] only if substantially more than one-half (that is, at least 65 percent[16]) of its assets are (1) devoted directly to the active conduct of its tax-exempt activities or to functionally related businesses[17] or to a combination thereof, (2) stock of a corporation which is controlled[18] by the foundation and substantially all (85 percent) of the assets of which are so devoted, or (3) in part assets described in (1) and part stock described in (2).[19] The assets test is particularly applicable to organizations such as nonpublicly supported museums.

An asset, to qualify under this test, must actually be used by the organization directly for the active conduct of its tax-exempt purpose. This type of asset includes the real estate, physical facilities or objects (for example, museum assets, classroom fixtures and equipment, and research facilities), and intangible assets (for example, patents, copyrights, and trademarks), but does not include assets held for the production of income, for investment, or for some other similar use. Property used both for tax-exempt purposes and other purposes will meet the assets test (assuming it otherwise qualified) as long as the tax-exempt use represents at least 95 percent of total use.[20]

For purposes of the assets test, all assets of an organization are valued at their fair market value.[21] However, in the case of assets which are properly devoted and for which neither a ready market nor standard valuation method exists (for example, art works or historical buildings), fair market value is considered equal to historical costs, unless the organization can demonstrate otherwise.[22]

Endowment Test

An organization will satisfy the endowment test[23] only where it normally expended its funds, in the form of qualifying distributions, directly for the active conduct of its tax-exempt activities, in an amount equal to at least two-thirds of its minimum investment return.[24] Thus, the private operating foundation payout requirement obligates the organization to distribute annually an amount equal to at least 3 $\frac{1}{3}$ ($\frac{2}{3} \times 5$) percent of the value of its noncharitable assets.

---

[15]Code § 4942(j)(3)(B)(i).
[16]Reg. § 53.4942(b)-2(a)(5).
[17]See Code § 4942(j)(5).
[18]See Code § 368(c).
[19]Reg. § 53.4942(b)-2(a)(1).
[20]Reg. § 53.4942(b)-2(a)(2).
[21]Reg. §§ 53.4942(b)-2(a)(4), 53.4942(a)-2(c)(4).
[22]Reg. § 53.4942(b)-2(a)(4).
[23]Code § 4942(j)(3)(B)(ii).
[24]Code § 4942(e); Reg. § 53.4942(b)-2(b)(1). See Chapter 26.

The concept of expenditures directly for the active conduct of tax-exempt activities under the endowment test is the same as that under the income test.[25] The endowment test is appropriate for organizations which actively conduct charitable activities (for example, research), but the services of which are so great in relationship to assets that the cost of these services cannot be met out of their endowment.

An organization which, on May 26, 1969, and at all times thereafter before the close of the tax year, operated and maintained, as its principal functional purpose, facilities for the long-term care, comfort, maintenance, or education of permanently and totally disabled persons, elderly persons, needy widows, or children, qualifies as an operating foundation, pursuant to Code § 4942(j)(6), if the organization meets the requirements of the endowment test.[26] This rule applies only for purposes of the foundation distribution requirements and therefore the rules for deductibility of contributions to such an organization are determined as if the organization is not an operating foundation (unless it meets a definition of a public charity or otherwise qualifies as an operating foundation).[27]

Support Test

An organization will satisfy the support test[28] only if (1) substantially all (85 percent[29]) of its support[30] (other than gross investment income[31]) is normally received from the general public and from at least five tax-exempt organizations which are not disqualified persons[32] with respect to each other or the recipient foundation, (2) not more than 25 percent of its support (other than gross investment income) is normally received from any one such organization, and (3) not more than one-half of its support is normally received from gross investment income.[33]

The support received by an organization from any one tax-exempt organi-

---

[25]Reg. § 4942(b)-2(b)(2).

[26]Code § 4942(j)(6).

[27]While formulating the Senate's version of the Tax Reform Act of 1976, the Senate Finance Committee concluded that the two-thirds expenditure requirement applicable to operating foundations, the status of which is based on the income and endowment tests, "may be onerous in light of the existing requirement that they distribute substantially all of their income" for the charitable purposes. S. Rep. No. 94-938 (Part 2), 94th Cong., 2d Sess. (1976) at 89. Consequently, the 1976 Senate bill would have lowered the endowment test requirement to a flat three percent of the average value of the assets of the operating foundation which are not used in the active conduct of its charitable activities. However, this revision did not survive to enactment.

[28]Code § 4942(j)(3)(B)(iii).

[29]Reg. § 53.4942(b)-2(c)(2)(ii).

[30]See Code § 509(d).

[31]See Code § 509(e).

[32]See Code § 4946(a)(1)(H); see Chapter 24.

[33]Reg. § 53.4942(b)-2(c)(1).

zation may be counted toward satisfaction of the support test only if the organization receives support from at least four other tax-exempt organizations. The regulations permit an organization to receive support from five tax-exempt organizations and no support from the general public,[34] although the statute appears to require both. Support received from an individual, trust, or corporation (other than an exempt organization) is taken into account as support from the general public only to the extent that the total amount received from any such source (including attributed sources) during the computational period (see below) does not exceed one percent of the organization's total support (other than gross investment income) for the period. However, support from a governmental unit, while treated as from the general public, is not subject to this one percent limitation.[35]

Organizations meeting the support test often have developed an expertise in an area and thus are targets for charitable contributions and grants by private foundations to enable them to sustain programs in their areas of specialization.

Other Requirements

An organization may satisfy the income test and either the assets, endowment, or support test by meeting the requirements (1) for any three tax years during a four-year period consisting of the tax year in question and the three immediately preceding tax years or (2) on the basis of an aggregation of all pertinent amounts of income or assets held, received, or distributed during the four-year period. The same method must be used for satisfying the income test and one of the three other tests for a particular tax year, although the methods may be alternated as respects a subsequent tax year.[36]

Generally, the status of grants or contributions made to an operating foundation are not affected until notice of change of status of the organization is communicated to the general public. This is not the case, however, if the grant or contribution was made after (1) the act or failure to act that resulted in the organization's inability to satisfy the requirements of one or more of the above tests, and the grantor or contributor was responsible for or was aware of the act or failure to act, or (2) the grantor or contributor acquired knowledge that the IRS had given notice to the organization that it would be deleted from classification as an operating foundation.[37] However, a grantor or contributor will not be deemed to have the requisite responsibility or awareness under (1) above if the grantor or contributor made his or her grant or contribution in reliance upon a written statement by the grantee organization containing sufficient facts to the effect that the grant or contribution would not result in the inability of the grantee organization to qualify as an operating foundation.[38]

[34]Reg. § 53.4942(b)-2(c)(2)(iii).
[35]Reg. § 53.4942(b)-2(c)(2)(iv).
[36]Reg. § 53.4942(b)-3.
[37]Reg. § 53.4942(b)-3(d)(1).
[38]Reg. § 53.4942(b)-3(d)(2).

Because an operating foundation is required to spend or use substantially all of its income for the active conduct of charitable purposes, it is not subject to the minimum payout requirements nor required to expend its entire income. Moreover, an operating foundation can be the recipient of grants from a "standard" private foundation without having to spend the funds so received within one year (see conduit foundations, below), with the funds nevertheless qualifying as expenditures of income by the donating foundation for purposes of its mandatory distribution requirements. Further, charitable contributions to private operating foundations are eligible for the 50 percent and 30 percent limitations.[39] In addition, a donor may contribute appreciated property to a private operating foundation without having to reduce the deduction by 40 percent of the appreciated value of the property, as is the case with appreciated property gifts to private nonoperating foundations.[40]

§ 23.2　Conduit Foundations

The "conduit foundation" is a private nonoperating foundation which makes qualifying distributions,[41] which are treated[42] as distributions out of corpus,[43] in an amount equal in value to 100 percent of all contributions received in the year involved, whether as cash or property.[44] The distributions must be made not later than the 15th day of the third month after the close of the foundation's tax year in which the contributions were received, and the foundation must not have any remaining undistributed income for the year.

The qualifying distribution may be of the contributed property itself or of proceeds of the sale of contributed property. In making the calculation in satisfaction of the 100 percent requirement, the original rule was that the amount distributed must be equal to the fair market value of the contributed property on the date of its contribution. However, effective March 1, 1980, the amount of this fair market value may be reduced by any reasonable selling expenses incurred by the foundation in the sale of the contributed property. Also, at the choice of the foundation, if the contributed property is sold or distributed within 30 days of its receipt by the foundation, the amount of the fair market value is either the gross amount received on the sale of the property (less reasonable selling expenses) or an amount equal to the fair market value of the property on the date of its distribution to a public charity.[45]

[39]Code §§ 170(b)(1)(A)(vii), 170(b)(1)(D)(i). See Chapter 3 § 2.
[40]Code § 170(e)(1)(B)(ii).
[41]See Code § 4942(g), other than Code § 4942(g)(3). In general, see Chapter 26.
[42]Such treatment is after the application of Code § 4942(g)(3). This means that every contribution described in Code § 4942(g)(3) (see Chapter 26 § 2, *infra*) received by the conduit foundation in a particular tax year must be distributed by it by the 15th day of the third month after the close of that year in order for any other distribution by the foundation to be counted toward the 100-percent requirement.
[43]See Code § 4942(h).
[44]Code § 170(b)(1)(D)(ii); Reg. § 1.170A-9(g)(1).
[45]Reg. § 1.170A-9(g)(2)(iv).

These distributions are treated as made first out of contributions of property and then out of contributions of cash received by the foundation in the year involved. The distributions cannot be made to an organization controlled directly or indirectly by the foundation or by one or more disqualified persons[46] with respect to the foundation or to a private foundation which is not an operating foundation.

These rules may be illustrated by the following example:

X is a private foundation on the calendar year basis. As of January 1, 1979, X had no undistributed income for 1978. X's distributable amount for 1979 was $600,000. In July, 1979, A, an individual, contributed $500,000 of appreciated property (which, if sold, would give rise to long-term capital gain) to X. X did not receive any other contribution in either 1978 or 1979. During 1979, X made qualifying distributions of $700,000, which were treated as made out of the undistributed income for 1979 (of $600,000) and the balance ($100,000) out of corpus. X will qualify as a conduit foundation for 1979 if it makes additional qualifying distributions of $400,000 out of corpus by March 15, 1980.

If the facts were as stated above, except that as of January 1, 1979, X had $100,000 of undistributed income for 1978, the $700,000 distributed by X in 1979 would be treated as made out of the undistributed income for 1978 and 1979 ($700,000). X would, therefore, have to make additional qualifying distributions of $500,000 out of corpus between January 1, 1980, and March 15, 1980, if X is to qualify as a conduit foundation for 1979.[47]

If the facts were as stated in the foregoing paragraph, but the calendar years involved were 1981 and 1982, the qualifying distributions which would otherwise have to total $500,000 may be less than that amount if the contributed property is sold or distributed within 30 days of its receipt by the foundation.

Charitable contributions to conduit foundations qualify as deductible items eligible for the 50 percent and 30 percent limitations.[48] The contributor must obtain adequate records or other sufficient evidence from the foundation showing that the foundation made the qualifying distributions.[49]

§ 23.3 "Common Fund" Foundations

A special type of private nonoperating foundation is one which pools contributions received in a common fund but allows the donor or his or her spouse (including substantial contributors) to retain the right to designate annually the organizations to which the income attributable to the contributions is given (as long as the organizations qualify as certain types of entities that are not private foundations[50]) and to direct (by deed or will) the organizations to which the

[46]See Chapter 24.
[47]Reg. § 1.170A-9(g)(4).
[48]Code § 170(b)(1)(A)(vii). See Chapter 3 § 2.
[49]Reg. § 1.170A-9(g)(1), Examples (1) and (2).
[50]Code § 509(a)(1). See Chapter 22 §§ 1 and 2.

corpus of the contributions is eventually to be given. Moreover, this type of foundation must pay out its adjusted net income to public charities by the 15th day of the third month after the close of the tax year in which the income is realized by the fund and the corpus must be distributed to the charities within one year after the death of the donor or his or her spouse.[51]

In the sole instance of the IRS to publicly rule on the status of a private foundation as a "common fund" foundation, the Service considered an exempt trust that is operated, supervised, and controlled by the distribution committee of a community trust.[52] Its function is to receive and pool contributions, and to distribute its income to publicly supported charities. Every donor has the right to designate the charitable recipients of the trust's income and of the corpus of the fund attributable to his or her contribution. All of the other requirements of the common fund foundation rules were satisfied in this instance and therefore the Service concluded that the trust qualifies as a common fund foundation.[53] Were it not for the fact that the donors have the right to designate the recipients, the trust would have qualified as a supporting organization[54] and not as a private foundation.

Contributions to this type of foundation also qualify for the 50 and 30 percent limitations on the charitable deduction.[55]

§ 23.4   Research and Experimentation Funds

One of the purposes of Congress in enacting the Economic Recovery Tax Act of 1981 was to provide incentives for an increase in the conduct of research and experimentation. Consequently, a 25 percent tax credit was created for certain research and experimental expenditures paid in carrying on a trade or business.[56] The credit is allowable to the extent that current-year expenditures exceed the average amount of research expenditures in a base period (generally, the preceding three tax years). Subject to certain exclusions, the term "qualified research" used for purposes of the credit is the same as that used for purposes of the deduction rules for research expenses.[57]

[51]Code § 170(b)(1)(D)(iii).
[52]See Chapter 22 § 1.
[53]Rev. Rul. 80-305, 1980-2 C. B. 71.
[54]See Chapter 22 § 3.
[55]Code § 170(b)(1)(A)(vii). See Chapter 3 § 2.
[56]Code § 44F. This change in the law was occasioned by enactment of § 221 of the 1981 Act and the new rules apply to amounts paid or incurred after June 30, 1981, and before January 1, 1986.
[57]A taxpayer may elect to deduct currently the amount of research or experimental expenditures incurred in connection with the taxpayer's trade or business or may elect to amortize certain research costs over a period of at least 60 months (Code § 174). These rules apply to the costs of research conducted on behalf of the taxpayer by a research firm, university, or the like.

Research expenditures qualifying for this new credit consist of two basic types: "in-house research" expenses and "contract research" expenses.

In-house research expenditures are those for research wages and supplies, along with certain lease or other charges for research use of computers, laboratory equipment, and the like. Contract research expenditures are 65 percent of amounts paid to another person (for example, a research firm or university) for research.

A tax credit is also available for 65 percent of an amount paid by a corporation to a qualified organization for basic research to be performed by the recipient organization, where the relationship is evidenced by a written research agreement. (This research is a form of "contract research.") The term "basic research" means "any original investigation for the advancement of scientific knowledge not having a specific commercial objective, except that such term shall not include (A) basic research conducted outside the United States, and (B) basic research in the social sciences or humanities."

For purposes of the rules concerning basic contract research, a "qualified organization" is either (1) an institution of higher education[58] that is a tax-exempt educational organization[59] or (2) any other type of charitable, educational, scientific, or like tax-exempt organization[60] that is organized and operated primarily to conduct scientific research and is not a private foundation.[61]

A special provision allows certain "funds" organized and operated exclusively to make basic research grants to institutions of higher education to be considered as "qualifying organizations," even though the funds do not themselves perform the research. To qualify, a fund must be a charitable, educational, scientific, or like tax-exempt organization, not be a private foundation, be established and maintained by an organization that is a public charity and was created prior to July 10, 1981, and make its grants under written research agreements. Moreover, a fund must elect to become this type of a "qualified fund"; by making the election, the fund becomes treated as a private foundation, except that the investment income excise tax[62] is not applicable.[63]

[58]Code § 3304(f).
[59]Code § 170(b)(A)(ii). See Chapter 22 § 1.
[60]Code § 501(c)(3).
[61]One of the questions thus posed by this provision is whether private operating foundations (see § 1) are eligible to participate in this contract research program. Certainly these types of foundations that conduct their own research should be qualified organizations for this purpose, notwithstanding the general prohibition against the involvement of private foundations (Code § 44F(e)(2)(B)(iii)). By contrast, for purposes of the new provision allowing an estate and gift tax charitable contribution deduction for the transfer of a work of art to a qualified charitable organization, irrespective of whether the copyright therein is simultaneously transferred to the charitable organization, a private operating foundation is expressly included as a qualified organization (Code § 2055(e)(4)(D)) even though "private foundations" are excluded.
[62]Code § 4940. See Chapter 30.
[63]Once this election is made, it can be revoked only with the consent of the IRS.

Thus, Congress has created a category of organizations that, because of the nature of their programs (rather than the nature of their support or degree of public involvement), are regarded as private foundations. Apparently this status as a private foundation continues only as long as the fund makes the qualified basic research grants and the fund can revert to some form of public charity when and if it ceases making the grants.

§ 23.5　Other Types of "Foundations"

The community foundation is in essence a fund created by contributions to support charitable activities primarily in a single geographical area. This type of organization may not be a "private foundation" at all but rather a public charity.[64]

Many corporations have associated foundations which perform charitable activities (for example, research, community development) which are related to the business of or undertaken with use of the name of the corporation.

Most public colleges and universities have related "foundations," usually public charities, which are used to attract charitable contributions for activities of the respective institutions.[65] Comparable organizations are often created for private educational institutions, hospitals, and other institutions but, in the absence of a special provision, must find their nonprivate foundation designation under the general rules.[66]

Trusts which are not exempt from federal tax are generally subjected to the same requirements and restrictions that are applicable to private foundations if the trust has any unexpired interests that are devoted to charitable purposes.[67] The reason for this rule is to prevent such a trust from being used to avoid the requirements and restrictions imposed on private foundations.

[64]See Chapter 22.

[65]Code § 170(b)(1)(A)(iv). See Chapter 22.

[66]Such an organization would find its public charity status under Code § 170(b)(1)(A)(vi), 509(a)(2), or 509(a)(3).

[67]Code § 4947. See Chapter 33.

24

Disqualified Persons

A basic concept of the tax laws relating to private foundations is that of the "disqualified person." An understanding of the meaning of this term, as defined in Code § 4946(a)(1), is essential to appreciation of the scope of the rules defining "permitted sources"[1] and against "self dealing"[2] and other private foundation rules. Essentially, a disqualified person is a person[3] (including an individual, corporation, partnership, trust, estate, or other foundation) standing in one or more particular relationships with respect to a private foundation.

§ 24.1 Substantial Contributor

One category of disqualified person[4] is a "substantial contributor" to the foundation.[5] The term means any person who contributed[6] or bequeathed an aggregate amount of more than $5,000 to the private foundation, where the amount is more than two percent of the total contributions and bequests received by the foundation before the close of its tax year in which the contribution or bequest is received by the foundation from that person. In computing against the $5,000/two percent tests, all contributions and bequests to the foundation since its creation are taken into account. The following example illustrates this rule:

> Throughout its existence through December 31, 1979, private foundation M (which has a calendar tax year) received $250,000 in contributions and bequests from all sources. Two percent of that amount is $5,000. On January 1, 1978, individual A made a first-time gift to M of $4,500. On January 1, 1979, A gave M $600. A became a substantial contributor to M on January 1, 1979.

[1]See Chapter 22.
[2]See Chapter 25.
[3]See Code § 7701(a)(1).
[4]Code § 4946(a)(1)(A).
[5]Code § 507(d)(2)(A).
[6]See Reg. § 1.507-6(c).

In the case of a trust, the term "substantial contributor" also means the creator of the trust.[7] The term "person" includes tax-exempt organizations[8] (except as discussed below) but does not include governmental units.[9] Once a person becomes a substantial contributor to a private foundation, he, she, or it can never escape that status,[10] even though he, she, or it might not be so classified if the determination were first made at a later date.[11]

For certain purposes,[12] the term "substantial contributor" does not include most organizations that are not private foundations[13] or an organization wholly owned by a public charity. Moreover, for purposes of the self-dealing rules, the term does not include any "charitable" organization,[14] since to require inclusion of such an organization would preclude private foundations from making large grants to or otherwise dealing with other private foundations.[15] However, in computing the support fraction for purposes of one category of publicly supported organization[16] the term "substantial contributor" includes public charities where the $5,000/two percent test is exceeded, although the support may qualify as a material change in support or an unusual grant. For support test purposes, contributions and bequests made before October 9, 1969, are taken into account in the year when they are actually made.[17]

In determining whether a contributor is a substantial contributor, the total of the amounts received from the contributor and the total contributions and bequests received by the foundation must be ascertained as of the last day of each tax year commencing with the first year ending after October 9, 1969.[18] Generally, all contributions and bequests made before October 9, 1969, are deemed to have been made on that date, and each contribution or bequest made thereafter is valued at its fair market value on the date received, with an individual treated as making all contributions and bequests made by his or her spouse.[19]

Thus, each private foundation must maintain a running tally of contributions and bequests from persons, taking into account the attribution rules (see below). For a private foundation with a calendar tax year, it should have determined

[7]See Reg. § 1.507-6(a)(1).

[8]That is, organizations encompassed by Code § 501(a).

[9]That is, entities described in Code § 170(c)(1).

[10]Code § 507(d)(2)(B)(iv).

[11]Reg. § 1.507-6(b)(1).

[12]Code §§ 170(b)(1)(D)(iii), 507(d)(1), 508(d), 509(a)(1) and (3), and Code Chapter 42.

[13]That is, organizations described in Code § 509(a)(1),(2) or (3). See Chapter 22.

[14]For these purposes, an organization described in Code § 501(c)(3), other than an organization that tests for public safety (Code § 509(a)(4)).

[15]Reg. § 1.507-6(a)(2). This exception also applies to Code § 4947(a)(1) trusts (see Chapter 33). Rev. Rul. 73-455, 1973-2 C. B. 187.

[16]Code § 509(a)(2)(A). See Chapter 22.

[17]Reg. § 1.507-6(b)(1).

[18]*Ibid.*

[19]Code § 507(d)(2)(B)(i)-(iii).

the total contributions and bequests received by it from all persons and the aggregate contributions and bequests made by a particular person as of December 31, 1969, and should thereafter make a similar determination as of the end of each succeeding tax year using accumulating totals.

A donor becomes a substantial contributor as of the first date when the foundation received from him, her, or it an amount sufficient to make him, her, or it a substantial contributor,[20] so the foundation should tabulate accumulating totals as the contributions and bequests are received, lest the foundation inadvertently commit an act of self-dealing or otherwise violate one or more of the other rules regulating the activities of private foundations.[21] However, the determination as to substantial contributor status is not made until the last day of the tax year, so that contributions and bequests made subsequent to the gifts of the contributor in question but within the same tax year may operate to keep him, her, or it out of substantial contributor status even though that status was temporarily obtained at an earlier point during the year. These rules may be illustrated as follows:

> On July 21, 1964, X Corporation gave Y Foundation (which has a calendar tax year) $2,000. As of December 31, 1969, Y had received $150,000 in contributions and bequests from all sources. On September 17, 1970, X gave Y an additional $3,100. As of September 17, 1970, Y had received a total of $245,000 in contributions and bequests from all sources. Between September 17, 1970, and December 31, 1970, Y received another $50,000 in contributions and bequests from others. X "temporarily" was a substantial contributor to Y on September 17, 1970, because X's gifts totaling $5,100 were at that time over the two percent maximum ($2\% \times \$245{,}000 = \$4{,}900$), although X is not a substantial contributor as of December 31, 1970, since the two percent maximum is $5,900 ($2\% \times \$295{,}000$).

§ 24.2   Foundation Manager

Another category of disqualified person[22] is a "foundation manager," defined to mean an officer, director, or trustee of a private foundation, or an individual having powers or responsibilities similar thereto.[23] A person is considered an "officer" of a private foundation if he or she is specifically so designated under the constitutive documents of the foundation or he or she regularly exercises general authority to make administrative or policy decisions on behalf of the foundation. Independent contractors, such as lawyers, accountants, and investment managers and advisers, acting in their capacity as such, are not "officers."[24] However, in one case, the IRS determined that employees of a bank which was the trustee of a private foundation were foundation managers, be-

---

[20]Reg. § 1.507-6(b)(1).
[21]In general, see Code Chapter 42.
[22]Code § 4946(a)(1)(B); Reg. § 53.4946-1(f)(1).
[23]Code § 4946(b)(1).
[24]Reg. § 53.4946-1(f)(2).

cause "they are free, on a day-to-day basis, to administer the trust and distribute the funds according to their best judgment."[25]

Certain foundation managers are excluded from disqualified person status.[26]

§ 24.3   Certain 20 Percent Owners

An owner of more than 20 percent of the total "combined voting power" of a corporation, the "profits interest" of a partnership, or the "beneficial interest" of a trust or unincorporated enterprise, any of which is (during the ownership) a substantial contributor to the private foundation, is a disqualified person.[27]

The term "combined voting power"[28] includes voting power represented by holdings of voting stock, actual or constructive,[29] but does not include voting rights held only as a director or trustee.[30] Thus, for example, an employee stock ownership trust[31] that held 30 percent of the stock of a corporation that was a substantial contributor to a private foundation on behalf of the corporation's participating employees (who direct the manner in which the trust votes the shares), was held to have merely the voting power of a trustee and not the ownership of the stock and thus to not be a disqualified person with respect to the foundation.[32]

The term "voting power" includes outstanding voting power and does not include voting power obtainable but not obtained, such as voting power obtainable by converting securities or nonvoting stock into voting stock, by exercising warrants or options to obtain voting stock, and voting power which will vest in preferred stockholders only if and when the corporation has failed to pay preferred dividends for a specified period of time or has otherwise failed to meet specified requirements.[33]

The "profits interest"[34] of a partner is that equal to his or her distributive share of income of the partnership as determined under special federal tax rules.[35] The term "profits interest" includes any interest that is outstanding but not any interest that is obtainable but has not been obtained.[36]

The "beneficial interest" in an unincorporated enterprise (other than a trust or estate) includes any right to receive a portion of distributions from profits of the enterprise or, in the absence of a profit-sharing agreeement, any right

---

[25]Rev. Rul. 74-287, 1974-1 C. B. 327.
[26]Code § 4946(b)(2); Reg. § 53.4946-1(f)(4).
[27]Code § 4946(a)(1)(C).
[28]Code § 4946(a)(1)(C)(i).
[29]See Code § 4946(a)(3).
[30]Reg. § 53.4946-1(a)(5). See, e.g., IRS Private Letter Ruling 8027078.
[31]Code § 4975(e).
[32]Rev. Rul. 81-76, 1981-1 C. B. 516.
[33]Reg. § 53.4946-1(a)(6).
[34]Code § 4946(a)(1)(C)(ii).
[35]Code §§ 707(b)(3), 4946(a)(4), Reg. § 53.4946-1(a)(2).
[36]Reg. § 53.4946-1(a)(6).

to receive a portion of the assets (if any) upon liquidation of the enterprise, except as a creditor or employee.[37] A right to receive distributions of profits includes a right to receive any amount from the profits other than as a creditor or employee, whether as a sum certain or as a portion of profits realized by the enterprise. Where there is no agreement fixing the rights of the participants in an enterprise, the fraction of the respective interests of each participant therein is determined by dividing the amount of all investments or contributions to the capital of the enterprise made or obligated to be made by the participant by the amount of all investments or contributions to capital made or obligated to be made by all of them.[38]

A person's beneficial interest in a trust is determined in proportion to the actuarial interest of the person in the trust.[39]

The term "beneficial interest" includes any interest that is outstanding but not any interest that is obtainable but has not been obtained.[40]

Constructive ownership of such rights and interests must be determined in accordance with the applicable attribution rules (see below).

§ 24.4 Family Members

Another category of disqualified person is a member of the family of an individual who is a substantial contributor, a foundation manager, or a 20 percent owner.[41] The term "member of the family" is defined to include an individual's spouse, ancestors, lineal descendants, and spouses of lineal descendants.[42] Thus, these family members are themselves disqualified persons, a result which becomes more troublesome the older the foundation, inasmuch as this rule can produce some bizarre situations and inadvertent acts of self-dealing. For example:

> X established a private foundation 50 years ago. X, now deceased, was a substantial contributor to the foundation. Z, X's grandson, is insane and never had any dealings with the foundation. Z's wife Q has become estranged from Z and the foundation's managers have not heard of or from her in over a decade. Yet Q is a disqualified person with respect to the foundation.

A legally adopted child of an individual is treated for these purposes as a child of the individual by blood. However, a brother or sister of an individual is not a "family member."[43]

---

[37]Code § 4946(a)(1)(C)(iii).
[38]Reg. § 53.4946-1(a)(3).
[39]Reg. § 53.4946-1(a)(4).
[40]Reg. § 53.4946-1(a)(6).
[41]Code § 4946(a)(1)(D).
[42]Code § 4946(d).
[43]Reg. § 53.4946-1(h).

§ 24.5   Corporation

A corporation is a disqualified person if more than 35 percent of the total combined voting power therein (including constructive holdings[44]) is owned by substantial contributors, foundation managers, twenty percent owners, or members of the family of any these individuals.[45]

In one situation, a corporation made an exchange offer to a private foundation concerning certain shares of the corporation's nonvoting stock. The corporation was once a disqualified person with respect to the foundation solely because an individual who was a manager of the foundation owned more than 35 percent of the total combined voting power of the corporation. Five years before the exchange took place, the foundation manager resigned that position. The IRS ruled that the resignation of the foundation manager terminated the status of the corporation as a disqualified person with respect to the foundation, noting that all aspects of the exchange occurred after the separation of the foundation manager and that he was not connected with the proposed exchange while serving in that capacity.[46]

§ 24.6   Partnership

A partnership is a disqualified person if more than 35 percent of the profits interests therein (including constructive holdings[47]) is owned by substantial contributors, foundation managers, twenty percent owners, or members of the family of any of these individuals.[48]

§ 24.7   Trust or Estate

A trust or estate is a disqualified person if more than 35 percent of the beneficial interest therein (including constructive holdings[49]) is owned by substantial contributors, foundation managers, twenty percent owners, or members of the family of any of these individuals.[50]

§ 24.8   Private Foundation

A private foundation may be a disqualified person with respect to another private foundation but only for purposes of the excess business holdings rules.[51]

---

[44]See Code § 4946(a)(3).

[45]Code § 4946(a)(1)(E).

[46]Rev. Rul. 76-448, 1976-2 C. B. 368. This ruling enabled the exchange to take place without causing an act of self-dealing under Code § 4941(d)(1)(A). See Chapter 26.

[47]See Code § 4946(a)(4).

[48]Code § 4946(a)(1)(F).

[49]See Code § 4946(a)(4).

[50]Code § 4946(a)(1)(G).

[51]Code § 4946(a)(1)(H). See Chapter 27.

The disqualified person private foundation must be effectively controlled,[52] directly or indirectly, by the same person or persons (other than a bank, trust company, or similar organization acting only as a foundation manager) who control the foundation in question, or must be the recipient of contributions substantially all of which were made, directly or indirectly, by substantial contributors, foundation managers, twenty percent owners, and members of their families who made, directly or indirectly, substantially all of the contributions to the foundation in question.[53] One or more persons are considered to have made "substantially all" of the contributions to a private foundation for these purposes if the persons have contributed or bequeathed at least 85 percent of the total contributions and bequests which have been received by the foundation during its entire existence, where each person has contributed or bequeathed at least two percent of such total.[54] For example:

> Foundation A has received contributions of $100,000 throughout its existence, as follows: $35,000 from X, $51,000 from Y (X's father), and $14,000 from Z (an unrelated person). During its existence, Foundation B has received $100,000 in contributions, as follows: $50,000 from X and $50,000 from Q (X's wife). For excess business holdings purposes, A is a disqualified person as to B and B is a disqualified person as to A.

§ 24.9 Governmental Official

A governmental official may be a disqualified person with respect to a private foundation but only for purposes of the self-dealing rules.[55] The term "governmental official" means (1) an elected public official in the U.S. Congress or executive branch, (2) presidential appointees to the U.S. executive or judicial branches, (3) certain higher compensated or ranking employees in one of these three branches, (4) House of Representatives or Senate employees earning at least $15,000 annually, (5) elected or appointed public officials in the U.S. or D.C. governments (including governments of U.S. possessions or political subdivisions or areas of the U.S.) earning at least $15,000 annually, or (6) the personal or executive assistant or secretary to any of the foregoing.[56]

In defining the term "public office" for purposes of the fifth category of governmental officials, this term must be distinguished from mere public employment. Although holding a public office is one form of public employment, not every position in the employ of a state or other governmental subdivision[57] constitutes a "public office." Although a determination as to whether a public employee holds a public office depends on the facts and circumstances of the

[52]See Reg. § 1.482-1(a)(3).
[53]Reg. § 53.4946-1(b)(1).
[54]Reg. § 53.4946-1(b)(2).
[55]Code § 4946(a)(1)(I). See Chapter 25.
[56]Code § 4946(c).
[57]See Code § 4946(c)(5).

case, the essential element is whether a significant part of the activities of a public employee is the independent performance of policy-making functions. Several factors may be considered as indications that a position in the executive, legislative, or judicial branch of the government of a state, possession of the United States, or political subdivision or other area of any of the foregoing, or of the District of Columbia, constitutes a "public office." Among the factors to be considered, in addition to that set forth above, are that the office is created by Congress, a state constitution, or the state legislature, or by a municipality or other governmental body pursuant to authority conferred by Congress, state constitution, or state legislature, and the powers conferred on the office and the duties to be discharged by the official are defined either directly or indirectly by Congress, a state constitution, or a state legislature, or through legislative authority.[58]

Further, in applying the rules concerning the fifth category of governmental officials, the $15,000 amount is the individual's "gross compensation."[59] This term refers to all receipts attributable to public office that are includible in gross income for federal income tax purposes. For example, an elected member of a state legislature may receive a salary of less than $15,000 each year, but also receive an expense allowance that, when added to the salary, results in a total amount of more than $15,000 per year; where the expense allowance is a fixed amount given to each legislator regardless of actual expenses and there is no restriction on its use and no requirement that an accounting for its use be made to the state, the expense allowance is part of the legislator's gross compensation and the legislator becomes a disqualified person.[60]

§ 24.10 Special Rules

For certain purposes,[61] the term "disqualified person" does not include most organizations that are not private foundations[62] or any other organization which is wholly owned by a public charity.

For purposes of the self-dealing rules only, the term "disqualified person" does not include any charitable organization.[63]

For the purpose of determining the combined voting power, profits interest, or beneficial interest of an individual, there are certain attribution rules.[64]

With respect to combined voting power,[65] stock (or profits or beneficial interests) owned directly or indirectly by or for a corporation, partnership,

[58]See Reg. § 53.4946-1(g)(2).
[59]Code § 4946(c)(5).
[60]Rev. Rul. 77-473, 1977-2 C. B. 421.
[61]See n. 12, *supra*.
[62]See n. 13, *supra;* Reg. § 53.4946-1(a)(7).
[63]See n. 14, *supra;* Reg. § 53.4946-1(a)(8).
[64]Code § 4946(a).
[65]Code § 4946(a)(1)(C)(i), (a)(1)(E).

estate, or trust is considered as being owned proportionately by or for its shareholders, partners, or beneficiaries.[66] Also, an individual is considered as owning the stock owned by members of his or her family, as discussed.[67] Any stockholders which have been counted once (whether by reason of actual or constructive ownership) in applying these rules[68] are not counted a second time.[69] Essentially, the attribution rules are the same as the federal tax rules generally[70] and there is a special rule for constructive ownership of stock.[71] With respect to profits or beneficial interests, ownership thereof is similarly taken into account in determining whether an individual is a disqualified person.[72]

[66]Code § 267(c)(1); Reg. § 53.4946-1(d)(1).
[67]Code § 267(c)(4), as modified by Code § 4946(a)(4); Reg. § 53.4946-1(d)(1)(i).
[68]Code § 4946(a)(1)(E).
[69]Reg. § 53.4946-1(d)(1)(ii).
[70]Code § 267(c) is applied without regard to Code § 267(c)(3).
[71]Stock constructively owned by an individual by reason of the application of Code § 267(c)(2) is not treated as owned by him or her if he or she is described in Code § 4946(a)(1)(A), (B), or (C). See Reg. § 53.4946-1(d)(1).
[72]Reg. § 53.4946-1(e).

25

Self-Dealing

The general federal tax rules pertaining to "charitable" organizations impose upon each of them, including private foundations, the requirement that no part of the net earnings of the organization may inure to the benefit of any private shareholder or individual.[1]

§ 25.1 Background

Prior to enactment of the Tax Reform Act of 1969, Code § 503(b) specified a number of prohibited self-dealing transactions applicable to several categories of tax-exempt organizations, including many "charitable" organizations. Arms'-length standards were imposed with regard to loans, payments of compensation, preferential availability of services, substantial purchases or sales, and substantial diversions of income or corpus to or from creators (of trusts) and substantial donors, their families, and controlled corporations. The sanctions were loss of tax exemption for at least one tax year and, perhaps, loss of the ability to attract deductible charitable contributions.

This statutory scheme was deemed ineffective by Congress with respect to private foundations, as the following indicates:

Arm's-length standards have proved to require disproportionately great enforcement efforts, resulting in sporadic and uncertain effectiveness of the provisions. On occasion the sanctions are ineffective and tend to discourage the expenditure of enforcement effort. On the other hand, in many cases the sanctions are so great in comparison to the offense involved, that they cause reluctance in enforcement, especially in view of the element of subjectivity in applying arm's-length standards. Where the Internal Revenue Service does seek to apply sanctions in such circumstances, the same factors encourage extensive litigation and a noticeable reluctance by the courts to uphold severe sanctions.

Consequently, as a practical matter, prior law did not preserve the integrity of private foundations. Also, the Congress concluded that compliance with arm's-

[1]See Chapter 12.

439

length standards often does not in itself prevent the use of a private foundation to improperly benefit those who control the foundations. This is true, for example, where a foundation (1) purchases property from a substantial donor at a fair price, but does so in order to provide funds to the donor who needs cash and cannot find a ready buyer; (2) lends money to the donor with adequate security and at a reasonable rate of interest, but at a time when the money market is too tight for the donor to readily find alternate sources of funds; or (3) makes commitments to lease property from the donor at a fair rental when the donor needs such advance leases in order to secure financing for construction or acquisition of the property.

To minimize the need to apply subjective arm's-length standards, to avoid the temptation to misuse private foundations for noncharitable purposes, to provide a more rational relationship between sanctions and improper acts, and to make it more practical to properly enforce the law, the Act generally prohibits self-dealing transactions and provides a variety and graduation of sanctions, as described below. This is based on the belief by the Congress that the highest fiduciary standards require complete elimination of all self-dealing rather than arm's-length standards.[2]

Consequently, Code § 503(b) was repealed by Congress when it enacted the Tax Reform Act of 1969.

Any determination that the sanctions with respect to self-dealing are to be imposed requires the existence of three elements: (1) a private foundation, (2) a disqualified person, and (3) an act of self-dealing between the two. Whether an organization may be a private foundation has been previously discussed, as have the various types of disqualified persons. Hence, the purpose of this chapter is to analyze what transactions between the two constitute prohibited self-dealing, pursuant to Code § 4941.

It is immaterial whether a self-dealing transaction results in a benefit or a detriment to the foundation.[3] However, a self-dealing transaction does not include a transaction between a private foundation and a disqualified person where the disqualified person status arises only as a result of the transaction.[4]

§ 25.2 Indirect Self-Dealing

An act of self-dealing may be direct or indirect. An indirect act of self-dealing generally is a self-dealing transaction between a disqualified person and an

[2]Joint Committee on Internal Revenue Taxation, *General Explanation of Tax Reform Act of 1969*, 91st Cong., 2d Sess. (1970), at 30–31. For instances of application by the IRS of prior Code § 503, see Rev. Rul. 73-609, 1973-2 C. B. 187; Rev. Rul. 73-586, 1973-2 C. B. 186; Rev. Rul. 72-352, 1972-2 C. B. 395; Rev. Rul. 72-494, 1972-2 C. B. 249; Rev. Rul. 71-546, 1971-2 C. B. 239; Rev. Rul. 71-462, 1971-2 C. B. 238; Rev. Rul. 71-479, 1971-2 C. B. 238; Rev. Rul. 70-131, 1970-1 C. B. 135; Rev. Rul. 70-82, 1970-1 C. B. 134.

[3]See *Leon A. Beeghly Fund* v. *Commissioner*, 35 T. C. 490 (1960), aff'd 310 F.2d 756 (6th Cir. 1962).

[4]Reg. § 53.4941(d)-1(a).

organization controlled by a private foundation.[5] There are two basic tests for determining whether an organization is controlled by a private foundation for these purposes.[6] The following is an illustration of an indirect self-dealing transaction:

> Private foundation P owns the controlling interest of the voting stock of corporation X, and as a result of this interest, elects a majority of the board of directors of X. Two of the foundation managers, A and B, who are also directors of corporation X, form corporation Y for the purpose of building and managing a country club. A and B receive a total of 40 percent of Y's stock, making Y a disqualified person with respect to P. In order to finance the construction and operation of the country club, Y requested and received a loan in the amount of $4,000,000 from X. The making of the loan by X to Y constitutes an indirect act of self-dealing.

The first self-dealing case under the private foundation rules to be decided by a court involved acts of indirect self-dealing.[7] The individual involved wholly owned a corporation (Corporation A) which transferred two encumbered properties to another corporation (Corporation B), which was a wholly owned subsidiary of a private foundation (C), of which the individual was a trustee. This individual was a foundation manager by virtue of being a trustee of foundation C and thus a disqualified person with respect to the foundation, as was Corporation A because the individual owned more than 35 percent of the total combined voting power therein.[8] Therefore, the court ruled that the sale of one of the properties by Corporation A to Corporation B constituted an act of self-dealing.[9] (The transfer of the other property was deemed to not be an act of self-dealing because, as to that property, Corporation A was acting merely as a nominee for Corporation B.) Another act of self-dealing was found,[10] by reason of the fact that even though the properties conveyed were encumbered, Corporation B paid the full purchase price for them, with the understanding that either the individual involved or Corporation A would satisfy the outstanding mortgage liabilities on the properties; the court agreed with the government's contention that the failure by Corporation A to immediately satisfy the liabilities upon receipt of the funds from Corporation B gave rise to an implied loan to Corporation A from private foundation C in the amount of the outstanding mortgage liabilities.

The term "indirect self-dealing" does not include a transaction, which is one of the enumerated types of self-dealing transactions (see below), between a disqualified person and an organization controlled by a private foundation if (1) the transaction results from a business relationship which was established before

[5]See Reg. § 53.4941(d)-1(b).
[6]See Reg. § 53.4941(d)-1(b)(5); Rev. Rul. 76-158, 1976-1 C. B. 354.
[7]*Adams* v. *Commissioner*, 70 T. C. 373 (1978).
[8]See Chapter 24.
[9]Code § 4941(d)(1)(A).
[10]Code § 4941(d)(1)(B).

the transaction constituted an act of self-dealing under the federal tax rules, (2) the transaction was at least as favorable to the foundation-controlled organization as an arms'-length transaction with an unrelated person, and (3) either (a) the foundation-controlled organization could have engaged in the transaction with someone other than a disqualified person only at a severe economic hardship to the organization or (b) because of the unique nature of the product or services provided by the foundation-controlled organization, the disqualified person could not have engaged in the transaction with anyone else or could have done so only by incurring severe economic hardship.[11]

Also, the term "indirect self-dealing" does not include a transaction engaged in by an intermediary organization with a governmental official where the organization is a recipient of a grant from a private foundation if (1) the private foundation does not control the organization, (2) the foundation does not earmark the use of the grant for any named governmental official, and (3) there does not exist an agreement, oral or written, whereby the foundation may cause the selection of the governmental official by the intermediary organization. A grant by a private foundation will not constitute an indirect act of self-dealing even though the foundation had reason to believe that certain governmental officials would derive benefits from the grant as long as the intermediary organization exercises control, in fact, over the selection process and actually makes the selection completely independently of the foundation.[12]

Further, the term "indirect self-dealing" does not include a transaction involving one or more disqualified persons to which a private foundation is not a party, in any case in which the private foundation, by reason of certain rules,[13] could itself engage in the transaction. Thus, for example, even if a private foundation has control of a corporation, the corporation may pay to a disqualified person, except a governmental official, reasonable compensation for personal services.[14]

The term "indirect self-dealing" also does not include any transaction between a disqualified person and an organization controlled by a private foundation or between two disqualified persons where the foundation's assets may be affected by the transaction if:

(1) The transaction arises in the normal and customary course of a retail business engaged in with the general public,

(2) In the case of a transaction between a disqualified person and an organization controlled by a private foundation, the transaction is at least as favorable to the organization controlled by the foundation as an arms'-length transaction with an unrelated person, and

---

[11]Reg. § 53.4941(d)-1(b)(1).
[12]Reg. § 53.4941(d)-1(b)(2).
[13]Code § 4941(d)(2).
[14]Reg. § 53.4941(d)-1(b)(7).

(3) The total of the amounts involved in the transactions with respect to any one such disqualified person in any one tax year does not exceed $5,000.[15]

§ 25.3 Self-Dealing Transactions

The following transactions between a private foundation and one or more disqualified persons generally are acts of self-dealing: (1) sale or exchange, or leasing, of property, (2) lending of money or other extensions of credit, (3) furnishing of goods, services, or facilities, (4) payments of compensation or expenses, (5) transfer to or use by or for the benefit of a disqualified person, of the private foundation's income or assets, and (6) payments to government officials.[16]

Sale or Exchange of Property

The sale or exchange of property between a private foundation and a disqualified person generally constitutes an act of self-dealing.[17] For example, this type of an act of self-dealing would include the sale of (1) incidental supplies by a disqualified person to a private foundation, regardless of the amount paid to the disqualified person for the supplies and (2) stock or other securities by a disqualified person to a foundation in a "bargain sale," regardless of the amount paid for the securities.[18] The IRS has ruled that the sale of a private foundation's art objects at public auction, by an auction gallery which took the objects on consignment, to a disqualified person who proposed to be the highest bidder would constitute an act of self-dealing.[19] By contrast, an act of self-dealing under these rules does not occur where a private foundation purchases property from a trust, merely because a bank is trustee of both entities.[20]

An installment sale may be an act of self-dealing either as a sale of property[21] or an extension of credit.[22]

The transfer of real or personal property by a disqualified person to a private foundation is treated as a sale or exchange for these purposes if the private foundation assumes a mortgage or similar lien which was placed on the property prior to the transfer or takes the property subject to a mortgage or similar lien which a disqualified person placed on the property within the ten-year period ending on the date of transfer.[23] A "similar lien" includes, but is not limited

[15]Reg. § 53.4941(d)-1(b)(6). See also Reg. § 53.4941(d)-1(b)(3),(4).
[16]Code § 4941(d)(1).
[17]Code § 4941(d)(1)(A).
[18]Reg. § 53.4941(d)-2(a)(1).
[19]Rev. Rul. 76-18, 1976-1 C. B. 355.
[20]Rev. Rul. 78-77, 1978-1 C. B. 378.
[21]Code § 4941(d)(1)(A).
[22]Code § 4941(d)(1)(B).
[23]Code § 4941(d)(2)(A). See Reg. § 53.4941(d)-2(a)(2); Rev. Rul. 78-395, 1978-2 C. B. 270.

to, deeds of trust and vendors' liens, but does not include any other lien if it is insignificant in relation to the fair market value of the property transferred.

Leasing of Property

The leasing of property between a private foundation and a disqualified person generally constitutes self-dealing.[24] However, the leasing of property by a disqualified person to a private foundation without charge is not an act of self-dealing. A lease is considered to be without charge even though the foundation pays for janitorial services, utilities, or other maintenance costs, as long as the payment is not made directly or indirectly to a disqualified person.[25]

In one instance, a disqualified person transferred to a private foundation a parcel of real property that was subject to a lien placed on the property by the disqualified person within the ten-year period ending on the transfer date. When the property was originally acquired, the lien created by the deed of trust executed in conjunction with the purchase of the property was placed upon the property prior to the ten-year period. However, within the ten-year period, the disqualified person obtained a loan, and the lien created by the deed of trust executed in conjunction with this loan was placed on the land within the ten-year period. The IRS said that, for purposes of the self-dealing rules, "it does not matter that the taxpayer placed the second lien on the property as part of a multi-phased financing program begun more than ten years before the date of transfer."[26]

The IRS accords these rules broad application, as evidenced by its determination that the contribution to a private foundation by a disqualified person of a life insurance policy subject to a policy loan is an act of self-dealing. This conclusion was rested upon the analysis that a life insurance policy loan is sometimes characterized as an advance of the proceeds of the policy, with the loan and the interest thereon considered charges against the property, rather than amounts which must be paid the insurer.[27] The Service concluded that the effect of the transfer is essentially the same as the transfer of property subject to a lien, in that the transfer of the policy relieves the donor of the obligation to repay the loan, pay interest on the loan as it accrues, or suffer continued diminution in the value of the policy. Application of the self-dealing rules to this type of transaction was completed by a finding that the amount of the loan is not insignificant in relation to the value of the policy.[28]

---

[24]Code § 4941(d)(1)(A), Reg. § 53.4941(d)-2(b)(1). See, e.g., IRS Private Letter Ruling 7839061.

[25]Reg. § 53.4941(d)-2(b)(2).

[26]Rev. Rul. 78-395, *supra*, n. 23.

[27]For example, *Dean* v. *Commissioner*, 35 T. C. 1083 (1961).

[28]Rev. Rul. 80-132, 1980-1 C. B. 255.

Extension of Credit

The lending of money or other extension of credit between a private foundation and a disqualified person generally constitutes an act of self-dealing.[29] For example, this type of self-dealing occurs where a third party purchases property and assumes a mortgage, the mortgagee of which is a private foundation, and subsequently the third party transfers the property to a disqualified person who assumes liability under the mortgage or takes the property subject to the mortgage, or where a note, the obligor of which is a disqualified person, is transferred by a third party to a private foundation which becomes the creditor under the note.[30]

These rules do not apply to the lending of money or other extension of credit by a disqualified person to a private foundation if the loan or other extension of credit is without interest or other charge and the proceeds of the loan are used exclusively for tax-exempt purposes.[31] However, this exception is voided where the foundation cancels the debt by transferring property (e.g., securities) to the disqualified person-lender, because the IRS takes the position that the transfer, when viewed together with the making of the loan, is tantamount to a sale or exchange of property between the foundation and the disqualified person (see above) and thus constitutes an act of self-dealing.[32]

The making of a promise, pledge, or similar arrangement to a private foundation by a disqualified person, whether evidenced by an oral or written agreement, a promissory note, or other instrument of indebtedness, to the extent motivated by charitable intent and unsupported by consideration, is not an "extension of credit" before the date of maturity.[33]

Thus, the performance by a bank or trust company which is a disqualified person of trust functions and certain general banking services for a private foundation is not an act of self-dealing, where the banking services are reasonable and necessary to carrying out the tax-exempt purposes of the private foundation, if the compensation paid to the bank or trust company, taking into account the fair interest rate for the use of the funds by the bank or trust company for the services, is not excessive.[34] The general banking services not

[29]Code § 4941(d)(1)(B).

[30]Reg. § 53.4941(d)-2(c)(1).

[31]Code § 4941(d)(2)(B); Reg. § 53.4941(d)-2(c)(2). A cost-sharing arrangement between a disqualified person/for-profit corporation and a private foundation, concerning reimbursements for an employee's group health insurance expenses, was determined not to be self-dealing because the transaction is an extension of credit without charge. IRS Private Letter Ruling 7952117.

[32]Rev. Rul. 77-379, 1977-2 C. B. 387.

[33]Reg. § 53.4941(d)-2(c)(3). For example, the satisfaction by donors (who are disqualified persons) of their pledges to a foundation before their due date at amounts less than face value was held not to be self-dealing. IRS Private Letter Ruling 8003134.

[34]Reg. § 53.4941(d)-2(c)(4).

constituting self-dealing are (1) checking accounts, as long as the bank does not charge interest on any overwithdrawals or a service fee in excess of the actual expense of processing the amount overdrawn,[35] (2) savings accounts, as long as the foundation may withdraw its funds on no more than 30 days' notice without subjecting itself to a loss of interest on its money for the time during which the money was on deposit,[36] and (3) safekeeping activities.[37] However, the purchase by a private foundation of a mortgage from a bank, a disqualified person that in the normal course of its business acquires and sells mortgages, was held to be an act of self-dealing because the bank, as the mortgage-holder, was not performing personal services as an agent for the foundation when it sold the mortgage and because the sale of the mortgage is not a general banking function.[38] Likewise, the IRS determined that the purchase of certificates of deposit by a private foundation from a banking institution that is a disqualified person is an act of self-dealing since—as is the case generally—the certificates provide for a reduced rate of interest (and thus a "loss" of interest) if they are not held to the full maturity date.[39] The Service considered the sale of these certificates of deposit to not constitute permissible "general banking services."

Furnishing of Goods, Services, or Facilities

The furnishing of goods, services, or facilities between a private foundation and a disqualified person generally constitutes an act of self-dealing.[40] This type of self-dealing includes the furnishing of office space, automobiles, auditoriums, secretarial help, meals, libraries, publications, laboratories, or parking lots.[41] As an example, the IRS ruled that the rental of a charter aircraft by a private foundation from a disqualified person aircraft company constituted an act of self-dealing, even though the rental rate was substantially the same as that charged by other aircraft companies.[42]

The furnishing of goods, services, or facilities to a foundation manager, to an employee, or to an unpaid worker in recognition of his or her services is not self-dealing if the value of whatever is furnished is reasonable and necessary to the performance of his or her tasks in carrying out the tax-exempt purposes of the foundation and (taken in conjunction with any other payment of com-

[35]Rev. Rul. 73-546, 1973-2 C. B. 384.
[36]Rev. Rul. 73-595, 1973-2 C. B. 384.
[37]Reg. § 53.4941(d)-2(c)(4).
[38]Rev. Rul. 77-259, 1977-2 C.B. 387.
[39]Rev. Rul. 77-288, 1977-2 C. B. 388.
[40]Code § 4941(d)(1)(C).
[41]Reg. § 53.4941(d)-2(d)(1).
[42]Reg. Rul. 73-363, 1973-2 C. B. 383.

pensation or payment or reimbursement of expenses to him or her by the foundation) is not excessive.[43]

The furnishing of goods, services, or facilities by a disqualified person to a private foundation is not an act of self-dealing if they are furnished without charge and used exclusively for tax-exempt purposes.[44] A furnishing of goods is considered to be without charge even though the private foundation pays for transportation, insurance, or maintenance costs it incurs in obtaining or using the property, so long as the payment is not made directly or indirectly to a disqualified person.[45]

The furnishing of goods, services, or facilities by a private foundation to a disqualified person is not self-dealing if they are made available to the general public on at least as favorable a basis as they are made available to the disqualified person.[46] However, there must be a substantial number of persons other than disqualified persons who are actually utilizing the goods, services, or facilities, and the furnishing of goods, services, or facilities must be functionally related[47] to the exercise or performance by a private foundation of its tax-exempt purposes.[48]

For example, the IRS ruled that the use of a private foundation's meeting room by a disqualified person was not an act of self-dealing inasmuch as the room was made available to the disqualified person on the same basis that it was made available to the general public and was functionally related to the performance of an exempt purpose of the foundation.[49] Similarly, the IRS held that it was not an act of self-dealing for a foundation-museum to allow a disqualified person-corporation to use its private road for access to the corporation's headquarters, since the road was made available to the general public on a comparable basis, a substantial number of (nondisqualified) persons actually used the road, and the use of the road as an entrance to the museum was functionally related to the foundation's tax-exempt purpose; the corporation had agreed to maintain the road, although that did not entitle it to any special privileges with respect to the use of the road.[50] However, in one instance, because the rental of office space (to disqualified persons) did not contribute importantly to a private foundation's tax-exempt purpose of conducting agricultural research and experimentation, the rental was held to be self-dealing, even though the disqualified persons conducted business activities in the same subject area of the foundation's research.[51]

---

[43]Reg. § 53.4941(d)-2(d)(2). See also Reg. § 53.4945-6(b)(2).
[44]Code § 4941(d)(2)(C).
[45]Reg. § 53.4941(d)-2(d)(3).
[46]Code § 4941(d)(2)(D).
[47]See Code § 4942(j)(5).
[48]Reg. § 53.4941(d)-3(b).
[49]Rev. Rul. 76-10, 1976-1 C. B. 355.
[50]Rev. Rul. 76-459, 1976-2 C. B. 369.
[51]Rev. Rul. 79-374, 1979-2 C. B. 387.

Payment of Compensation

The payment of compensation (or payment or reimbursement of expenses) by a private foundation to a disqualified person generally constitutes an act of self-dealing.[52]

However, except in the case of a government official, the payment of compensation (or payment or reimbursement of expenses) by a private foundation to a disqualified person for the performance of personal services which are reasonable and necessary to carrying out the foundation's tax-exempt purpose is not self-dealing if the compensation (or payment or reimbursement) is not excessive.[53] Under this exception, the making of a cash advance to a foundation manager or employee for expenses on behalf of the foundation is not an act of self-dealing, as long as the amount of the advance is reasonable in relation to the duties and expense requirements of the foundation manager.[54] Thus, the IRS ruled that the payment by a private foundation of legal fees, which were not excessive, awarded by a court to the lawyer for one of the foundation's managers (a disqualified person), who had filed suit against the other managers to require them to carry on the foundation's charitable program, does not constitute an act of self-dealing, since the service performed by the manager in filing the suit was reasonable and necessary to carry out the foundation's tax-exempt purpose.[55]

Transfer to or Use of Income and Assets

The transfer to, or use by or for the benefit of, a disqualified person of the income or assets of a private foundation generally constitutes self-dealing.[56] For example, the payment by a foundation of any tax imposed on a disqualified person by reason of the private foundation rules[57] is treated as a transfer of the income or assets of a private foundation for a disqualified person's benefit.[58] Similarly, the payment by a foundation of the premiums for an insurance policy providing liability insurance to a foundation manager in connection with the

---

[52]Code § 4941(d)(1)(D); Reg. § 53.4941(d)-2(e).

[53]Code § 4941(d)(2)(E). As to whether the compensation is "excessive," see Reg. § 1.162-7.

[54]Reg. § 53.4941(d)-3(c)(1).

[55]Rev. Rul. 73-613, 1973-2 C. B. 385. A pension paid by a private foundation to one of its directors (a disqualified person), whose total compensation including the pension is not excessive, is not an act of self-dealing. Rev. Rul. 74-591, 1974-2, C. B. 385. Also, a cost-sharing arrangement between a disqualified person/for-profit corporation and a private foundation, concerning the expenses of employees, was determined not to be self-dealing because the services of the employee satisfy the "reasonable and necessary" standard. IRS Private Letter Ruling 7952117.

[56]Code § 4941(d)(1)(E).

[57]In general, Code Chapter 42.

[58]Reg. § 53.4941(d)-2(f).

private foundation taxes is self-dealing, unless such premiums are treated as being part of the manager's compensation.[59] Thus, the payment of premiums by a private foundation for insurance indemnifying a disqualified person against liability for claims, in connection with his assistance in preparing a registration statement and prospectus for the foundation's public offering of stock issued by a corporation of which he is a principal officer, under the Securities Act of 1933, is treated as part of his compensation for such services and does not constitute self-dealing as long as the compensation is not excessive.[60] Likewise, the IRS ruled that a private foundation committed an act of self-dealing when it placed paintings owned by it in the residence of a substantial contributor.[61] However, one court held that the making of a charitable contribution to a private foundation by one of its trustees, on the condition that any nondeductible portion of the gift would be returned to him, was not an act of self-dealing.[62]

The IRS ruled that a private foundation that pays a legally enforceable charitable pledge incurred by a disqualified person with respect to the foundation engages in an act of self-dealing, in that the transaction is a transfer of the assets or income of a private foundation to or for the benefit of a disqualified person.[63] The matter involved a private foundation, created by several corporations to be a conduit for their contributions, that was to receive support from the corporations on the condition that the foundation use the funds to pay certain charitable pledges which the corporations had previously incurred. The Service's ruling is based upon a provision in the regulations[64] stating that, if a private foundation makes a payment that satisfies a legal obligation of a disqualified person, the payment will be an act of self-dealing.[65]

The fact that a disqualified person receives an incidental or tenuous benefit

---

[59]*Ibid.*

[60]Rev. Rul. 74-405, 1974-2 C. B. 384. See Reg. § 53.4941(d)-2(f)(2), (3); Rev. Rul. 77-6, 1977-1 C. B. 350. In Rev. Rul 82-223, 1982-51 I.R.B. 29, the IRS held that a private foundation may, without engaging in an act of self-dealing, indemnify, and/or purchase insurance to cover its managers for liabilities arising under state law concerning mismanagement of funds but that the foundation would commit an act of self-dealing if it indemnified a foundation manager for an amount paid in settlement of a state proceeding.

[61]Rev. Rul. 74-600, 1974-2 C. B. 385.

[62]*Underwood* v. *United States,* 461 F. Supp. 1382 (N.D. Tex. 1978). Presumably the returned portion of the original gift becomes gross income to the donor-recipient in the year of the restoration, pursuant to the "tax benefit rule." See, e.g., *Rosen* v. *Commissioner,* 71 T.C. 226 (1978).

[63]IRS Private Letter Ruling 8128072.

[64]Reg. § 53.4941(d)-2(f)(1).

[65]The regulations (*supra,* n. 64) contain an exception for the payment by a private foundation of a charitable pledge where the pledgor is a disqualified person and where the pledge is made prior to April 16, 1973; under the facts upon which the ruling is based, all of the pledges were incurred subsequent to that date.

from the use by a foundation of its income or assets will not, by itself, make the use an act of self-dealing. The IRS ruled that

> An incidental or tenuous benefit occurs when the general reputation or prestige of a disqualified person is enhanced by public acknowledgment of some specific donation by such person, when a disqualified person receives some other relatively minor benefit of an indirect nature, or when such a person merely participates to a wholly incidental degree in the fruits of some charitable program that is of broad public interest to the community.[66]

Thus, the public recognition a person may receive, arising from the charitable activities of a private foundation as to which the person is a substantial contributor, does not in itself result in an act of self-dealing.[67] For the same reason, a private foundation grant to an exempt hospital for modernization, replacement, and expansion was deemed not an act of self-dealing even though two of the trustees of the foundation served on the board of trustees of the hospital.[68] Similarly, a contribution by a private foundation to a public charity does not constitute an act of self-dealing even though the contribution is conditioned upon the agreement of the public charity to change its name to that of a substantial contributor to the foundation.[69] Likewise, a grant by a private foundation to a university to establish an educational program providing instruction in manufacturing engineering is not an act of self-dealing where a disqualified person corporation intends to hire graduates of the program and encourage its employees to enroll in the program, as long as the corporation does not receive preferential treatment in recruiting graduates or enrolling its employees.[70]

By contrast, a private foundation engages in an act of self-dealing when it pays membership dues or fees on behalf of a disqualified person, because the disqualified person is being relieved of the obligation; this benefit is not incidental or tenuous but direct and economic in nature. In one instance, a private foundation paid the dues of a disqualified person to a church, thereby enabling him to maintain his membership in and otherwise participate in the religious activities of the congregation. The dues payment was ruled to constitute self-dealing, with the IRS concluding that the foundation's payment of the dues "results in a direct economic benefit to the disqualified person because that

[66]Rev. Rul. 77-331, 1977-2 C. B. 388.
[67]Reg. § 53.4941(d)-2(f)(2). A closely held corporation's donation of its debentures, representing 14 percent of the value of its net assets, to a private foundation, managed by the corporation's employees and shareholders for the promotion of charitable activities in the locality of the corporation and for which it receives public recognition, is not a constructive dividend to the shareholders. Rev. Rul. 75-335, 1975-2 C. B. 107. Cf. Rev. Rul. 68-658, 1968-2 C. B. 119; IRS Private Letter Ruling 8027078.
[68]Rev. Rul. 75-42, 1975-1 C. B. 359. The IRS also ruled that a grant by one private foundation to another private foundation is not an act of self-dealing even though a bank serves as the sole trustee of both foundations. Rev. Rul. 82-136, 1982-28 I.R.B. 14.
[69]Rev. Rul. 73-407, 1973-2 C. B. 383.
[70]Rev. Rul. 80-310, 1980-2 C. B. 319.

person would have been expected to pay the membership dues had they not been paid by the foundation."[71] (The IRS observed nonetheless that "any rights or benefits that the disqualified person receives from the church by reason of that person's membership status might be described as incidental or tenuous.")

Similarly, the IRS ruled that the guarantee of loans made to disqualified persons under a student loan guarantee program established by a private foundation for the children of its employees constitutes an act of self-dealing.[72] The program is operated by a public charity, which received a $10,000 grant from the foundation and agreed to guarantee $100,000 in loans to the children, including the children of a few of the foundation's employees who are disqualified persons. In so ruling, the Service based its position on the general rule that the indemnification (of a lender) or guarantee (of repayment) by a private foundation with respect to a loan to a disqualified person is treated as a use for the benefit of a disqualified person of the income or assets of the foundation, as is a private foundation grant or other payment that satisfies the legal obligation of a disqualified person.[73] Moreover, the Service held that this use of the foundation's income and assets involves more than an incidental or tenuous benefit for the disqualified persons involved, because an act of self-dealing occurs each time a loan involving a disqualified person is made.

Payments to Government Officials

An agreement by a private foundation to make any payment of money or other property to a government official generally constitutes self-dealing, unless the agreement is to employ a government official for a period after termination of his or her government service if he or she is terminating his or her service within a 90-day period.[74] An individual who otherwise meets the definition of government official is treated as such while on leave of absence from the government without pay.[75]

Additional Exceptions

Any transaction between a private foundation and a corporation which is a disqualified person is not an act of self-dealing if the transaction is engaged in pursuant to a liquidation, merger, redemption, recapitalization, or other corporate adjustment, organization, or reorganization.[76] However, for this excep-

---

[71]Rev. Rul. 77-160, 1977-1 C. B. 351. Cf. Rev. Rul. 70-47, 1970-1 C. B. 49, and Rev. Rul. 68-432, 1968-2 C. B. 104.

[72]Rev. Rul. 77-331, *supra*, n. 66.

[73]Reg. § 53.4941(d)-2(f)(1).

[74]Code § 4941(d)(1)(F).

[75]Reg. § 53.4941(d)-2(g). Cf. H. R. 2984, H. Rep. No. 94-1070, 94th Cong., 2d Sess. (1976).

[76]Code § 4941(d)(2)(F).

tion to apply, all the securities of the same class as that held (prior to the transaction) by the foundation must be subject to the same terms and the terms must provide for receipt by the foundation of no less than fair market value.[77] For example, the IRS has ruled that this transaction exception is available with respect to a reorganization,[78] where there is only one class of voting stock involved and the shares received will reflect a market value as determined by independent investment bankers.[79]

In the case of a government official, the self-dealing rules do not apply to the receipt of certain prizes and awards, scholarships and fellowship grants, annuities, gifts, and traveling expenses.[80]

With respect to this last item, the exception operates only with respect to expenses for travel from one point in the United States to another point in the United States.[81] Consequently, reimbursement by a private foundation for travel expenses incurred by a member of Congress it selects to participate in a conference it co-sponsors in a foreign country constitutes an act of self-dealing.[82] Taking the position that the term "United States" is used only in a "geographical" sense in this context, the IRS ruled that the Commonwealth of Puerto Rico is not a "point in the United States."[83]

Still another requirement with respect to reimbursement of traveling expenses by a private foundation to a government official is that the payment or reimbursement may not exceed the actual cost of transportation involved plus an amount for all other traveling expenses not in excess of 125 percent of the maximum amount payable[84] for like travel by employees of the United States (at the present, $35).[85] The IRS was asked to rule in a situation involving a foundation that wanted to provide a $50 per diem allowance (plus reimbursement of actual transportation costs) for a government official traveling from Washington, D.C., to New York City to participate in a three-day seminar. A special federal law[86] provides for an allowance of up to $50 for travel to so-

---

[77]See Reg. § 53.4941(d)-3(d); IRS Private Letter Ruling 8004006. Also IRS Private Letter Ruling 7835059.

[78]Code § 368(a)(1)(C).

[79]IRS Private Letter Ruling 7847049.

[80]Code § 4941(d)(2)(G); Reg. § 53.4941(d)-3(e).

[81]Reg. § 53.4941(d)-3(e)(7).

[82]Rev. Rul. 74-601, 1974-2 C. B. 385.

[83]Rev. Rul. 76-159, 1976-1 C. B. 356. Legislation once under consideration would permit a private foundation (other than a foundation supported by any one business enterprise, trade association, or labor organization) to pay or reimburse government officials for certain expenses of foreign travel under similar types of limitations as apply under present law in the case of expenses for domestic travel. H. R. 810, 95th Cong., 1st Sess. (1977). An identical bill (H. R. 2984) passed the House of Representatives in 1976 but failed to clear the Senate Committee on Finance.

[84]5 U.S.C. § 5702(a).

[85]Code § 4941(d)(2)(G)(vii).

[86]5 U.S.C. § 5702(c).

called "high rate geographical areas," which includes New York City. Reasoning that since Congress referred only to the general reimbursement rules and not to the special provision when it enacted the self-dealing rules, the IRS held that the foundation can only pay a per diem allowance of $43.75 (125 percent of $35) and not the desired $50.[87]

Further, the Tax Reform Act of 1969 contains five "savings provision"[88] or transitional rules rendering the self-dealing rules inapplicable to various pre-1969 and other transactions.[89]

One of these provisions embodied in the 1969 Act excluded from the proscriptions of the self-dealing rules the disposition of a private foundation's excess and nonexcess business holdings, owned by the foundation on May 26, 1969, to a disqualified person where the foundation was required to dispose of the property in order to avoid the taxes on excess holdings,[90] the foundation received an amount which at least equaled the fair market value of the property, and (in the case of nonexcess holdings) the transaction occurred before January, 1975.[91] This exception was allowed in recognition of the fact that in the case of many closely held companies the only ready market for a foundation's holdings is one or more disqualified persons. (The transitional rule governing the sale of pre-1969 excess holdings to disqualified persons for fair value has no termination date.)

Another "transitional rule" adopted in 1969[92] enables a private foundation to lease (through 1979) property under certain circumstances to a disqualified person without violating the self-dealing rules.

Congress, in 1980, created a permanent exemption from the self-dealing rules for office space leasing arrangements between a private foundation tenant and a disqualified person where (1) the lease is pursuant to a binding contract in effect on October 9, 1969, even though it has been renewed, (2) at the time of execution the lease was not a prohibited transaction,[93] (3) the space is leased to the foundation on a basis no less favorable than that on which the space would be made available in an arms'-length transaction, and (4) the leased space must be in a building in which there are tenants who are not disqualified persons. These rules are effective for tax years beginning after December 31, 1979.[94]

To enable foundations to sell property presently being leased to a disqualified

---

[87]Rev. Rul. 77-251, 1977-2 C. B. 389.

[88]Tax Reform Act of 1969 § 101(1)(2).

[89]See Reg. § 53.4941(d)-4. But see, e.g., IRS Private Letter Ruling 8038049.

[90]Code § 4943. See Chapter 27.

[91]Tax Reform Act of 1969 § 101(1)(2)(B); see Rev. Rul. 75-25, 1975-1 C. B. 359; IRS Private Letter Rulings 7941006 and 7948051.

[92]Tax Reform Act of 1969 § 101(1)(2)(C).

[93]See § 1 *supra*.

[94]P.L. 96-608, 96th Cong., 2d Sess. (1980). The intended beneficiary of these rules is the Moody Foundation in Galveston, Texas.

person at its maximum value, Congress in 1976 approved another transitional rule allowing a foundation to dispose of nonexcess property to a disqualified person if at that time it is leasing substantially all of the property under the lease transitional rule and it receives an amount which at least equals the property's fair market value.[95] This rule applied to dispositions occurring before January 1, 1978, and after October 4, 1976.

§ 25.4   Definitions

An act of self-dealing "occurs" on the date on which all the terms and conditions of the transaction and the liabilities of the parties have been fixed.[96]

As respects a self-dealing act, the "amount involved" is the greater of the amount of money and the fair market value of the other property given or the amount of money and the fair market value of the other property received.[97] In the case of the payment of compensation for personal services to persons other than government officials, the "amount involved" is only the excess compensation paid by the private foundation.[98] Where the use of money or other property is involved, the "amount involved" is the greater of the amount paid for the use or the fair market value of the use for the period for which the money or other property is used.[99]

The fair market value of property or the use thereof, as the case may be, is determined as of the date on which the act of self-dealing occurred in the case of the initial taxes (see below) and is the highest fair market value during the correction period[100] in the case of the additional taxes (see below).[101]

"Correction" of an act of self-dealing must be accomplished by undoing the transaction which constituted the act to the extent possible but in no case may the resulting financial position of the private foundation be worse than would be the case if the disqualified person was dealing under the highest fiduciary standards.[102]

Thus, in the case of a sale of property by a private foundation to a disqualified person for cash, undoing the transaction includes rescission of the sale where possible and payment to the foundation of any net profits that were realized from the property while in the disqualified person's possession. If a disqualified person uses property owned by a foundation, undoing the transaction includes terminating the use of the property and payment by the disqualified person of

---

[95]Tax Reform Act of 1969 § 101(1)(2)(F).
[96]Reg. § 53.4941(e)-1(a)(2).
[97]Code § 4941(e)(2); Reg. § 53.4941(e)-1(b)(1).
[98]Reg. § 53.4941(e)-1(b)(2)(i).
[99]Reg. § 53.4941(e)-1(b)(2)(ii). See also Reg. § 53.4941(e)-1(b)(2)(iii).
[100]Code § 4941(e)(4); Reg. § 53.4941(e)-1(d).
[101]Code § 4941(e)(2); Reg. § 53.4941(e)-1(b)(3).
[102]Code § 4941(e)(3). See Reg. 53.4941(e)-1(c).

any excess of the fair market value of the use of the property over the amount actually paid. The payment of excessive compensation by a foundation to a disqualified person for the performance of personal services which are reasonable and necessary to carry out the foundation's tax-exempt purposes may be corrected by repaying the foundation the excessive portion of the payment; termination of the employment or independent contractor relationship is not required. Corrections of acts of self-dealing which meet the minimum standards of correction are not themselves acts of self-dealing.

Caution must be exercised in an attempt to effect correction of an act of self-dealing, so that the attempt is not itself regarded as an act of self-dealing. This nearly occurred when a disqualified person, in attempting to correct a self-dealing act in the form of a loan to him from a private foundation,[103] proposed to transfer to the foundation a parcel of real estate with a fair market value equal to the amount of the loan. The IRS held that (1) the transfer would constitute self-dealing because, since the self-dealer's indebtedness to the foundation would be cancelled, the transaction would be a sale of property by the disqualified person to the foundation, which would be an act of self-dealing[104] and (2) the minimum standards for an authentic correction[105] would not be met because "it will be generally less advantageous to the foundation to receive the property than to have the loan repaid since it may be both difficult and costly for the foundation to convert the property to cash and thus restore its position." The IRS noted that a transfer of property could be an acceptable correction of a self-dealing loan transaction, where the property had substantially appreciated in value and could be readily converted into an amount of money in excess of the debt.[106]

If joint participation in a transaction by two or more disqualified persons constitutes self-dealing (for example, a joint sale of property to a private foundation), the transaction is generally treated as a separate act of self-dealing with respect to each disqualified person.[107]

§ 25.5 Sanctions

The prohibitions against self-dealing—like the other foundation rules—are enforced by excise taxes that are in reality penalties for what Congress has characterized as wrongful conduct. One court has described these sanctions as follows:

> The language of the [Tax Reform] Act [of 1969], its legislative history, the graduated levels of the sanctions imposed, and the almost confiscatory level of the

[103]See Code § 4941(d)(1)(B), discussed *supra*.
[104]See Code § 4941(d)(1)(A), discussed *supra*.
[105]Reg. § 53.4941(e)-1(c)(4).
[106]Rev. Rul. 81-40, 1981-1 C. B. 508.
[107]Reg. § 53.4941(e)-1(e).

exactions assessed, convince us that the exactions in question were intended to curb the described conduct through pecuniary punishment.[108]

An initial tax is imposed on each act of self-dealing between a disqualified person and a private foundation, on the self-dealer at a rate of 5 percent of the amount involved with respect to the act for each year in the taxable period[109] or part thereof. This tax must be paid by the disqualified person (other than a foundation manager acting only as such) who participated in the act. This tax is imposed upon a government official who participates in an act of self-dealing only if he or she knows[110] that the act is an act of self-dealing.[111]

Where this initial tax is imposed, a tax of 2½ percent of the amount involved is imposed on the participation[112] of any foundation manager in the act of self-dealing, but only if the manager knowingly participated in the act.[113] However, this tax is not imposed where the participation is not willful and is due to reasonable cause. This tax, which must be paid by the foundation manager, may not exceed $10,000.[114]

In one instance, a trustee of a private foundation (and hence a disqualified person, as a foundation manager), acting on his own behalf and as trustee of the foundation, sold property he owned to the foundation, knowing that the transaction was an act of self-dealing. His participation in the transaction was willful and was not due to reasonable cause. Inasmuch as the disqualified person did not act solely in his capacity as a foundation manager, he was liable for the initial tax on a self-dealer and, because he participated in the transaction in part as a trustee, he was liable for the 2½ percent tax imposed on him as a foundation manager.[115]

Where an initial tax is imposed and the self-dealing act is not timely corrected, an additional tax is imposed in an amount equal to 200 percent of the amount involved. This tax must be paid by the disqualified person (other than a foundation manager) who participated in the act of self-dealing.[116]

In one case, the need to correct an act of self-dealing gave rise to a peculiar series of transactions. Upon being advised by the IRS that a sale of real estate in 1971 by a disqualified person to a private foundation was an act of self-dealing

---

[108]*In re Unified Control Systems, Inc.*, 586 F.2d 1036 (5th Cir. 1978). Also *Farrell v. United States*, 80-1 U.S.T.C. ¶ 9220 (E.D. Ark. 1980).

[109]See Code § 4941(e)(1). A private foundation loaned money to a disqualified person with a tax year different from that of the foundation; the disqualified person must compute the tax payable under Code § 4941 on account of self-dealing based on his or her own taxable year. Rev. Rul. 75-391, 1975-2 C. B. 446.

[110]See Reg. § 53.4941(a)-1(b)(3).

[111]Code § 4941(a)(1); Reg. 53.4941(a)-1(a).

[112]See Reg. § 4941(a)-1(b)(2).

[113]Code § 4941(a)(2).

[114]Code § 4941(a)(2). See, in general, Reg. § 4941(a)-1(b), (c).

[115]Rev. Rul. 78-76, 1978-1 C. B. 377.

[116]Code § 4941(b)(1); Reg. § 53.4941(b)-1(a).

that required correction, the foundation in 1973 sold the land back to the disqualified person for the original sale price. Immediately thereafter, the disqualified person transferred the property to a straw man for the same price, who in turn sold it back to the foundation for the same price. In 1975, the land was transferred by the foundation to the straw man for the same price. The court rejected the disqualified person's assertion that the transfers in 1973 were shams and thus should be ignored for tax purposes, and that any taxes applicable with respect to the 1971 transaction are barred by the statute of limitations. Instead, the court held that the 1973 transfer of the land back to the disqualified person was intended to correct the initial act of self-dealing in 1971, and thus was separate from the other 1973 transaction. The court did not, at the time, rule on the question as to whether the retransfer of the land to the foundation in 1973 via the straw man constituted an act of self-dealing.[117]

An additional tax equal to 50 percent of the amount involved, up to $10,000,[118] is imposed on any foundation manager (where the above additional tax is imposed) who refuses to agree to part or all of the correction.[119]

The effectiveness of these additional taxes was temporarily in jeopardy as the result of U.S. Tax Court decisions holding that the court lacks the jurisdiction to ascertain whether these taxes should be imposed. The matter first arose in 1978, in connection with the Tax Court's first self-dealing case,[120] where the court ordered the submission of briefs by the parties as to its authority to determine the 200 percent additional tax.[121] Thereafter, the court found that it did not have jurisdiction to determine whether this second-level tax should be imposed.[122]

The Tax Court reasoned that its jurisdiction[123] is generally confined to authority to redetermine the correct amount of a "deficiency,"[124] which is the amount by which the tax *imposed* (in this instance, by the various private foundation excise taxes[125]) exceeds the tax shown on the return.[126] However, in these cases, said the court, there is yet no deficiency for the court to re-

---

[117]*Dupont* v. *Commissioner*, 74 T.C. 498 (1980).

[118]Code § 4941(c)(2).

[119]Code § 4941(b)(2); Reg. § 53.4941(b)-1(b). The U.S. Court of Appeals for the Fifth Circuit has held that the self-dealing excise taxes imposed by Code §§ 4941(a)(1) (n. 111, *supra*) and 4941(b)(2) are penalties for purposes of the Bankruptcy Act and thus that these taxes are not enforceable by the federal government against the trustee in bankruptcy of the self-dealer's estate. *In re Unified Control Systems, Inc.*, *supra*, n. 108. Also *In re Kline*, 403 F. Supp. 974 (D. Md. 1975), aff'd 547 F.2d 823 (4th Cir. 1977).

[120]*Adams* v. *Commissioner*, *supra*, n. 7.

[121]*Adams* v. *Commissioner*, 70 T.C. 466 (1978).

[122]*Adams* v. *Commissioner*, 72 T.C. 81 (1979).

[123]See Code § 7442.

[124]See Code § 6214(a).

[125]In general, see Code Chapter 42.

[126]See Code § 6211(a).

determine, since the second-level tax cannot be imposed until the first-level tax is imposed and the act of self-dealing is corrected, and since the correction period does not expire until the court's decision is final.[127] By the time the second-level tax deficiency arises, the court held, the IRS has already mailed a deficiency notice as respects the act of self-dealing. But, since the IRS is precluded from issuing a second deficiency notice for the same self-dealing act,[128] it is, the court held, barred from issuing a deficiency notice for a second-level tax.[129]

Legislation to resolve this unintended void in Tax Court jurisdiction was introduced in 1979[130] and passed Congress on December 13, 1980.[131] Under this approach, the second-tier excise tax will be imposed before any litigation begins (to ensure that the Tax Court will have jurisdiction) but is to be forgiven if the prohibitied act is corrected within a correction period.

Subsequently, the Tax Court decided that the 1980 revisions in the statutory law revising the second-tier tax rules are applicable to a docketed and untried case where the second-tier taxes have not been assessed.[132] The new rules apply with respect to taxes assessed after the date of enactment of the 1980 law, which was December 24, 1980; the statutory notice of deficiency was mailed to the person, alleged to be a self-dealer with a private foundation, on May 14, 1980. The court said that the petitioner in the case "confused two distinct events by equating the mailing of the notice of deficiency with the assessment of the tax." Noting that "no assessment can be made where a petition has been timely and validly filed in this Court until the decision of this Court becomes final,"[133] the court decided that the 1980 amendments "are applicable in this case to the second tier taxes imposed by section 4941 because such taxes have not been 'assessed' and the doctrine of res judicata clearly does not apply where the case has not yet been tried and decided on its merits."[134]

Willful repeated violations of these prohibitions will result in involuntary

[127]See Code § 4941(a)(4).

[128]See Code § 6212(c).

[129]Presumably, this line of reasoning also precluded Tax Court jurisdiction over cases involving similar taxes in Code §§ 4942, 4943, 4944, 4945, 4947, 4951, and 4952. As respects Code § 4945, the Tax Court so held. *Larchmont Foundation, Inc.* v. *Commissioner*, 72 T.C. 131 (1979).

[130]H. R. 5391, 96th Cong., 1st Sess. (1979).

[131]P.L. 96-596, 94 Stat. 3469.

[132]*Howell* v. *Commissioner*, 77 T.C. 916 (1981).

[133]See Code § 6213(a).

[134]The opinion also rejects the contention that this interpretation of the 1980 law gives it a retroactive effect and that it is being applied in a manner violative of due process requirements because its retroactivity is not clearly expressed by the setting of a fixed date. Cf. Judge Fay's "dissent." Also see *The Barth Foundation* v. *Commissioner*, 77 T.C. 1008 (1981).

termination of the private foundation's status and the imposition of additional taxes.[135]

In any case where more than one person is liable for any initial or additional tax with respect to any one act of self-dealing, all of the persons are jointly and severally liable for the tax(es).[136]

[135]See Chapter 32.

[136]Code § 4941(c)(1); Reg. § 53.4941(c)-1(a)(1). In general, see Geske, "Indirect Self-Dealing and Foundations' Transfers for the Use or Benefit of Disqualified Persons," 12 *Houston L. Rev.* 379 (1975); Mulreany and Duncan, "Self-Dealing and Disqualified Persons under Chapter 42 of the Internal Revenue Code," 10 *N.Y.U. Conf. Char. Fdns.* 265 (1971); Lehrfeld, "Private Foundations and Tax Reform: Disqualified Persons and Self-Dealing" (Part 1), 1 *Tax Adviser* 662 (1970); (Part 2) 1 *Tax Adviser* 688 (1970).

26

Mandatory Distributions

Prior to enactment of the Tax Reform Act of 1969, Code § 504(a)(1) provided that a private foundation (and many other "charitable" organizations) would lose its tax-exempt status if its aggregate accumulated income was "unreasonable in amount or duration in order to carry out the charitable, educational, or other purpose or function constituting the basis for [its] exemption . . ."

This statutory sanction was deemed ineffective by Congress with respect to private foundations, as the following indicates:

> Under prior law, if a private foundation invested in assets that produced no current income, then it needed to make no distributions for charitable purposes. As a result, while the donor may have received substantial tax benefits from his contribution currently, charity may have received absolutely no current benefit. In other cases, even though income was produced by the assets contributed to charitable organizations, no current distribution was required until the accumulations became "unreasonable." Although a number of court cases had begun to set guidelines as to the circumstances under which an accumulation became unreasonable, in many cases the determination was essentially subjective. Morecover, as was the case with self-dealing, it frequently happened that the only available sanction (loss of exempt status) either was largely ineffective or else was unduly harsh.[1]

Consequently, Congress, in enacting the Tax Reform Act of 1969, repealed Code § 504 and substituted rules, embodied in Code § 4942, requiring certain distributions, for charitable purposes, by private foundations.

§ 26.1 Distribution Requirement—In General

The purpose of the mandatory distribution rules is to require a private foundation to distribute, each year, at least a minimum amount of cash and/or

[1]Joint Committee on Internal Revenue Taxation, *General Explanation of Tax Reform Act of 1969*, 91st Cong. 2d Sess. (1970), at 36; also see Rev. Rul. 67-5, 1967-1 C. B. 123.

property for charitable purposes. The definition of the minimum amount that must be distributed by a private foundation (other than a private operating foundation) was originally enacted in 1969 and was revised in 1976 and 1981.

The law defines the amount that must annually be distributed by a private foundation as the "distributable amount."[2] For tax years beginning after December 31, 1981, the "distributable amount" for a private foundation is an amount equal to 5 percent of the value of the noncharitable assets of the foundation (the "minimum investment return").[3] Prior law required a private foundation to distribute all of its adjusted net income for its tax-exempt purposes each year. However, under prior law, if for any year the adjusted net income of a private foundation was not equal to the minimum investment return amount, a portion of the principal (assets) of the foundation had to be combined with its income so that the total annual distribution (principal and income) equaled the mandatory payout requirement.

Specifically, the "distributable amount,"[4] with respect to a private foundation for any tax year beginning before 1982, is an amount equal to the greater of the foundation's minimum investment return or its adjusted net income,[5] re-

---

[2] Code § 4942(d).

[3] Code § 4942(d)(1). This change in the law was occasioned by enactment of § 822 of the Economic Recovery Tax Act of 1981.

[4] Code § 4942(d).

[5] Code § 4942(f) In computing its annual distributable amount under the pre-1982 rules, a private foundation had to determine its adjusted net income. The term "adjusted net income" means the excess (if any) of the gross income for the tax year determined with certain income modifications (Code § 4942(f)(2); Reg. § 53.4942(a)-2(d)(2), (3)) over the sum of the deductions determined with the deduction modifications (Code § 4942(f)(3); Reg. § 53.4942(a)-2(d)(4)) which would be allowed to a taxable corporation for the tax year (Code § 4942(f)(1)). Gross income does not include gifts, grants, or contributions received by a private foundation but does include income from a functionally related business (Reg. § 53.4942(a)-2(d)(1)).

Repayments of principal received by a private foundation in tax years beginning after 1969 on loans made in prior years to individuals for charitable purposes are not includible in its gross income to determine its adjusted net income for these purposes; however, payments of interest on the loans are items of adjusted net income (Rev. Rul. 75-443, 1974-2 C. B. 449). Repayments of a loan made by a foundation need not be treated as gross income where the loan amounts were not used in meeting the foundation's distribution obligations, and the repayments may be returned to corpus (Rev. Rul. 77-252, 1977-2 C. B. 390).

The IRS has issued two other rulings in this context. In one case, a private foundation receiving annual payments as a beneficiary of a decedent's deferred incentive compensation income plan was advised to include each payment as gross income to the extent that it exceeds the amount attributable to the value of the right to receive the payment on the decedent's date of death (Rev. Rul. 75-442, 1975-2 C. B. 448). In the other instance, the IRS ruled that capital gain dividends received by a private foundation from a regulated investment company (Code § 851) are excluded from the foundation's adjusted net income, because the dividends are statutorily treated as long-term capital

duced by any taxes on unrelated income and the tax on the foundation's investment income.[6] Also, the distributable amount must have been increased by the income portion of any distributions from nonexempt split-interest trusts with respect to amounts placed in trust after May 26, 1969.[7] Thereafter, as noted, the distributable amount with respect to a private foundation is equal to its minimum investment return.

In a pre-1982 ruling, a private foundation that made a valid election to change its accounting period, which resulted in a short tax year, and that had undistributed income at the end of its prior tax year was advised by the IRS to distribute the income before the close of the short tax year to avoid the penalty tax.[8]

A foundation's minimum investment return for any tax year is the amount determined by multiplying (1) the excess of the aggregate fair market value of all assets of the foundation, other than those being used or held for use directly in carrying out the foundation's tax-exempt purpose, over the amount of the acquisition indebtedness[9] with respect to the assets (without regard to the tax year in which the indebtedness was incurred), by (2) 5 percent.[10] The aggregate

---

gains (Code § 852(b)(3)(B); Rev. Rul. 73-320, 1973-2 C. B. 385). (Only net short-term capital gains are included in foundations' gross income for this purpose (Code § 4942(f)(2)(B).) Interest on government obligations which is normally excludable from gross income under Code § 103 is included within private foundation gross income. Generally, deductions are limited to ordinary and necessary expenses paid or incurred for the production or collection of gross income, or for the management, conservation, or maintenance of property held for the production of income. Amortizable bond premiums are deductible to the extent permitted by Code § 171 (Rev. Rul. 76-248, 1976-1 C. B. 353).

Imputed interest (Code § 483) is included within this concept of adjusted gross income. However, some private foundations sold property, prior to the enactment of the foundation rules in 1969, on an installment sales basis that did not call for a stated rate of interest. The Senate Finance Committee, when developing its version of the Tax Reform Act of 1976, regarded as "onerous" the fact that a foundation had to distribute income imputed to it as the result of pre-1969 sales, thereby causing it to drastically expand its ongoing active program or force it to make one-time grants (which, in the case of a private operating foundation, could cause it to fail to meet the income test, since grant-making does not constitute the "active conduct" of tax-exempt activities) (S. Rep. No. 94-938 (Part 2), 94th Cong., 2d Sess. (1976) at 89).

Accordingly, Congress in 1976 changed the definition of adjusted net income for purposes of Code § 4942 to exclude imputed interest in the case of sales made before 1969. However, imputed income from pre-1969 transactions is included in the net investment income of private foundations for purposes of the investment income tax. See Chapter 31.

[6]Reg. § 53.4942(a)-2(b)(1). See Chapter 30.
[7]Reg. § 53.4942(a)-2(b)(2). See Chapter 33.
[8]Rev. Rul. 74-315, 1974-2 C. B. 386. See § 6, *infra*.
[9]See Code § 514(c)(1). See Chapter 43.
[10]Code § 4942(e)(1).

fair market value of all assets of a foundation must include the average of the fair market values on a monthly basis of securities for which market quotations are readily available,[11] the average of the foundation's cash balances on a monthly basis, and the fair market value of all other noncharitable assets for the period of time during the year for which such assets are held by the foundation.[12]

The following assets are not taken into account in determining minimum investment return: (1) any future interest (such as a vested or contingent remainder, whether legal or equitable) of a private foundation in the income or corpus of any real or personal property until all intervening interests in, and rights to the actual possession or enjoyment of, the property have expired, or, although not actually reduced to the foundation's possession, until the future interest has been constructively received by the foundation, as, for example, where it has been credited to the foundation's account, set apart for the foundation, or otherwise made available so that the foundation may acquire it at any time or could have acquired it if notice of intention to acquire had been given, (2) the assets of an estate until such time as such assets are distributed to the foundation or, due to a prolonged period of administration, the estate is considered terminated for federal income tax purposes, (3) present interests in any trust created and funded by another person, (4) any pledge of money or property, whether or not the pledge is legally enforceable, and (5) any assets used or held for use directly in carrying out the foundation's tax-exempt purposes.[13]

An asset is "used (or held for use) directly in carrying out the foundation's exempt purpose" if the asset is actually used by the private foundation in the carrying out of the chartiable, educational, or other purpose which gives rise to the tax-exempt status of the foundation, or if the foundation owns the asset and establishes to the satisfaction of the IRS that its immediate use for tax-exempt purposes is not practical and that definite plans exist to commence the use within a reasonable period of time. Consequently, assets which are held for the production of income or for investment (for example, stocks, bonds, interest-bearing notes, endowment funds, or generally, leased real estate) must be taken into account in determining minimum investment return.[14] Where property is used for both tax-exempt purposes and for other purposes, it is considered to be used exclusively for exempt purposes where the exempt use represents 95 percent or more of the total use; otherwise, a reasonable allocation between tax-exempt and nonexempt uses must be made.[15]

---

[11]Code § 4942(a)(2)(A).

[12]Reg. § 53.4942(a)-2(c)(1).

[13]Reg. § 53.4942(a)-2(c)(2). See Rev. Rul. 75-392, 1975-2 C. B. 447.

[14]Code § 4942(e)(1)(A).

[15]Reg. § 53.4942(a)-2(c)(3). In the case of a building owned by a private foundation, the percentage of "exempt use" of the building should be determined by dividing the fair rental value of the portion of the building used for tax-exempt purposes by the fair rental value of the entire building, rather than by dividing the portion of the square footage of the building used for exempt purposes by the total area of the building. Rev. Rul. 82-137, 1982-28 I.R.B. 14.

Foundation assets which are considered used or held for use for tax-exempt purposes include (1) administrative assets, such as office equipment and supplies, used by foundation employees and consultants to the extent these assets are devoted to or used in exempt activities, (2) real estate or the portion of a building used by the foundation directly in exempt activities, (3) physical facilities used in exempt activities, such as paintings and other art work owned by the foundation on public display, classroom fixtures and equipment, and research facilities and related equipment, which serve a useful purpose in exempt activities, (4) any interest in a functionally related business or in a program-related investment, (5) the reasonable cash balances necessary to cover current administrative expenses and other normal and current disbursements directly connected with the foundation's exempt activities, and (6) any property leased by a foundation in carrying out its exempt purposes at no cost, or at nominal rent to the lessee, or for a program-related purpose, such as the leasing of renovated apartments to low-income tenants at a low rental as part of the lessor-foundation's program for rehabilitating a blighted portion of a community.[16]

As illustration of the foregoing, the IRS has ruled, with respect to a private foundation maintaining a program of loaning paintings for display in museums, universities, and similar institutions, that the value of the paintings need not be taken into account in computing the foundation's minimum investment return.[17] Similarly, as respects a foundation dedicated to preserve the natural ecosystems and historical and archaelogical remains on an island that has no residential use and to which present access is limited to invited researchers, the IRS determined that the value of the island may be excluded in ascertaining the foundation's minimum investment return.[18] In both of these instances, the assets were being used or held for use directly in carrying out the foundation's tax-exempt purpose. As noted, this requirement is also met with respect to a foundation's interest in a functionally related business, such as a trade or business for which substantially all of the work is performed without compensation and thus is not an unrelated trade or business.[19]

The percentage used to determined minimum investment return was originally set at 6 percent of noncharitable assets, for tax years beginning in 1970 or 1971, in the case of private foundations created after May 26, 1969. The Secretary of the Treasury was authorized to adjust this rate prospectively from time to time based on changes in money rates and investment yields using as

---

[16]Reg. § 53.4942(a)-2(c)(3).

[17]Rev. Rul. 74-498, 1974-2 C. B. 387.

[18]Rev. Rul. 75-207, 1975-1 C. B. 361. Also IRS Private Letter Ruling 7839104. In one instance, real property contributed to a private foundation that promotes health care, for the purpose of holding it until an organization to operate a hospital is formed and qualified and then granting the land to the organization, was held not includible in making the foundation's minimum investment return calculations. IRS Private Letter Ruling 8040042.

[19]Rev. Rul. 76-85, 1976-1 C. B. 357.

the standard the 6 percent rate, given rates and yields for 1969.[20] The subsequent applicable percentages were 5.5 percent for tax years beginning in 1972,[21] 5.25 percent for 1973,[22] and 6 percent for 1974[23] and 1975.[24]

To afford private foundations organized before May 27, 1969, an opportunity to revise their investment and payout practices, a phase-in period with respect to the 6 percent rule was instituted.[25] The minimum investment return rules did not apply to these foundations until 1972. The minimum payout was 4.125 percent for tax years beginning in 1972, 4.375 percent for tax years beginning in 1973, 5.5 percent for 1974, and 6 percent in 1975.[26] The Treasury Department set the applicable percentage for 1976 at 6.75 percent.[27]

However, Congress, in enacting the Tax Reform Act of 1976, reduced the private foundation mandatory payout rate. The 1976 measure lowered this minimum payout requirement, for years beginning after December 31, 1975, to the greater of adjusted net income or a minimum investment return of 5 percent and eliminated the Treasury's authority to annually adjust the rate. An effect of this change was to nullify the increase in the percentage to 6.75 percent. Thereafter, enactment of the Economic Recovery Tax Act of 1981 caused the private foundation payout rules to solely utilize the 5 percent minimum investment return.

§ 26.2 Qualifying Distributions

As originally enacted in 1969, the mandatory payout requirement did not forbid a private foundation from making low-yield investments, such as investments in growth stock or nonproductive land, if it wished. However, if the foundation did so, it periodically may have had to sell some assets to meet the distribution requirements or distribute property to public charities in partial satisfaction of the requirements. In either instance, the foundation would be chipping away at its corpus—its endowment—thereby merely postponing the day when its heedless investment policies caused its decline and subsequent extinction. For this reason the supporters of the mandatory distribution rules as finally developed in 1969 abandoned the "death knell" approach to foundations—adopted by the Senate in its version of the tax reform legislation—by which foundations would be forced to terminate after a stated period of years.[28] The mandatory payout requirement was seen as a strategem for elim-

[20]Reg. § 53.4942(a)-2(c)(5)(i).

[21]Rev. Rul. 72-625, 1972-2 C. B. 604.

[22]Rev. Rul. 73-235, 1973-1 C. B. 519.

[23]Rev. Rul. 74-238, 1974-1 C. B. 326.

[24]Rev. Rul. 75-270, 1975-2 C. B. 449.

[25]Code § 4942(e)(4); Reg. § 53.4942(a)-2(c)(5)(ii).

[26]See notes 21–24, *supra*.

[27]Rev. Rul. 76-193, 1976-1 C. B. 357.

[28]See, e.g., Fritchey, "Should Foundations Be Granted Immortality?," *Washington Star*, Aug. 4, 1969, at A-7.

inating foundations with foolhardy or private interest investment philosophies. However, during the 1970s, the real value of most foundations' assets was eroded and the income yield of many debt investments rose dramatically, so the total income payout requirement was abandoned to enable foundations to revise their investment strategies to assure their continued existence.[29]

Amounts expended by a private foundation to meet the mandatory payout must be in the form of "qualifying distributions."[30] The excise tax which is levied on failure to make the requisite distribution[31] is imposed on the "undistributed income," defined as the "distributable amount" for a tax year less "qualifying distributions" made out of the distributable amount.[32]

The term "qualifying distribution" means (1) any amount (including reasonable and necessary administrative expenses) paid to accomplish one or more tax-exempt purposes, other than a contribution to an organization controlled[33] by the distributing private foundation or by one or more disqualified persons with respect to the foundation or to a private foundation which is not an operating foundation[34] (except as noted below), (2) any amount paid to acquire an asset used or held for use directly in carrying out one or more tax-exempt purposes, or (3) any amount the subject of a qualified set-aside (see below).[35] The amount of a qualifying distribution of property is the fair market value of the property as of the date the distribution is made. The amount of a foundation's qualifying distribution is determined solely on the cash receipts and disbursements method of accounting.[36]

A private foundation that treats an outlay as a qualifying distribution cannot thereafter take another qualifying distribution for an amount that represents the same expenditure. However, it is possible for more than one qualifying distribution to be made involving a single asset. For example, a private foundation may purchase a building for tax-exempt use (a form of qualifying distribution) and subsequently donate the building to a public charity for use in

---

[29]See, e.g., Reilly and Skadden, *Private Foundations: The Payout Requirement and Its Effect on Investment and Spending Policies* (1981); Charles Stewart Mott Foundation, "Foundations: Scheduled for Extinction?" (1981); Williamson, "Investment Expectations and the Foundation Payout Rate," 171 *Foundation News* 13 (Jan./Feb. 1976).

[30]Code § 4942(g)(1).

[31]See § 6, *infra*.

[32]Code § 4942(c); Reg. § 53.4942(a)-2(a).

[33]See Reg. § 53.4942(a)-3(a)(3).

[34]See Chapter 23. Legal fees paid by a private foundation to determine the proper distributee are a reasonable and necessary expense to accomplish the foundation's tax-exempt purpose and, therefore, the payment is a qualifying distribution within the meaning of Code § 4942(g)(1). Rev. Rul. 75-495, 1975-2 C. B. 449. Also IRS Private Letter Ruling 7835057.

[35]Reg. § 53.4942(a)-3(a)(2).

[36]Reg. § 53.4942(a)-3(a)(1). A private foundation cannot treat an amount equal to straight-line depreciation on a building it constructed for charitable purposes as a qualifying distribution. Rev. Rul. 74-560, 1974-2 C. B. 389.

accomplishing the donee's exempt purposes. The contribution of the building is also a qualifying distribution but only to the extent that the fair market value of the property on the contribution date exceeds the amount of the first qualifying distribution.[37]

If a private foundation borrows money to make expenditures for an exempt purpose, a qualifying distribution out of the borrowed funds is deemed to have been made only at the time that the funds are actually distributed for the tax-exempt purpose.[38] Hovever, a private foundation cannot "borrow" from itself, as demonstrated by the unsuccessful attempt by a foundation to offset one year's large grant, treated as made out of its corpus, with its income as received in subsequent years being applied as qualifying distributions to restore its corpus.[39]

If an asset not used or held for use directly in carrying out one or more tax-exempt purposes is subsequently converted to an exempt use, the foundation may treat the conversion as a qualifying distribution. The amount of the qualifying distribution is the fair market value of the converted asset as of the date of its conversion.[40] This value is determined by making a valuation of the converted asset as of the date the property is effectively committed to an exempt use, not the date that the property becomes actually usable for tax-exempt purposes.[41]

A "qualifying distribution" can include a contribution to a "charitable" organization which is a controlled organization or a private nonoperating foundation if (1) not later than the close of the first tax year after the donee organization's tax year in which the contribution is received, the donee organization makes a distribution equal to the full amount of the contribution and the distribution is a qualifying distribution which is treated as a distribution out of corpus[42] (or would be so treated if the donee organization were a private nonoperating foundation), and (2) the private foundation making the contribution obtains adequate records or other sufficient evidence from the donee organization that the qualifying distribution has been made.[43] In the event that a donee organization redistributes less than an amount equal to the total contributions from donor organizations which are required to be redistributed by the donee organization by the close of the first tax year following the tax year in which the contributions were received, any distributions of the contributions are deemed to have been made pro rata out of all of the contributions received in the prior tax year, regardless of any earmarking or identification made by the donee organization with respect to the source of the distributions. Amounts

---

[37]Rev. Rul. 79-375, 1979-2 C. B. 389.
[38]Reg. § 53.4942(a)-3(a)(4).
[39]*H. Fort Flowers Foundation, Inc.* v. *Commissioner*, 72 T.C. 399 (1979).
[40]Reg. § 53.4942(a)-3(a)(5).
[41]Rev. Rul. 78-102, 1978-1 C. B. 379.
[42]See Code § 4942(h).
[43]Code § 4942(g)(3); Reg. § 53.4942(a)-3(c). See, e.g., Rev. Rul. 78-45, 1978-1 C. B. 378.

which are not so distributed must be taken into account in computing the donor foundation's gross income for the appropriate tax year.[44]

The other form of distribution from one foundation to another which can constitute a qualifying distribution is a distribution by a private foundation to a private operating foundation. Generally, because of the nature of the private operating foundation, there is no necessity for a requirement under the mandatory distribution rules for subsequent disbursement of distributed funds. However, if the private operating foundation is deemed to be an organization directly or indirectly controlled by the granting foundation or one or more of its disqualified persons, the one-year pass through rule, discussed previously, will apply.

A private foundation may have excess qualifying distributions in a tax year, namely, the amount by which the total qualifying distributions, treated as made out of undistributed income for any year after 1969 or out of corpus for the year, exceed the distributable amount for that tax year. (Any qualifying distribution made during the tax year is treated as made, first, out of the undistributed income of the immediately preceding tax year, to the extent thereof; second, out of undistributed income for the tax year to the extent thereof; and, finally, out of corpus.[45]) An excess qualifying distribution for any one tax year may be carried forward to reduce subsequent distributable amounts, but not for more than five years (the "adjustment period").[46]

§ 26.3   Set-Aside

An exception to the timing of distributions by a private foundation for mandatory payout purposes is the so-called "set-aside."[47] An amount set aside in one year for a specific project which is for an exempt purpose or purposes may be treated as a qualifying distribution, if payment for the project is to be subsequently made over a period not to exceed 60 months and if the the project can be better accomplished by a set-aside than by the immediate payment of funds. The funds set aside are credited, for purposes of the qualifying distribution requirements, as if paid in the tax year the set-aside is made, thus reducing the actual amount of the mandatory payout in that year.

---

[44]Reg. § 53.4942(a)-2(d)(2). See Reg. § 53.4942(a)-3(c)(2).

[45]Code § 4942(h)(1); Reg. § 53.4942(a)-3(d)(1). In the case of any qualifying distribution which is not treated as being made out of undistributed income of the immediately preceding tax year, the foundation may elect to treat any portion of the distribution as made out of undistributed income for a designated prior tax year or out of corpus. Code § 4942(h)(2); Reg. § 53.4942(a)-3(d)(2); Rev. Proc. 74-41, 1974-2 C. B. 495.

[46]Code § 4942(i); Reg. § 53.4942(a)-3(e). See Rev. Rul. 78-387, 1978-2 C. B. 270. In general, see Koch, "How to best utilize excess qualifying distributions of private foundations," 42 *J. Tax.* 180 (1975).

[47]Code § 4942(g)(2).

The amount set aside may be that amount by which a private foundation's minimum investment return for its immediately preceding taxable year exceeds its adjusted gross income for that year. The amount set aside need not reflect an accumulation of income but may be a bookkeeping entry that will require funding out of corpus by the end of the set-aside period.[48]

A "specific project" includes but is not limited to situations where relatively long-term grants or expenditures must be made in order to assure the continuity of particular projects or program-related investments or where grants are made as part of a matching-grant program.[49] The concept of this type of a project may encompass, for example, a plan to erect a building to house an exempt activity of the foundation (e.g., a museum building in which paintings are to be hung), a plan to purchase an additional group of paintings offered for sale only as a unit which requires an expenditure of more than one year's income, or a plan to fund a specific research program which is of such magnitude as to require an accumulation prior to commencement of the research.[50] For example, conversion by a private foundation of newly acquired land partially to its existing wildlife sanctuary and partially to a park for public use under a four-year construction contract, under which no payment is required until years three and four, was ruled to be a "specific project" and the amounts set aside will be treated as a qualifying distribution as long as a timely justifying application is filed.[51] By contrast, a private foundation, which makes renewable scholarships and fixed-sum research grants that usually run for three years, proposed to set aside the full amount to be given to each grantee and make annual payments to them from a set-aside account, rather than take the payments out of its current income. However, the IRS ruled that the amounts are not qualifying distributions within the meaning of the set-aside rules.[52]

An advance ruling is necessary for the foregoing type of set-aside, requiring a written request to the IRS, including a detailed description of the project, the amount of the intended set-aside, and the reasons why the project can be better accomplished by the set-aside than by the immediate payment of funds.[53]

According to the IRS, a private foundation's desire to retain control over

[48]Rev. Rul. 78-148, 1978-1 C. B. 380.
[49]Reg. § 53.4942(a)-3(b)(1).
[50]Reg. § 53.4942(a)-3(b)(2). See Rev. Rul. 77-7, 1977-1 C. B. 540.
[51]Rev. Rul. 74-450, 1974-2 C. B. 388.
[52]Rev. Rul. 75-511, 1975-2 C. B. 450. Cf. IRS Private Letter Rulings 7823033, 7823060, 7832030, and 7835071. Similarly, in Private Letter Ruling 8002037, the IRS determined that amounts accumulated by a charitable trust, equivalent to the sums for student loans that the trust would like to make but cannot because of restrictions in its governing instrument, pending judicial reformation proceedings, do not qualify under the set-aside rules because of the absence of a "specific project."
[53]Reg. § 53.4942(a)-3(b)(3)-(5). See "Point to Remember" No. 10, 26 *Tax Lawyer* 571 (1973); IRS Private Letter Ruling 8038067.

the funds so as to receive the income therefrom is not a persuasive reason for utilizing a qualified set-aside, where the foundation can make the grants out of current or future income.[54]

For good cause shown, the period for paying an amount set aside may be extended by the IRS.[55] For example, an organization that was permitted a set-aside to construct or acquire a youth camp was granted a two-year extension to pay out the funds, because of the institution of a building moratorium that caused a delay in acquiring the necessary property.[56]

Congress, in 1976, somewhat relaxed the "set-aside" requirements. The problem was that the IRS has been reluctant to approve set-asides that are repeatedly used by a private foundation in making grants. The dilemma was particularly severe for new foundations, or existing foundations experiencing a significant increase in assets, which were attempting to institute long-term supervised projects in the face of IRS inaction.

Consequently, Congress approved special set-aside rules, designed to be of particular aid to private foundations created after 1971 and existing foundations completing a qualifying five-year set-aside project in 1976. These rules permit foundations to set aside for subsequent payment amounts which might otherwise be required to be paid out immediately to avoid penalty. This type of set-aside, which can be utilized without obtaining prior IRS approval, is applicable to years beginning on or after January 1, 1975.

Congress did not change the basic set-aside rule, which requires advance IRS approval, in the 1976 tax law revision.[57] Rather, it created an alternative, whereunder a set-aside is to be allowed if the private foundation satisfies five requirements: (1) it establishes to the satisfaction of the IRS, at the time of the set-aside, that the amount will be paid for the specific project within five years, (2) the set-aside is for a project which will not be completed before the end of the foundation's year in which the set-aside is made, (3) the foundation will disburse, in each year beginning after December 31, 1975 (or, if later, after the end of the fourth tax year following the year of its creation) no less than its required annual distributable amount[58] for charitable purposes, (4) the foundation has distributed (including payments with respect to set-asides treated as qualifying distributions in prior years) during the four tax years immediately preceding the foundation's first tax year beginning after December 31, 1975 (or, if later, the fifth tax year after the year of the foundation's creation) an aggregate amount at least equal to the sum of certain percentages of preceding years' distributable amounts, and (5) the foundation correctly complies with certain delyaed delayed distribution requirements where it in good faith has

---

[54]Rev. Rul. 79-319, 1979-2 C. B. 388.

[55]Reg. § 53.4942(a)-3(b)(2).

[56]IRS Private Letter Ruling 7821141.

[57]Code § 4942(g)(2)(A), (B)(i).

[58]Code § 4945(d).

failed to make an adequate distribution.[59] The percentages in item (4) are as follows: 80 percent of the first preceding tax year's distributable amount, 60 percent of the second preceding tax year's distributable amount, 40 percent of the third preceding tax year's distributable amount, and 20 percent of the fourth preceding tax year's distributable amount. Also, in connection with this alternative, a foundation has a five-year carryover, for purposes of the distribution required in item (3), of any excess disbursements it may make in any tax year beginning after December 31, 1975, and immediately preceding the tax year.[60]

§ 26.4   Valuation of Assets

In computing its annual distributable amount, a private foundation must determine its minimum investment return, which requires in part computation of the "aggregate fair market value of all assets of the foundation."[61]

The fair market value of securities for which market quotations are readily available[62] must be determined on a monthly basis.[63] The regulations contain rules for the valuation of participating interests in certain common trust funds[64] and cash.[65] Generally, the fair market value of other assets must be determined annually.[66] Commonly accepted methods of valuation[67] must be used in making an appraisal.[68]

A private foundation may have among its assets a "unique asset" for which neither a ready market nor a standard valuation method exists, in which case different valuation rules may apply. For example, if a foundation can establish that the value of certain of its securities determined on the basis of the selling or the bid and asked prices does not reflect fair market value, than some reasonable modification of that basis or other relevant facts and elements of value should be allowable in determining "fair market value."[69] Thus, where a foundation's unique asset is securities, it may be appropriate for the foundation to take into account the fact that the block of securities is unusually large. In this instance, the foundation would have to demonstrate that the block to be valued is so large in relation to actual sales in the existing securities markets

[59]Code § 4942(g)(2)(B)(ii) and (C).
[60]Code § 4942(g)(2)(D), (E).
[61]Code § 4942(e)(1)(A).
[62]See Reg. § 53.4942(a)-2(c)(4)(i).
[63]Code § 4942(e)(2)(A). See Watts, "The Fair Market Value of Actively Traded Securities," 30 *Tax Lawyer* 51 (1976).
[64]See Code § 584.
[65]Reg. § 53.4942(a)-2(c)(4)(ii), (iii).
[66]Reg. § 53.4942(a)-2(c)(4)(iv)-(vii).
[67]See the regulations accompanying Code § 2031.
[68]Reg. § 53.4942(a)-2(c)(4)(iv).
[69]See Brody and Berger, "A Guide to Valuation of Closely Held Corporations for Federal Estate and Gift Tax Purposes," 13 *Law Notes* 49 (1977); Comment, "Valuation of Shares in a Closely Held Corporation," 47 *Miss. L. J.* 715 (1976).

that it could not be liquidated within a reasonable time without depressing the market ("blockage").[70] If so, the price at which the block could be sold outside the market may be a more accurate indication of value than market quotations.[71]

In writing the final version of the Tax Reform Act of 1976, the House–Senate conferees refined the general securities valuation rule[72] by adding a provision restricting the use of a "blockage" or discount factor in determining the fair market value of private foundations' securities for payout purposes.[73] The provision prohibits a reduction in value, unless and only to the extent that the securities could not be liquidated within a reasonable period of time, except at a price less than fair market value, due to (1) the size of the block of the securities, (2) the fact that the securities are those of a closely held corporation, or (3) the fact that the sale of the securities would result in a forced or distress sale. However, even where one or more of the foregoing criteria are met, the reduction in value of a foundation's securities may not exceed 10 percent of their otherwise determined fair market value.[74]

This restriction on the use of a discount factor is applicable only to securities for which market quotations are readily available. It does not apply to securities that are restricted from trade on an exchange because of the federal securities laws and thus "other assets." These restricted securities may be valued annually, with use of a blockage discount where appropriate, and the valuation may be made by employees of the private foundation or others.[75]

---

[70]See *Amerada Hess Corp.* v. *Commissioner*, 517 F.2d 75 (3rd Cir. 1975); *Estate of Christie* v. *Commissioner*, 33 T.C.M. 476 (1974); *Rushton* v. *Commissioner*, 498 F.2d 88 (5th Cir. 1974); *Maytag* v. *Commissioner*, 187 F.2d 962 (10th Cir. 1951); *Helvering* v. *Maytag*, 125 F.2d 55 (8th Cir. 1942); *Bolles* v. *Commissioner*, 69 T.C. 342 (1977); *Hirsch* v. *Commissioner*, 51 T.C. 121 (1968). In general, see Holzman, "The 'Blockage' Rule," 46 *Taxes* 292 (1968).

[71]See Reg. § 53.4942(a)-2(c)(4)(i)(b), 20.2031-2(e). The IRS has promulgated guidelines for the valuation of securities that cannot be immediately resold because they are restricted from resale pursuant to the federal securities laws, in Rev. Rul. 77-287, 1977-2 C. B. 319. Also see Rev. Rul. 78-367, 1978-2 C. B. 249.

[72]Code § 4942(e)(2).

[73]Code § 4942(e)(2)(B).

[74]This provision has a unique legislative history, in that it was added by the House–Senate conferees, as noted, even though neither house had previously considered the issue—a probable violation of House and Senate rules. During the conference, some legislators learned of a certain private foundation practice that angered them considerably. This concerned the fact that some foundations, in valuing their assets for purposes of computing their annual mandatory payout amount, were taking a sizable blockage discount in valuing securities for which market quotations are readily available (thereby reducing the required distributable amount), while at the same time distributing the securities to charity in satisfaction of their distribution obligation and for that purpose according them full market value.

[75]IRS Private Letter Ruling 7933084. Pursuant to the rules of the Securities and Exchange Commission (Rule 144), a holder of restricted securities may periodically sell a small portion of the securities without regard to the general restriction. Specifically, the holder may sell, in a six-month period on an exchange, a number of shares equal

§ 26.5 Exception for Certain Accumulations

The mandatory payout rules do not apply to a private foundation to the extent that its income is required to be accumulated pursuant to the mandatory terms (as in effect on May 26, 1969, and at all times thereafter) of an instrument executed before May 27, 1969, with respect to the transfer of income-producing property to the foundation.[76] The exception to this exception, however, is that the rules are applicable where the organization would have been denied tax exemption by reason of former law if that law had not been repealed by the Tax Reform Act of 1969.[77]

The payout rules also do not apply to a foundation which is prohibited by its governing instrument or other instrument from distributing capital or corpus to the extent the requirements of the section are inconsistent with the prohibition.[78] However, this exception only applies, for taxable years beginning after December 31, 1971, during the pendency of any judicial proceeding by the private foundation which is necessary to reform or to excuse it from compliance with its instrument (in effect on May 26, 1969) in order to comply with the mandatory payout rules.[79]

The nonapplicability of these two exceptions was illustrated by the IRS in 1977.[80]

§ 26.6 Sanctions

An initial tax of 15 percent is imposed on the undistributed income of a private foundation for any tax year which has not been distributed as qualifying

---

to the lesser of 1 percent of the outstanding stock or an amount equal to the average of trading volume for the four weeks immediately preceding notification to the SEC of a proposed sale. The amount of securities that can be freely sold under Rule 144 is restricted to securities for which market quotations are readily available, thus subjecting them to the 10 percent limitation on discount; the balance of the securities may be valued without regard to that limitation. See, in general, Hopkins, "Rule 144: The Applicability of the Restricted Securities Requirements to Colleges and Universities," 1 *J. Coll. Univ. Law* (No. 2) 136 (1974); Hopkins and Marx, "Charitable Organizations and the New Restricted Securities Requirements of Rule 144," 26 *Tax Lawyer* (No. 2) 247 (1973).

[76]Tax Reform Act of 1969 § 101(1)(3)(B); Reg. § 53.4942(a)-2(e)(1)(i).

[77]Old Code § 504 provided, in general, that an organization described in Code § 501(c)(3) would be denied exemption under Code § 501 for the taxable year if amounts accumulated out of income during the taxable year or any prior taxable year and not actually paid out by the end of the taxable year are unreasonably in amount or duration in order to carry out the charitable purpose or function constituting the basis for the organization's tax exemption. For instances of unreasonable accumulation, see Rev. Rul. 67-108, 1967-1 C. B. 127; Rev. Rul. 67-106, 1976-1 C. B. 126.

[78]Reg. § 53.4942(a)-2(e)(1)(ii).

[79]Reg. § 53.4942(a)-2(e)(3).

[80]Rev. Rul. 77-74, 1977-1 C. B. 352.

distributions before the first day of the second (or any succeeding) tax year following the tax year (if the first day falls within the taxable period[81]).[82] This tax does not apply to the undistributed income of a private foundation for any tax year for which it is an operating foundation or to the extent that the foundation failed to distribute any amount solely because of incorrect valuation of assets if certain criteria are satisfied.[83]

In any case in which an initial tax is imposed on the undistributed income of a private foundation for any tax year, an additional tax is imposed on any portion of the income remaining undistributed at the close of the correction period.[84] This tax is equal to 100 percent of the amount remaining undistributed at the close of the correction period.[85]

Payment of these taxes is in addition to, rather than in lieu of, making the required distribution.[86]

[81]See Code § 4942(j)(1); Reg. § 53.4942(a)-1(c)(1).

[82]Code § 4942(a); Reg. § 53.4942(a)-1(a)(1).

[83]Reg. § 53.4942(a)-1(b).

[84]Code §§ 4942(b), 4942(j)(2); Reg. § 53.4942(a)-1(c)(3).

[85]Reg. § 53.4942(a)-1(a)(2). The U.S. Tax Court, by reason of a special enactment, possesses the jurisdiction to determine whether this additional tax should be imposed. See Chapter 25, text accompanying nn. 123–131 *supra*.

[86]Reg. § 53.4942(a)-1(a)(3). In general, see American Bar Association Committee on Charitable Giving, Trusts and Foundations, "Deduction Modifications and Section 4942— Some Problems of Allocation," 10 *Real Property, Probate Trust J.* 687 (1975); Traini, "Some Constitutional Aspects of Section 4942 of the Internal Revenue Code," 9 *New England L. Rev.* 207 (1974); Gregory and Moorehead, "Final regs provide comprehensive rules for foundation distribution requirements," 38 *J. Tax.* 370 (1973); Moorehead, "Qualifying Distributions: Do Your Grants and Activities Qualify?," 11 *N.Y.U. Conf. on Char. Fdns.* 203 (1973); Wright, "Grantee Selection and Supervision: Legal Requirements and Practical Problems," 10 *N.Y.U. Conf. on Char. Fdns.* 127 (1971); Shrekgast, "Problems on Internal Revenue Service Audit of Foundations," 10 *N.Y.U. Conf. on Char. Fdns.* 207, 223–226 (1971); Kurz, "The Private Foundation Provisions: The Purpose and Effects of Sections 4941, 4942, 4943," 31 *N.Y.U. Inst. on Fed. Tax.* 1311, 1320–1325 (1973); Lehrfeld, "Private Foundations and Tax Reform: Mandatory Pay-Outs of Income and Corpus" (Part 1), 2 *Tax Adviser* 213 (1971), (Part 2) 2 *Tax Adviser* 274 (1971), (Part 3) 2 *Tax Adviser* 337 (1971).

27

Excess Business Holdings

Prior to enactment of the Tax Reform Act of 1969, there was nothing in statutory law dealing directly with private foundation ownership of business interests, although some courts had held that business involvement by foundations could become so extensive as to result in loss of tax-exempt status.

Congress, in 1969, decided that the time had come to institute limitations on the ability of private foundations to maintain holdings in business enterprises, as the following explains:

> Those who wished to use a foundation's stock holdings to acquire or retain business control in some cases were relatively unconcerned about producing income to be used by the foundation for charitable purposes. In fact, they might have become so interested in making a success of the business, or in meeting competition, that most of their attention and interest was devoted to this with the result that what was supposed to be their function, that of carrying on charitable, educational, etc., activities was neglected. Even when such a foundation attains a degree of independence from its major donor, there is a temptation for its managers to divert their interest to the maintenance and improvement of the business and away from their charitable duties. Where the charitable ownership predominates, the business may be run in a way which unfairly competes with other businesses whose owners must pay taxes on the income that they derive from the businesses. To deal with these problems, Congress concluded it is desirable to limit the extent to which a business may be controlled by a private foundation.[1]

These limitations became the subject of Code § 4943.

§ 27.1   General Rules

The excess business holdings rules generally limit to 20 percent the permitted ownership of a corporation's voting stock or other interest in a business

---

[1]Joint Committee on Internal Revenue Taxation, *General Explanation of the Tax Reform Act of 1969*, 91st Cong. 2d Sess. (1970) at 41.

enterprise which may be held by a private foundation and all disqualified persons combined.[2] If effective control of the corporation can be shown to be elsewhere (that is, other than by the foundation and disqualified persons), a 35 percent limit may be substituted for the 20 percent limit.[3] Effective control means possession of the power, whether direct or indirect, and whether or not actually exercised, to direct or cause the direction of the management and policies of a business enterprise.[4] It is the actual control which is decisive and not its form or the means by which it is exercisable.

Generally, excess business holdings must be promptly disposed of, in the face of a series of graduated sanctions,[5] with an exception in the case of businesses at least 95 percent of the gross income of which is derived from passive sources.[6] Gross income from passive sources includes (1) dividends, interest, and annuities, (2) royalties (including overriding royalties), whether measured by production or by gross or taxable income from the property, (3) rents from real property and from personal property leased with real property if the rents attributable to the personal property are an incidental amount of the total rents under the lease, (4) gains from sales, exchanges, or other dispositions of property, other than stock in trade or property held primarily for sale to customers in the ordinary course of business, and (5) income from the sale of goods if the seller does not manufacture, produce, physically receive or deliver, negotiate sales of, or maintain inventories in the goods.[7]

Another exception from the tax on excess business holdings exists for holdings in a functionally related business.[8] This is a business or activity (1) the conduct of which is substantially related (aside from the mere provision of funds for the tax-exempt purpose) to the exercise or performance by the foundation of its charitable, educational, or other exempt purpose, (2) in which substantially all the work is performed for the foundation, without compensation,[9] (3) carried on by the foundation primarily for the convenience of its employees, (4) which consists of the selling of merchandise, substantially all of which has been received by the foundation as gifts or contributions, or (5) carried on within a larger aggregate of similar activities or within a larger complex of other en-

[2]Code § 4943(c)(2)(A); Reg. §§ 53.4943-1, 53.4943-3(b)(1).

[3]Code § 4943(c)(2)(B); Reg. § 53.4943-3(b)(3).

[4]Reg. § 53.4943-3(b)(3)(ii). According to the IRS, for the 35 percent rule to apply, a private foundation must demonstrate by affirmative proof that some unrelated third party, or a group of third parties, does in fact exercise control over the business enterprise involved. Rev. Rul. 81-111, 1981-1 C. B. 509.

[5]Code §§ 4943(a), (b), 4943(d)(2), (3).

[6]Code § 4943(d)(4)(B).

[7]Reg. § 53.4943-10. See, e.g., IRS Private Letter Ruling 7820038, holding that the commercial lease by a private foundation of office space in a building owned by it and in which it is the primary occupant, where only usual and customary services will be provided to tenants (see Chapter 41 § 3), is not a business enterprise inasmuch as at least 95 percent of the gross income from the leases is derived from passive sources.

[8]Code §§ 4943(d)(4)(A), 4942(j)(5).

[9]See Rev. Rul. 76-85, 1976-1 C. B. 357.

deavors which is related to the tax-exempt purposes of the foundation (other than the need to simply provide funds for these purposes).

If a private foundation obtains holdings in a business enterprise after May 26, 1969, other than by purchase by the foundation or by disqualified persons (presumably, that is, by gift or bequest), and the additional holdings result in the foundation having excess business holdings, the foundation in effect has five years to reduce its gifts or bequest holdings or those of the disqualified persons to permissible levels.[10] The excess business holdings (or the increase in excess business holdings) resulting from the gift or bequest are treated as being held by a disqualified person, rather than by a foundation, during the five-year period beginning on the date the foundation obtains the holdings.

Thus, where the stock is held in excess of the applicable percentage, the foundation must reduce its holdings to the extent necessary to bring its holdings in relation to those of disqualified persons down to the requisite level. A *de minimus* rule permits a foundation to retain up to 2 percent of the voting stock of a corporation, although the holdings of related foundations[11] are aggregated for the purpose of computing the 2 percent amount,[12] so as to preclude the use of multiple foundations to convert the *de minimus* rule into a method of evading the excess business holdings rules.[13]

For determining the holdings in a business enterprise of either a private foundation or a disqualified person, any stock or other interest owned directly or indirectly by or for a corporation, partnership, estate, or trust is considered owned proportionately by or for its shareholders, partners, or beneficiaries.

§ 27.2　Permitted and Excess Holdings

The phrase "excess business holdings" means the amount of stock or other interest in a business enterprise that a private foundation would have to dispose of to a person other than a disqualified person in order for the remaining holdings of the foundation in the enterprise to constitute "permitted" holdings.[14]

An interest in a business enterprise owned either by a private foundation or a disqualified person includes an interest in a business enterprise constructively owned by the persons under rules established for partnerships and their partners, estates, and trusts and their beneficiaries, and corporations and their stockholders.[15] The term "business enterprise" includes the active conduct of

---

[10]Code § 4943(c)(6); Reg. § 4943-6.

[11]See Code § 4946(a)(1)(H).

[12]Code § 4943(c)(2)(C): Reg. § 53.4943-3(b)(4).

[13]Although the foregoing summary of the excess business holdings rules has stressed holdings in the form of stock in business corporations, corresponding limitations apply to partnerships and other entities. Code § 4943(c)(3); Reg. § 53.4943-3(c)(1), (2), and (4). A private foundation is not permitted to own a business as a sole proprietorship. Code § 4943(c)(3)(B); Reg. § 53.4943-3(c)(3).

[14]Code § 4943(c)(1); Reg. § 53.4943-3.

[15]Code § 4945(d)(1); Reg. § 53.4943-8.

a trade or business, including any activity which is carried on for the production of income from the sale of goods or the performance of services and which constitutes an unrelated trade or business.[16]

§27.3   Present Holdings and Delayed Divestiture

The excess business holdings rules requiring timely divestiture where the combined business holdings of a private foundation and all disqualified persons exceed 20 (or 35) percent do not apply to "present holdings," i.e., holdings as of May 26, 1969.[17] In these instances, a 50 percent limitation applies, unless the present holdings amount to less than 50 percent, in which case the actual percentage applies.[18] If a foundation organized before May 26, 1969, reduces its present percentage holdings of a business enterprise, it may not again increase these holdings (the so-called "downward rachet rule"), except that if they fall below the levels applicable for future holdings (that is, 20 or 35 percent) they may be increased to those levels.[19]

Where "present holdings" were in excess of 50 percent but not in excess of 75 percent, a ten-year period was available (i.e., to May 26, 1979) before the holdings had to be reduced to 50 percent.[20] If the combined present holdings are more than 75 percent, the reduction to 50 percent need not occur for a fifteen-year period (i.e., until May 26, 1984).[21] However, the fifteen-year period is expanded to twenty years (i.e., to May 26, 1989) if the foundation itself holds more than 95 percent of a business' stocks or other interest.[22] In the case of present holdings acquired under the terms of a trust which was irrevocable on May 26, 1969, or under the terms of a will executed on that date and thereafter unchanged, the foregoing ten- and fifteen-year periods commence on the date of distribution therefrom, rather than on the May 26, 1969, date.[23]

The foregoing, ten-, fifteen-, or twenty-year periods are known as the "first phase."[24] The first phase is suspended during the time a judicial proceeding is pending, for the purpose of reforming (or excusing the foundation from complying with) its governing instrument or any other instrument (in effect on May

---

[16]Code § 4943(d)(4); Reg. § 53.4943-10.

[17]See, in general, Reg. § 53.4943-4.

[18]Code § 4943(c)(4)(A)(i). See Rev. Rul. 75-25, 1975-1 C. B. 359.

[19]Code § 4943(c)(4)(A)(ii); Reg. § 53.4943-4(d)(4).

[20]Code § 4943(c)(4)(B)(iii).

[21]Code § 4943(c)(4)(B)(ii).

[22]Code § 4943(c)(4)(B)(i). This fifteen-year period is reduced to ten years if substantial contributors or members of their families having 15 percent or more of the interest in the enterprise objected, before January 1, 1971, to the additional five years for disposition of the excess holdings and elected not to have the fifteen-year period apply. Code § 4943(c)(4)(E).

[23]Code § 4943(c)(5); Reg. § 53.4943-5. See Rev. Rul. 81-119, 1981-1 C. B. 512.

[24]See Reg. § 53.4943-4(a).

26, 1969) to allow disposition of excess business holdings.[25] During the first phase, business interests owned by the foundation on May 26, 1969, are treated as held by a disqualified person, rather than by the foundation.

The fifteen-year period immediately following the first phase is the "second phase."[26] Thus, the holdings of a pre-May 26, 1969, private foundation and its disqualified persons in a business enterprise generally must be down to at least 50 percent by the close of the first phase. However, if at any time during the second phase all disqualified persons with respect to a pre-May 26, 1969, foundation together have holdings in a business enterprise in excess of 2 percent of the enterprise's voting stock, the 50 percent limitation is modified in that the foundation may only hold up to 25 percent of the stock.[27]

Thus, if at the close of the first phase, a pre-May 26, 1969, private foundation and all disqualified persons together have holdings not in excess of 50 percent and the foundation has holdings of not more than 25 percent, no further divestiture is required. If the disqualified persons together hold no more than 2 percent of the stock, the foundation is not subject to the foregoing 25 percent limit, although the 50 percent total still applies to the combined holdings at the end of the first phase. Instead, the foundation in this instance has another fifteen years (the scope of the second phase) to bring the combined holdings of the stock down to 35 percent.[28]

If a private foundation enters the "third phase"[29] with not more than 2 percent of the voting stock held by all disqualified persons, and any time after the beginning of the third phase these holdings exceed 2 percent, the foregoing 25 percent rule applies.

The regulations generally permit an active corporation, in which a private foundation has excess stock held since May 26, 1969, to acquire new subsidiaries or assets without creating excess business holdings for the foundation.[30]

§ 27.4 Transitional Rule

Congress, in adopting the Tax Reform Act of 1976, extended a private foundation transitional rule adopted in 1969,[31] relating to the sale of excess and nonexcess business holdings to disqualified persons. This rule, as originally enacted, permits a private foundation to sell excess and nonexcess business holdings (held or treated as held by the foundation on May 26, 1969) to a disqualified person without causing an act of self-dealing if the sales price equals

[25]Code § 4943(c)(4)(C).
[26]Code § 4943(c)(4)(D)(iii)Reg. § 53.4943-4(d)(5).
[27]Code § 4943(c)(4)(D)(i). An example of application of this 25 percent limitation appears in Rev. Rul. 81-22, 1981-1 C. B. 510.
[28]Code § 4943(c)(4)(D)(ii).
[29]See Reg. § 53.4943-4(d)(6).
[30]Internal Revenue News Release IR-2175 (Nov. 5, 1979).
[31]Tax Reform Act of 1969 § 101(1)(2)(B).

or exceeds the fair market value of the property being sold. This exception was allowed in recognition of the fact that in the case of many closely held companies the only ready market for a foundation's holdings is one or more disqualified persons. This rule applied to dispositions occurring before January 1, 1977.

The Senate Finance Committee, in approving this rule, stated its view "generally that it is still desirable to encourage private foundations to divest themselves of holdings in enterprises in which disqualified persons have a significant interest provided that the foundation receives fair market value for the business holdings."[32]

§ 27.5   Sanctions

An initial excise tax is imposed on the excess business holdings of a private foundation in any business enterprise for each tax year which ends during the taxable period.[33] The amount of this tax is 5 percent of the total value of all of the foundation's excess holdings in each of its business enterprises.[34] If the excess holdings are not disposed of during the correction period,[35] an additional tax is imposed upon the foundation.[36] The amount of this tax is 200 percent of the value of the excess holdings.[37]

[32]S. Rep. No. 94-938 (Part 2), 94th Cong., 1st Sess. (1976) at 87. See Rev. Rul. 75-336, 1975-2 C. B. 110.

[33]Code §§ 4943(a)(1), 4943(d)(2).

[34]See, in general, Reg. § 53.4943-2(a).

[35]Code § 4943(d)(3); Reg. § 53.4943-9.

[36]Code § 4943(b).

[37]Reg. § 53.4943-2(b). The U.S. Tax Court, by reason of a special enactment, possesses the jurisdiction to determine whether this additional tax should be imposed. See Chapter 25, text accompanying nn. 123–131, *supra*. In general, see Kauder, "Excess and Permitted Business Holdings of Private Foundations: A Critique of the Treasury's Construction of Section 4943," 30 *Tax L. Rev.* 101 (1974); Hasson, Jr., and Duffney, Jr., "Are redemptions of stock by private foundations being blocked by regs.?," 40 *J. Tax.* 300 (1974); Geske, "Excess business holdings can be disposed of to disqualified persons without penalty," 41 *J. Tax.* 296 (1974); Smith, "Planning for Private Foundations under Section 4943," 60 *A.B.A.J.* 969 (1974); Bandy, "Avoiding limits on private foundation business holdings: Planning possibilities," 38 *J. Tax.* 136 (1973); Reiner, "Excess Business Holdings and Unrelated Business Income," 10 *N.Y.U. Conf. on Char. Fdns.* 257 (1971); Plumb, "Avoiding the 200% tax on excess holdings for 20 to 50%-owned private foundations," 34 *J. Tax.* 296 (1971).

28

Jeopardizing Investments

Prior to enactment of the Tax Reform Act of 1969, Code § 504(a)(3) provided that a private foundation (and many other "charitable" organizations) would lose its tax-exempt status if its aggregate accumulated income was "invested in such a manner as to jeopardize the carrying out of the charitable, educational, or other purpose or function constituting the basis for [its] exemption . . ." No similar specific limitations applied with respect to investment of principal.

The statutory sanction was deemed ineffective by Congress with respect to private foundations, as the following explanation indicates:

> The grant of current tax benefits to donors and exempt organizations usually is justified on the basis that charity will benefit from the gifts. However, if the organization's assets are used in a way which jeopardizes their use for the organization's exempt purpose this result is not obtained. Prior law recognized this concept in the case of income, but not in the case of an organization's principal.

> Under prior law a private foundation manager might invest the assets (other than accumulated income) in warrants, commodity futures, and options, or might purchase on margin or otherwise risk the corpus of the foundation without being subject to sanction. (However, in one case a court held that the consistent practice of making such investments constituted operation of the foundation for a substantial non-exempt purpose and would result in loss of tax-exemption.)

> The Congress determined that investments which jeopardize the foundation's corpus should not be permitted. Here, as in other sections, the Congress concluded that, to achieve this objective, limited sanctions were preferable to the loss of exemption.[1]

Consequently, the Tax Reform Act of 1969 repealed Code § 504 and introduced rules, as Code § 4944, pertaining to "jeopardizing investments" by private foundations.

---

[1]Joint Committee on Internal Revenue Taxation, *General Explanation of Tax Reform Act of 1969*, 91st Cong., 2d Sess. (1970) at 46.

§ 28.1   General Rules

Under the rules concerning jeopardizing investments by private foundations, a foundation cannot invest any amount (income or principal) in a manner which would jeopardize the carrying out of any of its tax-exempt purposes.[2] The statute is silent as to what constitutes this type of an investment, other than to exclude from the concept the "program-related" investment (see below). However, the regulations state that an investment is considered to jeopardize the carrying out of the tax-exempt purposes of a private foundation if it is determined that the foundation managers, in making the investment, failed to exercise ordinary business care and prudence, under the facts and circumstances prevailing at the time the investment was made, in providing for the long- and short-term financial needs of the foundation to carry out its exempt purposes.[3] Congress contemplated that the determination as to whether investments jeopardize the carrying out of a foundation's charitable purposes is to be made as of the time of the investment, in accordance with the "prudent trustee" approach,[4] and not subsequently on the basis of hindsight.

A determination as to whether the making of a particular investment jeopardizes the tax-exempt purposes of a private foundation is to be made on an investment-by-investment basis, in each case taking into account the foundation's portfolio as a whole. It is permissible for the foundation managers to take into account expected returns, risks of rising and falling price levels, and the need for diversification within the investment portfolio. But to avoid the application of the applicable penalty tax, a careful analysis of potential investments must be made and good business judgment must be exercised.

The IRS has ruled that "approval of an investment procedure governing investments to be made in the future is not possible."[5] This position is in reflection of the fact that advance approval of investment procedures would constitute a determination prior to the investment, would not be on an investment-by-investment basis, and would necessarily preclude application of the "prudent trustee" approach.

No category of investments is treated as a *per se* violation of these rules. However, the types or methods of investment that are scrutinized closely to determine whether the foundation managers have met the requisite standard of care and prudence include trading in securities on margin, trading in commodity futures, investments in oil and gas syndications, the purchase of "puts," "calls," and "straddles," the purchase of warrants, and selling short. Once it has been ascertained that an investment does not jeopardize the carrying out of a foundation's tax-exempt purposes, the investment is never considered to jeopardize the carrying out of exempt purposes, even though, as a result of the investment, the foundation subsequently realizes a loss.[6]

[2] Code § 4944(a)(1).
[3] Reg. § 53.4944-1(a)(2)(i).
[4] See S. Rep. No. 91-552, 91st Cong., 1st Sess. (1969) at 46.
[5] Rev. Rul. 74-316, 1974-2 C. B. 389.
[6] Reg. § 53.4944-1(a)(2)(i). See, e.g., IRS Private Letter Ruling 8027078.

The IRS has made only one published determination as to whether an investment constitutes a jeopardizing investment. This occurred where the Service considered a situation involving the contribution to a private foundation of a whole-life insurance policy, which was subject to a policy loan, by a donor (the insured) who at the time of the gift had a life expectancy of ten years. The foundation did not surrender the policy for its cash value but continued to pay the annual premiums and interest due on the policy and the loan. Finding that the combined premium and interest payments were such that, by the end of eight years, the foundation would have invested a greater amount in premiums and interest than it could receive as a return on the investment (as insurance proceeds upon the death of the insured), the IRS concluded that "the foundation managers, by investing at the projected rate of return prevailing at the time of the investment[,] failed to exercise ordinary business care and prudence in providing for the long-term and short-term financial needs of the foundation in carrying out its exempt purposes." Therefore, under the circumstances, the Service held that each payment made by the foundation for a premium on the policy and interest on the policy loan was a jeopardizing investment.[7]

The jeopardizing investment rules do not exempt or relieve any person from compliance with any federal or state law imposing any obligation, duty, responsibility, or other standard of conduct with respect to the operation or administration of an organization or trust to which the provision applies. Nor does any state law exempt or relieve any person from any obligation, duty, responsibility, or other standard of conduct provided in these rules.[8]

The tax on jeopardizing investments does not apply to investments originally made by a person who later transferred them as gifts to the private foundation or to investments which are acquired by the foundation solely as a result of a corporate reorganization.[9] Nor does the tax apply to investments made before January 1, 1970, unless the form or terms of the investments are later changed or they are exchanged for other investments.[10]

§ 28.2 Program-Related Investments

A "program-related investment" is not a jeopardizing investment. A program-related investment is an investment the primary purpose of which is to accomplish one or more charitable purposes and no significant purpose of which is the production of income or the appreciation of property.[11] The regulations add a third characteristic, in that no purpose of the investment may be the furthering of substantial legislative or political activities.[12] Conspicuously absent from the elements of the program-related investment is the proscription on

[7]Rev. Rul. 80-133, 1980-1 C.B. 258.
[8]Reg. § 53.4944-1(a)(2)(i).
[9]Reg. § 53.4944-1(a)(2)(ii).
[10]Reg. § 53.4944-6.
[11]Code § 4944(e).
[12]Reg. § 53.4944-3(a)(1). See Code § 170(c)(2)(D); Chapters 13 and 14.

private inurement,[13] simply because private individuals necessarily do benefit from the investment, albeit in the course of achieving a larger (charitable) purpose.

An investment is considered as made primarily to accomplish one or more charitable purposes if it significantly furthers the accomplishment of the private foundation's tax-exempt activities and if the investment would not have been made but for the relationship between the investment and the activities.[14] An investment in a functionally related business[15] is considered as made primarily to accomplish one or more charitable purposes.[16] In determining whether a significant purpose of an investment is the production of income or the appreciation of property, it is relevant to determine whether investors for profit would be likely to make the investment on the same terms as the foundation. However, the fact that an investment produces significant income or capital appreciation is not, in the absence of other factors, conclusive evidence of such a significant purpose.[17]

Illustrations of program-related investments include (1) low-interest or interest-free loans to needy students, (2) high-risk investments in nonprofit low-income housing projects, (3) low-interest loans to small businesses owned by members of economically disadvantaged groups, where commercial funds at reasonable interest rates are not readily available, (4) investments in businesses in deteriorated urban areas under a plan to improve the economy of the area by providing employment or training for unemployed residents, or (5) investments in nonprofit organizations combating community deterioration. Likewise, the IRS has ruled that low-interest rate loans by a foundation, established to aid the blind in securing employment, that are made to blind persons who desire to establish themselves in business but who are unable to obtain funds through commercial sources, constitute program-related investments.[18]

Once it has been determined that an investment is program-related, it does not cease to qualify as such, provided that any changes in the form or terms of the investment are made primarily for tax-exempt purposes and not for any significant purpose involving the production of income or the appreciation of property. A change made in the form or terms of a program-related investment for the prudent protection of the foundation's investment ordinarily will not cause the investment to cease to qualify as program-related.[19] A program-related investment constitutes a qualifying distribution for the foundation.[20]

An investment which jeopardizes the carrying out of a private foundation's

---

[13]Code § 170(c)(2)(C). See Chapter 12.

[14]Reg. § 53.4944-3(a)(2)(i).

[15]See Code § 4942(j)(5)(B).

[16]Reg. § 53.4944-3(a)(2)(ii).

[17]Reg. § 53.4944-3(a)(2)(iii).

[18]Rev. Rul. 78-90, 1978-1 C. B. 380. Also see IRS Private Letter Ruling 7823072.

[19]Reg. § 53.4944-3(a)(3).

[20]See Chapter 26.

tax-exempt purposes is considered to be removed from jeopardy when the foundation sells or otherwise disposes of the investment and the proceeds therefrom are not themselves investments which jeopardize the carrying out of exempt purposes.[21]

§ 28.3 Sanctions

If a private foundation invests any amount in such a manner as to jeopardize the carrying out of any of its tax-exempt purposes, an initial tax is imposed on the foundation on the making of the investment, at the rate of 5 percent of the amount so invested for each tax year or part thereof in the taxable period.[22] In any case in which this initial tax is imposed, a tax is imposed on the participation of any foundation manager in the making of the investment, knowing that it is jeopardizing the carrying out of any of the foundation's exempt purposes, equal to 5 percent of the amount so invested for each tax year of the foundation (or part thereof) in the taxable period.[23] With respect to any one investment, the maximum amount of this tax is $5,000.[24] This tax, which must be paid by any participating foundation manager, is not imposed where the participation is not willful and is due to reasonable cause.[25]

A foundation manager's participation in making an investment is willful if it is voluntary, conscious, and intentional; however, it is not willful if the manager does not knowingly participate in a jeopardizing investment. A manager's action will be considered due to reasonable cause if the manager relies on advice of legal counsel expressed in a reasoned written opinion. In addition, a foundation manager may rely on the advice of a qualified investment counselor, given in writing in accordance with generally accepted practices, that a particular investment will provide for the long- and short-term financial needs of the foundation.[26]

An additional tax is imposed in any case in which this initial tax is imposed and the investment is not removed from jeopardy within the correction period.[27] This tax, which is to be paid by the private foundation, is at the rate of 25 percent of the amount of the investment.[28] In any case in which this additional tax is imposed and a foundation manager has refused to agree to part or all of the removal of the investment from jeopardy, a tax is imposed at the rate of 5 percent of the amount of the investment. This tax is payable by any foundation manager who has refused to agree to the removal of part or all of the investment

---

[21]Code § 4944(e)(2); Reg. § 53.4944-5(b).
[22]Code § 4944(a)(1); Reg. § 53.4944-1(a)(1).
[23]Code § 4944(e)(1); Reg. § 53.4944-5(a).
[24]Code § 4944(d)(2).
[25]Code § 4944(a)(2); Reg. § 53.4944-1(b)(1).
[26]Reg. § 53.4944-1(b)(2).
[27]Code § 4944(e)(3); Reg. § 53.4944-5(d).
[28]Code § 4944(b)(1); Reg. § 53.4944-2(a).

from jeopardy.[29] With respect to any one investment, the maximum amount of this tax is $10,000.[30]

Where more than one foundation manager is liable for an initial or additional tax with respect to any one jeopardizing investment, all of the managers are jointly and severally liable for the taxes.[31]

---

[29]Code § 4944(b)(2); Reg. § 53.4944-2(b).

[30]Code § 4944(d)(2). The U.S. Tax Court, by reason of a special enactment, possesses the jurisdiction to determine whether this additional tax should be imposed. See Chapter 25, text accompanying nn. 123–131, *supra*.

[31]Code § 4944(d)(1); Reg. § 53.4944-4(a). In general, see Morris, "Public Charities: Maintaining Their Favored Public Status," 11 *N.Y.U. Conf. on Char. Fdns.* 179, 190–199 (1973); Shrekgast, "Problems on Internal Revenue Service Audit of Foundations," 11 *N.Y.U. Conf. on Char. Fdns.* 207, 226–228 (1973); Lehrfeld, "Private Foundations and Tax Reform: Jeopardy Investments," 1 *Tax Adviser* 492 (1970); Denny, "Investments Which Jeopardize Charitable Purpose," 24 *Tax Lawyer* 113 (1970).

29

Impermissible Expenditures

The general federal tax rules pertaining to "charitable" organizations require that no substantial part of the activities of "charitable" organizations, including private foundations, may consist of the carrying on of propaganda or otherwise attempting to influence legislation, and that these organizations may not participate in or intervene in any political campaign on behalf of any candidate for public office.[1] Prior to enactment of the Tax Reform Act of 1969, Code § 504(a)(2) provided that a private foundation (and many other "charitable" organizations) would lose its tax-exempt status if its aggregate accumulated income was "used to a substantial degree for purposes or functions other than those constituting the basis for [its] exemption."

The statutory sanctions were deemed ineffective by Congress with respect to private foundations, as the following explanation indicates:

> As is the case with the other limitations described above (self-dealing, accumulation of income, etc.), the only sanction available under prior law with respect to political activity by a foundation was loss of exemption and denial of charitable contribution deduction status; a large organization, merely because of the substantiality test, might engage without consequence in more lobbying than a small organization; a heavily endowed organization might engage in lobbying and, if it lost its exempt educational or charitable status, might avoid tax on its investment income by becoming exempt under another provision of the law; also, the standards as to the permissible level of activities under prior law were so vague as to encourage subjective application of the sanction.

> Another problem arose from the fact that the absolute prohibition upon involvement in political campaigns on behalf of any candidate for public office frequently resulted in the alternatives of unreasonably severe punishment or unreasonably light punishment. As a practical matter, many organizations often found ways of making clear their views regarding opposing political candidates without fear that their exempt status would be revoked. Also, there was no prohibition against taking sides as to referendum issues. The latter activity was regarded as influencing

[1]See Chapters 13 and 14.

legislation, but, as indicated above, that was specifically permitted to a limited extent.

In recent years, private foundations had become increasingly active in political and legislative activities. In several instances called to the Congress' attention, funds were spent in ways clearly designed to favor certain candidates. In some cases, this was done by financing registration campaigns in limited geographical areas. In other cases contributions were made to organizations that then used the money to publicize the views, personalities, and activities of certain candidates. It also appeared that officials of some foundations exercised little or no control over the organizations receiving the funds from the foundations.

It also was called to the Congress' attention that prior law did not effectively limit the extent to which foundations could use their money for "educational" grants to enable people to take vacations abroad, to have paid interludes between jobs, and to subsidize the preparation of materials furthering specific political viewpoints.

The Congress concluded that more effective limitations must be placed on the extent to which tax-deductible and tax-exempt funds can be dispensed by private persons and that these limitations must involve more effective sanctions. Accordingly, the Congress determined that a tax should be imposed upon expenditures by private foundations for activities that should not be carried on by exempt organizations (such as lobbying, electioneering, and "grass roots" campaigning). The Congress also believes that granting foundations should take substantial responsibility for the proper use of the funds they give away.

In general, the Congress' decisions reflect the concept that private foundations are stewards of public trusts and their assets are no longer in the same status as the assets of individuals who may dispose of their own money in any lawful way they see fit.[2]

Consequently, the Tax Reform Act of 1969 repealed Code § 504(a)(2) and introduced Code § 4945 in an effort to further restrict the purposes and activities for which private foundations may expend their funds. This section, in effect, forbids a private foundation from expending or incurring any amount for various purposes or activities, discussed below. Improper and, in effect, prohibited expenditures are termed "taxable expenditures."

§ 29.1 Legislative Activities

The term "taxable expenditure" includes any amount paid or incurred by a private foundation to carry on propaganda, or otherwise attempt, to influence legislation.[3] Thus, the general test of "substantiality" in the rules for charitable organizations generally is inapplicable to private foundations in this regard, although the test governs as to tax-exempt status in general.

Attempts to influence legislation may include communications with a mem-

---

[2]Joint Committee on Internal Revenue Taxation, *General Explanation of Tax Reform Act of 1969*, 91st Cong., 2d Sess. (1970)) at 47-48.

[3]Code § 4945(d)(1).

ber or employee of a legislative body or with an official or employee of an executive department of government who may participate in formulating the legislation or efforts to affect the opinion of the general public or any segment thereof with respect to legislation being considered by, or to be submitted imminently to, a legislative body.[4] For these purposes, a proposed treaty required to be submitted by the President to the Senate for its advice and consent is considered "legislation being considered by, or to be submitted imminently to a legislative body" at the time the President's representative begins to negotiate its position with the prospective parties to the proposed treaty.[5] The term "legislation" also includes action by the U.S. Congress, any state legislature, any local council or similar governing body, or the public in a referendum, initiative, constitutional amendment, or similar procedure. This term does not include actions by executive, judicial, or administrative bodies, such as school boards, housing authorities, sewer and water districts, zoning boards, and other similar federal, state, or local special purpose bodies, whether elective or appointive. The term "action" includes the introduction, enactment, defeat, or repeal of legislation.[6]

A private foundation is not treated as having made taxable expenditures of amounts paid or incurred in carrying on discussions with officials of governmental bodies provided that (1) the subject of the discussions is a program which is jointly funded by the foundation and the government or is a new program which may be jointly funded by the foundation and the government, (2) the discussions are undertaken for the purpose of exchanging data and information on the subject matter of the program, and (3) the discussions are not undertaken by foundation managers in order to make any direct attempt to persuade governmental officials or employees to take particular positions on specific legislative issues other than the program.[7]

Any amount paid or incurred by a recipient of a program-related investment in connection with an appearance before, or communication to, any legislative body with respect to legislation or proposed legislation of direct interest to the recipient is not attributed to the investing foundation if the foundation does not earmark its funds to be used for any legislative activities and a business expense deduction[8] is allowable to the recipient for the amount.[9]

A grant by a private foundation to an organization that is not a private foundation[10] does not constitute a taxable expenditure by the grantor foundation

[4]Code § 4945(e); Reg. § 53.4945-2(b), (c).
[5]Reg. § 53.4945-2(a)(1).
[6]Reg. § 53.4945-2(a)(2).
[7]Reg. § 53.4945-2(a)(3).
[8]Code § 162.
[9]Reg. § 53.4945-2(a)(4).
[10]For this purpose, an organization described in Code § 509(a)(1), (2), or (3). See Chapter 22.

if the grant by the private foundation is not earmarked to be used for any legislative, electioneering, or noncharitable activity,[11] is not earmarked to be used in a manner which would violate the rules concerning grants to individuals or "expenditure responsibility,"[12] and there does not exist an agreement, oral or written, whereby the grantor foundation may cause the grantee to engage in any prohibited activity or to select the recipient to which the grant is to be devoted.[13]

With the advent of the liberalized rules enacted in 1976, concerning permissible legislative activities by public charities,[14] it may be presumed that the scope and extent of these activities by public charities will increase. The introduction of these rules and the prospects of substantial increases in lobbying gave private foundations some pause; they feared that the legislative activities of a grantee public charity electing to come under the rules would be attributed to the grantor private foundation, thereby converting the grant to a taxable expenditure.[15] However, late in 1978, the IRS privately ruled that a private foundation may—without running afoul of the taxable expenditures rule—make a grant to a lobbying public charity as long as the grant is not earmarked for use in legislative efforts.[16]

Engaging in nonpartisan analysis, study, or research and making available to the general public or segment thereof or to governmental bodies, officials, or employees the results of the work does not constitute carrying on propaganda, or otherwise attempting, to influence legislation.[17] "Nonpartisan analysis, study or research," which means an independent and objective exposition of a particular subject matter, may advocate a particular position or viewpoint so long as there is a sufficiently full and fair exposition of the pertinent facts to enable the public or an individual to form an independent opinion or conclusion. On the other hand, the mere presentation of unsupported opinion does not qualify.[18]

Normally, whether a publication or broadcast qualifies as "nonpartisan analysis, study, or research" will be determined on a presentation-by-presentation basis. However, if a publication or broadcast is one of a series prepared or supported by a private foundation and the series as a whole meets the standards of this exception, then any individual publication or broadcast within the series will not result in a taxable expenditure even though the individual broadcast

[11]See Code § 4945(d)(1), (2) and (5).

[12]See Code § 4945(d)(3) and (4).

[13]Reg. § 53.4945-2(a)(5).

[14]See Chapter 13 § 4.

[15]The prospects of this result were present before adoption of the 1976 rules but they were heightened following their enactment and the foundation community's perception of them.

[16]See Troyer, "Lobbying and Nonprofits: What's the Experience So Far?," 20 *Foundation News* (No. 3) 20 (1979).

[17]Code § 4945(e).

[18]Reg. § 53.4945-2(d)(1). See Chapter 7.

or publication does not, by itself, meet the standards. Whether a broadcast or publication is considered part of a series will ordinarily depend on all the facts and circumstances of each particular situation.[19]

A private foundation may choose any suitable means, including oral or written presentations, to distribute the results of its nonpartisan analysis, study, or research, with or without charge. These means include distribution of reprints of speeches, articles and reports; presentation of information through conferences, meetings and discussions; and dissemination to the news media, including radio, television and newspapers, and to other public forums. For these purposes, the presentations may not be limited to or directed toward persons who are interested solely in one side of a particular issue.[20]

Amounts paid or incurred in connection with providing technical advice or assistance to a governmental body or committee, or subdivision of either, in response to a written request therefrom do not constitute taxable expenditures.[21] The request for assistance or advice must be made in the name of the requesting governmental body, committee, or subdivision thereof rather than by an individual member thereof and the response must be available to every member of the requesting entity. Because the assistance or advice may be given only at the express request of a governmental entity, the oral or written presentation of the assistance or advice need not qualify as nonpartisan analysis, study, or research. The offering of opinions or recommendations will ordinarily qualify under this exception only if the opinions or recommendations are specifically requested by the governmental body, committee, or subdivision or are directly related to the materials so requested.[22]

A third exception is that the taxable expenditure rules do not apply to any amount paid or incurred in connection with an appearance before, or communication to, any legislative body with respect to a possible decision of the body which might affect the existence of the private foundation, its powers and duties, its tax-exempt status, or the deductibility of contributions to the foundation.[23] Under this exception, a foundation may communicate with the entire legislative body, committees or subcommittees of the legislative body, individual congressmen or congresswomen or legislators, members of their staff, or representatives of the executive branch, who are involved in the legislative process, if the communication is limited to the prescribed subjects. Similarly, the foundation may make expenditures in order to initiate legislation if the legislation concerns only matters which might affect the existence of the private foundation, its powers and duties, its tax-exempt status, or the deductibility of contributions to the foundation.[24]

---

[19]Reg. § 53.4945-2(d)(1)(iii).
[20]Reg. § 53.4945-2(d)(1)(iv).
[21]Code § 4945(e)(2).
[22]Reg. § 53.4945-2(d)(2).
[23]Code § 4945(e) (last sentence).
[24]Reg. § 53.4945-2(d)(3)(i).

Expenditures for examinations and discussions of broad social, economic, and similar issues are not taxable even if the problems are of the types with which government would be expected to deal ultimately. Thus, the term "any attempt to influence any legislation" does not include public discussion, or communications with members of legislative bodies or governmental employees, the general subject of which is also the subject of legislation before a legislative body, so long as the discussion does not address itself to the merits of a specific legislative proposal.[25] For example, a private foundation may, without having made a taxable expenditure, present discussions or problems such as environmental pollution or population growth which are being considered by Congress and various state legislatures, but only if the discussions are not directly addressed to specific legislation being considered.

§ 29.2 Electioneering

The term "taxable expenditure" includes any amount paid or incurred by a private foundation to influence the outcome of any specific public election or to carry on, directly or indirectly, any voter registration drive.[26]

A private foundation is considered to be influencing the outcome of any specific public election if it participates or intervenes, directly or indirectly, in any political campaign on behalf of or in opposition to any candidate for public office. The term "candidate for public office" means an individual who offers himself or herself, or is proposed by others, as a contestant for an elective public office, whether the office be national, state, or local. Such activities include (1) publishing or distributing written or printed statements or making oral statements on behalf of or in opposition to a candidate, (2) paying salaries or expenses of campaign workers, and (3) conducting or paying the expenses of conducting a voter registration drive limited to the geographic area covered by the campaign.[27] The prohibition on electioneering applicable to charitable organizations generally is expanded by these rules to apply to efforts to influence the outcome of referenda as well as campaigns by individuals for public office. This prohibition is limited to expenditures for the purpose of influencing the outcome of any specific election because of concern that otherwise the contention might be raised that nearly any statement, study, or general education activity could at a future date become an issue in an election, depending upon the views of the candidates at that time.

A private foundation may engage in electioneering activities, including voter registration drives, without making taxable expenditures, if (1) the activities of the foundation are nonpartisan, not confined to one specific election period, and carried on in five or more states, (2) it expends at least 85 percent of its income directly for the active conduct of its tax-exempt activities, (3) it receives

---

[25]Reg. § 53.4945-2(d)(4).
[26]Code § 4945(d)(2); Reg. § 53.4945-3(a)(1).
[27]Reg. § 53.4945-3(a)(2).

at least 85 percent of its support (other than gross investment income[28]) from tax-exempt organizations, the general public, governmental units,[29] or any combination of the foregoing, it does not receive more than 25 percent of such support from any one tax-exempt organization, and not more than half of its support is received from gross investment income, and (4) contributions to it for voter registration drives are not subject to conditions that they may be used only in specified states, possessions of the United States, or political subdivisions or other areas of any of the foregoing or the District of Columbia, or that they may be used in only one specific election period.[30]

§ 29.3   Grants to Individuals

The term "taxable expenditure" means any amount paid or incurred by a private foundation as a grant to an individual for travel, study, or other similar purposes.[31] The term "grants" includes but is not limited to scholarships, fellowships, internships, prizes, awards, and loans for charitable purposes, "program related investments," and payments to tax-exempt organizations to be used in furtherance of their exempt purposes. Conversely, the term "grants" does not ordinarily include salaries or other payments to persons for personal services rendered to the private foundation.[32] Thus, the IRS ruled that payments by a private foundation to consultants for services performed in the development of model curricula and design of educational materials to aid the foundation in its program activity of assisting educators to employ improved educational methods were not grants.[33] Likewise, the IRS ruled that amounts paid by a foundation's grantees to their research assistants, who are selected independently of the foundation, do not constitute grants.[34]

However, a grant to an individual for travel, study, or other similar purposes is not a "taxable expenditure" if the grant is awarded on an objective and nondiscriminatory basis pursuant to a procedure approved in advance by the IRS and it is demonstrated to the satisfaction of the IRS that (1) the grant constitutes a scholarship or fellowship grant which is excluded from gross income[35] and is to be used for study at an educational institution which normally maintains a regular faculty and curriculum and normally has a regularly organized body of students in attendance at the place where the educational activities are carried on, (2) the grant constitutes a prize or award which is excluded from gross income,[36] if the recipient of the prize or award is selected from the general

---

[28]See Code § 509(e).
[29]See Code § 170(c)(1).
[30]Reg. § 53.4945-3(b).
[31]Code § 4945(d)(3).
[32]Reg. § 53.4945-4(a)(2).
[33]Rev. Rul. 74-125, 1974-1 C. B. 327.
[34]Rev. Rul. 81-293, 1981-2 C. B. 218.
[35]Code § 117(a).
[36]Code § 74(b).

public, or (3) the purpose of the grant is to achieve a specific objective, produce a report or other similar product, or improve or enhance a literary, artistic, musical, scientific, teaching, or other similar capacity, skill, or talent of the grantee.[37]

A matter of some controversy has been the extent to which grants made by a private foundation under an employer-related grant program[38] to an employee or to a child of an employee of the particular employer constitute qualifying scholarships or fellowship grants. The IRS has promulgated guidelines[39] for use in determining whether the grants so qualify (and hence are not taxable expenditures).[40] Since these guidelines became effective as of December 27, 1976, the Service has set forth rules under which foundations may continue to rely on ruling letters approving their employer-related scholarship programs that were issued prior to that date.[41]

The IRS has issued guidelines for determining whether educational loans made by a private foundation under an employer-related loan program are taxable expenditures. These rules provide in general that educational loans made by a foundation to employees of a particular company or to their children are made for a purpose inconsistent with the foundation's tax-exempt purposes if the loans serve the private interests of the employer rather than serve charitable purposes. Where certain conditions are satisfied, the Service will assume that employer-related educational loans are made on the requisite objective and nondiscriminatory basis, and otherwise are not taxable expenditures. These conditions include no use of the loan program by the employer to recruit employees, selection of loan recipients by an independent selection committee, imposition of identifiable minimum requirements for loan eligibility, selection of loan recipients on the basis of objective standards unrelated to the employment, use of the loan proceeds for courses of study that are not of particular benefit to the employer, and making of the loan for the purpose of enabling the recipients to obtain an education solely for their personal benefit. Still other

[37]Code § 4945(g); Reg. § 53.4945-4(a)(3)(ii). See, e.g., Rev. Rul. 77-380, 1977-2 C. B. 419. The IRS has ruled that grants by a foundation to college students who plan to adhere to a "moral commitment" to teach in a particular state after graduation are not scholarships under Code § 117(a) and hence are not Code § 4945(g)(1) grants but are instead Code § 4945(g)(3) grants. Rev. Rul. 77-44, 1977-1 C. B. 355. This position stems from the insistence of the IRS that a tax-excludable scholarship cannot exist where there is a requirement of a substantial *quid pro quo* from the recipient. See *Bingler* v. *Johnson*, 394 U.S. 741 (1969); Rev. Rul. 73-256, 1973-1 C. B. 56, as modified by Rev. Rul. 74-540, 1974-2 C. B. 38; *Miss Georgia Scholarship Fund, Inc.* v. *Commissioner*, 72 T.C. 267 (1979).

[38]See Rev. Rul. 79-131, 1979-1 C. B. 368; Rev. Rul. 79-365, 1979-2 C. B. 389.

[39]See Sanders, "New guidelines tell when IRS will approve company foundation scholarship grants," 46 *J. Tax.* 212 (1977); Sacher, "Rev. Proc. 76-47: Guidelines for Advance Approval of Company Foundation Grants," 116 *Trusts & Estates* 541 (1977).

[40]Rev. Proc. 76-47, 1976-2 C. B. 670. See, e.g., IRS Private Letter Ruling 8038085.

[41]Rev. Proc. 77-32, 1977-2 C. B. 541.

rules impose percentage limitations on the number of employees, or children of employees, that may annually receive loans under the program, although where the program satisfies a facts-and-circumstances test in lieu of the applicable percentage test, the loans may not be regarded as taxable expenditures.[42]

Notwithstanding these guidelines, the IRS subsequently indicated its understanding "that for an employer-related educational grant or loan program to fulfill its intended purpose, it is necessary to inform the eligible employees of its availability." Thus, the Service ruled that a foundation's employer-related grant or loan program may be publicized in the employer's newsletter without causing a violation of either the rules promulgated in 1976 or 1980,[43] if the foundation is "clearly identified" as the grantor of the awards. The Service also ruled that "making public announcements of the grants or loans in the employer's newsletter" is not a violation of either set of rules[44] if the foundation or the independent selection committee is "clearly identified" as the grantor of the awards.[45]

A grant by a private foundation to an individual for purposes other than travel, study, or similar purposes is not a taxable expenditure even if the requirements described previously[46] are not met.[47] For this reason, grants by a foundation to individuals were ruled to not be taxable expenditures where they were made in recognition of past achievements (winning a competition among students), not intended to finance any future activities of an individual grantee, and under circumstances where no conditions were imposed on the manner in which the awards may be expended by the recipients.[48] For the same reason, an award by a foundation to the person who has written the best work of literary criticism during the preceding year was held not to be a taxable expenditure.[49] Likewise, private foundation grants made in recognition of past achievements in the field of journalism were ruled to not constitute taxable expenditures.[50] By contrast, as respects a foundation cash prize to a high school senior whose exhibit receives top honors in a local science fair, the award constitutes a taxable expenditure (unless the rules described previously[51] apply) where it is intended to finance future educational activities of the grantee and conditions are imposed on the manner in which the award may be expended by the recipient.[52]

---

[42]Rev. Proc. 80-39, 1980-2 C. B. 772.
[43]Rev. Proc. 76-47, *supra*, n. 40, at § 4.01; Rev. Proc. 80-39, *supra*, n. 42 at § 4.03.
[44]Rev. Proc. 76-47, *supra*, n. 40, at § 4.02; Rev. Proc. 80-39, *supra*, n. 42, at § 4.04.
[45]Rev. Proc. 81-65, 1981-2 C. B. 69.
[46]See n. 37, *supra*.
[47]Reg. § 53.4945-4(a)(3)(i).
[48]Rev. Rul. 76-460, 1976-2 C. B. 371.
[49]Rev. Rul. 75-393, 1975-2 C. B. 451; IRS Private Letter Ruling 8038119.
[50]Rev. Rul. 77-434, 1977-2 C. B. 420; Rev. Rul. 77-380, *supra*, n. 37.
[51]See n. 37, *supra*.
[52]Rev. Rul. 76-461, 1976-2 C. B. 371.

A renewal of a grant which satisfied the foregoing requirements is not treated as a grant to an individual which is subject to the requirements of these rules if (1) the grantor has no information indicating that the original grant is being used for any purpose other than that for which it was made, (2) any reports due at the time of the renewal decision pursuant to the terms of the original grant have been furnished, and (3) any additional criteria and procedures for renewal are objective and nondiscriminatory. An extension of the period over which a grant is to be paid is not itself regarded as a grant or a renewal of a grant.[53]

A grant by a private foundation to another organization, which the grantee organization uses to make payments to an individual for purposes described in these rules, is not regarded as a grant by the private foundation to the individual grantee if the foundation does not earmark the use of the grant for any named individual and there does not exist an agreement, oral or written, whereby the grantor foundation may cause the selection of the individual grantee by the grantee organization. A grant is not regarded as a grant by the foundation to an individual grantee even though the foundation has reason to believe that certain individuals would derive benefits from the grant so long as the grantee organization exercises control, in fact, over the selection process and actually makes the selection completely independently of the private foundation.[54]

A grant by a private foundation to an organization that is not a private foundation,[55] which the grantee organization uses to make payments to an individual for purposes encompassed by these rules, is not regarded as a grant by the private foundation to the individual grantee (regardless of the application of the rules in the preceding paragraph) if the grant is made for a project which is to be undertaken under the supervision of the public charity and the grantee organization controls the selection of the individual grantee. This rule applies regardless of whether the name of the individual grantee was first proposed by the private foundation, but only if there is an objective manifestation of control by the public charity over the selection process, although the selection need not be made completely independently of the private foundation.[56]

An illustration of the foregoing rules was provided in the case of a private foundation which makes grants to vocational high schools (all operating educational organizations[57]) in a certain geographical area, to be used to purchase the basic tools of a trade for students to enable them to better learn their trades and to enter into those trades upon graduation. Because the individual grant recipients are selected by representatives of the foundation, rather than the schools, the grants were deemed to be made directly to the individual stu-

---

[53]Reg. § 53.4945-4(a)(3)(iii).

[54]Reg. § 53.4945-4(a)(4)(i).

[55]For these purposes, an organization described in Code § 509(a)(1), (2) or (3). See Chapter 22.

[56]Reg. § 53.4945-4(a)(4)(ii). See, e.g., IRS Private Letter Ruling 8027104.

[57]That is, organizations described in Code § 170(b)(1)(A)(ii) and 509(a)(1).

dents.[58] Since the purpose of the grants is to aid needy and talented students in the completion of their vocational education, the grants are to individuals for study or similar purposes within the meanings of these rules and constitute taxable expenditures unless the foundation's grant-making procedures satisfy the requirements of the exception to the general rules.[59]

A grant by a private foundation to an individual, which meets the requirements of these general rules yet satisfies the rules constituting the above-discussed exception, is a taxable expenditure[60] only if (1) the grant is earmarked to be used for any legislative, electioneering, or noncharitable activity,[61] or is earmarked to be used in a manner which would violate the rules concerning grants to individuals or "expenditure responsibility,"[62] (2) there is an agreement, oral or written, whereby the grantor foundation may cause the grantee to engage in any prohibited activity and the grant is in fact used in a manner which violates these rules, or (3) the grant is made for a noncharitable purpose.[63]

In order for a private foundation to establish that its grants to individuals are made on an objective and nondiscriminatory basis, the grants must be awarded in accordance with a program which, if it were a substantial part of the foundation's activities, would be consistent with (1) the existence of the foundation's tax-exempt status, (2) the allowance of deductions to individuals for contributions to it, and (3) the following three additional requirements, relating to candidates for grants, selection of potential grantees, and the persons making selections.[64]

Ordinarily, selection of grantees on an objective and nondiscriminatory basis requires that the group from which grantees are selected be chosen on the basis of criteria reasonably related to the purposes of the grant. Furthermore, the group must be sufficiently broad so that the making of grants to members of such group would be considered to fulfill a charitable purpose. For example, the IRS has ruled that a trust is fostering discrimination by confining its scholarship grants to students of "Finnish extraction" and therefore that the scholarships are taxable expenditures.[65] Thus, ordinarily the group must be sufficiently large to constitute a charitable class. However, selection from a group is not necessary where, taking into account the purposes of the grant, one or several persons are selected because they are exceptionally qualified to carry

[58]Rev. Rul. 77-212, 1977-1 C. B. 356.
[59]See n. 37, *supra*.
[60]See Code § 4945(d).
[61]See Code § 4945(d)(1), (2), and (5).
[62]Code § 4945(d)(3) and (4).
[63]Reg. § 53.4945-4(a)(5).
[64]Reg. § 53.4945-4(b)(1). See Rev. Rul. 76-340, 1976-2 C. B. 370.
[65]IRS Private Letter Ruling 7851096. Yet the IRS has ruled that a scholarship fund for deserving Jewish students is charitable (IRS Private Letter Ruling 7744005), as is a scholarship fund for deserving male Protestant students (IRS Private Letter Ruling 7744007).

out these purposes or it is otherwise evident that the selection is particularly calculated to effectuate the charitable purpose of the grant rather than to benefit particular persons or a particular class of persons. Therefore, the foundation may impose reasonable restrictions on the group of potential grantees. For example, selection of a qualified research scientist to work on a particular project does not violate the requirements of these rules merely because the foundation selects him or her from a group of three scientists who are experts in that field.[66]

The criteria used in selecting grant recipients from the potential grantees should be related to the purpose of the grant. Thus, for example, proper criteria for selecting scholarship recipients might include (but are not limited to) the following: prior academic performance, performance on tests designed to measure ability and aptitude for college work, recommendations from instructors, financial need, and the conclusions which the selection committee might draw from a personal interview as to the individual's motivation, character, ability, and potential.[67]

The person or group of persons who select recipients of grants should not be in a position to derive a private benefit, directly or indirectly, if certain potential grantees are selected over others.[68]

Grants to individuals be made pursuant to a procedure approved in advance.[69] To secure such approval, a private foundation must demonstrate to the satisfaction of the IRS that (1) its grant procedure includes an objective and nondiscriminatory selection process, (2) the procedure is reasonably calculated to result in performance by grantees of the activities that the grants are intended to finance, and (3) the foundation plans to obtain reports to determine whether the grantees have performed the activities that the grants are intended to finance. No single procedure or set of procedures is required. Procedures may vary depending upon such factors as the size of the foundation, the amount and purpose of the grants, and whether one or more recipients are involved.[70]

Generally, with respect to any scholarship or fellowship grants, a private foundation must make arrangements to receive a report of the grantee's work in each academic period. In cases of grantees whose study at an educational institution does not involve the taking of courses but the preparation of research papers or projects, such as the writing of a doctoral thesis, the foundation must receive a brief report on the progress of the paper or project at least once a year. Upon completion of a grantee's study at an educational institution, a final report must also be obtained. With respect to a grant, the foundation must

[66]Reg. § 53.4945-4(b)(2).
[67]Reg. § 53.4945-4(b)(3).
[68]Reg. § 53.4945-4(b)(4).
[69]Code § 4945(g).
[70]Reg. §§ 53.4945-4(c)(1), 53.4945-4(d). See, e.g., Private Letter Rulings 7823026, 7823030, 7832021, 7832042, 7832051, 7832055, 7832090, 7832095, 7835031, 7835049, 7835051, 7835061, 7835106, 7839022, 7839093, 7839112, and 7839115.

require reports on the use of the funds and the progress made by the grantee toward achieving the purposes for which the grant was made on an annual and final basis.[71]

Where the reports submitted under these requirements or other information (including the failure to submit the reports) indicates that all or any part of a grant is not being used in furtherance of the purposes of the grant, the foundation is under a duty to investigate.[72] While conducting its investigation, the foundation must withhold further payments to the extent possible until any delinquent reports have been submitted. In cases in which the grantor foundation determines that any part of a grant has been used for improper purposes and the grantee has not previously diverted grant funds to any use not in furtherance of a purpose specified in the grant, the foundation will not be treated as having made a taxable expenditure solely because of the diversion so long as the foundation (1) is taking all reasonable and appropriate steps either to recover the grant funds or to ensure the restoration of the diverted funds and the dedication of other grant funds held by the grantee to the purposes being financed by the grant, and (2) withholds any further payments to the grantee after the grantor becomes aware that a diversion may have taken place (hereinafter referred to as "further payments") until it has received the grantee's assurances that future diversions will not occur and required the grantee to take extraordinary precautions to prevent future diversions from occurring.[73]

In cases where a grantee has previously diverted funds received from a grantor foundation and the grantor foundation determines that any part of a grant has again been used for improper purposes, the foundation is not treated as having made a taxable expenditure solely by reason of the diversion so long as the foundation (1) is taking all reasonable and appropriate steps to recover the grant funds or to ensure the restoration of the funds and the dedication of other grant funds held by the grantee to the purposes being financed by the grant, and (2) withholds further payments until the funds are in fact so recovered or restored, has received the grantee's assurance that future diversions will not occur, and requires the grantee to take extraordinary precautions to prevent future diversions from occurring. If a foundation is treated as having made a taxable expenditure in a case to which these rules apply, then unless the foundation meets the requirements as discussed in item (1) above, the amount of the taxable expenditure is the amount of the diversion plus the amount of any further payments to the same grantee. However, if the foundation complies with the requirements of item (1), but fails to withhold further payments until the requirements of item (2) are met, the amount of the taxable expenditure is the amount of the further payments.[74]

The above-discussed rules relating to supervision of scholarship and fellow-

[71]Reg. § 53.4945-4(c)(2), (3).
[72]Reg. § 53.4945-4(c)(4)(i).
[73]See Reg. § 53.4945-4(c)(5).
[74]Reg. § 53.4945-4(c)(4)(iii).

ship grants and investigations of jeopardized grants are considered satisfied with respect to scholarship or fellowship grants under the following circumstances: (1) the scholarship or fellowship grants are described in the rules described previously,[75] (2) the grantor foundation pays the scholarship or fellowship grants to an operating educational institution,[76] and (3) the educational institution agrees to use the grant funds to defray the recipient's expenses or to pay the funds (or a portion thereof) to the recipient only if the recipient is enrolled at the educational institution and his or her standing at the educational institution is consistent with the purposes and conditions of the grant.[77]

A private foundation must retain records pertaining to all grants to individuals made in accordance with these rules. There records must include (1) all information the foundation secures to evaluate the qualification of potential grantees, (2) identification of grantees (including any relationship of any grantee to the foundation sufficient to make the grantee a disqualified person of the private foundation[78]), (3) specification of the amount and purpose of each grant, and (4) the follow-up information which the foundation obtains in complying with the above-discussed requirements.[79]

Requests for approval of grant-making procedures should be submitted to the appropriate IRS district director. If, by the 45th day after a request for approval of grant procedures has been properly submitted, the foundation has not been notified that the procedures are unacceptable, they may be considered approved from the date of submission until receipt of actual notice from the IRS that they do not meet the requirements.[80]

A private foundation may find itself in the position of considering its grant-making procedures approved because of passage of the 45-day period, make grants accordingly, and then subsequently receive notification from the IRS that the procedures do not conform to the statutory requirements. In this situation, a grant made prior to the adverse notice is not a taxable expenditure. Even where the grant is structured as installment payments of a fixed amount, payments of the installments remaining after the notification will not result in taxable expenditures—the payments are considered merely the satisfaction of the foundation's obligation under the grants that were deemed approved. However, a renewal of a grant made during the prenotification period would be a taxable expenditure—this type of a payment would be within the discretion of the foundation and hence a new grant.[81]

---

[75]Code § 4945(g)(1).

[76]See Code § 170(b)(1)(A)(ii); Chapter 22.

[77]Reg. § 53.4945-4(c)(5).

[78]See Chapter 24.

[79]Reg. 53.4945-4(c)(6).

[80]Reg. § 53.4945-4(d)(3); IRS Private Letter Ruling 7943010. A foundation can trigger the start of the 45-day review period by submitting the requisite information as part of its application for recognition of exemption. IRS Private Letter Ruling 8038017.

[81]Rev. Rul. 81-46, 1981-1 C. B. 514.

Application of the rules concerning private foundation grants for individuals where the grants are made to a public charity,[82] as they interrelate to the rules concerning employer-related grants,[83] is illustrated by the case of a foundation program whereby the private foundation makes grants to a public charity in partial funding of a scholarship program, with the stipulation that the grants be expended on behalf of children of employees of a particular company who are finalists as determined by the public charity. As a variation of this program, a similar approach requires that any excess funds be made available as grants to the next most highly rated children of employees of the company even though they are not finalists. The IRS concluded that the grants are amounts paid to individuals for study and are taxable expenditures unless made pursuant to a procedure approved in advance by the Service.[84] The exception for foundation grants to public charities[85] was deemed inapplicable, in that the public charity does not select the scholarship recipients completely independently of the foundation and merely functions as an evaluator of the grant program of the foundation.

§ 29.4 Expenditure Responsibility

The term "taxable expenditure" includes any amount paid or incurred by a private foundation as a grant (or loan or program-related investment) to an organization (other than an organization that is not a private foundation[86]), unless the private foundation exercises "expenditure responsibility" with respect to the grant.[87] However, the granting foundation does not have to exercise expenditure responsibility with respect to amounts granted to organizations pursuant to the above-discussed voter registration drive rules.[88]

A private foundation may make a grant to a foreign charitable organization that does not have a determination from the IRS that it is a public charity, without the necessity of exercising expenditure responsibility, where the foundation has made a "good faith determination" that the grantee is a public charity.[89] The requisite "good faith determination" may be based on an affidavit of the grantee organization or a legal opinion that the grantee is a public charity. Also, the foundation may elect to secure a ruling or determination letter from the Service on the point.[90]

---

[82]See notes 55–56, *supra*.

[83]See notes 39–41, *supra*.

[84]Rev. Rul. 81-217, 1981-2 C. B. 217. To give foundations time to secure the necessary advance approval, the effective date of this ruling was set at March 8, 1982.

[85]Notes 54 and 56, *supra*.

[86]For these purposes, an organization described in Code § 509(a)(1), (2), or (3).

[87]Code § 4945(d)(4).

[88]Reg. § 53.4945-5(a)(1).

[89]Reg. § 53.4945-5(a)(5).

[90]See, e.g., IRS Private Letter Ruling 8030104.

For purposes of the expenditure responsibility rules exception, an organization is treated as a public charity[91] if it is an organization described in the charitable giving rules concerning contributions to governmental units[92] or if it is a foreign government or any agency or instrumentality thereof, even if (in either case) it is not considered a charitable organization under the rules pertaining to tax-exempt organizations,[93] as long as the grant by the foundation is made exclusively for charitable purposes.[94] In the case of a grant by a private foundation, made exclusively for charitable purposes, to a wholly owned instrumentality of a political subdivision in a state, the IRS reasoned that, if a grant to an instrumentality of a foreign government is treated as a grant to a public charity, a grant to an instrumentality of a domestic political subdivision should likewise be treated as a grant to a public charity.[95] Therefore, the foundation was held to not be required to exercise expenditure responsibility with respect to the grant.

A grant by a private foundation to a grantee organization which the grantee organization uses to make payments to another organization (the secondary grantee) is not regarded as a grant by the private foundation to the secondary grantee if the foundation does not earmark the use of the grant for any named secondary grantee and there does not exist an agreement, oral or written, whereby the grantor foundation may cause the selection of the secondary grantee by the organization to which it has given the grant. A grant is not regarded as a grant by the foundation to the secondary grantee even though the foundation has reason to believe that certain organizations would derive benefits from the grant so long as the original grantee organization exercises control, in fact, over the selection process and actually makes the selection completely independently of the private foundation.[96]

Since a private foundation is not an insurer of the activity of the organization to which it makes a grant, satisfaction of the expenditure responsibility requirements ordinarily means it has not violated these rules.[97] A private foundation is considered to be exercising "expenditure responsibility"[98] as long as it exerts all reasonable efforts and establishes adequate procedures to (1) see that the grant is spent solely for the purpose for which it is made, (2) obtain full and complete reports from the grantee on how the funds are spent, and (3) make full and detailed reports with respect to the expenditures to the IRS.

Before making a grant to an organization with respect to which expenditure responsibility must be exercised, a private foundation should conduct a limited

[91]Code § 509(a)(1).
[92]Code § 170(c)(1).
[93]Code § 501(c)(3).
[94]Reg. § 53.4945-5(a)(4).
[95]Rev. Rul. 81-125, 1981-1 C. B. 515.
[96]Reg. § 53.4945-5(a)(6)(i).
[97]Code § 4945(d)(1) or (2).
[98]Code § 4945(h).

inquiry concerning the potential grantee.[99] The inquiry should be complete enough to give a reasonable person assurance that the grantee will use the grant for the proper purposes. The inquiry should concern itself with matters such as the identity, prior history, and experience (if any) of the grantee organization and its managers, and any knowledge which the private foundation has (based on prior experience or otherwise) of, or other information which is readily available concerning, the experience, management, activities, and practices of the grantee organization. The scope of the inquiry may vary from case to case depending upon the size and purpose of the grant, the period over which it is to be paid, and the prior experience which the grantor has had with respect to the capacity of the grantee to use the grant for the proper purposes.[100]

Except with respect to program-related investments,[101] in order to meet the expenditure responsibility requirements, a private foundation must require that each grant to an organization, with respect to which expenditure responsibility must be exercised, be made subject to a written commitment signed by an appropriate officer, director, or trustee of the grantee organization. The commitment must include an agreement by the grantee (1) to repay any portion of the amount granted which is not used for the purpose of the grant, (2) to submit full and complete annual reports on the manner in which the funds are spent and the progress made in accomplishing the purposes of the grant, except as respects capital endowment grants,[102] (3) to maintain records of receipts and expenditures and to make its books and records available to the grantor at reasonable times, and (4) not to use any of the funds (a) to carry on propaganda, or otherwise to attempt, to influence legislation, (b) to influence the outcome of any specific public election, or to carry on, directly or indirectly, any voter registration drive, (c) to make any grant to an individual or organization, or (d) to undertake any activitiy for any noncharitable purpose, to the extent that use of the funds would be a taxable expenditure if made directly by the foundation. The agreement must also clearly specify the purposes of the grant. These purposes may include contributing for capital endowment, for the purchase of capital equipment, or for general support provided that neither the grants nor the income therefrom may be used for noncharitable purposes.[103]

In order to meet the expenditure responsibility requirements with regard to the making of a program-related investment, a private foundation must require that each investment with respect to which expenditure responsibility must be exercised be made subject to a written commitment signed by an appropriate officer, director, or trustee of the recipient organization. The commitment must specify the purpose of the investment and must include an agreement to the following practices by the organization.

[99]Reg. § 53.4945-5(b)(1).
[100]Reg. § 53.4945-5(b)(2).
[101]See Reg. § 53.4945-5(b)(4).
[102]See Reg. § 53.4945-5(c)(2).
[103]Reg. § 53.4945-5(b)(3).

(1) To use all the funds received from the private foundation only for the purposes of the investment and to repay any portion not used for those purposes, provided that, with respect to equity investments, the repayment shall be made only to the extent permitted by applicable law concerning distributions to holders of equity interests.

(2) At least once a year during the existence of the program-related investment, to submit full and complete financial reports of the type ordinarily required by commercial investors under similar circumstances and a statement that it has complied with the terms of the investment,

(3) To maintain books and records adequate to provide information ordinarily required by commercial investors under similar circumstances and to make the books and records available to the private foundation at reasonable times, and

(4) Not to use any of the funds to make a taxable expenditure.[104]

In the case of certain grants,[105] except as respects capital endowment grants, the granting private foundation must require reports on the use of the funds, compliance with the terms of the grant, and the progress made by the grantee toward achieving the purposes for which the grant was made. The grantee must make the reports as of the end of its annual accounting period within which the grant or any portion thereof is received and all subsequent periods until the grant funds are expended in full or the grant is otherwise terminated. The reports must be furnished to the grantor within a reasonable period of time after the close of the annual accounting period of the grantee for which the reports are made. Within a reasonable period of time after the close of its annual accounting period during which the use of the grant funds is completed, the grantee must make a final report with respect to all expenditures made from the funds (including salaries, travel, and supplies) and indicating the progress made toward the goals of the grant. The grantor need not conduct any independent verification of the reports unless it has reason to doubt their accuracy or reliability.[106]

To satisfy the report-making requirements,[107] a granting foundation must provide the required information on its annual information return (Form 990-PF) for each tax year with respect to each grant made during the tax year which is subject to the expenditure responsibility requirements. These reports must include the following data with respect to each grant: (1) the name and address of the grantee, (2) the date and amount of the grant, (3) the purpose of the grant, (4) the amounts expended by the grantee (based on the most recent report received from the grantee), (5) whether, to the knowledge of the grantor

---

[104]Reg. § 53.4945-5(b)(4).
[105]That is, those described in Code § 4945(d)(4).
[106]Reg. § 53.4945-5(c)(1), (3).
[107]Code § 4945(h)(3).

foundation, the grantee has diverted any funds from the purpose of the grant, (6) the dates of any reports received from the grantee, and (7) the date and results of any verification of the grantee's reports undertaken by or at the direction of the grantor foundation.

Information must also be provided on such return with respect to each grant subject to the requirements upon which any amount or any report is outstanding at any time during the tax year. However, with respect to any grant made for endowment or other capital purposes, the grantor must provide the required information only for any tax year for which the grantor must require a report from the grantee under the capital endowment grant rules.[108] These requirements with respect to any grant may be satisfied by submission with the foundation's information return of a report received from the grantee, if the requisite information[109] is contained in the report.[110]

Any diversion of grant funds (including the income therefrom in the case of an endowment grant) by the grantee to any use not in furtherance of a purpose specified in the grant may result in the diverted portion of such grant being treated as a taxable expenditure of the grantor. However, for these purposes, the fact that a grantee does not use any portion of the grant funds as indicated in the original budget projection is not treated as a diversion if the use to which the funds is committed is consistent with the purpose of the grant as stated in the grant agreement and does not result in a violation of the required terms of such agreement.[111]

In any event, a grantor will not be treated as having made a taxable expenditure solely by reason of a diversion by the grantee, if the grantor has complied with the next-discussed requirements.[112]

In cases in which the grantor foundation determines that any part of a grant has been used for improper purposes and the grantee has not previously diverted grant funds, the foundation will not be treated as having made a taxable expenditure solely by reason of the diversion so long as the foundation

(1) Is taking all reasonable and appropriate steps either to recover the grant funds or to ensure the restoration of the diverted funds and the dedication of the other grant funds held by the grantee to the purposes being financed by the grant, and

(2) Withholds any further payments to the grantee after the grantor becomes aware that a diversion may have taken place until it has received the grantee's assurances that future diversions will not occur and required the grantee to take extraordinary precautions to prevent future diversions from occurring. If a foundation is treated as having made a taxable ex-

[108]Reg. § 53.4945-5(c)(2).
[109]Reg. § 53.4945-5(d)(2)-(4).
[110]Reg. § 53.4945-5(d)(1).
[111]Reg. § 53.4945-5(e)(1)(i).
[112]Reg. § 53.4945-5(e)(1)(ii).

penditure in a case to which these rules apply, then, unless the foundation meets the requirements of item (1) above, the amount of the taxable expenditure is the amount of the diversion plus the amount of any further payments to the same grantee. However, if the foundation complies with the requirements of item (1) above but not the requirements of item (2), the amount of the taxable expenditure is the amount of the further payments.[113]

In cases where a grantee has previously diverted funds received from a grantor foundation, and the grantor foundation determines that any part of a grant has again been used for improper purposes, the foundation will not be treated as having made a taxable expenditure solely by reason of the diversion so long as the foundation

(1) Is taking all reasonable and appropriate steps to recover the grant funds or to ensure the restoration of the diverted funds and the dedication of other grant funds held by the grantee to the purposes being financed by the grant, except that if, in fact, some or all of the diverted funds are not so restored or recovered, then the foundation must take all reasonable and appropriate steps to recover all of the grant funds, and

(2) Withholds further payments until the funds are in fact so recovered or restored, it has received the grantee's assurances that future diversions will not occur, and it requires the grantee to take extraordinary precautions to prevent future diversions from occurring. If a foundation is treated as having made a taxable expenditure in a case to which these rules apply, then, unless the foundation meets the requirements of item (1) above, the amount of the taxable expenditure is the amount of the diversion plus the amount of any further payments to the same grantee. However, if the foundation complies with the requirements of item (1) but fails to withhold further payments until the requirements of item (2) are met, the amount of the taxable expenditure is the amount of such further payments.[114]

A failure by the grantee to make the required reports (or the making of inadequate reports) will result in treatment of the grant as a taxable expenditure by the grantor unless the grantor (1) has made the grant in accordance with the expenditure responsibility requirements, (2) has complied with the applicable reporting requirements, (3) makes a reasonable effort to obtain the required report, and (4) withholds all future payments on this grant and on any other grant to the same grantee until the report is furnished.[115]

In addition to the situations described above, a grant which is subject to the

[113]Reg. § 53.4945-5(e)(1)(iii).
[114]Reg. § 53.4945-5(e)(1)(iv).
[115]Reg. § 53.4945-5(e)(2).

expenditure responsibility requirements will be considered a taxable expenditure of the granting foundation if the grantor (1) fails to make a pre-grant inquiry as above-described, (2) fails to make the grant in accordance with a procedure consistent with the above requirements, or (3) fails to report to the IRS as discussed above.[116]

The IRS has assumed a very strict position on this point relating to timely reporting of expenditure responsibility grants to the Service. In one instance, a foundation made a grant but failed to include it among the list of grants made during that year required to be supplied as part of its annual information return. Later, the foundation discovered the omission of the grant from the return and filed a corrected amended return. The failure to comply with the reporting requirement caused the grant to be a taxable expenditure (although the foundation was able to correct the expenditure).[117] Nonetheless, the penalty tax[118] was levied, because "[w]hile the subsequent filing of the amended return may have accomplished correction . . ., the untimeliness of such filing precluded it from nullifying the foundation's failure to exercise expenditure responsibility in connection with the grant."[119]

§ 29.5 Noncharitable Purposes

The term "taxable expenditure" includes any amount paid or incurred by a private foundation for any noncharitable purpose.[120] The purposes that are considered "charitable" are those that are religious, charitable, scientific, literary, or educational purposes, the fostering of national or international sports competition, or the prevention of cruelty to children or animals (but not testing for public safety). Thus, ordinarily only an expenditure for an activity which, if it were a substantial part of the organization's total activities, would cause loss of tax exemption is a taxable expenditure.[121]

Expenditures ordinarily not treated as taxable expenditures under these rules are (1) expenditures to acquire investments entered into for the purpose of obtaining income or funds to be used in furtherance of charitable purposes, (2) reasonable expenses with respect to investments, (3) payment of taxes, (4) any expenses which qualify as deductions in the computation of unrelated business

---

[116]Reg. § 53.4945-5(e)(3).

[117]See Reg. § 53.4945-1(d)(2) and § 6, *infra*.

[118]See § 6, *infra*.

[119]Rev. Rul. 77-213, 1977-1 C. B. 357.

[120]Code § 4945(d)(5). For these purposes, the term "charitable purposes" means purposes encompassed by Code § 170(c)(2)(B).

[121]Reg. § 53.4945-6(a). See, e.g., Rev. Rul. 80-97, 1980-1 C. B. 257, where the IRS held that an unrestricted grant from a private foundation to a cemetery company exempt under Code § 501(c)(13) is a taxable expenditure because the grantee is not described in Code § 170(c)(2)(B), even though contributions to it are deductible under Code § 170(c)(5).

income tax,[122] (5) any payment which constitutes a qualifying distribution[123] or an allowable deduction pursuant to the investment income tax rules,[124] (6) reasonable expenditures to evaluate, acquire, modify, and dispose of program-related investments, or (7) business expenditures by the recipient of a program-related investment. Conversely, expenditures for unreasonable administrative expenses, including compensation, consultants' fees, and other fees for services rendered, are ordinarily taxable expenditures, unless the foundation can demonstrate that the expenses were paid or incurred in the good faith belief that they were reasonable and that the payment or incurrence of such expenses in amounts was consistent with ordinary business care and prudence.[125]

A private foundation may utilize these rules even where the expenditure constitutes an act of self-dealing.[126] In one instance, a private foundation made a loan to a disqualified person to generate income to be used solely for the foundation's charitable purposes—an act of self-dealing.[127] However, because the loan was made to the disqualified person at a reasonable rate of interest, was adequately secured, and otherwise met prudent investment standards, and was designed solely to provide income for the foundation's charitable purposes, the IRS concluded that it was not a taxable expenditure.[128]

Since a private foundation cannot make an expenditure for a noncharitable purpose, a private foundation may not make a grant to an organization other than a "charitable" organization unless the making of the grant itself constitutes a direct charitable act or the making of a program-related investment, or the grantor is reasonably assured that the grant will be used exclusively for charitable purposes.[129]

More than any other section of the private foundation rules, the rules described in this chapter portray the nearly unbridled antifoundation emotionalism that gripped Congress as it legislated in this area in 1969. Several of these provisions are directly traceable to specific events which fomented the legislators' unhappiness, many of which came to widespread public attention in the wake of the testimony early in 1969 by Ford Foundation president McGeorge

[122]See Chapter 41.
[123]Code § 4942(g). See Chapter 26.
[124]Code § 4940. See Chapter 30.
[125]Reg. § 53.4945-6(b). In Rev. Rul. 82-223, 1982-51 I.R.B. 29, the IRS held that a private foundation may, without making a taxable expenditure, indemnify, and/or purchase insurance to cover its managers for liabilities arising under state law concerning mismanagement of funds but that the foundation would make a taxable expenditure if it indemnified a foundation manager for an amount paid in settlement of a state proceeding.
[126]See Chapter 26.
[127]Code § 4941(d)(1)(B). See Chapter 25.
[128]Rev. Rul. 77-161, 1977-1 C.B. 358. In this ruling, the IRS observed that "[a] given set of facts can give rise to taxes under more than one provision of Chapter 42 of the Code," citing Reg. § 53.4944-1(a)(2)(iv).
[129]Reg. § 53.4945-6(c)(1).

Bundy before the House Committee on Ways and Means.[130] The restrictions on individual grants trace their heritage to the "travel and study awards" that the Ford Foundation made to staff assistants to Sen. Robert F. Kennedy following his assassination.[131] The rules concerning foundations' involvement in public elections and voter registration drives are a reflection of Ford Foundation financing of voter registration projects, including a grant to Cleveland CORE, travel grants to members of Congress, and the school decentralization experiments in New York (the subject of citywide teachers' strikes),[132] and of the spending interests of the Frederick W. Richmond Foundation at the time Mr. Richmond was seeking election to Congress.[133] These and similar incidents triggered many critical commentaries on private foundations in the general media,[134] which added to the reaction against foundations in Congress.

§ 29.6 Sanctions

An excise tax is imposed on each taxable expenditure of a private foundation, which is to be paid by the foundation at the rate of 10 percent of the amount on each taxable expenditure.[135] An excise tax is imposed on the agreement of any foundation manager to the making of a taxable expenditure by a foundation.[136] This initial tax is imposed only where the foundation initial tax is imposed, the manager knows that the expenditure to which he or she agreed was a taxable expenditure, and the agreement is not willful and not due to reasonable cause. A manager's reliance on the advice of counsel, given in a reasoned, written legal opinion, may avoid the tax.[137] This initial tax, which is at the rate of 2½ percent of each taxable expenditure, must be paid by the foundation manager.[138]

An excise tax is imposed in any case in which an initial tax is imposed on a private foundation because of a taxable expenditure and the expenditure is not

---

[130]See "Many in Congress Ready to Tax All Foundations, Curb Their Operations," *Wall Street Journal*, Feb. 28, 1969, at 1.

[131]See, e.g., "5 RFK Aides Defend Grants," *Washington Post*, Feb. 27, 1969, at G1.

[132]See, e.g., "Ford Fund Hints No Retreat on Financing of Disputed Projects, No Fear on Taxes," *Wall Street Journal*, March 3, 1969, at 12.

[133]See "Rooney Cites Tax-Free Aid Used by Foe," *Washington Star*, February 19, 1969, at A-1.

[134]See, e.g., White, "Congress Girding to Reduce Vast Power of Foundations," *Washington Post*, February 22, 1969, at A15; McGrory, "Stylist Bundy Sprinkles Snow," *Washington Star*, February 2, 1969, at A-3.

[135]Code § 4945 (a)(1); Reg. § 53.4945-1(a)(1).

[136]Code § 4945(a)(2).

[137]See *Burress Land & Lumber Co., Inc.* v. *United States*, 349 F. Supp. 188 (W.D. Va. 1972); IRS Private Letter Ruling 7902019 (issue no. 12).

[138]Reg. § 53.4945-1(a)(2).

timely corrected.[139] This additional tax is to be paid by the foundation and is at the rate of 100 percent of the amount of each taxable expenditure.[140] An excise tax in any case in which an initial tax has been levied is imposed on a foundation manager because of a taxable expenditure and the manager has refused to agree to part or all of the correction of the expenditure.[141] This additional tax, which is at the rate of 50 percent of the amount of the taxable expenditure, is to be paid by the manager.[142]

Where more than one foundation manager is liable for an excise tax with respect to the making of a taxable expenditure, all the managers are jointly and severally liable for the tax.[143] The maximum aggregate amount collectible as an initial tax from all foundation managers with respect to any one taxable expenditure is $5,000 and the maximum aggregate amount so collectible as an additional tax is $10,000.[144]

[139]Code § 4945(b)(1), (i); Reg. 53.4945-1(d), (e).

[140]Reg. § 53.4945 1(b)(1).

[141]Code § 4945(b)(2).

[142]Reg. § 53.4945-1(b)(2). The U.S. Tax Court, by reason of a special enactment, possesses the jurisdiction to determine whether these additional taxes should be imposed. See Chapter 25, text accompanying nn. 123–131, *supra*.

[143]Code § 4545(c)(1); Reg. § 53.4945-1(c)(1).

[144]Code § 4545(c)(2); Reg. § 53.4945-1(c)(2). In general, see Sacher, "How IRS' internal rules work for advance approval of company foundation grants," 40 *J. Tax.* 363 (1974); Sanders, "Final Regs on Section 4945; working with the new rules restricting foundations' activities," 38 *J. Tax.* 130 (1973); Sanders, "Private foundations: Final Regs on 4945 clarify and bring order to operating rules," 38 *J. Tax.* 246 (1973); Sanders, "How grants to organizations by private foundations are affected by the final Regs," 38 *J. Tax.* 299 (1973); Gregory and Moorehead, "Suggestions for Preventing Taxable Expenditures by Foundations," 19 *Prac. Lawyer* (No. 6) 45 (1973); Moorehead, "Qualifying Distributions: Do Your Grants and Activities Comply?," 11 *N.Y.U. Conf. on Char. Fdns.* 203 (1973); Treitler, "Prop. Regs on 'taxable expenditures': Useful guidelines for foundation managers," 34 *J. Tax.* 338 (1971); Wright, "Grantee Selection and Supervision: Legal Requirements and Practical Problems," 10 *N.Y.U. Conf. on Char. Fdns.* 127 (1971); Schilling and Thomson, "Tax Problems of Private Foundations in Receiving and Making Grants," 10 *N.Y.U. Conf. on Char. Fdns.* 277 (1971).

30

Tax on Investment Income

Prior to enactment of the Tax Reform Act of 1969, the investment income of private foundations was not subject to any tax. However, in that year, Congress decided that foundations should become subject to an excise tax on investment income, as the following explains:

> The Congress has concluded that private foundations should share some of the burden of paying the cost of government, especially for more extensive and vigorous enforcement of the tax laws relating to exempt organizations.

> However, the Congress believes that private foundations should continue to be exempt from income tax. Accordingly, the Act casts the charge or audit fee for private foundations in the form of an excise tax with respect to the carrying on of the organization's activities rather than as a tax under chapter 1 of the Internal Revenue Code.[1]

Consequently, Congress enacted Code § 4940.

Ideologically, a tax on the investment income of private foundations may be viewed as a serious encroachment on the principle that philanthropic undertakings should be exempt from taxation. Little consolation is to be found in its characterization as an excise tax in the nature of an audit fee,[2] since it is in effect an income tax. Moreover, the receipts from this tax exceeded the actual costs of the enforcement efforts of the IRS, until the tax was halved in 1978 (see below). Further, the foundation taxes are not earmarked for auditing and supervisory purposes but are commingled with the general revenues of the Treasury. At any rate, the foundation excise tax burden is borne most heavily by those foundations that have a profitable investment portfolio and reduces the flow of funds for charitable purposes.

An "excise tax" of 2 percent is imposed on the net investment income of all

[1]Joint Committee on Internal Revenue Taxation, *General Explanation of Tax Reform Act of 1969*, 91st Cong., 2d Sess. (1970) at 29.

[2]See H. Rep. No. 91-413 at 18, S. Rep. No. 91-552 at 27, 91st Cong., 2d Sess. (1969).

domestic tax-exempt private foundations (including operating foundations) for each tax year beginning after September 30, 1977.[3] A tax on nonexempt private foundations is imposed, equal to the amount (if any) by which the sum of the tax on domestic foundations (if it applied) and any unrelated business income tax exceeds the income tax imposed on the foundation for the tax year.[4] The purpose of this latter tax is to ensure that a private foundation will not attempt to reduce its tax liability by intentionally losing its tax-exempt status.

A private foundation's net investment income is the amount by which the sum of its gross investment income and the net capital gain exceeds the allowable deductions.[5] A private foundation's gross investment income is the gross amount of income from interest (excluding tax-exempt interest on governmental obligations), dividends, rents, payments with respect to securities loans, and royalties (including overriding royalties) received from all sources but does not include any income to the extent included in computing the tax on unrelated business income. Interest, dividends, rents, and royalties derived from assets devoted to charitable activities (e.g., interest on student loans) are includible in gross investment income.[6] The redemption of stock from a private foundation to the extent necessary for the foundation to avoid the excess business holdings tax is a sale or exchange not equivalent to a dividend[7] and the proceeds will not be taxed as investment income.[8] Similarly, a conversion of shares of a corporation owned by a foundation for shares of another corporation, where the conversion occurs pursuant to a tax-free corporate reorganization[9] does not constitute net investment income.[10]

In the case of a distribution to a private foundation of income from an estate, the distribution does not retain its character in the hands of the foundation for purposes of computing the investment income tax,[11] so that investment income received by and taxed to an estate is not again taxed when it is received by a private foundation. However, where a foundation receives from an estate Series E United States savings bonds, and no part of the periodic increase in the value of the bonds was reported as income by the estate,[12] the foundation receives the right to receive income upon redemption of the bonds, which is treated as income in respect of a decedent and taxed to the foundation,[13] rather than any distribution of income from the estate. Therefore, the interest income derived by the private foundation upon redemption of the bonds received from the

---

[3]Code § 4940(a), Reg. § 53.4940-1(a).
[4]Code § 4940(b), Reg. § 53.4940-1(b).
[5]Code § 4940(c)(1), Reg. § 53.4940-1(c)(1), (2).
[6]Code § 4940(c)(2), Reg. § 53.4940-1(d).
[7]See Code § 320(b)(1).
[8]Rev. Rul. 75-336, 1975-2 C. B. 110; IRS Private Letter Rulings 7839077, 7839113, and 7839114.
[9]See Code § 368.
[10]IRS Private Letter Ruling 7847049.
[11]Reg. § 53.4940-1(d)(2).
[12]See Code § 454.
[13]Rev. Rul. 64-104, 1964-1 (Part 1) C. B. 223.

estate is gross investment income, as is all the interest income accrued on the bonds from the date of purchase by the decedent until the date of redemption by the foundation.[14]

For purposes of computing net investment income, there is allowed, as a deduction from gross investment income, all the ordinary and necessary expenses paid or incurred for the production or collection of gross investment income or for the management, conservation, or maintenance of property held for the production of income,[15] These expenses include that portion of a private foundation's operating expenses which is paid or incurred for the production or collection of gross investment income. Not every expenditure associated with the receipt of income by a foundation is deductible in determining net investment income, such as the trustee's termination fee where the foundation is the sole remainder beneficiary of a trust.[16]

A foundation's operating expenses include compensation of officers, other salaries and wages of employees, outside professional fees, interest, and rent and taxes upon property used in the foundation's operations. Where a foundation's officers or employees engage in activities on behalf of the foundation for both investment purposes and for tax-exempt purposes, compensation and salaries paid to them must be allocated between the investment activities and the exempt activities.[17] Moreover, all other operating expenses of a private foundation are subject to an allocation where paid or incurred for both investment and other purposes.[18]

These deductions must be determined in accordance with certain modifications.[19] That is, the depreciation deduction is allowed but only on the basis of the straight-line method and the deduction for depletion is allowed but the deduction must be determined without regard to the percentage depletion rules (that is, the cost depletion method must be used).[20] The deduction for expenses paid or incurred in any tax year for the production of gross investment

---

[14]Rev. Rul. 80-118, 1980-1 C. B. 254.

[15]Code § 4940(c)(3)(A).

[16]*Lettie Pate Whitehead Foundation, Inc.* v. *United States*, 79-2 U.S.T.C. ¶ 9706 (5th Cir. 1979), aff'g (on the issue) 77-1 U.S.T.C. ¶ 9157 (N.D. Ga. 1977).

[17]Reg. § 53.4940-1(e)(1).

[18]See *Julia R. & Estelle L. Foundation, Inc.* v. *Commissioner*, 70 T.C. 1 (1978), aff'd 598 F. 2d 755 (2d Cir. 1979).

[19]Code § 4940(c)(3)(B).

[20]In the case of a private foundation that held royalty interests in oil and gas properties, that (prior to 1970) did not claim a depletion deduction, and that recorded depletion on its books using the percentage method (of Code § 613), the IRS advised the foundation to determine the basis of its depletable property as of January 1, 1970, and reduce its basis therein by an amount equal to the potential cost depletion (as provided by Code § 611). See *Beal Foundation* v. *United States*, 76-1 U.S.T.C ¶ 9149 (W.D. Tex. 1975), aff'd 559 F.2d 359 (5th Cir. 1977). However, since the foundation did not claim any depletion deduction on this royalty interest, the Service held that foundation did not have to further reduce the basis by the amount of the percentage of depletion recorded on its books (see Reg. § 53.4940-1(e)(2)(iii)). Rev. Rul. 79-200, 1979-2 C. B. 364.

income earned as an incident to a charitable function may be no greater than the income earned from the function which is includible as gross investment income for the year.[21] These expenses, to be deductible, must be related to the possibility of earning future income and cannot relate to the maintenance of and taxes on property held for tax-exempt purposes.[22] A foundation which amortizes bond premiums[23] may deduct the amortized amount in computing any tax.[24]

There are rules for determining a private foundation's net capital gain.[25] In computing the tax, a foundation must include any gains and losses from the sale or other disposition of property used for the production of interest, dividends, rents, and royalties.[26] This includes capital gain dividends received from a regulated investment company. If the foundation disposes of property that is used in the production of income that is subject to the unrelated business income tax, any gain or loss from the sale of that property must be included in net investment income, but only to the extent that it is not included in the computation of unrelated business income tax.[27] For tax years beginning after December 31, 1972, property is treated as held for investment purposes even though the property is disposed of by the foundation immediately upon its

---

[21]Reg. § 53.4940-1(e)(2).

[22]See *Historic House Museum Corp.* v. *Commissioner*, 70 T.C. 12 (1978).

[23]See Code § 171.

[24]Rev. Rul. 76-248, 1976-1 C. B. 353.

[25]Code § 4940(c)(4).

[26]Code § 4940(c)(4)(A). The regulation to accompany this provision states that net capital gains are capital gains and losses from the sale or other disposition of property held by a private foundation for investment purposes or for the production of income. Reg. § 53.4940-1(f)(1). One court held that this regulation is "overly broad" in three respects: (1) while the statute employs the term "used," the regulation utilizes the term "held," so that the regulation wrongfully "allows taxation of gains from the sale of property regardless of whether that property was used for the production of interest, dividends, rents, or royalties," (2) the regulation would subject to taxation the disposition of property momentarily in a foundation's possession even though it was never used for investment purposes, and (3) the regulation improperly includes property which produces "gains through appreciation" with the types of property the sale of which results in taxable capital gains. Consequently, the court concluded that the property at issue in the case (an undivided one-half interest in a tract of land, subject to a usufruct, that generated income from timber sales paid solely to the usufructuary) was not used by the foundation to produce any interest, dividends, rents, or royalties and thus that the sale of the property did not produce investment income subject to the Code § 4940 tax. *Zemurray Foundation* v. *United States*, 509 F. Supp. 976 (E.D. La. 1981). However, this decision was overruled by the U.S. Court of Appeals for the Fifth Circuit, which concluded that the regulation "is not perceived as unreasonable or plainly inconsistent with the statute." *Zemurray Foundation* v. *United States*, 82-2 U.S.T.C. ¶ 9609 (5th Cir. 1982).

[27]A similar rule operates for nonexempt charitable trusts described in Code § 4947 (see Chapter 33). Rev. Rul. 74-497, 1974-2 C. B. 383.

receipt, if it is property of the type which generally produces interest, dividends, rents, royalties, or capital gains.[28]

Any gain or loss from the sale or other disposition of property used for the tax-exempt purposes of a private foundation is excluded from the computation of the tax on net investment income. If the foundation uses property for its exempt purposes, but also incidentally derives income from the property which is subject to the net investment income tax, any gain or loss from the disposition of the property is not subject to the tax. However, if a foundation uses property both for exempt purposes and (other than incidentally) for investment purposes, the portion of the gain or loss from the sale or disposition of the property that is allocable to the investment use of the property must be taken into account in computing the net investment income tax.[29]

For purposes of determining net investment income, a private foundation cannot deduct the interest it pays on borrowed funds where they are loaned interest-free to an exempt university and the debt has been forgiven.[30]

The basis for determining gain from the sale or other disposition of property in the case of property held by a foundation on December 31, 1969, and continuously thereafter to the date of its disposition is not less than the fair market value of the property on that date.[31] Losses from sales or other dispositions of property are allowed only to the extent of gains from the sales or dispositions during the same tax year and the capital loss carryover rules do not apply.

Subsequent to enactment of the Tax Reform Act of 1969, which set the administration tax on foundations at 4 percent for each tax year beginning after December 31, 1969 (through 1977), representatives of the foundation community urged reduction of the foundation tax to the actual level of the cost of auditing and supervision, and an earmarking of the receipts for such purposes. The late Rep. Wright Patman, a long-time foe of foundations, proposed the establishment of an account in the Treasury for excise tax revenues, with at least 50 percent of the receipts used by the IRS for supervision of foundations and the remainder for the states for independent oversight of foundations' activities.[32] However, this approach was never seriously entertained. The Senate version of the Tax Reform Act of 1976 would have lowered the private foundation net investment income tax to 2 percent but that approach was not taken at that time because Congress lowered the mandatory payout percentage

---

[28]Code § 4940(c)(4)(A); Reg. § 53.4940-1(f)(1). Also *Balso Foundation* v. *United States*, 80-2 U.S.T.C ¶ 9581 (D. Conn. 1980); *Ruth E. and Ralph Friedman Foundation, Inc.* v. *Commissioner*, 71 T.C. 40 (1978); Rev. Rul. 74-404, 1974-2 C. B. 382.

[29]Cf. Rev. Rul. 75-410, 1975-2 C. B. 446, concerning a similar allocation of deductible audit fees.

[30]Rev. Rul. 74-579, 1974-2 C. B. 383.

[31]See Rev. Rul. 74-403, 1974-2 C. B. 381; Rev. Rul. 76-424, 1976-2 C. B. 367.

[32]H. R. 5728, 93rd Cong., 2d Sess. (1973).

to a flat 5 percent[33] and did not want to have too much legislation favorable to private foundations in one act. The reduction in the private foundation investment income tax was delayed until adoption of the Revenue Act of 1978.

Notwithstanding the alteration of the excise tax rate, the tax law-writing committees of Congress remain concerned that the IRS devote adequate resources to the administration of the law of tax-exempt organizations.[34] This is relevant in this context because this tax was instituted to assure the availability of these resources. In 1974, Congress made a permanent authorization of appropriations to further assure the availability of sufficient resources to administer this law.[35] However, the change in the foundation tax rate does not affect the amount of that permanent authorization.

In discussing this law change, the tax committees expressed their expectation that the IRS will annually report to Congress on (1) the extent to which audits are conducted as to the tax liabilities of tax-exempt organizations, (2) the extent to which examinations are made as to the continued qualification of exempt organizations for their exempt statuses, (3) the extent to which IRS personnel are given initial and refresher instruction in the relevant portions of the law and administrative procedures, (4) the extent to which the IRS cooperates with and receives cooperation from state officials with regard to supervision of exempt organizations, (5) the costs of maintaining the programs at levels which would produce proper compliance with the laws, (6) the amounts requested by the executive branch for the maintenance of the programs, and (7) the reasons for any difference between the needed funds and the requested amounts. Also, these committees have required the IRS to notify Congress "of any administrative problems that [are] experienced in the course of this enforcement of the internal revenue laws with respect to exempt organizations."[36]

[33]See Chapter 26.

[34]See H. Rep. No. 95-842, 95th Cong., 2d Sess. (1978), to accompany H. R. 112, which is the original legislation containing the foundation excise tax reduction that was made a part of the Revenue Act of 1978.

[35]Employee Retirement Income Security Act of 1974, 88 Stat. 829 § 1052.

[36]H. Rep. No. 95-842, *supra*, n. 34; S. Rep. No. 94-938, 94th Cong., 2d Sess. (1976) at 598-599. In general, see Lehrfeld, "Private Foundations and Tax Reform: Excise Tax on Investment Income," 2 *Tax Adviser* 73 (1971); Gregory, "The Congress and Private Foundations—Will the Patient Survive the Operation?," *Proceedings of the 1971 Annual Conference on Taxation, National Tax Association,* at 189–190.

31

Organizational Rules

An organization cannot achieve tax-exempt status unless the applicable organizational test is satisfied. Code § 508 provides specific organizational test rules for private foundations, which must be met in addition to the organizational test applicable for "charitable" organizations generally.[1]

A private foundation cannot be exempt from tax (nor will contributions to it be deductible as charitable gifts) unless its governing instrument includes provisions the effects of which are to require distributions at such time and in such manner as to comply with the payout rules and prohibit the foundation from engaging in any act of self-dealing, retaining any excess business holdings, making any jeopardizing investments, and making any taxable expenditures.[2] Generally, these elements must be in the foundation's articles of organization and not solely in its bylaws.[3]

The provisions of a foundation's governing instrument must require or prohibit, as the case may be, the foundation to act or refrain from acting so that the foundation, and any foundation managers or other disqualified persons with respect thereto, will not be liable for any of the private foundation excise taxes.[4] The governing instrument of a nonexempt split-interest trust[5] must make comparable provision as respects any of the applicable private foundation excise taxes.[6] Specific reference in the governing instrument to the appropriate sections of the Code is generally required, unless equivalent language is used which is deemed by the IRS to have the same full force and effect. However, a governing instrument which contains only language sufficient to satisfy the

---

[1]See Chapter 5.
[2]Code § 508(e)(1). See Chapters 25–29.
[3]Reg. § 1.508–3(c).
[4]Rev. Rul. 70–270, 1970–1 C. B. 135, contains sample governing instrument provisions.
[5]See Chapter 33.
[6]See Reg. § 1.508–3(e). Rev. Rul. 74–368, 1974–2 C. B. 390, contains sample governing instrument provisions.

requirements of the organizational test for "charitable" entities generally does not meet the specific requirements applicable with respect to private foundations, regardless of the interpretation placed on the language as a matter of law by a state court, and a governing instrument does not meet the organizational requirements if it expressly prohibits the distribution of capital or corpus.[7]

A foundation's governing instrument is deemed to conform with the organizational requirements if valid provisions of state law have been enacted which require the foundation to act or refrain from acting so as not to subject it to any of the private foundation excise taxes or which treat the required provisions as contained in the foundation's governing instrument.[8] The IRS has ruled as to which state statutes contain sufficient provisions in this regard.[9]

Any provision of state law is presumed valid as enacted, and in the absence of state law provisions to the contrary, applies with respect to any foundation that does not specifically disclaim coverage under state law (either by notification to the appropriate state official or by commencement of judicial proceedings).[10] If a state law provision is declared invalid or inapplicable with respect to a class of foundations by the highest appellate court of the state or by the U. S. Supreme Court, the foundations covered by the determination must meet certain requirements[11] within one year from the date on which the time for perfecting an application for review by the Supreme Court expires. If such an application is filed, these requirements must be met within a year from the date on which the Supreme Court disposes of the case, whether by denial of the application for review or decision on the merits. In addition, if a provision of state law is declared invalid or inapplicable with respect to a class of foundations by any court of competent jurisdiction, and the decision is not reviewed by the highest state appellate court of the Supreme Court, and the IRS notifies the general public that the provision has been so declared invalid or inapplicable, then all foundations in the state must meet these requirements, without reliance upon the statute to the extent declared invalid or inapplicable by the decision, within one year from the date such notice is made public. These rules do not apply to any foundation that is subject to a final judgment entered by a court of competent jurisdiction, holding the law invalid or inapplicable with respect to the foundation.[12]

---

[7]Reg. § 1.508–3(b).

[8]Reg. § 1.508–3(d)(1).

[9]Rev. Rul. 75–38, 1975–1 C. B. 161.

[10]See Reg. § 1.508–3(b)(6).

[11]See Code § 508(e).

[12]Reg. § 1.508–3(d)(2). See Brorby, "Using state law to amend foundations' governing instruments under 508(e)," 34 *J. Tax.* 170 (1971); Anthony, Jr., "Private Foundation Governing Instrument Requirements: Connecticut Public Acts Nos. 219 and 220," 46 *Conn. B. J.* 287 (1972).

32

Termination of Status

Congress, in its deliberations which concluded with the Tax Reform Act of 1969, decided that private foundations should not be able to receive tax benefits in exchange for the promise of use of their assets for charitable purposes, and subsequently avoid the carrying out of these responsibilities. The following is an explanation of the rationale underlying the termination requirements:

> Under prior law, an organization was exempt if it met the requirements of the code, whether or not it sought an "exemption certificate" from the Internal Revenue Service.
>
> If an organization did not continue to meet the requirements for exemption, if it committed certain specifically prohibited acts (sec. 503), or if it dealt in certain prohibited ways with its accumulated earnings (sec. 504), it lost its exempt status. This loss of exempt status might relate back to the time the organization first violated the code's requirements. However, if the violation occurred after the contributions had been made to the organization, no deductions were disallowed to such contributors. Also, the organization's income tax exemption was not disturbed for years before the organization's first violation.
>
> *   *   *
>
> Congress was concerned that in many cases under prior law the loss of exempt status would impose only a light burden on many foundations. This was true in those circumstances, for example, where the foundation had already received sufficient charitable contributions to provide its endowment and where the foundation could retain its exemption as to its current income by qualifying under an exemption category other than section 501(c)(3).[1]

The consequence was enactment of Code § 507.

The status of an organization as a private foundation may be terminated only if it properly transfers its assets to a public charity, notifies the IRS of its intent to accomplish termination, or as respects the organization there have either

---

[1]Joint Committee on Internal Revenue Taxation, *General Explanation of Tax Reform Act of 1969*, 91st Cong., 2d Sess. (1970) at 54–55.

519

been willful repeated acts (or failures to act) or a willful and flagrant act (or failure to act) giving rise to liability for one or more of the private foundation excise taxes and the IRS notifies the organization that, by reason of the acts, it is liable for the termination tax.[2] To terminate in this fashion, the organization must pay the tax imposed,[3] or any portion not abated,[4] or achieve abatement of the entire amount of the tax.[5]

§ 32.1   Voluntary Termination

In order to voluntarily terminate its private foundation status, an organization must submit a statement to the IRS of its intent to terminate the status, stating in detail the computation and amount of the termination tax.[6] Unless the organization requests abatement (see below), full payment of the termination tax must be made at the time this statement is filed. Voluntary termination of status does not relieve a private foundation or any disqualified person with respect thereto of liability for any of the foundation excise taxes with respect to acts or failures to act prior to termination or for any additional taxes imposed for failure to correct the acts or failures to act.[7] If any liability for a private foundation excise tax is incurred by a foundation before or in connection with a transfer, transferee liability may be applied against the transferee organization for payment of the taxes.

If a private foundation transfers all or part of its assets to another private foundation, to one or more foundations and one or more public charities, or to an organization operated for testing for public safety, pursuant to a liquidation, merger, redemption, recapitalization, or other adjustment, organization, or reorganization, the transferor foundation will not have accomplished a voluntary termination.[8] Neither a transfer of all of the assets of a private foundation nor a significant disposition of assets[9] by it will result in a termination of the transferor foundation unless it elects to terminate under the voluntary termination provision or the involuntary termination rules apply.[10]

§ 32.2   Involuntary Termination

An organization's private foundation status may be involuntarily terminated if the IRS notifies the organization that, because of willful, flagrant, or repeated

---

[2]Code § 507(a). Thus, this latter rule (Code § 507(a)(2)) is a third-level penalty in addition to the initial and additional taxes of Code Chapter 42.

[3]Code § 507(c).

[4]Code § 507(g).

[5]See Reg. § 1.507–1(a).

[6]Code § 507(a)(1), Reg. § 1.507–1(b)(1).

[7]Reg. § 1.507–1(b)(2).

[8]Reg. § 1.507–1(b)(6).

[9]See Reg. § 1.507–3(e)(2).

[10]Reg. § 1.507–1(b)(7),(8).

acts or failures to act giving rise to one or more of the private foundation excise taxes, the organization is liable for the termination tax.

Under the involuntary termination rule, the phrase "willful repeated acts (or failures to act)" means at least two acts or failures to act, which are voluntary, conscious, and intentional.[11] Such an act (or failure to act) means one which is voluntarily, consciously, and knowingly committed in violation of any of the private foundation rules[12] and which appears to a reasonable person to be a gross violation thereof.[13] An act or failure to act may result in termination of the foundation's status even though the tax is imposed on the foundation's managers rather than on the foundation itself. A failure to timely correct the act or acts, or failures to act, which gave rise to liability for tax under any of the foundation rules may be a willful and flagrant act (or failure to act).[14]

No motive to avoid legal restrictions or the incurrence of tax is necessary to make an act or failure to act willful. However, a foundation's act or failure to act is not willful if the foundation, or its manager if applicable, does not know that the act or failure to act is an act of self-dealing, a taxable expenditure, or other act or failure to act giving rise to liability for one or more of the private foundation taxes.

§ 32.3   Transfer of Assets to a Public Charity

A private foundation, with respect to which there has not been any act or acts described in the involuntary termination rules, may voluntarily terminate its foundation status by distributing all of its net assets to one or more "public" organizations and institutions,[15] each of which has been in existence and so described for a continuous period of at least 60 calendar months immediately preceding the distribution.[16] The IRS has ruled that, in measuring this 60-month period, the recipient organization may be an organization which has been in existence for less than 60 months where it was formed as a result of a consolidation of two organizations, both of which would have qualified as eligible public entities and would have been in existence for the requisite 60 months had the consolidation not occurred; the successor organization was formed for the same purposes and carried on the same activities as the two consolidating organizations.[17]

---

[11]Code § 507(a)(2), Reg. § 1.507–1(c)(1).

[12]Other than Code §§ 4940 (Chapter 30) or 4948 (Chapter 34).

[13]Reg. § 1.507–1(c)(2).

[14]Reg. § 1.507–1(c)(4).

[15]See Chapter 22; Reg. § 1.507–2(a)(2)(ii),(3).

[16]Code § 507(b)(1)(A). This technique was used, for example, to terminate the Richard Nixon Foundation (formed to establish a Nixon library and museum) following the former president's resignation from office; the assets were transferred to Whittier College. See "End Sought for Nixon Foundation," *Washington Post*, Dec. 26, 1974, at Al.

[17]Rev. Rul. 75–289, 1975–2 C. B. 215.

A private foundation terminating in this manner is not required to notify the IRS and does not incur a termination tax, thereby obviating the necessity of any abatement.[18] An organization which terminates its private foundation status by transferring its assets to a qualified public charity remains subject to the private foundation rules until the required distribution of all of its net assets has been completed.[19] Likewise, an organization that remains in existence after terminating its private foundation status under these rules must file an application for recognition of exemption[20] (unless excepted from that requirement) if it wishes to be regarded as a "charitable" organization, since it is treated as a newly created organization.[21]

A private foundation meets the requirement that it "distribute all of its net assets" within the meaning of these rules only if it transfers all of its right, title, and interest in and to all of its net assets to one or more qualified public charities.[22]

In order to effectuate this type of transfer, a transferor foundation may not impose any material restrictions or conditions that prevent the transferee public charity from freely and effectively employing the transferred assets, or the income derived therefrom, in furtherance of its tax-exempt purposes. Whether or not a particular condition or restriction imposed upon a transfer of assets is "material" must be determined from all of the facts and circumstances of the transfer. Some of the more significant facts and circumstances to be considered in making this determination are whether the public charity is the owner in fee of the assets it receives from the private foundation, whether the assets are held and administered by the public charity in a manner consistent with one or more of its exempt purposes, and whether the governing body of the public charity has the ultimate authority and control over the assets, and the income derived therefrom, for its exempt purposes.[23]

The presence of some or all of the following factors is not considered as preventing the transferee "from freely and effectively employing the transferred assets, or the income derived therefrom, in furtherance of its exempt purposes":

(1) The fund is given a name or other designation which is the same as or similar to that of the transferor private foundation or otherwise memorializes the creator of the foundation or his or her family.

(2) The income and assets of the fund are to be used for a designated purpose or for one or more particular organizations that are not private founda-

---

[18]Reg. § 1.507–2(a)(1).
[19]Reg. § 1.507–2(a)(4).
[20]See Chapter 37.
[21]Rev. Rul. 74–490, 1974–2 C. B. 171.
[22]Reg. § 1.507–2(a)(7).
[23]Reg. § 1.507–2(a)(8)(i).

tions, and the use is consistent with the charitable, educational, or other basis for the exempt status of the public charity.

(3) The transferred assets are administered in an identifiable or separate fund, provided that the public charity is the legal and equitable owner of the fund and exercises ultimate and direct authority and control over the fund, as, for example, a fund to endow a chair at a university or a medical research fund at a hospital.

(4) The transferor private foundation transfers property the continued retention of which by the transferee is required by the transferor and is important to the achievement of charitable or other similar purposes in the community.[24]

The presence of any of the following factors is considered as preventing the transferee "from freely and effectively employing the transferred assets, or the income derived therefrom, in furtherance of its exempt purposes":

(1) The transferor foundation, or any person or committee designated by the governing body of, or pursuant to the terms of an agreement with, the transferor foundation reserves the right to direct (other than by direction only in the instrument of transfer) the particular public organizations to which the transferee public charity must distribute the transferred assets, or the income derived therefrom, or both, or the timing of the distributions (as, for example, by a power of appointment).

(2) The terms of the transfer agreement, or any express or implied understanding between the transferor and the transferee, require the public charity to take or withhold action with respect to the transferred assets which is not designed to further one or more of the tax-exempt purposes of the public charity, and the action or withholding of action would, if performed by the transferor private foundation with respect to the assets, have subjected the transferor to one or more of the private foundation excise taxes.[25]

(3) The public charity assumes leases, contractual obligations, or liabilities of the transferor private foundation, or takes the assets thereof subject to the liabilities (including obligations under commitments or pledges to donees of the transferor private foundation), for purposes inconsistent with the purposes or best interests of the public charity.

(4) The transferee public charity is required by any restriction or agreement (other than a restriction or agreement imposed or required by law or regulatory authority), express or implied, to retain, or not to dispose of,

---

[24]Reg. § 1.507–2(a)(8)(ii).
[25]Other than with respect to Code § 4942(e). See Chapter 26.

any securities or other investment assets transferred to it by the private foundation, either permanently or for an extended period of time.

(5) An agreement is entered into between the transferor private foundation and the transferee public charity in connection with the transfer of securities or other property which grants to persons connected with the transferor private foundation a first right of refusal to purchase at fair market value the transferred securities or other property, when and if disposed of by the public charity, unless the securities or other property were purchased or otherwise received by the transferor private foundation subject to the right of first refusal prior to October 9, 1969.

(6) An agreement is entered into between the transferor private foundation and the transferee public charity which establishes irrevocable relationships with respect to the maintenance or management of assets transferred to the public charity, such as continuing relationships with banks, brokerage firms, investment counselors, or other advisors with regard to the investments or other property transferred to the public charity.

(7) Any other condition is imposed on action by the public charity which prevents it from exercising ultimate control over the assets received from the private foundation for purposes consistent with its tax-exempt purposes.[26]

A private foundation which terminates its status under these rules must file with the IRS,[27] setting forth the name and address of the organization and all other information as is prescribed by the requirements. A foundation seeking to terminate its status under these rules may rely on a ruling issued to a potential distributee that the distributee is a public charitable organization.

§ 32.4   Operation as a Public Charity

An organization, as to which there has not been any act or acts described in the involuntary termination rules, can voluntarily terminate its private foundation status if the organization (1) meets the requirements of one or more of the sets of rules concerning organizations that are not private foundations for a continuous period of 60 calendar months,[28] (2) properly notifies the IRS before the commencement of the 60-month period that it is terminating its private foundation status, and (3) properly establishes immediately after the expiration of such period that it has complied with the requirements of the rules whereby an organization can qualify as not being a private foundation.[29]

The IRS is authorized to issue an advance ruling that an organization can

---

[26]Reg. § 1.507–2(a)(8)(iii).
[27]Form 966–E.
[28]See Reg. § 1.507–2(d).
[29]Code § 507(b)(1)(B), Reg. § 1.507–2(b)(1).

be expected to satisfy the requirements of these rules during a 60-month termination period where that expectation is reasonable.[30] This type of a ruling was issued in the case of a foundation that is operating as a supporting organization,[31] being supportive of another foundation which was itself operating during a 60-month termination period as a publicly supported organization.[32] Once the supporting organization's termination period ends, it must establish to the satisfaction of the Service that the supported organization was in fact a public charity during the supporting organization's termination period.[33]

A private foundation which terminates its private foundation status by commencing operation as a public charity does not incur a termination tax and, therefore, no abatement of the tax is required.[34]

The regulations state the information that must be contained in the requisite notification[35] but require only information "as is necessary" to cause this type of termination.[36]

In one instance, a private foundation filed the requisite notice with the IRS that it was terminating its foundation status by operating as a public charity for a continuous 60-month period beginning with the first day of its next taxable year. In conjunction with that notice, filed on February 1, the foundation also gave notice[37] that it was changing its annual accounting period from a calendar year to a fiscal year beginning April 1. The IRS ruled that the foundation may begin the 60-month period required for termination of its foundation status with its tax year beginning April 1, rather than postpone the commencement of that period to January 1.[38]

§ 32.5 Termination Tax

There is imposed on each organization, the private foundation status of which is terminated, a tax equal to the lower of (1) the amount which the organization substantiates by adequate records or other corroborating evidence as the aggregate tax benefit resulting from the tax-exempt status of the organization as a "charitable" entity or (2) the value of the net assets of the organization.[39]

The aggregate tax benefit resulting from the tax-exempt status of a private

[30]Reg. § 1.507–2(e).
[31]See Chapter 22 § 1.
[32]See Chapter 22 § 3.
[33]Rev. Rul. 78–386, 1978–2 C. B. 179.
[34]Reg. § 1.507–2(b)(2). The IRS has ruled that a Code § 4947(a)(2) trust (see Chapter 33) must terminate its private foundation status pursuant to Code § 507 before it can acquire public charity status under Code § 509(a)(3). Rev. Rul. 76–92, 1976–1 C.B. 160.
[35]Reg. § 1.507–2(b)(3),(5).
[36]Reg. § 1.507–2(b)(4),(5).
[37]See Reg. § 1.442–1(c).
[38]Rev. Rul. 77–113, 1977–1 C.B. 152.
[39]Code § 507(c), Reg. § 1.507–4.

foundation is the sum of (1) the aggregate increases in income, estate, and gift taxes which would have been imposed with respect to all substantial contributors to the foundation if deductions for all contributions made by the contributors to the foundation after February 28, 1913, had been disallowed, (2) the aggregate increases in income taxes which would have been imposed with respect to the income of the foundation for tax years beginning after December 31, 1912, if it had not been exempt from tax (or, if a trust, the amount by which its income taxes were reduced because it was permitted to deduct charitable contributions in excess of 20 percent of its taxable income), (3) any amounts succeeded to from transferor private foundations,[40] and (4) interest on the foregoing increases in tax from the first date on which each increase would have been due and payable to the date on which the organization ceases to be a private foundation.[41]

In computing the amount of the aggregate increases in tax under item (1), all deductions attributable to a particular contribution for income, estate, or gift tax purposes must be included. Thus, the aggregate tax benefit as respects a single contribution may exceed the fair market value of the property transferred.[42]

As respects the amount of the tax benefit as stated in item (2) in the case of a trust, the U.S. Court of Claims found the provision "ambiguous."[43] Specifically, the applicable law[44] describes the tax benefit of a trust as including the aggregate increases in tax which would be imposed if "deductions under section 642(c) . . . had been limited to 20 percent of the taxable income of the trust (computed without the benefit of section 642(c) but with the benefit of section 170(b)(1)(A)). . . ." The court reached the conclusion that the provision requires a two-step calculation. The first step is to apply the pertinent charitable contribution deduction rule, which is the charitable deduction available to individuals for up to 50 percent of the donor's "contribution base."[45] The second step is to apply a deduction of 20 percent of the trust's taxable income, rather than the full (100 percent) deduction normally allowed,[46] against the trust income remaining after the charitable deduction. This interpretation thus produces a 60 percent (50 percent plus 20 percent of 50 percent) deduction, which in turn produces the amount retained by the trust in calculating the tax benefit to be recaptured. Pursuant to this reading of the statute, this portion of the termination tax equals 40 percent of the value of the trust's deduction, namely, the 100 percent deduction taken by the trust minus the 60 percent deduction the trust can retain.

In computing the value of the net assets of a private foundation, the amount

---

[40]See Code § 507(b)(2).
[41]Code § 507(d), Reg. § 1.507–5(a).
[42]Reg. § 1.507–5(b).
[43]*Peters* v. *United States*, 80–2 U.S.T.C.¶9510 (Ct.Cl. 1980).
[44]Code § 507(d)(1)(B)(ii).
[45]Code § 170(b)(1)(A). See Chapter 3 § 2.
[46]See Code § 642(c).

of the value is determined at whichever time the value is higher: the first day on which action is taken by the organization which culminates in its ceasing to be a foundation (i.e., the date the organization submitted notice it was terminating its private foundation status) or the date on which it ceases to be a foundation (i.e., the date a willful and flagrant act, failure to act, or a series of repeated acts or failures to act first occurred).[47] The term "net assets" means the gross assets of a private foundation reduced by all its liabilities, including appropriate estimated and contingent liabilities (such as any private foundation excise taxes or winding-up expenses).[48]

§ 32.6   Abatement

The IRS has discretion to abate an unpaid portion of the assessment of a termination tax or any liability in respect thereof, if the private foundation distributes all of its net assets to one or more eligible "public" organizations, each of which has been in existence and so described for a continuous period of at least 60 calendar months, or the foundation gives effective assurance to the IRS that its assets will be used for charitable purposes.[49]

Abatement of the unpaid portion of the assessment of a termination tax will occur only where the IRS determines that the requisite corrective action has been taken.[50] The appropriate state officer has one year from the date of notification[51] that a notice of deficiency of termination tax has been issued to advise the IRS that corrective action has been initiated (by the state officer or a recipient public charity) pursuant to state law as may be ordered or approved by a court of competent jurisdiction.[52] Upon receipt of certification from the state officer that corrective action has been taken, the IRS may abate the termination tax assessment, unless the Service determines that the action is not sufficiently corrective, in which case action on the assessment and collection of the tax may be suspended until corrective action[53] is obtained or assessment and collection of the tax may be resumed.[54]

---

[47]Code § 507(e), Reg. § 1.507–7(a)–(c).

[48]Reg. § 1.507–7(d).

[49]Code § 507(g), Reg. § 1.507–9(a).

[50]Reg. § 1.507–9(b)(1).

[51]See Code § 6104(c).

[52]Reg. § 1.507–9(b)(2).

[53]Reg. § 1.507–9(c).

[54]Reg. § 1.507–9(b)(3). In general, see Paluska, "Transforming a private foundation to a supporting organization: Why and how," 42 *J. Tax.* 248 (1975); Liles, "Operating and Terminating Private Foundations," 50 *Taxes* 851 (1972); Bromberg and Sugarman, "Termination of Private Foundations," 50 *Taxes* 388 (1972).

33

Nonexempt Trusts

Pursuant to Code § 4947, many of the private foundation rules are applicable to certain nonexempt trusts, in which all or part of the unexpired interests are devoted to one or more charitable purposes—certain "charitable trusts" and "split-interest trusts." The basic purpose of this requirement is to prevent these trusts from being used to avoid the requirements and restrictions applicable to private foundations.[1]

§ 33.1   Charitable Trusts

For certain purposes,[2] a nonexempt charitable trust is treated as an organization that is a "charitable" entity. Such a trust[3] is a trust which is not tax-exempt, all of the unexpired interests in which are devoted to one or more charitable purposes, and for which a deduction was allowed.[4]

This rule for charitable trusts usually applies to trusts in which all unexpired interests consist only of charitable income and remainder interests (regardless of whether the trustee is required to distribute corpus to, or hold corpus in trust for the benefit of, any remainder beneficiary) or to trusts in which all unexpired interests consist of charitable remainder interests where the trustee is required to hold corpus in trust for the benefit of any charitable remainder beneficiary. An estate from which the executor or administrator is required to distribute all of the net assets (free of trust) to charitable beneficiaries is generally not considered to be a charitable trust during the period of estate administration or settlement. However, in the case of an estate from which the

---

[1]Reg. § 53.4947–1(a). See, e.g., the discussion in *Peters* v. *United States*, 80–2 U.S.T.C.¶9510 (Ct.Cl. 1980).

[2]Code §§ 507–509 (except Code § 508(a)–(c)), 4940–4948.

[3]Code § 4947(a)(1).

[4]The deduction is that allowed by Code §§ 170, 545(b)(2), 556(b)(2), 642(c), 2055, 2106(a)(2), or 2522. Reg. § 53.4947–1(b)(1).

executor or administrator is required to distribute all of the net assets (free of trust) to charitable beneficiaries, if the estate is considered terminated for federal income tax purposes,[5] then the estate will be treated as a charitable trust between the date on which the estate is considered terminated and the date on which final distribution of all of the net assets is made to the charitable beneficiaries. Similarly, in the case of a trust in which all of the unexpired interests are charitable remainder interests which have become entitled to distributions of corpus (free of trust) upon the termination of all intervening noncharitable interests, if after the termination of the intervening interests the trust is considered terminated for federal income tax purposes,[6] then the trust will be treated as a charitable trust, rather than a split-interest trust (see below), between the date on which the trust is considered terminated and the date on which final distribution (free of trust) of all of the net assets is made to the charitable remainder beneficiaries.[7]

As noted, a nonexempt charitable trust is treated as a "charitable" organization. As discussed,[8] an organization that is a "charitable" entity is a private foundation unless it meets the requirements of one or more rules by which private foundation classification is avoided. Therefore, a nonexempt charitable trust is considered to be a private foundation unless it meets one of these requirements. A nonexempt charitable trust which was originally a private foundation and subsequently became qualified as a public charity must first terminate its foundation status[9] before it can be excluded from private foundation status as a "public" entity.[10]

§ 33.2   Split-Interest Trusts

Certain of the private foundation rules likewise apply to nonexempt split-interest trusts.[11] A split-interest trust is a trust which is not tax-exempt, not all of the unexpired interests in which are devoted to one or more charitable purposes, and which has amounts in trust for which a deduction was allowed.[12] This type of trust is subject to the termination rules, the organizational requirements to the extent applicable, the self-dealing rules, the excess business

---

[5]See Reg. § 1.641(b)–3(a).

[6]See Reg. § 1.641(b)–3(b).

[7]Reg. § 53.4947–1(b)(2). By enactment of legislation in 1980 (P.L. 96–603, 96th Cong., 2d Sess. (1980)), Congress has subjected nonexempt charitable trusts to the same reporting and disclosure requirements as are imposed upon tax-exempt charitable organizations (see Chapter 38 § 3). See, in general, Appert, "Nonexempt Charitable Trusts Under the Tax Reform Act of 1969," 25 *Tax Lawyer* 99 (1971).

[8]See Chapter 22.

[9]See Chapter 32.

[10]Rev. Rul. 76–92, 1976–1 C.B. 92.

[11]Code § 4947(a)(2).

[12]See n.4, *supra*.

holdings rules, the jeopardizing investments rules, and the prohibited expenditures rules as if it were a private foundation.[13]

The foregoing rule is inapplicable to any amounts payable under the terms of a split-interest trust to income beneficiaries, unless a charitable deduction was allowed[14] with respect to the income interest of any beneficiary.[15] The foregoing rule is inapplicable to any assets held in trust (together with the income and capital gains derived from the assets), other than assets held in trust with respect to which a deduction was allowed,[16] if the other amounts are segregated from the assets for which no deduction was allowable.[17] For these purposes, a trust with respect to which amounts are segregated must separately account for the various income, deduction, and other items properly attributable to each segregated asset in the books of account and separately to each of the beneficiaries of the trusts.[18] If any amounts held in trust are segregated, the value of the net assets for purposes of the termination rules[19] is limited to the segregated amounts.[20] The foregoing is inapplicable to any amounts transferred in trust before May 27, 1969.[21]

Notwithstanding the foregoing, the excess business holdings and jeopardizing investment rules do not apply to a split-interest trust if:

(1) All the income interest[22] (and none of the remainder interest) of the trust is devoted solely to one or more charitable purposes and all amounts in the trust for which a deduction was allowed[23] have an aggregate value (at the time the deduction was allowed) of not more than 60 percent of the aggregate fair market value of all amounts in the trust (after the payment of estate taxes and all other liabilities), or

(2) A deduction was allowed under one of these provisions for amounts payable under the terms of the trust to every remainder beneficiary but not to any income beneficiary.[24]

Once all of the noncharitable interests in a split-interest trust expire, the trust becomes a (nonexempt) charitable trust.

---

[13]Reg. § 53.4947–1(c)(1). For these rules, see Chapters 33, 32, 26, 28, 29, and 30, respectively.

[14]See Code §§ 170(f)(2)(B), 2055(e)(2)(B), or 2522(c)(2)(B).

[15]Code § 4947(a)(2)(A), Reg. § 53.4947–1(c)(2).

[16]See n.4, *supra*.

[17]Code § 4947(a)(2)(B), Reg. § 53.4947–1(c)(3).

[18]Code § 4947(a)(3), Reg. § 53.4947–1(c)(3).

[19]Code § 507(c)(2),(g). See Chapter 32.

[20]Reg. § 53.4947–2(a).

[21]Code § 4947(a)(2)(C), Reg. § 53.4947–1(c)(5).

[22]See Reg. § 53.4947–2(b)(2)(i).

[23]See n.4, *supra*.

[24]Reg. § 53.4947–2(b)(1). The term "income beneficiary" is defined in Reg. § 53.4947–2(b)(2)(ii).

34

Foreign Foundations

In lieu of the tax on the net investment income of private foundations,[1] Code § 4948(a) imposes for each tax year on the gross investment income[2] derived from sources within the United States[3] by every foreign organization which is a private foundation for the year a tax equal to 4 percent of income. A "foreign organization," for these purposes, means any organization which was not created or organized in the U.S. or any U.S. possession, or under the law of the U.S., any State, the District of Columbia, or any possession of the U.S.[4]

Whenever there exists a tax treaty between the United States and a foreign country, and a foreign private foundation subject to these rules is a resident of that country or is otherwise entitled to the benefits of the treaty, if the treaty provides that any item or items of gross investment income is exempt from income tax, the item or items need not be taken into account by the foundation in computing the foreign foundation tax.[5] Thus, Canadian private foundations, exempt from the Canadian income tax and qualifying under the rules for "charitable" organizations generally, are exempt from the foreign foundation tax by virtue of the U.S.–Canada Income Tax Convention.[6] By contrast, a Belgian foundation, which derived only interest income from the U.S., was ruled to not be exempt from the foreign foundation tax because neither the U.S.–Belgium Income Tax Convention nor the Treaty of Friendship, Establishment and Navigation with the Kingdom of Belgium provides the requisite exemption.[7]

However, the termination of private foundation status rules,[8] the special organizational rules,[9] and the general private foundation rules are inapplicable

---

[1]See Chapter 30.
[2]See Code § 4940(c)(2). Also see Rev. Rul. 72–244, 1972–1 C.B. 282.
[3]See Code § 861.
[4]Reg. § 53.4948–1(a)(1). See Code § 170(c)(2)(A).
[5]Reg. § 53.4948–1(a)(3).
[6]Rev. Rul. 74–183, 1974–1 C.B. 328.
[7]Rev. Rul. 76–330, 1976–2 C.B. 488. Also Rev. Rul. 77–289, 1977–2 C.B. 490.
[8]See Chapter 32.
[9]See Chapters 31 and 37.

to any foreign organization which, from the date of its creation, has received substantially all (i.e., at least 85 percent) of its support (other than gross investment income) from sources outside the United States.[10] For this purpose, gifts, grants, contributions, or membership fees directly or indirectly from a United States person[11] are from sources within the United States.[12]

Nonetheless, a foreign private foundation is not regarded as a tax-exempt organization if it has engaged in a prohibited transaction after December 31, 1969.[13] A "prohibited transaction"[14] is any act or failure to act (other than as respects the minimum investment return requirements[15]) which would subject the foundation or a disqualified person[16] with respect thereto to a penalty with respect to any private foundation excise tax liability[17] or a termination tax[18] if the foundation were a domestic private foundation.[19]

A foreign private foundation will be denied exemption from taxation for all tax years beginning with the tax year during which it is notified by the IRS that it has engaged in a prohibited transaction.[20] In the case of an act or failure to act, before giving notice, the IRS will warn the foreign private foundation that the act or failure to act may be treated as a prohibited transaction. However, the act or failure to act will not be treated as a prohibited transaction if it is corrected within 90 days after the making of the warning. The organization may, with respect to the second tax year following the tax year in which it was given a prohibited transaction notice, apply for tax exemption. If the IRS is satisfied that the organization will not knowingly again engage in a prohibited transaction and that the organization has satisfied all other applicable requirements for tax exemption, the organization will be so notified in writing. In that case, the organization will not, with respect to tax years beginning with the tax year with respect to which a claim for exemption is filed, be denied exemption from taxation by reason of any prohibited transaction which was engaged in before the date on which notice was given.[21]

No gift, bequest, legacy, devise, or transfer will give rise to a charitable contribution deduction if made to a foreign foundation after the date on which the IRS publishes notice that it has notified the organization that it has engaged in a prohibited transaction and in a tax year of the organization for which it is not exempt from taxation by reason of having engaged in a prohibited transaction.[22]

---

[10]Code § 4948(b).
[11]See Code § 7701(a)(30).
[12]Reg. § 53.4948–1(b).
[13]Code § 4948(c)(1).
[14]Code § 4948(c)(2).
[15]See Chapter 26.
[16]See Chapter 23.
[17]See Code § 6684.
[18]See Chapter 32.
[19]See Reg. § 53.4948–1(c)(2).
[20]Code § 4948(c)(3).
[21]Reg. § 53.4948–1(c)(3).
[22] Code § 4948(c)(4), Reg. § 53.4948–1(d).

35

Prospective Regulation of
Public Charities

In the wake of little more than one decade of experience in strenuously regulating the operations and activities of private foundations, many in the IRS and the Department of the Treasury and some in Congress are seriously contemplating comparable regulation of the affairs of one or more categories of charitable entities other than private foundations.

Unlike the alleged scandals that preceded the revolution in the federal tax laws pertaining to private foundations, which culminated in a major portion of the Tax Reform Act of 1969, there has been no parade of ostensible abuses warranting such strict supervision of public charities. Rather, it appears that this is a last frontier for reformers in the field of charitable organizations and that most of the reforms are being advocated because the statutory basis for the rules is already in place and because the imposition of these rules on public charities strikes many as the thing to do as a logical extension of existing regulation. Hence, the not-too-far-distant future may well see extension of many of the private foundation restrictions to some or all public charaities: most likely, the prohibitions (perhaps in some modified form) on self-dealing, excess business holdings, and jeopardizing investments, and the rules mandating minimum payout of funds and restricting the uses of funds. Also, as discussed below, the recent attention to the matter of government supervision or regulation of solicitations for charitable contributions may bring some new federally enforced rules to govern the activities of public charities.

§ 35.1 Filer Commission Recommendations

The Commission on Private Philanthropy and Public Needs[1] advanced a catalog of recommendations in this area, which may serve as a framework for

[1]See Chapter 1.

533

legislation. A summary of these recommendation for "improving the philan-thropic process"[2] follows:

The social benefit that flows from giving and nonprofit activity results from a process of interaction—between donors and donees and between both and the society at large. In order to function properly—and to reassure a public grown skeptical of its institutions—this "philanthropic process" requires considerable openness between donors and donees and the public; it requires open minds as well as open doors. The tax-exempt status of nonprofit organizations, moreover, entails an obligation to openness, an accountability to the public for actions and expenditures.

Yet the Commission's research, including meetings with and reports from rep-resentatives of donee organizations, indicates that the process is operating im-perfectly at best. So a number of recommendations were decided upon with the aim of improving the philanthropic process; the following are among the major ones. They fall into four categories: accountability, accessibility, personal or in-stitutional self-benefiting, and influencing legislation.

A. ACCOUNTABILITY

Demands for accountability that have been heard in the business and government worlds of late are also being sounded in the voluntary sector, reflecting the haphazard procedures for accountability that exist in the sector, the increasing use of public funds by nonprofit organizations, and the perception by some that private nonprofit organizations are too private. The Commission agrees that, with notable individual exceptions, the overall level of accountability in the voluntary sector is inadequate, and the Commission therefore recommends:

That all larger tax-exempt charitable organizations except churches and church affiliates be reqired to prepare and make readily available detailed annual reports on their finances, programs and priorities.

Annual reporting requirements that now apply to private foundations would, in effect, be extended to tax-exempt organizations with annual budgets of more than $100,000—including corporate giving programs but excluding religious organi-zations. These reports would have to be filed with appropriate state and federal agencies and be made readily available to interested parties upon request. Uniform accounting measures for comparable types of nonprofit organizations are rec-ommended, and an accounting model is provided in the compendium of Com-mission research, which is published separately.

That larger grant-making organizations be required to hold annual public meetings to discuss their programs, priorities and contributions.

This requirement would apply mainly to foundations, corporations and federated fund-raising groups such as United Ways, those with contribution budgets of $100,000 or more. Like the above requirement it would not apply to churches or church affiliates.

[2]*Giving in America: Toward a Stronger Voluntary Sector*, Report of the Commission on Private Philanthropy and Public Needs (1975) at 21–26.

B. Accessibility

Greater accessibility by potential donees to donor institutions has frequently been espoused as a goal in the nonprofit sector, yet the evidence suggests that it has been a goal honored more in preachments than in practical pursuit. The Commission believes that greater accessibility can only enrich the philanthropic process, and it is concerned that because of insufficient accessibility, the process may not be fluid enough to respond to new needs. So, with the aim of encouraging and facilitating wider access to and greater venturesomeness by institutional philanthropy, the Commission recommends:

That legal responsibility for proper expenditure of foundation grants, now imposed on both foundations and recipients, be eliminated and that recipient organizations be made primarily responsible for their own expenditures.

The 1969 Tax Reform Act places on foundations and their officers "expenditure responsibility" for any grant that a foundation makes. This provision serves as a restraint on the openness and venturesomeness of foundations. It also puts foundations in a policing and surveillance role and thus undermines the autonomy of grantees. The provision creates both an unnecessary and undesirable duplication of responsibility, and should be repealed.

That tax-exempt organizations, particularly funding organizations, recognize an obligation to be responsive to changing viewpoints and emerging needs and that they take steps such as broadening their boards and staffs to insure that they are responsive.

All exempt organizations, especially those that serve to channel funds to other nonprofit groups, have a public obligation to be aware of and responsive to new attitudes and needs of all segments of society, and each organization should periodically broaden its board and staff if need be so that a wide range of viewpoints is reflected in the organization's governance and management.

The Commission rejects the notion that all voluntary organizations should be "representative" but observes that as more government funds flow into or through voluntary organizations they may have to consider inviting "public" members on their boards as an element of public access and control.

In addition to broadening existing organizations the Commission urges the establishment of new funding organizations and structural changes to broaden the spectrum of institutional philanthropy in general. An example is the "People's Trust" plan currently being explored in Atlanta; it would raise money in modest monthly pledges for projects close to the donors' homes.

C. Personal or Institutional Self-Benefiting

While tax-exempt charitable organizations are now allowed to make profits, situations have been uncovered in which personal money-making appeared to be the main purpose of the organization or of certain transactions made by the organization. Most notorious, perhaps, have been discoveries of instances where fund-raising and administrative costs have used as much as four out of every five dollars raised. The 1969 tax reform law placed stringent restrictions on self-benefiting by foundation personnel. The Commission believes that other tax exempt organizations may be as open to such abuses, however, and it therefore favors extending the 1969 restriction to all exempt organizations, with appropriate modifications. Other remedies and restraints are considered desirable as well to insure public confidence that charitable nonprofit organizations do indeed serve only charitable nonprofit causes. The Commission recommends:

That all tax-exempt organizations be required to maintain "arms-length" business relationships with profit-making organizations or activities in which any principal of the exempt organization has a financial interest.

That a system of federal regulation be established for interstate charitable solicitations and that intrastate solicitations be more effectively regulated by state governments.

The Commission believes that the vast majority of charitable solicitations are conscientiously and economically undertaken. Nonetheless, cases of unduly costly or needless fund raising point to the absence of any focused mechanism for overseeing such activity and, if need be, applying sanctions. State regulation is weak and should be strengthened, but because many solicitations are spread over a number of states at once, federal regulation is needed.

The Commission recommends fuller disclosure requirements on solicitation costs and proposes that a special federal office be established to oversee solicitations and to take legal actions against improper, misleading or excessively costly fund raisings.

As the foregoing indicates, any further regulation of "public" charitable organizations is likely to come in the form of some extension of the private foundation rules and/or some type of federal law regulating the solicitation of contributions for charitable purposes. As to the latter, the follies of a few unscrupulous organizations in the pursuit of money by means of solicitations of the general public for ostensibly charitable purposes and the intense scrutiny being given to the matter of appropriate fund-raising costs may eventually usher in one or more statutes regulating solicitations at the federal level and imposing some additional requirements and restrictions on the activities of public charities. Developments in recent years have increased the likelihood that it is only a matter of time before a federal statute is enacted to regulate interstate solicitations of charitable contributions. At the present, this regulation is the subject of widely varying statutes in many states and the District of Columbia and innumerable city and county ordinances.

For a variety of reasons (including heavy media exposure), there has been increasing concern among the general public about the validity of many charitable organizations and the solicitations by them. The alleged "abuses" in this area fall basically within three categories: seemingly insufficient disclosure of meaningful information to prospective donors, excessive administrative and fund-raising costs, and insufficient portions of the proceeds of the solicitation passing for charitable purposes.[3]

One of the recommendations of the Filer Commission was that a "system of federal regulation be established for interstate charitable solicitations and

[3]A separate volume by the author discusses existing and prospective federal and state law concerning fund raising for charitable purposes. See Hopkins, *Charity Under Siege: Government Regulation of Fund Raising*, John Wiley & Sons, 1980.

that intrastate solicitations be more effectively regulated by state government."[4] The Commission's specific recommendations for federal regulation of charitable solicitations are as follows:

In the Commission's sample survey of taxpayers, 30 percent of those questioned said they did not like the way their contributions were used and one out of seven respondents specifically complained of excessive fund-raising or administrative costs. This wariness undoubtedly has been heightened in many minds by recent cases, including those uncovered in congressional investigations, where some costs of charitable fund raising absorbed most of the funds raised, leaving the impression that some charitable solicitations are more for the benefit of the solicitors than for the charitable causes involved. In some other instances, contributions have been recurrently solicited and raised that are far in excess of the organizations's operating outlays.

The Commission believes that the vast majority of charitable solicitations are conscientiously and economically undertaken. Nonetheless, cases of unduly costly or needless fund raising point to the absence of any focused mechanism for overseeing such activity and, if need be, applying sanctions. One Commission study finds, in fact, that only one half of the 50 states regulated the solicitation of funds and that "the coverage and scope of" those that do regulate "vary widely." State regulation of intrastate solicitations, the Commission believes, should be strengthened, but because many solicitations spread over many states at once, state regulation is inevitably limited in its effectiveness. Clearly, the federal government and federal law must play the major role in assuring the integrity of charitable solicitations, a role that they just as clearly do not play today. The Commission recommends specifically that all charitable organizations should be required by law to disclose all solicitation costs to the Internal Revenue Service, in accordance with accepted accounting principles; that all solicitation literature should be required to carry a notice to the effect that full financial data can be obtained from the soliciting organization on request; that any such requests be required to be rapidly answered; and that a special office be established in the Internal Revenue Service or in some other federal agency or regulatory body, such as the Federal Trade Commission, to oversee charity solicitaion and take action against improper, misleading or excessively costly fund raisings. This special office might be supplemented by and guided by an accrediting organization, which would review the finances of and certify all exempt organizations whose solicitation practices are found to merit approval.

The Commission considered but rejected proposals that solicitation costs be legally limited to a fixed percentage of receipts because, unless such a ceiling were so high as to be an ineffective restraint on most fund raising, it would risk being too low to account for the often justifiably high costs of solicitation for new or unpopular causes. On the other hand, state as well as federal agencies concerned with regulating solicitations should be required to establish clear qualitative criteria as to what constitutes "excessively costly" fund raising (or improper or misleading solicitation, as well). Such criteria should be widely publicized so that both soliciting organizations and the contributing public would clearly understand the limits within which fund raisers operate.[5]

[4] *Giving in America, supra,* n. 2.
[5] *Ibid.* at 176–178.

These recommendations, however, drew the following dissent from Commissioner member Raymond J. Gallagher:

> State governments already adequately police the solicitations of charitable contributions. There is no hard data in the material collected by this Commission that warrants a recommendation that the federal government assume a new policy role in this area. The Commission indicates that it believes that the vast majority of charitable solicitations are conscientiously and economically undertaken. The Commission, however, is concerned about the impression of many taxpayers that charity solicitations cost more than they should. I do not believe that the effective remedy for this impression is the creation of a new federal bureaucracy or the expansion of an existing one. Potential donors who have doubts about the efficiency of charitable solicitations can inquire directly of the organizations they are concerned about; and if they are not satisfied with the answers they are given, they have the most effective remedy of all: not making the contribution.[6]

§ 35.2 Ford Administration Treasury Proposals

When outgoing Treasury Secretary William E. Simon, on January 14, 1977, sent a package of legislative proposals to Congress to "improve public accountability and prevent abuses" in private philanthropy, the proposals included a recommendation that interstate solicitations be subject to federal legislation that would be administered by the Treasury Department. The Treasury also recommended disclosure of financial information about the soliciting organization, particularly with respect to its fund-raising and administrative costs.[7]

The Treasury proposals contain the observation that [t]here is no supervision or monitoring of interstate solicitation [of charitable contributions] by the Federal Government, and the State laws affecting it vary considerably, making it easy, particularly for large fund-raising drives, to circumvent tough enforcement by any one state."

This is a curious statement. In fact, the application for recognition of tax exemption[8] filed by charitable organizations requests information concerning charitable solicitation activities. Also, the IRS and Treasury are fully empowered to request more information about solicitation activities in the application for recognition of exemption and in an organization's annual information return[9] than is presently required. Further, it is an understatement to state that the state laws relating to charitable solicitations "vary considerably." In fact, they vary widely and the accompanying regulations, forms, and enforcement efforts are even more divergent. However, it does not follow from this observation that this variance contributes to lack of enforcement of these laws. Additionally, "large fund-raising drives" are able to "circumvent tough enforcement by any one state" only by refraining from soliciting contributions in that jursidiction

[6]*Ibid.* at 220–221.
[7]Department of the Treasury News Release, Jan. 18, 1977.
[8]See Chapter 37.
[9]See Chapter 38.

(unless the state law is simply violated); at the same time, the trade-off resulting from such a decision is that the organization deprives itself of the financial support otherwise available to it from the citizens of the particular state.

In connection with its recommendations, the Treasury Department suggested that Congress (specifically, the House Committee on Ways and Means and the Senate Committee on Finance) conduct hearings on the "appropriate methods" for regulating charitable solicitations, with "emphasis on the following issues":

(1) The extent of financial data concerning the soliciting organization that must be supplied with the solicitation material;

(2) The need for administrative review of solicitation material prior to dissemination (as opposed to relying solely on criminal and equitable sanctions for misleading or incomplete material);

(3) The appropriate method for regulating oral solicitations (e.g., by telephone or television) and the extent of disclosure required for them;

(4) The need for limitations on fund-raising and administrative costs; and

(5) The preemption of varying State reporting requirements for interstate solicitations, with a uniform Federal report to be filed with all requesting states.

The Treasury Department recommendations went far beyond the supervision and monitoring of charitable solicitations. In related areas, the recommendations also included a proposal that every private foundation, every public charity that makes grants, and every public charity or social welfare organization with annual gross receipts of at least $100,000 (other than a church or integrated auxiliary thereof or a convention or association of churches) be required to make available to the public an annual report on its finances, programs and priorities. Also, the Treasury recommended that certain of the restrictions on private foundations be extended to public charities. These restrictions involve the present requirements with respect to self-dealing, minimum payout, jeopardy investments, and taxable expenditures.

This proposal for an annual report by most public charities dovetails with recommendations tendered by others. Such a report could be the document which a soliciting charity would have to send to the public upon request and also file with the Postal Service and perhaps in the states where the solicitation is to take place. However, the prospects of preparation of another major document for filing with the federal tax authorities (in addition to the annual information return) are certain to generate protests if only because of the increased costs of compliance. Another reason that such a proposal will likely stimulate unhappiness is the scope of further disclosure that will be inevitable, particularly if the reporting requirements extend to the names and amount of compensation paid to top employees, consultants, contractors, and the like.

As respects other aspects of federal involvement in the private philanthropic processes, the Treasury recommended a variety of revisions of the tax laws with respect to the charitable contribution deduction and an investment of U.S. district courts with equity powers sufficient to remedy any violation of the substantive rules concerning philanthropic organizations in such a way as to minimize any financial detriment to the organization and to preserve its assets for its philanthropic purposes.

*   *   *

Thus it is that, due to a convergence of a number of trends and developments, public charities seem destined for greater governmental involvement in their affairs. To recapitulate: the converging forces are (1) the movements toward increasing "consumer protection," "disclosure," and "public accountability," (2) those who wish to encompass nearly all types of charitable organizations within the scope of the existing private foundation rules, and (3) those who are seeking to expand government regulation of the process of soliciting financial support. The outcome of all this will say much about the nature of philanthropy in the country in the coming years.

PART V

QUALIFICATION OF EXEMPT ORGANIZATIONS: SUBSTANCE AND PROCEDURE

36

Form of Organization and Governing Instruments

§ 36.1 Considerations of Form

Generally, the Internal Revenue Code does not prescribe a specific organizational form for entities to qualify for tax exemption. Basically, the choices are nonprofit corporation, trust (inter vivos or testamentary), or unincorporated association.[1] However, some Code provisions expressly reference, in whole or in part, the corporate form,[2] and other Code provisions reference the trust form.[3] Throughout the categories of tax-exempt organizations are such additional terms as "clubs," "associations," "societies," "leagues," "companies," "boards," "orders," "posts," and "units." For tax purposes, an organization may be deemed a "corporation" even though it is not formally incorporated.[4]

The federal tax provision, which describes charitable, educational, and like organizations[5] provides that an organization described therein must be a corporation, community chest, fund or foundation. An "unincorporated association" or "trust" can qualify under this provision, presumably as a "fund" or "foundation" or perhaps, as noted, as a "corporation."[6] However, a "partnership" cannot be tax-exempt as a "charitable" organization.[7]

[1]See Rev. Proc. 82–2, 1982–3 I.R.B. 9.
[2]Code §§ 501(c)(1), (2), (3), (14), and (16).
[3]Code §§ 501(c)(17), (18), (19), and (20), and 401 (a).
[4]See Code § 7701(a)(3).
[5]Code § 501(c)(3).
[6]*Fifth-Third Union Trust Co.* v. *Commissioner*, 56 F.2d 767 (6th Cir. 1932).
[7]IRS Exempt Organizations Handbook (IRM 7751) § 315.1. See *Emerson Institute* v. *United States*, 356 F.2d 824 (D.C. Cir. 1966), cert. den. 385 U. S. 822 (1966). Cf. Stoner and Pineo, "Tax-Exempt Organizations and Limited Partnerships," 54 *Taxes* 339 (1976).

An organization already exempt from federal taxation may establish a separate "fund" or like entity which is itself an exempt organization.[8] The attributes of such a "fund" include a separate category of tax exemption (for example, an educational research and scholarship fund established by a bar association[9]), a separate governing body, and separate books and accounts.[10] However, a mere bank deposit cannot amount to a requisite "fund," and a contribution to it would be considered a nondeductible gift to an individual rather than a possibly deductible gift to a qualified organization.[11]

For purposes of the rules concerning "charitable" organizations,[12] an organization exempt thereunder may be a unit of government[13] or a foreign organization,[14] or may conduct all or part of its activities in foreign countries.[15]

The formalities of organization of an entity may have a bearing on the tax exemption. This is not only the case in connection with the sufficiency of the governing instruments,[16] but also, and more fundamentally, as to whether there is a separate organization in the first instance. An individual may perform worthwhile activities, such as providing financial assistance to needy students, but will receive no tax benefits from his or her beneficence, unless he or she establishes and funds a qualified organization which in turn renders the charitable works, such as scholarship grants. The U. S. Tax Court has observed, in the process of denying a charitable contribution deduction, that the federal tax law makes no provision for a charitable deduction in the context of "personal ventures," however praiseworthy in character. The court noted that "[t]here is no evidence of such enterprise being a corporation, community chest, fund, or foundation and little information, if any, as to its organization or activities."[17] However, assuming the organization is not operated to benefit private interests, its tax exemption will not be endangered because its creator serves as the sole trustee and exercises complete control,[18] although state law may preclude close control.

It is the position of the IRS that a "formless aggregation of individuals" cannot be exempt as "charitable" entities.[19] At a minimum, the entity must

---

[8]See, e.g., Code § 509(a), last sentence.

[9]See Rev. Rul. 58–293, 1958–1 C. B. 146.

[10]See Rev. Rul. 54–243, 1954–1 C. B. 92.

[11]See *Bolton* v. *Commissioner*, 1 T. C. 717 (1943); *Pusch* v. *Commissioner*, 39 T. C. M. 838 (1980).

[12]Code § 501(c)(3).

[13]See Rev. Rul. 60–384, 1960–2 C. B. 172.

[14]See Rev. Rul. 66–177, 1966–1 C. B. 132.

[15]See Rev. Rul. 71–460, 1971-2 C. B. 231.

[16]See *Cone* v *McGinnes*, 63–2 U.S.T.C. ¶ 9551 (E. D. Pa. 1963). Also see § 2, *infra*.

[17]*Hewitt* v. *Commissioner*, 16 T.C.M. 468, 471 (1957). Also see *Doty, Jr.* v. *Commissioner*, 62 T. C. 587 (1974); *Walker* v. *Commissioner*, 37 T. C. M. 1851 (1978).

[18]Rev. Rul. 66–219, 1966–2 C. B. 208.

[19]IRS Exempt Organizations Handbook (IRM 7751) §§ 315.1, 315.2(3), 315.4(2).

have an organizing instrument, some governing rules, and regularly chosen officers.[20]

Among the nontax factors to be considered in selecting an organizational form are legal liabilities in relation to the individuals involved (the corporate form can limit such liabilities), local law requirements, necessities of governing instruments, local annual reporting requirements, organizational expenses, and any membership requirements.[21] Federal law, other than the tax laws, may also have a bearing on the choice, such as the organization's comparable status under the postal laws.[22]

A change in form may require an exempt organization to reapply for recognition of tax-exempt status. For example, an unincorporated organization that has been recognized by the IRS as a "charitable" entity must commence the application process anew if it incorporates.[23]

§ 36.2   Governing Instruments

An organization must have governing instruments to qualify for tax exemption, if only to satisfy the appropriate organizational test. This is particularly the case for "charitable" organizations, for which the federal tax law imposes specific organizational requirements,[24] which are even more stringent if the organization is a private foundation.[25]

If the corporate form is used, the governing instruments will be articles of incorporation and bylaws. An unincorporated organization will have articles of organization, perhaps in the form of a constitution, and undoubtedly, also bylaws. If a trust, the basic document will be a declaration of trust or trust agreement.

The articles of organization should contain provisions stating the organization's purposes; whether there will be members and, if so, the qualifications and classes thereof; the initial board of directors or trustee(s); the registered agent and incorporators (if a corporation); the dissolution or liquidation procedure; and the required language referencing the appropriate tax law (federal and state) requirements and prohibitions. If the organization is a corporation, particular attention need be given the appropriate state nonprofit corporation statute, which will contain requirements that may supersede the provisions of the articles and bylaws or may apply where the governing instruments are silent.

---

[20]*Trippe* v. *Commissioner*, 9 T. C. M. 622 (1950). Cf. *Morey* v. *Riddell*, 205 F. Supp. 918 (S. D. Cal. 1962).

[21]See Henn and Pfeifer, "Nonprofit Groups: Factors Influencing Choice of Form," 11 *Wake Forest L. Rev.* 181 (1975).

[22]See 39 C. F. R. Part 132 (second class), Part 134 (third class).

[23]See Chapter 38.

[24]See Chapter 5.

[25]See Chapter 31

The bylaws may also contain the provisions of the articles of organization and, in addition, should contain provisions amplifying or stating the purposes of the organization; the terms and conditions of membership (if any); the manner of selection and duties of the directors or trustees, and officers; the voting requirements; the procedure for forming committees; the accounting period; any indemnification provisions; the appropriate tax provisions; and the procedure for amendment of the bylaws.[26]

[26]In general, see Oleck, *Non-Profit Corporations, Organizations, and Associations* (3d ed. 1974); Webster, *The Law of Associations*; Chaffe, "The Internal Affairs of Associations Not For Profit," 43 *Harv. L. Rev.* 993 (1930).

37

Exemption Application Process

Under the law of federal income taxation in the United States, every element of gross income received by a person, corporate or individual, is subject to tax[1] unless there is a statutory provision that exempts from tax either that person or element. Thus, the U.S. Supreme Court has said that "[t]he starting point in the determination of the scope of 'gross income' is the cardinal principle that Congress in creating the income tax intended 'to use the full measure of its taxing power.' "[2]

For nonprofit organizations desiring federal tax exemption, the requisite statutory exemption provision generally will be Code § 501(a).

An organization is not exempt from tax merely because it is not organized and operated for profit. Organizations are formally tax-exempt where they meet the requirements of the particular statutory provision.[3] However, in order for an organization to secure recognition of its tax exemption as a "charitable" entity, the organization claiming the exemption must file an application for recognition of the exemption with the IRS. As a general rule, an organization desiring tax-exempt status pursuant to any other provision of federal tax law should (but is not required to) secure an IRS ruling to that effect.

Subject only to the authority in the IRS to revoke a ruling for good cause (for example, a change in the law), an organization that has been recognized by the Service as being tax-exempt can rely on the determination as long as there are no substantial changes in its character, purposes, or methods of operation.[4] Upon the occurrence of any such changes, the organization should notify the IRS and obtain a reevaluation of its tax status.

The IRS cannot "grant" tax exemption to an organization nor does it "revoke"

---

[1]Code § 61(a).

[2]*Commissioner* v. *Kowalski*, 434 U.S. 77, 82 (1977), quoting from *Helvering* v. *Clifford*, 309 U.S. 331, 334 (1940).

[3]For the most part, a subsection of Code § 501(c).

[4]Reg. §§ 1.501(a)-1(a)(2), 601.201(n)(3)(ii).

tax exemption of an organization. Whether an organization is entitled to tax exemption, on an initial or continuing basis, is a matter of law. Thus, it is Congress that defines the categories of organizations that are eligible for tax exemption[5] and it is Congress that decides whether an exemption should be continued.[6] Rather, the function of the IRS in this regard is to "recognize" tax exemption. Consequently, when an organization makes application to the Service for a ruling or determination as to tax-exempt status, it is requesting the IRS to recognize its tax exemption, not to grant tax exemption. Similarly, the IRS may determine that an organization is no longer entitled to tax exemption and act to revoke its prior recognition of exempt status.[7]

§ 37.1   Application Procedure

The IRS has promulgated specific rules by which a ruling or determination letter[8] may be issued to an organization in response to the filing of an application for recognition of its tax-exempt status. These rules are in addition to those concerning requests for rulings or determination letters generally.[9]

The procedures for filing applications for recognition of exemption generally discussed herein[10] are those that apply to most charitable and like organizations.[11] Such an organization seeking recognition of tax-exempt status[12] must file an application with the IRS key district director in the district in which the

[5]See, e.g., *HCSC-Laundry* v. *United States*, 450 U.S. 1 (1981).

[6]See, e.g., *Maryland Savings-Share Insurance Corp.* v. *United States*, 400 U.S. 4 (1970).

[7]See § 2, *infra*.

[8]A "ruling" is a letter issued by the National Office of the IRS. A "determination letter" is a letter issued by a key district director, or an appeals office in the case of an application for recognition of exemption, in response to a written inquiry by an individual or an organization that applies to the particular facts involved, and to the principles and precedents previously announced by the National Office, including a letter issued on the basis of advice secured from the National Office. Rev. Proc. 80-25, 1980-1 C. B. 667, § 3.02.

[9]See Rev. Proc. 80-24, 1980-1 C. B. 658.

[10]Rev. Proc. 80-25, *supra*, n. 8, superseding Rev. Proc. 72-4, 1972-1 C. B. 706. Also see Rev. Proc. 72-3, 1972-1 C. B. 698.

[11]The rules of Rev. Proc. 80-25, *supra*, n. 8, apply with regard to tax exemption under Code §§ 501 and 521 (except in instances involving pension, annuity, profit-sharing, and stock bonus plans, in which cases Rev. Proc. 80-30, 1980-1 C. B. 685, superseding Rev. Proc. 72-6, 1972-1 C. B. 710, applies). Also, Rev. Proc. 72-5, 1972-1 C. B. 709, states information on applications for recognition of exemption filed by certain religious and apostolic organizations (see Chapter 8 § 3) and Rev. Proc. 72-50, 1972-2 C. B. 830, states general instructions for issuance of determination letters on the private foundation-public charity status, under Code § 509(a)(3), and of nonexempt charitable trusts described in Code § 4947(a)(1) (see Chapter 33).

[12]This requirement relates to applications for *recognition* of tax-exempt status. As noted, only organizations desiring Code § 501(c)(3) status *must* file exemption applications with the IRS.

principal place of business or principal office of the organization is located. The seventeen key district offices that process applications, the Internal Revenue districts covered by each, and the regional office designations are reproduced as an Appendix.[13]

A ruling or determination letter will be issued to an organization, as long as the application and supporting documents establish that it meets the particular statutory requirements. Any oral representation of additional facts or modification of facts as represented or alleged in the application must be reduced to writing over the signature of an authorized representative of the organization.

In most instances, an organization seeking recognition of tax exemption by the IRS must file a particular form of application. For example, an organization desiring recognition as a charitable entity[14] must file Form 1023 and an organization seeking one of a variety of tax-exempt statuses[15] must file Form 1024.[16]

The exemption application must usually include, *inter alia*, a statement describing the organization's activities,[17] a conformed copy[18] of its articles of organization and bylaws or other code of regulations,[19] and current financial statement(s) showing the assets, liabilities, receipts, and disbursements of the organization.[20]

For a charitable organization, the application for recognition of exemption also requests information concerning its sources of financial support, its fundraising program, the composition of its governing body, its relationship with any other organizations, the nature of its services or products, the basis for imposing any charges for its services or products, its membership (if any), and a variety of other matters.

In addition, the IRS may require other information deemed necessary for proper determination as to whether a particular organization may be eligible for tax exemption.[21]

---

[13]Rev. Proc. 80-25, *supra*, n. 8, superseding Rev. Proc. 7-33, 1976-2 C. B. 655. See Rev. Proc. 80-25 § 4.

[14]That is, an organization described in Code § 501(c)(3).

[15]Those encompassed by Code §§ 501(c)(2),(4),(5),(6),(7),(8),(9),(10),(12),(13),(15),(17), and (19).

[16]Reg. § 1.501(a)-1(a)(3). For some categories of organization, there is no form by which to seek recognition of tax exemption; instead, a qualified representative of the organization makes the request by letter, as is done, for example, in the case of multiemployer pension plan trusts (see Chapter 20 § 22). Ann. 80-163, 1980-52 I.R.B. 50. Forms 1023 and 1024 were revised in 1981. See Ann. 81-145, 1981-39 I.R.B. 14.

[17]See Reg. §§ 1.501(a)-1(b)(1) and 1.501(c)(3)-1(b)(1)(v). Cf. *Draper* v. *Commissioner*, 32 T.C. 545 (1959).

[18]See Rev. Proc. 68-14, 1968-1 C. B. 768.

[19]Reg. § 1.501(a)-1(a)(3).

[20]*Ibid.*

[21]Reg. §§ 1.501(a)-1(b)(2), 601.201(h)(1)(ii),(iii). A Form 1023 must be "substantially completed" before it will be accepted by the IRS and made subject to the declaratory judgment rules of Code § 7428. See Chapter 38 § 6.

The proper preparation of an application for recognition of exemption involves far more than merely filling in the blanks in a government form. It is a process much akin to the preparation of a prospectus in conformance with the federal securities laws requirements, in that every statement made in the application should be carefully considered. The prime objective must be to be accurate; it is essential that all material facts be fully and fairly disclosed. Of course, the determination as to which facts are material and the marshaling of these facts requires judgment. Also, the manner in which the answers are phrased can be extremely significant; in this regard, the exercise is far more one of "art" than "science." The advisor should be able to anticipate the concerns the application may cause the IRS and to see that the application is drawn properly and yet so as to minimize the likelihood of conflict with the Service. Many organizations that are entitled to tax exemption have been denied exemption because inartful phraseologies in the application have enabled the Service to build a case that the organization cannot qualify for exemption. Therefore, as a general rule, the application for recognition of exemption should be regarded as an important legal document and prepared accordingly.

The IRS also expects, where an application for recognition of exemption involves an issue where contrary authorities exist, the organization involved to disclose and distinguish significant contrary authorities.[22] Failure to do so can result in requests for additional information and delay in action on the application.[23]

Tax-exempt status for an organization can be recognized by the IRS in advance of actual operations. The Service will do this where proposed operations can be described in sufficient detail to permit a conclusion that the organization will clearly meet the particular statutory requirements. However, the Service will not accept a mere restatement of purposes or a statement that proposed activities will be in furtherance of the organization's purposes. The organization must fully describe the activities in which it expects to engage, including the standards, criteria, procedures, or other means adopted or planned for carrying out the activities, as well as its anticipated sources of receipts and the nature of contemplated expenditures. Where the organization cannot demonstrate, to the satisfaction of the IRS, that its proposed activities will be exempt, a record of actual operations may be required before a ruling or determination letter will be considered an adverse determination from which administrative appeal rights will be afforded.[24]

If an application for recognition of exemption does not contain the required information, it is likely that the application will be returned to the organization (and not to anyone on any power of attorney) without being considered on its merits.[25] In the case of a charitable organization, where an application is so returned, the IRS will inform the organization of the time within which the

---

[22]See Rev. Proc. 80-24, *supra*, n. 9, § 6.06.

[23]Rev. Proc. 80-25, *supra*, n. 8, § 5.07.

[24]See § 2, *infra*.

[25]Rev. Proc. 80-25, *supra*, n. 8, § 5.

completed application must be resubmitted in order for it to be considered as a timely notice.[26]

A ruling or determination letter recognizing tax exemption will not ordinarily be issued where an issue involving the organization's exempt status is pending in litigation or is under consideration within the IRS.

An application for recognition of exemption may be withdrawn, upon the written request of an authorized representative of the organization, at any time prior to the issuance of the ruling or determination letter. Where an application is withdrawn, it and all supporting documents are retained by the IRS and are not returned to the organization.[27]

As a general rule, an organization acquiring recognition of tax-exempt status will do so by means of the issuance of a determination letter by the appropriate IRS key district director.[28] However, a key district director must refer to the IRS National Office an application that (1) presents questions, the answers to which are not specifically covered by the Internal Revenue Code, the Department of the Treasury regulations, a public IRS ruling, or court opinion or decision published in the *Internal Revenue Bulletin*, or (2) has been specifically reserved by revenue procedures and/or Internal Revenue Manual instructions for National Office handling for purposes of establishing uniformity or centralized control of designated categories of cases. In this instance, the National Office considers the application, issues a ruling directly to the organization, and sends a copy of the ruling to the key district director. In the event of a conclusion unfavorable to the applicant organization, it is informed of the basis for the conclusion and of its right to file a protest with, and for a conference in, the National Office.

If a key district director proposes to recognize tax exemption of an organization to which the National Office had issued a previous contrary ruling or technical advice, the key district director must seek technical advice from the National Office before issuing the determination letter.[29]

If, during the course of consideration of an exemption application, an organization believes that its case involves an issue on which there is no published precedent or there is nonuniformity between districts, the organization should ask the key district director involved to request technical advice from the National Office.[30]

As regards most categories of tax-exempt organizations, the Exempt Organizations Division in the IRS National Office reviews key district determination

---

[26]See §§ 4 and 5, *infra.*

[27]Rev. Proc. 80-25, *supra*, n. 8, § 7.01.

[28]See Reg. § 601.201(n)(2)(i).

[29]The procedures by which technical advice regarding tax-exempt organizations is requested and furnished are stated at Rev. Proc. 80-26, 1980-1 C. B. 671. Pursuant to these procedures, the right to seek technical advice from the IRS National Office has been expanded to include requests from both district and appeals offices, and, in certain instances, is now mandatory. Also see Rev. Proc. 83-2, 1983-1 I.R.B. 28.

[30]Rev. Proc. 80-25, *supra*, n. 8, § 6.

letters after issuance to assure uniformity in application of the Internal Revenue Code, regulations, rulings, opinions, or court decisions published in the *Internal Revenue Bulletin*.[31] Where the National Office takes exception to a key district determination letter, the key district director is advised. If the organization protests the exception taken, the file and protest will be returned to the National Office, with the referral treated as a request for technical advice.[32]

A ruling or determination letter recognizing tax exemption is usually effective as of the date of formation of the organization if its purposes and activities during the period prior to the date of the ruling or determination letter were consistent with the requirements for exemption.[33] If the organization is required to alter its activities or to make substantive amendments to its enabling instruments, the ruling or determination letter recognizing its tax-exempt status will be effective as of the date specified therein.[34]

The application forms contain general instructions for making the application. Reference may also be made to IRS Publication No. 557 entitled "How to Apply for Recognition of Exemption for an Organization."

An organization seeking a ruling as to recognition of its tax-exempt status has the burden of proving that it satisfies all the requirements of the particular exemption statute.[35]

The IRS, generally supported by the courts, usually will refuse to recognize an organization's tax-exempt status unless the entity tenders sufficient information to the government regarding its operations and finances.[36] A 1982 case illustrates the point that an organization is to be denied tax-exempt status where it cannot or will not sufficiently explain how it will operate in furtherance of tax-exempt purposes. An organization submitted an application for recognition of exemption, stating its "long-range plan" to form a "traditional Catholic School." The organization lacked students, faculty, facilities, state school charter, or any assets or liabilities; it was unable to substantively respond to any of the requests from the IRS for additional information. The court agreed with the IRS, holding that the organization "has failed to supply such information as would enable a conclusion that when operational, if ever, petitioner will conduct all of its activities in a manner which will accomplish its exempt purposes."[37] The court chided the entity for having only "vague generalizations" of its ostensibly planned activities and strongly suggested the organization had "no plan to operate a

---

[31]In instances involving farmers' cooperatives (see Chapter 20 § 16), this function is performed by the Corporate Tax Division in the IRS National Office.

[32]Rev. Proc. 80-25, *supra*, n. 8, § 8.

[33]For special rules regarding organizations formed after October 9, 1969, see §§ 4 and 5, *infra*.

[34]Rev. Proc. 80-25, *supra*, n. 8, § 12.01.

[35]See, e.g., *Harding Hospital, Inc.* v. *United States*, 505 F.2d 1068 (6th Cir. 1974).

[36]See, e.g., *The Basic Unit Ministry of Alma Karl Schurig* v. *United States*, 511 F. Supp. 166 (D.D.C. 1981).

[37]*Pius XII Academy, Inc.* v. *Commissioner*, 43 T.C.M. 634 (1982).

school in the foreseeable future." Indeed, the tenor of the opinion is that the court believed that the principal purpose underlying establishment of the organization is to secure a license to conduct bingo games.

Generally, until ruled exempt, an ostensibly "charitable" organization is considered a taxable entity and may be required to file one or more corporate tax returns (Form 1120).[38]

§ 37.2   Procedure where Determination is Adverse

The filing of an application for recognition of exemption with the IRS can, of course, lead to the issuance of an adverse determination. In this instance, or in the case of the issuance of a letter proposing revocation or modification of tax-exempt status,[39] the key district director involved will advise the organization of its right to protest the determination by requesting appeals office consideration.[40] Each of the appeals offices is under the direction of a Regional Director of Appeals, who reports directly to the Regional Commissioner. To initiate an appeal, the organization must submit to the key district director, within 30 days from the date of the letter, a statement of the facts, law, and arguments in support of its position. At this time, the organization must also state whether it wishes an appeals office conference.

Upon receipt of an organization's request for appeals office consideration, the key district person with responsibility for the case will (assuming the key district director maintains his or her position) forward the request and case file to the chief of the appropriate appeals office. However, any determination letter that is issued on the basis of IRS National Office technical advice may not be appealed to an appeals office as regards issues that were the subject of the technical advice.

The appeals office, after considering the organization's protest and any additional information developed in conference, will advise the organization of its decision and issue the appropriate determination letter to the organization.

An organization is expected to make full presentation of the facts, circumstances, and arguments at the initial level of consideration by the appeals office, since submission of additional facts, circumstances, and arguments may result in suspension of appeal procedures and referral of the case back to the key district for additional consideration. Any oral representation of additional facts or modification of facts originally represented or alleged must be reduced to writing.

If an appeals office believes that an exemption or private foundation status issue is not covered by published precedent or that there is nonuniformity,

---

[38]Reg. § 1.6012-2. In general, see Buratt, "Procedures for Securing Tax Exemption for Exempt Organizations," 34 *N.Y.U. Inst. Fed. Tax.* 181 (1976).

[39]See Reg. § 601.201(n)(6).

[40]The procedural rules concerning the protest of adverse determination letters are contained in Rev. Proc. 80-25, *supra*, n. 8.

the appeals office must request technical advice from the IRS National Office. Unless the appeals office believes that the conclusions reached by the National Office should be reconsidered and promptly requests the reconsideration, the case will be disposed of by the appeals office on the basis of the decision in the technical advice memorandum.

If at any time during the course of appeals office consideration, the organization believes that its case involves an issue as to which there is no published precedent or there is nonuniformity between districts, the organization should ask the appeals office to request technical advice from the National Office.[41]

If the proposed disposition by the appeals office is contrary to a prior National Office technical advice or ruling concerning tax exemption, the proposed disposition will be submitted through the Office of the Regional Director of Appeals to, in the case of charitable organizations, the Assistant Commissioner (Employee Plans and Exempt Organizations) or, in the case of farmers' cooperatives, the Assistant Commissioner (Technical).[42] Unless the appeals office believes that the conclusions reached by the National Office should be reconsidered and promptly requests that consideration, the decision of the National Office must be followed by the appeals office.[43] In any event, it is clear that the appropriate Assistant Commissioner will make the final decision.[44]

Once the IRS has acted to revoke recognition of the tax exemption of an organization, it will expect the entity to begin paying income taxes. Should the organization not do so, however, the IRS may be expected to commence proceedings to assess and collect the tax due. This activity is commenced by the mailing to the organization of a "statutory notice of deficiency." This the IRS is authorized to do following a determination that there is a tax deficiency.[45] However, because there cannot be general income tax liability for a tax-exempt organization, it is essential to the government's efforts to collect the tax that the statutory notice of deficiency be preceded by a valid letter of revocation. To have such a letter, the IRS is required to act in conformance with certain procedures[46] and at least generally apprise the organization of the basis for the revocation. However, the revocation itself must be in conformance with all requirements of law, so that if, for example, the grounds upon which the

[41]See Reg. §§ 601.201(n)(2)(iv) and 601.201(n)(9).

[42]See Reg. § 601.201(n)(5)(iii). In general, see Rev. Proc. 80-21, 1980-1 C.B. 646, mod. and clar. by Rev. Proc. 81-33, 1981-2 C.B. 564.

[43]These procedures became effective in 1978. Earlier, an organization could appeal an adverse decision (by the assistant regional commissioner affirming the key district director) to the IRS National Office. However, when these procedures were adopted, this "certiorari" appeal was eliminated. See, e.g., Webster, "Changes Possible in Way IRS Reviews Tax-Exempt Determination Cases," 30 *Association Management* 16 (July 1978).

[44]In general, see "New Procedures to Resolve Tax Disputes," remarks by the then-Commissioner of the IRS, reproduced at BNA *Daily Report for Executives* (No. 183), J-5 (Sept. 20, 1978).

[45]Code § 6212.

[46]Internal Revenue Manual § 7(10)(12).

revocation is based were erroneous, the revocation is not proper.[47] Likewise, if the letter of revocation was prompted by political or similar considerations that demonstrate lack of objectivity at the IRS, the revocation becomes null and void.[48] Thus, a letter of revocation can be shown to be void *ab initio* because of the considerations governing its issuance. Also, subsequent actions by the IRS indicating a continuing recognition of tax-exempt status can operate to make a prior revocation of recognition nugatory. In either event, the letter of revocation is not valid, so that the tax exemption has not been properly revoked, meaning that any notice of deficiency based upon the letter of revocation is of no force and effect.

Still other procedures have been promulgated for appeals from the attempted imposition of certain taxes on most tax-exempt organizations[49] and on certain individuals under the private foundation rules.[50] These taxes are (1) the excise taxes imposed by the federal tax law pertaining to private foundations,[51] (2) the unrelated income tax,[52] (3) the private foundation termination tax,[53] (4) the political activities tax,[54] (5) the tax on farmers' cooperatives,[55] (6) the tax on taxable private foundations,[56] and (7) the tax[57] on charitable and split-interest trusts.[58]

§ 37.3 Group Exemption

A subordinate organization (such as a chapter, local, post, or unit) that is affiliated with and is subject to the general supervision or control of a central organization (usually, a state, regional, or national organization) may be recognized as an exempt organization solely by reason of its relationship with the parent organization. Tax-exempt status acquired in this manner is referred to as tax exemption on a "group basis." The advantage of the group exemption is that each of the subordinate organizations covered by a group exemption letter is relieved from filing its own application for recognition of tax exemption.

The procedures by which a group exemption may be recognized by the IRS[59]

---

[47]See *A. Duda & Sons Cooperative Assn v. United States*, 504 F.2d 970, 975 (5th Cir. 1974).

[48]See *Center on Corporate Responsibility, Inc. v. Shultz*, 368 F. Supp. 863, 871–873 (D.D.C. 1973).

[49]Those described in Code §§ 501 or 521.

[50]Rev. Proc. 80-25, *supra*, n. 8.

[51]See Chapters 25–29.

[52]See Chapter 40.

[53]See Chapter 32.

[54]See Chapter 20 § 18.

[55]See Chapter 20 § 16.

[56]Code § 11.

[57]Code § 641.

[58]See Chapter 33.

[59]Rev. Proc. 80-27, 1980-1 C. B. 677. Also Reg. § 601.201(n)(7).

contemplate a functioning of the parent organization as an agent of the IRS, requiring that the parent organization responsibly and independently evaluate the tax-exempt status of its subordinate organizations from the standpoint of the organizational and operational tests applicable to them. A parent organization is required to record with the IRS on an annual basis its qualifying exempt subordinate organizations; such a listing amounts to an attestation by the central organization that the subordinate organizations qualify as tax-exempt organizations so that the IRS need not carry out an independent evaluation as to the tax-exempt status of the organizations. Therefore, it is essential that the central organization, in performing this agency function, exercise responsibility in evaluating the tax status of its subordinates.

Assuming that the general requirements for recognition of tax-exempt status[60] are satisfied, a group exemption letter will be issued to a central organization where (1) the above requirements as to subordinate organizations are met, (2) the exemption to be recognized is under the general exemption rules,[61] and (3) each of the subordinate organizations has an organizing document (although they do not have to be incorporated). If a subordinate organization is a private foundation, it may not be included in a group exemption letter. Further, a subordinate that is organized and operated in a foreign country may not be included in a group exemption letter.

Thus, a central organization applying for a group exemption letter must first obtain recognition of its own tax-exempt status and establish that all of the subordinate organizations to be included in the group exemption letter are (1) affiliated with it, (2) subject to its general supervision or control, (3) exempt under the same paragraph of the general exemption rules (although not necessarily the section under which the central organization is tax-exempt), (4) not private foundations, (5) on the same accounting period as the central organization if they are not to be included in group returns, and (6) formed within the 15-month period prior to the date of submission of the group exemption application (assuming this is the case and these entities are claiming "charitable" status and are subject to the requirements for application for recognition of tax exemption).[62] For example, as respects this third requirement, a central organization may be tax-exempt as a "charitable" entity with all of the subordinates thereof exempt as social welfare organizations. Concerning the sixth requirement, the procedures state that if one or more of the subordinates have not been organized within the fifteen-month period, the group exemption letter will be issued only if all of the subordinates agree to be recognized as tax-exempt from the date of the application rather than the date of their creation.

Each subordinate organization must authorize, in writing, the central organization to include it in the application for the group exemption letter.

---

[60]See Rev. Proc. 80-25, *supra*, n. 8.

[61]Code § 501(c). Thus, the group exemption procedures are unavailable to organizations described in Code §§ 521, 527, and 528.

[62]See § 6, *infra*.

A central organization may be involved in more than one group exemption arrangement, such as a "charitable" parent organization having both "charitable" and social welfare/civic organization subordinates. Also, a central organization may be a subordinate organization with respect to another central organization, such as a state organization that has subordinate units and is itself affiliated with a national organization.

An instrumentality or agency of a political subdivision that exercises control or supervision over a number of organizations similar in purposes and operations, each of which may qualify for tax exemption under the same category of exempt organizations, may obtain a group exemption letter covering the organizations in the same manner as a central organization. In this manner, the group exemption for organizations such as federal credit unions, state chartered credit unions, and federal land bank associations may be established.[63]

A central organization must submit to the appropriate IRS key district office, in addition to certain information about itself, the following information on behalf of its group exemption subordinates: (1) a letter signed by a principal officer of the central organization setting forth or including as attachments (a) information verifying the existence of the foregoing six relationships and requirements, (b) a detailed description of the principal purposes and activities of the subordinates, including financial information, (c) a sample copy of a uniform or representative governing instrument adopted by the subordinates, (d) an affirmation that, to the best of the officer's knowledge, the subordinates are operating in accordance with the stated purposes, (e) a statement that each subordinate to be included within the group exemption letter has furnished the requisite written authorization, (f) a list of subordinates to be included in the group exemption letter to which the IRS has issued an outstanding ruling or determination letter relating to exemption, and (g), if relevant, an affirmation that no subordinate organization is a private foundation, and (2) a list of the names, addresses, and employer identification numbers of subordinates to be included in the group exemption letter (or, in lieu thereof, a satisfactory directory of subordinates). Certain additional information is required if a subordinate is claiming tax-exempt status as a school.

Once a group exemption letter is issued,[64] certain information must be submitted annually by the central organization (at least 90 days before the close of its annual accounting period) to the IRS so as to maintain the letter. This information consists of (1) information regarding any changes in the purposes, character, or method of operation of the subordinates, (2) lists of (a) subordinates that have changed their names or addresses during the year, (b) subordinates no longer to be included in the group exemption letter (for whatever reason), and (c) subordinates to be added to the group exemption letter (for whatever reason), and (3) the information summarized in the foregoing paragraph (items

---

[63]For a discussion of these organizations, see Chapter 20 §§ 1, 10, and 22.
[64]See Chapter 6 § 9.

(1)(a) through (g)) with respect to subordinates to be added to the group exemption letter.

There are two ways in which a group exemption letter may be terminated. When a termination occurs, the tax-exempt status of the subordinate organizations is no longer recognized by the IRS, thereby requiring (where continuing recognition of exempt status is required or desired) each subordinate to file an application for recognition of exemption, the central organization to file for a new group exemption letter, or the subordinates (or a portion thereof) to become exempt by reason of their status with respect to another qualifying central organization. Termination of a group exemption letter will be occasioned where (1) the central organization dissolves or otherwise ceases to exist, (2) one or more of the subordinates fail to fulfill the qualification requirements, or (3) the central organization fails to qualify for tax exemption, to submit the information required to obtain such a letter, to file the annual information return or to otherwise comply with the reporting requirements.[65]

Of course, if the IRS revokes the tax-exempt status of the central organization, the group exemption letter involved is also revoked, thereby simultaneously revoking the exempt status of all of the subordinates. To reobtain recognition of exemption in such case, each subordinate would have to file an exemption application or a new group exemption would have to be applied for.

Where a subordinate organization has an outstanding ruling of tax exemption and becomes included in a group exemption letter, the prior exemption letter is superseded.[66] The central organization, in such a circumstance, is obligated to notify the affected subordinate organization(s) of this supersession.

Where the subordinates are "charitable" organizations, their public charity status must be considered. Oddly, the IRS pronouncements with regard to the group exemption do not address this point except to require that they be public charities. However, judging from the standard paragraphs promulgated by the National Office for use by key district offices in issuing group exemption letters, the IRS may contemplate that all subordinates must have the same public charity classification.

If this is in fact the policy of the IRS, it seems unduly narrow and may cause an otherwise qualifying group exemption to be withheld or terminated. The theory underlying such a policy presumably would be that the subordinates of a central organization are mere components of the parent and partake of all of its characteristics, including (where applicable) its public charity classification. However, since the central organization can be tax-exempt under a different paragraph of the general exemption rules than are the subordinates, then so too should the central organization be able to have a public charity designation different from that of the subordinates. For example, a publicly supported organization should be able to have qualifying subordinates that are supporting

[65]Code §§ 6001, 6033.
[66]See Exempt Organizations Handbook, Chapters (54)00 and 200 (as modified by Manual Supplement, dated May 24, 1976).

entities. Likewise, as among the subordinates, there is no reason why, for example, some of them could not have status as a publicly supported organization under the rules for "Type I" entities and some under the rules for "Type II" entities.[67]

Nonetheless, the answer to this question remains unknown. The form group exemption letter used by the IRS (at least the Mid-Atlantic Region) requests only a statement from the central organization that "none of the subordinates are private foundations as defined in section 509(a) of the Code."

§ 37.4   Organizations with "Tax-Exempt" Integral Components

Many tax-exempt organizations have component entities that, while they may appear to the outside world to be separate organizations, are not, in law, separate but are instead "integral parts" of the larger organization. For example, a university may have scholarship funds, a hospital may have research funds, and a charity may have an endowment fund; these "funds" may have separate names and may be recipients of contributions made in these names. These component entities may be little more than one of several accounts carried on an exempt organization's financial records. By analogy to the terminology of for-profit organizations, these component entities are akin to "divisions" (as is the case with the "schools" of a university or the "departments" of a hospital), while by contrast the organizations that are tax-exempt by reason of the group exemption procedures[68] are comparable to a for-profit organization's "subsidiaries." The principal distinction from a tax standpoint is that the entity that is an "integral part" of a tax-exempt organization is itself tax-exempt solely by virtue of the larger organization's tax status, without the need for any application for recognition of tax exemption, whether on an individual or group basis.[69]

An organization may be viewed as a composite of integrated parts—being

---

[67]See Chapter 22.

[68]See § 3 hereof, *supra.*

[69]This assumes that the attributes of such a component entity do not cause it to become considered a separate organization, although an entity with the minimal characteristics of an "organization" for tax purposes is not thereby precluded from qualifying as an integral part of another organization. In this regard, the chief attribute of an entity that is an integral part of an organization is that it is unincorporated—inasmuch as it is conceptually impossible for a corporation to be an "integral part" of another organization, whether the latter organization is incorporated or not. However, one IRS ruling suggests that a set of "activities" may be an integral part of a larger set of activities, rather than one organization being an integral part of another—an approach that may enable the activities of one corporate entity to be regarded as an integral part of the activities of another corporate entity. Rev. Rul. 81-19, 1981-1 C.B. 353. In general, see Chapter 36 § 1. Where the entity is a separate organization, tax exemption may be available (as noted in n. 68, *supra*) under the group exemption procedures and/or public charity classification may be available as a "supporting organization" (Chapter 22 § 3).

"composed of constituent parts making a whole."[70] In comparable instances, the law regards an item of property as an "integral part" of a larger property or process, such as a telephone set being an integral part of a telephone system for purposes of telephone rate regulations,[71] bottles and cartons being an integral part of manufactured beer for purposes of use tax exemptions,[72] and executed contracts being an integral part of a baseball team for purposes of defining the team's "raw materials."[73] Although the concept is infrequently recognized in the law of tax-exempt organizations, some recent examples include recognition of a high school as an integral part of a county high school system,[74] a vending machine management organization as an integral part of a university,[75] and schools that do not have a separate legal existence (i.e., are not incorporated) as an integral part of a church or a convention or association of churches.[76]

It has been held that a principal element leading to a finding that one organization functions as an integral part of another organization is the fact that the function of the integrated organization is "essential" to the operation of the larger organization, and is an "ordinary and proper" function of the larger organization.[77] While this may be the case in general, in the tax-exempt organizations context it is largely an irrelevant criterion, inasmuch as the decision as to whether to establish the putative integrated organization will nearly always be that of the larger organization.

Thus, the use of the integral part doctrine can be an efficient manner in which to acquire tax exemption for an organization, being a considerably speedier approach than the conventional exemption application process and even more rapid than the group exemption approach.

---

[70]*Application of Larson*, 340 F.2d 965, 967 (U.S. Ct. Cust. Pat. App. 1965).

[71]*New York Telephone Co.* v. *Maltbie*, 288 N.Y.S. 71 (Sup. Ct. N.Y. 1936).

[72]*Zoller Brewing Co.* v. *State Tax Commission*, 5 N.W. 2d 643 (Sup. Ct. Ia. 1942).

[73]*Hollywood Baseball Assn.* v. *Commissioner*, 423 F.2d 494 (9th Cir. 1970), cert. den., 400 U.S. 848 (1970).

[74]*Nellie Callahan Scholarship Fund* v. *Commissioner*, 73 T.C. 626 (1980).

[75]Rev. Rul. 81-19, *supra*, n. 69. In this ruling, the IRS harked back to a 1958 ruling holding that an organization operating a book and supply store and a cafeteria and restaurant on the campus of a university for the convenience of the student body and faculty qualified as a charitable and/or educational organization (Rev. Rul. 58-194, 1958-1 C. B. 240) and observed that because the organization "is performing functions for their [students and faculty] benefit and convenience and in furtherance of the university's educational program, it is for all intents and purposes an integral part of the university."

[76]*St. Martin Evangelical Lutheran Church* v. *South Dakota*, 451 U.S. 772 (1981).

[77]E.g., *Schwarz* v. *United States*, 284 F. Supp. 792, 797 (U.S. Customs Ct. 1968); also *Matczak* v. *Secretary of Health, Education and Welfare*, 299 F. Supp. 409 (E.D.N.Y. 1969).

§ 37.5   Special Rules for Charitable Organizations

An organization established after October 9, 1969, which desires status as a "charitable" organization[78] as of the date of its establishment, must notify the IRS that it is applying for recognition of exemption on that basis within 15 months from the end of the month in which it was organized.[79] This notice requirement does not apply to churches, their integrated auxiliaries, interchurch organizations, local units of a church, and conventions or associations of churches, or to any organization which is not a private foundation[80] and the gross receipts of which in each tax year are normally not more than $5,000.[81] Also, the notice requirement is inapplicable to subordinate organizations covered by a group exemption letter as long as the central organization has submitted a notice covering the subordinates. The IRS is authorized to exempt from the notice requirement operating educational institutions and any other class of organizations as to which full compliance with the requirement is not necessary to the efficient administration of the private foundation rules.[82]

The exception in the notification rules for organizations with gross receipts that are normally under $5,000 can operate to relieve an organization from the requirement of filing an application for recognition of exemption during the initial years of its operation but expire as the organization begins to receive greater amounts of financial support. Such an organization, to be assured of status as a charitable entity (assuming it otherwise continues to qualify) throughout its existence, must timely ascertain when to file the application.

The gross receipts of an organization are normally not more than $5,000 if (1) during its first tax year, it received gross receipts of no more than $7,500, (2) during its first two tax years, it received gross receipts of no more than $12,000, and (3) in the case of an organization that has been in existence for three tax years, the gross receipts received by it during its immediately preceding two tax years plus the current year are not more than $15,000. Once an organization fails to meet the foregoing rules for its formative years, it is required to file the notice (application for recognition of exemption) within 90 days after the end of the tax year(s) in which its gross receipts exceeded the amounts permitted under the exemption. Thus, this threshold period is used instead of the general 15-month period.[83]

---

[78]That is, one described in Code § 501(c)(3).

[79]Code § 508(a), Reg. § 1.508-1(a)(2)(i). See, e.g., *Peek* v. *Commissioner*, 73 T.C. 912 (1980). However, an organization that qualifies for tax exemption under Code § 501(c)(3) but files for exemption after the fifteen-month period usually can acquire tax exemption as a social welfare organization (see Chapters 15 and 16) for the period commencing as of the date of its inception to the date the Code § 501(c)(3) exemption becomes effective. See Rev. Rul. 80-108, 1980-1 C. B. 119.

[80]See Chapter 22.

[81]Code § 508(c)(1).

[82]Code § 508(c)(2). See Reg. § 1.508-1.

[83]Reg. § 1.508-1(a)(3)(ii).

In one instance, a charitable organization (not a private foundation) that was formed on January 1, 1973, and is on the calendar year basis, filed, on March 1, 1979, an application for recognition of tax-exempt status as a charitable entity. Its gross receipts during its initial years were as follows:

Taxable Year Ending	Gross Receipts
1973	$ 3,600
1974	2,900
1975	400
1976	12,600
1977	76,400
1978	96,200
1979	142,400

Because the organization's aggregate gross receipts during 1973, 1974, and 1975 were $6,900, it was not required to file the application within 90 days after the close of 1975. Therefore, the organization is tax-exempt as a charity through 1975. However, inasmuch as the aggregate gross receipts of the organization during 1974, 1975, and 1976 totaled $15,900, the exception is not available and it should have filed the application within 90 days after the close of 1976. Consequently, the organization is not tax-exempt as a charity during the period January 1, 1976, through February 28, 1979.[84]

In another instance, a charitable organization (also not a private foundation) that was formed on January 1, 1977, and is on the calendar year basis, filed, on April 1, 1979, an application for recognition of tax-exempt status as a charitable entity. For 1977, its gross receipts were less than $7,500 but its aggregate gross receipts for 1977 and 1978 exceeded $12,000. Under these circumstances, the organization was required to file the application within 90 days after the close of 1978. Consequently, the organization is not tax exempt as a charitable entity during the period January 1, 1977, through March 31, 1979.[85]

In general, if any return, claim, statement, or other document is required to be filed before a specified date, and the document is delivered by United States mail after such date to the agency, officer, or office with which the document is required to be filed, it shall be deemed to have been filed on or before that date if the U.S. postmark stamped on the envelope or other cover in which the document is mailed is dated on or before the date prescribed for

[84]Rev. Rul. 80-259, 1980-2 C. B. 192. In this ruling, the IRS states that it "will give consideration" to application of its discretionary authority (under Reg. § 1.9100-1) to extend the time for satisfying the Code § 508(a) notice requirement. See Rev. Proc. 79-63, 1979-2 C. B. 578; Rev. Proc. 80-24, *supra*, n. 9, § 3.02. The Application for Recognition of Exemption under Code § 501(c)(3) (Form 1023) was revised in 1981 to provide for a request for such relief (see Part III, question 13(c) and (d)). Ann. 81-145, 1981-39 I.R.B. 14.

[85]Rev. Rul. 81-177, 1981-2 C. B. 132.

filing.[86] On the basis of this rule, the IRS has ruled that the date of notice for purposes of these rules is the date of the U.S. postmark stamped on the cover in which the exemption application is mailed or, in the absence of a postmark, the date of notice is the date the application is stamped as received by the IRS.[87]

Where the Service recognizes the tax exemption which is the subject of a timely filing, the exemption will be effective as of the date the organization was created. In determining the date on which a corporation is organized, the IRS looks to the date the corporation comes into existence under the law of the state in which it is incorporated, which is usually the date its articles of incorporation were filed in the appropriate state office.[88] The date is not the date the organizational meeting was held, bylaws adopted, or actual operations began. Once notice is given after the pertinent date, the exemption (if recognized) and the organization's ability to attract deductible charitable contributions will only operate prospectively.[89] A timely filed application for recognition of tax exemption will satisfy both the notice and proof-of-status requirements (see below).

§ 37.6 Private Foundation Status

Generally, every "charitable" organization (would-be or otherwise), regardless of when created, must timely notify the IRS that it is not a private foundation (if that is the case) or else be presumed a private foundation.[90] The time for the giving of the notice is the same as for the notice requirement with respect to tax exemption and the same exceptions (see above) also apply.

However, this presumption is rebuttable. Thus, an organization which in fact is not a private foundation but fails to timely file a notice for that purpose may nonetheless be recognized by the IRS as a nonprivate foundation. The organization must establish that status by submitting a request for a determination letter to that effect to the appropriate district director.[91]

In one instance, a charitable corporation (organized after October 9, 1969, and not exempt from the notice requirements) did not apply for recognition of exemption until after the expiration of the fifteen-month deadline. The application of this organization, in which it claimed private foundation status, was subsequently approved. However, since the organization cannot be treated as a charitable corporation until the date of its application, it cannot be classified

---

[86]Code § 7502(a)(1).
[87]Rev. Rul. 77-114, 1977-1 C. B. 152.
[88]Rev. Rul. 75-290, 1975-2 C. B. 215.
[89]Code §§ 508(a)(2), 508(d)(2)(B); Reg. § 1.508-2.
[90]Code § 508(b).
[91]Rev. Rul. 73-504, 1973-2 C. B. 190.

as a private foundation until that date.[92] The same result obtains as respects applications for public charity status.[93]

Therefore, an organization (not exempt from the notice requirements) that has had no financial support and that filed its notice after expiration of the fifteen-month period can obtain an advance ruling that it is a publicly supported charitable organization as of the date it acquires its tax exemption.[94]

Charitable organizations established prior to 1969 should have given notice of nonprivate foundation status on Form 4653. Organizations applying for exemption as "charitable" entities after 1969 claim nonprivate foundation status in Parts IV and VII of the application for recognition of tax exemption.[95]

The IRS has promulgated rules with respect to (1) the issuance of rulings and determination letters as to private foundation status and private operating foundation status, and (2) revocations, modifications, and reconsiderations of rulings and determination letters.[96] Thereunder, key district directors are authorized to issue determination letters as to private foundation status, subject to the protest and conference procedures.[97]

As to private foundation status, the IRS (assuming a favorable determination) will issue a "definitive" or "advance" ruling. A definitive ruling is a permanent determination, absent a material change in the facts or the law. However, a newly created organization deemed tax-exempt as a "charitable" entity and seeking nonprivate foundation status as a publicly supported organization is entitled to only an advance ruling where the first tax year is less than eight months (assuming the organization can reasonably be expected to meet the appropriate requirements).[98] An advance ruling must be requested by an organization as to its status as a publicly supported entity where it has an advance ruling period of two tax years or three tax years if its first tax year is less than eight months.[99] (These rules contemplate eight full months.) However, where

[92]Rev. Rul. 77-207, 1977-1 C. B. 152.
[93]Rev. Rul. 77-208, 1977-1 C. B. 153. Similarly, the services performed by employees of an organization are not entitled to the FICA and FUTA exemptions available to services for Code § 501(c)(3) entities until this notice is given by the organization. Rev. Rul. 76-262, 1976-2 C. B. 310.
[94]Rev. Rul. 80-113, 1980-1 C. B. 58.
[95]See Sugarman, "New procedures available for establishing foundation status," 33 J. Tax. 236 (1970). Rev. Proc. 72-50, supra, n. 11, states procedures to be used by nonexempt charitable trusts described in Code § 4947(a)(1) (see Chapter 33) to obtain determinations of their status under Code § 509(a)(3) (see Chapter 22). As to the administrative procedures for change in tax-exempt organizations' annual accounting periods, see Rev. Proc. 76-9, 1976-1 C. B. 547, as modified by Rev. Proc. 79-2, 1979-1 C. B. 482, and Rev. Proc. 76-10, 1976-1 C. B. 548, as modified by Rev. Proc. 79-3, 1979-1 C. B. 483.
[96]Rev. Proc. 76-34, 1976-2 C. B. 656, as modified by Rev. Proc. 80-25, supra, n. 8.
[97]See § 2, infra.
[98]Reg. §§ 1.170A-9(e)(5)(i); 1.509(a)-3(d)(1).
[99]See Rev. Rul. 77-407, 1977-2 C. B. 77; Rev. Rul. 76-27, 1976-1 C. B. 64; Rev. Rul. 75-211, 1975-1 C. B. 86; Rev. Rul. 74-487, 1974-2 C. B. 82.

an incorporated "charitable" organization is claiming qualification as a publicly supported entity, and it is the successor to an unincorporated organization and incorporation was the only significant change in the organization, the period of time that the predecessor organization has operated may be taken into consideration in determining qualification under the time requirements[100] of the rules concerning publicly supported charity classification.[101] At the close of the advance ruling period, the IRS will determine if the organization has met the statutory tests for publicly supported organizations from its history of operations during the period (the organization having been treated as a public charity in the interim). An organization may also elect nonprivate foundation treatment for an "extended advance ruling period" consisting of its first five tax years (six, where the first tax year is less than eight months);[102] in this instance, the period of limitations for assessment of the private foundation investment income tax[103] must be extended one year beyond the expiration date of the last tax year within the extended advance ruling period (this is done by the filing of an IRS form[104]).[105]

If an organization, at the end of its advance ruling period, fails to support its claim that it is a publicly supported organization, it can have more time to satisfy the public charity requirements if it requested an extended advance ruling. (Generally, an advance ruling may not be extended in any other manner.) However, a degree of foresight is required in this regard, inasmuch as it is the position of the IRS that a newly created "charitable" organization that wishes to obtain an extended advance ruling must submit a request for the ruling at the *same time* as its request for an initial advance ruling.[106]

An organization that is related to a state college or university[107] is not subject to the foregoing eight-month requirement.[108] Thus, a newly created organization, prior to the close of its first taxable year consisting of at least eight months, may be issued a definitive ruling that it is described in the rules for such related "foundations" if it otherwise meets the statutory requirements and demonstrates that it will "normally" receive a substantial part of its support from contributions from governmental units or the general public.

Although nothing has been written on the point, the IRS takes the position that an organization that has been accorded an advance ruling that it is a publicly supported organization,[109] and that has received no funds during that period,

[100]Reg. §§ 1.170A-9(e)(4)(vi), 1.509(a)-3(c)(1)(iv).
[101]Rev. Rul. 73-422, 1973-2 C. B. 70. But see Rev. Rul. 77-116, 1977-1 C. B. 155, discussed in Chapter 22 §§ 1 and 2, *infra*.
[102]Reg. §§ 1.170A-9(e)(5)(iv), 1.509(a)-3(d)(4).
[103]See Chapter 30.
[104]Form 872-C.
[105]Code § 6501(c)(4).
[106]Rev. Rul. 77-115, 1977-1 C. B. 154.
[107]Code § 170(b)(1)(A)(iv). See Chapter 22 § 1, *supra*.
[108]Rev. Rul. 77-407, *supra*, n. 99.
[109]I.e., an organization described in Code §§ 170(b)(1)(A)(vi) and 509(a)(1), or 509(a)(2).

will automatically be classified as a private foundation until such years as public charity status can be achieved, even where there is great likelihood that the organization will receive the requisite amount of public support during the balance of the first four years of its existence.[110] This can occur, for example, where an organization was formally established (such as by incorporation) but no financial activity occurred until some time during the third year of its existence, and the organization filed its application for recognition of exemption late into the fifteen-month period.[111] As practical matter, however, this problem can be resolved by causing the organization to receive a small amount of funds, as long as the necessary public support is provided. This position of the Service is also followed in cases where some funds are received by an organization but the applicable public support test is not met, even though the organization fully anticipates meeting the test before the first four years of its existence are concluded. The Service's position in this regard appears incorrect, in that the Code specifies a four-year testing period, which means that the IRS lacks the authority to administratively classify an organization as a private foundation on the basis of only two years of experience.[112] At the most, failure of an organization to satisfy a public charity test should only raise a presumption that it is a private foundation.[113]

[110]Such four-year period is that referenced by the term "normally." See Chapter 22 § 3, pp. 395–396.

[111]See § 4, infra.

[112]The concept of the "advance ruling period" is wholly a creation of the IRS rather than being a statutory requirement.

[113]See this section, supra.

38

Maintenance of
Tax-Exempt Status

Basically, once an organization achieves tax-exempt status, that status may be maintained as long as the organization does not materially change its character, purposes, or methods of operation. Of course, an organization's tax status may also be affected by a subsequent change in the law. In addition, a tax-exempt organization may have annual reporting requirements with which it must comply.

§ 38.1 Material Changes

A determination of tax exemption remains operative as long as there are no substantial changes in the organization's character, purposes, or methods of operation.[1] A material change should be communicated to the IRS as soon as possible after the change is made or becomes effective. Other changes should be reflected in due course in the organization's annual information return.[2]

A substantial change may result in modification or revocation of the organization's tax-exempt status.

A change in the law may also afford the IRS a basis for modifying or revoking an organization's tax-exempt status.

Occasionally, the Service attempts to make a revocation of tax exemption operate retroactively. The government's procedural regulations state that a revocation of tax exemption may be retroactive in three instances: where (1)

[1] Reg. § 1.501(a)-1(a)(2). Also see Rev. Proc. 80-25, 1980-1 C. B. 667, § 12-02; Rev. Rul. 68-217, 1968-2 C. B. 260. The IRS may revoke a ruling letter which recognized an organization's tax exemption, without retroactive effect, pursuant to Code § 7805(b), but in such case the organization would be subject to taxation on any unrelated business taxable income (see Chapters 40–42) during the Code § 7805(b) relief period. Rev. Rul. 78-289, 1978-2 C. B. 180.

[2] See § 3 *infra*.

the organization omitted or misstated a material fact in the process of acquiring exemption, (2) the organization operates in a manner materially different from that originally represented, or (3) the organization engaged in a "prohibited transaction."[3] A prohibited transaction is one in which the organization entered into the process of pursuing tax exemption for the purpose of diverting substantial corpus or income from its exempt purpose.[4]

One of the infrequent cases on the point was decided in 1979. A nonprofit organization was recognized as an educational entity, in 1959, because its function is to operate a school. In 1970, when the rules prohibiting schools from maintaining racially discriminatory policies were introduced,[5] the IRS advised the school of its concerns that the school may be engaging in discriminatory practices. In 1976, the Service commenced a revocation procedure, which culminated in loss by the organization of its tax exemption by court order. However, the court upheld revocation retroactively to 1970, inasmuch as the IRS had expressly provided the organization with notice of the law change in that year, rather than to 1959.[6]

Thereafter, the same court upheld a retroactive revocation of tax exemption, effective as of the date the IRS determined that the exempt functions had ceased. The case involved an organization that was granted tax exemption in 1936 as a religious organization engaging in missionary activities, with the exemption upheld in 1953. In 1976, the IRS proposed to revoke the exemption on the grounds that the missionary activities had ceased and were replaced by commercial publishing operations, with the revocation retroactive to 1963, the year in which the exempt functions were determined to have stopped. The court agreed with the IRS and held that the organization failed to meet its burden of showing that the Service's action of retroactive revocation of exemption was erroneous. The IRS had also determined that the organization's records showed drastic increases in salaries and accumulated surplus by 1970 and ordered the filing of tax returns by the organization as of that year; this determination was also upheld by the court.[7]

A comparable line of law holds that the IRS has the power to retroactively revoke a determination if it becomes contrary to law.[8] However, the cases involve situations where the "change in the law" was made by Congress in

---

[3]Reg. § 601.201(n)(6)(i).

[4]Reg. § 601.201(n)(6)(vii); Rev. Proc. 80-25, *supra*, n. 1, § 13.01.

[5]See Chap. 6 § 9.

[6]*Prince Edward School Foundation v. United States*, 80-1 U.S.T.C. ¶ 9295 (D.D.C. 1979).

[7]*The Incorporated Trustees of the Gospel Worker Society v. United States*, 510 F. Supp. 374 (D.D.C. 1981), aff'd 672 F.2d 894 (D.C. Cir. 1981).

[8]This authority is predicated upon the authority of the IRS to apply withdrawal of an acquiescence retroactively. E.g., *Dixon v. United States*, 381 U.S. 68 (1965).

revising the statute.[9] Also, retroactivity of tax exemption may occur where the law was clear at the time the ruling was issued and the issuance was an error.[10]

An aspect of this subject that is by no means clear is the authority of the IRS to retroactively revoke the tax exemption of an organization solely for the reason that the Service has prevailed in a case of first impression. While such a victory for the government may be a basis for revocation, it does not appear to be a "change" in the law that would trigger retroactive revocation of exemption. Even a decision by the U.S. Supreme Court should not lead to automatic revocation of exemption of all similarly situated organizations, retroactive to the date they were established. In part, the rationale for a more reasoned approach is that an organization receiving a favorable ruling is permitted, in most circumstances, to rely upon the position stated in the ruling in planning and/or consummating a transaction.[11]

Retroactive revocation of tax exemption usually produces harsh results, particularly where the period embraced by the revocation covers several years. For example, comparable adverse tax consequences may result under state law. Also, for nearly all "charitable" organizations, retroactive revocation of tax exemption would operate to likewise retroactively revoke the organization's eligibility to receive deductible contributions, which could lead to disallowance of the tax deductions taken by the organization's donors.

The facts and circumstances of a given case determine whether, in retroactively revoking an organization's tax exemption, the IRS has abused its discretion[12] and thus has caused the government to be estopped from causing a revocation to be retroactive.[13]

§ 38.2 Change in Form

A mere change in organizational form is regarded by the IRS as a material change in an organization's character. The Service has determined that a change in form has the effect of creating a new legal entity requiring the filing of an application for recognition of exemption for the successor entity, even though the organization's purposes, methods of operation, sources of support, and accounting method remain the same as they were in its predecessor form.[14] In

[9]E.g., *Bornstein v. United States*, 345 F.2d 558 (Ct. Cl 1965), where a ruling was issued one month after a statute was enacted, the matter was reconsidered months later, and the ruling was retroactively revoked.

[10]E.g., *Automobile Club of Michigan v. Commissioner*, 353 U.S. 180(1957).

[11]See Rev. Proc. 62-28, 1962-2 C.B. 496.

[12]See Code § 7805.

[13]E.g., *Lesavoy Foundation v. Commissioner*, 238 F.2d 589 (3d Cir. 1957). In one case, a court held that the IRS abused its discretion in attempting to cause retroactivity of tax exemption as far back as it proposed. *Presbyterian and Reformed Publishing Co. v. Commissioner*, 79 T.C. No. 69 (1982).

[14]Rev. Rul. 67-390, 1967-2 C. B. 179.

this determination, the IRS stated that, in each of the following changes in the structure of organizations, a new exemption application is warranted: (1) conversion of a trust to a corporation, (2) conversion of an unincorporated association to a corporation, (3) reincorporation of an organization, incorporated under state law, by an act of Congress, and (4) reincorporation of an organization, incorporated under the laws of one state, under the laws of another state. This determination has been explicitly endorsed by the U. S. Tax Court.[15]

Absent a change in the law or in the policy of the IRS, the tax-exempt status of the predecessor entity will, in effect, be transmitted to the successor entity. This assumes, however, that the predecessor entity itself was an exempt organization and, in the case of a "charitable" entity, held a ruling from the IRS to that effect. Where the predecessor lacks such a ruling, the organization is treated as a "charitable" entity only as of the date of formation of the successor entity (assuming a ruling to that effect is timely secured).[16]

However, it should not be assumed that the tax status of a predecessor entity will automatically be transmitted to a successor entity. For example, as noted, the policies and views of the IRS may change, and the Service may deny tax exemption to an organization even though it granted tax exemption to a predecessor organization and the material facts did not differ.[17]

The law also imposes comparable requirements in other areas. Thus, an organization that remains in existence after terminating its private foundation status[18] must file a new application for recognition of exemption if it wishes to be treated as a "charitable" organization, since the IRS regards it as a newly created entity.[19] Similarly, a tax-exempt corporation formed to take over the operations of an exempt unincorporated association is regarded as a new organization for purposes of filing the Social Security (FICA) tax waiver certificate.[20]

By reason of enactment of the Tax Reform Act of 1969, the continuity of existence of a "charitable" organization is of extreme importance, notwithstanding a change in form. This is particularly the case where the organization has its nonprivate foundation status predicated on classification as a publicly supported organization, which classification contemplates a history of required financial support. To accommodate this change in law, the IRS continues to adhere to its position as to a form change requiring a new exemption application but allows, where certain requirements are met, the financial history of the predecessor entity to be used in establishing a public support record for the successor entity.[21]

---

[15]*American New Covenant Church* v. *Commissioner*, 74 T.C. 293 (1980).

[16]Rev. Rul. 77-469, 1977-2 C. B. 196; Rev. Rul. 77-208, 1977-1 C. B. 153.

[17]See *National Right to Work Legal Defense and Education Foundation, Inc.* v. *United States*, 80-1 U.S.T.C. ¶ 9155 (E.D. N. Car. 1979).

[18]See Chapter 32.

[19]Rev. Rul. 74-490, 1974-2 C. B. 171.

[20]Rev. Rul. 77-159, 1977-1 C. B. 302. Also Rev. Rul. 71-276, 1971-1 C. B. 289.

[21]See Rev. Rul. 73-422, 1973-2 C. B. 70, discussed in Chapter 36 § 5, *supra*.

§ 38.3   Reporting Requirements

Nearly every organization exempt from federal taxation must file an annual return.[22] This return is generally on Form 990; private foundations meet this requirement by the filing of a Form 990-PF. The annual return must state specifically the items of gross income, receipts and disbursements, and such other information must keep such records, render under oath such statements, make such other returns, and comply with such other requirements as the regulations may prescribe.[23]

This reporting requirement does not apply to (1) churches (including an interchurch organization of local units of a church), their integrated auxiliaries, and conventions or associations of churches, (2) certain organizations (other than private foundations[24]) the gross receipts[25] of which in each tax year are normally not more than $5,000, or (3) the exclusively religious activities of any religious order.[26] The second category of these organizations[27] embraces (1) religious organizations,[28] (2) educational organizations,[29] (3) charitable organizations or organizations for the prevention of cruelty to children or animals,[30] if the organizations are supported by funds contributed by the federal or a state government or are primarily supported by contributions from the general public, (4) organizations operated, supervised, or controlled by or in connection with a religious organization, (5) certain fraternal beneficiary organizations,[31] and (6) a corporation organized under an act of Congress if it is wholly owned by the United States or any agency or instrumentality thereof or a wholly owned subsidiary thereof.[32] Other organizations may be relieved from filing where a filing by them is not necessary to the efficient administration of the internal revenue laws, as determined by the IRS.[33] In the exercise of this discretionary authority, the IRS announced that organizations, other than private foundations, with gross receipts not normally in excess of $25,000 will not

[22]Code § 6033(a)(1). The filing requirements for charitable trusts are the subject of Rev. Proc. 73-29, 1973-2 C. B. 474.

[23]See Reg. § 1.6033-2.

[24]See Chapter 22.

[25]The term "gross receipts" means total receipts without any reduction for costs or expenses, including costs of goods sold (Form 990, part 1, line 8). For this purpose, insurance premiums collected by the local lodge of an exempt fraternal beneficiary society from its members, maintained separately without use or benefit, and remitted to its parent organization which issued the insurance contracts, are not "gross receipts" of the local lodge. Rev. Rul. 73-364, 1973-2 C. B. 393.

[26]Code § 6033(a)(2)(A).

[27]Code § 6033(a)(2)(C).

[28]Code § 501(c)(3). See Chapter 8.

[29]Code § 170(b)(1)(A)(ii). See Chapters 7 and 22.

[30]Code § 501(c)(3). See Chapters 6 and 10.

[31]Code § 501(c)(8). See Chapter 20.

[32]Code § 501(c)(1). See Chapter 21.

[33]Code § 6033(a)(2)(B).

have to file a Form 990 for tax years ending on or after December 31, 1982.[34] The Service stated that "[t]his change was made to relieve relatively small organizations from the filing requirement." This discretion in the IRS also has been exercised to except from the filing requirement (1) a school below college level that is affiliated with a church or operated by a religious order and that is not an integrated auxiliary of a church,[35] (2) mission societies sponsored by or affiliated with one or more churches or church denominations, more than one-half of the activities of which are conducted in, or directed at persons in, foreign countries, and (3) state institutions, the income of which is excluded[36] from gross income.[37]

An organization that has not been recognized by the IRS as a tax-exempt organization, but believes it qualifies for tax exemption, must nonetheless file a Form 990 (or, if it claims to be a private foundation, Form 990-PF).[38]

This definitions (or lack thereof) given to the terms "church" and "convention or association of churches" are discussed elsewhere.[39] The term "integrated auxiliary of a church" means an organization (1) which is a "charitable" entity and thus exempt from federal income taxation, (2) which is "affiliated" with a church, and (3) the principal activity of which is exclusively religious.[40] However, an organization's principal activity is not considered to be exclusively religious if that activity is of a nature other than religious that would serve as a basis for tax exemption (such as charitable, educational, or scientific).[41] It is for this reason that most institutions such as schools, colleges, universities, hospitals, orphanages, and old age homes do not qualify as integrated auxiliaries even though all of the other requirements of the definition are met.

---

[34]Ann. 82-88, 1982-25 I.R.B. 23. Previously, the IRS created such an exemption for organizations with gross receipts not normally in excess of $10,000, for tax years ending on or after December 31, 1976. Ann. 77-62, 1977-17 I.R.B. 22. For purposes of the exemption for organizations with annual gross receipts that are normally not more than $10,000, it was available if (1) in the case of an organization that has been in existence for one year or less, the organization had received, or donors have pledged to give, gross receipts of $15,000 or less during the first tax year of the organization, (2) in the case of an organization that had been in existence for more than one year, but less than three years, the average of the gross receipts received by the organization in its first two tax years was no more than $12,000, and (3) in the case of an organization that had been in existence for three years or more, the average of the gross receipts received by the organization in the immediately preceding three years, including the year for which the return would be filed, was no more than $10,000. Rev. Proc. 80-44, 1980-2 C.B. 777.

[35]Reg. § 1.6033-2(g)(1)(vii). See Chapter 8 § 1. Also see Rev. Rul. 78-316, 1978-2 C. B. 304.

[36]Code § 115.

[37]Rev. Proc. 80-44, *supra*, n. 34.

[38]Reg. § 1.6033-2(c); Rev. Rul. 79-30, 1979-1 C.B. 454.

[39]See Chapter 8 § 1.

[40]Reg. § 1.6033-2(g)(5)(i).

[41]Reg. § 1.6033-2(g)(5)(ii).

For these purposes, the term "affiliated" means "either controlled by or associated with a church or with a convention or association of churches."[42] The control requirement is satisfied where a majority of the auxiliary organization's officers or directors are appointed by a church's governing board or by officials of a church. The "association" requirement is satisfied where the auxiliary organization "shares common religious bonds and convictions" with a church or with a convention or association of churches.

Qualifying integrated auxiliaries include a men's or women's organization, a religious school (such as a seminary), a mission society, or a youth group.[43] For example, a church-affiliated college that trains ministers and lay workers to serve religious functions in the church was determined to qualify as an integrated auxiliary of the church.[44]

By virtue of the adoption of this definition of an "integrated auxiliary," a variety of church-related institutions were made subject to the Form 990 filing requirement for tax years beginning after December 31, 1976.[45] Church-related organizations that are not integrated auxiliaries of churches and that are covered by a group exemption letter[46] issued by the IRS to a church central or parent organization were given an extension of time within which to file Forms 990 in 1977, "to enable these organizations to establish adequate record-keeping systems."[47]

The Forms 990 or 990-PF as filed by "charitable" organizations must include the following items: (1) the organization's gross income for the year, (2) its expenses attributable to income and incurred within the year, (3) its disbursements within the year for tax-exempt purposes, (4) a balance sheet showing its assets, liabilities, and net worth as of the beginning of the year, (5) the total of the contributions and gifts received by it during the year, and the names and addresses of all substantial contributors,[48] (6) the names and addresses of its managers[49] and highly compensated employees, (7) the compensation and other payments made during the year to each of its managers and highly compensated employees, and (8) certain information concerning lobbying activities by those organizations that have elected[50] to come within the "safe haven" lobbying rules.[51]

The Form 990 was substantially revised, effective for tax years beginning on

---

[42]Reg. § 1.6033-2(g)(5)(iii).

[43]Reg. § 1.6033-2(g)(5)(iv).

[44]Rev. Rul. 77-381, 1977-2 C. B. 462. In general, see Reed, "Integrated Auxiliaries, Regulations and Implications," 23 *Cath. Lawyer* 211 (Summer 1978).

[45]See Ann. 77-64, 1977-18 I. R. B. 25.

[46]See Chapter 37 § 3.

[47]Ann. 77-74, 1977-18 I. R. B. 26.

[48]See Chapter 24.

[49]*Ibid.*

[50]Code § 501(h). See Chapter 13.

[51]Code § 6033(b).

or after January 1, 1979.[52] The filing requirements were simplified for small organizations, in that organizations with gross receipts (as defined) that are normally between $10,000 and $25,000 need only complete certain portions of the form, while organizations with gross receipts that are normally less than $10,000 are merely required to file the identification part of the form. A major alteration of the form reflected adoption by the IRS of the functional method of accounting as the means by which tax-exempt organizations report expenses. This approach requires not only the identification, line by line, of expenses as before, but also the allocation of expenses by function, namely, the categories of "program service," "management and general," and "fund raising." Organizations must identify their sources of "program service revenue" and have the option of distinguishing between revenue that is restricted and unrestricted.

This revision of Form 990 has special ramifications for fund-raising organizations, inasmuch as the IRS utilized the opportunity of promulgating the revised form to intensify its monitoring and regulation of fund-raising. The requirement that any fund-raising cost component of each expenditure be separately identified may reveal some indirect fund-raising costs that, when combined with the direct costs reported under the previous system, result in the reporting of higher fund-raising costs. This could have repercussions as respects the organization's status under state charitable solicitation acts, particularly those with percentage ceilings on allowable fund-raising costs.[53] Also, contributions and grants had to be segmented as between those received "[d]irectly from the public," "[t]hrough professional fundraisers," "[a]s allotments from fundraising organizations," "[a]s government grants," and from other sources. Further, the form requires an organization to report its receipts and expenses from special fund-raising activities by event, and uses only the net receipts from such events in computing the $25,000 of gross receipts that dictates the extent of the organization's reporting obligations. Moreover, the IRS has expressed its hope that the state regulatory authorities will accept the Form 990 in lieu of the individual state charitable solicitation act annual reports.

Form 990 was revised again, effective for tax years beginning on or after January 1, 1982.[54] The purpose of the revisions was to make the form acceptable to state regulatory officials so that it can be filed in satisfaction of the reporting requirements imposed by the state charitable solicitation acts and charitable trust laws. Consequently, both the Charitable Trusts and Solicitations Subcommittee of the National Association of Attorneys General and the Executive Committee of the National Assoication of State Charity Officials endorsed the use of the revised annual information return for this purpose. While the revision

---

[52]This form and accompanying instructions are published at 44 *Fed. Reg.* 43563 (July 25, 1979).

[53]See Hopkins, *Charity Under Siege: Government Regulation of Fund Raising* at 96–98, 108–139 (1980).

[54]The draft of this Form and accompanying instructions are published at 46 *Fed. Reg.* 24769 (May 1, 1981).

has been touted as "a move to cut the paperwork burden" for thousands of nonprofit charitable organizations, in fact the states are requiring items of information to supplement the Form 990 filing, so that the likelihood of a significant reduction in the totality of the "paperwork burden" is not great.

In many ways, the new and preexisting Form 990 are the same. The features that continue include functional accounting, breakdown of program service revenue, and a list of questions about the organization's activities and expenditures. (Fund-raising organizations and consultants were pleased to note that the Form drops the distinction between contributions received "directly from the public" and "through professional fund-raisers," and treats all of these receipts as "direct public support."[55])

The aspects of the present form that are most noteworthy are the following: (1) the (sometimes inequitable) practice of not allowing tax-exempt organizations to include as public support the value of any gifts of the use of facilities and equipment, and services, is perpetuated,[56] (2) "payments to affiliates" must be separately identified as a category of expenses,[57] (3) sources of interest income must be segregated,[58] (4) organizations will no longer have to identify special fund-raising events on the face of the return, although a schedule of these activities is required,[59] (5) expenses will have to be stated in greater detail, such as "specific assistance to individuals," accounting fees, legal fees, publications, and conferences, conventions, and meetings[60] (6) the statement of program services is expanded considerably,[61] and (7) an organization will have to identify the states with which a copy of the return is filed.[62] The instructions suggest that the solicitation of contributions may constitute "doing business" in one or more states, with the consequence that reporting pursuant to state nonprofit corporation acts may be required.[63]

The filing date for an annual information return (Form 990 or Form 990-PF) may fall due while the organization's application for recognition of exempt status is pending with the IRS. In that instance, the organization should nonetheless file the information return and indicate thereon that the application is pending.

---

[55]Form 990, Part I, line 1(a).

[56]The value of these gifts may be reported in Part VII, line 82, but may not be included in receipts or expenses.

[57]Form 990, Part I, line 16.

[58]Form 990, Part I, lines 4 and 5.

[59]Form 990, Part I, line 9.

[60]Form 990, Part II.

[61]Form 990, Part III.

[62]Form 990, Part VII, line 87.

[63]General instruction D.I. For analysis and commentary on the revised Form 990, see, e.g., "The Revised Charitable Organization Reporting Form: IRS 990," *The Philanthropy Monthly* 29 (Nov. 1981); Larkin, "Form 990 Becomes the Uniform Annual Report," *The Philanthropy Monthly* 29 (April 1981).

An organization with unrelated business taxable income[64] must file, in addition to the Form 990 (or, in the case of a private foundation, the Form 990-PF), a Form 990-T. It is on this separate form that the source (or sources) of unrelated income is reported and any tax computed.[65]

Some tax-exempt organizations were once permitted to file substitute financial information in lieu of Part II of the Form 990 (the income statement and balance sheet portion of the form), such as colleges and universities many of which follow fund accounting principles in maintaining their books and records. The IRS in 1975 announced that it generally would no longer accept these substitutes for years beginning on or after January 1, 1975.[66] Later, the IRS relented somewhat and allowed a college or university that follows fund accounting principles an extension of up to six months for filing the Form 990 for the tax year beginning in 1975, to enable these institutions to make the transition.[67] However, under certain guidelines.[68] tax-exempt labor organizations may file copies of U. S. Department of Labor forms in lieu of Form 990, Part II, and tax-exempt employee benefit plans may file for that purpose copies of forms otherwise filed with the IRS pursuant to the requirements of the Employee Retirement Income Security Act.

For tax years beginning after November 10, 1978, the Form 990 (or Form 990-PF) and any Form 990-T are due on or before the 15th day of the fifth month following the close of the tax year.[69] Thus, the return for a calendar year organization should be filed by May 15 of each year. For prior tax years, the Form 990 (or Form 990-PF) was due by the fifteenth day of the fifth month following the close of the organization's tax year, while the Form 990-T was due by the fifteenth day of the third month following the close of the organization's tax year.

Failure to timely file the information return, absent reasonable cause, can give rise to a $10 penalty, payable by the organization, for each day the failure continues, with a maximum of $5,000.[70] An additional penalty is imposed at the same rate and maximum on the individual(s) responsible for the failure to

---

[64]See Chapter 39.

[65]Reg. § 1.6012-2(e). See Parker, "Instructions for Filling Out Form 990-T," 22 *Cath. Lawyer* 262 (1976).

[66]Ann. 75-18, 1975-10 I. R. B. 62.

[67]Ann. 76-105, 1976-33 I. R. B. 41. For additional information on these filing requirements for colleges and universities, see the annual National Association of College and University Business Officers Special Report entitled "Guidelines For Completing IRS Information Returns."

[68]Rev. Proc. 79-6, 1979-1 C.B. 485.

[69]Code § 6072(e).

[70]Code § 6652(d)(1). See, e.g., IRS Private Letter Ruling 7902019 (issue no. 12). A private foundation is deemed to have reasonable cause for failure to comply with the requirements of Code § 6033, as well as §§ 6011, 6056, 6104 and 6151 (see *infra*), for filing of returns and payment of taxes until ninety days after it is issued a letter containing a determination of private foundation status from the IRS, thereby immunizing it from

file, absent reasonable cause, where the return remains unfiled following demand for the return by the IRS.[71] An addition to tax for failure to timely file a federal tax return, including a Form 990-T, may also be imposed.[72]

In one instance, an organization required to file a Form 990 submitted an incomplete return by omitting material information from the form, and failed to supply the missing information after being requested to do so by the IRS and did not establish a reasonable cause for its failure to file a complete return. Under these circumstances, the filing of the incomplete return is a failure to file the return for purposes of the penalty.[73] The IRS has observed that the legislative history underlying the pertinent law "shows that Congressional concern was to ensure that information requested on exempt organization returns was provided timely and completely so that the Service would be provided with the information needed to enforce the tax laws."[74] The IRS added:

> Form 990 and accompanying instructions issued by the Service request information that is necessary in order for the Service to perform the duties and responsibilities placed upon it by Congress for proper administration of the revenue laws. These duties and responsibilities include making exempt organization returns available for public inspection as well as conducting audits of exempt organizations to determine their compliance with statutory provisions. When a return is submitted that has not been satisfactorily completed, the Service's ability to perform its duties is seriously hindered, and the public's right to obtain meaningful information is impaired. Thus, when material information is omitted, a return is not completed in the manner prescribed by the form and instructions and the organization has not met the filing requirements of section 6033 (a) (1) of the Code.

A related point is that, in the case of failure to file a return, the tax may be assessed, or a proceeding in court for the collection of the tax may be begun without assessment, at any time.[75] In the above-discussed situation, the or-

---

application of penalty provisions Code §§ 6651 and 6652 with respect to a tax year for which, prior to the due date for filing Form 990-PF, the organization has filed notice (on Form 1023) claiming not to be a private foundation. Rev. Proc. 79-8, 1979-1 C.B. 487.

[71]Code § 6652(d)(2). Reg. § 301.6652-2. Two or more organizations exempt from taxation under Code § 501, one or more of which is described in Code § 501(c)(2) (see Chapter 20) and the other(s) of which derive income from Code § 501(c)(2) organization(s), are eligible to file a consolidated return Form 990 (and/or Form 990-T) in lieu of separate returns. Code § 1504(e); Prop. Reg. § 1.1502-100. In general, see Myers, "Preparation of Forms 990 and 990-T," 22 *Cath. Lawyer* 256 (1976); Buratt, Completing and Filing Form 990: Accounting and Legal Issues and Determinations," 10 *N. Y. U. Conf. on Char. Fdns.* 155 (1971).

[72]Code § 6651(a)(1).

[73]Rev. Rul. 77-162, 1977-1 C. B. 400.

[74]*Ibid.*, citing S. Rep. No. 91-552, 91st Cong., 1st Sess. (1969) at 52.

[75]Code § 6501(c)(3).

ganization was considered[76] to have failed to file any return at all and, therefore, the period of limitations on assessment and collection of the tax[77] was ruled to have not started.[78]

Certain other categories of tax-exempt organizations need not file annual information or income tax returns. This is the case, for example, with states and their political subdivisions, including municipalities. However, the filing requirements become unclear when a tax-exempt organization simultaneously satisfies the definition of an exempt organization required to file and one not required to file. As an illustration, this can occur when a state university has a ruling that it qualifies as a tax-exempt educational organization.[79]

Private foundations were once required to file an annual report in addition to an annual information return.[80] However, as the result of legislation enacted in 1980, the annual reporting requirements imposed upon private foundations have been consolidated so that only one return must be filed to furnish the information previously required in the information return and in the annual report. Also, the reporting requirement has been simplified in that disclosure

---

[76]Code § 6652(d)(1).

[77]Code § 6501(c)(3).

[78]In general, reliance on the advice of a competent tax advisor can constitute reasonable cause for a failure to file a return, for purposes of the Code § 6651(a)(1) addition to tax, and the Code § 6652(d)(1) or (2) penalty. See, e.g., *Waco Lodge No. 166, Benevolent & Protective Order of Elks* v. *Commissioner*, 42 T.C.M. 1202 (1981); *Coldwater Seafood Corp.* v. *Commissioner*, 69 T.C. 966 (1978); *West Coast Ice Co.* v. *Commissioner*, 49 T.C. 345 (1968).

[79]Rev. Rul. 78-316, *supra*, n. 35, clarifying Rev. Rul. 77-261, 1977-2 C.B. 45, holds that the income of an investment fund established by a state is excludable from gross income under Code § 115(1) but that the fund is required to annually file a federal income tax return pursuant to Code § 6012(a)(2). Enactment of the Tax Reform Act of 1969 (P.L. 91-172, 83 Stat. 487) introduced Code § 6050, which required a person who transfers income-producing property having a fair market value in excess of $50,000 to a tax-exempt organization (as described in Code § 511(a) or (b)) to file an information return. This section was repealed for transfers occurring after December 29, 1979 (P.L. 96-167, 93 Stat. 1275). Consequently, Form 4629 is obsolete with respect to transactions occurring after that date (Ann. 80-30, 1980-9 I.R.B. 21).

[80]Former Code § 6056. The report was made on Form 990-AR. The IRS was authorized, pursuant to Reg. § 1.6056-1(b)(2), to designate depositories to which copies of private foundation annual reports must be furnished. The Service, in 1979, proposed that The Foundation Center in New York City, which provides the public with information on private foundations, be so designated. 44 *Fed. Reg.* 60128 (1979). Under this proposal, only managers of foundations with assets of at least one million dollars or those that annually make grants of at least $100,000 would be required to comply with this filing obligation. However, in 1980, the IRS decided not to implement the proposal, on the ground that the designation would confer a "private benefit on a non-governmental entity at the expense of other private organizations" and would not appreciably speed up the process of disseminating the reports. 45 *Fed. Reg.* 10501 (1980).

of the name and address of a needy recipient of a grant of less than $1,000 in any year is not required.[81]

§ 38.4   Private Foundation Publicity Requirements

A copy of the private foundation annual return must be made available to any citizen for inspection at the foundation's principal office during regular business hours for at least 180 days of its availability.[82] Notice of the availability of the annual return must be published in a newspaper having general circulation in the county in which the principal office of the private foundation is located. Failure to properly publicize the availability of the annual return results in the same sanction as does the failure to file it.[83]

The IRS must, in the case of a "charitable" organization or an organization having applied for recognition as a "charitable" entity, make available to appropriate state officials upon request, for inspection and copying, any returns, statements, records, reports, or other information relating to a determination by the IRS that the organization does not qualify or no longer qualifies as a "charitable" entity or has been mailed a notice of deficiency regarding the imposition of a termination tax[84] or one or more of the other private foundation taxes[85] as are relevant to any determination under state law.[86] The IRS is also required to notify state officials as to either of these developments.[87]

§ 38.5   Publicity of Information in General

As the foregoing indicates, the following general categories of documents containing information about tax-exempt organizations must be filed with the IRS: the application for recognition of tax exemption and supporting documents (such as governing instruments, exhibits, and legal memoranda), any statements as to changes in material facts, and annual information returns. Another document on file at the IRS is, of course, a copy of the ruling as to tax-exempt (and, where applicable, private foundation) status. These several documents are likely to collectively comprise a wealth of information about the organization.

The application for recognition of exemption filed by an organization seeking classification as a charitable entity requests a variety of information, including data pertaining to the organization's fund-raising efforts. Virtually one-third of the space on the cover page of the application is reserved for a statement

---

[81]P.L. 96-603, 96th Cong., 2d Sess. (1980).
[82]Code § 6104(d).
[83]See Reg. § 301.6104-4.
[84]See Chapter 32.
[85]See Part IV.
[86]Code § 6104(c).
[87]See Reg. § 301.6104-3. In general, see "Lurie calls for cooperation with states in regulating charitable organizations," 43 *J. Tax.* 58 (1975).

describing the organization's fund-raising program and an explanation of the extent to which it has been put into effect. This question also requests inclusion of the "details of fund-raising activities such as selective mailings, formation of fund-raising committees, use of professional fund raisers, etc." Still another cover page question asks that representative copies of solicitations for financial support be attached as part of the application. The statement of expenditures in the form specifically requires a break-out of fund-raising outlays.

The annual information return, as part of the expense and disbursements financial portion, requires the organization to identify "direct fees paid for raising contributions, gifts, grants, etc." The functional accounting requirements mandate that the fund-raising component of every expense be separately stated. Schedule A of the Form 990 requires the organization to list the names, addresses and compensation of the five highest persons paid by it for "professional services" (including fund-raising advice and assistance), where these persons were each paid more than $30,000. A like requirement is contained in the Form 990-PF.

The application for recognition of tax exemption and any supporting documents filed by most tax-exempt organizations[88] are open to public inspection at the National Office of the IRS,[89] as long as the organization has been exempt in any tax year.[90] A copy of an application for recognition of tax exemption (but not the supporting documents) is open to inspection at the appropriate IRS regional service center and district director's office. Any person making inquiry in writing is to be informed as to which provision of the federal tax law has been determined to be descriptive of the organization and whether the organization is currently exempt from federal income tax.

The exemption application, supporting documents, and tax status of an organization which has been denied tax exemption will not be divulged by the IRS. Also, there will be withheld from public inspection any information relating to a trade secret, patent, process, style of work, or apparatus of an exempt organization if it is determined that public disclosure would adversely affect the organization or the national defense.[91]

The law also provides for public inspection of the information an exempt organization must file as part of its annual information return.[92] The same general procedures operate as to public access to information returns.

Information furnished on the public portion of returns and annual reports is publicly available in the office of any district director of the IRS.[93] (Under the rules in effect prior to the change in 1981, the returns and reports were

---

[88]Those described in Code § 501(c) or (d).
[89]See Reg. § 301.6104-1(a).
[90]Code § 6104(a)(1)(A).
[91]Code § 6104(a)(1)(D).
[92]Code § 6104(b), Reg. § 301.6104-2.
[93]Reg. § 301.6104-2(b).

locally available only in the office of the director of the IRS district in which the principal office of the organization is located.)

An individual desiring to inspect an exempt organization's application for recognition of exemption and supporting documents and/or information returns at the National Office (Public Information Division) must first make a written request to that effect to the Assistant to the Commissioner (Public Affairs).[94] The IRS is to subsequently notify the individual as to when the material will be available for inspection. The public inspection is allowed only in the presence of an internal revenue officer or employee and only during the regular hours of business of the IRS.

Notes may be taken of the material open for public inspection and copies thereof may be made manually. A procedure is available whereby, at $1 per page, the information will be copied and furnished to an individual making the request.

These rules may be seen as somewhat of an exception to the general rule of nondisclosure of tax records, the enactment of the Freedom of Information Act of 1966 notwithstanding.[95] Also, the Privacy Act of 1974 generally bars the disclosure of tax information to outside parties without the taxpayer's consent.[96] Pursuant to the law[97] prior to its revision in 1976, tax returns were open to inspection, albeit only under rather limited cicumstances. (Unauthorized disclosure of tax information is a criminal offense.[98]) The law was rewritten in 1976, as part of the Tax Reform Act of 1976, to provide that returns and return information are confidential and not subject to disclosure except as specifically provided by statute. Disclosure is permitted in a limited fashion to Congress, to the government in criminal cases, for statistical use, and for other defined purposes.

It was once the policy of the IRS to not disclose private letter rulings, technical advice memoranda, and the like (in the tax-exempt organizations field or otherwise).[99] However, recent court decisions have held that private rulings and the like are subject to public disclosure by reason of the Freedom of Information Act,[100] with the issue once pending before the U.S. Supreme

---

[94]Reg. § 301.6104-1(e).

[95]See Rosenbloom, "More IRS information may become public due to amended Freedom of Information Act," 45 *J. Tax.* 258 (1976).

[96]See Bowe, "The Privacy Act of 1974: How it affects taxpayers, practitioners and the IRS," 45 *J. Tax.* 74 (1976).

[97]Code § 6103.

[98]Code § 7213.

[99]See *Belisle* v. *Commissioner*, 78-1 U.S.T.C. ¶ 9459 (W.D. Okl. 1978), holding that results of an IRS investigation of a tax-exempt organization are within the ambit of Code § 6103 and are exempt from disclosure under the Freedom of Information Act (by reason of 5 U.S.C. § 552(b)(3)). Likewise, see *Virginia Independent Schools Ass'n* v. *Commissioner*, 76-1 U.S.T.C. ¶ 9322, ¶ 9360 (D.D.C. 1976).

[100]See *Tax Analysts and Advocates* v. *Internal Revenue Service*, 505 F.2d 350 (D.C. Cir. 1974).

Court.[101] This litigation prompted the IRS to issue proposed regulations in 1974 concerning the public availability of rulings.[102]

Congress, by the Tax Reform Act of 1976, enacted rules for the public disclosure of IRS determinations (including "background file documents") issued after November 1, 1976.[103] Names and identifying details are not normally to be disclosed, nor are certain types of commercial or financial information which is privileged or confidential. Internal IRS memoranda or communications between the IRS and the Department of Justice are not to be disclosed under this law.

However, it is clear that these disclosure rules are inapplicable to any matter to which the more specific rules requiring disclosure of information in the tax-exempt organizations context[104] apply.[105] Thus, the elaborate procedures concerning disclosure of IRS rulings are inapplicable where the information involved is provided by an exempt organization. For this reason, Congress in 1976 amended the specific rules for tax-exempt organizations by expanding it to also encompass "any letter or other document issued by the Internal Revenue Service with respect to such application."[106]

Consequently, as respects applications for recognition of exemption filed after October 31, 1976, the application, most supporting documents, the annual information returns, and the ruling issued to the tax-exempt organization must be made accessible to the public under the above-discussed procedures. However, adverse rulings and technical advice memoranda unrelated to a request for tax exemption will continue to remain undisclosed, unless made available by reason of the outcome of the litigation concerning the Freedom of Information Act.[107]

The excise tax return filed by private foundations (Form 4720) is disclosable to the public.[108] However, this return as filed by a person other than a foundation is not disclosable. Therefore, if disclosure of the return filed by a person other than a private foundation is not desired, the person should file separately rather than jointly with the foundation, inasmuch as the joint filing is disclosable.[109]

---

[101]See *Fruehauf Corp.* v. *Internal Revenue Service*, 522 F.2d 284 (6th Cir. 1975), remanded for reconsideration in light of Tax Reform Act of 1976, 429 U.S. 1085 (1977).

[102]See Corey, "The public availability of private rulings: How will it affect tax practice?," 42 *J. Tax.* 225 (1975).

[103]Code § 6110. See Thompson, "The Disclosure of Private Rulings," 59 *Marq. L. Rev.* 529 (1977).

[104]Code § 6104.

[105]Code § 6110(k)(1).

[106]Code § 6104(a)(1)(A).

[107]The procedural requirements for requesting rulings and determination letters from the IRS after November 1, 1976, are the subject of I. R. 1683 (Oct. 22, 1976). Also see Reg. § 601.201(c).

[108]Reg. § 1.6033-2(a)(2)(ii)(j).

[109]See T.D. 7785, 1981-36 I.R.B. 18.

The IRS in 1982 consented to the publication of documents used in preparing revenue rulings and other interpretations of the federal tax laws.[110] The documents involved are general counsel memoranda, actions on decisions, and technical memoranda. This publication of documents, which arises out of a consent order in a Freedom of Information Act case,[111] will involve materials dating back to 1967. The first group of documents became available on April 24, 1982, and all documents are to be released by December 24, 1983; the material is being released in reverse chronological order. As with published private rulings, these documents are not to be relied upon or cited as precedent.

§ 38.6   Revocation of Exemption: Judicial Alternatives

If an organization's tax-exempt (or, where applicable, nonprivate foundation) status is revoked (or adversely modified) by the IRS, its administrative remedies are much the same as if the original application for that status had been denied.[112]

Facing revocation of tax-exempt status and having exhausted its administrative remedies, an organization's initial impulse may be to seek injunctive relief in the courts, to restrain the IRS from taking such action. However, the Tax Injunction Act[113] provides that, aside from minor exceptions, "no suit for the purpose of restraining the assessment or collection of any tax shall be maintained in any court by any person. . . ." Despite the explicitly inflexible language of the statute, the U.S. Supreme Court has carved out a narrow exception, in that a preenforcement injunction against tax assessment or collection may be granted only if it is clear that under no circumstances could the government ultimately prevail and if equity jurisdiction otherwise exists (that is, a showing of irreparable injury, no adequate remedy at law, and advancement of the public interest).[114] Generally, loss of tax-exempt status will not bring an or-

---

[110]Ann. 82-17, 1982-5 I.R.B. 18.

[111]*Tax Analysts* v. *Internal Revenue Service*, 81-2 U.S.T.C. ¶ 9784 (D.D.C. 1981).

[112]See Rev. Proc. 80-25, *supra*, n. 1, § 13.02; Chapter 37 § 2. The protest and conference rights before a final revocation notice is issued are not applicable to matters where delay would be prejudicial to the interests of the IRS (such as in cases involving fraud, jeopardy, or the imminence of the expiration of the statute of limitations, or where immediate action is necessary to protect the interests of the federal government). Rev. Proc. 80-25, *supra*, n. 1, § 13.03. In general, see Sanders, "What to do About the Loss of Exemption: Effect Upon the Organization and Its Members," 24 *N.Y.U. Inst. Fed. Tax.* 167 (1966).

[113]Code § 7421(a).

[114]*Enochs* v. *Williams Packing & Navigation Co.*, 370 U. S. 1 (1962). See, e.g., *Investment Annuity* v. *Blumenthal*, 437 F.Supp. 1095 (D.D.C. 1977); *State of Minnesota, Spannaus* v. *United States*, 525 F.2d 231 (8th Cir. 1975). Also see Notes at 30 *Wash. & Lee L. Rev.* 573 (1973), 73 *Col. L. Rev.* 1502 (Part 2) (1973), and 1 *Tulsa L. J.* 88 (1964).

ganization within the ambit of this exception, under Supreme Court rulings[115] and other cases.[116] The exception may be available in this context but success will require rather unusual factual circumstances.[117]

An organization facing loss of tax-exempt status or similar adverse treatment from the IRS may petition the U.S. Tax Court for relief following the issuance of notice of tax deficiency (if one can be found)[118] or may pay the tax and sue for a refund in federal district court or the U.S. Claims Court following expiration of the statutory six-month waiting period.[119] However, the organization may well become defunct before any relief can be obtained in this fashion, particularly where the ability to attract charitable contributions is a factor, since denial of tax-exempt status also means (where applicable) loss of advance assurance by the IRS of deductibility of contributions. The U.S. Supreme Court has recognized the seriousness of this dilemma but concluded that "although the congressional restriction to postenforcement review may place an organization claiming tax-exempt status in a precarious financial position, the problems presented do not rise to the level of constitutional infirmities, in light of the powerful governmental interests in protecting the administration of the tax system from premature judicial interference. . . and of the opportunities for review that are available."[120]

---

[115]*Bob Jones University* v. *Simon*, 416 U. S. 725 (1974), aff'g 472 F.2d 903 (1973), reh. den. 476 F.2d 259 (4th Cir. 1973); *Alexander* v. *"Americans United," Inc.*, 416 U. S. 752 (1974), rev'g 477 F.2d 1169 (D. C. Cir. 1973). See Note, 46 *Temp. L. Q.* 596 (1974). For subsequent cases, see e.g., *United States* v. *American Friends Service Committee*, 419 U.S. 7 (1974); *Cattle Feeders Tax Committee* v. *Shultz*, 504 F.2d 462 (10th Cir. 1974); *Vietnam Veterans Against the War, Inc.* v. *Voskuil*, 389 F.Supp. 412 (E. D. Mo. 1974). In general, see Colvin, "Contesting Loss of Exemption Under I. R. C. Section 501(c)(3) After *Bob James University* and *'Americans United,' Inc.*," 34 *Fed. B. J.* 182 (1975); Note, 40 *Mo. L. Rev.* 176 (1975).

[116]See, e.g., *Crenshaw County Private School Foundation* v. *Connally*, 474 F.2d 1185 (5th Cir. 1973); *National Council on the Facts of Overpopulation* v. *Caplin*, 224 F.Supp. 313 (D. D. C. 1963); *Israelite House of David* v. *Holden*, 14 F.2d 701 (W. D. Mich. 1926).

[117]See *Center on Corporate Responsibility, Inc.* v. *Shultz*, 368 F.Supp. 863 (D. D. C. 1973).

[118]Code §§ 6212, 6213. See, e.g., *Golden Rule Church Association*, v. *Commissioner*, 41 T. C. 719 (1964). The role and responsibilities of the Chief Counsel of the IRS in tax-exempt organization cases docketed in the U. S. Tax Court is the subject of Rev. Proc. 78-9, 1978-1 C. B. 563.

[119]Code § 7422; 28 U. S. C. §§ 1346(a)(1), 1491. In the absence of the timely filing of a claim for refund (a jurisdictional prerequisite to this type of court action), such a suit may not be maintained. See *The American Association of Commodity Traders* v. *Department of the Treasury*, 79-1 U.S.T.C. ¶9183 (D.N.H. 1978), aff'd 79-1 U.S.T.C. ¶9408 (1st Cir. 1979).

[120]*Bob Jones University* v. *Simon, supra*, n. 115 at 747–748.

As part of the Tax Reform Act of 1976, Congress enacted a new law providing for declaratory judgments as to the tax status of "charitable" organizations.[121] Specifically, this law authorizes federal court jurisdiction in cases of actual controversy involving determinations (or failures to make a determination) by the IRS with respect to the tax status of "charitable" organizations. Resolving a matter of brief controversy, Congress decided to vest such jurisdiction in the U.S. District Court for the District of Columbia, the U.S. Claims Court, and the U.S. Tax Court.

This declaratory judgment procedure is designed to facilitate relatively prompt judicial review of four categories of tax-exempt organizations issues.[122] However, this procedure is not intended to supplant the preexisting avenues available for exempt organizations for judical review.

These rules[123] create a remedy in a case of actual controversy involving a determination by the IRS with respect to the initial qualification or classification or continuing qualification or classification of an entity as a "charitable" organization for tax exemption purposes[124] and/or charitable contribution deduction purposes,[125] a private foundation,[126] or a private operating foundation.[127] The remedy is also available in the case of a failure by the IRS to make a determination as respects one or more of these issues.[128] The remedy is pursued in one of the three above-noted courts, which is authorized to "make a declaration" with respect to the issues.

A "determination" within the meaning of these rules[129] is a final decision by the IRS affecting the tax qualification of a "charitable" organization. The term does not encompass an IRS ruling passing on an organization's proposed transactions. Such a ruling does not constitute a denial or revocation of an organization's tax-exempt status nor does it jeopardize the deductibility of contributions to it. Thus, absent a final determination, a declaratory judgment is

---

[121]Code § 7428.

[122]Congress in 1974 enacted a similar declaratory judgment procedure for ascertaining the tax qualifications of employee retirement plans, as part of the Employee Retirement Income Security Act. Code § 7476. See, e.g., *Federal Land Bank Association of Asheville, North Carolina* v. *Commissioner*, 67 T. C. 29 (1976).

[123]Code § 7428.

[124]Code § 501(c)(3).

[125]Code § 170(c)(2).

[126]Code § 509(a).

[127]Code § 4942(j)(3).

[128]Thus, the rulings and determination letters in cases subject to the declaratory judgment procedure of Code § 7428 are those issued pursuant to the procedures stated in Rev. Proc. 80-25, *supra*, n. 1. See Chapter 37 §§ 1, 2, and 5.

[129]Code § 7428(a)(1).

premature.[130] The same principle applies to an IRS ruling concerning an organization's public charity classification.[131]

A topic of some controversy is whether an organization can litigate, under the declaratory judgment rules, its public charity classification where the IRS accords public charity status to it but in a category different from that requested by the organization. In the first case on the point, the U.S. Tax Court held that it is a justiciable issue[132] for an organization to assert that it is not a private foundation because it is a church rather than a publicly supported organization.[133] The court said that, in such an instance, the organization has received the requisite "adverse" ruling, if only because the organization had requested a definitive ruling yet received only an advance ruling[134]; the Service unsuccessfully asserted that the declaratory judgment jurisdiction becomes available only where the ruling is "fully adverse."[135]

However, the U.S. Court of Appeals for the Fifth Circuit has endeavored to narrow the reach of this Tax Court decision.[136] While the appellate court agreed that "the receipt of a favorable ruling on a non-private [foundation] status that is a different and less advantageous status that [sic] the one which is the subject of the ruling request will not defeat" declaratory judgment jurisdiction,[137] the court said it would "not. . . [interpret] the statute to allow court review of an adverse holding by the Service which has no present effect on a taxpayer's classification" as a private foundation or nonfoundation.[138] The principal issue before the court of appeals concerned an organization that was ruled to be a "Type I" publicly supported organization; however, the IRS had also ruled, contrary to the position of the organization, that contributions from another organization were subject to the 2 percent limitation on allowable "public" contributions.[139] The court rejected the contention that the Tax Court had jurisdiction to entertain the action, concerning proper application of the 2 percent limitation, since the organization was accorded initial classification as a publicly supported charity and since the IRS had not failed to make the

---

[130]*New Community Senior Citizen Housing Corp.* v. *Commissioner,* 72 T.C. 372 (1979). In one case, the U.S. Tax Court held that the requirement that there be a final adverse determination means that the court lacks jurisdiction to review a determination issued by the IRS only after the organization agreed to not conduct a certain activity in consideration of receipt of the otherwise favorable determination, because the ruling is not "adverse" in relation to the proposed activity. *AHW Corporation* v. *Commissioner,* 79 T.C. 390 (1982).

[131]*Urantia Foundation* v. *Commissioner,* 77 T.C. 507 (1981).

[132]Under Code § 7428(a)(1)(B).

[133]See Chapter 22 § 1.

[134]See Chapter 37 § 5.

[135]*Friends of the Society of Servants of God* v. *Commissioner,* 75 T.C. 209 (1980).

[136]*CREATE, Inc.* v. *Commissioner,* 634 F.2d 803 (5th Cir. 1980).

[137]*Ibid.* at 813.

[138]*Id.* at 812.

[139]See Chapter 22 § 1.

requisite determination. Thus, the court concluded that the necessary "actual controversy" was not present and that the organization can litigate the applicability of the 2 percent rule when and if that rule causes the IRS to attempt to adversely classify the organization under the public charity classification rules.[140] Likewise, the U.S. Court of Appeals for the Sixth Circuit has held that the courts lack declaratory judgment jurisdiction where an organization is seeking reclassification under the public charity rules.[141]

A pleading may be filed under these rules "only by the organization the qualification or classification of which is at issue."[142] Prior to utilizing the declaratory judgment procedure, an organization must have exhausted all administrative remedies available to it within the IRS. For the first 270 days after a request for a determination is made, an organization is deemed to not have exhausted its administrative remedies, assuming no determination is actually made during that period.[143] After this 270-day period has elapsed, the organization may initiate an action for a declaratory judgment. However, if the IRS makes an adverse determination during the jurisdictional period, an action could be initiated immediately thereafter. Nonetheless, all actions under these rules must be initiated within 90 days after the date on which the final determination by the IRS is made.[144]

A "determination" can, in this context, include a proposed revocation of an organization's tax-exempt status or public charity classification. In one case, an organization received a letter in which the IRS proposed to revoke its public charity status; in response, it filed a written protest and thereafter filed a petition for a declaratory judgment (under the 270-day rule). After the court petition was filed, the IRS issued a final determination letter revoking the classification of the organization. At issue was whether the U.S. Tax Court had jurisdiction as the result of the filing of the petition. The IRS contended the court did not, inasmuch as the petition was filed before the final adverse letter was issued. The court disagreed, finding that the proposed revocation is sufficient to create the necessary "actual controversy" and that the written protest constitutes the requisite request for a determination.[145]

---

[140]Inherent in the opinion is the court's concern about overburdening the judicial system with too many Code § 7428 declaratory judgment cases, for it speaks of a contrary holding giving rise to "a significant volume of § 7428 litigation, some of which would be needless." *CREATE, Inc.* v. *Commissioner, supra,* n. 136, at 812.

[141]*Ohio County & Independent Agriculture Societies* v. *Commissioner,* 610 F.2d 448 (6th Cir. 1979).

[142] Code § 7428 (b) (1). Thus, for example, as regards an unincorporated organization that applied for tax exemption and subsequently, during the administrative process, incorporated, when the IRS denied tax exemption for the unincorporated entity, the corporation (being a separate legal entity) was held to lack standing to seek a declaratory judgment on the qualification as an exempt organization of the unincorporated organization. *American New Covenant Church* v. *Commissioner, supra,* n. 15.

[143]Code § 7428(b)(2).

[144]Code § 7428(b)(3).

[145]*J. David Gladstone Foundation* v. *Commissioner,* 77 T.C. 221 (1981).

According to the IRS, this 270-day period does not begin until the date a "substantially completed" application for recognition of tax exemption is sent to the appropriate key district director.[146] This type of a form is defined as one that:

(1) Is signed by an authorized individual;

(2) Includes an employer identification number or a completed application for such a number (Form SS-4);

(3) Includes (a) a statement of receipts and expenditures and a balance sheet for the current year and the three preceding years (or the years the organization was in existence, if less) or (b), if the organization has not yet commenced operations, or has not completed one accounting period, a proposed budget for two full accounting periods and a current statement of assets and liabilities;

(4) Includes a statement of proposed activities and a description of anticipated receipts and contemplated expenditures;

(5) Includes a copy of the organizing or enabling document that is signed by a principal officer or is accompanied by a written declaration signed by an officer authorized to sign for the organization certifying that the document is a complete and accurate copy of the original; and

(6) Includes a copy of its bylaws (if any) that is signed or otherwise verified as current by an authorized officer.

An application that is not substantially completed will likely be returned to the applicant for completion, in which case the 270-day period will not be considered as starting until the date the application is remailed to the IRS with the requested information or, if a postmark is not evident, on the date the Service receives a substantially completed application.[147]

As respects the exhaustion of administrative remedies requirements, the IRS has determined that the following steps and remedies must be exhausted prior to proper initiation of a declaratory judgment action:

(1) The filing of a substantially completed application for recognition of tax exemption, or the filing of a request for a determination of private foundation status;

(2) The timely submission of all additional information requested to perfect an exemption application or request for determination of private foundation status; and

---

[146]Rev. Proc. 80-25, *supra*, n. 1 at § 5.05.
[147]*Ibid.* at § 5.06. Also see Rev. Rul. 77-114, 1977-1 C.B. 152.

(3) Exhaustion of all administrative appeals available within the IRS,[148] as well as appeal of a proposed adverse ruling in National Office original jurisdiction exemption application cases.[149]

According to the IRS, an organization cannot be deemed to have exhausted its administrative remedies prior to the earlier of (1) the completion of the foregoing three steps and the sending of a notice of final determination by certified or registered mail or (2) the expiration of the 270-day period in a case where the IRS has not issued a notice of final determination and the organization has taken, in a timely manner, all reasonable steps to secure a ruling or determination.[150]

Further, the IRS states that the foregoing steps "will not be considered completed until the Service has had a reasonable time to act upon the appeal or request for consideration, as the case may be."[151] (As noted, nonetheless, once the statutory 270 days have elapsed, the action can be initiated, without regard to the pace of the Service in relation to these steps.)

To protect the financial status of an allegedly charitable organization during the litigation period, the law provides for circumstances under which contributions made to the organization during that period are deductible[152] even though the court ultimately decides against the organization.[153] Basically, this relief can only be accorded where the IRS is proposing to revoke, rather than initially deny, an organization's charitable status. However, the total deductions to any one organization from a single donor to be so protected during this period may not exceed $1,000.[154] (Where an organization ultimately prevails in a declaratory judgment case, this $1,000 limitation on deductibility becomes inapplicable, so that all gifts are fully deductible within the general limitations of the charitable deduction rules.) Further, this benefit is not available to any individual who was responsible, in whole or in part, for the actions (or failures to act) on the part of the organization which were the basis for the revocation of tax-exempt status.[155]

---

[148]See Rev. Proc. 80-25, *supra*, n. 1, §§ 9 and 10.

[149]*Ibid*. at § 11.01.

[150]*Id*. at § 11.02.

[151]*Id*. at § 11.03. The U.S. District Court for the District of Columbia, in *New York County Health Services Review Organization, Inc.* v. *Commissioner*, 80-1 U.S.T.C. ¶ 9398 (D.D.C. 1980), has held that the court lacks subject matter jurisdiction until the IRS makes an adverse determination or the 270-day period (commenced by the filing of a substantially completed application for recognition of exemption) has elapsed.

[152]Code § 170(c)(2).

[153]Code § 7428(c)(1).

[154]Code § 7428(c)(2).

[155]Code § 7428 (c)(3). In general see Kittrell, "Administrative prerequisites for declaratory judgments about tax issues," 66 *A.B.A.J.* 1570 (1980); Roady, "Declaratory judgments for 501(c)(3) Status Determinations: End of a 'Harsh Regime'," 30 *Tax Lawyer* 765 (1977).

In connection with this procedure and as an aid to proper oversight and to subsequent decision-making in the tax-exempt organizations field, the Senate Committee on Finance instructed the IRS to annually report to Congress on the activities of the Service regarding most tax-exempt organizations.[156] These reports are to include (1) the number of organizations that applied for recognition of tax-exempt status, (2) the number of organizations the applications of which were accepted and the number denied, (3) the number of organizations the prior favorable rulings of which were revoked, (4) the number of organizations audited during the year, and (5) the number of organizations the IRS regards as exempt from taxation.

In addition, the Finance Committee indicated that these data should be categorized by type of exempt organization, such as charitable organizations, social welfare organizations, fraternal beneficiary associations, and veterans' organizations. Also, the Committee wants the statistics on charitable organizations to reflect whether they are public charities or private foundations. Further, the IRS is expected to provide the amount of its expenditures for the year, the amount of its requested appropriations for the following two years, the amounts appropriated for each of the years, and the amounts authorized to be appropriated under the Employee Retirement Income Security Act of 1974.[157]

The first date on which an action could have been commenced under the declaratory judgment rules was April 5, 1977. The pleadings must relate to IRS determinations or requests by organizations for determinations made after January 1, 1976.

The U.S. Tax Court is the only of the three jurisdictions to adopt procedural rules for actions filed under these rules.[158] The singlemost significant feature of these rules is the decision of the court to generally confine its role to review of the denial by the IRS of a request for a determination of exemption based solely on the facts contained in the "administrative record," that is, not to conduct a trial *de novo* at which new evidence may be adduced.[159] (This approach does not apply where the tax exemption has been revoked.) Thus, in one case, the court refused to permit information orally furnished to IRS representatives during a conference at the administrative level to be introduced in evidence during the pendency of the case before the court.[160] Similarly, the

---

[156]S. Rep. No. 94-938, 94th Cong., 2d Sess. (1976) at 587.

[157]Specifically, § 1052 of such Act.

[158]Rules of Practice and Procedure, U. S. Tax Court, Title XXI.

[159]*Ibid.*, Rule 217(a). The U.S. Tax Court has allowed supplementation of the administrative record in only one denial case. *First Libertarian Church* v. *Commissioner,* 74 T.C. 396 (1980). Because the Tax Court will render a declaratory judgment in a nonrevocation case upon the petition, the answer, and the administrative record, it has held that a motion for summary judgment in that court is "superfluous" and "pointless." *Pulpit Resource* v. *Commissioner,* 70 T. C. 594, 602 (1978).

[160]*Houston Lawyer Referral Service, Inc.* v. *Commissioner,* 69 T. C. 570 (1978). Also *Church In Boston* v. *Commissioner,* 71 T.C. 102 (1979).

court is to base its decision upon only theories advanced in the IRS notice or at trial, and not upon arguments advanced anew by the Service during the litigation.[161]

The U.S. Tax Court has suggested that, if an organization that has been denied tax exemption and did not prevail before it has material information previously excluded from the administrative record, the organization may file a new application for recognition of exemption and that the principles of *res judicata* would not preclude the court from reviewing a denial of the subsequent application.[162]

The general Tax Court scheme for the processing of these declaratory judgment cases is being adopted, on a case-by-case basis, by both the U.S. District Court for the District of Columbia and the U.S. Claims Court. This approach includes basic reliance upon the "administrative record," with court review *de novo* only in unusual cases.[163]

An organization's fate before a court may well depend on the quality of the contents of the administrative record. It is highly significant that the applicant organization generally controls what comprises the administrative record. Even when the record includes responses to IRS inquiries, it is the organization that decides the phraseology of the answers and what, if anything, to attach as exhibits. It is, therefore, highly important that the administrative record be carefully crafted, particularly in instances where there is a reasonable likelihood that an initial determination case will be unsuccessful at the IRS level and thus ripen into a declaratory judgment case.

As an illustration, a court had before it the issue as to whether an organization that operates a mountain lodge as a retreat facility could qualify as a religious organization. The opinion in the case clearly reflects the court's view that this type of an organization can so qualify under appropriate circumstances, yet the particular organization involved lost the case primarily because the administrative record did not show that the recreational facilities were used for tax-exempt purposes or otherwise used only in an insubstantial manner.[164]

---

[161]*Peoples Translation Service/Newsfront International* v. *Commissioner*, 72 T.C. 42 (1979); *Goodspeed Scholarship Fund* v. *Commissioner*, 70 T.C. 515, 520–525 (1978); *Schuster's Express, Inc.* v. *Commissioner*, 66 T.C. 588, 593 (1976), aff'd 562 F.2d 39 (2d Cir. 1977).

[162]*Houston Lawyer Referral Service, Inc.* v. *Commissioner, supra*, n. 160 at 577–578.

[163]See *Southwest Virginia Professional Standards Review Organization, Inc.* v. *United States*, 78-2 U.S.T.C. ¶ 9747 (D.D.C. 1978); *Animal Protection Institute, Inc.* v. *United States*, 78-2 U.S.T.C. ¶ 9709 (Ct. Cl. 1978).

[164]*The Schoger Foundation* v. *Commissioner*, 76 T.C. 380 (1981). The organization attempted the argument that the administrative record did not show that the recreational facilities were used in more than an insubstantial manner but this failed because, under the U.S. Tax Court Rules of Practice and Procedure (Rule 217 (c)(2)(i)), the organization has the burden of showing that the determination of the IRS is incorrect. See Chapter 37 § 1.

The impact of this declaratory judgment procedure on the administrative practice before the IRS cannot be underestimated. In the past, the Service could be confident that, with rare exception, its determination as to a charitable organization's status was the final one. That is, because of the large amount of legal fees, expenses, and time required to litigate, the IRS knew that judicial review of one of its decisions in this area would be highly unlikely.

With the advent of the declaratory judgment rules, all this has dramatically changed. No longer can the IRS make its decisions with the luxury of assuming their finality. Now, the Service, in approaching this decision-making process, must do so with awareness of the greatly increased possibility of a challenge in court. This means that the IRS, obviously reluctant to have a total rebuff in the casebooks as precedent, may well be forced to issue favorable rulings in instances where the contrary would otherwise be the case. Also, these procedures force the IRS to act more quickly than it may otherwise be disposed to do.

Instances of this happening are on the rise. In a 1979 episode, the IRS refused to rule on an exemption request, saying that the issue raised was under study. Once the 270-day administrative remedies period expired, the organization launched a lawsuit. Within 60 days after the complaint was filed, the Department of Justice made it known that the IRS was willing to issue a favorable ruling (thereby mooting the case). Thus, within 2½ months after instituting a declaratory judgment request, the organization came into possession of a favorable ruling, under circumstances where, if this form of relief were not available, the IRS probably would not have acted for some time or would have issued an unfavorable determination.[165]

The growing interest in and popularity of this declaratory judgment procedure are fostering desire that its scope will be expanded to encompass other tax-exempt organization questions. For example, the private foundation excise taxes, other tax-exempt organization categories (such as trade associations, social clubs, and labor organizations), and issues of unrelated income taxation could all be made reviewable by the courts by means of a declaratory judgment procedure. Likewise, there is desire to subject the qualification of pooled income funds and charitable remainder trusts to a declaratory judgment procedure. At the same time, however, the corresponding workload on the courts must be considered.

These procedures are not solely of consequence to the new organization that is struggling to obtain its tax exemption and/or its private foundation/public charity status. They are also of immense significance to the established charitable (including educational, religious, and scientific) organization or institution, the tax status of which is, or appears to be, immune from revocation or other disturbance. This declaratory judgment provision is having a considerable impact on development of the law applicable to charitable organizations.

---

[165]*Infant Formula Action Coalition* v. *United States* (C.A. No. 79-0129, D.D.C.); also *Fair Campaign Practices Committee, Inc.* v. *United States* (C.A. No. 77-0830, D.D.C.).

The courts are holding a variety of organizations to be tax-exempt entities, in total rejection of IRS positions. As illustrations, the courts have concluded, notwithstanding the opposition of the IRS, that health maintenance organizations,[166] professional standards review organization foundations,[167] consumer credit counseling agencies,[168] and private schools providing custodial services for young pupils[169] can qualify for tax exemption. Not surprisingly, courts are also upholding the IRS position, such as in the case of genealogical societies,[170] communal groups,[171] and certain scholarship funds.[172] Interpretations of the private foundation definition rules have likewise gone for and against the government.[173]

Consequently, the growing use of these procedures is having an important impact on the law encompassing the reach of the tax exemption for "charitable" organizations. This can be of considerable importance in the continuing preservation of organizations' tax-exempt and/or private foundation classifications.

Moreover, the breadth of the issues being raised by these cases is fostering the rapid development of law in areas related to tax exemption other than as respects the exemption categories themselves. Chief among these areas being explored and expounded upon is the doctrine of private inurement.[174] Many of these cases under review and being decided are turning on the question of whether private interests are being unduly served. Thus, two courts have found that genealogical societies improperly (for tax exemption purposes) provide personal services to members when the societies help their members research their ancestry.[175] One set of cases has resulted in opinions that there is unwarranted private inurement with respect to a religious organization because of its communal structure, where meals, lodging, and other life necessities are provided to the ministers.[176] Other decisions contain analyses as to why particular facts may concern educational efforts,[177] or may involve private inure-

---

[166]*Sound Health Association* v. *Commissioner*, 71 T.C. 158 (1978).

[167]*Virginia Professional Standards Review Foundation* v. *Blumenthal*, 79-1 U.S.T.C. ¶ 9167 (D.D.C. 1979).

[168]*Consumer Credit Counseling Service of Alabama, Inc.* v. *United States*, 78-2 U.S.T.C. ¶9660 (D.D.C. 1978).

[169]*San Francisco Infant School, Inc.* v. *Commissioner*, 69 T.C. 957 (1978); *Michigan Early Childhood Center, Inc.* v. *Commissioner*, 37 T.C.M. 808 (1978).

[170]*The Callaway Family Association, Inc.* v. *Commissioner*, 71 T.C. 340 (1978); *Benjamin Price Genealogical Association* v. *Internal Revenue Service*, 79-1 U.S.T.C. ¶ 9361 (D.D.C. 1979).

[171]*Beth-El Ministries, Inc.* v. *United States*, 79-2 U.S.T.C. ¶ 9412 (D.D.C. 1979).

[172]*Miss Georgia Scholarship Fund, Inc.* v. *Commissioner*, 72 T.C. 267 (1979).

[173]E.g., *William F., Mabel E., and Margaret K. Quarrie Charitable Fund* v. *Commissioner*, 70 T.C. 182 (1978), aff'd 79-2 U.S.T.C. ¶ 9534 (7th Cir. 1979).

[174]See Chapter 12.

[175]*Supra*, n. 170.

[176]*Supra*, n. 171.

[177]*Big Mama Rag, Inc.* v. *United States*, 79-1 U.S.T.C. ¶ 9362 (D.D.C. 1979); *Afro-American Purchasing Center, Inc.* v. *Commissioner*, 37 T.C.M. 184 (1978).

ment, or why the inurement that is present is either insubstantial or unavoidable and incidental.[178]

These cases are also triggering examinations of the requirement that charitable organizations be organized and operated "exclusively" for tax-exempt purposes. The parameters of this requirement are being tested by cases that involve such questions as whether, or the extent to which, a charitable organization can operate at a profit or can provide services to members.[179]

The courts in these declaratory judgment cases are also paying close attention to the technical essentials of the "organizational test." This test looks to the sufficiency of an organization's governing instruments (articles of incorporation, constitution, bylaws, etc.) in light of the requirements of the income tax regulations. In one case, a court ruled that an organization could not qualify for tax exemption because of a defect in its articles of organization, in that the articles did not expressly preclude the possibility of a violation of the test by operation of state law.[180]

These developments and others to come are massively infusing new principles and interpretations in revision and expansion of the federal tax law applicable to charitable organizations. All indications are that representatives of charitable organizations are acquiring more understanding of the declaratory judgment procedures—not only the basics, but the planning aspects, such as shaping the administrative record, timely (albeit prudent) introduction at the administrative level of the possibility of a declaratory judgment action, and selection of the proper forum. These procedures are rewriting federal tax law affecting charitable organizations on many fronts, and the organizations and their advisors should monitor these cases to glean applicable legal principles—and not be reluctant to initiate a declaratory judgment action where the organization's interests warrant doing so.

Other, less feasible options, are open to the organization confronted with revocation of tax-exempt status. Where charitable contributions are involved, a "friendly donor" may bring suit attacking the legality of the IRS determi-

---

[178]*Christian Stewardship Assistance, Inc.* v. *Commissioner*, 70 T.C. 1037 (1978); *est of Hawaii* v. *Commissioner*, 71 T.C. 1067 (1979); *Federation Pharmacy Services, Inc.* v. *Commissioner*, 72 T.C. 687 (1979).

[179]*Pulpit Resource* v. *Commissioner*, n. 159, *supra*; *National Association for the Legal Support of Alternative Schools* v. *Commissioner*, 71 T.C. 118 (1978); *Aid to Artisans, Inc.* v. *Commissioner*, 71 T.C. 202 (1978); *Christian Manner International, Inc.* v. *Commissioner*, 71 T.C. 661 (1979); *Peoples Translation Service/Newsfront International* v. *Commissioner*, n. 161, *supra*; *Industrial Aid for the Blind* v. *Commissioner*, 73 T.C. 96 (1979); *The Schoger Foundation* v. *Commissioner*, *supra*, n. 164.

[180]*General Conference of the Free Church of America* v. *Commissioner*, 71 T.C. 920 (1979).

nation.[181] An organization may also sue for refund of FICA taxes,[182] FUTA taxes,[183] excise taxes,[184] or even wagering taxes.[185] But these avenues of review also can take substantial time, and the donor suit requires a plaintiff who is willing to be subjected to a general tax audit.

Also, conventional declaratory judgment suits[186] are of no avail in this setting, as the Declaratory Judgment Act expressly excludes controversies over federal taxes from its purview.[187]

Once an organization has secured a final determination from the courts that it is tax-exempt, and if the material facts and law have not changed since court consideration, the IRS will, upon request, issue a ruling or determination letter recognizing the tax exemption. However, if the organization did not previously file an application for recognition of exempt status, the Service will not issue a ruling or determination letter until the application is submitted.[188]

Absent relief administratively or in the courts, an organization facing loss of tax-exempt status may have no choice but to accept the revocation, discontinue the disqualifying activity (if its activities are sufficiently separable), and reestablish its exemption,[189] or spin the disqualifying activity off into a taxable subsidiary[190] or auxiliary exempt organization[191] and reestablish its exemption. Or, the organization may attempt an alternative to formal tax-exempt status, such as by operating as a nonexempt cooperative.[192]

---

[181]See, e.g., *Teich v. Commissioner*, 48 T. C. 963 (1967), aff'd 407 F.2d 815 (7th Cir. 1969); *Krohn v. United States*, 246 F.Supp. 341 (D. Col. 1965); *Kuper v. Commissioner*, 332 F.2d 562 (3d Cir. 1964), cert. den. 379 U. S. 902 (1964); *Bolton v. Commissioner*, 1 T. C. 717 (1943).

[182]See Code § 3121(b)(8)(B). See *Emerson Institute v. United States*, 336 F.2d 824 (D. C. Cir. 1966), cert. den. 385 U. S. 822 (1966).

[183]See Code § 3306(c)(8).

[184]See Code § 4253(h).

[185]See Code § 4421. See *Rochester Liederkranz, Inc. v. United States*, 456 F.2d 152 (2d Cir. 1972); *Hessman v. Campbell*, 134 F.Supp. 415 (S. D. Ind. 1955).

[186]28 U. S. C. §§ 2201-2202.

[187]See, e.g., *Mitchell v. Riddell*, 401 F.2d 842 (9th Cir. 1968), cert. den. 394 U. S. 456 (1969); *In re Wingreen Co.*, 412 F.2d 1048 (5th Cir. 1969); *Jolles Foundation, Inc. v. Moysey*, 250 F.2d 1966 (2d Cir. 1957); *International Telephone and Telegraph Corp. v. Alexander*, 396 F.Supp. 1150 (D. Del. 1975); *Kyron Foundation v. Dunlop*, 110 F.Supp. 428 (D. D. C. 1952).

[188]Rev. Proc. 80-28, 1980-1 C.B. 680.

[189]Compare *Danz v. Commissioner*, 18 T. C. 454 (1952), aff'd 231 F.2d 673 (9th Cir. 1955), cert. den. 352 U. S. 828 (1956), reh. den. 353 U. S. 951 (1957), with *John Danz Charitable Trust v. Commissioner*, 32 T. C. 469 (1959), aff'd 284 F.2d 726 (9th Cir. 1960).

[190]See *American Institute for Economic Research, Inc. v. United States*, 302 F.2d 934 (Ct. Cl. 1962), cert. den. 372 U. S. 976 (1963); Rev. Rul. 54-243, 1954-1 C. B. 92.

[191]See *Center on Corporate Responsibility, Inc. v. Shultz, supra*, n. 117.

[192]See Chapter 2.

§ 38.7 Third-Party Litigation

As noted at the outset, an organization's tax-exempt status may be maintained absent a material change in the pertinent facts or a change in the law. The organization generally will have control over the former circumstances but relatively little opportunity to affect the latter. The vulnerability as respects a law change was once heightened in light of the rash of third-party "ideological" or "policy" suits in the early 1970s.

Essentially, a third-party suit in this context is an action brought by one or more plaintiffs as a challenge to an IRS policy in administering the exempt organizations or other tax law. Rarely is such a plaintiff litigating as a "taxpayer" and such a suit is not framed as a conventional U.S. Tax Court or refund suit. Depending upon the outcome of the suit, the change in law wrought thereby can have considerable implications for one or more categories of tax-exempt organizations.

The present-day third-party "policy" suit challenging a principle of the law of tax-exempt organizations is an amalgam of a series of "public interest" suits in the tax field[193] and a variety of tax suits raising constitutional questions. As respects the latter, in the principal case, the courts involved concluded that racially discriminatory private schools are not entitled to tax federal exemption.[194] Comparable cases, with fainter relationships to constitutional principles, led to decisions that racially discriminatory fraternal organizations are not entitled to tax exemption,[195] although racially discriminatory social clubs[196] are not barred from tax-exempt status,[197] that "charitable" organizations will not lose such categorization because they discriminate in their membership policies on the basis of sex,[198] and that unions that expend membership dues for partisan political campaigns do not for that reason forfeit their tax-exempt status.[199]

These cases have given rise, however, to cases which strictly involve "policy" questions—questions heretofore answered only by the Department of the Treasury in its regulations, the IRS in its rulings, or the courts in passing on the tax status of particular organizations who were parties to the suit. The most prominent case in this category caused·the U.S. Court of Appeals for the District

---

[193]See, e.g., *Tax Analysts and Advocates* v. *Shultz*, 376 F. Supp. 889 (D. D. C. 1974); *Tax Analysts and Advocates* v. *Internal Revenue Service*, 362 F. Supp. 1298 (D. D. C. 1973); *Common Cause* v. *Shultz*, 73-2 U. S. T. C. ¶ 9592 (D. D. C. 1973).

[194]*Green* v. *Kennedy*, 309 F.Supp. 1127 (D. D. C. 1970); app. dis. sub nom. *Cannon* v. *Green*, 398 U. S. 956 (1970), cont. sub nom. *Green* v. *Connally*, 330 F.Supp. 1150 (D. D. C. 1971), aff'd on intervenors' appeal sub nom. *Coit* v. *Green*, 404 U. S. 997 (1971). See Chapter 7.

[195]Code § 501(c)(8).

[196]Code § 501(c)(7).

[197]*McGlotten* v. *Connally*, 338 F.Supp. 448 (1972).

[198]*McCoy* v. *Shultz*, 73-1 U. S. T. C. ¶ 9233 (D. D. C. 1973).

[199]Code § 501(c)(5). *Marker* v. *Connally*. 485 F.2d 1003 D. C. Cir. 1973), affg 337 F.Supp. 1301 (D. D. C. 1972).

of Columbia Circuit to consider IRS policy as to the criteria for an exempt hospital and pronounce a revision of that policy valid.[200] A comparable case initiated in 1974 sought to enjoin Treasury and IRS officials from granting "charitable" status to otherwise charitable organizations that substantially provide commercial travel services and from refusing to enforce the unrelated business income tax provisions.[201]

The viability of these types of cases is now somewhat questionable, inasmuch as the U.S. Supreme Court has sought to extinguish the so-called "third-party" litigation.[202] It has chosen to accomplish this end by the issuance of yet another opinion articulating its conception of the law of standing. The court, in a case initiated by indigents and organizations of indigents seeking judicial review of IRS criteria for exempting nonprofit hospitals from income tax, held that the plaintiffs lacked standing to bring the suit within the framework of Article III of the U.S. Constitution, which requires the existence of an authentic "case or controversy." Nonetheless, the court stated that "[w]e do not reach. . . .the question of whether a third party *ever* may challenge the IRS treatment of another. . . " (emphasis added).[203]

Still, the standing test as formulated in this decision is designed to curb the type of litigation represented by that case. The Court summarized the standing requirement as follows:". . . when a plaintiff's standing is brought into issue the relevant inquiry is whether, assuming justiciability of the claim, the plaintiff has shown an injury to himself that is likely to be redressed by a favorable decision."[204] The court's interpretation of that requirement in this context means that "an organization's abstract concern with a subject that could be affected by an adjudication does not substitute for the concrete injury required by Article III."[205] Thus, the plaintiffs in the case lost becuase they could not demonstrate the needed "concrete injury" (stated in a previous decision as the requisite "personal stake in the outcome of the controversy"[206]) and because, even if the hospitals had caused injury, the plaintiffs proceeded not against those institutions but against federal officials. (The second, "nonconstitutional" standing requirement that the interest of a plaintiff be "arguably within the

---

[200]*Eastern Kentucky Welfare Rights Organization* v. *Simon*, 560 F.2d 1278 (D. C. Cir. 1974), rev'g 370 F.Supp. 325 (D. D. C. 1973). Also see *Penn v. San Juan Hospital, Inc.*, 528 F.2d 1181 (10th Cir. 1975).

[201]*American Society of Travel Agents* v. *Simon*, 75-1 U.S.T.C. ¶ 9484 (D. D. C. 1975), aff'd 556 F.2d 145 (D. C. Cir. 1977), cert. den. 435 U.S. 947 (1978). Also see *Council of British Societies in Southern California* v. *United States*, 78-2 U.S.T.C. ¶ 9744 (D. C. Cal. 1978).

[202]*Simon v. Eastern Kentucky Welfare Rights Organization*, 426 U. S. 26 (1976).
[203]*Ibid*. at 37.
[204]*Id*. at 38.
[205]*Id*. at 40, citing *Sierra Club* v. *Morton*, 405 U.S. 727 (1972).
[206]*Warth* v. *Seldin*, 422 U.S. 490, 498 (1975).

zone of interests to be protected or regulated" by the statutory framework within which his or her claim arises[207] went unconsidered in the opinion.[208]

Consequently, the lifespan of general third-party suits under pre-1976 statutory law was action-packed but brief. Justice Stewart, in a concurring opinion in the case, was moved to observe that "I cannot now imagine a case, at least outside the First Amendment area, where a person whose own tax liability was not affected ever could have standing to litigate the federal tax liability of someone else."[209] However, this gratuitous comment is unduly broad. For example, an organization ruled by the IRS to be a supported organization pursuant to the public charity/private foundation rules[210] would have standing to bring suit against the Secretary of the Treasury and Commissioner of Internal Revenue contesting the legality of the determination on the ground that the alleged supporting organization was not in compliance with the statute's essentials (thereby depriving the alleged supported organization of funds) and hence is liable for the taxes imposed on private foundations.

Justice Brennan, joined by Justice Marshall, criticized his brethren for not deciding the case against the plaintiffs on the grounds that the case involved largely hypothetical situations and hence not a ripe controversy. He also complained that the majority unnecessarily and erroneously treated the "injury-in-fact" standing requirement in a manner in direct conflict with prior decisions of the court, in part by laying down a standard of pleading of facts not "in keeping with modern notions of civil procedure."[211]

On this latter point, Brennan stated that, in Administrative Procedure Act cases "standing is not to be denied merely because the ultimate harm alleged is a threatened future one rather than an accomplished fact."[212] (The "ultimate harm" alleged in the case was that tax-exempt hospitals, as encouraged by the IRS, would cease providing medical services to indigents.) The justice did some hypothecizing of his own,[213] wondering if, as the result of the opinion, "minority school children [will] now have to plead and show that in the absence of illegal governmental 'encouragement' of private segregated schools, such schools would

---

[207]*Association of Data Processing Service Organizations* v. *Camp*, 397 U. S. 150, 153 (1969). In *Wright* v. *Regan*, 81-2 U.S.T.C. ¶ 9504 (D.C. Cir. 1981), the U.S. Court of Appeals for the District of Columbia Circuit held that the parents of black public school children had standing to bring a class action suit claiming that Code § 501(a) promotes discrimination by permitting recognition of tax exemption of racially discriminatory private schools. Also *Tax Analysts* v. *Blumenthal*, 566 F.2d 130 (D. C. Cir. 1977).

[208]For commentary on the *Eastern Kentucky* case, see Note, 30 *Tax Lawyer* 490 (1977); Note, 1977 *Wis. L. Rev.* 247 (1977); Note, 29 *Tax Lawyer* 361 (1976); Note, 7 *Univ. of Toledo L. Rev.* 278 (1975); Note, 73 *Col. L. Rev.* 1502 (1973).

[209]426 U.S. 26, 46 (1976).

[210]See Chapter 22.

[211]426 U.S. 26, 62 (1976).

[212]*Ibid.* at 61.

[213]*Id.* at 63.

not 'elect to forego' their favorable tax treatment, and that this will 'result in the availability' to complainants of an integrated educational system"[214] or if "black Americans [will] be required to plead and show that in the absence of illegal government encouragement, private institutions would not 'elect to forego' favorable tax treatment, and that this will 'result in the availability' to complain[an]ts of services previously denied."[215]

Justice Brennan found the "most disturbing aspect" of the opinion to be the court's "insistence on resting its decision regarding standing squarely on the irreducible Art. III minimum of injury in fact, thereby effectively placing its holding beyond congressional power to rectify."[216] He added: "Thus, any time Congress chooses to legislate in favor of certain interests by setting up a scheme of incentives for third parties, judicial review of administrative action that allegedly frustrates the congressionally intended objective will be denied, because any complainant will be required to make an almost impossible showing."[217] What this augers for the future is unclear. Brennan stated the ultimate objective well: "In our modern-day society, dominated by complex legislative programs and large-scale governmental involvement in the everyday lives of all of us, judicial review of administrative action is essential both for protection of individuals illegally harmed by that action. . . .and to ensure that the attainment of congressionally mandated goals is not frustrated by illegal action."[218]

The impact of the U.S. Supreme Court's pronouncement on this subject has been somewhat moderated as the result of enactment by Congress of the declaratory judgment procedures for contesting loss or denial of tax-exempt and similar status. Although "third-party" suits are not involved as such, these new procedures are greatly enhancing the likelihood and frequency of court review of IRS determinations in the tax-exempt organizations field.

Although generally outside the scope of this work, it may be helpful to briefly summarize the jurisdictional and related issues raised by these third-party cases. Despite the government's attempts to invoke the doctrine of sovereign immunity, the courts have generally held that the doctrine does not bar actions against government officials who allegedly are acting in excess of their statutory authority or discretion or in an unconstitutional manner.[219] The general prohibition on injunctive relief[220] has been held not to be a bar to these

---

[214]Citing *Green* v. *Kennedy, supra,* n. 194. See Chapter 6.

[215]Citing *McGlotten* v. *Connally, supra,* n. 197, and *Pitts* v. *Wisconsin Department of Revenue,* 333 F.Supp. 662 (E. D. Wis. 1971).

[216]426 U.S. 26, 64 (1976).

[217]*Ibid.* at 64.

[218]*Id.* at 65. In general, see Sheldon and Bostock, "Supreme Court severely limits third party's right to contest exempt status," 45 *J. Tax.* 140 (1976).

[219]See, e.g., *Dugan* v. *Rank,* 372 U.S. 609 (1963); *State Highway Commission of Missouri* v. *Volpe,* 479 F.2d 1099 (8th Cir. 1973). So held in *Eastern Kentucky Welfare Rights Organization* v. *Simon, supra,* n. 200; *McGlotten* v. *Connally, supra,* n. 197.

[220]Code § 7421(a).

suits because they bear no relation to assessment or collection of taxes.[221] The Declaratory Judgment Act has likewise been found not a bar to jurisdiction, on the ground that its scope is coterminous with the injunctive relief rule.[222]

Aside from these and other alleged bars to jurisdiction, the courts have held that various statutes provide jurisdiction. Thus, jurisdiction in these cases has been fully asserted on the basis of the Administrative Procedure Act[223] and the Declaratory Judgment Act, the pendent jurisdiction rules,[224] and the more conventional jurisdictional basis.[225] Still another hurdle these suits, in many instances, have cleared is standing, which, of course, is a prerequisite of any action. Basically, a plaintiff must be able to demonstrate a direct injury and the requisite personal stake in the controversy.[226] The focus of these principles is far from clear,[227] as the above-discussed U.S. Supreme Court decision indicates.

The future of third-party suits in the tax-exempt organizations field is uncertain, in view of the above-discussed Supreme Court opinion and the decision of Congress to confine the tax-exempt organizations declaratory judgment procedure to use "by the organization the qualification or classification of which is at issue." In the first case to be considered by a court of appeals following the Supreme Court's ruling, the appellate court had deferred its consideration of the case pending the Supreme Court's determination and, once the Supreme Court acted, affirmed the lower court's dismissal of the case but on the ground of lack of standing.[228] The court concluded that the plaintiff organization failed to demonstrate any actual injury resulting from the administration of the tax laws, with respect to third parties, governing tax-exempt organizations.

Certainly this line of litigation produced much uncertainty about the appropriate tax treatment of particular activities and programs of tax-exempt organizations.[229] Moreover, these cases generated considerable controversy as

---

[221]*Eastern Kentucky Welfare Rights Organization* v. *Simon, supra*, n. 200; *McGlotten* v. *Connally, supra*, n. 197.

[222]See, e.g., *Jules Hairstylists of Maryland* v. *United States*, 268 F.Supp. 511 (D. Md. 1967), aff'd 389 F.2d 389 (4th Cir. 1968), cert. den. 391 U.S. 934 (1968). So held in, e.g., *Eastern Kentucky Welfare Rights Organization* v. *Simon, supra*, n. 200; "*Americans United*" v. *Walters, supra*, n. 115, at 447 F.2d 1176.

[223]5 U.S.C. §§ 702, 703. See *Eastern Kentucky Welfare Rights Organization* v. *Simon, supra*, n. 200.

[224]28 U.S.C. §§ 2282, 2284. See, e.g., *Zemel* v. *Rusk*, 381 U.S. 1 (1965).

[225]28 U.S.C. §§ 1331, 1340, 1361.

[226]*Frothingham* v. *Mellon*, 262 U.S. 447 (1923); *Flast* v. *Cohen*, 392 U.S. 83 (1968); *Association of Data Processing Service Organizations* v. *Camp, supra*, n. 207; *Tax Analysts and Advocates* v. *Simon*, 390 F.Supp. 927 (D. D. C. 1975). In general, see "Standing To Sue" (panel discussion), 26 *Tax Lawyer* 27 (1974).

[227]See *United States* v. *Richardson*, 418 U.S. 166 (1974); *Schlesinger* v. *Reservists Committee to Stop the War*, 418 U.S. 208 (1974); *United States* v. *Students Challenging Regulatory Agency Procedures*, 412 U.S. 669 (1973).

[228]*American Society of Travel Agents, Inc.* v. *Simon, supra*, n. 201.

[229]See, e.g., *Jackson* v. *Statler Foundation*, 496 F.2d 623 (2d Cir. 1974).

to the proper roles of the courts, the IRS and the Department of the Treasury in formulating the law of tax-exempt organizations.[230]

Recent developments, however, strongly suggest that third-party litigation over tax exemption issues is once again a viable litigation option. As illustrations, the debate over the tax status of private schools with racially discriminatory policies was resumed, in part, because the original litigation was reopened,[231] and the challenge on equal protection grounds to the disparate treatment of "charitable" and veterans' groups that lobby is—at least so far—successful.[232]

Yet the most striking example of the resurgence in the ability of third-party plaintiffs to leap the standing hurdle came in mid-1982 when the U.S. District Court for the Southern District of New York ruled that a variety of organizations and individuals have standing to challenge the constitutionality of the government's alleged refusal to enforce the restrictions in the general rules for "charitable" organizations on legislative and political campaign involvements against the Roman Catholic Church.[233]

The plaintiffs in the case sued the Secretary of the Treasury and the Commissioner of Internal Revenue for failing to revoke the tax-exempt status of the Catholic Church because of its legislative and electioneering activities. The Church has mounted an extensive campaign, involving both lobbying and political campaign efforts, to outlaw abortion. These efforts, claim the Abortion Rights Mobilization (ARM) and other plaintiffs, are in direct conflict with the limitations on lobbying and electioneering under which the Church and its affiliates continue to be tax-exempt. By contrast, the plaintiffs assert that the IRS has refused to grant to organizations with opposing views on the abortion controversy (such as ARM) tax exemption as "charitable" entities where they engage in comparable legislative and electioneering activities. The plaintiffs contend that this is discriminatory tax policy that is unconstitutional, illegal, and unfair.

Before considering the claims of these plaintiffs on their merits, the court had to dispose of a variety of motions, including the government's motion to dismiss for lack of standing. The court considered three bases for standing: establishment clause standing, voter standing, and equal protection standing. The essential elements for standing, said the court, are (1) a "distinct and palpable injury" to the plaintiff, (2) a "fairly traceable causal connection between the claimed injury and the challenged conduct," and (3) a showing that "the exercise of the Court's remedial powers would redress the claimed injuries."[234]

---

[230]See Tannenbaum, "Public Interest Tax Litigation Challenging Substantive I.R.S. Decisions," 27 *Nat'l Tax J.* 373 (1974); Worthy, "Judicial determinations of exempt status: Has the time come for a change of systems?," 40 *J. Tax.* 324 (1974).

[231]*Wright* v. *Regan*, 656 F.2d 820 (D.C. Cir. 1981).

[232]*Taxation With Representation of Washington* v. *Regan*, 676 F.2d 715 (D.C. Cir. 1982).

[233]*Abortion Rights Mobilization, Inc.* v. *Regan*, 82-2 U.S.T.C. ¶9477 (S.D. N.Y. 1982).

[234]*Ibid.* at p. 84,727.

As to establishment clause standing, most of the plaintiffs were found to have failed the "injury-in-fact" test. Said the court: "Plaintiffs' devotion to the pro-choice position does not identify an interest that the allegedly illegal activities have damaged; it only explains why plaintiffs have chosen to complain about a particular government impropriety—renewal of the church defendants' [Code] § 501 (c) (3) status. . . ."[235] However, the plaintiffs who are members of the clergy and one abortion clinic were found to have shown "compelling and personalized injuries flowing from the tacit government endorsement of the Roman Catholic Church position on abortion that are sufficient to confer standing on them to complain of the alleged establishment clause violations."[236] In language that suggests the government is going to lose this case on the merits in this court, the court ruled that the "causation" and "redressability" tests are also satisfied. As to the former, the court said: "The granting of a uniquely favored tax status to one religious entity is an unequivocal statement of preference that gilds the image of that religion and tarnishes all others."[237] As to the latter, the court observed: "A decree ordering the termination of this illegal practice and restoring all sects to equal footing will redress this injury."[238]

Concerning voter standing, the underlying issue is whether some arbitrary government action diluted the strength of voters in one group at the expense of those in another group. Finding this type of standing in the plaintiffs, the court concluded: "Plaintiffs claim that allegedly unconstitutional government conduct and illegal private conduct has distorted the electoral and legislative process by creating a system in which members of the public have greater incentive to donate funds to the Roman Catholic Church than to politically active abortion rights groups and in which each dollar contributed to the church is worth more than one given to non-exempt [i.e., noncharitable donee] organizations."[239] Once again, in language highly suggestive of victory to the plaintiffs (at least at the district court level), the court stated: "An injunction against that discriminatory policy will restore the proper balance between adversaries in the abortion debate."[240]

As to the equal protection basis for standing, the court rejected the contention that the plaintiffs can prevail on any Fifth Amendment grounds. The court also found that the litigation is outside the reach of the Anti-Injunction Act[241] and that conventional declaratory relief[242] is not available to the plaintiffs. The United States Catholic Conference and the National Conference of Catholic Bishops were dismissed as defendants.

[235]*Id.* at p. 84,728.
[236]*Id.* at p. 84,729.
[237]*Id.* at p. 84,730.
[238]*Id.*
[239]*Id.* at p. 84,731.
[240]*Id.* at pp. 84,731–84,732.
[241]Code § 7421.
[242]Code § 2201.

In any event, a somewhat functional equivalent of the third-party suit is available. The congressional committee reports constituting part of the legislative history of the Tax Reform Act of 1976 specifically state that Congress' silence on third party litigation "constitutes neither an implied endorsement nor an implied criticism of such 'third-party' suits."[243] Nonetheless, Congress indicated its intent that the courts should be reasonably "generous" in accepting amicus curiae briefs and permitting appearances by third parties in these suits.[244]

§ 38.8   The IRS Audit

The IRS is empowered to audit the affairs and records of tax-exempt organizations. In recent years, this audit activity has increased, in an effort to assure that exempt organizations are in compliance with all pertinent requirements, generally those enacted or imposed by reason of the Tax Reform Act of 1969.[245] Consequently, the likelihood of an IRS audit has become of increasing concern to organizations as a factor affecting continuation of their tax exemption (and, where applicable, their private foundation status), susceptibility to the tax on unrelated income, and proper administration of their payroll.

The audit is usually initiated in the field, under the auspices of the appropriate key district. The individuals involved are supposed to be specialists in tax-exempt organization matters and are under the direction of a supervisor in the district office. The Exempt Organization Division of the Office of Employee Plans and Exempt Organizations at the IRS National Office has the responsibility for establishing the procedures and policy for the conduct for exempt organization audit programs.

While there is some coordination within the IRS as to the timing and focus of audits, an exempt organization can generally expect one at any time, particularly if a significant period of time has elapsed since any prior audit.

The records that must be produced upon audit are likely to include all organizational documents (such as articles of organization, bylaws, resolutions, and minutes of meetings), documents relating to tax status (such as the application for recognition of exemption and IRS rulings as to exempt and private foundation status), financial statements (including underlying entry books and records), and newsletters and/or other publications. The items that must be

---

[243]E.g., S. Rep. No. 94-938, *supra*, n. 156 at 587, n. 6.

[244]*Ibid*.

[245]In general, see Bacon, "Working with the I. R. S. in the New Exempt Organizations Program in Audit," 1 *Tax Adviser* 69 (1970); Lehrfeld, "IRS' new large private foundation audit program: How to prepare for it," 33 *J. Tax.* 16 (1970). For pre-1970 audit practices, see Stratton, "A Guide to Dealing With The IRS," 31 *Association Management* 45 (August 1979); Wolfe, "Federal Policing of Exempt Organizations," *N. Y. U. 28th Ann. Inst. on Fed. Tax.* 1387 (1969); Lehrfeld, "Administration by the IRS of Nonprofit Organization Matters," 21 *Tax Lawyer* 591 (1968); Panel Discussion, "What To Do When The Revenue Agent Appears To Make An Audit," *N. Y. U. Sixth Ann. Inst. on Char. Fdns.* 251 (1963).

produced will depend upon the type of audit being conducted; the audit may or may not encompass payroll records, pension plan matters, returns of associated individuals or subsidiary organizations, and the like. A related element is the attitude and competence of the revenue agent(s), and the degree to which the organization is prepared to cooperate in the audit. In some circumstances, the organization may find it appropriate to produce information only upon the presentation of a subpoena.[246]

The techniques for coping with IRS personnel on the occasion of an audit are easily summarized but their deployment and success are likely to depend heavily on the personalities involved. Certainly, the key staff personnel and legal counsel of the audited organization should be in the process from the beginning, and it is advisable to select one person who will serve as liaison with the IRS during the audit. The duration of and the procedures to be followed during the audit should be ascertained at the outset and records should be carefully maintained as to information and documents examined or copies by the revenue agents. All interviews should be monitored by the liaison person, with appropriate records made; at least some of the questioning should occur only in the presence of legal counsel.

Where issues arise, one or both sides may decide to pursue the technical advice procedure (see above) or the matter may be taken up with the IRS by means of the conference(s) procedure.[247]

The IRS audit (and related) efforts in the tax-exempt organizations field during 1979 has been described as follows:

> The Exempt Organizations activity determines the qualifications of organizations seeking tax-exempt recognition, determines their private foundation status and examines returns to ensure compliance with the law. The number of active entities on the exempt organizations master file (EOMF) increased from 810,048 in 1978 to 824,536 in 1979.
>
> This year, 7 regulations, 25 revenue rulings and procedures, 340 technical advice memoranda and 21 announcements were issued or revised. An average of 433 field professional positions were used to examine 22,371 exempt organizations returns. Also, 114 field professional positions and 117 National Office technical positions were used for 50,568 applications, reapplications and requests for rulings on proposed transactions from organizations seeking a determination of tax-exempt status or of the effect of organizational or operational changes on their status. The development of the new formulas to select certain exempt organization returns for examination has been completed, using the taxpayer compliance measurement program (TCMP) file augmented by EOMF data. The result was improved formulas for selection of *Internal Revenue Code* subsection 501(c)(3) public charities and *IRC* 501(c)(4) organizations for examination.

---

[246]For a discussion of enforcement proceedings in connection with IRS administrative summonses, see *United States v. Church of Scientology of California*, 520 F.2d 818 (9th Cir. 1975). In general, the U.S. Supreme Court has broadly construed the IRS summons power. See *United States v. LaSalle National Bank*, 437 U.S. 298 (1978).

[247]Details of the IRS Audit Procedures for Exempt Organizations appear in the Internal Revenue Manual. IR Manual MT 4(11) 00-6.

The IRS is developing a TCMP survey for all *IRC* 501(c) subsections through (c)(8) having more than 5,000 filers. The survey, involving examinations of 20,000 returns filed in 1980 through 1983 will begin in October 1980.

Additional guidelines have been published providing instructions and procedures to examiners for the pre-examination of churches and related organizations. Guidelines were also issued providing uniform procedures for the identification, investigation and examination of organizations employing questionable claims of tax-exempt church status.

In 1979, IRS conducted a nationwide review of the exempt status under *IRC* 501(c)(4) and 501(c)(7) of certain homeowners associations. The IRS advised the homeowners associations revoked under the program of the availability of exempt status under *IRC* 528. The program resulted in 532 revocations under 501(c)(4) and 501(c)(7) and 479 conversions to *IRC* 528 status.[248]

[248]Commissioner of Internal Revenue 1979 Annual Report at 25.

PART VI

FEEDER ORGANIZATIONS AND UNRELATED INCOME TAXATION

39

Feeder Organizations

Federal tax law provides that "[a]n organization operated for the primary purpose of carrying on a trade or business for profit shall not be exempt from taxation under section 501 on the ground that all of its profits are payable to one or more organizations exempt from taxation under section 501."[1] This type of entity is known as a "feeder" organization, inasmuch as it is a business operation that "feeds" monies to a tax-exempt organization. In determining the primary purpose of an organization, all pertinent circumstances are considered, including the size and extent of the trade or business and the size and extent of the activities of the tax-exempt organization.[2] If an organization carries on a trade or business but not as a primary function, the organization may be tax-exempt, although the income from the trade or business may be taxed as unrelated business taxable income.[3]

The feeder organization rules were added to the law in 1950, as a legislative overturning of the "destination of income" test.[4] Under the destination of income test, the destination of an organization's income was considered of greater consequence than the source and use of its income (the emphasis now as the result of enactment of the feeder rules) for purposes of determining exemption from taxation. However, the principal problem with this approach was that exempt business operations were able to competitively undercut businesses which were not related to tax-exempt organizations.

The House Committee on Ways and Means report accompanying the Revenu Act of 1950 stated that the feeder organization provision was intended to—

[1]Code § 502 (a).
[2]Reg. § 1.502-1(a).
[3]Reg. § 1.502-1(c). See Chapters 40–42.
[4]See *Trinidad* v. *Sagrada Orden De Predicadores*, 263 U.S. 578, 581 (1924); *Roche's Beach, Inc.* v. *Commissioner*, 96 F.2d 776, 778 (2d Cir. 1938); *Consumer-Farmer Milk Cooperative* v. *Commissioner*, 186 F.2d 68, 70 (2d Cir. 1950); *Universal Oil Products Co.* v. *Campbell*, 181 F.2d 451 (7th Cir. 1950); *Willingham* v. *Home Oil Mill*, 181 F.2d 9 (5th Cir. 1950).

609

prevent the exemption of a trade or business organization under. . .[the predecessor to Code § 501(c)(3)] on the grounds that an organization actually described
in. . .[that section] receives the earnings from the operations of the trade or
business organization. In any case it appears clear to your committee that such
an organization is not itself carrying out an exempt purpose. Moreover, it obviously
is in direct competition with other taxable businesses.[5]

The impact of the feeder organization rules may be vividly seen in the case
of the SICO Foundation, which was a nonstock corporation owning controlling
interests in several corporations engaged in the business of selling and distributing petroleum products.[6] Its net income was distributed to teachers' colleges
for scholarship purposes. The SICO Foundation was before the Court of Claims
for tax years prior to 1951, seeking tax-exempt status, in 1952. Following the
destination of income test, the court found the organization to be "educational"
in nature and hence tax-exempt.[7] But, when its tax status for years 1951, 1952,
and 1953 was litigated in the Court of Claims, the court held that enactment
of the feeder organization rules in 1950[8] caused the organization to lose its tax-
exempt status. Concluded the court: "That it gave all its profits to an educational
institution availeth it nothing [except presumably a charitable contribution
deduction] in the mundane field of taxation, however much the children in our
schools have profited from its beneficence."[9]

One vestige of the destination of income test remains, however. Under the
rules defining the meaning of the term "gross income,"[10] the value of services
is not includible in gross income when the services are rendered directly and
gratuitously to a charitable organization.[11] Thus, a parimutuel race track corporation was able to distribute charity day race proceeds to a charitable organization, which agreed to absorb any losses arising from the event and to
assume all responsibility for the promotion, and not include any of the proceeds
in its gross income for federal income tax purposes.[12] Where, by contrast, the
race track corporation is the promoter of the charity day racing event, rather
than the agent of the charity, the proceeds from the event are taxable to the
corporation.[13]

[5]H. Rep. No. 2319, 81st Cong., 2d Sess. (1950) at 41. Also S. Rep. No. 2375, 81st
Cong., 2d Sess. (1950) at 35.
[6]SICO Foundation v. United States, 295 F.2d 924 (Ct. Cl. 1961), reh. den. 297 F.2d
557 (Ct. Cl. 1962).
[7]The SICO Co. v. United States, 102 F. Supp. 197 (Ct. Cl. 1952).
[8]26 U.S.C. § 101.
[9]Supra, n. 6 at 925.
[10]Code § 61(a).
[11]See Reg. § 1.61-2(c).
[12]Rev. Rul. 77-121, 1977-1 C. B. 17.
[13]Rev. Rul. 72-542, 1972-2, C. B. 37. In this instance, however, the corporation
receives a business expense deduction under Code § 162 or a charitable contribution
deduction under Code § 170 for the proceeds turned over to charity. Rev. Rul. 77-124,
1977-1 C. B. 39; Rev. Rul. 72-542, supra.

The distinctions at play in the feeder organization context are frequently difficult to initially discern. For example, the IRS accorded tax-exempt status to a nonprofit corporation controlled by a church, where the organization's function was to print and sell educational and religious material to the church's parochial system at a profit, with the profits returned to the system.[14] But, an organization formed by a church to operate a commercial printing business (which generated a substantial profit) and to print religious materials for the church at cost (about 10 percent of its activities), where all net income was paid over to the church, was ruled a feeder organization and thus not tax-exempt.[15] The distinguishing feature here is the fact that an overwhelming percentage of the organization's activities in the latter instance was the provision of commercial services to other than the related tax-exempt organization.

The government's position is that where a subsidiary organization of a tax-exempt parent would itself be exempt, because its activities are an "integral part" of the activities of the parent, the exempt status of the subsidiary will not be lost because the subsidiary derives a profit from its dealings with the parent.[16] For example, the income tax regulations contain an illustration of a subsidiary organization operated for the sole purpose of furnishing electric power used by the parent organization (an exempt educational institution) in carrying on its tax-exempt activities; the subsidiary is itself a "charitable" entity. However, where a subsidiary of a tax-exempt parent is operated for the primary purpose of carrying on a trade or business which would be an unrelated trade or business if regularly carried on by the parent, the subsidiary would not be tax-exempt.[17] The regulations contain the example of a subsidiary of an exempt parent which is not exempt because it is operated primarily for the purpose of furnishing electric power to consumers other than the parent.

The income tax regulations accompanying the feeder organizations law contain an observation which has no basis in statutory law and which has nothing to do with that rule. This is the comment that "if the [subsidiary] organization is owned by several [i.e., more than one] unrelated exempt organizations, and is operated for the purpose of furnishing electric power to each of them, it is not exempt since such business would be an unrelated trade or business if regularly carried on by any one of the tax-exempt organizations."[18] On this point, the regulations have it backwards, for the feeder organization rules do not even apply until there is an organization "operated for the primary purpose of carrying on a trade or business for profit." Thus, the Senate Finance Committee report accompanying the Senate version of the measure that became

[14]Rev. Rul. 68-26, 1968-1 C. B. 272. Also *Pulpit Resource* v. *Commissioner*, 70 T. C. 594 (1978).

[15]Rev. Rul. 73-164, 1973-1 C. B. 223.

[16]Reg. § 1.502-1(b). A technical parent–subsidiary relationship need not be present. See Rev. Rul. 68-26, *supra*, n. 14.

[17]*Ibid.* Cf. IRS Private Letter Ruling 7902019 (Issue no. 1).

[18]*Ibid.*

the Revenue Act of 1950 states that the provision "applies to organizations operated for the primary purpose of carrying on a trade or business for profit, as for example, a feeder corporation whose business is the manufacture of automobiles for the ultimate profit of an educational institution."[19] These rules do not purport to define such an organization and nothing in its history indicates that it was intended to denominate as a feeder an organization controlled by and serving only tax-exempt organizations. As discussed,[20] this statement is one of the rationales of the IRS for denying tax-exempt status to consortia and other organizations performing "joint activities" for exempt organizations,[21] even though this rationale has been explicitly rejected in the first cases where it was considered.[22] In one of these cases, the court first questioned the relationship of this regulation to the statute: "Charitably put (no pun intended), the Court has difficulty in finding any basis in the statute, 26 U.S.C. sec. 502, for . . .[this] portion of the regulations."[23] Secondly, the court dismissed the applicability of these rules in the context of "shared services" organizations (consortia): "What does this [the feeder organization rule] have to do with two or more such [tax-exempt] organizations setting up a not-for-profit corporation, wholly controlled by them, and not serving the public, in order to effect economies in their own charitable operations? The Court in. . .[a prior case] gave no effect to the regulation, nor does this Court."[24]

As the government progressed to ultimate success in defeating tax exemption for cooperative hospital laundry organizations,[25] it abandoned its argument against consortia based on this interpretation of the feeder rules. The argument was rejected by the federal district court,[26] jettisoned by the government on appeal to the U.S. Court of Appeals for the Third Circuit,[27] and thus not considered by the U.S. Supreme Court.[28] Therefore, it is not clear whether the argument has been abandoned altogether or just for purposes of litigation strategy; probably the latter is the case. As noted,[29] however, the U.S. Tax Court has accepted this argument.[30]

With the increasing emphasis on determination of unrelated business taxable income, rather than deprivation of tax-exempt status, the IRS has retreated

[19]S. Rep. No. 2375, *supra*, n. 5, at 116.
[20]See Chapter 6.
[21]See Rev. Rul. 69-528, 1969-2 C. B. 127.
[22]*Hospital Bureau of Standards & Supplies* v. *United States*, 158 F.Supp. 560, 563 (Ct. Cl. 1958); *United Hospital Services, Inc.* v. *United States*, 384 F.Supp. 776 (S. D. Ind. 1974).
[23]*United Hospital Services, Inc.* v. *United States*, *supra*, n. 22, at 782.
[24]*Ibid.*
[25]See Chapter 10 § 4.
[26]*HCSC-Laundry* v. *United States*, 473 F.Supp. 250 (E.D. Pa. 1979).
[27]*HCSC-Laundry* v. *United States*, 624 F.2d 428, 432, n. 6 (3d Cir. 1980).
[28]*HCSC-Laundry* v. *United States*, 450 U.S. 1 (1981).
[29]Chapter 6 § 9 at 90.
[30]*Associated Hospital Services, Inc.* v. *Commissioner*, 74 T.C. 213 (1980).

somewhat as concerns vigorous assertion of the feeder organization rules.[31] Also, the courts have infrequently construed the feeder rules against the affected organizations.[32]

For purposes of these rules,[33] the term "trade or business" does not include (1) the derivation of most types of rents,[34] (2) any trade or business in which substantially all the work in carrying on the trade or business is performed for the organization without compensation, or (3) any trade or business which consists of the selling of merchandise, substantially all of which has been received by the organization as gifts or contributions.[35] For example, a thrift shop may avoid feeder organization status because the work is performed by volunteers[36] or because the merchandise was received as gifts.[37]

[31]See, e.g., Rev. Rul. 66-296, 1966-2 C. B. 215; Rev. Rul. 66-295, 1966-2 C. B. 207.

[32]For cases where Code § 502 was not applied, see, e.g., *Industrial Aid for the Blind v. Commissioner*, 73 T.C. 96 (1979); *E. Orton, Jr. Ceramic Foundation v. Commissioner*, 56 T. C. 147 (1971); *Duluth Clinic Foundation v. United States*, 67-1 U.S.T.C. ¶9226 (D. Minn. 1967); *Bright Star Foundation v. Campbell*, 191 F.Supp. 845 (N. D. Tex. 1960). Code § 502 was applied in, e.g., *Veterans Foundation v. United States*, 281 F.2d 912 (10th Cir. 1960); *Disabled Veterans Service Foundation, Inc. v. Commissioner*, 29 T. C. M. 202 (1970).

[33]See Code § 502(b).

[34]See Code § 512(b)(3)(a), Chapter 41.

[35]See Reg. § 1.502-1 (d)(2).

[36]Rev. Rul. 80-106, 1980-1 C. B. 113.

[37]Rev. Rul. 71-581, 1971-2 C. B. 236.

40

Taxation of Unrelated Income

Even though a nonprofit organization achieves general exemption from the federal income tax,[1] it nonetheless remains potentially taxable on any unrelated business income.[2] This tax[3] is generally levied at the corporate rates,[4] in the case of charitable trusts,[5] it is imposed at the individual rates.[6]

§ 40.1 Introduction

The taxation of unrelated income, a feature of the federal tax law since 1950, is based on the concept that the approach is a more effective and workable sanction for authentic enforcement of the law of tax-exempt organizations than total denial of exempt status.[7] It is basically a simple concept: the unrelated business income tax only applies to active business income which arises from activities which are "unrelated" to the organization's tax-exempt purposes.

Of course, if a substantial portion of an organization's income is from unrelated sources, the organization will not qualify for tax exemption in the first instance.[8] However, an organization may satisfy the requirements of the rules pertaining to "charitable" organizations,[9] although it operates a trade or business as a substantial part of its activities, where the operation of the trade or business

---

[1]Code § 501(a).
[2]Code § 501(b).
[3]Code § 511(a)(1).
[4]Code § 11.
[5]Code § 511(b).
[6]Code § 1(d).
[7]For an analysis of developments leading to enactment of the unrelated business income tax provisions, see Myers, "Taxing the Colleges," 38 *Cornell L. Q.* 388.
[8]See, e.g., *Indiana Retail Hardware Association* v. *United States*, 366 F.2d 998 (Ct. Cl. 1966); *People's Educational Camp Society, Inc.* v. *Commissioner*, 331 F.2d 923 (2d Cir. 1964); Rev. Rul. 69-220, 1969-1 C. B. 154.
[9]Code § 501(c)(3).

is in furtherance of the organization's tax-exempt purposes[10] and where the organization is not organized or operated for the primary purpose of carrying on a trade or business. In determining the existence or nonexistence of a primary purpose, all the circumstances must be considered, including the size and extent of the trade or business and of the activities which are in furtherance of one or more tax-exempt purposes.[11] For example, an organization that purchases and sells at retail products manufactured by blind persons was held by the U.S. Tax Court to qualify as a charitable organization because its activities result in employment for the blind, notwithstanding its receipt of net profits and its distribution of some of these profits to qualified workers.[12]

At the other end of the spectrum, incidental trade or business activity will not alone cause an organization to lose or be denied tax exemption, although the income derived from the activity may be taxable.[13]

Prior to enactment of the Tax Reform Act of 1969, the unrelated business income tax applied only to certain tax-exempt organizations, including charitable, educational, some religious, and comparable organizations; labor, agricultural, and horticultural organizations; and business leagues and similar organizations. However, the tax on unrelated business income is now imposed on nearly all exempt organizations, its coverage having been extended by the Tax Reform Act of 1969.[14] Congress decided to broaden the applicability of the unrelated business income tax for the following reason:

> In recent years, many of the exempt organizations not subject to the unrelated business income tax—such as churches, social clubs, fraternal beneficiary societies, etc.—began to engage in substantial commercial activity. For example, numerous business activities of churches were brought to the attention of the Congress. Some churches are engaged in operating publishing houses, hotels, factories, radio and TV stations, parking lots, newspapers, bakeries, restaurants, etc. Furthermore, it is difficult to justify taxing a university or hospital which runs a public restaurant or hotel or other business and not tax a country club or lodge engaged in similar activity.[15]

The unrelated business income tax now applies to nearly all tax-exempt organizations, including churches and conventions or associations of churches, social welfare organizations, social clubs, and fraternal societies. This tax applies to any college or university which is an agency or instrumentality of any government or political subdivision thereof, or which is owned or operated by a

---

[10]In general, see Horvitz, "Financing Related Commercial Activities of Exempt Universities," 55 *Taxes* 457 (1977); Note, "Profitable Related Business Activities and Charitable Exemption Under Section 501(c)(3)," 44 *Geo. Wash. L. Rev.* 270 (1976).

[11]Reg. § 1.501(c)(3)-1(e)(1).

[12]*Industrial Aid for the Blind v. Commissioner*, 73 T.C. 96 (1979).

[13]See, e.g., Rev. Rul. 66-221, 1966-2 C. B. 220.

[14]Code § 511(a)(2)(A).

[15]Joint Committee on Internal Revenue Taxation, *General Explanation of Tax Reform Act of 1969*, 91st Cong., 2d Sess. (1970) at 66–67.

government or any political subdivision thereof, or by any agency or instrumentality of one or more governments or political subdivisions, and applies to any corporation wholly owned by one or more of these colleges or universities.[16] Excepted from the tax are federal government instrumentalities, certain religious and apostolic organizations, farmers' cooperatives, and shipowners' protection and indemnity associations.

The primary objective of the unrelated business income tax is to eliminate a source of unfair competition by placing the unrelated business activities of covered tax-exempt organizations on the same tax basis as the nonexempt business endeavors with which they compete.[17] The House Ways and Means Committee report on the Revenue Act of 1950 observes:

> The problem at which the tax on unrelated business income is directed here is primarily that of unfair competition. The tax-free status of . . . [Code § 501] organizations enables them to use their profits tax-free to expand operations, while their competitors can expand only with the profits remaining after taxes. Also, a number of examples have arisen where these organizations have, in effect, used their tax exemption to buy an ordinary business. That is, they have acquired the business with no investment on their own part and paid for it in installments out of subsequent earnings—a procedure which usually could not be followed if the business were taxable.[18]

(The problem discussed by the Committee in the latter portion of the foregoing quotation was further addressed by enactment of the unrelated debt-financed income rules.[19]) The Senate Finance Committee reaffirmed this position in the context of enactment of the Tax Reform Act of 1976 when it noted that one "major purpose" of the unrelated income tax "is to make certain that an exempt organization does not commercially exploit its exempt status for the purpose of unfairly competing with taxpaying organizations."[20]

§ 40.2   Tax Structure

As Congress adjusts the federal income tax rates from time to time, as is its wont, the taxation of unrelated income likewise becomes affected. Undoubtedly, the unrelated income rates payable by most tax-exempt organizations are the corporate rates.

The corporate rate reductions provided by the Economic Recovery Tax Act

---

[16]Code § 511(a)(2)(B).

[17]Reg. § 1.513-1(b). In general, see IRS Pub. No. 598, "Tax on Unrelated Business Income of Exempt Organizations"; Steinfeld, "Unrelated business income tax: An increased hazard for qualified trusts," 36 *J. Tax*. 110 (1972); Webster, "Unrelated Business Income Tax," 48 *Taxes* 844 (1970); Newland, "Profit in Nonprofit Corporations," 22 *Tax L. Rev*. 687 (1967); Rogovin, "Charitable Enigma: Commercialism," 17 *So. Cal. Tax Inst*. 61 (1965).

[18]H. Rep. No. 2319, 81st Cong., 2d Sess. (1950) at 36–37. Also S. Rep. No. 2375, 81st Cong., 2d Sess. (1950) at 28–29.

[19]See Chapter 44.

[20]S. Rep. No. 94-938, 94th Cong., 2d Sess. (1976) at 601.

of 1981[21] were intended for the benefit of business corporations, as part of the overall program of incentives for economic recovery. The reductions, while not enacted for the benefit of tax-exempt organizations, nonetheless reduced the unrelated income tax rates to which tax-exempt corporations are subject.

Under the law antedating the revisions caused by the 1981 Act, the corporate income tax was imposed at the following rates:

Taxable Income	Rate (percent)
Less than $25,000	17
$25,000–$50,000	20
$50,000–$75,000	30
$75,000–$100,000	40
Over $100,000	46

The 1981 Act decreased the tax rates on the two lowest corporate tax brackets, namely, those imposing tax on taxable income below $50,000. The changes went into effect in 1982 and 1983.[22]

The brackets below $50,000 will be adjusted as follows:

Taxable Income	Rate (percent)
In 1982	16
Less than $25,000	
$25,000–$50,000	19
1983 and later years	15
Less than $25,000	
$25,000–$50,000	18

Thus, for example, the same unrelated income that was taxable at the 17 percent rate in 1981 is taxable at a 16 percent rate in 1982 and a 15 percent rate in 1983.

§ 40.3 Deduction Rules

Generally, the term "unrelated business taxable income" means the gross income derived by an organization from any unrelated trade or business, regularly carried on by the organization, less business deductions which are directly connected with the carrying on of the trade or business.[23] For purposes of computing unrelated business taxable income, both gross income and business deductions are computed with certain modifications.[24]

Generally, to be "directly connected with" the conduct of unrelated business, an item of deduction must have a proximate and primary relationship to the

---

[21]P. L. 97-34, 95 Stat. 172 (1981).

[22]These changes in the law were occasioned by enactment of §§ 101 and 231 of the 1981 Act.

[23]Code § 512(a)(1).

[24]See Chapter 42 § 1.

carrying on of that business. In the case of an organization which derives gross income from the regular conduct of two or more unrelated business activities, unrelated business taxable income is the aggregate of gross income from all unrelated business activities, less the aggregate of the deductions allowed with respect to all unrelated business activities.[25] Expenses, depreciation, and similar items attributable solely to the conduct of unrelated business are proximately and primarily related to that business and therefore qualify for deduction to the extent that they meet the requirements of relevant provisions of the federal income tax law.[26]

Where facilities or personnel are used both to carry on tax-exempt functions and to conduct unrelated trade or business, the expenses, depreciation, and similar items attributable to the facilities or personnel (as, for example, items of overhead) must be allocated between the two uses on a reasonable basis. The portion of any item so allocated to the unrelated trade or business must be proximately and primarily related to that business, and is allowable as a deduction in computing unrelated business income in the manner and to the extent permitted by federal income tax law.[27] Gross income may be derived from an unrelated trade or business which exploits an exempt function. Generally, in this case, expenses, depreciation, and similar items attributable to the conduct of the tax-exempt function are not deductible in computing unrelated business taxable income. Since the items are incident to a function of the type which is the chief purpose of the organization to conduct, they do not possess a proximate and primary relationship to the unrelated trade or business. Therefore, they do not qualify as being directly connected with that business.[28]

[25]Reg. § 1.512(a)-1(a).

[26]E.g., Code §§ 162,167. Reg. § 1.512(a)-1(b).

[27]Reg. § 1.512(a)-1(c).

[28]Reg. § 1.512(a)-1(d). See IRS Private Letter Ruling 7902019 (Issue No. 5 and 11).

In *Rensselaer Polytechnic Institute* v. *Commissioner*, 79 T.C. No. 60 (1982), the issue was the proper allocation of indirect expenses incurred in the operation of a fieldhouse that was used both for exempt and unrelated functions. The Institute contended that it is entitled to allocate all indirect expenses on the basis of relative time of actual use. The IRS claimed that fixed expenses should be allocated on the basis of available use and that variable expenses can be based on actual use time but disagreed with the Institute's method of computing total hours of use. Generally agreeing with the Institute, the court held that the allocation with respect to all indirect expenses can be made on the basis of actual use, as being reasonable. In reaching this decision, the court relied on prior tax cases upholding allocations based on time of actual use when the dual use of a facility is involved. The court observed that the college totally controlled the operation of the fieldhouse and that the fieldhouse was at all times equally available for both educational and commercial activities. Thus, concluded the court, "as long as the facility is equally available for either purpose during hours of nonuse, expenses are to be allocated in proportion to actual use." To allocate the indirect expenses on the basis of total hours of availability for use would, said the court, be the result of an "erroneous and distorting assumption that a dual-use facility is not, when unused, just as much available for business use as it is for non-business use."

§ 40.4 Special Rules

Federal tax law provides a definition of unrelated business taxable income specifically applicable to foreign organizations that are subject to the tax on unrelated income.[29] Basically, such an organization is taxed on its unrelated business taxable income "effectively connected" with the conduct of a trade or business within the United States and on unrelated income derived from sources within the United States even though not so effectively connected.

In the case of certain veterans' organizations,[30] the term "unrelated business taxable income" does not include any amount attributable to payments for life, sick, accident, or health insurance with respect to members of the organizations or their dependents which is set aside for the purpose of providing for the payment of insurance benefits or for a charitable purpose.[31]

Special rules are applicable to social clubs[32] and employees' beneficiary associations.[33] These rules[34] apply the unrelated business income tax to all of these organizations' income other than "exempt function income."[35]

§ 40.5 Partnership Rule

If a trade or business regularly carried on by a partnership, of which an exempt organization is a member, is an unrelated trade or business with respect to the organization, in computing its unrelated business taxable income the organization must include its share (whether or not distributed) of the gross income of the partnership from the unrelated trade or business and its share of the partnership deductions directly connected with the gross income.[36] This rule applies irrespective of whether the tax-exempt organization is a general or limited partner.[37]

---

[29]Code § 512(a)(2).
[30]See Chapter 20.
[31]Code § 512(a)(4).
[32]See Chapter 18.
[33]See Chapter 20.
[34]Code § 512(a)(3).
[35]Interest on obligations of a state (see Code § 103(a)) received by a tax-exempt social club is not included in gross income for purposes of Code § 512(a)(3). Rev. Rul. 76-337, 1976-2 C. B. 177.
[36]Code § 512(c), Reg. § 1.512(c)-1. See, e.g., IRS Private Letter Ruling 7934008.
[37]Rev. Rul. 79-222, 1979-2 C. B. 236. In general, see Myers and Myers, Jr., "How art-oriented exempt organizations can skirt the unrelated business income tax," 49 *J. Tax.* 150 (1978); Warren, "Taxable Income of Qualified Trusts," 61 *A. B. A. J.* 981 (1975); Webster, "Unrelated Business Income," 23 *Tax Lawyer* 471 (1970); Note, "Unrelated Business Income of Tax Exempt Organizations," 19 *De Paul L. Rev.* 525 (1970); Note, "The Macaroni Monopoly: The Developing Concept of Unrelated Business Income of Exempt Organizations," 81 *Harv. L. Rev.* 1280 (1968).

41

Unrelated Trade or Business

The term "unrelated trade or business" means any trade or business, the conduct of which is not substantially related to the exercise or performance by the tax-exempt organization of its exempt purpose or function.[1] The conduct of a trade or business is not substantially related to an organization's tax-exempt purpose solely because the organization may need the income or because of the use the organization makes of the profits derived from the business. There are special rules in this area for certain trusts.[2]

§ 41.1 Introduction

Therefore, absent one of the specific exceptions,[3] gross income of a tax-exempt organization subject to the tax on unrelated income is includible in the computation of unrelated business taxable income if three factors are present: (1) it is income from a trade or business, (2) the trade or business is regularly carried on by the organization, and (3) the conduct of the trade or business is not substantially related to the organization's performance of its tax-exempt functions.[4]

An illustration of these precepts is the case of the Iowa State University of Science and Technology, which operated a television station.[5] Seeking recovery of income taxes paid on allegedly unrelated business income, the University contended that operation of the station was in furtherance of its exempt, educational purposes, by training students in the broadcasting industry, closed circuit transmissions to classrooms, and the like. However, operation of the

[1]Code § 513(a).
[2]Code § 513(b).
[3]See Chapter 42.
[4]Reg. § 1.513-1(a).
[5]*Iowa State University of Science and Technology* v. *United States*, 500 F.2d 508 (Ct. Cl. 1974).

station was found to be an unrelated trade or business, in that the station was operated as a commercial enterprise (it was an ABC affiliate) and as a profit-making enterprise. Finding the "primary question here involved . . . [to be] close and perplexing," the Court of Claims concluded that, on balance, the "television revenues constitute unrelated business income to the University."[6]

§ 41.2　Definition of "Trade or Business"

Generally, any activity which is carried on for the production of income from the sale of goods or the performance of services and which otherwise possesses the characteristics required to constitute "trade or business" within the meaning of general federal income tax principles[7] is a "trade or business" for purposes of the unrelated income tax.[8] The cases contain illustrations of activities considered not to be a trade or business.[9]

It is not necessary, for an activity to be considered an unrelated trade or business for these purposes, that the tax-exempt organization engage in the activity with a profit motive. In assessing the application of the technical criteria for imposition of the unrelated income tax, the profit motivation factor is irrelevant.

Pursuant to the statutory law, "an activity does not lose identity as trade or business merely because it is carried on within a larger aggregate of similar activities or within a larger complex of other endeavors which may, or may not, be related to the exempt purposes of the organization."[10] Additionally, the law states that "[w]here an activity carried on for profit constitutes an unrelated trade or business, no part of such trade or business shall be excluded from such classification merely because it does not result in profit."[11]

By enactment of these rules (in 1969), Congress confirmed the government's prior contention that income from a particular activity can be taxed as unrelated business income even where the activity is an integral part of a larger activity that is in furtherance of an exempt purpose. This provision was initially directed at, but is by no means confined to, activities of soliciting, selling, and publishing commercial advertising, even where the advertising is published in an exempt organization publication which contains editorial matter related to the tax-exempt purposes of the organization.[12] With this authority, the IRS is empowered to fragment a tax-exempt organization's operation, run as an integrated

---

[6]*Ibid.* at 516. Cf. Reg. § 1.513-2(a)(4); Rev. Rul. 55-676, 1955-2 C.B. 266.

[7]Code § 162.

[8]Code § 513(c), Reg. § 1.513-1(b).

[9]See, e.g., *Adirondack League Club* v. *Commissioner*, 55 T.C. 796 (1971), aff'd 72-1 U.S.T.C. ¶ 9402 (2d Cir. 1972); *Oklahoma Cattlemen's Association, Inc.* v. *United States*, 310 F.Supp. 320 (W.D. Okla. 1969); *The Marion Foundation* v. *Commissioner*, 19 T.C.M. 99 (1960). But see Rev. Rul. 69-278, 1969-1 C.B. 148.

[10]Code § 513(c).

[11]*Ibid.*

[12]See § 5 hereof, *infra.*

whole, into its component parts in search of an unrelated trade or business. The significance of this fragmentation rule cannot be overstated, inasmuch as it is the basis for most of the development of the law in this field. The fragmentation rule is carrying this aspect of the law far beyond the concepts contemplated by Congress when these rules were initially framed in 1950.

The absence or presence of unfair competition also is not among the technical criteria for assessing whether a particular activity is subject to the tax on unrelated income. Thus, it is theoretically possible for an activity of a tax-exempt organization to be wholly uncompetitive with a taxpaying organization activity and nonetheless be treated as an unrelated trade or business.[13] Yet, on occasion, the IRS has taken the position that, where an activity constitutes a trade or business and is not substantially related to the performance of tax-exempt functions, there is sufficient likelihood (something akin to an irrebuttable presumption) that unfair competition is present.

Not every activity of an exempt organization that generates a financial return is a "trade or business" for purposes of the unrelated income tax or otherwise. As the U. S. Supreme Court has observed, the "narrow category of trade or business" is a "concept which falls far short of reaching every income or profit-making activity."[14] This is well-illustrated by the practice engaged in by many tax-exempt organizations of lending securities to brokerage houses.[15]

In the typical securities lending transaction, the tax-exempt organization lends securities (stocks and bonds) from its investment portfolio to a brokerage house, to enable the broker to make delivery of the securities to cover either a short sale or a failure to receive securities. In this type of transaction, the broker receiving the certificates posts cash collateral with the lending institution in an amount equivalent to or exceeding the then-fair market value of the particular securities. This collateral may be available to the lending organization in the interim for the purpose of short-term investment as it deems appropriate.

---

[13]See, e.g., *Clarence LaBelle Post No. 217* v. *United States*, 78-2 U.S.T.C. ¶ 9496 (8th Cir. 1978), holding (in a case finding that the operation of a bingo game by a social welfare organization gives rise to unrelated business income) that "the tax on unrelated business income is not limited to income earned by a trade or business that operates in competition with taxpaying entities." In general, the conduct of bingo games has been held to constitute a trade or business. See, e.g., *Waco Lodge No. 166, Benevolent & Protective Order of Elks* v. *Commissioner*, 42 T.C.M. 1202 (1981); *Smith-Dodd Businessman's Association, Inc.* v. *Commissioner*, 65 T.C. 620 (1975); *Porter* v. *Commissioner*, 437 F.2d 39 (2d Cir. 1970); *Hirsch* v. *Commissioner*, 315 F.2d 731 (9th Cir. 1963); *Help the Children, Inc.* v. *Commissioner*, 28 T.C. 1128 (1957).

[14]*Whipple* v. *Commissioner*, 373 U.S. 193, 197, 201 (1963). Also *Blake Construction Co., Inc.* v. *United States*, 572 F.2d 820 (Ct. Cl. 1978); *Monfore* v. *United States*, 77-2 U.S.T.C. ¶ 9528 (Ct. Cl. 1977); *McDowell* v. *Ribicoff*, 292 F.2d 174 (3d Cir. 1961), cert. den. 368 U.S. 919 (1961).

[15]See Stern and Sullivan, "Exempt organizations which lend securities risk imposition of unrelated business tax," 45 *J. Tax.* 240 (1976). Legislation to preclude unrelated business tax treatment of securities lending income was signed into law in 1978, as P.L. 95-345, 95th Cong., 2d Sess. (1978). See Chapter 42 § 2.

Under this arrangement, either the lending organization or the broker can terminate the lending relationship upon notice. In this instance, the broker becomes obligated to return the identical securities to the organization, which has retained the beneficial interest therein, and the organization becomes obligated to return the collateral to the broker. In the event of default on the part of the broker, the organization is required to use the collateral to purchase replacement securities and has a claim against the borrowing broker for any deficiency. Any excess funds derived in the process of securing replacement securities must be returned to the broker. Thus, the organization's portfolio position cannot be improved by virtue of any default by a broker-borrower. An amount equivalent to any dividend or interest which comes due during the course of the lending period must be paid by the particular broker to the organization whether or not he or she holds the securities. The brokerage house also pays the lending organization additional compensation for entering into the arrangement, either as a predetermined premium computed as a percentage of the value of the loaned securities or, as noted, by allowing the organization to invest the collateral and retain the income.

Looking to the pertinent requirements under the general tax rules defining a "business" activity,[16] it is clear that the management of an investment portfolio comprised wholly of the manager's own securities should not constitute the carrying on of a trade or business. For example, the U.S. Supreme Court has held that the mere keeping of records and collection of interest and dividends from securities, through managerial attention to the investments, is not the operation of a business.[17] On that occasion, the court sustained the government's position that "mere personal investment activities never constitute carrying on a trade or business."[18] Subsequently, the Supreme Court stated that "investing is not a trade or business."[19] Likewise, the U. S. Court of Appeals for the Ninth Circuit has observed that "the mere management of investments . . . is insufficient to constitute the carrying on of a trade or business."[20]

It is likewise clear that investment activities do not constitute the carrying on of a trade or business in the tax context. Thus, the IRS ruled that the receipt of income by an exempt employees' trust from installment notes purchased from the employer-settlor is not income derived from the operation of an unrelated trade or business.[21] The Service noted that the trust "merely keeps the records and receives the periodic payments of principal and interest collected for it by the employer." Consequently, it may be regarded as settled

---

[16]Code § 162.

[17]*Higgins* v. *Commissioner*, 312 U.S. 212, 218 (1941).

[18]*Ibid.* at 215.

[19]*Whipple* v. *Commissioner*, *supra*, n. 14, at 202.

[20]*Continental Trading, Inc.* v. *Commissioner*, 265 F.2d 40, 43 (9th Cir. 1959), cert. den. 361 U.S. 827 (1959). Also see *Van Wart* v. *Commissioner*, 295 U.S. 112, 115 (1935); *Deputy* v. *duPont*, 308 U.S. 488, 499 (concurring opinion) (1940); *Commissioner* v. *Burnett*, 118 F.2d 659, 660–661 (5th Cir. 1941); Rev. Rul. 56-511, 1956-2 C.B. 170.

[21]Rev. Rul. 69-574, 1969-2 C.B. 130.

that mere record-keeping and income collection for a person's own investments are not to be regarded as the carrying on of a trade or business.

Until late in 1977, when a private ruling was issued to a college, it was not clear as to whether the IRS would regard the practice of securities lending as a trade or business. This matter was further clarified by the Service's determination, published in 1978,[22] that securities lending is a form of "ordinary or routine investment activities" and thus not a business. As noted,[23] this matter was rectified by statute in 1978.[24]

Also, funds received by a tax-exempt organization as an agent for another organization are not taxable income to the exempt organization and thus cannot be unrelated business income.[25]

§ 41.3 Definition of "Regularly Carried On"

In determining whether a trade or business from which a particular amount of gross income is derived by a tax-exempt organization is "regularly carried on," within the meaning of these rules,[26] regard must be had to the frequency and continuity with which the activities productive of the income are conducted and the manner in which they are pursued. This requirement must be applied in light of the purpose of the unrelated business income tax to place tax-exempt organization business activities upon the same tax basis as the nonexempt business endeavors with which they compete. Hence, for example, specific business activities of a tax-exempt organization will ordinarily be deemed to be "regularly carried on" if they manifest a frequency and continuity, and are pursued in a manner generally similar to comparable commercial activities of nonexempt organizations.[27]

An illustration of this principle is the case of a tax-exempt organization which publishes a yearbook for its membership. The publication contains advertising, and the organization contracts on an annual basis with a commercial firm for solicitation of advertising sales, printing, and collection of advertising charges. Although the editorial materials were prepared by the organization's staff, the organization, by means of its contract with the commercial firm, was ruled to be "engaging in an extensive campaign of advertising solicitation" and thus to

---

[22]Rev. Rul. 78-88, 1978-1 C.B. 163. Also IRS Private Letter Ruling 7902019 (issue no. 2).

[23]See n. 15, *supra*.

[24]For further discussion of the securities lending technique, see S. Rep. No. 95-762, 95th Cong., 2d Sess. (1978) at 3-9; also H. Rep. No. 94-1266, 94th Cong., 2d Sess. (1976). As is the case with any nonexempt activity, securities trading and lending can be such a large part of the activities of an organization that it fails to satisfy the operational test (see Chapter 5 § 2; see *Randall Foundation, Inc.* v. *Riddell*, 244 F.2d 803 (8th Cir. 1957)).

[25]See IRS Private Letter Ruling 7823048.

[26]Code § 512.

[27]Reg. § 1.513-1(c)(1).

be "conducting competitive and promotional efforts typical of commercial endeavors." Therefore, in this instance, the income derived by the organization from the sale of advertising in its yearbook was deemed unrelated business taxable income.[28]

By contrast, a one-time sale of property (as opposed to an ongoing income-producing program) is not an activity that is regularly carried on and thus does not give rise to unrelated income. For example, a tax-exempt organization that was formed to deliver diagnostic and medical health care and that developed a series of computer programs concerning management and administrative matters, such as patient admissions and billings, payroll, purchases, inventory, and medical records, sold some or all of the programs to another exempt organization composed of three teaching hospitals affiliated with a university. The income derived from the sale was held to be from a "one-time-only operation" and thus not taxable as unrelated income.[29]

Where income-producing activities are of a kind normally conducted by nonexempt commercial organizations on a year-round basis, the conduct of the activities by a tax-exempt organization over a period of only a few weeks does not constitute the regular carrying on of a trade or business. For example, the operation of a sandwich stand by a hospital auxiliary for only two weeks at a state fair would not be the regular conduct of a trade or business. Similarly, if a charitable organization gives an occasional dance to which the public is admitted for a charge, hiring an orchestra and entertainers for the purpose, the activity would not be a trade or business regularly carried on.[30] However, the conduct of year-round business activities for one day each week would constitute the regular carrying on of a trade or business. Thus, the operation of a commercial parking lot on one day of each week would be the regular conduct of a trade or business. Where income-producing activities are of a kind normally undertaken by nonexempt commercial organizations only on a seasonal basis, the conduct of the activities by an exempt organization during a significant portion of the season ordinarily constitutes the regular conduct of trade or business. For example, the operation of a track for horse racing for several weeks of a year would be considered the regular conduct of trade or business because it is usual to carry on the trade or business only during a particular season.[31]

In determining whether or not intermittently conducted activities are regularly carried on, the manner of conduct of the activities must be compared with the manner in which commercial activities are normally pursued by nonexempt organizations. In general, exempt organization business activities which are engaged in only discontinuously or periodically will not be considered regularly carried on if they are conducted without the competitive and pro-

[28]Rev. Rul. 73-424, 1973-2 C.B. 190.
[29]IRS Private Letter Ruling 7905129.
[30]S. Rep. No. 2375, 81st Cong., 2d Sess. (1950) at 106-107.
[31]Reg. § 1.513-1(c)(2)(i). See Rev. Rul. 68-505, 1968-2 C.B. 248.

motional efforts typical of commercial endeavors. For example, the publication of advertising in programs for sports events or music or drama performances will not ordinarily be deemed to be the regular carrying on of business. On the other hand, where the nonqualifying sales are not merely casual but are systematically and consistently promoted and carried on by the organization, they meet the requirement of regularity.[32]

Certain intermittent income-producing activities occur so infrequently that neither their recurrence nor the manner of their conduct will cause them to be regarded as trade or business regularly carried on. For example, income-producing or fund-raising activities lasting only a short period of time will not ordinarily be treated as regularly carried on if they recur only occasionally or sporadically. Furthermore, activities will not be regarded as regularly carried on merely because they are conducted on an annually recurrent basis. Accordingly, income derived from the conduct of an annual dance or similar fund-raising event for charity would not be income from trade or business regularly carried on.[33]

§ 41.4   Definition of "Substantially Related"

Gross income derives from "unrelated trade or business," within the meaning of these rules,[34] if the conduct of the trade or business which produces the income is not substantially related (other than through the production of funds) to the purposes for which tax exemption is granted. The presence of this requirement necessitates an examination of the relationship between the business activities which generate the particular income in question—the activities, that is, of producing or distributing the goods or performing the services involved—and the accomplishment of the organization's exempt purposes.[35]

Trade or business is "related" to tax-exempt purposes, in the relevant sense, only where the conduct of the business activity has causal relationship to the achievement of an exempt purpose (other than through the production of income) and it is "substantially related" only if the causal relationship is a substantial one. Thus, for the conduct of trade or business from which a particular amount of gross income is derived to be substantially related to the purposes for which tax exemption is granted, the production or distribution of the goods or the performance of the services from which the gross income is derived must contribute importantly to the accomplishment of those purposes.[36] Where the production or distribution of the goods or the performance of the services does not contribute importantly to the accomplishment of the tax-exempt purposes

---

[32]Reg. § 1.513-1(c)(2)(ii). Also IRS Private Letter Rulings 7826063 and 7839047.

[33]Reg. § 1.513-1(c)(2)(iii). See *Orange County Builders Association, Inc.* v. *United States*, 65-2 U.S.T.C. ¶ 9679 (S.D. Cal. 1965); IRS Private Letter Ruling 7905129.

[34]Code § 513(a).

[35]Reg. § 1.513-1(d)(1).

[36]See, e.g., Rev. Rul. 75-472, 1975-2 C.B. 208.

of an organization, the income from the sale of the goods or the performance of the services does not derive from the conduct of related trade or business. For example, the sale at a profit of standard legal forms by a local bar association to its member attorneys, which purchases the forms from the state bar association, was ruled to be an unrelated trade or business because the activity does not contribute importantly to the accomplishment of the association's tax-exempt functions.[37] The same rationale was used to characterize as an unrelated trade or business the publication and sale, by an association of credit unions to its members, a consumer-oriented magazine designed as a promotional device for distribution to the numbers' depositors.[38] Likewise, the presentation of commercial programs and the sale of air time were ruled to be activities not substantially related to the tax-exempt purposes of an exempt broadcasting station;[39] a charitable organization operating to promote physical fitness of young persons was held to have unrelated activity in the form of a health club, since the dues and fees charged are sufficiently high so as to restrict the club's use to a limited number of the members of the community;[40] and the operation of a miniature golf course in a commercial manner, by a charitable organization operating to provide for the welfare of young people, was determined by the IRS to constitute an unrelated business.[41] By contrast, an organization that promotes professional auto racing was held to not receive unrelated business income from the conduct of a product certification program, because the program is part of the organization's regulatory activities designed to prevent trade abuses in the auto racing business.[42]

Whether activities productive of gross income contribute importantly to the accomplishment of any purpose for which an organization is granted tax-exemption depends in each case upon the facts and circumstances involved.[43]

In determining whether activities contribute importantly to the accomplishment of an exempt purpose, the size and extent of the activities involved must be considered in relation to the nature and extent of the tax-exempt function which they purport to serve. Thus, where income is realized by a tax-exempt organization from activities which are in part related to the performance of its exempt functions, but which are conducted on a larger scale than is reasonably

---

[37]Rev. Rul. 78-51, 1978-1 C.B. 165. However, a court subsequently held that the sale at a profit of standard real estate legal forms to lawyers and law students by a bar association is not an unrelated trade or business but rather is an exempt activity because it promotes the common business interests of the legal profession and improves the relationship among the bench, bar, and public. *San Antonio Bar Association* v. *United States*, 80-2 U.S.T.C. ¶ 9594 (W.D. Tex. 1980).

[38]Rev. Rul. 78-52, 1978-1 C.B. 166.

[39]Rev. Rul. 78-385, 1978-2 C.B. 174.

[40]Rev. Rul. 79-360, 1979-2 C.B. 236.

[41]Rev. Rul. 79-361, 1979-2 C.B. 237.

[42]IRS Private Letter Ruling 7922001.

[43]Reg. § 1.513-1(d)(2). See *Huron Clinic Foundation* v. *United States*, 212 F.Supp. 847 (D.S. Dak. 1962).

necessary for performance of the functions, the gross income attributable to that portion of the activities in excess of the needs of tax-exempt functions constitutes gross income from the conduct of unrelated trade or business. Such income is not derived from the production or distribution of goods or the performance of services which contribute importantly to the accomplishment of any tax-exempt purpose of the organization.[44] For example, a trade association had a membership of business concerns in a particular state. One of its activities was to supply businesses (members and nonmembers) with job injury histories on prospective employees for a profit. Despite the organization's contention that this service contributed to accomplishment of its tax-exempt purposes, the IRS ruled that the operation is an unrelated trade or business, in that the services went "well beyond" any mere development and promotion of efficient business practices.[45] The IRS adopted a similar posture in ruling that a retail grocery store operation, formed to sell food in a poverty area at lower-than-usual prices and to provide job training for unemployed residents of the area, could not qualify for tax exemption because the operation was conducted "on a much larger scale than reasonably necessary" for the training program.[46] Yet a tax-exempt organization that was formed to provide a therapeutic program for emotionally disturbed adolescents was advised that a retail grocery store operation, almost fully staffed by adolescents to secure their emotional rehabilitation, was not an unrelated trade or business because it was operated on a scale no larger than reasonably necessary for its training and rehabilitation program.[47]

Gross income derived from charges for the performance of tax-exempt functions does not constitute gross income from the conduct of unrelated trade or business. This principle encompasses income generated by functions such as performances by students enrolled in a school for training children in the performing arts, the conduct of refresher courses to improve the trade skills of members of a trade union, and the presentation of a trade show for exhibiting industry products by a trade association to stimulate demand for the products.[48]

Ordinarily, gross income from the sale of products which result from the performance of tax-exempt functions does not constitute gross income from the conduct of unrelated trade or business if the product is sold in substantially the same state it is in upon completion of the exempt functions. Thus in the case of a "charitable" organization engaged in a program of rehabilitation of handicapped persons, income from the sale of articles made by these persons as a part of their rehabilitation training would not be gross income from conduct of an unrelated trade or business. The income in this case would be from the sale of products, the production of which contributed importantly to the ac-

---

[44]Reg. § 1.513-1(d)(3).
[45]Rev. Rul. 73-386, 1973-2 C.B. 191.
[46]Rev. Rul. 73-127, 1973-1 C.B. 221.
[47]Rev. Rul. 76-94, 1976-1 C.B. 171.
[48]Reg. § 1.513-1(d)(4)(i).

complishment of purposes for which tax exemption is granted the organization—namely, rehabilitation of the handicapped. Conversely, if a product resulting from an exempt function is utilized or exploited in further business endeavors beyond that reasonably appropriate or necessary for disposition in the state it is in upon completion of tax-exempt functions, the gross income derived therefrom would be from the conduct of unrelated trade or business. Thus, in the case of an experimental dairy herd maintained for scientific purposes by a tax-exempt organization, income from sale of milk and cream produced in the ordinary course of operation of the project would not be gross income from conduct of unrelated trade or business. However, if the organization were to utilize the milk and cream in the further manufacture of food items such as ice cream, pastries, and the like, the gross income from the sale of the products would be from the conduct of unrelated trade or business unless the manufacturing activities themselves contribute importantly to the accomplishment of an exempt purpose of the organization.[49]

The IRS can become enmeshed in considerable detail in evaluating an exempt organization's sales activities in the light of these rules. The best illustration of this is the case of the tax-exempt blood bank that sells blood plasma to commercial laboratories. The blood bank maintains inventories of blood and blood products which are furnished to hospitals for patient use. Because medical techniques have been perfected whereby red blood cells are transfused into a patient in lieu of whole blood, the blood bank is left with a large supply of plasma after these cells are removed. Since the hospitals serviced by the blood bank require little of this by-product plasma, most of it is sold to commercial laboratories. The blood bank also obtains plasma from three other sources: (1) from donors by means of a procedure called "plasmapheresis," where blood is drawn, the red cells are separated and replaced in the donors, and the plasma collected, (2) from unused whole blood maintained in the bank's inventory which is nearing the end of its shelf life (known as "salvage plasma"), and (3) from plasma purchased from other blood banks. The IRS ruled that "where the blood bank is merely disposing of products which result from the performance of its exempt functions, it will not be considered to be engaging in unrelated trade or business." Consequently, the sale of byproduct plasma was determined to not be unrelated trade or business, and the same treatment was accorded the sale of salvage plasma. However, the sale of plasmapheresed plasma was ruled to be an unrelated business since this plasma is not a product resulting from the performance of the bank's tax-exempt functions, as was the sale of plasma acquired from other blood banks.[50]

In another instance, the IRS considered the activities of an organization the primary purpose of which is to retain and stimulate trade in a city's downtown area where adequate parking facilities are lacking. This organization, formed by businesspersons, civic leaders, and professional people, operates fringe park-

[49]Reg. § 1.513-1(d)(4)(ii).
[50]Rev. Rul. 78-145, 1978-1 C.B. 169.

ing facilities and a shuttle bus service to and from the downtown area. No
merchant or group of merchants is favored by the manner in which the fringe
parking lot and shuttle bus are operated or in the selection of discharge and
pickup points, nor are they able to offer patrons free or discount parking or
bus fares. The organization—as an insubstantial part of its activities[51]—operates
a park-and-shop plan whereby patrons of particular downtown member merchants are able to park free at certain parking lots. Merchants participating in
this plan purchase parking stamps, which are distributed to their customers
and subsequently surrendered to the parking lot management in lieu of cash.
The IRS ruled that the operation of the fringe parking lot and shuttle bus
service contributes importantly to the accomplishment of the organization's tax-
exempt purposes because it provides "easy and convenient access to the downtown area and, thus, stimulates and improves business conditions in the downtown area generally." But, the IRS also ruled, the operation of the park-and-
shop plan "constitutes the provision of a particular service to individual members of the organization" and therefore does not further the organization's tax-
exempt purposes and consequently is an unrelated trade or business.[52]

In certain cases, an asset or facility necessary to the conduct of tax-exempt
functions may also be employed in a commercial endeavor. In these cases, the
mere fact of the use of the asset or facility in exempt functions does not, by
itself, make the income from the commercial endeavor gross income from
related trade or business. The test, instead, is whether the activities productive
of the income in question contribute importantly to the accomplishment of tax-
exempt purposes. Assume, for example, that a tax-exempt museum has a theater
auditorium which is specially designed and equipped for showing of educational
films in connection with its program of public education in the arts and sciences.
The theater is a principal feature of the museum and is in continuous operation
during the hours the museum is open to the public. If the organization were
to operate the theater as an ordinary motion picture theater for public entertainment during the evening hours when the museum was closed, gross income
from that operation would be gross income from conduct of unrelated trade or
business.[53]

This concept has particular application to colleges and universities, which
not infrequently utilize facilities in what some may view as for a "dual" use. A
prime example in this regard is an institution's athletic facilities, which, while
primarily used for educational (student) purposes, may also be made available
for faculty, other of the institution's employees, and perhaps outsiders. Income
derived from the use of the facilities by outsiders may, to some, be regarded
as from the conduct of an unrelated trade or business. For example, the IRS
ruled that the operation of a ski facility by a school for the general public is
the conduct of an unrelated trade or business, while use of the facility by the

[51]See Rev. Rul. 78-86, 1978-1 C.B. 151; Rev. Rul. 64-108, 1964-1 (Part I) C.B. 189.
[52]Rev. Rul. 79-31, 1979-1 C.B. 206.
[53]Reg. § 1.513-1(d)(4)(iii). See Rev. Rul. 68-550, 1968-2 C.B. 249.

school's students for recreational purposes and in its physical education program are related activities.[54] Likewise, a college that makes available its facilities and personnel, to an individual not associated with the institution, for the conduct of a summer tennis camp was ruled to be conducting an unrelated trade or business.[55]

However, it may be that the provision of athletic (or other) facilities by a school, college, or university to outsiders is an exempt function, inasmuch as the instruction of individuals in sports can be an educational activity.[56] For example, the IRS held that the conduct of a summer hockey camp for youths by a college was an exempt educational activity,[57] as was the conduct of four summer sports camps by a university[58] and the operation of a summer sports camp by a university-affiliated athletic association.[59]

Similarly, the IRS has determined that a college may operate a professional repertory theater on its campus that is open to the general public[60] and that a college may make its facilities available to outside organizations for the conduct of conferences,[61] both activities being in furtherance of tax-exempt purposes.

Another way in which a seemingly "dual use" arrangement involving a college or university may be structured so as to avoid taxation is to cast the income received by the institution as passive rent.[62] For example, a college may lease its facilities to a professional football team for the conduct of a summer camp and receive nontaxable lease income, as long as the college does not provide food or maid service to the team.[63] By contrast, where the institution provides

---

[54]Rev. Rul. 78-98, 1978-1 C.B. 167. Subsequently, the IRS distinguished an arrangement where the educational institution itself undertakes the operation involving use of facilities (in the ruling, summer sports camps) from that where the institution leases its facilities to independent operators of the facilities (as was the case in Rev. Rul. 76-402, 1976-2 C.B. 177), holding that in the former arrangement the institution is engaging in its tax-exempt function of instructing individuals (see Rev. Rul. 77-365, 1977-2 C.B. 192) so that no unrelated activity is involved (IRS Private Letter Ruling 7908009). Also IRS Private Letter Ruling 7840072.

[55]Rev. Rul. 76-402, n. 54, *supra*. In IRS Private Letter Ruling 7902019 (issue no. 5), the Service ruled that the sale of computer time by a university to outsiders is an unrelated trade or business as a dual use of facilities. Also, in IRS Private Letter Ruling 8020010 (issue nos. 1 and 2), the Service concluded that the sale of memberships in its recreational facility to the general public and the sale of ice time at its ice skating rink to alumni by a university constitutes an unrelated trade or business. Also see IRS Private Letter Ruling 7747054.

[56]E.g., Rev. Rul. 77-365, *supra*, n. 54. In general, see Chapter 7 § 2.

[57]IRS Private Letter Ruling 8024001.

[58]IRS Private Letter Ruling 7908009.

[59]IRS Private Letter Ruling 7826003.

[60]IRS Private Letter Ruling 7840072.

[61]IRS Private Letter Rulings 8024001 and 8020010 (issue no. 3).

[62]See Chapter 42 § 1.

[63]IRS Private Letter Ruling 8024001.

services such as room cleaning, food, laundry, security, and grounds maintenance, the exclusion for rent will be defeated.[64]

This dichotomy is reflected in the treatment the Service has accorded a school that uses its tennis facilities, which are employed during the regular academic year in the school's educational program, in the summer as a public tennis club operated by employees of the school's athletic department. Because the school not only furnishes its facilities, but operates the tennis club through its own employees who render substantial services for the participants in the club, the Service held that the operation of the club is an unrelated trade or business and that the income derived therefrom is not sheltered by the exclusion for rental income. However, the Service also observed that if the school had furnished its tennis facilities to an unrelated individual without services (leaving it to the lessee to hire the club's administrators) and for a fixed fee not dependent on the income or profits derived from the leased property, the rental income exclusion would be available.[65] In a comparable ruling, the IRS determined that, when a tax-exempt university that leases its stadium to a professional football team for several months of the year and provides the utilities, grounds maintenance, and dressing room, linen, and stadium security services, it is engaged in an unrelated trade or business and is not entitled to the rental income exclusion.[66]

In certain cases, activities carried on by an organization in the performance of tax-exempt functions may generate good will or other intangibles which are capable of being exploited in commercial endeavors. Where an organization exploits such an intangible in commercial activities, the mere fact that the resultant income depends in part upon an exempt function of the organization does not make it gross income from related trade or business. In these cases, unless the commercial activities themselves contribute importantly to the accomplishment of an exempt purpose, the income which they produce is gross income from the conduct of unrelated trade or business.[67]

Here again, the operation of athletic or other facilities by a college or university for other than instructional (in the strictest sense of the term) purposes may give rise to unrelated trade or business gross income—but by virtue of the "exploitation" rule rather than the "dual use" rule. (The regulations with respect to taxation of advertising revenue received by tax-exempt organizations[68] treat advertising as an "exploitation" of exempt publication activity.) Where access to athletic facilities by students is covered by a general student fee, outside use may amount to "exploitation," whereas, if separate charges for use

---

[64]IRS Private Letter Ruling 7840072. Also IRS Private Letter Rulings 7902019 (issue nos. 6 and 7) and 7852007 (issue no. 7).

[65]Rev. Rul. 80-297, 1980-2 C.B. 196.

[66]Rev. Rul. 80-298, 1980-2 C.B. 197.

[67]Reg. § 1.513-1(d)(4)(iv); IRS Private Letter Rulings 8115125 and 7930001.

[68]See § 5, *infra*.

of the facilities are made of students, faculty, outsiders, and others, any unrelated income is treated under the "dual use" rule.[69]

The cases and rulings provide several other examples of instances where a trade or business was deemed unrelated to an exempt organization's purpose or function. Thus, unrelated activities include the provision of pet boarding and grooming services, for pets owned by the general public, by an organization operated to prevent cruelty to animals,[70] carrying on of commercially sponsored research, where the publication of which is withheld or delayed significantly beyond the time reasonably necessary to establish ownership rights,[71] weekly operation of a bingo game by a social welfare organization,[72] sale of membership lists to commercial companies by educational organizations,[73] publication of academic works,[74] receipt of commissions from sales of cattle by an agricultural organization for its members,[75] maintenance of excessive reserve funds,[76] sale of certain blood and blood components by an exempt blood bank to commercial laboratories,[77] management of health and welfare plans by a business league for a fee,[78] the sale of heavy-duty appliances to senior citizens by a senior citizens' center,[79] the conduct of a language translation service by a trade association that promotes international trade relations,[80] and furnishing of laborers by a religious organization (usually members thereof) to forest owners to plant seedlings on cleared forest land.[81]

---

[69]See, e.g., IRS Private Letter Ruling 7823062.

[70]Rev. Rul. 73-587, 1973-2 C.B. 192.

[71]Rev. Rul. 76-296, 1976-2 C.B. 141.

[72]*Clarence LaBelle Post No. 217* v. *United States*, 78-2 U.S.T.C. ¶ 9496 (8th Cir. 1978); *Smith-Dodd Businessman's Association, Inc.* v. *Commissioner*, 65 T.C. 620 (1975). Also see Rev. Rul. 59-330, 1959-2 C.B. 153.

[73]Rev. Rul. 72-431, 1972-2 C.B. 281.

[74]IRS Private Letter Ruling 7839042. Also *Oklahoma Dental Association* v. *United States*, 75-2 U.S.T.C. ¶ 9682 (W.D. Okl. 1975); *Western Catholic Church* v. *Commissioner*, 73 T.C. 196 (1979), aff'd 631 F.2d 736 (7th Cir. 1980), cert. den. 450 U.S. 981 (1981).

[75]Rev. Rul. 69-51, 1969-1 C.B. 159; IRS Private Letter Ruling 8112013.

[76]*San Antonio District Dental Society* v. *United States*, 340 F. Supp. 11 (W.D. Tex. 1972).

[77]Rev. Rul. 66-323, 1966-2 C.B. 216, as modified by Rev. Rul. 78-145, *supra*, n. 50.

[78]Rev. Rul. 66-151, 1966-1 C.B. 152. Also see *Cooper Tire & Rubber Co. Employees' Retirement Fund* v. *United States*, 306 F.2d 20 (6th Cir. 1962); Rev. Rul. 69-633, 1969-2 C.B. 121; Rev. Rul. 69-69, 1969-1 C.B. 159; Rev. Rul. 68-505, 1968-2 C.B. 248; Rev. Rul. 68-267, 1968-1 C.B. 284; *Duluth Clinic Foundation* v. *United States*, 67-1 U.S.T.C. ¶ 9226 (D. Minn. 1967); Rev. Rul. 66-47, 1966-1 C.B. 149; Rev. Rul. 62-191, 1962-2 C.B. 146; Rev. Rul. 60-228, 1960-1 C.B. 200; Rev. Rul. 60-86, 1960-1 C.B. 198; Rev. Rul. 58-482, 1958-2 C.B. 273; Rev. Rul. 57-466, 1957-2 C.B. 311; Rev. Rul. 57-313, 1957-2 C.B. 316; Rev. Rul. 55-449, 1955-2 C.B. 599.

[79]Rev. Rul. 81-62, 1981-1 C.B. 355.

[80]Rev. Rul. 81-75, 1981-1 C.B. 356.

[81]Rev. Rul. 76-341, 1976-2 C.B. 307.

Similarly, other cases and rulings provide illustrations where a trade or business was considered a related activity. Thus, related activities include operation of a dining room, cafeteria, and snack bar by an exempt art museum for use by its staff, employees, and visiting members of the public,[82] income from championship tournaments by an association organized to promote a sport,[83] the operation of a beauty shop and barber shop by a senior citizens' center,[84] the sale of members' horses by a horsebreeders' association,[85] the sale of greeting cards and art reproductions by a museum,[86] the conduct of weekly dances by a volunteer fire company,[87] and the charging of activity fees to libraries of profit corporations for computer-stored library cataloging services.[88]

For example, the sales (or rental) of reproductions of works by an art museum are recognized by the IRS to contribute importantly to the achievement of the museum's tax-exempt purposes by enhancing the understanding and appreciation of art by the general public. Nonetheless, the IRS will separately consider sales of particular lines of merchandise to determine the relationship to an exempt purpose.[89] Thus a tax-exempt art museum was found to be engaging in an unrelated trade or business to the extent it is selling scientific books and souvenir items relating to the city in which it is located.[90] By contrast, a national conservation education organization was ruled to be engaging in related activities, by the sale of stationery items, serving items, desk accessories, nature gift items, emblem items, toys, and wearing apparel, because each of the product lines serves to stimulate the public about wildlife preservation.[91]

Occasionally, a situation will arise where monies are paid to an agent of a tax-exempt organization, who in turn pays the monies over to the organization, with the monies taxable as unrelated business income. This situation occurs, for example, in connection with a religious order, which requires its members to provide services for a component of the supervising church and to turn over their remuneration to the order under a vow of poverty. Under these circumstances, the payments for services are income to the order and not to the

[82]Rev. Rul. 74-399, 1974-2 C.B. 172. Cf. Rev. Rul. 69-268, 1969-1 C.B. 160.

[83]Rev. Rul. 58-502, 1958-2 C.B. 271, as clarified by Rev. Rul. 80-294, 1980-2 C.B. 187. Cf. *Mobile Arts and Sports Association* v. *United States*, 148 F.Supp. 315 (S.D. Ala. 1957).

[84]Rev. Rul. 81-61, 1981-1 C.B. 355.

[85]IRS Private Letter Ruling 8112013.

[86]Rev. Rul. 73-104, 1973-1 C.B. 263.

[87]Rev. Rul. 74-361, 1974-2 C.B. 159. Also see Rev. Rul. 68-225, 1968-1 C.B. 283; Rev. Rul. 67-296, 1967-2 C.B. 212; Rev. Rul. 67-219, 1967-2 C.B. 210; Rev. Rul. 64-182, 1964-1 (Part 1) C.B. 186; Rev. Rul. 56-152, 1956-1 C.B. 56; *Maryland State Fair and Agricultural Society, Inc*. v. *Chamberlin*, 55-1 U.S.T.C. ¶ 9399 (D. Md. 1955).

[88]IRS Private Letter Ruling 7816061.

[89]See Reg. § 1.513-1(d)(2), Code § 513(c).

[90]Rev. Rul. 73-105. 1973-1 C.B. 264.

[91]IRS Private Letter Ruling 8107006.

member.[92] However, where the individual is not acting as agent for the order and is performing services (as an employee) of the type ordinarily required by members of the religious order, the income is to the individual, and the unrelated income tax is avoided, because the monies are received by the orders as charitable contributions.

As indicated, the unrelated income rules apply to a wide variety of tax-exempt organizations other than charitable entities. For example, the operation of dining facilities for the general public by a social welfare organization[93] or by a veterans' organization[94] would be an unrelated trade or business.[95] (However, the operation of a restaurant and cocktail lounge by such organizations for their members is an activity that is in furtherance of their tax-exempt purposes, so that the unrelated income rules would come into play only to the extent the facilities are unduly patronized by persons other than the organizations' members and their guests.[96]) Likewise, the certification of the accuracy and authenticity of export documents by a tax-exempt chamber of commerce, for the purpose of providing an independent vertification of the origin of exported goods, was ruled to not be an unrelated business because the activity "stimulates international commerce by facilitating the export of goods and, thus, promotes and stimulates business conditions in the community generally."[97]

§ 41.5   Special Applications of Unrelated Income Rules

There are a variety of types of tax-exempt organizations, and of activities of tax-exempt organizations, that present special applications of the rules concerning the operation of "trades or businesses" that may or may not generate taxable unrelated business income.

Educational Institutions

Tax-exempt colleges, universities, and schools traditionally have been the chief targets of the unrelated business income tax and the application (or non-application) of this tax to their operations serve as good examples of the distinctions made in this area. In a larger sense, however, some of these distinctions are artificial when viewed in light of the principal purpose of the unrelated business tax—elimination of a source of unfair competition—inasmuch as these institutions have their proprietary counterparts.[98]

---

[92]Rev. Rul. 76-323, 1976-2 C.B. 18, clarified by Rev. Rul. 77-290, 1977-2 C.B. 26. Also Rev. Rul. 77-436, 1977-2 C.B. 25; Rev. Rul. 68-123, 1968-1 C.B. 35.
[93]See Chapter 18.
[94]See Chapter 20 § 15.
[95]See Rev. Rul. 68-46, 1968-1 C.B. 260.
[96]See IRS Private Letter Ruling 8120006.
[97]Rev. Rul. 81-127, 1981-1 C.B. 357. Also Rev. Rul. 70-187, 1970-1 C.B. 131.
[98]See, e.g., "GWU [George Washington University] a Thriving Business," *Washington Post*, Sept. 19, 1976, at A1.

Thus, a tax-exempt college or university is not taxable on its tuition and dormitory rental receipts from students. The legislative history of the Revenue Act of 1950 states that income of an exempt educational institution from charges for admissions to athletic events is not income from an unrelated business since the activities are substantially related to the educational program.[99] This history provides additional examples: a wheat farm operated by an exempt agricultural college as part of its educational program is a related business and income from a university press is exempt "in the ordinary case" since it is derived from an activity that is substantially related to the purposes of the university.[100]

By contrast, an activity such as the manufacture and sale of automobile tires by a college would ordinarily be considered an unrelated business; this type of an activity would not become substantially related even though some students performed some minor clerical or bookkeeping functions as part of their educational program.[101] Yet the IRS has determined that the sale of handicraft articles by an exempt vocational school, made by its students as part of their regular courses of instruction, is a related trade or business.[102]

A college or university may provide dormitory facilities to persons other than its students, such as for programs for nonstudents during the summer months. The income derived from the provision of the facilities in these circumstances is likely to be regarded by the IRS as unrelated business income, particularly where the institution is providing collateral services such as meals or maintenance; a mere leasing of facilities would generate passive rental income excluded from taxation.[103] However, the provision of dormitory space may be an activity that is substantially related to an exempt purpose, as the IRS ruled in an instance of rental of dormitory rooms primarily to people under the age of 25 by an exempt organization the purpose of which is to provide for the welfare of young people.[104]

In 1977, the National Office of the IRS, in a technical advice memorandum, ruled that the travel tour program conducted by the alumni association of the University of North Carolina at Greensboro is an unrelated trade or business. The program is available to all members of the association and their families; in the year at issue, the association made four mailings announcing nine tours to between 27,500 to 34,900. The memorandum states that "[al]though the tours include sightseeing, there is no formal educational program conducted in connection with them; nor is there any program for contacting and meeting with alumni in the countries visited." The IRS determined that (1) the activities

---

[99]H. Rep. No. 2319, 81st Cong., 2d Sess. (1950) at 37, 109; S. Rep. No. 2375, *supra*, n. 30 at 107.

[100]*Ibid.*

[101]S. Rep. No. 2375, *supra*, n. 30 at 107.

[102]Rev. Rul. 68-581, 1968-2 C.B. 250.

[103]See Chapter 42 § 1.

[104]Rev. Rul. 76-33, 1976-1 C.B. 169. Also IRS Private Letter Ruling 7840072; Behrsin, "College and University Leasing Activities Evoke IRS Scrutiny," 57 *Taxes* 431 (1979).

of the alumni association in working with commercial travel agencies in the planning and preparation of the tours, mailing out the tour announcements, and receiving reservations constitute a trade or business, (2) the travel tours are inherently recreational, not educational,[105] and thus do not contribute importantly to an exempt (educational) purpose, (3) the unrelated business is regularly carried on, and (4) this commercial endeavor exploits an intangible, namely, the association's membership.[106] It remains clear, however, that an alumni association travel tour program that is structured as an educational activity is not an unrelated trade or business.[107]

In 1977, the IRS advised Texas Christian University, Southern Methodist University, the University of Kansas, the University of Southern California, and the Cotton Bowl Athletic Association that the revenue derived by the universities from the telecasting and radio broadcasting of athletic events constitutes unrelated trade or business income. TCU was told that its share of revenue from the Southwest Athletic Conference from the televising and radio broadcasting of football and basketball games was taxable. This controversial position was challenged by the Cotton Bowl Association and the National Collegiate Athletic Association. However, the Service subsequently reversed its position, as indicated in a 1978 technical advice memorandum issued by the IRS National Office of the IRS to the CBAA.[108]

This initial determination by the IRS was unwarranted as a practical matter, although the law afforded the Service a reasonably good technical argument in support of its position. The legislative history underlying the unrelated income rules states that

> Athletic activities of schools are substantially related to their educational functions. For example, a university would not be taxable on income derived from a basketball tournament sponsored by it, even where the teams were composed of students from other schools.[109]

Since the imposition of the unrelated business income tax in 1950, there had been no attempt to tax this type of university revenue. Certainly, revenue from this source is akin to income received by tax-exempt organizations for the

[105]See Rev. Rul. 67-327, 1967-2 C. B. 187.

[106]This technical advice memorandum is the basis of Rev. Rul. 78-43, 1978-1 C. B. 164. This position of the IRS was challenged in *The Alumni Association of the University of North Carolina at Greensboro, Inc.* v. *United States* (No. 442-78, Ct. Cl.), with the Association contending, *inter alia*, that the operation of travel tours is an exempt function because they enhance the relationship among the Association, the university, and the alumni, but the Association subsequently dismissed the suit on April 25, 1980, in the face of burdensome discovery proceedings. Also see IRS Private Letter Ruling 7944018.

[107]See Rev. Rul. 70-534, 1970-2 C. B. 113; IRS Private Letter Ruling 8115125. In general, see Chapter 7 § 2.

[108]IRS Private Letter Ruling 7851004.

[109]S. Rep. No. 2375, *supra*, n. 30 at 29; H. Rep. No. 2319, *supra*, n. 94 at 37.

presentation of educational activities such as plays, musicals, symphonies, and the like.[110] It may be contended, therefore, that the broadcasting of these activities is merely a means of expanding access to the educational activities to the public at large and that no adverse tax consequences should result.[111]

At the same time, it seems clear that this legislative history is referring to revenues from admissions to athletic events, not from the sale of radio and, more particularly, television rights to commercial broadcasting companies. (As noted, the unrelated income tax scheme was adopted in 1950; the Cotton Bowl game was first covered by television in 1953 and the NCAA assumed control of college football television with the 1961 season.)

As discussed, the IRS now possesses the authority to fragment an exempt organization's operation and treat a portion of it as an unrelated trade or business. Therefore, it was not baseless for the IRS to assert that the CBAA, for example, has as one of its activities the business of selling television rights to CBS for coverage of the Cotton Bowl Classic. (The principal purpose of the CBAA is to stage the annual Cotton Bowl football game.) The broadcasting of college athletic events may be considered as an activity in competition with the broadcasting of professional athletic events. Also, since taxable businesses purchase advertising on these broadcasts, the argument can be made that the broadcasting of college athletic events is in competition with other programs being broadcast simultaneously on other networks.

In the technical advice memorandum, the IRS held that the sale of broadcast rights is a trade or business, inasmuch as it is profit-motivated. In so doing, the Service observed that "the amount of activity employed by an exempt organization in generating income is not relevant to the question of whether it is engaged in trade or business." The IRS also concluded that this trade or business is regularly carried on. The Service combined the sale of broadcast rights and the concomitant broadcasts of the games, and viewed the collective activity as "systematic and consistent," not "discontinuous or periodic." However, the IRS determined that the conduct of these trade or business activities is related to the CBAA's (and the universities') tax-exempt educational functions. The Service observed that "an audience for a game may contribute importantly to the education of the student-athlete in the development of his/her physical and inner strength." Further, "[a]ttending the game enhances student interest in education generally and in the institution because such interest is whetted by exposure to the school's athletic activities." Finally, "the games (and the opportunity to observe them) foster those feelings of identification, loyalty, and participation typical of a well-rounded educational experience."[112]

---

[110]See Chapter 6 § 8.

[111]See Rev. Rul. 58-502, *supra*, n. 83, as clarified by Rev. Rul. 80-294, *supra*, n. 83; IRS Private Letter Ruling 7845029.

[112]See IRS Private Letter Ruling 7930043.

In defending against the initial stance of the IRS, the CBAA asserted that (1) the production of the Cotton Bowl game is the performance of an exempt function, the exempt function includes the broadcasting of it, and the revenue received by the participating universities amounts to a charge for the performance of an exempt function as permitted by the regulations,[113] and (2) since income from the sale of products is not unrelated income where the product sold is done so in substantially the same state it is in on completion of the tax-exempt functions,[114] the income from the Cotton Bowl broadcasts is merely the sale of a product (the football game) in its original state, i.e., a simultaneous extension of the exempt function-game to the general public.

At the outset, it appeared that the best argument the CBAA and the universities had was that the income from the sale of the game broadcast rights is not unrelated business income because the activity is not regularly carried on. The Cotton Bowl game is played and broadcast once each year. As discussed above, an event occasioned only once each year is simply not regularly carried on and thus any income therefrom is not unrelated business income even if all of the other factors are resolved against the organization. In 1969, the Senate Finance Committee expressly stated that the unrelated income tax does not apply "unless the business is 'regularly' carried on and therefore does not apply, for example, in cases where income is derived from an annual athletic exhibition."[115]

In the face of this argument, the IRS retorted that the CBAA's unrelated business activities extend beyond the mere staging and televising of the Cotton Bowl and include the entire process of negotiating the television contract. The IRS relied on an analogy to a 1973 ruling, involving the sale of advertising in an annual yearbook, to contend that this process involves a business that is regularly carried on.[116] In response, the CBAA invoked a subsequent refinement of this published ruling, wherein the fact that the advertising solicitation was undertaken by volunteers and did not continue for an "extended period" was relied upon in holding that the sale of advertising was not an unrelated activity.[117]

One collateral issue relates to the "regularity" concept, in that the IRS was not looking only to the period in which the event in question transpired but used the period including the time span in which preparations for it are made. Also, if the broadcast rights income was held to be unrelated business income,

---

[113]Reg. § 1.513-1(d)(4)(i).

[114]See Reg. § 1.513-1(d)(4)(ii).

[115]S. Rep. No. 91-552, 91st Cong., 1st Sess. (1969) at 68.

[116]Rev. Rul. 73-424, *supra*, n. 28.

[117]Rev. Rul. 75-201, 1975-1 C. B. 164. This ruling was expressly upheld by the U. S. Tax Court in *Suffolk County Patrolmen's Benevolent Association, Inc.* v. *Commissioner*, 77 T. C. 1314 (1981). See "University TV receipts not unrelated business income," 50 *J. Tax.* 184 (1979).

then related types of income—such as that realized from concession and parking facilities—would have been susceptible to tax.

In subsequent determinations, the IRS ruled that an organization that sponsors a post-season all-star college football game for the benefit of a state university does not jeopardize its tax-exempt status because of nor realize unrelated income from the sale of television broadcast rights of the games since broadcasting of the games "contributes importantly" to the accomplishment of its tax-exempt purposes,[118] that payments received by a state university for the sale of radio and television broadcasting rights to its basketball and football games are not unrelated business income because the carrying on of the sporting events is substantially related to the university's tax-exempt purposes,[119] that income received by an organization that promotes professional auto racing from the sale of television broadcast rights to the races it sanctions does not constitute unrelated income because the television coverage effectively popularizes automobile racing,[120] that income derived from the sale by an organization that sponsors and sanctions amateur athletics of television rights to broadcast its athletic events is not unrelated income because the television medium is used to disseminate its goals and purposes to the public,[121] that an organization promoting interest in a particular sport that sells television rights to championship golf tournaments that it sponsors does not incur unrelated income because the grant of the rights is directly related to its tax-exempt purposes,[122] and that payments to be received from the sale of radio and television broadcasting rights to an athletic events are not items of unrelated income because the promotion of the event (the organization's tax-exempt purpose) is furthered by the broadcasting of it.[123]

Thereafter, the IRS issued a public ruling, holding that the sale of exclusive television and radio broadcasting rights to athletic events to an independent producer by an exempt national governing body for amateur athletics is not unrelated business because the "broadcasting of the organization's sponsored, supervised, and regulated athletic events promotes the various amateur sports, fosters widespread public interest in the benefits of its nationwide amateur athletic program, and encourages public participation" and, therefore, the sale of the broadcasting rights and the broadcasting of the events is an exempt function.[124] The Service issued a similar ruling with respect to the sale of broadcasting rights to a national radio and television network by an organization

---

[118]IRS Private Letter Rulings 7948113 (which also holds that the proceeds from admissions to the game, sales of the program of the game, and sales of advertising in the program are not taxable as unrelated income) and 7851004.

[119]IRS Private Letter Rulings 7930043, 7851011, 7851006, and 7851005.

[120]IRS Private Letter Ruling 7922001.

[121]IRS Private Letter Ruling 7851003.

[122]IRS Private Letter Ruling 7845029.

[123]IRS Private Letter Ruling 7919053.

[124]Rev. Rul. 80-295, 1980-2 C. B. 194.

created by a regional collegiate athletic conference composed of tax-exempt universities to hold an annual athletic event.[125]

Another contemporary tax issue confronting colleges, universities, and schools in the unrelated trade or business context also involves application of the fragmentation rule: sales by their bookstores. As a general rule, while these stores are tax-exempt,[126] all types of sales income are not necessarily exempt from tax. The IRS employs the fragmentation rule to isolate the sales that it believes are subject to the tax on unrelated business income. Thus, the Service conceives of these bookstore operations as embodying three types of business: two related and one unrelated.

The first of the related businesses is the sale of items that are directly educational in nature, such as books, supplies, phonograph records, tapes, and accessories. The other related business is the sale of items that probably would be unrelated activity but for the convenience doctrine,[127] such as sundry items, items embossed with the university emblem, items used in school activities, novelty items, film, pipes and smoking materials, cards, and health and beauty aids. All other sales are thus regarded as unrelated activity. One of the lines of demarcation between the second and third categories of sales is whether the items have a useful life of more than one year; if they do, the position is that the convenience rule cannot apply, so that the sales are unrelated. Under this approach, taxable sales include sales of items such as clothing and plants.[128]

Hospitals

Along these same lines, in the case of a tax-exempt hospital, the income from patients is considered related income.[129]

Further, hospitals operate businesses which are necessary in relation to their tax-exempt function. Thus, a hospital may operate a gift shop, which is patronized by patients, visitors making purchases for patients, and its employees, without incurring the unrelated business income tax.[130] The IRS observed: "By providing a facility for the purchase of merchandise and services to improve the physical comfort and mental well-being of its patients, the hospital is carrying on an activity that encourages their recovery and therefore contributes importantly to its exempt purposes." The same rationale has been extended to

---

[125]Rev. Rul. 80-296, 1980-2 C. B. 195. These two public rulings, along with Rev. Rul. 80-294, 1980-2 C. B. 187, captures the essence of the foregoing (ns. 113–118) and like private letter rulings. In general, see Thompson and Young, "Taxing the Sale of Broadcast Rights to College Athletics—An Unrelated Trade or Business?," 8 *J. Coll. & U. L.* 331 (1981–2).

[126]*Squire v. Students Book Corp.*, 191 F.2d 1018 (9th Cir. 1951); Rev. Rul. 58-194, 1958-1 C. B. 240.

[127]See Chapter 42 § 2.

[128]IRS Private Letter Rulings 8025222 and 8004010.

[129]S. Rep. No. 2375, *supra*, n. 30 at 107.

[130]Rev. Rul. 69-267, 1969-1 C. B. 160.

the hospital operation of a cafeteria and coffee shop primarily for its employees and medical staff[131] and the hospital operation of a parking lot for its patients and visitors.[132]

Similarly, an exempt hospital has as its primary activity the operation of a clinic that provides various rehabilitation services to handicapped persons, including those with hearing deficiencies. The hospital tests and evaluates the hearing of its patients with the deficiencies and recommends types of hearing aids as may be necessary in each case. Also, the hospital sells hearing aids and fits them to ensure maximum assistance to the patients in the correction or alleviation of their hearing deficiencies. The IRS ruled that the sale of hearing aids as an integral part of the hospital's program is not an unrelated trade or business because it "contributes importantly to the organization's purpose of promoting the health of such persons."[133] Likewise, the IRS has determined that a hospital is not conducting an unrelated business when it allows its physicians and facilities to be used in reading and diagnosing electrocardiogram tests for a hospital that lacks the physicians and facilities to provide the service.[134]

However, the sale of pharmaceutical supplies by an exempt hospital to private patients of physicians who have offices in a medical building owned by the hospital is considered by the IRS to constitute the conduct of an unrelated business.[135] The IRS has also outlined the circumstances in which an exempt hospital derives unrelated business income from the sale of pharmaceutical supplies to the general public.[136] By contrast, the sale of pharmaceutical supplies by a hospital pharmacy to its patients is not the conduct of an unrelated trade or business; the IRS has ruled on varying situations whereunder an individual is a "patient" in a hospital.[137]

By contrast, one court held that income received by a teaching and research hospital for the performance of pathological diagnostic tests on samples submitted by physicians associated with the hospital is not unrelated business

---

[131]Rev. Rul. 69-268, *supra*, n. 82. In one instance, a tax-exempt medical center provided diagnostic testing services for the private patients of physicians, yet was held to generate no unrelated income from the testing services because the activity "contributes importantly to the improvement of the health of the community" and the instruments involved are "unique to the particular testing community" (IRS Private Letter Ruling 8124076). Similarly, a tax-exempt hospital was ruled to receive no unrelated income from the provision of laboratory services for physicians' private patients because the facility was the only one available in the community (IRS Private Letter Ruling 8124006). Also IRS Private Letter Ruling 8121098.

[132]Rev. Rul. 69-269, 1969-1 C. B. 160. Also *Ellis Hospital* v. *Fredette*, 279 N. Y. S. 2d 925 (Sup. Ct. N.Y. 1967); Rev. Rul. 81-29, 1981-1 C. B. 329. Cf. IRS Private Letter Ruling 7841061.

[133]Rev. Rul. 78-435, 1978-2 C. B. 181.

[134]IRS Private Letter Ruling 8004011.

[135]Rev. Rul. 68-375, 1968-2 C. B. 245. Cf. Rev. Rul. 69-463, 1969-2 C. B. 131; IRS Private Letter Rulings 7841061 and 7729002.

[136]Rev. Rul. 68-374, 1968-2 C. B. 242.

[137]Rev. Rul. 68-376, 1968-2 C. B. 246.

taxable income.[138] The court found that the performance and interpretation of these outside pathology tests by the hospital's pathology department are substantially related to the performance by the hospital of its tax-exempt functions because the tests contribute importantly to the teaching functions of the hospital. Further, the court concluded that the testing is a related activity because it increases the doctors' confidence in the quality of the work performed by the pathology department and it is convenient in the event of surgery, in that the pathologist who interpreted the test could interpret the biopsy.[139]

The U.S. Court of Appeals for the Seventh Circuit has considered this issue and concluded that sales of pharmaceuticals by a hospital to members of the general public give rise to unrelated business taxable income.[140] The concept of the "general public" encompasses the private patients of the hospital-based physicians, on the rationale that sales by the pharmacy to the patients are related to the purchaser's visit to his or her private physician at offices rented from the hospital and are not related to the use of services provided by the hospital. Another consideration is that tax-exempt hospital-operated pharmacies unfairly compete with commercial pharmacies.[141]

Museums

Museums, like other operating educational institutions, are by no means immunized from unrelated trade or business concerns. Some museum business operations are nontaxable by reason of the lines of law referenced above, pertaining to parking lots, snack bars, and the like.

The most difficult issues in the unrelated trade or business context presented by museum operations relate to sales to the general public. Where, for example, a museum sells to the general public greeting cards that display printed reproductions of selected works from the museum's collection and from other art collections, the sales activity is deemed to be substantially related to the museum's tax-exempt purpose.[142] The rationale for this conclusion is twofold: (1) the sale of the cards "contributes importantly to the achievement of the museum's exempt educational purposes by stimulating and enhancing public awareness, interest, and appreciation of art" and (2) "a broader segment of the public may be encouraged to visit the museum itself to share in its educational functions and programs as a result of seeing the cards."[143]

---

[138]*St. Luke's Hospital of Kansas City* v. *United States*, 80-2 U. S. T. C. ¶ 9533 (W. D. Mo. 1980).

[139]Also *Anateus Lineal 1948, Inc.* v. *United States*, 366 F.Supp. 118 (W. D. Ark. 1973). In general, see Kannry, "How hospitals can minimize their potential exposure to the unrelated business income tax," 43 *J. Tax.* 166 (1975).

[140]*Carle Foundation* v. *United States*, 611 F.2d 1192 (7th Cir. 1979).

[141]The reasoning in the *Carle Foundation* case has been followed in *Hi-Plains Hospital* v. *United States*, 81-1 U. S. T. C. ¶ 9214 (N. D. Tex. 1981).

[142]Rev. Rul. 73-104, *supra*, n. 86.

[143]*Ibid.*

Of course, the IRS applies the fragmentation rule, to segment the retailing activities of tax-exempt museums, in this setting as well.[144] In so doing, the IRS has evidenced a readiness to isolate a particular type of sale and presume it is an unrelated activity because of one or more characteristics of the items being sold.[145] For example, museums traditionally have sold greeting cards, slides, instructional literature, and metal, wood, and ceramic copies of art works. In recent years, some museums have begun selling novelty items, clothing, and the like. To the extent that the items being sold are "expensive," "lavish," or otherwise "luxury" items, there is a greater likelihood that the IRS will presume the sales activity to be unrelated.

Where an item sold by a museum is priced at a "low cost,"[146] and bears the museum's logo, the IRS generally finds the sales activity to be related, because it enhances public awareness and encourages greater visitation at a museum. Again, however, as the price of items bearing a museum's logo increases, so too will the likelihood that the IRS will find the sales activity to be substantially unrelated to the museum's tax-exempt purposes. Nonetheless, the sale of, for example, clothing bearing a reference to a museum is arguably *per se* substantially related to the museum's tax-exempt purposes—since it publicizes the museum and attracts visitors—irrespective of the price paid for the clothing.

One of the most difficult issues in this context lies in the distinction drawn by the IRS between museum "reproductions" and "adaptations." For the most part, the IRS considers the sales of reproductions to be sales that are related to the museum's tax-exempt purposes, although the Service may resist that conclusion where the items, while copies of items originally created by master period craftsmen, are not contemporaneously made in a manner commensurate with the period. The IRS is much more likely to question the relatedness of sales of adaptations, which are items that may incorporate or reflect original art but differ significantly in form from the original work. Nonetheless, an adaptation may have intrinsic artistic merit or historical significance in its adaptive form (so that a sale of it by a museum is a related activity) or it may bear a museum's logo or otherwise reference the museum (so that it enhances public awareness of the museum and encourages the public to visit the museum, thereby making the sale of it a related activity).[147]

Trade Associations

A tax-exempt trade association (or "business league"[148]) is subject to the unrelated income rules. Therefore, all of the general rules described in the

---

[144]Rev. Rul. 73-105, *supra*, n. 90.

[145]See, e.g., "Exempt Organizations Annual Technical Review Institute for 1979," Training 3177-01 and 02 (3-79).

[146]See Reg. § 1.513-1(b). See discussion at ns. 194 and 213–215, *infra*.

[147]Cf. IRS Private Letter Rulings 8107006, 8024111, and 8004010.

[148]See Chapter 17.

foregoing sections of this chapter and in the related chapters are applicable to trade associations.

However, in recent years, the IRS has devoted an increasing amount of effort to the analysis of the activities of trade groups, both as regards unrelated income taxation and basic tax exemption. For the IRS, the springboard in this area was the enactment of the rule which enables the Service to evaluate "[a]ctivities of producing or distributing goods or performing services from which a particular amount of gross income is derived," notwithstanding the fact that the activities are carried on within a host of other tax-exempt or nonexempt endeavors.[149]

Armed with this authority since 1969, the IRS has repeatedly ruled, publicly and privately, that a variety of services performed by trade associations for their members are unrelated trades or businesses.[150] Illustrations of this approach include the sale of legal forms by a bar association to its members,[151] the sale of equipment by an association to its members,[152] the management of health and welfare plans for a fee by a business league,[153] the provision of insurance for its members,[154] and the publication of ordinary commercial advertising for products and services used by the legal profession in a bar association's journal.[155]

In one instance, the IRS carefully examined seven activities of a tax-exempt trade association and found all of them to be productive of unrelated income. These activities are the sale of vehicle signs to members, the sale to members of embossed tags for inventory control purposes, the sale to members of supplies and forms, the sale to members of kits to enable them to retain sales tax information, the sale of price guides, the administration of a group insurance program, and the sale of commercial advertising in the association's publications. In fact, since the majority of the income of the organization was derived from these activities and the majority of the time of the organization's employees was devoted to them, the IRS revoked the association's tax exemption.[156]

Of this range of trade association activities, none is attracting more attention than the extent to which—without loss of tax exemption or exposure to the unrelated income tax—an association may provide insurance for its members. The evolving position of the IRS is that the provision of insurance is an unrelated activity and thus will cause deprivation of tax-exemption if substantial, or otherwise will be an unrelated trade or business.

---

[149]Code § 513(c); see § 2, *supra*.
[150]See Chapter 17 § 6.
[151]Rev. Rul. 78-51, *supra*, n. 37.
[152]Rev. Rul. 66-338, 1966-2 C. B. 226.
[153]Rev. Rul. 66-151, *supra*, n. 78.
[154]Rev. Rul. 74-81, 1974-1 C. B. 135.
[155]Rev. Rul. 82-139, 1982-29 I. R. B. 6. In this ruling, the IRS also held that the publication of legal notices by a bar association is not an unrelated trade or business.
[156]IRS Private Letter Ruling 7902006.

An association can become involved in a variety of insurance programs in several ways. An association may have little relationship to an insurance offering except to make its name and membership records available to the insurer. By contrast, the association may be directly involved in the management of an insurance program or may operate a self-insurance fund. And the insurance coverage (on a group basis or otherwise) may range over life, health, disability, legal liability, workmen's compensation, product liability, and similar subjects. The insureds may be the association's employees, members, and/or employees of members.

Where an insurance company provides insurance coverage for an association's members (and/or its employees) and the association is the mere sponsor, there may not be the operation of an unrelated trade or business. In one instance, an association provided an insurance company with information about its membership, mailed a letter about the insurance coverage, and allowed the insurer to use the association's name and insignia on brochures. For this, the association received a percentage of the premiums paid by its members to the insurance company. The IRS litigated the issue and the court concluded that the association was merely passively involved and thus that the activity did not become a trade or business.[157]

However, where an association actively and regularly manages an insurance program for its members, for a fee, and a substantial portion of its income and expenses is traceable to the activity, the management undertaking will be regarded by the IRS as an unrelated trade or business.[158] If the provision of insurance is an association's sole or principal activity, the IRS will deny or deprive it of tax exemption, as illustrated by the denial of exemption to an organization that provides group workmen's compensation insurance to its members[159] and to an organization that provided insurance and similar plans for its members.[160]

The approach of the courts in this area is somewhat the same as that of the IRS. The courts, like the IRS, have a tendency to consolidate a variety of association activities—including but not limited to the provision of insurance—and to evaluate the bundle of services as one trade or business. The Court of Claims has adhered to this approach in finding that a significant portion of an association's income was from the performance of services to members, including billing and collecting insurance premiums and distributing claim forms (with the association's income set as a percentage of premiums collected), and therefore held the association to not qualify for tax exemption.[161] The U.S. Tax Court has adopted a like rationale, combining insurance activities with the sale

---

[157]*Oklahoma Cattlemen's Association* v. *United States, supra* n. 9.

[158]Rev. Rul. 66-151, *supra*, n. 78. Also Rev. Rul. 60-228, *supra*, n. 78.

[159]Rev. Rul. 76-81, 1976-1 C. B. 156.

[160]Rev. Rul. 67-176, 1967-1 C. B. 140.

[161]*Indiana Retail Hardware Association* v. *United States*, 366 F.2d 998 (Ct. Cl. 1966).

of educational materials, jewelry, emblems, and supplies to conclude that an association failed to qualify for tax exemption.[162]

Thus, the remaining major substantive issue for the IRS in this area is no longer whether an association can have its tax status adversely affected by, or must treat as an unrelated trade or business, the active conduct of an insurance program but whether there is a way for an association to be only passively involved in an insurance activity. The IRS does not believe the court decision finding this passive involvement[163] to be correct; rather, the Service holds that initiation of an insurance program by an association, negotiation with the broker, and general support of and promotion of the program are services to the association's members and thus an unrelated trade or business.[164] Consequently, in the view of the IRS, once the insurance activity rises to the level of a trade or business,[165] it is a nonexempt activity, and all association insurance activities constitute more than mere passive involvements.

One solution may be to have the insurance program conducted by a separate entity, such as a trust or corporation, albeit controlled by the parent association. This approach requires care that the separate entity is in fact a true legal entity, with its own governing instruments, governing board, and separate tax return filing obligation. If it is a mere trusteed bank account or the like of the association, the IRS will regard the program as an integral part of the association itself.[166] If it is an authentic separate legal entity, any tax liability would be confined to that imposed on the net income of the entity, which presumably would have no basis for securing tax exemption.[167] However, if the entity transfers funds to the parent association, such funds may be taxable to it as unrelated income.[168]

The extent to which the courts will uphold the position of the Service in this regard is not clear. One case recognizes that the acquisition and provision of insurance can be an exempt function of a business league.[169] In this instance, the organization's purposes included counseling governmental agencies with regard to insurance programs, accepting and servicing insurance written by the agencies, and otherwise acting as insurance broker for the governmental

---

[162]*Associated Master Barbers and Beauticians of America, Inc.* v. *Commissioner,* 69 T.C. 53 (1977).

[163]See n. 157, *supra.*

[164]See IRS Private Letter Rulings 7840014, 7841004, 7841031, 7847001, 7847006, 7847101, and 7849003.

[165]See Chapter 41 § 2.

[166]IRS Private Letter Ruling 7847001.

[167]See *North Carolina Oil Jobbers Association, Inc.* v. *United States,* 78-2 U.S.T.C. ¶ 9658 (E. D. N. C. 1978); *New York State Association of Real Estate Boards Group Insurance Fund* v. *Commissioner,* 54 T. C. 1325 (1970).

[168]See Code § 512(b)(13); Chapter 42 § 1.

[169]*Independent Insurance Agents of Northern Nevada, Inc.* v. *United States,* 79-2 U.S.T.C. ¶ 9601 (D. Nev. 1979).

agencies. Finding this function to be "an important public service" (because the activity results in the best comprehensive insurance program for each agency and eliminates political corruption in the procurement of insurance), the court held that the net brokerage commissions received are not taxable as being from an unrelated trade or business. In so holding, the court placed some reliance on an IRS ruling that the provision for equitable distribution of high-risk insurance policies among member insurance companies is an exempt undertaking.[170] However, one of the first courts to rule directly on the point has upheld the IRS position. The court determined that a commission paid a tax-exempt organization upon the writing of new and renewal insurance policies by an insurance company the coverage plans of which the organization endorses is unrelated income.[171]

If the association provides insurance for its own employees, it can do so without adverse tax consequences by contracting with an insurance provider or by establishing a "voluntary employees beneficiary association," which is itself tax-exempt.[172] This type of organization is one that provides "for the payment of life, sick, accident, or other benefits to the members of such association or their dependents or designated beneficiaries. . . ."[173]

Separate consideration must be given the insurance programs of tax-exempt fraternal beneficiary societies,[174] inasmuch as their exempt purpose is to provide for the payment of qualifying benefits to their members and their dependents.[175] The IRS has recognized that these benefits are in the nature of insurance, in holding that a society may keep the benefits in effect after membership is terminated but that a society may not, as an exercise of an exempt function, provide additional insurance for terminated members.[176]

Advertising Activities

Under the rules defining what is a "trade or business,"[177] income from the sale of advertising in publications of tax-exempt organizations (even where the publications are related to the exempt purpose of the organization) generally constitutes unrelated business income, taxable to the extent it exceeds the expenses directly related to the advertising. However, if the editorial aspect

[170]Rev. Rul. 71-155, 1971-1 C. B. 152.

[171]*Louisiana Credit Union League* v. *United States*, 80-2 U.S.T.C. ¶ 9805 (E. D. La. 1980).

[172]Code § 501(c)(9). See Chapter 20 § 5.

[173]In general, see Greif and Goldstein, "Rulings holding insurance plans of exempt orgs. taxable may threaten exemptions," 50 *J. Tax*. 294 (1979); Claytor, "When will business activities cause trade associations to forfeit their exempt status?," 49 *J. Tax*. 104 (1978).

[174]Code § 501(c)(8). See Chapter 20 § 4.

[175]See Chapter 20 § 4.

[176]IRS Private Letter Ruling 7937002.

[177]Code § 513(c). See § 2, *supra*.

of the publication is carried on at a loss, the editorial loss may be offset against the advertising income from the publication. Thus, there will be no taxable unrelated trade or business income because of advertising where the publication as a whole is published at a loss. This rule embodies a preexisting regulation[178] which was promulgated in an effort to carve out (and tax) income from advertising and other activities in competition with taxpaying businesses, even though the advertising may appear in a periodical related to the educational or other tax-exempt purpose of the organization.

These rules are not intended to encompass the publication of a magazine with little or no advertising, which is distributed free or at a nominal charge not intended to cover costs. This type of publication would likely be published basically as a source of public information and not for the production of income. For a publication to be considered an activity carried on for the production of income, it must be contemplated that the revenues from advertising in the publication or the revenues from sales of the publication, or both, will result in net income (although not necessarily in a particular year). Nonetheless, for the tax on unrelated business income to apply, the advertising activity must also constitute a trade or business that is regularly carried on. Also, the tax is inapplicable where the advertising activity is an exempt function.[179]

As an example, an association of law enforcement officials publishes a monthly journal containing conventional advertising featuring the products or services of a commercial enterprise. The IRS ruled that the regular sale of space in the journal for the advertising is carried on for the production of income and constitutes the conduct of trade or business, which is not substantially related to the organization's tax-exempt functions. "The controlling factor in this case," said the Service, is that the "activities giving rise to the income in question constitute the sale and performance of a valuable service on the part of the publisher, and the purchase of that service on the part of the other party to the transaction."[180]

In a similar situation, the IRS ruled that income derived by a tax-exempt membership organization from the sale of advertising in its annual yearbook is unrelated business taxable income. Preparation of the editorial materials in the yearbook was largely done by the organization's staff, which also distributed it. However, an independent commercial firm was used, under a full year

---

[178]Reg. § 1.513-1(b). This regulation became effective on December 13, 1967. Code § 513(c) became effective on December 31, 1969. As respects tax years beginning between these dates, the regulation is of no effect, as an impermissible administrative enlargement of the scope of the statutory unrelated business income law, according to two court decisions. *Massachusetts Medical Society* v. *United States*, 514 F.2d 153 (1st Cir. 1975); *American College of Physicians* v. *United States*, 530 F.2d 930 (Ct. Cl. 1976).

[179]See, e.g., IRS Private Letter Ruling 7948113, holding that proceeds from the sale of advertising in the program published in promotion of a post-season all-star college football game are not unrelated income.

[180]Rev. Rul. 74-38, 1974-1 C. B. 144. Also see Rev. Rul. 76-93, 1976-1 C. B. 170.

contract, to conduct an intensive advertising solicitation campaign in the organization's name and the firm was paid a percentage of the gross advertising receipts for selling the advertising, collecting from advertisers, and printing the yearbook. The IRS stated that "[b]y engaging in an extensive campaign of advertising solicitation, the organization is conducting competitive and promotional efforts typical of commercial endeavors."[181]

This determination should be contrasted with the situation involving a "charitable" organization which raised funds for a tax-exempt symphony orchestra. As part of this effort, the organization published an annual concert book which was distributed at the orchestra's annual charity ball. The IRS ruled that the solicitation and sale of advertising by volunteers of the organization was not an unrelated taxable activity because the activity was not regularly carried on and because it was conducted as an integral part of the process of fund-raising for charity.[182] Thus, part of a successful contention that the unrelated income tax should not apply in the advertising context would seem to be a showing that the advertising activity ties in with other organization activity. Yet the same type of organization which engaged in the sale of advertising over a four-month period by its paid employees, for publication in concert programs distributed free at symphony performances over an eight-month period, was found by the IRS to be carrying on an unrelated business.[183] In that ruling, the IRS observed:

> It is a matter of common knowledge that many non-exempt organizations make a regular practice of publishing and distributing a seasonal series of special interest publications covering only a portion of each year with a format that includes substantial amounts of advertising matter. It would not be unusual for such an organization to concentrate its efforts to sell the advertising space thus made available during similar periods of intensive activity that would frequently last for no more than three or four months of each year. Since it is likewise further apparent that the activities giving rise to the advertising income here in question do not otherwise substantially differ from the comparable commercial activities of nonexempt organizations, those activities of the subject organization are regularly carried on within the meaning of section 512 of the Code.

Similarly, a business league that sells a membership directory, but only to its members, was held not to be engaged in an unrelated trade or business. The directory was considered to contribute importantly to the achievement of the organization's tax-exempt purposes by facilitating communication among its members and encouraging the exchange of ideas and expertise, resulting in greater awareness of collective and individual activities of the membership.

---

[181]Rev. Rul. 73-424, *supra*, n. 28. This attribution of income generated by an independent advertising activity to a tax-exempt organization does not necessarily work in reverse, as illustrated by the IRS ruling that allowed an organization to receive from an independent advertising effort a fee characterized as a royalty, which is excluded from unrelated income taxation (see Chapter 42 § 1). IRS Private Letter Ruling 7926003.

[182]Rev. Rul. 75-201, *supra*, n. 117.

[183]Rev. Rul. 75-200, 1975-1 C. B. 163.

The principal aspect governing the outcome of this matter, however, was the fact that the sale of the directory, done in a noncommercial manner, does not confer any private benefit on the organization's members.[184]

Income attributable to a publication of a tax-exempt organization basically is regarded as either "circulation income" or (if any) "gross advertising income."[185] Circulation income is the income attributable to the production, distribution, or circulation of a publication (other than gross advertising income), including amounts realized from the sale of the readership content of the publication. Gross advertising income is the amount derived from the unrelated advertising activities of an exempt organization publication.

Likewise, the costs attributable to a tax-exempt organization publication are characterized as "readership costs" and "direct advertising costs."[186] A reasonable allocation may be made as between cost items attributable both to an exempt organization publication and to its other activities (such as salaries, occupancy costs, and depreciation). Readership costs are, therefore, the cost items directly connected with the production and distribution of the readership content of the publication, other than the items properly allocable to direct advertising costs. Direct advertising costs include items which are directly connected with the sale and publication of advertising (such as agency commissions and other selling costs, art work and copy preparation), the portion of mechanical and distribution costs attributable to advertising lineage, and any other element of readership costs properly allocable to the advertising activity.

As noted, a tax-exempt organization (assuming it is subjected to the unrelated business income rules in the first instance) is not taxable on its advertising income where its direct advertising costs equal such (gross) income. Even if gross advertising income exceeds direct advertising costs, costs attributable to the readership content of the publication qualify as costs deductible in computing (unrelated) income from the advertising activity, to the extent that the costs exceed the income attributable to the readership content.[187] There are limitations on this rule, however, including the conditions that its application may not be used to realize a loss from the advertising activity nor to give rise to a cost deductible in computing taxable income attributable to any other unrelated activity. Of course, if the circulation income of the publication exceeds its readership costs, any unrelated business taxable income attributable to the publication is the excess of gross advertising income over direct advertising costs.

An example of the foregoing rules may be of assistance (this assumes that the production and distribution of the readership content of the publication is a related activity). A trade association publication carrying advertising generated, in one tax year, $40,000 in gross advertising income and $60,000 in

---

[184]Rev. Rul. 79-370, 1979-2 C. B. 238.
[185]Reg. § 1.512(a)-1(f)(3).
[186]Reg. § 1.512(a)-1(f)(6).
[187]Reg. §§ 1.512(a)-1(f)(2)(ii), 1.512(a)-1(d)(2).

circulation income (total publication income is thus $100,000). Readership costs were $40,000 and direct advertising costs were $50,000 (total periodical costs thus were $90,000). Since circulation income was in excess of readership costs (resulting in $20,000 in related income), the unrelated income rules look only to advertising income and costs, which in the example produce a $10,000 loss attributable to the advertising activity. Moreover, the loss can be offset in computing taxable income from any other unrelated activity.[188]

Carrying this further, assume the same facts, except for $100,000 in circulation income, $40,000 in gross advertising income, $65,000 in readership costs, and $25,000 in direct advertising costs. Since the circulation income again exceeds readership costs, the unrelated taxable advertising income is $15,000— the excess of the gross advertising income over direct advertising costs.

Further, assume $60,000 in circulation income, $40,000 in gross advertising income, $70,000 in readership costs, and $20,000 in direct advertising costs. In this case, unrelated taxable income from the advertising is not $20,000 ($40,000 minus $20,000). Rather, since the readership costs are in excess of the circulation income, the unrelated business taxable income from advertising is the amount of total income attributable to the publication ($100,000), less the total costs of the publication ($90,000), or $10,000.

Again, assume $60,000 in circulation income, $40,000 in gross advertising income, $90,000 in readership costs, and $30,000 in direct advertising costs. Because the readership costs exceed the circulation income, any unrelated business taxable income from advertising would be the net total income attributable to the publication (as in the previous example). Here, however, there is no unrelated taxable income because the total publication costs ($120,000) exceed total publication income ($100,000). Moreover, in computing unrelated business taxable income in general, only $70,000 of the readership costs are deductible, by reason of the above-noted rules that such costs may be deducted only to the extent they exceed circulation income and only to the extent they do not result in a loss from the advertising activity. Therefore, in this example, no amount is deductible on this account in computing taxable income from any other unrelated activity.

Another set of rules requires an allocation of membership dues to circulation income where the right to receive the publication is associated with membership status in the tax-exempt organization for which dues, fees, or other charges are received.[189] There are three ways of determining the portion of membership dues which constitute a part of circulation income ("allocable membership receipts"):

(1) If 20 percent or more of the total circulation of the publication consists of sales to nonmembers, the subscription price charged to the nonmembers is the amount allocated from each member's dues to circulation income.

---

[188]Reg. § 1.512(a)-1(f)(2)(i).
[189]Reg. § 1.512(a)-1(f)(4). See IRS Private Letter Ruling 7822003.

(2) If rule (1) is inapplicable and if the membership dues from 20 percent or more of the members of the organization are less than the dues received from the remaining members because the former category of members does not receive the publication, the amount of the dues reduction is the amount used in allocating membership dues to circulation income.

(3) Otherwise, the portion of membership receipts allocated to the publication is an amount equal to the total amount of the receipts multiplied by a fraction, the numerator of which is the total costs of the publication and the denominator of which is these costs plus the costs of the other tax-exempt activities of the organization.[190] For example, assuming that rules (1) and (2) are inapplicable, that total publication costs are $30,000 and other exempt activity costs are $70,000, and that membership receipts are $60,000, $18,000 is the amount allocable to circulation income ($60,000 times $30,000/$100,000).

The following examples of the foregoing three rules assume that the tax-exempt organization publication contains advertising and that the production and distribution of the readership content of the publication is a related activity.

A tax-exempt scientific organization has 10,000 members who pay annual dues of $15. Its monthly publication is distributed to all of its members and it also distributes an additional 5,000 copies of the publication to nonmembers at an annual subscription cost of $10. Rule (1) is applicable because the nonmember circulation of the publication is 33⅓ percent of total circulation. Thus, the organization's allocable membership receipts are $100,000 ($10 times 10,000 members) and its total circulation income from the publication is $150,000 ($100,000 from members and $50,000 from nonmembers).

Another example assumes the facts of the previous illustration, except that the organization sells only 500 copies of its publication to nonmembers at a price of $10 annually and the organization's members may elect not to receive the publication, in which case their annual dues are reduced to $6. Three thousand members elect to receive the publication. The stated subscription price to members of $9 consistently results in an excess of total income attributable to the publication over its total costs. Since the 500 copies of the publication distributed to nonmembers represents only 14 percent of the 3,500 copies distributed, the $10 subscription price is not used to determine allocable membership receipts. Rather, rule (2) applies inasmuch as 70 percent of the members elect not to receive the publication and pay $9 less per year in dues; the $9 price is used to determine the subscription price charged to members. Thus, the organization's allocable membership receipts are $9 per member or

---

[190]The reference to the "costs of the other exempt activities" means the total costs or expenses incurred by an organization in connection with its other tax-exempt activities, not offset by any income earned by the organization from the activities. Rev. Rul. 81-101, 1981-1 C. B. 352.

$27,000 ($9 times 3,000 copies) and its total circulation income is $32,000 ($27,000 plus $5,000).

Still another example concerns a tax-exempt trade association having 800 members who pay annual dues of $50. The association's monthly journal is distributed to all of its members and no receipts are derived from nonmembers. The association's total receipts are $100,000 of which $40,000 ($50 times 800) is membership receipts and $60,000 is gross advertising income. Its total costs for the journal and other tax-exempt activities are $100,000; its total publication costs are $76,000, of which $41,000 is direct advertising costs and $35,000 is readership costs. Rule (3) applies; based upon pro rata allocation of membership receipts ($40,000) by a fraction, the numerator of which is total publication costs ($76,000) and the denominator of which is the total costs of the journal and other tax-exempt activities ($100,000), its circulation income is $30,400 ($40,000 times $76,000/$100,000).

These rules become even more intricate where a tax-exempt organization publishes more than one publication for the production of income. (A publication is published for the production of income if the organization generally receives gross advertising income from the publication equal to at least 25 percent of its readership costs and the publication activity is engaged in for profit.) In this case, the organization may treat the gross income from all (but not just some) of the publications and the deductible items directly connected with the publications on a consolidated basis in determining the amount of unrelated business taxable income derived from the sale of advertising. (Thus, an organization cannot consolidate the losses of a publication not published for the production of income with the "profit" of other publications which are so published.) This treatment must be followed consistently and, once adopted, is binding, unless the organization obtains the requisite permission from the IRS to change the method.[191]

Fund-Raising Activities

It would be a substantial understatement to say that charitable organizations do not regard their fund-raising activities as unrelated business endeavors. Yet, unbeknownst to most in the philanthropic community, fund-raising practices

---

[191]Code § 446(e); Reg. § 1.446-1(e). In general, see Kannry, "Taxing Advertising," IX *The Philanthropy Monthly* (No. V) 26 (1976); Kannry, "How to mitigate the impact of new Regs. on exempt organization's advertising income," 45 *J. Tax.* 304 (1976); Sugarman and Vogt, "The New Advertising Regulations and Their Application to Exempt Organizations," 54 *Taxes* 196 (1976); Spevack, "Taxation of Advertising Income of Exempt Organizations' Publications," 21 *Cath. Lawyer* 268 (1975); Endicott, "Proposed Changes in the Taxation of Advertising Income of Exempt Organization Publications," 2 *Tax Adviser* 710 (1971); Lehrfeld, "The Unfairness Doctrine: Commercial Advertising Profits as Unrelated Business Income," 23 *Tax Lawyer* 349 (1970); Weithorn and Liles, "Unrelated Business Income Tax: Changes Affecting Journal Advertising Revenues," 45 *Taxes* 791 (1967).

and the unrelated trade or business rules have been enduring a precarious relationship for years.

Traditionally, the IRS has exercised suitable restraint by refraining from applying the unrelated income rules to charitable gift solicitation efforts. However, this restraint is seemingly being abandoned, with the IRS now beginning to utilize the unrelated income rules to characterize the receipts from certain fund-raising activities as taxable income. In fact, this utilization of these rules is one of the chief means by which the IRS is embarking upon regulation of fund-raising for charity.

At the outset, it must be conceded that some fund-raising practices possess all of the technical characteristics of an unrelated trade or business. Reviewing the criteria for unrelated income taxation,[192] some fund-raising activities are (1) trades or businesses, (2) regularly carried on, and (3) not efforts that are substantially related to the performance of tax-exempt functions. Further, applying some of the tests often used by the IRS and the courts, there is no question but that some fund-raising endeavors (4) have a commercial counterpart and they are being conducted in competition with that counterpart, and (5) are being undertaken with the objective of realizing a profit.[193] Treatment of a fund-raising effort as an unrelated business certainly is not consistent with the intent of Congress when it enacted the unrelated income rules in 1950, but nonetheless can be a logical and technically accurate application of the rules.

In the past, the IRS appears to have basically avoided application of the unrelated income rules to the fund-raising endeavors of charitable organizations. Even if the matter was given much thought, the rationale seems to have been that either the fund-raising activity is not a trade or business or is not regularly carried on.

The rationale that fund-raising activities are not "businesses" was expressed by the Senate Committee on Finance in 1969, when it stated that "where an activity does not possess the characteristics of a trade or business within the meaning of IRC [§] 162, such as when an organization sends out low-cost articles incidental to the solicitation of charitable contributions, the unrelated business income tax does not apply since the organization is not in competition with taxable organizations."[194] However, an examination of this rationale reveals two

---

[192]See §§ 2–4, *supra*.

[193]The fact that the "profits" of an activity are destined for use in furtherance of tax-exempt functions cannot be taken into consideration in assessing whether an activity is an unrelated one. See Code §§ 502 and 513(a).

[194]S. Rep. No. 91-522, 91st Cong., 1st Sess. 71 (1969), quoted as part of the IRS Exempt Organizations Handbook (IRM 7751, Nov. 14, 1975) at (36) 21 (2), and Reg. § 1.513-1(b). In an application of this rule, an association with sponsoring associate members that pay an annual fee for a bronze shield of the association's insignia was advised by the IRS that the fee is not unrelated income. IRS Private Letter Ruling 7938003. This ruling is in error on this point, inasmuch as the tax exemption is available only in relation to the solicitation of *charitable* contributions, while the association involved is a Code § 501(c)(6) business league.

elements that substantially undermine its widespread application: (1) the funds received by the organization are in the form of gifts, not payments for the articles or services provided, and (2) the activity is not in competition with commercial endeavors. These two elements are frequently absent in a fund-raising endeavor.

Thus, a tax-exempt organization may well engage in fund-raising efforts that have their commercial counterparts. Some of these activities are sheltered by law from consideration as businesses, such as a business (1) in which substantially all of the work is performed for the organization by volunteers,[195] (2) carried on primarily for the convenience of the organization's members, students, patients, officers, or employees,[196] or (3) which consists of the sale of merchandise, substantially all of which has been received by the organization as gifts.[197] Also, a statute exempts from unrelated business income taxation the receipts from certain types of bingo games. [198]

Perhaps the beginning of serious regard of fund-raising activities as businesses can be traced to the Tax Reform Act of 1969, whereby Congress authorized the taxation of revenue from the acquisition and publication of advertising in the magazines of tax-exempt organizations.[199] To accomplish this result, Congress codified two rules previously contained in the income tax regulations: it enacted laws which state that (1) the term "trade or business" includes any activity carried on for the production of income from the sale of goods or the performance of services, and (2) an activity of producing or distributing goods or performing services from which gross income is derived does not lose identity as a trade or business merely because it is carried on within a larger aggregate of similar activities or within a larger complex of other endeavors which may or may not be related to the exempt purposes of the organization.[200]

Needless to say, this definition of the term "trade or business" is extremely encompassing. The IRS, for example, has observed that the definition of the term "is not limited to integrated aggregates of assets, activities, and good will which comprise businesses" for purposes of other tax rules.[201] In addition to the breadth of this definition, the IRS is, as noted, authorized by statute to examine the activities of a tax-exempt organization one-by-one (rather than as a single bundle of activities) and fragment its operations in search of unrelated business endeavors. As the result of both of these rules, the fund-raising prac-

---

[195]Code § 513(a)(1). See Chapter 42 § 2.

[196]Code § 513(a)(2). See Chapter 42 § 2.

[197]Code § 513(a)(3). See, e.g., Rev. Rul. 71-581, 1971-2 C. B. 236. See Chapter 42 § 2.

[198]Code § 513(f). See Chapter 42 § 2.

[199]See § 5(d), *supra*.

[200]Code § 513(c); also Reg. § 1.513-1(b). See § 2, *supra*.

[201]Exempt Organizations Handbook, *supra*, n. 194 at (36) 21 (1).

tices of charitable organizations are now, more than ever, exposed and thus more vulnerable to the charge that they are unrelated businesses.

More directly, in somewhat of the fund-raising context, the IRS has held that the regular sales of membership mailing lists by a tax-exempt educational organization to colleges and business firms for the production of income is an unrelated trade or business.[202] By contrast, the IRS has privately ruled that the exchange of mailing lists by an exempt organization with similar exempt organizations does not give rise to unrelated business income (namely, barter income of an amount equal to the value of the lists received).[203] In this ruling, the Service ruled that the activity is not a business because it is not carried on for profit but rather to obtain the names of potential donors. Likewise, this exchange function was held to be substantially related to the organization's exempt function as being a "generally accepted method used by publicly supported organizations to assist them in maintaining and enhancing their active donor files." Nonetheless, where a tax-exempt organization exchanges mailing lists so as to produce income, it is the position of the IRS that the transaction is economically the same as a rental and thus is an unrelated trade or business.[204]

The rationale that fund-raising activities are not taxable businesses because they are not regularly carried on also finds support in the early IRS literature. The basic position of the Service is that "exempt organization business activities which are engaged in only discontinuously or periodically will not be considered regularly carried on if they are conducted without the competitive and promotional efforts typical of commercial endeavors."[205] For example, the operation of a sandwich stand by a hospital auxiliary for two weeks at a state fair is not the regular conduct of a trade or business,[206] while the operation of a parking lot for commercial purposes one day each week on a year-round basis is the regular conduct of a trade or business.[207] Thus, the Service has observed that "[a]n annually recurrent dance or similar fund-raising event for charity would not be regular since it occurs so infrequently."[208]

In one case, the U.S. Tax Court concluded that the annual fund-raising activity of a charitable organization, consisting of the presentation and sponsoring of a professional vaudeville show (one weekend per year), is not regularly carried on. The court concluded: "The fact that an organization seeks to insure the success of its fundraising venture by beginning to plan and prepare for it

---

[202]Rev. Rul. 72-431, *supra*, n. 73.

[203]IRS Private Letter Ruling 8127019. Also IRS Private Letter Ruling 8128004.

[204]IRS Private Letter Ruling 8216009.

[205]Exempt Organizations Handbook, *supra*, n. 194 at (36)30(2)(d).

[206]*Ibid*. at (36)30(2)(a).

[207]*Id*. at (36)30(2)(b).

[208]*Id*. at (36)30(2)(f). However, a charity may be found to be engaged in an unrelated trade or business for conducting such a fund-raising event where it is done for the benefit of another charity. Rev. Rul. 75-201, *supra*, n. 117; IRS Private Letter Ruling 7902019 (issue no. 7).

earlier should not adversely affect the tax treatment of the income derived from the venture."[209]

However, just as many fund-raising practices are technically "trades or businesses," so are many "regularly carried on." Inasmuch as the other rationales for avoiding unrelated income taxation (principally, the contention that the activity is "substantially related" or that the income is "passive") are unlikely to apply in the fund-raising context, it is today quite possible for a fund-raising activity to be deemed a trade or business that is regularly carried on and an undertaking that is not substantially related to the exercise of a charitable organization's tax-exempt purposes.

At this writing, there are only three known instances of the assumption by the IRS of this position. One is a 1979 private letter ruling concerning a case involving a religious organization that conducted, as its principal fund-raising activity, bingo games and related concessions.[210] Players were charged a fixed amount for the use of bingo cards, the games were held on three nights each week, and the receipts from the expenses of the games were substantial. The IRS concluded that "the bingo games constitute a trade or business with the general public, the conduct of which is not substantially related to the exercise or the performance by the organization of the purpose for which it was organized other than the use it makes of the profits derived from the games."[211]

Also, the U.S. Court of Appeals for the Seventh Circuit has held that a solicitation of charitable contributions by means of the mailing of greeting cards to potential contributors does not constitute the conduct of an unrelated trade or business.[212] The case concerned a school that unsuccessfully attempted to raise funds from foundations and other organizations, so it turned to a program of mailing packages of greeting cards to prospective donors, with information about the school and a request for contributions. An outside firm printed, packaged, and mailed the greeting cards and the accompanying solicitation letter. The court rejected the government's contention that the solicitation is a trade or business, finding that the greeting cards were not being sold but were distributed incidental to the solicitation of charitable contributions. As noted, the income tax regulations provide that "an activity does not possess the characteristics of a trade or business . . . when an organization sends out

---

[209]*Suffolk County Patrolmen's Benevolent Association, Inc.* v. *Commissioner, supra,* n. 117. The court took the opportunity of this case to observe: "Respondent [IRS] apparently believes that all fundraisers of exempt organizations are conducted by amateurs in an amateurish manner. We do not believe that this is, nor should be, the case. It is entirely reasonable for an exempt organization to hire professionals in an effort to insure the success of a fundraiser . . . ."

[210]IRS Private Letter Ruling 7946001.

[211]The organization was unable to utilize the exemption from unrelated income taxation afforded by Code § 513(f) because, under the law of the state in which it is organized (Texas), the bingo games constituted, at that time, an illegal lottery. See Chapter 42 § 2.

[212]*The Hope School* v. *United States,* 612 F.2d 298 (7th Cir. 1980).

low cost articles incidental to the solicitation of charitable contributions."[213] The government argued that this rule was inapplicable in this case because the funds involved are not "gifts," but the court said that to read the law in that narrow manner would "completely emasculate the exception."[214] The court held that the case turned on the fact that the unrelated income rules were designed to prevent nonprofit organizations from unfairly competing with for-profit companies, and that the school's fund-raising program did not give it "an unfair competitive advantage over taxpaying greeting card businesses."[215]

Thirdly, the U.S. Court of Claims subsequently examined application of the unrelated income rules as they relate to certain fund-raising efforts of a national veterans organization.[216] The case focuses on two fund-raising practices of the organization. The first was its practice of offering items ("premiums") to potential donors as part of its semiannual direct mail solicitation. The premiums, offered in exchange for contributions of $2, $3, or $5, were maps, charts, calendars, and books. The rationale for this use of premiums was that it gained the attention of the recipients so that more initial responses were obtained or, in instances involving prior donors, the level of contributions was upgraded. The second practice was the rental of names on the organization's mailing list to both tax-exempt and commercial organizations. The court found that certain of the organization's solicitation activities using premiums constituted a trade or business because they were conducted in a competitive and commercial manner. In making the differentiation, the court ruled that "if the contribution required for any one premium was set at an amount greatly in excess of the retail value of the premium concerned, a competitive situation would not be present." Because the $2 premium items were valued at $0.85 to $1 and the $3 items were valued at $1.50, the court concluded that there was not trade or business. But, because the $5 premium items were valued at $2.95 to $5.45, the court found the requisite trade or business, noting that the sending of a $5 contribution "may well have formed a contract binding . . . [the organization] to furnish the premium item." Also finding that the solicitation was regularly carried on (because of "sufficient similarity to a commercial endeavor") and was not an activity related to the organization's tax-exempt purposes (notwithstanding the utility of the premiums as attention-getting devices), the court declared the presence of an unrelated trade or business.

The court also determined that the rental of the organization's donor list is a trade or business that is regularly carried on and that is not substantially related to the accomplishment of its tax-exempt purposes.[217]

It is clear, from these two court cases, that there is much less of a likelihood

---

[213]*Supra*, n. 194.

[214]*The Hope School* v. *United States, supra*, n. 212 at 302.

[215]*Id*. at 304.

[216]*Disabled American Veterans* v. *United States*, 80-2 U.S.T.C. ¶ 9568 (Ct. Cl. 1980).

[217]This determination thus upholds the IRS policy on the point proclaimed in Rev. Rul. 72-431, *supra*, n. 202.

that the use of premium items as part of a fund-raising activity will be considered an unrelated trade or business if the items are mailed with the solicitation. That is, where the recipients are informed that the premiums can be retained without any obligation to make a contribution, the activity is not conducted in a competitive manner and hence presumably is not a trade or business. But, as the Court of Claims observed, "when premiums are advertised and offered only in exchange for prior contributions in stated amounts, the activity takes on much more of a commercial nature."[218] The activity also will take on some tax liability.

Subsequently, the full Court of Claims (per curiam) adopted the trial judge's report, with some modifications but none concerning the substantive unrelated business income issues. Thus, the position of the entire court in the case is that the amounts received by this veterans' organization from a semiannual solicitations program utilizing premium items constituted unrelated business income and that the amounts received by the organization from the rental of its mailing list constituted unrelated business income. Consequently, the emerging law appears to be that "when premiums are advertised and offered only in exchange for prior contributions in stated amounts,"[219] the activity becomes a commercial one, but if the organization "had mailed the premiums with its solicitations and had informed the recipients that the premiums could be retained without any obligation arising to make a contribution," the activity is not a business because it is not a competitive practice.[220]

A related issue can arise in characterizing a direct mail effort as being grass-roots lobbying rather than being fund raising, with the IRS perhaps inclined to treat it as the former for purposes of regulation, particularly where the fund-raising literature has a legislative theme. In a technical advice memorandum interpreting the limitation on charitable organizations on attempts to influence legislation,[221] the IRS held that the facts and circumstances of the mail appeal for funds will determine whether it is merely a fund-raising appeal or whether it is a disguised attempt at grass-roots lobbying. Some of the factors the IRS considered important in determining that a direct mail solicitation was not grass-roots lobbying include the use of an outside fund-raising consultant; the consultant's preparation of the text of the letter, its graphics and design, and the type of postage used going out and coming in; the design of the involvement devices included in the mailing; the use of standard fund-raising techniques such as the number of times paragraphs asking for more money were included in the text (usually 30 percent of the total text); whether the consultant ever consulted with lobbyists or policy analysts of the soliciting organization to assure uniformity or correctness in the discussion of the legislative topic or theme;

---

[218]*Disabled American Veterans v. United States, supra,* n. 216.

[219]*Disabled American Veterans v. United States,* 650 F.2d 1179, 1187 (Ct. Cl. 1981).

[220]*Ibid.*at 1186. See *Hope School v. United States, supra,* n. 212. For subsequent applications of these rules, see IRS Private Letter Rulings 8203134 and 8232011.

[221]See Chapter 13.

whether there was any direct request in the letter that the solicitee do anything other than send money or return a poll card; if the poll card used involved an opinion on the legislative topic, whether the poll card was disregarded or not used in some legislative format by the soliciting organization; whether the soliciting organization had an institutional point of view, expressed through its publications or otherwise, which publicly favored or opposed pending or proposed legislation consistent with the theme of the solicitation letter; the type of mailing lists used by the fund-raising consultant and whether the mailing lists had a political orientation; and finally, whether the fund-raising appeal was a financial success.

Thus it is that, since the raising of funds by a charitable organization is not in itself an exempt function, many types of fund-raising activities are vulnerable to the claim that they are unrelated trades or businesses.

The likelihood of occurrence of this result is substantially reduced where the activity is more akin to an "administrative" or "management" activity, rather than an active "business enterprise." In this category of fund-raising efforts somewhat comparable to administrative or management undertakings are the writing of charitable remainder trusts and charitable gift annuity agreements, the offering of participations in pooled income funds, and the administration of charitable bequest programs. Yet a 1978 U.S. Tax Court case raises some questions about these activities as well.

A fundamental precept of the federal tax law concerning charitable organizations is that they may not, without imperiling their tax-exempt status, be operated in a manner that causes persons to derive a private benefit from their operations.[222] Yet the provision of services that amount to personal financial and tax planning—an essential element of the appreciated property and planned gift techniques[223]—may not be considered an exempt activity but rather the provision of private benefit. While it would seem nearly inconceivable to contend that, when a charitable organization works with a donor to effect a sizable gift that will generate significant tax savings for the donor by reason of a charitable contribution deduction and other benefits, the organization is jeopardizing its tax-exempt status because it is providing a "private benefit," such a conclusion is the import of this case.

The case concerned the tax status of an organization that engages in financial counseling by providing tax planning services (including charitable giving considerations) to wealthy individuals referred to it by subscribing religious organizations. The counseling given by the organization consists of advice on how a contributor may increase current or planned gifts to the religious organizations, including the development of a financial plan which, among other objectives, results in a reduction of federal income and estate taxes. The position of the IRS was that this organization cannot qualify for federal income tax exemption because it serves the private interests of individuals by enabling

[222]See Chapter 12.
[223]See Chapter 13 § 2.

them to reduce their tax burden. The organization's position was that it was merely engaging in activities that tax-exempt organizations may themselves undertake without loss of their tax exemption.[224] The court agreed with the government, finding that the organization's "sole financial planning activity, albeit an exempt purpose furthering . . . [exempt] fundraising efforts, has a nonexempt purpose of offering advice to individuals on tax matters that reduces an individual's personal and estate tax liabilities."[225] As the court dryly stated, "We do not find within the scope of the word charity that the financial planning for wealthy individuals described in this case is a charitable purpose."[226]

In this opinion, the court singled out the planned giving techniques for portrayal as methods that give rise to unwarranted private benefit. Thus, the court observed:

> For example, when petitioner advises a contributor to establish a charitable unitrust gift, the contributor ultimately forfeits the remainder. Nevertheless, this loss is voluntarily exchanged for considerable lifetime advantages. Unitrusts generate substantial income and estate and gift tax benefits, such as retained income for life, reduced capital gains tax, if any, on the exchange of appreciated investments, favorable tax rates for part or all of the income payments on certain investments, and lower probate costs. Consequently, there are real and substantial benefits inuring to the contributors by the petitioner's activities.[227]

Concluded the court: "We think the tax benefits inuring to the contributors are . . . substantial enough to deny exemption."[228]

Subsequently, the U.S. Tax Court again evinced a lack of understanding of fund raising for charity and thus issued an opinion that raises anew questions about the imposition of the unrelated income tax in the fund-raising context.[229] At issue was the tax status of a membership organization for citizens' band radio operators, that uses insurance, travel and discount plans to attract new members. The organization contended that it is only doing what many tax-exempt organizations do to raise contributions, analogizing these activities to fund-raising events such as rallies and dinners. The court rejected this argument, defining a "fund raising event" as "a single occurrence that may occur on limited occasions during a given year and its purpose is to further the exempt activities of the organization." These events were contrasted with activities that "are continuous or continual activities which are certainly more pervasive a part of the organization than a sporadic event and [that are] . . . an end in themselves." Of course, there are a wide variety of fund-raising methods other than special

---

[224]This rationale has ample support in the law. See Chapter § 9, pp. 112–119.

[225]*Christian Stewardship Assistance, Inc.* v. *Commissioner*, 70 T. C. 1037, 1041 (1978).

[226]*Ibid.* at 1043.

[227]*Ibid.* at 1044.

[228]*Id.*

[229]*U. S. CB Radio Association, No. 1, Inc.* v. *Commissioner*, 42 T. C. M. 1441 (1981).

events that are "continuous" and "pervasive," and that are intended "to further the exempt activities of the organization." Also, no legitimate fund-raising activity is an end in itself, yet many tax-exempt organizations and institutions have major, ongoing fund-raising and development programs that are permanent fixtures among the totality of the entities' activities. This decision, then, is another in a series of cases that is forming the foundation for the contention that certain types of fund-raising endeavors are unrelated businesses.

Thus it is that the IRS may be embarking on a new approach for regulating charitable fund-raising, by characterizing it as unrelated business, [230] while the courts may be trending toward a line of thinking that equates charitable giving and associated tax planning with private benefit, thereby causing denial or loss of tax exemption. Either way, it appears that the basic rules governing federal income tax exemption are being applied in a very restrictive manner in relation to fund-raising endeavors, so that fund-raising charitable groups may be facing a new wave of regulation, with their exempt status or the extent thereof as the government's leverage.

[230]The Internal Revenue Manual §331(2), as amended in 1982, directs internal revenue agents to, as part of their examination of public charities, "[c]onsider the [charities'] method of raising funds and whether such income is subject to unrelated business income tax."

42

Exceptions to Unrelated Income Taxation

Notwithstanding the fact that a particular activity may otherwise constitute an unrelated trade or business, the activity may escape taxation under one of the "modification" rules or one of the other specific statutory exceptions. The rules concerning "passive" income are also encompassed by the "modification rules.

§ 42.1 Modifications

In determining unrelated business taxable income, both gross income derived from an unrelated trade or business and business deductions are computed with certain "modifications."[1]

Passive income, namely, dividends, interest, payments with respect to securities loans, annuities, royalties, certain rents (generally of real estate), and gain from the disposition of property, is generally excluded from unrelated business taxable income, along with directly connected deductions.[2]

---

[1]Code § 512(b).

[2]Code §§ 512(b)(1), (2), (3), and (5). See Reg. § 1.512(b)-1(a)-(d). Also see *State National Bank of El Paso* v. *United States,* 509 F.2d 832 (5th Cir. 1975); Rev. Rul. 69-430, 1969-2 C. B. 129; Rev. Rul. 69-178, 1969-1 C. B. 158; Rev. Rul. 69-69, 1969-1 C. B. 159; Rev. Rul. 67-218, 1967-2 C. B. 213; Rev. Rul. 60-206, 1960-1 C. B. 201; *Louis W. Hill Family Foundation* v. *United States,* 347 F. Supp. 1225 (D. Minn. 1972); IRS Private Letter Ruling 7728060. In general, see Greif, "Tax implications of an exempt organization constructing and operating a building," 6 *Tax Adviser* 354 (1975); Reed, "Exemptions From Unrelated Business Tax—Rental Income," 21 *Cath. Lawyer* 282 (1975); Johnson, "Rental and investment income of many exempt organizations may be taxable," 41 *J. Tax.* 170 (1974).

Mineral royalties, whether measured by production or by gross or taxable income from the mineral property, are excludable in computing unrelated business taxable income. However, where an exempt organization owns a working interest in a mineral property, and is not relieved of its share of the development costs by the terms of any agreement with an operator, income received is not excludable.[3] The holder of a mineral interest is not liable for the expenses of development (or operations) for these purposes where the holder's interest is a net profit interest not subject to expenses which exceed gross profits. Thus, a university was ruled to have excludable royalty interests, where the interests it holds in various oil and gas producing properties are based on the gross profits from the properties reduced by all expenses of development and operations.[4] The result would undoubtedly be different (namely, imposition of the unrelated income tax) if the university was obligated to and did pay its pro rata share of expenses in excess of gross profits.

The IRS ruled that patent development and management service fees deducted from royalties collected from licensees by an exempt charitable organization for distribution to the beneficial owners of the patents are not within this exception for royalties; the Service said that "although the amounts paid to the [tax-exempt] organization are derived from royalties, they do not retain the character of royalties in the organization's hands" for these purposes.[5] Similarly, the Service decided that income derived by a tax-exempt organization from the sale of advertising in publications produced by an independent firm was properly characterized as royalty income.[6] By contrast, the IRS determined that amounts received from licensees by an exempt organization, which was the legal and beneficial owner of patents assigned to it by inventors for specified percentages of future royalties, constitute excludable royalty income.[7] The U. S. Court of Appeals for the Fifth Circuit has held that income consisting of 100 percent of the net profits in certain oil properties, received by an exempt organization from two corporations controlled by it, constituted income from overriding royalties and thus is excluded from taxation.[8]

A matter of some concern to the IRS has been the proper tax treatment of payments to an exempt organization, the principal purpose of which is the development of a U. S. team for international amateur sports competition, in

---

[3]Reg. § 1.512(b)-1(b).

[4]IRS Private Letter Ruling 7741004.

[5]Rev. Rul. 73-193, 1973-1 C. B. 262. Also Rev. Rul. 69-179, 1969-1 C. B. 158.

[6]IRS Private Letter Ruling 7926003.

[7]Rev. Rul. 76-297, 1976-2 C. B. 178; IRS Private Letter Ruling 7841001. See *J. E. and L. E. Mabee Foundation, Inc.* v. *United States*, 533 F.2d 521 (10th Cir. 1976), aff'g 389 F. Supp. 673 (N. D. Okl. 1975).

[8]*United States* v. *The Robert A. Welch Foundation*, 334 F.2d 774 (5th Cir. 1964), aff'g 228 F. Supp. 881 (S. D. Tex. 1963). The IRS does not follow this decision, as stated in Rev. Rul. 69-162, 1969-1 C. B. 158. In general, see Holloman, "Are Overriding Royalties Unrelated Business Income?," 24 *Oil and Gas Tax Q.* 1 (1975).

return for the right to commercially use the organization's name and logo. The organization enters into licensing agreements that, in consideration of the annual payment of a stated sum, authorize use of the organization's name and logo in connection with the sale of products. The initial position of the IRS was that payments must be measured according to the use made of a valuable right to be characterized as a royalty and thus be excludable from unrelated income taxation. However, the Service became sufficiently persuaded, on the basis of caselaw precedent,[9] that fixed-sum payments for the right to use an asset qualify as excludable royalties, although it continues to adhere to the position that, absent the statutory exclusion, the income would be taxable as being from an unrelated trade or business.[10]

Subsequently, the IRS ruled that certain payments a labor organization receives from various business enterprises for the use of its trademark and similar properties are royalties.[11] This conclusion was reached even though the organization retained the right to approve the quality or style of the licensed products and services and the payments were sometimes set as flat annual payments.[12]

The legislative history of these provisions indicates that Congress believed that "passive" income should not be taxed under these rules "where it is used for exempt purposes because investments producing incomes of these types have long been recognized as proper for educational and charitable organizations."[13]

The exclusion relating to gains and losses from the disposition of property does not extend to dispositions of inventory or property held primarily for sale to customers in the ordinary course of a business.[14] Congress in 1976 expanded this rule to also exclude "all gains on the lapse or termination of options, written by the [tax-exempt] organization in connection with its investment activities, to buy or sell securities . . . ." Under prior law, the income from the writing of options (premiums) was generally treated as ordinary income—and thus was

---

[9]*Commissioner* v. *Affiliated Enterprises, Inc.*, 123 F.2d 665 (10th Cir. 1941), cert. den. 315 U. S. 812 (1942). Also *Commissioner* v. *Wodehouse*, 337 U. S. 369 (1949); *Rohmer* v. *Commissioner*, 153 F.2d 61 (2d Cir. 1946); *Sabatini* v. *Commissioner*, 98 F.2d 753 (2d Cir. 1938).

[10]IRS Private Letter Ruling 8006005.

[11]Rev. Rul. 81-178, 1981-2 C. B. 135. By contrast, other payments were held to not be royalties because the personal services of the organization's members are required.

[12]The IRS cited the following authority for its conclusion: *Uhlaender* v. *Henrickson*, 316 F. Supp. 1277 (D. Minn. 1970); *Cepeda* v. *Swift & Co.*, 415 F.2d 1205 (8th Cir. 1969); *Commissioner* v. *Wodehouse*, supra, n. 9; *Rohmer* v. *Commissioner*, supra, n. 9; *Sabatini* v. *Commissioner*, supra, n. 9; and *Commissioner* v. *Affiliated Enterprises, Inc.*, supra, n. 9.

[13]H. Rep. No. 2319, 81st Cong., 2d Sess. (1950) at 38. Also S. Rep. No. 2375, 81st Cong., 2d Sess. (1950) at 30-31.

[14]Reg. § 1.512(b)-1(d).

subject to the unrelated business income tax.[15] (Premiums received for options which are exercised are treated as part of the gain or loss on the sale of the property involved, that is, usually as capital gain or loss.) In the opinion of the Senate Committee on Finance, the law change was necessary because "[t]axing such income is inconsistent with the generally tax-free treatment accorded to exempt organizations' income from investment activities."[16]

The exclusion from unrelated business taxable income for rents is frequently misunderstood, since not all income labeled "rent" will qualify for the exclusion. Where the tax-exempt organization carries on activities that constitute an activity carried on for trade or business, even though the activities involve the leasing of real estate, the exclusion will not be available.[17] For example, a tax-exempt organization may own a building and lease space therein and the income from this activity will constitute excludable rent even where the organization performs normal maintenance services, such as the furnishing of heat, air conditioning, and light, the cleaning of public entrances, exits, stairways, and lobbies, and the collection of trash. Where, however, the organization undertakes functions beyond these maintenance services, such as services rendered primarily for the convenience of the occupants (for example, the supplying of maid service), the payments will not be considered as being from a passive source but instead from an unrelated trade or business (assuming that the activity is regularly carried on and is not substantially related to the organization's tax-exempt purposes).[18]

If a payment is termed "rent" by the parties but is in fact a return of profits by a person operating the property for the benefit of the tax-exempt organization, the payment will not be properly treated as excludable "rent."[19] This rule is apparently intended to apply to the situation where the tax-exempt organization is actively operating a trade or business (which may involve more than rental of property) and has employed or retained a person to manage the business, and where the organization is attempting to characterize its share of the profits of such business as "rent." That is, the rule is inapplicable where there is a valid landlord–tenant relationship between the parties and the land-

---

[15]Rev. Rul. 66-47, 1966-1 C. B. 137. In general, see Oifer and Coleman, "Option writing by exempt organizations: An analysis of the tax problems," 44 *J. Tax.* 42 (1976).

[16]S. Rep. No. 94-1172, 94th Cong., 2d Sess. (1976) at 3, accompanying P. L. 94-396.

[17]In general, the rental of real estate can constitute the carrying on of a trade or business. *Hazard* v. *Commissioner*, 7 T. C. 372 (1946).

[18]Reg. § 1.512(b)-1(c)(5); Rev. Rul. 69-69, *supra*, n. 2; Rev. Rul. 58-482, 1958-2 C. B. 273; IRS Private Letter Rulings 7817124, 7820057, and 7820058. The distinction between such "permitted" and "impermissible" services is discussed in Rev. Rul. 69-178, *supra*, n. 2; see, in general, IRS Private Letter Rulings 7852001, 7841061, 7841005, 7833055, and 7820038.

[19]Reg. § 1.512(b)-1.

lord receives nothing more than net rental payments (gross rents less operating expenses).[20]

Further, the exclusion for rental payments is inoperative where the ostensible "rent" is a share of the profits retained by the organization as a partner or joint venturer.[21] As noted above, the reference to "a share of the profits" is apparently intended to apply to a situation where the recipient of monies is actively involved in the business operation of property and the monies are labeled "rent" when in fact they are a return of profits. Thus, one commentator made reference to a tax-exempt charity that is "participating in a joint business venture for profit, and is not merely passively collecting rent."[22] This provision seems to embody, at least in part, the frequent position of the IRS that receipts measured by a percentage of the operating business' net income are not "rent."

The term "partnership" is defined as including "a syndicate, group, pool, joint venture, or other unincorporated organization, through or by means of which any business financial operation, or venture is carried on, and which is within the meaning of this title, a trust or estate or a corporation."[23] In the broadest sense, co-owners of income-producing real estate that operate real estate (either through an agent or one of their own number) for their joint profit are operating as a partnership.[24] Similarly, two or more parties (including one or more tax-exempt organizations) may operate a business enterprise as a joint venture.[25] In both instances, however, there is a profit motive. Thus, one court defined a "partnership" as a "contract of two or more persons to place their money, efforts, labor, and skill, or some or all of them, in lawful commerce or business, and to divide the profit and bear the loss in definite proportions."[26] This same court defined a "joint venture" as an "association of two or more persons with intent to carry out a single business venture for joint profit, for which purpose they combine their efforts, property, money, skill and knowledge, but they do so without creating a formal partnership or corporation."

Consequently, where the requisite profit motive is absent, even if the arrangement is a partnership or joint venture in the broad sense of ownership of property and sharing of net rents, there presumably is no partnership or joint venture for federal tax purposes because of the lack of an intent of a return of profits and because the relationship does not involve a working interest or operational control of the "business." Thus, where the income is truly rent and

---

[20]See *The State National Bank of El Paso* v. *United States*, 75-2 U.S.T.C. ¶ 9868 (W. D. Tex. 1975). Cf. Rev. Rul. 54-420, 1954-2 C. B. 128.

[21]Reg. § 1.512(b)-1.

[22]Berl, "Boot-Strap and Contingent Sales: The Implications of Clay Brown: Problems of the Tax Exempt Organizations: Proposed Legislation," *25 N. Y. U. Inst. Fed. Tax.* 701, 711 (1967).

[23]Code § 7701(a)(2).

[24]Rev. Rul. 54-369, 1954-2 C. B. 364; Rev. Rul. 54-170, 1954-1 C. B. 213.

[25]*Stevens Bros. Foundation, Inc.* v. *Commissioner*, 324 F.2d 633 (8th Cir. 1963).

[26]*Whiteford* v. *United States*, 61-1 U.S.T.C. ¶ 9301 (D. Kan. 1960).

where the relationship is a passive one (of investor only), the exclusion for rental income is available.[27]

The exclusion from unrelated business taxable income for rents of personalty leased with realty is limited to instances where the rent attributable to the personalty is "incidental" (no more than 10 percent).[28] Moreover, the exclusion is not available where the rent attributable to personalty is tied into the user's income or profits or if more than 50 percent of the total rent is attributable to the personalty leased. Thus, where the rent attributable to personalty is between 10 and 50 percent of the total, only the exclusion with respect to personalty is lost.[29]

However, unrelated debt-financed income is not subject to these exclusions.[30]

Income derived from research for government is excluded, as is income derived from research for anyone in the case of a college, university, or hospital and "of fundamental research" units.[31] According to the legislative history, "research" includes "not only fundamental research but also applied research such as testing and experimental construction and production."[32] As respects the separate exemption for college, university, or hospital research, it is clear that "funds received for research by other institutions [do not] necessarily represent unrelated business income," such as a grant by a corporation to a foundation to finance scientific research if the results of the research were to be made freely available to the public.[33] Without defining the term "research," the IRS was content to find applicability of this rule because the studies are not "merely quality control programs or ordinary testing for certification purposes, as a final procedural step before marketing."[34]

In employing the term "research" in this context, the IRS generally looks

---

[27]*United States* v. *Myra Foundation*, 382 F.2d 107 (8th Cir. 1967), where it was held that a foundation that was a lessor of farmland and received a portion of the crops produced by the tenant as rent was not subject to the unrelated business tax on the rent. Also Rev. Rul. 67-218, *supra*, n. 2; IRS Letter Ruling 7905010. Cf. Reg. § 1.512(c)-1.

[28]Code § 512(b)(3).

[29]See Reg. § 1.512(b)-1(c)(2). Also see Rev. Rul. 67-218, *supra*, n. 2; Rev. Rul. 60-206, *supra*, n. 2. In IRS Private Letter Ruling 7938003, the Service held that an association's fund-raising practice of levying an annual fee on its sponsoring associate members during the term of their membership, for which they receive a bronze shield of the association's insignia, does not constitute the rental of personal property.

[30]Code § 512(b)(4). See Chapter 43.

[31]Code § 512(b)(7), (8), and (9). See Reg. § 1.512(b)-1(f). Also see Rev. Rul. 54-73, 1954-1 C. B. 160.

[32]H. Rep. No. 2319, *supra*, n. 13 at 37. See e.g., IRS Private Letter Ruling 7924009, where the IRS applied the Code § 512(b)(7)(A) exclusion to income received by an educational institution for contract work for the federal government in the field of rocketry.

[33]S. Rep. No. 2375, *supra*, n. 13 at 30.

[34]IRS Private Letter Ruling 7936006.

to the body of law defining the term in relation to what is considered tax-exempt "scientific" research.[35] Thus, the issue is usually whether the activity is being carried on as an incident to commercial or industrial operations; if it is, it will almost assuredly be regarded by the IRS as an unrelated trade or business.[36] In one instance, the Service found applicability of the exclusion because the studies undertaken by a medical college in the testing of pharmaceutical products under contracts with the manufacturers were held to be more than "mere quality control programs or ordinary testing for certification purposes, as a final procedural step before marketing."[37] In another instance, the exclusion was held applicable to contract work done by an educational institution for the federal government in the field of rocketry.[38]

There are limitations on the availability of the charitable contribution deduction, as allowed in the unrelated income tax context.[39]

In computing unrelated business taxable income, there is a specific deduction of $1,000.[40] The specific deduction is allowed, in the case of a diocese, province of a religious order, or a convention or association of churches, with respect to each parish, individual church, district, or other local unit.[41] This deduction is intended to eliminate imposition of the unrelated income tax in cases where to do so would involve excessive costs of collection and payment.[42]

Payments of interest, annuities, royalties, and rents (but not dividends) by a controlled corporation (80 percent interest) to an exempt organization are taxable, at a ratio depending on whether the controlled corporation is exempt or not.[43] The purpose of this provision, which was added by the Tax Reform Act of 1969, is to prevent an exempt organization from "renting" its physical plant to a wholly owned taxable corporation for 80 or more percent of all the net profits (before taxes and rent deduction), thereby enabling the taxable corporation to escape nearly all income taxation.

---

[35]Rev. Rul. 76-296, 1976-2 C. B. 141. Cf. Code § 44F; Kertz, "Tax Exempt Organizations and Commercially Sponsored Scientific Research," 9 *J. Coll. & U. L.* 69 (1982–3). In general, see Chapter 9.

[36]Rev. Rul. 68-373, 1968-2 C. B. 206; IRS Private Letter Rulings 8020009, 8016010, 7852007 (issues nos. 1, 3, and 4), and 7902019 (issue no. 3).

[37]IRS Private Letter Ruling 7936006.

[38]IRS Private Letter Ruling 7924009.

[39]See Reg. § 1.512(b)-1(g). The 5 percent limitation on deductible charitable contributions under Code § 512(b)(10) was not revised when Congress, in 1981, expanded the general limitation on deductible corporate charitable contributions to 10 percent (see Chapter 3 § 2). However, this 5 percent limitation was subsequently increased to 10 percent upon enactment of the Technical Corrections Act of 1982.

[40]Code § 512(b)(12).

[41]See Reg. § 1.512(b)-1(h). Also see Rev. Rul. 68-536, 1968-2 C. B. 244.

[42]H. Rep. No. 2319, *supra*, n. 13 at 37; S. Rep. No. 2375, *supra*, n. 13 at 30.

[43]Code § 512(b)(13). See Reg. § 1.512(b)-1(l); *J. E. and L. E. Mabee Foundation, Inc.* v. *United States*, *supra*, n. 7; *United States* v. *The Robert A. Welch Foundation*, *supra*, n. 8; IRS Private Letter Ruling 8244114.

In the case of a church or a convention or association of churches (unless debt-financed property is involved), gross income derived from a trade or business was excluded until 1976, if the trade or business was carried on by the organization or its predecessor before May 27, 1969.[44] In the case of churches, related businesses, such as cemeteries, conduct of charitable institutions, sale of religious articles, and the printing, distribution, and sale of religious pamphlets, tracts, calendars, papers, books, and magazines with a substantial religious content, are tax-exempt as long as these activities are carried on in connection with the church. No examination to determine unrelated business income can be made of a church unless the Secretary of the Treasury or his or her delegate—no lesser official than the principal internal revenue officer for an internal revenue region—believes that such organization is engaged in unrelated business or is not a church, and so notifies the organization in advance of the examination.[45]

The unrelated business income tax will not apply to a religious order or educational institution maintained by the order, with respect to a trade or business, even though the business is unrelated, if the business provides services under license issued by a federal regulatory agency, if less than 10 percent of its net income is used for unrelated activities, and if the business was carried on before May 27, 1969.[46]

However, the "deadwood" amendments of the Tax Reform Act of 1976 deleted a provision which excluded from the definition of unrelated business taxable income certain income received by tax-exempt trusts created by the wills of individuals who died between August 16, 1954, and January 1, 1957, if that income is received by such trusts as limited partners.[47] Also deleted was a provision which provided a similar exclusion for income used by tax-exempt labor, agricultural, or horticultural organizations to establish, maintain, or operate a retirement home, hospital, or similar facility, if the income is derived from agricultural pursuits on grounds contiguous to the facility and if the income does not provide more than 75 percent of the cost of operating or maintaining the facility.[48] Nonetheless, the Tax Reform Act of 1976 contains a savings provision continuing both of these exclusions.[49]

---

[44]Code § 512(b)(14).

[45]See Reg. § 301.7605-1(c). See Ellis, "Tax on unrelated business income of churches," 7 *Tax Adviser* 270 (1976); Shaw, "Tax Audits of Churches," 22 *Cath. Lawyer* 247 (1976); Nolan, "Application of Unrelated Business Income Tax to Churches," 21 *Cath. Lawyer* 247 (1976). For general discussion of the question of "taxation" of churches, see Bittker, "Churches, Taxes and the Constitution," 78 *Yale L. J.* 1285 (1969); Note, "Tax Code Loopholes: Business Income of Religious Organizations," 23 *N. Y. U. Intra. L. Rev.* 70 (1967).

[46]Code § 512(b)(15).

[47]Pre-1969 Code § 512(b)(13).

[48]Pre-1969 Code § 512(b)(14).

[49]Tax Reform Act of 1976 § 1951(b)(8).

In assessing the modification for "passive income," it is useful to focus on the lending of securities transaction,[50] which generates passive income to the lending organization,[51] in light of the state of the law on this point before 1978. That is, the interest earned on the collateral and the interim dividend and interest payments are excludable from unrelated trade or business income tax consideration. The IRS issued a ruling to this effect in 1978[52] and Congress legislated on the subject in that year.[53]

It is clear that the interest earned by the lending organization as the result of its independent investment of the collateral posted by the brokers is "interest" as that term is employed for these purposes. The accepted rule is that the amounts received through independent investment are characterized in accordance with the nature of the investment. Therefore, the income derived from an investment of this collateral by the organization in bank certificates of deposit or a form of short-term investment would without question be excludable "interest". Similarly, an investment of the collateral by the organization in stocks or bonds would unquestionably produce excludable "dividends" or "interest." (Any gain realized by the organization by reason of a sale of the securities would also be excludable from unrelated business income[54].)

The amounts paid by the brokers to the lending organization in reflection of any dividends or interest earned in respect of the securities on loan are excludable from unrelated business taxable income. Certainly the dividends or interest if paid to the organization while it was in physical possession of the certificates would be excluded by reason of this rule. It would exalt form over substance to treat the pass-through payments from the broker for dividends and interest any differently. The substance of the transaction should and does prevail.[55]

The term "interest," as noted below, is frequently defined as compensation paid for the use or forebearance of money.[56] Of course, in the above-described transaction, the income received by the organization derives from an arrangement involving the use of property. However, courts have utilized a collateral definition of interest, that being an amount paid which is contingent upon

[50]See § 2, *supra.*

[51]Code § 512(b)(1).

[52]Rev. Rul. 78-88, 1978-1 C. B. 163. Cf. *Council of British Societies in Southern California* v. *United States,* 78-2 U. S. T. C. ¶ 9744 (C. D. Cal. 1978).

[53]Code § 512(a)(5). See § 2, *supra.*

[54]Code § 512(b)(5).

[55]See *McBride* v. *Commissioner,* 44 B. T. A. 273 (1941); *Kell* v. *Commissioner,* 31 B. T. A. 212 (1934); *Peck* v. *Commissioner,* 31 B. T. A. 87 (1934).

[56]See, e.g., Rev. Rul. 69-188, 1969-1 C. B. 54, holding "points" to be interest in certain circumstances; Rev. Rul. 67-297, 1967-2 C. B. 87, holding fees attributable to loan services to not be interest; and Rev. Rul. 79-349, 1979-2 C. B. 233, holding service fees from mortgage loans to not be interest for purposes of unrelated income taxation, with all three rulings based on this definition.

having some relationship to an indebtedness.[57] The term "indebtedness" is defined as "something owed in money which one is unconditionally obligated or bound to pay, the payment of which is enforceable."[58]

Therefore, these amounts paid by the brokers to the organization may constitute "interest," inasmuch as they are amounts paid in conjunction with an enforceable indebtedness, namely, the obligation of the broker to return the securities or in lieu thereof work a forfeiture of the collateral. Hence, these payments could be regarded as "interest" excludable from unrelated income taxation.

Even if these payments were not regarded as "interest" as such, they nonetheless retain their character as "interest," "dividends," or other form of passive income for purposes of the exclusion.

In the above-described transaction, the income paid to the lending organization by brokers should not lose its character as "interest" or "dividends." Authority for this assertion may be found in an IRS ruling,[59] where the Service distinguished between "sale" and "purchase" transactions and "loan" transactions. The facts underlying the ruling are that bank customers "sell" securities to the bank in return for loans from the bank, agreeing to "repurchase" the identical securities at the close of the loan period. The Service ruled that this transaction did not constitute a sale or exchange but instead a loan of money upon collateral security (that is, the securities).

The pertinence of this ruling is enhanced by dint of the fact that the securities in question there were state or municipal bonds the interest of which is exempt from federal income taxation.[60] At issue was the appropriate party to have the benefit of the exclusion: the lender-customer or the borrower-bank. Concurrent with its finding that the transaction was a loan and not a sale, the IRS ruled that the tax-exempt interest is the income of the customer who submitted the securities to the bank for collateral and that the bank is not entitled to treat the interest paid by the customers as exempt from tax.[61]

The analogy between that ruling and the securities lending transaction is unmistakable. Just as the bank in that ruling was unable to treat customer-paid interest as tax-exempt, having to "leave" that tax feature with its customers'

[57]*Commissioner* v. *Wilson*, 163 F.2d 680, 682 (9th Cir. 1947), aff'g 5 T. C. M. 647 (1946), cert. den. 332 U. S. 842 (1947); *Commissioner* v. *Park*, 113 F.2d 352 (3rd Cir. 1940), aff'g 38 B. T. A. 1118 (1938).
[58]*Gilman* v. *Commissioner*, 53 F.2d 47 (8th Cir. 1931).
[59]Rev. Rul. 74-27, 1974-1 C. B. 24.
[60]Code § 103.
[61]Reliance for the Service's position in this regard was placed on *First American National Bank of Nashville* v. *United States*, 467 F.2d 1098 (6th Cir. 1972), and *American National Bank of Austin* v. *United States*, 421 F.2d 442 (5th Cir. 1970), cert. den. 400 U. S. 819 (1970).

holdings, so too may the broker-paid amounts to the organization be treated as interest or dividends (as the case may be) rather than as interest or dividends paid to the broker. This parallel is underscored by the characterization by the IRS of the transaction as a loan rather than a sale or exchange, which is the correct characterization to be given the organization's transaction with the brokers. It is the organization, not the broker, that retains the debt or equity position in the issuer-corporation.

The courts also have recognized the concept of "equivalency payments," with the result that the payments are regarded as "interest," "dividends," or the like even though the technical elements of the definitions of those terms may not be wholly satisfied. As an illustration, the U.S. Court of Appeals for the Fifth Circuit, in characterizing oil and gas lease bonus payments for personal holding company purposes, concluded:

> Our conclusion is reached with respect to a hybrid category of income not expressly provided for in the statute, which, as a matter of semantics, is not clearly either rent or royalty, and as to which the legislative history of the statute is unrevealing.
>
> *   *   *
>
> Because it seems to us that the type of lease bonus here under consideration is precisely the sort of passive investment income with which the statute is concerned . . . we have no doubt that the lease bonus falls within one category or another.[62]

Similarly, the income received by the organization from the brokers reflecting interest or dividends paid by the issuer is properly regarded as "interest" or "dividends" for these purposes—even if it is treated as a "hybrid category of income" that cannot fully meet all of the semantical definitional requirements.

However, it is not necessary for these purposes to resolve the question as to whether or not a "pass-through" theory is pertinent. This is because, regardless of whether or not the payments are considered of "interest" or "dividends" by virtue of a "pass-through" or equivalency approach, they should nonetheless be so characterized for purposes of the unrelated income rules. In other words, regardless of the availability of the "pass-through" theory, the payments by brokers to the lending organization are still appropriately characterized as coming within the exclusions for passive income.

The monies paid by the brokers to the organization perhaps may not satisfy the precise doctrinal requirements of the terms used in these rules, such as "interest," "dividends," or "rents." Nonetheless, these monies clearly constitute passive income to the organization and accordingly warrant treatment as being within the scope of the intention of the exclusion. The U.S. Supreme Court has defined the term "interest" as follows: "In the business world 'interest or indebtedness' means compensation for the use or forebearance of money."[63] Similarly, "interest" is defined in the Treasury regulations for personal holding

---

[62]*Bayou Verret Land Co.* v. *Commissioner*, 450 F.2d 840, 855, 854 (5th Cir. 1971).
[63]*Deputy* v. *Dupont*, 308 U. S. 488, 498 (1940).

company income purposes as amounts received for the use of money loaned.[64] These regulations define "rent" as compensation for the use of, or right to use, property of the lessor.

It may technically be advanced, as noted above, that payments by borrowing brokers to the organization cannot qualify as "interest" inasmuch as the payments are for the use of securities, which is property not money. These payments may not constitute "rent" because the securities recovered by the organization are different from those that were borrowed, the right to sell the property becomes vested in the borrower, and the borrower has the authority to sell the securities to a third party—features of a transaction usually antithetical to the typical lease arrangement.

Nonetheless, the strict definitional classifications of the types of passive income are not dispositive of the question as to their treatment in relation to these rules. Rather, "[w]hether a particular item of income falls within any of the modifications provided in section 512(b) shall be determined by all of the facts and circumstances of each case."[65]

In the factual setting here, the income generated by the above-described securities lending transaction is clearly passive in nature, thereby warranting treatment as being within these modifications. That is, from the standpoint of the lending organization, there is no additional activity necessitated to procure the income (the only activity at all is the "investment" effort in entering into the contracts with brokers) and the amount remains the same (albeit the source is different).

The legislative history of the unrelated business income tax provisions is amply clear on the point that Congress, in enacting these rules, did not intend and has not authorized taxation of the passive receipt of income by tax-exempt organizations, and that a technical satisfaction of the definitional requirements of the terms used in the passive income rules is not required. Thus, the Senate Finance Committee observed in 1950 that the unrelated income tax was to apply to "so much of . . . [organizations'] income as rises from *active business enterprises* which are unrelated to the exempt purposes of the organizations" (emphasis supplied).[66] The Committee added: "The problem at which the tax on unrelated business income is directed is primarily that of unfair competition."[67] Speaking of the exclusion for passive sources of income, the Committee stated:

> Dividends, interest, royalties, most rents, capital gains and losses and *similar items* are excluded from the base of the tax on unrelated income because your committee believes that they are "passive" in character and are not likely to result in serious competition for taxable businesses having similar income. Moreover,

[64]Reg. § 1.543-1(b)(2).
[65]Reg § 1.512(b)-1.
[66]S. Rep. No. 2375, *supra*, n. 13 at 27.
[67]*Ibid.* at 28.

investment-producing incomes of these types have long been recognized as a proper source of revenue for educational and charitable organizations and trusts (emphasis supplied).[68]

Therefore, it seems unmistakable that passive income, regardless of type, is properly includible within the exclusion.[69]

The validity of the foregoing is borne out by the line of law that holds that payments made by a broker-borrower in a securities lending transaction are the functional equivalent of interest paid in connection with a business loan and therefore are deductible by the broker as an ordinary and necessary business expense. Thus the U.S. Supreme Court held that the taxpayer, engaged in extensive short sales transactions, properly deducted the payments to the lender, which were in amounts equal to dividends declared during the period the seller is "short," as business expenses.[70] Similarly, on like facts, the court first noted that "interest" is an amount having some relationship to an indebtedness, in turn defined as "something owed in money which one is unconditionally obligated or bound to pay, the payment of which is enforceable."[71] Recognizing that the securities transaction under examination necessarily involves a borrower and a lender, the court concluded:

> The payment of the dividend here represents a sum of money unconditionally owed by the borrower to the lender of stock; it arises out of the relationship of debtor and creditor and is a customary expense in a "short" sale incident to obtaining and using the stock. It is ordinary and necessary in this type of transaction.[72]

The acceptance by the IRS of this rationale was memorialized in an IRS ruling involving an investor who paid loan premiums and amounts equal to cash dividends to the lenders of securities to him. The dividend equivalency and other payments were ruled by the IRS to be deductible under these rules.[73]

Therefore, the correct conclusion in this regard (even if securities lending was treated as a trade or business in the first instance) is to treat the brokers' payments to the lending organization as "interest" or "dividends" (as the case may be), excludable from unrelated income taxation by operation of the rules encompassing passive income or as income items so functionally equivalent to interest and dividends by virtue of their nature as passive income as to be similarly excludable.

The point of the foregoing in this context is that there may be "passive income" incurred by an exempt organization which may not be strictly within

---

[68]*Ibid.* at 30–31.

[69]Also see H. Rep. No. 2319, *supra*, n. 13 at 36–38.

[70]*Commissioner v. Wiesler*, 161 F.2d 997 (6th Cir. 1947), cert. den. 322 U. S. 842 (1947), aff'g 6 T. C. 1148 (1946).

[71]*Commissioner v. Wilson*, *supra*, n. 57 at 163 F.2d 682.

[72]*Ibid.*

[73]Rev. Rul. 72-521, 1972-2 C. B. 178.

the technical meaning of the terms of the passive income rules, yet which should be outside the framework of unrelated income taxation.

§ 42.2 Exceptions

Exempt from the scope of unrelated trade or business is a business in which substantially all of the work in carrying on the business is performed for the tax-exempt organization without compensation.[74] An example involving this exception is a tax-exempt orphanage operating a second-hand clothing store and selling to the general public, where substantially all of the work in running the store is performed by volunteers.[75] As to the scope of this exception, Congress apparently intended to provide an exclusion from the definition of unrelated trade or business only for those unrelated business activities in which the performance of services is a material income-producing factor in carrying on the business and substantially all of the services are performed without compensation.[76] In reliance upon the legislative history underlying this rule, the IRS ruled that the rental of heavy machinery under long-term lease agreements requiring the lessees to provide insurance, pay the applicable taxes, and make and pay for most repairs, with the functions of securing leases and processing rental payments performed without compensation, was not an unrelated trade or business excluded under this exception since "there is no significant amount of labor regularly required or involved in the kind of business carried on by the organization" and thus the performance of services in connection with the leasing activity is not a material income-producing factor in the business.[77] In one case, the exemption was held defeated in part because free drinks provided to the collectors and cashiers in connection with the conduct of a bingo game were considered "liquid compensation."[78]

Also excluded is a business, in the case of a "charitable" organization or a state college or university, which is carried on by the organization primarily for the convenience of its members, students, patients, officers, or employees.[79] An example involving this exception is a laundry operated by a college for the purpose of laundering dormitory linens and the clothing of students.[80] (However, a laundry operated by a college apart from its campus primarily for the

---

[74]Code § 513(a)(1). See *Greene County Medical Society Foundation* v. *United States*, 345 F. Supp. 900 (W. D. Mo. 1972); Rev. Rul. 56-152, 1956-1 C. B. 56.

[75]S. Rep. No. 2375, *supra*, n. 13 at 108.

[76]H. Rep. No. 2319, *supra*, n. 13 at 37, and S. Rep. No. 2375, *supra*, n. 13 at 107-108.

[77]Rev. Rul. 78-144, 1978-1 C. B. 168.

[78]*Waco Lodge No. 166, Benevolent & Protective Order of Elks* v. *Commissioner*, 42 T. C. M. 1202 (1981).

[79]Code § 513(a)(2). See Rev. Rul. 69-268, 1969-1 C. B. 160; Rev. Rul. 55-676, 1955-2 C. B. 266. But see *Carle Foundation* v. *United States*, 611 F.2d 1192 (7th Cir. 1979).

[80]S. Rep. No. 2375, *supra*, n. 13 at 108.

purpose of making a profit from laundering the clothing of the general public would be an unrelated business and outside the scope of this limitation.) One court expanded this concept by holding that physicians on the staff of a teaching hospital are "members" of the hospital, in that the term "refers to any group of persons who are closely associated with the entity involved and who are necessary to the achievement of the organization's purposes.[81]

Likewise excluded is a business, in the case of a local association of employees[82] organized before May 27, 1969, which is the selling by the organization of items of work-related clothing and equipment and items normally sold through vending machines, through food-dispensing facilities or by snack bars, for the convenience of its members at their usual places of employment.[83] Further, unrelated trade or business does not include a business which is the selling of merchandise, substantially all of which has been received by the organization as gifts or contributions.[84] This last exception is available for thrift shops which sell donated clothes and books to the general public.[85]

Payments to an exempt organization for the lending of securities to a broker and the return of identical securities are not items of unrelated business taxable income.[86] For this nontaxation treatment to apply, the security loans must be fully collateralized and must be terminable on five business days' notice by the lending organization. Further, an agreement between the parties must provide for reasonable procedures to implement the obligation of the borrower to furnish collateral to the lender with a fair market value on each business day the loan is outstanding in an amount at least equal to the fair market value of the security at the close of business on the preceding day.

Congress, in enacting the Tax Reform Act of 1976, authored three additional exceptions, namely, the conduct of entertainment at fairs and expositions and of trade shows by tax-exempt organizations, and the performance of certain services for small hospitals.

The rule with respect to entertainment at fairs and expositions,[87] applies to charitable, social welfare, labor, agricultural, and horticultural organizations[88]

---

[81]*St. Luke's Hospital of Kansas City* v. *United States*, 80-2 U. S. T. C. ¶ 9533 (W. D. Mo. 1980).

[82]Code § 501(c)(4). See Chapter 15.

[83]Code § 513(a)(2).

[84]Code § 513(a)(3). See *Disabled Veterans Service Foundation* v. *Commissioner*, 2 T. C. M. 202 (1970). As respects notes 74–84, see Reg. § 1.513-1(e). In general, see "Panel Discussion on Unrelated Business Income Tax," 21 *Cath. Lawyer* 287 (1975); Cooper, "Trends in the Taxation of Unrelated Business Activity," 29 *N. Y. U. Inst. Fed. Tax.* 1999 (1971).

[85]See Rev. Rul. 71-581, 1971-2 C. B. 236.

[86]Code § 512(a)(5).

[87]Code § 513(d)(1), (2).

[88]Code § 501(c)(3), (4) or (5).

which regularly conduct, as a substantial tax-exempt purpose, an agricultural and educational fair or exposition.[89] This exemption from the unrelated income tax, which applies to tax years beginning after December 31, 1962, overrides an earlier IRS pronouncement.[90]

The term "unrelated trade or business" does not include qualified "public entertainment activities" of an eligible organization.[91] This term is defined to mean "any entertainment or recreational activity of a kind traditionally conducted at fairs or expositions promoting agricultural and educational purposes, including, but not limited to, any activity one of the purposes of which is to attract the public to fairs or expositions or to promote the breeding of animals or the development of products or equipment."[92]

No unrelated income taxation is to occur with respect to the operation of a "qualified public entertainment activity" that meets one of the following conditions: the public entertainment activity is conducted (1) in conjunction with an international, national, state, regional, or local fair or exposition, (2) in accordance with state law which permits that activity to be conducted solely by an eligible type of tax-exempt organization or by a governmental entity, or (3) in accordance with state law which permits that activity to be conducted under license for not more than 20 days in any year and which permits the organization to pay a lower percentage of the revenue from this activity than the state requires from other organizations.[93]

To qualify under this rule, the organization must regularly conduct, as a substantial tax-exempt purpose, a fair or exposition which is both agricultural and educational. The Senate Finance Committee report states that a book fair held by a university does not come within this provision since this type of a fair is not "agricultural" in nature.[94]

A charitable, social welfare, labor, agricultural, or horticultural organization is not to be considered as not entitled to tax exemption solely because of qualified public entertainment activities conducted by it.

The rule with respect to trade show activities[95] applies to labor, agricultural, and horticultural organizations, and business leagues,[96] which regularly conduct, as a substantial tax-exempt purpose, shows which stimulate interest in and demand for the products of a particular industry or segment thereof.[97] This provision, which applies to tax years beginning after December 31, 1969, ef-

---

[89]Code § 513(d)(2)(C).
[90]Rev. Rul. 68-505, 1968-2 C. B. 248.
[91]Code § 513(d)(1).
[92]Code § 513(d)(2)(A).
[93]Code § 513(d)(2)(B).
[94]S. Rep. 94-938, 94th Cong., 2d Sess. (1976), at 602.
[95]Code § 513(d)(1), (3).
[96]Code § 501(c)(5), (6).
[97]Code § 513(d)(3)(C).

fectively overrules (except as to "charitable" and social welfare organizations) contrary IRS determinations.[98]

The term "unrelated trade or business" does not include qualified "convention and trade show activities" of an eligible organization.[99] This term is defined to mean "any activity of a kind traditionally conducted at conventions, annual meetings, or trade shows, including but not limited to, any activity one of the purposes of which is to attract persons in an industry generally (without regard to membership in the sponsoring organization) as well as members of the public to the show for the purpose of displaying industry products or services, or to educate persons engaged in the industry in the development of new products and services or new rules and regulations affecting the industry."[100]

No unrelated income taxation is to occur with respect to the operation of a "qualified convention and trade show activity" that meets all of the following conditions: (1) it must be conducted in conjunction with an international, national, state, regional, or local convention or show, (2) one of the purposes of the organization in sponsoring the activity must be the promotion and stimulation of interest in and demand for the industry's products and services in general, and (3) the show must be designed to promote that purpose through the character of the exhibits and the extent of the industry products displayed.[101]

A tax-exempt organization may sponsor and perform educational and supporting services for a trade show (such as use of its name, promotion of attendance, planning of exhibits and demonstrations, and provision of lectures for the exhibits and demonstrations) without having the compensation for its efforts taxed as unrelated income, as long as the trade show is not a sales facility.[102] The IRS has ruled that this type of activity both stimulates interest in and demand for services of the profession involved in the ruling (the organization being a business league) and educates the members on matters of professional interest.

As respects the third of these items, it has been the position of the IRS that income which a tax-exempt hospital derives from providing services to other tax-exempt hospitals constitutes unrelated business income to the hospital providing the services, on the theory that the providing of services to other hospitals

---

[98]Rev. Ruls. 75-516 through 75-520, 1975-2 C. B. 220-226. Also see Rev. Rul. 67-219, 1967-1 C. B. 210; Rev. Rul. 58-224, 1958-1 C. B. 242. For an analysis of these rulings, see Kannry, "Trade shows must bar all selling to avoid unrelated business income tax," 44 *J. Tax.* 300 (1976).

Legislation (H. R. 12828, 95th Cong., 2d Sess. (1978)), which passed the House in 1978 but not the Senate, would exclude income derived from conventions and trade shows sponsored by Code § 501(c)(3) organizations where the purpose of the show or convention is to educate the attendees about new products, services, and rules and regulations.

[99]Code § 513(d)(1).

[100]Code § 513(d)(3)(A).

[101]Code § 513(d)(3)(B).

[102]Rev. Rul. 78-240, 1978-1 C. B. 170.

is not an activity which is substantially related to the tax-exempt purpose of the hospital providing the services.[103] Congress acted to reverse this attitude in the case of small hospitals.

Congress enacted a special rule[104] to overrule the IRS position taxing income as from an unrelated trade or business where a hospital[105] provides services only to other tax-exempt hospitals, as long as each of the recipient hospitals has facilities to serve not more than 100 inpatients and the services would be consistent with the recipient hospitals' tax-exempt purposes if performed by them on their own behalf. The services provided must be confined to certain ones.[106]

This law change was implemented to enable a number of small hospitals to receive services from a single institution instead of providing them directly or creating a separate organization to provide the services. However, language in the legislative history is somewhat broader than the specifics of the statutory rule, inasmuch as the Senate Finance Committee explanation states that "a hospital is not engaged in an unrelated trade or business simply because it provides services to other hospitals if those services could have been provided on a tax-free basis, by a cooperative organization consisting of several tax-exempt hospitals."[107]

Congress, in enacting the Revenue Act of 1978, added a provision[108] which provides that bingo game income realized by most tax-exempt organizations is not subject to the unrelated business income tax. This exclusion would apply where the bingo game[109] is not conducted on a commercial basis and where the games do not violate state or local laws.[110] By virtue of the way the organizations are taxed, the bingo game rule is not applicable to social clubs, employees' beneficiary associations, political organizations, and homeowners' associations.[111]

---

[103]Rev. Rul. 69-633, 1969-2 C. B. 121.

[104]Code § 513(e).

[105]Code § 170(b)(1)(A)(iii).

[106]See Code § 501(e)(1)(A), Chapter 10.

[107]S. Rep. No. 94-938 (Part 2), 94th Cong., 2d Sess. (1976) at 76.

[108]Code § 513(f).

[109]Code § 513(f)(2)(A).

[110]See H. Rep. No. 95-1608, 95th Cong., 2d Sess. (1978); IRS Private Letter Rulings 7832089 and 7946001. See, e.g., *Waco Lodge No. 166, Benevolent & Protective Order of Elks* v. *Commissioner*, 42 T. C. M. 1202 (1981), where this exception was held unavailable because the bingo game was illegal under state law (Texas) as being a "lottery."

[111]See Chapters 18 and 20. Cf. *Clarence LaBelle Post No. 217* v. *United States*, 78-2 U. S. T. C. ¶ 9496 (8th Cir. 1978); *Smith-Dodd Businessman's Association, Inc.*, v. *Commissioner*, 65 T. C. 620 (1975).

43

Unrelated Debt-Financed Income

§ 43.1 Introduction

Prior to the enactment of the Tax Reform Act of 1969, most "charitable" organizations and certain other tax-exempt organizations were subject to the unrelated business income tax on rental income from real property to the extent the property was acquired with borrowed funds. However, there was an important exception which excluded rental income from a lease of five years or less and, further, the tax was not applicable to all exempt organizations. Moreover, there was a question as to whether the tax applied to income from the leasing, by an exempt organization, of assets constituting a going business.

In the years immediately preceding enactment of the Tax Reform Act of 1969, some tax-exempt organizations were using their tax privileges to purchase businesses and investments on credit, frequently at what was more than the market price, while contributing little or nothing themselves to the transaction other than their tax exemption. A typical factual situation in this regard has been described as follows:

> A sells an incorporated business to B, a charitable foundation, which makes a small (or no) down payment and agrees to pay the balance of the purchase price only out of profits to be derived from the property. B liquidates the corporation and then leases the business assets to C, a new corporation formed to operate the business. A (collectively, the stockholders of the original business) manages the business for C and frequently holds a substantial minority interest in C. C pays 80 percent of its business profits as "rent" to B, who then passes on 90 percent of those receipts to A until the original purchase price is paid in full. B has no obligation to pay A out of any funds other than the "rent" paid by C.[1]

The tax results of this type of transaction provided capital gain to the seller, a rent deduction for the operator, and no tax on the tax-exempt organization.

In this manner, a business was able to realize increased after-tax income

---

[1]H. Rep. 91-413 (Part 1), 91st Cong., 1st Sess. (1969) at 45.

and a tax-exempt organization was able to acquire the ownership of a business valued at $1.3 million without the investment of its own funds.[2] Immediately prior to the 1969 Tax Reform Act, the U.S. Tax Court upheld the acquisition of 24 businesses by the University Hill Foundation in this manner in the period 1945 to 1954.[3]

The response of Congress to the problems in this area was enactment of the unrelated debt-financed income rules by means of a revamped Code § 514. In 1969, Congress acted to impose a tax on the investment income of tax-exempt institutions which is traceable in one way or another to borrowed funds. This was done by the addition to the Code of rules which impose a tax on "unrelated debt-financed income."[4]

In computing a tax-exempt organization's unrelated business taxable income, there must be included with respect to each debt-financed property which is unrelated to the organization's exempt function—as an item of gross income derived from an unrelated trade or business—an amount of income therefrom, subject to tax in the proportion in which the property is financed by the debt.[5] Basically, deductions are allowed with respect to each debt-financed property in the same proportion.[6] The allowable deductions are those which are directly connected with the debt-financed property or its income, although any depreciation may only be computed on the straight-line method.[7] For example, if a business property is acquired by a tax-exempt organization subject to an 80 percent mortgage, 80 percent of the income and 80 percent of the deductions are taken into account for these tax purposes. As the mortgage is paid off, the percentage taken into account usually diminishes.[8] Capital gains on the sale of debt-financed property are also taxed in the same proportions.[9]

§ 43.2 Debt-Financed Property

The term "debt-financed property" means, with certain exceptions, all property (e.g., rental real estate, tangible personalty, corporate stock) which is held to produce income (e.g., rents, royalties, interest, dividends) and with respect

[2]*Commissioner* v. *Brown*, 380 U. S. 563 (1965).

[3]*University Hill Foundation* v. *Commissioner*, 51 T. C. 548 (1969), rev'd 446 F.2d 701 (10th Cir. 1971), cert. den. 405 U. S. 965 (1972).

[4]For an example of an interpretation of pre-1969 Code § 514, see Rev. Rul. 70-132, 1970-1 C. B. 138.

[5]Code §§ 514(a)(1), 512(b)(4).

[6]Code § 514(a)(2).

[7]Code § 514(a)(3).

[8]Cf. "Point to Remember" no. 8, 25 *Tax Lawyer* 181 (1971).

[9]See Reg. § 1.514(a)-1. A special rule enacted in 1980 (P. L. 96-608, 96th Cong., 2d Sess. (1980)), for the benefit of the Tillamook County YMCA in Tillamook, Oregon, allows certain sales of real property in 1976 to be made free of the unrelated income tax if the property had been acquired prior to 1952 and the indebtedness was incurred before 1965.

to which there is an "acquisition indebtedness" (see below) at any time during the tax year (or during the preceding 12 months, if the property is disposed of during the year).[10]

Excepted from the term "debt-financed property" is (1) property where substantially (at least 85 percent) all of its use is substantially related (aside from the need of the organization for income or funds) to the exercise or performance by the organization of its tax-exempt purpose or, if less than substantially all of its use is related, to the extent that its use is related to the organization's exempt purpose,[11] (2) property to the extent that its income is already subject to tax as income from the conduct of an unrelated trade or business,[12] (3) property to the extent that the income is derived from research activities and therefore excluded from unrelated business taxable income,[13] and (4) property to the extent that its use is in a trade or business exempted from tax because substantially all the work is performed without compensation, the business is carried on primarily for the convenience of members, students, patients, officers, or employees, or the business is the selling of merchandise, substantially all of which was received as gifts or contributions.[14] For purposes of item (1), substantially all of the use of property is considered substantially related to the exercise or performance of an organization's exempt purpose if such property is real property subject to a lease to a medical clinic, where the lease is entered into primarily for purposes which are substantially related to the lessor's exempt purposes. For purposes of items (1), (3), and (4), the use of any property by a tax-exempt organization which is related to an organization is treated as use by such organization.[15]

An illustration of a situation where property that is debt-financed does not yield unrelated debt-financed income because the use of the property is substantially related to an exempt use is provided by the case of an exempt organization, created to encourage business development in a particular area, that constructed a building to lease, at below-market rates, to an industrial tenant for the purpose of attracting new industry to the area. Once the lease was executed, the organization completed the building (which was initially financed by the business community) to suit the needs of the tenant; the completion of the building was financed by subjecting the property to a mort-

---

[10]Code § 514(b)(1).

[11]Code § 514(b)(1)(A). In reliance upon this exception, the IRS determined that an educational organization may purchase a golf course and lease it back to the seller, which is financing the acquisition, without causing the property to be debt-financed for purposes of Code § 514, inasmuch as the golf course will be used by the organization's students, staff, and faculty. IRS Private Letter Ruling 7823062.

[12]Code §§ 512(b)(7), (8), or (9), 514(b)(1)(B). This rule does not apply in the case of income excluded under Code § 512(b)(5).

[13]Code § 514(b)(1)(C). See Chapter 42 § 1.

[14]Code § 514(b)(1)(D). See Chapter 42 § 2.

[15]Code § 514(b)(2).

gage. Because the leasing of the building under these circumstances is an activity designed to attract industry to the community, the IRS concluded that the activity contributes importantly to the organization's exempt purpose and hence does not constitute debt-financed property subject to these tax rules.[16]

Also, for purposes of the foregoing item (1), the principles established under the general unrelated income rules[17] are applicable in determining whether there is a substantial relationship between the property and the tax-exempt purposes of the organization.[18] These principles were adversely applied to an organization that was operated for educational purposes essentially in the same manner as a museum in that it promotes the appreciation of history and architecture by acquiring, restoring, and preserving buildings of historical and/or architectural significance and opens the restored buildings to the general public for a nominal admission fee. The organization acquired certain historically or architecturally significant buildings by assumption of outstanding mortgages and leased them at a fair rental value, subject to a covenant to ensure that the historical architecture of the buildings is maintained by the lessees, for uses that neither bear any relationship to the buildings' historical or architectural significance nor accommodate viewing by the general public. Because this leasing does not contribute importantly to the accomplishment of the organization's educational purpose and has no causal relationship to the achievement of that purpose, the Service found that substantially all the use of the buildings is not substantially related to the organization's exempt purposes and thus that the leased buildings constitute debt-financed property.[19]

Property owned by a tax-exempt organization and used by a related tax-exempt organization or by an exempt organization related to the related exempt organization is not treated as debt-financed property to the extent the property is used by either organization in furtherance of its tax-exempt purpose.[20] Two tax-exempt organizations are related to each other if more than 50 percent of the members of one organization are members of the other organization.[21] In one instance, the IRS held that a "charitable" organization may acquire a building, use a portion of it, and lease the other portions to a related "charitable" organization and a related business league for their offices and activities, and that the building will not be treated as debt-financed property.[22] The organi-

---

[16]Rev. Rul. 81-138, 1981-1 C. B. 358, amplifying Rev. Rul. 70-81, 1970-1 C. B. 131. Also IRS Private Letter Ruling 8246006. Cf. Rev. Rul. 58-547, 1958-2 C. B. 275.

[17]Code § 513.

[18]Reg. § 1.514(b)-1(b)(1). See Chapter 42 § 3.

[19]Rev. Rul. 77-47, 1977-1 C. B. 157.

[20]Reg. § 1.514(b)-1(c)(2)(i).

[21]Reg. § 1.514(b)-1(c)(2)(ii)(c).

[22]IRS Private Letter Ruling 7833055. The IRS cautioned that the "charitable" organization should charge the business league a fair market value rent, for if it did not it would be conferring a financial benefit upon a non-Code § 501(c)(3) organization, which might adversely affect its tax-exempt status.

zation acquiring the building has as its membership all of the active members of the business league who have contributed to it, and the membership of the other "charitable" organization consists of those active members of the business league who are elected to and serving on the governing body of the business league; the members of one of the "charitable" organizations would not necessarily be members of the other.

The "neighborhood land" rule provides an exemption from the debt-financed property rules for interim income from neighborhood real property acquired for an exempt purpose. The tax on unrelated debt-financed property does not apply to income from realty, located in the neighborhood of the tax-exempt organization, which it plans to devote to exempt uses within 10 years of the time of acquisition.[23] A more liberal 15-year rule is established for churches and it is not required that the property be in the neighborhood of the church.[24]

If debt-financed property is sold or otherwise disposed of, a percentage of the total gain or loss derived from the disposition is to be included in the computation of unrelated business taxable income.[25] The IRS recognizes, however, that the unrelated debt-financed income rules do not render taxable a transaction which would not be taxable by virtue of a nonrecognition provision of the federal tax law if it were carried out by an entity which is not tax exempt.[26] The occasion was a transfer, subject to an existing mortgage, of an appreciated apartment complex by a tax-exempt hospital to its wholly owned taxable subsidiary in exchange for additional stock in the subsidiary. Because of the operation of federal tax rules which provide for the nonrecognition of gain or loss in certain circumstances,[27] including those involving this hospital, the transaction did not result in a taxable gain for the hospital.

§ 43.3 Acquisition Indebtedness

Income-producing property is considered to be debt-financed property (making income from it, less deductions, taxable) only where there is an "acquisition indebtedness" attributable to it. Acquisition indebtedness, with respect to debt-financed property, means the unpaid amount of (1) the indebtedness incurred by the organization in acquiring or improving the property, (2) the indebtedness incurred before any acquisition or improvement of the property if the indebtedness would not have been incurred but for the acquisition or improvement, and (3) the indebtedness incurred after the acquisition or improvement of the property if the indebtedness would not have been incurred but for the acquisition or improvement and the incurrence of the indebtedness was reasonably foreseeable at the time of the acquisition or improvement.[28] Debt incurred

[23]Code § 514(b)(3)(A)-(C)).
[24]Code § 514(b)(3)(E). In general, see Reg. § 1.514(b)-1.
[25]Reg. § 1.514(a)-1(a)(1)(v).
[26]Rev. Rul. 77-71, 1977-1 C. B. 156.
[27]Code §§ 351 and 357.
[28]Code § 514(c)(1).

prior to June 28, 1966, was not taken into account until tax years beginning after December 31, 1971.

If property is acquired by a tax-exempt organization subject to a mortgage or other similar lien, the indebtedness thereby secured is considered an acquisition indebtedness incurred by the organization when the property is acquired, even though the organization did not assume or agree to pay the indebtedness.[29] However, some relief is provided with respect to mortgaged property acquired as a result of bequest or devise. That is, the indebtedness secured by this type of mortgage is not treated as acquisition indebtedness during the ten-year period following the date of acquisition. A similar rule applies to mortgaged property received by gift, where the mortgage was placed on the property more than five years before the gift and the property was held by the donor more than five years before the gift.[30]

A "charitable" organization acquired an undivided interest in income-producing rental property subject to a mortgage; the property was leased for purposes unrelated to the organization's tax-exempt purposes. To liquidate its share of the mortgage, the organization prepaid its proportionate share of the mortgage indebtedness, thereby receiving releases of liability from the mortgagee and the co-owners. The lien securing payment of the mortgage nonetheless extended to the entire rental property and the mortgagee is not to release the lien until the entire principal of the mortgage is paid by the co-owners. The IRS ruled that the organization, by satisfying the full amount of its indebtedness under the mortgage, has no acquisition indebtedness.[31]

By contrast, a "charitable" organization purchased mineral production payments with borrowed funds to obtain income for its grant-making program, receiving from each payment the difference between the aggregate amount payable to the lender of the borrowed funds and the total amount of the production payment, with the difference generally amounting to one-sixteenth of one percent of each payment purchased. The IRS held that the indebtedness incurred to purchase the production payment was an acquisition indebtedness and that, accordingly, the payments are debt-financed property.[32]

The regulations accompanying the statutory unrelated debt-financed income rules provide, in effect, a special rule for debts for the payment of taxes, stating that "in the case where State law provides that a tax lien attaches to property prior to the time when such lien becomes due and payable, such lien shall not be treated as similar to a mortgage until after it has become due and payable and the organization has had an opportunity to pay such lien in accordance with State law."[33] However, prior to enactment of the Tax Reform Act of 1976, the IRS had been taking the position that a lien arising from a special assessment imposed by a state or local government on land for the purpose of making

[29]Code § 514(c)(2)(A).
[30]Code § 514(c)(2)(B).
[31]Rev. Rul. 76-95, 1976-1 C. B. 172. Also see IRS Private Letter Ruling 7852001.
[32]Rev. Rul. 76-354, 1976-2 C. B. 179.
[33]Reg. § 514(c)-1(b)(2).

improvements thereon, with the improvements financed by the sale of bonds secured by the lien, constitutes acquisition indebtedness, even though (like the property tax lien) the installment payments are due in future periods. In 1976, Congress took action to reverse this position so that, as respects tax years which began after December 31, 1969, where state law provides that a lien for taxes or for assessments made by the state or a political subdivision thereof attaches to property prior to the time when the taxes or assessments become due and payable, the indebtedness does not become "acquisition indebtedness" (that is, the lien is not regarded as similar to a mortgage[34]) until and to the extent that the taxes or assessments become due and payable and the organization has had an opportunity to pay the taxes or assessments in accordance with state law.[35] The Senate Finance Committee noted that it is not intended-that this provision apply to special assessments for improvements which are not of a type normally made by a State or local governmental unit or instrumentality in circumstances in which the use of the special assessment is essentially a device for financing improvements of the sort that normally would be financed privately rather than through a government."[36]

Other exemptions from the scope of acquisition indebtedness are as follows:

(1) The term does not include indebtedness which was necessarily incurred in the performance or exercise of an organization's tax-exempt purpose or function, such as the indebtedness incurred by a tax-exempt credit union[37] in accepting deposits from its members.[38]

(2) The term does not include an obligation to pay an annuity which (a) is the sole consideration issued in exchange for property if, at the time of the exchange, the value of the annuity is less than 90 percent of the value of the property received in the exchange, (b) is payable over the life of one individual who is living at the time the annuity is issued, or over the lives of two individuals living at that time, and (c) is payable under a contract which does not guarantee a minimum amount of payments or specify a maximum amount of payments and does not provide for any adjustment of the amount of the annuity payments by reference to the income received from the transferred property or any other property.[39]

(3) The term does not include an obligation to finance the purchase, rehabilitation, or construction of housing for low and moderate income persons to the extent that it is insured by the Federal Housing Administration.[40]

[34]See Code § 514(c)(2)(A).
[35]Code § 514(c)(2)(C).
[36]S. Rep. No. 94-938 (Part 2), 94th Cong., 2d Sess. (1976) at 86.
[37]See Chapter 20 § 10.
[38]Code § 514(c)(4).
[39]Code § 514(c)(5). Cf. IRS Private Letter Ruling 7902019 (issue no. 10).
[40]Code § 514(c)(6). In general, see Reg. § 1.514(c)-1.

(4) The term does not include an exempt organization's obligation to return collateral security pursuant to a securities lending arrangement, thereby making it clear that, in ordinary circumstances, payments on securities loans are not debt-financed income.[41]

The IRS ruled that a tax-exempt employees' trust (which is, in general, subject to tax on unrelated business taxable income[42]), which was a partner in a partnership that was organized to make investments in securities, could experience unrelated debt-financed income.[43] The partnership borrows money to invest in securities and becomes primarily liable for repayment of the debt and for payment of interest thereon, with the partners secondarily liable on a pro rata basis. The Service held that the indebtedness was an acquisition indebtedness because it was incurred to acquire property for investment purposes, its incurrence was not inherent in the performance of the trust's tax-exempt function (namely, to receive employer and employee contributions and to use them and increments thereon to provide retirement benefits to the plan participants[44]), and the investment property was not substantially related to the exercise of the trust's exempt purposes. Thus, whether the trust's investment activity can result in unrelated business taxable income under these rules is determined by whether its share of any partnership income[45] is derived from or on account of debt-financed property.[46] Subsequently, the U.S. Tax Court held that the income from securities purchased on margin by a qualified profit-sharing plan is unrelated debt-financed income, in that this type of indebtedness is not inherent in the exercise of the trust's exempt function.[47]

By contrast, the IRS examined similar practices engaged in by a trust forming part of a leveraged employee stock ownership plan.[48] An ESOP is a technique of corporate finance designed to build beneficial equity ownership of shares in an employer corporation into its employees substantially in proportion to their relative income without requiring any cash outlay on their part, any reduction in pay or other employee benefits, or the surrender of any rights on the part of the employees.[49] This type of trust generally acquires stock of the employer with the proceeds of a loan made to it by a financial institution. Consequently, the IRS concluded that a leveraged ESOP's capital growth and stock ownership

[41]Code § 514(c)(8).

[42]See Rev. Rul. 71-311, 1971-2 C. B. 184. For a discussion of life insurance policy loans constituting an indebtedness for these purposes, see IRS Private Letter Ruling 7918095.

[43]Rev. Rul. 74-197, 1974-1 C. B. 143.

[44]See Reg. § 1.401-1(a)(2)(i).

[45]See Reg. § 1.702-1(a).

[46]Cf. "Point to Remember" no. 12, 27 *Tax Lawyer* 523 (1974).

[47]*Elliot Knitwear Profit Sharing Plan* v. *Commissioner*, 71 T. C. 765 (1979).

[48]Code § 4975(e)(7).

[49]See S. Rep. No. 94-938, 94th Cong., 2d Sess. (1976).

objectives are part of its tax-exempt function[50] and "borrowing to purchase employer securities is an integral part of accomplishing these objectives." Thus, the borrowing is not acquisition indebtedness and the securities thereby purchased are not debt-financed property. But the IRS cautioned that these circumstances are "distinguishable from a situation in which a pension or profit-sharing plan that satisfies the requirements of [Code] section 401(a) borrows money to purchase securities of the employer; in the latter situation the exempt trusts' borrowing to purchase employer securities could result in unrelated business income within the meaning of [code] section 512."[51]

Rules enacted in 1980 provide that, with certain exceptions, debt incurred by a tax-exempt employee trust with respect to real estate investments is not acquisition indebtedness, so that the income from the investments is not subject to the tax on unrelated business income. However, debt does not qualify for this exception where it is incurred with respect to real property if (1) the purchase price is not a fixed amount determined as of the date of acquisition, (2) the purchase price (or the amount or timing of any payment) is dependent, in whole or in part, upon the future revenues, income, or profits derived from the property, (3) the property is leased to the transferor (or to a party related to the transferor), (4) the property is acquired from, or leased to, certain persons who are disqualified persons with respect to the trust, or (5) the debt is nonrecourse debt owed to the transferor (or a related party) which either is subordinate to any other indebtedness secured by the property or bears a rate of interest significantly less than that which would apply if the financing had been obtained from a third party.[52]

An example of the "flexibility" of the potential application of the unrelated debt-financed income rules was the suggestion made by some within the IRS that such income is realized by tax-exempt organizations in the conventional lending of securities transaction.[53] This conclusion was arrived at by the way of the contention that the exempt institution is not really lending the securities but is "borrowing" the collateral, thereby making—so the argument goes—the entire interest (and perhaps the dividend or interest equivalent) taxable.

However, this matter was clarified by the enactment of a special rule[54] and earlier by an IRS ruling that the income from the investment of the collateral posted by the broker is not unrelated debt-financed income, since the organization did not incur the indebtedness "for the purpose of making additional investments."[55]

The intent of these rules is to treat an otherwise tax-exempt organization in the same manner as an ordinary business enterprise to the extent that the

---

[50]See Code § 401(a).

[51]Rev. Rul. 79-122, 1979-1 C. B. 204. Cf. Rev. Rul. 79-349, 1979-2 C. B. 233. See Point to Remember No. 4, 33 *Tax Lawyer* 909 (1980).

[52]Code § 514(c)(9).

[53]See discussions in Chapters 39 and 42.

[54]N. 41, *supra*.

[55]Rev. Rul. 78-88, 1978-1 C. B. 163.

exempt organization purchases property through the use of borrowed funds.[56] The IRS recalled this intent in passing on the tax status of indebtedness owed to a labor union by its wholly owned subsidiary title-holding company resulting from a loan to pay debts incurred to acquire two income-producing office buildings. The Service ruled that this "interorganizational indebtedness" was not an acquisition indebtedness because "the very nature of the title-holding company as well as the parent-subsidiary relationship show this indebtedness to be merely a matter of accounting between the organizations rather than an indebtedness as contemplated by" these rules.[57]

§ 43.4 Computation of Unrelated Debt-Financed Income

The computation of unrelated debt-financed income (the amount subject to tax) is made by applying to the total gross income and deductions attributable) to debt-financed property the following fraction: the average acquisition indebtedness for the tax year over the average adjusted basis of the property during the tax year.

For purposes of the numerator of this fraction, acquisition indebtedness is to be averaged over the tax year.[58] This averaging mechanism precludes an exempt organization from avoiding a tax by using other available funds to pay off the indebtedness immediately before any fixed determination date. If debt-financed property is disposed of during the year, "average acquisition indebtedness" would mean the highest acquisition indebtedness during the preceding twelve months. Absent this rule, an exempt organization could avoid tax by using other resources to discharge indebtedness before the end of one tax year and dispose of property after the beginning of the next tax year.

For purposes of the denominator of the fraction, adjusted basis is the average adjusted basis for the portion of the year during which the property is held by the tax-exempt organization. The use of average adjusted basis is only for purposes of determining the fraction. Where property is disposed of, gain or loss will, as usual, be computed with reference to adjusted basis at the time of disposition.

The essence of the foregoing rules[59] may be illustrated by the following example:

An exempt organization acquires property for the production of income on July 1, 1979, for $100,000, of which $80,000 is financed (i.e., there is an $80,000 acquisition indebtedness). As of December 31, 1979, the organization has satisfied $10,000 of the debt, by one payment (on September 1, 1979) and has claimed $2,500 in straight-line depreciation. For 1979, 75.9 percent of the income (less appropriate deductions) from the property is taxable.

---

[56]See H. Rep. No. 91-413, 91st Cong., 1st Sess. (1969), at 46.
[57]Rev. Rul. 77-72, 1977-1 C. B. 157; IRS Private Letter Ruling 7841005.
[58]Code § 514(c)(7).
[59]Code § 514(a)–(c).

To determine this percentage, the average acquisition indebtedness for 1979 must be computed. This amount is $75,000, ascertained as follows:

(1) Debt	(2) Months Outstanding	(3) (1) × (2)
$80,000	3	$240,000
70,000	3	210,000
	6	$450,000

(3) divided by (2) equals $75,000, which is the weighted average for the six-month period involved.

To determine the average adjusted basis, it is necessary to compute the basis at the beginning (here, $100,000) and at the end of the tax year ($97,500, i.e., original basis less depreciation). The average adjusted basis ($100,000 divided by $97,500 divided by 2) is $98,750.

The applicable percentage thus becomes 75.9 precent ($75,000/$98,750).

If property is distributed by a corporation in liquidation to an exempt organization, the exempt organization uses the basis of the distributing corporation, with adjustment for any gain recognized on the distribution either to the exempt organization or to the taxable corporation. An example of the former would be where a tax-exempt organization had an acquisition indebtedness applicable to its stock in the distributing corporation and an illustration of the latter would be an instance of recapture of depreciation.[60] This rule prevents an exempt organization from acquiring the property in a taxable subsidiary to secure accelerated depreciation during the first several years of the life of the property, enabling the subsidiary to pay off a large part of the indebtedness during those years, after which the exempt organization would obtain a stepped-up basis on liquidation of the subsidiary.[61] If property is used partly for tax-exempt and partly for nonexempt purposes, the income and deductions attributable to the exempt uses are excluded from the computation of unrelated debt-financed income and allocations are made, where appropriate, for acquisition indebtedness, adjusted basis, and deductions assignable to the property.[62]

[60]See Code §§ 1245, 1250.

[61]Code § 514(d); Reg. § 1.514(d)-1.

[62]Code § 514(e); Reg. § 1.514(e)-1. See *Florida Farm Bureau Federation* v. *Commissioner,* 65 T. C. 1118 (1975). In general, see Beller, "Exempt Organizations: Taxation of Debt-Financed Income," 24 *Tax Lawyer* 489 (1971).

Afterword

As noted, all too many regard tax-exempt organizations as a quaint anachronism of another era—forms of institutional life not suited for future organization of U.S. society.[1] Some see tax-exempt organizations disappearing as a result of tax policy, such as by the adoption of a pure "flat tax" that recognizes no exemptions at all.[2] Others prophesy the demise of tax-exempt organizations because of an evolving absence of necessity for them.

Aside from tax policy aspects, the thought that tax-exempt (or, in any absence of tax exemption, nonprofit) organizations are destined for extinction may be tested against the thinking of futurists. Probably the most popular of the thinkers about the future is Alvin Toffler, author of *Future Shock* (about change, and the personal and social costs of it) and, more pertinently, *The Third Wave*.

In *The Third Wave*, Toffler divides civilization into three parts: an agricultural phase that began around 8000 B.C. and closed about A.D. 1650–1750 (the "First Wave"), an industrial phase that evolved out of the agricultural era and dominated until the 1950s (the "Second Wave"), and a postindustrial phase that is now underway (the "Third Wave").[3] Obviously, Toffler uses as his "grand metaphor" the concept of "colliding waves of change"[4]—a "social 'wave-front' analysis" that "looks at history as a succession of rolling waves of change."[5]

Toffler envisions a "world that is fast emerging" and that "demands wholly new ideas and analogies, classifications and concepts."[6] Regarding classifications, he concludes that a civilization has a "techno-sphere," a "socio-sphere," an "info-sphere," a "power-sphere," a "bio-sphere," and a "psycho-sphere."

Except for religious institutions, there is little in the First Wave (and certainly

[1]See Chapters 1 and 3.
[2]See Chapter 3 §§ 3–7.
[3]Toffler, *The Third Wave*, xxii, 8 (1980).
[4]*Ibid.* at xxiii.
[5]*Id.* at 7.
[6]*Id.* at xx.

far less in the preagricultural era) that resembles today's nonprofit organization. It is, however, during the Second Wave (particularly as it was manifested in the United States, as aptly described by Alexis de Tocqueville) that the nonprofit entity—and, with the advent of taxation, the tax-exempt entity—appears. This appearance came as part of the organization of society (the socio-sphere), which witnessed a shift of functions out of the agrarian family (the principal First Wave unit) and to "new, specialized institutions," such as schools, poor-houses, old-age homes, and nursing homes.[7] Moreover, around the three core institutions of Second Wave society (the nuclear family, the factory, and the corporation) sprang up a host of other institutions, including "sports clubs, churches, chambers of commerce, trade unions, professional organizations, political parties, libraries, ethnic associations, [and] recreational groups."[8]

Toffler's analysis pictures the First Wave society as essentially composed of church, state, and the individual. But, he writes, the wave of industrialism (the Second Wave) "broke society into thousands of interlocking parts,"[9] such as churches, schools, hospitals, trade unions, trade associations, and recreational groups.[10]

Toffler's view of the waves of change does not project the future as a linear extension of the present (the underlying thesis of writings such as *1984* and *Brave New World*). Instead, the "thrust of Third Wave change is toward increased diversity" in "ideas, political convictions, sexual proclivities, educational methods, eating habits, religious views, ethnic attitudes, musical tastes, fashions, and family forms."[11] This, in turn, he predicts, will produce (indeed, is producing), "a maelstrom of conflicting, confusing, and cacophonous ideas."[12] It is out of "the collapse of the industrial era mind-structure, [and] its growing irrelevance in the face of the new technological, social, and political realities"[13] that tax-exempt (nonprofit) organizations are to find their future.

The key term in this regard is "diversity," stimulated in part by what Toffler labels the "de-massification" of society. This development, he believes, will lend to a splintering and/or reshaping of many of society's institutions—both a decentralizing and a fragmenting process. He writes: "As the mass society of the industrial era disintegrates under the impact of the Third Wave, regional, local, ethnic, social, and religious groups grow less uniform."[14] If nothing else, this result would mean more tax-exempt organizations. For example, Toffler sees this de-massification phenomenon occurring in U.S. political life, in de-

---

[7]*Id*. at 22.
[8]*Id*. at 24–25.
[9]*Id*. at 54.
[10]*Id*. at 54, 57.
[11]*Id*. at 242.
[12]*Id*. at 274.
[13]*Id*. at 294.
[14]*Id*. at 300.

scribing "the sudden, bewildering proliferation of high-powered splinter groups."[15] He continues:

> . . . The latest buzzword in Washington is "single-issue group," referring to the political organizations springing up by the thousands, usually around what each perceives as a single burning issue: abortion, gun control, gay rights, school busing, nuclear power, and so on. So diverse are these interests at both the national and local levels that politicians and officials can no longer keep track of them.
>
> Mobile home owners organize to fight for county zoning changes. Farmers battle power transmission lines. Retired people mobilize against school taxes. Feminists, Chicanos, strip miners, and anti-strip miners organize, as do single parents and anti-porn crusaders. A midwest magazine even reports formation of an organization of "gay Nazis"—an embarrassment, no doubt, to both the heterosexual Nazis and the Gay Liberation Movement.
>
> Simultaneously, national mass organizations are having trouble holding together. Says a participant at a conference of voluntary organizations, "Local churches are not following the national lead any more." A labor expert reports that instead of a single unified political drive by the AFL–CIO, affiliated unions are increasingly mounting their own campaigns for their own ends.[16]

As far as the future of tax-exempt (or, at least, nonprofit) organizations is concerned, Toffler clearly expects not only more of them but an expanded role for them. A brief survey of *The Third Wave* by category of institutions partially illustrates this vision.

Religious Organizations

Religious organizations are probably the oldest form of tax-exempt organization. Toffler acknowledges the centralizing influence of churches during the First Wave[17] and the role of religion in spreading Second Wave civilization.[18]

Toffler predicts, however, a greater diversity in organized religion and the emergence of new religions. For example, when writing of the "maelstrom of conflicting, confusing, and cacophonous ideas," he notes (with exaggeration for effect) that "[e]very day brings some new fad, scientific finding, religion, movement, or manifesto."[19] He writes of "a wildfire revival of fundamentalist religion,"[20] the spread of Eastern religions in the United States,[21] "[w]aves of

[15]*Id.* at 388.
[16]*Id.*
[17]*Id.* at 49.
[18]*Id.* at 77, 90, 146.
[19]*Id.* at 274. Also 293–294, 346.
[20]*Id.*
[21]*Id.* at 286, 346.

religious revivalism,"[22] religious views that "are becoming less uniform and standardized,"[23] a "clash of cultures, religions, and traditions in the world,"[24] and the rise of religious cults.[25] He expects that "[a] host of new religions, new conceptions of science, new images of human nature, new forms of art will arise—in far richer diversity than was possible or necessary during the industrial age."[26]

Clearly, then, Toffler visualizes an extensive role in Third Wave society for organizations that are tax-exempt because they are "religious."

Educational Institutions

Toffler discusses at some length the mainstay role of educational institutions, particularly schools, during the Second Wave.[27] He writes vividly of mass public education as being essential to Second Wave society, inasmuch as it taught standardization, punctuality, and synchronization.[28] But he believes that the educational system suited to serve industrial society is inadequate for post-industrial (Third Wave) society.

This does not mean abolishment of schools, colleges, universities, museums, and the like. At the same time, Toffler dismisses the prediction that "the university will replace the factory as the central institution of tomorrow" as being "little more than a professorial wish-fulfillment fantasy"[29] (he suggests instead that that institution will be the home).

Rather, as part of Toffler's general thesis that the new "society is likely to be built around a network rather than a hierarchy of new institutions,"[30] coupled with "increased diversity" throughout Third Wave civilizations,[31] he foresees new educational organizations and new educational methods.[32] In the realm of formal education, he predicts restructuring of curricula, revisions in the concept of grading, increased parental influence on the schools,[33] and a lessening in the number of years of compulsory schooling.[34]

His views on a broader scale, however, entail a wide range of new approaches

[22]*Id.* at 11.

[23]*Id.* at 241.

[24]*Id.* at 309.

[25]*Id.* at 346. Toffler explains the growth of religious cults as a response to individuals' needs for community, life structure, and meaning, elements that are elusive in a disintegrating Second Wave System. *Id.* at 354–356.

[26]*Id.* at 338.

[27]*Id.* at 22–23.

[28]*Id.* at 41, 45.

[29]*Id.* at 335.

[30]*Id.* at 336.

[31]*Id.* at 242.

[32]*Id.* at 328–329, 333.

[33]*Id.* at 349–351.

[34]*Id.* at 364.

in instruction. He calls for new forms of consultancies, particularly in fields where assistance can be provided to enable persons to cope with the transition from Second Wave to Third Wave life (these he terms "structure-providers" and "life organizers").[35]

The advent of word processors, home computers, and telecommunications, predicted by Toffler and already obvious today, is certain to work massive changes in the modes of educational instruction.[36] He foresees an increase in the type of education that requires active participation in the process by those receiving the instruction.[37]

The most massive single change in education may derive from what Toffler perceives as a radical shift in the economy, "a progressive blurring of the line that separates producer from consumer."[38] Second Wave industrial society is economically based on production of goods and services for exchange (for the "market"), while First Wave agricultural society is economically predicated on production for use. Toffler contends that Third Wave society brings with it a rising significance of production for use again—a new arrival of the "prosumer."[39]

In the context of tax-exempt educational organizations, the new age of pro-suming has many applications, two of which illustrate the point.

One of these is the self-help movement, described by Toffler as follows:

In Britain in 1970, a Manchester housewife named Katherine Fisher, after suffering for years from a desperate fear of leaving her own home, founded an organization for others with similar phobias. Today that organization, The Phobics Society, has many branches and is one of thousands of new groups cropping up in many of the high-technology nations to help people deal directly with their own problems—psychological, medical, social, or sexual.

In Detroit, some 50 "bereavement groups" have sprung up to aid people suffering from grief after the loss of a relative or friend. In Australia an organization called GROW brings together former mental patients and "nervous persons." GROW now has chapters in Hawaii, New Zealand, and Ireland. In 22 states an organization called Parents of Gays and Lesbians is in formation to help those with homosexual children. In Britain, Depressives Associated has some 60 chapters. From Addicts Anonymous and the Black Lung Association to Parents Without Partners and Widow-to-Widow, new groups are forming everywhere.

Of course, there is nothing new about people in trouble getting together to talk out their problems and learn from one another. Nonetheless, historians can find little precedent for the wildfire speed with which the self-help movement is spreading today.

Frank Riessman and Alan Gartner, co-directors of the New Human Services Institute, estimate that in the United States alone there are now over 500,000 such groupings—about one for every 435 in the population—with new ones

[35]*Id*. at 356.
[36]*Id*. at 158–161.
[37]*Id*. at 268.
[38]*Id*. at 253.
[39]*Id*. at 252–253.

forming daily. Many are short-lived, but for each one that disappears several seem to take its place.

These organizations vary widely. Some share the new suspicion of specialists and attempt to work without them. They rely entirely on what might be termed "cross-counseling"—people swapping advice based on their own life experience, as distinct from receiving traditional counseling from the professionals. Some see themselves as providing a support system for people in trouble. Others play a political role, lobbying for changes in legislation or tax regulations. Still others have a quasi-religious character. Some are intentional communities whose members not only meet but actually live together.

Such groups are now forming regional, even transnational linkages. To the extent that professional psychologists, social workers, or doctors are involved at all, they increasingly undergo a role change, shifting from the role of impersonal expert who is assumed to know best to that of listener, teacher, and guide who works with the patient or client. Existing voluntary or nonprofit groups—originally organized for the purpose of helping others—are similarly struggling to see how they fit in with a movement based on the principle of helping oneself.

The self-help movement is thus restructuring the socio-sphere. Smokers, stutterers, suicide-prone people, gamblers, victims of throat disease, parents of twins, overeaters, and other such groupings now form a dense network of organizations that mesh with the emerging Third Wave family and corporate structures.[40]

The other illustration is the do-it-yourself movement, which Toffler translates as opening up new opportunities in instruction and publishing.[41] This development will be enhanced with the increase in leisure time and the advances in microprocessing, microcomputing, and telecommunications.

Consequently, the universe of organizations that are tax-exempt because they are educational is expanding.

Health and Scientific Institutions

The forces discussed above are, of course, at work in the fields of health and science. As with the educational institutions, Toffler does not write of any particular decline in the number of entities such as hospitals and research laboratories but instead predicts new advances and diversification of organizations.

Thus, in science, Toffler writes of the coming impact of the electronics and computer industries, outer space exploration, ocean exploration, and genetic engineering.[42] As noted earlier, he writes that "[e]very day brings some new fad, scientific finding, religion, movement, or manifesto."[43] He observes that "[n]ature worship, ESP, holistic medicine, sociobiology, anarchism, structuralism, neo-Marxism, the new physics, Eastern mysticism, technophilia, technophobia, and a thousand other currents and crosscurrents sweep across the

---

[40]*Id*. at 254–255.
[41]*Id*. at 258.
[42]*Id*. at 129–138.
[43]*Id*. at 274.

screen of consciousness, each with its scientific priesthood or ten-minute guru."[44] In general, he predicts "[f]antastic scientific advances,"[45] and there should be little doubt that tax-exempt organizations will be directly in the forefront of these advances.

At the same time, there will be considerable resistance to new technology. Thus, Toffler also writes of "the dangers of electronic smog, information pollution, combat in outer space, genetic leakage, climatic intervention, and what might be called 'ecological warfare'. . . ."[46] He describes a "fast-growing army of people" who are "well-organized and articulate" and who are opposed to the "uncontrolled technological thrust."[47] He terms these individuals "techno-rebels" and notes that "[t]hey publish their own technical journals and propaganda" and they "file lawsuits and draft legislation, as well as picket, march, and demonstrate."[48] As this techo-rebellion unfolds, as it "provides the basis for humanizing the technological thrust,"[49] tax-exempt organizations are certain to be in this forefront as well.

In health, Second Wave society brought a number of "specialized institutions," such as hospitals, nursing homes, and homes for the aged.[50] But paralleling and reflecting the advances in science, there will be significant changes in health-care delivery systems. One illustration of this is related to the rise of the prosumers—who, in the health care setting, are the ones who are performing for themselves tasks previously conducted for them by physicians, nurses, and laboratories.[51] Thus, Toffler observes that "a number of health problems (like those deriving from smoking, for example) cannot be solved by doctors alone but require instead the active participation of the patient."[52] Likewise, he writes of the "holistic health" movement, based "on the notion that the well-being of the individual depends on an integration of the physical, the spiritual, and the mental."[53] Once again, tax-exempt organizations are very much a part of these developments.

Community Organizations

While community organizations obviously were (and are) a part of Second Wave society, they were incompatible with many of its forces. Among these forces are the transient nature of much of the population due to transfers

---

[44]*Id.*

[45]*Id.* at 273.

[46]*Id.* at 138–139.

[47]*Id.* at 139.

[48]*Id.* at 139–140.

[49]*Id.* at 142.

[50]*Id.* at 22, 25, 204.

[51]*Id.* at 251–252. Also 43.

[52]*Id.* at 268.

[53]*Id.* at 287.

dictated for employment reasons and the standardized practice of work being done in factories and office buildings, often many miles from home. For several reasons (including the availability of the requisite technology and the force of decentralization), Toffler believes that the evolving production system is going to shift much work into the home—the "electronic cottage."[54] One of the consequences of home work on a significant scale may, he asserts, be "greater community stability" which in turn could generate "greater participation in community life."[55] The potential impact of a work-at-home situation on the future of tax-exempt organizations has been captured by Toffler:

> The electronic cottage could help restore a sense of community belonging, and touch off a renaissance among voluntary organizations like churches, women's groups, lodges, clubs, athletic and youth organizations."[56]

Political Organizations

The de-massification phenomenon is also affecting the nation's political system, according to Toffler. As discussed, the Second Wave system of "a few well-recognized and clearly organized constituencies" is splintering, giving way to "countless new constituencies, fluidly organized, [that] demand simultaneous attention to real but narrow and unfamiliar needs."[57] While these constituencies are obviously housed in tax-exempt organizations, they are, in Toffler's view, among the reasons that Second Wave "representative democracy" is under severe strain and challenge.[58]

Toffler calls for nothing less than "the design of new, more appropriate political structures."[59] One of the pathways to this objective is "imaginative new arrangements for accommodating and legitimating diversity—new institutions that are sensitive to the rapidly shifting needs of changing and multiplying minorities."[60] Tax-exempt organizations will certainly be a part of this process, both as entities that help to design the new political process and that are participatory elements of it. As to the latter, for example, two Toffler quotations are illustrative:

- We shall almost certainly have to discard our obsolete party structures, designed for a slowly changing world of mass movements and mass merchandizing, and invent temporary modular parties that service changing configurations of minorities—plug-in/plug-out parties of the future.

[54]*Id*. at 181–193.
[55]*Id*. at 191.
[56]*Id*.
[57]*Id*. at 389.
[58]*Id*. at 389–390.
[59]*Id*. at 397.
[60]*Id*. at 401.

• We may have to create quasi-political institutions to help minorities—whether professional, ethnic, sexual, regional, recreational, or religious—to form and break alliances more quickly and easily.[61]

New Organizations

In his wide-ranging analysis of Third Wave life, Toffler has ample opportunity to speculate on some of the needs of tomorrow and on ways to satisfy them. Many of these ways would require the use of tax-exempt organizations.

For example, Toffler discusses some of the problems that cannot be solved by national governments alone (such as inflation, activities of transnational corporations, arms trade, outer space governance, and interlocking currencies). He states that "[w]e desperately need, therefore, to invent imaginative new institutions at the transnational level to which many decisions can be transferred" and calls for "consortia and teams of nongovernmental organizations to attack various global problems."[62]

Likewise, he writes of the need to enable a variety of minorities to regulate more of their own affairs. To this end, he speculates, "[w]e might, for example, help the people in a specific neighborhood, in a well-defined subculture, or in an ethnic group, to set up their own youth courts under the supervision of the state, disciplining their own young people rather than relying on the state to do so."[63] He rationalizes this suggestion in terms embodying some well-recognized tax law doctrines for such groups: "Such institutions would build community and identity, and contribute to law and order, while relieving the overburdened government institutions of unnecessary work."[64]

In still another example of new tax-exempt organization life forms, Toffler postulates the use of "semi-cults"—organizations that "lie somewhere between [the application of] structureless freedom and tightly structured regimentation."[65] These groups are envisioned by him as a means to impose a certain degree of structure where and as long as it is required, yet enabling persons to freely return to productive life in society. He also suggests a variant of these entities to provide community services.[66]

The point of the foregoing is not to endorse any particular vein of futurist thinking or the necessary evolution of any particular form of tax-exempt organization but to suggest that unfolding societal needs are likely to heavily entail the active involvement of tax-exempt (nonprofit) organizations. Irrespective of Toffleresque terminology, his prognostications indicate an exciting

[61]*Id.* at 402.
[62]*Id.* at 410.
[63]*Id.* at 403.
[64]*Id.*
[65]*Id.* at 357.
[66]*Id.* at 357–358.

and meaningful future, replete with a large dosage of the American tendency to create "associations." The Toffler premise suggests that nonprofit, tax-exempt organizations are an integral part of the American societal and political structure, and that the concern for the immediate future is not whether nonprofit groups are a dying breed but whether they are to be seriously endangered by evolving tax policy.[67]

[67]Toffler, in *The Third Wave*, does not directly address the question of the existence and role of nonprofit organizations in the postindustrial age, but certainly assumes their ongoing function. Therefore, he does not write of any need to preserve tax exemption for nonprofit organizations—this he apparently assumes also will continue. He clearly is not opposed to such a utilization of the tax system, however, as in his book he calls for the application of tax incentives to help accomplish particular objectives.

APPENDICES

Internal Revenue
Code Sections

Following are the various provisions of the Internal Revenue Code which comprise the statutory framework for the field of tax-exempt organizations:

Section 48(a)(4)—denial of investment tax credit for exempt organization used property.

Section 84—tax on appreciated property gifts to political organizations.

Section 103—exclusion for interest on governmental obligations.

Section 115—tax "exemption" for political subdivisions and the like.

Section 120—prepaid group legal services.

Section 162(e)—business expense deduction for legislative activities.

Section 170—income tax deduction for charitable contributions.

Section 192—deduction for contributions to Black Lung Benefit Trusts.

Section 216(b)—cooperative housing corporations.

Section 277—deductions incurred by certain non-exempt membership organizations.

Section 403(b)—treatment of annuity contracts of charitable organizations-employers.

Section 501—general requirements for income tax exemption.

Section 502—feeder organizations.

Section 503—denial of tax exemption to certain organizations engaged in prohibited transactions.

Section 504—special legislative activities rules.

Section 507—termination of private foundation status.

Section 508—special rules for section 501(c)(3) organizations.

Section 509—definition of private foundation.

Section 511—imposition of tax on unrelated business income.

Section 512—definition of unrelated business taxable income.

Section 513—definition of unrelated trade or business.

Section 514—unrelated debt-financed income.

Section 521—farmers' cooperatives.

Section 526—shipowners' protection and indemnity associations.

Section 527—political organizations.

Section 528—homeowners' and condominium owners' associations.

Section 542(b)(2)—charitable contribution deduction in computing undistributed personal holding company income.

Section 556(b)(2)—charitable contribution deduction in computing undistributed foreign personal holding company income.

Section 642(c)—charitable contribution deduction for certain estates or trusts; definition of pooled income fund.

Section 642(j)—cemetery perpetual care fund deduction.

Section 664—rules concerning charitable remainder trusts.

Section 681—limitations on estate or trust charitable contribution deduction.

Sections 1245(b)(7), 1250(d)(9)—recapture of depreciation postponed where controlled subsidiary operating unrelated business is liquidated into parent exempt organization.

Section 1504(e)—tax-exempt organizations eligible to file a consolidated return.

Sections 1381-1388—tax treatment of non-exempt cooperatives.

Section 2055—estate tax deduction for charitable contributions.

Section 2106(a)(2)(A)—estate tax deduction for charitable contributions for estate of nonresidents not citizens.

Section 2501(a)(5)—gift tax exemption for political gifts.

Section 2522—gift tax deduction for charitable contributions.

Section 3121(b)—exclusion from social security taxes (FICA), particularly subsections (8) and (10).

Section 3306(c)(8)—exclusion from unemployment taxes (FUTA).

Section 4057(a)—exemption of non-profit educational organizations from retailers excise tax.

Sections 4221(a)(5) and (d)(5)—exemption of non-profit educational organizations from manufacturers excise tax.

Section 4294—exemption of non-profit educational organizations from excise tax on communications.

Section 4911—excise tax on excess lobbying amounts.

Section 4940—excise tax on investment income of private foundations.

Section 4941—private foundation self-dealing rules.

Section 4942—private foundation mandatory distribution rules.

Section 4943—private foundation excess business holdings rules.

Section 4944—private foundation rules concerning jeopardizing charitable purpose.

Section 4945—private foundation rules concerning taxable expenditures.

Section 4946—private foundations rules definitions.

Section 4947—application of private foundation rules to certain non-exempt trusts.

Section 4948—application of foundation rules to foreign organizations.

Section 4951—taxes on self-dealing with Black Lung Benefit Trusts.

Section 4952—taxes on taxable expenditures by Black Lung Benefit Trusts.

Section 4953—taxes on excess contributions to Black Lung Benefit Trusts.

Sections 6033, 6034—annual information returns.

Section 6043(b)—returns of exempt organizations concerning liquidation, dissolution, termination or substantial contraction.

Section 6050—requirement of information return for certain charitable transfers.

Section 6056—annual reports by private foundations.

Section 6072(e)—time for filing returns.

Section 6104—required publicity of information from certain exempt organizations and trusts.

Section 6213—restrictions applicable to deficiencies and petitions to U. S. Tax Court (see especially section 6213(e)).

Section 6501(n)—limitations on assessment or collections; special rule for Chapter 42 taxes.

Section 6511(f)—limitations on credit or refund—special rule for Chapter 42 taxes.

Section 6652(d)—late filing penalties for failure to file returns.

Section 6684—assessable penalties with respect to liability for Chapter 42 taxes.

Section 7421(a)—prohibition of restraint on assessment or collection of taxes.

Section 7428—declaratory judgment provision for charitable organizations.

Section 7454(b)—burden of proof in foundation manager cases.

Section 7476—declaratory judgment provision for employee plans.

Section 7478—declaratory judgment provision for political subdivisions.

Section 7605(c)—restriction on examination of churches for Code sections 511-514 purposes.

Section 7701(a)(3)—tax law definition of "corporation."

Table of Cases

Table of IRS Rulings and Other Items

IRS Key District Offices

Atlanta, Greensboro, Columbia, Nashville	Internal Revenue Service EP/EO Division, P.O. Box 632 Atlanta, Georgia 30301
Austin, Cheyenne, Denver, Albuquerque, New Orleans	Internal Revenue Service EP/EO Division, P.O. Box 2135 Austin, Texas 78767
Baltimore, Pittsburgh, Richmond, any U.S. possession, or a foreign country	Internal Revenue Service EP/EO Division, P.O. Box 13163 Technical and Service Staff Baltimore, Maryland 21203
Boston, Burlington, Portsmouth Augusta, Hartford, Providence	Internal Revenue Service EP/EO Division, P.O. Box 9081, J.F.K. Post Office Boston, Massachusetts 02203
Brooklyn, Albany, Buffalo	Internal Revenue Service EP/EO Division, P.O. Box 1680 General Post Office Brooklyn, New York 11202
Chicago	Internal Revenue Service EP/EO Division, P.O. Box A-3617 Chicago, Illinois 60690
Cincinnati, Indianapolis, Louisville	Internal Revenue Service EP/EO Division, P.O. Box 2508 Cincinnati, Ohio 45201
Cleveland, Parkersburg	Internal Revenue Service EP/EO Division, P.O. Box 99187 Cleveland, Ohio 44199
Dallas, Little Rock, Oklahoma City, Wichita	Internal Revenue Service EO2, Code 309, 1100 Commerce St. Dallas, Texas 75242
Detroit	Internal Revenue Service EP/EO Division, P.O. Box 32509 Detroit, Michigan 48232

Jacksonville, Birmingham, Jackson	Internal Revenue Service EP/EO Division, P.O. Box 35045 Jacksonville, Florida 32202
Los Angeles, Honolulu, Phoenix	Internal Revenue Service EP/EO Division, P.O. Box 2350 Los Angeles, California 90053
Manhattan	Internal Revenue Service EP/EO Division, P.O. Box 3200 Church Street Station New York, New York 10008
Newark	Internal Revenue Service EP/EO Division, P.O. Box 260 Newark, New Jersey 07101
Philadelphia, Wilmington	Internal Revenue Service EP/EO Division, P.O. Box 12821 Philadelphia, Pennsylvania 19106
San Francisco, Reno, Salt Lake City	Internal Revenue Service EP/EO Division 620 Folsom Street San Francisco, Calif. 94107
Seattle, Anchorage, Boise, Helena, Portland	Internal Revenue Service EP/EO Division, P.O. Box 21224 Seattle, Washington 98111
St. Louis, Des Moines, Omaha, Springfield	Internal Revenue Service EP/EO Division, Group 7206 P.O. Box 1123, Central Station St. Louis, Missouri 63188
St. Paul, Aberdeen, Fargo, Milwaukee	Internal Revenue Service EP/EO Division, Group 1902 316 N. Robert Street St. Paul, Minnesota 55101

Index

Matching grant argument, 38
Means-to-charitable-end principle, 62–63, 65, 255–258
Medicaid program, 81, 89, 91, 124, 125
Medical research organizations, 28, 95, 384
Medical societies, 145, 285–286, 287
Medicare program, 81, 89, 91, 124, 125, 332
Membership organizations, 13, 156, 298–299
Mental health, 90–91
Mentally incompetent, trust for, 371
Mill, John Stuart, 7
Mineral clubs, 155, 303
Minimum investment return, 417, 419, 420, 422, 461–465, 532
Miss Georgia Pageant, 76
Missionaries, as beneficiaries of charity, 85, 179, 568
Missions, 114, 183
Model Cities demonstration project, 89
Modifications, in computing unrelated income, 664–677
Monasteries, 173
Moody Foundation, 453
Moynihan, Daniel P., 20–21
Multiemployer Pension Plan Amendments Act of 1980, 363
Multiemployer pension plan trusts, 363, 549
Museums, 8, 10, 85, 86, 104, 115–116, 150, 382, 386, 391, 421, 422, 447, 464, 469, 521, 630, 634, 643–644, 685
Muskie, Edmund, 236–237
Mutual or cooperative telephone companies, 335–339
Mutual ditch or irrigation companies, 335–339
Mutual insurance companies, 344–345
Mutual organizations, 328, 334–339, 343–344
Mutual reserve funds, 343–344
Mutual savings banks, 4

National Alliance, 131–133
National Association for the Advancement of Colored People, 132
National Association of Attorneys General, 574
National Association of College and University Business Officers, 576
National Association of State Charity Officials, 574
National Collegiate Athletic Association, 637
National Conference of Catholic Bishops, 602
National Cooperative Dairy Herd Improvement Program, 320
National Economy League, 232
National Organization for Women, 254

National Park Service, 155
National Theater, 108
Nazis, 131–133, 695
Neighborhood community associations, 297
Neighborhood corporations, 371
Neighborhood land rule, 686
Neo-American Church, 181
"Net earnings," meaning of, 211, 229–230
Net investment income, tax on, 26, 357, 428, 507, 511–516, 531
New Human Services Institute, 697
Newsletter funds, 356
New York State Housing Finance Agency, 368
Nixon, Richard, Foundation, 521
Noncharitable purposes, of private foundations, 471–473
Nontheistic beliefs, 177
"Normally," concept of, 388, 395
North Carolina, University of, 636–637
Notice of deficiency, 554–555
Nunneries, 173
Nursing organizations, 95, 225–226, 292, 314

Office for Church in Society, 252–253
Office of Employee Plans and Exempt Organizations, 369, 554, 603
Ohio Deposit Guaranty Fund, 344
Operational tests, 75–78, 302, 392, 402–403, 556, 624
Options, writing of, by exempt organizations, 666–667
Orchestras, 104, 150, 386, 391, 638, 650
Organizational rules, of private foundations, 481–483, 496, 517–518, 529, 531, 545
Organizational tests, in general, 68–74, 302, 392, 402, 404, 545, 556, 594
Organized Crime Control Act, 27–28
Orphans, as beneficiaries of charity, 28, 80, 102, 179, 183, 572, 677

Packwood, Bob, 21
Parent organizations, 555–559, 611–613
Parents of Gays and Lesbians, 697
Parents Without Partners, 697
Parent-teacher associations, 11
Parks, 89, 90, 155, 230, 266, 418, 421, 469
Partnership, as disqualified person, 435
  as tax-exempt organization, 370, 543
Passive income, 664–677
Pass-through rule, 425–426, 468
Patman, Wright, 376, 515
Patriotism, promotion of, as charitable purpose, 98, 102
Peer review boards, 287